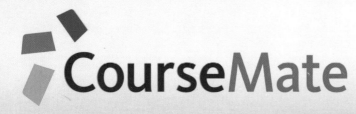

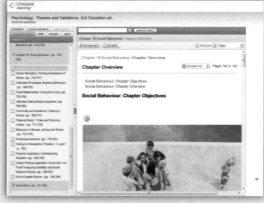

The Future of Business

FOURTH EDITION

Norm R. Althouse
University of Calgary

Laura A. Allan
Wilfrid Laurier University

Christopher M. Hartt
Dalhousie University

NELSON EDUCATION

NELSON / EDUCATION

The Future of Business, Fourth Edition

by Norm R. Althouse, Laura A. Allan, and Christopher M. Hartt

Vice President, Editorial Higher Education:
Anne Williams

Acquisitions Editor:
Alwynn Pinard

Marketing Manager:
Dave Stratton

Developmental Editor:
Lacey McMaster

Photo Researcher and Permissions Coordinator:
Matthew Maloney: Strand Acquisitions

Senior Content Production Manager:
Natalia Denesiuk Harris

Production Service:
Integra

Copy Editor:
Joan Bondar

Proofreader:
Integra

Indexer:
Jeanne Busemeyer

Manufacturing Manager:
Joanne McNeil

Design Director:
Ken Phipps

Managing Designer:
Franca Amore

Interior Design:
Dianna Little

Interior Design Modifications:
Peter Papayanakis

Cover Design:
Courtney Hellam

Cover Image:
Olas de Viento by Yvonne Domenge

Compositor:
Integra

Printer:
RRDonnelley

Additional credits for recurring images:
globe, Bananaboy/Shutterstock; green footprints, Arsen/Shutterstock; road signs, Nataliia Natykach/Shutterstock

Library and Archives Canada Cataloguing in Publication Data

Althouse, Norm
    The future of business / Norm R. Althouse, Laura A. Allan, Christopher M. Hartt. — 4th ed.

Rev. ed. Future of business/ Norm R. Althouse ... [et al.], 3rd Canadian ed., 2011.
Includes bibliographical references and index.
ISBN 978-0-17-650963-7

    1. Management—Textbooks.
2. Business—Textbooks. I. Allan, Laura A II. Hartt, Christopher M., 1961– III. Title.

HD70.C3F88 2013   658
C2012-907793-3

ISBN-13: 978-0-17-650963-7
ISBN-10: 0-17-650963-1

About the Cover

Olas de Viento (Wind Waves) was installed at Garry Point Park in Richmond, British Columbia, as part of Vancouver's Biennale celebrations. This striking work by Mexican artist Yvonne Domenge creates a sense of motion and interaction within a contained form. This piece was chosen for the cover of *The Future of Business* as a visual representation of the integrative model of business. While a business is a defined entity, the way in which its units work together and operate as a whole in its external environment is fluid and constantly changing. *Olas de Viento*, an international work featured in a Canadian celebration, is a powerful visual representation of how international trade and global business can create vibrant partnerships in our global community.

For more information on *Olas de Viento*, please visit http://www.richmond.ca/culture/publicart/biennale/windwaves.htm

To my family, friends, and colleagues that have helped me so much with this work.

To my students, who continue to inspire me every day. Remember what Gandhi said: "Live as if you were to die tomorrow. Learn as if you were to live forever."

LAURA A. ALLAN

To my wife, Gretchen Pohlkamp.

CHRISTOPHER M. HARTT

brief contents

contents

Part 4 Functional Areas of Business 331

an integrative approach to business

INTEGRATED LEARNING SYSTEM

The Integrated Learning System helps students learn quickly by driving home key chapter concepts and providing a framework for studying. It links all of the instructor and student materials to each chapter's learning outcomes.

Learning outcomes are listed at the beginning of each chapter, and then major headings within the chapter are identified by the relevant chapter learning outcome. Each section of the chapter ends with **Concept Checks** that can be used to self-test understanding of the material.

The **Summary of Learning Outcomes at the end of the chapter** provides easy review of the chapter's content.

LEARNING OUTCOMES

1 Describe the world of business.

2 Understand the responsibilities of the three levels of government in Canada.

3 List some of the roles governments play in Canada and how they affect business.

4 Explain some of the Canadian laws that protect businesses and consumers.

5 List the most common taxes paid by businesses.

6 List some of the trends that are reshaping the political environment.

GOVERNMENT—MORE THAN ONE LEVEL **LO2**

Canada is a diverse country with a large land mass and a very small population (approximately 34.5 million). There are three levels of government in Canada: federal, provincial/territorial, and municipal. Each has different responsibilities and regulations that affect business and society. Some of those responsibilities are listed below.

Federal Government—Overseeing the Well-Being of Canada

The federal government has the authority for money and banking, trade regulation, external relations, defence, criminal law, employment insurance, copyrights, and transportation, just to name a few responsibilities. Through the use of the fiscal policy (taxation and spending—discussed in Chapter 2) and the Bank of Canada (monetary policy—discussed in Chapter 2) Canada's financial system is regulated and wealth is collected, transferred, and spent to provide Canadians with one of the highest standards of living in the world. Although the Bank of Canada is not a government department (it is actually a Crown corporation) and operates with considerable independence, we introduce it here because of its impact on our economy (see Chapter 2).

Although the majority of Canada's workforce is regulated by the provincial/territorial legislation, approximately 10 percent of Canada's workforce is regulated by the federal government's Canada Labour Code. The Code regulates employment standards in industries such as banking, marine shipping, ferry and port service, air transportation, railway, and road transportation.

Provincial/Territorial Governments—Protecting Rights

Some of the responsibilities of the provinces/territories are the administration of labour laws (other than that mentioned above), education, health and welfare, protection of property and civil rights, natural resources, and the environment. One of the most significant provincial/territorial jurisdictions is labour law. This includes minimum working standards such as minimum wages, vacations, statutory holidays, overtime, etc.

Concept *Check*

Define business and differentiate between goods and services.

What is standard of living and how is it measured?

What are revenues and costs?

Summary of Learning Outcomes

LO1 Explain what economics is and how the three sectors of the economy are linked.

Economics is the study of how individuals, businesses, and governments use scarce resources to produce and distribute goods and services. The two major areas in economics are macroeconomics, the study of the economy as a whole, and microeconomics, the study of households and businesses. The individual, business, and government sectors of the economy are linked by a series of two-way flows. The government provides public goods and services for the other two sectors and receives income in the form of taxes. Changes in one flow affect the other sectors.

LO2 Understand the primary features of the world's economic systems.

An economic system is the combination of policies, laws, and choices made by a nation's government to establish the systems that determine what goods and services are produced and how they are allocated. The main economic systems in the world today include market economies (capitalism), command (planned) economies, socialism, and mixed economies.

LO3 Explain the four types of market structure.

Market structure is the number of suppliers in a market. Perfect competition is characterized by a large number of buyers and sellers, very similar products, good market information for both buyers and sellers, and ease of entry into and exit from the market. In monopolistic competition, many companies sell close substitutes in a market that is fairly easy to enter. In an oligopoly, a few companies produce most or all of the industry's output. An oligopoly is also difficult to enter, and what one company does will influence others. In a pure monopoly, there is a single seller in a market.

LO4 Discuss the basic microeconomic concepts of demand and supply, and how they establish prices.

Demand is the quantity of a good or service that people will buy at a given price. Supply is the quantity of a good or service that companies will make available at a given price. When the price increases, the quantity demanded falls but the quantity supplied rises. A price decrease leads to increased demand but a lower supply. At the point where the quantity demanded equals the quantity supplied, demand and supply are in balance. This equilibrium point is achieved by market adjustments of quantity and price.

LO5 Show how economic growth, full employment, and price stability indicate a nation's economic health.

A nation's economy is growing when the level of business activity, as measured by gross domestic product, is rising. GDP is the total value of all goods and services produced in a year. The goal of full employment is to have a job for all who can and want to work. How well a nation is meeting its employment goals is measured by the unemployment rate. There are four types of unemployment: frictional, structural, cyclical, and seasonal.

With price stability, the overall prices of goods and services are not moving either up or down very much. Inflation is the general upward movement of prices. When prices rise, purchasing power falls. The rate of inflation is measured by changes in the consumer price index (CPI) and the producer price index (PPI). There are two main causes of inflation. If the demand for goods and services exceeds the supply, prices will

THE INTEGRATIVE MODEL OF BUSINESS

The Integrative Perspective in *The Future of Business* helps students understand the important connections of business and prepares them for the intricacies of working in an ever more interconnected world. The **Introduction** to the text sets up this perspective, and it is reinforced before each chapter in the **Making the Connection** feature. Making the Connection introduces each chapter; this section shows how the chapter concepts relate to the "Integrative Model," helping students connect the chapter concepts to the external and internal business environments.

PART 1 illustrates the relationship of each chapter to the Political, Economic, Social, Technological, and International (PESTI) model.

PART 2 shows the impact of different forms of business on the PESTI model and the functional areas of the business.

PART 3 connects strategic decisions of management, structure, and motivation to the business's goals in the external environment.

PART 4 shows the impact of the external environment on each business unit through the PESTI model and how those business units both influence and are influenced by other functional areas.

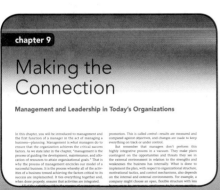

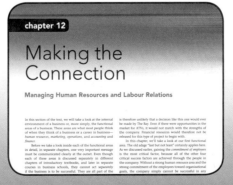

CHAPTER FEATURES THAT CONNECT

Four Thematic Boxes

EXPANDING AROUND THE GLOBE This boxed feature demonstrates how globalization is important in today's marketplace and its impact on real companies.

MAKING ETHICAL CHOICES The ethical activities in these boxes present real-world ethical challenges to stimulate discussion about ethical issues faced by organizations.

Opening Vignettes

Opening Vignettes teach key principles through real-life examples.

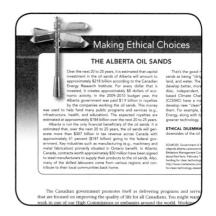

SUSTAINABLE BUSINESS, SUSTAINABLE WORLD These boxes highlight the growing importance of sustainability in today's business practices.

CREATING THE FUTURE OF BUSINESS This new boxed feature profiles young Canadian entrepreneurs who have been successful in their business ventures.

Hot Links

The **Hot Links** feature appears in the margin to provide an opportunity to connect to relevant websites that expand on chapter information.

bankruptcy
The legal procedure by which individuals or businesses that cannot meet their financial obligations are relieved of some, if not all, of their debt.

HOT Links

For more information on corporate bankruptcy, see the website that helps people and businesses get a fresh financial start at
www.bankruptcycanada.com

Concept in Action

Interesting companies, business leaders, and ideas are featured in our "Concept in Action" photo essays. Many of these conclude with a critical thinking question to spark further discussion and study about a business topic.

Concept *in Action*

PPP Canada is a Crown corporation created to improve the delivery of public infrastructure to Canadians. The private sector assumes a major share of the responsibility in the public–private partnerships (P3). One example is the $11 million the Government of Canada contributed towards a new biosolids management facility in Sudbury, Ontario.

Key Terms

Business terms are carefully defined and conveniently located in the text margins beside the section where the term is first introduced. A complete glossary of all key terms is included at the end of the text.

END-OF-CHAPTER SKILL-BUILDING ACTIVITIES, EXERCISES, AND RESOURCES

Experiential Exercises

This feature allows students to practise and apply the chapter concepts and to expand on the chapter topics. These exercises can be used as assessments or assignments and to add a real-world application.

Review Questions

Review questions confirm students' learning and understanding of chapter topics.

Creative Thinking Cases

These chapter-ending cases encourage the exploration and analysis of business strategies.

patent
A form of protection (limited monopoly) established by the government for inventors; it gives an inventor the exclusive right to manufacture, use, and sell an invention for 20 years.

copyright
A form of protection established by the government for creators of works of art, music, literature, or other intellectual property; it gives the creator the exclusive right to use, produce, and sell the creation during the lifetime of the creator and extends these rights to the creator's estate for 50 years thereafter.

trademark
The legally exclusive design, name, or other distinctive mark that a manufacturer uses to identify its goods in the marketplace.

Experiential Exercises

1. Find out what's happening in Canadian business at www.canadianbu
2. Check out the latest on the world's ranking of highest quality of countries at www.mapsofworld.com/world-top-ten/world-top-ten-life-map.html.
3. Search for any not-for-profit organization. See what challenges the funding, volunteerism, etc.
4. Check out what is new in the federal government at www.gc.ca.
5. Search your provincial/territorial government's website to see the latest
6. Search how your local government impacts business activities through
7. What is new at the Office of the Auditor General of Canada? See ww gc.ca.
8. Learn more about our legal system at www.blakes.com/DBIC/guide/b system.html.
9. How are our courts organized, both federally and provincially/territo www.justice.gc.ca/eng/dept-min/pub/ccs-ajc/.
10. What patents, copyrights, and trademarks are expiring? Search the Inte out!
11. Check out Health Canada to see the latest advisories, warnings, and products at www.hc-sc.gc.ca/cps-spc/advisories-avis/index-eng.php

Review Questions

1. What is a business?
2. Products consist of goods and services. List some of the differe and services.
3. What impact do our governments have on our standard of liv life?
4. Explain the relationship between revenues, costs, and profits.
5. What are the responsibilities of the three levels of governm
6. What roles do the governments play in our economy?
7. Explain our legal system in terms of public and private law.
8. What laws govern business operations?
9. What are the conditions of a valid contract?
10. What remedies are available for the breach of a contract?
11. What are the most common taxes paid by businesses and governments?
12. What trends are occurring in politics and governments today?

CREATIVE THINKING CASE

Inside Intel: It's about Copying—Exactly

Intel Corporation has more than 82,000 employees worldwide, but innovation depends on people like Tmib Roughgarden, an Air Force veteran whose job is to copy slavishly. Ms. Roughgarden is known inside Intel as a "seed," an unofficial title for technicians who transfer manufacturing know-how from one Intel chip factory to another. Her job to help ensure that Intel's latest plant works just like identical plants around the world. If there is a problem at one plant, production may be slowed but not stopped—other plants pick up the slack. So when an earthquake interrupts a plant in China, a plant in Oregon may increase production.

It is all part of a major Intel strategy known as "Copy Exactly," which discourages experimentation at individual factories. Instead, engineers and technicians painstakingly clone proven Intel manufacturing techniques from one plant to the next—down to the colour of workers' gloves and wall paint, or other features that would seem to have no bearing on efficiency. New plants fall into two basic categories: model plants that will be copied and those that are copies.

The strategy emerged after a production disaster in the 1980s, when maddening variations between factories hurt productivity and product quality. Japanese competitors nearly drove Intel out of business. Today, Copy Exactly shapes Intel's response to the latest economic downturn, helping accelerate the relentless pace of technology improvements known as Moore's Law, after former Intel chairman Gordon Moore. Moore predicted that the number of transistors that could be placed on a computer chip (of the same size) would double every two years.

Although it prohibits willy-nilly changes, the Copy Exactly methodology encourages Intel workers to come up with ideas to boost productivity or make chip features smaller. But the ideas must pass a committee called the Process Change Control Board, which requires workers to come up with tests to prove the value of their suggestions.

The idea of Copy Exactly comes into the planning of new plants such as the $3 billion facility expected to open in 2013. Located in Chandler, Arizona, near several other Intel facilities, this plant will employ 1,000 and Intel executives project that it will be the most advanced high-volume semiconductor manufacturing facility anywhere in the world. This project received significant tax incentives from the state of Arizona, but the government saw the value of the high-paying jobs coming to or staying in the state. The innovations for the Chandler plant are evolutions of the ongoing improvements at other plants and, as the new processes are developed, seeds will take them out to the other Intel plants and continue the "Copy Exactly" process.

Thinking Critically

1. Explain the link between quality and "Copy Exactly."

preface

YOUR FUTURE IS OUR BUSINESS

The Future of Business, Fourth Edition, provides a personal road map for understanding and navigating the future of business. The fourth edition builds on the success of the first three editions with thorough coverage of business principles and leading-edge practices adopted by business innovators, all illustrated with relevant and interesting business examples. *The Future of Business*, Fourth Edition, takes an integrative approach to business, highlighting how functional areas work together and how innovation fuels new forms of collaboration. The text is written in a friendly and conversational style and helps prepare students of all interests and abilities for future achievements with the information, skills, and techniques they need to get to work and jump on the fast-track to success.

THE INTEGRATIVE PERSPECTIVE: MAJOR BUSINESS TOPICS UP CLOSE

Business and business units do not work in isolation; they work within the external and internal environments. Our approach has been to discuss the various topics with a focus on the integrative nature of business. The Integrative Perspective in *The Future of Business* helps students understand these connections and prepares them for the intricacies of working in an ever-interconnected world. The introduction to the text sets up this perspective, and it is reinforced before each chapter in the **Making the Connection** feature.

Making the Connection

Making the Connection introduces each chapter. This section shows how the chapter concepts relate to "The Integrative Model" to help students connect the chapter concepts to the external and internal business environments.

> **Part 1:** Illustrates the relationship of each chapter to the Political, Economic, Social, Technological, and International (PESTI) model.
>
> **Part 2:** Shows the impact of different forms of business on the PESTI model and the functional areas of the business.
>
> **Part 3:** Connects strategic decisions of management, structure, and motivation to the business's goals in the external environment.
>
> **Part 4:** Shows the impact of the external environment on each business unit through the PESTI model and how those business units both influence and are influenced by other functional areas.

The **Making the Connection** feature helps students contextualize the chapter content within the framework of business as a whole, and allows them to begin to see the bigger picture.

WHAT'S NEW IN THE FOURTH EDITION

Today's most important business topics and trends are thoroughly covered in the fourth edition—this means more insight into the key economic and business developments that shape the future. Topics at the forefront of business, covered in this edition, include

- integration of business practices;
- globalization and global management skills;
- sustainable business;
- changing Canadian demographics;
- corporate ethical standards;
- managing multinational cultures in the workplace;
- virtual teams and corporations;
- nurturing knowledge workers; and
- entrepreneurship.

Through extensive reviews, we discovered that instructors teaching the Introduction to Business course place considerable importance on the topics of ethics, the role of technology in business, e-commerce, entrepreneurship and small business management, global business opportunities, and careers. Therefore, we gave these topics special emphasis.

The Future of Business is supported by real-world examples to introduce today's students to tomorrow's business careers. Highlights of new content to the fourth edition include the following:

Reorganization

In response to reviewers' suggestions, the following organizational changes were incorporated:

- more discussion of sustainability and entrepreneurship;
- an UPDATED chapter on International Business to expand our PEST model to the new PESTI model;
- a NEW chapter that offers advice on "Analyzing the Business";
- new and updated chapter-opening vignettes and closing creative-thinking cases; and
- a reorganization of the chapters to make the flow easier for students.

New Features

Two new boxed features have been added or expanded.

CREATING THE FUTURE OF BUSINESS This new boxed feature profiles young Canadian entrepreneurs who have been successful in their business ventures.

SUSTAINABLE BUSINESS, SUSTAINABLE WORLD To supplement the "Making Ethical Choices" boxes, we have included "Sustainable Business, Sustainable World" boxes in all chapters. These boxes highlight the growing importance of sustainability in today's business practices.

New Canadian Examples

Some of the many Canadian examples profiled in this edition include Lululemon Athletica's move to global markets; SMART Technologies' interactive SMART Board's appearance in classrooms, meeting rooms, and training centres around the country; ProSkate's small business built on clear values; Oasis Bags' management and leadership; Contact North's organizational structure; and Encana Corporation's sustainability practices.

Prologue

An updated prologue, "A Quick Guide to Your Future Success in Business," offers practical and inspiring advice for developing test-taking, interpersonal, time management, and planning skills. The prologue also features suggestions for finding the right career and succeeding in that first professional job. Not only will students find up-to-date guidelines for finding a job using the Internet, they can also gain insights into their own readiness for the job market. Fun Self-Tests explore the following topics:

- Can You Persuade Others?
- Can You Play the Political Game?
- How Well Do You Manage Your Time?
- Are You Good at Managing Money?
- Do You Have Good Study Habits?
- How Assertive Are You?
- Are You a Good Listener?

GREAT FEATURES RETAINED FROM THE PREVIOUS EDITIONS

Chapter Organization

Organization matters! Each chapter of *The Future of Business,* Fourth Edition, has been organized into a unique three-part structure that links principles, trends, and ideas:

PRINCIPLES OF BUSINESS Gives students a comprehensive overview of current business practices, and teaches key principles through real-world examples from the largest global corporate giants to the smallest family startups.

TRENDS IN BUSINESS Explores the fundamental factors and emerging trends that are reshaping today's business world and altering tomorrow's competitive environment. This preview of the future gives students a keen advantage when entering the workplace.

GREAT IDEAS TO USE NOW Brings chapter topics to life with relevant and interesting tips for making the most of a professional career or becoming a smart consumer. Students develop skills that are applicable immediately.

Structure of Content

INTRODUCTION In the **Introduction**, students learn the basic terms that are associated with organizations and business. They are given the foundation of what a business is, how risk can affect the business, revenues, expenses and profits, etc. Here, too, the students are first introduced to the "Integrated Model of a Successful Business."

SUSTAINABILITY BOXES In each chapter is a "Sustainable Business, Sustainable World" feature. This feature was first introduced in select chapters of the third edition and proved to be very popular with both the students and the reviewers.

MAKING ETHICAL CHOICES BOXES These ethical activities boxes present real-world ethical challenges to stimulate discussion of ethical issues faced by organizations.

CONCEPT IN ACTION In each chapter you will find interesting companies and business leaders profiled in our "**Concept in Action**" photo essays. The photos and accompanying essays are fun, contemporary, insightful, and a super learning tool for the visual learner. Many of these conclude with a critical thinking question to spark further discussion and study about a business topic.

HOT LINKS **Hot Links** give the student an opportunity to connect to various websites to expand on the information presented in the chapter. Instructors may also choose to send students to the website links to fulfill assignments.

ORGANIZATION

In Part One of *The Future of Business,* Fourth Edition, students learn how the PESTI (political, economic, social, technology, international) model works and its impact on any business. In these first four chapters, to either introduce or refresh the students' awareness of certain elementary—but critical—components, the book discusses "Politics: Governments' Roles" (Chapter 1), "Economics: Evolving Systems" (Chapter 2), "Social: Society, Corporate Responsibility, and Making Ethical Decisions" (Chapter 3), "Technology: Managing Information for Business Success" (Chapter 4), and "International: The Global Marketplace" (Chapter 5).

Part Two introduces the concepts of Canadian business by discussing "Entrepreneurship and Small Business" (Chapter 6), "Analyzing the Business" (Chapter 7), and "Forms of Business Ownership" (Chapter 8).

Business Management (Part Three) examines "Management and Leadership in Today's Organizations" (Chapter 9), "Designing Organizational Structures" (Chapter 10), and "Motivating Employees" (Chapter 11).

The final section, Part Four, gives the students a basic understanding of the functional areas of business. The seven chapters cover "Managing Human Resources and Labour Relations," "Marketing: The Customer Focus," "Creating Marketing Strategies," "Achieving World-Class Operations Management," "Accounting for Financial Success," "Understanding Money and the Canadian Financial System," and "Finance: Maximizing the Value."

SUPPLEMENTS FOR SUCCESS

Reliable and Easy-to-Use Instructor Ancillaries

Business success is stimulated by access to and mastery of vital resources. The same is true for the classroom. Whether teaching an online course or simply enhancing your course with Web resources, *The Future of Business,* Fourth Edition, offers a vast, complementary system of teaching and learning resources.

The **Nelson Education Teaching Advantage (NETA)** program delivers research-based instructor resources that promote student engagement and higher-order thinking to enable the success of Canadian students and educators.

Instructors today face many challenges. Resources are limited, time is scarce, and a new kind of student has emerged: one who is juggling school with work, has gaps in his or her basic knowledge, and is immersed in technology in a way that has led to a completely new style of learning. In response, Nelson Education has gathered a group of dedicated instructors to advise us on the creation of richer and more flexible ancillaries that respond to the needs of today's teaching environments.

The members of our editorial advisory board have experience across a variety of disciplines and are recognized for their commitment to teaching. They include

Norman Althouse, Haskayne School of Business, University of Calgary

Brenda Chant-Smith, Department of Psychology, Trent University

Scott Follows, Manning School of Business Administration, Acadia University

Jon Houseman, Department of Biology, University of Ottawa

Glen Loppnow, Department of Chemistry, University of Alberta

Tanya Noel, Department of Biology, York University

Gary Poole, Senior Scholar, Centre for Health Education Scholarship, and Associate Director, School of Population and Public Health, University of British Columbia

Dan Pratt, Department of Educational Studies, University of British Columbia

Mercedes Rowinsky-Geurts, Department of Languages and Literatures, Wilfrid Laurier University

David DiBattista, Department of Psychology, Brock University

Roger Fisher, Ph.D.

In consultation with the editorial advisory board, Nelson Education has completely rethought the structure, approaches, and formats of our key textbook ancillaries. We've also increased our investment in editorial support for our ancillary authors. The result is the Nelson Education Teaching Advantage and its key components: *NETA Engagement, NETA Assessment,* and *NETA Presentation.* Each component includes one or more ancillaries prepared according to our best practices, and a document explaining the theory behind the practices.

NETA Engagement presents materials that help instructors deliver engaging content and activities to their classes. Instead of Instructor's Manuals that regurgitate chapter outlines and key terms from the text, NETA Enriched Instructor's Manuals (EIMs) provide genuine assistance to teachers. The EIMs answer questions like *What should students learn?, Why should students care?,* and *What are some common student misconceptions and stumbling blocks?* EIMs not only identify the topics that cause students the most difficulty, but also describe techniques and resources to help students master these concepts. Dr. Roger Fisher's *Instructor's Guide to Classroom Engagement (IGCE)* accompanies every Enriched Instructor's Manual. (Information about the NETA Enriched Instructor's Manual prepared for *The Future of Business* is included in the description of the IRCD below.)

NETA Assessment relates to testing materials. Under *NETA Assessment,* Nelson's authors create multiple-choice questions that reflect research-based best practices for constructing effective questions and testing not just recall but also higher-order thinking. Our guidelines were developed by David DiBattista, a 3M National Teaching Fellow whose recent research as a professor of psychology at Brock University has focused on multiple-choice testing. All Test Bank authors receive training at workshops conducted by Prof. DiBattista, as do the copyeditors assigned to each Test Bank. A copy of *Multiple Choice Tests: Getting Beyond Remembering,* Prof. DiBattista's guide to writing effective tests, is included with every Nelson Test Bank/Computerized Test Bank package. (Information about the NETA Test Bank prepared for *The Future of Business* is included in the description of the IRCD below.)

NETA Presentation has been developed to help instructors make the best use of PowerPoint® in their classrooms. With a clean and uncluttered design developed by Maureen Stone of StoneSoup Consulting, NETA Presentation features slides with improved readability, more multimedia and graphic materials, activities to use in class, and tips for instructors on the Notes page. A copy of *NETA Guidelines for Classroom Presentations* by Maureen Stone is included with each set of PowerPoint slides. (Information about the NETA PowerPoint prepared for *The Future of Business* is included in the description of the IRCD below.)

IRCD Key instructor ancillaries are provided on the *Instructor's Resource CD* (ISBN 978-0-17-661728-8), giving instructors the ultimate tool for customizing lectures and presentations. (Downloadable Web versions are also available at www.nelson.com/futureofbusiness4e.) The IRCD includes the following:

NETA Engagement. The Enriched Instructor's Manual was written by Norm Althouse, University of Calgary. It is organized according to the textbook chapters, and addresses key educational concerns such as typical stumbling blocks students face and how to address them. Other features include classroom activity and discussion suggestions, lesson plans, and additional exercises.

NETA Assessment. The Test Bank was revised by Mike Wade, Seneca College. It includes over 1300 multiple-choice questions written according to NETA guidelines for effective construction and development of higher-order questions. Also included are approximately 465 True/False and 260 short-answer questions. Test Bank files are provided in Word format for easy editing and in PDF format for convenient printing, whatever your system.

The Computerized Test Bank by ExamView® includes all the questions from the Test Bank. The easy-to-use ExamView software is compatible with Microsoft Windows and Mac OS. Create tests by selecting questions from the question bank, modifying these questions as desired, and adding new questions you write yourself. You can administer quizzes online and export tests to WebCT, Blackboard, and other formats.

NETA Presentation. Microsoft PowerPoint lecture slides for every chapter have been created by Norm Althouse, University of Calgary. There is an average of 30 slides per chapter, many featuring key figures, tables, and photographs from *The Future of Business*. NETA principles of clear design and engaging content have been incorporated throughout.

Image Library. This resource consists of digital copies of figures, short tables, and photographs used in the book. Instructors may use these jpegs to create their own PowerPoint presentations.

DayOne. Day One—Prof InClass is a PowerPoint presentation that you can customize to orient your students to the class and their text at the beginning of the course.

ADDITIONAL RESOURCES

TurningPoint®. Another valuable resource for instructors is **TurningPoint classroom response software** customized for *The Future of Business*. Now you can author, deliver, show, access, and grade, all in PowerPoint … with no toggling back and forth between screens! JoinIn on Turning Point is the only classroom response software tool that gives you true PowerPoint integration. With JoinIn, you are no longer tied to your computer. You can walk about your classroom as you lecture, showing slides and collecting and displaying responses with ease. There is simply no easier or more effective way to turn your lecture hall into a personal, fully interactive experience for your students. If you can use PowerPoint, you can use JoinIn on TurningPoint! (Contact your Nelson publishing representative for details.)

DVD to accompany *The Future of Business*, Fourth Edition, and DVD Guide (ISBN 978-0-17-662886-4). Designed to enrich and support chapter concepts, each of the 23 video segments presents real business issues faced by a variety of service and manufacturing organizations. The video cases, which have been written by textbook author Christopher Hartt, challenge students to study business issues and develop solutions to business problems. The instructor's DVD guide, included in the instructor's manual, suggests answers to the critical thinking questions that accompany each video segment.

CourseMate. CourseMate brings course concepts to life with interactive learning and exam preparation tools that integrate with the printed textbook. Students activate their knowledge through quizzes, games, and flashcards, among many other tools.

CourseMate provides immediate feedback that enables students to connect results to the work they have just produced, increasing their learning efficiency. It encourages contact between students and faculty: You can choose to monitor your students' level of engagement with CourseMate, correlating their efforts to their outcomes. You can even use CourseMate's quizzes to practise "Just in Time" teaching by tracking results in the Engagement Tracker and customizing your lesson plans to address their learning needs.

Watch student comprehension and engagement soar as your class engages with CourseMate. The website can be found at www.nelsonbrain.com. Ask your Nelson representative for a demo today.

Engaging Student Ancillaries

INFOTRAC® COLLEGE EDITION With InfoTrac, students can receive anytime, anywhere online access to a database of full-text articles from hundreds of popular and scholarly periodicals, such as *Canadian Business, Canadian Business Review, BusinessWeek, Canadian Labour, HR Magazine,* and *HR Professional,* among others. Students can use its fast and easy search tools to find relevant news and analytical information among the tens of thousands of articles in the database—updated daily and going back as far as four years—all at a single website. InfoTrac is a great way to expose students to online research techniques, with the security that the content is academically based and reliable. An InfoTrac College Edition subscription card is packaged free with all new copies of *The Future of Business.*

COURSEMATE The more you study, the better the results. Make the most of your study time by accessing everything you need to succeed in one place. Read your textbook, take notes, review flashcards, watch videos, and take practice quizzes—online with CourseMate, which can be purchased at www.nelsonbrain.com.

ACKNOWLEDGMENTS

We are exceedingly grateful to the many reviewers who offered suggestions and recommendations for enhancing the coverage, pedagogy, and support package of *The Future of Business.* The feedback from these instructors helped guide our efforts and ensures that the textbook surpassed expectations for customer satisfaction and quality. We are deeply appreciative of the insights of the following reviewers:

Colin Boyd, University of Saskatchewan

Sunil Kaplash, University of Victoria

Michael Khan, University of Toronto

Puneet Luthra, Seneca College

Valerie Miceli, Seneca College

Barb Neil, Northern Alberta Institute of Technology

Frank Saccucci, Grant MacEwan University

Charles Scott, University of Northern British Columbia

Drew Smylie, Centennial College

Kent Walker, University of Windsor

We would also like to recognize the contribution of Lawrence Gitman and Carl McDaniel, authors of the U.S. editions of *The Future of Business.* Their original work served as the foundation for our writing and set a standard of excellence we conscientiously followed.

We have benefited from the detailed and constructive contributions of many individuals. Specifically, we would like to thank the following people for their insight and contributions to *The Future of Business*:

Cindy Anderson

Bruce Byford

Victoria Calvert

Gordon Campbell

Michael Corbeil

David B. Crawford

Joan Dauter

Doug Dokis

Katherine Drewes

Janice Eliasson

Jeff Everett

Christopher Halpin

Karina Hope
Wayne Irvine
Sharaz Khan
Rafik Kurji
Ryan B. Lee
David Lertzman
Robin Lynas
Robert L. Malach
Sandra E. Malach
Arden Matheson
Leanne McDonald
Doug McDonnell
Fred (Scoop) McKay
Katrina Montgomery

Ron Munaweera
Ron Murch
Albert Nasaar
Gino Panucci
Karen Parsons
Joan Reidulff
Barry Sadrehashemi
Christine Stark
Frank Thirkettle
Elizabeth Watson
Justine Wheeler
Kim Wilson
Claire Wright

Norm would like to express his sincere gratitude to all those who helped with this project. He would like to thank Janice Eliasson, Sharaz Khan, and Wayne Irvine for giving advice from their subject knowledge, and the Haskayne School of Business Library staff for all the information they provided. A special thanks to a great colleague and friend, Shirley Rose, whose work on the first three editions helped lay the groundwork for the fourth edition.

Laura Allan would like to send a sincere thanks to all of the young entrepreneurs who have agreed to be featured in this book—many of whom have been students of hers—for their help, but mostly their inspiration to students as they enter the business world. But most of all she would like to thank her teaching assistants for all of their hard work and dedication toward the students as they learn the material, and for all of their advice and feedback to help make the material more useful to the students.

Chris would like to thank his wife, Gretchen Pohlkamp, and his sons, Joshua and Noah, who have assisted him by being supportive and giving feedback on the materials he has created. He would also like to thank his students at Saint Mary's and Dalhousie Universities. In particular, he thanks each of the teaching assistants who have worked with him, especially Sheila Sutherland, who has been invaluable in discussing the practical application of the text.

And, of course, our talented and patient editorial and production staff at Nelson Education Limited.

Norm R. Althouse
Laura A. Allan
Christopher M. Hartt

ABOUT THE AUTHORS

Norm R. Althouse

Norm Althouse received his Bachelor of Business Administration (Accounting) and worked in the public sector for ten years before returning to continue studies in the Master of Business Program. He has studied in Canada, Australia, Ireland, and Hungary. Currently, Norm teaches at the Haskayne School of Business at the University of Calgary. He has also taught at the University of Lethbridge and Mount Royal College.

After several years of teaching in the Human Resource area at the University of Calgary, Norm transferred to the Strategy and Global Management area, where he currently teaches. Initially, Norm's primary responsibility was to develop a required core-course in business for first- and second-year business students. His commitment to

COURTESY OF NORM ALTHOUSE

"continuous improvement" has resulted in many new developments, including the integration of materials and changes in the pedagogy of the course.

Norm's research activities include team building, the changing nature of management and managers, and, most currently, studying values and diversity in the workplace. Additionally, Norm has presented at conferences such as the Administrative Sciences Association of Canada ("The Gendering Component of Diversity: How Is It Faring?") and the Academy of Management ("Success in the Classroom, Grading Strategies, and Group Work for New Instructors"), and has been published in a book of readings from the Global Business and Technology Association—Budapest, Hungary ("Hierarchies in Transition: Hungary and Canada").

Laura A. Allan

Laura Allan received her Honours Bachelor of Business Administration from Wilfrid Laurier University and, after a brief stint in the private sector working for an advertising agency, went on to earn her Master of Business Administration in Marketing at York University. Laura went back to her alma mater to teach in 1984 and, apart from taking brief time off to have her two children, has been there ever since. Laura teaches primarily first-year undergraduate classes, but has also taught a second-year decision-making course. She also conducts executive development seminars and consults on the topic of emotional intelligence. Laura has been academic editor on another introductory text, written a study guide, and contributed chapters for two introductory textbooks. She has also coauthored the lab manual for the two first-year courses since 1998, and has developed an online version of both courses for the university's distance education department.

Laura's commitment to the integrative approach to teaching business led to a complete redesign of the first-year courses. She also developed the annual New Venture and Pitch Competitions for first-year students. Currently, Laura serves as co-coordinator for the first year functional area course at Wilfrid Laurier University, with over 2000 students and 40 TAs. She has been recognized as one of the "most popular profs" in *Maclean's* magazine since 2000.

Christopher M. Hartt

In 2012 Chris returned to Dalhousie University as an Assistant Professor, 29 years after his graduation with a Bachelor of Arts in Political Science in 1983. That graduation was followed by a year in the workforce and then a Master of Business Administration (MBA) degree, majoring in Finance, at Saint Mary's University. Chris then spent 22 years in the business world, first as an intrapreneur and Director of Finance and Administration for a large hospital foundation for 11 years and then 11 years as an entrepreneur owning such varied businesses as an amusement park and a sporting goods franchise. In 2008 Chris decided to return to his studies and began a PhD in Management at the Sobey School of Business at Saint Mary's University in Halifax, N.S. He is currently a PhD candidate nearing the completion of his dissertation studying the role of Actor-Network theory and sensemaking on a key event in the history of Air Canada. Chris has presented his work at conferences on three continents; over the past four years he has contributed to four journal publications and given more than 25 conference presentations, including such prestigious conferences as the Academy of Management, International Federation of Scholarly Associations of Management, European Group for Organizational Studies, Eastern Academy of Management, and Standing Conference on Organizational Symbolism. In addition to this textbook, Chris has contributed a chapter to another book and continues to write and research. As a father of two university students, Chris tries to ensure that his textbook contributions will connect with today's learners and takes the same approach to the classes he teaches.

prologue

A Guide to Your Future Success in Business

YOUR FUTURE IN BUSINESS: BEGIN WITH A DEGREE, DIPLOMA, OR CERTIFICATE

What makes someone successful in life? Successful people are those who go through the various stages of life content in knowing that they have done their best: their best at work, at home, and in all pursuits of life. And a big part of having a happy life is pursuing a career that offers job satisfaction and financial rewards. If you are going to "be all that you can be," you need a good education and experience.

A degree, diploma, or certificate unlocks doors to economic opportunity. Why get a degree, diploma, or certificate?

- *Get and keep a better job.* Because the world is changing rapidly, and many jobs rely on new technology, more jobs require education beyond high school. With a postsecondary education, you will have more jobs from which to choose.
- *Earn more money.* People who go to postsecondary institutions usually earn more than those who do not.
- *Get a good start in life.* A postsecondary education helps you acquire a wide range of knowledge in many subjects as well as an advanced understanding of your specialized area, for example, business. Postsecondary institutions also train you to express your thoughts clearly in speech and in writing and to make informed decisions.

Simply stated, a degree, diploma, or certificate gives you the chance to achieve the quality of life you desire and deserve. The lifestyle, the new friends, the purchasing power of a degree, diploma, or certificate won't guarantee happiness but will put you well on the road to finding it.

Learning the Basics of Business

You might want to pursue a career as a physician, lawyer, executive assistant, florist, information technology (IT) specialist, or any of a thousand other opportunities. One thing that all careers have in common is that you need to have a basic understanding of business. Your success in whatever you choose will depend partially on your basic business skills. And that is why this course is so important.

Few courses present all the fundamental areas of business and then link them together the way this course does. This is where you get the big picture as well as an introduction to fundamental components of business. Learn it well, because it will be invaluable throughout your life.

Choosing a Career

Because this course gives you a detailed overview of all of the areas of business, it will guide you in selecting a major should you decide to pursue a degree, diploma, or certificate in business. Choosing a major is one of life's true milestones. Your major essentially determines how you will spend the next four decades of your life! A marketing major will find a career in sales, marketing research, advertising, or other marketing-related field. An accounting major (you guessed it) will become an accountant. Never take selecting a major lightly; working 40 hours a week for the next 45 years (less vacations), you will put in about 90,000 hours on the job. Don't you think that you should choose something that you will enjoy?

DEVELOPING INTERPERSONAL SKILLS IS KEY TO YOUR SUCCESS

A degree, diploma, or certificate in business is going to offer you many great career opportunities. Once you take your first job, how rapidly you move up the corporate ladder is up to you. People with great interpersonal skills will always do better on and off the job than those who lack them. It has been estimated that up to 95 percent of our workplace success depends on an understanding of other people.[1] The interpersonal skills become more valuable as you move up the corporate ladder. Here's how to enhance your interpersonal skills:

1. **Build your people skills.** Learn to build alliances in a group and establish harmony. Make a concerted effort to know what is happening in the lives of those on your team at school and work. About once a month, get together with your group and pass out a list of issues, concerns, fears, and potential problems. Then invite everyone to give input to solve little problems before they become big. If something goes wrong, try to find out where things are not running smoothly and improve them. Be sure to compliment someone in your group who is doing an exemplary job.

   Become a good listener. When you listen well, you are in effect telling the other person that he or she is worth listening to. Listening well includes listening to both what is said and what is not said. Learn to read unspoken gestures and expressions. When giving feedback, plan what you will say in advance. Be positive and be specific. Ask the person receiving the feedback if whether he or she would like to discuss your comments further.

2. **Understand how to persuade others.** Remember, we all must sell ourselves and ideas to get ahead in life and business. Influencing others means overcoming objections, igniting passions, or changing minds. The first step is to build esprit de corps, a shared enthusiasm and devotion to the group. Make your vision their vision so that everyone is working toward a common goal. Praise the team as a whole, but recognize the unique contributions different team members have made. The trick is to praise everyone, yet for different reasons. When you and your team successfully solve a problem, change will result.

   Persuasion rests on trust. You can build trust by being honest, fulfilling your commitments, being concerned about others, and minimizing problems and pain for others whenever possible. In short, if you have integrity, building trust becomes a simple task.

   When people raise objections to your plans or ideas, try to fully understand their comments and the motivation for making them. When you feel that you understand the true objection, answer the objection in the form of a benefit: "Yes, you will need to work next Saturday, but then you can have compensatory time off anytime you wish next month." Determine your persuasion skills by taking the quiz in Exhibit P.1.

Rate your level of agreement with the statements below using the following scale:

STRONGLY AGREE	AGREE	NEITHER AGREE NOR DISAGREE	DISAGREE	STRONGLY DISAGREE

1. I prefer to work in a team rather than individually.
2. I enjoy motivating others to help accomplish objectives.
3. I avoid working with difficult people or trying to resolve group differences.
4. I can learn more working in a team rather than working by myself.
5. I would prefer to work with individuals I have known previously.
6. I give up if my team members do not agree with me.
7. I may not always convince my team members to agree with my opinions, but I will go ahead and do what I feel is correct.
8. I think people who can persuade others always possess sound judgment.
9. I will do the work myself if others do not agree to do it.
10. To get the work done, I will listen to a person to understand how he/she wants it to be done.
11. I can get people to voluntarily make commitments and get the work done.[2]

See the scoring guidelines at the end of the prologue to obtain your score.

3. **Learn to think on your feet.** Top executives, such as former automobile chairman Lee Iacocca, say that "speaking well on your feet" is the best thing that you can do for your career. If you cannot quickly express yourself with confidence, others will lose confidence in you.

It will not happen overnight, but you can become an outstanding thinker and speaker. A simple technique is to set a timer for two minutes and ask a friend to begin speaking. When the timer goes off, your friend stops speaking and you begin talking. The challenge is to use the final thought that your friend spoke as the first word of your two-minute talk. Another technique is to have someone supply you with a series of quotes. Then, without hesitation, give your interpretation.

4. **Empower yourself.** No matter who you are, what position you will hold, or where you will work, you probably will have to report to somebody. If you are fortunate enough to work in a culture of empowerment, you are allowed control over your job (not complete control, but enough control to make you feel your opinion matters). When you are not given an opportunity to provide input, you will eventually lose interest in your job. When empowered, you have the confidence to do something to alter your circumstances. On the job, empowerment means that you can make decisions to benefit the organization and its customers.

If you want to gain empowerment in your life and work, here are a few tips: be assertive, ask for credit for yourself when it is due, propose ideas to your group and your supervisor, initiate projects without being asked, tie your personal goals to those of the organization, develop your leadership skills, plan to learn on a continuous basis, be informed, don't let others intimidate you, and don't complain about a bad situation. Instead, take action to improve it.

5. **Acquire political savvy.** Politics is an inevitable part of every organization in Canada, including your school. Politics has always been a part of the workplace and always will be. The trick is to learn to play the political game to your own advantage and to the advantage of others without causing harm to anyone else. Being political means getting along with others in order to move them toward accomplishing a specific goal. It does not mean manoeuvring for selfish purposes, manipulating in order to deceive, or scheming so others lose while you win.

Here are some tips and techniques to be an effective player in the political game:
- *Think about what you say.* Understand the effect your words will have on others before you say or write them.
- *Empathize.* Try to think of a situation from the other person's perspective.

- *Suggest a trial period, if you meet opposition to an idea you're proposing.* If you are as successful as you are confident, you can then ask to have the trial period extended.
- *Learn about the political climate in which you are working.* This means knowing, among other things, what actions have led to failure for others, knowing who is "in" and why, determining who is "out" and why, and learning what behaviours lead to promotion.
- *Volunteer to do the jobs no one else wants to do.* Occasionally pitching in shows your willingness to get the job done. However, do not make this your trademark; you do not want others to think they can take advantage of you.
- *Work hard to meet the needs of those in authority.* Make certain you fully understand management's requirements; then go out of your way to meet them. If in time you do not think you are getting the recognition or respect you deserve, make your own needs known.
- *Give credit.* You never know who may be in a position to hurt or harm you. Consequently, the best policy is to treat everyone with respect and dignity. Show your appreciation to everyone who has helped you. Do not steal credit that belongs to someone else.
- *Learn your supervisor's preferences.* The more you are in sync with your supervisor's style, wishes, and preferences, the better you can do your job. However, do not be a rubber stamp. Rather, work the way your manager works. When necessary, suggest better ways of doing things.
- *Keep secrets—your own and others'.* Resist the temptation to tell all. Not only do you run the risk of being labelled a gossip, if you share too much about yourself, your words can come back to haunt you. If you are revealing information told to you in confidence, you are bound to lose the trust and respect of those who originally confided in you.

Find out how well you play the political game by taking the quiz in Exhibit P.2.

6. **Become a team builder.** Throughout your education and business career you will participate on teams. Most Canadian organizations employ teamwork. An effective team is one that meets its goals on time and, if a budget is involved, within

---

Exhibit P.2   Fun Self-Test—Can You Play the Political Game?

Rate your level of agreement with the statements below using the following scale:

STRONGLY AGREE	AGREE	NEITHER AGREE NOR DISAGREE	DISAGREE	STRONGLY DISAGREE

1. To be successful, you should have a strong relationship with your boss and subordinates.
2. Office politics is not very challenging.
3. Tough people give you a tough time but also teach you tough lessons.
4. Networking and observation plays a major role in being good at office politics.
5. There are no ethics or morals in office politics.
6. Corporate politics is not about the individuals, it is about the survival of the corporation.
7. Office politics is the only way you gain real access to your boss's ear.
8. Those who avoid being political at work may not move forward in their careers, may find themselves resentful and frustrated, and run the risk of being isolated.
9. If you do all of the work on a project, you won't tell the boss because you don't want your coworkers to get in trouble.
10. When faced with gossip and rumours, you prefer to be silent but aware.
11. To master office politics, you should seek a win-lose situation.
12. If a person in authority is out to get rid of you, a good tactic would be to establish allies and position yourself for another job in the company.
13. If you have made any significant contribution to a project, you always make sure that others know about it which, in turn, adds to your reputation.[3]

See the scoring guidelines at the end of the prologue to obtain your score.

1. What are the goals? (What is the vision?)
2. Who provides the mission statement?
3. What are our limits?
4. Where will support come from? Who will be our sponsor, our champion?
5. Who will be team leader? How is he or she selected?
6. What are the deadlines we face?
7. What resources are available?
8. What data will we need to collect?
9. For how long will our team exist?
10. Who are the customers for our team results? What do they expect of us?
11. Will our team responsibilities conflict with our regular jobs?
12. What is the reward for success?
13. How will decisions be made?
14. How will our efforts be measured?
15. Will our intended success be replicated? If so, how and by whom?

budget. The first step in creating an effective team is to have goals that are clear, realistic, supported by each team member, and parallels the larger organization goals. Exhibit P.3 lists the questions that teams should answer to ensure their success.

7. **Handle conflict well.** The world is not a perfect place, and there are no perfect people inhabiting it. The best we can hope for is people's willingness to improve life's circumstances. Whenever there is more than one person, conflict is most likely to arise. Conflict should not be thought of as bad or good, but how we deal with it will make it so. Conflict, if not dealt with properly, can cause breakdowns in relationships (both professional and personal) and have negative outcomes. But if dealt with correctly, conflict can challenge us to look at different perspectives and make better decisions.

When conflicts occur, try the K-I-N-D technique. The letters stand for

K = Kind
I = Informed
N = New
D = Definite

The technique involves having a discussion with the others affected by the conflict—preferably collectively—regardless of whether they recognize that there is an issue or not. Start off with kind words, words that encourage cooperation, words that show your determination to make the situation better.

Next, demonstrate that you have taken the time to learn more about those involved, what is important to them, what they prefer in terms of work. Show by your words that you have taken the time to become informed about the others.

The third step requires you to do something novel, something you have not tried before. Put your creativity to work, and discover a plan to which all can subscribe (for example, keeping a journal regarding the issue and possible solutions).

Finally, do not permit the exchange to conclude until you have made a definite overture to ensure future success. What can you promise the others that you will do differently? What are you asking them to do differently? Set a time to meet again and review your individual attempts to achieve collective improvement.

MAKE YOUR FUTURE HAPPEN: LEARN TO PLAN[4]

There is a natural conflict between planning and being impulsive, between pursuing a long-range goal and doing what you feel like doing right now. If you have ever had to study while the rest of the family was in the living room watching television, you know what that conflict feels like. If you have ever been invited to go to the mall to eat pizza and hang out with friends but stayed home to work on a class assignment, you know that sticking to a plan is not easy.

Of course, planning and being impulsive are both good. Each has a place in your life; you need to balance them. Having a plan does not mean that you can't act on the spur of the moment and do something that was not planned. Spontaneous events produce some of the happiest, most meaningful times of your life. Problems arise only when you consistently substitute impulsive actions for goal-oriented planning. Success in life requires a balance between the two.

If you do not engage in long-range planning and lack the discipline for it, you might limit your opportunities to be impulsive. You are not going to take a weekend fun trip just because you need a break, if you haven't saved the money to do it. In the short run, planning involves sacrifice, but in the long run, it gives you more options.

What Is a Plan?

A plan is a method or process worked out in advance that leads to the achievement of some goal. A plan is systematic, which means it relies on using a step-by-step procedure. A plan also needs to be flexible, so that it can be adapted to gradual changes in your goal.

The Planning Process

Whether choosing a postsecondary institution or finding financial aid, you should understand how the planning process helps you accomplish your goals. The following steps outline the planning process.

Step 1: Set a goal. Identify something you want to achieve or obtain: your goal. The goal, which is usually longer term in nature, will require planning, patience, and discipline to achieve. Just living in the present moment is not a goal.

Step 2: Acquire knowledge. Gain an understanding of your goal and what will be required to achieve it. Gather information about your goal through research, conversation, and thought.

Step 3: Compare alternatives. Weigh your options, which are the different paths you might take to achieve your goal. Analyze the pluses and minuses of each—the costs, the demands, and the likelihood of success.

Step 4: Choose a strategy. Select one option as the best plan of action. The choice is based on sound information, the experience of others, and your own interests and abilities.

Step 5: Make a commitment. Resolve to proceed step-by-step toward achieving your goal. Keep your eyes on the prize.

Step 6: Stay flexible. Evaluate your progress and, when necessary, revise your plan to deal with changing circumstances and new opportunities.

An Example of Planning

The following example illustrates the process of buying a tablet using this planning process.

Step 1: Set a goal. To purchase a tablet.

Step 2: Acquire knowledge. Ask others about their experiences with tablets and the various models. Study standards and specifications. Check on dealers, brands, models, and prices. Consult various consumer reports.

Step 3: Compare alternatives.

Alternative 1: Purchase a used tablet online.
Pro: Affordable good quality. Can buy right now.
Con: Uncertain condition of equipment. Limited warranty.
Alternative 2: Buy a new, lower cost tablet.
Pro: Can afford now. New equipment with warranty.
Con: Unsuitable for adding extras. Not the best quality.
Alternative 3: Buy a high-quality, more expensive new tablet.
Pro: Excellent sound. Greatest flexibility. New equipment with warranty.
Con: Costs more than prepared to pay now.

Concept *in Action*

Life requires planning, and the more important your goals, the more important planning is to achieve those goals. Whether the objective is to graduate from a university or college, develop a professional career, or build a brighter future for one's family and community, personal success depends on a good plan. How can the six steps of the planning process help individuals achieve their educational, personal, and career dreams?

Step 4: Choose a strategy. Decide to buy the high-quality, more expensive tablet but, rather than use a credit card and paying interest, delay the purchase for six months to save for it.

Step 5: Make a commitment. Give up going to the movies for the six-month period, pack lunches and stop eating out, and place the savings in a tablet fund.

Step 6: Keep flexible. Four months into the plan, a model change sale provides an opportunity to buy a comparable tablet for less than was originally planned. Make the purchase, paying cash.

Planning for Your Life

Using the planning process to make a buying decision is a simple exercise. Making a decision about major parts of your life is far more complex. You will see that no part of life is exempt from the need for planning. It is important to apply thought, creativity, and discipline to all the interrelated phases of our lives. These phases include the following:

Career. Choosing a field of work and developing the knowledge and skills needed to enter and move ahead in that field. We will offer you some tips to get started on a great career later in the Prologue.

Self. Deciding who you are and what kind of person you want to be, working to develop your strengths and overcome your weaknesses, and refining your values.

Lifestyle. Expressing yourself in the nature and quality of your everyday life, your recreation and hobbies, and how you use your time and money.

Relationships. Developing friendships and learning to get along with people in a variety of contexts. Building family and community ties.

Finances. Building the financial resources and the economic security needed to pursue all the other dimensions of your life.

Dreams and Plans

People are natural dreamers. Dreams give us pleasure. They are also part of making a future. If you don't have dreams or think that you are not worthy of dreaming, something very important might be missing from your life. You have a right to your dreams, and you need them—even if there is little possibility that they will ever come true.

Planning is not the same as dreaming, but it uses dreams as raw materials. It translates them into specific goals. It tests them. It lays out a course of action that moves you toward realizing these goals and sets up milestones you need to achieve. Planning brings dreams down to earth and turns them into something real and attainable. For example, assume you have a dream to visit Spain as an exchange student. To translate this dream into a specific goal, you will need to follow the planning process—gather information about the exchange process, discuss the program with parents and teachers, and improve your Spanish-language skills.

Directions for Your Life

One of the best things about pursuing your dreams is that even when you fall short, the effort leads to growth and opens a path to other opportunities. The person who practises the piano every day might not achieve the dream of becoming a concert pianist but might eventually put appreciation of music to work as the director of an arts organization. A hockey player might not make it to a professional team but might enjoy a satisfying career as a coach or a sportswriter. Without a plan, dreams simply dissolve. With a plan, they give shape and direction to our lives.

Planning involves a lot of thinking and finding answers to lots of questions. The answers, and even the plan, will change over time as you gain more knowledge and life experience. Planning is a skill that is useful in every area of your life. It is something you have to pursue consciously and thoughtfully. When you plan, you translate your goals and dreams into step-by-step strategies, specific things you can do to test your goals and bring them to reality. You often have to revise your plans, but even when your plans are not fulfilled, planning will have a positive effect on the course of your life.

GOING TO A POSTSECONDARY INSTITUTION IS AN OPPORTUNITY OF A LIFETIME—GRAB IT, AND DON'T LET GO[5]

You have already had one of your dreams come true—you are in a postsecondary institution. It is, indeed, a rare privilege, because far less than one percent of traditional postsecondary-age people around the world get to attend a postsecondary institution. You're lucky! So make the best of it by learning the following skills:

Learn to Concentrate

Concentration is the art of being focused, the ability to pay attention. Without concentration, you have no memory of what you hear, see, and read. Concentration is a frame of mind that enables you to stay centred on the activity or work you are doing. You know when you're concentrating, because time seems to go by quickly, distractions that normally take you off task don't bother you, and you have a lot of mental or physical energy for the task.

You are ultimately in charge of how well you concentrate. Here are some ways to make it happen.

- *Choose a workplace.* Avoid the bed—you associate it with relaxing or sleeping. Try a desk or table for studying; you will concentrate better and accomplish more in less time. You will also have a convenient writing space and plenty of space to spread out. Be sure to have good lighting.
- *Feed your body right.* What you eat plays an important role in how well or how poorly you concentrate. Low-quality carbohydrates (such as pasta, bread, processed sugars, and most junk foods) make you sleepy.
- *Avoid eating while studying.* Food and serious learning don't mix well. Think about it. When you try to eat and study at the same time, which gets more of your concentration? The food, of course! You will be more effective if you eat first and then study.
- *Listen to your thoughts.* Listening to anything but your own thoughts interferes with good concentration. Eliminating distractions such as music, television, cellphones, e-mail notifications, and other people can greatly increase the amount of studying you can accomplish. Hold all calls, and let e-mail wait.
- *Make a to-do list.* If you are trying to study but get distracted by all of the things you need to do, take time to make a to-do list. Keeping track of your thoughts on paper and referring to the paper from time to time can be very effective for clearing your mind and focusing on your task.
- *Take short, frequent breaks.* Since people concentrate for about 20 minutes or less at a time, it would make sense to capitalize on your natural body rhythms and take a short break every 20 to 30 minutes. If you feel you are fully concentrating and involved in a task, then work until a natural break occurs.

Learn to Manage Your Time

There are two ways to make sure you have more time in a day. *The first and most important way to gain more time is to plan it!* It's like getting in a car and going somewhere. You need to know where you are going and have a plan to get there. Without a plan, you will waste your time and take longer to get to your destination—if you get there at all!

Rate your level of agreement with the following statements using the scale below:

STRONGLY AGREE	AGREE	NEITHER AGREE NOR DISAGREE	DISAGREE	STRONGLY DISAGREE

1. I rarely feel driven by the urgencies that come my way.
2. I keep a log of each activity to be performed in a day. I prioritize them accordingly.
3. I prioritize not by the importance of the work but by its nature.
4. I can manage my schedule without preparing a weekly plan that includes specific activities.
5. I always want to do all the work myself, thinking I can do it better than anyone else.
6. I plan my weekends with my family and friends.
7. I can delegate work to people so that the work gets done on time and the people feel they are a part of the team.
8. I allow time for the unexpected things I cannot control.
9. If something doesn't happen as per my schedule, it doesn't get done.
10. To accomplish a set of objectives doesn't mean to avoid other unexpected problems.
11. I seldom work after office hours.
12. I would never work by hand if a machine could do it faster.
13. I feel it is easier and time-saving to try new ways of doing things.
14. I always find time to do what I want to do and what I should do.[6]

See the scoring guidelines at the end of the prologue to obtain your score.

A **weekly project planner** will allow you to keep track of your assignments in more detail. It contains a to-do list specific to one day. It looks like a calendar but is divided into five one-day periods with plenty of space to write. Using a weekly project planner is an effective way of keeping track of assignments and planning study time according to the school calendar.

A second way to gain more time in a day is to do more in less time. This can be as simple as doubling-up on activities. For example, if you have three errands, you might try to combine them instead of doing one at a time, making one round-trip instead of three. If you commute on a bus or train, or carpool, you can study during your ride. At lunch, you can review notes. Use your imagination as to how you can get more done in less time.

Here are some ideas to help you master your time.

- *Prepare for the morning the evening before.* Put out your clothes, make lunch, and pack your books.
- *Get up 15 minutes earlier in the morning.* Use the time to plan your day, review your assignments, or catch up on the news.
- *Schedule a realistic day.* Avoid planning for every minute. Leave extra time in your day for getting to appointments and studying.
- *Leave room in your day for the unexpected.* This will allow you to do what you need to do, regardless of what happens. If the unexpected never happens, you will have more time for yourself.
- *Do one thing at a time.* If you try to do two things at once, you become inefficient. Concentrate on the here and now.
- *Learn to say "No."* Say no to social activities or invitations when you don't have the time or energy.

Use Your Money Wisely

You can get postsecondary money from three different sources.

- *Grants and scholarships.* This refers to aid you do not have to repay. Grants are usually based on need, whereas scholarships are frequently based on academic merit and other qualifying factors.

- *Student loans.* The mission of the Canada Student Loans Program (CSLP) is to promote accessibility to postsecondary education for students with a demonstrated financial need by lowering financial barriers through the provision of loans and grants, and to ensure that Canadians have an opportunity to develop the knowledge and skills to participate in the economy and society.
- *Working.* Working, whether on or off campus, will bring in some money that you can use. Not only will you make money, but you can gain more experience as well.

There are many ways to cut the cost of going to a postsecondary institution. Consider the following:

- going to a community college for the first two years and then transferring to a four-year institution;
- attending a nearby postsecondary institution and living at home;
- enrolling in one of the postsecondary institutions that offer cooperative educational programs that alternate between full-time studies and full-time employment; or
- taking a full-time job at a company that offers free educational opportunities as a fringe benefit.

Check with your postsecondary institution for the various sources of financial aid that are available to you.

Gain some insight into your money management skills by taking the quiz in Exhibit P.5.

Study Smart

The first key to doing well in a subject is completing your assignments on time. Most instructors base their assignments on what they will be discussing in class on a given day. Therefore, if you read the pages you are assigned for the day they are due, you will understand the day's lecture better. If you don't complete an assignment when it is due, not only will you be at a disadvantage in the class, you will also have twice as much work to do for the following class.

Second, know what material to study. This might sound simple, but all too often, students don't ask what material they should study and find out too late that they studied the wrong information. The easiest and most accurate way to learn what will be covered on a test is to ask your instructor or read the syllabus.

Exhibit P.5 Fun Self-Test—Are You Good at Managing Money?

Rate your level of agreement with the following statements, using the scale below:

STRONGLY AGREE	AGREE	NEITHER AGREE NOR DISAGREE	DISAGREE	STRONGLY DISAGREE

1. I eagerly wait for the day I get my paycheque, because my bank balance is generally below the minimum.
2. I have set my savings and spending priorities and have a budget.
3. When I go shopping, I don't buy anything unless it is on sale or is required.
4. I can easily spend money when I am in school.
5. I can differentiate between what I want and what I truly need.
6. I always max out my credit cards.
7. I don't need to plan for my child's education because there will be plenty of government programs.
8. I don't have or plan to open a savings account.
9. I was raised in a family where I always felt that money was quite tight.
10. Credit cards have been useful to me during times of emergency.
11. It is easy for me to resist buying on credit.[7]

See the scoring guidelines at the end of the prologue to obtain your score.

If you are studying alone, choose a study location that is free from distractions, so you can concentrate better and accomplish more in less time. If you are involved in a study group, make sure that the location is appropriate for group interaction. How do you think study groups can be used to enhance your learning?

ANDRESR/SHUTTERSTOCK

Tests measure your working memory and knowledge base. To help yourself remember, you can use several **memory devices** to recall the information you need to study. Here are a few that have been proven to work:

- *Recite information using your own words.* You will learn more when you reinforce your learning in as many ways as possible. You can reinforce your learning through hearing, writing, reading, reviewing, and reciting.
- *Develop acronyms.* **Acronyms** are words or names formed from the first letters or groups of letters in a phrase. Acronyms help you remember, because they organize information according to the way you need or want to learn it. When you study for a test, be creative and make up your own acronyms. For example, COD means "cash on delivery," and GDP refers to "gross domestic product."
- *Try mnemonic sentences, rhymes, or jingles.* **Mnemonic sentences** are similar to acronyms; they help you organize your ideas, but instead of creating a word, you make up a sentence. Creating a rhyme, song, or jingle can make the information even easier to remember. The more creative and silly the sentence, the easier it is to remember. For example, if you are learning to read sheet music, the notes on the lines of the treble clef are EGBDF—you could remember this as Every Good Boy Deserves Fudge.
- *Visualize.* Visualization refers to creating or recalling mental pictures related to what you are learning. Have you ever tried to remember something while taking a test and visualized the page the information was on? This is your visual memory at work. Approximately 90 percent of your memory is stored visually in pictures, so visualizing what you want to remember is a powerful study tool.

Study Groups

Using study groups can increase your marks considerably. It is one of the most effective ways for preparing for classes and exams by reinforcing concepts. It is an easy approach that gives immediate feedback regarding your individual study habits. Study groups are most effective with a small group—four to six people.

Answer "yes" or "no" to the following questions:

1. Do you usually spend too much time studying for the amount that you are learning?
2. Do you spend hours cramming the night before an exam?
3. Do you find it easy to balance your social life with your study schedule?
4. Do you prefer to study with sound (TV or radio) around you?
5. Can you study for several hours without getting distracted (although taking short breaks)?
6. Do you always borrow notes/materials from your friends before the exam?
7. Do you review your class notes periodically throughout the semester while preparing for the tests?
8. Is it easy for you to recall what you studied at the beginning of the semester?
9. Do you need to change your reading/learning style in response to the difficulty level of the course?
10. Do you normally write your papers or prepare for your presentations the night before they are due?
11. Do you feel comfortable contacting the instructor and asking questions or for help whenever you need it?
12. Do you prefer to study lying on a bed or couch rather than at a desk or table?[8]

See the scoring guidelines at the end of the prologue to obtain your score.

Study groups benefit all the group members because, as you share ideas, you are forced to think out loud. Each of us has our own particular individual study habits. Study groups provide a support system that allows the group to cover more material, especially when the material is difficult. With four or more people working on the same problem, talent can be shared and synergy created.

Study sessions should not exceed two to three hours. Each group member must come prepared, preparing the readings prior to the meeting. Participation by all is very important for the study group to maximize the benefits. With groups, especially smaller ones, getting off-track is easy; the group must stay focused.

The study group starts with individual studying: preparation for the group meeting. If the group is working on difficult problems, the group members share their ideas, out loud, with the other group members until the solution is found. If the group is preparing for class discussions or an exam, group members should take turns asking questions. Individual group members are asked to answer the questions until someone gives the correct response. If none of the group members can answer the question, the person who asked the question reads the answer from the book. Exhibit P.6 helps you evaluate your study skills.

Become a Master at Taking Tests

Taking a formal test is like playing a game. The object is to get as many points as possible in the time that you are allowed. Tests are evaluations of what you know and what you can do with what you know. Here are the rules of the test-taking game:

Rule 1: Act as if you will succeed. Thought is powerful. When you think negative thoughts, your stress level rises. Your confidence level might drop, which often leads to feelings of failure. When this happens, think about success. Smile and take deep, slow breaths. Close your eyes, and imagine getting the test back with a good grade written at the top.

Rule 2: Arrive ahead of time. Being on time or early for a test sets your mind at ease. You will have a better chance of getting your favourite seat, relaxing, and preparing yourself mentally for the game ahead.

Rule 3: Bring the essential testing tools. Don't forget to bring the necessary testing tools along with you, including extra pens, sharpened pencils, erasers, a calculator, a dictionary, and other items you might need.

Rule 4: Ignore panic pushers. Some people become nervous before a test and hit the panic button, afraid they don't know the material. **Panic pushers** are people who ask you questions about the material they are about to be tested on. If you know the answers, you will feel confident; however, if you don't, you might panic and lose your confidence. Instead of talking with a panic pusher before a test, spend your time concentrating on what you know, not on what you don't know.

Rule 5: Preview the playing field. Here's how to do a preview:

- Listen to instructions, **and** read directions carefully.
- Determine the point spread. Look at the total number of questions and the point value of each. Decide how much time you can spend on each question and still finish the test on time.
- Budget your time. If you budget your time and stick to your time limits, you will always complete the test in the amount of time given.
- Use the test as an information tool. Be on the lookout for clues that answer other questions. Frequently, instructors will test you on a single topic in more than one way.

Rule 6: Write in the margin. Before you begin the test, write key terms, formulas, names, dates, and other information in the margin, so you don't forget them.

Rule 7: Complete the easy questions first. Answering easy questions first helps build your confidence. If you come across a tough question, mark it so you can come back to it later. Avoid spending so much time on a challenging question that you run out of time to answer the questions you do know.

Rule 8: Know if there is a guessing penalty. Chances are your tests will carry no penalty for guessing. If your time is about to run out and there is no penalty, take a wild guess. On the other hand, if your test carries a penalty for guessing, choose your answers wisely, and leave blank the answers you do not know.

Rule 9: Avoid changing your answers. Have you ever chosen an answer, changed it, and learned later that your first choice was correct? Research indicates that three out of four times, your first answer will be correct; therefore, you should avoid changing an answer unless you are absolutely sure the answer is wrong.

Rule 10: Write clearly and neatly. If you are handwriting your test (versus using a computer), imagine your instructor reading your writing. Is it easy to read or difficult? The easier your test is for the instructor to read, the better your chances of getting a higher grade.

GETTING YOUR CAREER OFF ON THE RIGHT TRACK

Mark this section of the text with a permanent bookmark, because you are going to want to refer back to it many times during the remainder of your postsecondary institution career. Yes, we are going to give you a roadmap to find, keep, and advance in that job that is perfect for you.

Think Positively

To be successful in life and in a career, you need to be positive. Positive thinking is making a conscious effort to think with an optimistic attitude and to anticipate positive outcomes. *Positive behaviour* means purposely acting with energy and enthusiasm. When you think and behave positively, you guide your mind toward your goals and generate matching mental and physical energy.

Positive thinking and behaviour are often deciding factors in landing top jobs: your first job, a promotion, a change of jobs—whatever career step you are targeting. That's because the subconscious is literal; it accepts what you regard as fact.

Follow these steps to form a habit of positive thinking and to boost your success:

1. *Deliberately motivate yourself every day.* Think of yourself as successful, and expect positive outcomes for everything you attempt.
2. *Project energy and enthusiasm.* Employers hire people who project positive energy and enthusiasm. Develop the habit of speaking, moving, and acting with these qualities.
3. *Practise this positive expectation mind-set until it becomes a habit.* Applicants who project enthusiasm and positive behaviour generate a positive chemistry that rubs off. Hiring decisions are influenced largely by this positive energy. The habit will help you reach your peak potential.
4. *Dwell on past successes.* Focusing on past successes to remind yourself of your abilities helps in attaining goals. For example, no one is born knowing how to ride a bicycle or how to use a computer software program. Through training, practice, and trial and error, you master new abilities. During the trial-and-error phases of development, remind yourself of past successes; look at mistakes as part of the natural learning curve. Continue until you achieve the result you want, and remind yourself that you have succeeded in the past and can do so again. You fail only when you quit trying![9]

Take a Good Look at Yourself

Once you've developed a positive, "can do" attitude, the next step is to understand yourself better. Ask yourself two basic questions: "Who am I?" and "What can I do?"

Who Am I? The first step is to ask "Who am I?" This question is the start of *self-assessment*, examining your likes and dislikes and basic values. You might want to ask yourself the following questions:

- Do I want to help society?
- Do I want to help make the world a better place?
- Do I want to help other people directly?
- Is it important for me to be seen as part of a big corporation?
- Do I prefer working indoors or outdoors?
- Do I like to meet new people, or do I want to work alone?

Are you assertive? Assess your assertiveness by taking the quiz in Exhibit P.7.

What Can I Do? After determining what your values are, take the second step in career planning by asking, "What can I do?" This question is the start of *skill assessment*, evaluating your key abilities and characteristics for dealing successfully with problems, tasks, and interactions with other people. Many skills—for instance, the ability to speak clearly and strongly—are valuable in many occupations.

Be sure to consider the work experience you already have, including part-time jobs while going to school, summer jobs, volunteer jobs, and internships (short-term jobs for students, related to their major field of study). These jobs teach you skills and make you more attractive to potential employers. It's never too early or too late to take a part-time job in your chosen field. For instance, someone with an interest in accounting would do well to try a part-time job with an accounting firm.

In addition to examining your job-related skills, you should also look at your leisure activities. Some possible questions: Am I good at golf? Do I enjoy sailing? Tennis? Racquetball? In some businesses, transactions are made during leisure hours. In that case, being able to play a skilful, or at least adequate, game of golf or tennis might be an asset.

Concept *in Action*

Part-time jobs can teach you valuable business skills that will make you more attractive to employers. Choose a job, if possible, that gives you experience related to your chosen field. What advantages do you think those with work experience have over those who have no work experience?

ACESTOCK/GETSTOCK

Rate your level of agreement with the following statements, using the scale below:

STRONGLY AGREE	AGREE	NEITHER AGREE NOR DISAGREE	DISAGREE	STRONGLY DISAGREE

1. I don't easily agree to work for others.
2. There are some people who make jokes about the way I communicate and put me down repeatedly.
3. I speak up without fear of what others will think of me.
4. I rarely have to repeat my thoughts to make people understand.
5. I sound like I am asking a question, when I am making a statement.
6. I'm more reluctant to speak up on the job than in other situations.
7. I can always think of something to say when faced with rude remarks.
8. I tend to suffer in silence when unfairly criticized or insulted.
9. I tend to respond aggressively when criticized unfairly.
10. People don't listen when I am speaking.
11. If I say "no," I feel guilty.
12. When I have a conflict with someone, the results seem to always go their way.
13. When I speak, people listen.[10]

See the scoring guidelines at the end of the prologue to obtain your score.

It's hard to like your job if you don't like the field that you're in. Most career counsellors agree that finding work you're passionate about is one of the critical factors behind career success. That's why so many career counsellors love all those diagnostic tools that measure your personality traits, skill levels, professional interests, and job potential.

Understand What Employers Want[11]

Employers want to hire people who will make their businesses more successful. The most desirable employees have the specific skills, transferable career competencies, work values, and personal qualities necessary to be successful in the employers' organizations. The more clearly you convey your skills as they relate to your job target, the greater your chance of landing your ideal job.

Job-specific skills. Employers seek job-specific skills (skills and technical abilities that relate specifically to a particular job). Two examples of job-specific skills are using specialized tools and equipment and using a custom-designed software program.

Transferable skills and attitudes. Change is a constant in today's business world. Strong transferable career skills are the keys to success in managing your career through change. The most influential skills and attitudes are the abilities to

- work well with people;
- plan and manage multiple tasks;
- maintain a positive attitude; and
- show enthusiasm.

Employers need workers who have transferable career competencies—basic skills and attitudes that are important for all types of work. These skills make you highly marketable, because they're needed for a wide variety of jobs and can be transferred from one task, job, or workplace to another. Examples include

- planning skills;
- research skills;
- communication skills;
- human relations and interpersonal skills;
- critical thinking skills; and
- management skills.

Take, for example, a construction supervisor and an accountant. Both must work well with others, manage time, solve problems, read, and communicate effectively—all transferable competencies. They both must be competent in these areas, even though framing a house and balancing a set of books (the job-specific skill for each field, respectively) are not related. In every occupation, transferable competencies are as important as technical expertise and job-specific skills.

Finding My First Professional Job

The next step is landing the job that fits your skills and desires. You need to consider not only a general type of work but also your lifestyle and leisure goals. If you like to be outdoors most of the time, you might be very unhappy spending eight hours a day in an office. Someone who likes living in small towns might dislike working at the headquarters of a big corporation in Toronto, Calgary, or Vancouver. But make sure that your geographic preferences are realistic. Some parts of the country will experience much greater growth in jobs than others.

You might start answering the question "What will I do?" by searching various Internet sites that offer job counselling or job offers.

Using the Internet to Jump-Start Your Job Search

You must start with a great résumé—a written description of your education, work experience, personal data, and interests. Professional Web résumé software (available through www.webresume.com) can make the task a lot easier. WebResume software not only helps you format your résumé but also lets you control who sees it. A "confidential" option enables you to create a two-tiered résumé. The first tier offers professional information but doesn't include your name or address. The second contains contact information but is password protected—and you decide who gets the password. WebResume understands what's different about looking for a job online. Its "Search Engine Keywords" function inserts the "tags" that major search engines use to index résumés.

Once you have created a great résumé, the next step is to get it noticed. Here are seven tips for building résumé traffic.

- Post a digital version of your résumé, with examples of past work experience, on your own home page. Many postsecondary institutions and professional associations offer free or low-cost Web space and resources for posting résumés.
- Place the word *résumé* in the website address to increase your chances of being caught by Internet recruiters.
- Place plenty of links to websites of present and former employers, postsecondary institutions, professional associations, and publications on your digital résumé.
- Create a simpler version of your résumé to send to a recruiter or potential employer, and let them know a longer version is available.
- Read the privacy policies of online job boards to prevent unwanted eyes from viewing your résumé. Some companies have "Web scavengers" who check for their own employees' résumés online. In turn, some job boards let users "block" certain companies from seeing their postings.
- Use niche job boards in your field. Smaller, targeted boards can sometimes be more effective than the big brand-name sites.[12]

There are thousands of places to send your résumé. Don't neglect using the Internet; 83 percent of corporate recruiters use the Internet to advertise their jobs.[13]

Oh My Gosh—I've Got a Job Interview

If some of the companies you contacted want to speak with you, your résumé achieved its goal of getting you a job interview. Look at the interview as a chance to describe your knowledge and skills and interpret them in terms of the employer's specific needs.

- Use key words to define your skills, experience, education, professional affiliations, and so on.
- Use concrete words rather than vague descriptions to describe your experience. For example, use "managed a team of software engineers" rather than "responsible for managing and training."
- Be concise and truthful.
- Use jargon and acronyms specific to your industry (spell out the acronyms for a human reader).
- Increase your list of key words by including specifics. For example, list the names of software that you use, such as Microsoft Word.
- Use common headings, such as Objective, Experience, Work History, Skills, Education, Professional Affiliations, Licenses, and References.
- Describe your interpersonal traits and attitude. Key words can include *dependable, high energy, leadership, sense of responsibility,* and *good memory.*

SOURCE: "Resume Tool Kit," http://www. thespectrum.com, accessed January 2003.

Concept *in Action*

iSTOCKPHOTO/THINKSTOCK

For today's grads, preparation for a job interview should include taking time out to Google oneself. The Internet is an easy way for recruiters to learn about prospective employees, and what job candidates post on blogs or on social networking sites could convey an undesirable impression. Do a thorough search on popular search engines to make sure the Web is free of unflattering self-revelations. What can employers learn about you online?

To make this kind of presentation, you need to do some research on the company. There are many electronic databases and sources that provide company information. Ask your librarians for assistance to access company profiles and information.

As you do your information search, you should build your knowledge in these three areas.

1. *General information about the industry.* Learn about the current and predicted industry trends, general educational requirements, job descriptions, growth outlook, and salary ranges in the industry.
2. *Information about prospective employers.* Learn whether the organization is publicly or privately owned. Verify company names, addresses, products or services (current and predicted, as well as trends); history; culture; reputation; performance; divisions and subsidiaries; locations (Canada and global); predicted growth indicators; number of employees; company philosophies and procedures; predicted job openings; salary ranges; and listings of managers of your targeted department within the organization. Also learn about competitors and customers.
3. *Information about specific jobs.* Obtain job descriptions; identify the required education and experience; and determine prevalent working conditions, salary, and fringe benefits.[14]

Interview Like a Pro

An interview tends to have three parts: icebreaking (about five minutes), in which the interviewer tries to put the applicant at ease; questioning (directly or indirectly) by the interviewer; and questioning by the applicant. Almost every recruiter you meet will be trying to rate you in 5 to 10 areas. The questions will be designed to assess your skills and personality.

Many companies start with a *screening interview,* a rather short interview (about 30 minutes) to decide whether to invite you back for a second interview. Only about 20 percent of job applicants are invited back. The second interview is a half day or a day of meetings set up by the human resource department with managers in different departments. After the meetings, someone from the human resource department will discuss other application materials with you and tell you when a letter of acceptance or rejection is likely to be sent. (The wait might be weeks or even months.) Many applicants send follow-up letters in the meantime to show they are still interested in the company.

For the interview, you should dress conservatively. Plan to arrive about 10 to 15 minutes ahead of time. Try to relax. Smile and make eye contact with (but do not stare at) the interviewer. Body language is an important communicator. The placement of your hands and feet and your overall posture say a good deal about you. Here are some other tips for interviewing like a pro.

1. *Concentrate on being likable.* As simplistic as it seems, research proves that one of the most essential goals in successful interviewing is to be liked by the interviewer. Interviewers want to hire pleasant people that others will like working with on a daily basis. Pay attention to the following areas to project that you are highly likable:

   - Be friendly, courteous, and enthusiastic.
   - Speak positively.
   - Smile.
   - Use positive body language.
   - Make certain your appearance is appropriate.

2. *Project an air of confidence and pride.* Act as though you want and deserve the job, not as though you are desperate.

3. *Demonstrate enthusiasm.* The applicant's level of enthusiasm often influences employers as much as any other interviewing factor. The applicant who demonstrates little enthusiasm for a job will never be selected for the position.

4. *Demonstrate knowledge of and interest in the employer.* "I really want this job" is not convincing enough. Explain why you want the position and how the position fits your career plans. You can cite opportunities that might be unique to a company or emphasize your skills and education that are highly relevant to the position.

5. *State your name and the position you're seeking.* When you enter the interviewer's office, begin with a friendly greeting, and state the position you're interviewing for: "Hello, Ms. Levine, I'm Bella Reyna. I'm here to interview for the accounting position." If someone has already introduced you to the interviewer, simply say, "Good morning, Ms. Levine." Identifying the position is important, because interviewers often interview for many different positions.

6. *Focus on how you fit the job.* Near the beginning of your interview, as soon as it seems appropriate, ask a question similar to this: "Could you describe the scope of the job and tell me what capabilities are most important in filling the position?" The interviewer's response will help you focus on emphasizing your qualifications that best match the needs of the employer.

7. *Speak correctly.* Grammatical errors can cost applicants the job. Use correct grammar, word choice, and a businesslike vocabulary, not an informal, chatty one. Avoid slang. When under stress, people often use pet phrases (such as *you know*) too often. This is highly annoying and projects immaturity and insecurity. Don't use *just* or *only*. "I just worked as a waiter." Don't say "I guess." Avoid the word *probably*, because it suggests unnecessary doubt. Ask a friend or family member to help you identify any speech weaknesses you have. Begin eliminating these speech habits now.[15]

In addition, you should avoid these "disqualifiers" at all costs. Any one of these blunders could cost you your dream job:

1. Don't sit down until the interviewer invites you to; waiting is courteous.
2. Don't bring anyone else to the interview; it makes you look immature and insecure.
3. Don't put anything on or read anything on the interviewer's desk; it's considered an invasion of personal space.
4. Don't chew gum or have anything else in your mouth; this projects immaturity.
5. If you are invited to a business meal, don't order alcohol. When ordering, choose food that's easy to eat while carrying on a conversation.
6. Don't offer a limp handshake; it projects weakness. Use a firm handshake.[16]

Selecting the Right Job for You

Hard work and a little luck can pay off with multiple job offers. Your happy dilemma is deciding which one is best for you. Start by considering the FACTS:

- *Fit.* Do the job and the employer fit your skills, interests, and lifestyle?
- *Advancement and growth.* Will you have the chance to develop your talents and move up within the organization?
- *Compensation.* Is the employer offering a competitive salary and benefits package?
- *Training.* Will the employer provide you with the tools needed to be successful on the job?
- *Site.* Is the job location a good match for your lifestyle and your pocketbook?

A great way to evaluate a new location is through HOMEFAIR, www.homefair.com. This site offers tools to help you calculate the cost of moving, the cost of living, and the quality of life in various places in Canada and the United States. The Moving Calculator helps you figure out how much it will cost to ship your worldly possessions to a particular city. The Relocation Crime Lab compares crime rates in various locations. The City Snapshots feature compares demographic, economic, and climate information for two cities of your choosing. The Salary Calculator computes cost-of-living differences between hundreds of Canadian and international cities and tells you how much you'd need to make in your new city to maintain your current standard of living.

Starting Your New Job

No time is more crucial, and possibly nerve-racking, than the first few months at a new job. During this breaking-in period, the employer decides whether a new employee is valuable enough to keep and, if so, in what capacity. Sometimes the employee's whole future with the company rides on the efforts of the first few weeks or months.

Most companies offer some sort of formal orientation, but generally speaking, they expect employees to learn quickly—and often on their own. You will be expected to become familiar with the company's goals; its organization, including your place in the company; and basic personnel policies, such as coffee breaks, overtime, and parking.

Here are a few tips on making your first job rewarding and productive.

LISTEN AND LEARN When you first walk into your new job, let your eyes and ears take everything in. Do people refer to one another by first names, or is the company more formal? How do people dress? Do the people you work with drop into one

---

Exhibit P.9 Fun Self-Test—Are You a Good Listener?

Rate your level of agreement with the statements below using the following scale:

STRONGLY AGREE	AGREE	NEITHER AGREE NOR DISAGREE	DISAGREE	STRONGLY DISAGREE

1. A person who takes time to ask for clarification about something that might be unclear is not a good listener.
2. While listening, I am distracted by the sounds around me.
3. I try to understand not only what is being said, but also analyze the strength of any ideas that are being presented.
4. I ask questions, make observations, or give opinions when necessary for clarifications.
5. While I am listening, I avoid eye contact but am polite.
6. I am tempted to judge a person whether or not he or she is a good speaker.
7. I feel more comfortable when someone talks to me about a topic that I find interesting.
8. I always jot down key phrases/points that strike me as important points of concern that require a response.
9. My listening style varies depending on the speaker's style of communication.
10. A good listener requires a good speaker.

See the scoring guidelines at the end of the prologue to obtain your score.

another's open offices for informal chats about business matters? Or have you entered a "memo mill," where anything of substance is put on e-mail and talks with other employees are scheduled through secretaries? Size up where the power lies. Who seems to assume a leadership role most often? Who is the person others turn to for advice? Why has that person achieved that position? What traits have made this person a "political leader"? Don't be misled by what others say, but also don't dismiss their evaluations. Make your own judgments based on what you see and hear.

Take the quiz in Exhibit P.9 to see if you are a good listener.

DO UNTO OTHERS Be nice. Nice people are usually the last to be fired and among the first to be promoted. Don't be pleasant only with those who can help you in the company. Be nice to everyone. You never know who can help you or give you information that will turn out to be useful. Genuinely nice people make routine job assignments, and especially pressure-filled ones, more pleasant. And people who are dealt with pleasantly usually respond in kind.

DON'T START OUT AS A MAVERICK If every new employee tried to change tried-and-true methods to suit his or her whims, the company would quickly be in chaos. Individual needs must take a back seat to established procedures. Devote yourself to getting things done within the system. Every manager realizes that it takes time for a new person to adjust. But the faster you start accomplishing things, the faster the boss will decide that you were the right person to hire.

FIND A GREAT MENTOR The leading cause of career unhappiness is working for a bad boss. Good jobs can easily be ruined by supervisors who hold you back. In contrast, your career will soar (and you will smile every day) when you have a great mentor helping you along the way. If you find a job with a super mentor, jump at the chance to take it.

Movin' On Up

Once you have been on the job for a while, you will want to get ahead and be promoted. We offer several suggestions for improving your chances of promotion. The first item might seem a bit strange, yet it's there for a practical reason. If you don't really like what you do, you won't be committed enough to compete with those who do. The passionate people are the ones who go the extra mile, do the extra work, and come up with fresh outside-the-box ideas.

So there you have it! In the following chapter, we will begin our journey through the world of business so that you can determine what areas are most interesting to you. Remember, it's never too early to begin planning your career—the future is now.

Concept in Action

Finding a mentor can be especially helpful when starting a new career. Whether assigned through a corporate mentorship program or sought out on one's own, mentors have inside access to the company and can help protégés learn the ropes. A good mentor is a seasoned veteran who offers insight and advice, boosts morale, and makes networking contacts—while steering mentees away from pitfalls. What lessons can a mentor pass on that aren't necessarily taught in school but are essential to career success?

Exhibit P.10 How to Move Up

- Love what you do, which entails first figuring out who you are.
- Never stop learning about new technologies and new management skills.
- Try to get international experience, even if it is only a short stint overseas.
- Create new business opportunities—they could lead to a promotion.
- Be really outstandingly terrific at what you're doing now, this week, this month.

scoring guidelines

After you answer the questions in each of the fun self-tests that appear in the "Prologue: A Guide to Your Future Success in Business," determine your score and evaluate your skills using the following scoring guidelines.

EXHIBIT P.1 FUN SELF-TEST: CAN YOU PERSUADE OTHERS?

For questions 1, 2, 4, 8, 10 and 11, use the following to calculate your score:

STRONGLY AGREE	AGREE	NEITHER AGREE NOR DISAGREE	DISAGREE	STRONGLY DISAGREE
2 points	1 point	0 points	0 points	0 points

For questions 3, 5, 6, 7, and 9 use the following to calculate your score:

STRONGLY AGREE	AGREE	NEITHER AGREE NOR DISAGREE	DISAGREE	STRONGLY DISAGREE
0 points	0 point	0 points	4 points	5 points

If your score is between 40–55, you have an excellent ability to persuade others. A score between 30–39 means you have reasonably good persuasion skills. However, you may need to improve your listening and communicating skills. A score below 30 means that you should consider reading a book or taking a short course on "how to persuade others."

EXHIBIT P.2 FUN SELF-TEST: CAN YOU PLAY THE POLITICAL GAME?

For questions 1, 3, 4, 7, 8, 10, 12 and 13, give yourself 1 point if you said "true." For questions 2, 5, 6, 9 and 11, give yourself 1 point if you said "false." If your score is 9 or below, you may be good at managing your work, but you need to improve your political skills. Being political means getting along with others in order to move them toward accomplishing a specific goal. If your score is low, consider reviewing the tips offered in the Prologue on how to be an effective political player.

EXHIBIT P.4 FUN SELF-TEST: HOW WELL DO YOU MANAGE YOUR TIME?

For questions 2, 6, 8, 9, 11, 13, 14 and 15, use the following to calculate your score:

STRONGLY DISAGREE	DISAGREE	NEITHER DISAGREE NOR AGREE	AGREE	STRONGLY AGREE
0 points	0 point	0 points	4 points	5 points

For questions 1, 3, 4, 5, 7, 10 and 12, use the following to calculate your score:

STRONGLY DISAGREE	DISAGREE	NEITHER DISAGREE NOR AGREE	AGREE	STRONGLY AGREE
5 points	4 points	0 points	0 points	0 points

If your score is 60 or above, you have excellent time management skills. Congratulations—you use your time well! If your score is below 60, consider reading a book on time management, taking a course on time management, or investing in time management tools such as a weekly project planner. The Prologue has additional tips that may be useful in improving your time management skills.

EXHIBIT P.5 FUN SELF-TEST: ARE YOU GOOD AT MANAGING MONEY?

For questions 2, 3, 5, 6, 10 and 11, use the following to calculate your score:

STRONGLY DISAGREE	DISAGREE	NEITHER AGREE NOR DISAGREE	AGREE	STRONGLY AGREE
0 points	0 points	0 points	4 points	5 points

For questions 1, 4, 7, 8 and 9, use the following to calculate your score:

STRONGLY DISAGREE	DISAGREE	NEITHER AGREE NOR DISAGREE	AGREE	STRONGLY AGREE
5 points	4 points	0 points	0 points	0 points

If your score is 44 or higher, you are able to manage money while balancing your expenses and income. You will be ready to handle financial emergencies without turning to friends or relatives. If your score is 36–43, your savings habits may be inconsistent. To achieve better savings, control your expenses and avoid unnecessary purchases. If your score is 35 or below, you spend too much! Remember it's a lot more painful to earn money than to spend it. You need to gain control of your finances by limiting your spending, paying off credit cards, or investing in a good personal finance book or course. You may also need to meet with a financial advisor to seek direction on your spending and saving habits.

EXHIBIT P.6 FUN SELF-TEST: DO YOU HAVE GOOD STUDY HABITS?

If you answered "yes" to questions 3, 5, 7, 8 and 11, give yourself 1 point for each correct answer.

If you answered "no" to questions 1, 2, 4, 6, 9, 10 and 12, give yourself 1 point for each correct answer.

If your score is 10 or above, congratulations! You have good study habits. If your score is below 10, read the tips offered in the Prologue on improving your study skills. You may also meet with someone at your school to help maximize your study time.

EXHIBIT P.7 FUN SELF-TEST: HOW ASSERTIVE ARE YOU?

For questions 1, 3, 4, 7, 9 and 13, use the following to calculate your score:

STRONGLY AGREE	AGREE	NEITHER AGREE NOR DISAGREE	DISAGREE	STRONGLY DISAGREE
5 points	4 points	0 points	0 points	0 points

For questions 2, 5, 6, 8, 10, 11 and 12, use the following to calculate your score:

STRONGLY AGREE	AGREE	NEITHER AGREE NOR DISAGREE	DISAGREE	STRONGLY DISAGREE
0 points	0 points	0 points	4 points	5 points

If your score is 44 or higher, you stand up for your rights while showing respect for others. You quickly respond to unfair criticism. You should be able to fare well in office politics. If your score is 43 or lower, you may want to consider ways to become more comfortable communicating your ideas and opinions and managing your relationships with others.

EXHIBIT P.9 FUN SELF-TEST: ARE YOU A GOOD LISTENER?

For questions 3, 4, 8 and 9, use the following to calculate your score:

STRONGLY AGREE	AGREE	NEITHER AGREE NOR DISAGREE	DISAGREE	STRONGLY DISAGREE
5 points	4 points	0 points	0 points	0 points

For questions 1, 2, 5, 6, 7 and 10, use the following to calculate your score:

STRONGLY AGREE	AGREE	NEITHER AGREE NOR DISAGREE	DISAGREE	STRONGLY DISAGREE
0 points	0 points	0 points	4 points	5 points

Part 1

The Business Environment

introduction

This text on business is important whether you are working in a business today or hope to work in one in the future. Even if your major is in the arts or sciences, you will likely work in an organization that is considered to be a business or run on business principles. Profit or not-for-profit, the same principles apply. The only difference with a not-for-profit organization is that it is operated to sustain itself rather than to make a profit.

I'm going to assume that you want to be as successful as you can be, and make your business as successful as it can be. In that case, it is critical that you understand how a successful business works. Most introductory textbooks and courses do a good job of introducing you to the different elements of a business, but often fail to show you how these elements fit together. This objective is achieved mostly in senior business courses. The problem is that by that point, you are so used to studying each piece separately that it's very difficult to see them working together to create the business entity as a whole. And what's important to see is that "the whole" really is greater than the sum of its parts. To truly understand what makes a business successful, you must accept it as a fully integrated entity and, as you study each of its parts, study them with the whole in mind.

To this end, we have used an integrative model (shown on page xx) of a successful business as the framework, or basis, of this book. Each chapter will focus on a specific part of this model, and you will be reminded of where and how each piece fits with the other aspects of the model at the beginning of each chapter.

Before we get into the model in detail, take a look at the title—The Integrative Model of a Successful Business. Why is this important? What does it tell you?

It Is Integrative

All the elements of the model work together to create a unified whole. Each piece depends on the others, and they all affect one another. One of the most important lessons to learn about business is that you can't make a decision in one area of a business without considering the impact of the external environment, the impact on the stakeholders of the business, and the impact the decision will have on other areas of the business.

Let's look at an example. According to Report on Business magazine's 2012 ranking of the Top 1000 public companies by profit (www.theglobeandmail.com/report-on-business/rob-magazine/top-1000), Toronto-Dominion Bank (which along with its subsidiaries is known as the TD Bank Group), was the number one-ranked publicly listed company in Canada. In fact, half of the top ten of the Top 1000 were financial institutions; with the other half, not surprisingly, being resource companies. The external environment had a great deal to do with that. According to the Report on Business " … since the 2008–2009 (economic) collapse … surplus-rich China and a handful of other big emerging countries shifted into aggressive stimulus mode … The result was booming demand for the stuff Canadians dig up or pump out … and new opportunities for the banks."[1] But if you think that the performance of these companies was predetermined based on external environmental factors alone, take note: of the ten companies that saw the biggest drop from their previous year's ranking, three were financial institutions and three were resource companies. What is important to note about the top ranked companies, relative to our model of a successful business, is that they were not only successful in terms of achieving financial performance. TD for example, among many other awards, was recognized (in 2012) as being the Highest in Customer Satisfaction Among the Big Five Retail Banks by J.D. Power and

Associates for the seventh year in a row (www.jdpower.com), was identified (in 2011) as among the Global 100 Most Sustainable Organizations by Corporate Knights (www.global100.org), was acknowledged (in 2012) as one of the Top 100 Employers in Canada by Mediacorp (www.canadastop100.com), and was awarded (in 2012) Grand Prix for best overall investor relations (for a large cap company) by IR Magazine (www.insideinvestorrelations.com). TD clearly appreciates the need to balance the needs of all of its *stakeholders*—in this case customers, society, employees, and shareholders— to be successful.

TD is an organization that provides us with an excellent example of the need to act in an integrative fashion to achieve the critical success factors. For example, if those who manage the *operations* for TD at the branch level, for example, decided that they should reduce the number of tellers during key times of the day, could they do so without any impact on other areas of the business? This move would undoubtedly provide a lower quality of service due to higher wait times, affecting the image of the product in the mind of the consumer, and making it difficult for the *marketing* area to promote TD. This, in turn, would impact the *finance* area, as it would affect the expected income of the company for the year, which might then mean that future salaries negotiated by the *human resources* area might be lower, and so on. All the elements of the business or areas of its internal environment (shown by the green circle on the model) affect one another.

By the same token, what if new *technology* was developed that would allow TD to provide banking services with absolutely no human input? Then layoffs would likely result and affect the *economy* of the cities and towns where bank branches were located. This, in turn, would have an impact on the *social* environment of the company with respect to the relationship it has with the residents of the community, and might lead to the government stepping in to enact a *political* solution for the community. And if TD were to make these changes outside Canada, in its *international* operations, the impacts would be magnified.

All the areas of the external environment also have an impact on each other as well as on the business as a whole. These areas of the external environment together are often referred to by the acronym PEST—for political, economic, social, and technological. The external environment can, indeed, be a pest to business! But it can also create enormous opportunities, as you will see. We have chosen to add one more area to our study of the external environment—I for international environment—resulting in the acronym PESTI. In today's world, it is impossible to forget that business is global and, as a result, businesses have to consider the political, economic, social and technological factors of each country in which they operate in the broader international environment.

To make our model more fully integrated, changes in this external environment set off other chain reactions inside the internal environment of the business, just as society's increasing demands for business to be more responsible in the social environment have led to strategic changes within TD that have made it into the sustainable business that it is today. The interactions are endless. It's not necessary that you see all these connections. What is necessary is that you understand, as we go through the material section by section, that these sections of material cannot be treated as if they are separate areas of a business that can act on their own. They all work together.

It Is a Model

This means several things. A model represents reality—this is how a real business works! A model simplifies reality—you are learning how a successful business works, and that's very complicated. A model summarizes the essential elements in a simple form to give you a base on which to build your knowledge. A model integrates ideas into a whole, as we discussed. And finally, a model provides a framework, so that you can see how the pieces fit together and how you can build on it in later business courses.

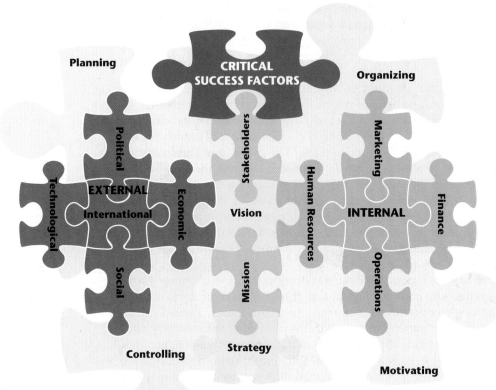

SOURCE: Reprinted with permission of Captus Press Inc. <http://www.captus.com>

It Is a Model of a Successful Business

We're not discussing what all businesses do. We are discussing what successful businesses do that makes them successful over time—not just one year but consistently outperforming year after year. That's how we learn about business—by studying those successful businesses that are leaders in their fields.

What does it mean to be truly successful? Is it simply making money? What does it take to make money? The critical success factors for any business, or the factors that indicate success, are:

- achieving financial performance;
- meeting and exceeding customer needs;
- providing value—quality products at a reasonable price;
- encouraging creativity and innovation; and
- gaining employee commitment.[2]

SOURCE: Adapted from Fred L. Fry, Charles R. Stoner, and Richard E. Hattwick. *Business: An Integrative Framework*, New York: Mc-Graw-Hill Higher Eduction, 2001.

Most businesses exist to make money, but what is often left out of the discussion is how a business becomes successful in the first place. Can a business be truly successful at generating income if it ignores the other four factors? For example, can it make money by selling products that do not satisfy customers' needs, with inferior quality at an unreasonable price, using yesterday's ideas (when the competition is 10 steps ahead), while displaying a negative attitude toward the customer as demonstrated by its employees? Even one of these points would result in lower income and a less successful business. Using TD again as an example, according to its website (www.td.com): "We want our employees to feel engaged in what they do, empowered to make a difference, excited by opportunities to develop and grow to their full potential, and recognized for their unique contributions." Clearly TD appreciates the importance of the critical success factors of gaining employee commitment in order to encourage the innovation and creativity so important to its success.

ACHIEVING SUCCESS

It's important to remember as well that these critical success factors are also integrative— they all affect one another. It is virtually impossible to find a successful business in which all of these factors have not been achieved. They work together to make the company truly successful. For example, let's consider a completely different company in a different industry; one that produces a good vs providing a service—Toyota. To *meet customer needs*, Toyota was the first to mass-produce a hybrid vehicle, but it took creativity and *innovation* to come up with the technology, a *committed workforce* to follow through, and a commitment to providing *value* through *quality* at a reasonable price to achieve success. Because of these factors, the company is able to achieve *financial performance*.

Achieving financial performance is measured in three ways: profit, cash flow, and net worth. A company needs to have a healthy profit, or "bottom line," but it also needs to earn a good profit relative to the money it has invested – that is, the equity of the owners or shareholders. But this means nothing, of course, if it can't pay its bills. It's important to understand that a company that is profitable can still go bankrupt. For instance, while it is waiting for its customers to pay for the products they have purchased, it still has to pay its bills. The timing of the cash flows can put an otherwise profitable business into a very precarious position. And finally, the net worth of the company is important, measured either by its stock price multiplied by the number of shares outstanding, or in terms of its assets (what it owns) relative to its liabilities (what it owes).

Meeting and exceeding customer needs means that companies must be sensitive to the needs of customers, anticipate changes in their needs, and, of course, work to meet these needs in a proactive fashion—before a customer complains. However, today companies cannot just provide what the customer wants. They need to satisfy customers beyond their expectations, or the competition will.

Providing value means that a business must constantly strive to improve the quality of its products and services, and do so at a reasonable cost. Customers demand quality and will stand for nothing less, but they want value for their dollar as well. They will pay a price that gives them value for their money—the quality that they demand at a price that makes it worthwhile or valuable to them.

Encouraging creativity and innovation involves the process of being creative (or "thinking outside the box"), as well as harnessing that creativity to generate the innovations that keep the company one step ahead of the competition. Danger exists when the company becomes comfortable with its level of success, as it might resist the change needed to stay ahead. But remember, there are only two kinds of businesses— those that constantly innovate and those that go out of business. In today's business world, one of the only constants is change. The status quo doesn't work anymore. Companies need to become "learning organizations," proactively seeking to learn and move ahead every day in everything they do.

And finally, probably the most important success factor is gaining employee commitment. Employees need to be empowered to act and be motivated to meet the company's objectives in each of the first four factors, or those objectives won't be met. Therefore, every company needs to understand the needs of its employees. Only then can it gain their commitment, for they will be committed to meeting the goals of the company only if their own goals are met at the same time. It is, again, an integrative relationship.

Underneath the critical success factors in our model are the stakeholders of the business. These are individuals and groups that have a "stake" in what the business does, as we discussed earlier in our discussion of TD. They are affected by the decisions that the business makes, and therefore the business has a responsibility to consider them in those decisions.

The three most critical and obvious stakeholder groups are the owners of the business (or shareholders in the case of a corporation), the employees of the business (and their union if represented by one), and the customers. But there is a much wider world out there that must be considered—the government, special interest groups, the community surrounding the business, its suppliers, and so on. All of these groups interact with the business and keep it operating.

The business cannot operate in a vacuum, as if these groups did not exist. They must be considered in every decision the business makes. If we change this material, how will our customers react? Will they keep buying our product? If we move the business, how will it affect the community? How many employees will we lose? If we cut down these trees to build the new plant, how will the environmentalist groups respond? How will the community and the local government respond? If earnings drop in the fourth quarter as expected, will our shareholders sell their shares, making the share price fall even lower? Achieving the critical success factors clearly depends on an intimate knowledge of and relationship with the stakeholders of the business.

It is primarily top management's external focus that keeps the business looking at the stakeholders. It is the responsibility of the top management of the company to look outward and chart a course for the company. They examine the external environment of the business and match the threats and opportunities in the external environment with both the expectations of the stakeholders and the strengths and weaknesses of the company internally, to determine the direction the company should take in the future—their *vision* for the future of the company. This is further refined into a *mission* statement for the company. Next they determine the *strategy* for the company to pursue to achieve this mission—how to go about achieving the company's goals in the future.

For example, perhaps opportunities exist in the external environment to take the company global. Perhaps needs exist within foreign countries for the type of product the company sells, and little competition exists from other firms at the present time. If the company has the internal marketing, operations, human, and financial strength to achieve this objective, then top management might determine that the vision for the future of the company is to make it a strong global competitor. The strategy would then need to take into account such decisions as what countries to enter first, whether to search out foreign firms with which to form a joint venture, and whether to pursue a licensing arrangement with a foreign firm or build its own plants.

It is then middle management's job within each of the functional areas of the business to determine and plan out what each area needs to do to help achieve this overall corporate strategy. For example, what type of marketing campaigns will be most successful in these new foreign markets? Do we build new plants or lease/purchase and renovate existing plants? What new skills and attributes are needed to staff our operations in these new foreign markets? Where will the money come from, and how will the budgets be realigned?

First-line management manages the workers who do the actual work in each of the functional areas. It is their job to make sure the higher level plans are implemented—and, most important—by committed workers who are motivated to achieve the goals of the company.

Top managers, middle managers, and first-line managers are responsible for managing the company and its employees to ensure that all five of the critical success factors are achieved. They do this by

- *planning* what the goals are (to achieve the critical success factors) and how to achieve them;
- *organizing* the resources of the company—human, physical, and financial—to achieve the goals;

- *motivating* the workers to gain their commitment to the goals; and then
- measuring results and making any changes necessary to continue to steer the company in the direction of the goals, thus maintaining *control* over the achievement of these five critical success factors.

This is the model we will use in this text to help you integrate the different topics covered into an understanding of how a successful business works as a whole. By studying the topics presented in this textbook using this framework, you will gain a solid foundation on which to build your further understanding of successful business practices.

Making the Connection

Politics: Governments' Roles

In this chapter, you'll learn about the role of government in business. But first, you might be wondering, "Where does all this fit into our understanding of a successful business?"

Take a peek back at the model introduced in Framework for Business Success. The most obvious relationship between this chapter and the model of a successful business is in the external environment. The PESTI model of the external environment is an acronym for the **p**olitical, **e**conomic, **s**ocial, **t**echnological, and **i**nternational environments that interact with business.

The *political* environment is thus a part of our PESTI model of the external environment. In this chapter, we will describe the role of government and how it affects the external environment that businesses operate in. Remember, this is an integrative model. As you'll see throughout the chapter, the political environment has an impact on all the other aspects of the external environment, as well as on the internal environment of a business and how it operates.

Take, for example, any of the new hybrid cars, such as the first electric vehicle with extended range, the Chevrolet Volt (introduced in the 2012 model year). You might have seen these trendy machines racing around your neighbourhood. As a result of pressure from governments (political environment) and *society* to reduce fuel emissions that cause pollution and increase the threat of global warming, as well as *economic* pressure from foreign oil companies (*international* environment) raising gas prices, business has worked to create the *technology* for hybrid cars that run on gasoline and electricity. This in turn affects the economic environment, because it is an action that other companies need to respond to if they are going to remain competitive—and many have. Interestingly, the global financial crises of 2008 and 2011 pointed out sharply that competing automotive companies hadn't responded sufficiently. The Big Three—General Motors, Ford, and Chrysler—were already in trouble as oil prices skyrocketed leading into the economic crisis, because a large part of their market was gas-guzzling SUVs and pickup trucks. This position put them in even more serious financial trouble when credit tightened up, and had General Motors and Chrysler running to governments for bail-out money. Many groups in society felt that the automakers put themselves into that position by not sufficiently responding to the environment by building fuel-efficient cars in the first place. This is an example of how the integrative nature of business can cause a large number of complex spinoff effects.

Ideally, the internal environment of the business interacts by creating products to *meet the needs of the customer*—a critical success factor. *Marketing* works with *operations* to design and build the product through the *human resources* of the company and with the *financial* resources of the company. In Chevrolet's case, this was a very *innovative* move on the part of the company that would take several years to create a return on investment. But it is this commitment to innovation in response to an environmental threat that has allowed companies like Chevrolet to remain competitive and turn what would have been a threat into an opportunity for the business. That is what competition and success are all about.

As in the above example, the external environment presents many opportunities and threats for a business. The business considers these opportunities and threats when determining its *strategy* for the future. Government and the political environment certainly present threats to business, and this in fact is the way most businesspeople view the government. However, it also presents opportunities. As you read through the chapter, watch for the different opportunities that are presented by government policy—such as the "Summer Company" program—which may interest some of you who are considering entrepreneurship as a career or who are just considering running your own business to fund school.

Also look for the impact government plays in the different aspects of a company's internal environment—how government policies affect decisions made in these areas. Choosing where to operate a business is a good example of a decision affected by government policy—property taxes can be either high or low, which, along with supportive or restrictive municipal government bylaws, will either attract or dissuade a company from operating in a certain location. Another obvious attractive government policy mentioned in the chapter is clean technology incentives. These will hopefully attract a lot of companies to move their strategies in a more sustainable direction.

Marketing decisions are greatly affected by government laws in the areas of patent protection—affecting which products will have a sustainable competitive advantage—and consumer protection—affecting how products are designed, packaged, and marketed so that product liability risks are minimized.

Government laws and regulations are often seen as the most restrictive and threatening aspect of the political environment for business, but again they need not be—they simply represent the framework within which companies must operate. More examples of these regulations that affect decisions in different areas of the business include laws governing international trade, and thus how businesses compete globally, regulations on domestic trade such as the Competition Act, as well as labour laws in the human resource area. As shown in the hybrid car example, it is up to business to turn these threats (or what appear as threats) into opportunities, or at least neutralize them so as to succeed despite them.

Hopefully you will see that every business must consider the framework the political environment lays out for it, as it must consider all aspects of the external environment; and if it works within this framework in a positive way, every business can achieve the critical success factors. It can *achieve financial performance* by meeting the needs of its customers with innovative products of value that also protect the customer from harm. And it can do this through a diverse *workforce* whose rights are protected and respected and thus is *committed* to achieving its company's goals.

chapter 1

Politics: Governments' Roles

LEARNING OUTCOMES

1 Describe the world of business.

2 Understand the responsibilities of the three levels of government in Canada.

3 List some of the roles governments play in Canada and how they affect business.

4 Explain some of the Canadian laws that protect businesses and consumers.

5 List the most common taxes paid by businesses.

6 List some of the trends that are reshaping the political environment.

GOVERNMENT GRANTS—STUDENT JOBS

Instead of finding a summer job in 2011, Melanie Mirza of Brantford, Ontario, started a business called Adirondeck Art. Her attention-getting Adirondack chairs are hand-painted with unique designs, some commissioned at client request.

This business was made possible with a grant from the "Summer Company" program of the Ontario government. Melanie received $1500 to start her company; a second $1500 was available to student firms that stayed in business all summer.

Not everyone is aware of the many government programs created to reduce economic difficulties such as student unemployment and graduate debt.

Some not-for-profits are eligible for federal grants that pay 100 percent of the cost of employing a student, including wages and all mandatory employment-related expenses such as Employment Insurance and Canada Pension Plan. This program may be supported by donations encouraged through income tax credits.

Public sector employers and businesses with fewer than 51 employees may also access federal grants that pay up to 50 percent of the cost of employing a student. Larger firms cannot access these programs. The government recognizes small business as the creator of most new jobs and, for that reason, many government programs support small businesses.

Employers can also access other grant programs to help support student positions. For example, infrastructure grants may provide the facilities, and program grants may fund equipment and services that the students use to do their jobs.

Frequently, government also provides matching grants that are paid in proportion to donations received from private citizens.

Government interventions in the economy serve more than one purpose. Creating employment is just one objective. Another purpose is to support other government priorities, such as increasing diversity in the workplace or supporting the work of not-for-profits by funding summer jobs.

Student job creation is supported both directly and indirectly. Indirect support includes setting up student employment centres or making exceptions in visa regulations to permit international students to work on-campus.

Directly, federal, provincial/territorial, and municipal governments also hire students. Seasonal needs such as parks and recreation or environmental research lend themselves well to summer jobs. And sometimes, students are fortunate enough to find work in their chosen area of study.

COURTESY OF MELANIE MIRZA

According to the Canadian Federation of Students, the average student graduates after four years with $27,000 in debt, with interest ranging from 5 to 9 percent. Since many students need grants and loans to pay for tuition and living costs, being gainfully employed each summer serves to reduce that need.

Perhaps in 2012, Melanie will hire a student to help her … and access a Canada Summer Jobs grant to fund half the cost.[1]

THINKING CRITICALLY

As you read this chapter consider the following questions:

1. How does government influence business operations?

2. How can governments help businesses?

3. What impact do governments' agendas have on their policies that relate to business?

business
An organization that strives for a profit by providing goods and services desired by its customers.

goods
Tangible items manufactured by businesses.

services
Intangible offerings of businesses that can't be touched or stored.

standard of living
A country's output of goods and services that people can buy with the money they have.

In Canada, all three levels of government play very important roles in business. They are tax agents, regulators, providers of essential services and incentives, customers, and competitors. Each level of government has unique responsibilities and controls that affect business in Canada and Canadian businesses doing business globally.

Canada has had a history of strong government and laws that have been instrumental in providing us with a very high standard of living. Organizations, associations, industry, and government are increasingly working together to protect the stakeholders (those with a vested interest) to ensure that business is governed in an ethical and legal manner.

In this chapter, we will start by discussing the world of business. We will then look at the three levels of government, discuss their responsibilities, and discuss some of the laws and regulations that affect business and protect consumers.

LO1

THE WORLD OF BUSINESS

quality of life
The general level of human happiness based on such things as life expectancy, educational standards, health, sanitation, and leisure time.

A **business** is an organization that strives for a profit by providing goods and services desired by its customers. Businesses meet the needs of consumers by providing movies, medical care, vehicles, and countless other goods and services. **Goods** are tangible items manufactured by businesses, such as tablets and BlackBerry devices. **Services** are intangible offerings that can't be touched or stored. Governments, accountants, lawyers, restaurants, car washes, and airlines all provide services. Businesses also serve other organizations—such as hospitals, retailers, and governments—by providing machinery, goods for resale, computers, and thousands of other items.

Thus, governments and businesses create the goods and services that are the basis of our **standard of living**. The standard of living of any country is measured by the output of goods and services people can buy with the money they have. This includes not only privately purchased goods and services but also collectively consumed goods and services, such as those provided by public utilities and governments.

Governments and businesses play a key role in determining our quality of life by providing jobs and goods and services to society. **Quality of life** refers to the general level of human happiness of a society. Although there are various criteria used to measure the quality of life, some of the common criteria include *material well-being* (GDP per person), *health* (life expectancy and access to health care), *political stability and security*, community life (involvement in social activities), *job security, political freedom,* and *gender equality.* Canada and many of its cities are consistently ranked in the top 10. Building a high quality of life is a combined effort of government, businesses, and not-for-profit organizations.

Creating a high quality of life is not without risks, however. **Risk** is the potential for losing resources, most commonly time and money, or otherwise not being able to accomplish an organization's goals. Without enough blood donors, for example, Canadian Blood Services faces the risk of not meeting the demand for blood by victims of disaster. Businesses such as Bell Canada Enterprises face the risk of falling short of their revenue goals if resources are not properly managed. **Revenue** is the money a company earns from providing services or selling goods to customers. **Costs** are expenses for rent, salaries, supplies, transportation, and many other items that a company incurs from creating and selling goods and services. Some of the costs incurred by Research In Motion (developer of the BlackBerry) include expenses for research and development, building

Concept *in Action*

Governments in Canada provide their citizens with many of the services that we use on a daily basis, including education and health care. As well, our high standard of living is in large part due to the political stability and security we enjoy in Canada. What else contributes to our high standard of living?

rental or purchase, advertising, and transportation. **Profit** is the money left over after all expenses are paid.

When a company such as Research In Motion uses its resources intelligently, it can often increase sales, hold costs down, and earn a profit. Not all companies earn a profit, but that is the risk of being in business. In Canadian business today, there is generally a direct relationship between risks and profit: the greater the risks, the greater the potential profit (or loss).

Not all organizations strive to make a profit. A not-for-profit organization is an organization that exists to achieve some goal other than the usual business goal of profit. The United Way, the Canadian Cancer Society, and Greenpeace are all not-for-profit organizations.

Successful not-for-profit organizations follow sound business principles. These groups have goals they hope to accomplish, but the goals are not focused on profits. For example, a not-for-profit organization's goal might be feeding the poor, stopping destruction of the environment, increasing attendance at the ballet, or preventing drunk driving. Reaching such goals takes good planning, management, and control. Not-for-profit organizations do not compete directly with each other like businesses such as Shoppers Drug Mart, Rexall, and Value Drug Mart do, but not-for-profit organizations do compete for people's scarce volunteer time and donations.

risk
The potential for losing resources, most commonly time and money, or otherwise not being able to accomplish an organization's goals.

revenue
The money a company earns from providing services or selling goods to customers.

costs
Expenses incurred in creating and selling goods and services.

profit
The money left over after all expenses are paid.

not-for-profit organization
An organization that exists to achieve some goal other than the usual business goal of profit.

GOVERNMENT—MORE THAN ONE LEVEL

LO2

Canada is a diverse country with a large land mass and a very small population (approximately 34.5 million). There are three levels of government in Canada: federal, provincial/territorial, and municipal. Each has different responsibilities and regulations that affect business and society. Some of those responsibilities are listed below.

Federal Government—Overseeing the Well-Being of Canada

The federal government has the authority for money and banking, trade regulation, external relations, defence, criminal law, employment insurance, copyrights, and transportation, just to name a few responsibilities. Through the use of the fiscal policy (taxation and spending—discussed in Chapter 2) and the Bank of Canada (monetary policy—discussed in Chapter 2) Canada's financial system is regulated and wealth is collected, transferred, and spent to provide Canadians with one of the highest standards of living in the world. Although the Bank of Canada is not a government department (it is actually a Crown corporation) and operates with considerable independence, we introduce it here because of its impact on our economy (see Chapter 2).

Although the majority of Canada's workforce is regulated by the provincial/territorial legislation, approximately 10 percent of Canada's workforce is regulated by the federal government's Canada Labour Code. The Code regulates employment standards in industries such as banking, marine shipping, ferry and port service, air transportation, railway, and road transportation.

Provincial/Territorial Governments— Protecting Rights

Some of the responsibilities of the provinces/territories are the administration of labour laws (other than that mentioned above), education, health and welfare, protection of property and civil rights, natural resources, and the environment. One of the most significant provincial/territorial jurisdictions is labour law. This includes minimum working standards such as minimum wages, vacations, statutory holidays, overtime, etc.

Concept *Check*

Define business and differentiate between goods and services.

What is standard of living and how is it measured?

What are revenues and costs?

Municipal Governments—Delivering the Services

Municipalities deliver such services as water, sewer, and waste collection; encourage economic development; and use bylaws to regulate, for example, how businesses operate.

Serving the Public's Interest—The Audit

All three levels of government are held accountable to you and me through the audit system. For example, the Auditor General of Canada is responsible for ensuring that public resources have been properly allocated. The Auditor is independent of the government and performs the following duties:

- ensures management's information is reliable and complete;
- identifies opportunities for improving control for and use of public resources; and
- makes recommendations to improve systems and practices.

LO3

THE GOVERNMENTS' OTHER ROLES

Governments' roles include tax agent, regulator, provider of essential services, provider of incentives, customer (purchasing materials to deliver the services), and competitor (e.g., the governments compete for workers with the private sector).

Governments as Tax Agents

There are many types of taxes that businesses and individuals are responsible for, for example, income taxes, sales taxes, property taxes, sin taxes, etc. The federal government, for example, collects the taxes from businesses and individuals and then redistributes some of it to the provinces/territories. Some of this distribution is the taxes collected on behalf of the provinces/territories (i.e., the federal government is responsible for collecting the provinces'/territories' portion of taxes). The federal government also provides significant financial support to assist the provinces/territories to provide the programs and services they are responsible for in the form of transfer payments.[2] Transfer payments are not only used for specific purposes, but also to help equalize the wealth across our country. Two of these specific programs are the Canada Health Transfer (CHT) and the Canada Social Transfer (CST). These support specific areas such as health care and education (all levels), as well as child care. See Exhibit 1.1, which

transfer payments
Payments made to the provinces and territories by the federal government to help to deliver required services such as health and education, and to help equalize the wealth across Canada.

Exhibit 1.1   Federal Support to the Provinces and Territories 2011–2012 Fiscal Year

PROVINCE/TERRITORY	TOTAL DISTRIBUTION (IN MILLIONS OF DOLLARS)	PER CAPITA DISTRIBUTION	PERCENTAGE OF TOTAL PROVINCIAL/ TERRITORIAL REVENUES
Newfoundland and Labrador	$ 1,200	1,171	15%
Prince Edward Island	$ 495	3,418	33%
Nova Scotia	2,600	2,740	31%
New Brunswick	2,500	3,322	33%
Québec	17,300	2,187	26%
Ontario	17,400	1,325	16%
Manitoba	3,400	2,715	25%
Saskatchewan	1,200	1,175	11%
Alberta	3,400	922	9%
British Columbia	5,300	1,183	13%
Yukon	745	21,494	67%
Northwest Territories	1,000	23,812	76%
Nunavut	1,200	36,682	88%

SOURCE: Adapted from *Federal Support to Provinces and Territories*, (Department of Finance Canada, 2012), <http://www.fin.gc.ca/fedprov/mtp-eng.asp> (24 February 2012).

shows the distribution for each of the provinces/territories for the fiscal year 2011–2012. Also included is the per capita distribution and the estimated value of total revenue. A more detailed discussion of taxes is presented in Learning Outcome 5 on page 21.

Governments as Regulators

Each of the three government levels has different responsibilities and regulations. For example, the federal government controls international trade (discussed in Chapter 5), provincial/territorial governments control most labour laws, and municipalities control bylaws (e.g., where retail stores can operate or where manufacturing facilities can be located). Regulations are used to protect Canadian interests (e.g., trading embargos), creating competition (e.g., Competition Bureau), protect the consumer (e.g., the Canadian Radio-television Telecommunications Commission), promote social programs (e.g., universal health care), and protect the environment (e.g., Environment Canada).

Governments as Providers of Essential Services

In Canada, we look to our governments to provide certain services that we expect. These include the federal government providing a reliable national defence, and transportation means such as roads. We expect that our provincial/territorial governments will provide us with hospitals so that we can maintain a healthy life, and education facilities to expand our knowledge and skills. We expect our municipalities to promote economic development, deliver safe drinking water, and have an effective police service.

Governments as Providers of Incentives

There are numerous government programs that help individuals, businesses, and economic development. The incentive programs are intended to stimulate economic growth, development, and employment. For example, some people can qualify for

HOT *inks*

Find the latest news about Environment Canada at www.ec.gc.ca

Concept *in Action*

PPP Canada is a Crown corporation created to improve the delivery of public infrastructure to Canadians. The private sector assumes a major share of the responsibility in the public–private partnerships (P3). One example is the $11 million the Government of Canada contributed towards a new biosolids management facility in Sudbury, Ontario.

COURTESY OF RV ANDERSON AND THE CITY OF SUDBURY

employment insurance from the federal government if they are taking courses or training programs that will make them more employable. Another example is the many students who receive student loans or grants to make post-secondary education possible, which can lead to better job opportunities.

The governments also help businesses. In 2011, the federal government committed $53 million to fund 17 clean technology projects.[3]

Governments as a Customer and Competitor

Governments purchase thousands of different products from businesses to carry out their functions. Some businesses (e.g., road construction companies) rely on governments for most, if not all, of their revenues. Businesses that want to sell their products to the governments usually must register their business with them. The governments are also a competitor, for example, competing with the private sector for employees—maybe you'll work for government when you graduate, let's say, as a commercial attaché!

Sustainable Business, Sustainable World

WHAT DOES IT MEAN?

The term "sustainable development" was coined in 1972 at the United Nations Conference on Human Development. It was popularized through *Our Common Future* (1987), the report of the UN *World Commission on Environment and Development*, also known as the Brundtland Commission. One feature of the Brundtland Commission was its challenge that business be part of the solution rather than part of the problem. Since then, sustainable development has been commonly understood as "development that meets the needs of the present without compromising the ability of future generations to meet their needs." Thus, linking social and environmental variables within economic agendas is a hallmark of sustainable development. Sustainable development provides a framework to describe the bigger picture within which human activities occur, the intention of which is to preserve or enhance the systems—ecological, socioeconomic and cultural—upon which humans and other species depend.[4] This bigger picture frames the business environment for the 21st century.

Humans have an increasing impact on the planet. Along with various forms of pollution and toxic waste, climate change and loss of habitat, we are responsible for the greatest rate of species extinction since the demise of the dinosaurs in the Mesozoic era 65 million years ago.[5] As a single species, humans have already exceeded the ecological capacity of the biosphere.[6] The wealthiest 20 percent of the world's human population uses some 80 percent of the resources. The wealthiest 25 percent of the world gets 75 percent of the income, even after adjustment for the parity of purchasing power.[7] Thus, along with addressing our collective and individual impacts on the biosphere—which has led, amongst other things, to the dwindling of natural resources—sustainable development must also address issues of equity in sharing those resources.

The business environment of the 21st century is ecologically uncertain, socially complex, financially unpredictable and ethically challenging. From a business ethics point of view, sustainable development provides an opportunity to achieve the greatest good or least harm to the Earth's human and non-human inhabitants.[8] Does business have a *moral obligation* to see that its practices are socially just and ecologically sustainable? Markets operate within certain constraints. While business is free to pursue profits, there is a *moral minimum* within which business operates and companies have the *responsibility* to operate within these limits. Traditional models of social responsibility include legal and moral constraints; the sustainable development approach also includes ecological constraints.[9]

Corporate responsibility can be seen to encompass a set of tools for achieving goals and assessing the performance of individuals and organizations within the larger context of the sustainable development business environment. This might include ecological, social, financial, governance and cross-cultural performance. Corporate leaders in the 21st century innovate strategic capabilities, achieving competitive advantage through sustained, responsible performance in these areas.

Thinking Critically

1. What do you think is the responsibility of companies to protect our environment?
2. What responsibilities do consumers have to ensure that the products and services they are purchasing and using contribute to sustainability?

SOURCE: David Lertzman, Ph.D. The University of Calgary, September 2011. Used with permission.

Expanding Around the Globe

MAGNA INTERNATIONAL INC.—AN INTERNATIONAL SUCCESS STORY

Magna International is the world's most diversified automobile supplier in the world. Today, it has 275 manufacturing operations in 26 countries on five continents and employs more than 100,000 people.

Its founder, Frank Stronach, started a tool and die company (a company which makes tools used in the manufacturing business) called Multimatic Investments Limited, and eventually expanded to the production of automobile parts. In 1969, Multimatic merged with Magna Electronics Corporation becoming Magna International Inc.

The company is proud of its "Fair Enterprise" philosophy that builds ownership and inspires pride in its employees. The company believes that its continued success is dependent on the skills, knowledge, and commitment of its employees. The "Employees'

Charter" is built on the premise that employees and management share the responsibility to ensure the success of the company.

Some of the principles in the "Employees' Charter" are job security, fair treatment, a safe and healthful workplace, competitive wages and benefits, communication and information, and employee and profit participation.

Today Magna is developing green technologies, fuel and process efficiencies, and lightweight products with a concern for safety, comfort, and convenience. Since its beginnings in Ontario to its international presence today, Magna is just one example of a Canadian success story.

SOURCE: Adapted from "Employee's Charter," Magna International Inc., <http://www.magna.com/for-employees/employee's-charter>.

PROTECTING BUSINESSES AND CONSUMERS

LO4

The legal environment is meant to not only protect citizens in everyday life, but also to provide protection to owners and consumers alike. Below is a brief discussion of some of these protections.

Patents, Copyrights, and Trademarks

Canadian law protects authors, inventors, and creators of other intellectual property by giving them the rights to their creative works. Patents, copyrights, and registration of trademarks are legal protection for key business assets.

A **patent** gives an inventor the exclusive right to manufacture, use, and sell an invention for 20 years. The Patent Act grants patents for ideas that meet its requirements of being new, unique, and useful. The physical process, machine, or formula is what is patented. Patent rights—pharmaceutical companies' rights to produce drugs they discover, for example—are considered intangible personal property (i.e., they do not have physical form but are of value).

The government also grants copyrights. A **copyright** is an exclusive right, shown by the symbol © (which does not necessarily need to be shown), that is given to a writer, an artist, a composer, or a playwright to use, produce, and sell her or his creation. This protection is automatic. Works protected by copyright include printed materials (books, magazine articles, lectures), works of art, photographs, and movies. Under current copyright law, the copyright is issued for the life of the creator plus 50 years after the creator's death. Patents and copyrights, which are considered intellectual property, are the subject of many lawsuits today.

A **trademark** is a design, name, or other distinctive mark that a manufacturer uses to identify its goods in the marketplace. Tim Hortons oval-shaped logo (symbol) is an example of a trademark.

Trademarks are valuable because they create uniqueness in the minds of customers. At the same time, companies don't want a trademark to become so well known that it is used to describe all similar types of products. For instance, Coke is often used to refer to any cola soft drink, not just those produced by the Coca-Cola Company. Companies spend millions of dollars each year to keep their trademarks from becoming generic

patent
A form of protection (limited monopoly) established by the government for inventors; it gives an inventor the exclusive right to manufacture, use, and sell an invention for 20 years.

copyright
A form of protection established by the government for creators of works of art, music, literature, or other intellectual property; it gives the creator the exclusive right to use, produce, and sell the creation during the lifetime of the creator and extends these rights to the creator's estate for 50 years thereafter.

trademark
The legally exclusive design, name, or other distinctive mark that a manufacturer uses to identify its goods in the marketplace.

words, terms used to identify a product class rather than the specific product. Coca-Cola employs many investigators and files 70 to 80 lawsuits each year to prevent its trademarks from becoming generic words.

Once a trademark becomes generic (which a court decides), it is public property and can be used by any person or company. Names that were once trademarked but are now generic include Kleenex, Aspirin, thermos, linoleum, and zipper.

Bankruptcy and Insolvency Act

It might be possible to save a business, even though it is insolvent, by using the provisions under the Bankruptcy and Insolvency Act. **Bankruptcy** is the legal act by which individuals or businesses that cannot meet their financial obligations are relieved of some, if not all, of their debt. Working through a Trustee in Bankruptcy, the company (or individual) files a Proposal ("offer") to the company's creditors asking them to accept less than the actual monies owed so that the company can survive or the person can rebuild.

Deregulation of Industries

Since the 1980s, the Canadian governments (federal and provincial/territorial) have actively promoted deregulation—the removal of rules and regulations governing business competition. **Deregulation** has drastically changed some once-regulated industries (especially the transportation, telecommunications, and financial services industries) and created many new competitors. The result has been companies entering some industries while governments exit these industries.

Tort Law

A **tort** is a civil, or private, act that harms other people or their property. The harm might involve physical injury, emotional distress, invasion of privacy, or defamation (injuring a person's character by publication of false statements). The injured party may sue the wrongdoer to recover damages for the harm or loss. A tort is not the result of a breach of contract, which would be settled under contract law. Torts are part of common law. Examples of tort cases are medical malpractice, slander (an untrue oral statement that damages a person's reputation), libel (an untrue written statement that damages a person's reputation), product liability (discussed in the next section), professional negligence, and fraud.

A tort is generally not a crime, although some acts can be both torts and crimes. (Assault and battery, for instance, is a criminal act that would be prosecuted by the government and is also a tort because of the injury to the person.) Torts are private wrongs and are settled in courts. Crimes are violations of public law punishable by the government in the criminal courts. The purpose of criminal law is to punish the person who committed the crime. The purpose of tort law is to provide remedies to the injured party.

For a tort to exist and damages to be recovered, the harm must be done through either negligence or deliberate intent. Negligence occurs when reasonable care is not taken for the safety of others. For instance, a woman attending a baseball game was struck on the head by a foul ball that came through a hole in the screen behind home plate. The court could rule that a sports team charging admission has an obligation to provide structures free from defects and seating that protects spectators from danger. Therefore, the baseball organization could be found negligent. Negligence does not apply when an injury is caused by an unavoidable accident, an event that was not intended and could not have been prevented even if the person used reasonable care. This area of tort law is quite controversial, because the definition of negligence leaves much room for interpretation.

HOT links

For more information about patents, copyrights, and trademarks, go to Canada One's website and search for information at
www.canadaone.com

bankruptcy
The legal procedure by which individuals or businesses that cannot meet their financial obligations are relieved of some, if not all, of their debt.

HOT links

For more information on corporate bankruptcy, see the website that helps people and businesses get a fresh financial start at
www.bankruptcycanada.com

deregulation
The removal of rules and regulations governing business competition.

tort
A civil or private act that harms other people or their property.

Concept in Action

© MOODBOARD/PHOTOSHOT

Patents, copyrights, and trademarks protect those with the ideas. What are some of the issues in the music industry regarding copyrights?

Creating the Future of Business

YOUNG ENTREPRENEURS

So you think you want to start your own business. That is exciting! You truly are the "future of business" as you will be the ones running the businesses that shape tomorrow.

Start by thinking about what it means to be an entrepreneur. There is a great video—www.youtube.com/watch?v=lZKhZmvJuZY— put together for *New York Entrepreneur Week* that describes in very real, concrete terms what it means to be an entrepreneur. If that describes you, then read on …

So what does it mean to be a "young entrepreneur"? Is it really possible to start a business at your age? Absolutely. Just look at Mark Zuckerberg of *Facebook*, Chad Hurley of *YouTube*, or Blake Ross and David Hyatt of *Mozilla*, all of whom are on *The 50 Richest Young Entrepreneurs Under 30* list. Or check out Blake Mycoskie's story of how he created TOMS shoes in the book *Start Something That Matters*. Inc. Magazine puts together a list of the *Top 30 Under 30* young entrepreneurs every year. There are lots of lists and lots of examples. These particular examples may seem like anomalies to you. We have, however, profiled a number of very real, accessible examples for you; many of whom have graduated from your own schools. Read their stories, contact them, and ask your questions. They all had a dream, a vision, and went for it. And they will all inspire you. You *can* do it too.

You will see that a number of the young entrepreneurs we have profiled for you have also won awards. One such award is the FUEL Awards for Canada's best young entrepreneurs. These awards were launched recently, in 2011, to "promote entrepreneurship in Canada by identifying forward-thinking role models for youth and illustrating the many benefits of venturing out on one's own." The awards are sponsored by Rogers, KPMG, TD Bank, Filemobile, *Profit* Magazine, and Impact Entrepreneurship Group.

The Impact Entrepreneurship Group was started as a one-day event at University of Waterloo in 2004 and has grown into a national organization run by 100 volunteers at 35 universities and colleges across Canada. Its aim is to "foster a spirit of entrepreneurship among high school and university students" with a view that "entrepreneurship embodies something bigger than just starting a business—a mindset towards life that can help achieve any dream." Sounds pretty great to us. How about you? If you want to get started on your journey, check out their program called Impact Apprentice Competition, inspired by Donald Trump's *The Apprentice* at http://apprentice.impact,org.

As quoted in *Career Options* Magazine, Canada's National Youth Entrepreneur Social Attitude and Innovation Study, conducted in January 2008, showed that "close to 50 percent of youth between the ages of 16 and 24 would like to start their own business." If you are one of the 50 percent, there are lots of resources and networks available for you to get started, from the Impact Entrepreneurship Group (www.impact.org), to Youth Canada (www.youthcanada.ca), ACE (www.acecanada.ca), and Young Social Entrepreneurs of Canada (www.ysec.org). Good luck. Remember, you are the "future of business."

Thinking Critically

1. If youth did not start businesses, what would the "future of business" look like?
2. Do you think that youth today have a different perspective than those who started businesses 20 or 30 years ago? Will the "future of business" look different because of it?
3. What different perspectives and priorities do the youth of today bring to new businesses?

SOURCES: Entrepreneur Week website, http://www.entrepreneurweek.net; http://www.retireat21.com/top-youngentrepreneurs; Blake Mycoskie, "How I Did It: The TOMS Story," Entrepreneur.com, September 20, 2011, http://www.entrepreneur.com/article/220350; "30 Under 30," Inc.com, http://www.inc.com/30under30/2011/index.html; Fuel Awards: Celebrating the Best Young Entrepreneurs in Canada, http://www.fuelawards.ca; Vinod Rajasekaran and Despina Sourias, "Entrepreneurship: The Path of Change Makers," Career Options Magazine online, http://www.careeroptionsmagazine.com/1394/entrepreneurship-the-path-of-change-makers.

Consumer Protection

Consumerism reflects the struggle for power between buyers and sellers. Specifically, it is a movement seeking to increase the rights and powers of buyers vis-à-vis sellers, often resulting in consumer protection laws. Sellers' rights and powers include the right

- to introduce into the marketplace any product, in any size and style, that is not hazardous to personal health or safety, or, if it is hazardous, to introduce it with the proper warnings and controls;
- to price the product at any level they wish, provided they do not discriminate among similar classes of buyers;
- to spend any amount of money they wish to promote the product, so long as the promotion does not constitute unfair competition;
- to formulate any message they wish about the product, provided that it is not misleading or dishonest in content or execution; and
- to introduce any buying incentives they wish.

Meanwhile, buyers have the rights and powers to

- refuse to buy any product that is offered to them (right of choice);
- expect products to be safe (right of safety);

consumerism
A movement that seeks to increase the rights and powers of buyers vis-à-vis sellers.

Concept *in Action*

Consumers in Canada have the right of choice, safety, honesty, and to be informed. If these are violated, legal action is one course to take against a business. What are some recent incidents that have occurred recently where consumer rights have been violated?

HOT *Links*

Learn more about what is happening regarding consumer rights at
www.consumer.ca

product liability
The responsibility of manufacturers and sellers for defects in the products they make and sell.

strict liability
A concept in product-liability laws under which a manufacturer or seller is liable for any personal injury or property damage caused by defective products or packaging that does not meet industry standards.

HOT *Links*

Learn more about consumer protection and legal action at
www.canadian-lawyers.ca

- expect a product to be essentially as the seller represents it (right to be heard and action taken); and
- receive adequate information about the product (right of information).

Warranties

Express warranties are specific statements of fact, or promises about a product by the seller. This form of warranty is considered part of the sales transaction that influences the buyer. Express warranties appear in the form of statements that can be interpreted as fact. The statement "This machine will process 3800 litres of paint per hour" is an express warranty, as is the printed warranty that comes with a new iPad.

Implied warranties are neither written nor oral. These guarantees are imposed on sales transactions by statute or court decision. They promise that the product will perform up to expected standards. For instance, a man bought a used car from a dealer, and the next day the transmission fell out as he was driving on the highway. The dealer fixed the car, but a week later the brakes failed. The man sued the car dealer. The court ruled in favour of the car owner, because any car without a working transmission or brakes is not fit for the ordinary purpose of driving. Similarly, if a customer asks to buy a copier to handle 5000 copies per month, she relies on the salesperson to sell her a copier that meets those needs. The salesperson implicitly warrants that the copier purchased is appropriate for that volume.

Product-Liability Law

Product liability refers to manufacturers' and sellers' responsibility for defects in the products they make and sell. It has become a specialized area of law combining aspects of contracts, warranties, torts, and statutory law.

An important concept in product-liability law is **strict liability**. A manufacturer or seller is liable for any personal injury or property damage caused by defective products or packaging that does not meet industry standards.

Competition Act

The Competition Act was enacted to protect consumers and provide provisions that can be grouped under three categories: conspiracies, monopolies, and mergers. Each of these three categories is briefly discussed below.

Many measures have been taken to try to keep the marketplace free from influences that would restrict competition. The Competition Act sets out the basic prohibition against cartels (the expression that is often used is *antitrust law*), among other issues. A **cartel** is an agreement between enterprises to lessen competition. If it can be proven that enterprises entered into an agreement or arrangement (a conspiracy) to lessen competition, they can be charged with a criminal offence.

Some of the more common methods of reducing or eliminating competition are

- *parallel pricing*—competing firms adopt similar pricing strategies;
- *quota setting*—imposing limits of production;
- *market sharing*—dividing the market based on a geographical basis; and
- *product specialization*—whereby each firm agrees to specialize its products.

According to the free market economy (as discussed in this chapter), the essential characteristic of an efficient market is competition. If customers have a choice of products to purchase (i.e., competition), prices will be generally lower, and quality will be better, or both. A **monopoly** is a situation when there is no competition and the benefits of a free market are lost.

For various reasons (e.g., small population, large geographical area) some monopolies are allowed to exist in Canada. Some examples have been utilities and telecommunications services, but these were governed by regulatory agencies (e.g., utility boards) that protected consumers' rights. These *natural monopolies* have been disappearing in the past decade as government regulations have promoted more competition in reaction to the stronger move to increased competition.

The third area where the Competition Act protects the consumer is mergers and acquisitions. As discussed in Chapter 8, mergers and acquisitions are often an important means of seeking efficiencies in business. The Competition Act allows the government to stop any mergers and acquisitions that might lessen competition.

Concept *Check*

What are patents, copyrights, and trademarks? What does each do?

What is a tort?

List how consumers are protected?

cartel
An agreement between enterprises to lessen competition.

monopoly
A situation where there is no competition and the benefits of a free market are lost.

TAXATION OF BUSINESS

Taxes are sometimes seen as the price we pay to live in this country. Taxes are assessed by all levels of government on both businesses and individuals, and they are used to pay for the services provided by government.

Income Taxes

Income taxes are based on the income received by businesses and individuals. Most personal income taxes are progressive, meaning that rates increase as income increases (one exception is the flat tax for individuals in Alberta). The tax rates for the federal government apply to all Canadians (with few exceptions) equally, but the provinces are free to set their own rates. Income taxes for businesses are flat (i.e., the same rate regardless of income).

As we will discuss in Chapter 8, the net income for sole proprietorships and partnerships are included in the personal income of the owners. For corporations, taxes are the responsibility of the corporation.

income taxes
Taxes that are based on the income received by businesses and individuals.

Other Types of Taxes

Besides income taxes, individuals and businesses pay a number of other taxes. The four main types are property taxes, payroll taxes (only as a remittance), sales taxes, and excise taxes.

Property taxes are assessed on real property, based on its assessed value. Most jurisdictions tax land and buildings. Property taxes may be based on fair market value (what a buyer would pay), a percentage of fair market value, or replacement value (what it would cost today to rebuild or buy something like the original). The value on which the taxes are based is the *assessed value.*

Any individual that is employed is required to pay income taxes—federal and provincial/territorial taxes on the money that he or she earns (after the personal exemption is deducted). These taxes must be paid on wages, salaries, and commissions. The employer deducts the income taxes from the employee's pay and remits them to the federal government, where they are called payroll taxes.

Sales taxes are levied on goods and services when they are sold and are a percentage of the sales price. These taxes are imposed by the federal government (the goods and services tax, or GST) and most provincial governments in the form of a provincial sales tax (PST). (Provincially, one exception is that there is no provincial sales tax in Alberta and there are no territorial sales taxes in any of the three territories.) Some provinces now have a harmonized sales tax (HST), which is a combination of the GST and the PST (e.g., Ontario, New Brunswick, and Nova Scotia). The PSTs vary in amount and in what is considered taxable. Sales taxes increase the cost of goods to the consumer. Businesses are responsible for collecting sales taxes and remitting them to the government.

property taxes
Taxes that are imposed on real and personal property based on the *assessed value* of the property.

payroll taxes
Income taxes that are collected by the employer and remitted to the federal government, usually in the form of a deduction from the employee's pay.

sales taxes
Taxes that are levied on goods and services when they are sold; calculated as a percentage of the price.

excise taxes
Taxes that are imposed on specific items such as gasoline, alcoholic beverages, and tobacco.

Learn more about the Government of Canada's guidelines for procurement at
www.pwgsc.gc.ca

Excise taxes are placed on specific items, such as gasoline, alcoholic beverages, and tobacco. They can be assessed by federal and provincial governments. In many cases, these taxes help pay for services related to the item taxed. For instance, gasoline excise taxes are often used to build and repair highways. Other excise taxes—like those on alcoholic beverages and tobacco—are used to control practices that can cause harm.

LO6 THE FUTURE OF POLITICS AND GOVERNMENTS' ROLES

Governments are more proactive in environmental issues, Canada is seeking more skilled workers, and governments in Canada are demanding more transparency in business and government activities.

Clean Technology Projects

As a reaction to the concerns of Canadians regarding environmental issues, the Canadian government has increased its investment in clean energy projects. For example, in 2011 the federal government committed $53 million to fund 17 clean technology projects.[10] The money was provided by Sustainable Development Technology Canada, which offers funding to create technology to deal with climate change issues, clean air, clean water, or soil quality. Alberta, for example, received $11.8 million of the money. It plans to use the bulk of the funding ($10 million) to test using solvent instead of water to recover oil sands that are too deep to mine.

Canada—Looking for Skilled Labour

Except for our First Nations Peoples, Canada's population has been one of immigration. Canada has struggled in recent years with a lack of skilled labour. One of the priorities of the government is the economy. To maintain our high standard of living, we need to produce more than we can consume (see Chapter 5). To accomplish this, Canada must continue to attract more skilled labour and educate Canadians.

The Federal Skilled Worker Program is an initiative of the federal government that is the primary stream for skilled immigrants to Canada. In 2011, approximately 47,000 skilled immigrants were admitted under the program. The total immigration for 2011 was approximately 240,000.

More Transparency

Governments are expecting more transparency in marketing, operations, and corporate social responsibility (see Chapter 3) from Canadian businesses and themselves. The Government of Canada, for example, spends billions of dollars a year to procure goods and services and its actions are mandated by *The Code of Conduct for Procurement* for both public servants and vendors alike. This policy reflects the principles of the Financial Administration Act and the Federal Accountability Act.

GREAT IDEAS TO USE NOW

Government—Is It Your Career Choice?

Are you interested in working for the government? There are many exciting career opportunities with all three levels, although they are often challenging because of the political element.

Making Ethical Choices

THE ALBERTA OIL SANDS

Over the next 20 to 25 years, it is estimated that capital investment in the oil sands of Alberta will amount to approximately $218 billion according to the Canadian Energy Research Institute. For every dollar that is invested, it creates approximately $8 dollars of economic activity. In the 2009–2010 budget year, the Alberta government was paid $1.9 billion in royalties by the companies working the oil sands. This money was used to help fund many public programs and services (e.g., infrastructure, health, and education). The expected royalties are estimated at approximately $184 billion over the next 20 to 25 years.

Alberta is not the only financial beneficiary of the oil sands. It is estimated that, over the next 20 to 25 years, the oil sands will generate more than $307 billion in tax revenue across Canada with approximately 61 percent ($187 billion) going to the federal government. Key industries such as manufacturing (e.g., machinery and metal fabrication) primarily situated in Ontario benefit. In Atlantic Canada, contracts worth approximately $50 million have been signed to steel manufacturers to supply their products to the oil sands. Also, many of the skilled labourers come from various regions and contribute to their local communities back home.

That's the good news. The bad news is the reputation of the oil sands as being "dirty oil," damaging our environment including air, land, and water. The petroleum producers are working frantically to develop better, more environmentally friendly production methods. Also, independent, not-for-profit organizations such as Alberta-based Climate Change and Emissions Management Corporation (CCEMC) have a mandate to expand climate change knowledge, develop new "clean" technologies, and explore ways to implement them. For example, in July 2010 CCEMC provided funds to Suncor Energy, along with its industry partners, for two projects to develop greener technology.

ETHICAL DILEMMA: How can we balance the benefits with the downsides of the oil sands?

SOURCES: Government of Alberta, "Economic and Investment Information," http://www.oilsands.alberta.ca/economicinvestment.html, December 6, 2011; Climate Change and Emissions Management Corporation (CCEMC), http://ccemc.ca/about and http://ccemc.ca/about/fast-facts, February 14, 2012; Suncor Energy, "Suncor Energy and partners receive funding for clean technology research projects," *MarketWire*, July 02, 2010, http://www.marketwire.com/press-release/Suncor-Energy-and-partners-receive-funding-for-clean-technology-researchprojects-TSX-SU-1285337.htm, February 14, 2012.

The Canadian government promotes itself as delivering programs and services that are focused on improving the quality of life for all Canadians. You might want to work in one of our High Commissions or embassies around the world. Working with Foreign Affairs and International Trade Canada can be quite rewarding.

The Government of Canada's training provider for foreign service is the Canadian Foreign Service Institute (CFSI). It provides top-quality learning programs that cover international affairs, foreign language training, intercultural effectiveness, and professional and management development. You can learn specialized skills such as negotiation, policy analysis, international business development, and so on.

Provincially (and federally) you might choose a career that will lead to a deputy minister position (the senior civil servant in a government department). In this position, you would be responsible for your department's day-to-day operations, overseeing your department in a way similar to any department head in a non-government organization.[11]

Think about it. Governments can offer many opportunities and career choices for you.

HOT *links*

See the opportunities with Foreign Affairs and International Trade Canada at
www.dfait-maeci.gc.ca

Summary of Learning Outcomes

A business is an organization that strives to make a profit by providing goods and services. Not-for-profit organizations operate for other reasons such as social causes or charity work. Governments also provide services that contribute to Canada's high standard of living and quality of life. Businesses sell their product, receive revenue, and pay their expenses (costs), hopefully realizing a profit in the process.

LO1 Describe the world of business.

LO2 Understand the responsibilities of the three levels of government in Canada.

The federal government has the authority for money and banking, trade regulation, external relations, defence, criminal law, employment insurance, copyrights, and transportation, just to name a few responsibilities. Approximately 10 percent of Canada's workforce is regulated by the federal government's Canada Labour Code. The Code regulates employment standards in industries such as banking, marine shipping, ferry and port service, air transportation, railway, and road transportation.

Some of the responsibilities of the provinces/territories are the administration of labour laws (other than those mentioned above), education, health and welfare, protection of property and civil rights, natural resources, and the environment. One of the most significant provincial/territorial jurisdictions is labour law. This includes minimum working standards such as minimum wages, vacations, statutory holidays, overtime, etc.

Municipalities deliver such services as water, sewer, and waste collection; encourage economic development; and use bylaws to regulate, for example, how businesses operate.

LO3 List some of the roles governments play in Canada and how they affect business.

Governments are tax agents, regulators (e.g., laws), providers of essential services (e.g., national defence and transportation), and providers of incentives used to simulate the economy (e.g., student loans), but they are also customers and competitors.

LO4 Explain some of the Canadian laws that protect businesses and consumers.

Laws protect patents, copyrights, and trademarks and provide mechanisms for bankruptcy and insolvency. Tort law provides a means for someone or a business to correct harm done to them. Consumers are protected by warranties, product-liability law, and the Competition Act.

LO5 List the most common taxes paid by businesses.

Income taxes are based on the income received by businesses and individuals. They are paid to both the federal and provincial/territorial governments—the latter are each responsible for setting their own rates. In addition to income taxes, individuals and businesses also pay property taxes (assessed on real property), payroll taxes (employers are responsible for collecting the income taxes from their employees and remitting them to the federal government), sales taxes (e.g., GST and HST, which are levied on goods and services), and excise taxes (levied on specific products such as gasoline, alcoholic beverages, and tobacco).

LO6 List some of the trends that are reshaping the political environment.

Governments are more proactive in environmental issues, Canada is seeking more skilled workers, and governments in Canada are demanding more transparency in business and government activities.

Key Terms

bankruptcy 18
business 12
cartel 21
consumerism 19
copyright 17
costs 13
deregulation 18
excise taxes 22
goods 12
income taxes 21
monopoly 21
not-for-profit organization 13
patent 17
payroll taxes 21

product liability 20
profit 13
property taxes 21
quality of life 12
revenue 13
risk 13
sales taxes 21
services 12
standard of living 12
strict liability 20
tort 18
trademark 17
transfer payments 14

Experiential Exercises

1. Find out what's happening in Canadian business at www.canadianbusiness.com.

2. Check out the latest on the world's ranking of highest quality of life among countries at www.mapsofworld.com/world-top-ten/world-top-ten-quality-of-life-map.html.

3. Search for any not-for-profit organization. See what challenges they have in funding, volunteerism, etc.

4. Check out what is new in the federal government at www.gc.ca.

5. Search your provincial/territorial government's website to see the latest news.

6. Search how your local government impacts business activities through bylaws.

7. What is new at the Office of the Auditor General of Canada? See www.oag-bvg.gc.ca.

8. Learn more about our legal system at www.blakes.com/DBIC/guide/html/legal_system.html.

9. How are our courts organized, both federally and provincially/territorially? See www.justice.gc.ca/eng/dept-min/pub/ccs-ajc/.

10. What patents, copyrights, and trademarks are expiring? Search the Internet to find out!

11. Check out Health Canada to see the latest advisories, warnings, and recalls of products at www.hc-sc.gc.ca/cps-spc/advisories-avis/index-eng.php.

Review Questions

1. What is a business?

2. Products consist of goods and services. List some of the differences between goods and services.

3. What impact do our governments have on our standard of living? Our quality of life?

4. Explain the relationship between revenues, costs, and profits.

5. What are the responsibilities of the three levels of government in Canada?

6. What roles do the governments play in our economy?

7. Explain our legal system in terms of public and private law.

8. What laws govern business operations?

9. What are the conditions of a valid contract?

10. What remedies are available for the breach of a contract?

11. What are the most common taxes paid by businesses and individuals to the governments?

12. What trends are occurring in politics and governments today?

CREATIVE THINKING CASE

Inside Intel: It's about Copying—Exactly

Intel Corporation has more than 82,000 employees worldwide, but innovation depends on people like Trish Roughgarden, an Air Force veteran whose job is to copy slavishly. Ms. Roughgarden is known inside Intel as a "seed," an unofficial title for technicians who transfer manufacturing know-how from one Intel chip factory to another. Her job: to help ensure that Intel's latest plant works just like identical plants around the world. If there is a problem at one plant, production may be slowed but not stopped—other plants pick up the slack. So when an earthquake interrupts a plant in China, a plant in Oregon may increase production.

It is all part of a major Intel strategy known as "Copy Exactly," which discourages experimentation at individual factories. Instead, engineers and technicians painstakingly clone proven Intel manufacturing techniques from one plant to the next—down to the colour of workers' gloves and wall paint, or other features that would seem to have no bearing on efficiency. New plants fall into two basic categories: model plants that will be copied and those that are copies.

The strategy emerged after a production disaster in the 1980s, when maddening variations between factories hurt productivity and product quality. Japanese competitors nearly drove Intel out of business. Today, Copy Exactly shapes Intel's response to the latest economic downturn, helping accelerate the relentless pace of technology improvements known as Moore's Law, after former Intel chairman Gordon Moore. Moore predicted that the number of transistors that could be placed on a computer chip (of the same size) would double every two years.

Although it prohibits willy-nilly changes, the Copy Exactly methodology encourages Intel workers to come up with ideas to boost productivity or make chip features smaller. But the ideas must pass a committee called the Process Change Control Board, which requires workers to come up with tests to prove the value of their suggestions.

The idea of Copy Exactly comes into the planning of new plants such as the $5 billion facility expected to open in 2013. Located in Chandler, Arizona, near several other Intel facilities, this plant will employ 1,000 and Intel executives project that it will be the most advanced high-volume semiconductor manufacturing facility anywhere in the world. This project received significant tax incentives from the state of Arizona, but the government sees the value of the high-paying jobs coming to or staying in the state. The innovations for the Chandler plant are evolutions of the ongoing improvements at other plants and, as the new processes are developed, seeds will take them out to the other Intel plants and continue the "Copy Exactly!" process.

Thinking Critically

1. Explain the link between quality and "Copy Exactly."

2. How important is technology to a global competitor like Intel? What about product quality?

3. Most management consultants claim that employees are happiest when they have freedom to make decisions in the work environment. How does this fit with Copy Exactly? What can be done to let employees exercise their creativity?

SOURCES: Clark, D. "In Setting up Its New Plants, Chip Maker Clones Older Ones Down to the Paint on the Wall." *Wall Street Journal*, October 28 2002, B1, B4; Intel, "Annual Report." 2010; Intel, "Copy Exactly!" http://www.intel.com; Randazzo, R., E. Jensen, and M. Pitzl, "Intel's New Chandler Plant to Bring Construction, High-Tech Positions," *The Arizona Republic*, February 19 2011.

chapter 2

Making the Connection

Economics: Evolving Systems

In this chapter, you'll learn about another element of our PESTI model of the external environment. You will learn about the *economic* environment—about the different economic systems that exist, and the basic economic concepts you need to know to understand how the economy works and how business decisions are made within the context of this environment. These concepts are very important for businesses to understand, as they are intricately connected to the decisions that businesses make every day—for example, pricing levels affect *marketing* decisions, interest rates affect *financing* decisions, and employment rates affect *human resource* decisions.

The chapter will also describe the economic system of a country as a combination of policies, laws, and choices made by its government. Remember, this is an integrative model. Here we see a direct link between the *political* and economic environments. But as you'll see throughout the chapter, the economy has an impact on all the other aspects of the external environment, as well as on the internal environment of a business and how it operates as described above.

You'll find that economies differ based on how they manage the factors of production—the resources needed to produce a company's products. These factors are provided by the *stakeholders* of the business: employees provide human resources, and owners provide financial resources, for example. The economic system that exists in a society depends partly on the relationship between the stakeholders, business, and the government. This stakeholder relationship to the economic environment can also be seen in the discussion of economics as a "circular flow": resources are provided by the stakeholders who then receive something in return from the business. This circular flow clearly demonstrates the integrative nature of a business, as changes in one flow affect the others. A really good example of that in today's

businesses is the trend toward sustainability in *operations*. Natural resources are one of the factors of production and businesses are understanding more and more that, to succeed long-term, they need to take care of this factor of production.

Another integrative example discussed in the chapter is the "crowding out" that occurs when government spending replaces private sector spending. This is an excellent example of how the political and economic environments affect each other and affect the internal environments of companies. When the government spends more on libraries, for example, and individuals spend less on books, how does that affect all the different functional areas of a company? As described in this chapter, this crowding out also occurs when the government raises funds for spending, making corporate financing more expensive and thus crowding out private investment, which in turn slows economic growth in the private sector.

You'll also see many examples in the chapter of how the economic environment creeps into the daily workings of a business. As you read through the chapter, think of how different economic events affect company decisions. Consider the following:

- *"The Bank of Canada lowers interest rates."* This would affect the financial decisions of the company, perhaps making it more feasible financially to expand operations—affecting the company's overall strategy, as well as its ability to meet the needs of the customer by offering better financing packages.
- *"The Minister of Finance proposes a cut in income taxes."* Lower personal income taxes result in customers having more disposable income to spend on the company's products. Lower corporate taxes make the economic environment more favourable to business investment domestically and make it easier for Canadian enterprises to compete with companies from countries with lower taxes.

Many factors in the economy affect business decisions in the internal environment. They affect what companies decide to produce (marketing and operations), how they price these products (marketing and finance), and how many people they decide to employ and how much to pay them (human resources and finance). On a macroeconomic level, the rate of inflation that exists and where the economy is in the business cycle affect business decisions. And on a microeconomic level, if you look at the factors that cause demand and supply curves to shift, you can see many other aspects of the environment at play; for example, *technology* shifts the supply curve, while buyers' preferences (*social environment*) shift the demand curve. Everything is related.

The economy also affects how companies meet the critical success factors of the business. For example, the chapter describes a trend toward companies "building, maintaining, and enhancing interactions with customers and other parties to develop long-term satisfaction through mutually beneficial partnerships." This trend toward relationship management comes as a result of the demands of today's economic environment, but also as a result of better educated and more demanding customers from the social environment, new technology that allows customers to find companies that *meet their needs* and switch to them at the click of a mouse, and the globalization of markets *internationally*, creating more competition. These environmental factors, combined with an understanding that financially it's better on the bottom line to keep an existing customer than find a new one, results in a trend toward meeting the critical success factors in a much longer-term way. This leads to companies improving training and utilizing technology to improve worker productivity in order to build a *workforce committed* to meeting the *quality* needs of the customer in an *innovative* way and to building long-term relationships with them. And, of course, satisfied long-standing customers and more productive and committed workers result in both higher revenues and cost savings, helping the company achieve better *financial performance*.

chapter 2

Economics: Evolving Systems

LEARNING OUTCOMES

1 Explain what economics is and how the three sectors of the economy are linked.

2 Understand the primary features of the world's economic systems.

3 Explain the four types of market structure.

4 Discuss the basic microeconomic concepts of demand and supply, and how they establish prices.

5 Show how economic growth, full employment, and price stability indicate a nation's economic health.

6 Describe how the Bank of Canada uses monetary policy, and how governments use fiscal policy to achieve their macroeconomic goals.

7 List some of the trends that are reshaping micro- and macroeconomic environments.

BEANIE BABIES

Peanut the Elephant is a very popular Beanie Baby to give to newborn baby boys, probably because of its light blue colour. The original Peanut, introduced in 1995 by manufacturer TY Inc., was royal blue and is among the most expensive for collectors since it was only produced for three months before the colour change.

The light blue Peanut sells for about $12, but in the 1990s the royal blue eventually sold for more than $5,000. In 2011, eBay reported an original royal blue Peanut selling for $1,767.78; a Princess Diana Memorial Beanie Baby bear was listed for $245,525.06 on a "Buy it now" price.

The price of Peanut and the other rare Beanie Babies has varied significantly over the years since the Beanie craze began. In 1993, the company first produced the PVC-pellet-filled toys that can be placed in poses because of a bendable core. Beanie Babies are sold unpackaged, but with very specific and somewhat delicate tags attached. Collectors look for intact tags and pay accordingly.

Despite large-scale success, TY Inc. did not raise prices or widely advertise. By keeping prices down and employing an almost secret distribution system, the cachet of the toys was maintained and copy-cats were kept to a minimum. Beanies were distributed through small toy shops, or to large corporations as special editions created for them. McDonald's restaurants bought miniature replicas of a few designs, called Teenie Beanies, to include them in Happy Meals. Beanies even hit the ballpark! One giveaway at Yankee Stadium occurred on the night David Wells pitched a perfect game; the toy valued at $7 in the first inning was worth more than $200 when the last out was recorded.

TY began a process of "retiring" Beanies, which made them even more valuable. Beanie Babies went from cute toy to collector craze in just three years. By 1996, more than 100 million had been produced and resale prices began to rise. In 1998, some parents found that the toy they just bought for their child at the local store for $5 could be sold to a collector for $2,000. The rare royal blue Peanut had climbed to $5,200 at auction.

Only 2000 of the royal blue Peanut were produced. Many were not in mint condition, so they were valued lower.

COURTESY OF CHRIS HARTT

The small number of top condition royal blues represents a limited supply. The combination of their original popularity and the profits made from resale increased demand. This is a classic economic example—when demand exceeds supply, price goes up. But like all toy crazes, the Beanie Baby bull market has seen a decline. Special Beanies, such as the bear made to honour Princess Diana a few months after her death, and rare ones such as Peanut and #1 Bear (given to employees at staff parties) have maintained value. But, most have dropped back to their original price or less.

The 2011 price of more than $1,000 for a royal blue Peanut demonstrates a renaissance in the Beanie Baby market, but who can say how high it will go, or how long any fad will last?[1]

THINKING CRITICALLY

As you read this chapter consider the following questions:

1. How do different economic systems work?

2. What role does supply and demand play in consumer products?

Economics is an analytical science that will help you understand the world around you. As you study this chapter, remember that economics is not something you should learn for an exam and then forget. It can help you be more imaginative and insightful in everyday life. You will understand why prices are going up or down, when interest rates will fall, and when and why the unemployment rate will fall. A knowledge of basic economic concepts can help you decide whether to change jobs (and how much money to ask for) and whether to buy a car now or wait until next year. When you hear that a car dealership has 115 days of inventory, your understanding of the forces of supply and demand will tell you that now may be the time to buy that new car.

Similarly, economics will help you become a better-informed citizen. Almost every political issue is, in some way, grounded in economic concepts. Economics can also help you understand what is happening in other countries and raise your awareness of opportunities in those countries. Understanding economics and how changes in an economy affect business is important to be successful. Recently we have experienced many changes, from nations changing economic systems to world-wide economic challenges. These have created opportunities for some and threats to others.

Reading this chapter will help you understand how economies provide jobs for workers and also create and deliver products to consumers and businesses. Next, we discuss how supply and demand determine prices for goods and services. You will also learn how governments attempt to influence economic activity through policies such as lowering or raising taxes. As well, you will see how the Bank of Canada uses the Monetary Policy to ensure economic stability. The chapter concludes by examining trends in evolving economic systems and competition.

LO1 BUSINESS AND ECONOMIES WORKING TOGETHER

economics
The study of how a society uses scarce resources to produce and distribute goods and services.

Economics is the study of how a society uses scarce resources to produce and distribute goods and services. The resources of a person, a company, or a nation are limited. Hence, economics is the study of choices—what people, companies, or nations choose from among the available resources. Every economy is concerned with what types and amounts of goods and services should be produced, how they should be produced, and for whom. These decisions are made by the marketplace, the government, or both. In Canada, the government and the free-market system together guide the economy.

You probably know more about economics than you realize. Every day, many news stories deal with economic matters: A union wins wage increases at Company X; the Bank of Canada raises/lowers interest rates; Toronto Stock Exchange has a record day; the federal government proposes a cut in income taxes; consumer spending rises as the economy grows; or retail prices are on the rise, to mention just a few examples.

Microeconomics and Macroeconomics

microeconomics
The sub-area of economics that focuses on individual parts of the economy, such as households or businesses.

macroeconomics
The sub-area of economics that focuses on the economy as a whole by looking at aggregate data for large groups of people, companies, or products.

The state of the economy affects both people and businesses. How you spend your money (or save it) is a personal economic decision. Whether you continue in school and whether you work part-time are also economic decisions. Every business also operates within the economy. Based on their owners' and managers' economic expectations, businesses decide what products to produce, how to price them, how many people to employ, how much to pay these employees, how much to expand the business, and so on.

Economics has two main sub-areas. Microeconomics focuses on individual parts of the economy, such as households or businesses. In contrast, macroeconomics is the

After many setbacks, the first flight of the Boeing 787 Dreamliner was on October 26, 2011, by All Nippon Airways (ANA). Made from lightweight composites, the jet aircraft's ultra-efficient design reduces fuel consumption by 20 percent per flight. How does the economy affect the types of goods and services that are produced?

EVERETT KENNEDY BROWN/EPA/LANDOV

study of the economy as a whole. It looks at *aggregate* data—data for large groups of people, companies, or products—considered as a whole.

Both micro- and macroeconomics offer valuable outlooks on the economy. For example, Honda might use both to decide whether to introduce a new line of cars. From a microeconomic viewpoint, Honda would judge consumer demand for new cars versus the existing supply, competing models, labour and material costs and availability, and current prices and sales incentives. The company would consider such macroeconomic factors as the national level of personal income, the unemployment rate, interest rates, fuel costs, and the national level of sales of new cars.

More about micro- and macroeconomics later in the chapter.

Factors of Production: The Building Blocks of Business

Factors of production are the resources used to create goods and services. By using the factors of production efficiently, a company can produce more output with the same resources. Four traditional factors of production are common to all productive activity: natural resources, labour, capital, and entrepreneurship. Many experts now include knowledge as a fifth factor, acknowledging its key role in business success.

Commodities that are useful inputs in their natural state are known as natural resources. They include farmland, forests, mineral and oil deposits, and water. Sometimes natural resources are simply called *land*, although, as you can see, the term means more than just land. Today, urban sprawl, pollution, and limited resources have raised questions about resource use. Conservationists, ecologists, and government bodies are proposing laws to require land use planning and resource conservation.

The economic contributions of people working with their minds and muscles are called labour. This input includes the talents of everyone—from a restaurant cook to a nuclear physicist—who performs the many tasks of manufacturing and selling goods and services. The tools, machinery, equipment, and buildings used to produce goods and services and get them to the consumer are known as capital. Sometimes the term *capital* is also used to mean the money that buys machinery, factories, and other production and distribution facilities. However, because money itself produces nothing, it is *not* one of the basic inputs. Rather, it is a means of acquiring the inputs. Therefore, in this context, capital does not include money.

Entrepreneurs are people who combine the inputs of natural resources, labour, and capital to produce goods or services with the intention of making a profit. These people make all the decisions that set the course for their companies; they create products and production processes. Because they are not guaranteed a profit in return

factors of production
The resources used to create goods and services, including natural resources, labour, capital, entrepreneurship, and knowledge.

natural resources
Commodities that are useful inputs in their natural state.

labour
Economic contributions of people.

capital
The inputs, such as tools, machinery, equipment, and buildings, used to produce goods and services and get them to the customer.

entrepreneurs
People who combine the inputs of natural resources, labour, and capital to produce goods or services with . the intention of making a profit or accomplishing a not-for-profit goal.

for their time and effort, they must be risk takers. Of course, if their companies succeed, the rewards can be great.

Today, many Canadians want to start their own businesses. They are attracted by the opportunity to be their own bosses and reap the financial rewards of owning successful business. For those working within an organization, they are often expected to use **entrepreneurial thinking**. That is, think like an entrepreneur, but within the company.

A number of outstanding managers and noted academics are now emphasizing a fifth factor of production—knowledge. **Knowledge** is the combined talents and skills of the workforce. As the world becomes ever more uncertain, the very nature of work, organizations, and management is changing. The new competitive environment places a premium on knowledge and learning. Lester Thurow, a leading world expert on economic issues, says, "The dominant competitive weapon of the 21st century will be the knowledge of the work force."[2] The companies that will become and remain successful will be the ones that can learn quickly, assimilate this learning, and develop new insights.

Economics as a Circular Flow

Another way to see how the sectors of the economy interact is to examine the circular flow of inputs (factors of production) and outputs among households, businesses, and governments, as shown in Exhibit 2.1. Let's review the exchanges by following the purple circle around the inside of the diagram. Households provide inputs (natural resources, labour, capital, entrepreneurship) to businesses, which convert these inputs into outputs (goods and services) for consumers. In return, consumers receive income from rent, wages, interest, and ownership profits (green circle). Businesses receive income from consumer purchases of goods and services.

The other important exchange in Exhibit 2.1 takes place between governments (federal, provincial, and municipal) and both individuals and businesses. Governments supply many types of publicly provided goods and services (highways, schools, police, courts, health services, employment insurance, Canada Pension Plan) that benefit individuals and businesses. Government purchases from businesses also contribute to business profits. The contractor who repairs a local stretch of highway, for example, is paid by government for the work. As the diagram shows, government receives taxes from individuals and businesses to complete the flow.

Changes in one flow affect the others. If the government raises taxes, households have less to spend on goods and services. Lower consumer spending causes businesses to reduce production, and economic activity declines; unemployment might rise. In contrast, cutting taxes can stimulate economic activity. Keep the circular flow in mind as we continue our study of economics. The way economic sectors interact will become more evident as we explore macroeconomics and microeconomics.

LO2 ## GLOBAL ECONOMIC SYSTEMS

A nation's **economic system** is the combination of policies, laws, and choices made by its government to establish the systems that determine what goods and services are produced and how they are allocated. Economic systems found in the world today include market economy (private enterprise or market system), command economies (planned economies), socialism, and mixed economies.

The major differentiator among economic systems is whether the government or individuals decide how to allocate limited resources—the factors of production—to individuals and organizations to

- best satisfy unlimited societal needs;
- choose what goods and services to produce, and in what quantities;
- determine how to produce these goods and services and who will produce them; and
- distribute goods and services to consumers.

---

entrepreneurial thinking
Thinking like an entrepreneur—even those who work in a company.

knowledge
The combined talents and skills of the workforce.

circular flow
The movement of inputs and outputs among households, businesses, and governments; a way of showing how the sectors of the economy interact.

Concept *Check*

What is economics?

What is the difference between macroeconomics and microeconomics?

What are the five factors of production?

How do resources flow among the household, business, and government sectors?

Exhibit 2.1 Economics as a Circular Flow

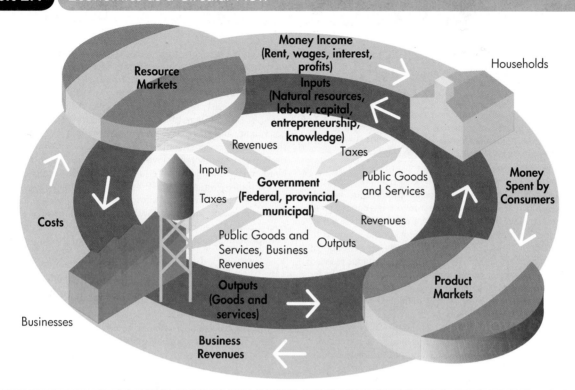

Money Income (Rent, wages, interest, profits)

Inputs (Natural resources, labour, capital, entrepreneurship, knowledge)

Resource Markets

Households

Revenues

Taxes

Inputs

Taxes

Government (Federal, provincial, municipal)

Public Goods and Services

Money Spent by Consumers

Costs

Public Goods and Services, Business Revenues

Outputs

Revenues

Product Markets

Outputs (Goods and services)

Businesses

Business Revenues

Companies that do business internationally may discover that they must adapt production and selling methods to accommodate the economic system of another country. Additionally, managers must understand and adapt to the factors of production and the economic system or systems in which they operate to be successful.

Market Economy

In the last decade of the 20th century, many countries shifted toward market economic systems. Sometimes, as in the case of the former East Germany, the transition to a market economy was painful but fairly quick. In other countries, such as Russia, the movement was characterized by false starts and backsliding. A **market economy**, also known as the *private enterprise system* or *capitalism*, is based on competition in the marketplace and private ownership of the factors of production (resources). In a competitive economic system, a large number of people and businesses buy and sell products freely in the marketplace. In a pure market economy, all the factors of production are owned privately and the government does not try to set prices or coordinate economic activity.

A market economy guarantees certain economic rights: the right to own property, the right to make a profit, the right to make free choices, and the right to compete. The right to own property is central to a market economy. The main incentive in this system is profit, which encourages entrepreneurship. Profit is also necessary for producing goods and services, building plants, paying dividends and taxes, and creating jobs. The freedom to choose whether to become an entrepreneur or to work for someone else means that people have the right to decide what they want to do on the basis of their own drive, interest, and training. The government does not create job quotas for each industry or give people tests to determine what they will do.

In a market economy, competition is good for both businesses and consumers. It leads to better and more diverse products, keeps prices stable, and increases the efficiency of producers. Producers try to produce their goods and services at the

economic system
The combination of policies, laws, and choices made by a nation's government to establish the systems that determine what goods and services are produced and how they are allocated.

market economy
An economic system based on competition in the marketplace and private ownership of the factors of production (resources); also known as the *private enterprise system* or *capitalism*.

Creating the Future of Business

PATRICK LOR, iSTOCKPHOTO

After immigrating to Canada from Hong Kong as a small child, Patrick Lor went from mopping floors and stocking shelves in his parents' grocery store to helping pioneer the microstock photography industry, co-founding the world's first microstock agency in 2001, which was sold to Getty Images for US$50 million just 5 years later!

This company was none other than iStockphoto, the world's leading Web 2.0 stock photography company based on the innovative use of crowdsourcing and a credit-based purchasing system. Crowdsourcing, made possible through the Internet, is a concept that has revolutionized the economic models of a number of industries. The crowdsourcing business model used by iStockphoto is similar to that used by Wikipedia and eBay, who rely on the contribution of users. iStockphoto basically created a marketplace for images created by amateur photographers at prices that are next to impossible for professional photographers to compete with, and the rest is history.

According to Patrick, when his family immigrated to Canada, it was a huge sacrifice for his parents as they had solid careers in Hong Kong, but did not have the English language skills to continue those careers in Canada. They saved up the money to purchase a grocery store in Calgary, Alberta, and taught Patrick the value of hard work, telling him he could be anything he wanted to be—as long as it was a doctor, engineer, or lawyer! Patrick did his undergraduate degree in sociology, after which he worked for Image Club Graphics, which was acquired by Adobe on the day he joined the company. There, he managed the product development department, responsible for creating digital photography, fonts, clip art, etc. They operated out of a converted warehouse much like an entrepreneurial venture, but with the marketing clout of a billion-dollar company.

Image Club was later chopped from Adobe's portfolio, but it left Patrick with the roots of what was to come. Shortly after completing his MBA in 2001, he met up with an old Adobe colleague by the name of Bruce Livingstone. Bruce had started a stock photography community and was giving away digital images for free. At the time, there was no low-cost photography available on the Internet to speak of. Patrick instantly fell in love with the idea and convinced Bruce to hire him in exchange for an equity stake in the company.

Currently Patrick is the President of Fotolio.com, one of the world's leading providers of affordable stock imagery, with a database of over 5 million images on websites in 10 languages and used by over 1 million members around the world. Patrick's is truly a story of entrepreneurial success.

Thinking Critically

1. How important was iStockphoto's use of crowdsourcing to its success? Do you think another business model could have worked as well?
2. Patrick Lor seemed destined to be an entrepreneur, with all the events in his life conspiring to make sure he did not become a "doctor, engineer, or lawyer." Do you think entrepreneurs are born or made? Are there personality characteristics that entrepreneurs share that other business people do not?

SOURCES: http://www.fotolio.com and http://www.patricklor.typepad.com, used with permission from Patrick Lor; "The Rise of Crowdsourcing," *Wired* Magazine, Issue 14.06, June 2006, http://www.wired.com.

---

lowest possible cost and sell them at the highest possible price. But when profits are high, more companies enter the market to seek those profits. The resulting competition among companies tends to lower prices. Producers must then find new ways of operating more efficiently if they are to keep making a profit—and stay in business.

The Command Economy

command economy
An economic system characterized by government ownership of virtually all resources and economic decision making by central-government planning; also known as *planned economy* and *central planning*.

At the other end of the economic spectrum is the command economy. In a command economy, also called a planned economy or central planning, the government owns virtually all resources and controls all markets. Economic decision making is centralized (hence the term, central planning): the government, rather than the market's competitive force, decides what and how much to produce, where to locate production facilities, where to acquire raw materials and supplies, who will get the output, and what the prices will be. This form of centralized economic system offers little if any choice to a country's citizens.

In the 20th century, countries such as China and Cuba chose the command economic system, believing that it would raise their standards of living. In practice, however, the tight controls over most aspects of people's lives, such as what careers they could choose, where they could work, and what they could buy, led to lower productivity. Workers had no reasons to work harder or produce quality goods because there were no rewards for excellence. Errors in planning and resource allocation led to shortages of even basic items.

These factors were among the reasons for the 1991 collapse of the Soviet Union into multiple independent nations. The reforms have moved many economies—most notably in former Central European countries such as Hungary, Czech Republic, and Russia—toward more capitalistic, market-oriented economic systems. North Korea and Cuba are the best remaining examples of command economic systems.

Socialism

Socialism is an economic system in which the basic industries are owned by the government (social ownership) or by the private sector under strong government control. A socialist state controls critical large-scale industries such as transportation, communications, and utilities. Smaller businesses may be privately owned. To varying degrees, the state also determines the goals of businesses, the prices and selection of goods, and the rights of workers. Socialist countries typically provide their citizens with a higher level of services, such as health care and unemployment benefits, than do most market-oriented countries. As a result, taxes and unemployment can also be quite high in socialist countries. Sweden is often cited as one of the primary socialist countries in the world.

socialism
An economic system in which the basic industries are owned either by the government or by the private sector under strong government control.

Mixed Economic Systems

Canada and Great Britain, among others, are called mixed economies; that is, they use more than one economic system. Sometimes, the government is essentially socialist and owns basic industries. In Canada, some industries are at least partly owned or controlled by the various levels of government (e.g., communications, education, health care, transportation, and utilities), but most activities are carried on by private enterprises, as in a market system.

The few factors of production owned by the government include some public lands, Canada Post, and some water resources. But the government is extensively involved in the economic system through taxing, spending, and social (welfare) activities. The economy is also mixed in the sense that the country tries to achieve many social goals—income redistribution (transfer payments) and Canada Pension Plan, for example—that might not be attempted in purely market-oriented systems. Exhibit 2.2 summarizes key factors of the world's economic systems.

mixed economies
Economies that combine several economic systems; for example, an economy in which the government owns certain industries but the private sector owns others.

Concept *in Action*

Since joining the World Trade Organization in 2001, China has continued to embrace tenets of a market economic system and grow its economy. China is the world's largest producer of mobile phones, PCs, and cameras, and the country's over 1.3 billion citizens constitute an enormous emerging market. What are some of the benefits that China has experienced by moving toward a market economy?

Exhibit 2.2 The Basic Economic Systems of the World

	MARKET ECONOMY	COMMAND ECONOMY	SOCIALISM	MIXED ECONOMY
Ownership of Business	Businesses are privately owned with minimal government ownership or interference	Governments own all or most enterprises	Basic industries such as railroads and utilities are owned by government; very high taxation as government redistributes income from successful private businesses and entrepreneurs	Private ownership of land and businesses but government control of some enterprises; the private sector is typically large
Control of Markets	Complete freedom of trade; no or little government control	Complete government control of markets	Some markets are controlled and some are free; significant central-government planning; state enterprises are managed by bureaucrats; these enterprises are rarely profitable	Some markets, such as nuclear energy and the post office, are controlled or highly regulated
Worker Incentives	Strong incentive to work and innovate because profits are retained by owners	No incentive to work hard or produce quality products	Private-sector incentives the same as a market economy; public-sector incentives the same as a planned economy	Private-sector incentives the same as capitalism; limited incentives in the public sector
Management of Enterprises	Each enterprise is managed by owners or professional managers with little government interference	Centralized management by the government bureaucracy; little or no flexibility in decision making at the factory level	Significant government planning and regulation; bureaucrats run government enterprises	Private-sector management similar to capitalism; public sector similar to socialism
Forecast for 2020	Continued steady growth	No growth and perhaps disappearance	Stable with probable slight growth	Continued growth

MARKET STRUCTURES

One of the characteristics of a free-market system is that suppliers have the right to compete with one another. The number of suppliers in a market is called **market structure**. Economists identify four types of market structures: (a) perfect competition, (b) monopolistic competition, (c) oligopoly, and (d) pure monopoly. Exhibit 2.3 illustrates the four types of market structures and Exhibit 2.4 summarizes the primary types of market structures.

Perfect Competition

Characteristics of **perfect (pure) competition** include the following:

- A large number of small businesses are in the market.
- The businesses sell similar products—that is, each business' product is very much like the products sold by other companies in the market.
- Buyers and sellers in the market have good information about prices, sources of supply, and so on.
- It is easy to open a new business or close an existing one.

In a perfectly competitive market, companies sell their products at prices determined solely by forces beyond their control. Because the products are very similar, and because each company contributes only a

market structure
The number of suppliers in a market.

perfect (pure) competition
A market structure in which a large number of small businesses sell similar products, buyers and sellers have good information, and businesses can be easily opened or closed.

Concept *Check*

What is an economic system?

What is a market economy, and why is the system becoming more pervasive worldwide?

What is socialism, and why is it still popular?

Why are most economies mixed?

Exhibit 2.3 Types of Market Structure

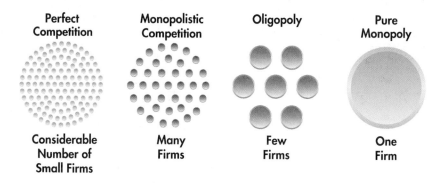

small amount to the total quantity supplied by the industry, price is determined by supply and demand. A company that raised its price even a little above the going rate would lose customers.

Monopolistic Competition

Three characteristics define the market structure known as monopolistic competition:

- Many businesses are in the market.
- The businesses offer products that are close substitutes but still differ from one another.
- It is relatively easy to enter the market.

Under monopolistic competition, companies take advantage of product differentiation. Industries in which monopolistic competition occurs include clothing, food, and similar consumer products. Companies under monopolistic competition have more control over pricing than do companies under perfect competition because consumers do not view the products as exactly the same. Nevertheless, companies must demonstrate those product differences to justify their prices to customers. Consequently, companies use advertising to distinguish their products from others. Such distinctions may be significant or superficial. For example, Nike says, "Just Do It," and Tylenol is advertised as being easier on the stomach than Aspirin.

monopolistic competition
A market structure in which many businesses offer products that are close substitutes, and in which entry is relatively easy.

Oligopoly

An oligopoly has two characteristics:

- A few companies produce most or all of the output.
- Large capital requirements or other factors limit the number of companies.

Bombardier Inc. of Québec, U.S. Steel Canada of Ontario (Canada's largest and most diversified Canadian steel producer, previously Stelco Inc.), and WestJet Airlines of Alberta are major companies in different oligopoly industries.

With so few companies in an oligopoly, what one company does has an impact on the others. Thus, the companies in an oligopoly watch one another closely for new technologies, product changes and innovations, promotional campaigns, pricing, production, and other developments. Sometimes they go as far as coordinating their pricing and output decisions, which is illegal. Many antitrust cases—legal challenges arising out of laws designed to control anticompetitive behaviour—occur in oligopolies.

oligopoly
A market structure in which a few companies produce most or all of the output, and in which large capital requirements or other factors limit the number of companies.

Exhibit 2.4 Primary Types of Market Structures

CHARACTERISTICS	PERFECT COMPETITION	PURE MONOPOLY	MONOPOLISTIC COMPETITION	OLIGOPOLY
Number of companies in market	Many	One	Many, but fewer than perfect competition	Few
Company's ability to control price	None	High	Some	Some
Barriers to entry	None	Subject to government regulation	Few	Many
Product differentiation	Very little	No products that compete directly	Emphasis on showing perceived differences in products	Some differences
Examples	Farm products such as wheat and corn	Utilities gas, water, cable television	Retail such as clothing stores, specialty automobiles, airlines, aircraft manufacturers	Steel

Pure Monopoly

pure monopoly
A market structure in which a single company accounts for all industry sales and in which there are barriers to entry.

barriers to entry
Factors, such as technological or legal conditions, which prevent new companies from competing equally with a monopoly.

At the other end of the spectrum is pure monopoly, the market structure in which a single company accounts for all industry sales. The company is the industry. This structure is characterized by barriers to entry—factors that prevent new companies from competing equally with the existing company. Often the barriers are technological or legal conditions. Polaroid, for example, has held major patents on instant photography for years. When Kodak tried to market its own instant camera, Polaroid sued, claiming patent violations. Polaroid collected millions of dollars from Kodak. Another barrier might be one company's control of a natural resource. De Beers Group, for example, controls most of the world's supply of uncut diamonds.

Concept *in Action*

Each hotel offers essentially the same product, with information about pricing easily accessible. Entry into the hotel market is relatively simple, and competition can change with the entry of a new operation. To which one of the four types of market structure do hotels belong?

© JNBAZINET/ALAMY

Sustainable Business, Sustainable World

TORONTO-DOMINION BANK

In Toronto-Dominion Bank's 2010 Corporate Responsibility Report and Public Accountability Statement, it describes its vision to be "The Better Bank." It would appear that it is on target. Regardless of current economic turmoil, TD held to its commitments with respect to sustainability and was able to rank #92 on the 2011 list of the Global 100 Most Sustainable Corporations in the World—one of eight Canadian companies to make the list.

Part of the reason for TD's solid performance is its goal "to be an environmental leader in the financial services industry across North America … working to make a positive impact through our operations, our products and our employees." A huge milestone for the company came when it reached its 2008 goal of becoming carbon-neutral on February 18, 2010, the first large North American–based bank to achieve this. It also learned lessons about the renewable energy business—through the process of purchasing renewable energy to meet its carbon reduction goal—that allowed it to launch a program to finance renewable energy projects for homeowners and small businesses—helping its customers go green.

Moving forward, TD has developed "four pillars" to its environmental program—focusing on its operational footprint, responsible financing, green products such as paperless record keeping and the TD Global Sustainability Fund, and stakeholder engagement. One of its key stakeholders is, of course, its employees. In April 2011, TD was named one of *Maclean's* magazine's "Green 30" based on how employees perceive their employer's environmental efforts. Paperless record keeping was one of the green services offered by TD that led the company to be included in this prestigious list. Chosen by 8.9 million of its customers, the program saves about 10,000 trees a year. One of TD's greatest challenges is in reducing its operational footprint. It has made improvements to reduce energy use and greenhouse gas emissions, develop green building design standards, and green its supply chain, but paper use and paper waste remains a big challenge. Paper usage per employee in TD's Canadian operations actually increased from 2009 to 2010, although being below the industry average. TD has committed to tackle the issue "through all stages of the paper life cycle, from sourcing through usage and disposal." One of the problems is that some bank account paperwork is required by law but, where possible, TD is offering paperless options, and in 2010 it announced participation in the "Closed Loop System" of paper manufacture that diverts paper waste from landfills and reuses it in the production of recycled office paper. This system will divert 1,500 metric tonnes of paper from landfills every year.

Tough economic times and demanding industry requirements have challenged TD to hold to its commitment to be an environmental leader, and so far it has met the challenge.

Thinking Critically

1. Are tough economic times a reasonable excuse for a company to slow down its efforts towards sustainability? Or do these efforts actually help it weather the storm by improving its bottom line?
2. Do different industries have different challenges with respect to sustainability, and should we therefore expect more, less, or the same from companies in different industries?

SOURCES: TD Bank Group, http://www.td.com; The Global 10, http://www.global100.org; and Macleans.ca, http://www2.macleans.ca.

Public utilities such as natural gas and water are pure monopolies (although many public utilities are being privatized, and competition is being encouraged). Some monopolies have been created by government regulations that prohibit competition. Canada Post Corporation's direct mail service is one such monopoly.

MICROECONOMICS: BUSINESSES, INDUSTRIES, AND CONSUMERS

LO4

Now let's shift our focus to *microeconomics*, the study of households, businesses, and industries. This field of economics is concerned with how prices and quantities of goods and services behave in a free market. It stands to reason that people, companies, and governments try to get the most from their limited resources. Consumers want to buy the best quality at the lowest price. Businesses want to keep costs down and revenues high to earn larger profits. Governments also want to use their revenues to provide the most effective public goods and services possible. These groups choose among alternatives by focusing on the prices of goods and services.

As consumers in a free market, we influence what is produced. If Vietnamese food is popular, the high demand attracts entrepreneurs who open more Vietnamese restaurants. They want to compete for our dollars by supplying Vietnamese food at a lower price, of better quality, or with different menu choices. This section explains how business and consumer choices influence the price and availability of goods and services.

Concept *Check*

What is meant by market structure?

Describe the four types of market structure.

Exhibit 2.5   Demand Curve for Snowboarder Jackets

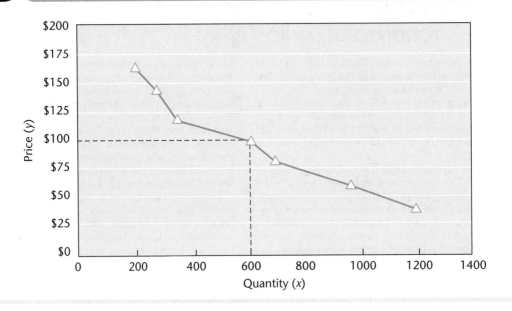

The Nature of Demand

demand
The quantity of a good or service that people are willing to buy at various prices.

demand curve
A graph showing the quantity of a good or service that people are willing to buy at various prices.

Demand is the quantity of a good or service that people are willing to buy at various prices. The higher the price, the lower the quantity demanded, and vice versa. A graph of this relationship is called a demand curve.

Let's assume you own a store that sells jackets for snowboarders. From experience, you know how many jackets you can sell at different prices. The demand curve in Exhibit 2.5 depicts this information. The *x*-axis (horizontal axis) shows the quantity of jackets, and the *y*-axis (vertical axis) shows the related price of those jackets. For example, at a price of $100, customers will buy (demand) 600 jackets.

In the graph, the demand curve slopes downward and to the right. This means that as the price falls, people will want to buy more jackets. Some people who were not going to buy a jacket will purchase one at the lower price. Also, some snowboarders who already have a jacket will buy a second one. The graph also shows that if you put a large number of jackets on the market, you will have to reduce the price to sell all of them.

Understanding demand is critical to businesses. This is because demand tells you how much you can sell and at what price—in other words, how much money the business will take in that can be used to cover costs and hopefully earn a profit. Predicting demand is often difficult, even for the very largest corporations, but is particularly challenging for small businesses.

The Nature of Supply

supply
The quantity of a good or service that businesses will make available at various prices.

supply curve
A graph showing the quantity of a good or service that a business will make available at various prices.

Demand alone is not enough to explain how the market sets prices. We must also look at **supply**, the quantity of a good or service that businesses will make available at various prices. The higher the price, the greater the amount a jacket manufacturer is willing to supply, and vice versa. A graph of the relationship between various prices and the quantities a manufacturer will supply is a supply curve.

We can again plot the quantity of jackets on the *x*-axis and the price on the *y*-axis. As Exhibit 2.6 shows, 800 jackets will be available at a price of $100. Note that the supply curve slopes upward and to the right, the opposite of the demand curve. If snowboarders are willing to pay higher prices, manufacturers of jackets will buy more inputs (Gore-Tex, dye, machinery, labour, etc.) and produce more jackets. The quantity supplied will be greater at higher prices, because producers can earn higher profits.

Exhibit 2.6 Supply Curve for Snowboarder Jackets

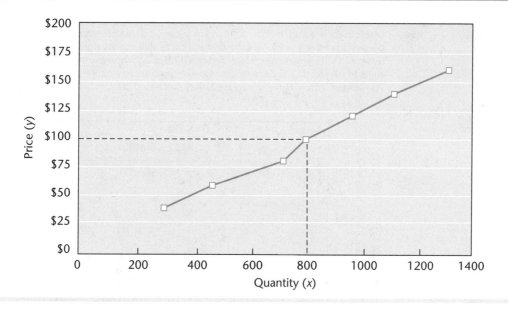

How Demand and Supply Interact to Determine Prices

In a stable economy, the number of jackets that snowboarders demand depends on the jackets' price. Likewise, the number of jackets that suppliers provide depends on price. But at what price will consumer demand for jackets match the quantity suppliers will produce?

To answer this question, we need to look at what happens when demand and supply interact. By plotting both the demand curve and the supply curve on the same graph (Exhibit 2.7), we see that they cross at a certain quantity and price. At that point, labelled E, the quantity demanded equals the quantity supplied. This is the point of **equilibrium**. The equilibrium price is $80; the equilibrium quantity is 700 jackets. At that point, there is a balance between the amount consumers will buy and the amount the manufacturers will supply.

Market equilibrium is achieved through a series of quantity and price adjustments that occur automatically. If the price increases to $160, suppliers produce more jackets than consumers are willing to buy, and a surplus results. To sell more jackets, prices will have to fall. Thus, a surplus pushes prices downward until equilibrium is reached. When the price falls to $60, the quantity of jackets demanded rises above the available supply. The resulting shortage forces prices upward until equilibrium is reached at $80.

equilibrium
The point at which quantity demanded equals quantity supplied.

Changes in Demand

A number of things can increase or decrease demand. For example, if snowboarders' incomes go up, they might decide to buy a second jacket. If incomes fall, a snowboarder who was planning to purchase a jacket might wear an old one instead. Changes in fashion or tastes can also influence demand. If snowboarding were suddenly to go out of fashion, demand for jackets would decrease quickly. A change in the price of related products can also influence demand. For example, if the average price of a snowboard rises to $1,500, some people will quit snowboarding, and jacket demand will fall.

Another factor that can shift demand is expectations about future prices. If you expect jacket prices to increase significantly in the future, you might decide to go ahead and get one today. If you think prices will fall, you will postpone your purchase. Finally, changes in the number of buyers will affect demand. Snowboarding is a young person's sport. The number of teenagers will increase in the next few years. Therefore, the demand for snowboarding jackets should increase.

Exhibit 2.7   Equilibrium Price and Quantity

The number of snowboarder jackets produced and bought at $80 will tend to rest at equilibrium unless there is a shift in either demand or supply. If demand increases, more jackets will be purchased at every price, and the demand curve shifts to the right (as illustrated by line D$_2$ in Exhibit 2.8). If demand decreases, fewer will be bought at every price, and the demand curve shifts to the left (D$_1$). If demand decreased, snowboarders bought 500 jackets at $80 instead of 700 jackets. When demand increased, they purchased 800.

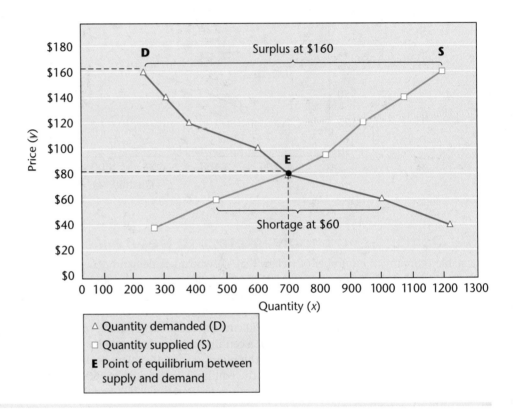

Exhibit 2.8   Shifts in Demand

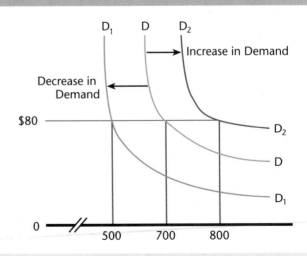

Changes in Supply

Other factors influence the supply side of the picture. New technology typically lowers the cost of production. For example, North Face, a manufacturer of ski and snowboarder jackets, purchased laser-guided pattern-cutting equipment and computer-aided pattern-making equipment. After implementing the new equipment, each jacket was cheaper to produce, resulting in a higher profit per jacket. This became an incentive to supply more jackets at every price. On the other hand, if the price of resources, such as labour or fabric, goes up, North Face will earn a smaller profit on each jacket, and the amount supplied will decrease at every price. Changes in the prices of other goods can also affect supply.

Let's say that snow skiing becomes a really hot sport. The number of skiers jumps dramatically, and the price of ski jackets soars. North Face can use its machines and fabrics to produce either ski or snowboard jackets. If the company can make more profit from ski jackets, it will produce fewer snowboarding jackets at every price. Also, simply a change in the number of producers will shift the supply curve. If the number of manufacturers increases, more jackets will be placed on the market at every price, and vice versa. Taxes can also affect supply. If the government decides, for some reason, to tax the manufacturer for every snowboard jacket produced, then profits will fall and fewer jackets will be offered at every price. Exhibit 2.9 summarizes the factors that can shift demand and supply curves.

Concept Check

What is the relationship between prices and demand for a product?

How is market equilibrium achieved?

Draw a graph that shows an equilibrium point.

MACROECONOMICS: THE BIG PICTURE

LO5

Have you ever looked at CBC Newsworld on the Internet (cbc.ca) or turned on the radio or television and heard something similar to, "Today, the government reported that, for the second straight month, the unemployment rate has risen"? Statements like this are macroeconomic news. Understanding the national economy and how changes in government policies affect households and businesses is a good place to begin our study of economics.

Let's look first at macroeconomic goals and how they can be met. Canada and most other countries have three main macroeconomic goals: economic growth, full employment, and price stability. A nation's economic well-being depends on carefully defining these goals and choosing the best economic policies to reach them.

HOT *links*

The Canadian government follows national and regional economic statistics, including the GDP. For the latest economic overview of the Canadian economy, visit
www.statcan.gc.ca

Exhibit 2.9 — Factors That Cause Demand and Supply Curves to Shift

SHIFT DEMAND

FACTOR	TO THE RIGHT IF:	TO THE LEFT IF:
Buyers' incomes	increase	decrease
Buyers' preferences/tastes	increase	decrease
Prices of substitute products	increase	decrease
Expectations about future prices	will rise	will fall
Number of buyers	increases	decreases

SHIFT SUPPLY

FACTOR	TO THE RIGHT IF:	TO THE LEFT IF:
Technology	lowers cost	increases cost
Resource prices	fall	increase
Changes in prices of other products that can be produced with the same resources	profit of other product falls	profit of other product increases
Number of suppliers	increases	decreases
Taxes	lowered	increased

Striving for Economic Growth

economic growth
An increase in a nation's output of goods and services.

Perhaps the most important way to judge a nation's economic health is to look at its production of goods and services. The more the nation produces, the higher its standard of living. An increase in a nation's output of goods and services is economic growth.

Economic growth is usually a good thing, but it also has a bad side. Increased production yields more pollution. Growth can strain public facilities, such as roads, electricity, schools, and hospitals. Thus, the government tries to apply economic policies that will keep growth to a level that does not reduce the quality of life.

gross domestic product (GDP)
The total market value of all final goods and services produced within a nation's borders in a year.

The most basic measure of economic growth is the gross domestic product (GDP). GDP is the total market value of all final goods and services produced within a nation's borders each year. It is reported quarterly and is used to compare trends in national output. When GDP rises, the economy is growing.

The *rate* of growth in real GDP (GDP adjusted for inflation) is also important. For example, if the Canadian economy has been growing at about 3 percent annually, this growth rate has meant a steady increase in output of goods and services. When the growth rate slides toward zero, the economy begins to stagnate and decline. Canada's average annual GDP growth rate for the years 1962 to 2011 was 3.37 percent. In the past few years, we have generally experienced growth except for the period from late 2008 to beginning of 2011 where we saw a decline.[3]

gross national product (GNP)
The total market value of all final goods and services produced by a country regardless of where the factors of production are located.

Another measurement often used by economists is the gross national product (GNP). Unlike the GDP, which calculates what is produced within the country's borders, the GNP measures what is produced by the nation regardless of where the factors of production are located. Therefore, the Canadian GNP includes the value of the goods and services produced by Canadian companies in Canada and profits from capital held abroad.

One country that continues to grow more rapidly than most is China. Today, there are few things in the global marketplace that are not or cannot be made in China. The primary contributor to China's rapid growth has been technology. For example, most laptop computers are now produced in China, as the Expanding Around the Globe box explains.

business cycles
Upward and downward changes in the level of economic activity.

The level of economic activity is constantly changing. These upward and downward changes are called business cycles. Business cycles vary in length, in how high or low the economy moves, and in how much the economy is affected. Changes in GDP trace the patterns as economic activity expands and contracts. An increase in business activity results in rising output, income, employment, and prices. Eventually, these all peak—and output, income, and employment decline. A decline in GDP that lasts for two consecutive quarters (each a three-month period) is called a recession. It is followed by a recovery period, when economic activity once again increases. The global recession of 2008 reduced consumer confidence, loss of personal wealth, increased unemployment, etc. Some countries we less affected by the recession than other countries, for example, China and Australia. In 2008, the majority of the Canadian manufacturing industries experienced lower sales compared to past years (e.g., auto sales decreased by 22 percent). Exceptions included those provinces that have significant energy, chemical, and aerospace industries.[4]

recession
A decline in GDP that lasts for at least two consecutive quarters.

Businesses must monitor and react to the changing phases of business cycles. When the economy is growing, companies often have a difficult time hiring good employees and finding scarce supplies and raw materials. When a recession hits, many companies find they have more capacity than the demand for their goods and services requires. During the recession of the early 1990s, many companies operated at 75 percent or less of their capacity. When plants use only part of their capacity, they operate inefficiently and have higher costs per unit produced. Let's say that Nestlé has a plant that can produce one million Aero chocolate bars a day, but because of a recession, Nestlé can sell only half a million candy bars a day. Nestlé has a huge plant with large, expensive machines designed to produce a million candy bars a day. Producing Aero chocolate bars at 50 percent capacity does not use Nestlé's investment in the plant and equipment efficiently.

Concept Check

What are Canada's three main macroeconomic objectives?

What is GDP? GNP?

What are business cycles?

Expanding Around the Globe

YOUR TABLET—YOUR LAPTOP: CITIZEN OF THE WORLD

Your new tablet or laptop has already travelled across the world—before you even open the box! Probably assembled in China, it contains parts from many countries. The power supply may have come from China, the microprocessor from the United States, the hard drive and display from Japan, and the memory chips from South Korea. The graphics processor was probably designed in the United States—but manufactured in Taiwan.

Tablets and laptops are a good example of how companies and countries cooperate in today's global economic environment. Taiwanese companies manufacture 80 percent of the world's tablets and laptops. Dell, Apple, Gateway, and Acer outsource 100 percent of their tablet and laptop production (Dell does final assembly in its own offshore factories), and Hewlett-Packard outsources 95 percent. Japanese companies such as NEC, Sony, and Toshiba also outsource, but to a lesser degree—between 35 percent and 60 percent.

Moving tablet and laptop production offshore is not a new strategy for computer companies who needed to reduce costs and find more efficient production methods to stay competitive. Until the 1990s, many laptops were assembled in Japan and Singapore. In the 1990s, Taiwanese companies became the major recipients of the production because of their lower labour costs and high quality.

The rising demand for laptops brought new companies into the market. Although total industry revenues are still rising because of higher demand, profits on laptops have fallen sharply. Low-cost producers such as Acer and Averatec are willing to accept low profit margins to gain market share. With increased competition came sharply lower prices.

To stay competitive despite continuing cost pressures, most Taiwanese contract manufacturers shifted their production facilities to China after Taiwan's government lifted a ban on manufacturing in China in 2001. Quanta, the world's largest notebook manufacturer, employs 20,000 workers at its factory complex in Shanghai, China.

Today, China assembles 68 percent of the world's tablets and laptops, followed by Taiwan with 17 percent, and Japan with 8 percent. The Chinese government recognizes the importance of foreign investment to its economic future, especially in technology, and is encouraging companies to locate production facilities there. Producers of hard drives, displays, memory chips, and other components are already setting up shop in China.[5]

Thinking Critically

1. What are the benefits and disadvantages to computer companies of using offshore contract manufacturers to produce their laptops? Are there any risks in this strategy?
2. How would you describe the market structure of the laptop industry (see the section "Competing in a Free Market" later in this chapter), and why?

Keeping People on the Job

Another macroeconomic goal is **full employment**, or having jobs for all who want to and can work. Full employment doesn't actually mean 100 percent employment. Some people choose not to work for personal reasons (attending school, raising children) or are temporarily unemployed while they wait to start a new job. Thus, the government defines full employment as the situation when about 94 to 96 percent of those available to work actually have jobs.

full employment
The condition when all people who want to work and can work have jobs.

Concept *in Action*

The housing industry is a leading economic indicator. A rise in new home construction typically translates into a robust economy.

What is the current state of Canada's economy?

© KIM STEELE/PHOTODISC/GETTY IMAGES

To determine how close we are to full employment, the government measures the **unemployment rate**. This rate indicates the percentage of the total labour force that is not working but is actively *looking for work*. It excludes "discouraged workers," those not seeking jobs because they think no one will hire them. Each month the government releases statistics on employment. These figures help us understand how well the economy is doing.

unemployment rate
The percentage of the total labour force that is actively looking for work but is not actually working.

Economists classify unemployment into four types: frictional, structural, cyclical, and seasonal. The categories are of small consolation to someone who is unemployed, but they help economists understand the problem of unemployment in our economy.

Frictional unemployment is short-term unemployment that is not related to the business cycle. It includes people who are unemployed while waiting to start a better job, those who are reentering the job market, and those entering for the first time, such as new university and college graduates. This type of unemployment is always present and has little impact on the economy.

frictional unemployment
Short-term unemployment that is not related to the business cycle.

Structural unemployment is also unrelated to the business cycle but is involuntary. It is caused by a mismatch between available jobs and the skills of available workers in an industry or a region. For example, if the birthrate declines, fewer teachers will be needed. Or the available workers in an area might lack the skills that employers want. Retraining and skill-building programs are often required to reduce structural unemployment.

structural unemployment
Unemployment that is caused by a mismatch between available jobs and the skills of available workers in an industry or a region; it is not related to the business cycle.

Cyclical unemployment, as the name implies, occurs when a downturn in the business cycle reduces the demand for labour throughout the economy. In a long recession, cyclical unemployment is widespread, and even people with good job skills can't find jobs. The government can partly counteract cyclical unemployment with programs that boost the economy.

cyclical unemployment
Unemployment that occurs when a downturn in the business cycle reduces the demand for labour throughout the economy.

In the past, cyclical unemployment affected mainly less skilled workers and those in heavy manufacturing. Typically, they would be rehired when economic growth increased. Since the 1990s, however, competition forced many Canadian companies to downsize so they could survive in the global marketplace.

The last type is **seasonal unemployment**, which occurs during specific seasons in certain industries. Employees subject to seasonal unemployment include retail workers hired for the December buying season, road construction, and restaurant employees in winter ski areas.

seasonal unemployment
Unemployment that occurs during specific seasons in certain industries.

Keeping Prices Steady

The third macroeconomic goal is to keep overall prices for goods and services fairly steady. The situation in which the average of all prices of goods and services is rising is called **inflation**. Inflation's higher prices reduce **purchasing power**, the value of what money can buy. If prices go up but income doesn't rise or rises at a slower rate, a given amount of income buys less. For example, if the price of a basket of groceries rises from $30 to $40 but your salary remains the same, you can buy only 75 percent as many groceries ($30 ÷ $40). Your purchasing power declines by 25 percent ($10 ÷ $40).

inflation
The situation in which the average of all prices of goods and services is rising.

purchasing power
The value of what money can buy.

Inflation affects both personal and business decisions. When prices are rising, people tend to spend more—before their purchasing power declines further. Businesses that expect inflation often increase their supplies, and people often speed up planned purchases of cars and major appliances.

There are two types of inflation. **Demand-pull inflation** occurs when the demand for goods and services is greater than the supply. In this case, would-be buyers have more money to spend than the amount needed to buy available goods and services. Their demand, which exceeds the supply, tends to pull

demand-pull inflation
Inflation that occurs when the demand for goods and services is greater than the supply.

prices up. This situation is sometimes described as "too much money chasing too few goods." The higher prices lead to greater supply, eventually creating a balance between demand and supply.

Cost-push inflation is triggered by increases in production costs, such as expenses for materials and wages. These increases push up the prices of final goods and services. Wage increases are a major cause of cost-push inflation, creating a "wage-price spiral." For example, assume the Canadian Auto Workers Union negotiates a three-year labour agreement that raises wages 3 percent per year and increases overtime pay. Car makers will then raise car prices to cover their higher labour costs. These higher wages will also give auto workers more money to buy goods and services, and this increased demand might pull up other prices. Workers in other industries will demand higher wages to keep up with the increased prices, and the cycle will push prices even higher.

HOW INFLATION IS MEASURED Economists most commonly measure the rate of inflation by looking at changes in the consumer price index (CPI), an index of the prices of a "shopping basket" of goods and services purchased by consumers. It tracks the retail price of a representative shopping basket of approximately 600 goods and services that an average household would purchase and is published monthly by Statistics Canada. Some of the expenditures include food, housing, transportation, furniture, clothing, and recreation. The index is weighted to reflect typical spending patterns. For instance, greater importance is given to housing than to recreation. Statistics Canada updates the CPI basket to reflect broad changes in consumer spending habits and to acknowledge changes in products and services.

The CPI sets prices in a base period at 100, currently using the base period of 2002. Current prices are then expressed as a percentage of prices in the base period. A rise in the CPI means prices are increasing. For example, the CPI in September 2011 was measured at 120.6, meaning that the same basket of goods that cost $100.00 in 2002 cost $120.60 in September 2011.[6]

Changes in wholesale prices are another important indicator of inflation. The producer price index (PPI) measures the prices paid by producers and wholesalers for such commodities as raw materials, partially finished goods, and finished products.

cost-push inflation
Inflation that occurs when increases in production costs push up the prices of final goods and services.

consumer price index (CPI)
An index of the prices of a "shopping basket" of goods and services purchased by consumers.

For historical and current information on the CPI, visit Statistics Canada's website at
www.statcan.ca

producer price index (PPI)
An index of the prices paid by producers and wholesalers for various commodities such as raw materials, partially finished goods, and finished products.

Concept *in Action*

The consumer price index (CPI) provides a broad measure of the cost of living in Canada. Currently, the base year is 2002 and subsequent years are compared to the prices in 2002. What is the current rate of inflation in your area, in your province or territory, and in Canada?

The PPI is actually a family of indexes for many different product categories. Examples of PPI indexes are raw materials and industrial products. Because the PPI measures prices paid by producers for raw materials, energy, and other commodities, it might foreshadow subsequent price changes for businesses and consumers.

THE IMPACT OF INFLATION Inflation has several negative effects on people and businesses. For one thing, it penalizes people who live on fixed incomes. Let's say that a couple receives $1,000 a month retirement income beginning in 2012. If inflation is 10 percent in 2013, then the couple can buy only about 90 percent of what they could purchase in 2012. Similarly, inflation hurts savers. As prices rise, the real value, or purchasing power, of savings deteriorates.

LO6 ACHIEVING MACROECONOMIC GOALS

To reach macroeconomic goals, countries must often choose among conflicting alternatives. Sometimes political needs override economic ones. For example, bringing inflation under control might call for a politically difficult period of high unemployment and low growth. Or, in an election year, politicians might resist raising taxes to curb inflation. Still, the federal government and the Bank of Canada must try to guide the economy to a sound balance of growth, employment, and price stability. The two main tools used are the fiscal policy and monetary policy. By having a separation of fiscal and monetary policymakers (i.e., the federal government and the Bank of Canada, respectively), Canada has separated the power to spend money (i.e., fiscal policy) from the power to create money (i.e., monetary policy).

Bank of Canada
Canada's central bank, whose objective is the economic and financial well-being of Canada by creating a sound balance of growth, employment, and price stability.

Monetary Policy

Monetary policy refers to the Bank of Canada's programs for controlling the amount of money circulating in the economy and controlling interest rates. Changes in the money supply affect both the level of economic activity and the rate of inflation. According to the Bank of Canada Act of 1934, the Bank of Canada is the central banking system that prints money and controls how much of it will be in circulation to "promote the economic and financial well-being of Canada."

monetary policy
The measures taken by the Bank of Canada to regulate the amount of money in circulation in order to influence the economy.

As the Bank of Canada increases or decreases the amount of money in circulation, these decisions affect interest rates (the cost of borrowing money and the reward for lending it). The Bank of Canada can change the interest rate (also called the bank rate and target for the overnight rate) on money it lends to banks, signalling to the banking system and financial markets that it has changed its monetary policy. Banks, in turn, may pass along this change to consumers and businesses that receive loans from the banks. If the cost of borrowing increases, the economy slows because interest rates affect consumer and business decisions to spend or invest. The housing industry, business, and investments react the most strongly to changes in interest rates.

contractionary policy
The use of monetary policy by the Bank of Canada to tighten the money supply by selling government securities or raising interest rates.

expansionary policy
The use of monetary policy by the Bank of Canada to increase the growth of the money supply.

As you can see, the Bank of Canada can use monetary policy to contract or expand the economy. With contractionary policy, the Bank of Canada restricts, or tightens, the money supply by selling government securities or raising interest rates. The result is slower economic growth and higher unemployment. Thus, contractionary policy reduces spending and, ultimately, lowers inflation. With expansionary policy, the Bank of Canada increases, or loosens, growth in the money supply. An expansionary policy stimulates the economy. Interest rates decline, so business and consumer spending go up. Unemployment rates drop as businesses expand. But increasing the money supply also has a negative side: More spending pushes prices up, increasing the inflation rate. There is more discussion of the monetary policy in Chapter 17.

Fiscal Policy

The other economic tool used by the government is **fiscal policy**, its program of taxation and spending. By increasing government spending or by cutting taxes, the government can stimulate the economy. Look again at Exhibit 2.2 on page 38. The more government buys from businesses, the greater business revenues and output are. Likewise, if consumers or businesses have to pay less in taxes, they will have more income to spend for goods and services. Tax policies in Canada therefore affect business decisions. High corporate taxes can make it harder for Canadian companies to compete with companies in countries with lower taxes. As a result, companies may choose to locate facilities in other countries to reduce their tax burden

If the government spends more for programs (social services, education, etc.) than it collects in taxes, the result is a **federal budget deficit**. To balance the budget, the government can cut its spending, increase taxes, or do some combination of the two. When it cannot balance the budget, the government must make up any shortfalls by borrowing (just like any business or household). The accumulated total of all of the federal government's annual budget deficits is known as the **national debt**.

Although fiscal policy has a major impact on businesses and consumers, continual increases in government spending raise another important issue. When government takes more money from businesses and consumers (the private sector) and uses these funds for increased government spending (the public sector), a phenomenon known as **crowding out** occurs. Here are three examples of crowding out:

1. The government spends more on public libraries, and individuals buy fewer books at bookstores.
2. The government spends more on public education, and individuals spend less on private education.
3. The government spends more on public transportation, and individuals spend less on private transportation.

In other words, government spending is crowding out private spending.

CROWDING OUT PRIVATE INVESTMENT Of concern is the effect of the national debt on private investment. If, to sell its **bonds**, the government raises the interest rate on the bonds it offers, it forces private businesses, which must stay competitive as suppliers of bonds in the bond market, to raise the rates they offer on their corporate bonds (long-term debt obligations issued by a company). In other words, financing government spending by government debt makes it more costly for private industry to finance its own investment. As a result, government debt can end up crowding out private investment and slowing economic growth in the private sector.

Another concern is that there is limited supply of investment capital. If the government borrows heavily, there is less for private investment and, therefore, private growth.

Economic Crises of 2008 and 2011

The economic crisis that started in 2008 changed the way that businesses and governments thought about the economy; the first critical recession in Canada since 1990. The crisis of 2008 was primarily caused by ineffective regulations, a careless regulating agency, and bad corporate governance. The situation in 2011 was primarily the result of government and fiscal irresponsibility. We still see the effects of these crises today and their future impact is still not fully understood.

In many countries, industries and the financial institutions were bailed out by governments, taken over by governments, or simply closed their doors. In Canada, we were not immune to the crisis but were less

fiscal policy
The government's use of taxation and spending to affect the economy.

federal budget deficit
The condition that occurs when the federal government spends more for programs than it collects in taxes.

national debt
The accumulated total of all of the federal government's annual budget deficits.

HOT|inks

Want to know the current budget deficit and national debt? Head to
www.fin.gc.ca

crowding out
The situation that occurs when government spending replaces spending by the private sector.

Concept *in Action*

The interest rate set by the Bank of Canada is passed on to consumers and businesses by the banking system. What is the current overnight rate and how has it changed over the last few years?

DAVID EVISON/SHUTTERSTOCK

bonds
Securities that represent long-term debt obligations (liabilities) issued by corporations and governments.

affected than many countries in part because of our strong financial regulations. Yet our governments were forced to respond with sometimes unfavourable decisions. Some of these decisions are discussed below.

STEADY GROWTH In response to business and consumers opting to reserve spending because of the uncertainty in the economy, the government increased spending for capital infrastructure projects and other initiatives. For example, the government introduced home renovation credits to encourage people to spend money to upgrade or make their homes more energy efficient.

FULL EMPLOYMENT The manufacturing industries, especially those that rely on exports, were greatly affected by the economic crisis, as were commodities and tourism. The government responded by lending money to industries and encouraging upgrades to existing capital assets.

STEADY PRICES The Bank of Canada responded to the financial crisis by reducing the overnight rate to record lows. In March 2008 the overnight rate was set at 3.50 percent, and by March 2009 the overnight rate was set at 0.50 percent. The Bank of Canada used monetary policy to try to return to a consumer price index of 2 percent (its target).

LO7   THE FUTURE OF ECONOMICS

Trends in business occur at several levels. Never before have the economies of the world been more connected—a "domino effect" is being felt around the world as we experience economic changes, especially the legacy of the economic crises of 2008 and 2011. Three of the major trends are lack of confidence in the markets, meeting competitive challenges, and increasing entrepreneurship worldwide.

Making Ethical Choices

PURCHASING POWER

As a child, you treasured your weekly allowance and delighted in seeking out the best deals. You ended up with more toys than your friends while spending the same amount of money. Your keen sense of the price of goods and ability to buy more quality products for the same money made your university friends envious. Finally, they convinced you to take their money to purchase needed items. You were a natural purchasing agent.

You understood the relationship between supply and demand and the price you were willing to pay for goods. Shortly after graduating, you accepted a position as chief purchasing agent for a hospital.

At the hospital, you became concerned that prices paid for pharmaceutical goods seemed out of alignment with the laws of supply and demand. No more best deals. Perhaps even "a crisis with regard to the cost of prescription drugs." Two pharmaceutical companies seemed to be inflating their drug prices. Your sense about overcharging proved correct. The provincial government

filed a lawsuit against the companies, accusing them of offering drugs to pharmacists at deeply discounted prices as a way of selling more. Part of the issue involved the government's wholesale price system. Could the government be impeding your purchasing power at the hospital? The companies' pricing policies seem to involve inflating the price reported to the government and then offering the pharmacists an opportunity to make money on the difference between the higher reimbursements and promised lower prices from the companies.

All of this is troubling because you haven't been able to identify manufacturers of equivalent drugs at competitive prices.

ETHICAL DILEMMA: Would you purchase drugs that were not exactly the same to save the hospital money?

SOURCES: Christopher Bowe, "NY Attorney General Targets Drugmakers," *Financial Times*, February 23, 2003, http://www.FT.com; and Hollister H. Hovey, "New York State Sues Pharmacia, Glaxo, Alleging Pricing Scheme," *Wall Street Journal*, February 14, 2003. Note: This case has been amended from its earlier publication.

Waning Confidence in the Markets

According to TD Bank chief economist Craig Alexander, the three areas of concern that have lowered confidence in the markets are the ability of the European governments to deal with fiscal and financial problems, the ability of the United States to deal with its deficits, and the sustainability of the global economic recovery (especially in the United States).[7]*

EUROPE The problems are the result of a flawed introduction of the Euro as a common currency for 17 members of the European Union. It was introduced with a common central bank (similar to the Bank of Canada) and common monetary policy, but without a common treasury and common fiscal mandatory arrangements. This led to irresponsible financial behaviours by many of the countries, Greece leading the way.

UNITED STATES The United States has shown no willingness to eliminate its annual deficit (difference between what the government revenues are and its spending) and start to pay down its national debt (accumulated annual deficits). Currently, the national debt is approximately $15 trillion USD. The difference between Greece, for example, and the United States is that the latter has the ability to pay, but not the political willingness.

GLOBAL ECONOMIC RECOVERY In 2011, there were disasters, including the tsunami in Japan, that ruined its supply chain for global manufacturing, unrest in the Middle East, and unusual weather, all contributing to slow economic recovery. According to Craig Alexander, Canada is fundamentally sound but housing debt is a concern here.

Meeting Competitive Challenges

Companies are turning to many different strategies to remain competitive in the global marketplace. One of the most important is relationship management, which involves building, maintaining, and enhancing interactions with customers and other parties to develop long-term satisfaction through mutually beneficial partnerships. Relationship management includes both supply chain management, which builds strong bonds with suppliers, and relationship marketing, which focuses on customers. (We'll discuss supply chain management in greater detail in Chapter 15 and return to relationship marketing in Chapter 13.) In general, the longer a customer stays with a company, the more that customer is worth. Long-term customers buy more, take less of a company's time, are less sensitive to price, and bring in new customers. Best of all, they require no acquisition or start-up costs. Good long-standing customers are worth so much that, in some industries, reducing customer defections by as little as five points—from, say, 15 percent to 10 percent per year—can double profits.

Another important way companies stay competitive is through strategic alliances (also called strategic partnerships). The trend toward forming these cooperative agreements between companies is accelerating rapidly, particularly among high-tech companies. These companies have realized that strategic partnerships are more than just important—they are critical. Strategic alliances can take many forms. Some companies enter into strategic alliances with their suppliers, who take over much of their actual production and manufacturing. Nike, the largest producer of athletic footwear in the world, does not manufacture a single shoe. Gallo, the largest wine company on earth, does not grow a single grape.

Others with complementary strengths team up. For example, computer manufacturer Hewlett-Packard (HP) and retail giant Walmart partnered to improve sales at both. HP provided Walmart with low-cost electronic products. The two companies worked together to develop special products for Walmart, such as desktop

relationship management
The practice of building, maintaining, and enhancing interactions with customers and other parties to develop long-term satisfaction through mutually beneficial partnerships.

strategic alliance
A cooperative agreement between companies; sometimes called a *strategic partnership*.

*Material reprinted with the express permission of: **Postmedia News**, a division of Postmedia Network Inc.

Concept *in Action*

Tim Hortons strives to build strong customer relationships and retain loyal customers with the Quickpay TimCard. How do loyalty cards build customer relations?

and notebook computers for about $400, digital cameras for $100, and all-in-one printers for $50. HP was eager to satisfy Walmart, one of its biggest retail partners. For Walmart, HP's products would lure customers who might otherwise shop for electronics at Best Buy and Circuit City into Walmart where they could spend more of their holiday gift dollars.[8]

Companies in the same industry often form alliances. Smaller companies with unique products or technologies may partner with larger companies who can provide wider distribution in exchange for access to the technology. Even rivals find strategic alliances advantageous. South Korean electronics manufacturer Samsung competes with Sony and a few other companies for the top spot in global television sales. Yet since 2003, the two companies have worked together on producing television display panels. Sony, in search of a supplier for its new line of flat-panel televisions, arranged to become a partner in Samsung's new liquid crystal display factory. The result has benefited both companies in many ways. Their engineers now cooperate on panel technologies, leading to speedier improvement cycles. With Samsung's approval, Sony introduced some of Samsung's LCD technologies before Samsung did—and sold significantly more models equipped with the new technology than Samsung. Why would Samsung want to continue working with Sony? Whereas Samsung had the edge in developing LCD technologies, Sony excelled at applying technology to consumer products, especially televisions. Teaming up with and at the same time competing with Sony has pushed Samsung to new technological breakthroughs and better product design. "If we learn from Sony, it will help us in advancing our technology," says Jang Insik, a Samsung engineer. Other Asian electronics manufacturers are pooling resources to their mutual benefit, despite struggles to overcome concerns about helping rivals and working with companies in other countries.[9]

Entrepreneurship Spreads Worldwide

A key trend in macroeconomics and competition is the rising entrepreneurial spirit in former command economies and other developing nations such as India. As Russia and China have shifted away from centralized economic controls towards greater competitive freedom, many people have embraced the opportunity to start businesses that meet the needs of local consumers.

China itself has been called "the world's largest startup" as it goes through many of the same eras in the history of business that Canada experienced—but in a greatly compressed time frame. The development of modern business occurred over about 150 years in Canada; China is attempting to accomplish the same thing in about 25 years. A key element in China's economic transformation is setting free the as-yet-untapped entrepreneurial power of its citizens. The Chinese government recognizes the potential of this huge untapped resource and its role in creating new products and a world-class economy that will rival others in the world.[10]

Concept *Check*

What are three major economic issues troubling the world?

How does relationship management make a business more competitive?

Explain the entrepreneurial movement in former command economies.

GREAT IDEAS TO USE NOW

As you study micro- and macroeconomics, remember that economics is not something you should learn for an exam and then forget. Economics is an analytical science that will help you understand the world around you. It can help you be more imaginative and insightful in everyday life. You should now better understand why prices are going up or down, when interest rates will fall, and when and why the unemployment rate will fall.

Understanding these basic economic concepts can help you decide whether to change jobs (and how much money to ask for) and whether to buy a car now or wait until next year. When you hear that an automobile manufacturer has 115 days of inventory, understanding supply and demand will tell you that now might be the time to buy that new car.

Similarly, economics will help you become a better informed citizen. Almost every political issue is, in some way, grounded in economic concepts. You should now know what it means to balance the budget and what problems occur with monopoly power. In short, economics can help you make more thoughtful and informed decisions.

Economics not only can help you understand what is happening in other countries but also can help raise your awareness of opportunities in those countries. As more and more countries have moved away from command economies, Canadian and foreign multinational companies are moving in to take advantage of ground-floor opportunities. Consider accepting a foreign assignment. It's a wonderful way to experience other cultures and, at the same time, get ahead in your career. More and more large organizations are requiring that their middle and upper level managers have foreign field experience. When you have an opportunity for a foreign assignment, don't let it slip by.

In today's business world, if a company doesn't deliver customer value, it doesn't survive. Companies that provide customer value end up with satisfied customers. Some companies that are especially good at satisfying customers are SaskTel, TD Canada Trust, T-Mobile, Mercedes-Benz, H. J. Heinz, Lexus, Colgate-Palmolive, Mars, Maytag, Quaker Oats, Hershey Foods, Toyota, and Cadbury Schweppes. All of the companies have won either quality or customer satisfaction awards at one time or another.

Summary of Learning Outcomes

LO1 Explain what economics is and how the three sectors of the economy are linked.

Economics is the study of how individuals, businesses, and governments use scarce resources to produce and distribute goods and services. The two major areas in economics are macroeconomics, the study of the economy as a whole, and microeconomics, the study of households and businesses. The individual, business, and government sectors of the economy are linked by a series of two-way flows. The government provides public goods and services for the other two sectors and receives income in the form of taxes. Changes in one flow affect the other sectors.

LO2 Understand the primary features of the world's economic systems.

An economic system is the combination of policies, laws, and choices made by a nation's government to establish the systems that determine what goods and services are produced and how they are allocated. The main economic systems in the world today include market economies (capitalism), command (planned) economies, socialism, and mixed economies.

LO3 Explain the four types of market structure.

Market structure is the number of suppliers in a market. Perfect competition is characterized by a large number of buyers and sellers, very similar products, good market information for both buyers and sellers, and ease of entry into and exit from the market. In monopolistic competition, many companies sell close substitutes in a market that is fairly easy to enter. In an oligopoly, a few companies produce most or all of the industry's output. An oligopoly is also difficult to enter, and what one company does will influence others. In a pure monopoly, there is a single seller in a market.

LO4 Discuss the basic microeconomic concepts of demand and supply, and how they establish prices.

Demand is the quantity of a good or service that people will buy at a given price. Supply is the quantity of a good or service that companies will make available at a given price. When the price increases, the quantity demanded falls but the quantity supplied rises. A price decrease leads to increased demand but a lower supply. At the point where the quantity demanded equals the quantity supplied, demand and supply are in balance. This equilibrium point is achieved by market adjustments of quantity and price.

LO5 Show how economic growth, full employment, and price stability indicate a nation's economic health.

A nation's economy is growing when the level of business activity, as measured by gross domestic product, is rising. GDP is the total value of all goods and services produced in a year. The goal of full employment is to have a job for all who can and want to work. How well a nation is meeting its employment goals is measured by the unemployment rate. There are four types of unemployment: frictional, structural, cyclical, and seasonal.

With price stability, the overall prices of goods and services are not moving either up or down very much. Inflation is the general upward movement of prices. When prices rise, purchasing power falls. The rate of inflation is measured by changes in the consumer price index (CPI) and the producer price index (PPI). There are two main causes of inflation. If the demand for goods and services exceeds the supply, prices will rise. This is called demand-pull inflation. With cost-push inflation, higher production costs, such as expenses for materials and wages, increase the final prices of goods and services.

Monetary policy refers to actions by the Bank of Canada to control the money supply. When the Bank of Canada restricts the money supply, interest rates rise, the inflation rate drops, and economic growth slows. By expanding the money supply, the Bank of Canada stimulates economic growth.

The government uses fiscal policy—changes in levels of taxation and spending—to control the economy. Reducing taxes or increasing spending stimulates the economy; raising taxes or decreasing spending does the opposite. When the government spends more than it receives in tax revenues, it must borrow to finance the deficit. Some economists favour deficit spending as a way of stimulating the economy; others worry about our high level of national debt.

LO6 Describe how the Bank of Canada uses monetary policy, and how governments use fiscal policy to achieve their macroeconomics goals.

Three of the major trends are lack of confidence in the markets, meeting competitive challenges, and increasing entrepreneurship worldwide. The lack of confidence has been primarily caused by the European crisis of 2011, United States' reluctance to pursue fiscal responsibility, and slow global economic recovery. Companies are establishing long-term relationships with both customers and suppliers. At the macro level, budding entrepreneurial spirit is sparking wealth among individual business owners and fuelling the growth of market economies.

LO7 List some of the trends that are reshaping micro- and macroeconomic environments.

Key Terms

Bank of Canada   50
barriers to entry   40
bonds   52
business cycles   46
capital   33
circular flow   34
command economy (planned economy or central planning)   36
consumer price index (CPI)   49
contractionary policy   50
cost-push inflation   49
crowding out   51
cyclical unemployment   48
demand   42
demand curve   42
demand-pull inflation   48
economic growth   46
economic system   35
economics   32
entrepreneurial thinking   34
entrepreneurs   33
equilibrium   43
expansionary policy   50
factors of production   33
federal budget deficit   51
fiscal policy   51
frictional unemployment   48
full employment   47

gross domestic product (GDP)   46
gross national product (GNP)   46
inflation   48
knowledge   34
labour   33
macroeconomics   32
market economy   35
market structure   38
microeconomics   32
mixed economies   37
monetary policy   50
monopolistic competition   39
national debt   51
natural resources   33
oligopoly   39
perfect (pure) competition   38
producer price index (PPI)   49
purchasing power   48
pure monopoly   40
recession   46
relationship management   53
seasonal unemployment   48
socialism   37
strategic alliance   53
structural unemployment   48
supply   42
supply curve   42
unemployment rate   48

Experiential Exercises

1. Understand your tax commitment. Soon you will enter the permanent job market, if you are not there already. Typically, your earnings will rise over the next 35 years, but as your earnings increase, so will your taxes. The average Canadian works five to six months out of every year just to cover taxes. Are taxes too high in our country? As taxes will be a major part of your financial life for the next 35 to 45 years, you need to be informed. Visit the websites of a few organizations that advocate tax reform, such as the Canadian Taxpayers Federation at www.taxpayer.com.

2. Learn a new language. Consider taking a job outside of Canada for a while. If you decide to work overseas, having basic skills in a second language will go a long way toward ensuring that you have a rewarding and pleasant experience. Learning a second language can also bring a lot of self-satisfaction. Go to www.learnalanguage.com and find out more about learning a foreign language.

3. Use the Internet or go to the library and determine the current trends in GDP growth, unemployment, and inflation. What do these trends tell you about the level of business activity and the business cycle? If you owned a personnel agency, how would this information affect your decision making?

4. As a manufacturer of in-line skates, you are questioning your pricing policies. You note that over the past five years, the CPI increased an average of 2 percent per year, but the price of a pair of skates increased an average of 8 percent per year for the first three years and 2 percent for the next two years. What does this information tell you about demand, supply, and other factors influencing the market for these skates?

5. Write a paper describing an occasion on which you received outstanding customer value and an occasion when you received very poor customer value.

6. Divide the class into four teams. One pair of teams will debate the pros and cons of airline deregulation. The other pair will debate electric-utility deregulation. One team should take the pro and the other the con for each issue. If you have Internet access, use the Dow Jones news service, ABI, or another database to obtain current articles on the subjects.

Review Questions

1. Explain economics as a circular flow.

2. What are the factors of production? How do they work together to produce goods and services?

3. What are the four types of economies? How do they differ regarding the ownership and allocation of the factors of production?

4. What are the four market structures?

5. Distinguish between micro- and macroeconomics. What are the three main macro goals?

6. How do GDP and GNP differ?

7. What are the various types of unemployment?

8. What are monetary policy and fiscal policy? Who is responsible for each?

9. What are contractionary policy and expansionary policy?

10. What is relationship management? How can it be achieved?

11. What is a strategic alliance? What are its benefits to the companies involved?

12. Why is it important for companies to create a competitive workforce?

13. How can understanding economics help you as a consumer? As a business manager or owner?

CREATIVE THINKING CASE

We Want Our MTV (International)

Viacom Inc.'s most popular brand, MTV, is just as popular in Shanghai, China as it is in Sydney, Australia; or in Lagos, Nigeria, as it is in Los Angeles, USA. London-based MTV Networks International (MTVNI), the world's largest global network, has taken its winning formula to 167 foreign markets on six continents, including urban and rural areas. It broadcasts in 18 languages to 430 million homes, or about 1.3 billion people, through locally programmed and operated TV channels and websites. While the United States currently generates about 80 percent of MTV's profits, 80 percent of the company's subscriber base lives outside the U.S. "The development of our international business is a major priority ... All of this builds on the growing strength of our domestic brands and businesses, which will continue to provide fuel and momentum for our international ambitions," said Viacom President and CEO Philippe Dauman.

Viacom was originally a spin-off from CBS, but it has spread from its television roots into a multimedia lifestyle entertainment and culture brand for all ages. In addition to MTV and MTV2, its channel lineup includes BET, Nickelodeon, VH1, Comedy Central, LOGO, Spike, TMF (The Music Factory), Game One, and several European music, comedy, and lifestyle channels. Viacom serves over 700 million subscribers (over two billion channel subscriptions worldwide). Revenue will top $15 billion in 2011. Adding to the complexity is MTV's multimedia and interactive nature, with gaming, texting, and websites, as well as television. The technology changes nearly every day and the corporate partnerships continue to expand into new markets.

The company prefers to hire local employees rather than import staff. According to Brent Hansen, president and chief executive of MTV Networks Europe until his retirement in 2006, getting the local perspective is invaluable in helping the network understand its markets, whether in terms of musical tastes or what children like. For example, Alex Okosi, a Nigerian who went to college in the United States, is chief executive for MTV Base, which launched in sub-Saharan Africa in 2005. Okosi recommended that MTV consider each country as an individual market, rather than blending them all together.

One reason for MTVNI's success is "glocalization"—its ability to adapt programs to fit local cultures while still maintaining a consistent, special style. "When we set a channel up, we always provide a set of parameters in terms of standards of things we require," Hansen explains. "Obviously an MTV channel that doesn't look good enough is not going to do the business for us, let alone for the audience. There's a higher expectation." The local unit can tailor content to its market. MTV India conveys a "sense of the colourful street culture," explains Bill Roedy, former MTV International's President, while MTV Japan has "a sense of technology edginess; MTV Italy, style and elegance." In Africa, MTV Base features videos from top African artists as well as from emerging African music talent. The goal, according to Brent Hansen, is to "provide a unique cultural meeting point for young people in Africa, using the common language of music to connect music fans from different backgrounds and cultures."

Thinking Critically

1. Do you agree with Philippe Dauman that MTV's future lies mostly in its international operations, and why?

2. What types of political, economic, and competitive challenges does MTV Networks International face by operating worldwide?

3. How has MTVNI overcome cultural differences to create a world brand?

SOURCES: MTV Africa website, www.MTVbase.com, (December 18, 2012); MTV International website, www.mtv.com/international, (January 18, 2006); "Now, Africa Gets MTV Base," Africa News Service, February 25, 2005, www.comtexnews.com; Johnnie L. Roberts, "World Tour'" Newsweek, June 6, 2005, pp. 34–35; Robin D. Rusch, "MTV Networks Internationally," Brandchannel.com, July 26, 2004, www.brandchannel.com; Finke, N. "Robert Bakish Named President & CEO of Viacom International Media Networks," Deadline (2011), published electronically January 19, http://www.deadline.com/2011/01/robert-bakish-named-president-ceo-of-viacom-international-media-networks/. Viacom, "4th Quarter Earnings Release," 2011. Viacom, "Pulse," 2011.

chapter 3

Making the Connection

Social: Society, Corporate Responsibility, and Making Ethical Decisions

In this chapter, you'll be learning about some very important trends in the *social* environment. One such trend is the changing demographic composition of the Canadian population, resulting in changing patterns in the workforce and in consumer wants and needs. Another is the trend toward better ethics or, at least, higher expectations with regard to business ethics and increased corporate responsibility.

Just as the other trends in the PESTI environment model affect one another, so do social trends. For example, demographic changes in the population—both in age and in multicultural diversity—lead to changing consumer wants and needs (another social trend), and to changes in government/*political* policy. For example, extending the mandatory retirement age will delay the damage to the Canada Pension Plan that will occur as the large bulge of boomers retires. Increasing immigration to offset a shrinking labour force is another good example. Demographic changes also lead to changes in *technology* as businesses look for ways to make up for labour shortages. This has even helped lead to the *economic* trend toward entrepreneurship (which we'll discuss in Chapter 6), as those born at the end of the baby boom have difficulty finding jobs at higher levels in companies because the early boomers have taken all of those jobs, and the numbers of visible minorities starting their own businesses increase. This trend toward increased diversity is one that can have a very positive impact on a business if it embraces this diversity in its hiring, making it much more capable of understanding and meeting its increasingly varied customer base.

Business ethics and corporate responsibility also have integrative implications for businesses. Market forces and market failures in the economic environment have motivated greater corporate responsibility for organizations wishing to promote consumer confidence. And of course the political factor is always present; if business does not act ethically and accept its social responsibility voluntarily, governments are likely to step in and enact legislation, as we have seen in response to the Enron and WorldCom scandals in the United States.

On its website, www.ic.gc.ca, Industry Canada presents a "Business Case for CSR" that demonstrates how a company's commitment to corporate social responsibility affects its success by helping it meet the critical success factors in our model. For example, it leads to "operational efficiency gains" that reduce costs to help the company *achieve financial performance*; "improved reputation and branding" that increases sales and customer loyalty (helping to achieve financial success, because the company gains customer trust and better *meets their needs* in the long term); and "enhanced employee relations" that help to gain *employee commitment*.

Recent events would also support the notion that corporate responsibility is necessary to achieving the critical success factors in the long term: a global recession brought on by a focus on short-term wealth, increasing evidence of human-accelerated climate change, and a loss of trust in the private sector brought about by recent scandals. All of these have combined to create a new reality for businesses that, if nothing else, has shed light on the dangers of short-term thinking. BSR (Business for Social Responsibility, www.bsr.org), in its 2008 Report, describes the situation facing business today as one that "future generations are likely to view … as a pivot point, when old frameworks were discarded and new ones began to emerge … a 'reset,' when business as usual was no longer possible, and new ways of thinking and acting were needed."

In fact, acting in an ethical and responsible fashion creates a key opportunity for businesses to be more financially successful; whereas not doing so creates enormous threats to the survival of the business—just look at the famous cases of WorldCom and Enron, as mentioned earlier. Actually, all environmental trends create threats that can be turned into opportunities if seen early enough and acted on proactively. For example, the social trend of the growth of dual-income families has resulted in the economic effect of increased purchasing power. As we indicate in this chapter, the "phenomenon of working women has probably had a greater effect on *marketing* than has any other social change." As women's earnings have grown, so has their impact on purchase decisions, particularly big-ticket items. Working women create opportunities for items such as childcare and eldercare, home-cleaning services, and other convenience items and services. The impact on items such as car sales, however, has created huge market opportunities that many companies have taken advantage of, changing their sales messages to attract female customers.

An interesting and challenging opportunity discussed in this chapter is the trend toward component lifestyles. This makes meeting customer needs very difficult but full of opportunities. Businesses must use technology to track customer needs, and then focus on *innovation* to develop products of value to customers while keeping *operations* extremely flexible. Changes can be met as they occur, and the business can adjust to the differing demands of the consumer.

Another major social trend discussed in this chapter is the shift in the demographic composition of the Canadian population created by the baby boom. As this chapter indicates, demographic changes definitely affect the market for products, as well as the size and composition of the workforce, so shifts in demographics have implications for the overall *strategy* of a business as well as its functional areas. Some products will find demand declining, whereas others will experience increased demand as demographics shift—important concerns for marketing. The size and composition of the workforce will change, and that's important for *human resources* to understand and plan for. This changing composition of the workforce might necessitate moving operations to other countries in search of labour with the required skills. Clearly, all of these implications have a direct impact on the *finance* area of business, but the demographic shifts we are experiencing in Canada, coupled with a declining birth rate, have also caused the government to respond with changes in economic policy (as discussed earlier) and this inevitably affects finance.

Without a doubt, there is also a connection between functional areas, and ethical and responsible corporate behaviour. According to Canadian Business for Social Responsibility (CBSR, www.cbsr.ca), companies that practise corporate social responsibility develop and put into practice policies and programs in areas such as employee relations (human resources), *international* relations (operations), marketplace practices (marketing), and fiscal responsibility and accountability (finance). But if a business is to be truly responsible, commitment must come from the top; it must be part of the *mission* and culture of the company, and therefore part of the decisions made within all functional areas.

Behaving ethically and responsibly involves operating in a manner that recognizes and balances the competing expectations of all the various *stakeholders* of the business, and building a relationship of trust with them. Furthermore, meeting the company's obligations to its stakeholders helps the company achieve its critical success factors. For example, meeting its responsibility to employees helps gain employee commitment, meeting its responsibility to customers helps meet customer needs, and meeting its responsibility to investors helps achieve financial performance by providing needed capital. In fact, social investing theory would suggest that this is a very big factor. More and more investment funds are moving toward socially responsible companies and, if you follow the Jantzi Social Index or JSI, www.jantziresearch.com—created by Jantzi Research, one of the leading independent, socially responsible investing research companies in the world—you can see they are doing very well.

chapter 3

Social: Society, Corporate Responsibility, and Making Ethical Decisions

LEARNING OUTCOMES

1 Identify some of the current social factors that have an impact on business.

2 Illustrate how businesses meet their social responsibilities to stakeholders.

3 Explain corporate governance and why it is important.

4 Discuss the philosophies and concepts that shape personal ethical standards.

5 Show how organizations can encourage ethical business behaviour.

6 List some of the trends in society, corporate responsibility, and ethics.

BULLFROG POWER—CONNECTING ELECTRICITY USERS TO A GREEN GRID

As a young student, Tom Heintzman developed a school project on the environment, which revolved around the question of how energy projects would affect future generations. Today, Heintzman is president and co-founder of Bullfrog Power, a company whose goal is to offer electricity from clean, renewable sources. You could say he's now helping to make the planet a better place for those future generations, and his efforts have been recognized with numerous awards. He's been named a Green Hero and one of Canada's Clean16, among others.

Founded in 2004, Bullfrog Power connects individuals and companies with green-sourced electricity and natural gas. Its electricity is generated at regional wind and hydro facilities that meet or exceed Environment Canada's standards for renewable energy; the natural gas comes from methane collection at locations such as the landfill gas project at Rive-Nord, Québec. Bullfrog has wind-electric projects from Prince Edward Island to British Columbia and is adding new ones regularly, and the potential for gas collection at landfills or composting facilities is enormous, as CO_2 is released into the atmosphere when organic matter rots in landfills or composters.

The company doesn't use special lines or facilities to bring the power to homes or workplaces—it simply puts its green electricity into the existing system. Customers who sign up with Bullfrog pay the price of generating the power they use at the renewable source closest to their location. Renewable energy costs more, but most of that increase is to cover the capital expense of building renewable generation facilities. Users pay Bullfrog an extra fee—about 60 cents a day in Nova Scotia, for example—above their regular utility company's bill. Once the capital costs are covered, the fee is used to fund new projects and help reduce Canada's reliance on fossil fuels. It amounts to an extra two to three cents per kilowatt hour, which may seem like a pittance, but it adds up when many businesses and homeowners get involved.

Well-known individuals such as Tragically Hip singer Gord Downie have become proud Bullfrog customers. Downie's family sat at the dinner table, kids and all, to discuss a commitment to green power, and it's become a family project. "Now, when a light bulb in the house is turned on, suddenly it means something," Downie says. Like the thousands of families listed on Bullfrog's founders' page, the Downies have put the environment ahead of their pocketbooks.

Bullfrog clients feel they are demonstrating a commitment to the environment that sets them apart from other energy users, but that green image doesn't come without detractors. Corporate users are given the right to use Bullfrog's logo to tell the world they are doing something for the environment, and critics say Bullfrog may be running

MARIUSZ SZCZYGIEL/SHUTTERSTOCK

a risk of being a passive participant in "greenwashing." They point out that companies with poor environmental practices can sign up with Bullfrog and then market themselves as eco-friendly. When a company contracts with Bullfrog, it can claim that 100 percent of the power it uses is produced from renewable sources (this is verified by a Deloitte audit). That's a marketing tool that has attracted companies like RIM, Walmart, Unilever, and major banks.

Bullfrog sees this in a positive light, as a commitment to part of the "triple bottom line" philosophy of business. For most organizations, the first bottom line is profit; the second is societal impact, and the third is environmental impact. Bullfrog dedicates itself to having a positive effect on the environment, so that Tom Heintzman, and all those who work with him, can look back at his school scrapbook and say: "We are doing something to help future generations."[1]

THINKING CRITICALLY

As you read this chapter consider the following questions:

1. How have society's expectations changed regarding the behaviour of corporations?

2. How can organizations create a balance between the financial bottom line and acting in a socially responsible manner?

3. Could companies use a contract with Bullfrog Power to try to silence criticism of their environmental practices? How? Would it work?

No one business is large or powerful enough to create major changes in the external environment. Thus, managers are basically adapters to, rather than agents of, change. In this chapter, we examine the social trends in the business environment that are reshaping today's business landscape. Most important are the trends for companies to consider their social responsibility and the expectation that they will act in an ethical manner.

Every day, managers and business owners make business decisions based on what they believe to be right or wrong. Through their actions, they demonstrate to their employees what is and is not acceptable behaviour and shape the moral standard of the organization. Ethics *is a set of moral standards for judging whether something is right or wrong. As you will see in this chapter, personal and professional ethics are important cornerstones of an organization and shape its ultimate contributions to society. Let's consider first the important social trends and then how individual business ethics are formed.*

ethics
A set of moral standards for judging whether something is right or wrong.

LO1 SOCIAL TRENDS—OUR CHANGING SOCIETY

Social change is perhaps the most difficult environmental factor for owners and managers to forecast, influence, or integrate into business plans. Social factors include our attitudes, values, and lifestyles. Attitudes include our beliefs about such varied topics as religion, family, and the role of government in providing social services. Whereas some attitudes have an indirect impact on business, others—for example, how we feel about work—directly affect businesses. Examples of values include honesty, job satisfaction, materialism, convenience, and simplicity. Lifestyles are the ways in which consumers and families live, use time, and spend money. Because such social factors are very subjective, they are often difficult to define and measure. They change as we move through different life stages. Recent university and college graduates may value job success most for several years until they establish their careers. Family often becomes their primary concern after they marry.

Social factors influence the products people buy, the prices they pay, the effectiveness of specific promotions, and how, where, and when people expect to purchase products. They are closely tied to and affected by demographics. For example, the living and spending patterns of the young single and empty nester lifestyles relate to those specific age groups. Young singles may spend a higher proportion of their income on entertainment, such as eating out, while empty nesters may travel more.

Companies that track customer attitudes, values, and interests have a competitive advantage. They can use their knowledge of what's in or out to develop goods and services that address changing consumer needs and desires.

Different Lifestyles, Different Choices

The lifestyles we choose have a significant impact on business decisions. If we choose the simple life as a way to reduce stress, we will buy less. If we choose a component lifestyle, one made up of a complex set of interests, needs, and choices, we become multidimensional rather than following a stereotype. Whereas in the past a person's profession—for instance, accountant—defined that person's lifestyle, today a person can be an accountant as well as a gourmet, fitness enthusiast, dedicated single parent, and conservationist—all at once. Each of these component lifestyles is associated with different goods and services and represents a unique market, increasing the complexity of consumers' buying habits. For example, this accountant may respond to advertisements for cookware, wines, and exotic foods in magazines like *Bon Appétit*

component lifestyle
A lifestyle made up of a complex set of interests, needs, and choices.

and *Gourmet,* and for mutual funds in *Canadian Business* magazine. She may buy Adidas equipment and special jogging outfits to suit her fitness needs and read *Runner's World* magazine, eat fast-food for lunch but drink French wine for dinner, own sophisticated photographic equipment but drive a less expensive vehicle, and shop for hosiery at Target and suits at Holt Renfrew.

Today's fast paced lifestyles create a "poverty of time." Overworked, tired, and stressed out, we look for ways to gain control of our time. For example, more employees are asking for flex-time and part-time schedules. On-site daycare and fitness centres are popular employee benefits. Consumers place a high priority on convenience and healthier lifestyles—and some products meet both needs. Frozen dinners from Healthy Choice, Lean Cuisine, and South Beach Diet make it easy to stay on a low-fat diet. Recently Nabisco introduced 100-calorie "packages of cookies and chips to help calorie-counters limit their portions of snack foods." They were an immediate hit. "We live harried lives," says Stephanie Childs of the Grocery Manufacturers Association. "It's much easier to have somebody else count for you."[2]

Women in the Workforce

A contributing factor to the evolution of component lifestyles is the number of women in the workforce, including those in dual-income families, and the resulting increase in purchasing power. Women make a tremendous contribute to the Canadian economy but women's paid work lags behind what men in similar positions earn (women make approximately 63 percent of what similarly educated men earn[3]). The disparity of income between women and men can be partly explained by women often choosing less lucrative occupations than men (e.g., social work versus finance). The career opportunities for women are changing as more women are opting for the better paying jobs (e.g., in business, engineering, medicine).

The phenomenon of working women has probably had a greater effect on marketing than has any other social change. As women's earnings grow, so do their levels of expertise, experience, and authority. Working-age women are not the same group businesses targeted 30 years ago. They expect different things in life—from their jobs, from their spouses, and from the products and services they buy—and they want

Concept *in Action*

SMART Technologies is a Canadian company that creates products that enrich the lives of millions of students, teachers, and business professionals. It is the maker of the SMART Board™, the interactive whiteboard now common in classrooms, meeting rooms and training centres. In its headquarters in Calgary they offer employees an in-house fitness facility and daycare centre to help support a healthy work-life balance. Why have more companies begun to offer such benefits as SMART Technologies?

© NAJLAH FEANNY/CORBIS

demography
The study of people's vital statistics, such as their age, gender, race and ethnicity, and location.

a say in major economic decisions. Trend expert Faith Popcorn believes that women influence or make 80 percent of all purchasing decisions. "If men and women are different (mentally), why do we market to them in the same way?" she asks. She adds that businesses must target their marketing to women and build relationships, regardless of the type of product they sell.[4]

Demographic Trends

Demographic factors are another uncontrollable factor in the business environment and extremely important to managers. **Demography** is the study of people's vital statistics, such as their age, gender, race and ethnicity, and location. Demographics help companies define the markets for their products and also determine the size and composition of the workforce. You'll encounter demographics as you continue your study of business. For example, later in this chapter and in Chapter 12, we'll examine the challenges of managing a diverse workforce. In Chapter 13, you'll learn how marketers use demographics to segment markets and select target markets.

At the end of May 2012, Statistics Canada released the latest demographic information. The major census is conducted every five years and these latest data are from the 2011 survey (the following data reflect the changes from the 2006 to the 2011 census). The results were very interesting in that Canadians are getting older and younger at the same time. There was an 11 percent increase in the number of children aged four and under compared to the numbers in 2006. However the largest increase was in the 60 to 64 age group, with an increase of 29.1 percent.[5]

What does this all mean? If we look deeper into the data, we find that there is an increasing older population in Eastern Canada and a younger population in Western Canada. This will impact the ability of the provincial governments in the East to honour their responsibilities to social programs. Other potential impacts are to pensions, provincial health care, and consumer spending.

Concept in Action

The tremendous influx of women into the workforce has created a new class of female consumers with enormous purchasing power and unique lifestyle characteristics. Today's working women are busy multitaskers who must balance home, career, and personal needs—they are as preoccupied with home decorating and school supplies as with PDAs and personal fitness. Why do companies that tailor their promotional messages directly to women gain a competitive advantage over those that don't?

IAN LISHMAN/JUICE IMAGES/GLOW IMAGES

THE CONNECTED ONES OF GENERATION Z Generation Z, also known as Generation M (multitasking) or the iGeneration, are those born somewhere between the late 1990s and the present. This generation has been brought up with the full use of technology, as were most of Generation Y, and will enter into the workforce in the near future.

Generation Z
Canadians born from the late 1990s onward.

THE DIGITAL KIDS OF GENERATION Y Those designated by demographers as Generation Y were born between about 1977 and 1997 (demographers have reached no consensus as to exact dates, with some starting in 1979 and some ending as late as 2000); also called the Echo Boomers or the Millennium Generation. In Canada there are approximately 34,500,000 people, of which about 9.3 million are Generation Y. See Exhibit 3.1 for the population breakdown by age.

Generation Y
Canadians born between about 1977 and 1997.

According to Neil Howe and William Strauss, authors of *Millennials Rising: The Next Great Generation,* Generation Y is the most ethnically and socially diverse generation in history.[6]

The marketing impact of Generation Y has been immense—and they haven't yet reached their peak income and spending years. These technologically sophisticated consumers are the first to grow up with digital technology and the Internet. "They actually go online to be with each other," comments Melissa Payner, chief executive of Bluefly Inc., an online retailer. "It's a different kind of life."[7] Cell phones, iPhones, etc., are loaded with features and come in many colour combinations, allowing Gen Yers to keep up with their peers yet express their individuality through their gadgets.[8] Their spending habits reflect their love of technology, therefore electronic commerce—for example, websites with online ordering capabilities, e-mail newsletters, and sale announcements—becomes an important tool to reach them. The best marketing approaches position brands as cutting-edge, fashionable, and popular, but avoid the hard sell.

Exhibit 3.1	Population by Sex and Age Group, 2011

AGE GROUP	CANADA	MALE	FEMALE	CANADA	MALE	FEMALE
	PERSONS (THOUSANDS)			PERCENTAGE OF TOTAL OF EACH GROUP		
Total	34,482.8	17,104.1	17,378.7	100.0	100.0	100.0
0 to 4	1,921.2	982.9	938.3	5.6	5.7	5.4
5 to 9	1,824.0	938.8	885.2	5.3	5.5	5.1
10 to 14	1,899.7	975.7	923.9	5.5	5.7	5.3
15 to 19	2,196.4	1,123.8	1,072.7	6.4	6.6	6.2
20 to 24	2,402.2	1,234.2	1,168.0	7.0	7.2	6.7
25 to 29	2,419.3	1,227.5	1,191.7	7.0	7.2	6.9
30 to 34	2,348.1	1,173.5	1,174.6	6.8	6.9	6.8
35 to 39	2,290.4	1,149.0	1,141.4	6.6	6.7	6.6
40 to 44	2,396.7	1,206.2	1,190.5	7.0	7.1	6.9
45 to 49	2,750.7	1,385.0	1,365.7	8.0	8.1	7.9
50 to 54	2,668.2	1,333.3	1,334.8	7.7	7.8	7.7
55 to 59	2,354.2	1,161.1	1,193.1	6.8	6.8	6.9
60 to 64	2,038.3	998.4	1,039.9	5.9	5.8	6.0
65 to 69	1,534.5	744.2	790.3	4.4	4.4	4.5
70 to 74	1,142.6	538.8	603.7	3.3	3.2	3.5
75 to 79	918.3	415.4	502.9	2.7	2.4	2.9
80 to 84	703.0	293.3	409.7	2.0	1.7	2.4
85 to 89	439.0	157.3	281.8	1.3	0.9	1.6
90 and older	236.0	65.6	170.4	0.7	0.4	1.0

SOURCE: **Population by Sex and Age Group** http://www40.statcan.gc.ca/l01/cst01/demo10a-eng.htm Reproduced with the permission of the Minister of Public Works and Government Services Canada, 2012.

Note: Population as of July 1, 2011.

In the fall of 2012, Apple launched the new iPhone 5. It was the thinnest, lightest, and fastest iPhone to date, yet had a larger display and faster chip that incorporated the latest technology. What characteristics of Generation Y made it the ideal target demographic for Apple's iPhone 5?

Generation X
Canadians born between 1964 and about 1977.

baby boomers
Canadians born between 1946 and 1964.

GENERATION X REACHES MIDDLE AGE Although they are highly educated, Generation X—people born between 1964 and 1977—have been overshadowed by the very large baby boomer generation that preceded them (until recently). As the first Gen Xers are now in their mid 40s, they are finding their place and entering the mainstream. In the process, they are exhibiting different characteristics from earlier generations.

It is the first generation of latchkey children—products of dual-career households or, in roughly half of the cases, of divorced or separated parents. This influences their decisions to marry and start families later than their parents. Family and friends, rather than the career success and wealth accumulation that drove their parents, come first. Bombarded by multiple media since their cradle days, Gen Xers are savvy and cynical consumers. "The Xers are the first generation that will not live as well as their parents," says one marketing researcher. They've lived through several rounds of corporate downsizings and spend cautiously, planning for retirement.[9]

PRIME TIME FOR BABY BOOMERS AND BEYOND In 2006 the first baby boomers, born between 1946 and 1964, turned 60, and in 2011 more than half were over 47 years of age. This powerful age demographic represents approximately 23 percent of the Canadian population and has significant spending power. Because some boomers are in their peak earning years while others are nearing retirement, it's useful to divide boomers into two subgroups:

- younger boomers between their late 40s and early 50s, whose spending is still directed by their children and have the highest average household incomes and spending of any group
- older boomers, ages 55 and above, most of whom are empty nesters

The two groups exhibit different spending patterns. For younger boomers, home and family are still priorities. Two-thirds of this group own their homes and allocate a larger share of their budgets to home-related expenditures than other ages. Spending on their children and financing their secondary educations is a high priority for young boomers.

Marketers who chased after the youth market are now catering to the needs of this wealthy and diverse generation of consumers. Research from Home Depot indicates that those over 50 will account for half the growth in home-improvement spending as they remodel their existing homes and buy second homes for investment and retirement purposes. In response, the company introduced in-store kiosks in many of its stores to provide information on making improvements that accommodate the needs of older people. Other industry sectors are courting the older consumer as well. Revlon and L'Oreal recently launched a new line of "age defying products" targeted towards women over 50 years of age.

The automotive industry is also taking notice of the over-50 group, which makes more than half of all automobile purchases and will drive auto sales for the next 10 to 15 years. Boomers value quality finishes, safety features and luxury touches, and stylish rather than stodgy vehicles. Muscle cars that were popular with the baby boomer generation have regained their popularity. "They still are caught up in a car-culture mentality where a vehicle is really a primary means of defining who you are," says Art Spinella, president of CNW Marketing Research.[10]

Other industry sectors will be heavily influenced by the extended lifespans and active lives of the boomers and their parents. Many are pursuing new passions as they look forward to another 20 to 30 years of life, from hobbies to travel and even new careers. The aging population also places increased demands on health care and related services, and companies are already preparing to meet these needs.

Although many retirees live on fixed incomes, they are still a force in the marketplace. They like convenience and will pay for services, such as home delivery of groceries and prescriptions.

NOT OVER THE HILL YET As the huge baby boomer generation ages, so does the workforce.[11] In 2010, 25 percent of all employees were of retirement age—but the number of people who choose to retire at age 62 or 65 has been declining. Health advances make it possible for them to continue working if they so desire. No longer is retirement an all-or-nothing proposition. Many Canadians expect to work full- or part-time after "retirement," and most would work longer if phased retirement programs were available at their companies.

Financial reasons motivate some of these older workers, who worry that their longer life expectancies will mean outliving their money. Fewer companies offer traditional pension plans, so workers need to supplement social benefits (e.g., Canada Pension Plan payments and Old Age Security payments) and retirement funds. For many, however, the satisfaction of working and feeling productive is more important than money alone. Some stay on with their former companies as consultants or with part-time schedules.

In addition, the number of new entrants to the labour market is not sufficient to replace the retirees, creating resource shortages. Younger workers have different approaches and attitudes to work than their elders.

These converging dynamics create major challenges. Companies must focus not only on recruiting employees to replace retiring workers and track where employees fall in their career lifecycles, but to determine when, whether, and how to replace them. Many companies are developing special programs to retain older workers and benefit from their practical knowledge and problem-solving abilities: employers such as RONA and Home Depot actively seek out older workers because they are disciplined, reliable, and loyal. When older employees do choose to retire, companies discover that they are taking with them vast amounts of knowledge that is difficult—if not impossible—to replace.

Diversity Matters—Canada's Strength

Diversity has been an important factor in developing Canada. Initially, inhabited by the members of the First Nations, Canada later experienced different waves of immigration. Today diversity continues to play a significant role as trade becomes more global and has certainly shaped some of our international policies. According to the 2006 census, of the 1.1 million immigrants that arrived in Canada between 2001 and 2006, 58.3 percent were born in Asian countries.[12]

Multiculturalism is fundamental to Canada and our belief that all citizens are equal regardless of their racial and ethnic backgrounds. Canada was the world's first country to enact an official Multiculturalism Policy in 1971, later affirmed by the Multiculturalism Act in 1988. Multiculturalism encourages racial cross-cultural understanding and discourages hatred, discrimination, and violence.[13] Because of the current demographic transition, the trend in Canada is toward greater multiculturalism, although the degree varies in different parts of the country. The majority of the residents of both Toronto and Vancouver might be members of what are now considered visible minorities by 2017.[14]

multiculturalism
The fundamental belief that all citizens are equal regardless of their racial or ethnic backgrounds.

Changing demographics affect the marketing of goods and services. As Canadians are becoming more health conscious, for instance, companies should promote the "healthiness" of goods and services. As our population ages and becomes more technically sophisticated, organizations need to search for new marketing streams that will encourage the target market to purchase goods and services.

Organizations need to be responsive to customers and, as these buyers change, the organizations need to adjust their marketing efforts. This includes the goods and services they are providing, their price points, their place of availability, and how the organizations promote the goods and services.

If organizations fail to monitor the changing demographics of their customers, they will not be able to respond to these changes and will most likely lose sales.

Concept *in Action*

Employees from different ethnic and racial backgrounds will continue to enrich the workplace with their diverse views and ideas. What can the various governments in Canada do to promote immigration?

LES AND DAVE JACOBS/CULTURA/GLOW IMAGES

The Impact of Immigration

Part of the reason for the tremendous shift in Canadian demographics is immigration. Canada's relativity small population simply cannot maintain the current high standard of living. From July 2010 to June 2011, there were approximately 386,000 births in Canada.[15] This rate cannot sustain our economic growth. The federal government—along with the provinces—is trying to determine both the level of need for immigration and various ways to encourage people to move to Canada. One initiative to encourage immigration is the increased use of migrant workers in Canada.

There is no doubt that immigrant entrepreneurs, from the corner grocer to the local builder, are creating jobs for other immigrants and for those born in Canada. Vibrant immigrant communities are revitalizing cities and older suburbs that would otherwise be suffering from a shrinking tax base. And the immigrants' links to their countries of origin are boosting Canadian exports to fast-growing regions such as Asia and Latin America.

Canada is also reaping a bonanza of highly educated foreign-born citizens. High-tech industries, which deal in everything from semiconductors to biotechnology, are depending on immigrant scientists, engineers, and entrepreneurs to remain competitive.

social responsibility
The concern of businesses for the welfare of society as a whole; consists of obligations beyond those required by law or contracts.

LO2 MANAGING A SOCIALLY RESPONSIBLE BUSINESS

Concept *Check*

Explain the impact Generation X, Generation Y, and the baby boomers have on our economy.

How is diversity changing the marketplace?

What has been the impact of immigration in Canada?

Acting in an ethical manner is one of the four components of the pyramid of corporate social responsibility (CSR). **Social responsibility** is the concern of businesses for the welfare of society as a whole. It consists of obligations beyond those required by law or union contract. This definition makes two important points. First, social responsibility is voluntary. Beneficial action required by law, such as cleaning up factories that are polluting air and water, is not voluntary. Second, the obligations of social responsibility are broad. They extend beyond investors in the company to include workers, suppliers, consumers, and communities.

Exhibit 3.2 The Pyramid of Corporate Social Responsibility

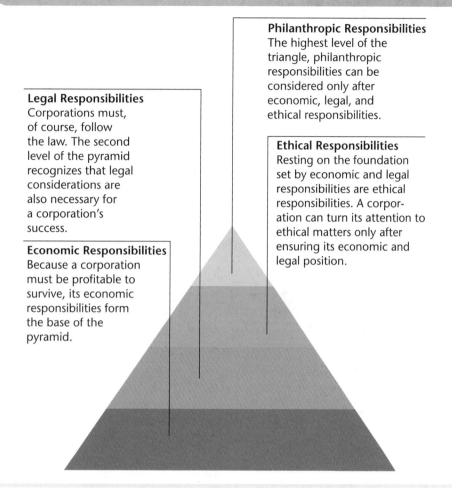

Philanthropic Responsibilities
The highest level of the triangle, philanthropic responsibilities can be considered only after economic, legal, and ethical responsibilities.

Legal Responsibilities
Corporations must, of course, follow the law. The second level of the pyramid recognizes that legal considerations are also necessary for a corporation's success.

Ethical Responsibilities
Resting on the foundation set by economic and legal responsibilities are ethical responsibilities. A corporation can turn its attention to ethical matters only after ensuring its economic and legal position.

Economic Responsibilities
Because a corporation must be profitable to survive, its economic responsibilities form the base of the pyramid.

Exhibit 3.2 portrays economic performance as the foundation for the other three responsibilities. At the same time that a business pursues profits (economic responsibility), however, it is expected to obey the law (legal responsibility); to do what is right, just, and fair (ethical responsibility); and to be a good corporate citizen (philanthropic responsibility). These four components are distinct but together constitute the whole.

Another belief is that social policy should be market-driven and stress the efficiencies of private enterprises. Known as neoliberalism, this approach believes that by transferring control of the economy from the governments to the corporate sector, governments would be more efficient and there would be an improvement in the economic health of the country.

A third belief argues that only under exceptional circumstances are markets efficient and therefore social policy should be regulated by the governments.

neoliberalism
A set of economic policies that believes that the economy (and therefore social policy) should be market-driven, not government-driven.

Understanding Social Responsibility

Peter Drucker, a management expert, says to look first at what an organization does to society and second at what it can do for society. This idea suggests that social responsibility has two basic dimensions: legality and responsibility.

The vast majority of business activities fall into the category of behaviour that is both legal and responsible. Most companies act legally, and most try to be socially responsible. Sometimes companies act irresponsibly, yet their actions are legal

Find out which companies test their products on animals and which don't in the campaign section of the People for the Ethical Treatment of Animals (PETA) website:
www.peta.org

(e.g., companies that create harm to our environment but are within the acceptable levels of pollutants).

The idea of social responsibility is so widespread today that it is hard to conceive of a company continually acting in illegal and irresponsible ways. Nevertheless, such actions do sometimes occur. In the aftermath of the financial crisis of 2008, we saw acts by those in companies who created financial ruin for their organizations, extreme financial hardships for many existing and former employees and investors, and general hardships for the communities in which they operated. Yet top executives walked away with millions. Some, however, will ultimately pay large fines and be sentenced to jail. Federal, provincial/territorial, and local laws determine whether an activity is legal or not.

Corporate Responsibility to Stakeholders

stakeholders
Individuals, groups, or organizations to whom a business has a responsibility: employees, customers, suppliers, investors, and the general public.

What makes a company admired or perceived as socially responsible? This type of company meets its obligations to its stakeholders. Stakeholders are the individuals, groups, or organizations to whom a business has a responsibility. In a broader view, stakeholders are considered to be anyone or any organization that has a vested interest

Creating the Future of Business

GREG OVERHOLT, STUDENTS OFFERING SUPPORT

Greg Overholt, founder and Executive Director of Students Offering Support, has always been a go-getter; full of energy and a desire to direct that energy towards helping others. Being a double degree business and computer science student at university, and seeing fellow students struggle with content in some of their courses, Overholt decided that he could help. Along with a fellow student, Stewart McKendry, he started tutoring sessions through the Business and Computer Science Association (called BUCS) to help students prepare for exams. They decided to charge a small fee that would go towards helping students in developing countries gain access to a quality education. Thus the humble beginning of what has developed into an award-winning multi-national charitable organization called Students Offering Support, or SOS for short.

The first Exam-AID sessions were led by a team of 25 passionate volunteers, who tutored 200 students in 2004, and have grown to 1,200 even more passionate volunteers tutoring over 25,000 students all over North America in 2011. Now that's growth! Actually, SOS has seen a consistent average annual growth rate of 80 to 100 percent each year, starting at one Canadian university and extending to 28 Canadian university chapters, as well as 5 chapters across the US. More importantly, it has been growth with a purpose, fuelled by this purpose.

The business model of the organization, which was "uniquely designed *by* students *for* students," according to Greg, is to raise funds to build schools in Latin America through Exam-AID review sessions taught and coordinated by student volunteers. This unique model, primarily designed to give back to the community in an effective and meaningful manner, also gives the student leaders practical entrepreneurial experience as each chapter operates as a micro-enterprise managed by each campus' executive team. SOS

volunteers gain experience in growing sustainable businesses to create self-sufficient communities.

Its motto says it all: "Raising Marks. Raising Money. Raising Roofs." Greg's social entrepreneurial drive, and the passion of the student volunteers, has generated more than $700,000 in Exam-AID revenue to fund more than 35 sustainable development projects in rural communities within 10 Latin American countries. But perhaps the coolest part of the business model is that the volunteers not only assist in the funding and coordination of the development projects, they also travel to the rural communities at their own expense and literally help in the physical building process of their selected project, see the impact that they have made first hand, and change their own lives in the process.

What an incredible journey it is, to "engage student volunteers in becoming innovative entrepreneurs and active social agents"—and it's a journey that has been praised many times over. Greg was the 2011 winner in the Social Entrepreneurship category of the Ernst & Young Entrepreneur of the Year competition, recipient of the Top 40 Under 40 Award in Waterloo Region, first place in the University of New Brunswick business plan competition, first place in the Ontario Regionals of the UBC Sauder Enterprize business plan competition, second place in the Queen's Entrepreneur competition, and second place in the Wake Forest Social Entrepreneurship business plan competition.

Thinking Critically

1. What role do you think student attitude and organizational culture play in making something like this work?
2. Do you think the same business principles to run a for-profit venture apply to running a social venture?
3. According to Greg: "Our world will be transformed by social entrepreneurs who apply business principles to enable social change." Does Greg's story motivate you to get more involved in making a difference?

SOURCE: http://www.studentsofferingsupport.ca and information supplied by Greg Overholt personally.

COURTESY OF GREG OVERHOLT

in the business. The primary stakeholders of a business are its employees, its customers, the investors, its suppliers, and the general public (i.e., government and society).

RESPONSIBILITY TO EMPLOYEES An organization's first responsibility is to provide jobs for employees. Keeping people employed and letting them have time to enjoy the fruits of their labours is the finest thing business can do for society. Beyond this fundamental responsibility, employers must provide a clean and safe working environment that is free from all forms of discrimination. Companies should also strive to provide job security whenever possible.

Enlightened companies are also empowering employees to make decisions on their own and suggest solutions to company problems. Empowerment contributes to an employee's self-worth, which, in turn, increases productivity and reduces absenteeism.

RESPONSIBILITY TO CUSTOMERS A central theme of this text is that to be successful today, a company must satisfy its customers. A company must deliver what it promises. It must also be honest and forthright with its clients. When the *Listeria* outbreak occurred at Maple Leaf Foods in 2008, the company took measures to minimize the effect on customers by recalling products and cleaning the machinery.

RESPONSIBILITY TO INVESTORS Companies' relationships with investors also entail social responsibility. Although a company's economic responsibility to make a profit might seem to be its main obligation to its shareholders, many investors increasingly are putting emphasis on other aspects of social responsibility. This includes such actions as the company acting within its legal responsibilities and, at times, doing more than the law mandates.

Some investors are limiting their investments to securities that fit within their beliefs about ethical and social responsibility. This is called social investing (also called ethical investing, green investing, and sustainable investing). It is important for these investors to look for companies that evaluate the risks, including environmental, social, and corporate governance. For example, a social investment fund might eliminate from consideration the securities of all companies that make tobacco products or liquor, manufacture weapons, or have a history of polluting.

Investors who are dissatisfied with corporate managers tend to be less passive than in the past. They are pressuring corporations with tactics such as exposés on television and in other media, and calling government attention to perceived wrongdoings. Groups of owners are pressuring companies to increase profits, link executive pay to performance, and oust inefficient management. Consequently, executives and managers are giving more weight to the concerns of owner stakeholders in the decision-making process.

RESPONSIBILITY TO SUPPLIERS Many companies rely on other companies for their survival. Often companies hire other companies to provide products or perform services for them. These suppliers (or business partners) are usually contracted because they can provide the products or perform the services more cheaply. Mark's Work Wearhouse, for example, does not produce its own line of clothing for resale but instead contracts it out to its suppliers. These suppliers are employing people, in turn providing more money to fuel the economy. It is important that businesses support their suppliers (e.g., giving contracts, paying supplier invoices). As we will see in Chapter 4, many companies are tying the e-business technology to their suppliers to realize many efficiencies.

RESPONSIBILITY TO GOVERNMENTS Governments in Canada rely on tax dollars to operate and provide their services to Canadians. Much

social investing
The practice of limiting investments to securities of companies that act in accordance with the investor's beliefs about ethical and social responsibility.

Concept *in Action*

CIBC's sponsorship of the Run for the Cure represents a legal and socially responsible activity that also enhances the image of the bank in the eyes of many consumers. What other examples can you cite of companies being socially responsible?

TORONTO STAR/THE CANADIAN PRESS/STUART NIMMO)

Each year the *Financial Post* lists the best companies to work for. See the latest at

www.working.canada.com

Want to see how the global environment is changing and learn the latest about global warming? Check out

www.climatehotmap.org

of the tax revenue that the governments collect is in the form of corporate taxes. Corporations are responsible for accurately reporting their earnings and fulfilling their tax obligations. Another expectation, for example is that the company operates in a safe and reasonable manner.

RESPONSIBILITY TO SOCIETY A business must also be responsible to society. A business provides a community with jobs, goods, and services. It also pays taxes that go to support schools, hospitals, and better roads. Most companies try to be good citizens in their communities.

Business must also be good stewards of the environment. This includes water, land, and air. In late 2011 Tim Hortons launched the new "Cup-to-Tray" recycling program. Announced during National Waste Reduction Week, Tim Hortons teamed up with its Nova Scotia recycling partners to find an effective way to recycle the hot beverage cups into Tim Horton take-out trays – trays that can be recycled into more trays.

Responsibility to society doesn't end at our shores. Global enterprises are attempting to help around the world, as explained in the Expanding Around the Globe box.

Business is also responsible for protecting and improving the world's fragile environment. The world's forests are rapidly being destroyed. Every second, an area the size of a football field is laid bare. Plant and animal species are becoming extinct at the rate of 17 per hour. A continent-sized hole is opening in the earth's protective ozone shield. Each year we throw out more refuse; as a result, more of our landfills are filled to capacity. To maintain sustainable development, business must be more sensitive to our environment (e.g., recycling, land management, pollution controls).

To slow the erosion of the world's resources, many companies are becoming more environmentally responsible. Canadian Tire, for example, strives to divert as much waste as possible from landfills. Since 1990, it has implemented aggressive pallet reuse and packaging recycling programs.[16]

Expanding Around the Globe

CLEAN WATER, NO PROFIT

Like plenty of multinationals, Procter and Gamble (P&G) rushed to offer aid to tsunami victims in Asia, shipping 15 million packets of water purifier to affected countries and pledging 13 million more if needed. What's less known is that the product P&G airlifted was a commercial bust.

Called Pur, the powder was envisioned as a revolutionary way to clean the world's drinking water. P&G spent four years and $10 million (USD) for research and development before launching Pur. But the packets of chlorine salt and iron sulfate are relatively complicated to mix and, at about 10 cents each, expensive for many of the world's poor.

Just over a year later, Pur still hadn't caught on as a profitable venture. In virtually every market where it was available, Pur gained early interest but not broad acceptance. Later, P&G abandoned plans to sell the product for profit in developing countries and dramatically cut back its water-purification ambitions.

P&G wondered how it would unload the millions of packets of Pur sitting in the company's factory in Manila. Then, shortly after the tsunami, the phone started ringing with calls from AmeriCares, UNICEF, and the International Federation of the Red Cross with orders for Pur.

The company added a third shift to its factory and had orders to ship 15 million packets of the product to areas hit by the tsunami. Initially, P&G sold the packets to aid organizations at cost—3½ cents, but later decided to donate them because of the enormity of the disaster.

In order to keep the product going, management has examined a list of 40 countries with the highest rates of infant mortality due to unsafe drinking water. P&G has pledged to introduce Pur to two new countries a year. P&G is selling Pur in Haiti and Uganda for 8 or 9 cents a packet and Kenya is the next market to be served.[17]

Thinking Critically

1. After the tsunami, should P&G have given Pur away at the beginning?
2. Should Pur be given away in Haiti, Uganda, and Kenya? Why?

SOURCE: Sarah Ellison and Eric Bellman, "Clean Water, No Profit," *Wall Street Journal*, February 3, 2005, B1, B2. Dow Jones & Co Copyright 2005 Reproduced with permission of DOW JONES & COMPANY, INC. via Copyright Clearance Center.

Companies also display their social responsibility through corporate philanthropy, which includes cash contributions, donations of equipment and products, and support for the volunteer efforts of company employees. For example, in 2005, Manulife Financial assisted approximately 500 non-profit companies with community building in four main areas: health care, education, community services, and local volunteerism. Its contribution was not only in the form of cash donations and sponsorship but also included more than 44,000 hours of employees' time globally.[18]

CORPORATE GOVERNANCE

LO3

Corporate governance refers to the way in which an organization is governed, directed, and administered.[19] As discussed in Chapter 8, the board of directors (also known simply as directors) is responsible for the organization being managed in the best interest of the corporation. As such, directors of corporations need to be concerned about their responsibilities and potential liabilities. Canadian society is very concerned about proper corporate governance and the accountability of the board of directors. As such Canada has a complex system of regulations and closely analyzes the actions of the board of directors.

Recent experiences in Canada, the United States, and around the world have highlighted the outcome of poor corporate governance on the organization's performance and survival. Increasingly, stakeholders are looking at the corporate governance and control systems of businesses to ensure that they are being managed with the interests of the stakeholders in mind. Although the debate has focused primarily on the financial position and reporting of companies, other concerns are being discussed (honesty in other information, respect for the environment, etc.).

Since the early 1990s, the debate on corporate governance has been flourishing, and regulators in Canada have been setting guidelines to address this issue. This has been in response to worldwide incidents that have raised questions about boards of directors' performance and alleged management incompetence. Companies are expected to be socially responsible in their investing. According to Brian A. Schofield and Blair W. Feltmate in Sustainable Development Investing, stakeholders now require that companies be committed to minimizing environmental disruptions and to contribute to the economic and social advancement of the communities in which they operate, known as sustainable development.[20]

In July 2002, the Canadian Institute of Chartered Accountants, the Canadian Securities Administrators, and the Office of the Superintendent of Financial Institutions announced the creation of the Canadian Public Accountability Board (CPAB). Its mission is "to contribute to public confidence in the integrity of financial reporting of public companies in Canada by promoting high quality, independent auditing."[21]

So what has brought about the need to create the CPAB? There have been many successful attempts by associations to regulate their industries. The provincial legal associations, medical associations, faculty associations, accounting associations, and others have developed strict guidelines that control the responsibilities and actions of their members, but this does not guarantee that every member will follow the guidelines. Typically, when there are serious violations, government bodies react and enact regulations (in the form of laws) to protect society, or, in some cases, governments have been proactive in anticipation of violations.

corporate philanthropy
The practice of charitable giving by corporations; includes contributing cash, donating equipment and products, and supporting the volunteer efforts of company employees.

corporate governance
The way in which an organization is governed, directed, and administered.

For more news and updated events, search the Office of the Superintendent of Financial Institutions' website at
www.osfi-bsif.gc.ca

ETHICS—IT'S A PERSONAL CHOICE

LO4

Individual business ethics are shaped by personal choices and the environments in which we live and work. In addition, the laws of our society are guideposts for choosing between right and wrong. In this section, we describe personal philosophies and legal factors that influence the choices people make when confronting ethical dilemmas.

THE GLOBAL 100

In Chapter 1 you were introduced to the concept of sustainability, and in Chapter 2 we discussed Toronto-Dominion Bank as an example of a sustainable organization operating in the financial sector of the economic environment. TD Bank was a good example because it was named to the 2011 list of the Global 100 Most Sustainable Corporations in the World.

What is the Global 100? For a quick lesson search YouTube for "The Global 100 in 100 seconds." This short video will tell you that essentially the Global 100 is the definitive corporate sustainability benchmark. It was created in 2005 by an independent Canadian-based social enterprise called Corporate Knights who formed the Global Responsible Investment Network with three partners—Inflection Point Capital Management, www.inflectionpointcm.com; Global Currents Investment Management, www.globalcurrents.com; and Phoenix Global Advisors, www.fxpga.com, to launch the Global 100.

The Global 100 are picked from a universe of 3,500 stocks. The top 10 percent are ranked on a set of key performance indicators, including energy productivity (sales/energy consumption), carbon productivity (sales/CO_2 emissions), water productivity (sales/water use), waste productivity (sales/waste produced), leadership diversity (percentage of women on the board of directors), ratio of CEO to average worker pay, percentage of tax paid, safety productivity (sales/lost time incidents), whether at least one senior officer has his/her pay linked to sustainability, and innovation capacity (R&D/sales). The final 125 are then reviewed to identify the Global 100 list that is announced each year during the World Economic Forum Annual Meeting in Davos-Klosters, Switzerland.

The idea behind the Global 100 is to "mainstream sustainability in the business world." Basically by "applying objective corporate social and environmental measures that clearly show which companies stand above their peers, (the aim of the Global 100) … is to create a virtuous cycle where the most sustainable companies attract the most capital and earn the best returns." So virtue does have its rewards! According to the Global 100 these companies "deserve to be recognized, because they are models for the art of the possible, living proof of how billion dollar entities can squeeze more wealth from less material resources while honouring the social contract." I can't agree more.

In the mission statement of the Global 100 it outlines how a company's ability to manage its sustainability is a strong indicator of overall management quality, which in turn is the "single greatest determinant" of a company's financial performance. Therefore the goal is to "promote better managed and better performing corporations regarding sustainability issues," and give stakeholders a way to "pick out the true leaders from the pack … those most willing and able to deal with key social and environmental factors they face in their everyday operations."

So we're going to start you on your way to understanding what makes a true leader in sustainability by profiling in each chapter some of those that made the list, and some that didn't but that we think are worth mentioning.

Thinking Critically

1. Do you agree that "a company's ability to manage its sustainability is a strong indicator of overall management quality"?
2. What impact do you think making the Global 100 has on a company? Does it matter what the impact is, or is helping create a more sustainable world its own reward?
3. Without looking at the list, what companies do you think are on the 2011 list?

SOURCES: The Global 100, http://www.global100.org; and Corporate Knights website, http://www.corporateknights.ca.

Utilitarianism—Seeking the Best for the Majority

utilitarianism
A philosophy that focuses on the consequences of an action to determine whether it is right or wrong, and holds that an action that affects the majority adversely is morally wrong.

One of the philosophies that might influence choices between right and wrong is utilitarianism, which focuses on the consequences of an action taken by a person or an organization. The notion that "people should act so as to generate the greatest good for the greatest number" is derived from utilitarianism. When an action affects the majority adversely, it is morally wrong. One problem with this philosophy is that it is nearly impossible to determine accurately how a decision will affect a large number of people.

Another problem is that utilitarianism always involves both winners and losers. If sales are slowing, and a manager decides to release five people rather than putting everyone on a 30-hour workweek, the 20 people who keep their full-time jobs are winners, but the other five are losers.

A final criticism of utilitarianism is that some "costs," although small relative to the potential good, are so negative that some segments of society find them unacceptable. Reportedly, the backs of up to 3000 animals a year are deliberately broken so that scientists can conduct research that might someday lead to a cure for spinal cord injuries. To a number of people, however, the "costs" are simply too horrible for this type of research to continue.

Individual Rights

In our society, individuals and groups have certain rights that exist under certain conditions regardless of the external circumstances. These rights serve as guides when individuals make ethical decisions. The term *human rights* implies that certain rights are conveyed at birth and cannot be arbitrarily taken away. Denying the rights of an individual or a group is considered to be unethical and illegal in most, though not all, parts of the world. Certain rights are guaranteed by the various levels of government and their laws, and these are considered legal rights. The Canadian Charter of Rights and Freedoms was enacted in 1982 to guarantee the rights and freedoms of Canadians and is superordinate to any other laws that affect Canadians' rights and freedoms.

Some of the freedoms listed in the Charter include

- freedom of conscience and religion;
- freedom of thought, belief, opinion, and expression (e.g., press and other communications media);
- freedom of peaceful assembly; and
- freedom of association.

Charter rights include

- democratic rights (right to vote at the age of majority);
- mobility rights (the right to enter, remain in, and leave Canada);
- legal rights (the right to life, liberty, and security);
- equality rights (everyone is equal under the law); and
- minority language educational rights (the right to be educated in either English or French).

Justice—The Question of Fairness

A factor that influences individual business ethics is justice, or what is fair according to prevailing standards of society. We all expect life to be reasonably fair. You expect your exams to be fair, the grading to be fair, and your wages to be fair, based on the type of work being done.

In the 21st century, we take justice to mean an equitable distribution of the burdens and rewards that society has to offer. The distributive process varies from society to society. Those in a democratic society believe in the "equal pay for equal work" doctrine, in which individuals are rewarded based on the value that the free market places on their services. Because the market places different values on different occupations, the rewards, such as wages, are not necessarily equal. Nevertheless, many regard the rewards as just. At the other extreme, communist theorists have argued that justice would be served by a society in which burdens and rewards were distributed to individuals according to their abilities and their needs, respectively.

Stages of Ethical Development

We can view an individual's ethical development as having reached one of three levels: preconventional, conventional, or postconventional. The behaviour of a person at the level of preconventional ethics is childlike in nature; it is calculating, self-centred, and even selfish, and is based on the possibility of immediate punishment or reward. Thus, a student might not cheat on an exam because he or she is afraid of getting caught and therefore receiving a failing grade for the course. The student's behaviour is based not on a sense of what's right or wrong but, instead, on the threat of punishment.

Conventional ethics moves from an egocentric viewpoint toward the expectations of society. Loyalty and obedience to the organization (or society) become paramount. At the conventional ethics level, a businessperson might say, "I know that our advertising is somewhat misleading, but as long as it will increase sales we should continue the campaign." Right or wrong is not the issue; the only question is whether the campaign will benefit the organization.

For more about the Canadian Charter of Rights and Freedoms and other Canadian legislation, go to www.laws-lois.justice.gc.ca/eng/charter/

Canadian Charter of Rights and Freedoms
Legislation that guarantees the rights and freedoms of Canadians.

justice
What is considered fair according to the prevailing standards of society; in the 21st century, an equitable distribution of the burdens and rewards that society has to offer.

preconventional ethics
A stage in the ethical development of individuals in which people behave in a childlike manner and make ethical decisions in a calculating, self-centred, selfish way, based on the possibility of immediate punishment or reward; also known as self-centred ethics.

conventional ethics
The second stage in the ethical development of individuals in which people move from an egocentric viewpoint to consider the expectations of an organization or society; also known as social ethics.

postconventional ethics
The third stage in the ethical development of individuals in which people adhere to the ethical standards of a mature adult and are less concerned about how others view their behaviour than about how they will judge themselves in the long run; also known as principled ethics.

Postconventional ethics represents the ethical standards of the mature adult. At the postconventional level, businesspeople are concerned less about how others might see them and more about how they see and judge themselves over the long run. A person who has attained this ethical level might ask, "Even though this action is legal and will increase company profits, is it right in the long run? Might it do more harm than good in the end?" A manager at a fast-food restaurant might refuse to offer Styrofoam cups because they are non-biodegradable. An advertising agency manager might refuse a tobacco account because of the health hazards of smoking. A lab technician might refuse to recommend a new whitener for a detergent because it could harm the environment. All of these individuals are exhibiting postconventional morality.

Many people believe that the Internet is a vast anonymous place where they can say and do just about anything. When they think that they can't be caught, they sometimes revert to preconventional ethics. Yet e-mail servers owned by businesses and governmental agencies can quickly tell what is being sent and to whom.

Computers and Ethics

The Canadian Information Processing Society is a professional association providing leadership in information systems and technologies fields. Find out more about their code of ethics at
www.cips.ca

The Computer Ethics Institute (CEI) is a research, education, and policy study organization focusing on the interface of information technologies, ethics, and corporate and public policy. Its objective is to undertake research about the actual and potential effects of information technology, and to provide advice to various interested parties (individuals, organizations, communities, etc.) regarding ethical and social responsibilities.

Until recently, there has been a very laissez-faire approach to ethics when it comes to cyberspace, coupled with a great reluctance to restrict information on the Internet, but this is changing in the 21st century. The increased use of the information highway has encouraged more policing. First presented in Dr. Ramon C. Barquin's paper "In Pursuit of a 'Ten Commandments' for Computer Ethics," the CEI has created the "Ten Commandments of Computer Ethics," shown in Exhibit 3.3.

Recognizing Unethical Business Activities

Researchers from Brigham Young University state that all unethical business activities will fall into one of the following categories:

1. *Taking things that don't belong to you.* The unauthorized use of someone else's property or taking property under false pretences is taking something that does not belong to you. Even the smallest offence, such as using the postage meter at

---

Exhibit 3.3 Ten Commandments of Computer Ethics

1. Thou shalt not use a computer to harm other people.
2. Thou shalt not interfere with other people's computer work.
3. Thou shalt not snoop around in other people's computer files.
4. Thou shalt not use a computer to steal.
5. Thou shalt not use a computer to bear false witness.
6. Thou shalt not copy or use proprietary software for which you have not paid.
7. Thou shalt not use other people's computer resources without authorization or proper compensation.
8. Thou shalt not appropriate other people's intellectual output.
9. Thou shalt think about the social consequences of the program you are writing or the system you are designing.
10. Thou shalt always use a computer in ways that ensure consideration and respect for your fellow humans.

SOURCE: The Computer Ethics Institute, "The Ten Commandments of Computer Ethics," September 1, 2011, http://cpsr.org/issues/ethics/cei/. Used with permission from The Brookings Institution.

your office for mailing personal letters or exaggerating your travel expenses, belongs in this category of ethical violations.

2. *Saying things you know are not true.* When trying for a promotion and advancement, employees might be tempted to discredit their coworkers. Falsely assigning blame or inaccurately reporting conversations is lying. Although "This is the way the game is played around here" is a common justification, saying things that are untrue is an ethical violation.

3. *Giving or allowing false impressions.* The salesperson who permits a potential customer to believe that cardboard boxes will hold tomatoes for long-distance shipping when the salesperson knows the boxes are not strong enough has given a false impression. A car dealer who fails to disclose that a car has been in an accident is misleading potential customers.

4. *Buying influence or engaging in a conflict of interest.* A conflict of interest occurs when the official responsibilities of an employee or a government official are influenced by the potential for personal gain. Suppose a company awards a construction contract to a company owned by the father of a provincial politician while the attorney general's office is investigating that company. If this construction award has the potential to shape the outcome of the investigation, a conflict of interest has occurred.

5. *Hiding or divulging information.* Failing to disclose the results of medical studies that indicate your company's new drug has significant side effects is the ethical violation of hiding information that the product could be harmful to purchasers. Taking your company's product development or trade secrets to a new place of employment constitutes the ethical violation of divulging proprietary information.

6. *Taking unfair advantage.* Many current consumer protection laws were passed because so many businesses took unfair advantage of people who were not educated or were unable to discern the nuances of complex contracts. Credit disclosure requirements, truth-in-lending provisions, and new regulations on auto leasing all resulted because businesses misled consumers who could not easily follow the jargon of long, complex agreements.

7. *Committing improper personal behaviour.* Although the ethical aspects of an employee's right to privacy are still debated, it has become increasingly clear that personal conduct outside the job can influence performance and company reputation. Thus, a company driver must abstain from substance abuse because of safety issues. Even the traditional company December party and summer picnic have come under scrutiny because of the possibility that employees at and following these events might harm themselves or others through alcohol-related accidents.

8. *Abusing another person.* Suppose a manager sexually harasses an employee or subjects employees to humiliating corrections in the presence of coworkers or customers. In some cases, laws protect employees. Many situations, however, are simply interpersonal abuse that constitutes an ethical violation.

9. *Permitting organizational abuse.* Many companies with operations outside of their own country have faced issues of organizational abuse. The unfair treatment of workers in international operations appears in the form of child labour, demeaning wages, and excessive work hours. Although a business cannot change the culture of another country, it can perpetuate—or stop—abuse through its operations there.

10. *Violating rules.* Many organizations use rules and processes to maintain internal controls or to respect the authority of managers. Although these rules might seem burdensome to employees trying to serve customers, a violation might be considered an unethical act.

11. *Condoning unethical actions.* What if you witnessed a fellow employee embezzling company funds by changing the payee to her own name on a cheque that was to be voided? Would you report the violation? A winking tolerance of others' unethical behaviour is itself unethical.[22]*

*From JENNINGS, *Case Studies in Business Ethics*, 2E. © 1995 Cengage Learning.

HOT *Links*

Visit the Canadian Resources for Business Ethics site at
www.businessethics.ca

Concept *Check*

How are individual business ethics formed?

How can you recognize unethical activities?

HOW ORGANIZATIONS INFLUENCE ETHICAL CONDUCT

People choose between right and wrong based on their personal code of ethics. Ethical behaviours (or unethical behaviours) are also influenced by the ethical environment created by their employers. Consider the following newspaper headlines:

- CEO gets paid millions of dollars in salary and bonuses, but when times are tough, it is the middle class taxpayers who bail big companies out of their problems.
- Canadian Bank Note Company, Limited Fined $75,000 After Worker Injured.

As these headlines illustrate, poor business ethics can be very expensive for a company. Organizations can reduce the potential for these types of liability claims by educating their employees about ethical standards through various informal and formal programs. The first step in making a good ethical decision, however, is to recognize unethical business activities when they occur.

Leading by Example

Employees often follow the examples set by their managers. That is, leaders and managers establish patterns of behaviour that determine what's acceptable and what's not within the organization. While Ben Cohen was president of Ben & Jerry's ice cream, he followed a policy that no one could earn a salary more than seven times that of the lowest-paid worker. He wanted all employees to feel that they were equal. At the time he resigned, company sales were $140 million (USD) and the lowest-paid worker earned $19,000 (USD) per year. Ben Cohen's salary was $133,000 (USD) based on the "seven times" rule. A typical top executive of a $140 million (USD) company might have earned 10 times Cohen's salary. Ben Cohen's actions helped shape the ethical values of Ben & Jerry's.

Offering Ethics Training Programs

code of ethics
A set of guidelines prepared by a company to provide its employees with the knowledge of what the company expects in terms of their responsibilities and behaviour toward fellow employees, customers, and suppliers.

In addition to providing a system to resolve ethical dilemmas, organizations also provide formal training for employees to help them develop an awareness of questionable business activities and practise appropriate responses. Many Canadian companies have some type of ethics training program. The ones that are most effective begin with techniques for solving ethical dilemmas such as those discussed earlier. Next, employees are presented with a series of situations and are asked to come up with the "best" ethical solution. One of these ethical dilemmas is shown in Exhibit 3.4. Some companies have tried to add a bit of excitement and fun to their ethics training programs by presenting them in the form of games.

Establishing a Formal Code of Ethics

Most large companies and thousands of smaller ones have created, printed, and distributed codes of ethics. In general, a code of ethics provides employees with the knowledge of what their company expects in terms of their responsibilities and behaviour toward fellow employees, customers, and suppliers. Some ethical codes offer a lengthy and detailed set of guidelines for employees. Others are not really codes at all but rather summary statements of goals, policies, and priorities. Some companies have their codes framed and hung on office walls or printed on cards to be carried at all times by executives.

HOT *inks*

See Parks Canada's Code of Ethics at
www.pc.gc.ca/docs/pc/guide/code.aspx

Concept *Check*

What is the role of top management in organizational ethics?

What is a code of ethics?

Exhibit 3.4 An Ethical Dilemma Used for Employee Training

Bill Gannon was a middle manager of a large manufacturer of lighting fixtures in Newark, New Jersey. Bill had moved up the company ladder rather quickly and seemed destined for upper management in a few years. Bill's boss, Dana Johnson, had been pressuring him about the semi-annual reviews concerning Robert Talbot, one of Bill's employees. Dana, it seemed, would not accept any negative comments on Robert's evaluation forms. Bill had found out that a previous manager who had given Robert a bad evaluation was no longer with the company. As Bill reviewed Robert's performance for the forthcoming evaluation period, he found many areas of substandard performance. Moreover, a major client had called recently, complaining that Robert had filled a large order improperly and then had been rude to the client when she called to complain.

Thinking Critically

1. What ethical issues does the situation raise?
2. What courses of action could Bill take? Describe the ethics of each course.
3. Should Bill confront Dana? Dana's boss?
4. What would you do in this situation? What are the ethical implications?

THE FUTURE OF SOCIETY, CORPORATE RESPONSIBILITY, AND ETHICS

LO6

Four important trends are the baby boomers and retirement, the growth of social responsibility, the Occupy Movement that focuses on economic and social inequities, and global ethics.

Experienced Workers in High Demand

In 2011, PriceWaterhouseCoopers (PwC) released a study that showed Canadian CEOs are more likely to recruit older employees and retain them than the CEOs in other countries.[23] The study showed that these CEOs are looking at older works as important human capital and a way to maintain knowledge as a competitive advantage.

Today, many are choosing, for various reasons, some form of employment after retirement. Many companies are offering older workers flexibility (working part-time or setting their own hours) and opportunities to maintain lifestyles that they may not be able to without some supplementary income. Whether it is for social interaction or financial issues, the reality is that many baby boomers are opting to keep working beyond the typical 65 years of age.

The Growth of Social Responsibility—Just Keeps on Growing

CORPORATE TRANSPARENCY Public corporations are being encouraged to be more transparent regarding many issues. One of the primary issues is that of executive compensation; shareholders are asking tough questions about this. In 2007, the Canadian Securities Administration standardized the guidelines for disclosure requirements by public companies. Since this guideline was introduced companies, have become more transparent regarding executive compensation.

MORE PROTECTION FOR WHISTLEBLOWERS In the recent past there have been many instances of whistle blowing in Canada. A **whistleblower** is an employee, a former employee, or any other stakeholder of an organization who reports misconduct, or harmful or illegal acts by others in the organization.

In Canada, various federal and provincial statutes are designed to protect employees who provide information to law enforcement offices (especially related to health and

whistleblower
An employee, a former employee, or any other member of an organization who reports misconduct by others in the organization to those who have the power to take corrective action.

safety standards). However, little has been done until recently to protect those that have "blown the whistle" on corrupt and/or unethical behaviours of an organization or its employees or directors.

CHANGES IN CORPORATE PHILANTHROPY Corporate philanthropy has typically involved seeking out needy groups and then giving them money or company products. Today the focus is shifting to **strategic giving**, which ties philanthropy more closely to the corporate mission or goals and targets donations to regions where a company operates. For example, The Forzani Group supports the Sport Chek Mother's Day Run & Walk each year in Alberta.

strategic giving
The practice of tying philanthropy closely to the corporate mission or goals and targeting donations to regions where a company operates

A NEW SOCIAL CONTRACT TREND BETWEEN EMPLOYER AND EMPLOYEE
Another trend in social responsibility is the effort by organizations to redefine their relationship with their employees. Many people have viewed social responsibility as a one-way street that focuses on the obligations of business to society, employees, and others. Now companies are telling employees that they also have a responsibility when it comes to job security. The new contract reads somewhat like this: "There will never be job security. You will be employed by us as long as you add value to the organization, and you are continually responsible for finding ways to add value. In return, you have the right to demand interesting and important work, the freedom and resources to perform it well, pay that reflects your contribution, and the experience and training needed to be employable here or elsewhere."

Occupy Movement—Financial and Social Inequities

In the summer of 2011, a new and very visible movement began that would become worldwide, the Occupy Movement, which was sparked and branded by Kalle Lasn and his colleagues at the Vancouver-based Adbusters Media Foundation. The primary goals of these protesters were to spotlight corporate greed and social inequities. The movement started in Kuala Lumpur, Malaysia, and quickly moved to North America, first in New York City and the spreading across the United States and Canada. Overall, the movement spread to 95 cities in 82 countries.

Concept *in Action*

Computer companies that link their product donations with their corporate goals, for example, those that donate to schools, represent the corporate trend of strategic giving. How can other forms of business engage in corporate philanthropy?

MASKOT/GLOW IMAGES

The economic downturn of 2011 and the extreme inequities provided the catalyst for this movement. Not all Occupy movements focused on the same issues. For some it was the political elites (e.g., Syria and Libya) along with their supporters, while for others it was financial-based (Canada and the United States) and the influence corporations had over the politics of the day. In other countries, it was concerned with austerity measures (e.g., Greece), mass youth unemployment (e.g., Spain), or the rising cost of living (e.g., Israel).[24]

Global Ethics and Social Responsibility

As Canadian businesses expand into global markets, their corporate codes of ethics and policies on social responsibility must travel with them. As a citizen of several countries, a multinational corporation has several responsibilities. These include respecting local practices and customs, ensuring that there is harmony between the organization's staff and the host population, providing management leadership, and developing a cadre of local managers who will be a credit to their community. When a multinational makes an investment in a foreign country, it should commit to a long-term relationship. That means involving all stakeholders in the host country in decision making. Finally, a responsible multinational will implement ethical guidelines within the organization in the host country. By fulfilling these responsibilities, the company will foster respect for both local and international laws.

Multinational corporations often must balance conflicting interests of stakeholders when making decisions regarding social responsibilities, especially in the area of human rights. Questions involving child labour, forced labour, minimum wages, and workplace safety can be particularly difficult. Levi Strauss was strongly praised when it announced it was leaving China because of the country's poor human rights record. However, China is an inexpensive place to manufacture clothing, and the temptation to stay there was simply too great. In fact, Levi Strauss never stopped making clothes in China; its Hong Kong subsidiary continues to manufacture clothes on a contract basis. Levi recently announced

HOT *links*

How is the International Business Ethics Institute working to promote business ethics worldwide? Find out at www.business-ethics.org

Concept *Check*

What value added do older workers give companies?

What are some of the trends in corporate social responsibility?

What were the various focuses of the Occupy Movement?

How do multinational corporations demonstrate social responsibility in a foreign country?

Making Ethical Choices

TOO DELICIOUS TO RESIST

We are constantly bombarded with media reports claiming that many people are becoming dangerously overweight. A recent medical study also just classified obesity as a disease in its own right, unconnected to such symptoms as high blood pressure, cholesterol, or heart problems. So perhaps it is not surprising that a recent lawsuit claimed that McDonald's is responsible for the obesity of two teenagers by "getting them hooked" on their burgers and fries.

You are the lawyer approached by the teens' parents to bring suit against McDonald's. You ask yourself some soul-searching questions. Does McDonald's market and sell food in such a manner that it poses a health danger to unsuspecting consumers? And what about personal accountability? Shouldn't the teens and/or their parents be held responsible for their food choices? You wonder whether if this were a local mom and pop restaurant, would the teens' parents be suing? Or are the deep pockets of McDonald's too delicious to resist?

Using a Web search tool, locate articles about this topic and then write responses to the following questions. Be sure to support your arguments and cite your sources.

ETHICAL DILEMMA: Do you tell the teens' parents to go home, cook healthful meals, and put their kids on a diet? Or do you take the case—believing that McDonald's has not acted in a socially responsible way—while recognizing the potential for some serious money?

SOURCES: Dave Carpenter, "DIET: McDonald's to post nutrition facts on packaging next year," *The America's Intelligence Wire*, October 26, 2005, http://www.galenet.thomsonlearning.com; Pallavi Gogoi, "McDonald's New Wrap," *Business Week* Online, February 17, 2006, www.businessweek.com; Richard Martin, "Revived McD Obesity Lawsuit Still Suggests Personal-Responsibility Defense—for Now," *Nation's Restaurant News*, February 14, 2005, http://www.galenet.thomsonlearning.com; Wendy Melillo, "Bringing Up Baby: Where's the Line, and Who Should Draw It, In Advertising to Children?" *ADWEEK*, February 13, 2006, p.14; Libby Quaid, "House Votes to Block Lawsuits Blaming Food Industry for Obesity," *The America's Intelligence Wire*, October 19, 2005, http://www.galenet.thomsonlearning.com.

that it would begin selling clothes in China. One might argue that Levi Strauss must remain competitive and profitable, or it will not be able to be a leader in the cause of social responsibility. When the announcement came, however, human rights activists quickly set up a picket at Levi's San Francisco headquarters.

GREAT IDEAS TO USE NOW

In many situations, there are no right or wrong answers. Instead, organizations must provide a process to resolve the dilemma quickly and fairly. Two approaches for resolving ethical problems are the "three-question test" and the newspaper test.

Resolving Ethical Problems in Business

In evaluating an ethical problem, managers can use the three-question test to determine the most ethical response: "Is it legal?" "Is it balanced?" and "How does it make me feel?" Many companies such as Texas Instruments, Marriott, and McDonald's rely on this test to guide employee decision-making. If the answer to the first question is "no," then don't do it. Many ethical dilemmas, however, involve situations that aren't illegal. For example, the sale of tobacco is legal in Canada, but given all the research that shows that tobacco use is dangerous to one's health, is it an ethical activity?

The second question, "Is it balanced?" requires you to put yourself in the position of other parties affected by your decision. For example, as an executive, you might not favour a buyout of your company because you will probably lose your job. Shareholders, however, might benefit substantially from the price to be paid for their shares in the buyout. At the same time, the employees of the business and their community might suffer economically if the purchaser decides to close the business or focus its efforts in a different product area. The best situation, of course, is when everybody wins or shares the burden equally.

The final question, "How does it make me feel?" asks you to examine your comfort with a particular decision. Many people find that after reaching a decision on an issue, they still experience discomfort that can manifest itself in a loss of sleep or appetite. Those feelings of conscience can serve as a guide in resolving ethical dilemmas.

"Front Page of the Newspaper" Test

Many managers use the "front page of the newspaper test" for evaluating ethical dilemmas. The question to be asked is how a critical and objective reporter would report your decision in a front-page story. Some managers rephrase the test for their employees: How will the headline read if I make this decision? This test is helpful in spotting and resolving potential conflicts of interest.

Summary of Learning Outcomes

Identify some of the current social factors that have an impact on business.

The business environment consists of social, demographic, economic, technological, and competitive trends. Managers cannot control environmental trends. Instead, they must understand how the environment is changing and the impact of those changes on the business. Several social trends are currently influencing businesses. First, people choose different lifestyles based on such factors as economics, interests, and resources. Second, the phenomenon of working women has probably had a greater effect on marketing than has any other social change. Increasing financial resources have given more opportunities for a component lifestyle.

Stakeholders are individuals or groups to whom business has a responsibility. Businesses are responsible to employees, customers, investors, suppliers, governments, and society. They should provide a clean and safe working environment. Organizations can build employees' self-worth through empowerment programs. Businesses also have a responsibility to customers to provide good, safe products and services. Companies are responsible to investors. They should earn a reasonable profit for the owners. Suppliers are another stakeholder—knowing that they will have a customer and be paid for their products and services. Governments want to know that the companies are following the rules and regulations and reporting their tax obligation correctly. Organizations are responsible to the general public to be good corporate citizens. Companies must help protect the environment and provide a good place to work. Companies also engage in corporate philanthropy, which includes contributing cash, donating goods and services, and supporting volunteer efforts of employees.

LO2 Illustrate how businesses meet their social responsibilities to stakeholders.

Corporate governance refers to the way in which an organization is governed, directed, and administered.[25] As discussed in Chapter 8, the board of directors (also known simply as directors) is responsible for the organization's being managed in the best interest of the corporation. As such, directors of corporations need to be concerned about their responsibilities and potential liabilities. Canadian society is very concerned about proper corporate governance and the accountability of the board of directors. As such Canada has a complex system of regulations and closely analyses the actions of the board of directors.

LO3 Explain corporate governance and why it is important.

Ethics is a set of moral standards for judging whether something is right or wrong. A utilitarianism approach to setting personal ethical standards focuses on the consequences of an action taken by a person or an organization. According to this approach, people should act so as to generate the greatest good for the greatest number. Every human is entitled to certain rights such as freedom and the pursuit of happiness. Another approach to ethical decision making is justice, or what is fair according to accepted standards.

LO4 Discuss the philosophies and concepts that shape personal ethical standards.

Top management must shape the ethical culture of the organization. They should lead by example, offer ethics training programs, and establish a formal code of ethics.

LO5 Show how organizations can encourage ethical business behaviour.

Four of the trends are baby boomers retiring later either for social interaction or for financial reasons; an increase in the expectation by stakeholders that businesses will be more socially responsible; the Occupy Movement that highlighted such issues as corporate greed, political elitism, mass unemployment, and financial and social inequities; and an increase of business ethics.

LO6 List some of the trends in society, corporate responsibility, and ethics.

Key Terms

baby boomers   68
Canadian Charter of Rights and
   Freedoms   77
code of ethics   80
component lifestyle   64
conventional ethics   77
corporate governance   75
corporate philanthropy   75
demography   66
ethics   64
Generation X   68
Generation Y   67

Generation Z   67
justice   77
multiculturalism   69
neoliberalism   71
postconventional ethics   78
preconventional ethics   77
social investing   73
social responsibility   70
stakeholders   72
strategic giving   82
utilitarianism   76
whistleblower   81

Experiential Exercises

1. **Support a good cause.** You don't have to wait until you graduate to start demonstrating your social responsibility. It will also look good on your résumé when you need to differentiate yourself from all of the other job seekers. Go to www.volunteer.ca/index-eng.php and find organizations in your area looking for volunteers. Find one that meets your interest and that is related to your career goals, and go to work.

2. **Know your ethical values.** To get a better idea of your own level of ethical development, think about various actions and how you would respond to them.

3. If you are thinking about giving money to a charity, check it out first. Find out what charities are registered in Canada at www.cra-arc.gc.ca/chrts-gvng/lstngs/menu-eng.html.

4. **Work for a company that cares about its social responsibilities.** When you enter the job market, make certain that you are going to work for a socially responsible organization. Ask a prospective employer "how the company gives back to society." If you plan to work for a large company, check out the current list of Canada's most admired corporations in the *Financial Post*.

5. The Canadian Institute of Chartered Accountants (CICA) is actively promoting ethical behaviours among its membership. The CICA's "Guidance on Control" states, "An organization should provide guidance for all its people to promote their understanding of the organization's principles of integrity and ethical values, and it should provide support to help them deal with dilemmas and uncertainty...."* Check out what is new regarding ethics at the CICA's website, www.cica.ca.

6. Your company has decided to create a new position for an ethics officer and has asked you to be part of the team that is writing the job description. Using resources such as the website of the Ethics and Compliance Officer Association (ECOA), www.theecoa.org, and other materials, draft a list of job responsibilities for this new role.

7. The Boeing Company makes business ethics a priority, asking employees to take refresher training every year. It encourages employees to take the Ethics Challenge with their work groups and to discuss the issues with their peers. You can take the challenge, too, by going to www.boeing.com/companyoffices/-aboutus/ethics/education.htm. Each question presents an ethical dilemma, together with three or four potential answers. Taking the challenge will show you how Boeing approaches workplace ethics. Summarize your findings. Did any answers surprise you?

8. You'll find a comprehensive list of business ethics sites at www.web-miner.com/busethics.htm. Once at the site, go to the section on Corporate Codes of Ethics. Look at three examples of codes in different industries. What elements do they have in common? How are they different? Suggest how one of the codes could be improved.

9. What ethical issues arise as companies add e-business to their operations? Go to the *Information Week* website, www.informationweek.com, and perform a search for business ethics. What topics did you find? Identify three areas where the potential for ethical breaches could occur, and briefly discuss each.

10. Visit the Fur Is Dead website from the People for the Ethical Treatment of Animals (PETA), www.furisdead.com. Read about PETA's view of the fur industry. Do you agree with this view? Why or why not? How do you think manufacturers of fur clothing would justify their actions to someone from PETA? Would you work for a store that sold fur-trimmed clothing? Explain your answer.

11. *Green Money Journal*, www.greenmoneyjournal.com, is a bimonthly online journal that promotes social responsibility investing. What are the current topics of concern in this area? Visit the archives to find articles on socially responsible investing and find two areas of corporate social responsibility. Summarize what you have learned.

* Reprinted [or adapted] with permission from The Canadian Institute of Chartered Accountants, Toronto, Canada. Any changes to the original material are the sole responsibility of the author (and/or publisher) and have not been reviewed or endorsed by the CICA.

Review Questions

1. What are some of the social trends affecting Canadian business? Discuss how each of these is affecting business.

2. What are the major demographic groups by age? What are some characteristics of each group?

3. How do diversity and multiculturalism impact Canadian business?

4. Define social responsibility.

5. Give examples of legal but irresponsible business behaviours.

6. List the various stakeholders of an organization.

7. What responsibilities does a company have to the various stakeholders?

8. How can being philanthropic help the bottom line of a company?

9. What is utilitarianism?

10. What are some of the individual rights we enjoy in Canada?

11. How does the idea of justice affect business?

12. What are some unethical business activities discussed in the chapter?

13. What can organizations do to influence ethical conduct?

CREATIVE THINKING CASE

Helping Those to Develop Their Potential

Cosmopolitan Industries Ltd. (Cosmo) in Saskatoon, Saskatchewan is a not-for-profit corporation focused on creating opportunities for individuals with intellectual challenges. They support and challenge participants to reach their full potential while respecting the dignity and needs of each individual. They started back in 1970 and over time have developed partnerships with businesses and government to provide employment for up to 100 persons and programs for approximately 400 participants. Cosmo provides lifestyle and skills training, works with employers to design sustainable work environments for their participants, and raises funds to support their program costs.

Cosmo has a reputation as a value-based ethical organization. The organizations that partner with Cosmo benefit from this reputation. Cosmo produces and sells more than $5 million per annum in clubs and other golf accessories, making them one of the largest manufacturers in Canada. Sports stores like Source for Sports sell the Cosmo golf club lines. This is one way Cosmo has expanded the work opportunities for the intellectually challenged beyond the traditional button making and newspaper recycling. Opportunities have substantially changed for this segment of society who once were relegated to institutions away from the public, before companies such as Cosmo formed.

Cosmo serves a diverse population. As services and programs for the intellectually challenged have improved, life expectancy and quality of life have both increased. Cosmo now serves senior citizens who have been participants in their programs for as long as 40 years. Those seniors expect to continue an active life and Cosmo keeps them moving. A partnership with a local school gives Cosmo the facilities to provide ongoing programs for those who have developed multiple needs as they age. For the younger participant, Cosmo provides the opportunity to learn and work. Some jobs, such as recycling, confidential shredding, and the manufacture of golf clubs, take place within a Cosmo-operated facility, supervised by Cosmo's staff of professionals. Other jobs are within an unsheltered work environment, working with the staff of an organization. Cosmo provides support and sometimes transportation for those workers. All participants have access to literacy, fitness and skills programs. Companies who hire Cosmo participants can usually rely on those workers to be at work and on time. When medical or other needs come up, the Cosmo staff and volunteers are there to coordinate and support.

Cosmo is operated by a professional staff augmented by volunteers and supervised by a volunteer board. Incorporation provides some protection for the Board members from litigation, which helps them recruit top-notch volunteers. Some come from corporate partners like the Saskatchewan Lottery Commission, others from the health field and the community. Corporate partners achieve both a social goal and corporate goals. By sponsoring a team in the "Bowl 'n Cruise," Source for Sports gets some positive publicity, builds staff cohesiveness among those who form the team, provides those staff with an opportunity to work with their Captain (a Cosmo participant), and reinforces their corporate message of fitness for all.

Private companies have choices. They can hire a company like Cosmo to provide them with workers and/or services or they can deal with turnover issues among unsupported hires in these types of jobs. They can buy inexpensive golf clubs from overseas or from Cosmo. They can participate in events with Cosmo and build employee sensitivity or try to accomplish this through workshops alone. Organizations such as Cosmo give corporate citizens opportunities to model social responsibility and ethics for their staff and client base.

Thinking Critically

1. Some employers meet with resistance among their employees when they bring in a worker supported by Cosmo. How would you explain this resistance? What steps should the employer take to avoid or prevent this problem?

2. How do organizations such as Source for Sports benefit from their association with Cosmo?

3. Are there similar programs in your town or a nearby large city? If you were an employee, would you encourage your employer to seek an alliance with a Cosmo-like organization?

SOURCES: Cosmo, "About Us," Cosmopolitan Industries, http://www.cosmoindustries.com/html/about_contact_us.html; Cosmo, "Bowl N' Cruise Gives 14,854 Reasons to Smile," Cosmopolitan Industries, http://www.cosmoindustries.com/index.html; Cosmopolitan Industries Ltd. - Complete Profile, (Ottawa: Industry Canada, 2012), http://www.ic.gc.ca/app/ccc/srch/nvgt.do?lang=eng&prtl=1&sbPrtl=&estblmnt No=123456111229&profile=cmpltPrfl&profileId=501&app=sold; Manta, "Cosmopolitan Industries Golf Canada Ltd," Manta Inc., http://www.manta.com/ic/mvsgyzt/ca/cosmopolitan-industries-golf-canada-ltd; Tammy Robert, "Saskatoon and Curbside Recycling: A Political Minefield," *Scene in Saskatchewan*, 2011; Government of Saskatchewan, "Cosmopolitan Industries Expands Recycling Facility with Federal, Provincial and Municipal Funding," Government of Saskatchewan, 2007; Government of Saskatchewan, "Increase for Funding for Cosmopolitan Industries," Publications Centre, 2011; Troy Stewart, "Cosmopolitan Industries: Chapter 2 - Organizational Stakeholders, Management, and Ethics." 8. Halifax, N.S.: Saint Mary's University, 2011.

Making the Connection

Technology: Managing Information for Business Success

In this chapter, you'll learn about the next piece of our PESTI model puzzle—the *technological* environment.

This is a wonderful example of the integrative nature of business, because technology permeates just about every aspect of our model. To begin with, it affects a company's ability to meet its critical success factors. *Financial performance* is affected by technology, because a company can operate more efficiently and, therefore, increase its bottom line by using technology. Technology also allows us to better *meet customer needs* by giving businesses quicker and better access to information on their buyers' needs. Consequently, these needs are better met through the speed of technology, helping us deliver on our promises and provide customer service. In fact, as you'll see in the chapter, a company's technology-based information system can "track new orders" to speed order processing; "determine what products are selling best," which can help a company to develop products to meet customer needs; "identify high-volume customers" to focus on enhancing those relationships; "or contact customers about new or related products" to help form relationships. In fact, even greater needs can be met with expanded product offerings because the Internet does not have the physical limitations of a typical store—any number of items can be sold through a single website. *Quality* is also enhanced through the use of technology. In fact, *innovations* have allowed us to improve quality and make it a priority at all levels of an organization. The rate of these and other innovations has been boosted to "warp speed" because of technology. Finally, employees are more *committed* to meeting company goals, because companies can make their jobs more interesting; the most repetitive and monotonous jobs can be completed through the use of technology instead of valuable *human resources*. So technology can definitely help a business be more successful, and since the rapid pace of technological change is a reality for today's business, it is, in fact, a necessity for success.

Technology as an environmental factor affects the other aspects of our PESTI model as well. For example, in the *political* environment, the government issues patents on new technology, preventing other companies from copying that technology. This gives a company an advantage over other companies for years to come. From the point of view of *economics*, we saw during the "tech bubble" how the rapid growth of technological companies can fuel the stock market to the point of overvalue and then rapid adjustment, to the shock of many investors. Technology also changes the nature of competition. The same dominant company, for example, IBM, served the same customers for decades. Lower technical barriers have opened many commercial opportunities. There has been substantial new entry into the computer industry, but not into direct competition with the established leader. Instead, entrants have opened up new market segments in social media, e-business, and global trading. The Internet has removed the geographic and time-related limits to doing business. Customers no longer have to visit a store during business hours—companies don't even need to have a store! And the traditional relationship between manufacturers, distributors, and retailers has changed because companies can bypass these channels, selling directly over the Internet. From a *social* perspective, it is clear that technology has changed how we, as consumers, see the world—it has given us much more access to information, making us better equipped to make buying decisions and more demanding in our speed-of-fulfillment expectations. It is also important to understand that, as new technologies are adopted, they promote other waves of technological innovation and disruption. In this way, technology enhances our ability to create more technology.

Technology also affects how companies operate. As we emphasize in this chapter, it affects the way businesses communicate and share information in all areas of the company. The company's information system can gather and provide information on what customers want directly to the *marketing* department to enhance its sales efforts. The order information can then be provided directly to *operations* so that managers can obtain the correct inventory needed, when it's needed, and schedule production to meet the customer's needs exactly and on time. Information is also provided to human resources to ensure skilled workers are available as the production schedule requires. The final sales information can also be provided directly to *finance* to prepare financial statements. This integration of information brings together the functional areas in an essential way so that they can work together more efficiently to achieve the company's goals and ensure its success.

Technology also affects each specific functional area. For example, on the operational side, it affects *how* products are built (using computers to help design products and guide manufacturing) as well as *what* products are built (as technology allows for greater customization to meet customer needs). It affects how products are marketed (such as through the Internet, using e-commerce) and financed. (The "bursting of the tech bubble" has had such an impact on capital markets that it's difficult for new technology companies to sell their stock to the public and generate much-needed funds for expansion.) Even the human resource function is affected by technology, because computers can take over many tasks done by humans, and companies therefore have the added demand of finding the best people with the necessary skills to use the technology, and to manage technology workers.

The very nature of business has changed dramatically with technology. E-business has revolutionized the way business is done, affecting the overall *strategies* of many organizations because it has created a new paradigm for business. We have moved beyond the individual enterprise to an interconnected economy through interconnected information systems. As businesses become more interconnected between suppliers, manufacturers, and retailers, they operate more as one company. This allows them to meet the needs of the customer better, providing a seamless integration from the beginning of the business chain to the ultimate consumer.

chapter 4

Technology: Managing Information for Business Success

LEARNING OUTCOMES

1 Explain why information is so important in business.

2 Explain how information technology has transformed business and managerial decision making.

3 Give examples of the types of systems that make up a typical company's management information system.

4 Discuss why computer networks are an important part of today's information technology systems.

5 Describe how technology management and planning can help companies optimize their information technology systems.

6 Identify some of the best ways to protect computers and the information they contain.

7 List some of the leading trends in information technology.

SABIAN—THAT CRASH IS FROM CANADA

Not many music fans can find Meductic, New Brunswick, on a map, but they hear its sounds when they listen to their MP3s. Meductic, a village of 155 residents, 80 kilometres north of Fredericton, is home to Sabian Cymbal, the world's second largest cymbal producer (by volume), selling in approximately 120 countries.

"Meductic" means "the end of the trail" in Maliseet, exactly where Mike Wengren, drummer for Disturbed, probably thought he was when he visited the factory in June 2009. But his visit let him meet the artisans who make his cymbals and listen to thousands of sounds in the vault where sounds are designed and discovered. Many top percussionists make the pilgrimage to meet with Mark Love, Master Product Specialist, and tour the factory.

Afterwards, they keep in touch via the Internet—that's how Sabian stays connected with its worldwide network of wholesalers, dealers, and high profile customers (www.sabian.com), including such greats as Neil Peart (Rush) and Ian Wright (Royal Liverpool Philharmonic). So if you hear Rush in Rotterdam, you can head downtown to Feedback Music and buy the same brand, perhaps the same model, of cymbal Peart played.

Sabian embraced the Internet in 1996 and now draws 12,000 to 15,000 page views per day. The challenge for the Web development team is to keep the material fresh and relevant. But the website isn't Sabian's only technology—in 1997, Sabian linked its five buildings via fibre optic cable with Fast Ethernet backbone; adding a remote Internet link to an office in Marshfield, Massachusetts; and company-wide e-mail to connect satellite offices in France, Canada, and the USA.

Employees who travel stay in touch via e-mail and intranet. Sales reps visit Sabian's thousands of dealers around the world and submit reports to Meductic via the Internet. Manufacturing gets feedback on products; marketing hears what's working in different countries, cultures, and segments of the music industry; and distribution can address inventory needs. Time zones no longer matter—customers around the world send in queries at their convenience and get prompt responses to everything, including special orders, factory tour bookings, and requests for personalized cymbals.

These kinds of interactions require serious Internet speed. In 2009, Sabian increased its bandwidth to 20 Mb, which supports a network of Small Office/Home Office (SOHO) sites in Europe, Canada, and the United States, as well as several warehouse locations around the world. Not only Sabian thrives in this rural setting—its staff can use home offices and travel to dealers rather than commute from big cities. All of these remote offices can now be supported from Meductic.

All this technology and the fast pace of change means that Greg Hartt, manager of the Information Systems

PHOTO COURTESY OF SABIAN LTD.

A secret formula of molten metals starts the cymbal-making process.

department, and his staff must constantly upgrade their knowledge. Greg says, "I'm always reading up on new hardware and software, trying things out and looking for a better way. It is a fun area if you're willing to do the work to stay on top of new trends."

Sabian keeps growing—from 11 staff at the plant in the 1960s to more than 100 today, plus many reps working as independent contractors worldwide; from a few dedicated artists, to a long list of satisfied customers. The Internet and strong commitment to technology has enabled this growth. [1]

THINKING CRITICALLY

1. Do some Internet research on Sabian. Would you describe their business as e-business or e-commerce? Why?

2. Do you think there are new innovations in IT that will affect Sabian's business model? What steps should Greg take to stay ahead?

3. Would you want to work for a company like Sabian? What disadvantages do you see in their structure?

4. Outline some of the security threats created by linking remote offices.

SOURCES: http://www.city-data.com/canada/Meductic-Village.html; Sabian.com; http://www.historicplaces.ca/en/rep-reg/place-lieu.aspx?id=14831; http://www.native-artifact-consulting.com/treasures.html; http://www.trafficoutlook.com/sabian.com; http://www.webmator.com/sabian.com; http://bizinformation.co/www.sabian.com; Interview with Greg Hartt

According to the Merriam-Webster online dictionary, www.merriam-webster.com/dictionary/technology, technology is "the practical application of knowledge." Knowledge is applied for practical purposes every day in the business world, and technology has become one of the fastest changing and most influential factors in the business environment. Just looking at the headlines in a recent issue of Technology Review *(published by MIT, www.technologyreview.com, August 16, 2012), you can see a number of practical applications of technology in the business world:*

- *Disney researchers are using a new computer interface to create the sensation of texture when touching an object on a computer screen.*
- *The future of nuclear power is being brought into question because of cheap and abundant natural gas.*
- *A new mathematical technique developed at Cornell University could offer a way for personal data gathered on the Internet to be shared and analyzed by companies, while guaranteeing individual privacy.*
- *A camera-equipped ring is being developed by researchers at MIT that helps visually impaired people identify objects and read text.*

It's mind-boggling really, isn't it? The use of technology can be seen in every aspect of a business, as discussed in Making the Connection. Because it is such a vast area, this chapter will focus on one specific aspect of technology that is gaining momentum and importance in the business world—the technology of information.

Harnessing the power of information technology gives a company a significant competitive advantage. **Information technology (IT)** *includes the equipment and techniques used to manage and process information.*

The centrepiece for businesses, large or small, lies in the coordination of information. Information is at the heart of all organizations. Without information about the processes of and participants in an organization—including orders, products, inventory, scheduling, shipping, customers, suppliers, and employees—a business cannot operate.

Because most jobs today depend on information—obtaining, using, creating, managing, and sharing it—we begin this chapter with a discussion of the business value of information, transformation of the business through information, linking up the technology behind the information, technology management and planning, ways to protect computers, securing of information, and finally, trends in information technology.

Throughout the chapter, we will use examples to show how managers and their companies are using computers to make better decisions in a highly competitive world.

information technology (IT)
The equipment and techniques used to manage and process information.

HOT *L* inks

If you want to know the definition of an information technology or information system term, or more about a particular topic, the following are some resources that have answers to particular areas:
www.webopedia.com
www.ciocan.ca
www.backbonemag.com

LO1 IS THERE BUSINESS VALUE IN INFORMATION?

Management of Information Systems (MIS)
A discipline that involves the management of people, process, and technology around the care of information.

Management of Information Systems (MIS) is a discipline that involves the management of people, process, and technology around the care of information (the information systems or IS). MIS involves handling, classifying, holding, arranging, managing, and having the mastery to structure information through systems and technology. The management of information provides decision-making support at various levels of the organization.

Exhibit 4.1   MIS Integration

Information System

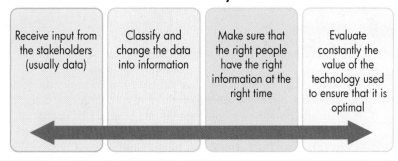

| Receive input from the stakeholders (usually data) | Classify and change the data into information | Make sure that the right people have the right information at the right time | Evaluate constantly the value of the technology used to ensure that it is optimal |

As seen in Exhibit 4.1, management of information *systems* specialists focus on integrating information technology solutions and business processes to meet the information needs of businesses and other enterprises, enabling them to achieve their objectives in an effective, efficient way. In complement, information *technology* specialists focus on the technology itself more than on the information it conveys. These systems must work properly, be secure, and be upgraded, maintained, and replaced as appropriate. MIS gathers data and information over time, structures it using information system specialists, and utilizes the technology and computer systems with the help of computer technologists to deliver the resources to various destinations to support business planning, strategy, efficiency and effectiveness of an organization.

There are many types of MIS: transaction-processing systems, operators information systems, decision support systems, and expert systems. This will be discussed in Learning Outcome 2.

When analyzing the values of its information, an organization analyzes its strategic importance of its information for a competitive advantage. Is the information being utilized by its employees in an efficient manner? Is the information available and organized? Is the information easily accessible and affordable to retrieve?

information system (IS)
The combination of technology, people, and process that an organization uses to produce and manage information.

The Value of E-Commerce

The business value of information technology in e-business or e-commerce (EC) environments is categorized into business-to-consumer (B2C), business to business (B2B), government to citizens (G2C), government to business (G2B), customer to customer (C2C), and mobile commerce (m-commerce). Because of today's technology, EC is seen as very appealing in many industries because it is available anywhere, at anytime, by anyone. Economically, there is tremendous transactional value from EC.

More and more traditional brick and mortar businesses are incorporating EC into their way of conducting business and connecting with their customers. Generally, labour and and other costs are minimized. Both factors—labour and general costs—when decreased make EC very attractive to conduct current business and attract new opportunities. According to Forrester research, by the year 2016, e-commerce sales will grow to \$327 billion dollars; moreover, it predicts an annual growth rate of 10.1 percent.[2] The growth of EC is largely influenced by the introduction of mobile devices and the availability of broadband networks that enable easy and efficient Internet access. With this environment (constant innovation

Concept *Check*

What is information technology?

What is MIS?

What is e-commerce?

Why is EC an attractive alternative to the traditional "brick"?

in mobile communication devices), consumers are enticed to explore the power of the Internet and harness processing power with mobile devices that few PCs two decades ago could top. EC has barely been tapped.

LO2 TRANSFORMING BUSINESSES THROUGH INFORMATION

In less than 60 years, we have shifted from an industrial society to a knowledge-based economy driven by information. More companies are collecting and storing data about you and providing recommendations or solutions every time you "connect" with your device, use the Internet, and even when you use your loyalty cards. The more data that is collected, the better the company understands your purchasing behaviour and can better compete for your time and resources.

Information Technology

Businesses depend on information technology for everything from running daily operations to making strategic decisions. Computers are the tools of this information age, performing or helping workers perform extremely complex operations and everyday jobs like word processing and creating spreadsheets. Change has been rapid since the personal computer became a fixture on most office desks. Individual units became part of small networks, followed by more sophisticated enterprise-wide networks. Now the Internet makes it effortless to connect quickly to almost any place in the world. A manager can share information with hundreds of thousands of people worldwide almost as easily as with a colleague on another floor of the same office building. The Internet and the Web have become indispensable business tools that facilitate communication within companies as well as with customers. The rise of electronic trading hubs, discussed in the Expanding Around the Globe box, is just one example of how technology is facilitating the global economy.

Canadian companies have made considerable contributions to technology use in the world. For example, CGI Group Inc. successfully competes in the competitive IT services industry, with over 100 offices in 16 countries. CGI has partnered with many companies across many industries that include banking, distribution, government, healthcare, insurance, retail, oil and gas, etc. CGI has been ranked by Mediacorp as one of Canada's "Top 100 Employers" and is among the Corporate Knights' listing of Best 50 Corporate Citizens. Many companies entrust an executive called the chief information officer (CIO) with the responsibility of managing all information resources and processes. This is the person in an organization who is responsible for the information technology and computer systems that support enterprise goals. As information management, technology, and systems have become more important, the CIO have come to be viewed in many organizations as key contributors in formulating strategic goals. They are a key stakeholder in the utilization and dissemination of internal and external information for competitive advantage. In many companies, the CIO reports directly to the chief executive officer (CEO). In some companies, the CIO sits on the executive board. The importance of this responsibility is immense. As Jerry McElhatton, the retired CIO of MasterCard, points out, "Next to actual cash itself, data is probably the most precious asset a financial institution has, and for good reason." Companies such as MasterCard, banks, and insurance companies don't sell tangible products. "There is nothing to look at in a showroom, nothing to ship, nothing that will make a noise if you drop it. There is simply an agreement that something will happen, such as funds will become available if the customer signs on the dotted line. That's what makes data so precious

 HOT _inks_

To see the different kinds of objects and places you can search by using Google Goggles, go to www.google.com/mobile/goggles/#text

chief information officer (CIO)
An executive responsible for managing all information resources and processes in an organization.

to us and why we're more protective of it than the average mother lioness is with her cubs," McElhatton explains.

Today most of us are knowledge workers who create, develop, and use knowledge. Knowledge workers contribute to and benefit from information they use in performing various tasks, including planning, acquiring, searching, analyzing, organizing, storing, programming, producing, distributing, marketing, or selling functions. The knowledge worker captures, codifies, and transfers knowledge across organizations for competitive advantage. We must know how to gather and use information from the many resources available to us. What differentiates knowledge work from other forms of work, especially in a knowledge economy, is its primary task of "non-routine" problem solving that requires a combination of convergent, divergent, and creative thinking (Reinhardt et al., 2011).[3]

Data and Information Systems

Businesses collect a great deal of *data*—quantities, characters, or symbols that are raw, unorganized facts that can be moved and stored—in their daily operations. Only through well-designed IT systems and the power of computers can managers process these data into meaningful and useful *information*, which they can use for specific purposes such as making business decisions. One such form of business information is the database, a collection of data organized to facilitate accessing, searching, updating, and deleting data. Using software called a *database management system (DBMS)*, you can quickly and easily enter, store, organize, select, and retrieve data in a database. These data are then turned into information to run the business and to perform business analysis.

Databases are at the core of business information systems. Databases should be simple, stable, and secure. For example, pictured in Exhibit 4.2 is Microsoft's Access®, which keeps track of and organizes similar data, such as customers or suppliers, and provides information to many departments. Similarly, a data collection of test scores is another example of a database.

Marketing teams track new orders and determine what products are selling best, salespeople identify high-volume customers or contact customers about new or related products, operations managers source order information to obtain inventory and schedule production of the ordered products, and financial personnel mine sales data to prepare financial statements. Information within databases provides tremendous opportunities for e-commerce success. Later in the chapter, we will see how companies use very large databases called data warehouses and data marts. Data warehouses help retailers in many ways, from cutting inventory costs to identifying market trends more quickly.

Companies are discovering that they can't operate well with a series of separate information systems geared to solving specific departmental problems. It takes a team effort to integrate the systems throughout the company. Company-wide *enterprise resource planning (ERP)* systems that bring together human resources, operations, and technology are becoming an integral part of business strategy. So is managing the collective knowledge contained in an organization by using data warehouses and other technology tools. Technology experts are learning more about the way the business operates, and business managers are learning to use information systems technology effectively to create new opportunities and reach their goals.

Concept *in Action*

In today's high-tech world, CIOs must possess not only the technical smarts to implement global IT infrastructures, integrate communications systems with partners, and protect customer data from insidious hackers, but also strong business acumen. FedEx's acclaimed tech chief Rob Carter manages the technology necessary to deliver more than six million packages daily, with an eye toward greater business efficiency, growth, and profits. Why is it important for CIOs to possess both technological and business expertise?

knowledge worker
A worker who develops or uses knowledge, contributing to and benefiting from information used in performing various tasks, including planning, acquiring, searching, analyzing, organizing, storing, programming, producing, distributing, marketing, or selling functions.

database
An electronic filing system that collects and organizes data and information.

Concept *Check*

How has the use of information changed in business?

What is a knowledge worker?

Why are databases important?

Exhibit 4.2   Customer Database

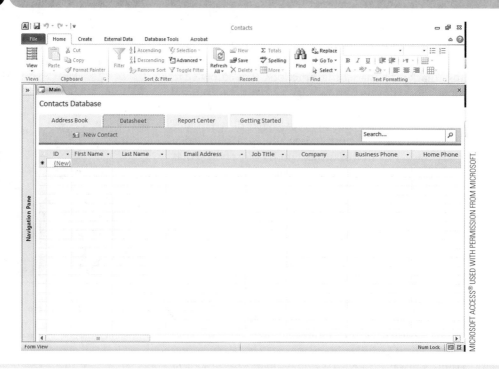

MICROSOFT ACCESS® USED WITH PERMISSION FROM MICROSOFT.

Expanding Around the Globe

ELECTRONIC HUBS INTEGRATE GLOBAL COMMERCE

Thanks to the wonders of technological advancement, global electronic trading now goes far beyond the Internet retailing and trading that we are all familiar with. Special websites known as trading hubs, or e-marketplaces, facilitate electronic commerce between businesses in specific industries such as automotive manufacturing, retailing, telecom provisioning, aerospace, financial products and services, and more.

The trading hub functions as a means of integrating the electronic collaboration of business services. Each hub provides standard formats for the electronic trading of documents used in a particular industry, as well as an array of services to sustain e-commerce between businesses in that industry. Services include demand forecasting, inventory management, partner directories, and transaction settlement services. And the payoff is significant—lowered costs, decreased inventory levels, and shorter time to market—resulting in bigger profits and enhanced competitiveness. For example, large scale manufacturing procurement can amount to billions of dollars. Changing to "just-in-time purchasing" on the hub can save a considerable percentage of these costs.

Electronic trading across a hub can range from the collaborative integration of individual business processes to auctions and exchanges of goods (electronic barter). Global content management is an essential factor in promoting electronic trading agreements on the hub. A globally consistent view of the "content" of the hub must be available to all. Each participating company handles its own content, and applications such as content managers keep a continuously updated master catalogue of the inventories of all members of the hub. The transaction manager application automates trading arrangements between companies, allowing the hub to provide aggregation and settlement services.

Ultimately, trading hubs for numerous industries could be linked together in a global e-commerce Web—an inclusive "hub of all hubs." One creative thinker puts it this way: "The traditional linear, one-step-at-a-time supply chain is dead. It will be replaced by parallel, asynchronous, real-time marketplace decision making. Take manufacturing capacity as an example. Enterprises can [put up for] bid their excess production capacity on the world e-commerce hub. Offers to buy capacity trigger requests from the seller for parts bids to suppliers who, in turn, put out requests to other suppliers, and this whole process will all converge in a matter of minutes."[4]

Thinking Critically

1. How do companies benefit from participating in an electronic trading hub?
2. What impact does electronic trading have on the global economy?

SOURCES: "Electronic Trading Hubs," http://www.com-met2005.org.uk, April 4, 2006; David Luckham, "The Global Information Society and the Need for New Technology," http://www.informit.com, April 4, 2006; "Trading Hubs," http://www.investni.com, April 4, 2006; "Trading Hubs in Asia," Oikono, December 6, 2005, http://www.oikono.com.

MANAGEMENT INFORMATION SYSTEMS   **LO3**

Companies typically have several types of information systems; two common branches of systems are management support systems and transaction-processing systems. Management support systems are dynamic systems that allow users to analyze data to make forecasts, identify business trends, and model business strategies. Transaction-processing systems are systems in which the computer responds immediately to user requests. The availability of this type of a system maintains and improves the flow of data throughout all information systems in the organization. Each type of information system serves a particular level of decision making: operational, tactical, or strategic. Exhibit 4.3 shows the relationship between transaction-processing and management-support systems as well as the management levels they serve. Let's now take a more detailed look at how companies and managers use transaction-processing and management support systems to manage information.

Transaction-Processing Systems

A company's integrated information system starts with its transaction-processing system (TPS). The TPS receives raw data from internal and external sources and prepares these data for storage in a database similar to a microcomputer database but vastly larger. In fact, all the company's key data are stored in a single, huge database that becomes the company's central information resource. As noted earlier, the *database management system* tracks the data and allows users to query the database for the information they need.

The database can be updated in two ways: batch processing, whereby data are collected over some time period but processed together, and online (or real-time), processing, in which data are processed as they become available. Batch processing uses computer resources very efficiently and is well suited to applications such as payroll processing that require periodic rather than continuous processing. Online processing keeps the company's data current. When you make an airline reservation, the agent enters your reservation directly into the airline's computer and quickly receives confirmation. Online processing is more expensive than batch processing, so companies must weigh the cost versus the benefit. For example, a factory that

transaction-processing system (TPS)
An information system that handles the daily business operations of a company. The system receives and organizes raw data from internal and external sources for storage in a database using either batch or online processing.

batch processing
A method of updating a database in which data are collected over some time period, but processed together.

online (real-time) processing
A method of updating a database in which data are processed as they become available.

Exhibit 4.3   A Company's Integrated Information System

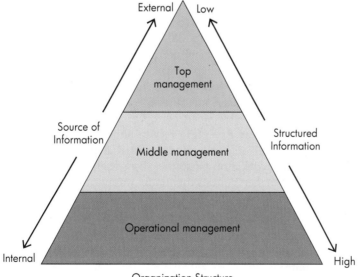

EXPERTSMIND IT EDUCATIONAL PVT. LTD.

Computer modelling helps Sanofi-Aventis, a major pharmaceutical company, save time and money on later-stage clinical drug trials. When simulation results in one study indicated that a drug's side effects outweighed its benefits, Aventis saved approximately $50 million to $100 million by stopping the trial and using that funding for another project with greater potential for success. What are some other applications for computer modelling?

management support system (MSS)
An information system that uses the internal master database to perform high-level analyses that help managers make better decisions.

data warehouse
An information technology that combines many databases across a whole company into one central database that supports management decision making.

data mart
A special subset of a data warehouse that deals with a single area of data and is organized for quick analysis.

decision support system (DSS)
A management support system that helps managers make decisions by using interactive computer models that describe real-world processes.

operates around the clock might use real-time processing for inventory and other time-sensitive requirements, but process accounting data in batches overnight.

The accounting information system diagrammed in Exhibit 4.4 is a typical TPS. It has subsystems for order entry, accounts receivable (for billing customers), accounts payable (for paying bills), payroll, inventory, and general ledger (for determining the financial status and profitability of the business). The accounting information system provides input to and receives input from the company's other information systems, such as manufacturing (production planning data, for example) and human resources (data on hours worked and salary increases to generate paycheques).

Decisions, Decisions: Management Support Systems

Transaction-processing systems automate routine and tedious back-office processes such as accounting, order processing, and financial reporting. They reduce clerical expenses and provide basic operational information quickly. Management support systems (MSSs) use the internal master database to perform the higher-level analyses that help managers make better decisions.

Information technologies such as data warehousing are part of more advanced MSSs. A data warehouse combines many databases across the whole company into one central database that supports management decision making as seen in Exhibit 4.5. With a data warehouse, managers can easily access and share data across the enterprise, to get a broad overview rather than just isolated segments of information. Data warehouses include software to extract data from operational databases, maintain the data in the warehouse, and provide data to users. They can analyze data much faster than transaction-processing systems. Data warehouses may contain many data marts, special subsets of a data warehouse that each deal with a single area of data. A data mart is a repository of data, gathered from operational data and other sources, that is designed to serve a particular community of knowledge workers. Data marts are organized for quick analysis.

Companies use data warehouses to gather, secure, and analyze data for many purposes, including customer relationship management systems, fraud detection, product line analysis, and corporate asset management. Retailers might wish to identify customer demographic characteristics and shopping patterns to improve direct-mailing responses. Banks can more easily spot credit-card fraud, as well as analyze customer usage patterns.

At the first level of an MSS is an *information-reporting system*, which uses summary data collected by the TPS to produce both regularly scheduled and special reports. The level of detail would depend on the user. A company's payroll personnel might get a weekly payroll report showing how each employee's paycheque was determined. Higher-level managers might receive a payroll summary report that shows total labour cost and overtime by department, and a comparison of current labour costs with those in the prior year. Exception reports show cases that fail to meet some standard. An accounts receivable exception report that lists all customers with overdue accounts would help collection personnel focus their work. Special reports are generated only when a manager requests them; for example, a report showing sales by region and type of customer can highlight reasons for a sales decline.

Decision Support Systems

A decision support system (DSS) helps managers make decisions by using interactive computer models that describe real-world processes. The DSS also uses data from the internal database but looks for specific data that relate to the problems at hand. It is a tool

Exhibit 4.4 Accounting Information System

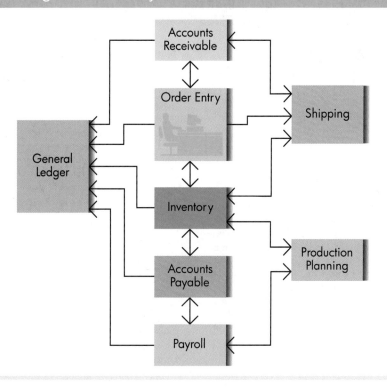

for answering "what if" questions about what would happen if the manager made certain changes. In simple cases, a manager can create a spreadsheet and try changing some of the numbers. For instance, a manager could create a spreadsheet to show the amount of overtime required if the number of workers increases or decreases. With models, the manager enters into the computer the values that describe a particular situation, and the program computes the results. Marketing executives at a furniture company could run DSS models that use sales data and demographic assumptions to develop forecasts of the types of furniture that would appeal to the fastest-growing population groups.

Executive Information Systems

Although similar to a DSS, an executive information system (EIS) is customized for an individual executive. These systems provide specific information for strategic

executive information system (EIS)
A management support system that is customized for an individual executive; it provides specific information for strategic decisions.

Exhibit 4.5 Data Warehouse

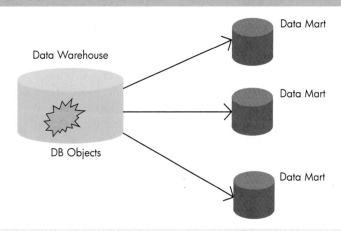

Creating the Future of Business

MATT INGLOT, TILTED PIXEL

Matt Inglot first found his entrepreneurial spirit in high school, when he says he "realized that although I really enjoyed computer programming, I didn't actually like the idea of working in a cubicle for a big company and the things that came with it … Having 9:00 to 5:00 set aside for work for the rest of my life, and having to code for a living instead of for fun, just didn't seem as fun." But before you run to your nearest bank for a start-up loan, finish your degree first! A lot of Matt's success has come from marrying the lessons he learned in school with those learned through building his business.

It started when a high school friend began selling products on eBay, and Matt asked "why not me?" and decided to start writing his own software program to sell online. It was his first real foray into running his own business, and after over a year of work, met with some success. But most importantly, he says he "learned important business fundamentals, such as the need to continuously get feedback from your target market to make sure that what is being built is in fact what people want and are willing to pay for." In fact, a lot of Matt's customers (this author included!) will tell you that one of Matt's rare gifts is his ability to understand not just the tech side but also the business side, and to translate that into solutions that make real sense for a business.

Matt followed this first experience by starting a Web hosting business before entering a combined business and computer science program at university. He admits it was originally "simply so that I could have control over my own dedicated Web server, since I couldn't afford my own at the time." But it wound up turning a profit and some of its customers are still with him today. Matt's current business, Tilted Pixel, is a website development business that he started in 2005 while in his second year at university. According to Matt, what differentiates his company is the ability to make "the confusing process of website development easy for people who don't necessarily have any experience building websites." And here we are back to the importance of understanding your target market.

Matt continued to build the company while finishing his degree officially in 2011. One of the key lessons he learned was that the connections he built early on in school proved invaluable in securing his first few clients, essentially using networking in lieu of a marketing budget. One of his first jobs was actually building the course management system for the first-year business courses at Wilfrid Laurier University, which is still in use today.

Tilted Pixel has grown to a team of seven core people. It leased its first space in 2008, but has since moved out "in favour of the power and flexibility of a virtual infrastructure, making it possible to serve clients in a wider geographical area, as well as providing access to a much larger pool of talent"—another one of the many lessons he has learned on his journey.

You can visit Matt at his blog, www.mattinglot.com, which he started back up in 2012, and read the books that influenced him most—*E-Myth, Built to Last,* and *Four Hour Work Week*—all of which he says push the idea of building businesses that are self-sustaining and not dependent on the owner for their survival, businesses that can scale and grow.

Thinking Critically

1. Do you think it's enough to start a business based on something that you understand and are passionate about, or do you really need to understand your customer as well? Do you believe that "if you build it, they will come"?
2. What impact do you think Matt's business degree had on his success?

SOURCES: Tilted Pixel website, www.tiltedpixel.com; and information supplied by Matt Inglot personally.

---

decisions. For example, a CEO's EIS might include special spreadsheets that present financial data comparing the company to its principal competitors, and graphs showing current economic and industry trends.

Expert Systems

expert system
A management support system that gives managers advice similar to what they would get from a human consultant; it uses artificial intelligence to enable computers to reason and learn to solve problems in much the same way that humans do.

An **expert system** gives managers advice similar to what they would get from a human consultant. Artificial intelligence enables computers to reason and learn to solve problems in much the same way humans do, using what-if reasoning. Although they are expensive and difficult to create, expert systems are finding their way into more companies as more applications are found. Top-of-the-line systems help airlines appropriately deploy aircraft and crews, critical to the carriers' efficient operations. The cost of hiring enough people to do these ongoing analytical tasks would be prohibitively expensive. Expert systems have also been used to help explore for oil, schedule employee work shifts, and diagnose illnesses. Some expert systems take the place of human experts, whereas others assist them.

Office Automation Systems

office automation system
An information system that uses information technology tools such as word-processing systems, e-mail systems, cellphones, smartphones, pagers, and facsimile (fax) machines to improve communications throughout an organization.

Today's **office automation systems** make good use of the computer networks in many companies to improve communications. Office automation systems assist all levels of employees and enable managers to handle most of their own communication. Many

Medical professionals use expert systems to analyze patients' medications, ensuring that they do not cause allergic reactions or potentially dangerous interactions with the patients' other prescriptions. How can the use of expert systems minimize human error?

© MICHAEL NEWMAN/PHOTOEDIT

of the newer devices now combine multiple functions. The key elements (many of which have been around for years while others are fairly new) include

- word-processing systems for producing written messages;
- e-mail systems for communicating directly with other employees and customers, and transferring computer files;
- departmental scheduling systems for planning meetings and other activities;
- smartphones, such as the BlackBerry or iPhone, which allow wireless e-mail access, Internet access, detailed contact lists, personal planners/calendars, and a variety of business-related applications;
- pagers, which notify employees of phone calls and prompt on-call workers to report in, often with a displayed code or contact number;
- voice mail systems for recording, storing, and forwarding phone messages;
- fax systems for delivering messages on paper within minutes; and
- electronic bulletin boards and computer conferencing systems for discussing issues with others who are not present.

Office automation systems also make telecommuting and home-based businesses possible. Instead of spending time on the road twice a day, telecommuters work at home two or more days a week. This can save time for workers while increasing their flexibility. Companies can save costs by eliminating the need to provide a physical space for employees.

LINKING UP: TECHNOLOGY BEHIND THE INFORMATION

We now understand the importance of information, now let's see how this information gets from point A to B with the use of technology.

Today most businesses use networks to deliver information to employees, suppliers, and customers. A **computer network** is a group of two or more computer systems linked together by communications channels to share data and information. Today's

---

Concept *Check*

What are the main types of management information systems, and what does each do?

Discuss how the different types of management support systems can be used in companies.

How can office automation systems help employees work more efficiently?

LO4

computer network
A group of two or more computer systems, as well as devices (such as printers, external hard drives, modems, and routers), linked together by communications channels to share data, commands, information, and other resources.

networks, with their bandwidth power, often link thousands of users and can transmit data, images, audio, and video.

Networks include clients and servers. The *client* is the application that runs on a personal computer or workstation. It relies on a *server*, which manages network resources or performs special tasks, such as storing files, managing one or more printers, or processing database queries. Any user on the network can access the server's capabilities.

By making it easy and fast to share information, networks have created new ways to work and increase productivity. They provide more efficient use of resources, permitting communication and collaboration across distance and time. With file sharing (e.g., www.dropbox.com), all employees, regardless of location, have access to the same information. Shared databases also eliminate duplication of effort. Employees at different sites can "screen share" computer files, working on data as if they were in the same room (e.g., www.yuuguu.com, www.teamviewer.com, www. unyte.net).

Their computers are connected by phone or cable lines, they all see the same thing on their display, and anyone can make changes, which are seen by the other participants. The employees can also use the networks for videoconferencing.

Networks make it possible for companies to run enterprise software, large programs with integrated modules that manage all of the corporation's internal operations. Enterprise resource planning systems run on networks. Typical subsystems include finance, human resources, engineering, sales and order distribution, and order management and procurement. These modules work independently and then automatically exchange information, creating a company-wide system that includes current delivery dates, inventory status, quality control, and other critical information. There are three basic types of networks companies use to transmit data—local area, wide area, and metropolitan networks—and popular networking applications like intranets and extranets. Intranets and extranets are communication tools designed to enable easy information sharing within workgroups.

Connecting Near and Far with Networks

local area network (LAN)
A network that connects computers at one site, enabling the computer users to exchange data and share the use of hardware and software from a variety of computer manufacturers.

A local area network (LAN) lets people at one site exchange data and share the use of hardware and software from a variety of computer manufacturers. LANs offer companies a more cost-effective way to link computers than linking terminals to a mainframe computer. The most common uses of LANs at small businesses, for example, are office automation, accounting, and information management. LANs can help companies reduce staff, streamline operations, and cut processing costs. LANs can be set up with wired or wireless connections.

wide area network (WAN)
A network that connects computers at different sites via telecommunications media such as phone lines, satellites, and microwaves.

A wide area network (WAN) connects computers at different sites via telecommunications media such as phone lines, satellites, and microwaves. A modem connects the computer or a terminal to the telephone line and transmits data almost instantly, in less than a second. The Internet is essentially a worldwide WAN. Long-distance telephone companies operate very large WANs. Companies also connect LANs at various locations into WANs. WANs make it possible for companies to work on critical projects around the clock by using teams in different time zones.

Several forms of WANs—intranets, virtual private networks (VPNs), and extranets—use Internet technology. Here we'll look at intranets (internal corporate networks that are widely available in the corporate world) and VPNs.

Although wireless networks have been around for more than a decade, they are increasing in use because of falling costs, faster and more reliable technology, and improved standards. They are similar to their wired LAN and WAN cousins except that they use radio frequency signals to transmit data. You probably use a wireless WAN (WWAN) regularly when you use your cellular phone.

Exhibit 4.6 | LAN vs MAN vs WAN

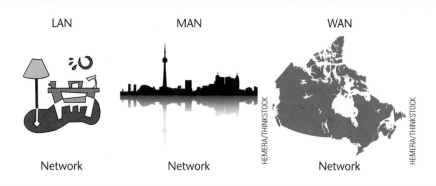

LAN MAN WAN

Network Network Network

HEMERA/THINKSTOCK

HEMERA/THINKSTOCK

SOURCE: Soltechnology.com

Metropolitan area network (MAN) is a network which covers a larger geographic area than a LAN, but generally smaller than a WAN. It's the interconnection of networks within a city, generally spanning many buildings. Examples of this would be running optical fibres through subway tunnels within a city, although there are wireless MANs now that require no cabling and perform the same activities. A MAN is owned by either a consortium of users or by a single network provider who sells the service to the users.

See Exhibit 4.6 for a visual of the difference between the LAN, WAN, and MAN.

metropolitan area network (MAN)
A network that covers a larger geographic area than a LAN, but generally smaller than a WAN.

An Inside Job: Intranets

Like LANs, intranets are private corporate networks. Many companies use both types of internal networks. However, because they use Internet technology to connect computers, intranets are WANs that link employees in many locations and with different types of computers. Essentially mini-Internets that serve only the company's employees, intranets operate behind a *firewall*, which prevents unauthorized access. Employees navigate using a standard Web browser, which makes the intranet easy to use. They are also considerably less expensive to install and maintain than other network types and can take advantage of the Internet's interactive features, such as chat rooms and team work spaces. Many software providers now offer off-the-shelf intranet packages so that companies of all sizes can benefit from the increased access to and distribution of information.

intranet
An internal, corporate-wide area network that uses Internet technology to connect computers and link employees in many locations and with different types of computers.

Companies now recognize the power of intranets to connect employers and employees in many ways, promoting a central communication hub, teamwork and knowledge sharing. Intranets act as a "self-service" model. They deliver true information value to the organization if managed and maintained efficiently. Intranets can also act as a way of providing feedback to management by way of ideas, suggestions, and perceptions on various company initiatives. Intranets have many applications, from human resource (HR) administration to logistics. The benefits-administration intranet at a major insurance company quickly became a favourite with employees: instead of having to contact an HR representative to make any changes in personnel records, change retirement plan contributions, or submit time sheets, staff members simply log on to the intranet and update the information themselves. The intranet proved to be especially valuable after a merger. With more than 9000 employees in multiple locations, the insurance company expanded its intranet, which had been used mostly for marketing and client services, to handle more HR functions and improve communications. Managers can now process staffing updates, performance reviews, and incentive payments without filing paperwork with human resources. Employees regularly check an online job board for new positions. Shifting routine administrative tasks to the intranet brought the company additional benefits: it reduced the size of the HR department by 30 percent, and HR staff members can now turn their attention to more substantive projects.[5]

Making Ethical Choices

ETHICS ACTIVITY

As the owner of a small but growing business, you are concerned about employees misusing company computers for personal matters. Not only does this cost the company in terms of employee productivity, but it also ties up bandwidth that may be required for company operations and exposes the company's networks to increased risks of attacks from viruses, spyware, and other malicious programs. Installing e-mail monitoring and Web security and filtering software programs would allow you to track e-mail and Internet use, develop use policies, block access to inappropriate sites, and limit the time employees can conduct personal online business. At the same time, the software will protect your IT networks from many types of security concerns, from viruses to

Internet fraud. You are concerned, however, that employees will take offence and consider such software an invasion of privacy.

Using a Web search tool, locate articles about this topic and then write responses to the following questions. Be sure to support your arguments and cite your sources.

ETHICAL DILEMMA: Should you purchase employee monitoring software for your company, and on what do you base your decision? If you install the software, do you have an obligation to tell employees about it? Explain your answers and suggest ways to help employees understand your rationale.

SOURCES: Lindsay Gerdes, "You Have 20 Minutes to Surf. Go," *Business Week*, December 26, 2005, p. 16; "Nothing Personal," Global Cosmetic Industry, August 2005, p. 19; "Tips on Keeping Workplace Surveillance from Going too Far," *HR Focus*, January 2006, p. 10.

Sustainable Business, Sustainable World

NOKIA

This chapter is about the technological environment of business. What better company to feature than a company based around its technology—Nokia. Not only did the Finnish company rank fourth on the 2011 list of the Global 100 Most Sustainable Corporations in the World, but in 2010 it was chosen as the "Global Technology Supersector Leader" in the Dow Jones Sustainability Index Review for the second year in a row, and ranked first in the 16th edition of the quarterly *Greenpeace Guide to Greener Electronics* for the eighth consecutive time, among many other awards and accolades it has received. In fact, of the top 30 green mobile devices listed in the "Good Guide," the top 26 are made by Nokia. The Nokia C7-00 was the first in the industry to use bio-paints, the C6-01 was the first to use recycled materials, and 100 percent of the materials in Nokia phones can be used to make new products or generate energy so that nothing needs to go to a landfill.

So what's its secret? According to Stephen Elop, President and CEO of Nokia: "sustainability is embedded in everything we do at Nokia ... sustainability is not a trend for Nokia, but rather it is our way of conducting business." This philosophy has resulted in what may in fact be the most impressive use of the company's technology—to help its customers live more sustainably. As stated in the company's 149 page (!) 2010 Sustainability Report: "Mobile technologies are in the hands of billions, and it is by working together that we can truly change the world." This is something Nokia calls "the power of we."

Nokia wants to help customers reduce their own carbon footprint by developing solutions to enable mobile phones to replace several other products (converging several devices into one to cut the amount of resources used), developing mobile services that could replace physical products (helping to dematerialize the economy as

increased consumption of new phones just increases resource use), and developing services that could reduce unnecessary travel and commuting and therefore cut down on CO_2 emissions. The impact of this action is best described this way: "Assume, for example, that just 10 percent of the people using Nokia devices would do the following ... for one year: use their mobile device for attending a meeting once instead of travelling to the meeting by plane; use their mobile device to work remotely once a week instead of driving to work; use their mobile device instead of buying a separate music player, camera, video camera, PC, fixed line telephone and a car navigator ... The combined impact of these actions could reduce global CO_2 emissions by over 220 million tonnes. That represents nearly the same amount as the annual fossil fuel-based CO_2 emission of the countries of Sweden, Chile, and Vietnam combined." Just imagine.

What a great example of a company using technology to expand its reach to not just do less harm, but actually have a net positive impact by harnessing the exponential "power of we."

Thinking Critically

1. Would knowing this about Nokia affect your choice of cellphone? Do you think enough customers are looking for ways to be part of the solution or do you think it's more of a corporate responsibility? If your answer is that it's a corporate responsibility, why?
2. As a customer, how responsive would you be to a company making suggestions on how you should use its products to help the environment?

SOURCES: Nokia Canada website, www.nokia.com; The Global 100, www.global100.org; Dow Jones Sustainability Indexes, www.sustainability-index.com; Greenpeace International website, www.greenpeace.org; and GoodGuide website, www.goodguide.com.

Enterprise Portals Open the Door to Productivity

Intranets that take a broader view serve as sophisticated knowledge management tools. One such intranet is the enterprise portal, an internal website that provides proprietary corporate information to a defined user group. Portals can take one of three forms: business to employee (B2E), business to business (B2B), and business to consumer (B2C). Unlike a standard intranet, enterprise portals allow individuals or user groups to customize the portal home page to gather just the information they need for their particular job situations into one place and deliver it through a single webpage. Because of their complexity, enterprise portals are typically the result of a collaborative project that brings together designs developed and perfected through the joint effort of HR, corporate communications, and information technology departments.

More companies are turning to portal technology to provide

- single, consistent, simple user interface across the company;
- integration of disparate systems and multiple sets of data and information;
- a single unified source for accurate and timely information that integrates internal and external information;
- a shorter time to perform tasks and processes;
- cost savings through the elimination of "information intermediaries";
- improved communications within the company and with customers, suppliers, dealers, and distributors;
- a single-sign feature that allows employees to use one username/one password to access the myriad of company software applications.

At Intercontinental Hotels Group (IHG), a new enterprise portal will connect staff at the group's 3500 hotels around the world while supporting marketing, human resources, finance, and IT functions. A major goal is to eliminate duplication of efforts. "All of these departments are tackling similar problems independently," says David House, IHG's senior vice president for global human resources. "For example, you might have marketing efforts going on in one part of the world and someone doing a similar kind of thing in another without knowing it." The portal will facilitate collaboration and teamwork throughout the organization. "We want people to use the intranet to bridge these gaps, to improve availability of information, and to better exploit the intellectual capital in the organization," explains House.[6]

enterprise portal
A customizable internal website that provides proprietary corporate information to a defined user group, such as employees, supply chain partners, or customers.

No More Tangles: Wireless Technologies

Wi-Fi, WiMAX, WMM, Bluetooth Wireless—terms that are common place in technology to describe wireless technology. We routinely use such devices as smartphones, garage door openers, and television remote controls without thinking of them as examples of wireless technology. Businesses use wireless technologies to improve communications with customers, suppliers, and employees. You might have seen the term Wi-Fi, which refers to wireless fidelity. When products carry the "Wi-Fi Certified" designation, they have been tested and certified to work with each other, regardless of manufacturer. Usage of wireless technologies in today's business world is essential. Nowadays, each and every type of business desires to get more profit from their business and wireless network helps to do this. Because now, no matter what size the business is—big or small—everyone wants to know about the business, and what technologies are used by the business to serve their customers. Because of this, the first priority of each business is a wireless network.

One example of wireless technology is Radio Frequency Identification (RFID). RFID is a technology used to track items as they move from point A to point B. Large companies have used this technology very effectively by tracking their supply trucks across geographic boundaries. RFID are small tags that emit signals that can be tracked and automatically identified.

One way to see how this can affect all of our lives is to look at a simple shopping example. As we wait in line at a local grocery store to pay the cashier for our items, time is of the essence. RFID can help by having items already bar-coded and tagged and emitting a signal. Therefore, as you exit the store, sensors identify all the items in your shopping cart and "checks" them in and your bill shows up on your credit card. This is the advantage of RFID wireless technology.

Companies in the package delivery industry were among the first users of wireless technology. Delivery personnel use handheld computers to send immediate confirmation of package receipt. These companies consider the investment in wireless technology a good one. Not only do customers get better service, the company can also keep expenses down. Without wireless technology, delivery companies would have to hire more call centre and service representatives. You might also have seen meter readers and repair personnel from utility and energy companies sending data from remote locations back to central computers.[7]

Bluetooth short-range wireless technology is a global standard that improves personal connectivity for users of mobile phones, portable computers, stereo headsets, and MP3 players. Bluetooth wirelessly connects keyboards and mice to computers and headsets to phones and music players. A Bluetooth-enabled mobile phone, for example, provides safer hands-free cellphone use while driving. The technology is finding many applications in the auto industry as well. "Bluetooth wireless technology will start to become standard in cars in the near future," predicts David McClure, head of Telematics Research at SBD automotive technology consultants. Many car and cellphone manufacturers—among them Audi, BMW, Honda, Saab, Toyota, Volkswagen, Motorola, and Nokia—already offer Bluetooth hands-free solutions. Other uses include simplifying the connection of portable digital music players to the car's audio system and of transferring music to the system.[8]

Private Lines: Virtual Private Networks

virtual private networks (VPNs)
Private corporate networks connected over a public network, such as the Internet. VPNs include strong security measures to allow only authorized users to access the network.

Many companies use virtual private networks (VPNs) to connect two or more private networks (such as LANs) over a public network, such as the Internet. VPNs include strong security measures to allow only authorized users to access the network and its sensitive corporate information. By using a VPN, businesses ensure security—anyone intercepting the encrypted data can't read it. Companies with widespread offices might find that a

Concept *in Action*

In today's ever-changing technological world, communication devices are becoming increasing smaller, user friendly, and sophisticated. These "ultra-mobile" devices are allowing businesses more opportunities to connect with customers and suppliers. How are these devices impacting business today?

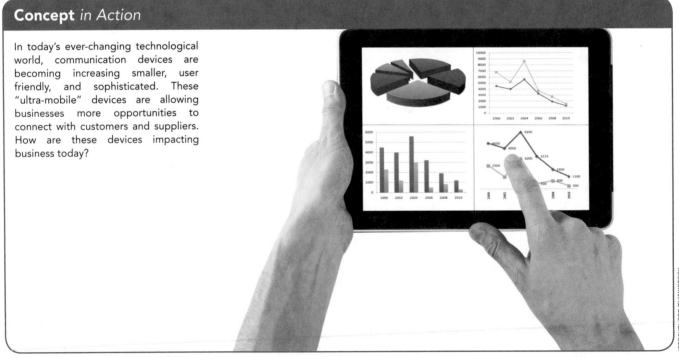

iSTOCKPH-0T0/THINKSTOCK

Exhibit 4.7 | Virtual Private Networks (VPNs)

VPN is a more cost-effective option than purchasing equipment and private lines for that purpose alone. A private line network is more limited than a VPN because it doesn't allow users to connect to the corporate network when they are at home or travelling.

As Exhibit 4.7 shows, the VPN uses existing Internet infrastructure and equipment to connect remote users and offices almost anywhere in the world—without long-distance charges. In addition to saving on telecommunications costs, companies using VPNs don't have to buy or maintain special networking equipment and can outsource management of remote access equipment. VPNs are useful for salespeople and telecommuters—they can access the company's network as if they were onsite in the office. On the downside, the VPN's availability and performance, especially when it uses the Internet, depend on factors largely outside of an organization's control.[9]

Software on Demand: Application Service Providers

As software developers release new types of application programs and updated versions of existing ones every year or two, companies have to analyze whether they can justify buying or upgrading to the new software in terms of both cost and implementation time. Application service providers (ASPs) offer a different approach to this problem. Companies subscribe to an ASP and use the applications much like you'd use telephone voice mail, the technology for which resides at the phone company. In essence, ASPs are a way for organizations to outsource some or almost all aspects of their information technology needs. They may be commercial ventures that cater to customers, or not-for-profit or government organizations, providing service and support to end users. Exhibit 4.8 shows how the ASP interfaces with software and hardware vendors and developers, the IT department, and users. The software on demand is a subscription model that has become a popular low-cost alternative for companies. The only disadvantage is that this software cannot be customized for the company's requirements, therefore, the use of traditional on-premises software, will never quite disappear.

The simplest ASP applications are automated. For example, a user might use one to build a simple e-commerce site. ASPs provide three major categories of applications to users:

- enterprise applications, including customer relationship management, enterprise resource planning (ERP), e-commerce, and data warehousing;
- collaborative applications for internal communications, e-mail, groupware, document creation, and management messaging; and
- applications for personal use, such as games, entertainment software, and home office applications.

The basic idea behind subscribing to an ASP is compelling. Users can access any of their applications and data from any computer, and IT can avoid purchasing, installing, supporting, and upgrading expensive software applications. ASPs buy and maintain the software on their servers

application service providers (ASPs)
A service company that buys and maintains software on its servers and distributes it through high-speed networks to subscribers for a set period and price.

HOT *links*

For more information about the benefits of ASPs, see MarketWeb at www.marketweb.ca

Concept *Check*

What is a computer network? What benefits do companies gain by using networks?

How do LANs and WANs differ? Why would a company use a wireless network?

What advantages do VPNs offer a company? ASPs and MSPs?

Exhibit 4.8 Structure of an ASP Relationship

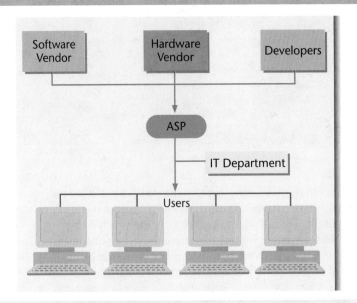

and distribute it through high-speed networks. Subscribers rent the applications they want for a set period and price. The savings in infrastructure, time, and staff could be significant.

managed service providers (MSPs)
The next generation of ASPs, offering customization and expanded capabilities such as business processes and complete management of the network servers.

Managed service providers (MSPs) represent the next generation of ASPs, offering greater customization and expanded capabilities that include business processes and complete management of the network servers. Companies who utilize MSP are outsourcing some of their technology services that were delivered internally. For example, Bell Canada offered its VoIP Managed Services for large companies such as Cisco and Nortel in 2005. The Global Voice over Internet Protocol can manage customers' voice and data traffic over a single integrated network anywhere in the world.[10]

LO5 TECHNOLOGY MANAGEMENT AND PLANNING

With the help of computers, people have produced more data in the past 30 years than in the previous 5000 years combined. Companies today make sizable investments in information technology to help them manage this overwhelming amount of data, convert the data into knowledge, and deliver it to the people who need it. In many cases, however, the companies do not reap the desired benefits from these expenditures. Among the typical complaints from senior executives are that the company is spending too much and not getting adequate performance and payoff from IT investments, that these investments do not relate to business strategy, that the company seems to be buying the latest technology for technology's sake, and that communications between IT specialists and IT users are poor.

Optimize IT!

Managing a company's enterprise-wide IT operations, especially when those often stretch across multiple locations, software applications, and systems, is no easy task. Not only must IT managers deal with on-site systems, they must also oversee the networks that connect staff working at locations ranging from the next town to another continent. What makes the IT manager's job even more difficult is providing this technology for remote employees in the face of time constraints and lower budgets, while maintaining a cohesive corporate culture.[11] Add to these concerns the increasing use by employees of handheld devices like smartphones that handle e-mail messaging, and you have an overwhelming management task!

Growing companies might find themselves with a decentralized IT structure that includes many separate systems and much duplication of efforts. A company that wants to enter or expand into e-commerce needs systems that are flexible enough to adapt to this changing marketplace. Security for equipment and data, which we will cover later in the chapter, is another critical area.

The goal is to develop an integrated, company-wide technology plan that balances business judgment, technology expertise, and technology investment. IT planning requires a coordinated effort among a company's top executives, IT managers, and business-unit managers to develop a comprehensive plan. Such plans must take into account the company's strategic objectives and how the right technology will help managers reach those goals.

Technology management and planning are not just about buying new technology. Today, companies are cutting IT budgets, so managers are being asked to do more with less. They are implementing projects that leverage their investment in the technology they already have, finding ways to maximize efficiency and optimize utilization.

Managing Knowledge Resources

As a result of information proliferation, we are seeing a major shift from information management to a broader view that focuses on finding opportunities in and unlocking the value of intellectual rather than physical assets. Whereas *information management* involves collecting, processing, and condensing information, the more difficult task of **knowledge management (KM)** focuses on researching, gathering, organizing, and sharing an organization's collective knowledge to improve productivity, foster innovation, and gain a competitive advantage. Some companies have even created a new position, *chief knowledge officer*, to head up this effort. The goal of KM is to allow organizations to generate value from their intellectual assets—not just documents but also the knowledge in their employees' heads.[12]

As discussed in LO1, there are two large categories of information that an organization holds: structured and tacit. Structured is organized information that is easily accessed and retrieved—algorithms within information systems facilitate the order of this information. Tacit information presents itself in an implied, inferred, and less than accessible manner. The goal of knowledge management is to bring together these two types of information so individuals, departments, and the organization can maximize on the intelligence that exists, in turn gaining competitive advantage and the ability to work in a collaborative manner.

Companies use their IT systems to facilitate the physical sharing of knowledge. But better hardware and software are not the answer to KM. KM is not technology based, but rather a business practice that uses technology. Technology alone does not constitute KM, nor is it the solution to KM. Rather, it facilitates KM. Executives with successful KM initiatives understand that KM is not simply a matter of buying a major software application that serves as a data depository and coordinates all of a company's intellectual capital.

Effective KM calls for an interdisciplinary approach that coordinates all aspects of an organization's knowledge. It requires a major change in behaviour as well as technology to leverage the power of information systems, especially the Internet, and a company's human capital resources. The first step is creating an information culture, through organizational structure and rewards, which promotes a more flexible, collaborative way of working and communicating. However, moving an organization toward KM is no easy task, but well worth the effort in terms of creating a more collaborative environment, reducing duplication of effort, and increasing shared knowledge. The benefits can be significant in terms of growth, time, and money.

knowledge management (KM)
The process of researching, gathering, organizing, and sharing an organization's collective knowledge to improve productivity, foster innovation, and gain competitive advantage.

Exhibit 4.9 The Technology Plan

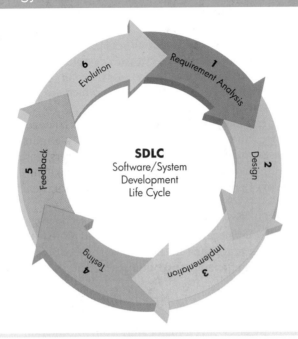

Technology Planning

A good technology plan provides employees with the tools they need to perform their jobs at the highest levels of efficiency. The first step, as seen in Exhibit 4.9, is a general requirements analysis that includes needs assessment, ranking of projects, and the specific choices of hardware and software. Next follows a design phase, then implementation, testing, and a feedback phase. SDLC[13] is only one example of a technology planning tool utilized. Exhibit 4.10 poses some basic questions departmental managers and IT specialists should ask when planning technology purchases.

Once managers identify the projects that make business sense, they can choose the best products for the company's needs. The final step is to evaluate the potential benefits of the technology in terms of efficiency and effectiveness. For a successful project, you must evaluate and restructure business processes, choose technology, develop and implement the

Concept Check

What are some ways in which a company can manage its technology assets to its advantage?

Differentiate between information management and knowledge management. What steps can companies take to manage knowledge?

List the key questions managers need to ask when planning technology purchases.

Exhibit 4.10 Questions for IT Project Planning

- What are the company's overall objectives?
- What problems does the company want to solve?
- How can technology help meet those goals and solve the problems?
- What are the company's IT priorities, both short- and long-term?
- What type of technology infrastructure (centralized or decentralized) best serves the company's needs?
- Which technologies meet the company's requirements?
- Are additional hardware and software required? If so, will they integrate with the company's existing systems?
- Does the system design and implementation include the people and process changes, in addition to the technological ones?
- Does the company have the in-house capabilities to develop and implement the proposed applications, or should an outside specialist be brought in?

system, and manage the change processes to serve your organizational needs in the best possible way. Installing a new IT system on top of inefficient business processes is a waste of time and money.

PROTECTING COMPUTERS AND SECURING INFORMATION

LO6

As systems, technology, and information are ubiquitous today, it is possible to either advertently or inadvertently view data and information that doesn't belong to you or the company you work for. Therefore, millions of dollars are spent by companies and individuals to keep devices and information safe and secure. From employing software or a hardware solution, to protecting computers and securing information, companies must reduce the risk of data and information being compromised.

For example, have you ever lost a term paper you'd worked on for weeks because your hard drive crashed or you deleted the file by mistake? You were upset, angry, and frustrated. Multiply that paper and your feelings hundreds of times over, and you can understand why companies must protect computers, networks, and the information they store and transmit, from a variety of potential threats. For example, security breaches of corporate information systems—from human hackers or electronic assailants such as viruses and worms—are growing in number at an alarming rate. The ever-increasing dependence on computers requires plans that cover human error, power outages, equipment failure, and as we experienced at the beginning of this century, terrorist attacks. To withstand natural disasters such as major fires, earthquakes, and floods, for example, many companies install specialized fault-tolerant computer systems.

Disasters are not the only threat to data. A great deal of data, much of it confidential, can easily be tapped into or destroyed by anyone who knows technology. Keeping your networks secure from unauthorized access—from internal as well as external sources—requires formal security policies and enforcement procedures. The increasing popularity of mobile devices—laptops, handheld computers, smartphones, and digital cameras—and wireless networks calls for new types of security provisions.

In response to mounting security concerns, companies have increased spending on technology to protect their IT infrastructure and data. Along with specialized hardware and software, companies need to develop specific security strategies that take a proactive approach to prevent security and technical problems before they start.

Data Security Issues

Virus attacks, hardware corruption, accidental deletion, natural disasters, lost or stolen devices, hacking, firmware corruption, and break-ins are some of the more common breaches of data security issues a company faces. Unauthorized access to a company's computer systems can be expensive, and not just in monetary terms. Cybercriminals are becoming more sophisticated all the time, finding new ways to get into ultra-secure sites. "As companies and consumers continue to move towards a networked and information economy, more opportunity exists for cybercriminals to take advantage of vulnerabilities on networks and computers," says Chris Christiansen, program vice president at technology research company IDC. Whereas early cybercrooks were typically amateur hackers working alone, the current ones are more professional and often work in gangs to commit large-scale Internet crimes for large financial rewards. The Internet, where criminals can hide behind anonymous screen names, has increased the stakes and expanded the realm of opportunities to commit identity theft and similar crimes. Catching such cybercriminals is difficult— fewer than 5 percent are caught.[14]

Companies are taking steps to prevent these costly computer crimes and problems, which fall into several major categories.

- *Unauthorized access and security breaches.* Whether from internal or external sources, unauthorized access and security breaches are a top concern of IT managers. These can create havoc with a company's systems and damage customer relationships. Unauthorized access also includes employees, who can copy confidential new-product information and provide it to competitors or use company systems for personal business that may interfere with systems operation. Networking links also make it easier for someone outside the organization to gain access to a company's computers.

- *Hackers* are a very serious problem. There are white hat and black hat hackers. White hat hackers are employed legitimately by a company and paid to hack into their own systems to test their vulnerabilities. This in turn gets reported and fixed. Black hat hackers are trying to get into (hack) unauthorized systems. Therefore, companies find the best means to protect themselves by keeping up-to-date with anti-virus/spyware programs and firewalls.

- *Keylogging.* One of the latest forms of cybercrime involves secretly installing keylogging software via software downloads, e-mail attachments, or shared files. This software then copies and transmits a user's keystrokes—passwords, PINs, and other personal information—from selected sites, such as banking and credit card sites, to thieves.

- *Computer viruses, worms, and Trojan horses.* Computer viruses and related security problems such as worms and Trojan horses are among the top threats to business and personal computer security. A computer program that copies itself into other software and can spread to other computer systems, a computer virus can destroy the contents of a computer's hard drive or damage files. Another form is called a worm because it spreads itself automatically from computer to computer. Unlike a virus, a worm doesn't require e-mail to replicate and transmit itself into other systems. It can enter through valid access points.

  Trojan horses are programs that appear to be harmless and from legitimate sources but trick the user into installing them. When run, they damage the user's computer. For example, a Trojan horse may claim to get rid of viruses but instead infects the computer. Other forms of Trojan horses provide a "trap door" that allows undocumented access to a computer, unbeknown to the user. Trojan horses do not, however, infect other files or self-replicate.[15]

  Viruses can hide for weeks or months before starting to damage information. A virus that "infects" one computer or network can be spread to another computer by sharing infected files or downloading them over the Internet. To protect data from virus damage, virus protection software automatically monitors computers to detect and remove viruses. Program developers make regular updates available to guard against newly created viruses. In addition, experts are becoming more proficient at tracking down virus authors, who are subject to criminal charges.

- *Deliberate damage to equipment or information.* For example, an unhappy employee in the purchasing department could get into the computer system and delete information on past orders and future inventory needs. The sabotage could severely disrupt production and the accounts payable system. Wilful acts to destroy or change the data in computers are hard to prevent. To lessen the damage, companies should back up critical information.

- *Spam.* Although you might think that spam, or unsolicited and unwanted e-mail, is just a nuisance, it also poses a security threat to companies. Viruses spread through e-mail attachments that can accompany spam e-mails. On most days, spam accounts for 70 to 80 percent of all e-mail sent, according to Postini, a message filtering company. In contrast, legitimate e-mail that carries viruses represents just 1.5 percent of all messages on average. The volume of spam has increased five times since 2003. Spam is now clogging blogs, instant messages,

computer virus
A computer program that copies itself into other software and can spread to other computer systems.

and cellphone text messages as well as e-mail inboxes. Spam presents other threats to a corporation, such as lost productivity and expenses from dealing with spam (like opening the messages), and searching for legitimate messages that special spam filters keep out. Spam filters can greatly reduce the amount of spam that gets through, but spammers continually find new ways to bypass them.[16]

- *Software and media piracy.* The copying of copyrighted software programs, games, and movies by people who haven't paid for them is another form of unauthorized use. Piracy, defined as using software without a licence, takes revenue away from the company that developed the program—usually at great cost. It includes making counterfeit CDs to sell and personal copying of software to share with friends.
- *Cloud computing and the protection of data.* Cloud computing enhances the ability to collect and centrally store consumer data and to share that data with third parties. For example, Canadians are worried that US companies that host Canadian data could turn data over to the US government if required, violating individual privacy. In some countries, for example the Netherlands, the Dutch government has banned US cloud supplier companies from doing business in the country.

Preventing Problems with Governance

Considerable emphasis is placed on using technology to protect company data from unauthorized personnel and software/hardware intrusions. Companies that take a proactive approach can prevent security and technical problems before they start. Creating formal, written security policies—to set standards and provide the basis for enforcement—is the first step in a company's security strategy. Unfortunately, a recent survey of 8200 IT executives worldwide revealed that only 37 percent have such plans, and just 24 percent of the other companies intend to develop one within a year. Without information security strategies in place, companies spend too much time in a reactive mode—responding to crises—and don't focus enough on prevention.[17]

Security plans should be discussed in the boardroom with the support of top management, and be implemented with technical personnel in the back room. For example, there are governance frameworks such as COBIT (Control Objectives for Information Technology), COSO (Committee of Sponsoring Organizations), ITIL (Information Technology Infrastructure Library), or Sarbanes-Oxley Act for compliance. These frameworks act as overall guidelines for technology best practices and processes that handle high volumes, and the sensitive and meaningful data of an organization. The type of governance model depends on the strategies of the organization, and if top management can decide on an approach, then this guideline can assist network architects and security practitioners with the appropriate placement of security services, thus protecting the data and information of the organization.

Because IT is a dynamic field with ongoing changes to equipment and processes, it's important to review security policies often. Some security policies can be handled automatically, by technical measures, whereas others involve administrative policies that rely on humans to perform them. Examples of administrative policies are "Users must change their passwords each quarter," and "End users will update their virus signatures at least once a week."[18]

Preventing costly problems can be as simple as regularly backing up applications and data. Companies should have systems in place that automatically back up the company's data every day and store copies of the backups off-site. In addition, employees should back up their own work regularly. Another good policy is to maintain a complete and current database of all IT hardware, software, and user details to make it easier to manage software licences and updates and to diagnose problems. In many cases, IT staff can use remote access technology to automatically monitor and fix problems, as well as update applications and services.

Companies should never overlook the human factor in the security equation. One of the most common ways that outsiders get into company systems is by posing as an employee, first getting the staffer's full name and username from an e-mail message, then calling the help desk to ask for a forgotten password. Crooks can also get passwords by viewing them on notes attached to a desk or computer monitor, using machines that employees leave logged on when they leave their desks, and accessing laptop computers with sensitive information that have been left unsecured in public places.[19]

Portable devices, from tablets and smartphones to tiny plug-and-play flash drives and other storage devices (including MP3 players), pose security risks as well. They are often used to store sensitive data such as passwords, bank details, and calendars. Mobile devices can spread viruses when users download virus-infected documents to their company computers. Research company Gartner Inc. reports that only about 10 percent of companies have policies covering security for these portable devices. "It's actually a fairly big problem," says Eric Ouellet, Gartner's vice president of research for security. "You've got so much space on these things now. You can go for an iPod or MP3 player and you've got 60 GB or more on them. You can put a small database on them. It's just a matter of time before we hear about someone losing data because of this."[20]

Imagine the problems that could arise if an employee saw a calendar entry on a smartphone like "meeting re: layoffs," an outsider saw "meeting about merger with ABC Company," or an employee lost a flash drive containing files about marketing plans for a new product. Manufacturers are responding to IT managers' concerns about security by adding password protection and encryption to flash drives. Companies can also use flash drive monitoring software that prevents unauthorized access on PCs and laptops.

Companies have many ways to avoid an IT meltdown, as Exhibit 4.11 demonstrates.

Exhibit 4.11　Procedures to Protect IT Assets

- Protect the equipment with stringent physical security measures on the premises.
- Protect data by using special encryption technology to encode confidential information, so only the recipient can decipher it.
- Secure your wireless transmissions. Always have a password to access your wireless connection. Leaving open access to your wireless makes your data vulnerable to hacking.
- Always back up your data. Whether you are working from home or at work, ensure that either you or someone in the organization is constantly backing up your data on a regular basis. It's important to keep a copy of your backup off-site (away from home or office) in case of fire, or other natural disaster that can destroy your backup.
- Stop unwanted access from inside or outside with special authorization systems. These can be as simple as a password or as sophisticated as fingerprint or voice identification.
- Install *firewalls*—hardware or software designed to prevent unauthorized access to or from a private network.
- Monitor network activity with intrusion-detection systems that signal possible unauthorized access and document suspicious events.
- Train employees to troubleshoot problems in advance rather than just react to them.
- Hold frequent staff training sessions to teach correct security procedures, such as logging out of networks when they go to lunch and changing passwords often.
- Make sure employees choose sensible passwords, of at least six and ideally eight characters long or more, containing numbers, letters, and punctuation marks. Avoid dictionary words and personal information.
- Establish a database of useful information and FAQs (frequently asked questions) for employees so they can solve problems themselves.
- Develop a healthy communications atmosphere.

Keep IT Confidential: Privacy Concerns

The very existence of huge electronic file cabinets full of personal information presents a threat to our personal privacy. Until recently, our financial, medical, tax, and other records were stored in separate computer systems. Computer networks make it easy to pool these data into data warehouses. Companies also sell the information they collect about you from sources like warranty registration cards, credit card records, registration at websites, personal data forms required for online purchases, and grocery store discount club cards. Telemarketers can combine data from different sources to create fairly detailed profiles of consumers. With information about their buying habits, advertisers can target consumers for specific marketing programs. Data about individuals or groups are constantly being sold and bought in the "underbelly" of the Internet, meaning that there are individuals who do this for a profitable living, without getting noticed, so it is very important to be vigilant about what you share about yourself on the Internet.

Increasingly, consumers are fighting to regain control of personal data and how that information is used. Privacy advocates are working to block sales of information collected by governments and corporations. For example, they want to prevent governments from selling driver's licence information, and supermarkets from collecting and selling information gathered when shoppers use bar-coded plastic loyalty cards.

The challenge to companies is to find a balance between collecting the information they need and protecting individual consumer rights. Most registration and warranty forms that ask questions about income and interests have a box for consumers to check to prevent the company from selling their names. Many companies now state their privacy policies to ensure consumers that they will not abuse the information they collect.

In Canada, the Personal Information Protection and Electronic Documents Act, which was enacted in 2000, is intended to support and promote electronic commerce by protecting personal information. In an era of technology that is used to facilitate the exchange of information, the Government of Canada recognized a need for rules that governed the collection, use, and disclosure of personal information in a manner that recognizes the right of privacy of individuals with respect to their personal information.[21]

Concept *in Action*

At the heart of the computer-privacy dilemma is the trade-off between confidentiality and convenience. Today's tech-savvy consumers are increasingly willing to give out personal information in exchange for enhanced shopping, more downloads, and user benefits. Entrusting personal data to online merchants eliminates repeat data entry, enables greater personalization of websites, and produces remarkably relevant cross-selling and search results. Can consumers have both convenience and privacy, or will they ultimately have to choose one or the other?

THE FUTURE OF INFORMATION TECHNOLOGY

Information technology is a continually evolving field. The fast pace and amount of change, coupled with IT's broad reach, make it especially challenging to isolate industry trends. From the time we write this chapter to the time you read it—as little as six months—new trends will appear and those that seemed important may fade. However, some trends that are reshaping today's IT landscape are digital forensics, the shift to a distributed workforce, and the increasing use of grid computing.

Cyber-Sleuthing: A New Style of Crime Busting

Digital evidence taken from an individual's computer or a corporate network—Web pages, pictures, documents, and e-mails—are part of a relatively new science called digital forensics. Digital forensics software safeguards electronic evidence used in investigations by creating a duplicate of a hard drive that an investigator can search by keyword, file type, or access date. Clients can have professional investigators, from

For more information about personal information protection in Canada, see the website of the Office of the Privacy Commissioner of Canada
www.privcom.gc.ca

For the latest in technology news, see www.zdnet.com or www.news.cnet.com

a company like Guidance Software, access suspect hard drives—Guidance makes EnCase, a forensic software tool used by 17,000 clients, including 90 percent of all law-enforcement investigators—or they can buy the software for around $2400 and do it themselves.[22]

Today, digital sleuthing is not limited to the police. Companies like Microsoft have their own secret in-house digital forensics teams. And what if you're in Toronto and need to seize a hard drive in Hong Kong? No problem. Over 75 members of the Fortune 500 now use technology that allows them to search hard drives remotely over their corporate networks.[23] Digital forensics makes it possible to track down those who steal corporate data and intellectual property.

However, there is a downside to having these advanced capabilities. If this kind of software falls into the wrong hands, sophisticated hackers could access corporate networks and individual computers as easily as taking candy from a baby—and the victims would not even know it was happening. In an age of corporate wrongdoing, sexual predators, and cyberporn, your hard drive will tell investigators everything they need to know (and even things they don't) about your behaviour and interests, good and bad. Cyber-sleuthing means we are all potential targets of digital forensics. As evidenced by the huge increase in identity theft, personal privacy—once an unassailable right—is no longer as sacred as it once was.

The Distributed Workforce

When companies shut the doors to some of their operations, it may seem that they are in financial trouble. Not necessarily—in fact, far from it. Instead of maintaining expensive offices in multiple locations, many companies are sending employees home to work and adopting a new model for their employees: the distributed workforce. Employees have no permanent office space and work from home or on the road. By shifting to virtual workers, companies save considerable overhead costs and often see more productive employees. Virtual computing is less expensive for the organization in the long run and employees are more flexible and happier. According to Virtualteambuilders.com, people are more productive and creative working in their pajamas!

Grid Computing Offers Powerful Solutions

How can smaller companies that occasionally need to perform difficult and large-scale computational tasks find a way to accomplish their projects? They can turn to grid computing, also called utility computing or peer-to-peer computing. Grid technology provides a way to divide the job into many smaller tasks and distribute them to a virtual supercomputer consisting of many small computers linked into a common network. Combining multiple desktop machines results in computing power that exceeds supercomputer speeds. A hardware and software infrastructure clusters and integrates computers and applications from multiple sources, harnessing unused power in existing PCs and networks. The grid structure distributes computational resources but maintains central control of the process. A central server acts as a team leader and traffic monitor. The controlling cluster server divides a task into subtasks, assigns the work to computers on the grid with surplus processing power, combines the results, and moves on to the next task until the job is finished. Exhibit 4.12 shows how a typical grid setup works.

With utility computing, any company—large or small—can access the software and computer capacity on an as-needed basis. As John Meyer, vice president of brand strategy at software company Computer Associates, asks, "Why should manufacturers pay millions of dollars to run their computer infrastructure, when they can pay on demand for the amount of IT resources they actually consume?"[24]

Exhibit 4.12 How Grid Computing Works

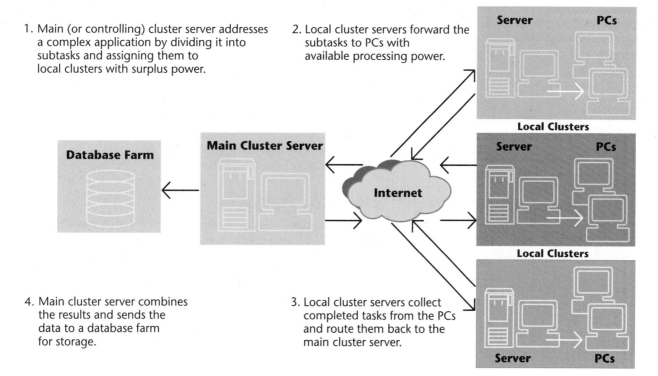

1. Main (or controlling) cluster server addresses a complex application by dividing it into subtasks and assigning them to local clusters with surplus power.

2. Local cluster servers forward the subtasks to PCs with available processing power.

Database Farm

Main Cluster Server

Internet

Server **PCs**

Local Clusters

Server **PCs**

Local Clusters

Server **PCs**

4. Main cluster server combines the results and sends the data to a database farm for storage.

3. Local cluster servers collect completed tasks from the PCs and route them back to the main cluster server.

SOURCE: Adapted from Sami Lais, "Grid Computing," *Computerworld*, December 23, 2002.

Oracle Grid Computing, IBM, and Hewlett-Packard are among the companies providing as-needed grid services. Although grid computing appears similar to outsourcing or on-demand software from ASPs, it has two key differences:

- Pricing is set per-use, whereas outsourcing involves fixed-price contracts.
- Grid computing goes beyond hosted software and includes computer and networking equipment as well as services.

Grids provide a very cost-effective way to provide computing power for complex projects in areas such as weather research and financial and biomedical modelling. Because the computing infrastructure already exists—grids tap into computer capacity that is otherwise unused—the cost is quite low. The increased interest in grid technology will contribute to high growth.

Concept *Check*

How are companies and other organizations using digital forensics to obtain critical information?

Why do companies find that productivity rises when they offer employees the option of joining the virtual workforce?

What advantages does grid computing offer a company? What are some of the downsides to using this method?

GREAT IDEAS TO USE NOW

Computer literacy is no longer a luxury. To succeed in business today, almost everyone must develop technological competence. Whether you have a part-time job in a fast-food restaurant that uses computerized ordering systems, or perform financial analyses that guide the future of your company, you will depend on computers. The more you increase your knowledge of technology, the more valuable you will be as an employee in today's information-driven businesses. In addition, the shortage of qualified IT personnel opens up new career avenues to those who enjoy working with technology. You will also have the knowledge required to take steps to protect your privacy.

For a more complete list of recommendations of the Office of the Privacy Commissioner of Canada, see www.privcom.gc.ca

Preparation Pays Off

Whether you are an employee or a business owner, you need to be aware of how technology affects the way your company operates. New applications can change fundamental company operations and employees' roles. For example, companies that install ERP systems want individual employees to make more strategic, far-reaching decisions than before. This requires a dramatic shift in employees' roles and the way they should view their jobs. For example, an accountant's responsibilities might now include analyzing budgets, not just auditing expenses. A salesperson's role might expand to include more strategic decision making about customer issues. Your company will see the business benefits sooner if you prepare for these changing roles. A manager should begin teaching employees operational procedures before implementing the new system and help them acquire the necessary analytical skills. As an employee, you can take the initiative to learn as much as possible about the new technology and how it operates.

Protect Your Good Name

Identity theft is on the rise. Recent developments in telecommunications and computer processing make it easier for companies and the public to reach each other; they also cause your personal information to be more widely circulated. If identity theft happens, you could be held responsible for bills and other charges.

Often, you have no idea that your identity has been stolen, and you might not be able to prevent it. The Office of the Privacy Commissioner of Canada has compiled the "Top 10 Ways Your Privacy Is Threatened":

1. Surveillance cameras, swipe cards, Internet searches—you leave a trail of data as you go about your daily life.
2. Freely sharing your personal information.
3. Personal information being posted on social networking sites.
4. Governments collecting personal data in the name of national security and public safety.
5. Businesses collecting more and more information without having the necessary means to protect it.
6. Data breaches in both the public and private sectors.
7. Fraudsters from all over the globe able to access your personal information through devious, technologically savvy means.
8. Identity theft.
9. Information flows internationally. Not all countries have privacy protection laws, and even if they do, the laws are not necessarily created equal.
10. People become complacent about their privacy and share too much, too freely.[25]

Summary of Learning Outcomes

 LO1 **Explain why information is so important in business.**

Management of Information Systems (MIS) is a discipline that involves the management of people, process, and technology around the care of information (the information systems or IS). The environment of MIS is about handling, classifying, holding, arranging, managing, and having the mastery to structure information through systems and technology. The management of information provides decision-making support at various levels of the organization.

When an organization determines the value of its information, it analyzes its strategic importance for competitive advantage. Is the information being utilized by its employees in an efficient manner? Is the information available and organized? Is the information easily accessible and affordable to retrieve?

The business value of information technology in e-business or e-commerce (EC) environments is categorized into business-to-consumer (B2C), business to business (B2B), government to citizens (G2C), government to business (G2B), customer to customer (C2C), and mobile commerce (m-commerce). All these forms of EC are ubiquitous, meaning that EC is available anywhere and at anytime.

Businesses depend on information technology for everything from running daily operations to making strategic decisions. Companies must have management information systems that gather, analyze, and distribute information to the appropriate parties, including employees, suppliers, and customers. These systems collect data and process it into usable information for decision making. Managers tap into databases to access the information they need, whether for placing inventory orders, scheduling production, or preparing long-range forecasts. They can compare information about the company's current status to its goals and standards. Company-wide enterprise resource planning systems that bring together human resources, operations, and technology are becoming an integral part of business strategy.

LO2 Explain how information technology has transformed business and managerial decision making.

A management information system consists of a transaction-processing system, management support systems, and an office automation system. The transaction-processing system (TPS) collects and organizes operational data on the company's activities. Management support systems help managers make better decisions. They include an information-reporting system, which provides information based on the data collected by the TPS to the managers who need it; decision support systems, which use models to assist in answering "what if" types of questions; and expert systems, which give managers advice similar to what they would get from a human consultant. Executive information systems are customized to the needs of top management. All employees benefit from office automation systems that facilitate communication by using word processing, e-mail, fax machines, and similar technologies.

LO3 Give examples of the types of systems that make up a typical company's management information system.

Computer networks link computers so they can share. Today, companies use networks of computers that share data and expensive hardware to improve operating efficiency. Types of networks include local area networks (LANs), wide area networks (WANs), and wireless local area networks (WLANs). Intranets are private WANs that allow a company's employees to communicate quickly with each other and work on joint projects, regardless of their location. Companies are finding new uses for wireless technologies, such as tablets, cellphones, and e-mail devices. Virtual private networks (VPNs) give companies a cost-effective, secure connection between remote locations using public networks such as the Internet.

LO4 Discuss why computer networks are an important part of today's information technology systems.

To get the most value from information technology (IT), companies must go beyond simply collecting and summarizing information. Technology planning involves evaluating the company's goals and objectives, and using the right technology to reach them. IT managers must also evaluate existing infrastructure to get the best return on the company's investment in IT assets. Knowledge management (KM) focuses on sharing an organization's collective knowledge to improve productivity and foster innovation. Some companies establish the position of chief knowledge officer to head up KM activities.

LO5 Describe how technology management and planning can help companies optimize their information technology systems.

Because companies are more dependent on computers than ever before, they need to protect data and equipment from natural disasters and computer crime. Types of computer crime include unauthorized use and access, software piracy, malicious damage, and computer viruses. To protect IT assets, companies should prepare written security policies. They can use technology, such as virus protection and firewalls, and employee training in proper security procedures. They must also take steps to protect customers' personal privacy rights.

LO6 Identify some of the best ways to protect computers and the information they contain.

LO7 List some of the leading trends in information technology.

IT is a dynamic industry, and companies must stay current in the latest trends to identify ones that help them maintain their competitive edge, such as digital forensics, the distributed workforce, and grid computing. With digital forensics techniques, corporations, government agencies, lawyers, and lawmakers can obtain evidence from computers and corporate networks—Web pages, pictures, documents, and e-mails. Many knowledge workers now work remotely rather than from an office. Companies adopting the distributed workforce model gain many benefits, such as cost savings, more satisfied and productive employees, and increased employee retention. Grid computing harnesses the idle power of desktop PCs and other computers to create a virtual supercomputer. A company can access the grid on an as-needed basis instead of investing in its own supercomputer equipment. Outsourcing a portion of the company's computing needs provides additional flexibility and cost advantages. Companies can also set up internal grids.

Key Terms

application service providers (ASPs)   109
batch processing   99
chief information officer (CIO)   96
computer network   103
computer virus   114
database   97
data mart   100
data warehouse   100
decision support system (DSS)   100
enterprise portal   107
executive information system (EIS)   101
expert system   102
information system (IS)   95
information technology (IT)   94

intranet   105
knowledge management (KM)   111
knowledge worker   97
local area network (LAN)   104
managed service providers (MSPs)   110
Management of Information
    System (MIS)   94
management support system (MSS)   100
metropolitan area network (MAN)   105
office automation system   102
online (real-time) processing   99
transaction-processing system (TPS)   99
virtual private networks (VPNs)   108
wide area network (WAN)   104

Experiential Exercises

1. **Stay current.** Keeping up with the fast pace of technology change is a real challenge, but it is necessary if you wish to remain up-to-date on the latest IT developments. The Internet has simplified this task, however. Get into the habit of visiting news sites such as ZDNet, www.zdnet.com, for current tech news. You can also link to Ziff Davis publications such as *PC Magazine*, read product reviews, find online classes, and even compare prices on technology products. Another excellent site is CNet's News www.news.com, which updates the technology news headlines throughout the day. It has sections on enterprise computing, e-business, communications, media, personal technology, and investing, among others.

2. **What jobs are hot?** Managing information is an emerging career area. There are jobs for people to enter the information; for people to "mine" it to find the best markets, as well as to assess the interest and need for new products; and for specialists who understand the complex hardware and software needed to facilitate the loading, maintenance, and use of information. As a result of the increase in outsourcing of some IT functions, and the shift of many IT jobs overseas (where labour costs are lower), companies are now hiring business analysts (BAs), also called subject area experts, or SAEs. BAs serve as business liaisons, interfacing with the company to which the project is outsourced and with offshore personnel. To learn more about these areas and the wide range of other IT positions currently available, read the classified employment ads in your local newspaper and *The Wall Street Journal*. Go online to browse the employment ads from almost any

major newspaper and surf through the websites with job listings. Many technology company websites also post job openings. Make a list of jobs that interest you. In addition, read the general job listings to see how many require computer skills.

3. How has information technology changed your life? Describe at least three areas (both personal and school/work related) where having access to better information has improved your decisions. Are there any negative effects? What steps can you take to manage information more effectively?

4. Should companies outsource IT? According to an interview in the December 9, 2002, San Jose *Mercury News*, Craig Conway, president and chief executive of PeopleSoft, believes that IT is too important to outsource and that application service providers (ASPs) don't have a future. What's your position? Divide the class into groups designated "for" or "against" outsourcing and/or ASPs. Have them research the current status of ASPs using publications like *CIO* and *Computerworld* and websites like ASPnews.com, www.aspnews.com.

5. One of the fastest-growing areas of business software is enterprise resource planning (ERP) applications. Visit one of the following company's sites: SAP, www.sap.com, or PeopleSoft, www.oracle.com/index.html. Prepare a short presentation for the class about the company's ERP product offerings and capabilities. Include examples of how companies use the ERP software.

6. What can an intranet accomplish for a company? Find out by using such resources as Brint.com's Intranet Portal, www.brint.com/Intranets.htm, and *Intranet Journal*, www.intranetjournal.com. Look for case studies that show how companies apply this technology. Summarize the features an intranet provides.

7. Learn more about the CERT Coordination Center (CERT/CC), which serves as a centre of Internet security expertise. Explore its website, www.cert.org. What are the latest statistics on incidents reported, vulnerabilities, security alerts, security notes, mail messages, and hotline calls? What other useful information does the site provide to help a company protect IT assets?

8. Research the latest developments in computer security at Computerworld's site, www.computerworld.com/securitytopics/security. What types of information can you find here? Pick one area, such as security for mobility/wireless devices, and summarize your findings.

Review Questions

1. Why is information so valuable to an organization?

2. How has technology been incorporated to help manage business?

3. What is the role of the CIO?

4. What is an MIS, and what are its roles?

5. How do LANs, WANs, and MAN's help in business?

6. How does a transaction-processing system (TPS) help to manage information?

7. Compare data warehouses and data marts.

8. Discuss the role of decision support systems (DSS).

9. How have office automation systems helped businesses?

10. How can we manage knowledge resources?

11. Why is protecting computers and information so important?

12. What are some ways that computer and information security issues can be breached?

13. How can we prevent security and technical problems?

CREATIVE THINKING CASE

Canada Takes the Lead

The 2006 Canada Census information formed the basis for the February 2007 release of data by Statistics Canada. The census provided data for such important facts as characteristics of the population, households, dwellings, and families. This information is used to inform planning and decision making in government, and the public and private sector—both profit and not-for-profit.

Canada Post delivered census questionnaires to approximately 70 percent of households, with the remaining 30 percent receiving their questionnaires from one of the 20,000 census enumerators. Most households received the short questionnaire, with only about 20 percent receiving the longer questionnaire.

The census represented a massive project six years in the making; the census website, designed to handle online responses, was more successful than any other in the world. The system had the capacity to handle 15,000 respondents at once and did not go down even during the busiest time of the response activity. Then director-general Anil Arora stated that the security was so sophisticated that it exceeded even the level of security on most banking transactions. He also felt that the most important improvement was in the quality of the responses submitted. If respondents were unable to get through because of capacity problems, they were asked to try again later, and they did. About 20 percent of the 13 million households completed the census online, resulting in huge savings in labour, postage, and other costs. For example, having the data already in digital form when submitted eliminates the need for data entry and also eliminates the potential for error. The cost to the government for census administration is about $15 per person, whereas in the United States, it is more than $90 per household, six times the Canadian cost. Canadians also had access to a toll-free hotline number that handled one million calls over three days. The total cost for administering the census was approximately $567 million, a saving of over $11 million compared to the 2001 census.

The first release of information for the 2011 Census began in February 2012. This census built on the success of the 2006 edition. (The census is taken every five years.) A change for 2011 was the elimination of forms. Instead, each household was sent the information via Canada Post or hand delivery by an enumerator. (A sample of 20 percent was sent questionnaires.) These changes resulted in even greater savings. The long form questionnaire was completely eliminated in a controversial move by the government that, at least in part, resulted in the resignation of Arora. StatsCan reported a response rate of 98.1 percent on the 2011 Census. The northern territories of Nunavut and Yukon had response rates under 95 percent.

Thinking Critically

1. Given the importance of the data collected by the census, is there any way costs could be lowered further by using technology?

2. What technology could be used to improve the response rates in remote areas?

SOURCES: "Counter Spin," *The Ottawa Citizen*, May 21, 2006, pg. A7. Reprinted with permission; David Eadie, "2007... and still counting," *Summit*, Ottawa: April/May 2007, Vol. 10, Iss. 3, page 7; StatsCanada, "2011 Census Collection."

Making the Connection

International: The Global Marketplace

In this chapter, we will look at the final element in our PESTI model of the external environment of business—the *international* environment or global marketplace. This is a very important element of the model and is perhaps the most integrative, as it forces us to consider not only the external environment outside our immediate domestic markets, but also the political, economic, social, and technological (PEST) factors within each international market affecting the business—both in terms of creating opportunities with new customers and in terms of dealing with threats from global competition.

In this chapter, you will learn about the international environment, and see the very strong interrelationship between the *political* and *economic* environments and global trade. The most obvious connection is how critical international trade is to our economy. As stated in the chapter, about half of what we manufacture is exported. Trade imbalances can seriously affect the economic climate for business. And these trade imbalances are often a result of government policy in both the foreign and the domestic country.

There is no question that the international environment offers many opportunities for business, but it also presents a number of threats. A business needs to consider these opportunities and threats when determining its *strategy* for going global. Governments often help to create opportunities for business to expand internationally. How a business capitalizes on these political initiatives depends on its strategy, and you will learn about the different options for expanding in the global marketplace later in the chapter.

Other political initiatives result in threats to business. Tariff and non-tariff barriers are obvious examples. In an attempt to protect domestic trade, governments set up obstacles for foreign competition by making foreign goods more expensive through tariffs or by restricting the import of foreign goods through quotas. These barriers are meant to create opportunities for domestic companies to grow within a protected domestic environment; however, they may very well stifle these companies instead, because they don't have to *innovate* (one of the critical success factors) and improve their operations to compete with this foreign competition.

The economic infrastructure of a country is a large consideration for a business. Without a strong infrastructure, it is very difficult to do business in that country, and of course the stronger its economy the greater the purchasing power of its people—the customers. Currency differences also need to be taken into account and can seriously restrict a company, as discussed in the chapter.

Social and cultural differences also need to be taken into account. These differences will undoubtedly affect marketing—the products that are sold and how they are sold—but also will affect how business is done in that country. Therefore, acting without knowledge of the differences can seriously affect the success of a global strategy.

Technological factors, such as transportation improvements and the Internet, have actually made physical distances less of a barrier to global trade than they used to be. Companies such as Purolator and UPS, for example, can take advantage of both these factors, as transportation improvements have greatly increased the speed and efficiency with which packages are shipped, and advanced computerized tracking software can communicate where packages are at any time.

Businesses need to have a global *vision* to recognize and react to international business opportunities, as well as to remain competitive at home. In relation to our model of a successful business, what this means is that the vision created for the company must take the international environment into account to survive and prosper, as this environment affects the business whether or not it decides to pursue a strategy that involves selling in the global marketplace. It cannot ignore the fact that foreign companies can and will still compete in the domestic marketplace and this foreign competition presents a threat to a Canadian enterprise—one that, if ignored, can easily put it out of business.

All of these external environmental factors interact when a business enters the global marketplace. They affect the company's vision and its strategy for competing. They also affect the internal environment. The *marketing* department must consider the differing needs of customers in the different countries where the company sells product. The *operations* department must consider the logistics of operating in a global environment depending on the strategic option chosen—exporting to the country or investing in its own facilities in that country, for example. The *human resources* department must consider the skills needed of its employees to do business effectively in foreign countries, language being an obvious example. And the *finance* department must consider differences in exchange rates to maintain the company's profitability.

If a company considers its external environment carefully and develops a global vision for doing business, it can work toward achieving the critical success factors. It can achieve *financial performance* by *meeting the needs* of foreign customers with products of *value* to their unique tastes and circumstances. And whether its strategy is to expand into foreign markets or not, it will be forced to *innovate* to stay ahead of foreign competition. These critical factors of success are, of course, achieved through a *committed workforce* that understands the global marketplace.

chapter 5

International: The Global Marketplace

LULULEMON—CHIP WILSON

In 1997, Chip Wilson enrolled in a yoga class. He loved the class, but not the clothes. As a former competitive swimmer, he expected his clothes to stretch when he did, not get in the way of his workouts. This experience inspired him to create Lululemon, now known the world over for fashionable, yoga-inspired workout clothing.

Chip (real name Dennis) is from Calgary, but since his parents met in southern California, many family summers were spent back in the San Diego area soaking up the sun, surfing, and getting into all the latest fashions. When he returned home to Calgary each fall, his landlocked buddies all wanted the stuff he was bringing back: baggy shorts, tall Ts … cool surfwear no one else had.

So, in Vancouver in the early 1980s, Chip and two friends opened WestBeach Surfwear to sell the clothes and cash in on the surfing culture. And by the early 90s they had successfully sold the business.

Next, Chip merged his athletic clothing background with his first experience of a commercial yoga class, and his next project was born in 1998. The clothing design studio added nightly yoga classes to pay the Kitsilano rent. This was an ideal environment to perfect the product—initial testing was done by giving clothing samples to their yoga instructors for feedback, and the winning products were sold to the studio's yoga enthusiasts.

This participatory environment also helped name the store—Lululemon was chosen from a 100-person, 20-sample survey. Today, Lulu stores still follow this customer-centric model, staying in touch with their base—the contemporary yoga community.

Of course there are detractors, and no shortage of rumours. Some say Lulu sells pseudo-spirituality. Others claim the products are made in sweatshops in the developing world and aren't worth anywhere near their prices. The *New York Times* tested some of the clothes and indicated there was no seaweed in them as claimed, and the bags contained lead.

None of this has hurt Lululemon sales; both corporate and franchised growth continues worldwide. In fact, after being featured on Oprah's *Ultimate Favorite Things* list, sales soared and the stock price doubled in a month.

A big part of Lulu growth is due to its partnership with Advent, a private equity company. In 2005, Advent bought

REPRINTED WITH PERMISSION FROM THE HALIFAX HERALD LIMITED

48 percent of the company, and the capital infusion allowed growth into international markets and expansion from 36 to more than 100 stores. Advent insiders joined the Lululemon board and advised from their understanding of world markets.

It's a motivating story to see where interests can take you. The young Chip Wilson's penchant for surfing clothes planted the seed for his future in what is now a worldwide athletic wear company, making its mark in modern yoga everywhere.[1]

THINKING CRITICALLY

As you read this chapter, consider the following questions:

1. Why do nations trade?

2. How can governments and other institutions help Canadian companies compete in the international marketplace?

3. What are some of the obstacles in operating internationally?

SOURCES: "Lululemon athletica inc. corporate survey," retrieved from FP Advisor database, May 29, 2009, http://www.FPInfomart.ca; www.lululemon.com, modified November 18, 2011.

Today, global revolutions are under way in many areas of our lives: management, politics, communications, and technology, to name a few. Globalization of business is not an accident; it has been created by a forced effort. The word global has assumed a new meaning, referring to a boundless mobility and competition in social, business, and intellectual arenas. No longer just an option, having a global vision has become a business imperative. Having a global vision *means recognizing and reacting to international business opportunities, being aware of threats from foreign competitors in all markets, and effectively using international distribution networks to obtain raw materials and move finished products to the customer.*

Canadian managers must develop a global vision if they are to recognize and react to international business opportunities, as well as remain competitive at home. Often a Canadian company's toughest domestic competition comes from foreign companies. Moreover, a global vision enables a manager to understand that customer and distribution networks operate worldwide, blurring geographic and political barriers and making them increasingly irrelevant to business decisions. The purpose of this chapter is to explain how global trade is conducted. We also discuss the barriers to international trade and the organizations that foster global trade. We conclude the chapter with a discussion of trends in the global marketplace.

global vision
The ability to recognize and react to international business opportunities, be aware of threats from foreign competition, and effectively use international distribution networks to obtain raw materials and move finished products to customers.

LO1 CANADA GOES GLOBAL

Trade is very important to Canada: exports create Canadian employment and allow Canadian companies to focus on those activities where we have a competitive advantage; imports provide Canadian consumers with less expensive products. Global business is not a one-way street, where only Canadian companies sell their wares and services throughout the world. Foreign competition in the domestic market used to

Concept *in Action*

Maple Leaf Foods, headquartered in Toronto, is a leading consumer packaged food company. It has operations across Canada, as well as in the United States, United Kingdom, Asia, and Mexico. What are some of the considerations for companies expanding internationally?

MARK BLINCH/REUTERS/LANDOV

be relatively rare but now occurs in almost every industry. Nevertheless, the global market has created vast, new business opportunities for many Canadian companies. As mentioned above, globalization is no accident; it has been created by a forced effort.

The Importance of Global Business to Canada

One reason the United Nations has ranked Canada as one of the best countries in which to live is because of our ability to do business with the "outside world." According to the Department of Foreign Affairs and International Trade, "trade enhances the quality of Canadian life" and helps give Canadians the economic energy we need to create the nation we want.[2]

Just how important is international trade to Canada? Canada's population, at approximately 34.5 million, is relatively small versus the over seven billion people worldwide. This translates into roughly 200 times as many potential customers for Canadian business. Canada exports approximately half of what we manufacture. In terms of a dollar value, for each Canadian resident we export more than $15,000 in goods and services. Every $1 billion increase in Canada's exports translates into more than 10,000 jobs, and one fifth of all Canadian jobs are directly related to international trade. We can see that exports are vital to the Canadian economy.[3]

But can we maintain this advantage and keep our economy growing? The simple answer is no—not unless we continue to develop outside markets. Canada has seen international trade increase, helped in part by its proactive partnership between government and businesses/industries. In 2011, the federal minister responsible for international trade said that, "Success of Canadian companies abroad will be a key driver of prosperity at home."[4]

As mentioned above, international trade refers to exports and imports. If we expect countries to purchase our products, they will need the dollars that are generated by their exports to do so. Imports offer Canadians a wider range and choice of products and services to purchase. Our economy has become more sophisticated in recent decades (see Chapter 2), developing into a knowledge-based economy. Canada's technological potential is ranked first among nations according to the *Global Competitiveness Report*.[5] If Canada is to capitalize on its technical potential, we must convert this potential into global success.

Not only does international trade affect the Canadian economy and provide employment for Canadians, but other benefits have been identified. These include

- economies of scale in production and marketing;
- ease of the transfer of experience, technology, and know-how across borders;
- global recognition of products and brand names, allowing for easier introduction of new products and services; and
- the possibility of a uniform global image for the companies.

HOT Links

For more information about Foreign Affairs and International Trade Canada, visit
www.international.gc.ca/ media_commerce/comm/ news-communiques/2011/331. aspx?lang=eng&view=d

The Impact of Multinational Corporations

Corporations that move resources, goods, services, and skills across national boundaries without regard to the country in which their headquarters are located are multinational corporations. Some are so rich and have so many employees that they resemble small countries. The successful ones take political and cultural differences into account. Some examples of successful Canadian multinational companies are Magna International Inc., Cott Corporation, Bombardier Inc., and ScotiaBank.

THE MULTINATIONAL ADVANTAGE Large multinationals have several advantages over other companies. For instance, multinationals can often overcome trade problems. Taiwan and South Korea have long had an embargo against Japanese cars for political reasons and to help

multinational corporations
Corporations that move resources, goods, services, and skills across national boundaries without regard to the country in which their headquarters are located.

Concept *Check*

What is a global vision, and why is it important?

What impact does international trade have on the Canadian economy and Canadians?

domestic automakers. Yet Honda USA, a Japanese-owned company based in the United States, sends Accords to Taiwan and Korea.

Another advantage for multinationals is their ability to sidestep regulatory constraints. Pharmaceutical company SmithKline and Britain's Beecham decided to merge, in part so that they could avoid licensing and regulatory hassles in their largest markets. The merged company can say it's an insider in both Europe and North America. "When we go to Brussels, we're a member state (of the European Union)," one executive explains. "And when we go to Canada, we're a North American company."

Multinationals can also shift production from one plant to another as market conditions change or other situations warrant it. When Magna International suffered a fire in 2011 at one of its plants, it shifted production to other Magna plants.

Multinationals can also tap new technology from around the world. Xerox has introduced some 80 different office copiers in Canada that were designed and built by Fuji Xerox, its joint venture with a Japanese company. Versions of the super-concentrated detergent that Procter & Gamble first formulated in Japan in response to a rival's product are now being sold under the Ariel brand name in Europe and being tested under the Cheer and Tide labels in Canada. Also, consider Otis Elevator's development of the Elevonic 411, an elevator that is programmed to send more cars to floors where demand is high. It was developed at six research centres in five countries. The Otis group in the United States handled the systems integration, a Japanese group designed the special motor drives that make the elevators ride smoothly, a French group perfected the door systems, a German group handled the electronics, and a Spanish group took care of the small-geared components. Otis says the international effort saved more than $10 million (USD) in design costs and cut the process from four years to two.

Finally, multinationals can often save a lot in labour costs, even in highly unionized countries. For example, when Xerox started moving copier-rebuilding work to Mexico to take advantage of the lower wages, its union objected because it saw that members' jobs were at risk. Eventually, the union agreed to change work styles and to improve productivity to keep the jobs at home.

THE MULTINATIONAL CHALLENGES The multinationals also face many challenges. These include social and cultural issues (the need to understand diversity and the host country's customs), economic and financial issues (access to financial resources, foreign currency regulations, etc.), legal and regulatory issues (e.g., government regulations), and environmental issues (e.g., access to raw materials, labour). These are discussed in more detail later in the chapter (learning outcome 6).

Measuring Trade Between Nations

International trade improves relationships with friends and allies, helps ease tensions among nations, and—economically speaking—bolsters economies, raises people's standard of living, provides jobs, and improves quality of life. The value of international trade is more than $8 trillion (USD) a year and growing. In this section, we take a look at some key measures of international trade: exports and imports, the balance of trade, the balance of payments, and exchange rates.

exports
Goods and services produced in one country and sold in other countries.

imports
Goods and services bought from other countries.

EXPORTS AND IMPORTS The developed nations (those with mature communication, financial, educational, and distribution systems) are the major players in international trade, accounting for about 70 percent of the world's exports and imports. Exports are goods and services made in one country and sold to others. Imports are goods and services that are bought from other countries. Canada is both an exporter and importer. The main countries (based on dollar amounts) that Canada trades with are listed in Exhibit 5.1.

As Exhibit 5.1 illustrates, approximately 73.3 percent of Canada's exports are to the United States, and approximately 62.8 percent of imports come from the United States in 2010. This heavy reliance that Canada has on the United States for trade is one rationale for Canada's seeking other international trading partners. Recent studies have shown that the Canadian economy is relying less on trade with the United States. The same figures for the year 2005 were 81.8 percent (Canadian exports to the United States) and 63 percent (Canadian imports from the United States).

BALANCE OF TRADE The difference between the value of a country's exports and the value of its imports during a certain time is the country's balance of trade. A country that exports more than it imports is said to have a *favourable* balance of trade, called a trade surplus. A country that imports more than it exports is said to have an *unfavourable* balance of trade, or a trade deficit. When imports exceed exports, more money from trade flows out of the country than flows into it.

BALANCE OF PAYMENTS Another measure of international trade is called the balance of payments, which is a summary of a country's international financial transactions showing the difference between the country's total payments to and total receipts from other countries. The balance of payments includes imports and exports (balance of trade), long-term investments in overseas plants and equipment, government loans to and from other countries, gifts and foreign aid, military expenditures made in other countries, and money transfers into and out of foreign banks.

balance of trade
The difference between the value of a country's exports and the value of its imports during a certain time.

trade surplus
A favourable balance of trade that occurs when a country exports more than it imports.

trade deficit
An unfavourable balance of trade that occurs when a country imports more than it exports.

balance of payments
A summary of a country's international financial transactions showing the difference between the country's total payments to and total receipts from other countries.

| **Exhibit 5.1** | Chart of Canada's Main Trading Partners Based on Dollar Amounts |

(Balance-of-payments basis)

	2005	2006	2007	2008	2009	2010
	$ MILLIONS					
Exports	450,210.0	453,951.9	463,120.4	488,754.1	369,343.2	404,834.2
United States[1]	368,278.9	361,442.1	355,731.5	370,005.3	271,108.7	269,672.0
Japan	10,172.8	10,278.1	10,026.8	11,784.3	8,861.8	9,716.6
United Kingdom	9,360.5	11,282.2	14,152.3	14,029.3	13,046.0	16,958.8
Other European Union[2]	18,643.8	20,903.7	24,392.7	25,173.5	19,010.3	19,475.8
Other OECD[3]	14,545.6	16,808.1	19,743.6	20,748.6	16,690.6	17,908.3
All other countries	29,208.5	33,237.6	39,073.5	47,013.1	40,625.8	44,075.7
Imports	387,837.8	404,345.4	415,683.1	443,777.2	374,080.9	413,832.8
United States[1]	259,332.9	265,088.3	270,066.9	281,535.0	236,289.6	259,952.7
Japan	11,213.1	11,849.9	11,967.1	11,671.8	9,329.2	10,067.2
United Kingdom	9,066.5	9,547.1	9,962.9	11,232.9	8,529.6	9,560.6
Other European Union[2]	29,487.3	32,547.5	32,403.7	35,461.4	30,240.5	30,788.3
Other OECD[3]	24,282.1	23,680.1	25,159.8	27,380.4	25,961.7	29,012.9
All other countries	54,455.9	61,632.4	66,122.7	76,495.7	63,730.4	74,451.1
Balance	62,372.2	49,606.5	47,437.3	44,976.9	−4,737.7	−8,998.6
United States[1]	108,946.0	96,353.8	85,664.6	88,470.3	34,819.1	36,719.3
Japan	−1,040.3	−1,571.8	−1,940.3	112.5	−467.4	−350.6
United Kingdom	294.0	1,735.1	4,189.4	2,796.4	4,516.4	7,425.2
Other European Union[2]	−10,843.5	−11,643.8	−8,011.0	−10,287.9	−11,230.2	−11,312.5
Other OECD[3]	−9,736.5	−6,872.0	−5,416.2	−6,631.8	−9,271.1	−11,104.6
All other countries	−25,247.4	−28,394.8	−27,049.2	−29,482.6	−23,104.6	−30,375.4

[1] Also includes Puerto Rico and Virgin Islands.
[2] Other European Union includes Austria, Belgium, Bulgaria, Cyprus, Czech Republic, Denmark, Estonia, Finland, France, Germany, Greece, Hungary, Ireland, Italy, Latvia, Lithuania, Luxembourg, Malta, Netherlands, Poland, Portugal, Romania, Slovakia, Slovenia, Spain, and Sweden.
[3] Other countries in the Organisation for Economic Co-operation and Development (OECD) include Australia, Canada, Iceland, Mexico, New Zealand, Norway, South Korea, Switzerland, and Turkey.

SOURCE: Statistics Canada, CANSIM, table 228-0003, 09 June 2011; <http://www40.statcan.gc.ca/101/cst01/gblec02a-eng.htm> (07 November 2011).

The Impact of the 2008 and 2011 Economic Crises on Canada

In Chapter 2, you learned that the primary causes of the 2008 economic crisis were ineffective regulations, careless regulating agencies, and bad corporate governance. The crisis of 2011 was primarily the result of government and fiscal irresponsibility. As you can see in Exhibit 5.1, until recently, Canada had a favourable balance of payments. In 2009, Canada experienced its first trade deficit in many years, in large part because of the economic crisis of 2008.

The economic crises of 2008 and 2011 decreased the demand for Canada's exports and had serious implications for employment. Exports in January 2009 decreased by 9 percent from December 2008 and decreased by approximately 18 percent compared to January 2008.[6] Governments in Canada provided stimulus packages to keep Canadians working, including financing of public infrastructure projects and loans to some of the automobile manufacturers. In 2010, Canada experienced a growth in both exports and imports but still experienced a trade deficit.

The international crisis of 2011 that carried over into 2012 again impacted Canada, although not as seriously as many other countries. Canada's strong financial regulatory system, strong federal government, large pool of commodities (especially in the energy and mining sectors), and strong knowledge-based economy shielded Canada from much of the downside of this crisis.

The unemployment rate ranged from 5 percent in Alberta to 13.2 percent in Newfoundland and Labrador, with Canada's overall rate at 7.4 percent. From December 2011 to January 2012, employment in the goods sector changed little. There was considerable growth in the natural resources and construction sectors of our economy, but declines in utilities and manufacturing, all of which impacted our international trade balance.[7]

Today we still see the effects of the 2008 and 2011 economic crisis, but have yet to appreciate their full impact.

Concept in Action

Many Canadian exports and imports are transported between Canada and the United States by the rail systems. What other transportation methods are used to move products internationally? What are the advantages and disadvantages of each?

IMAGES ETC LTD/GETSTOCK

The Changing Value of Currencies

The exchange rate is the price of one country's currency in terms of another country's currency. If a country's currency *appreciates*, less of that country's currency is needed to buy another country's currency. If a country's currency *depreciates*, more of that currency will be needed to buy another country's currency.

How do appreciation and depreciation affect the prices of a country's goods? If, say, the Canadian dollar depreciates relative to the Japanese yen, Canadian residents will have to pay more dollars to buy Japanese goods. To illustrate, presume the dollar price of a yen is $0.012 and a Toyota is priced at 2 million yen. At this exchange rate, a Canadian resident pays $24,000 for a Toyota ($0.012 × 2 million yen = $24,000). If the dollar depreciates to $0.018 to one yen, then the Canadian resident will have to pay $36,000 for a Toyota.

As the dollar depreciates, the price of Japanese goods rises for Canadian residents, so they buy fewer Japanese goods—thus, Canadian imports decline. At the same time as the dollar depreciates relative to the yen, the yen appreciates relative to the dollar. This means prices of Canadian goods fall for the Japanese, so they buy more Canadian goods—and Canadian exports rise.

Currency markets operate under a system called floating exchange rates. Prices of currencies "float" up and down based upon the demand for and supply of each currency. Global currency traders create the supply of and demand for a particular currency based on that currency's investment, trade potential, and economic strength. If a country decides that its currency is not properly valued in international currency markets, the government may step in and adjust the currency's value. In a devaluation, a nation lowers the value of its currency relative to other currencies. This makes that country's exports cheaper and should, in turn, help the balance of payments.

WHY NATIONS TRADE

LO2

One might argue that the best way to protect workers and the domestic economy is to stop trade with other nations. Then the whole circular flow of inputs and outputs would stay within our borders. But if we decided to do that, how would we get resources like cotton and coffee beans? Canada simply can't produce some things, and it can't

Check out the current Canadian balance of trade with various countries by going to www.statcan.gc.ca and then, using the search menu, typing in "balance of trade" for the latest URL.

floating exchange rates
A system in which prices of currencies move up and down based on the demand for and supply of the various currencies.

devaluation
A lowering of the value of a nation's currency relative to other currencies.

Get up-to-the-minute exchange rates at www.xe.com/ucc

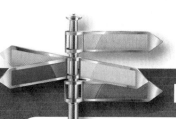

Making Ethical Choices

WHAT ARE ACCEPTABLE INTERNATIONAL BUSINESS PRACTICES?

The executives of a clothing manufacturer want to outsource some of their manufacturing to more cost-efficient locations in Indonesia. After visiting several possible sites, they choose one and begin to negotiate with local officials. They discover that it will take about six months to get the necessary permits. One of the local politicians approaches the executives over dinner and hints that he can speed up the process, for an advisory fee of $5,000.

Using a web search tool, locate articles about this topic and then write responses to the following questions. Be sure to support your arguments and cite your sources.

ETHICAL DILEMMA: Is paying the advisory fee a bribe or an acceptable cost of doing business in that area of the world? If the executives agree to pay the fee, what should they do beforehand?

SOURCES: Jane Easter Bahls, "Illicit Affairs? If You Do Business Overseas, Be Certain Your 'Administrative Fees' Aren't Really Illegal Bribes," *Entrepreneur*, September 2004, p. 80; Paul Burnham Finney, "Shaking Hands, Greasing Palms," *New York Times*, May 17, 2005, p. C10; Phelim Kyne, "Freeport- McMoRan Indonesia Payments Not Graft: Official," *FWN Financial News*, January 18, 2006.

Concept *Check*

What is the difference between balance of trade and balance of payments?

What impact does international trade have on the Canadian economy?

Explain the impact of a currency devaluation.

absolute advantage
The situation when a country can produce and sell a product at a lower cost than any other country or when it is the only country that can provide the product.

principle of comparative advantage
The concept that each country should specialize in the products that it can produce most readily and cheaply and trade those products for those that other countries can produce more readily and cheaply.

free trade
The policy of permitting the people of a country to buy and sell where they please without restrictions.

protectionism
The policy of protecting home industries from outside competition by establishing artificial barriers such as tariffs and quotas.

manufacture some products—such as steel and most clothing—at the low costs we're used to. The fact is that nations—like people—are good at producing different things: You might be better at balancing a ledger than repairing a car. In that case, you benefit by "exporting" your bookkeeping services and "importing" the car repairs you need from a good mechanic. Economists refer to specialization like this as *advantage*.

Absolute Advantage

A country has an absolute advantage when it can produce and sell a product at a lower cost than any other country or when it is the only country that can provide a product. Canada, for example, has an absolute advantage in softwood and certain technologies.

Assume that Canada has an absolute advantage in air traffic control systems for busy airports and that Brazil has an absolute advantage in coffee. Canada does not have the proper climate for growing coffee, and Brazil lacks the technology to develop air traffic control systems. Both countries would gain by exchanging air traffic control systems for coffee.

Comparative Advantage

Even if Canada had an absolute advantage in both coffee and air traffic control systems, it should still specialize and engage in trade. Why? The reason is the principle of comparative advantage, which says that each country should specialize in the products that it can produce most readily and cheaply and trade those products for goods that foreign countries can produce most readily and cheaply. This specialization ensures greater product availability and lower prices.

For example, Mexico and China have a comparative advantage in producing clothing because of low labour costs. Japan has long held a comparative advantage in consumer electronics because of technological expertise. The United States has an advantage in computer software, airplanes, some agricultural products, heavy machinery, and jet engines. Canada's advantages are numerous, including softwood lumber, oil and gas equipment and services, agricultural products, and technology.

Thus, comparative advantage acts as a stimulus to trade. When nations allow their citizens to trade whatever goods and services they choose without government regulation, free trade exists. Free trade is the policy of permitting the people of a country to buy and sell where they please without restrictions. The opposite of free trade is protectionism, in which a nation protects its home industries from outside competition by establishing artificial barriers such as tariffs and quotas. In the next section, we'll look at the various barriers, some natural and some created by governments, that restrict free trade.

The Fear of Trade and Globalization

The protests in Genoa and Seattle during meetings of the World Trade Organization, and the protests in New York during the convocation of the World Bank and the International Monetary Fund (the three organizations are discussed later in the chapter) showed that many people fear world trade and globalization. What do they fear? The negatives of global trade are as follows:

- Canadians have lost jobs because of imports or production shifts abroad. Most find new jobs, but those jobs often pay less.
- Others fear losing their jobs, especially at those companies operating under competitive pressure.
- Employers often threaten to export jobs if workers do not accept pay cuts.
- Service and white-collar workers are increasingly vulnerable to seeing their operations moving offshore.[8]

Benefits of Globalization

A closer look, however, reveals that globalization has been the engine that creates jobs and wealth. Benefits of global trade include the following:

- Productivity grows more quickly when countries produce goods and services in which they have a comparative advantage. Living standards can go up faster.
- Global competition and cheap imports keep prices down, so inflation is less likely to arrest economic growth.
- An open economy spurs innovation with fresh ideas from abroad.
- Export jobs often pay more than other jobs.[9]

Concept Check

Describe the policy of free trade and its relationship to comparative advantage.

Why do people fear globalization?

What are the benefits of globalization?

INTERNATIONAL ECONOMIC COMMUNITIES

LO3

Nations that trade with each other frequently might decide to formalize their relationship. In this case, their governments meet and work out agreements for a common economic policy. The result is an economic community or, in other cases, a bilateral trade agreement (an agreement between two countries to lower trade barriers). For example, two nations might agree on a preferential tariff, which gives advantages to one nation (or several nations) over others. When members of the British Commonwealth trade with Great Britain, for example, they pay lower tariffs than do other nations. In other cases, nations may form free trade associations. In a free trade zone, few duties or rules restrict trade among the partners, but nations outside the zone must pay the tariffs set by the individual members.

preferential tariff
A tariff that is lower for some nations than for others.

free trade zone
An area where the nations allow free, or almost free, trade with each other while imposing tariffs on goods of nations outside the zone.

North American Free Trade Agreement (NAFTA)

The North American Free Trade Agreement (NAFTA) created one of the world's largest free trade zones and has become an admirable example of the benefits of trade liberalization. It includes Canada, the United States, and Mexico, with a combined population of more than 450 million and an economy of approximately $16 trillion (USD). Canada and the United States entered a free-trade agreement in 1988. Thus, as NAFTA was established in 1994, most of the new long-run opportunities opened for Canadian business under NAFTA are in Mexico.

Since NAFTA came into effect, trade and investment levels have increased with strong economic growth, job creation, and better pricing. As well, the agreement has eliminated most tariff and non-tariff barriers to trade and investment in the three countries by creating an environment of confidence and stability. The real test of NAFTA will be whether it can continue to deliver rising prosperity to its three members. For Mexicans, NAFTA must provide rising wages, better benefits, and an expanding middle class with enough purchasing power to keep buying goods from Canada and the United States.

North American Free Trade Agreement (NAFTA)
A 1993 agreement creating a free-trade zone that includes Canada, Mexico, and the United States.

HOT|inks

Find out more about Canada's participation in NAFTA at
www.international.gc.ca

Mercosur

Mercosur, "The Common Market of the South," is the largest trading bloc in South America. The purpose of Mercosur is to allow for free trade between its member states, with the ultimate goal of full economic integration of South America. The member states include Argentina, Brazil, Paraguay, Uruguay, and Venezuela. Associate states, which do not have full voting rights or complete access to the markets of the full member states, are Bolivia, Chile, Colombia, Ecuador, and Peru. The collective GDP of the full member states (including Venezuela) is $2.4 trillion (USD) making it the fourth largest trading bloc in the world.[10]

Mercosur
Trade agreement between Brazil, Argentina, Uruguay, Paraguay, and Venezuela.

HOT|inks

See the latest news about Mercosur at
www.mercosur.int

The European Union

In 1993, the member countries of the European Community (EC) ratified the Maastricht Treaty, which proposed to take the EC further toward economic, monetary, and political union. Although the heart of the treaty deals with developing a unified European Market, Maastricht was also intended to increase integration among **European Union (EU)** members.

The EU has helped increase this integration by creating a borderless economy for these 27 European nations, shown on the map in Exhibit 5.2. The two newest members, Bulgaria and Romania, were admitted in 2007.

One of the principal objectives of the EU is to promote the economic progress of all member countries. The EU has stimulated economic progress by eliminating trade barriers, differences in tax laws, and differences in product standards, and by establishing a common currency. A new European Community Bank was created along

European Union (EU)
Trade agreement among 27 European nations.

| Exhibit 5.2 | The European Union Gets Bigger |

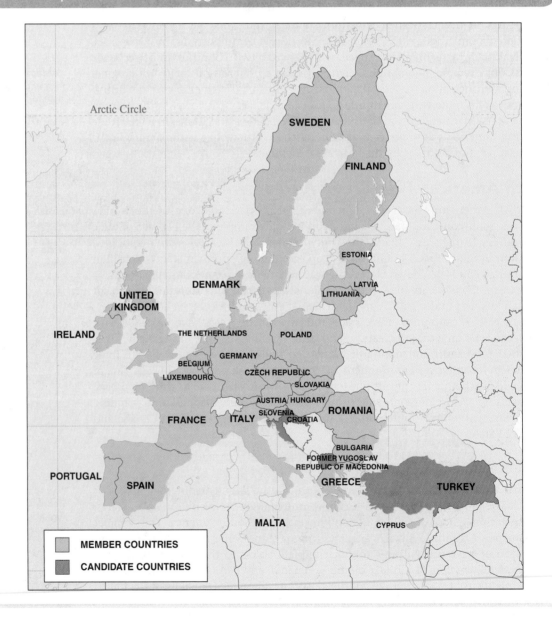

with a common currency called the Euro. Not all member countries have adopted the Euro as their official currency (e.g., Great Britain).

Starting in 2011, serious discussions were taking place in some of the individual countries as to the efficiency of the Union. With economic issues plaguing many of the member countries, Greece, Spain, Ireland, and Portugal, for example, some of the wealthier member states were debating whether or not membership was an advantage.

Concept Check

Explain the pros and cons of NAFTA.

What is Mercosur?

What is the European Union?

ASEAN

The Association of Southeast Asian Nations (ASEAN) was initially established in 1967, with the original members being Indonesia, Malaysia, the Philippines, Singapore, and Thailand. Today the association has 10 members, the original five plus Brunei Darussalam, Vietnam, Laos, Myanmar, and Cambodia. The region has a population of about 600 million, a combined GDP of $1.1 billion (USD), and a total trade of $1.4 billion (USD).[11]

In the summer of 2010, Canada signed the ASEAN-Canada Plan of Action to enhance our relationship with the ASEAN community in Ha Noi, which laid the foundation for an enhanced partnership and cooperation. The shared priorities of this agreement reflect Canada's strong commitment to promoting peace and stability in the region, as well as to fostering communication of political, security, economic, and social issues.

Association of Southeast Asian Nations (ASEAN)
The Association of Southeast Asian Nations, which, as of 2012, included 10 member states.

For further in-depth information on ASEAN see
www.aseansec.org

PARTICIPATING IN THE GLOBAL MARKETPLACE

LO4

Companies decide to "go global" for a number of reasons. Perhaps the most urgent is to earn additional profits. If a company has a unique product or technological advantage not available to other international competitors, this advantage should result in major business successes abroad. In other situations, management might have exclusive market information about foreign customers, marketplaces, or market situations not

Concept *in Action*

The Eurodollar replaced the individual currencies of many of the European Union nations. The common currency enables the countries to do business as a single trading bloc. What is the advantage of having a single currency?

known to others. In this case, although exclusivity can provide an initial motivation for going global, managers must realize that competitors will eventually catch up. Finally, saturated domestic markets, excess capacity, and potential for cost savings can also be motivators to expand into international markets. A company can enter global trade in several ways, as we describe in this section.

Exporting

exporting
The practice of selling domestically produced goods to buyers in another country.

When a company decides to enter the global market, usually the least complicated and least risky alternative is exporting, or selling domestically produced products to buyers in another country. A company, for example, can sell directly to foreign importers or buyers. Exporting is not limited to huge corporations.

Licensing and Franchising

licensing
The legal process whereby a company agrees to allow another company to use a manufacturing process, trademark, patent, trade secret, or other proprietary knowledge in exchange for the payment of a royalty.

One effective way for a company to move into the global arena with relatively little risk is to sell a licence to manufacture its product to a company in a foreign country. Licensing is the legal process whereby a company (the *licensor*) agrees to let another company (the *licensee*) use a manufacturing process, trademark, patent, trade secret, or other proprietary knowledge. The licensee, in turn, agrees to pay the licensor a royalty or fee agreed on by both parties.

Many companies have eagerly embraced the licensing concept. For instance, Philip Morris licensed Labatt Brewing Company to produce Miller High Life in Canada. The Spalding Company receives more than $2 million annually from licence agreements on its sporting goods. Fruit of the Loom lends its name through licensing to 45 consumer items in Japan alone, for at least 1 percent of the licensee's gross sales.

The licensor must make sure it can exercise sufficient control over the licensee's activities to ensure proper quality, pricing, distribution, and so on. Licensing might also create a new competitor in the long run, if the licensee decides to void the licence agreement. International law is often ineffective in stopping such actions. Two common ways in which a licensor can maintain effective control over its licensees are by shipping one or more critical components from Canada and by registering patents and trademarks locally in its own name.

Franchising, which we will discuss in Chapter 8, is a form of licensing that has grown rapidly in recent years. The Canadian Franchise Association publishes a bimonthly magazine for entrepreneurs wanting to establish a successful franchise and an annual comprehensive directory listing franchises available in Canada.

HOT *inks*

Find out more about the Canadian Franchise Association at www.cfa.ca

Contract Manufacturing

contract manufacturing
The practice in which a foreign company manufactures private label goods under a domestic company's brand name.

In contract manufacturing, a foreign company manufactures private label goods under a domestic company's brand. Marketing may be handled by either the domestic company or the foreign manufacturer.

The advantages of contract manufacturing is that it lets a company "test the water" in a foreign country and it does not have maintain production service facilities, purchase raw materials, or hire labour. For example, when Levi Strauss wanted to enter into the French market, it contracted with the French company Cacharel to produce a certain volume of products to specification and put Levi's name on them, allowing Levi to broaden its global marketing base without investing in overseas plants and equipment. After establishing a solid base, the domestic company may switch to a joint venture or direct investment, explained below.

Although, until recently, contract manufacturing has been limited to the production of goods, it now applies to services as well. Services such as telecommunications, Internet access, and cellphone services are some examples.

Joint Ventures

Joint ventures are somewhat similar to licensing agreements. In a joint venture, the domestic company buys part of a foreign company or joins with a foreign company to create a new entity. A joint venture is a quick and relatively inexpensive way to enter the global market. It can also be very risky. Many joint ventures fail; others fall victim to takeovers, in which one partner buys out the other.

Sometimes countries have required local partners in order to establish a business in their country. China, for example, had this requirement in a number of industries until recently. Thus, a joint venture was the only way to enter the market. Joint ventures help reduce risks by sharing costs and technology. Often joint ventures will bring different strengths together from each member. In a successful joint venture, both parties gain valuable skills from the alliance.

joint venture
An agreement in which a domestic company buys part of a foreign company or joins with a foreign company to create a new entity.

Foreign Direct Investment

Active ownership of a foreign company or of overseas manufacturing or marketing facilities is referred to as foreign direct investment (also referred to as direct foreign investment). Direct investors have either a controlling or a large minority interest in the company. Thus, they stand to receive the greatest potential reward but also face the greatest potential risks. A company may make a foreign direct investment by acquiring an interest in an existing company or by building new facilities. It might do so

foreign direct investment
Active ownership of a foreign company or of manufacturing or marketing facilities in a foreign country.

Creating the Future of Business

CHRIS AND MARTIN HERRINGTON, HERRINGTON TEDDY BEARS

Chris and Martin Herrington grew up in Montréal, Québec. From Montréal to international prominence, Chris and Martin Herrington have taken the world by storm with something as simple as plush teddy bears. In October 2011, the company announced an initial public offering of shares to raise capital to increase its already enormous Internet presence and grow the retail and distribution end of the business.

In the early 1980's Chris Herrington, then a waiter for The Cheesecake Factory in Marina del Rey, California, was asked to create t-shirts for the staff. When a co-worker asked if he would make a custom t-shirt to fit her teddy bear with the intent to display it as a mascot, his future changed. He dressed the teddy bear in a miniature version of one of his designs, and the idea for Herrington Teddy Bears was born. Chris was overwhelmed by how many people wanted to buy the bear. The operation soon expanded into a line of branded bears and other advertising and promotional items for companies like Giorgio Beverly-Hills, the Hard Rock Café, Mercedes-Benz, and Trump Hotels and Casinos. In 1992 his brother Martin joined him as Partner and CFO.

Martin Herrington embodies the same entrepreneurial spirit as his brother Chris. At only five years old, he started his first business selling plastic "milk bottles" of water in his neighbourhood. He helped pay for university to graduate with a Bachelor of Commerce degree by shoveling sidewalks and mowing lawns through high school. Martin helped Chris build the company from a small garage

in Venice, California, to its current 10,000 square foot facility in Irvine, California.

A truly international operation, Herrington Teddy Bears' products are manufactured with meticulous attention to quality and detail in a dedicated partner manufacturing facility in China. They are shipped to 51 different countries around the world as collectibles for a loyal following of collectors, and as powerful corporate brand-building tools. Beyond marketing strength, one of the other keys to the company's success is its ability to produce low minimum quantities with quick turnaround times, offering flexibility to its customer.

In 1997, Chris, the chief teddy bear designer for the company, introduced his own signature branded bears, Harry & Hannah Herrington, and even published his first children's book featuring Harry & Hannah. Clearly, global domination in branded teddy bears wasn't enough. In fact, the funds raised by taking the company public will allow it to introduce its "new state of the art, high tech line of social media interactive teddy bears and plush toys." There seems to be no end to what they can do!

Thinking Critically

1. To expand a company globally, there are a number of options. Herrington has chosen to partner with a manufacturing facility in China to produce its products. What might be the strategic reason(s) for doing this?
2. Typically when quality is a key product feature, outsourcing is risky. Can you think of other options?
3. The company's product line is expanding in exciting new areas. What other directions could they take the product line?

SOURCES: www.herringtonteddybears.com; www.prlog.com Oct 5, 2011. Used with permission from Herrington Teddy Bears.

Concept Check

Discuss several ways that a company can enter international trade.

Explain the concept of countertrade.

because it has trouble transferring some resources to a foreign operation or obtaining that resource locally. One important resource is personnel, especially managers. If the local labour market is tight, the company might buy an entire foreign company and retain all its employees instead of paying higher salaries than competitors.

Sometimes companies make direct investments because they can find no suitable local partners. Direct investments also help businesses avoid the communication problems and conflicts of interest that can arise with joint ventures. IBM, for instance, insists on total ownership of its foreign investments, because it does not want to share control with local partners.

Countertrade

countertrade
A form of international trade in which part or all of the payment for goods or services is in the form of other goods and services.

International trade does not always involve cash. Today, **countertrade** is a fast-growing way to conduct international business. In countertrade, part or all of the payment for goods or services is in the form of other goods or services. Countertrade is a form of barter (swapping goods for goods), an age-old practice whose origins have been traced back to cave dwellers.

Atwood Richards Inc. is the world's largest countertrade organization. Atwood reviews a client's unsold products and issues trade credits in exchange. The credits can be used to obtain other products and services. Atwood has acquired everything from hotel rooms and airline tickets to television advertising time, forklift trucks, carpeting, wood pulp, envelopes, steel castings, or satellite tracking systems.

LO5   FOSTERING GLOBAL TRADE

Governments and international financial organizations work hard to increase global trade, as we explain in this section.

Concept *in Action*

The Corruption of Foreign Public Officials Act has three offences, including bribing a foreign public official. The act allows for prosecution of anyone who bribes the official to obtain or retain an advantage in the course of doing business. If it is customary to bribe an official to do business in that country, how can a Canadian company compete without bribing?

THE CANADIAN PRESS(MARIO BEAUREGARD)

Concept *in Action*

In 2010, North America accounted for 37 percent of global tablet revenue, and its sales are expected to triple by 2015. By 2014, Asia-Pacific region will account for more than half (about 58 percent) of global tablet revenue.[12] What other consumer products have an international appeal?

Antidumping Laws

Canadian companies don't always get to compete on an equal basis with foreign companies in international trade. To level the playing field, the federal government has passed antidumping laws. Dumping is the practice of charging a lower price for a product (perhaps below cost) in foreign markets than in the company's home market. The company might be trying to win foreign customers, or it might be seeking to get rid of surplus goods.

When the variation in price can't be explained by differences in the cost of serving the two markets, dumping is suspected. Most industrialized countries have antidumping regulations. They are especially concerned about *predatory dumping*, the attempt to gain control of a foreign market by destroying competitors with impossibly low prices.

The legal test for product dumping is based on two criteria. First, the product must be priced unfairly low—either below its production costs or below the selling price in the home country. Second, the imported product must harm the domestic industry.

The World Trade Organization

The World Trade Organization (WTO) replaced the old General Agreement on Tariffs and Trade (GATT), which was created in 1948. The GATT contained extensive loopholes that enabled countries to evade agreements to reduce trade barriers. Today, all WTO members must comply fully with all agreements under the Uruguay Round. The WTO also has an effective dispute settlement procedure with strict time limits to resolve disputes.

The WTO has emerged as the world's most powerful institution for reducing trade barriers and opening markets. The advantage of WTO membership is that member countries lower trade barriers among themselves. Countries that don't belong must negotiate trade agreements individually with all their trading partners. In August of 2012, Russia was one of the last major global economies to become a member of the WTO.

dumping
The practice of charging a lower price for a product in foreign markets than in the company's home market.

World Trade Organization (WTO)
An organization established by the Uruguay Round in 1994 to oversee international trade, reduce trade barriers, and resolve disputes among member nations.

The World Trade Organization tracks the latest trade developments between countries and regions around the world. For the most recent global trading news, visit the WTO's site, www.wto.org

Sustainable Business, Sustainable World

COCA-COLA

If you go to www.coca-cola.com, you will see front and centre a large banner that reads: "Help Us Protect the Polar Bear's Arctic Home" with a link to "join us." The polar bear has been an iconic figure in Coca-Cola ads since 1922 and it has also long been a symbol of what is happening to our world because of global warming. The Coca-Cola Company has partnered with the World Wildlife Fund to raise awareness and funds to create an Arctic refuge for polar bears. As a symbol of its commitment, beginning in November 2011 Coca-Cola changed its red cans to polar bear white for the first time ever.

Why is an international company with the size and global reach of Coca-Cola interested in protecting polar bears? Is this a PR effort? Actually, it is a very small part of what Coca-Cola is doing to help create a more sustainable world. As an international company, its reach is very wide and thus the positive impact it can have is far-reaching as well. Coca-Cola was, in fact, named to the 2011 list of the Global 100 Most Sustainable Corporations in the World, ranking 78th, one of only 13 US and 21 North American companies.

On the Coca-Cola website you'll also see "Sustainability" as a prominent page link, second only to "Our Company." In its annual sustainability review, which is downloadable from the front page of the sustainability section of the website, it explains the system-wide sustainability framework, developed in 2007, that Coca-Cola uses to make a positive difference in the world. This framework is called "LIVE POSITIVELY" and consists of seven core areas: beverage benefits, active healthy living, community, energy efficiency and climate protection, sustainable packaging, water stewardship, and workplace. In its words: "We created LIVE POSITIVELY ... to bring structure and visibility to the sustainability programs that already existed in our company ... it is a way for us to holistically think about

sustainability and keep us focused on driving business growth while acting with future generations in mind."

One example of a Coca-Cola effort in an area where it clearly could otherwise have a very negative impact internationally, is in water stewardship. Lack of clean drinking water is a very real problem in many parts of the world, and making a beverage like Coca-Cola clearly uses a great deal of water. Their goal is to "work to safely return to nature and communities an amount of water equivalent to what we use in our beverages and their production." That's a big goal, but Coca-Cola uses its own 3Rs to reach this goal: Reducing water use by improving water efficiency; Recycling water through improved wastewater treatment; and Replenishing the water used through support of healthy watersheds and sustainable community water programs. In fact, it is again working with the WWF to help conserve seven of the world's most critical freshwater river basins.

This is the kind of effort that you'd hope for and expect from a company operating on an international scale—truly international sustainable efforts.

Thinking Critically

1. Is Coca-Cola a company that instantly comes to mind when you think of sustainability? Check out the websites of companies you wouldn't instantly think of—you may change your perception. If you don't see a commitment to sustainability, what actions do you feel they could be taking?
2. Is the company you work for making efforts to be sustainable? How do you feel about that?

SOURCES: http://www.thecoca-colacompany.com and http://www.global100.org.

The World Bank and International Monetary Fund

Two international financial organizations are instrumental in fostering global trade. The **World Bank** offers low-interest loans to developing nations. Originally, the purpose of the loans was to help these nations build infrastructure such as roads, power plants, schools, drainage projects, and hospitals. Now the World Bank offers loans to help developing nations relieve their debt burdens. To receive the loans, countries must pledge to lower trade barriers and aid private enterprise. In addition to making loans, the World Bank is a major source of advice and information for developing nations.

The **International Monetary Fund (IMF)** was founded in 1945, one year after the creation of the World Bank, to promote trade through financial cooperation and eliminate trade barriers in the process. The IMF makes short-term loans to member nations that are unable to meet their budgetary expenses and operates as a lender of last resort for troubled nations. In exchange for these emergency loans, IMF lenders frequently obtain significant commitments from the borrowing nations to address the problems that led to the crises. These steps can include curtailing imports or even devaluing the currency.

Some global financial problems do not have a simple solution. One option would be to pump a lot more funds into the IMF, giving it enough resources to bail out troubled countries and put them back on their feet. In effect, the IMF would be turned into a real lender of last resort for the world economy.

World Bank
An international bank that offers low-interest loans, as well as advice and information, to developing nations.

International Monetary Fund (IMF)
An international organization, founded in 1945, that promotes trade, makes short-term loans to member nations, and acts as a lender of last resort for troubled nations.

HOT _inks_

Gain additional insight into the workings of the International Monetary Fund at
www.imf.org

Concept *in Action*

Based in Toulouse, France, Airbus is one of the world's top commercial aircraft manufacturers, operating design and manufacturing facilities in Europe, Japan, China, and the United States. The airliner's current product lineup of 12 jet-aircraft types, ranging from 100 seats to 555 seats, is heavy competition for Boeing, a top U.S. airline company with which Airbus has ongoing subsidy-related disputes. What is the World Trade Organization's role in settling disputes between competing multinational corporations?

TIM JENNER/SHUTTERSTOCK

The danger of counting on the IMF, though, is the "moral hazard" problem. Investors would come to assume that the IMF would bail them out and might therefore be tempted to take bigger and bigger risks in emerging markets, leading to the possibility of even deeper financial crises in the future.

THREATS IN THE GLOBAL MARKETPLACE

LO6

To be successful in a foreign market, companies must fully understand the foreign environment in which they plan to operate. Politics, cultural differences, and the economic environment can often represent pitfalls in the global marketplace. International trade is carried out by both businesses and governments—as long as no one puts up trade barriers. In general, trade barriers keep companies from selling to one another in foreign markets. The major obstacles to international trade are natural barriers, tariff barriers, and non-tariff barriers.

Political Considerations

Governments can use many tools to restrict trade. The political structure of a country can jeopardize a foreign producer's success in international trade.

Intense nationalism, for example, can lead to difficulties. Nationalism is the sense of national consciousness that boosts the culture and interests of one country over those of all other countries. Strongly nationalistic countries, such as Iran and New Guinea, often discourage investment by foreign companies. In other, less radical forms of nationalism, the government may take actions to hinder foreign operations.

The Canadian Radio-television and Telecommunication Commission (CRTC) has established a quota system that requires Canadian content to air on AM/FM radio stations and television. For example, on AM/FM radio, the requirement is 35 percent of all music aired each week must be Canadian—specifically, 35 percent Canadian music broadcast between 6:00 a.m. and

nationalism
A sense of national consciousness that boosts the culture and interests of one country over those of all other countries.

Concept *Check*

Describe the purpose and role of the WTO.

What are the roles of the World Bank and the IMF in world trade?

Explain how political factors can affect international trade.

Describe several cultural factors that a company involved in international trade should consider.

How can economic conditions affect trade opportunities?

6:00 p.m from Monday to Friday. To be considered "Canadian," two of the following criteria of the MAPL system must be satisfied:

- Music—composed entirely by a Canadian
- Artist—the music and/or lyrics performed by a Canadian
- Production—live performance that is recorded entirely in Canada or performed entirely in Canada and broadcast live
- Lyrics—written wholly by a Canadian[13]

In a hostile climate, a government might *expropriate* a foreign company's assets, taking ownership and compensating the former owners. Even worse is *confiscation*, when the owner receives no compensation. This happened during rebellions in several African nations during the 1990s and 2000s.

Cultural Differences

Central to any society is the common set of values shared by its citizens that determine what is socially acceptable. Culture underlies the family, educational system, religion, and social class system. The network of social organizations generates overlapping roles and status positions. These values and roles have a tremendous effect on people's preferences and thus on marketers' options. Inca Kola, a fruity, greenish-yellow carbonated drink, is the largest-selling soft drink in Peru. It was invented in Peru and contains only fruit indigenous to the country. Despite being described as "liquid bubble gum," the drink has become a symbol of national pride and heritage. A local consumer of about a six-pack a day says, "I drink Inca Kola because it makes me feel like a Peruvian." He tells his young daughter, "This is our drink, not something invented overseas. It is named for your ancestors, the great Inca warriors."

Language is another important aspect of culture. Marketers must take care in selecting product names and translating slogans and promotional messages so as not to convey the wrong meaning. For example, Mitsubishi Motors had to rename its Pajero model in Spanish-speaking countries because in Spanish, the term refers to a sexual activity. The MR2 model from Toyota Motors dropped the number 2 in France because the combination sounds like a French swear word. The literal translation of Coca-Cola in Chinese characters means "bite the wax tadpole."

Each country has its own customs and traditions that determine business practices and influence negotiations with foreign customers. In many countries, personal relationships are more important than financial considerations. For instance, skipping social engagements in Mexico might lead to lost sales. Negotiations in Japan often include long evenings of dining, drinking, and entertaining; only after a close personal relationship has been formed do business negotiations begin. See Exhibit 5.3 for some cultural "dos and don'ts."

The Economic Environment

The level of economic development varies considerably worldwide, ranging from countries where everyday survival is a struggle (such as Sudan and Eritrea), to those that are highly developed (such as Switzerland and Japan). In general, complex, sophisticated industries are found in developed countries, and more basic industries are found in less developed nations. Average family incomes are higher in the more developed countries than in the least developed markets. Larger incomes mean greater purchasing power and demand not only for consumer goods and services but also for the machinery and workers required to produce consumer goods.

Business opportunities are usually better in countries that have an economic **infrastructure** in place. Infrastructure is the basic institutions and public facilities on which an economy's development depends. It includes the money and banking system that provides the major investment loans to our nation's businesses; the educational system that turns out the incredible variety of skills; fundamental research on the best production methods and their implementation; the extensive transportation and

infrastructure
The basic institutions and public facilities on which an economy's development depends.

Exhibit 5.3 Cultural Dos and Don'ts

DO:

- Always present your business card with both hands in Asian countries. It should also be right-side up and print-side showing so that the recipient can read it as it is being presented. If you receive a business card, accept it with gratitude and examine it carefully. Don't quickly put it into your pocket.

- Dress to the culture. If you are in Switzerland, always wear a coat and tie. In other countries, wearing a coat and tie might be viewed as overdressing and make you appear snobbish.

- Use a "soft sell" and subtle approach when promoting a product in Japan. Japanese people do not feel comfortable with North America's traditional hard-selling style.

- Understand the role of religion in business transactions. In Muslim countries, Ramadan is a holy month when most people fast. During this time, everything slows down, including business.

- Have a local person available to interpret culturally and linguistically any advertising that you plan to do. When American Airlines wanted to promote its new first-class seats in the Mexican market, it translated the "Fly in Leather" campaign literally, which meant "Fly Naked" in Spanish.

- In Chile, expect women to greet you with a kiss on the cheek even if you are a stranger. Offer a kiss on each cheek after you become friends with a French woman (this applies to males and females).

- In Switzerland, offer three kisses, starting on the left cheek and alternating.

- Run late for your appointment in some Latin American countries.

- Always be on time for your appointment in Germany.

DON'T:

- Glad-hand (greet too effusively), back-slap, or use first names on your first business meeting in Asia. If you do, you will be considered a lightweight.

- Fill a wine glass to the top if dining with a French businessperson. It is considered completely uncouth.

- Begin your first business meeting in Asia by talking business. Be patient. Let your clients get to know you first.

- Kiss someone on the cheek or pat them on the shoulder in Spain before you get to know them.

---

communications systems—highways, railroads, airports, canals, telephones, Internet sites, postal systems, television stations—that link almost every piece of our geography into one market; the energy system that powers our factories; and, of course, the market system itself, which brings our nation's goods and services into our homes and businesses. When we think about how our own economy works, we tend to take our infrastructure for granted.

Natural Barriers

Natural barriers to trade can be either physical or cultural. For instance, even though raising beef in the relative warmth of Argentina might cost less than raising beef in the bitter cold of Siberia, the cost of shipping the beef from South America to Siberia might drive the price too high. *Distance* is thus one of the natural barriers to international trade.

Some other natural barriers include

- *language differences*—people who can't communicate effectively might not be able to negotiate trade agreements or might ship the wrong goods;
- *cultural differences*—companies that wish to pursue business with countries whose culture is different from theirs must consider these differences and adjust their operations, products, services, and so on, to account for the differences; and
- *legal and regulatory differences*—Canadian companies have to consider not only Canadian laws and regulations but also the laws and regulations of the host country.

Expanding Around the Globe

DELL'S SUCCESS IN CHINA TELLS TALE OF A MATURING MARKET

In 2003, Dell Inc. rejected a plan to sell computers online in China. The personal-computer giant worried that most Chinese consumers didn't use credit cards and were too poor to become big web shoppers.

In 2004, Dell executives in China showed their bosses a startling statistic: More than 90 million people in the country's coastal cities have access to the Internet at home or work. "We're missing a great opportunity," William J. Amelio, Dell's top executive in Asia, recalls thinking.

Today, online sales account for about 6 percent of Dell's orders in China and are becoming a big part of the company's push to shake up the Chinese computer industry the way it did in the United States a decade ago. In China, Dell faced repeated warnings that its strategy—which relies on sophisticated computer buyers willing to purchase a product sight unseen—wouldn't work. But by first going after business customers and then pushing into the consumer market, Dell has become China's third-largest seller of PCs, behind two Chinese rivals, with an 8 percent market share.

Dell has learned some new tricks in China. Rather than create a joint venture with a Chinese company, it waited to form a wholly owned subsidiary that cultivated close ties with a regional government. And it boosted its reputation in the region by teaching quality-checking and just-in-time manufacturing skills to locals.

Dell stuck to its playbook, concentrating initially on business and institutional buyers who are most familiar with PCs and tend to be the most profitable clients. In China, as in Europe, it started out selling high-margin products, such as server computers, and gradually added less pricey desktop and notebook PCs. Most of its orders are taken by telephone sales representatives who work at a call centre in Xiamen, a city bigger than Dallas, Texas, on China's southeast coast. In nine other Chinese cities, Dell has sales representatives who visit large business and government customers, sending orders back to colleagues in Xiamen.

Thinking Critically

1. Do you think that Dell would have been more successful if it had entered into a joint venture with a Chinese company? Why?
2. Do you think that Dell should open a sales force to call on businesses in North America?

SOURCE: Evan Ramstad and Gary McWilliams, "For Dell, Success in China Tells Tale of Maturing Market," *Wall Street Journal*, July 5, 2005, pp. A1, A8. Dow Jones & Co Copyright 2005 Reproduced with permission of DOW JONES & COMPANY, INC. via Copyright Clearance Center.

Tariff Barriers

tariff
A tax imposed on imported goods.

A tariff is a tax imposed by a nation on imported goods. It might be a charge per unit, such as per barrel of oil or per new car; it might be a percentage of the value of the goods, such as 5 percent of a $500,000 shipment of shoes; or it might be a combination. No matter how it is assessed, any tariff makes imported goods more costly, so they are less able to compete with domestic products.

protective tariffs
Tariffs that are imposed to make imports less attractive to buyers than domestic products.

Protective tariffs make imported products less attractive to buyers than domestic products. The United States, for instance, has at times imposed protective tariffs on imported softwood from Canada. On the other side of the world, Japan imposes a tariff on U.S. cigarettes that makes them cost 60 percent more than Japanese brands. U.S. tobacco companies believe they could get as much as a third of the Japanese market if there were no tariffs on cigarettes. With tariffs, they have less than 2 percent of the market.

ARGUMENTS FOR AND AGAINST TARIFFS Tariffs are not a new concept. For centuries, industries have tried to protect their products and services and countries have used tariffs to protect employment. The main argument against tariffs is that they discourage free trade, and free trade lets the principle of comparative advantage work most efficiently. The main argument for tariffs is that they protect domestic businesses and workers.

One of the oldest arguments in favour of protectionism is the *infant industry argument*. By protecting new domestic industries from established foreign competitors, so this argument goes, a tariff can give a struggling industry time to become an effective competitor.

A second argument for tariffs is the *job protection argument*. Supporters—especially unions—say we should use tariffs to keep foreign labour from taking away Canadian jobs. Canadian jobs are lost, they say, when low-wage countries sell products at lower prices than those charged in Canada. The higher prices charged by the Canadian companies help pay the higher wages of Canadian workers.

An argument against tariffs is that they cause an increase in prices, thereby decreasing consumers' purchasing power. Over the long run, tariffs can also be too protective if they cause domestic companies to stop innovating and fall behind technologically. An example is the Italian car builder Fiat. Protective tariffs helped keep Fiat's Italian market share very high, but as Europe's trade barriers fell, foreign competitors moved in with cars that Italian drivers preferred. Fiat is now desperately spending billions of dollars to revamp its factories and design new models.

Non-Tariff Barriers

Governments use many tools in addition to tariffs to restrict trade. Among them are import quotas, embargoes, customs regulations, and exchange controls.

IMPORT QUOTAS One type of non-tariff barrier is the import quota, or limit on the quantity of a certain good that can be imported. The goal of setting quotas is to limit imports to the optimum amount of a given product.

EMBARGOES A complete ban against importing or exporting a product is an embargo. For instance, Canada does not allow the export of "military goods to countries that threaten Canada's security, are under UN (United Nations) sanction, are threatened by internal or external conflict, and/or abuse the human rights of their citizens."[14]

CUSTOMS REGULATIONS In a more subtle move, a country may make it hard for foreign products to enter its markets by establishing customs regulations that are different from generally accepted international standards, such as requiring bottles to be litre size rather than quart size. France seems particularly adept at using this tactic. For example, to reduce imports of foreign VCRs, at one time France ruled that all VCRs had to enter through the customs station at Poitiers. This customs house was located in the middle of the country, was woefully understaffed, and was open only a few days each week. What's more, the few customs agents at Poitiers opened each package separately to inspect the merchandise. Within a few weeks, imports of VCRs in France came to a halt.

EXCHANGE CONTROLS Exchange controls are laws that require a company earning foreign exchange (foreign currency) from its exports to sell the foreign exchange to a control agency, usually a central bank. For example, assume that Rolex, a Swiss company, sells 300 watches to a Canadian retailer for $120,000. If Switzerland had exchange controls, Rolex would have to sell its Canadian dollars to the Swiss central bank and would receive Swiss francs. If Rolex wants to buy goods from abroad, it must go to the central bank and buy foreign exchange (currency). By controlling the amount of foreign exchange sold to companies, the government controls the amount of products that can be imported. Limiting imports and encouraging exports helps a government to create a favourable balance of trade.

Concept in Action

Tariffs on the imported goods arriving on this foreign ship make the products more expensive than those of Canadian competitors. What are some reasons that countries would impose a tariff on an import?

import quota
A limit on the quantity of a certain good that can be imported; also known as a *quantitative restraint*.

embargo
A total ban on imports or exports of a product.

customs regulations
Regulations on products that are different from generally accepted international standards.

exchange controls
Laws that require a company earning foreign exchange (foreign currency) from its exports to sell the foreign exchange to a control agency, such as a central bank.

Concept Check

Discuss the concept of natural trade barriers.

Describe several tariff and non-tariff barriers to trade.

THE FUTURE OF THE GLOBAL MARKETPLACE

In this section, we will examine several underlying trends that will continue to propel the dramatic growth in world trade. These trends are Canada's expanding importance on the international stage; Canada's search for new and undertapped markets; and growth in the emerging markets of Brazil, Russia, India, and China.

Canada—Increasing Its Prominence in the World

Canada is one of the world's most affluent and dynamic countries. Its stable government, business-friendly restrictions that protect both business and consumers, and its relatively young population has increased its importance on the world stage. According to the International Monetary Fund, Canada's GDP per capita surpassed that of the United States by $3000 in 2011.[15]

Canada has outpaced most other countries, with energy, mining, and financial services leading the way. Our financial system is the most stable in the world. Unlike other countries that were negatively affected by the economic crises of 2008 and 2011/2012, Canada was relatively unscathed. Few people had their homes foreclosed, compared to the United States.

The governor of the Bank of Canada, Mark Carney, was appointed as the new chief of the Financial Stability Board (FSB) based in Switzerland. The FSB is the global banking regulator. This is a credit not only to Mr. Carney but also to the Canadian financial system and our regulatory system.

Canada—Seeking New Markets

For some time, Canada has been seeking new markets for its goods and services. The financial crisis of 2008 and 2011/12 gave greater momentum to this effort, specifically in the Asian markets. Shifting the trade from a north/south direction to a west/east direction has opened up new markets for Canada on a scale that has not been seen for over 60 years.

The emerging Asian markets of China and India (discussed below) have welcomed foreign investment in the manufacturing and technology industries. For example, China's exports have boomed, largely thanks to foreign investment: lured by low labour costs, big manufacturers have surged into China to expand their production base and push down prices globally. Now manufacturers of all sizes, making everything from windshield wipers to washing machines to clothing, are scrambling either to reduce costs at home or to outsource more of what they make in cheaper locales.[16]

With this increase in economic activity in Asia, especially in the manufacturing sector, one of the most important factors of production is natural resources (specifically oil and gas). Acquisitions, joint ventures, and partnerships between Asian companies and Canadian producers is becoming routine so that Asia can secure a low-risk and predictable source of energy. In 2011 alone there were five major deals announced.

The Emergence of BRIC Economic Power

Brazil, Russia, India, and China (BRIC) are the fastest growing and largest emerging market economies today. With approximately three billion people, they have contributed to most of the growth of GDP worldwide. Many economists predict that China will become the biggest economy in the world between 2030 and 2050.

Today, BRIC countries are seeing increasing investment. These countries have little in common other that their economic growth. If the analysts are correct, it is believed that China will lead in manufacturing, India in services, and Brazil and Russia in natural resources.

Concept *Check*

What are the reasons that Canada is increasing its importance in the world?

Why is it important for Canada to look for new markets?

What are opportunities and threats of the countries of BRIC to Canada?

GREAT IDEAS TO USE NOW

Continue Your Education

The writing is on the wall. Low-skilled jobs are rapidly disappearing in Canada. Canadian businesses know that to compete globally, they must find cheap labour for labour-intensive businesses. This means establishing plants in Mexico, Asia, or other places in the world where labour is inexpensive. It also means that unskilled or low-skilled Canadian workers will find it increasingly difficult to secure permanent jobs. By continuing your education, you can avoid falling into this very undesirable trap.

Study the Role of a Global Manager

Business is becoming more global, so chances are you might become a global manager. Start learning right now what this means and if it's right for you. The life of a global manager can be hectic, as these examples illustrate.

Top overseas performers at Secure Computing, a software developer, are treated to a dinner for two by Christine Hughes, senior vice-president of marketing and business development. Ms. Hughes supervises a 24-person staff in North and South America and Asia. One of her missions on trips is to combat the tendency of foreign-based employees to think the organization is "North American-centric," she says. Because they take much longer flights than the typical corporate road warrior, global managers wind up turning airplanes into offices. When she is overseas, Ms. Hughes has her office ship a package of paperwork overnight to her, so she can work on the flight home.

Indeed, a global manager's workday never really ends. Wherever he or she is, it's still business hours somewhere else. When she's working in Australia, Ms. Hughes usually ends her day in a hotel room, talking with someone at the home office. "I'm on the phone until two in the morning dealing with issues," she says. "You just have to accept that."[17]

Your position might not be as hectic as that of Hughes, but you can easily see the differences between a person who is a global manager and one who is not. Is this the life for you? Would you enjoy living abroad? Can you adapt easily to other cultures?

One way to see if you might be cut out to be a global manager is to spend some time abroad. The ideal situation is to find a job overseas during the summer months. This experience will help you decide if you want to be a global manager. Also, it will look good on your resumé. One source of international jobs information is www. internationaljobs.org.

If you can't find a job overseas, save your money and travel abroad. Seeing how others live and work will broaden your horizons and give you a more enlightened view of the world. Even international travel can help you decide what you want to do in the global marketplace.

Summary of Learning Outcomes

LO1 Show why global trade is important to Canada, and how it is measured.

International trade improves relations with friends and allies, eases tensions among nations, helps bolster economies, raises people's standard of living, and improves the quality of life. With Canada's small population, to meet the economies of scale, we must produce more than we can consume.

Two concepts important to global trade are the balance of trade (the difference in value between a country's exports and its imports over some period) and the balance of payments (the difference between a country's total payments to other countries and its total receipts from other countries). Canada currently has both a positive balance of trade and a positive balance of payments. Another import concept is the exchange rate, which is the price of one country's currency in terms of another country's currency. Currencies float up and down based upon the supply and demand for each currency. Sometimes a government steps in and devalues its currency relative to those of other countries.

Multinational corporations have several advantages. First, they can frequently sidestep restrictive trade and licensing restrictions because they have headquarters in more than one country. Multinationals can also move their operations from one country to the next, depending on which location offers more favourable economic conditions. In addition, multinationals can tap into a vast source of technological expertise by drawing on the knowledge of a global workforce.

LO2 Explain why nations trade.

Nations trade because they gain by doing so. The principle of comparative advantage states that each country should specialize in the goods it can produce most readily and cheaply and trade them for those that other countries can produce most readily and cheaply. The result is more goods at lower prices than if each country produced everything it needed. Free trade allows trade among nations without government restrictions.

LO3 List some of the international economic communities.

International economic communities reduce trade barriers among themselves while often establishing common tariffs and other trade barriers toward non-member countries. The best-known economic communities are the NAFTA, European Union, ASEAN, and Mercosur.

LO4 Explain how companies can enter the global marketplace.

There are a number of ways to enter the global market. The major ones are exporting, licensing, contract manufacturing, joint ventures, and direct investment.

The World Trade Organization created by the Uruguay Round has dramatically lowered trade barriers worldwide. For the first time, a trade agreement covers services, intellectual property rights, and exchange controls. The World Bank makes loans to developing nations to help build infrastructures. The International Monetary Fund makes loans to member nations that cannot meet their budgetary expenses. Despite efforts to expand trade, terrorism can have a negative impact on trade growth.

LO5 Discuss how governments and institutions foster world trade.

Domestic companies entering the international arena need to consider the politics, economies, and culture of the countries where they plan to do business. For example, government trade policies can be loose or restrictive, countries can be nationalistic, and governments can change. As well, many products fail because companies don't understand the culture of the country where they are trying to sell their products. Some developing countries also lack an economic infrastructure, which can make it very difficult to conduct business.

The three major barriers to international trade are natural barriers, such as distance and language; tariff barriers, or taxes on imported goods; and non-tariff barriers. The non-tariff barriers to trade include import quotas, embargoes, customs regulations, and exchange controls. The main argument against tariffs is that they discourage free trade and keep the principle of comparative advantage from working efficiently. The main argument for using tariffs is that they help protect domestic companies, industries, and workers.

LO6 Explain some of the threats in the global marketplace.

Three of the major trends are Canada's growing importance on the world's stage, Canada's search for new markets, and the emergence of BRIC.

LO7 List some of the trends in the global marketplace.

Key Terms

absolute advantage 136
Association of Southeast Asian Nations (ASEAN) 139
balance of payments 133
balance of trade 133
contract manufacturing 140
countertrade 142
customs regulations 149
devaluation 135
dumping 143
embargo 149
European Union (EU) 138
exchange controls 149
exporting 140
exports 132
floating exchange rates 135
foreign direct investment 141
free trade 136
free trade zone 137
global vision 130

import quota 149
imports 132
infrastructure 146
International Monetary Fund (IMF) 144
joint venture 141
licensing 140
Mercosur 137
multinational corporations 131
nationalism 145
North American Free Trade Agreement (NAFTA) 137
preferential tariff 137
principle of comparative advantage 136
protectionism 136
protective tariffs 148
tariff 148
trade deficit 133
trade surplus 133
World Bank 144
World Trade Organization (WTO) 143

Experiential Exercises

1. Know the exchange rate between the Canadian dollar and the currencies of the countries you plan to visit before you go. Go to www.cnnfn.com/markets/currencies for the latest quotations. Keep up with the changing rates by reading your local paper. Explain the implication in the change of the exchange rate for your next vacation to Mexico.

2. When you travel, avoid changing money at airports, train stations, and hotels. These places usually have the worst rates. Ask local people where they change money. Locals know where the best rates are.

3. Discuss the rise of the economies of the BRIC nations. Investigate what the future might hold for these countries from a political and economic perspective.

4. How can a country's traditions create barriers to trade? Ask foreign students to describe such barriers in their country. Students should give examples of problems that foreign businesspeople might experience with Canadian customs.

5. Should the United Kingdom be admitted to NAFTA? Why might Britain not wish to join?

6. Write a paper on how international economic communities might affect Canadian business.

7. What do you think is the best way for a small company to enter international trade? Why?

8. What impact have foreign multinationals had on the Canadian economy? Give some examples.

9. Identify some Canadian multinational companies that have been successful in world markets. How do you think they have achieved their success?

Review Questions

1. What is a global vision?

2. What is the importance of global business to Canada?

3. What impact has terrorism had on international trade?

4. Define exports and imports.

5. What is the balance of trade? What is the difference between a trade surplus and a trade deficit?

6. What is a country's balance of payments?

7. How do changing currency values affect imports and exports?

8. Why do nations trade? What is the principle of comparative advantage?

9. What are some natural barriers to trade?

10. What are tariffs? What are some arguments for and against tariffs?

11. What is the role of the World Bank and the International Monetary Fund?

12. What are some of the main international economic communities?

13. What are some options for Canadian companies that want to participate in the global marketplace?

CREATIVE THINKING CASE

Kobo in the International Market (Chapters/Indigo)

The book market is in significant flux; worldwide sales of physical books are decreasing and digital versions are becoming more popular. The Kobo e-reader was a Chapters/Indigo product, introduced in Toronto, in February 2009, by Indigo, and spun off as a separate company. Other investors included the Australian book and music seller RedGroup Retail and US chain Borders, both of which went bankrupt in 2011, and Cheung Kong Holdings (CKH) of Hong Kong. The Kobo e-reader has been battling with the Amazon Kindle and the Barnes & Noble Nook for market share. But the underlying companies have been struggling with the weight of their traditional business.

In 2011, Indigo Books & Music Inc. (Indigo) of Toronto made two major deals, ultimately selling their stake in the Kobo e-reader. In April, Indigo and CKH jointly invested $50 million (CAD) to fund a major international expansion for Kobo. CKH increased its ownership to 49 percent in the deal. Then in November, Indigo announced the selling of the assets of Kobo Inc. to Rakuten Inc. of Tokyo. Heather Reisman, CEO of Indigo, characterized the sale this way: "One big part of my decision to go ahead with the sale at this moment was because I believed firmly that the best future for Kobo would be with a partner of the scale of Rakuten."

It appears that the deal was primarily the result of cash needs at Indigo. Both their Indigo and Chapters stores posted reduced sales numbers for 2011 but in the second quarter alone, Kobo revenue was up 219 percent. Indigo retains a revenue stream from Kobo as part of the deal. Indigo has been moving its product mix away from books and toward gifts, games, and "lifestyle products." Indigo expected to net approximately $145 million from the sale of Kobo to invest in the new areas. Kobo appears poised for growth; Rakuten has the cash and long vision to compete in an increasingly tough market.

The big push for Kobo is in Europe, particularly Germany, which is the largest non-North American market for books. There, too, the trend has been away from paper books to electronic versions. Kobo not only battles the Amazon Kindle but also fights with tablets, such as the iPad, for market share. Kindle had the majority of the market in 2010 but the iPad 2 rewrote the category.

As of 2012, the e-reader market has become small potatoes compared to the tablet market, which is dominated by iPad. Both Kindle and Kobo have re-emphasized their product features and benefits. Now the web browser, which was originally a way of facilitating the downloading of books, has become a central feature. Kobo uses the Android operating system and essentially turns the Kobo Vox product into a low-priced tablet—not as good at all functions as the iPad 2, but much cheaper.

In the early days of the e-reader (the first was introduced in 1999), the products used a closed format, much like an early music player. If you owned a Kobo, you had to buy your books from Kobo. But, beginning with the Amazon Kindle App for iPhone, e-books have become increasingly open format. So far, the iPad operating system dominates the market, but Android systems have been making inroads. Much like the DOS vs Apple OS competition of the 1980s, Android appears to be relying on the open source advantage. The more manufacturers who have access to the Android operating system, the more innovations will be developed. Android phones had eclipsed the Apple iPhone in US market share by mid-2011.

Kobo pushes this envelope. Kobo books can be read on virtually any smartphone or tablet. By opening the context, Kobo becomes a bookseller to the world regardless of where the reader is or what technology is being used. Kobo e-readers are sold in 200 countries and books can be sold by Kobo to readers anywhere.

A quick scan of the job opportunities page at www.kobobooks.com gives a picture of the organization. Sales and service are worldwide, but the unit construction work is done in Toronto. Aside from marketing, sales reps, and vendor support staff, Kobo does its work from the home of Indigo and Kobo in Canada.

Physical devices such as the Kobo Vox must be supported locally, but this can be achieved through a network of retailers and independent technical companies. Manufacturing is achieved through international partnerships, but the business can be managed and developed from a hub city, such as Toronto.

Thinking Critically

1. What activities can be centralized when marketing a product globally? (Expand your list beyond those mentioned in the case.)

2. How is Kobo doing? Use Internet sources to investigate market penetration by number of countries and units sold. How has the e-book business done? (Differentiate from the e-reader.)

3. Has the sale of Kobo been good for Indigo?

SOURCES: Ashley, M. "Publishing Ebooks: Kindle, iPad, Nook, Kobo?" *Gizmodo*, July 13, 2010; CP, "E-Reader Kobo Closes $50 Million Financing to Aid International Growth," *Marketing, Advertising, Media and PR in Canada*, April 11, 2011; CP, "Kobo Needed a Bigger Investor to Grow, Reisman Says," *Marketing, Advertising, Media and PR in Canada*, November 9, 2011; Kobo, "About Kobo," Indigo Books and Music, http://www.kobobooks.com/about_us; Kobo, "Kobo Vox," Indigo Books and Music, http://www.kobobooks.com/about_us.

Part 2

Building a Business

Making the Connection

Entrepreneurship and Small Business

Now that we have looked at the different factors that make up the external environment of business—the context in which it operates—we can start to examine businesses themselves. We will start at the beginning of a business—with the people whose ideas create businesses. In this chapter, you will be learning about entrepreneurship and small business. What motivates people to start businesses, and what factors shape the business's success?

Individuals with a desire to start a business, whether they are people who simply want to start a small business of their own or entrepreneurs with a grander *vision*, need to see the big picture. Every business is affected by its external environment. All those environmental factors have an effect on each other, and they also affect whether the business meets its critical success factors. But it also works the other way around—entrepreneurs and small-business owners have a major effect on the economic environment as well. The decisions that these individuals make inside their businesses—whether marketing, finance, operations, or human resource decisions—will affect and be affected by the environment and, in turn, impact the degree to which the business achieves the critical success factors. This is their business—the whole integrative package. In fact, entrepreneurs and small-business owners experience the integrative nature of business more than other business people because, initially at least, they start off handling all aspects of the business and they are responsible for all of the critical success factors. They come up with the *innovative* idea that will *meet customer needs* and generate *value*; they need to find people to assist them who will be *committed* to its success and continue to encourage creativity. Everything is riding on them to achieve *financial performance*. And because this is so all-consuming, these individuals have to ensure that they put balance in their lives—to work hard but to still take care of their families and their health. This is a critical lesson for entrepreneurs: the integrative nature of business extends beyond their businesses to their personal lives as well. Since it creeps into life outside of work, the interconnections need to be viewed on a much broader level. You can't get more integrative than that! But you'd also have to look long and hard to find a job more rewarding than to see your own dreams come alive.

This chapter is full of examples of trends in the external environment affecting entrepreneurs and small-business owners—trends that provide the motivation and the ideas to fuel these businesses. Start by looking at why people start their own businesses. For example, in the *economic* environment, we see many corporations restructuring and downsizing their staff requirements, and so employees look to create their own businesses for greater job security. Many of these same corporations have begun to outsource various things they used to do in-house, thus creating an opportunity for small businesses (often the same people that were downsized!) to pick up the slack.

A trend that is both *social* and economic is the fact that there simply aren't as many advancement opportunities for women and minorities as there should be, despite the improvements made in this area, and so many of these people look to create their own opportunities in their own businesses. In fact, as you'll read in the chapter, women and minorities are increasing business ownership at a much faster rate than the national average. This, in turn, has led to many innovations in the workplace, such as more flexible scheduling, family-like environments, and more socially responsible business practices—changes favoured by women and, therefore, incorporated into their businesses. Furthermore, advancements in the *technological* environment have given people the ability to compete in areas previously inaccessible to them, giving rise to many new web-driven small businesses and entrepreneurial ventures. This trend in technology has, in turn, led to a social change in the demographics of small-business owners and entrepreneurs—they are often younger, as most technologically literate people are from a younger generation that grew up with this technology. Interestingly, as discussed in the chapter, Web-driven entrepreneurs are 25 percent more likely to be women.

The external environment also presents numerous ideas for new businesses. Often the competition isn't meeting customer needs sufficiently, and entrepreneurs see these holes and fill them. There are many examples of this in the chapter. One such example of this is Mike Pratt of OGIO International. Mike was frustrated with "trying to cram his gym bag into a too-small locker" and came up with a solution in The Original Locker Bag. At first, retailers weren't convinced of the product's appeal, but because it met the needs of the customer better than other products, the customer ensured its success through demand and forced the retailers' interest. Google is a similar example. The company's founders were not even looking to start a business—they just wanted to find a more efficient way than was currently available to search the infinite amount of information available on the Web. As we state later in the chapter, today's global economy rewards innovative, flexible companies that respond quickly to changes in the business environment. Because our economy today is so global, we have much more competition and, therefore, need to be more concerned with meeting customer needs. Smaller, more entrepreneurial businesses tend to be more flexible and innovative (one of our critical success factors, remember); they can respond more quickly as customer needs change in response to the external environment. But larger businesses can also encourage innovation and creativity by simulating this entrepreneurial environment within the organization through "intrapreneurship."

Thus, *marketing* decisions made by small-business owners and entrepreneurs tend to be innovative and responsive to customer needs; *human resource* decisions are also innovative and are often made to rectify problems these business owners saw in their previous jobs (see Christopher Halpin of Manna Catering Services in Chapter 8). But *financing* can be difficult for new businesses. However, with good ideas and well thought-out business plans that see the whole business in an integrative way, funds can be generated to cover *operations* and growth—just as Google was able to get their first $100,000 from a Sun Microsystems founder before Google Inc. even existed as a corporation. Perhaps the biggest challenge, though, is for small-business owners and entrepreneurs to handle adequately the first of the management functions—*planning*. As discussed in the chapter, economic factors, financial causes, and lack of experience are the most common reasons for business failure. These causes are interrelated and often directly related to poor management and inadequate planning. It is critical that, early on, the new business owner sees the integrative nature of all parts of the business, and plans accordingly.

chapter 6

Entrepreneurship and Small Business

LEARNING OUTCOMES

1 Explain entrepreneurship and the different types of entrepreneurs.

2 Describe the characteristics that successful entrepreneurs share.

3 Discuss how small businesses contribute to the Canadian economy.

4 Identify the opportunities and challenges facing owners of small businesses.

5 Summarize the first steps to take if you are starting your own business.

6 Discuss some of the programs available to help entrepreneurs and small-business owners.

7 List some of the trends that are shaping entrepreneurship and small-business ownership.

PROSKATE—VALUES ARE THE BUSINESS

A little girl trying on new skates looks up at Kenny Slywka. "My dad gets his skates here," she says, and Kenny smiles. That's ProSkate's success story in a nutshell—a reputation for customer service keeps customers and their families coming back. After well over a decade in the business, he's now putting the children of his early customers on skates.

When Slywka came from Waskatenau, Alberta, to Edmonton as a teenager to play hockey for the Sherwood Park Crusaders, he dreamed of playing in the NHL. But injuries held him back. When he couldn't play anymore, he turned his part-time job at ProSkate into a full-time career, eventually buying into the company and joining the management team. That was 1999; many years later, he still loves it. Slywka runs the operations, while majority partner Patrick Francey looks after marketing and strategy for their two stores. It's a small company of about 15 employees, but a major force in the market.

ProSkate is different from big-box chain sporting goods and hockey stores. It focuses on custom skate fitting and blade alignment to give its customers the best on-ice performance. The original owners of ProSkate brought ideas from figure skating to the hockey-skate business. Slywka and Francey have built on that foundation, evolving a set of core principles that centre on personal service, value, and product quality. (The ProSkate Service Values and Goals can be found on the company's website at www.proskate.ca/about.)

Focusing on goals sustains the entrepreneurial spirit and helps build a business. Entrepreneurs are motivated by an ideology, a reason for their businesses to exist, that guides them and their employees. At ProSkate, it's about listening and teaching to help customers get the best-fitting skates. Each skate brand is different, and every customer is different. Figure skating stores have recognized this for years, but hockey shops still sell brands by price, cachet, or endorser. ProSkate's niche is customers who want fit and performance.

Slywka often hears parents asking for bigger skates for their children when the problem is not the size of the skate, but its shape. All feet are shaped differently, and each brand builds its skates on a specific foot-shaped mould, called a "last." Kenny and his staff measure the customer's foot, then recommend a brand based on these measurements.

But the foot fit isn't the end of the conversation—staff members are taught to ask questions and be observant. High-end skates are stiff and need to be worn in. If a customer only plays once a week, stiff skates may never get broken in and fit well. The same goes for the smaller player trying to use a skate designed for a larger professional.

PHOTO COURTESY OF KENNY SLYWKA AND PROSKATE

With good fit, proper sizing and flex, the final discussion is about blade alignment. Unlike figure skates, where boots and blades are sold separately, hockey skates are sold as one piece. ProSkate removes the blades and adjusts them for optimal player performance. "Skates are manufactured on a production line; players aren't," Slywka says. "We will even go out to the rink with a screw gun and adjust figure or hockey skates on-site."

ProSkate maintains its business by educating its staff and its customers, and offering the experience of a perfectly fitted skate. The result: happy customers who spread the word.

THINKING CRITICALLY

As you read this chapter, consider the following questions:

1. What roles do entrepreneurs play in the Canadian economy?

2. What are the advantages and disadvantages of remaining a small business?

3. Are there other products that are, or could be, successfully sold based on a unique individual assessment of each customer?

SOURCE: Personal Interview with Kenny Slywka, 2011. Used with permission.

Many people catch the entrepreneurial bug; they are people from all backgrounds and age groups. Many recent graduates shun the "jacket and tie" corporate world to head out on their own. Downsized employees and mid-career executives form another large group of small-business owners. Retirees who worked for others all their lives might form the company they always wanted to own.

Companies started by entrepreneurs and small-business owners make significant contributions to the Canadian and global economies. These companies are hotbeds of innovation, taking leadership roles in technological change and the development of new goods and services. Small business is hard to define, because different agencies and researchers use different criteria. For our purposes, we define small businesses as being independently owned and operated, and not dominant in their market. Small businesses make a major contribution to our economy.

You might be one of the thousands of Canadians who are considering joining the ranks of business owners. As you read this chapter, you'll discover why entrepreneurship continues to be one of the hottest areas of business activity, as well as the characteristics you need to become a successful entrepreneur. We will offer guidelines for starting, managing, and growing a small business, and discuss their advantages and disadvantages. You will read about some of the programs available to help entrepreneurs and small-business owners, including the role of the Business Development Bank of Canada. Finally, we will explore the trends that are shaping entrepreneurship and small-business ownership.

Do you have what it takes to own a business? See the "Your Career as an Entrepreneur" section at the end of the chapter.

HOT *links*

Check out the Office of Small and Medium Enterprises on the Canadian government's website at
www.canada.gc.ca

LO1

ENTREPRENEURSHIP TODAY

From experiments with cardboard and tape, 20-something Mike Pratt pieced together a company that today is the top gear bag designer, OGIO. Frustrated with trying to cram his gym bag into a too-small locker, he went home and built a model of his ideal duffle bag. It fit into standard fitness-club lockers and kept all his supplies easily accessible in its rigid-framed interior. Retailers considered The Original Locker Bag too cumbersome. Customers, however, loved the bag that carried like a duffle bag and worked like a locker. In one weekend, they snapped up the 50 bags that Pratt convinced Foot Locker to take on consignment, and soon Pratt's bags were featured at various stores.

Not content to limit OGIO International's fortunes to one bag, Pratt and his employees "geared up" to produce duffles and backpacks with patented design features. His next breakthrough product was the Rig, a protective golf bag designed to go from airport to course that came to market just as golf's popularity began to rise. A complete line of golf bags followed, made in non-traditional colours and fabrics that appealed to younger players. "Today this cutting-edge company has revolutionized bag designs."[1]

Canada is blessed with a rich history of entrepreneurs. And their ranks continue to swell as up-and-coming entrepreneurs aspire to become the next Bill Gates. You may be familiar with some of the following: Grahame Ferguson (IMAX), Tim Horton (Tim Hortons), Christine Magee (Sleep Country Canada), Joe Mimran (Club Monaco), Heather Reisman (Chapters/Indigo), John McLaughlin (Canada Dry Ginger Ale), Thomas Ryan (five pin bowling), and Gideon Sundback (the zipper).[2]

Why has entrepreneurship remained a strong part of the foundation of the Canadian business system for so many years? Today's global economy rewards innovative, flexible companies that respond quickly to changes in the business environment. These companies are started by **entrepreneurs**, people with vision,

entrepreneurs
People with vision, drive, and creativity who are willing to take the risk of starting and managing a business to make a profit or greatly changing the scope and direction of an existing company.

drive, and creativity who are willing to take the risk of starting and managing a business to make a profit.

Entrepreneur or Small-Business Owner?

The term *entrepreneur* is often used in a broad sense to include most small-business owners. The two groups share some of the same characteristics, and we'll see that some of the reasons for becoming an entrepreneur or a small-business owner are very similar. But there is a difference between entrepreneurship and small-business management. Entrepreneurship involves taking a risk, either to create a new business or to greatly change the scope and direction of an existing one. Entrepreneurs typically are innovators who start companies to pursue their ideas for a new product or service. They are visionaries who spot trends.

Although entrepreneurs may be small-business owners, not all small-business owners are entrepreneurs. Small-business owners are managers, or people with technical expertise, who started a business or bought an existing business and made a conscious decision to stay small. For example, the proprietor of your local independent bookstore is a small-business owner. Jeff Bezos, founder of Amazon.com, also sells books. But Bezos is an entrepreneur: He developed a new model—a Web-based book retailer—that revolutionized the bookselling world and then moved on to change retailing in general. Entrepreneurs are less likely to accept the status quo and usually take a longer-term view than the small-business owner.

Creating the Future of Business

PAUL MAXWELL, MAXWELL'S MUSIC HOUSE

Paul Maxwell grew up loving music. He loved playing piano and guitar, and listening to his favourite rock bands playing live. He certainly had the talent to pursue music in university and even considered it, but decided to pursue a business degree instead. His motto, "Think of something you could do every day for the rest of your life, and find a way to make it profitable," sums up his career path perfectly. And isn't that what we all want out of life; to make a living doing what we love? Fortunately for Paul, his choices came together in perfect harmony (pardon the pun!) when he took an entrepreneurship course in 2007, in his fourth year of his business degree. It was then that he realized he had a passion for running his own business. "That's when it really started to come together, when I started to figure out what I wanted to do with my business degree," said Paul in an interview with his university alma mater.

Paul started off with a bang (or perhaps more appropriately, a cymbal clash), coming in 3rd place in the "LaunchPad $50K" Venture Creation Competition in 2007 with his new business idea, and was in the same year awarded the KPMG "Award in Entrepreneurship." His idea was to develop a space where musicians could practice and perform, and in May of 2008, after a lot of "blood, sweat and tears," he opened the doors of Maxwell's Music House, a licensed lounge near the Wilfrid Laurier University campus. The venue features live concerts and performances, as well as providing jam space, music lessons, workshops, and "rock star" music camps for aspiring musicians.

Paul has since been honoured with the Greater Kitchener-Waterloo Chamber of Commerce "Young Entrepreneur of the Year" award in both 2008 and 2010, the Junior Achievement "Best New

Business" award in 2010, the Impact "Arts Entrepreneur of the Year" award in 2010, and the KW Arts Awards "Leading Edge Arts" award in 2009. Not a bad start for a business student with a passion for music and an entrepreneurial spirit.

At the beginning, Paul could be found on location at all hours, putting in 100 hours per week in the first year (now about 60 hours per week) doing everything from booking classes and bands, to teaching piano, bartending during performances, and even carrying out janitorial duties. According to Paul: "Working 60 hours here is like working 30 hours at a regular job." Currently, Maxwell's Music House employs nine full-time staff and has several volunteers, including high school co-op students; it has hosted close to 1000 live performances, and has put over 300 students through its music school.

Paul regularly speaks at the university, inspiring other budding entrepreneurs to follow in his footsteps—take their passion and turn it into something profitable. In his words: "It's been very exciting to have all of my passions under one roof." See Paul, listen to his story in his own words, and get some valuable advice by checking out a recent CTV interview of Paul on YouTube: www.youtube.com/watch?v=mpXMoapZ7TQ.

Thinking Critically

1. Do you have a passion you could make profitable? What is it?
2. Do you believe Paul when he says that "working 60 hours" at his own business "is like working 30 hours at a regular job"? Why do you think he says that?
3. Do you have the drive to put in those long hours and take the risks necessary to see your passion come alive?

SOURCES: http://www.maxwellsmusichouse.ca, used with permission from Paul Maxwell; Wilfrid Laurier University website, http://www.wlu.ca.

Types of Entrepreneurs

Entrepreneurs fall into several categories: classic entrepreneurs, multipreneurs, and intrapreneurs.

CLASSIC ENTREPRENEURS Classic entrepreneurs are risk takers who start their own companies based on innovative ideas. Some classic entrepreneurs are *micro-preneurs*, who start small and plan to stay small. They often start businesses just for personal satisfaction and the lifestyle. Her passion for food led chemistry and psychology major Katrina Markoff to Paris to study at Le Cordon Bleu cooking school. She then took more classes while travelling in Europe, Asia, Australia, and Hawaii, attending cooking schools along the way. Intrigued by the many cultures and tastes she encountered, she returned home and started Vosges Chocolate, a specialty candy company that makes chocolates in unusual flavours, such as curry, spicy wasabi powder from Japan, sweet dulce de leche from Argentina, and a rare white honey from Hawaii. "People are traveling a lot more and wanting more interesting experiences with food," says Markoff. "I want people to take the time to appreciate what's going on in their mouth. What better way to do that than with curry and wasabi?"[3]

In contrast, *growth-oriented entrepreneurs* want their businesses to grow into major corporations. Most high-tech companies are formed by growth-oriented entrepreneurs. Jeff Bezos recognized that, with Internet technology, he could compete with large chains of traditional book retailers. Bezos' goal was to build his company into a high-growth enterprise—and he even chose a name that reflected this strategy: Amazon.com. Once his company succeeded in the book sector, Bezos applied his online retailing model to other product lines, from toys and house and garden items to tools, apparel, and services. In partnership with other retailers, Bezos is well on his way to making Amazon's motto—"Earth's Biggest Selection"—a reality.[4]

MULTIPRENEURS Then there are *multipreneurs*, entrepreneurs who start a series of companies. They thrive on the challenge of building a business and watching it grow. In fact, over half of the chief executives at *Inc. 500* companies say they would start another company if they sold their current one.

Jim Pattison is the Chairman, Chief Executive Officer, and sole owner of The Jim Pattison Group. The Jim Pattison Group started when Mr. Pattison purchased a General Motors automobile dealership. Today, the company has more than 30,000 employees with operations in various industries such as food services, packaging, distribution, manufacturing, communications, and entertainment, among others. The Jim Pattison Group, headquartered in Vancouver, BC, is Canada's third largest privately held company.[5]

intrapreneurs
Entrepreneurs who apply their creativity, vision, and risk taking within large corporations rather than starting companies of their own.

INTRAPRENEURS Some entrepreneurs don't own their own companies, but apply their creativity, vision, and risk taking within a large corporation. Called intrapreneurs, these employees enjoy the freedom to nurture their ideas and develop new products, while their employers provide regular salaries and financial backing. Intrapreneurs have a high degree of autonomy to run their own mini-companies within the larger enterprise. They share many of the same personality traits as classic entrepreneurs but take less personal risk. According to Gifford Pinchot, who coined the term *intrapreneur* in his book of the same name, many large companies now provide seed funds that finance in-house entrepreneurial efforts.

Why Become an Entrepreneur?

As the examples in this chapter show, entrepreneurs are found in all industries and have different motives for starting companies. The most common reason cited by CEOs listed in the *Inc. 500*, the magazine's annual list of fastest-growing private companies, is the challenge of building a business, followed by the desire to control

Have an idea for a business? Starting a new business is a lot of work and often requires a lot of cash. *Dragon's Den* on CBC television allows aspiring entrepreneurs to pitch their ideas to a panel of Canadian business moguls. These business moguls have the cash and the know-how to make a product successful, but it takes more than passion to convince one of them that your idea is worth their attention. How might a person's interests and passions lead to a life of successful entrepreneurship?

DRAGON'S DEN / CANADIAN BROADCASTING CORPORATION

Expanding Around the Globe

LULULEMON ATHLETICA INC.

Chip Wilson, a University of Calgary graduate, was in the first commercial yoga class offered in Vancouver, B.C., and found it very exhilarating. Chip had spent 20 years in the surf, skate, and snowboard businesses, and liked the post-yoga feeling to these activities. He could sense that yoga was going to boom! But Chip found the cotton clothing too sweaty and inappropriate for power yoga. With his enthusiasm for technical athletic fabrics and feedback from the yoga instructors wearing his new designs, the lululemon success story was born.

The company was founded in 1998 and its first real store was opened in November of 2000 in Vancouver. The goal was to train his people so that he could have a positive influence on their families, communities, and customers. Initially, the intent was to have one store, but soon it was obvious growth was necessary for success. In 2003, the Retail Council of Canada recognized the company as the "Innovative Retailer of the Year" in its small store classification.

The company's line of apparel includes fitness wear designed for athletic pursuits such as yoga, dance, running, and general fitness. To complement the apparel line, the company also offers other fitness related products. Today, lululemon has a global brand and is a good corporate citizen. Its stores have close ties to the local community and host in-store events ranging from self-defence to goal-setting workshops.

Thinking Critically

1. At what point do you think the owners of a company contemplate expanding the company outside of the domestic borders?
2. What considerations should a company pondering international expansion think about?

SOURCES: "Lululemon athletica inc. corporate survey," Retrieved from FP Advisor database, May 29, 2009, http://www.FPInfomart.ca; www.lululemon.com, modified November 18, 2011.

their own destiny. Other reasons include financial independence and frustration working for someone else. Two important motives mentioned in other surveys are a feeling of personal satisfaction with your work, and creating the lifestyle that you want. Do entrepreneurs feel that going into business for themselves was worth it? The answer is a resounding yes. Most say they would do it again. See the "Expanding Around the Globe" box for an example of how one successful Canadian company started.

LO2 # CHARACTERISTICS OF SUCCESSFUL ENTREPRENEURS

Do you have what it takes to become an entrepreneur? Being an entrepreneur requires special drive, perseverance, passion, and a spirit of adventure in addition to managerial and technical ability. Having a great concept is not enough. An entrepreneur must also be able to develop and manage the company that implements the idea. In addition, entrepreneurs *are* the company; they cannot leave problems at the office at the end of the day. Entrepreneurs tend to work longer hours and take fewer vacations once they have their own companies. They also share other common characteristics, as described in the next section.

The Entrepreneurial Personality

Studies of the entrepreneurial personality generally find that entrepreneurs share certain key traits. Most entrepreneurs are

- *ambitious.* Entrepreneurs have a high need for achievement and are competitive.
- *independent.* They are self-starters who prefer to lead rather than follow. They are also individualists.
- *self-confident.* They understand the challenges of starting a business but are decisive and have faith in their abilities to resolve problems.
- *risk taking.* Though they are not averse to risk, most successful entrepreneurs prefer situations with a moderate degree of risk, where they have a chance to control the outcome, over highly risky ventures that depend on luck.
- *visionary.* Entrepreneurs' abilities to spot trends and act on them sets entrepreneurs apart from small-business owners and managers.
- *creative.* To compete with larger companies, entrepreneurs need to have creative product designs, marketing strategies, and solutions to managerial problems.
- *energetic.* Starting a business takes long hours. Some entrepreneurs start companies while still employed full-time.
- *passionate.* Entrepreneurs love their work.
- *committed.* They make personal sacrifices to achieve their goals. Because they are so committed to their companies, entrepreneurs are persistent in seeking solutions to problems.

Most entrepreneurs combine many of the above characteristics. Sarah Levy, 23, loved her job as a restaurant pastry chef but not the low pay, high stress, and long hours of a commercial kitchen. So she found a new one—in her parents' home—and launched Sarah's Pastries and Candies. Part-time staffers now help her fill pastry and candy orders to the soothing sounds of music videos playing in the background.

University graduate Conor McDonough started his own Web design company, OffThePathMedia.com, after becoming disillusioned with the rigid structure of his job. "There wasn't enough room for my own expression," he says.

Concept *in Action*

The Boston Pizza concept was begun by Gus Agioritis, who immigrated to Canada from Greece in 1964. His strategy was to grow the Boston Pizza chain by franchising his concept (see Chapter 8 on franchising). Although no longer owned by Mr. Agioritis, his original dream has been realized: the chain is nationwide and has moved into the United States and Mexico. What do you think were Mr. Agioritis's entrepreneurial characteristics?

CPI/THE CANADIAN PRESS/MARIO BEAUREGARD)

"Freelancing keeps me on my toes," says busy graphic artist Ana Sanchez. "It forces me to do my best work because I know my next job depends on my performance."[6]

Managerial Ability and Technical Knowledge

A person with all the characteristics of an entrepreneur might still lack the necessary business skills to run a successful company. Entrepreneurs need the technical knowledge to carry out their ideas and the managerial ability to organize a company, develop operating strategies, obtain financing, and supervise day-to-day activities. Good interpersonal and communication skills are important in dealing with employees, customers, and other business associates such as bankers, accountants, and lawyers. As we will discuss later in the chapter, entrepreneurs believe they can learn these much-needed skills. Mike Becker learned how to manage Funko, Inc., www.funko .com, by trial and error. He started the company to bring back low-tech, nostalgia-based bobble-headed dolls he called Wacky Wobblers. His first character was Bob's Big Boy, the restaurant chain mascot. Putting his licensing background to work, he began producing cartoon, movie, and advertising character Wobblers—Mr. Magoo, Betty Boop, Charlie Tuna, Count Chocula, Pink Panther, and Austin Powers, for example. "(After my first order,) I still didn't understand what the heck I was doing," Becker says. "I didn't have any distribution networks, sales reps, employees, or even a place

Sustainable Business, Sustainable World

PATAGONIA, INC.

Patagonia, Inc. is a very large and successful company that started from very humble beginnings. Its founder, Yvon Chouinard, son of a French Canadian blacksmith, was a world-class mountain climber who discovered he could make higher quality and less environmentally damaging climbing equipment than what was currently available and "before he knew it his way of life became (his) business." As the book about his life and business *Let My People Go Surfing* explains: "This is not another tale of a successful businessman who manages to do good on the side and have grand adventures; it's the story of a man who brought doing good and having grand adventures into the heart of his business life—and who enjoyed even more business success as a result." Sustainability is at the very core of what Patagonia is.

Patagonia's mission statement is to "Build the best product, cause no unnecessary harm, (and) use business to inspire and implement solutions to the environmental crisis." The company is passionate in its belief that it must participate in the fight to maintain a beautiful and environmentally strong planet. These are words you might expect from a company like Patagonia, but what you might not expect is that it is also very clear and transparent about acknowledging the damage that its business activities have on the environment. And as Dr. Phil says, "You can't fix what you don't acknowledge." This acknowledgment further underscores Patagonia's commitment to sustainability.

This is a company that is so committed to what it stands for that it wants to make these issues public, but at the same time stay true to its core values to work to reduce those harms. In fact, since 1985 (long before it became fashionable to do so) Patagonia has pledged one percent of sales to preserving and restoring the natural environment. Its 1% for the Planet" program has led to cash and in-kind donations to grassroots environmental groups of over $40 million. Chouinard, and owner of Blue Ribbon Flies, Craig Matthews, even created a non-profit corporation (see www.onepercentfortheplanet.org) to encourage other businesses to do the same.

One of the other innovative initiatives that Patagonia has undertaken is the "Common Threads Initiative." This program extends the three Rs to five and asks customers to join the company in a pledge to: Reduce—it will make gear that lasts a long time and you will not buy what you don't need; Repair—it will repair your gear and you will fix what's broken; Reuse—it will help find a home for gear you no longer need and you will sell or pass your used gear to someone who needs it; Recycle—it will take back your worn-out gear and you will not throw it out; and lastly, Reimagine—"Together we reimagine a world where we take only what nature can replace." Sounds like a good plan.

In fact it all sounds too good to be true, but that's what happens when an entrepreneur creates a business based on sustainability vs. building a company and then looking for a way to make it sustainable.

Thinking Critically

1. What other organizations do you know of that would be similar to the Patagonia story—built on the values of the entrepreneur, and those values permeate the structure and decisions of the organization? Would Anita Roddick of The Body Shop, or Ben Cohen and Jerry Greenfield of Ben & Jerry's Ice Cream be examples?
2. Does knowing this about Patagonia make you more likely to buy its products or want to work for the company?

SOURCES: http://www.patagonia.com; Chouinard, Yvon, *Let My People Go Surfing*: The Education of a Reluctant Businessman (New York, NY: The Penguin Press).

Concept *Check*

Describe the personality traits and other skills characteristic of successful entrepreneurs.

What does it mean when we say that an entrepreneur should work on the business, not in it?

of business." He quickly had to become competent in every phase of the business, even tasks he hated, like accounting and paperwork.[7]

Entrepreneurs soon learn that they can't do it all themselves. Often they choose to focus on what they do best and hire others to do the rest. Becker learned to delegate many of the operational responsibilities so he could be "Chairman of Fun" and handle product creation and licensing.

LO3 SMALL BUSINESS: DRIVING CANADA'S GROWTH

Although large corporations dominated the business scene for many decades, in recent years small businesses have once again come to the forefront. Corporate greed and fraud have given large corporations a bad name. Downsizings that accompany economic downturns have caused many people to look toward smaller companies for employment, and they have plenty to choose from.

What Is a Small Business?

How many small businesses are there in the Canada? This is not that easy to answer because different institutions define small business differently. Some base it on the number of employees, others on revenues. For example, Industry Canada's definition of a small business is the number of employees and the sector it operates in—for a company in the goods-producing sector to be considered a small business it must have fewer than 100 employees; whereas in the service-producing sector it must have fewer than 50 employees.

There are approximately 2.4 million business locations in Canada. Using Industry Canada's definition of small business:

- small businesses account for 98 percent of all employers;
- small businesses employ 48 percent of the workforce;
- 54.6 percent of Canadian businesses employ 1 to 4 people, 20.4 percent employ 5 to 9, 12.3 percent employ 10 to 19, and 9.7 percent employ 20 to 99;
- only 0.2 percent of all Canadian businesses have more than 500 employees; and
- approximately 46.7 percent of all new jobs in the economy were created by the small-business sector.[8]

So what makes a business "small"? Many different criteria can be used to define a small business. It might be the value of its annual sales or revenues, value of its assets or the number of employees. In addition, a small business is

small business
A business that is independently managed, is owned by an individual or a small group of investors, is based locally, and is not a dominant company in its industry.

- independently managed;
- owned by an individual or a small group of investors;
- based locally (although the market it serves might be widespread); and
- not a dominant company (thus, it has little influence in its industry).

Small businesses in Canada can be found in almost every industry group. Services dominate small businesses, accounting for about 75 percent, with the balance of small businesses (25 percent) producing goods.[9] These companies provide everything from health care to computer consulting and food and lodging. Small businesses are found in all of the various sectors, as suggested below.

- *Services.* Service companies are the most popular category of small business, because they are easy and inexpensive to start. They are often small; very few service-oriented companies are national in scope. They include repair services, restaurants, specialized software companies, accountants, travel agencies, management consultants, and temporary help agencies.

- *Wholesale and retail trade.* Retailers sell goods or services directly to the end user. Wholesalers link manufacturers and retailers or industrial buyers; they assemble, store, and distribute products ranging from heavy machinery to produce. Most retailers also qualify as small businesses, whether they operate one store or a small chain.
- *Manufacturing.* This category is dominated by large companies, but many small businesses produce goods. Machine shops, printing companies, clothing manufacturers, beverage bottlers, electronic equipment manufacturers, and furniture makers are often small manufacturers. In some industries, small manufacturing businesses have an advantage because they can focus on customized products that would not be profitable for larger manufacturers.
- *Construction.* Companies employing fewer than 20 people account for many of Canada's construction companies. They include independent builders of industrial and residential properties and thousands of contractors in such trades as plumbing, electrical, roofing, and painting.
- *Agriculture.* Small businesses dominate agriculture-related industry, including forestry and fisheries.

HOT links

For information about starting and growing a business, visit www.canadaone.ca

SMALL BUSINESS, LARGE IMPACT

LO4

An uncertain economy has not stopped people from starting new companies. A poll conducted by Léger Marketing shows that two-thirds of Canadians believe that small business is making a very positive contribution to our economy.[10] This is not surprising when you consider the many reasons why small businesses continue to thrive in Canada:

- *Independence and a better lifestyle.* Large corporations no longer represent job security or offer as many fast-track career opportunities. Mid-career employees leave the corporate world—either voluntarily or as the result of downsizing—in search of new opportunities. Many new college and business school graduates shun the corporate world altogether and start their own companies or look for work in small businesses.
- *Personal satisfaction from work.* Many small-business owners cite this as one of the primary reasons for starting their companies. They love what they do.
- *Best route to success.* Small businesses offer their owners the potential for profit. Also, business ownership provides greater advancement opportunities for women and minorities, as we discuss later in this chapter.
- *Rapidly changing technology.* Advances in computer and telecommunications technology, as well as the sharp decrease in the cost of this technology, have given individuals and small companies the power to compete in industries that were formerly closed to them. The arrival of the Internet and World Wide Web is responsible for the formation of many small businesses, as we'll discuss in the trends section later in this chapter.
- *Outsourcing.* As a result of downsizing, corporations often contract with outside companies for services they used to provide in-house. This "outsourcing" creates opportunities for smaller companies, many of which offer specialized goods and services.
- *Major corporate restructurings and downsizings.* These force many employees to look for other jobs or careers. They can also provide the opportunity to buy a business unit that a company no longer wants.

Small businesses are resilient. They are able to respond fairly quickly to changing economic conditions by refocusing their operations.

Why Stay Small?

Owners of small businesses recognize that being small offers special advantages. Greater flexibility and an uncomplicated company structure allow small businesses to react more quickly to changing market forces. Innovative product ideas can be developed and

Making Ethical Choices

MINDING YOUR BUSINESS

As the owner of LT Designs, a small South African company, Lisa Taylor loves her work producing competitively priced, handcrafted home accessories. She is an advocate for the empowerment of women, recruiting and training workers from nearby towns. These poor rural women are often the sole supporters of their families, and they are grateful for the jobs and eager to learn new skills.

Taylor is thrilled when a Canadian textile wholesaler and distributor, attracted by her unique, well-priced products and socially responsible approach to doing business, starts buying from her. Her business triples, and she hires more workers to handle the extra load. The company is soon Taylor's single largest customer and plans an elaborate and costly marketing campaign to promote her products in Canada. The company assigns you to supervise production and work closely with Taylor on developing appropriate designs for the Canadian market.

At first Taylor welcomes your input, but her receptivity quickly turns into resentment of what she perceives as your company's attempt to "control" her business. Although she has signed an agreement with your company to approve new designs, her new sample ranges reflect none of the agreed-on design elements. After checking with your boss, you tell Taylor that unless she agrees to follow your design standards, you will have no choice but to terminate the relationship. Taylor insists the new designs fall within agreed design specifications and that you are trying to take advantage of the workers' need for jobs to force her to compromise her artistic integrity.

If your company does not buy the products, she will have to lay off the additional workers she hired, and their families will suffer. Everyone will blame the overbearing Canadian company for ruining the local economy. You are in a bind, because the company will lose its investment in the marketing campaign. It could also receive negative publicity, damaging its image as a good corporate citizen.

ETHICAL DILEMMA: The Canadian company can afford to buy LT's products and hold them in inventory, waiting for an appropriate marketing opportunity. Should they absorb the cost of doing this to protect workers' jobs?

SOURCE: Case based on experience of Linda Ravden, former owner of Bellissima Designs, as described in a personal interview, February 24, 2003.

Concept *in Action*

Brent Lane, an entrepreneurship student, is the force behind the growth of Golden Lane Honey, which now offers a wide range of products. Brent is assisted by his twin brother and marketing student, Bryce Lane. What do you think some of Brent's reasons were for starting the company?

COURTESY SHIRLEY A. ROSE

brought to market more quickly, using fewer financial resources and personnel than would be needed in a larger company. And operating more efficiently keeps costs down as well. Small companies can also serve specialized markets that may not be cost-effective for large companies. Another feature is the opportunity to provide a higher level of personal service. Such attention brings many customers back to small businesses like gourmet restaurants, health clubs, spas, fashion boutiques, and travel agencies.

Many small-business owners believe that, to respond to the dynamic tastes of their customers, they can best serve them by not growing too large.

On the other hand, being small is not always an asset. Many small businesses encounter difficulties in obtaining adequate financing. If the founders have limited managerial skills, they might have problems growing the company. As well, complying with regulations is more expensive for small businesses. Those with fewer than 20 employees spend about twice as much per employee compared to larger companies. In addition, starting and managing a small business requires a major commitment by the owner. According to Dun & Bradstreet's 21st Annual Small Business Survey, 37 percent of all entrepreneurs work more than 50 hours a week.[11] Long hours, the need for owners to do much of the work themselves, and the stress of being personally responsible for the success of the business can take a toll.

Managing a Small Business—Coping with the Challenges

Managing a small business is quite a challenge. Whether you start a business from scratch or buy an existing one, you must be able to keep it going. The small-business owner must be ready to solve problems as they arise and move quickly if market conditions change. A sound business plan is key to keeping the small-business owner in touch with all areas of his or her business. Hiring, training, and managing employees is another important responsibility because, over time, the owner's role may change. As the company grows, others will make many of the day-to-day decisions while the owner focuses on managing employees and planning for the company's long-term success. The owner must constantly evaluate company performance and policies in light of changing market and economic conditions and develop new policies as required. He or she must also nurture a continual flow of ideas to keep the business growing. The types of employees needed may change, too, as the company grows. For instance, a larger company may need more managerial talent and technical expertise.

USING OUTSIDE CONSULTANTS One way to ease the burden of managing a business is to hire outside consultants. Nearly all small businesses need a good accountant (e.g., CA, CMA, or CGA) who can help with financial record keeping, tax planning, and decision making. An accountant who works closely with the owner to help the business grow is a valuable asset. A lawyer who knows about small-business law can provide legal advice and draw up essential documents. Consultants in other areas, such as marketing, employee benefits, and insurance, can be hired as needed. Outside directors with business experience are another source of advice for small companies. Resources like these free the small-business owner to concentrate on planning and day-to-day operations.

Some aspects of the business can be outsourced, or contracted out to specialists in that area. Among the departments that most commonly use outsourcing are information technology, customer service, order fulfillment, payroll, and human resources. Hiring an outside company—in many cases another small business—can save money, because the purchasing company buys just the services it needs and has no investment in expensive technology. Management should review any outsourced functions as the business grows. At some point, it might be more cost-effective to bring it in-house.

HIRING AND RETAINING EMPLOYEES A small company might have to be creative to find the right employees and convince applicants to join their company. Coremetrics, a Web analytics company that tracks habits of site visitors, ran into problems when founder Brett Hurt hired the wrong person to fill a major role. "A big company won't go under because of one bad hire, but a start-up might," Hurt explains. "If you are starting your own business and you hire someone and they're not ethical, or their heart isn't in it, or they're not of the same frame of mind as you, it can crush your business."[12] Today, Coremetrics is owned by IBM.

Making the decision to hire the first employee is also a major one. Most realize it is time to hire the first employee when the business owner can no longer do it alone. The business might be held back because the owner is working a very long work week and still cannot keep up. In deciding when to hire an employee, it is important to identify all the costs involved in hiring an employee to make sure the business can afford it. Help wanted ads, extra space, employer responsibilities (e.g., CPP and EI), and employee benefits—these will easily add up to substantial costs in addition to the salary. Having an employee might also mean more work for you at first, in terms of training and management. It's a catch-22: To grow, you need to hire more people, but making the shift from solo worker to boss can be very stressful.[13]

Attracting good employees can be hard for a small business, which might not be able to match the higher salaries, better benefits, and advancement potential offered by many larger companies. Once they hire employees, small-business owners must promote employee satisfaction to retain them. Comfortable working conditions, flexible hours, employee benefit programs, opportunities to help make decisions, and a share in profits and ownership are some of the ways to do this.

GOING GLOBAL WITH EXPORTING Increasingly more small businesses are discovering the benefits of looking beyond Canada for markets. As we learned in

Concept *Check*

Why are small businesses becoming so popular?

Discuss the major advantages and disadvantages of small businesses.

Check out the Canadian Federation of Independent Business at
www.cfib.ca

Find out more about small business at
www.sbinfocanada.about.com

Want to know more about employment? See
www.employease.com

How does the small-business owner's role change over time?

What role do technology and the Internet play in creating small businesses and helping them grow?

What are the benefits to small companies of doing business internationally, and what steps can small businesses take to explore their options?

Chapter 5, the global marketplace represents a huge opportunity for Canadian businesses, both large and small. Small businesses decide to export because of foreign competition in Canada, new markets in growing economies, economic conditions in Canada, and the need for increased sales and higher profits. When the value of the Canadian dollar declines against other foreign currencies, Canadian goods become less expensive for overseas buyers, and this creates opportunities for Canadian companies to sell globally. Small businesses that choose to do business abroad might also face issues of social responsibility, as "Making Ethical Choices," on page 170, demonstrates.

Like any major business decision, exporting requires careful planning. Many online resources can help you decipher the complexities of preparing to sell in a foreign country and identify potential markets for your goods and services. Export Development Canada (EDC) helps companies grow their export business. Some services that EDC offers are insurance (including political risk insurance) and financing solutions (e.g., foreign customers can access financing through EDC or their partners). EDC recognizes that access to cash is one of the greatest barriers and has developed solutions that can help.

Many small businesses hire international-trade specialists to get started selling overseas. They have the time, knowledge, and resources that most small businesses lack. Export trading companies buy goods at a discount from small businesses and resell them abroad. Export management companies (EMCs) act on a company's behalf. For fees of 5 to 15 percent of gross sales and multi-year contracts, they handle all aspects of exporting, including finding customers, billing, shipping, and helping the company comply with foreign regulations.

LO5 READY, SET, START YOUR OWN BUSINESS

You have decided that you'd like to go into business for yourself. What is the best way to go about it? Start from scratch? Buy an existing business? Or buy a franchise? About 75 percent of business start-ups involve brand-new organizations, with the remaining 25 percent representing purchased companies or franchises. Franchising is discussed in Chapter 8, so we'll cover the other two options in this section.

Getting Started

The first step in starting your own business is a self-assessment to determine whether you have the personal traits you need to succeed and, if so, what type of business would be best for you. (See the exercise "Your Career as an Entrepreneur," featured on pages 186 and 187. It includes a questionnaire and other information to help you make these decisions.) Exhibit 6.1 provides a checklist to consider before starting your business.

FINDING THE IDEA Entrepreneurs get ideas for their businesses from many sources. It is not surprising that about 80 percent of *Inc. 500* executives got the ideas for their companies while working in the same or a related industry. Starting a business in a field where you have experience improves your chances of success. Other sources of inspiration are personal experiences as a consumer; hobbies and personal interests; suggestions from customers, family, and friends; and college courses or other education.

An excellent way to keep up with small-business trends is by reading entrepreneurship and small-business magazines and visiting their websites regularly. With articles on everything from idea generation to selling the business, they provide invaluable resources. For example, each year *Entrepreneur* publishes lists of the fastest-growing young, private companies. Reading about companies that are only a few years old but now have more than $1 million in sales will inspire you.

Interesting ideas are all around you. Many successful businesses get started because someone identifies needs and then finds a way to fill them. Do you have a problem

Exhibit 6.1 Checklist for Starting a Business

Before you start your own small business, consider the following checklist:

- Identify your reasons. (Why do I want to start a business?)

- Do a self-analysis. (Do I have the personality to start and operate a business?)

- Assess your personal skills and experience. (What skills do I bring to the business? What is my experience in business?)

- Find a niche. (What is my product offering and target market?)

- Complete a market analysis. (Will the market support my business?)

- Plan your start-up. (What are the steps needed to be successful?)

- Think about the finances. (How am I going to finance the business?)

SOURCE: Adapted from "Checklist for Starting a Business," March 20, 2006, www.sba.gov/survey/checklist.

that you need to solve or a product that doesn't work as well as you'd like? Maybe one of your coworkers has a complaint. Raising questions about the way things are done is a great way to generate ideas. Many business owners have difficulty filling jobs. On the other hand, many students have problems finding jobs. With websites such as monster.ca and canadajobs.com, employers and students (as well as others) can connect.

CHOOSING A FORM OF BUSINESS ORGANIZATION A key decision for a person starting a new business is whether it will be a sole proprietorship, partnership, corporation, or limited liability company. As discussed in Chapter 8, each type of business organization has advantages and disadvantages. The choice depends on the type of business, number of employees, capital requirements, tax considerations, and level of risk involved. Most important, though, is the entrepreneur's tolerance for liability.

DEVELOPING THE BUSINESS PLAN Once you have the basic concept for a product or service, you must develop a plan to create the business. This planning process, culminating in a sound business plan, is one of the most important steps in starting a business. It can help to attract appropriate loan financing, minimize the risks involved, and be a critical determinant in whether a company succeeds or fails. Many

HOT *links*

Are you interested in starting your own business? Learn how at
www.entrepreneur.com

business plan
A formal written statement that describes in detail the idea for a new business and how it will be carried out. It includes a general description of the company, the qualifications of the owner(s), a description of the product or service, an analysis of the market, and a financial plan.

Concept *in Action*

In their start-up stages, small-business owners have to be masters of multitasking. Home Hardware is a cooperative wholesaler (see Chapter 8) owned by over 1000 independent small business operators across Canada, with more than 100,000 different items available. What do you think are the characteristics of these business owners and what skills and attributes do they process?

THE CANADIAN PRESS(BORIS SPREMO)

people do not venture out on their own because they are overwhelmed with doubts and concerns. A comprehensive business plan lets you run various "what if" analyses and "operate" your business as a dry-run, without any financial outlay or risk. You can also develop strategies to overcome problems—well before the business actually opens.

Taking the time to develop a good business plan pays off. A venture that seems sound at the idea stage may not look so good on paper. A well-prepared, comprehensive, written business plan forces entrepreneurs to take an objective and critical look at their business venture and analyze their concept carefully; make decisions about marketing, production, staffing, and financing; and set goals that will help them manage and monitor its growth and performance.

The business plan also serves as the initial operating plan for the business; writing a good business plan can take several months. But many businesspeople neglect this critical planning tool in their eagerness to begin doing business, getting caught up in the day-to-day operations instead.

The key features of a business plan are a general description of the company, the qualifications of the owner(s), a description of the product or service, an analysis of the market (demand, customers, competition), and a financial plan. The sections should work together to demonstrate why the business will be successful, while focusing on the uniqueness of the business and why it will attract customers. Exhibit 6.2 provides an outline of what to include in each section of a business plan.

The most common use of a business plan is to persuade lenders and investors to finance the venture. The detailed information in the plan helps them assess whether to invest. Even though a business plan may take months to write, it must capture potential investors' interest within minutes. For that reason, the basic business plan should be written with a particular reader in mind. Then, you can fine-tune and tailor it to fit the investment goals of the investor(s) you plan to approach.

But don't think you can set aside your business plan once you obtain financing and begin operating your company. Entrepreneurs who think their business plans are only for raising money make a big mistake. Business plans should be dynamic documents, reviewed and updated on a regular basis—monthly, quarterly, or annually, depending on how the business progresses and the particular industry changes.

Owners should adjust their sales and profit projections up or down as they analyze their markets and operating results. Reviewing your plan on a constant basis will help you identify strengths and weaknesses in your marketing and management strategies, and help you evaluate possible opportunities for expansion in light of both your original mission and current market trends.

Financing the Business

Once the business plan is complete, the next step is to obtain financing to set up the company. The funding required depends on the type of business and the entrepreneur's own investment. Businesses started by lifestyle entrepreneurs require less financing than growth-oriented businesses, and manufacturing and high-tech companies generally require a large initial investment.

Who provides start-up funding for small companies? Some 94 percent of business owners raise start-up funds from personal accounts, family, and friends. Personal assets and money from family and friends are important for new businesses, whereas funding from financial institutions may become more important as companies grow. Three quarters of *Inc. 500* companies were funded on $100,000 or less.[14] The two forms of business financing are debt, borrowed funds that must be repaid with interest over a stated time period, and equity, funds raised through the sale of stock (i.e., ownership) in the business. Those who provide equity funds get a share of the business' profits. Because lenders usually limit debt financing to no more than a quarter to a third of the company's total needs, equity financing often amounts to about 65 to 75 percent of total start-up financing.

Two sources of equity financing for young companies are angel investors and venture-capital companies. Angel investors are individual investors or groups of

debt
A form of business financing consisting of borrowed funds that must be repaid with interest over a stated time period.

equity
A form of business financing consisting of funds raised through the sale of stock (i.e., ownership) in a business.

angel investors
Individual investors or groups of experienced investors who provide funding for start-up businesses.

Exhibit 6.2 Outline for a Business Plan

Title page: Provides names, addresses, and phone numbers of the venture and its owners and management personnel; date prepared; copy number; and contact person.

Table of contents: Provides page numbers of the key sections of the business plan.

Executive summary: Provides a one- to three-page overview of the total business plan. Written after the other sections are completed, it highlights their significant points and, ideally, creates enough excitement to motivate the reader to continue reading.

Vision and mission statement: Concisely describes the intended strategy and business philosophy for making the vision happen.

Company overview: Explains the type of company, such as manufacturing, retail, or service; provides background information on the company if it already exists; and describes the proposed form of organization—sole proprietorship, partnership, or corporation. This section should be organized as follows: company name and location, company objectives, nature and primary product or service of the business, current status (start-up, buyout, or expansion) and history (if applicable), and legal form of organization.

Product and/or service plan: Describes the product and/or service and points out any unique features; explains why people will buy the product or service. This section should offer the following descriptions: product and/or service; features of the product or service that provide a competitive advantage; available legal protection—patents, copyrights, and trademarks; and dangers of technical or style obsolescence.

Marketing plan: Shows who the company's customers will be and what type of competition it will face; outlines the marketing strategy and specifies the company's competitive edge. This section should offer the following descriptions: analysis of target market and profile of target customer; methods of identifying and attracting customers; selling approach, type of sales force, and distribution channels; types of sales promotions and advertising; and credit and pricing policies.

Management plan: Identifies the key players—active investors, management team, and directors—citing the experience and competence they possess. This section should offer the following descriptions: management team, outside investors and/or directors and their qualifications, outside resource people and their qualifications, and plans for recruiting and training employees.

Operating plan: Explains the type of manufacturing or operating system to be used; and describes the facilities, labour, raw materials, and product-processing requirements. This section should offer the following descriptions: operating or manufacturing methods, operating facilities (location, space, and equipment), quality-control methods, procedures to control inventory and operations, sources of supply, and purchasing procedures.

Financial plan: Specifies financial needs and contemplated sources of financing; presents projections of revenues, costs, and profits. This section should offer the following descriptions: historical financial statements for the last three to five years or as available; pro forma financial statements for three to five years, including Income Statements, Balance Sheets (or Statements of Financial Position), Statement of Cash Flows, and cash budgets (monthly for first year and quarterly for second year); breakeven analysis of profits and cash flows; and planned sources of financing.

Appendix of supporting documents: Provides materials supplementary to the plan. This section should offer the following descriptions: management team biographies, any other important data that support the information in the business plan, and the company's ethics code.

SOURCE: From Longenecker / Moore / Petty. *Small Business Management*, 11E. © 2000 South-Western, a part of Cengage Learning, Inc. Reproduced by permission. www.cengage.com/permissions

experienced investors who provide financing for start-up businesses by investing their own funds. This gives them more flexibility on what they can and will invest in, but because it is their own money, angels are careful. Angel investors often invest early in a company's development and they want to see an idea they understand and can have confidence in. Exhibit 6.3 offers some guidelines on how to attract angel financing.

Venture capital is financing obtained from venture capitalists—investment companies that specialize in financing small, high-growth companies. Venture capitalists receive an ownership interest and a voice in management in return for their money.

An Alternative—Buying a Small Business

Another route to small-business ownership is buying an existing business. Although this approach is less risky than starting a business from scratch, it still requires careful and thorough analysis. The potential buyer must answer several important

venture capital
Financing obtained from investment companies that specialize in financing small, high-growth companies and receive an ownership interest and a voice in management in return for their money.

HOT links

Check out the listing of venture capital companies at
www.cvca.ca

Exhibit 6.3 The Heavenly Deal

If you require financing for your start-up business, you need to find angel investors and create an interest for them. It is important to have a solid business plan and show the potential for a solid return on their investments. Here are some suggestions for success:

- Know who you are looking for (e.g., income level, age group, past history with success, etc.).
- Look close to home, they want to be included and often prefer businesses within their own community.
- Network, network, to find out who is out there and who do they know.
- Use connection services that are available on the Internet.
- Show them something they understand, ideally a business from an industry they've been associated with.
- Have respect for your prospective investors. They know things you don't.
- Hone your vision. Be able to describe your business—what it does and who it sells to—in less than a minute.
- Angels can always leave their money in the bank, so an investment must interest them. It should be something they're passionate about. And timing is important—knowing when to reach out to an angel can make a huge difference.
- They need to see management they trust, respect, and like. Present a mature management team with a strong, experienced leader who can withstand the scrutiny of the angel's inquiries.
- Angels prefer something they can bring added value to. Those who invest could be involved with your company for a long time, or perhaps take a seat on your board of directors. Show the angel investor that there is an opportunity for them to be actively involved.
- They are more partial to deals that don't require huge sums of money or additional infusions of angel cash.
- Emphasize the likely exits for investors and have a handle on who the competition is, why your solution is better, and how you are going to gain market share.

SOURCES: Rhonda Abrams, "What Does it Take to Impress an Angel Investor?", Inc.com, http://www.inc.com, March 2001. Copyright © 2005 Inc.com; Stacy Zhao, "9 Tips for Winning Over Angels," Inc.com, http://www.inc.com, June 2005. Copyright © 2005 Inc.com; Susan Ward, "How to Find an Angel Investor," About.com Small Business: Canada, http://sbinfocanada.about.com/od/financing/a/findangel.htm, accessed July 2012; Susan Ward, "Attracting Angel Investors," About.com Small Business: Canada, http://sbinfocanada.about.com/od/financing/a/angelinvestor.htm, accessed July 2012.

Concept *in Action*

TRAVEL CUTS VOYAGES CAMPUS

PHOTO COURTESY OF TRAVEL CUTS

Travel CUTS started in Ontario and operates from over 30 locations in Canada, with most of them either on university and college campuses or nearby. It began with the purpose of providing discounted travel to students but now has expanded to serve the general public as well. It has been profitable by offering unique products to its various target markets. Why do small businesses often fail?

questions: Why is the owner selling? Does he or she want to retire or move on to another challenge, or are there some problems with the business? Is the business operating at a profit? If not, can the problems be corrected? On what basis has the owner valued the company, and is it a fair price? What are the owner's plans after selling the company? Depending on the type of business, customers might be more loyal to the owner than to the product or service. They could leave the company if the current owner decides to open a similar business. To protect against this situation, many purchasers include a "non-compete clause" in the contract of sale.

Many of the same steps for starting a business from scratch apply to buying an existing company. You should prepare a business plan that thoroughly analyzes all aspects of the business. Get answers to all your questions, and determine, via the business plan, that the business is a good one. Then you must negotiate the purchase price and other terms and get financing. This can be a difficult process, and it might require the use of a consultant or a business broker.

Risky Business

Running your own business might not be as easy as it sounds. Despite the many advantages of being your own boss, the risks are great as well. Businesses close down for many reasons—and not all are failures. Some businesses that close are financially successful and close for nonfinancial reasons. But the causes of business failure can be interrelated. For example, low sales and high expenses are often directly related to poor management. Some common causes of business closure are

- economic factors—business downturns and high interest rates;
- financial causes—inadequate capital, low cash balances, and high expenses;
- lack of experience—inadequate business knowledge, management experience, and technical expertise; and
- personal reasons—the owners may decide to sell the business or move on to other opportunities.

Inadequate early planning is often at the core of later business problems. As described earlier, a thorough feasibility analysis, from market assessment to financing, is critical to business success. Yet even with the best plans, business conditions change and unexpected challenges arise. An entrepreneur may start a company based on a terrific new product only to find that a larger company with more marketing, financing, and distribution clout introduces a similar item.

The stress of managing a business can also take its toll. The business can consume your whole life. Owners may find themselves in over their heads and unable to cope with the pressures of business operations, from the long hours to being the main decision maker. Even successful businesses have to deal with ongoing challenges. Growing too quickly can cause as many problems as sluggish sales. Growth can strain a company's finances when additional capital is required to fund expanding operations, from hiring additional staff to purchasing more raw materials or equipment. Successful business owners must respond quickly and develop plans to manage its growth.

Concept *Check*

How can potential business owners find new business ideas?

Why is it important to develop a business plan? What should such a plan include?

What financing options do small-business owners have?

Summarize the risks of small-business ownership.

THERE'S HELP OUT THERE

LO6

There are many government agencies and private organizations that can help entrepreneurs and small-business owners to grow stronger. Many of these are visible during Global Entrepreneurship Week and Small Business Week, where people can network and share ideas. The Business Development Bank of Canada (BDC), Aboriginal Business Canada, Women Entrepreneurs of Canada, Youth Entrepreneur Programs, and Canada Business Network are just a few of the agencies and organizations that can help entrepreneurs and small-business owners.

The Business Development Bank of Canada

Many small-business owners turn to the Business Development Bank of Canada (BDC) for assistance. The BDC is a financial institution that is wholly owned by the Government of Canada. Its mission is to help people start and manage small businesses, help them win federal contracts, and speak on behalf of small business. Through its national network of local offices, the BDC advises and helps small businesses in the areas of finance and management.

Business Development Bank of Canada (BDC)
Bank that provides small- and medium-sized businesses with flexible financing, affordable consulting services, and venture capital.

Canada Business Network

Canada Business Network is a collaborative arrangement between federal and provincial/territorial government and not-for-profit organizations. Its goal is to provide businesses with the resources they need to prosper. Through its organized network of service centres across Canada, it promotes entrepreneurship and innovation.

The Canada Business Network strives to

- "reduce the complexity of dealing with multiple levels of government;
- consolidate business information in one convenient service;

Want to know more about government grants, loans, and financing? Go to
www.canadabusiness.ca/eng

- enable you to make well-informed business decisions in a global economy; and
- contribute to your success through sound business planning, market research and the use of strategic business information."[15]*

Canada Business Network has both print material and databases that provide not only insight into the industry and the competition, but also information on start-up regulations for each city and province. An interactive business planner is also available.

Financial Institutions

Many of Canada's financial institutions, including the chartered banks, offer advice from starting or buying an existing business, business planning, operating the business, growing the business, to selling the business. For example, TD Canada Trust offers advice to small businesses, including all the above, and provides other tools and resources. TD's advisers can help with understanding economic reports, conducting webinar workshops geared towards the small-business owner, and through its "My Business Planner" online site, can even help the small-business owner identify the business's competitive advantages and set goals.

LO7

THE FUTURE OF ENTREPRENEURSHIP AND SMALL-BUSINESS OWNERSHIP

What services does the Women Business Owners of Canada Inc. provide? See
www.wboc.ca

Much entrepreneurial opportunity comes from major changes in demographics, society, technology, and economic changes and, at present, there is a confluence of all four. A major demographic group, the baby boomers, is moving into a significantly different stage in life, and minorities are increasing their business ownership in remarkable numbers. We have created a society in which we expect to have our problems taken care of, and the technological revolution stands ready with already-developed solutions. Evolving social and demographic trends, combined with the challenge of operating in a fast-paced technology-dominated business climate, are changing the face of entrepreneurship and small-business ownership.

Changing Demographics Create Entrepreneurial Diversity

The baby boomers, discussed in Chapter 3, are no longer willing to retire simply to knitting and golf. The growing numbers of baby boomer entrepreneurs has prompted some forward-thinking companies to recognize business opportunities in technology. At one time, there was a concern that the aging of the population would create a drag on the economy. Conventional wisdom said that the early parenthood years were the big spending years. As we aged, we spent less, and because boomers are such a big demographic group, this was going to create a long-term economic decline. Not true, it now appears. The boomer generation has built sizable wealth, and they are not afraid to spend it to make their lives more comfortable.

"In the future, everything from cell phones to computers will be redesigned for users with limited manual dexterity, poor eyesight, and compromised hearing. Intel and other research centres are working on sensor-rich environments that can monitor inhabitants, helping people remember to complete tasks, and watching for sudden behavioural or physical changes," says Jeff Cornwall, who holds the Jack C. Massey Chair in Entrepreneurship at Belmont University in Nashville, Tennessee. "This could be a huge entrepreneurial pot of gold for the next 40 years."[16]

*SOURCE: About Canada Business Network, http://www.canadabusiness.ca/eng/page/about/. Reproduced with the permission of the Minister of Public Works and Government Services Canada, 2012.

MONKEY BUSINESS IMAGES/SHUTTERSTOCK

Minorities are also adding to the entrepreneurial mix. Minority groups and women are increasing business ownership at a much faster rate than the national average, reflecting their confidence in the Canadian economy.

The Growth of "Web-Driven Entrepreneurs"

Technology, of course, plays a large role in the Canadian economy. According to a survey of 400 small businesses conducted by MasterCard International and Warrillow & Co., a small-business consulting company, Web-driven entrepreneurs are 25 percent more likely to be women and 25 percent more likely to be university educated.[17]

Today's customers are more comfortable with technology, and many of the over two billion Internet users are either starting Internet-based businesses or buying from them. A relatively new marketing concept using technology is "Cyber Monday," started in November 2005. It is the Monday following what has been known in the United States as "Black Friday"; a concept that has moved to retail stores in Canada. Black Friday is the official start of the holiday buying season and many retailers offer considerable discounts on merchandise. Technology has allowed retailers to piggyback on the Black Friday concept of in-store shopping with the Internet-based Cyber Monday.

Economic Times—Motivation to Go It Alone?

Many would-be entrepreneurs chose to get hands-on experience first at larger companies. They recognize that developing their managerial and technical skills improves their chances of successful business ownership. Their employers benefit as well. These intrapreneurs are applying their entrepreneurial inclinations within existing companies; these employees open up new opportunities by creating new products and identifying new markets.[18]

The economic climate of late has prompted many of those with entrepreneurial aspirations to start their own businesses. They have benefited from the work experience, and many have lost positions and are now looking to live their dream. It is hard to say if these new entrepreneurs would have stayed within the safety of their employer if the economic situations of 2008 and 2011 had not happened. But what we do know is that many did take the risk.

GREAT IDEAS TO USE NOW

After reading this chapter, you might be ready to go into business. Perhaps you believe you have just the product the world needs. Maybe you want to be your own boss or seek financial rewards. On the other hand, quality-of-life issues might be your primary motive.

Whatever your reasons, you'll have to do a lot of groundwork before taking the plunge. Do you know what you want from life and how the business fits into your overall goals? Do you have what it takes to start a business, from personal characteristics, like energy and persistence, to money to fund the venture? You'll also have to research the market and financial feasibility of your product idea and develop a business plan. No question about it, becoming an entrepreneur or small-business owner is hard work.

Taking the First Steps

Maybe you know that you want to run your own business but don't know what type of business to start. In addition to the advice provided earlier in the chapter, here are some ways to gather possible ideas:

- *Brainstorm with family and friends*. Don't set any limits, and then investigate the best ideas, no matter how impossible they might seem at first.
- *Be observant*. Look for anything that catches your interest, wherever you are—in your hometown or when you travel. What's special about it? Is there a niche market you can fill? Look at products that don't meet your needs and find ways to change them. Pay attention to the latest fads and trends. Amy Wolf remembered how thrilled she was to find a music store at London's Heathrow airport. Six years later, she founded AltiTunes Partners LP, a $15 million chain of music stores for travellers, which was later sold to InMotion Pictures, a leader in portable DVD player and movie rentals in airports. Wolf knows her idea wasn't new. "I stole the idea, and then did some serious adapting," she says. She saw a need and filled it.[19]
- *Focus on your interests and hobbies*. Opportunities abound, from home-based crafts or consulting businesses to multimillion-dollar companies. Robert Tuchman turned his love of sports into a $10 million company. TSE Sports and Entertainment arranges special travel packages for corporations that want to entertain clients at major sporting and entertainment events.[20]
- *Use your skills in new ways*. Are you computer savvy? You could start a business providing in-home consulting to novices who don't know how to set up or use their computers.

Working at a Small Business

Working for a small company can be a wonderful experience. Many people enjoy the less structured atmosphere and greater flexibility that often characterize the small-business workplace. Several years' experience at a small company can be a good steppingstone to owning your own company. You'll get a better understanding of the realities of running a small business before striking out on your own. There are other potential benefits as well:

- *More diverse job responsibilities*. Small companies might not have formal job descriptions, giving you a chance to learn a wider variety of skills to use later. In a large company, your job might be strictly defined.
- *Less bureaucracy*. Small companies typically have fewer formal rules and procedures. This creates a more relaxed working atmosphere.
- *Greater sense of your contribution to the business*. Your ideas are more likely to count, and you'll see how your work contributes to the company's success. You'll have greater access to top management and be able to discuss your ideas.

However, you should also be aware of the disadvantages of being a small-business employee:

- *Lower compensation packages.* Although the gap between large and small businesses is narrowing, salaries are likely to be lower at small businesses. In addition, there might be few, if any, employee benefits, such as health insurance and retirement plans.
- *Less job security.* Small businesses might be affected more profoundly by changing economic and competitive conditions. A change in ownership can put jobs at risk as well. However, small businesses run lean to begin with and, as noted earlier, are at the forefront of job creation.
- *Greater potential for personality clashes.* Conflicts between employees are more apparent in a small company and can affect the rest of the staff. In addition, if your boss owns the company, you don't have anyone to go to if you have a problem with him or her.
- *Fewer opportunities for career advancement.* After a few years, you might outgrow a small company because there are no chances for promotion. As well, with fewer people within the company with whom to network, you'll have to join outside organizations for these connections.

Evaluating these factors will help you decide whether working at a small business is the right opportunity for you.

Summary of Learning Outcomes

Entrepreneurship involves taking the risk of starting and managing a business to make a profit. Entrepreneurs are innovators who start companies either to have a certain lifestyle or to develop a company that will grow into a major corporation. People become entrepreneurs for four main reasons: the opportunity for profit, independence, personal satisfaction, and lifestyle. Classic entrepreneurs may be micropreneurs, who plan to keep their businesses small, or growth-oriented entrepreneurs. Multipreneurs start multiple companies, whereas intrapreneurs work within large corporations.

LO1 Explain entrepreneurship and the different types of entrepreneurs.

Successful entrepreneurs are ambitious, independent, self-confident, creative, energetic, passionate, and committed. They have a high need for achievement and a willingness to take moderate risks. They have good interpersonal and communication skills. Managerial skills and technical knowledge are also important for entrepreneurial success.

LO2 Describe the characteristics that successful entrepreneurs share.

A small business is independently owned and operated, has a local base of operations, and is not dominant in its field. Small businesses play an important role in the economy. More than 95 percent of Canadian businesses have fewer than 50 employees. Small businesses are found in every field, but they dominate the construction, wholesale, and retail categories. Most new private sector jobs created in Canada over the past decade were in small companies. Small businesses also create about twice as many new goods and services as larger companies. Approximately 70 percent of all new jobs in the economy were created by the small-business sector.

LO3 Discuss how small businesses contribute to the Canadian economy.

Small businesses have flexibility to respond to changing market conditions. Because of their streamlined staffing and structure, they can be operated efficiently. Small businesses can serve specialized markets more profitably than large companies and provide a higher level of personal service. Disadvantages include limited managerial

LO4 Identify the opportunities and challenges facing owners of small businesses.

skill, difficulty in raising the capital needed for start-up and expansion, the burden of complying with increasing levels of government regulation, and the major personal commitment required on the part of the owner.

At first, small-business owners are involved in all aspects of the company's operations. Wise use of outside consultants can free up the owner's time to focus on planning and strategy in addition to day-to-day operations. Other key management responsibilities are finding and retaining good employees and monitoring market conditions. Expanding into global markets can be a profitable growth strategy for small businesses.

LO5 Summarize the first steps to take if you are starting your own business.

After finding an idea that satisfies a market need, the small-business owner should choose a form of business organization. The process of developing a formal business plan helps the business owner to analyze the feasibility of his or her idea. This written plan describes in detail the idea for the business and how it will be implemented. The plan also helps the owner obtain both debt and equity financing for the new business.

LO6 Discuss some of the programs available to help entrepreneurs and small-business owners.

The BDC is the main federal agency serving small businesses. It provides guarantees of private lender loans for small businesses. The BDC also offers a wide range of management assistance services, including courses, publications, and consulting.

The Canada Business Network is a collaborative arrangement between federal and provincial/territorial government and not-for-profit organizations. Its goal is to provide businesses with the resources they need to prosper. Through its organized network of service centres across Canada, it promotes entrepreneurship and innovation.

Many of Canada's financial institutions, including the chartered banks, offer advice, from starting or buying an existing business, business planning, operating the business, growing the business, to selling the business.

LO7 List some of the trends that are shaping entrepreneurship and small-business ownership.

Opportunities continue to exist for entrepreneurs of all ages and backgrounds. The numbers of women and minority business owners continue to increase. The number of start-ups in the technology sector has declined, but Internet technology is creating numerous opportunities for new types of small businesses and fuelling small-business growth by making it easier to open Web-based businesses. The economic crises of 2008 and 2011 resulted in many people without jobs; while for the most part this was devastating, for some it provided the motivation to live their dreams and start their businesses.

Key Terms

angel investors   174
Business Development Bank of Canada
   (BDC)   177
business plan   173
debt   174

entrepreneurs   162
equity   174
intrapreneurs   164
small business   168
venture capital   175

Experiential Exercises

1. After working in software development with a major food company for 12 years, you are becoming impatient with corporate "red tape" (regulations and routines). You have an idea for a new snack product for nutrition-conscious consumers and are thinking of starting your own company. What are the entrepreneurial characteristics you will need? What other factors should you consider before quitting your job? Working with a partner, choose one to be the entrepreneurial

employee and one to play the role of his or her current boss. Develop notes for a script. The employee will focus on why this is a good idea, reasons he or she will succeed, and so on, whereas the employer will play devil's advocate to convince him or her that staying on at the large company is a better idea. Then switch roles and repeat the discussion.

2. What does it really take to become an entrepreneur? Find out by interviewing a local entrepreneur or researching an entrepreneur you've read about in this chapter or in the business press. Get answers to the following questions, as well as any others you'd like to ask:

   • How did you develop your vision for the company?
   • What are the most important entrepreneurial characteristics that helped you succeed?
   • Where did you learn the business skills you needed to run and grow the company?
   • How did you research the feasibility of your idea?
   • How did you prepare your business plan?
   • What were the biggest challenges you had to overcome?
   • Where did you obtain financing for the company?
   • What are the most important lessons you learned by starting this company?
   • What advice do you have for would-be entrepreneurs?

3. A small catering business in your city is for sale for $150,000. The company specializes in business luncheons and smaller social events. The owner has been running the business for four years from her home but is expecting her first child and wants to sell. You will need outside investors to help you purchase the business. Develop questions to ask the owner about the business and its prospects and a list of documents you'd want to see. What other types of information would you need before making a decision to buy this company? Summarize your findings in a memo to a potential investor that explains the appeal of the business for you and how you plan to investigate the feasibility of the purchase.

4. Does it work? Select a type of business that interests you and go through the checklist presented at www.bizmove.com/starting/m1b.htm "Starting a Business: Determining the Feasibility of Your Business Idea." Given the results of your feasibility study, should you continue to investigate this opportunity?

5. Do you have what it takes to be an entrepreneur or small-business owner? See www.toolkit.com/small_business_guide/sbg.aspx?nid=P01_0001. What did your results tell you, and were you surprised by what you learned?

6. Your class decides to participate in a local business plan competition. Divide the class into small groups and choose one of the following ideas:

   • a new computer game based on the stock market;
   • a company with an innovative design for a skateboard; or
   • travel services for college and high school students.

   Prepare a detailed outline for the business plan, including the objectives for the business and the types of information you would need to develop product, marketing, and financing strategies. Each group will then present its outline for the class to critique.

7. Home base. Starting a business from your home is one of the easiest ways to become self-employed. Choose an idea that you feel is suited to this type of business. What other issues do you need to investigate before start-up? How feasible is your idea? Use a variety of research resources to answer these questions.

8. Visit Sample Business Plans at www.bplans.com to review sample plans for all types of businesses. Select an idea for a company in a field that interests you, and using information from this site, prepare an outline for its business plan.

9. You want to buy a business but don't know much about valuing small companies. Using the "Buy & Sell a Business" online at www.inc.com and resources on other small-business sites, including advertisements, develop a checklist of questions to ask when buying a business. Also summarize several ways in which businesses arrive at the sale price ("Business for Sale" includes the price rationale for each profiled business).

Review Questions

1. What is the definition of an entrepreneur? What is the definition of a small business?

2. Why do people become entrepreneurs?

3. What are some of the challenges for entrepreneurs?

4. What impact does small business have on the Canadian economy?

5. Why does small business thrive in Canada?

6. What are some sources of financing for a small business?

7. What role can outside consultants play in a small business?

8. Why does small business have to be creative in hiring and retaining employees?

9. What are some alternatives to starting your own business?

10. Why would a small business decide to remain small?

11. What needs to be included in a business plan? What is the business plan used for?

12. How does Export Development Canada help small businesses?

13. What services do the financial institutions provide to small-business owners?

14. What are some of the trends in entrepreneurship and small business?

CREATIVE THINKING CASE

180s Gives Old Products New Spin

People laughed when Ron Wilson and Brian Le Gette quit solid investment banking jobs with six-figure salaries to build a better earmuff. The buddies, both engineers, shared a vision based on a simple strategy: to innovate mundane products with redefined style and function.

It all started with the humble earmuff. Walking across campus at his university on a blustery winter day, Ron Wilson mused about keeping his ears warm without looking like a dork, conceptualizing what would later become the company's signature product, the Ear Warmer. Seven years later he and his business school buddy, Brian Le Gette (they both earned MBAs in Entrepreneurial Management), designed and developed prototypes of an expandable, collapsible, fleece-covered ear warmer that wraps around the back of the head.

They charged $7,500 in start-up expenses to credit cards and, in the following fall, sold their first ear warmers on a university campus—for $20 apiece. Two classmates persuaded Wilson and Le Gette to hawk their product on the Home Shopping Network, and the rest, as they say, is history. Their television debut sold 5,000 Ear Warmers in 8.5 minutes, and three years later home shoppers had bought 600,000 Ear Warmers. Their product was a winner.

Launched by this momentum, their business quickly grew into a booming product design and development company, a creator and marketer of innovative performance wear with 71 employees worldwide. The company's headquarters, known as the 180s Performance Lab, includes an interactive storefront where consumers can test new products. The building's architecture—"floating" conference rooms, a sailcloth roof, four huge windows to the sky—inspires the creative process taking place inside. World-class product design and development teams are constantly working on new innovations, the very core of the 180s culture. And nearly every product has multiple design and utility patents that reflect the unique design solutions the company creates.

Both founders left the company to pursue other interests in the early 2000s. They were the ones laughing, all the way to the bank. But the company did not thrive in their absence, so a new vision was necessary. In an odd twist, 180s has become a Lynn Tilton Company, named for the award-winning female entrepreneur who also left the investment banking world to make her mark on the world of Main Street. 180s has gone on to become a supplier to such masculine bastions as the NHL, the NFL, and the US Marine Corps—all while earning the Women Business Enterprise National Certification. 180s earmuffs can be found throughout Canada, the US, and many other countries. A couple of cold ears and some innovation helped bring an 1873 invention to the modern world and make some visionaries well-off.

Thinking Critically

1. What characteristics made Ron Wilson and Brian Le Gette successful entrepreneurs?

2. How did their partnership and shared vision serve their business goals?

3. Do you think their departure from the company affected its growth? Why or why not?

4. Research Lynn Tilton online. What characteristics set her apart from many investors?

SOURCES: Julekha Dash, "180s CEO Le Gette Departs," *Baltimore Business Journal*, July 15, 2005, http://www.bizjournals.com; "Winners Announced for Maryland's Business International Leadership Awards," World Trade Center Institute press release, March 9, 2004; "Brian Le Gette, CEO and co-founder, and Tim Hodge, Chief Legal Officer, of 180s, LLC," World Trade Center Institute, http://www.wtci.org/events/awards/leadership2004/legette.htm, November 9, 2005; 180s corporate website, http://www.180s.com, March 15, 2006; 180s corporate website, "News in 2011." 180s, December 2011.

your career

AS AN ENTREPRENEUR

Do you have what it takes to own your own company? Or are you better suited to working for a corporation? To find out, you need to determine whether you have the personal traits for entrepreneurial success. If the answer is yes, you need to identify the type of business that is best for you.

Know Yourself

Owning a business is challenging and requires a great deal of personal sacrifice. You must take a hard and honest look at yourself before you decide to strike out on your own. The quiz in Exhibit YC.1 can help you evaluate whether you have the personality traits to become a successful entrepreneur. Think about yourself and rate yourself—honestly!—on each of these characteristics.

Which Business Is for You?

If you are well suited to owning your own company, the next question is what type of business to start. You need to consider your expertise, interests, and financial resources. Start with a broad field; then choose a specific good or service. The business can involve a new idea or a refinement of an existing idea. It might also bring an existing idea to a new area.

To narrow the field, ask yourself the following questions:

- What do I like to do?
- What am I good at?
- How much can I personally invest in my business?

- Do I have access to other financial resources?
- What is my past business experience?
- What are my personal interests and hobbies?
- How can I use my experience and interests in my own business?
- Do I want or need partners?

Spending time on these and similar questions will help you identify some possible business opportunities and the resources you will need to develop them.

Prior job experience is the number one source of new business ideas. Starting a business in a field where you have specialized product or service experience improves your chances for success.

Personal interests and hobbies are another major source of ideas. Gourmet food enthusiasts have started many restaurants and specialty food businesses. For example, Eleni Gianopulos transformed the humble cookie into a specialty item, bringing in more than $1 million in sales each year. Eleni's unique, beautifully decorated cookies come in shapes for every season and occasion, such as several series featuring Academy Award nominees and movie quotes. Customers, who include corporate and celebrity clients, can also place special orders. One customer ordered a cookie model of Elton John's house! Business at Eleni's NYC is growing; the cookies are now sold online at www.elenis.com and featured in many specialty catalogues.

Each January, *Entrepreneur* magazines feature lists of top businesses and business trends for the coming year. Check out the current hot lists at www.entrepreneur.com/hotcenter.

SOURCES: Eleni's NYC website, http://www.elenis.com; and "Got ID?" *Entrepreneur*, November 2002, http://www.entrepreneur.com.

Exhibit YC.1 How Do You Rate?

The following quiz will help you to assess your personality and determine if you have what it takes to start your own company. Think about yourself and rate yourself—honestly!—on each of these characteristics.

PERSONALITY TRAIT	HIGH	ABOVE AVERAGE	AVERAGE	BELOW AVERAGE	LOW
Ability to handle uncertainty	○	○	○	○	○
Confidence	○	○	○	○	○
Discipline	○	○	○	○	○
Drive/ambition	○	○	○	○	○
Energy	○	○	○	○	○
Flexibility	○	○	○	○	○
Independence	○	○	○	○	○
Ability to seize opportunity	○	○	○	○	○
Persistence	○	○	○	○	○
Problem solving	○	○	○	○	○
TOTAL	___	___	___	___	___

Scoring
Give yourself 5 points for every "high," 4 points for every "above average," 3 points for every "average," 2 points for every "below average," and 1 point, for every "low."

Score results
- 46–50: You are already in business for yourself or should be!
- 40–45: Your entrepreneurial aptitude and desires are high.
- 30–39: A paid staff job and owning your own business rate equally.
- 20–29: Entrepreneurial aptitude is apparently not one of your strong suits.
- 10–19: You might find the going tough and the rewards slim if you owned your own business.

SOURCE: "Test your aptitude, attitude to see how you stack up," staff written that published September 24, 1997. Copyright © 1997. Los Angeles Times. Reprinted with Permission.

Making the Connection

Analyzing the Business

In this chapter, we will be looking at how to analyze a business by using different theories and tools. This analysis follows our integrative model of a successful business, analyzing the different factors in the model and requiring you to see the connections between the factors.

We have placed this chapter on analysis here because you have an understanding of the environment that the business operates in from the first 6 chapters, and can now use this analytical framework to build your understanding of business as you learn more about the internal workings of companies in later chapters.

We start by looking at the *critical success factors* in more detail—what they are and how to measure whether a company has achieved them. It is one thing to suggest they are important, but if that is the case, it is then critically important that you understand how to evaluate whether a company has achieved them.

Right under the critical success factors in our model are the *stakeholders*. Because these groups have such an important stake in the success of a business, they have to be analyzed so that the business really understands the nature of its relationship with them and how to best manage that relationship to ensure success.

Next in our model are the two major environments that the business operates within—the external environment surrounding the business, and its own internal environment. We have looked at each of the five elements of the *PESTI* model of the external environment already, but in this chapter we will also give you a framework for analyzing that environment and understanding the implications of it

for the business. Just as with the success factors, it is one thing to understand what they are, but it is also critically important to understand what they mean for your business, or the business you are analyzing.

You will also learn, in this chapter, how to use your understanding of the external environment and combine that with an understanding of the company's internal environment to see how they work together. Remember—everything is connected. The SWOT analysis will help you to see what the company's strengths and weaknesses are in its *marketing, financial, human resource*, and *operations* areas to compare them to the opportunities and threats in the external environment. This particular tool is one of the most integrative tools available and is fundamentally the premise that the integrative model of a successful business is built on. Ultimately, it is the company's *vision, mission* and *strategy* that determine the decisions it makes and the actions it takes; and the SWOT analysis helps to explain these decisions and actions, allowing you to analyze whether they make sense. A full analysis will also require that you look at how these decisions are implemented through the functions of management—specifically, does the *organizational* structure fit the strategy, and is the reward system designed to *motivate* the employees to implement the strategy in a *committed* way? Remember, this is the most critical of the success factors as it is the foundation upon which they all rest—nothing happens without people.

The chapter finishes off with a discussion of the future of analyzing a business—what to expect. A lot of the trends in the environment are further emphasized here as they become the focus for your analysis—what will be the expectations of stakeholders into the future? As we have brought up in earlier chapters, analysis needs to focus on changing customer expectations in terms of their wants and needs, but also changing societal expectations in terms of the environment—whether the company is operating in a sustainable fashion and, in terms of ethical behaviour, whether the company is operating in a socially responsible way, particularly as it expands internationally.

chapter 7

Analyzing the Business

LEARNING OUTCOMES

1 Describe the critical success factors and how to measure them.

2 Explain how to do a SWOT analysis, and how to use it.

3 Understand the basic framework for analyzing the business.

4 Discuss some methods for analyzing the financial position of the company.

5 List some of the trends in analyzing the business.

RIM VS iPHONE

In August of 2011, it was reported that, despite an increase in overall sales from the previous quarter, the BlackBerry smartphone, sold by industry pioneer Research In Motion (RIM) Canada, dropped to fourth among the world rankings with less than 12 percent of the market. Apple surged into first place, selling over 20 million of the iPhone compared to 12 million RIM smartphones. In the same quarter of 2010, RIM outsold Apple 11 to 8. The newer phones and tablets from RIM received poor reviews and the company lost competitive ground to Google, Motorola, and others.

RIM was started in 1984 by Mike Lazardis and his VP Operations, Douglas Fregin. They developed technology with Erickson, Motorola, and other partners in the pager, modem and other high-tech markets. In the early 1990s, RIM developed the first wireless point-of-sale systems. This technology seems to have developed alongside interactive pagers (pagers that can send back a response). It was a relatively short step to the device that was to become the BlackBerry in 1999 and revolutionize the working world.

Revenue at RIM doubled to nearly $50 million in 1999. By 2005, sales of the "Crackberry" propelled RIM sales over the $1 billion level. In 2011, sales were projected to be nearly $20 billion. This made billionaires of the founders, along with Jim Balsillie who joined in 1992 and became Co-CEO with Lazardis.

RIM initially saw the smartphone market as an opportunity, just like Apple had done with the MP3 player market in the 1990s. There had been several MP3 players before the iPod, but Steve Jobs and his design team saw many flaws in those products. The Apple team looked at customer complaints in the MP3 industry and developed the iPod to address as many of those complaints as possible. In 2005, just as BlackBerry was taking off, Apple started looking at the smartphone business.

The cellphone market in North America had been controlled by the service providers (the companies that own the towers and sell the phones). RIM used this to its benefit by limiting products and working with the companies. But the phones were slow, and expensive to use. Apple saw an unhappy user population that appeared to have little power in the marketplace.

The first iPhones were released in 2007, just as RIM was becoming the darling of the stock market. Apple customers, thrilled with the quality of the iPod and other Apple products, lined up to be the first owners of the iPhone. Prices were very high, with Apple netting $80 from each phone and over $200 from the sale of a two-year contract with AT&T in the US, and similar margins from later launches in Canada and abroad. RIM stock peaked at $148 in 2008 and, even though sales have continued to grow, the share price has dropped as market share declines.

THOMAS BARWICK/ICONICA/GETTY IMAGES

Apple saw a competitive opportunity as RIM stagnated and failed to provide users with new and exciting ways to use the Blackberry. The iPhone opened up the market for Android and others. The future will tell us if Apple can withstand competitive pressures as they have in the MP3 business or if the traditional players in the cellphone industry can fight back.[1]

THINKING CRITICALLY

As you read this chapter, consider the following questions:

1. How do companies analyze whether they have achieved the critical success factors?
2. What are some of the approaches to analyze a business?
3. How do companies use analyses of their operations to compete in the marketplace?

SOURCES: Porter's Five Forces Analysis, http://www.slideshare.net/jontymohta444/porters-5-forces-model-case-apple-inc; "Smartphone rankings," *Vancouver Sun*, February 24, 2011; P 21 http://www.vancouversun.com/technology/Apple+tops+global+smartphone+rankings+slides/5212449/story.html; Research In Motion Ltd (RIM.TO), http://ca.finance.yahoo.com/q?s=RIM. TO; J. Van Sack, "Analysts torch BlackBerry maker's smartphone move," *Boston Herald*, August 5, 2011, http://www.bostonherald.com/business/technology/general/view/2011_0805analysts_torch_blackberrymakers_smartphone_move/; "History of RIM, the BlackBerry smartphone," February 2, 2009, http://www.berryreview.com/2009/02/12/the-history-of-rim-the-blackberry-smartphone-part-1-the-origins/; F. Vogelstein, "The Untold Story: How the iPhone Blew Up the Wireless Industry," *Wired* Magazine, 16(2), 2008, http://www.wired.com/gadgets/wireless/magazine/16-02/ff_iphone; "Investing Money, RIM," http://investing.money.msn.com/investments/financial-statements?symbol=rimm; "RIM Financials 2010," BlackberryPlanetBook.com, http://blackberryplanetbook.com/index.php/BlackBerry_Planet_-_RIM_Financials; "RIM's Structure goes under the microscope," The Canadian Press, July 12, 2011, http://www.obj.ca/Technology/2011-07-12/article-2647413/RIMs-structure-goes-under-the-microscope/1.

Businesses are constantly evaluating their operations and reviewing whether they have met the critical success factors. Successful businesses review their operations to explain what makes them successful over time—not just one year but consistently outperforming year after year. That's how we learn about business—by studying those successful businesses that are leaders in their fields.

This chapter looks at what the critical success factors are and some ways to analyze the operations of companies as they work to meet those success factors. Not only is financial success important, but meeting and hopefully exceeding their customers' expectations is also required of successful companies. There are many tools to analyze the business—here we present a general overview.

LO1 ## THE CRITICAL SUCCESS FACTORS

What does it mean to be truly successful? Is it simply making money? What does it take to make money? *The critical success factors* for any business, or the factors that indicate success, are

- achieving financial performance;
- meeting and exceeding customer needs;
- providing value—quality products at a reasonable price;
- encouraging creativity and innovation; and
- gaining employee commitment.

Businesses need to evaluate these factors to determine if they are truly successful in all areas, and identify the areas where there are opportunities for improvement in order to increase success. See Exhibit 7.1 below.

Most businesses exist to make money and achieve financial performance, but what is often left out of the discussion is how a business becomes successful in the first place. Can a business be truly successful at generating income if it ignores the other four factors? For example, can it make money by selling products that do not satisfy customers' needs, with inferior quality at an unreasonable price, using yesterday's ideas (when the competition is 10 steps ahead), while displaying a negative attitude toward the customer as demonstrated by its employees? Even one of these points would result in lower income and a less successful business. For example, according to the Encana website at www.encana.com: "At the heart of Encana's success are the ingenuity,

Exhibit 7.1 Critical Success Factors

Encouraging Creativity and Innovation

Achieving Financial Performance

Successful Business

Gaining Employee Commitment

Meeting and Exceeding Customers' Needs

Providing Value—Quality Products at a Reasonable Price

SOURCE: Adapted from Fred L. Fry, Charles R. Stoner, and Richard E. Hattwick. *Business: An Integrative Framework*, New York: Mc-Graw-Hill Higher Education, 2001.

technical leadership and enthusiasm of [its] over 7,000 staff." Clearly Encana appreciates the importance of the critical success factors of gaining employee commitment in order to encourage the innovation and creativity so important to its success.

Achieving Success

It's also important to remember that these factors are integrative—they all affect one another. It is virtually impossible to find a successful business in which all of these factors have not been achieved. They work together to make the company truly successful. For example, consider Toyota. To meet customer needs, Toyota was the first to mass-produce a hybrid vehicle, but it took creativity and innovation to come up with the technology, a committed workforce to follow through, and a commitment to providing value through quality at a reasonable price to achieve success. Therefore, it is critically important, if a business wants to be truly successful, to measure its ability to achieve all the success factors—not just bottom-line performance. It is because of these other factors that the company is able to achieve financial performance—bottom-line performance is simply not possible without the other factors.

Achieving financial performance is measured in a number of ways, the primary ones being profit, return on investment, cash flow, and net worth. A company needs, to have a healthy profit, or "bottom line," but it also needs to earn a good profit relative to the money it has invested—in other words, a good return on the equity investment made by the owners or shareholders. But this means nothing, of course, if it can't pay its bills. It's important to understand that a profitable company can still go bankrupt. For instance, while it is waiting for its customers to pay for the products they have purchased, it still has to pay its own bills. The timing of the cash flows can put an otherwise profitable business into a very precarious position. And finally, the net worth of the company (what it owns less what it owes) is important. These concepts, and how they are measured, will be discussed later in this chapter and in more detail in the final chapters of the book.

Meeting and exceeding customer needs means that companies must be sensitive to the needs of customers, anticipate changes in those needs, and, of course, work to meet those needs in a proactive fashion; that is, before a customer complains. However, companies today cannot just provide what the customer wants. They need to satisfy customers beyond their expectations, or the competition will. This is difficult to measure because, unlike financial performance, it is subjective; there are no easily calculated figures in recognizable units like dollars, to measure whether a company has met its customers' needs. Also, there are standardized financial performance measures available for other companies that a business can use to compare itself against—that is not the case with meeting and exceeding customer needs. However, it is still critically important to measure, because if you don't measure it, problems are not identified and don't get corrected until it is often too late and the customer is lost.

One way to measure whether a business is meeting its customers' needs is through "second-level communications"—are customers going "above the heads" of sales people and customer service reps to complain? Companies that ignore this information do so at their own peril. Most people don't complain, they just go away and tell other people to stay away. When someone complains, that needs to be taken seriously and viewed as potentially symptomatic of a much larger problem.

Another very effective way of measuring whether a company has met customer needs is through "gap analysis." The steps for this type of analysis follow:

1. Determine the "real" gap that exists between customer expectations and customer perceptions. A good way to do this is by surveying your customers. Ask them what factors are important to them and what

Concept *in Action*

What makes a successful company? The answer depends on the criteria used to determine success. If it is based on profit, it would most likely be one of the Canadian Chartered Banks. If it is based on corporate social responsibility, certainly Brookfield Properties Corp would make the list. What other criteria could be used to determine if a company would make the list?

THE GLOBE AND MAIL/THE CANADIAN PRESS(DEBORAH BAIC)

their expectations are, and have them rate the company on those same factors—these are their perceptions. This way, you have a true measure of the gap between what they want and what they think they are getting. This gap in the customer's mind is what matters, not what *you* think it is.

2. Determine the sources and causes of the gap. It could simply be that the customer has incorrect expectations to begin with—likely because of miscommunication. A very common mistake of companies is to over-promise to get the sale and then under-deliver on what they have promised, which inevitably leads to dissatisfaction. It could also be a clear case of inadequate performance of the product or service, or it could be a case of inadequate follow-up by the company. As we've said earlier, it is easier and cheaper to keep customers than get customers, and inadequate follow-up is a sure-fire way to make a customer feel you don't care about keeping them.

3. Take corrective action—do something about it! It is critical to accept responsibility (even if you don't think it is the company's fault. Remember the old adage "the customer is always right"?) and take immediate action, showing that you are committed to a solution. It is also important to continue to communicate to show the customer they are important to you. Keeping that communication line open will also provide you with more useful information to improve your performance. Finally, it is important to reassess—commit to continuous improvement, don't just assume that everything is OK.

Customer loyalty is the ultimate indicator that you have met and exceeded customer needs. An article in the *Harvard Business Review* (July/August 2010) titled "Stop Trying to Delight Your Customers" suggested that there are three metrics that can be used to predict customer loyalty: CSAT, measuring customer satisfaction; NPS, the net promoter score; and CES, the customer effort score. These are very useful measures for determining whether a company is meeting and exceeding customer needs. However, the article further suggested that focusing on "delighting customers" doesn't build their loyalty; instead, a company should focus on reducing the effort (CES) that a customer must go through to get a problem solved. The research suggested that 94 percent of respondents with a low CES expressed an intention to repurchase and 88 percent would increase their spending, whereas 81 percent of those with a high CES intended to spread negative word of mouth. And that would definitely not help you to meet this critical success factor!

Providing value means that a business must constantly strive to improve the quality of its products and services, and do so at a reasonable cost. Customers demand quality and will stand for nothing less, but they want value for their dollar. They will pay a price that gives them value for their money—the quality that they demand at a price that makes it worthwhile or valuable to them. This can be measured by gap analysis as well.

Encouraging creativity and innovation involves the process of being creative (entrepreneurial thinking), as well as harnessing that creativity to generate the innovations that keep the company one step ahead of the competition. When a company becomes comfortable with its level of success, it often resists the change needed to stay ahead. This is dangerous for the company because there are only two kinds of businesses—those that constantly innovate and those that go out of business. In today's business world, one of the only constants is change. The status quo doesn't work anymore. Companies need to become "learning organizations," proactively seeking to learn and move ahead every day in everything they do.

Companies measure their ability to encourage creativity and innovation typically by the number of new ideas that come forward, the percentage that are followed-through on, and the percentage of sales that come from these new ideas. To build truly innovative organizations, it is critical that businesses build their reward systems around innovation and creativity to ensure that they are, in fact, encouraging their employees to take risks and experiment, as well as tolerating and learning from their mistakes. They also need to determine the degree to which they embrace diversity and differences in their hiring, because thinking differently fuels innovative thinking. And they need to deliberately employ creative personalities—both the "adaptor" types who always look for ways to improve how things are done, and the "innovators" who challenge the existing ways and look for new ones.

And finally, probably the most important success factor is *gaining employee commitment*. Employees need to be empowered to act and be motivated to meet the company's objectives in each of the first four factors, or those objectives won't be met. Therefore, every company needs to understand the needs of its employees. Only then can it gain their commitment, because they will commit to meeting company goals only if their own goals are met at the same time. It is, again, an integrative relationship. Measuring employee commitment is difficult because it is so subjective. One way a company can tell whether employees are committed is if they are going "above and beyond" what is expected. This indicates that they are intrinsically committed to the organization's goals versus just doing what is required for the extrinsic reward—the paycheque at the end of the day. Companies can also do "exit" interviews with departing employees. This often provides good information as to why commitment does not exist.

Stakeholder Analysis

Underneath the critical success factors in our model of a successful business are the stakeholders of the business (discussed in Chapter 3). These are individuals and groups that have a "stake" in what the business does. They are affected by the decisions that the business makes, and therefore the business has a responsibility to consider them in those decisions.

The three most critical and obvious stakeholder groups are the owners of the business (or shareholders in the case of a corporation), the employees of the business (and their union if represented by one), and the customers. But there is a much wider world out there that must be considered—the government, special interest groups, the community surrounding the business, its suppliers, and so on. All of these groups interact with the business and keep it operating.

Businesses cannot operate in a vacuum, as if these groups do not exist. These stakeholders must be considered in every decision the business makes. For example: If we change this material, how will our customers react? Will they keep buying our product? If we move the business, how will it affect the community? How many employees will we lose? If we cut down these trees to build the new plant, how will the environmentalist groups respond? How will the community and the local government respond? If earnings drop in the fourth quarter as expected, will our shareholders sell their shares, making the share price fall even lower? Achieving the critical success factors clearly depends on an intimate knowledge of, and relationship with, the stakeholders of the business. The question is, how does a company analyze its stakeholders?

A useful method for performing a stakeholder analysis was presented by Grant Savage et al. in an *Academy of Management Executive* article titled "Strategies for Assessing and Managing Organizational Stakeholders." The article suggested that a company assess each stakeholder along two dimensions—the potential to threaten the company and the potential to cooperate with the company. Once you determine whether the stakeholders are supportive (low potential for threat/high potential for cooperation), a mixed blessing (high potential for both), non-supportive (high potential for threat/low potential for cooperation), or marginal (low potential for both), the company can then develop strategies for dealing with each of the stakeholders and ultimately change the more threatening relationships into more cooperative ones.

Concept *Check*

What are the success factors?

How does a company analyze whether it has met the success factors?

Identify the stakeholders of a business.

CHAPTER 7 Analyzing the Business **195**

Creating the Future of Business

RAY CAO AND ADITYA SHAH, LOOSE BUTTON

Loose Button is a really cool name for a unique business created by two young entrepreneurs; they identified an opportunity in the business environment and used their strengths to capitalize on that opportunity. If you've ever made a purchase and later wished you could have tried it first to know it wasn't right for you before you spent your hard-earned money, then you'll understand the concept of Loose Button. According to Aditya Shah, Loose Button "is changing the face of how consumers discover and try products … our mission is to help customers discover, try, and purchase quality beauty products through a unique shopping experience."

Aditya Shah and Ray Cao, the founders of the company, have created a unique service where members receive, for a low fee, a chic box of brand-new, high-end seasonal beauty product samples delivered to their homes every three months so that they can try them out before buying them full-sized. Along with their membership, they also receive access to other exclusive samples of teas, coffees, chocolates, accessories, etc., as well as access to new product launches and gift cards to other shopping sites. The company also plans to launch an online retail store so members can buy full-sized products after sampling them. The result is a win-win for both the consumer and the manufacturer—current clients include Procter & Gamble, L'Oréal, and Coty. The manufacturer gets its samples out and receives invaluable information in return from the highly engaged users who create web videos and blog posts reviewing the products.

It didn't start out that way though. Loose Button started as an apparel e-commerce company. Eight months into it they realized that the space was too saturated, so they redirected Loose Button into the beauty space online. According to Ray, "You have to be passionate about your idea, but you can't be in love with it. You have to be willing to adapt." He says, "Building a high-growth business is one of the most difficult challenges that one can pursue in life. Be prepared for failure, and be prepared to fail many times. But don't ever give up. Just remember: if it's easy to do, then everyone would be doing it." In the future, Ray and Aditya would like to apply their subscription business model to other product lines.

Ray, a recipient of the Waterloo "Top 40 Under 40" award, pays forward his success to help other aspiring young entrepreneurs succeed. He serves as a board member of the Impact Entrepreneurship Group, is an advisory board member of New York's Entrepreneur Week, and sits on a steering committee of the Toronto-based DiverseCity initiative, whose aim it is to increase the number of visible minorities in leadership positions. Ray's networking savvy is one of the keys to the company's success. It has enabled Loose Button to attract an advisory board with a wealth of experience to offer—Harry Rosen for one—offering advice that has proven invaluable.

Aditya's advice for young budding entrepreneurs? "If students are interested in becoming entrepreneurs, they should start brainstorming and tinkering with ideas right now. Work with different people to see who would be ideal co-founders with complementary skill sets. If they can gain some momentum on a project before they graduate, they will be better poised to tackle a startup full time." Well there's your motivation—get going!

Thinking Critically

1. Many entrepreneurs fail because they believe too much in their vision and hold steadfast when all information would point them in a different direction. What qualities do these entrepreneurs possess that keep them flexible to change?
2. Was it these same qualities that allowed them to see outside the paradigm of how business is typically done in the beauty industry and to capitalize on the opportunities in e-commerce, technology, and social media to create such an amazing idea, or does it take something more?
3. What other qualities do they possess that have helped them succeed?

SOURCES: http://www.loosebutton.com, used with permission from Aditya Shah and Ray Cao; http://www.profitguide.com, December 6, 2011; http://www.notable.ca, June 12, 2011.

LO2 SWOT—A BASIC FRAMEWORK FOR ANALYZING THE BUSINESS

Examining the external environment by using the PESTI model, as we have done in the first five chapters, is the first step to analyzing a business by using a SWOT framework. SWOT stands for strengths, weaknesses, opportunities, and threats. Essentially it is a tool used to compare the opportunities and threats in the external environment to the strengths and weaknesses in the internal environment of a business. You take this information, along with your understanding of the key stakeholders, and analyze whether the vision, mission, and strategy of the business make sense in this context. Performing a SWOT analysis is important to understanding whether the entrepreneur's or CEO's vision is logical and feasible, and whether the strategies used to pursue the vision will lead to success.

Where Have We Been*

A good start to a SWOT analysis is to investigate how a company's past strategy and structure affect it in the present. This can be done by charting the critical incidents

*From unknown, *http://college.cengage.com/business/resources/casestudies/students/analyzing.htm.* © Cengage Learning

in its history—that is, the events that were the most unusual or the most essential for its development into the company it is today. Some of the events have to do with its founding, its initial products, how it makes new-product market decisions, and how it developed and chose functional competencies to pursue. Its entry into new businesses and shifts in its main lines of business are also important milestones to consider. This will help you to see why it is where it is today.

Where Are We Now—The SWOT*

IDENTIFY THE COMPANY'S INTERNAL STRENGTHS AND WEAKNESSES

Once the historical profile is completed, you can begin the SWOT analysis. Use all the incidents you have charted to develop an account of the company's strengths and weaknesses as they have emerged historically. The strengths and weaknesses come from the internal environment (e.g., financial, operations, marketing, and human resources). Examine each of the value creation functions of the company, and identify the functions in which the company is currently strong and currently weak. Some companies might be weak in marketing; some might be strong in research and development. Make lists of these strengths and weaknesses. Exhibit 7.2 lists some of the issues that may be considered when developing the strengths and weaknesses; the list will be specific to each company.

ANALYZE THE EXTERNAL ENVIRONMENT
The next step is to identify environmental opportunities and threats. These external factors are specific to each company, and there are different ways to analyze the external environment.

Two tools that are important to analyze the competitive environment and industry are Porter's Five Forces Model and the industry life cycle model. Porter's

SWOT analysis
A SWOT analysis looks at the Strengths and Weaknesses of the company itself and the Opportunities and Threats for the company in its external environment.

Porter's Five Forces Model
A model that focuses on the five forces that shape competition within an industry.

industry life cycle model
A useful tool for analyzing the effects of an industry's evolution on competitive forces.

Exhibit 7.2 The Strengths and Weaknesses Checklist

POTENTIAL INTERNAL STRENGTHS	POTENTIAL INTERNAL WEAKNESSES
Many product lines?	Obsolete, narrow product lines?
Broad market coverage?	Rising manufacturing costs?
Manufacturing competence?	Decline in R&D innovations?
Good marketing skills?	Poor marketing skills?
Good materials management systems?	Poor materials management systems?
R&D skills and leadership?	Loss of customer goodwill?
Many product lines?	Obsolete, narrow product lines?
Broad market coverage?	Rising manufacturing costs?
Manufacturing competence?	Decline in R&D innovations?
Good marketing skills?	Poor marketing skills?
Good materials management systems?	Poor materials management systems?
R&D skills and leadership?	Loss of customer goodwill?
Information system competencies	Inadequate information systems?
Human resource competencies?	Inadequate human resources?
Brand name reputation?	Loss of brand name capital?
Portfolio management skills?	Growth without direction?
Cost of differentiation advantage?	Bad portfolio management?
New-venture management expertise?	Loss of corporate direction?
Appropriate management style?	Infighting among divisions?
Appropriate organizational structure?	Loss of corporate control?
Appropriate control systems?	Inappropriate organizational structure and control systems?
Ability to manage strategic change?	High conflict and politics?
Well-developed corporate strategy?	Poor financial management?
Good financial management?	Others?
Others?	

SOURCE: http://college.cengage.com/business/ resources/casestudies/students/swot.htm © Cengage Learning.

*From unknown, *http://college.cengage.com/business/resources/casestudies/students/analyzing.htm.* © Cengage Learning.

Lululemon founder and University of Calgary graduate Chip Wilson stepped down from his executive position in 2012 to focus on his position as chairman of the board. The company grew to a point that having Chip hold both positions was working against the organization. He needed to focus on the opportunities presented by international expansion. What can companies do to monitor their strengths and weaknesses?

THE GLOBE AND MAIL/THE CANADIAN PRESS(JOHN LEHMANN)

Concept *Check*

What is a SWOT analysis?

What are some of the potential strengths and weaknesses of the company?

What is the importance of Porter's Five Forces Model?

What are some of the potential opportunities and threats to the company?

Five Forces Model, developed by Michael E. Porter of the Harvard Business Administration, focuses on the five forces that shape competition within an industry. Specifically, these five forces are

1. The risk of new entry by potential competitors
2. The degree of rivalry among established companies within an industry
3. The bargaining power of buyers
4. The bargaining power of suppliers
5. The threat of substitute products

Exhibit 7.3 illustrates some of the issues that should be looked at when using Porter's Five Forces Model

The industry life cycle model analyzes the effects of an industry's evolution on competitive forces. Using the industry life cycle model, we can identify what stage the industry is at. There are five stages of industry evolution

1. An embryonic industry environment
2. A growth industry environment
3. A shakeout industry environment
4. A mature industry environment
5. A declining industry environment*

This analysis will generate both an analysis of the company's environment and a list of opportunities and threats. Exhibit 7.4 lists some common environmental opportunities and threats that you may look for, but the list will be specific to each company.

 LO3 ANALYZING THE STRATEGY

Once you have identified the strengths and weaknesses of the company and the external opportunities and threats it is faced with, you need to consider what these findings mean. That is, you need to balance strengths and weaknesses against opportunities and threats to first see what the company's competencies and competitive advantages are;

*From unknown, *http://college.cengage.com/business/resources/casestudies/students/life_cycle.htm.* © Cengage Learning.

Exhibit 7.3   Porter's Five Forces Model of Competition

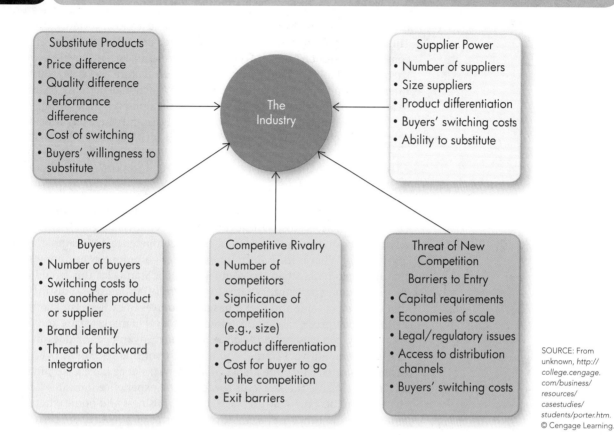

Substitute Products
- Price difference
- Quality difference
- Performance difference
- Cost of switching
- Buyers' willingness to substitute

The Industry

Supplier Power
- Number of suppliers
- Size suppliers
- Product differentiation
- Buyers' switching costs
- Ability to substitute

Buyers
- Number of buyers
- Switching costs to use another product or supplier
- Brand identity
- Threat of backward integration

Competitive Rivalry
- Number of competitors
- Significance of competition (e.g., size)
- Product differentiation
- Cost for buyer to go to the competition
- Exit barriers

Threat of New Competition
Barriers to Entry
- Capital requirements
- Economies of scale
- Legal/regulatory issues
- Access to distribution channels
- Buyers' switching costs

SOURCE: From unknown, *http://college.cengage.com/business/resources/casestudies/students/porter.htm.* © Cengage Learning.

Exhibit 7.4   The Opportunities and Threats Checklist

POTENTIAL ENVIRONMENTAL OPPORTUNITIES

Expand core business(es)?
Exploit new market segments?
Widen new market segments?
Extend cost or differentiation advantage?
Diversify into new growth businesses?
Expand into foreign markets?
Apply R&D skills in new areas?
Enter new related businesses?
Vertically integrate forward?
Vertically integrate backward?
Enlarge corporate portfolio?
Overcome barriers to entry?
Reduce rivalry among competitors?
Make profitable new acquisitions?
Apply brand name capital in new areas?
Seek fast market growth?
Others?

POTENTIAL ENVIRONMENTAL THREATS

Attacks on core business(es)?
Increases in domestic competition?
Increases in foreign competition?
Change in consumer taste?
Fall in barriers to entry?
Rise in new or substitute products?
Increase in industry rivalry?
New forms of industry competition?
Potential for takeover?
Existence for corporate raiders?
Increase in regional competition?
Changes in demographic factors?
Changes in economic factors?
Downturn in economy?
Rising labour costs?
Slower market growth?
Others?

SOURCE: From unknown, *http://college.cengage.com/business/resources/casestudies/students/swot.htm.* © Cengage Learning.

and then to determine whether its vision and mission are appropriate and, consequently, whether its overall strategy is appropriate. Ideally what a business should do is exploit the opportunities that exist, particularly in areas of strength; neutralize threats or ideally turn them into opportunities; build on its strengths; and avoid or, ideally, correct its weaknesses. The kinds of questions that need to be answered are, Is the company in an overall strong competitive position? Can it continue to pursue its current business- or corporate-level strategy profitably? What can the company do to turn weaknesses into strengths and threats into opportunities? Can it develop new functional, business, or corporate strategies to accomplish this change? Do its vision and mission even make sense?

You shouldn't generate the SWOT analysis and then put it aside. It provides a succinct summary of the company's situation, so it's key to all the analyses that follow.

Determine Competencies and Competitive Advantages

To understand a company's strategy, it is important to understand first what it has to compete with at its most basic level. What is its *core competence*?—a strength that it has, anything it can do very well. Starbucks core competence, for example, would be making great coffee. What is its *distinctive competence*?—a unique core competence, something that it can do better than the competition. For Starbucks, this would be making great coffee into an experience. What is its *competitive advantage*?—a distinctive competence that consumers value and that it has the resources to exploit. For Starbucks, that would definitely be the case, as demonstrated by its level of market share and financial success. And finally, what is its *sustainable competitive* advantage, or does it even have one? This is a competitive advantage that it can continue to exploit over time as it is not easily duplicated. It can be argued that Starbucks does have a sustainable competitive advantage because the key to its success is the experience it creates for its customers— the ability to become a "third place" outside business and home where you go to relax, and the culture it has for its employees in terms of how they are treated. Although the coffee itself could be copied, these intangible things are almost impossible to duplicate.

Analyze the Corporate-Level Strategy

Once you know what the company's competitive position is, you can better understand its vision statement and mission statement, and then understand the strategy it is pursuing to achieve this vision and mission. At its most basic level, the vision statement outlines why the company exists and where it going in the future. It clearly states the goals and objectives of the company and helps decision makers plan for future actions. The mission statement is used to differentiate an organization from its competition and further refines the direction articulated in the vision statement, answering such questions as, "Who are we, and what businesses are we in?" These two questions are closely linked by the values of the organization. Most times the vision and mission are stated explicitly, but there are times when they must be inferred from available information.

The company's corporate-level strategy outlines the different businesses it has decided to compete in to achieve its vision and mission. What are its SBUs or *strategic business units*? To determine the corporate-level strategy, you need to look at its line(s) of business and the nature of its subsidiaries and acquisitions. It is also important to analyze the relationship among the company's businesses. Do they trade or exchange resources? Are there gains to be achieved from synergy? Alternatively, is the company just running a portfolio of investments that are unrelated and therefore do not offer synergistic advantages?

This analysis should enable you to define the corporate strategy that the company is pursuing. Some possibilities:

- *Concentration* in one product, market, or technology.
- *Growth* through global expansion, penetration of existing markets, or product development.
- *Integration* vertically along the supply chain—either backward, such as Campbell's soup making its own cans; or forward, such as Sony operating its own stores.

---

vision statement
A clear, concise picture of the company's future direction in terms of its values and purpose that is used to guide and inspire.

mission statement
A clear, concise articulation of how the company intends to achieve its vision— how it is different from its competition and the keys to its success.

- *Integration* horizontally with a similar business, such as Wendy's buying Tim Hortons. This is often done through mergers or acquisitions—discussed in more detail in Chapter 8.
- *Diversification* of either the product line, or through entering different markets with the same or different products. This can be done in a related way to complement existing products and markets, or in an unrelated way with a "portfolio" strategy to spread the risks.

Of course, the company may choose a combination of strategies. Using the SWOT analysis, we can debate the merits of the chosen strategy. Is it appropriate, given the environment the company is in? Could the company capitalize on one of its areas of strength to pursue an opportunity in another line of business, or turn what might be a threat into an opportunity? A good example of this occurred when music downloading became available with technology, threatening the music industry and traditional record albums and CDs. What a great opportunity for a new form of distribution! If the industry had seen the signs and listened to what the consumer wanted, they would have seen the opportunity to use technology to enhance their businesses vs. reacting to the threat in a defensive, legalistic way. So the question needs to be, would a change in corporate strategy provide the company with new opportunities, transform a threat into an opportunity, or convert a weakness into a strength? For example, should the company diversify from its core business into new businesses?

Other issues should be considered as well. How and why has the company's strategy changed over time? What is the claimed rationale for any changes? Often, it is a good idea to analyze the company's businesses or products to assess its situation and identify which divisions contribute the most to, or detract from, its competitive advantage. It is also useful to explore how the company has built its portfolio over time. Did it acquire new businesses, or did it start new ventures? All these factors provide clues about the company and indicate ways of improving its future performance.

Analyze the Business-Level Strategy

Once you have done the SWOT analysis and know the company's corporate-level strategy, the next step is to identify the company's business-level strategy. The business-level strategy outlines how the company has decided to compete in the businesses it has

Concept *in Action*

Canadian Tire Corporation's vision is "to create sustainable growth by being a national champion and Canada's most trusted company. We will grow from our strengths—leveraging our brands, core capabilities, assets and extraordinary people." How do companies use their vision statement to help in the decision-making process?

GERRY THOMAS/NATIONAL HOCKEY LEAGUE/NHLI VIA GETTY IMAGES

chosen to be in. It describes its competitive position—the market, product, and service emphasis it has chosen to pursue. If the company is in many businesses, each business will have its own business-level strategy. Michael Porter (of the Five Forces Model discussed earlier) also outlined a number of generic competitive positions companies can take. They are cost leadership—for example, Walmart positions itself on its low prices; differentiation—for example, Ben & Jerry's ice cream positions itself on the uniqueness of the product; and focus—Long Tall Sally Girl positions itself toward a specific market niche of clothing for tall women. The company may market different products by using different business-level strategies. For example, it may offer a low-cost product range and a line of differentiated products. It is important to fully assess a company's business-level strategy to understand how it competes.

It's also important to identify the functional strategies the company uses internally to build competitive advantage in order to achieve its business-level strategy. Has it built the competencies it needs through superior efficiency, quality, innovation, or customer responsiveness in order to be successful in its chosen business-level strategy? The SWOT analysis will have provided information on the company's functional competencies—strengths and weaknesses. But further investigation is required regarding the company's operations, marketing, or research and development strategy to gain a picture of where the company is going and if it makes sense. For example, pursuing a low-cost strategy successfully requires a very different set of competencies from pursuing a differentiation strategy. Has the company developed the right ones? If it has, how can it exploit them further? Can it pursue both a low-cost and a differentiation strategy simultaneously?

It is useful to look at Porter's Five Forces Model in the context of business-level strategy. The model will have revealed threats to the company from the environment. The question is, can the company deal with these threats? How should it change its business-level strategy to counter them? Is the company's business-level strategy designed to properly deal with the opportunities and threats in its external environment.

Once you've completed the analysis, you will have a full picture of the way the company is operating and be in a position to evaluate the potential of its strategy. Thus, you will be able to make recommendations concerning the pattern of its future actions. However, first you need to consider strategy implementation, or the way the company tries to achieve its strategy. The strategy may make sense, but can it be implemented?

Making Ethical Choices

IS IT ETHICAL?—WHAT'S YOUR POSITION

It is not uncommon for issues to hit the media that offend our sensibilities. Because of the use of technology, including the social networks, reports of unethical behaviours by companies are widespread.

Globalization, although important to Canada and its standard of living, has its critics who say that many companies are taking advantage of poorer nations for production bases. Globalization is one of the most powerful trends of our time. It provides jobs often where jobs are needed and cheaper products (because of cheaper labour costs), but it has been argued that these companies are taking advantage of the poor nations.

Fair trade aims for equitable or better compensation for those who produce the goods. But it is not regulated by international trade laws. It can be argued that, regardless of the compensation that the producers receive, it is better than nothing, and some even go so far as to say that the producers don't need more. At the same time, others would argue that it is not fair to take advantage of these producers, and thereby the workers. It has also been said that these international companies exploit the developing nations only to seek increased profits; they provide poor working conditions and lack benefits.

Many people use the same arguments for child labour and feel that this is simply slavery.

Cigarette companies continue to produce tobacco products despite evidence of the health issues they cause. These companies employ workers and keep communities alive, but contribute in a negative way to the health of the nation and health-care costs.

ETHICAL DILEMMA: Companies are providing needed jobs at low wages and with poor working conditions. But without this pay there would be nothing. Some of these products are dangerous to consumers' health, yet demanded by them. Therefore, the companies are justified in what they are doing. What are your thoughts on this?

Analyze the Structure and Control Systems

The aim of this analysis is to identify what structure and control systems the company is using to implement its strategy and to evaluate whether that structure is the appropriate one for the company. Organizational structures will be explored in a more detailed way in Chapter 10. But for now it is important to recognize that different corporate and business strategies require different structures. For example, if there is a great deal of product diversification in the company's strategy, it would likely make sense for there to be more of a product than a functional structure. Similarly, is the company using the right integration or control systems to manage its operations? Are managers being appropriately rewarded? Are the right rewards in place for encouraging cooperation among divisions, for example? These are all issues that should be considered.

Obviously, in analyzing an organization it is important that the analysis is focused on its main issues. For example, organizational conflict, power, and politics will be important issues for some companies. Try to analyze why problems in these areas are occurring. Do they occur because of bad strategy formulation or because of bad strategy implementation?

Make Recommendations*

The last part of any analytical process involves making recommendations based on the analysis. Obviously, the quality of your recommendations is a direct result of the thoroughness with which you have prepared the analysis. Recommendations from a SWOT analysis should be directed at solving whatever strategic problem the company is facing in order to increase its future profitability, directly or indirectly, through the other success factors. Your recommendations should be in line with your analysis; that is, they should follow logically from the previous discussion. For example, your recommendations generally will focus on the specific ways of changing functional, business, and corporate strategy; and organizational structure and control, to improve business performance. These recommendations might include an increase in spending on specific research and development projects, the divesting of certain businesses, a change from a strategy of unrelated to related diversification, an increase in the level of integration among divisions by using task forces and teams, or a move to a different kind of structure to implement a new business-level strategy. Again, it is important to make sure the recommendations are mutually consistent and are written in the form of an action plan. The plan might contain a timetable that sequences the actions for changing the company's strategy and a description of how changes at the corporate level will necessitate changes at the business level and, subsequently, at the functional level.

FINANCIAL ANALYSIS

LO4

The financial health of a company is very important to understand. It is, of course, one of our critical success factors. The company must be in a good financial position in order to pay its suppliers, invest in new technology and research and development, and expand the company—ultimately to pursue its strategy to achieve its objectives. Financial analysis will also help you to better understand the financial strengths and weaknesses of the company for your SWOT analysis. There are many tools that can be used, and more will be discussed in Chapter 16—the accounting chapter. Here we will introduce only three basic themes: financial statements, ratios, and cost/benefit analysis.

Financial Statements

Financial statements are invaluable for understanding the financial health of a company. The three key statements are the balance sheet or statement of financial position (what

*From unknown, *http://college.cengage.com/business/resources/casestudies/students/analyzing.htm*. © Cengage Learning.

pro forma financial statements
Projected financial statements of future values.

is owned, what is owed, and the net worth of the company), the income statement (revenues, expenses, and profit or loss), and the statement of cash flows (money coming in and money going out).

We can use current and past financial information to "estimate" or project future accounting numbers for the company based on our recommended plans. These are called **pro forma financial statements**.

- The *pro forma income statement* can be determined from past expenses as a percentage of sales, and then projected forward based on your sales projections.
- The *pro forma balance sheet* can be created by applying existing ratio levels from the current statements. It's more complicated, so you need to make sure it is needed to make a point.
- The *pro forma statement of cash flows* is always critical for a business. The company can show profitability and still have a threat of bankruptcy because there is essentially no cash to pay the bills.

Ratio Analysis

One of the most obvious financial analysis tools is ratio analysis, discussed in more detail in Chapter 16. Ratios can help answer many questions, such as

- Does the company have sufficient cash, and is it managing its cash flows appropriately? Can it pay its debts? (*liquidity ratios*)
- How has the company been funded and what are the implications of this? (*stability ratios*)

Sustainable Business, Sustainable World

ANALYTICAL MODELS

When looking for models to follow when pursuing sustainability, the *Triple Bottom Line* by Andrew Savitz, former head of PricewaterhouseCooper's Sustainability Business Services practice, instantly comes to mind. The model of the triple bottom line measures business success not just by traditional bottom line financial performance, but as three performance indicators—economic (sales, profits, ROI, taxes paid, monetary flows, and jobs created), environmental (air and water quality, energy usage, and waste produced), and social performance (labour practices, community impacts, human rights, and product responsibilities). Savitz suggests that companies need to find their "sweet spot," where corporate and societal interests intersect in order to have a sustainable and profitable business in today's environment.

Another model, put forth by Bob Willard, speaker and author of *The Sustainability Advantage* in his July 20th, 2010, blog posting, suggests that those three factors—economy, society, and the environment—are not just three "legs of a stool," or three overlapping circles, but three "nested dependencies." He says: "If you ask a maritime fisherman whether the devastating collapse of the cod fishery off the east coast of Newfoundland was an environmental disaster, a social disaster, or an economic disaster, he would say, 'Yes.'" There is a co-dependent reality between the three factors—essentially "without food, clean water, fresh air, fertile soil, and other natural resources, we're cooked." Without the environment, society can't survive, nor can companies continue to operate. This explains clearly why today's business paradigm is unsustainable—we can't continue a "take-make-waste" model and assume it can go on forever. A "borrow-use-return" model is necessary to sustain our way of life, as outlined by Michael Braungart in *Cradle to Cradle*.

In his July 10th, 2010, blog, Willard suggests there are five criteria for creating a sustainable business model that is better for

the environment, society, and the company: 1) radical resource productivity—companies need to increase the productivity of the resources they consume and eliminate their dependencies on resources dug from the earth's crust; 2) investment in natural capital—companies need to work to restore, maintain, and expand ecosystems; 3) ecological redesign—companies need to use closed-loop production systems in which waste material is treated as a resource and reused vs. being sent to a landfill; 4) service and flow economy—companies need to replace their goods with services, leasing products and solutions and taking them back to recycle or remanufacture; and 5) responsible consumption—reduce the demand for "stuff" and its associated pollution and waste by educating consumers to make more informed decisions. Watch www.storyofstuff.com/movies-all/story-of-stuff.

There are a number of models to apply. The key is to apply them. Your challenge is to see if you can identify these models at work in the sustainable companies profiled in the different chapters.

Thinking Critically

1. Do you think it's necessary for a company to have a model to follow to become a sustainable business? Is it necessary that a model be used to measure sustainability so that companies can report on their sustainability efforts and be compared to other companies?

2. Do you agree that companies need to measure all three of the performance indicators—economic, social, and environmental performance? Can a company that focuses just on traditional bottom line be a success in today's business world?

SOURCES: http://www.sustainabilityadvantage.com; Andrew W. Savitz, 2006, *The Triple Bottom Line*. San Francisco, CA: John Wiley & Sons, Inc.; "The Triple Bottom Line," Sustainable Business Strategies, http://www.getsustainable.net/triple-bottom-line.html.

Ratios can also be used to analyze the impact of different decisions on profitability:

- What is the return we can expect on this investment? (*ROI—return on investment*)
- How long will it take to recoup our investment? (*Payback*)
- Net Investment/Net Annual Return = number of years to recover the initial investment

Cost/Benefit Analysis

The basic concept of doing a cost/benefit analysis is to compare the costs and benefits of a particular decision using a common unit of measurement such as money. These costs are generally tangible—such as land, labour, machinery, etc. However, benefits can be both tangible—such as revenue—and intangible—such as customer and employee satisfaction, brand awareness, etc. These intangibles are obviously more difficult to value.

THE FUTURE OF ANALYZING BUSINESS LO5

In today's competitive world, business needs to respond not only to financial performance and on-time deliveries but also to the customer, environment, and society. In short, business must respond to the more subjective issues. These stakeholders and the company's response to them can help or hinder achieving the success factors.

The Customers

Not only do customers demand quality products at reasonable prices, but they also expect the company to provide these products in a safe, ethical manner. Canadian companies are answerable not only to the shareholders but also to the other stakeholders, including the customers. The customers expect that the company is not only providing value but being good corporate citizens too.

It is imperative that the company is not only analyzing its operations and financial stability but also monitoring and analyzing its responsibility to its customers. For example, some companies have customer service departments, but they must determine if it is simply a name of a department or a philosophy of the company.

The Environment

As you have been reading in the Sustainable Business, Sustainable World boxes, companies can be analyzed based on their commitment to the environment and to sustainable business. Companies that demonstrate that they are good stewards of the environment are more likely to earn good publicity than those that are not.

A large sector of the Canadian economic activity has been in the commodity industries, which often have a negative impact on the environment to extract, refine, and transport these commodities. Nowadays, companies are expected to protect future generations by leaving a clean, safe, and protected environment. By doing so, they are proving to be good corporate citizens with a more attractive public image, and that can lead to better financial performance.

Society

Companies can be analyzed based on their operations and impact on society. As we saw in Chapter 5, international trade and globalization are very important to Canada. For those companies that operate internationally, there is an expectation that they will act in a manner consistent with operating in Canada. Issues such as fair trade, child labour, etc., are important issues for Canadians. Violating any values that we as a society appreciate can have a negative impact on a company.

Another important issue (first introduced in Chapter 3) is the expectation that companies will give back to the society that supports

> **Concept** *Check*
>
> How does responding to customers' expectations increase the opportunity for more profit?
>
> Why is it important that companies be good stewards of the environment?
>
> Why does Canadian society expect that companies will give back to society?

Expanding Around the Globe

In Canada, many of the products that we use on a daily basis are imported from around the world. As well, Canada exports many goods and services to other countries. Today, there is more interdependence between nations than ever before. In analyzing the international operations of a company, Canadians expect that corporate behaviour will be consistent with our values, human rights legislation, and environmentalism.

As discussed earlier in the chapter, financial performance is one of the critical success factors, but it must not be at the cost of violating what we believe is right. If companies are exporting to Canada, we expect that the goods are not produced using child labour. We promote the practice of fair trade where equal value is exchanged, not taking advantage of economic situations of a particular region.

Transparency is also highly regarded by Canadian companies operating globally, or by international companies that we do business with. We expect that the companies will provide for employees on the job, but there is often expectations for these companies to give opportunities to those who are less fortunate.

McCain Foods, with global operations headquartered in Toronto, is the world's largest manufacturer of frozen French fries and potato specialties (not to mention other foods). It has operations in most regions of the globe. According to its website, its core values are

- We work every day to make our customers and consumers **SMILE**
- We value **continuous improvement** in our people, our products and our business
- We cherish the "**Can Do**" spirit: Trying but failing is okay; failing to try is not
- We dare to be **different**: New ideas, innovation and differentiation matter
- We value **teamwork** and the sharing of ideas
- We **win** market by market, and create advantage by leveraging our **global scale**
- We believe that honesty, integrity and fair dealings are integral to our success—**good ethics** is good business
- We will "**drink the local wine**": We are multicultural and care about our people, our families and our local community
- We take pride in being a **family business**

McCain Foods is an excellent example of how a Canadian company, with an international presence, achieves the critical success factors.

SOURCE: http://www.mccain.com/GoodBusiness/Vision%20Strategy/Pages/values.aspx, accessed February 2, 2012. Used with permission of McCain Foods Limited.

Concept in Action

AMJ Campbell is Canada's largest and most reliable moving and relocation company, with 48 offices in Canada. Its international division has five regional offices in Canada and affiliates in 120 countries. What are some of the considerations to make sure that a company has a positive public image that is expanding internationally?

them without an expectation of financial gain. Being philanthropic is becoming more important, moving away from the traditional view of companies' primary responsibility being to make profits. Companies that are perceived to be philanthropic are valued much more highly than those that are not.

GREAT IDEAS TO USE NOW

Looking for a career? What do you need to know about the company to determine if it would be a good fit for you? Some of the questions you need to ask yourself are, Will the company give me the opportunities that I want? Is the company ethical in its operations? Is the company financially sound?

Knowing as much about the company as possible will help you decide if this is the company for you. Much of the information can be retrieved from reliable sources, including databases and the personal experiences of others. Specifically look at the following:

- What is the background of the company (e.g., history, the industry it operates in, and its business focuses)?
- What are the primary activities that have demonstrated the company's ethically and socially responsible actions?
- How does the company incorporate technology in its operations to make it more efficient and effective?
- What are the primary products/services of the company and how does the company ensure quality (e.g., in the production and delivery of the products/services)?
- How do the products/services benefit the company's customers and society?
- What has been the profitability of the company for the last three years (include a discussion of net income and earnings per share)? How have external factors impacted the profitability of the company's industry? How have internal factors impacted the company's profitability?

Now ask yourself, "Would I work for this company?"

Summary of Learning Outcomes

Companies need to achieve financial performance to pay their obligations (e.g., to employees and suppliers) and meet their obligations to their shareholders; they must understand their customer and provide the products (goods and services) that meet and hopefully exceed their customers' expectations. The customers must also believe that the benefits of the product are at least equal to, if not greater than, the sacrifice (e.g., the costs of acquiring the products)—that they provide value. Companies must always look for new and better ways to provide their goods and services by focusing on creativity and innovation. There is a direct correlation between morale (how a person feels about something) and productivity; motivated employees are productive employees, therefore, companies must gain employee commitment to achieve the other success factors.

LO1 Describe the critical success factors and how to measure them.

We begin by looking at where we have been. Then by completing the SWOT, we can identify our strengths, weaknesses, opportunities, and threats, in order to determine if our vision, mission, and strategy are appropriate. We can use models to help to develop the SWOT, such as Porter's Five Forces Model and the industry life cycle model.

LO2 Explain how to do a SWOT analysis, and how to use it.

We need to look at the vision and mission statement of the company. We can then analyze the company at the corporate and business level by identifying the strengths and weaknesses. The external environment provides us with the opportunities and threats for the company. Finally, analyze the structure and control systems that are in place and make recommendations for future activities.

LO4   Discuss some methods for analyzing the financial position of the company.

There are many ways to analyze the financial position of the company by using the statements in the financials: balance sheet, income statement, and statement of cash flows. Ratio analysis provides information as to the company's liquidity, stability, activities, etc.

LO5   List some of the trends in analyzing the business.

Three trends that have become very important are analyzing the company's responsiveness to its customers, the environment, and society. These include providing products that were produced in a safe and ethical manner, being good stewards of the environment, and responding appropriately to society's expectations.

Key Terms

industry life cycle model   197
mission statement   200
Porter's Five Forces Model   197

pro forma financial statements   204
SWOT analysis   197
vision statement   200

Experiential Exercises

1. Using database searches, analyze a company that you are familiar with (e.g., maybe you shop or work there) and see if it is meeting the critical success factors. Try to explain why or why not for each of the factors.

2. Look at a retail store that you are familiar with and try to determine who its customers are, and what their expectations of the products are (goods and services). Describe how the company provides value to its customers.

3. Choose a company and do some research regarding its internal factors (e.g., financial, operations, marketing, and human resources). What are some of the strengths and weakness of each?

4. Using the same company as in Question 3 above, look at the external environment (e.g., political (legal and regulatory), economic, social, and technical). What are some of the opportunities and threats that the external environment presents?

5. Pick a company that you are familiar with or interested in, and using Porter's Five Forces Model, determine its competitiveness.

6. Select a few companies and, using the industry life cycle model, determine at what stage they are at.

7. Look at various companies' websites and study their vision and mission statements. What do these tell you about the companies?

8. Start to look at the statement of position, statement of earnings, and cash flow statements of companies. Do you see how different the template can be for different companies? Can you recognize similarities?

9. Choose a few companies and go to their websites. What do they say about their commitment to their customers, environment, and society?

Review Questions

1. What are five success factors for a company?
2. Why is it important that companies make a profit?
3. What options do customers have if a company does not meet their expectations?
4. What does "providing value" mean?
5. Why is it important to be creative and innovative in business?
6. How is employee commitment beneficial to a company?
7. What does SWOT stand for?
8. In looking at the internal environment, what part of SWOT does it relate to?
9. The external environment relates to what part of SWOT?
10. What are the forces in Porter's model of competition?
11. What are the five stages of industry evolution?
12. What is a vision statement? What is the purpose of the mission statement?
13. What is the last stage in analyzing an organization?
14. What are pro forma statements?
15. What are the three statements in the financials?
16. What are some of the trends in analyzing a business?

CREATIVE THINKING CASE

Wind Cellphone Entry to Canada, Competitive Analysis

In 2009, Wind Mobile came to Canada; within six months it built a subscriber base of over 100,000. The customers primarily were dissatisfied clients of the big three cellphone companies: Bell Mobility, Rogers, and Telus. It appeared that Wind came flying out of the starting gate, but then things began to slow. The projected 1.5 million subscribers by December 2012 was not achieved. The total was under one-half million.

Wind has attempted to compete on price. Competing on price is a double-edged sword. Wind derived an average per-customer revenue of approximately $30, about half of what its competitors reap. This will attract price-conscious customers, but it also limits the funding of growth. Marketing strategies are constrained by low revenues. Combined with lower than expected subscriber sales, Wind has a hard time getting its message out.

On the good news side, government regulations have forced the tower owners (Bell and Rogers) to lease space on their towers to other service providers, at what they claim is below-cost pricing. The market is growing with more and more Canadians using cellphones, smartphones, tablets, and other cell-based devices. Many Canadians are getting rid of wired phones in their homes in favour of a one-number mobile approach. These changes should have helped Wind, but at the same time, the mobile market has become cluttered. In addition to the big three and their branded options (like Virgin Mobile, Koodo, and Fido), Wind has been joined by other new entrants: Mobilicity, Public Mobile, and Videotron.

Some manufacturers offer different models to the various service providers, but for the most part the product offerings are the same. A big exception is the iPhones, which tend to come to Rogers first, then Bell Mobility and Telus. Wind appears to be low on the Apple priority list, since Wind pushes a wide range of alternative smartphones and superphones.

As Wind has struggled to produce revenue, it has generated internal problems. In an effort to cut costs, it has moved some services overseas to its investment partners—which seems to have had an impact on employee morale. Promised growth has soured investor confidence and weakened the subscriber base.

Many customers switched to Wind because of the poor service reputations of the big three providers—this was a central strategy at Wind. Yet, Wind has begun to be the subject of the same complaints: long waits, faulty products, inaccurate information, and no refunds. One disgruntled customer made a list of pros and cons for Wind service after his very negative experience trying to provide his son with a cellphone. He could not come up with one pro and stopped his list of cons at six. In most cases, his complaints are the same as the ones we hear on CBC's *Marketplace* about the other providers. He tells us Wind is no different.

Thinking Critically

1. Using Porter's Five Forces, analyze the competitive environment surrounding Wind Mobile.

2. Who owns Wind Mobile? Does this affect the model you developed?

3. Are there new players in the cellphone market (or have some left) since we wrote this case? Make sure you check to see what brands, which appear to be separate companies, are actually the big three under different labels.

SOURCES: Marlow, I., "Wind Mobile shakes up top ranks," June 23, 2011, http://www.theglobeandmail.com/report-on-business/wind-mobile-shakes-up-top-ranks/article2072299/; Marketplace, "Canada's Worst Cellphone Bill," CBC, K. Couglin (Producer), *Marketplace*, 2011, Toronto; "Our team," 2011, http://www.windmobile.ca/en/pages/ourteam.aspx; Sturgeon, J., "Wind Mobile's subscriber growth falls short," November 14, 2011, http://www.canada.com/technology/Wind Mobile subscriber growth falls short/5708748/story.html; Thompson, H., "Wireless Nightmare: A Wind Mobile Review," January 19, 2011, http://www.digitalhome.ca/2011/01/wireless-nightmare-a-wind-mobile-review/ Dec 15, 2011; "Wind Mobile," August 17, 2011, http://www.ratemyemployer.ca/employer/employer.aspx?empID=6152&l=en; "Wind Mobile backer regrets Canadian launch," November 17, 2011, http://www.cbc.ca/news/business/story/2011/11/17/f-naguib-sawiris.html; "Wind Mobile doing better than expected?" August 12, 2010, http://thecellularguru.com/2010/08/12/wind-mobile-doing-better-than-expected/; "Wind Mobile reports 30% growth in wireless subscribers," May 13, 2011, http://www.thestar.com/business/article/990848--wind-mobile-reports-30-growth-in-wireless-subscribers.

Making the Connection

Forms of Business Ownership

In this chapter, you'll learn about the different forms of organizations used by business owners. How does an owner set up the business legally, and what does this imply for the business and its owner(s)? This is related directly to our *political* environment in the PESTI model, because the government regulates the options for business ownership and the rules to follow. However, you will see that the form of business ownership has implications for all aspects of the integrative business model and thus, ultimately, for the success of the business.

Let's look at the critical success factors. First, the form of business ownership chosen will affect the *financial performance* of the company, because it affects its costs (costs of setting up the organization, for example) and, most importantly, the level of taxes that it must pay. It also affects how much profit is available or distributed to the owner(s). The form of business ownership can also indirectly affect the business' ability to *meet customer needs*, as the degree of flexibility and control for the owner(s) tends to decrease as the business grows larger, which is often when the form of ownership is changed. More directly, the owner is restricted in terms of how to meet the needs of the customer if he or she is under a franchise agreement, for example, or has pressures from shareholders once the company has gone public. This, in turn, will affect the amount of *innovation and creativity* that is possible. Finally, it is perhaps easier to gain *employee commitment* in some forms of business organization, as they offer the possibility of direct ownership beyond purchasing a minority interest in the company's stock.

The issue of going public is one that gets a lot of attention in the press, as this is big news for a company, but it is also one that needs to be considered carefully, as there are implications in every area of the business. One very obvious implication is the impact of the financial markets on the value of the business. Although there are obvious financial advantages to going public in terms of access to capital, there is no certainty and little stability as the recent roller coaster in the markets have shown us, and so this is a big, if not a bigger, decision for the owners than the original form of ownership would be.

Clearly, the form of business ownership, like most decisions made in a business, has an integrative impact. It must be chosen with the company's overall goals and *strategy* in mind; for example, it would be difficult for a sole proprietorship to raise sufficient capital to build a chain of hotels worldwide. The form of business ownership also affects how the external environment treats the business and how that business, in turn, affects the environment, in addition to affecting the decisions that are made internally.

Looking back at the external environment, we can examine the effect that the form of business ownership has with regard to those dealing with the business from the outside. For example, within the political environment, the government tends to regulate larger businesses more heavily, especially large public corporations that have a greater impact on society. As well, the amount of legal liability that the owners have for business debts depends on the form of ownership. This might lead to a situation in which a loan is turned down because the lender doubts that the debt can be satisfied out of business assets alone; and if the business was incorporated, this would not allow for the debt to be satisfied from the personal assets of the owner(s) unless they are specifically used as collateral.

The form of business ownership chosen also affects the amount of taxes paid to the government as well, which, in turn, affects the *economic* environment: paying less tax allows for greater spending to grow the business. Within the *social* environment, society is becoming ever more demanding of businesses to be socially responsible and act ethically. This extends to all forms of business organization, but perhaps the highest expectations rest on the larger public corporations because of their visibility and resources. The trends in business ownership, as discussed later in this chapter, also have relationships to the social environment. For example, the changing demographics in society—the increasingly prominent role of women in business, and the influence women have over purchase decisions, along with political pressure from various groups—have led many franchisors to encourage women to own their own franchises and to facilitate the process for them.

The *technological* environment is perhaps the only area not directly affected by the form a business takes. Small and large organizations, whether sole proprietorships, partnerships, or corporations, have equal access to technology. This access to technology has allowed different forms of business to compete on more of a level playing field, leading to the creation of many new businesses. These new businesses usually start small, as sole proprietorships, partnerships, or small private corporations—creating a trend that was discussed in Chapter 6.

When looking at the advantages and disadvantages of each form of ownership, you will see many examples of the integration of the form of ownership on the decisions made within the functional areas. For example, in the *finance* area, the form of ownership directly affects the degree of capital that the business has access to, and the options it has to raise that capital. This, in turn, will affect the size of its operations. In the *human resource* area, taking the large corporation as an example, this form of ownership affects the organization's ability to find and keep quality employees, as well as the incentives available to them—the larger the company, the greater the opportunities for employees to advance and the greater the resources to attract and hold onto them.

In a broader sense, the form of ownership affects the ability of the business to make good decisions in all areas. It is very unlikely for a sole proprietor, for example, to be an expert at every function, and thus the business will be weak where he or she is weak unless expert assistance is brought in. This is why businesses often develop partnerships—preferably with people who have complementary skills—and/or create corporations that can, as they grow larger, attract professional talent to round out the company's needs. A good example is Research In Motion (RIM), the maker of the famous BlackBerry smartphone. The company was built on the strength of its technology, but a major weakness early on was in the area of *marketing*. Because of the success and visibility of this publicly traded corporation, it was able to attract very strong talent in that area to continue the success of the company. A smaller sole proprietorship would have had much more difficulty.

This issue is the same with respect to the basic tasks of a manager in any of the functional areas or levels of the company. A sole proprietor may be good at *planning*, but bad at executing (*organizing*, *motivating*, and *controlling*), or vice versa. Bringing other people into the company to balance those needs is important to the success of the company, and it is easier as the business grows, which often necessitates a change in the form of ownership.

Planning the future of the company is another issue discussed in this chapter and it connects to our discussion of strategy in the previous chapter. Often businesses change their "form of ownership" per se when they get involved in a merger or an acquisition to pursue a particular strategy. This takes the form of ownership to a whole new level and has far-reaching integrative consequences. Like going public, being involved in a merger or acquisition is a complex decision and set of actions, and one that has many integrative implications for the whole business.

chapter 8

Forms of Business Ownership

LEARNING OUTCOMES

1 Discuss the advantages and disadvantages of the sole proprietorship form of business organization.

2 Describe the advantages of operating as a partnership, and the downside risks partners should consider.

3 Explain the corporate structure and its advantages and disadvantages, and identify a special type of corporation.

4 Review some of the other business organization options in addition to sole proprietorships, partnerships, and corporations.

5 Understand why mergers and acquisitions can be important to a company's overall growth.

6 Identify when franchising is an appropriate business form and why it is growing in importance.

7 List some of the current trends that may affect the business organizations of the future.

MTY ACQUIRES JUGO JUICE

MTY Food Group of Montréal, the fourth-largest franchised food operator in Canada, gained even more presence in your local mall food court in April 2011 when it bought Jugo Juice of Calgary, another franchised company.

MTY, which owns restaurant franchises including such well-known brands as Yogen Früz, Taco Time, Thai Express and Country Style, was first listed on the TSX Venture Exchange in 1979. It gained market presence when principal Stanley Ma liquidated his $400,000 investment in a restaurant and started the Tiki Ming Chinese fast-food concept.

In franchising, the central company takes relatively little risk in the setup of each store. For example, Jugo Juice franchisees were required to have at least $100,000 in unencumbered capital (cash they could put into the operation) and a net worth of $250,000. These numbers went up depending on size and location of the store because of construction or renovation costs. Owners were expected to work 40 hours per week in the stores and have a passion for the business.

Jason Cunningham and Derek Brock had started Jugo Juice in 1998. The two continued to manage the Jugo system from a small office in Calgary, and by 2010 there were 133 stores. The parent company operated only one; the rest were run by franchisees who paid royalties of six percent of gross revenue and a four percent marketing fee. In 2010, system-wide sales were reported at $36.4 million, so those royalties and fees were a substantial sum. In return, franchise owners got a proven model (with fixed store design and menu) and training and support from head office.

Meanwhile, as the income trust bandwagon rolled through the Canadian equity market between 2000 and 2005, investment bankers had pushed Ma to follow the lead of several other restaurant chains and convert MTY to an income trust. He resisted. The company remained closely held, and when some of the other chains floundered in the face of looming changes to the income trust regulations, he bought them out. Expansion continued and finally, in 2010, a debt-free MTY moved onto the TSE through an IPO.

Jugo Juice's business was also expanding, but in 2010 Jugo began to fall behind rival Booster Juice of Edmonton. That's when MTY entered the picture. With Jugo's growth stalled, sale of the company to MTY for $15.5 million seemed like a good plan, and the deal went through on April 27, 2011.

MTY continues to forge ahead. In 2011, 19 million MTY shares were authorized, trading in the $15 range, and the company has a healthy price-to-equity ratio of over 16. The cash generated from the IPO, and the continued positive cash flow from operations, have opened the door to more acquisitions.[1]

PHOTO COURTESY OF JUGO JUICE

THINKING CRITICALLY

As you read this chapter, consider the following questions:

1. What are the different forms of business ownership?

2. What factors influence the form of business ownership chosen?

3. Why do the owners of companies change the form of business ownership?

So you've decided to start a business. You have a good idea and some cash in hand, have done your analysis, and thought through your strategy. But before you get going, you need to decide what form of business organization will best suit your needs.

So first ask yourself some questions. Would you prefer to go it alone as a sole proprietorship, or do you want others to share the burdens and challenges of a partnership, or do you prefer the limited liability protection of a corporation?

Here are some other questions you need to consider: How easy will it be to find financing? Can you attract employees? How will the business be taxed, and who will be liable for the business's debts? If you choose to share ownership with others, how much operating control will they want, and what costs will be associated with that or other forms of ownership? Most start-up businesses select one of the major ownership categories.

In the following pages, we will discover the advantages and disadvantages of each form of business ownership and the factors that might make it necessary to change from one form of organization to another as the needs of the business change. As your business expands from a small to midsize or larger venture, the form of business structure you selected in the beginning might no longer be appropriate. We will also look at specialized forms of business.

LO1

GOING IT ALONE: SOLE PROPRIETORSHIPS

Mike Robson was working full-time, just finishing a bachelor's degree and starting work on his master's, when having lunch with a fellow student changed everything. His friend mentioned that the company he worked for had trouble obtaining "toppers," metal boxes for ATM (automatic teller machine) modems. Before lunch was over, Robson decided to start a business—building toppers.

sole proprietorship
A business that is established, owned, operated, and often financed by one person.

Eight months after Robson had set up business as a sole proprietorship—a business established, owned, operated, and often financed by one person—his $20,000 home equity loan financing was gone without his having sold a single box! Then he made a fateful sales call at a local credit union, where it needed someone to spruce up a dilapidated ATM. Robson drew on his chemical engineering background to clean, polish, and paint the machine until it looked like new, and so his new business restoring and maintaining ATMs was born!

Robson thrived as a sole proprietor. He liked the independence of being his own boss and controlling all business decisions. When he realized that his initial idea was headed nowhere, he was able to change direction quickly when a new opportunity presented itself. Many businesses in your neighbourhood—including florists, dry cleaners, and beauty salons—are sole proprietorships, as are many service providers such as lawyers, accountants, and real estate agents.[2]

Advantages of Sole Proprietorships

Sole proprietorships have several advantages that make them popular:

- *Easy and inexpensive to form.* As Mike Robson discovered, sole proprietorships have few legal requirements and are not expensive to form, making them the business organization of choice for many small companies and start-ups.
- *Profits all go to the owner.* The owner of a sole proprietorship obtains the start-up funds and gets all the profits earned by the business.
- *Direct control of the business.* All business decisions are made by the sole proprietorship owner, without having to consult anyone else. This was beneficial for Mike Robson when he needed to change the direction of his business.

- *Relative freedom from government regulations.* Sole proprietorships have more freedom than other forms of business with respect to government controls.
- *No special taxation.* Sole proprietorships do not pay corporate taxes. Profits are taxed as personal income and are reported on the owner's individual tax return.
- *Ease of dissolution.* With no co-owners or partners, the sole proprietor can sell the business or close the doors at any time, making this form of business organization an ideal way to test new business ideas.

Concept *Check*

What is a sole proprietorship?

Why is this a popular form of business organization?

What are the drawbacks to being a sole proprietor?

Disadvantages of Sole Proprietorships

Along with the freedom to operate the business as they wish, sole proprietors face several disadvantages:

- *Unlimited liability.* From a legal standpoint, the sole proprietor and the business he or she owns are one and the same, making the business owner personally responsible for all debts the business incurs, even if they exceed the business's value. The owner might need to sell other personal property—his or her car, home, or other investments—to satisfy claims against the business.
- *Difficulty in raising capital.* Business assets are unprotected against claims of personal creditors, and business lenders view sole proprietorships as high risk because of the owner's unlimited liability. Owners often must use personal funds—borrowing on credit cards, securing assets (collateral) for loans or lines of credit, or selling investments—to finance their business, and expansion plans can also be affected by an inability to raise additional funding.
- *Limited managerial expertise.* The success of a sole proprietorship rests solely with the skills and talents of the owner, who must wear many different hats and make all decisions. Owners are often not equally skilled in all areas of running a business. A graphic designer might be a wonderful artist but may not know bookkeeping, how to manage production, or how to market his or her work.
- *Trouble finding qualified employees.* Sole proprietors often cannot offer the same pay, fringe benefits, and opportunities for advancement as larger companies can, making them less attractive to employees seeking the most favourable employment opportunities.
- *Personal time commitment.* Running a sole proprietorship business requires personal sacrifices and a huge time commitment, often dominating the owner's life with 12-hour workdays and 7-day workweeks.
- *Unstable business life.* The lifespan of a sole proprietorship can be uncertain. The owner might lose interest, experience ill health, retire, or die. The business will cease to exist unless the owner makes provisions for it to continue operating or puts it up for sale.
- *Losses are the owner's responsibility.* The sole proprietor is responsible for all losses, although tax laws allow these to be deducted from other personal income.

The sole proprietorship might be a suitable choice for a one-person start-up operation with no employees and little risk of liability exposure. For many sole proprietors, however, this is a temporary choice, and as the business grows, the owner might be unable to operate with limited financial and managerial resources. At this point, he or she might decide to take in one or more partners to ensure that the business continues to flourish.

PARTNERSHIPS: SHARING THE LOAD

LO2

Can partnerships, an association of two or more individuals who agree to operate a business together for profit, be hazardous to a business' health? Let's assume partners Ron and Liz own a stylish and successful hair salon. After a few years of operating the business they find they have contrasting visions for their company. Liz is happy with the status quo, while Ron wants to expand the business by bringing in investors and opening salons in other locations.

How do they resolve this impasse? By asking themselves some tough questions. Whose view of the future is more realistic? Does the business actually have the expansion potential Ron believes it does? Where will he find investors to make his dream of multiple locations a reality? Is he willing to dissolve the partnership and start over again on his own? And who would have the right to their clients?

Ron realizes that expanding the business in line with his vision would require a large financial risk, and that his partnership with Liz offers many advantages he would miss in a sole proprietorship form of business organization. After much consideration he decides to leave things as they are.

For those individuals who do not like to "go it alone," a **partnership** is simple to set up and offers a shared form of business ownership. It is a popular choice for professional service companies such as lawyers, accountants, architects, and real estate companies.

The parties agree, *either orally or in writing*, to share in the profits and losses of a joint enterprise. A *written partnership agreement*, spelling out the terms and conditions of the partnership, *is recommended* to prevent later conflicts between the partners. These agreements typically include the name of the partnership, its purpose, and the contributions of each partner (financial, asset, skill/talent), as well as outline the responsibilities and duties of each partner and their compensation structure (salary, profit sharing, etc.). It should contain provisions for the addition of new partners, the sale of partnership interests, and the procedures for resolving conflicts, dissolving the business, and distributing the assets.

There are *three basic types of partnerships: general, limited,* and *limited liability partnerships*. In a **general partnership**, all partners share in the management and the profits. They co-own the assets, and each can act on behalf of the company. Each partner also has unlimited liability for all business obligations of the company. A **limited partnership** has two types of partners: one or more **general partners**, who have unlimited liability, and one or more **limited partners**, whose liability is limited to the amount of their investment. In return for limited liability, limited partners agree not to take part in the day-to-day management of the business. They help to finance the business, but the general partners maintain operational control.

In the **limited liability partnership (LLP)**, each individual partner is protected from responsibility for the acts of other partners, and each partner's liability is limited to harm resulting from his or her own actions. Ontario was the first province to allow LLPs in 1998, followed by Alberta in 1999. Today most provinces allow LLPs to operate, and they are common in accounting and law firms.

Advantages of Partnerships

Some advantages of partnerships come quickly to mind:

- *Ease of formation.* Like sole proprietorships, partnerships are easy to form. For most partnerships, applicable laws are not complex. The partners agree to do business together and draw up a partnership agreement.
- *Availability of capital.* Because two or more people contribute financial resources, partnerships can raise funds more easily for operating expenses and business expansion. The partners' combined financial strength also increases the company's ability to raise funds from outside sources.
- *Diversity of skills and expertise.* Partners share the responsibility of managing and operating the business. Ideal partnerships bring together people with complementary backgrounds rather than those with similar experience, skills, and talents. Combining partner skills to set goals, manage the overall direction of the company, and problem solve increases the chances of the partnership's success. To find the right partner, however, you must examine your own strengths and weaknesses, and

---

partnership
An association of two or more individuals who agree to operate a business together for profit.

general partnership
A partnership in which all partners share in the management and profits. Each partner can act on behalf of the company and has unlimited liability for all its business obligations.

limited partnership
A partnership with one or more general partners who have unlimited liability, and one or more limited partners whose liability is limited to the amount of their investment.

general partners
Partners who have unlimited liability for all of the company's business obligations and who control its operations.

limited partners
Partners whose liability for the company's business obligations is limited to the amount of their investment. They help to finance the business but do not participate in the company's operations.

limited liability partnership (LLP)
In a limited liability partnership, each individual partner is protected from responsibility for the acts of other partners, and each party's liability is limited to harm resulting from that party's own actions.

know what you need from a partner. In Exhibit 8.1, you'll find some advice on choosing a partner.

- *Flexibility.* General partners are actively involved in managing their company and can respond quickly to changes in the business environment.
- *No special taxes.* Partnerships pay no income taxes. Each partner's profit or loss is reported on the partner's personal income tax return, with any profits taxed at personal income tax rates.
- *Relative freedom from government control.* Governments exercise little control over partnership activities.

Concept *Check*

How does a partnership differ from a sole proprietorship?

Describe the three main types of partnerships.

Explain the difference between a limited partner and a general partner.

What are the main advantages and disadvantages of a partnership?

Disadvantages of Partnerships

Business owners must consider the following disadvantages of setting up their venture as a partnership:

- *Unlimited liability.* All general partners have unlimited liability for the debts of the business. In fact, any one partner can be held personally liable for all partnership debts and legal judgments (such as malpractice)—regardless of who caused them. As with sole proprietorships, business failure can lead to a loss of the general partners' personal assets. To overcome this problem, most provinces now allow the formation of limited liability partnerships, which protect each individual partner from responsibility for the acts of other partners, and limit partners' liability to harm resulting from their own actions.
- *Potential for conflicts between partners.* Partners might have different ideas about how to run the business, which employees to hire, how to allocate responsibilities, and when to expand. Differences in personalities and work styles can cause clashes or breakdowns in communication, sometimes requiring outside intervention to save the business.
- *Complexity of profit-sharing.* Dividing the profits is relatively easy if all partners contribute equal amounts of time, expertise, and capital. But if one partner puts in more money and others more time, it might be difficult to arrive at a fair profit-sharing formula.
- *Difficulty exiting or dissolving a partnership.* As a rule, partnerships are easier to form than to leave. When one partner wants to leave, the value of his or her share must be calculated. To whom will that share be sold, and will that person be acceptable to the other partners? To avoid these problems, most partnership agreements include specific guidelines for transfer of partnership interests and buy-sell agreements that make provision for surviving partners to buy a deceased partner's interest. Partners can purchase special life insurance policies on each partner designed to fund such a purchase.

Business partnerships are often compared to marriages. As with a marriage, choosing the right partner is critical, so if you are considering forming a partnership, allow plenty of time to evaluate your and your potential partner's goals, personality, expertise, and working style. Exhibit 8.1 (page 220) lists questions that you and a potential business partner can ask each other.

HOT links

In Canada, the provinces have jurisdiction with respect to sole proprietorships and partnerships. To find out more, check your provincial/territorial government's website.

CORPORATIONS: LIMITING YOUR LIABILITY

LO3

When people think of corporations, they typically think of major, well-known companies such as Suncor, TD Canada Trust, Bell Canada Enterprises, Rogers Communications Inc. But corporations range in size from large multinationals, with thousands of employees and billions of dollars in sales, to midsize or even smaller companies, with few employees and little or no revenue.

Exhibit 8.1 Perfect Partners

Picking a partner is both an art and a science. Be prepared to talk about everything. On paper, someone might have all the right credentials, but does that person share your vision and the ideas you have for the business? Is he or she a straight shooter? Honesty, integrity, and ethics are equally important, as you might be liable for what your partner does. Trust your intuition and "your gut feelings—they're probably right," advises Irwin Gray, author of The *Perils of Partners*. So ask yourself the following questions, and then ask a potential partner and see how well your answers match up:

1. Why do you want a partner?
2. What characteristics, talents, and skills does each person bring to the partnership?
3. How will you divide responsibilities? Consider every aspect of the business, from long-range planning to daily operations. Who will handle marketing, sales, accounting, and customer service?
4. What is your long-term vision for the business (size, lifespan, financial commitment, etc.)?
5. What are your personal reasons for forming this business: Are you looking for a steady pay-cheque? For independence? To create a small business? Or to build a large one?
6. Are all parties willing to put in the same amount of time and, if not, is there an alternative arrangement that is acceptable to everyone?
7. What are your work ethics and values?
8. What requirements should be in the partnership agreement?

SOURCES: Julie Bawden Davis, "Buddy System," Business Startups, June 1998, http://www. entrepreneurmag.com; Azriela Jaffe, "Til Death Us Do Part' Is No Way to Start a Business," *Business Week* Online, October 23, 1998, http://www. businessweek.com/smallbiz; Jerry Useem, "Partners on the Edge," *Inc.*, August 1998, 54, 59.

corporation
A legal entity with its own rights and responsibilities separate from its shareholders, who therefore are not personally liable for the entity's actions and liabilities.

A corporation is a legal entity and is separate from its owners, who therefore are not personally liable for its debts. It is important that although shareholders of a corporation are protected by limited liability, directors and officers of a corporation are accountable for their action and can be sued in cases of wrongdoing or wilful negligence. A corporation is subject to the laws of the jurisdiction in which it is incorporated. A corporation can do what most people can do, such as own property, enter into contracts, sue and be sued, and engage in business operations and more. As corporations are separate legal entities, they have to file their own tax return, unlike the owners of sole proprietorships and partnerships, who are taxed personally.

In launching his company, eEye Digital Security, 21-year-old Marc Maiffret needed the limited liability protection of the corporate business organization model. Maiffret started hacking at age 15, learning how to mangle websites and breach net-works. When the authorities suspected him of breaching a military network, Maiffret and his boss Firas Bushnaq (Maiffret dropped out of school to work for a software company) decided to capitalize on his expertise. They launched eEye to outsmart the best hackers in the business by designing software to protect corporate network security.

With Maiffret bearing the title "Chief Hacking Officer," the growing company has offices around the world and includes, among its 100 employees, a team of engineering hackers whose efforts bring eEye an estimated $11 million annually. Its unusual background makes eEye an unconventional corporation.[3] Maiffret has since moved on to become the director of professional services of the Digi Trust Group, a company providing information security consultancy.[4]

Public versus Private Corporations

public corporation
A corporation whose shares are widely held and available to the general public.

Corporations can be either public or private. A public corporation's shares are widely held and available to the general public. Some public companies choose to list their shares on organized stock markets (e.g., Toronto Stock Exchange) or in the over-the-counter markets (e.g., NASDAQ) (discussed in detail in Chapter 17). Not all public companies' shares are traded on a stock exchange or in the over-the-counter markets. Companies that are traded on a stock exchange or in the over-the-counter markets are called listed companies; every listed company is a public company but not all public companies are listed. A **private corporation** normally has limited number of shareholders, and most of the time there are restrictions on the sale or transfer of shares to a third party (i.e., shares are not available to the general public). We come across many private corporations daily, examples would include small and professional corporations (e.g., your doctor or dentist are most likely a professional corporation). But not all private corporations are small; McCain Foods or Irving Oil are prime examples. Most corporations begin as a private corporation. If they choose, they may become public corporations as a means of raising extra money or as an exit strategy for the owners. Just as private corporations can become public corporations, public corporations can become private. This is normally called a leverage buyout and only happens when a group of investors or management of the company offers to buy shares of the others in the market and is successful in obtaining the required number of shares.

private corporation
A corporation whose number of shareholders is limited; there are normally restrictions on the transfer of shares to third parties, and its shares do not trade on a recognized stock exchange

Going Public

The main reason that a company would go "public" is to raise capital to expand or maintain its growth. In this case, one of the primary concerns for the original owners is the potential loss of control of the company. One strategy is to issue various classes of shares (discussed in Chapters 17 and 18) so that the control remains with the original owners while still attracting capital from the new investors; such was the case with Canadian Tire and Magna International Inc. Another reason for a private company to go public is as an exit strategy of the original owners. This would be the case if there were no one in the family wanting to take over the company.

The process of going public is complicated and involves considerable preparation. In a simplified explanation, once a private company decides to go public, it must first find a sponsor. This would typically be an investment bank (e.g., BMO Capital Markets or TD Waterhouse—see Chapter 17) and would represent the company. The company must then prepare the financial statements, answer questions as to past activities as well as future plans (both financial and operational) and then submit its application to one of the stock markets (e.g., TSX Venture or Toronto Stock Exchange—see Chapter 17). If the application is successful, the company is given its ticker symbol (unique identifier that is assigned to each type of share traded).The company is now a reporting entity to one or more of the Provincial Securities Commissions.

The Incorporation Process

Setting up a corporation is more complex than starting a sole proprietorship or partnership. If the business activity is primarily in only one province, it is necessary to incorporate only as a provincial company under that province's Companies Act (or other similarly named act), although there is no restriction for a provincially incorporated company to have operations in other provinces; it can even have most or even all of its operations in another province. A corporation can also be set up under the Canada Business Corporations Act if it is to operate in more than one province or across Canada. Either route of incorporation requires more steps than setting up a sole proprietorship or partnership.

Incorporating a company involves five main steps:

1. Selecting the company's name (including searching existing company names to confirm that you can use the name). If the company chooses not to have a name or if no name is selected, the registry will start a numbered company, a numbered company then can have a trade name or operate under the numbered company;
2. Writing the articles of incorporation (see below) and filing them with the appropriate government office (these are generally fairly standard);
3. Paying the required fees and taxes;
4. Holding an organizational meeting; and
5. Adopting bylaws, electing directors, and passing the first operating resolutions.

Exhibit 8.2 Articles of Incorporation

Articles of incorporation are prepared on a form authorized or supplied by the province, or the federal government if the corporation incorporated federally. Although they may vary slightly from province to province, all articles of incorporation include the following key items:

- the name of the corporation;
- the province in which the registered office is to be situated;
- the classes and any maximum number of shares that the corporation is authorized to issue;
- if the issue, transfer, or ownership of shares is to be restricted, a statement that clearly sets out the restrictions;
- the number of directors, or the minimum and maximum number of directors; and
- any restriction on the business in which the corporation may engage.

The province or federal government issues the corporate charter based on the information in the articles of incorporation. Once the corporation has its charter, it holds an organizational meeting to adopt bylaws, elect directors, and pass initial operating resolutions. Bylaws provide the legal and managerial guidelines for operating the company.

To distinguish a corporation from other forms of ownership, corporations must use Limited (Ltd./Ltée), Incorporated (Inc.), or Corporation (Corp.) at the end of the company name. This tells the customers, suppliers, and other shareholders that the owners have limited liability for the corporate obligations. See Exhibit 8.2 for a listing of what the Articles of Incorporation include.

The Corporate Structure

As Exhibit 8.3 shows, corporations have their own organizational structure, with three important components: shareholders, directors, and officers.

shareholders
The owners of a corporation who hold shares of stock that provide certain rights; also known as stockholders.

Shareholders, or stockholders, are the owners of a corporation, holding shares of stock that provide them with certain rights. They may receive a portion of the corporation's profits in the form of dividends, and they can sell or transfer their ownership—their shares of stock in the corporation—at any time. Common shareholders (discussed in more detail in Chapters 17 and 18) can attend annual meetings, elect the board of directors, and vote on matters that affect the corporation, in accordance with its charter and bylaws. Each share of stock generally carries one vote. It is possible for one person to own all the shares of a corporation.

board of directors
A group of people elected by the shareholders to handle the overall management of a corporation, such as setting major corporate goals and policies, hiring corporate officers, and overseeing the company's operations and finances.

The common shareholders elect a board of directors to govern and handle the overall management of the corporation. The board of directors is responsible for ensuring that the business is managed with the corporation's best interests in mind. The directors set major corporate goals and policies, hire corporate officers, and oversee the company's operations and finances.

The boards of large corporations typically include both corporate executives (inside directors) and independent directors (not employed by the organization) chosen for their professional and personal expertise. Independent directors often bring fresh viewpoints to the corporation's activities, because they are independent of the company. See "Making Ethical Choices" (page 225) for an insight at some of the decisions corporate boards make.

Hired by the board, the officers of a corporation are its top management and include the president and chief executive officer (CEO), vice presidents, the treasurer, and the secretary; they are responsible for achieving corporate goals and policies. Besides the CEO, other common titles of officers of a corporation include chief financial officer (CFO), chief information officer (CIO), and chief operating officer (COO). Officers may also be board members (inside directors) and/or shareholders.

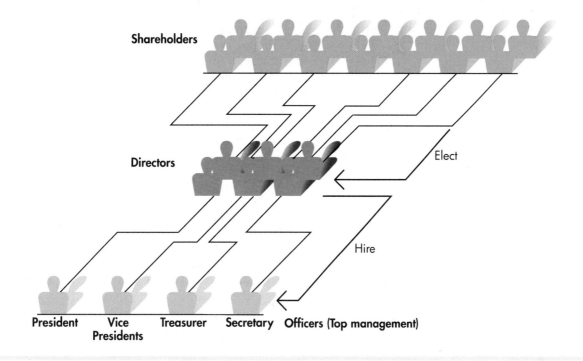

Shareholders

Directors

Elect

Hire

President | Vice Presidents | Treasurer | Secretary Officers (Top management)

Concept *in Action*

Maple Leaf Foods is a leading consumer packaged food company headquartered in Toronto. It has operations across Canada and in the United States, United Kingdom, Asia, and Mexico. Its three main consumer brands are Maple Leaf, Schneiders, and Dempster's, which are supplemented by many regional brands. What important tasks and responsibilities are entrusted to Maple Leaf's board of directors?

THE CANADIAN PRESS(NATHAN DENETTE)

Advantages of Corporations

The corporate structure allows companies to merge financial and human resources into enterprises with great potential for growth and profits:

- *Limited liability.* A key advantage of corporations is that they are separate legal entities that exist apart from their owners. An owner's (shareholder's) liability for the debts of the company is limited to the amount of the stock he or she owns. If the corporation goes bankrupt, creditors can look only to the assets of the corporation for payment. The main exception is when a shareholder personally guarantees a business obligation (most common in corporations with one or only a few owners).
- *Ease of transferring ownership.* Shareholders of public corporations can sell their shares at any time without affecting the status of the corporation.
- *Unlimited life.* The life of a corporation is unlimited. Because the corporation is an entity separate from its owners, the death or withdrawal of an owner does not affect its existence, unlike a sole proprietorship or partnership.
- *Ability to attract financing.* Corporations can raise money by selling new shares of stock. Dividing ownership into smaller units makes it affordable to more investors, who can purchase one or several thousand shares. The large size and stability of corporations also helps them get bank financing. All of these financial resources allow corporations to invest in facilities and human resources, and to expand beyond the scope of sole proprietorships and partnerships. It would be impossible for a sole proprietorship or partnership to make automobiles, provide nationwide telecommunications, or build oil or chemical refineries.
- *Ability to attract potential employees.* Corporations often offer better benefit plans and opportunities, which allows them to attract more potential employees. Larger companies also have the advantage of professional management opportunities (e.g., accounting managers).

Disadvantages of Corporations

Although corporations offer companies many benefits, they have some disadvantages:

- *Double taxation of profits.* Corporations must pay federal and provincial income taxes on their profits. The after-tax profit may then be distributed to the shareholders (dividends), and then the shareholders are taxed on the dividends as investment income.
- *Cost and complexity of formation.* As outlined earlier, forming a corporation involves several steps, and costs can run into thousands of dollars, including filing, registration, and licensing fees, as well as the cost of lawyers and accountants.
- *More government restrictions.* Unlike sole proprietorships and partnerships, corporations are subject to many regulations and reporting requirements.
- Business losses cannot be written off against the other income of the owners (shareholders) of the company.

Find out more about corporations and shareholder rights by searching for "Corporations Canada" at
www.ic.gc.ca

one-person corporation
A corporation with only one person as the shareholder; common in professional practices (e.g., medical doctors, accountants, or lawyers) and in trades (e.g., plumbers and electricians).

The One-Person Corporation

The one-person corporation offers certain personal liability protection to owners of a business. This is common in professional practices such as those of doctors, accountants, and lawyers and in the trades such as plumbers and electricians. Usually the personal assets of the shareholder are not at risk, except when the shareholder has personally guaranteed a business debt (this is quite common in small businesses, because the corporation does not have adequate financing or collateral) or when there is professional malpractice. It is important that the corporation has adequate business insurance to protect the company from overwhelming legal liabilities.

A one-person corporation might qualify for small-business tax rates, and the owner might be able to secure a dividend tax credit, which can result in lower corporate and personal taxes than in a sole proprietorship or partnership.

Exhibit 8.4 summarizes the advantages and disadvantages of each form of business ownership.

Making Ethical Choices

THE BOARD GAME

After completing your post-secondary education, you have found your place in the world of business. Everything clicks. You have a knack for seeing the big picture. You excel when working in multifaceted business environments—the more complex, the better. Companies value your fresh approach to structuring businesses for maximum productivity and profitability. Your adeptness has come to the attention of quite a few CEOs from a myriad of companies. In fact, you are one of the youngest people invited to serve on corporate boards of directors.

Wanting to focus most on your career, you accepted a seat on only one board—a young high-technology company, i2T, which has been losing money steadily. You're concerned that decisions about compensation for top executives that come before the board might further erode profitability and shareholder confidence. As a voting member, you must decide whether to approve awarding a

severance package, including a $500,000 consulting fee and a BMW Z-8, to Greg Brady, who was removed as CEO after a year of heavy losses. In addition to your concerns about the company's financial picture and shareholder loyalty, you wonder how your reputation as a young member of the board might be affected if you vote in favour of the award. Many fear boards will continue to play games. How will you play?

ETHICAL DILEMMA: With your expertise in structuring for maximum profitability, would you vote in favour of the severance package and the huge bonus in the face of the company's dismal financial condition?

SOURCES: "Corporate Power, Influence, Money and Interlocking Boards of Directors Page," http://www.verdant.net/corp.htm, February 18, 2003; and Arlene Weintraub and Ronald J. Grover, "Look Who's Still at the Trough," *Business Week*, September 9, 2002, 58.

Exhibit 8.4 — Advantages and Disadvantages of Major Types of Business Organization

SOLE PROPRIETORSHIP	PARTNERSHIP	CORPORATION
ADVANTAGES		
Owner receives all profits	More expertise and managerial skill available	Limited liability protects owners from losing more than they invest
Low organizational costs	Relatively low organizational costs	Can achieve large size because of marketability of stock (ownership)
Income taxed as personal	Income taxed as personal	Ownership is readily transferable
Income of proprietor	Income of partners	
Independence	Fundraising ability is enhanced by more owners	Long life of company (not affected by death of owners)
Secrecy		Can attract employees with specialized skills
Ease of dissolution		Greater access to financial resources allows growth
DISADVANTAGES		
Owner receives all losses	Owners have unlimited liability; may have to cover debts of other, less financially sound partners	Double taxation because both corporate profits and dividends paid to owners are taxed although the dividends are taxed at a reduced rate
Owner has unlimited liability; total wealth can be taken to satisfy business debts	Dissolves or must reorganize when partner dies	More expensive and complex to form
Limited fundraising ability can inhibit growth	Difficult to liquidate or terminate	Subject to more government regulation
Proprietor may have limited skills and management expertise	Potential for conflicts between partners	Financial reporting requirements make operations public
Few long-range opportunities and benefits for employees Lacks continuity when owner dies	Difficult to achieve large-scale operations	

A Special Type of Corporation: The Crown Corporation

Corporations that are owned by either a provincial or the federal government are called **Crown corporations**. They are structured similarly to private or independent corporations and are established to conduct regulatory, advisory, administrative, financial, or other services or to provide goods and services. Although Crown corporations generally have greater freedom from direct political control than government departments, they are ultimately accountable, through a cabinet minister, to Parliament. Some of the more recognizable Crown corporations are Canada Post Corporation, the Canadian Broadcasting Corporation (CBC), the Bank of Canada, and the Canada Science and Technology Museum.

Crown corporations
Companies that only the provincial and federal governments can set up.

LO4 SPECIALIZED FORMS OF BUSINESS ORGANIZATION

In addition to the three main forms, several specialized types of business organization play an important role in our economy. We will look at cooperatives and joint ventures in this section and take a detailed look at franchising in the following section.

Cooperatives

cooperative
A legal entity typically formed by people with similar interests, such as suppliers or customers, to reduce costs and gain economic power. A cooperative has limited liability, an unlimited life span, an elected board of directors, and an administrative staff; all profits are distributed to the member-owners in proportion to their contributions.

Cooperatives (co-ops) in Canada are a vital component in our economy; there are more than 9,000 cooperatives and credit unions (financial cooperatives) in Canada, servicing approximately 18 million Canadians in virtually every sector of the economy, and directly employ 150,000 people and are led by 100,000 volunteer directors and committee members.[5] Cooperatives are typically formed by people with similar interests, such as customers or suppliers (dealers), to reduce costs and gain economic power and are owned by the members who use the services.

Cooperatives differ from other business in three distinct areas:

1. *Purpose.* The primary focus is to meet the common needs of their members, whereas the primary purpose of investor-owned businesses is to maximize the value of the company.
2. *Control structure.* Unlike most businesses, with shares that typically give one vote for each share, cooperatives use the one member—one vote system to ensure that people, not capital, control the organization.
3. *Allocation of profit.* This is based on the extent to which members use the cooperative, not the number of shares held.[6]

A cooperative is a legal entity with several corporate features, such as limited liability for the membership, unlimited lifespan, an elected board of directors, and an administrative staff. Cooperatives distribute all profits to the members in proportion to their contributions. Cooperatives empower people to improve their quality of life and enhance their economic opportunities through self-help. Throughout the world, cooperatives are providing members with credit and financial services, energy, consumer goods, affordable housing, telecommunications, and other services that would not otherwise be available to them. Exhibit 8.5 outlines the basic principles of operation that cooperatives follow.

The Calgary Co-operative Association Limited, Credit Union of Central New Brunswick, Ontario Co-operative Association (OnCoop), and Mountain Equipment Co-op (MEC) are just a few of the cooperatives in Canada.

HOT Links

For more information about cooperatives in Canada, visit the Canadian Co-operative Association's website,
www.coopscanada.coop

PHOTO COURTESY OF MOUNTAIN EQUIPMENT CO-OP

Joint Ventures

In a **joint venture**, two or more companies form an alliance to pursue a particular project, usually for a specified time period. There are many reasons for joint ventures. The project might be too large for one company to handle on its own, and by forming joint ventures, companies can gain access to new markets, products, or technology. Both large and small companies can benefit from this type of endeavour.

For example, Syncrude Canada Ltd. is a joint venture of seven oil-producing companies, including Canadian Oil Sands Limited and Imperial Oil Resources. By

joint venture
Two or more companies that form an alliance to pursue a particular project for a specified time period.

Exhibit 8.5 Seven Internationally Recognized Principles Cooperatives Follow

- Voluntary and open membership
- Democratic member control
- Member economic participation
- Autonomy and independence
- Education, training, and information
- Cooperation among cooperatives
- Concern for community

SOURCE: NCBA, "Co-op Principles," http://www.ncba.coop/ncba/about-co-ops/co-op-principles. Used with permission from the National Cooperative Business Association.

Exhibit 8.6 Ownership of Syncrude Canada Ltd.

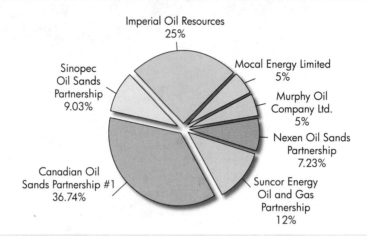

Imperial Oil Resources
25%

Mocal Energy Limited
5%

Murphy Oil
Company Ltd.
5%

Nexen Oil Sands
Partnership
7.23%

Suncor Energy
Oil and Gas
Partnership
12%

Canadian Oil
Sands Partnership #1
36.74%

Sinopec
Oil Sands
Partnership
9.03%

IMAGE COURTESY SYNCRUDE CANADA LTD.

HOT Links

For more information about direct selling in Canada, visit the Direct Sellers Association website at www.dsa.ca

creating the joint venture, infrastructure costs, production costs, and risks were spread out among the owners. The joint Venture Vision is "Creating wealth for our stakeholders from Canada's oil sands through the 21st century. This will be achieved by the safe, reliable, and profitable production of quality crude oil and other products in an environmentally safe and socially responsible manner." [7]

Exhibit 8.6 shows the ownership percentages of Syncrude Canada Ltd.

Direct Selling

direct selling
Direct selling is a popular marketing structure that connects the sellers "directly" with the customers.

Direct selling is a popular marketing structure that connects the sellers "directly" with the customers. Often referred to as network or referral marketing, direct selling does not use a fixed retail presence but instead uses such methods as one-on-one demonstrations, party plans, Internet sales, home shopping clubs, direct mail.

Direct selling can use multi-level marketing where a salesperson recruits others to sell the product and shares in the recruits' profits; for example, Mary Kay Inc. uses this structure. It can also use single-level marketing where the salesperson is paid only for her or his sales; an example is Avon Products Inc.

LO5

MERGERS AND ACQUISITIONS: MAKING IT BIGGER AND BETTER

merger
The combination of two or more companies to form a new company, which often takes on a new corporate identity.

acquisition
The purchase of one company by another company or by an investor group; the identity of the acquired company might be lost.

friendly takeover
A takeover that is supported by the management and board of directors of the targeted company.

A merger occurs when two or more usually similar-sized companies combine to form one new company, which often takes on a new corporate identity. In an acquisition, a corporation or an investor group buys a corporation, and the identity of the acquired company might be lost. (A company can also acquire divisions or subsidiaries of another company.) This happens more often when the buying company is larger than the acquired company. Normally, an acquiring company finds a target company and, after analyzing the target carefully, negotiates with its management or shareholders. Two noted acquisitions are Canadian Tire Corporation acquiring Mark's Work Wearhouse in 2001 (later rebranded as "Mark's") Forzani Group (Sport Chek, Sport Mart, Atmosphere, Nevada Bob's Golf, Hockey Experts, etc.) in 2011.

When there is a takeover that is supported by the target company's management and board of directors, it is called a friendly takeover. On the other hand, if the takeover goes against the wishes of the target company's management and board of directors, it is called a **hostile takeover**. Hostile takeovers are usually accomplished by the acquiring company buying controlling interest in the targeted company.

The interest of the companies to merge is not the only consideration, however. Some mergers require the approval of the Competition Bureau, which administers and enforces the Competition Act. This is intended to protect not only the general public but also the industry. The principal test is whether the merger is likely to reduce competition in Canada.

hostile takeover
A takeover that goes against the wishes of the target company's management and board of directors.

Types of Mergers and Acquisitions

The three main types of mergers and acquisitions are horizontal, vertical, and conglomerate. In a **horizontal merger or acquisition**, companies at the same stage of the supply chain (or production and sales process) in the same industry merge to reduce costs, expand product offerings, or reduce competition. Many of the recent large mergers were horizontal mergers to achieve economies of scale. This would be called a horizontal integration strategy, as discussed in Chapter 7.

Vertical mergers and acquisitions occur between companies in the same industry but involved in an earlier or later stage of the supply chain. Buying a supplier, a distribution company, or a customer gives the acquiring company more control over a source of supply, a distribution channel, or a market. This was also discussed in Chapter 7. When involving a supplier it would be called a backward vertical integration strategy, and when involving a distributor it would be called a forward vertical integration strategy.

A **conglomerate merger** or acquisition brings together companies in unrelated businesses to reduce risk. Combining with a company whose products have a different seasonal pattern or that responds differently to the business cycle can result in a more stable sales pattern.

A specialized, financially motivated type of merger or acquisition, the **leveraged buyout (LBO)**, became popular in the 1980s but is less common today. LBOs are corporate takeovers financed by large amounts of borrowed money—as much as 90 percent of the purchase price. LBOs can be started by outside investors or the corporation's own management.

Believing that the company is worth more than the value of all the stock, the investors buy the stock and expect to generate cash flow by improving operating efficiency or by selling off some units for cash that can be used to pay the debt. Although some LBOs did improve efficiency, many did not live up to investor expectations or generate enough cash to pay the debt.

horizontal merger or acquisition
A merger or an acquisition involving companies at the same stage of the supply chain in the same industry; done to reduce costs, expand product offerings, or reduce competition.

vertical merger or acquisition
Mergers or acquisitions involving companies at different stages of the supply chain in the same industry; done to gain control over supplies of resources or to gain access to different markets.

conglomerate merger or acquisition
A merger of acquisition involving companies in unrelated businesses; done to reduce risk.

leveraged buyout (LBO)
A corporate takeover financed by large amounts of borrowed money; can be done by outside investors or by a company's own management.

Merger and Acquisition Motives

Although the headlines tend to focus on mega-mergers, "merger mania" affects small companies as well. The motives for undertaking mergers and acquisitions are similar regardless of size. Often the goal is strategic: improving the overall performance of the merged companies through cost savings, elimination of overlapping operations, improved purchasing power, increased market share, or reduced competition. Growth, widening of product lines, and the ability to acquire technology or management skill quickly are other motives. Acquiring a company is often faster, less risky, and less costly than developing products internally or expanding internationally.

Another motive for acquisitions is financial restructuring—cutting costs, selling off units, laying off employees, or refinancing—to increase the value of the company to its shareholders. Financially motivated mergers are based not on the potential to achieve economies of scale but, rather, on the acquirer's belief that the target has hidden value that can be unlocked through restructuring. Most financially motivated mergers involve larger companies.

HOT *links*

For more information about the Competition Bureau and the Competition Act, see
www.competitionbureau.gc.ca

Concept *Check*

Differentiate between a merger and an acquisition.

What are the most common motives for corporate mergers and acquisitions?

Describe the different types of corporate mergers.

Sustainable Business, Sustainable World

TIMBERLAND

One of the major questions that needs to be answered as a business is created and begins to grow is "who are we?" and "what do we stand for?" Part of the process of creating a business is the development of a mission statement. Every company needs to have a mission, a purpose, a reason for being. Why was the business created in the first place? A company's mission statement puts this into words—the company's purpose, its business, and its values.

Businesses are created for many purposes, to achieve many different goals. Many businesses in today's environment have decided their purpose is higher than simply profit. Take Timberland, for example. Its mission is "to equip people to make a difference in their world … by creating outstanding products and by trying to make a difference in the communities where we live and work." Timberland's very reason for being involves sustainability—reducing its carbon footprint and being environmentally responsible, so that the outdoors, the environment in which its products are used, is made better by its actions. This is a philosophy that has permeated the organization for generations.

According to the company, its Earthkeepers line is in fact "grounded in a philosophy of reducing our impact on the planet while making premium gear." It incorporates recycled PET bottles in its linings, recycled rubber in its soles, leather components from tanneries that are silver-rated by external environmental auditors, and organic cotton. In a truly innovative move in 2006, Timberland even created a "nutritional label" for its footwear products that communicates information that helps customers know what goes into making the shoes they put on their feet and, therefore, make responsible choices about the products they buy. The label includes the climate impact of the product—the percentage of renewable energy used;

chemicals used—the percentage of PVC used in its footwear; and resource consumption—the percentage of eco-conscious materials and the percentage of recycled content in the shoebox, along with information on the number of trees planted by the company that year. Timberland also uses a "Green Index" rating system to measure aspects of the environmental impact of its products.

According to former CEO Swartz: "These are not commitments we make altruistically … As an outdoor company, we have a vested interest in protecting and preserving the environment; if there's no great outdoors, there's nowhere for our consumers to use our products." Makes pretty good sense to us. Timberland recognizes that in making its products it is part of the problem, but it also believes it can and will be part of the solution and puts its money where its mouth is. Its mission and its philosophy permeate everything it does.

Thinking Critically

1. Does every form of business organization need a mission statement, or just large corporations?
2. In today's business environment, can a business be truly successful ignoring sustainability in its mission statement and, hence, how it operates?
3. Do you think Timberland gains any economic benefit by its actions, or is there a necessary compromise when pursuing sustainability? Most importantly, what would happen if companies like Timberland didn't realize their impact and do something about it?

SOURCE: http://www.timberland.com. Reprinted with the permission of Timberland LLC. © TBL Licensing LLC.

LO6 FRANCHISING: A POPULAR TREND

franchising
A form of business organization based on a business arrangement between a *franchisor*, which supplies the product concept, and the *franchisee*, which sells the goods or services of the franchisor in a certain geographic area.

franchisor
In a franchising arrangement, the company that supplies the product concept to the *franchisee*.

franchisee
In a franchising arrangement, the individual or company that sells the goods or services of the franchisor in a certain geographic area.

Franchises come in all sizes, including McDonald's, the world's largest food service retailer, with 31,000 restaurants in 119 countries (70 percent of which are owned and operated by franchisees) and over 1,400 in Canada employing more than 77,000 Canadians.[8] Chances are, you deal with one of the more than 2,100 franchise systems in Canada and the United States almost every day. When you have lunch at Tim Hortons or Pizza Pizza, use the services of a UPS store, take your car for servicing at AAMCO or Mr. Lube, buy candles at A Buck or Two, or rent a car from Budget Rent A Car, in each case you are dealing with a franchised business. These and other familiar name brands have come to mean quality, consistency, and value to customers.

Providing a way to own a business without starting it from scratch, franchising is one of the fastest-growing segments of the economy. **Franchising** is a form of business organization that involves a business arrangement between a **franchisor**, the company supplying the product concept, and the **franchisee**, the individual or company selling those goods or services in a certain geographic area. The franchisee buys a package that includes a proven product, proven operating methods, and training in managing the business.

RYAN SMOLKIN, SMOKE'S POUTINERIE

How do you like your poutine? A simple question, but the answer is the key to Ryan Smolkin's success, and the motto of his concept for Smoke's Poutinerie. You can certainly get your poutine the way you like it, as Smoke's Poutinerie serves up 23 varieties of the Québécois classic—from its best-selling Pulled Pork, to Veggie Deluxe and Curry Chicken—not just your regular cheese curds and gravy, that's for sure.

According to the website, they've been "clogging arteries since 2008." In that time, Ryan has launched a rapidly expanding chain of franchised fast-food poutine restaurants starting in Toronto and quickly spreading to London, Ottawa, Kingston, and even Mont Tremblant. As reported in the *Financial Post*: "the problem isn't finding an appetite for his product, but rather finding enough money to fuel the rapid growth of his company." That won't likely remain a problem for long. Private equity financing is quite fond of franchising. According to the *Financial Post*, the increasing interest in franchising is because it is "relatively stable, the model has been proven and there is an opportunity for long-term cash flow."

Ryan is something of a born entrepreneur. As a business student, he ran a successful property development company that he slowly built up and sold for $4 million in 2002. Then, he started a branding and design company, Amoeba Corp., which he sold in 2007, after becoming a nationally recognized brand leader with clients that included Nike, Molson, Maple Leaf Sports + Entertainment, YTV, and SIMS Snowboards!

These startups paved the way for Ryan to start his "dream company" that he had envisioned a decade earlier, growing up in the Ottawa Valley bordering Québec. In just three short years, Ryan managed to open 31 Smoke's Poutinerie locations from Halifax to Vancouver, but his goal is to expand nationally with 80 to 100 locations across Canada, and then achieve "global domination." He is already in the process of setting up the business infrastructure in the U.S. and, not surprisingly,

has received over 1,500 calls from around the world asking about franchise opportunities.

This growth has been fuelled through the use of traditional media relations and social media. As Ryan told *The Globe and Mail*, "When I opened the first store, all I had to sell the product was my own excitement. I was convincing people one at a time to try the poutine—family, friends, even strangers on the street." However, once the word got out, the walls of the stores were lined with news clippings that were shared with the 18- to 25-year-old target customer through a tweet or Facebook link. Using social media to generate buzz at his Winnipeg franchise opening created a lineup out the door for most of the day, with 800 people stopping by. In the first five days they served over 5,000 customers. That's some powerful social media at work.

It's also about branding. There is no mistaking a Smoke's Poutinerie—with the "overwhelming use of lumberjack plaid and the glass bottles of Pop Shoppe stocked in the fridge to feel both patriotic and nostalgic." When does it work the best? The busiest time of the day is actually when the after-bar crowd descends on the restaurant locations from 1:30 to 3:00 a.m. As Ryan told *The Globe and Mail*, "We're doing back-to-back one hundred-plus servings an hour." He even once served 165 poutines in an hour—do the math—that's 2.5 per minute! The humble poutine is not so humble anymore.

Thinking Critically

1. Taking a simple idea and creating something no one ever thought of seems to be a winning formula for entrepreneurs. What have you enjoyed in your life that you are passionate about? Challenge yourself to see it in a new way. Could you build a business around it?

2. Could you create a business model around that idea that could be duplicated over and over again as a franchise?

3. Would you prefer to buy a franchise and operate your own business? Is it a different type of entrepreneur that starts a franchise than buys a franchise?

SOURCES: http://www.smokespoutinerie.com, used with permission from Ryan Smolkin; http://www.shalomlife.com, September 11, 2009; http://www.financialpost.com, July 27, 2010; www.theglobeandmail.com, June 30, 2011.

A **franchise agreement** is a contract allowing the franchisee to use the franchisor's business name, trademark, and logo. The agreement also outlines the rules for operating the franchise, the services provided by the franchisor, and the financial terms. The franchisee agrees to keep inventory at certain levels, buy a standard equipment package, keep up sales and service levels, follow the franchisor's operating rules, take part in franchisor promotions, and maintain a relationship with the franchisor. In return, the franchisor provides the use of a proven company name and symbols, help finding a site, building plans, guidance and training, management assistance, managerial and accounting procedures, employee training, wholesale prices for supplies, and financial assistance.

franchise agreement
A contract setting out the terms of a franchising arrangement, including the rules for operating the franchise, the services provided by the franchisor, and the financial terms. Under the contract, the franchisee is allowed to use the franchisor's business name, trademark, and logo.

Advantages of Franchises

Like other forms of business organization, franchising offers some distinct advantages:

- *Increased ability for the franchisor to expand.* Because franchisees finance their own units, franchisors can grow without making a major investment. Although franchisors give up a share of profits to their franchisees, they receive ongoing revenues in the form of royalty payments.

Considering buying a franchise? Check out the opportunities and costs at www.canada.franchiseopportunities.com

- *Recognized name, product, and operating concept.* The franchisee gets a widely known and accepted business with a proven track record, as well as operating procedures, standard goods and services, and national advertising. Consumers know they can depend on products from franchises such as Pizza Hut, Hertz, and Holiday Inn. As a result, the franchisee's risk is reduced and the opportunity for success increased.
- *Management training and assistance.* The franchisor provides a structured training program that gives new franchisees a crash course in how to start and operate their business. Ongoing training programs for managers and employees are another plus. In addition, franchisees have a peer group for support and sharing ideas.
- *Financial assistance.* Being linked to a nationally known company can help a franchisee obtain funds from a lender. The franchisor typically also gives the franchisee advice on financial management, referrals to lenders, and help in preparing loan applications. Many franchisors offer payment plans, short-term credit for buying supplies from the franchise company, and loans to purchase real estate and equipment.

Disadvantages of Franchises

Franchising also has some disadvantages:

- *Loss of control.* The franchisor has to give up some control over operations and has less control over its franchisees than over company employees.
- *Cost of franchising.* Franchising can be a costly form of business. Costs will vary depending on the type of business and might include expensive facilities and equipment. The franchisee also pays fees and/or royalties, which are usually tied to a percentage of sales. Fees for national and local advertising and management advice might also add to a franchisee's ongoing costs.
- *Restricted operating freedom.* The franchisee agrees to conform to the franchisor's operating rules and facilities design, as well as inventory and supply standards. Some franchises require franchisees to purchase from only the franchisor or approved suppliers. The franchisor may restrict the franchisee's territory or site, which could limit growth. Failure to conform to franchisor policies could mean the loss of the franchise.

Franchise Growth

Many of today's major names in franchising, such as McDonald's and Kentucky Fried Chicken (KFC), started in the 1950s, but franchising grew rapidly through the 1960s and 1970s, with more types of businesses—clothing, convenience stores, business services, and many others—using franchising to distribute their goods and services. Business owners found franchising to be a way to expand operations quickly into new geographic areas with limited capital investment, and many are turning to technology to further expand their businesses.

Changing demographics drive franchise industry growth, in terms of who, how, and what experiences the most rapid growth. The continuing growth and popularity of technology and personal computing is responsible for the rapidly multiplying number of eBay drop-off stores, and tech consultants like Geeks on Call are in greater demand than ever. Other growth franchise industries are the specialty coffee market, children's enrichment and tutoring programs, senior care, weight control, and fitness franchises.

And the savviest franchisees see multi-unit development as a great way to further expand franchise systems and increase profits. Multi-unit buyers tend to be white-collar workers who have been laid off from middle-management jobs. They are well qualified financially, and bring

Concept *in Action*

Franchises offer a recognized name, product, and operating concept and, in many cases, management training and financial assistance. What are the advantages and disadvantages of owning a franchise?

RICHARD LAUTENS/GETSTOCK.COM

Exhibit 8.7 Examples of Franchises in Canada

MR. SUB
Days Inn Canada
Keg Restaurants Ltd.
Kwik Kopy Printing Canada
M&M Meat Shops
McDonald's Restaurants Canada Limited
Mr. Lube Canada Inc.
Orange Julius Canada Limited

Pizza Hut
Quizno's Canada Corporation
Rent-A-Wreck
Royal LePage Real Estate Services
Second Cup Ltd., The
Shoppers Drug Mart
Swiss Chalet Chicken & Ribs

management skills, financial resources, business acumen, and a lot of drive to their franchise ventures. Exhibit 8.7 shows some of the franchises with a presence in Canada.

The Next Big Thing in Franchising

All around you, people are talking about the next big thing—"always fresh" at Tim Hortons; the half hour workout at Curves, the answer to North America's fitness needs—and you are ready to take the plunge and buy a trendy franchise. But consumers' desires can change with the tide, so how do you plan an entrance—and exit—strategy when purchasing a franchise that's a big hit today but could be old news by tomorrow? Exhibit 8.8 outlines some tips offered by Michael H. Seid, managing director of Michael H. Seid & Associates, a management consulting company specializing in the franchise industry.

International Franchising

Like other forms of business, franchising is part of our global marketplace economy. As international demand for all types of goods and services grows, most franchise systems are already operating internationally or planning to expand overseas. Restaurants, hotels, business services, educational products, car rentals, and non-food retail stores are popular international franchises.

Franchisors in foreign countries face many of the same problems as other companies doing business abroad. In addition to tracking markets and currency changes, franchisors must understand local culture, language differences, and the political environment. Franchisors in foreign countries also face the challenge of aligning their business operations with the goals of their franchisees, who may be located half a globe away. In the Expanding Around the Globe box on the next page, you will learn about a hugely successful North American company that attempted to replicate its success in the Chinese fast food market, with mixed results.

Concept *Check*

Describe franchising and the main parties to the transaction.

Summarize the major advantages and disadvantages of franchising.

Why has franchising proved so popular?

Exhibit 8.8 Franchise Purchase Tips

Act fast, yet proceed with caution. Normal trends tend to have a five-year lifespan, so it's important to get in early. Commit to a shorter term when the investment is not so secure.

Put the franchisor to the test. When you get into a franchise system that needs to be nimble, make certain it can respond quickly to change.

Know what you're getting into. Ask the franchisor what product(s) they plan to add if trends change. If they don't have an answer or aren't talking about research and development, you still might be able to buy into the trend but not with that franchisor.

Don't invest more than you can afford to lose. Bank your money and look at other investments.

Don't fall in love with a trend. Trends are fickle. Adored one day, they can become one-hit wonders the next. Buy on business sense, not on emotions.

SOURCE: Reprinted by permission of Michael H. Seid.

Expanding Around the Globe

SETTING UP (SANDWICH) SHOP IN CHINA

Lured by China's fast-food industry—estimated at $15 billion—Jim Bryant, 50, was not the only entrepreneur to discover it is hard to do business in China. In ten years, Bryant has opened 19 Subway stores in Beijing—only half the number he was supposed to have by now—while other companies like Chili's and Dunkin' Donuts have given up their Chinese operations altogether.

Subway, or Sai Bei Wei (Mandarin for "tastes better than others"), is now the third-largest North American fast-food chain in China, right behind McDonald's and KFC, and all its stores are profitable. Although Bryant had never eaten a Subway sandwich before, Jana Brands, the company Bryant worked for in China, sold $20 million in crab to Subway annually, so he knew it was big business. When Subway founder Fred DeLuca visited Beijing in 1994, Bryant took him to a place not on the official tour: McDonald's. It was Sunday night and the place was packed. "We could open 20,000 Subways here and not scratch the surface," Bryant remembers De Luca saying.

Two weeks later Bryant called Subway's headquarters in Milford, Connecticut, and asked to be the company representative in China. He would recruit local entrepreneurs, train them to become franchisees, and act as a liaison between them and the company. He would receive half the initial $10,000 franchise fee and one-third of their 8 percent royalty fees. He could also open his own Subway restaurants. Steve Forman, the founder of Jana Brands, invested $1 million in return for a 75 percent stake.

All foreign businesses in China had to be joint ventures with local partners, so Bryant used the Chinese business practice of relying on local relationships to find a manager for his first restaurant in Beijing. The project ran into problems immediately. Work on the store was delayed and construction costs soared. It didn't take Bryant long to realize that he and Forman had been swindled out of $200,000.

When it finally opened, the restaurant was a hit among Americans in Beijing, but the locals weren't sure what to make of it. They didn't know how to order and didn't like the idea of touching their food, so they held the sandwich vertically, peeled off the paper, and ate it like a banana. Most of all, the Chinese didn't seem to want sandwiches.

But Subway did little to alter its menu—something that still irks some Chinese franchisees. "Subway should have at least one item tailored to Chinese tastes to show they respect local culture," says Luo Bing Ling, a Beijing franchisee. Bryant thinks that with time, sandwiches will catch on in China. Maybe he's right: Tuna salad, which he couldn't give away at first, is now the number one seller.[9]

Thinking Critically

1. What are some of the main problems franchisors encounter when attempting to expand their business in a foreign country?
2. What steps can franchisors take to ensure a smooth and successful launch of a new franchise business in a foreign country?

LO7

THE FUTURE OF BUSINESS OWNERSHIP

As we learned earlier, an awareness of trends in the business environment is critical to business success. Many social, demographic, and technology trends affect how businesses organize. When reviewing options for organizing a business or choosing a career path, consider the trends. Three of these trends are mergers and acquisitions, the influence of the baby boomers, and increasing franchising innovations.

Joining Forces

Increasingly we are seeing mergers and acquisitions in Canada, with Canadian companies merging or acquiring Canadian and foreign-owned companies, and Canadian companies being taken over by foreign companies. The primary reasons are economies of scale and access to markets. Additionally, more strategic alliances (e.g., President's Choice Financial and CIBC) and joint ventures allow for shared risk and information.

Two other trends include employee ownership and institutional ownership, as many of the baby boomers who are owners of companies simply want an exit strategy. This is easily accomplished by allowing employees to participate in a stock ownership plan (ESOP). Institutional ownership, for example, mutual funds or pension funds, generally have larger resources and can therefore purchase more shares than an individual might be able to.

"Baby Boomers" Rewrite the Rules of Retirement

We all hear and read a great deal about the "greying of Canada," which refers to the "baby boomer" generation heading towards retirement age. This unprecedented demographic phenomenon—in 2006 the first members of the Baby Boom generation turned 60—is driving the ongoing battle to stay young, slim, and healthy. Boomers have transformed every life stage they've touched so far, and their demographic weight means that business opportunities are created wherever they go. With their interest in staying fit, boomers are contributing to the growth of fitness and weight-loss franchises.

Another area of boomer-driven franchise growth is eldercare. Founded in 1994, Home Instead Senior Care is recognized as one of the world's fastest growing franchise companies in the eldercare market, with a network of over 800 independently owned and operated franchises in 15 countries. And as the world's population continues to age, the need for its unique services will continue to increase.

Home Instead Senior Care provides a meaningful solution for the elderly who prefer to remain at home. Seniors' quality of life is enhanced by Home Instead Senior Care's part-time, full-time, and around-the-clock services, designed for people who are capable of managing their physical needs but require some assistance and supervision. Home Instead Senior Care provides meal preparation, companionship, light housekeeping, medication reminders, incidental transportation, and errands. These services make it possible for the elderly to remain in the familiar comfort of their own homes for a longer period of time.[10]

But the best deal yet may be adult day services, one of the top 10 fastest-growing franchises and "still one of the best-kept secrets around" according to *Entrepreneur* magazine. Based on the concept of daycare services for children, Sarah Adult Day Services, Inc. offers a franchising opportunity that meets the two criteria for a successful and socially responsible business: a booming demographic market with great potential for growth, and excellent eldercare.[11]

Franchise Innovations

As more franchise systems crowd into growing industry categories, established franchises must find ways to differentiate themselves, such as the following:

- *Multiple-concept franchises*. When franchisors can take the competency they have developed and bridge it over to another franchise (i.e., the skills are transferable), these multi-concept franchises improve efficiencies and save money. For example, combination franchise Molly Maid and Mr. Handyman benefit from shared marketing and promotion, hoping to appeal to a similar customer.[12]
- *Expanded product offerings*. When a company can offer its customers multiple products and services, the customers can enjoy reduced costs and one-stop shopping. An example is a business that will deliver and pick up the dry cleaning, go shopping for gifts and essentials, and so on.
- *Cross-branding*. Operating two or more franchises in one location generates more customer traffic and maximizes space, personnel, and management utilization. For instance, gas stations frequently offer fast food outlets.
- *New ideas*. Finding new and innovative products and services that can be offered by a franchise helps to expand its target market and provide better service to its customers. For example, a residential cleaning company might offer house- and pet-sitting services to its clients when they travel.

GREAT IDEAS TO USE NOW

It is important to understand the benefits of the different forms of business organization if you start your own company. Even if you decide to work for someone else, this information will help you match a business entity with your goals. Suppose you are considering two job offers for a computer-programming position: a two-year-old consulting company with 10 employees owned by a sole proprietor, or a publicly traded software developer with sales of $500 million. In addition to comparing the specific job responsibilities, consider the following:

- Which company offers better training? Do you prefer the on-the-job training you'll get at the small company, or do you want formal training programs as well?

- Which position offers the chance to work on a variety of assignments?
- What are the opportunities for advancement? Employee benefits?
- What happens if the owner of the young company gets sick or decides to sell the company?
- Which company offers a better working environment for you?

Answering these and similar questions will help you decide which job meets your particular needs.

Is Franchising in Your Future?

If the franchise route to business ownership interests you, begin educating yourself on the franchise process by investigating various franchise opportunities. You should research a franchise company thoroughly before making any financial commitment. Once you've narrowed your choices, you must research the franchisor, including its history, operating style, management, any past or pending litigation, the franchisee's financial obligations, and any restrictions on the sale of units. Interviewing current and past franchisees is another essential step.

Would-be franchisees should check recent issues of small-business magazines such as *Franchise Zone, Entrepreneur, Inc., Business Startups,* and *Success,* for industry trends, ideas on promising franchise opportunities, and advice on how to choose and run a franchise. The International Franchise Association website, www.franchise.org, has links to *Franchise World Magazine* and other useful sites.

Is franchising for you? Assertiveness, desire to be your own boss, willingness to make a substantial time commitment, passion about the franchise concept, optimism, patience, and integrity rank high on franchisors' lists. Prior business experience is also a definite plus, and some franchisors prefer or require experience in their field. The information in Exhibit 8.9 can help you make a realistic self-assessment to increase your chances of success.

Exhibit 8.9 Are You Ready to Be a Franchisee?

What can you to do to prepare when considering the purchase of a franchise? Doing your homework can spell the difference between success and failure, and some early preparation can help lay the groundwork for a successful launch of your franchised business.

Getting to know your banker at an early date should speed the loan process if you plan to finance your purchase with a bank loan. Stop by and introduce yourself. The proper real estate is another critical component for a successful retail/food franchise, so establish a relationship with a commercial real estate broker and begin scouting locations.

Professional guidance while evaluating franchise opportunities can prevent expensive mistakes, so interview advisers to find one that is right for you. Selecting a lawyer with franchise experience will speed the review of your franchise agreement. Most franchise systems use computers, so if you are not computer literate, take a class in the basics.

Then ask yourself some searching questions:

- Are you willing to work hard and put in long hours?
- Do you have the necessary financial resources?
- Are you excited about a specific franchise concept?
- Do you have prior business experience?
- Do your expectations and personal goals match the franchisor's?

SOURCES: Michael H. Seid and Kay Marie Ainsley, "Are You Ready to be a Franchisee?" *FranchiseZone*, December 9, 2002, http://www.entrepreneur.com; and Thomas Love, "The Perfect Franchisee," *Nation's Business*, April 1, 1998, http://www.ask.elibrary.com.

Summary of Learning Outcomes

The advantages of sole proprietorships include ease and low cost of formation, the owner's rights to all profits, the owner's control of the business, relative freedom from government regulation, absence of special taxes, and ease of dissolution. Disadvantages include the owner's unlimited liability for debts, difficulty in raising capital, limited managerial expertise, difficulty in finding qualified employees, large personal time commitment, unstable business life, and the owner's personal absorption of all losses.

LO1 Discuss the advantages and disadvantages of the sole proprietorship form of business organization.

Partnerships can be formed as either general or limited partnerships. In a general partnership, the partners co-own the assets and share the profits. Each partner is individually liable for all debts and contracts of the partnership. The operations of a limited partnership are controlled by one or more general partners with unlimited liability. Limited partners are financial partners whose liability is limited to their investment; they do not participate in the company's operations. The advantages of partnerships include ease of formation, availability of capital, diversity of managerial skills and expertise, flexibility to respond to changing business conditions, no special taxes, and relative freedom from government control. Disadvantages include unlimited liability for general partners, potential for conflict between partners, sharing of profits, and difficulty exiting or dissolving the partnership.

LO2 Describe the advantages of operating as a partnership, and the downside risks partners should consider.

A corporation is a legal entity chartered by a province. Its organizational structure includes stockholders who own the corporation, a board of directors elected by the stockholders to govern the company, and officers who carry out the goals and policies set by the board. Stockholders can sell or transfer their shares at any time, and are entitled to receive profits in the form of dividends. Advantages of corporations include limited liability, ease of transferring ownership, and ability to attract financing. Disadvantages include double taxation of profits at a somewhat reduced rate, the cost and complexity of formation, and government restrictions.

LO3 Explain the corporate structure and its advantages and disadvantages, and identify a special type of corporation.

A special type of corporation that is owned by either a provincial or the federal government is called a Crown corporation.

LO4 Review some of the other business organization options in addition to sole proprietorships, partnerships, and corporations.

Businesses can also organize as cooperatives, joint ventures, and franchises. Cooperatives are collectively owned by individuals or businesses with similar interests that combine to achieve more economic power. Cooperatives distribute profits to their members. Two types of cooperatives are buyer and seller cooperatives.

A joint venture is an alliance of two or more companies formed to undertake a special project. Joint ventures can be set up in various ways, through partnerships or special-purpose corporations. By sharing management expertise, technology, products, and financial and operational resources, companies can reduce the risk faced by new enterprises.

A franchise is based on a business arrangement between a *franchisor*, which supplies the product concept, and a *franchisee*, who sells the goods or services of the franchisor in a certain geographic area.

LO5 Understand why mergers and acquisitions can be important to a company's overall growth.

In a merger, two companies combine to form one. In an acquisition, one company or investor group buys another. Companies merge for strategic reasons, to improve overall performance of the merged company through cost savings, to eliminate overlapping operations, to improve purchasing power, to increase market share, or to reduce competition. Company growth, broadening product lines, and the ability to quickly acquire new markets, technology, or management skills are other motives. Another motive for merging is financial restructuring—cutting costs, selling off units, laying off employees, and refinancing the company to increase its value to stockholders.

There are three types of mergers. In a horizontal merger, companies at the same stage in the same industry combine to gain economic power, to diversify, or to win a greater market share. A vertical merger involves the acquisition of a company that serves an earlier or a later stage of the production or sales process, such as a supplier or sales outlet. In a conglomerate, unrelated businesses come together to reduce risk through diversification.

LO6 Identify when franchising is an appropriate business form and why it is growing in importance.

Franchising is one of the fastest-growing forms of business ownership. It involves an agreement between a franchisor, the supplier of goods or services, and a franchisee, an individual or company that buys the right to sell the franchisor's products in a specific area. With a franchise, the business owner does not have to start from scratch but instead buys a business concept with a proven product and operating methods. The franchisor provides management training and assistance; use of a recognized brand name, product, and operating concept; and financial assistance. Franchises can be costly to start and might restrict operating freedom, because the franchisee must conform to the franchisor's standard procedures. The growth in franchising is attributed to its ability to expand business operations quickly into new geographic areas with limited capital investment.

LO7 List some of the current trends that may affect the business organizations of the future.

Mergers, acquisitions, strategic alliances, employee ownership, and institutional ownership are becoming more common.

The baby boomers are demanding more products that enhance their lifestyles. They are living a healthier lifestyle and demanding more independence, which presents opportunities for new and innovative products (both goods and services). Many are delaying retirement, preferring instead to remain employed or self-employed. Many who do retire work as consultants on a part-time basis to supplement the shortage of experienced workers.

Another trend, as the franchise market starts to mature, is many franchise owners expanding their product lines, or cross-branding, to reach more customers with better service.

Key Terms

Experiential Exercises

1. **Learn the laws.** Before starting your own company, you should know the legal requirements in your area. Call the appropriate city or provincial departments, such as licensing, health, and zoning, to find out what licences and permits you need, and any other requirements you must meet. Do the requirements vary depending on the type of company? Are there restrictions on starting a home-based business? Then, check the Web for information on how to incorporate.

2. **Study franchise opportunities.** Franchising offers an alternative to starting your own business from scratch. Do you have what it takes to be successful? Start by making a list of your interests and skills, and do a self-assessment by using some of the suggestions in the last section of this chapter. Next, you need to narrow a field of thousands of different franchise systems. At Franchise Handbook Online, www.franchise1.com, you'll find articles with checklists to help you thoroughly research a franchise and its industry, as well as a directory of franchise opportunities. Armed with this information, you can develop a questionnaire to evaluate a prospective franchise.

3. Bridget Jones wants to open her own business selling her handmade chocolates over the Internet. Although she has some money saved and could start the business on her own, she is concerned about her lack of bookkeeping and management experience. A friend mentions he knows an experienced businessman seeking involvement with a start-up company. As Bridget's business consultant, prepare recommendations for Bridget regarding an appropriate form of business organization, including outlining the issues she should consider and the risks involved, supported by reasons for your suggestions.

4. You and a partner co-own Swim-Clean, a successful pool supply and cleaning service. Because sales have tapered off, you want to expand your operations to another town 100 kilometres away. Given the high costs of expanding, you decide to sell Swim-Clean franchises. The idea takes off, and soon you have 25 units throughout the region. Your success results in an invitation to speak at a local chamber of commerce luncheon. Prepare a brief presentation describing how you evaluated the benefits and risks of becoming a franchisor, the problems you have encountered, and how you've established good working relationships with your franchisees.

5. Find news of a recent merger using an online search or in a business periodical such as *Canadian Business* or *The Globe & Mail Report on Business*. Research the merger by using a variety of sources, including the company's website and news articles. Discover the motives behind the merger, the problems facing the new entity, and the company's progress toward achieving its objectives.

Review Questions

1. What are some of the considerations when choosing a form of business ownership to ensure that it suits your needs?

2. Why are proprietorships the most popular form of business ownership?

3. What should a partnership agreement include?

4. Considering some of the disadvantages of corporations, why do so many choose to use the corporation form?

5. When are joint ventures a good idea?

6. What are the various types of mergers? Give examples of each.

7. Why are franchise operations popular? What opportunities do they offer to the franchisor and franchisee?

CREATIVE THINKING CASE

Meet the Gore Family

Imagine an organization with more than $3 billion in sales, 9,500 employees working in 30 countries around the world—with no organizational charts. W. L. Gore & Associates, headquartered in Newark, Delaware, is a model of unusual business practices. Wilbert Gore, who left DuPont to explore new uses for Teflon, started the company in 1958. Best known for its breathable, weatherproof Gore-Tex fabric, Glide dental floss, and Elixir guitar strings, the company has no bosses, no titles, no departments, and no formal job descriptions. There is no managerial hierarchy at Gore, and top management treats employees, called associates, as peers. They call it "a team-based, flat lattice organization."

In April 2005, the company named 22-year associate Terri Kelly its new chief executive officer. Unlike large public corporations, Gore's announcement was made without much fanfare. "It's never about the CEO," she says. "You're an associate, and you just happen to be the CEO. We don't like anyone to be the center of attention." She considers the idea that the CEO of W. L. Gore manages the company a misperception. "My goal is to provide the overall direction. I spend a lot of time making sure we have the right people in the right roles.... We empower divisions and push out responsibility. We're so diversified that it's impossible for a CEO to have that depth of knowledge—and not even practical."

The company focuses on its products and company values rather than individuals. Committees, comprising employees, make major decisions such as hiring, firing, and compensation. They even set top executives' compensation. Employees work on teams, which are switched around every few years. In fact, all employees are expected to make minor decisions instead of relying on the "boss" to make them. "We're committed to how we get things done," Kelly says. "That puts a tremendous burden on leaders because it's easier to say, 'Just do it' than to explain the rationale. But in the long run, you'll get much better results because people are making a commitment."

The company tries to maintain a family-like atmosphere by dispersing its employees into more than 60 buildings on five continents. Because no formal lines of authority exist, employees can speak to anyone in the company at any time. This arrangement also forces employees to spend considerable time developing relationships. As one employee described it, instead of trying to please just one "boss," you have to please everyone. This doesn't work for everyone; new hires can get confused and some get frustrated. One contributor to www.glassdoor.com remarked on the challenge to get a raise when everyone you work with gets a vote. No doubt, those who don't fit, don't stay.

The informal organizational structure is working well. The company produces thousands of advanced technology products for the electronics, industrial, fabrics, and medical markets. Its corporate structure fosters innovation and has been a significant contributor to associate satisfaction. Employee turnover is a low 5 percent a year, and the company can choose new associates from the 38,000 job applications it receives annually. As of 2011, *Fortune* magazine has produced 14 "100 Best Companies to Work For" lists, and W. L. Gore has been near the top of the list every time.

Thinking Critically

1. Given the lack of formal structure, how important do you think the informal structure becomes? Does Gore's reliance on committee work slow processes down?

2. Is W. L. Gore a mechanistic or an organic organization (see pages 283–285)? Support your answer with examples from the case.

3. How do you think Gore's organizational structure affects the division of labour?

SOURCES: Alan Deutschman, "What I Know Now: Terri Kelly, CEO, W. L. Gore & Associates," *Fast Company*, September 2005, p. 96; "Gore Marks 9th Year as One of Nation's Best, Company Earns #5 Position on FORTUNE Magazine '100 Best Companies to Work For' List," W. L. Gore & Associates, press release, January 9, 2006, http://www.gore.com; Robert Levering and Milton Moskowitz, "And the Winners Are ...," *Fortune*, January 23, 2006, p. 89; Sara J. Welch, "GORE The Fabric of Success," *Successful Meetings*, May 2005, p. 49-51; W. L. Gore & Associates website, http://www.gore.com February 10, 2006 and December 19, 2011; "About Gore," http://www.gore.com/een_xx/aboutus/index.html, December 19, 2011; "W. L. Gore Reviews," http://www.glassdoor.com, December 19, 2011; and J. Huey, "The New Post-Heroic Leadership," 1994, http://money.cnn.com/magazines/fortune/fortune_archive/1994/02/21/78995/index.htm, November 23, 2011.

Part 3

Business Management

Making the Connection

Management and Leadership in Today's Organizations

In this chapter, you will be introduced to management and the first function of a manager in the act of managing a business—planning. Management is what managers do to ensure that the organization achieves the critical success factors. As we state later in the chapter, "management is the process of guiding the development, maintenance, and allocation of resources to attain organizational goals." That is why the process of management encircles our model of a successful business. It is the process whereby all of the activities of a business geared toward achieving the factors critical to its success are implemented. It ties everything together and, when done properly, ensures that activities are integrated.

All of the activities within the process of management—planning, organizing, motivating, and controlling—are highly integrated. As you'll read in this chapter, they form a tightly integrated cycle of thoughts and actions. They are highly interdependent and are performed in such a way that it is difficult, if not impossible, to separate them. Just watch a manager at work. Let's suppose that she has just made a decision to promote a particular individual and leave that person's previous position permanently vacant. You might say that this was a decision made to reward an individual for a job well done and therefore to *motivate* him to continue to work hard by recognizing his efforts. However, *planning* would have gone into that decision as well, because managers can't just move people around without looking ahead to the implications of those moves on other employees and the goals of the company. One of those implications is that a change would have occurred to the structure of the *organization*, as a position was left vacant, perhaps causing that individual's subordinates to change managers and the number of managers to be reduced at that level. It also would require that the performance of that individual had been monitored to determine that he was worthy of this

promotion. This is called *control*—results are measured and compared against objectives, and changes are made to keep everything on track or under control.

But remember that managers don't perform this highly integrative process in a vacuum. They make plans contingent on the opportunities and threats they see in the external environment in relation to the strengths and weaknesses the business has internally. What is done to implement the plan, with respect to organizational structure, motivational tactics, and control mechanisms, also depends on the internal and external environments. For example, a company might choose an open, flexible structure with less bureaucracy to encourage employees to be more creative, and to seek and pursue opportunities that exist in a rapidly changing, highly competitive *economic* environment. This would, in turn, be dependent on the types of employees the company has, whether they would grow and develop in that type of environment, and whether they would need more direction to be motivated to perform. In other words, the strengths and weaknesses of the employees would need to be considered.

The planning process itself is also highly integrative. As mentioned in the chapter, there are different levels of planning—the main ones being strategic, tactical, and operational—but they must all work together. Strategic planning is broad based and determines the goals and plans for the entire organization. Then, at the tactical level, each functional area determines its own goals and plans, which enables that area to fulfill its role in achieving the overall strategic plan. Finally, at the operational level, each unit within each functional area determines its goals and plans to implement those at the next higher level.

For example, if a company decided strategically to develop a new product line to compete with another company that is threatening to reduce its market share, then, at the tactical level, *marketing* would need to determine how to promote this new product line, and *operations* would need to determine the most efficient and cost-effective way to produce it. At the operational level, sales quotas, territories, and strategies for salespeople would then be set, and production schedules would be established in the plant. The important factor is that all of these plans are related to each other. They are connected as if by a string to the next higher level; each one helps to achieve the objectives of the next level, so ultimately, the company achieves its overall goals and the critical factors of success.

As we indicate in the chapter, there are many trends in the environment that affect management and leadership today. One of these is empowerment. Employees are being given more freedom to make decisions, which, in turn, increases *employee commitment* to the organization and its goals—our most important critical success factor. But this requires really solid communication and integration, so that when employees make decisions, they are in tune with other decisions that are being made, and everyone is moving in the same direction. This is improved by the impact of *technology*, which wires everyone in the organization together with instant, equal access to pertinent information.

This trend toward empowerment is linked to the discussion of leadership. Just as teams need coaches, organizations need leaders to keep everyone moving in the same direction. There are many different leadership styles, but as you'll see in the chapter, the most effective are those that result in individuals working together as a team. These styles result in the greatest commitment, which is, of course, our primary objective: to have employees take ownership of the results of the company as if it were their own. As mentioned by Max Messmer, Chairman and CEO of Robert Half International, "Most people will work harder … [if] they are trusted to be responsible to make their own decisions. Empowering your employees will likely pay off with … loyalty, and the high level of productivity that comes from effective teamwork." The leader and his or her style are critical to developing a *vision* for the company and inspiring employees to be committed to that vision, so that all the critical success factors can be achieved.

chapter 9

Management and Leadership in Today's Organizations

LEARNING OUTCOMES

1 Differentiate between management and leadership.

2 Discuss the four types of planning.

3 List the primary responsibilities of managers in organizing activities.

4 Describe how leadership styles influence a corporate culture.

5 Examine how organizations control activities.

6 Summarize the roles managers take on in different organizational settings.

7 Identify the set of managerial skills necessary for managerial success.

8 List some of the trends that will affect management in the future.

ROBIN MALONI AND OASIS BAGS—A VISION TO MAKE A DIFFERENCE

Today, when you pay for your purchase at a retail store, the question isn't "Paper or plastic?" It's more likely "Do you have a bag, or would you like to buy one?" This wasn't the case in 1989, when Robin Maloni co-founded Oasis Bags.

At the time, the problem was clear: there were shopping bags in the landfills, trees being cut down, and oil and energy used to manufacture and transport more and more bags. Public awareness was increasing, and some shoppers tried reusing plastic bags. But the disposable bags didn't last long. Others went without bags, but that wasn't a practical long-term solution. Oasis Bags was born from the idea that a viable reusable bag could make a difference in reducing waste.

Retailers scoffed at the idea that customers would pay for a cloth bag and reuse it. So Oasis Bags offered bags on consignment at small local shops—the merchants would pay Oasis Bags only if the bags sold. The idea soon took off, and Oasis Bags today makes and sells bags around the world from its head office in Vaudreuil, Québec.

Oasis Bags was the first company to be certified by the EcoLogo environmental standards program for cotton and polypropylene bags. And when consumer watchdogs went looking, Oasis Bags tested lead-free when many of its competitors' bags did not.

From the start, Maloni committed to a vision of a sustainable product that was good for the environment. This vision continues to resonate with people—reusing bags makes customers feel good, selling reusable bags helps support a green image for the retailer, and working for Oasis Bags makes its employees feel like they are making a difference.

The commitment has been recognized in areas that go beyond the income statement. In 2010, Maloni was honoured by the RBC Canadian Woman Entrepreneur Awards, in the Sustainability category. More than 2000 female entrepreneurs were nominated for this award, but only one was chosen. The size of the field shows the importance of female entrepreneurs, and Maloni's selection is a testimony to the lasting impact of reusable bags.

Beyond the products it produces, a green vision clearly permeates Oasis Bags. Its website contains pages of information that has no direct connection with reusable bags: tips for reducing waste, reports on international initiatives, and challenges to do more for the environment. The Oasis Bags vision is not product-centred—rather, the product is at the centre of the organization's environmental vision. The co-founders wanted to do something for the environment, and while the outcome was an environmentally friendly alternative to single-use plastic and paper bags, the overall goal remains to supply socially and environmentally responsible, certified products.

This vision extends to Earth Day activities, school support programs, and many initiatives, including a caring relationship with employees. Oasis Bags is a family-based company with a family-modelled culture; it supports staff

PHOTO COURTESY OF ROBIN MALONI

fundraising initiatives and celebrates a team concept of success. The company began with vision, and vision sustains it through worldwide growth.[1]

THINKING CRITICALLY

As you read this chapter, consider the following questions:

1. What is the difference between management and leadership?

2. How does a leader's vision affect an organization?

3. What can happen when a company grows too big for its leader to model the initial vision throughout all its operations?

SOURCES: Laurie Maloni, "Letter to Our Customers," http://www.oasisbags.com/blog/wp-content/uploads/2010/12/Letter-to-our-customers-2011.pdf; Oasis, "About Us," Oasis website, http://www.oasisbags.com/en/about_us.htm; Oasis Bags Blog, http://www.oasisbags.com/blog/; Oasis Bags, "Our Co-Founder Robin Maloni Wins the Sustainability Award at RBC Canadian Woman Entrepreneur of the Year," Oasis Bags Blog, December 1, 2010, http://www.oasisbags.com/blog/? p=254/; TPH Sustainability Award Finalist video of Robin Maloni, RBC Canadian Entrepreneur Awards, http://www.theawards.ca/cwea/robinmaloni_hq.mov/.

Developing consistency in top leadership is critical for the successful future of Canadian organizations. Today's companies rely on managers to guide the daily process using human, technological, financial, and other resources to create a competitive advantage. For many beginning business students, being in "management" is an attractive, but somewhat vague, future goal. This vagueness is due in part to an incomplete understanding of what managers do and how they contribute to organizational success or failure. In this chapter, we introduce the basic functions of management and the skills required by managers to drive an organization toward its goals. We will also discuss how leadership styles influence a corporate culture and highlight the trends that are shaping the future role of managers.

LO1 THE ROLE OF MANAGEMENT AND LEADERSHIP

management
The process of guiding the development, maintenance, and allocation of resources to attain organizational goals.

Management is the process of guiding the development, maintenance, and allocation of resources to attain organizational goals. Managers are the people in the organization responsible for developing and carrying out this management process (managing the tasks). Management is dynamic by nature and evolves to meet needs and constraints in the organization's internal and external environments. In a global marketplace where the rate of change is rapidly increasing, flexibility and adaptability are crucial to the managerial process. This process is based in four key functional areas of the organization: planning, organizing, motivating, and controlling. Although these activities are discussed separately in the chapter, they actually form a tightly integrated cycle of thoughts and actions.

From this perspective, the managerial process can be described as

1. Anticipating potential problems or opportunities and designing plans to deal with them
2. Coordinating and allocating the resources needed to implement plans
3. Guiding personnel through the implementation process
4. Reviewing results and making any necessary changes

This last stage provides information to be used in ongoing planning efforts, and thus the cycle starts over again.

As shown in Exhibit 9.1, the four functions are highly interdependent, with managers often planning, organizing, leading, and controlling. The four functions are highly interdependent, with managers often performing more than one of them at a time and each of them many times over the course of a normal workday. As you will learn in the following sections, all of the functions require sound decision-making and communication skills.

efficiency
Using the least amount of resources to accomplish the organization's goals (doing things right).

effectiveness
The ability to produce the desired results or goods (doing the right thing).

The four management functions can help managers increase organizational efficiency and effectiveness. Efficiency is using the least possible amount of resources to get work done, whereas effectiveness is the ability to produce a desired result. Managers need to be both efficient and effective in order to achieve organizational goals.

leadership
The relationship between a leader and the followers who want real changes, resulting in outcomes that reflect their shared purposes (leading people).

Leadership is a relationship between a leader and the followers who want real changes and outcomes that reflect their shared purposes (leading people). Managers and leaders are not inherently the same. While both are concerned with providing direction for the company, managers are concerned with managing the tasks, leaders with leading people. Leadership requires a vision of the future and developing strategies for producing the changes needed to reach that vision.

Exhibit 9.1 What Managers Do and Why

GOOD MANAGEMENT CONSISTS OF THESE FOUR ACTIVITIES: | | **WHICH RESULTS IN** | **AND LEADS TO**

Planning

- Set objectives and state mission
- Examine alternatives
- Determine needed resources
- Create strategies to reach objectives

Motivating

- Lead and motivate employees
- To accomplish organizational goals
- Communicate with employees
- Resolve conflicts
- Manage change

→ Organizational efficiency and effectiveness → Achievement of organizational mission and objectives

Organizing

- Design jobs and specify tasks
- Create organizational structure
- Staff positions
- Coordinate work activities
- Set policies and procedures
- Allocate resources

Controlling

- Measure performance
- Compare performance to standards
- Take necessary action to
- improve performance

The following is cited from an unknown author:

A Manager versus a Leader

The manager drives group members; the leader coaches them.
The manager depends upon authority; the leader on goodwill.
The manager inspires fear; the leader inspires enthusiasm.
The manager says "I"; the leader says "we."
The manager assigns the task; the leader sets the pace.
The manager says, "Get there on time"; the leader gets there ahead of time.
The manager fixes the blame for the breakdown; the leader fixes the breakdown.
The manager knows how it is done; the leader shows how.
The manager makes work drudgery; the leader makes it a game.
The manager says, "Go"; the leader says, "Let's go."

—Author unknown

There is more discussion of leadership later in this chapter.

Concept *Check*

Define the term management.

What are the four key functions of managers?

What is the difference between efficiency and effectiveness?

How are management and leadership different?

PLANNING

LO2

Planning begins with the anticipation of potential problems or opportunities that the organization might encounter. Managers then design strategies to solve current problems, prevent future problems, or take advantage of opportunities. These strategies serve as the foundation for goals, objectives, policies, and procedures. Put simply, planning is deciding what needs to be done to achieve organizational objectives, identifying when and how it will be done, and determining by whom it should be

planning
The process of deciding what needs to be done to achieve organizational objectives, identifying when and how it will be done, and determining by whom it should be done.

Creating the Future of Business

LAUREN FRIESE, TALENTEGG.CA

Lauren Friese is the Founder of Talentegg.ca, Canada's leading online career resource for students and recent graduates, and a company you definitely need to know as you work towards a career in business. If the name throws you a little, the slogan says it all: "hatching graduate careers," and that's exactly what she does. Lauren started TalentEgg in 2008, in order to create a better way for students to transition from school to work.

After graduating with a degree in economics, Lauren didn't really know what to do next, so she decided to get a master's degree from the London School of Economics. It was in the UK that Lauren happened on a career website designed for young people, www.milkround.com, and based on her own difficult transition experience, decided to try a similar model in Canada.

It is clear that there was a need in Canada just waiting for someone to fill it. TalentEgg was profitable from its very first sale—a short eight months after Lauren quit her "real job"—and has been profitable ever since. Taking a peek at the number and type of employers on the TalentEgg site, you can clearly see that she has definitely made the transition from school to work easier for a lot of young people—1.2 million users in 2011 alone, and 1.8 million in the 12 months before this was written!

Asked how she competes with sites like Monster.ca, Lauren described her site as "more like the evolution of a traditional campus career fair" than a job board. Besides being specifically for students and new grads as opposed to other job sites, it also, unlike a campus career fair, has the added bonus of connecting students with employers nationwide and, being on the Web, is always open.

On talentegg.ca you'll find "information about careers, companies, and the jobs they offer," as well as "a ton of editorial resources on everything, from writing a resume to how to use LinkedIn to how to ask for a reference letter."

This isn't Lauren's first website business—she was born to be an entrepreneur. After being inspired by a two-line part in *Macbeth* at age 15, she set her goal to be a "world-famous actress" and started a website for young actors called BigDreamers.com. Lauren has learned a lot since those early days.

According to Lauren, "being young and straight out of school is probably THE best time in your life to start a career as an entrepreneur." You have fewer responsibilities, there are tons of people willing to help young entrepreneurs, and the experiences you get make you "extremely hirable to another company." Lauren has learned that as an entrepreneur it is important "to surround yourself with good people and great support," but also feels that one of the most important strengths she possesses as an entrepreneur is "persistence, and the ability to persist past rejection," because at the end of the day: "Ideas are easy. Execution is hard." Good advice from someone who started young and made it work.

Thinking Critically

1. Lauren is a "self-described 'horrible manager' with no formal business training." This is not unusual for an entrepreneur, but how does someone without this skill set go on to run a successful business?
2. What traits does Lauren have that suggest she really is a better manager than she thinks?
3. Would you describe her more as a manager or a leader, and why?

SOURCES: http://www.talentegg.ca, used with permission from Lauren Friese; Arina Kharlamova, "Entrepreneur Lauren Friese talks starting your own business right out of university," January 3, 2012, http://www.arbitragemagazine.com/topics/studentresources/talentegg-lauren-friese-exclusive/; "Lauren Friese," Profit Guide, December 6, 2011, http://www.profitguide.com/opportunity/lauren-friese-30284; http://www.allentrepreneur.wordpress.com/2009/01/19/hatching-graduate-careers-withlauren-friese-founder-of-talentegg; alb, "Advisory Board Spotlight: Lauren Friese," Social Media Week website, December 2, 2011, http://www.socialmediaweek.org/toronto/2011/12/02/advisory-board-spotlight-lauren-friese.

PHOTO COURTESY OF LAUREN FRIESE

done. Effective planning requires extensive information about the external business environment in which the company competes, as well as its internal environment.

There are four basic types of planning: strategic, tactical, operational, and contingency. Most of us use these different types of planning in our own lives. Some plans are very broad and long term (more strategic in nature), such as planning to attend graduate school after earning a bachelor's degree. Some plans are much more specific and short term (more operational in nature), such as planning to spend a few hours in the library this weekend. Your short-term plans support your long-term plans. If you study now, you have a better chance of achieving some future goal, such as getting a job interview or attending graduate school. Like you, organizations tailor their plans to meet the requirements of future situations or events. A summary of the four types of planning appears in Exhibit 9.2.

strategic planning
The process of creating long-range (one to five years) broad goals for the organization and determining what resources will be needed to accomplish those goals.

Strategic planning involves creating long-range (one to five years) broad goals for the organization, and determining what resources will be needed to accomplish those goals. An evaluation of external environmental factors, such as economic, technological, and social issues, is critical to successful strategic planning. Strategic goals, such as the organization's long-term mission, are formulated by top-level managers and put into action at lower levels in the organization. For example, Carly Fiorina, when she was CEO of Hewlett-Packard, engineered the merger with Compaq to create a vast organization that could effectively compete with Dell Computer and IBM. She believed that the merger gave her a technology company with enough

			Exhibit 9.2	Types of Planning	

TYPE OF PLANNING	TIME FRAME	LEVEL OF MANAGEMENT	EXTENT OF COVERAGE	PURPOSE AND GOAL	BREADTH OF CONTENT	ACCURACY/ PREDICTABILITY
Strategic	1–5 years	Top management (CEO, vice-presidents, directors, division heads)	External environment and entire organization	Establish mission and long-term goals	Broad and general	High degree of uncertainty
Tactical	Less than 1 year	Middle management	Strategic business units	Establish mid-range goals for implementation	More specific	Moderate degree of certainty
Operational	Current	Supervisory management	Geographic and functional divisions	Implement and activate specific objectives	Specific and concrete	Reasonable degree of certainty
Contingency	When an event occurs or a situation demands	Top and middle management	External environment and entire organization	Meet unforeseen challenges and opportunities	Both broad and detailed	Reasonable degree of certainty once event or situation occurs

products and services to satisfy all customers. "We are betting on heterogeneity," she says. "We'll be the only systems provider to support everything."[2] Different types of strategic plans—corporate- and business-level strategies, for example, were discussed in Chapter 7, as were mergers and acquisitions in Chapter 8.

The vision statement (as discussed in Chapter 7) is a clear, concise picture of the company's future direction in terms of its values and purpose that is used to guide and inspire. An organization's **mission** is formalized in its **mission statement**, a document that states the purpose of the organization and its reason for existing. The mission statement is a clear, concise articulation of how the company intends to achieve its vision—how it is different from its competition and the keys to its success. For example, Ben & Jerry's mission statement addresses three fundamental issues and states the basic philosophy of the company (see Exhibit 9.3).

mission
An organization's purpose and reason for existing; its long-term goals.

mission statement
A clear, concise articulation of how the company intends to achieve its vision—how it is different from its competition and the keys to its success.

Concept *in Action*

In the summer of 2010, an oil pipeline that supplies refineries in Canada and the United States broke. The pipeline is owned by Enbridge Inc., a Canadian company and North America's leader in delivering energy. About 19,500 barrels of oil was released into a creek and Enbridge responded immediately to contain the damage and clean up the spill. What is the importance of contingency plans?

NATIONAL TRANSPORTATION SAFETY BOARD/REUTERS/LANDOV

Exhibit 9.3 Ben & Jerry's Mission Statement

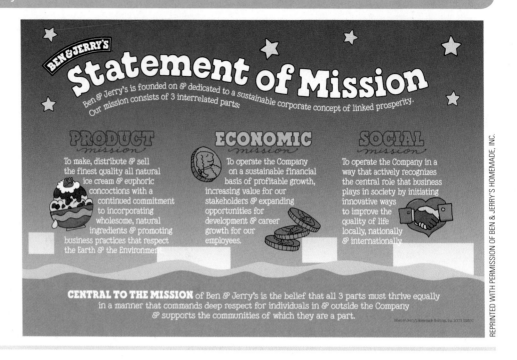

tactical planning
The process of beginning to implement a strategic plan by addressing issues of coordination and allocation of resources to different parts of the organization; has a shorter time frame (less than one year) and more specific objectives than strategic planning.

How does a company translate its mission statement into company action? Find out at Ben & Jerry's homepage,
www.benjerry.com

operational planning
The process of creating specific standards, methods, policies, and procedures that are used in specific functional areas of the organization; helps guide and control the implementation of tactical plans.

In all organizations, plans and goals at the tactical and operational levels should clearly support the organization's mission statement.

Tactical planning begins the implementation of strategic plans. Tactical plans have a shorter (less than one year) time frame than strategic plans and more specific objectives, designed to support the broader strategic goals. Tactical plans begin to address issues of coordination and allocation of resources to different parts of the organization.

For an example of how planning affects an organization, look at Procter & Gamble—makers of such products as Mr. Clean, Tide detergent, Zest, and Pringles.[3] Prior to the tenure of the former CEO, A. G. Lafley, P&G had lost $70 billion in market value in just 6 months. Following a strategy of aggressive new-product introduction and brand-name changes that contributed to the loss of market value, Mr. Lafley's mission was simple: turn around the current situation and grow the $40 billion company.

Unlike his predecessor, Mr. Lafley's strategy was straightforward and direct: refocus on the top brands. On a tactical level, he chose the top 10 brands and made them the highest priority. These products got most of the company's human resources and financial backing. The goal was to sell more of what were already winners instead of trying to invest in a new blockbuster product. Additionally, to reduce expenses, Mr. Lafley eliminated 9600 jobs, shut down weak product lines, and sold product lines that were not a good strategic fit. Even in day-to-day operations, Lafley is a very hands-on CEO. He frequently visits retail stores to talk directly to both employees and customers to find out exactly what they think about his company's products. He also likes to make suggestions to store owners on where Procter & Gamble's products will sell best.

Operational planning creates specific standards, methods, policies, and procedures that are used in specific functional areas of the organization. Operational objectives are current, narrow, and resource focused. They are designed to help guide and control the implementation of tactical plans.

In an industry where new versions of software have widely varying development cycles, Autodesk, maker of software tools for designers and engineers, has implemented new operational plans that are dramatically increasing profits. Former CEO Carol Bartz (now CEO of Yahoo!) shifted the company away from the erratic release schedule it had been keeping to regular, annual software releases. By releasing upgrades on a defined and predictable schedule, the company is able to use annual-subscription pricing, which is more affordable for small and mid-size companies. The new schedule keeps Autodesk customers on the most recent versions of popular software and has resulted in an overall increase in profitability.[4]

The key to effective planning is anticipating future situations and events. Yet even the best-prepared organization must sometimes cope with unforeseen circumstances, such as a natural disaster, an act of terrorism, or a radical new technology. Therefore, many companies have developed contingency plans that identify alternative courses of action for very unusual or crisis situations. The contingency plan typically stipulates the chain of command, standard operating procedures, and communication channels the organization will use during an emergency. An effective contingency plan can make or break a company.

contingency plans
Plans that identify alternative courses of action for very unusual or crisis situations; typically stipulate the chain of command, standard operating procedures, and communication channels the organization will use during an emergency.

ORGANIZING

A second key function of managers is organizing, which is the process of coordinating and allocating a company's resources to carry out its plans. Organizing includes developing a structure for the people, positions, departments, and activities within the company. Managers can arrange the structural elements of the company to maximize the flow of information and the efficiency of work processes. They accomplish this by

- dividing up tasks (division of labour);
- grouping jobs and employees (departmentalization); and
- assigning authority and responsibilities (delegation).

These and other elements of organizational structure are discussed in detail in Chapter 10. In this chapter, however, you should understand the three levels of a managerial hierarchy. This hierarchy is often depicted as a pyramid, as in Exhibit 9.4. The fewest managers are found at the highest level of the pyramid. Called top management, they are the small group of people at the head of the organization (such as the CEO, president, and vice president). Top-level managers develop *strategic plans* and address long-range issues, such as which industries to compete in, how to capture market share, and what to do with profits. These managers design and approve the company's basic policies and represent the company to other organizations. They also define the company's values and ethics and thus set the tone for employee standards of behaviour. For example, Clive Beddoe, the former CEO of WestJet (now Chairman of the board of Directors), was a role model for his managers and executives. Admirers say that he had an extraordinary capacity to inspire people. Following his leadership, WestJet executives and employees turned in impressive results.

The second and third tiers of the hierarchy are called middle management and supervisory management (also called operational management), respectively. Middle managers (such as division heads, departmental managers, and regional sales managers) are responsible for beginning the implementation of strategic plans. They design and carry out *tactical plans* in specific areas of the company. They begin the process of allocating resources to meet organizational goals, and they oversee supervisory managers throughout the company. Supervisors, the most numerous of the managers, are at the bottom of the managerial pyramid. These managers design and carry out *operational plans* for the ongoing daily activities of the company. They spend a great deal of their time guiding and motivating the employees who actually produce the goods and services.

organizing
The process of coordinating and allocating a company's resources to carry out its plans.

top management
The highest level of managers, including CEOs, presidents, and vice-presidents; they develop strategic plans and address long-range issues.

middle management
Managers who design and carry out tactical plans in specific areas of the company.

supervisory management (operational management)
Managers who design and carry out operational plans for the ongoing daily activities of the company.

Exhibit 9.4　The Managerial Pyramid

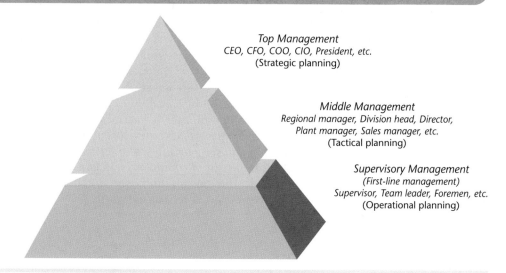

Top Management
CEO, CFO, COO, CIO, President, etc.
(Strategic planning)

Middle Management
Regional manager, Division head, Director,
Plant manager, Sales manager, etc.
(Tactical planning)

Supervisory Management
(First-line management)
Supervisor, Team leader, Foremen, etc.
(Operational planning)

LO4

LEADING, GUIDING, AND MOTIVATING OTHERS

leading
The process of guiding and motivating others toward the achievement of organizational goals.

power
The ability to influence others to behave in a particular way.

legitimate power
Power that is derived from an individual's position in an organization.

reward power
Power that is derived from an individual's control over rewards.

coercive power
Power that is derived from an individual's ability to threaten negative outcomes.

expert power
Power that is derived from an individual's extensive knowledge in one or more areas.

referent power
Power that is derived from an individual's personal charisma and the respect and/or admiration the individual inspires.

leadership style
The relatively consistent way in which individuals in leadership positions attempt to influence the behaviour of others.

Leading, the third key management function, is the process of guiding and motivating others toward the achievement of organizational goals. Managers are responsible for directing employees on a daily basis as the employees carry out the plans and work within the structure created by management. Organizations need strong, effective leadership at all levels to meet goals and remain competitive.

To be effective leaders, managers must be able to influence others' behaviour. This ability to influence others to behave in a particular way is called **power**. Researchers have identified five primary sources, or bases, of power:

- **legitimate power**, which is derived from an individual's position in an organization;
- **reward power**, which is derived from an individual's control over rewards;
- **coercive power**, which is derived from an individual's ability to threaten negative outcomes;
- **expert power**, which is derived from an individual's extensive knowledge in one or more areas; and
- **referent power**, which is derived from an individual's personal charisma and the respect and/or admiration the individual inspires.

Many leaders use a combination of all of these sources of power to influence individuals toward goal achievement. Clive Beddoe got his legitimate power from his position as CEO of WestJet. His reward power comes from reviving the company and making the company more valuable. Also, raises and bonuses for employees who meet their goals is another form of reward power. His referent power was derived by others wanting to model his behaviour.

Leadership Styles

Individuals in leadership positions tend to be relatively consistent in how they attempt to influence the behaviour of others, meaning that each individual has a tendency to react to people and situations in a particular way. This pattern of behaviour is referred to as **leadership style**. As Exhibit 9.5 shows, leadership styles can be placed on a continuum that encompasses three distinct styles: autocratic, participative, and free rein.

Exhibit 9.5 Leadership Styles of Manager

← Amount of authority held by the leader

AUTOCRATIC STYLE	PARTICIPATIVE STYLE (DEMOCRATIC, CONSENSUAL, CONSULTATIVE)	FREE-REIN (LAISSEZ-FAIRE) STYLE
• Manager makes most decisions and acts in authoritative manner.	• Manager shares decision making with group members and encourages teamwork.	• Manager turns over virtually all authority and control to group.
• Manager is usually unconcerned about subordinates' attitude toward decisions.	• Manager encourages discussion of issues and alternatives.	• Members of a group are presented with task and given freedom to accomplish it.
• Emphasis is on getting task accomplished.	• Manager is concerned about subordinates' ideas and attitudes.	• Approach works well with highly motivated, experienced, educated personnel.
• Approach is used mostly by military officers and some production line supervisors.	• Manager coaches subordinates and helps coordinate efforts.	• Approach is found in high-tech companies, labs, and colleges.
	• Approach is found in many successful organizations.	

Amount of authority held by group members →

Autocratic leaders are directive leaders, allowing for very little input from subordinates. These leaders prefer to make decisions and solve problems on their own and expect subordinates to implement solutions according to very specific and detailed instructions. In this leadership style, information typically flows in one direction, from manager to subordinate. The military, by necessity, is generally autocratic. When autocratic leaders treat employees with fairness and respect, they may be considered knowledgeable and decisive. But often autocrats are perceived as narrow-minded and heavy-handed in their unwillingness to share power, information, and decision making in the organization. The trend in organizations today is away from the directive, controlling style of the autocratic leader.

Instead, Canadian businesses are looking more and more for participative leaders, meaning leaders who share decision making with group members and encourage discussion of issues and alternatives. For example, they might enlist frontline workers to help design the assembly lines, or involve employees in programs to improve safety, quality, and process efficiency. The goal is to create a business where workers are passionately involved in their work. Participative leaders can be classified as either democratic, consensual, or consultative.

Democratic leaders solicit input from all members of the group and then allow the group members to make the final decision through a voting process. This approach works well with highly trained professionals. Consensual leaders encourage discussion about issues and then require that all parties involved agree to the final decision. This style is often used when consensus is necessary. Consultative leaders confer with subordinates before making a decision but retain the final decision-making authority. This technique has been used in some situations to increase productivity dramatically.

autocratic leaders
Directive leaders who prefer to make decisions and solve problems on their own with little input from subordinates.

HOT Links

Search for recent articles relating to business leaders who interest you.
www.canadianbusiness.com

participative leaders
Leaders that share decision making with group members and encourage discussion of issues and alternatives; includes democratic, consensual, and consultative styles.

democratic leaders
Leaders who solicit input from all members of the group and then allow the members to make the final decision through a vote.

consensual leaders
Leaders who encourage discussion about issues and then require that all parties involved agree to the final decision.

consultative leaders
Leaders who confer with subordinates before making a decision, but retain the final decision-making authority.

free-rein (laissez-faire) leadership
A leadership style in which the leader turns over all authority and control to subordinates.

empowerment
The process of giving employees increased autonomy and discretion to make decisions, as well as control over the resources needed to implement those decisions.

The third leadership style, at the opposite end of the continuum from the autocratic style, is **free-rein**, or **laissez-faire** (French for "leave it alone") **leadership**. Managers who use this style turn over all authority and control to subordinates. Employees are assigned a task and then given free rein to determine the best way to accomplish it. The manager doesn't get involved unless asked and then usually acts only as a facilitator. Under this approach, subordinates have unlimited freedom as long as they do not violate existing company policies. This approach is sometimes used with highly trained professionals, as in a research laboratory.

Although one might at first assume that subordinates would prefer the free-rein style, this approach can have several drawbacks. If free-rein leadership is accompanied by unclear expectations and lack of feedback from the manager, the experience can be frustrating for an employee. Employees might perceive the manager as being uninvolved and indifferent to what is happening or as unwilling or unable to provide the necessary structure, information, and expertise.

There is no one best leadership style. The most effective style for a given situation depends on elements such as the characteristics of the subordinates, the complexity of the task, the source of the leader's power, and the stability of the environment.

Employee Empowerment

Participative and free-rein leaders use a technique called empowerment to share decision-making authority with subordinates. **Empowerment** means giving employees increased autonomy and discretion to make their own decisions, as well as control over

Sustainable Business, Sustainable World

STATOIL

It seems fitting in a chapter on leadership to profile the number one sustainable company in the world in 2011, according to the 2011 *Global 100 Most Sustainable Corporations in the World*. That company is Statoil. Statoil is an international energy company based in Norway and with operations in 34 countries worldwide. Its operations in Canada include the acquisition in 2007 of 100 percent of the North American Oil Sands Corporation (NAOSC). It currently owns interests in 1129 km² of oil sands leases in the Athabasca region in Alberta, and a growing part of its Canadian operations is in offshore projects in Newfoundland.

Statoil is "committed to accommodating the world's energy needs in a responsible manner, applying technology and creating innovative business solutions." One of its aims is to "meet the demand for energy which is necessary for further economic and social development, while showing consideration for the environment and making an active effort to fight global climate change." The company's leadership in sustainability is clear from a number of its initiatives. Three of these initiatives with great promise for responsible energy production are CO₂ storage, subsea oil recovery, and the development of biofuels.

The company is a pioneer in CO₂ storage—or what is called carbon capture and storage (CCS)—being the first company, in 1996, to store CO₂ in a geological formation solely for environmental reasons. This technology involves removing CO₂ and storing it in the subsurface, keeping it out of the atmosphere permanently, and eliminating its detrimental impact on climate change. CCS technology has been reported to have the potential to reduce greenhouse gas emissions by 20 percent by 2050.

Being the world's largest operator of subsea technology at depths greater than 100 metres makes Statoil a leader in the use of new subsea technology for oil recovery. This technology provides opportunities for greater production efficiency, improved recovery and reduced environmental impact. The use of subsea technology reduces ship and helicopter traffic, thereby cutting emissions, and through remote operation of the technology, reduces the number of high-risk operations.

Statoil also has a "longstanding tradition as a pioneer in the use of eco-friendly fuels" such as biofuel, which has the largest near-term possibility of decreasing CO₂ emissions from transportation of any fuel source. The company's goal is to become a "significant provider of sustainable biofuels with a global production and trading position, and be in a first mover position" in retail markets. In fact it started sales of biofuels as far back as 1999.

These are just a few of the reasons Statoil is a worldwide leader in sustainability, being on the forefront of new, innovative technologies to fight global climate change.

Thinking Critically

1. What does it take for a company to be in a leadership position in an area such as sustainability?
2. What degree of top management commitment is necessary, and what kind of culture would it create?
3. Most importantly, what would happen if companies like Statoil didn't exist? Where would that leave us in such an energy-dependent world?

SOURCE: http://www.global100.org; http://www.statoil.com. Used with permission from Statoil.

Concept *in Action*

Toyota Motor Manufacturing Canada Inc. employs over 6000 people at its plants in Ontario. Each employee on the Toyota assembly line has been empowered to act as a quality control inspector, stopping the line if necessary to correct a problem. How can empowerment increase productivity and a company's profitability?

REX FEATURES/THE CANADIAN PRESS/CHRIS RATCLIFFE)

the resources needed to implement those decisions. When decision-making power is shared at all levels of the organization, employees feel a greater sense of ownership in, and responsibility for, organizational outcomes.

Max Messmer, Chairman and CEO of Robert Half International, says, "Most people will work harder and do a better job if they feel their opinions are respected and that they are trusted to be responsible to make their own decisions. Empowering your employees will likely pay off with respect, loyalty, and the high level of productivity that comes from effective teamwork."[5]

Concept *Check*

How do leaders influence other people's behaviour?

How can managers empower employees?

What is corporate culture

Expanding Around the Globe

LEADERSHIP IN FOREIGN SUBSIDIARIES

Canadian companies are often seeking new opportunities, and many of these are presented outside of our borders. These opportunities provide new markets to service and the potential of increased profits. But associated with these benefits are challenges, especially from a leadership perspective.

Many of these challenges result from cultural differences. For example, some cultures are more comfortable with autocratic leadership styles than participative or free rein styles. This can present problems for Canadian managers working internationally, especially when they are accustomed to allowing more autonomy for the employees. Suddenly they may have to use more "hands-on" management techniques that may seem insulting to employees in Canada.

When a Canadian company purchases an existing foreign company, another challenge may be adapting the Canadian corporate culture to those of the host country's company. Corporate culture evolves over time and based on the history of the organization, it will be most likely resistant to sudden changes in the new attitudes and standards of behaviours. Canadian managers assigned to foreign subsidiaries must understand the current corporate culture and modify their leadership styles accordingly.

Some other issues that may create challenges for Canadian managers in foreign subsidiaries include the decision-making process, timing of decisions, how to disseminate the decisions, etc.

Thinking Critically

1. Is it possible to change the attitudes of workers regarding the appropriateness of the leadership style? If so how?
2. How can managers assigned to foreign subsidiaries learn the corporate culture?

PHOTO COURTESY OF PORTER AIRLINES INC.

Innovative organizations empower their employees to present and implement new ideas. Porter Airlines' corporate culture, for example, encourages employees to solve problems and keep customers happy. What correlations do you see between corporate culture and corporate success?

corporate culture
The set of attitudes, values, and standards of behaviour that distinguishes one organization from another.

HOT/inks

HOT/inks

See Waterstone's complete list of Canada's 10 Most Admired Corporate Cultures™ list at
www.waterstonehc.com

controlling
The process of assessing the organization's progress toward accomplishing its goals; includes monitoring the implementation of a plan and correcting deviations from it.

See the Expanding Around the Globe box for a discussion of some of the challenges Canadian companies encounter when they decide to go global.

Corporate Culture

The leadership style of managers in an organization is usually indicative of the underlying philosophy, or values, of the organization. The set of *attitudes, values*, and *standards of behaviour* that distinguishes one organization from another is called corporate culture. A corporate culture evolves over time and is based on the accumulated history of the organization, including the vision of the founders. It is also influenced by the dominant leadership style within the organization. Evidence of a company's culture is seen in its heroes (e.g., Andy Grove of Intel), myths (stories about the company that are passed from employee to employee), symbols (e.g., the Nike swoosh), and ceremonies.

Although culture is intangible and its rules are often unspoken, it can have a strong impact on a company's success. Therefore, managers must try to influence the corporate culture so that it will contribute to the success of the company. Companies can most often match the competition on the spreadsheet, but they can create a competitive advantage with the corporate culture.

Since 2005, Waterstone Human Capital has interviewed hundreds of senior Canadian executives in a wide range of industries for their annual Canadian Corporate Culture Study™. Some of the companies that have been recognized as having an admirable corporate culture include: Aeroplan Canada Inc., Boston Pizza International Inc., Corus Entertainment, Flight Centre, RBC, Shoppers Drug Mart, and Tim Hortons. Some of the interesting findings from the interviews include the following:

- 93 percent of the executives see a correlation between their corporate culture and corporate performance;
- 37 percent say that company leadership creates the corporate culture; and
- 86 percent say that cultural fit is more important than skills in finding executive-level candidates.[6]

LO5 CONTROLLING

The fourth key function that managers perform is controlling. Controlling is the process of assessing the organization's progress toward accomplishing its goals. It includes monitoring the implementation of a plan and correcting deviations from that plan. As Exhibit 9.6 shows, controlling can be visualized as a cyclical process made up of five stages:

1. Setting performance standards (goals).
2. Measuring performance.
3. Comparing actual performance to established performance standards.
4. Taking corrective action (if necessary).
5. Using information gained from the process to set future performance standards.

Performance standards are the levels of performance the company wants to attain. These goals are based on its strategic, tactical, and operational plans. The most effective performance standards state a measurable behavioural objective that can be achieved in a specified time frame. For example, the performance objective for the sales division of

Making Ethical Choices

WAITING AND WAITING AND WAITING

You've always been in a hurry, whether it's to get to a party or to find a job. You were in a hurry to land a supervisory position immediately on college graduation and looked for an organization that satisfied your goals of providing community service and moving up quickly. As an adept organizer with an innate sense of the right number of people and amount of money necessary to complete a task, you wanted your ability to plan and stay focused on goals to be recognized.

Your search led you to the police department of a major metropolitan city, as the supervisor of 911—the perfect job for someone in a hurry. On taking over, you analyzed the department's requirements and determined you needed more operators to service the growing call volume. You shared your findings with the chief of police, who had to approve all staffing allocations, and he agreed with your evaluation. Human resources, however, repeatedly denied your requests for more operators, even though your department received numerous complaints from callers who were left waiting and

waiting. Even more serious, you knew people were dying because of missed calls and delayed responses.

Investigating further, you discovered that although he told you otherwise, the chief of police never, in fact, approved your proposal, which would have permitted human resources to hire the additional staff. When the mayor called to discuss complaints his office had received about poor 911 service, the chief told the mayor the call centre was fully staffed and placed the blame on your department's inefficiency. Based on current call volume, your department is short approximately 25 percent of the operators needed to service the 911 calls it receives efficiently.

ETHICAL DILEMMA: Once you realize your staffing proposal has been ignored and take into account the serious ramifications that result from this, do you report this to the mayor and the city's board of elected officials?

SOURCES: Mike Fitzgerald, "911 Problem Began Months Ago," *Belleville News-Democrat*, October 13, 2002, http://www.belleville.com; and Phil Mendelson, "Want an Explanation of D.C.'s 911 Deficiencies? Hold, Please," *The Washington Post*, March 9, 2003, B8.

---

a company could be stated as "$100,000 in gross sales for the month of January." Each individual employee in that division would also have a specified performance goal. Actual company, division, or individual performance can be measured against desired performance standards to see if a gap exists between the desired level of performance and the actual level of performance. If a performance gap does exist, the reason for it must be determined and corrective action taken.

Feedback is essential to the process of control. Most companies have a reporting system that identifies areas where performance standards are not being met. A feedback

---

Exhibit 9.6   The Control Process

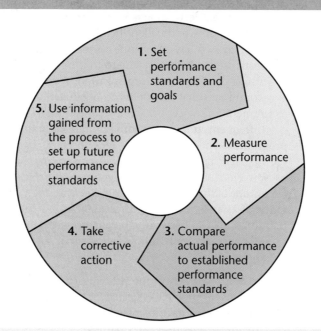

1. Set performance standards and goals
2. Measure performance
3. Compare actual performance to established performance standards
4. Take corrective action
5. Use information gained from the process to set up future performance standards

Concept *Check*

Describe the control process.

Why is the control process important to the success of the organization?

system helps managers detect problems before they get out of hand. If a problem exists, the managers take corrective action. Toyota uses a simple but effective control system on its automobile assembly lines. Each worker serves as the "customer" for the assembly process and is empowered to act as a quality control inspector. If a part is defective or not installed properly, the next worker won't accept it. Any worker can alert the supervisor to a problem by tugging on a rope that turns on a warning light (i.e., feedback). If the problem isn't corrected, the worker can stop the entire assembly line.

Why is controlling such an important part of a manager's job? First, it helps managers to determine the success of the other three functions: planning, organizing, and leading. Second, control systems direct employee behaviour toward achieving organizational goals. Third, control systems provide a means of coordinating employee activities and integrating resources throughout the organization.

Since there is no guarantee what will happen in the future, it is important that managers make sure that there are contingency plans. By having contingency plans developed in advance, managers can properly react to situations as they arise. If no contingency plans are in place, managers may have to make decisions without all relevant information; resulting in potential disastrous outcomes.

LO6

MANAGERIAL ROLES

In carrying out the responsibilities of planning, organizing, leading, and controlling, managers take on many roles. A role is a set of behavioural expectations, or a set of activities that a person is expected to perform. Managers' roles fall into three basic categories: *informational roles, interpersonal roles,* and *decisional roles.* These roles are summarized in Exhibit 9.7. In an **informational role,** the manager may act as an information gatherer, information distributor, or spokesperson for the company. A manager's **interpersonal roles** are based on various interactions with other people. Depending on the situation, a manager might need to act as a figurehead, company leader, or liaison. When acting in a **decisional role,** a manager might have to think like an entrepreneur, make decisions about resource allocation, help resolve conflicts, or negotiate compromises.

informational roles
A manager's activities as an information gatherer, information disseminator, or spokesperson for the company.

interpersonal roles
A manager's activities as a figurehead, company leader, or liaison.

decisional roles
A manager's activities as an entrepreneur, resource allocator, conflict resolver, or negotiator.

programmed decisions
Decisions made in response to frequently occurring routine situations.

non-programmed decisions
Responses to infrequent, unforeseen, or very unusual problems and opportunities where the manager does not have a precedent to follow in decision making.

Managerial Decision Making

In every function performed, role taken on, and set of skills applied, a manager is a decision maker. Decision making means choosing among alternatives. Decision making occurs in response to the identification of a problem or an opportunity. Managers make decisions in two basic categories: programmed and non-programmed. **Programmed decisions** are made in response to routine situations that occur frequently in a variety of settings throughout an organization. For example, the need to hire new personnel is a common situation for most organizations. Therefore, standard procedures for recruitment and selection are developed and followed in most companies.

Infrequent, unforeseen, or very unusual problems and opportunities require **non-programmed decisions** by managers. Because these situations are unique and complex, the manager rarely has a precedent to follow. For example, after Hurricane Katrina in New Orleans, many non-programmed decisions were needed. The overwhelming magnitude of the disaster was unforeseen, and rescue and emergency workers responded to the disaster to the best of their abilities but were unable to keep up with the needs. Had this situation been anticipated, more and better planning would have resulted.

Managers typically follow five steps in the decision-making process, as illustrated in Exhibit 9.8:

1. Recognize or define the problem or opportunity. Although it is more common to focus on problems because of their obvious negative effects, managers who do not take advantage of new opportunities might lose the company's competitive advantage over other companies.

Exhibit 9.7 The Many Roles that Managers Play in an Organization

ROLE	DESCRIPTION	EXAMPLE
Informational Roles		
Monitor	Seeks out and gathers information relevant to the organization.	Finding out about legal restrictions on new product technology.
Disseminator	Provides information where it is needed in the organization.	Providing current production figures to workers on the assembly line.
Spokesperson	Transmits information to people outside the organization.	Representing the company at a shareholders' meeting.
Interpersonal Roles		
Figurehead	Represents the company in a symbolic way.	Cutting the ribbon at ceremony for the opening of a new building.
Leader	Guides and motivates employees to achieve organizational goals.	Helping subordinates to set monthly performance goals.
Liaison	Acts as a go-between among individuals inside and outside the organization.	Representing the retail sales division of the company at a regional sales meeting.
Decisional Roles		
Entrepreneur	Searches out new opportunities and initiates change.	Implementing a new production process using new technology.
Disturbance handler	Handles unexpected events and crises.	Handling a crisis situation such as a fire.
Resource allocator	Designates the use of financial, human, and other organizational resources.	Approving the funds necessary to purchase computer equipment and hire personnel.
Negotiator	Represents the company at negotiating processes.	Participating in salary negotiations with union representatives.

Exhibit 9.8 The Decision-Making Process

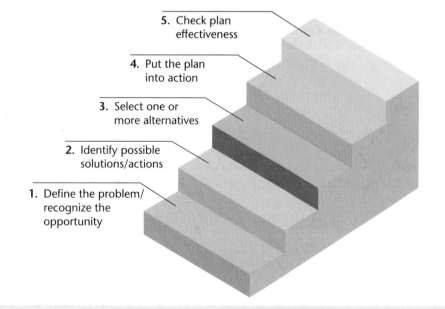

5. Check plan effectiveness

4. Put the plan into action

3. Select one or more alternatives

2. Identify possible solutions/actions

1. Define the problem/recognize the opportunity

2. Gather information so as to identify alternative solutions or actions.
3. Select one or more alternatives after evaluating the strengths and weaknesses of each possibility. This must be based not only on the ability to solve the problem or take advantage of the opportunity but also on the available resources.
4. Put the chosen alternative into action.
5. Gather information to obtain feedback on the effectiveness of the chosen plan.

LO7

MANAGERIAL SKILLS

To be successful in planning, organizing, leading, and controlling, managers must use a wide variety of skills. A *skill* is the ability to do something proficiently. Managerial skills fall into three basic categories: conceptual, human relations, and technical skills. The degree to which each type of skill is used depends on the level of the manager's position, as seen in Exhibit 9.9. Additionally, in an increasingly global marketplace, it pays for managers to develop a special set of skills to deal with global management issues.

Technical Skills

technical skills
A manager's specialized areas of knowledge and expertise, as well as the ability to apply that knowledge.

Specialized areas of knowledge and expertise and the ability to apply that knowledge make up a manager's **technical skills**. Preparing a financial statement, programming a computer, designing an office building, and analyzing market research are all examples of technical skills. These types of skills are especially important for supervisory managers, because they work closely with employees who are producing the goods and/or services of the company.

Human Relations Skills

human relations skills
A manager's interpersonal skills that are used to accomplish goals through the use of human resources.

Human relations skills are the interpersonal skills managers use to accomplish goals through the use of human resources. This set of skills includes the ability to understand human behaviour, to communicate effectively with others, and to motivate individuals to accomplish their objectives. Giving positive feedback to employees, being sensitive to their individual needs, and showing a willingness to empower subordinates are all examples of good human relations skills. Identifying and promoting managers with human relations skills is important for companies. A manager with little or no people skills can end up using an authoritarian leadership style and alienating employees.

At many service companies, one of the keys to success is genuinely friendly service. Achieving their service standards requires enthusiastic staff. The capacity for such enthusiasm must be determined before the employee is hired. Prospective employees might be asked to take a written test that measures skills and gives personality insights. Once an applicant is hired, the coaching process should begin almost immediately.

Conceptual Skills

conceptual skills
A manager's ability to view the organization as a whole, understand how the various parts are interdependent, and assess how the organization relates to its external environment.

Conceptual skills include the ability to view the organization as a whole, understand how the various parts are interdependent, and assess how the organization relates to its external environment. These skills allow managers to evaluate situations and develop alternative courses of action. Good conceptual skills are especially necessary for managers at the top of the management pyramid, where strategic planning takes place.

Global Management Skills

global management skills
A manager's ability to operate in diverse cultural environments.

Increasingly, Canadian companies are participating in the international marketplace, as discussed in Chapter 5; this has created a need for managers who have **global management skills**, that is, the ability to operate in diverse cultural environments. With more and more companies choosing to do business in multiple locations around

	Conceptual Skills	Human Skills	Technical Skills
Top Management			
Middle Management			
Supervisory Management			

Very important   Not as important

Concept *in Action*

For many managers, accepting an international position might mean helping their spouses and children adapt to the new environment. What special skills do you think Canadian managers need to be successful in international assignments?

RICK MADONIK/TORONTO STAR/GETSTOCK.COM

Concept Check

Define the basic managerial skills.

How important is each of these skill sets at the different levels of the management pyramid?

What new challenges do managers face due to increasing globalization?

the world, employees are often required to learn the geography, language, and social customs of other cultures. It is expensive to train employees for foreign assignments and pay their relocation costs; therefore, choosing the right person for the job is especially important. Individuals who are open-minded, flexible, willing to try new things, and comfortable in a multicultural setting are good candidates for international management positions.

Although a single manager might possess some or most of the skills described above, rarely does one person excel in all types of managerial skills. Every business needs a leader, but in today's marketplace things move too quickly, the need for specialization is too great, and competition is too fierce for a one-person show to survive.

LO8 THE FUTURE OF MANAGEMENT AND LEADERSHIP

Three important trends in management today are: crisis management, the growing use of information technology, and the increasing need for global management skills.

Crisis Management

Crises can occur in even the best-managed organizations. For example, the economic crises of 2008 and 2011 were, for the most part, unexpected in the business environment. Another example is power grid meltdowns, where the supply of electricity was suspended because of a system overload. No manager or executive can be completely prepared for these types of unexpected crises. However, how a manager handles the situation could mean the difference between disaster, survival, or even financial gain.

No matter what the crisis, there are some basic guidelines that managers should follow to minimize negative outcomes. Managers should not become immobilized by a problem, nor should they ignore it. Managers should face the problem head on. They should always tell the truth about the situation and then put the best people on the job to correct the problem. They should ask for help if they need it and, finally, managers must learn from the experience to avoid the same problem in the future.[7]

Managers and Information Technology

The second trend having a major impact on managers is the proliferation of information technology. An increasing number of organizations are selling technology, and an increasing number are looking for cutting-edge technology to make and market the products and services they sell. One particularly useful type of technology is dashboard software. Much like the dashboard in a car, dashboard software gives managers a quick look into the relevant information they need to manage their companies. Most large companies are organized in divisions (which you'll learn about in more detail in Chapter 10), and often each division relies on a particular type of application or database software. Dashboard software allows employees to access information from software they don't routinely use, for example, from an application used by a different division from their own. More important, however, is the ability of a dashboard to show up-to-the-minute information and to allow employees to see all the information they need—like financial and performance data—on a single screen. Such integrated functionality is making dashboards extremely popular.

Managing in Diverse Cultural Environments

The increasing globalization of the world market, as discussed in Chapter 5, has created a need for managers who have global management skills, that is, the ability

Marketing and sales professionals are increasingly turning to advanced software programs called "dashboards" to monitor business and evaluate performance. These computer tools help managers identify valuable customers, track sales, and align plans with company objectives—all in real time. A typical dashboard might include sales and bookings forecasts, end of month data, customer satisfaction data, and employee training schedules. How does information technology affect managerial decision making?

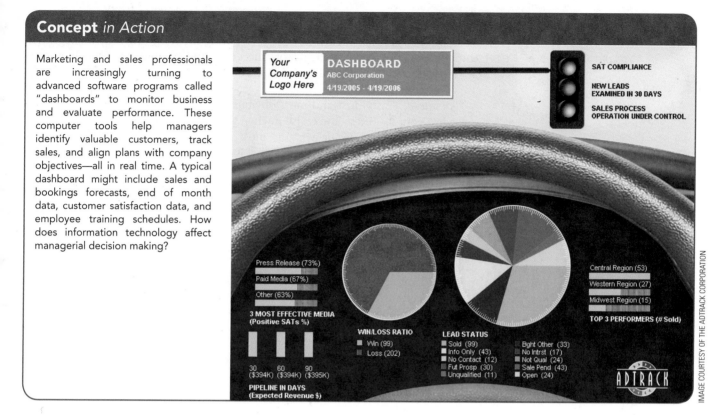

IMAGE COURTESY OF THE ADTRACK CORPORATION

to operate in diverse cultural environments. As companies expand around the globe, managers will face the challenges of directing the behaviour of employees around the world. They must recognize that because of cultural differences, people respond to similar situations in very different ways. The burden, therefore, falls on the manager to produce results while adapting to the differences among the employees he or she manages. How a manager gets results, wins respect, and leads employees varies greatly among countries, cultures, and individuals.

The best way to meet this challenge of managing international employees is to develop an individual-level program that is based on values and principles. Managers should apply three specific principles to this process: example, involvement, and trust. *Example* means that managers should set and live out the standard for others to follow. They must act as role models for all employees of the organization. Leaders must also create personal *involvement* in the organization for all members. Involvement brings the whole person into the company's operations. People are treated like valuable partners, not just as an expense to the company. Leaders must develop a culture of *trust*. This is essential to getting people to invest themselves for the mutual benefit of everyone. When these principles are applied, people are able to manage themselves, and they can release incredible talent and energy.[8]

Despite cultural differences, managing within a different culture is only an extension of what managers do every day. That is, working with differences in employees, processes and projects.

Concept *Check*

Describe several guidelines for crisis management.

How can information technology aid in decision-making?

What are three principles of managing in diverse cultural environments?

GREAT IDEAS TO USE NOW

Many of the skills managers use to accomplish organizational goals can be applied outside the organizational setting. You could be using these skills in your life right now to accomplish your personal goals.

Effective Time Management

Successful managers use their time wisely. Adopting the following time management techniques will help you become a more successful student now and will help prepare you for the demands of your future workplace:

- *Plan ahead.* This is first and most obvious. Set both long- and short-term goals. Review your list often, and revise it when your situation changes.
- *Establish priorities.* Decide what is most important and what is most urgent. Sometimes they are not the same thing. Keep in mind the 80–20 rule: 80 percent of the results are delivered by 20 percent of the effort.
- *Delegate.* Ask yourself if the task can be accomplished as effectively by someone else. Empower other people, and you might be surprised by the quality of the outcome.
- *Learn to say no.* Be stingy with your time. Be realistic about how long tasks will take. Don't feel guilty when you don't have the time, ability, or inclination to take on an additional task.
- *Batch.* Group activities together so they take up less of your day. For example, set aside a certain time to return phone calls, answer e-mail, and do any necessary written correspondence.
- *Stay on task.* Learn how to handle diversions. For example, let your answering machine take messages until you finish a particular task.
- *Set deadlines.* Don't let projects drag on. Reward yourself each time you cross a certain number of items off your "to do" list.

Stress Management

One of the things that can stop any career in its tracks is burnout. One way to prevent burnout is to examine how well you are dealing with the current stress you are experiencing and learn how to develop coping mechanisms. To start this process, look to see if you are exhibiting any of the warning signs of being overstressed. Students under stress can have a wide range of symptoms, including headaches, asthma attacks, nail biting, and sleep problems.[9]

More serious symptoms can include stomach problems and even depression.

If you feel that you are not coping with the stress in your life, now is the time to learn some stress management skills. Here are some helpful ideas:

- Make sure to include physical exercise in your schedule. Try some mind/body work, such as yoga or stretching.
- Find someone you trust and can confide in. Talking out your problems can help a lot.
- If there is no one you feel comfortable talking to, try keeping a diary to work out your stressful situations.
- For more information, visit the Canadian Institute of Stress website, www.stress-canada.org.*

*Used with permission from the Canadian Institute of Stress

Management is the process of guiding the development, maintenance, and allocation of resources to attain organizational goals (manage the tasks). Managers are the people in the organization responsible for developing and carrying out this management process. The four primary functions of managers are planning, organizing, leading, and controlling.

Leadership is the relationship between a leader and the followers who want real changes, resulting in outcomes that reflect their shared purposes (leading people).

LO1 Differentiate between management and leadership.

Planning is deciding what needs to be done, identifying when and how it will be done, and determining by whom it should be done. Managers use four types of planning: strategic, tactical, operational, and contingency planning. Strategic planning involves creating long-range (one to five years) broad goals and determining the necessary resources to accomplish those goals. Tactical planning has a shorter time frame (less than one year) and more specific objectives that support the broader strategic goals. Operational planning creates specific standards, methods, policies, and procedures that are used in specific functional areas of the organization. Contingency plans identify alternative courses of action for very unusual or crisis situations.

LO2 Discuss the four types of planning.

Organizing involves coordinating and allocating a company's resources to carry out its plans. It includes developing a structure for the people, positions, departments, and activities within the company. This is accomplished by dividing up tasks (division of labour), grouping jobs and employees (departmentalization), and assigning authority and responsibilities (delegation).

LO3 List the primary responsibilities of managers in organizing activities.

Leading is the process of guiding and motivating others toward the achievement of organizational goals. Managers have unique leadership styles that range from autocratic to free rein. The set of attitudes, values, and standards of behaviour that distinguishes one organization from another is called corporate culture. A corporate culture evolves over time and is based on the accumulated history of the organization, including the vision of the founders.

LO4 Describe how leadership styles influence a corporate culture.

Controlling is the process of assessing the organization's progress toward accomplishing its goals. The control process is as follows: set performance standards (goals), measure performance, compare actual performance to established performance standards, take corrective action (if necessary), and use information gained from the process to set future performance standards.

LO5 Examine how organizations control activities.

In an informational role, the manager may act as an information gatherer, an information distributor, or a spokesperson for the company. A manager's interpersonal roles are based on various interactions with other people. Depending on the situation, a manager might need to act as a figurehead, company leader, or liaison.

LO6 Summarize the roles managers take on in different organizational settings.

Managerial skills fall into three basic categories: technical, human relations, and conceptual skills. Specialized areas of knowledge and expertise, and the ability to apply that knowledge, make up a manager's technical skills. Human relations skills include the ability to understand human behaviour, to communicate effectively with others, and to motivate individuals to accomplish their objectives. Conceptual skills include

LO7 Identify the set of managerial skills necessary for managerial success.

the ability to view the organization as a whole, understand how the various parts are interdependent, and assess how the organization relates to its external environment.

LO8 List some of the trends that will affect management in the future.

Three important trends in management today are: crisis management, the increasing use of information technology, and the need for global management skills. Crisis management requires quick action, telling the truth about the situation, and putting the best people on the task to correct the situation. Management must learn from the crisis to prevent it from happening again. Using the latest information technology, managers can make quicker, better informed decisions. As more companies "go global," the need for multinational cultural management skills is growing. Managers must set a good example, create personal involvement for all employees, and develop a culture of trust.

Key Terms

autocratic leaders   255
coercive power   254
conceptual skills   262
consensual leaders   255
consultative leaders   256
contingency plans   253
controlling   258
corporate culture   258
decisional roles   260
democratic leaders   255
effectiveness   248
efficiency   248
empowerment   256
expert power   254
free-rein (laissez-faire) leadership   256
global management skills   262
human relations skills   262
informational roles   260
interpersonal roles   260
leadership   248
leadership style   254

leading   254
legitimate power   254
management   248
middle management   253
mission   251
mission statement   251
non-programmed decisions   260
operational planning   252
organizing   253
participative leaders   255
planning   249
power   254
programmed decisions   260
referent power   254
reward power   254
strategic planning   250
supervisory management (operational management)   253
tactical planning   252
technical skills   262
top management   253

Experiential Exercises

1. **Would you be a good manager?** Do a self-assessment that includes your current technical, human relations, and conceptual skills. What skills do you already possess, and which do you need to add? Where do your strengths lie? Based on this exercise, develop a description of an effective manager.

2. You are planning to start one of the companies listed below. Develop a mission statement that defines its vision, and give examples of how you would apply each of the four types of planning (strategic, tactical, operational, and contingency) in building the business. Choose one of the following:

   - Ethnic restaurant near your campus
   - Custom skateboard manufacturer
   - Computer training company
   - Boutique specializing in Latin American clothing and jewellery

3. Focusing on either your educational institution or a place where you have worked, prepare a brief report on its unique culture. How would you describe it? What has shaped it? What changes do you see occurring over time?

4. Strategic Advantage, www.strategy4u.com, offers many reasons why companies should develop strategic plans, as well as a strategy tip of the month, assessment tools, planning exercises, and resource links. Explore the site to learn the effect of strategic planning on financial performance, and present your evidence to the class. Then select a planning exercise and, with a group of classmates, perform it as it applies to your school.

5. Are you leadership material? Go to the HRWorld site at www.hrworld.com/features/top-10-leadership-qualities-031908/ to find out.

6. How do entrepreneurs develop corporate culture in their companies? Do a search on the term "corporate culture" on *Inc.*, www.inc.com, *Entrepreneur*, www.entrepreneur.com, or *Fast Company*, www.fastcompany.com. Prepare a short presentation for your class that explains the importance of corporate culture and how it's developed in young companies.

Review Questions

1. Briefly describe the four primary management functions.

2. How does proper planning help the organization to achieve its mission statement?

3. What are the impacts on a company that does not allocate its resources properly? (Relate this to their stakeholders.)

4. What are the various power bases? What determines the power in each of these?

5. How do the various leadership styles impact a corporate culture?

6. In what situation would each of the three leadership styles be appropriate?

7. Why is it important for leaders to set performance standards? After the performance standards have been set, what actions should follow?

8. As a manager what are the roles you have to play?

9. What skills are necessary to be an effective manager? How does the focus change between the various levels of management?

10. What are the trends that are becoming more important in leadership?

CREATIVE THINKING CASE

Leadership at Potash Corp—Diversity and Safety, Setting the Example

Potash Corporation of Saskatoon, Saskatchewan is the world's largest producer of potash fertilizer. Potash (a generic word for a variety of potassium salts) is mined like iron or coal, but its use is much different. Potash is an important mineral for growing crops. Much of the company's activity is in Saskatchewan where it was first formed as a crown corporation; however it also has operations in many countries.

Safety is very important to the company. In April 2011, the Trinidad plant celebrated 10 million person hours without a lost-time injury. That's the equivalent to one person working 1,100 years without missing work because of an accident on the job. Potash Corp. achieves these impressive results through a strong commitment to leadership principles.

The corporate health and safety manual outlines the role of leadership in safety. Leaders are instructed to lead by example, both on and off the job. Potash Corp's senior personnel (up to and including the CEO) are expected to set a personal example, recognizing and reinforcing positive behaviours in employees. The manual describes two-way communication, documented procedures and expectations.

Potash Corp. managers integrate safety, environmental, and ethical targets and goals with other targets for each of their business activities. Performance management reinforces the process and external sources are used to improve the measures. Rewards and compensation are tied to successful leadership in all areas. Training is also very important in safety management. Potash Corp. has an intensive training program attached to all of the key areas of organizational development.

Potash Corp. also sees itself as a corporate leader in the creation of a diverse workforce, and once again requires its leaders to set an example. The company expected labour shortages and saw an untapped labour pool in Western Canada of First Nations youth. A senior position was created to work with Aboriginal community leaders with the expressed intent of hiring as many as 800 Aboriginal workers over a five year period. The company collaborated with community leaders to develop training programs for potential workers and to develop a welcoming environment among their current staff. All senior staff are expected to participate in the training sessions and work with the Aboriginal leaders and employees to ensure the success of the programs. As with safety, goals and targets are used to measure and manage the success of the programs. When the company decided to recruit more Aboriginal workers, it not only developed programs to support schools in First Nations and Métis communities, which would develop potential employees, but also addressed any training issues within the existing workforce.

Being able to attract and keep employees is an important aspect of leadership. A safe and welcoming environment supports that objective. In these two key areas, Potash Corps uses leadership by example to achieve these goals.

Thinking Critically

1. What sort of managers does Potash Corporation appear to look for?

2. Assuming that the extra safety steps cost money and reduce productivity, why would a company such as Potash Corporation want to export their culture of safety to developing nations?

3. Research Potash Corp on the Internet. Has the company changed as a result of the attempted takeover by BHP Billington? How well has their Aboriginal hiring program gone? How many Aboriginal employees do they report having?

SOURCES: G. Chon, P. Dvorak, "BHP Weighs Next Move on Potash," *Wall Street Journal*, New York, 2010. L. Grebinski, "Potash Company Employs Aboriginal Hiring Strategy to Fill Labour Shortage," Saskatchewan Sage, 2011. PotashCorp., "Leadership and Accountability," Safety, Health and Environmental Guide for Managers, edited Saskatoon, SK, 2012, http://www.potashcorp.com/media/POT_SHE_manual.pdf. PotashCorp., "Safe Workers, Safe Work"; C. Steed, W. F. Bawden, A. M. Coode, and P. Mottahed, "Subsidence Prediction for Saskatchewan Potash Mines," 1985; S. Walker, "Potash: The New 'Hot' Commodity," *Engineering and Mining Journal* 212, no. 4, 2011; J.W. Warnock, "Saskatchewan as a Resource Hinterland Economy," 2010.

Making the Connection

Designing Organizational Structures

We saw in the previous chapter how all of the functions of a manager are highly integrated. They are done almost simultaneously, and they affect and are affected by one another. They are the glue that binds the organization together, because it is the process of management that guides the internal organization to achieve its critical success factors, within the external environment that it is faced with, and to the satisfaction of its *stakeholders*. Sounds complicated, doesn't it? Well, management isn't easy. The rewards of a successful business don't come without effort, but they are definitely worth it. To make it easier, we will examine each of the functions of a manager separately. Just remember that they are connected.

In this chapter, we will examine the design of organizational structures suitable for achieving the goals of the company. This is something we discussed back in Chapter 7—the organization's *strategy* and structure must be in line. Consider the case of Procter & Gamble (P&G) discussed in the previous chapter. Procter & Gamble made changes to its organizational structure in 2005 to better reach its goal of faster product *innovation*, and increased flexibility and response time. This goal came in reaction to today's rapidly changing business environment, which demands that businesses act more quickly to meet both competitive threats and changing customer needs. Innovation, we know, is a critical success factor, and P&G needed to be a step ahead of the competition. To achieve this goal, it shifted from a geographically based structure to a structure based on products. It also introduced a new compensation system to encourage innovation. This example demonstrates how integrative strategy and structure are. To meet its goals, a business needs to have the structure to follow through on its plans. We can see in this case that the strategic plan fits with the environment, that the organizational structure fits with the strategic plan, and that

the tactical plan, in the case of P&G for compensation, was changed to fit with the strategic plan as well.

In fact, you'll see that when organizations change their structures, they are attempting to increase their ability to *meet customer needs*, the central ingredient to organizational success—whether through centralizing some operations to improve customer service, reduce costs, and ultimately reduce price; decentralizing to be more responsive to customer needs; or using information *technology* to get closer to the customer.

One of the structural building blocks of the organization is the managerial hierarchy. The traditional configuration is a pyramid structure with employees at the bottom and top management at the top. However, some companies alter this to improve *employee commitment*. One such company is Halsall Associates. As discussed in the chapter, it is one of Canada's leading engineering companies and is considered one of the best places to work in Canada. Halsall has followed the trend that some companies have followed—inverting the pyramid and putting employees at the top. This demonstrates graphically that "employees are the priority within the company," in the same way that we understand how important a factor employee commitment is to a company's success.

As discussed in the chapter, the organizing or structuring process is accomplished by dividing the work to be done, grouping the parts together, and assigning authority and responsibility. A formal organizational structure is the result of this design process. In this chapter, we describe this formal organization as "human, material, financial, and information resources deliberately connected to form the business organization." In other words, the resources of each functional area are structured in such a way that even though they are in separate areas—*human resources, operations, finance, and marketing*—they are linked together so that the organization can achieve its goals. If the organization is not structured in this way, with all the parts working together in an integrative way, success is not possible. We know from our discussion in the introduction to the model that all of the critical success factors are connected. They are also connected to each of the functional areas. The most obvious connections are

- achieving *financial performance* (finance);
- meeting and exceeding customer needs (marketing);
- providing value—quality products at reasonable prices (operations and marketing);
- encouraging creativity and innovation (all areas); and
- gaining employee commitment (human resources).

However, the parts of the business can't work independently and achieve these success factors. It all starts, as we've said, with the customer. As you'll see in the chapter, every organization is structured with the customer as the central thread. With this in mind, operations and marketing must work together. Marketing determines customer needs and works with operations to design a product to meet those needs. Operations provide the product in a quality manner, and marketing prices it to reflect the level of quality, providing something of value to the customer. They can't do this without people committed to making it work, and they can't keep doing it without fresh ideas that keep the organization providing something that distinguishes it from the competition. All of these areas provide the income for the business, but that money must flow back to each of the areas as needed to fuel the plans. It is therefore necessary that whatever structure you design, you take into consideration the inseparable connections among the different areas of the business.

Certain structures specifically integrate the different functional areas intentionally, so that they are working together on specific projects. A matrix structure is one such example. All areas are represented so that conflicting objectives can be balanced and overall goals, rather than individual ones, become the priority. This structure also allows for other factors that contribute to success—different minds working together increases creativity and innovation, for example.

In a matrix structure, individuals work together on teams. As discussed in the chapter, team-based structures are increasingly being used in organizations today. They help the organization in many ways; in particular they help to integrate the different areas of the business and to gain employee commitment to the organization's goals. This integration is crucial, as we'll see in our discussion of the functional areas, and is achieved when the teams are cross-functional—made up of employees from different functional areas working together on a common task. Without this integration, and commitment of the employees toward this integration, the areas can't work together to achieve the overall company goals. We've also seen this through our discussion of *planning*. Different departments or areas within the organization have different roles to play in the overall plan, but they must work together in an integrative fashion to achieve these overall goals.

Another type of structure takes the topic of integration beyond the borders of the business, as is the case with most successful businesses today. As we describe in the chapter, the virtual corporation is a "network of independent companies linked by information technology," which allows them to take advantage of opportunities they couldn't act on alone and share each other's key competencies to become a truly integrative organization. Cisco is one such company at the forefront of this new type of structure. Cisco CEO John Chambers's beliefs reflect the essence of this integrative structure—organizations should be built on change, organized as networks, and based on interdependencies.

chapter 10

Designing Organizational Structures

LEARNING OUTCOMES

1 Identify the five structural building blocks that managers use to design organizations.

2 Examine the tools companies use to establish relationships within their organizations.

3 Show how the degree of centralization/decentralization can be altered to make an organization more successful.

4 Describe the differences between a mechanistic and organic organization.

5 Discuss the traditional and contemporary organizational structures companies are using.

6 Summarize why companies are using team-based organizational structures.

7 Explain how the informal organization affects the performance of the company.

8 List some of the trends that are influencing the way businesses organize.

RESTRUCTURING FOR SUCCESS: CONTACT NORTH ADDS A REGIONAL LAYER

Imagine you lived in a community where the nearest university, college, or even high school was so far away, and travel to it so difficult, that you and your friends never went beyond the elementary grades. This was the reality for people in many small and remote communities in northern Ontario, and it was compounded by the fact that even when students left home to attend higher education, it was offered only in English—a language unfamiliar to those who spoke First Nations languages and Francophone dialects.

In 1986, the Ontario provincial government began to address this problem by starting Contact North, a program with a goal of bringing educational opportunities from public colleges, universities, school boards, literacy and basic skills, and other training providers to these isolated areas. Some of the early Contact North participants were the very first post-secondary learners in their families. Classes were delivered in ways that are now familiar—forms of e-learning and distance education that were pioneered by Contact North.

The initiative was so successful that the government of Ontario established a similar program to serve small and rural communities in east central and southwestern regions of the province in 2007. With more than 100 online learning centres serving students in communities across Ontario, the government decided to bring them together under one guiding structure, with Contact North as the lead organization. The learners are served by online learning centres where they can attend classes; students are also able to participate in their classes from home by using Contact North learning technologies. All of the centres are housed in space donated by the local communities. Twenty-six of the 112 centres are in First Nations communities, with only 18 in east central and southwestern Ontario.

From its inception, Contact North was set up with departments running each of its operational functions from its central headquarters in Thunder Bay, Ontario. With the 2007 expansion, Contact North was now serving the entire province. As each region has its own unique needs and requirements, in 2011, Contact North introduced a regional

PHOTO COURTESY OF CONTACT NORTH

structure, while still maintaining its central office, reflecting the reality of the merged organizations and keeping the strengths of a single "command centre."

Each region and its online learning centre needed attention, and under the previous setup it wasn't practical for centralized staff to travel to all regions, so coordinated management of the various centres was virtually impossible. Contact North explains that the new structure "allows [members of the] management staff to continuously crisscross their respective regions, visit and support centre coordinators, monitor closely the student recruitment plans and strategies of centre coordinators, realistically manage all of the local centres and help link with major regional stakeholders."

The Contact North story is an example of how organizational structures need to change as organizations grow—if those organizations are to succeed in their key goals. Success at Contact North can be measured by the number of course registrations it supports for Ontario's public education and training providers, and by the decision of government to put it in charge of the province-wide initiative. But the success couldn't have been maintained unless the organization had changed.

Contact North continues to grow and succeed, and link with other organizations around the globe. It has become the world's largest distance education and training network. Its global reach was illustrated when, at a 2010 conference in Thunder Bay, Ontario, Contact North joined electronically with an Australian Aboriginal group 15,000 kilometres away in a live cultural sharing event, connecting the Woolyungah Indigenous Centre in Australia's Illawarra region and the Sioux Hudson Literacy Council in northwestern Ontario.[1]

THINKING CRITICALLY

As you read this chapter, consider the following questions:

1. What are some of the strengths of a centralized management structure? What are some weaknesses?

2. Can you think of any examples of organizations or businesses that have failed to change and restructure as they grew? What happened to them?

3. In the example above, what is the long-term economic benefit of a program like Contact North? To what resource does it give access?

SOURCES: http://www.mah.gov.on.ca/Page8772.aspx/; http://www.contactnorth.ca/; http://www.tonybates.ca/2011/04/09/new-web-site-design-for-contact-north/; http://www.northernc.on.ca/programs/coned/distance/contactnorth.html/; http://elearnnetwork.ca/?q=content/e-share-contact-north-connects-aboriginal-partners-15-hours-and-15000-km-apart/; http://www.downes.ca/cgi-bin/page.cgi?journal=Contact%20North/.

In today's dynamic business environment, organizational structures need to be designed so that the organization can respond quickly to new competitive threats and changing customer needs. Future success for companies will depend on the company's ability to be flexible and respond to the needs of customers. In this chapter, we'll look first at how companies build organizational structures. Then, we'll explore how managers establish the relationships within the structures they have designed, including determining lines of communication, authority, and power. We will examine some contemporary structures and the use of teams in organizations. Finally, we'll examine the new trends that are changing the choices companies make about organizational design.

 # BUILDING ORGANIZATIONAL STRUCTURES

As you learned in Chapter 9, the key functions that managers perform include planning, organizing, leading, and controlling. This chapter focuses specifically on the organizing function. Organizing involves coordinating and allocating a company's resources so that the company can carry out its plans and achieve its goals. This organizing, or structuring, process is accomplished by

- determining work activities and dividing up tasks (division of labour);
- grouping jobs and employees (departmentalization); and
- assigning authority and responsibilities (delegation).

formal organization
The order and design of relationships within a company; consists of two or more people working together with a common objective and clarity of purpose.

The result of the organizing process is a formal organizational structure. A **formal organization** is the order and design of relationships within the company. It consists of two or more people working together with a common objective and clarity of purpose. Formal organizations also have well-defined lines of authority, channels for information flow, and means of control. Human, material, financial, and information resources are deliberately connected to form the business organization. Some connections are long lasting, such as the links among people in the finance or marketing department. Others can be changed at almost any time, as when a committee is formed to study a problem.

Every organization has some kind of underlying structure. Traditional structures are more rigid and group employees by function, products, processes, customers, or regions,

Concept *in Action*

Founded in 1943, IKEA has grown from a small mail order operation into an international home furnishings retailer with over 230 stores in 33 countries throughout Europe, North America, and Asia. Best known for its intriguing modern furniture designs, highly trafficked store openings, and quirky advertising, the IKEA Group consists of multiple corporate divisions corresponding to the company's retail, purchasing, sales, and design and manufacturing functions. What factors likely influenced the development of IKEA's organizational structure as the company changed over the years?

as described in the next section. Contemporary and team-based structures are more flexible and assemble employees to respond quickly to dynamic business environments. Regardless of the structural skeleton a company chooses to implement, all managers must first consider what kind of work needs to be done within the company.

Division of Labour

The process of dividing work into separate jobs and assigning tasks to workers is called division of labour. In a fast-food restaurant, for example, some employees take or fill orders, others prepare food, a few clean and maintain equipment, and at least one supervises all the others. In an auto assembly plant, some workers install rear-view mirrors, whereas others mount bumpers on bumper brackets. The degree to which the tasks are subdivided into smaller jobs is called specialization. Employees who work at highly specialized jobs, such as assembly-line workers, perform a limited number and variety of tasks. Employees, who become specialists at one task, or a small number of tasks, develop greater skill in doing that particular job. This can lead to greater efficiency and consistency in production and other work activities. However, a high degree of specialization can also result in employees who are uninterested or bored because of the lack of variety and challenge. In Chapter 11, we will discuss ways managers can mitigate the disadvantages of a highly specialized workforce.

division of labour
The process of dividing work into separate jobs and assigning tasks to workers.

specialization
The degree to which tasks are subdivided into smaller jobs.

Departmentalization

After a company divides into jobs the work it needs to do, managers then group the jobs together so that similar or associated tasks and activities can be coordinated. This grouping of people, tasks, and resources into organizational units is called departmentalization and facilitates the planning, leading, and control processes. As Exhibit 10.1 shows, five basic types of departmentalization are commonly used in organizations:

1. **Functional departmentalization**, which is based on the primary functions performed within an organizational unit (marketing, finance, production, sales, and so on)

departmentalization
The process of grouping jobs together so that similar or associated tasks and activities can be coordinated.

functional departmentalization
Departmentalization that is based on the primary functions performed within an organizational unit.

product departmentalization
Departmentalization that is based on the goods or services produced or sold by the organizational unit.

process departmentalization
Departmentalization that is based on the production process used by the organizational unit.

customer departmentalization
Departmentalization that is based on the primary type of customer served by the organizational unit.

geographic departmentalization
Departmentalization that is based on the geographic segmentation of the organizational units.

2. **Product departmentalization,** which is based on the goods or services produced or sold by the organizational unit (such as outpatient/emergency services, paediatrics, cardiology, and orthopaedics)

3. **Process departmentalization,** which is based on the production process used by the organizational unit (such as lumber cutting and treatment, furniture finishing, shipping)

4. **Customer departmentalization,** which is based on the primary type of customer served by the organizational unit (such as wholesale or retail purchasers)

5. **Geographic departmentalization,** which is based on the geographic segmentation of organizational units (such as Canadian and U.S. marketing, European marketing, South American marketing)

Once companies choose a method of departmentalization, they must then establish the relationships within that structure. In other words, the company must decide how many layers of management it needs and who will report to whom. The company must also decide how much control to invest in each of its managers and where in the organization decisions will be made and implemented.

Creating the Future of Business

DAVE WILKIN, REDWOOD STRATEGIC

At 23 years old, Dave Wilkin is the founder of a national company that has recently launched in the U.S., and he is the second-youngest person to win the FuEL Future Entrepreneurial Leaders award (2011), which, sponsored by *PROFIT Magazine*, profiles Canada's top 20 entrepreneurs under 30 years of age. Need we say more?

Dave's company is called Redwood Strategic and it runs CommunityPerks.com—formerly known as "CampusPerks." The name was changed, according to Dave, because "students and youth are not just involved and active on campus; they are also active and influential in their communities." CommunityPerks is one of the fastest growing youth experiential and social media marketing agencies in Canada. As Dave describes it, with the largest network of youth influencers in Canada (over 25,000) CommunityPerks "connects brands to (these) influencers and advocates through their passion points." In other words, "youth tell us their passion points and what activities they're involved in, then CommunityPerks connects them with sponsorship and scholarship opportunities from the best companies." These companies can then run social media and experiential marketing programs through the networks of these influencers in a way that is lasting, is meaningful, and improves community life.

Instead of the traditional brand awareness campaigns that companies invest in, CommunityPerks offers companies a way to find opportunities to connect with students, young professionals, and parents to support initiatives that they care about—students get the support they need and, in turn, they become advocates for the brand, offering the companies the kind of emotional connection and long-term relationship building that is priceless. It's a win-win.

Dave's company is not structured like a traditional marketing company. Instead of using an organizational structure built around servicing its different accounts, CommunityPerks structure is unique because their service is unique. He does have the typical agency side that pitches to the brands and works with them to build the campaigns,

but it is his proprietary crowd-sourcing platform that is the difference. Apart from the agency side, there is a technology-based product team that manages the platform that connects these influencers with the opportunities around which to build the campaigns.

The idea for CommunityPerks came to Dave when studying biochemistry at university. He was very involved on campus, but noticed how difficult it was for under-funded clubs and societies to get support from companies, and how those companies in turn were restricted in how they could reach students. He wanted to work with those companies to improve student life on campus. Today, he works with brands like Virgin Mobile, Loblaws, PepsiCo and Microsoft.

Dave's advice for young entrepreneurs is that "it is important to turn criticism into positive energy and use it to help your company adapt to new situations." You'll face a lot of rejection and skepticism, put in long hours, and deal with a lot of pressure, but "it's what will make you and your company strong and resilient." In only his first two years in business, he has provided over $500,000 in sponsorship and opportunities to student leaders. Dave's advice is definitely worth listening to.

Thinking Critically

1. How important do you think CommunityPerks organizational structure is to its success?
2. How is CommunityPerks different from other marketing organizations in terms of what it does and how it does it?
3. Successful entrepreneurship requires the ability to spot trends and seize the opportunities created by them. What different external environmental trends were at work that created the opportunity that Dave saw for CommunityPerks?

SOURCES: http://www.redwoodstrategic.com, used with permission from Dave Wilkin; Laura Stricker, "Dave Wilkin makes Canadian Top 20 Entrepreneurs Under 30 List," November 21, 2011, http://uwaterloo.ca/science/news/dave-wilkin-makes-canadian-top-20-entrepreneurs-under-30-list; David Tal, "Dave Wilkin, CampusPerks founder," April 18, 2012, http://www.jobpostings.ca/article/dave-wilkin-campusperks-founder; "Dave Wilkin," *Profit Guide*, December 6, 2011, http://www.profitguide.com/manage-grow/leadership/dave-wilkin-30273; http://www.newswire.ca/en/story/876957/canada-s-topyoung-entrepreneurs-of-the-year-named-by-the-fuel-awards; telephone interview with D. Wilkin, June 28, 2012.

Exhibit 10.1 Five Traditional Ways to Organize

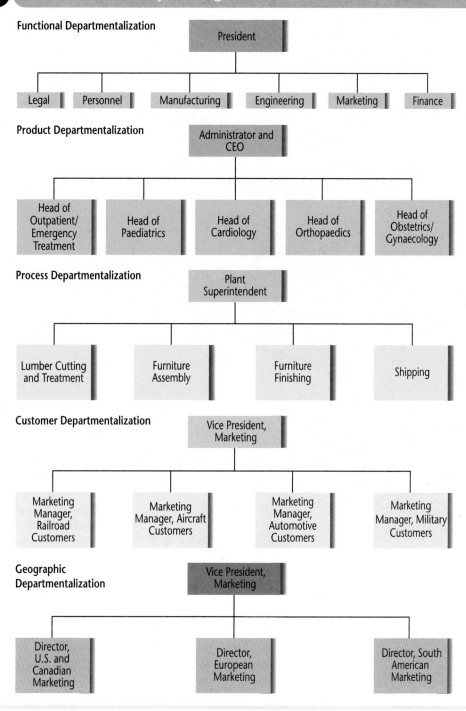

Functional Departmentalization

President

Legal | Personnel | Manufacturing | Engineering | Marketing | Finance

Product Departmentalization

Administrator and CEO

Head of Outpatient/Emergency Treatment | Head of Paediatrics | Head of Cardiology | Head of Orthopaedics | Head of Obstetrics/Gynaecology

Process Departmentalization

Plant Superintendent

Lumber Cutting and Treatment | Furniture Assembly | Furniture Finishing | Shipping

Customer Departmentalization

Vice President, Marketing

Marketing Manager, Railroad Customers | Marketing Manager, Aircraft Customers | Marketing Manager, Automotive Customers | Marketing Manager, Military Customers

Geographic Departmentalization

Vice President, Marketing

Director, U.S. and Canadian Marketing | Director, European Marketing | Director, South American Marketing

Organization Chart

An **organization chart** is a visual representation of the structured relationships among tasks, responsibilities, and the people given the authority to do those tasks. In the organization chart in Exhibit 10.2, each figure represents a job, and each job includes several tasks. The exhibit shows the executive as departmentalized by function. Reporting to the Chief Operating Officer are the District Managers (geographical) who are then responsible for the Sales Managers (by customer/consumer). The Sales Managers oversee the Sales Associates (by product).

organization chart
A visual representation of the structured relationships among tasks and the people given the authority to do those tasks.

Exhibit 10.2 Organization Chart for a Typical Retailer

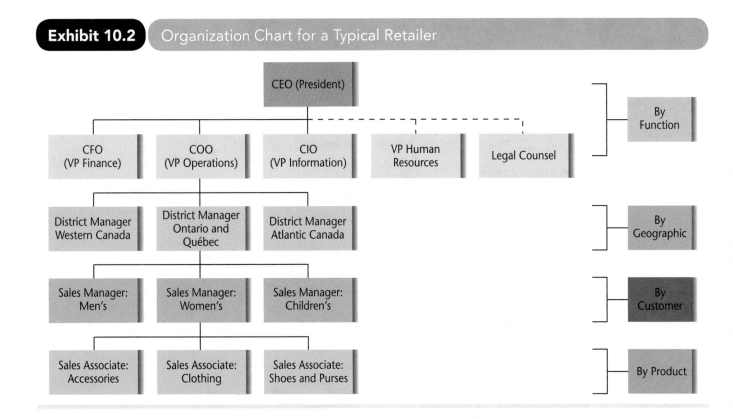

People are assigned to a particular organizational unit because they perform similar or related tasks, or because they are jointly responsible for a product, client, or market. Decisions about how to departmentalize affect the way in which management assigns authority, distributes resources, rewards performance, and sets up lines of communication. Many large organizations use several types of departmentalization. For example, a global company might be departmentalized first geographically (North American, European, and Asian units), then by product line (foods/beverages and health care), and finally by functional area (marketing, operations, finance, and so on).

LO2

MANAGERIAL HIERARCHY

managerial hierarchy
The levels of management within an organization; typically includes top, middle, and supervisory management.

Managerial hierarchy (also called the *management pyramid*), is defined by the levels of management within an organization. Generally, the management structure has three levels: top, middle, and supervisory management. These three levels were introduced in Chapter 9.

In a managerial hierarchy, each organizational unit is controlled and supervised by a manager in a higher unit. The person with the most formal authority is at the top of the hierarchy. The higher a manager, the more power he or she has. Thus, the amount of power decreases as you move down the management pyramid. At the same time, the number of employees increases as you move down the hierarchy.

Not all companies today are using this traditional configuration. An interesting trend in designing a company's management structure is the inverted pyramid. For instance, Toronto-based Halsall Associates Ltd., an engineering company, describes itself just that way.[2] When the president of the company, Peter Halsall, discusses his management structure, he draws an upside-down pyramid. At the bottom of the pyramid, he puts himself. Above him, he lists the layers of management and, finally, the frontline employees. The reason he does this is to show graphically that the employees are the priority within the company. He explains, "Decisions are made so these people maximize their opportunities." This unusual view must pay off: Halsall Associates is one of Canada's leading engineering companies and is considered one of the best places to work.

An organization with a well-defined hierarchy has a clear **chain of command**, which is the line of authority that extends from one level of the organization to the next, from top to bottom, and makes clear who reports to whom. The chain of command is shown in the organization chart and can be traced from the CEO all the way down to the employees producing goods and services. Under the *unity of command* principle, everyone reports to and gets instructions from only one boss. Unity of command guarantees that everyone will have a direct supervisor and will not be taking orders from a number of supervisors. Unity of command and chain of command give everyone in the organization clear directions and help coordinate people doing different jobs.

The growth of the global marketplace has led some companies to examine the traditional principle of unity of command with a single person at the top of the organization. These organizations are finding the need for quick decision making and flexibility in every worldwide location too difficult for any one individual to handle. Many companies are moving to alternative management models, including co-CEOs or even a committee model of leadership.

Individuals who are part of the chain of command have authority over other persons in the organization. **Authority** is legitimate power, granted by the organization and acknowledged by employees, that allows an individual to request action and expect compliance. Exercising authority means making decisions and seeing that they are carried out. Most managers delegate, or assign, some degree of authority and responsibility to others below them in the chain of command. The **delegation of authority** makes the employees accountable to their supervisor. *Accountability* means responsibility for outcomes. Typically, authority and responsibility move downward through the organization as managers assign activities to, and share decision making with, their subordinates. Accountability moves upward in the organization as managers in each successively higher level are held accountable for the actions of their subordinates.

chain of command
The line of authority that extends from one level of an organization's hierarchy to the next, from top to bottom, and makes clear who reports to whom.

authority
Legitimate power, granted by the organization and acknowledged by employees, that allows an individual to request action and expect compliance.

delegation of authority
The assignment of some degree of authority and responsibility to persons lower in the chain of command.

Span of Control

The fourth structural building block is the managerial span of control. Each company must decide how many managers are needed at each level of the management hierarchy to effectively supervise the work performed within organizational units. A manager's **span of control** (sometimes called *span of management*) is the number of employees the manager directly supervises. It can be as narrow as 2 or 3 employees or as wide as 50 or more. In general, the larger the span of control, the more efficient the organization is. As Exhibit 10.3 shows, however, both narrow and wide spans of control have benefits and drawbacks.

If hundreds of employees perform the same job, one supervisor might be able to manage a very large number of employees. Such might be the case at a clothing plant, where hundreds of sewing machine operators work from identical patterns. But if employees perform complex and dissimilar tasks, a manager can effectively supervise only a much smaller number. For instance, a supervisor in the research and development area of a pharmaceutical company might oversee just a few research chemists because of the highly complex nature of their jobs.

span of control
The number of employees a manager directly supervises; also called span of management.

The span of control is wide for employees who have highly specialized and similar skills like these memory chip technicians. A wide span of control means that managers can supervise more employees. Discuss what criteria determine how many subordinates a manager can manage.

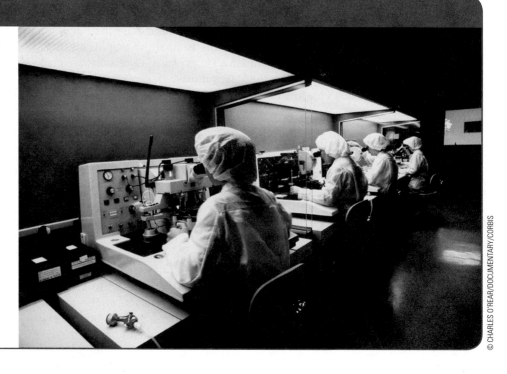

© CHARLES O'REAR/DOCUMENTARY/CORBIS

The optimal span of control is determined by the following five factors:

1. *Nature of the task.* The more complex the task, the narrower the span of control.
2. *Location of the workers.* The more locations, the narrower the span of control.
3. *Ability of the manager to delegate responsibility.* The greater the ability to delegate, the wider the span of control.
4. *Amount of interaction and feedback between the workers and the manager.* The more feedback and interaction required, the narrower the span of control.
5. *Level of skill and motivation of the workers.* The higher the skill level and motivation, the wider the span of control.

Exhibit 10.3 Narrow and Wide Spans of Control

	ADVANTAGES	DISADVANTAGES
Narrow span of control	• High degree of control • Fewer subordinates may mean manager is more familiar with each individual • Close supervision can provide immediate feedback	• More levels of management, therefore more expensive • Slower decision making because of vertical layers • Isolation of top management
Wide span of control	• Fewer levels of management means increased efficiency and reduced costs • Increased subordinate autonomy leads to quicker decision making • Greater organizational flexibility • Higher levels of job satisfaction because of employee empowerment	• Discouragement of employee autonomy • Less control • Possible lack of familiarity because of large number of subordinates • Managers spread so thinly that they can't provide necessary leadership or support • Lack of coordination or synchronization

DEGREE OF CENTRALIZATION

LO3

The final component in building an effective organizational structure is deciding at what level in the organization decisions should be made. **Centralization** is the degree to which formal authority is concentrated in one area or level of the organization. In a highly centralized structure, top management makes most of the key decisions in the organization, with very little input from lower-level employees. Centralization lets top managers develop a broad view of operations and exercise tight financial controls. It can also help to reduce costs by eliminating redundancy in the organization. But centralization can also mean that lower-level personnel don't get a chance to develop their decision making and leadership skills, and that the organization is less able to respond quickly to customer demands.

centralization
The degree to which formal authority is concentrated in one area or level of an organization.

Decentralization is the process of pushing decision-making authority down the organizational hierarchy, giving lower-level personnel more responsibility and power to make and implement decisions. Benefits of decentralization can include quicker decision making, increased levels of innovation and creativity, greater organizational flexibility, faster development of lower-level managers, and increased levels of job satisfaction and employee commitment. But decentralization can also be risky. If lower-level personnel don't have the necessary skills and training to perform effectively, they might make costly mistakes. Additionally, decentralization can increase the likelihood of inefficient lines of communication, incongruent or competing objectives, and duplication of effort.

decentralization
The process of pushing decision-making authority down the organizational hierarchy.

Several factors must be considered when deciding how much decision-making authority to delegate throughout the organization. These factors include the size of the organization, the speed of change in its environment, managers' willingness to give up authority, employees' willingness to accept more authority, and the organization's geographic dispersion.

Decentralization is usually desirable when the following conditions are met:

- The organization is very large, such as Magna, Petro-Canada, or Ford.
- The company is in a dynamic environment where quick, local decisions must be made, as in many high-tech industries.
- Managers are willing to share power with their subordinates.
- Employees are willing and able to take more responsibility.
- The company is spread out geographically, such as The Bay, Parmalat Canada, and Prudential Financial.

As organizations grow and change, they continually re-evaluate their structure to determine whether it is helping the company achieve its goals.

> **Concept** *Check*
>
> What factors determine the optimal span of control?
>
> What are the primary characteristics of a decentralized organization?
>
> What factors should be considered when choosing the degree of centralization?

ORGANIZATIONAL DESIGN CONSIDERATIONS

LO4

You are now familiar with the different ways to structure an organization, but as a manager, how do you decide which design will work the best for your business? What works for one company may not work for another. In this section, we'll look at two generic models of organizational design and briefly examine a set of contingency factors that favour each.

Mechanistic versus Organic Structures

Structural design generally follows one of the two basic models described in Exhibit 10.4: mechanistic or organic. A **mechanistic organization** is characterized by a relatively high degree of job specialization, rigid departmentalization, many

mechanistic organization
An organizational structure that is characterized by a relatively high degree of job specialization, rigid departmentalization, many layers of management, narrow spans of control, centralized decision making, and a long chain of command.

Sustainable Business, Sustainable World

JOHNSON & JOHNSON

Johnson & Johnson, headquartered in New Brunswick, New Jersey, is a family of more than 250 operating companies employing about 120,000 people in 57 countries worldwide. It is a world leader in consumer health, medical devices and diagnostics, biologics, and pharmaceuticals. In its Canadian operations alone there are six individual operating companies employing about 3,450 people. You probably know Johnson & Johnson as the maker of Tylenol. What you may not know is that, in 2009, it was the second largest producer of solar panels in the U.S., was the largest corporate user of hybrid vehicles, and got 30 percent of its energy from renewable sources. In fact, it was ranked as the number two most sustainable company in the world in 2011, according to the 2011 *Global 100 Most Sustainable Corporations in the World* and was number six on *Newsweek* magazine's *Green Ranking List* of the greenest companies in the U.S. that same year.

Johnson & Johnson's credo—which upholds its responsibility to the communities in which it operates and to the world community in general by committing to protect the environment—makes it clear how well the company understands how important the health of the environment is to human health. In fact, its Senior Director of Worldwide Environmental Health and Safety, Al Iannizzi, told a story at the 2009 *Net Impact Conference* about how he believed "corporations are evil" until he read J&J's credo, and he's been working for them for nearly 30 years since. J&J has been setting long-term environmental goals since 1990 and has reported on triple-bottom line sustainability since 2003, but in January 2011, J&J also launched a program called *Healthy Future 2015* that defines long-term goals and priorities for sustainability and ties social and transparency-related priorities to its overall sustainability strategy for the first time.

How does a company of this size manage to coordinate its operations at a level sufficient to attain such a high level of success in its efforts toward sustainability? Because it is committed to achieving its goals and backs that commitment with a management structure and a system of certification and assessment processes, and it holds its employees accountable company-wide, to ensure those goals are met. In short, it has developed an organizational structure to support its sustainability efforts.

J&J's Worldwide Environment, Health and Safety (EHS) department provides advice and assistance to local management teams responsible for environmental compliance in its facilities. It also has an EHS Leadership Council to coordinate efforts. Each of the key business segments is overseen by councils or executives responsible for the promotion of sustainability throughout the segments. In the Consumer Products group, there is a VP for Sustainability who guides efforts while the other sectors are overseen by Sustainability councils. Maybe that's why it doesn't hesitate to partner with NGOs to hold its products accountable and add credibility to what it does, and why it can say without hesitation that it does not "greenwash" in its advertising.

It can say this because Johnson & Johnson is committed to sustainability, and has backed up that commitment with a solid structure that will ensure its goals are reached and control is maintained to keep it on its course.

Thinking Critically

1. Is it necessary for a company to put such an extensive structure in place to support its sustainability efforts?
2. Do you think that a given strategy can be successfully executed without the appropriate organizational structure behind it? And do you agree that the "environment is the ultimate human health issue"?
3. Go to the Johnson & Johnson website and check out its Healthy Future 2015 goals. Ask yourself if our world can survive without this kind of commitment.

SOURCES: www.jnj.com; www.global100.org; www.triplepundit.com, November 14, 2009; www.thedailybeast.com, October 16, 2011.

Exhibit 10.4 Mechanistic versus Organic

STRUCTURAL CHARACTERISTIC	MECHANISTIC	ORGANIC
Job specialization	High	Low
Departmentalization	Rigid	Loose
Management hierarchy (levels of management)	Tall (many levels)	Flat (few levels)
Span of control	Narrow	Wide
Decision-making authority	Centralized	Decentralized
Chain of command	Long	Short

layers of management (particularly middle management), narrow spans of control, centralized decision making, and a long chain of command. This combination of elements results in what is called a tall organizational structure. The Canadian Armed Forces and the United Nations are typical mechanistic organizations.

In contrast, an organic organization is characterized by a relatively low degree of job specialization, loose departmentalization, few levels of management, wide spans of control, decentralized decision making, and a short chain of command. This combination of elements results in what is called a flat organizational structure. Colleges and universities tend to have flat organizational structures, with only two or three levels of administration between the faculty and the president. Exhibit 10.5 shows examples of flat and tall organizational structures.

organic organization
An organizational structure that is characterized by a relatively low degree of job specialization, loose departmentalization, few levels of management, wide spans of control, decentralized decision making, and a short chain of command.

Factors Influencing the Choice between Mechanistic versus Organic Structures

Although few organizations are purely mechanistic or purely organic, most tend more toward one type or the other. The decision to create a more mechanistic or a more organic structural design is based on factors such as the company's overall strategy, the size of the organization, the types of technologies used in the organization, and the stability of its external environment, among others. A company's organizational structure should enable it to achieve its goals, and because setting corporate goals is part of a company's overall strategy-making process, it follows that a company's structure depends on its strategy.

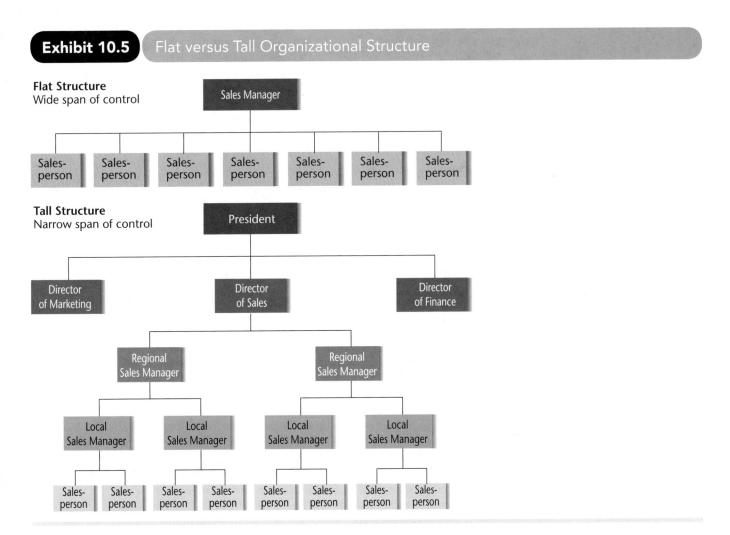

Exhibit 10.5 Flat versus Tall Organizational Structure

That alignment can be challenging for struggling companies trying to accomplish multiple goals. For example, a company with an innovation strategy will need the flexibility and fluid movement of information that an organic organization provides. But a company using a cost-control strategy will require the efficiency and tight control of a mechanistic organization. Often, struggling companies try to simultaneously increase innovation and reduce costs, which can be organizational challenges for managers. Such is the case at Sony, whose CEO (also the Chairman and President), Howard Stringer, cut 10,000 jobs, closed factories, and shuffled management in an attempt to control costs and improve efficiency. At the same time, he is also trying to encourage cross-divisional communication (like between the music and electronics divisions) and increase the pace of innovation. Stringer will need to balance these two strategies regardless of which organizational model he relies on most.[3]

Another factor that affects how mechanistic or organic a company's organizational structure is, is its size. Much research has been conducted that shows a company's size has a significant impact on its organizational structure.[4] Smaller companies tend to follow the more organic model, in part because they can. It is much easier to be successful with decentralized decision making, for example, if you have only 50 employees. A company with that few employees is also more likely, by virtue of its size, to have a lesser degree of employee specialization. That's because when there are fewer people to do the work, those people tend to know more about the entire process. As a company grows, it becomes more mechanistic, as systems are put in place to manage the greater number of employees. Procedures, rules, and regulations replace flexibility, innovation, and independence.

Lastly, the business in which a company operates has a significant impact on its organizational structure. In complex, dynamic, and unstable environments, companies need to organize for flexibility and agility. That is, their organizational structures need to respond to rapid and unexpected changes in the business environment. For companies operating in stable environments, however, the demands for flexibility and agility are not so great. The environment is predictable. In a simple, stable environment, therefore, companies benefit from the efficiencies created by a mechanistic organizational structure.

LO5 · TRADITIONAL AND CONTEMPORARY STRUCTURES

Line-and-Staff Organization

line organization
An organizational structure with direct, clear lines of authority and communication flowing from the top managers downward.

The line organization is designed with direct, clear lines of authority and communication flowing from the top managers downward. Managers have direct control over all activities, including administrative duties. An organization chart for this type of structure would show that all positions in the company are directly connected via an imaginary line extending from the highest position in the organization to the lowest (where production of goods and services takes place). This structure with its simple design and broad managerial control is often well suited to small, entrepreneurial companies.

line-and-staff organization
An organizational structure that includes both line and staff positions.

line positions
All positions in the organization directly concerned with producing goods and services and directly connected from top to bottom.

staff positions
Positions in an organization held by individuals who provide the administrative and support services that line employees need to achieve the company's goals.

As an organization grows and becomes more complex, the line organization can be enhanced by adding staff positions to the design. Staff positions provide specialized advisory and support services to line managers in the line-and-staff organization, shown in Exhibit 10.6. In daily operations, individuals in line positions are directly involved in the processes used to create goods and services. Individuals in staff positions provide the administrative and support services that line employees need to achieve the company's goals. Line positions in organizations are typically in areas such as production, marketing, and finance. Staff positions are found in areas such as legal counselling, managerial consulting, public relations, and human resource management.

Exhibit 10.6 | Line-and-Staff Organization

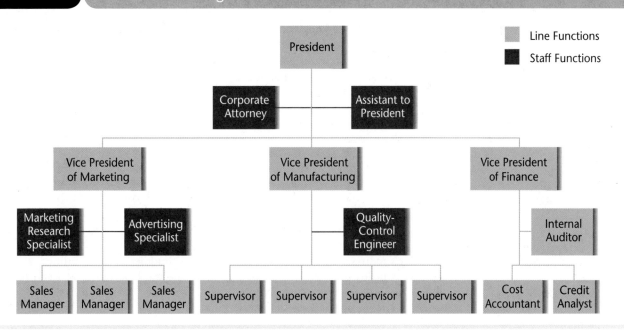

Line Functions
Staff Functions

Although traditional forms of departmentalization still represent how many companies organize their work, newer, more flexible organizational structures are in use at many companies. Let's look at matrix and committee structures, and how those two types of organizations are helping companies better leverage the diverse skills of their employees.

Matrix Structure

The **matrix structure** (also called the *project management* approach) is sometimes used in conjunction with the traditional line-and-staff structure in an organization. Essentially, this structure combines two different forms of departmentalization, functional and product, that have complementary strengths and weaknesses. The matrix structure brings together people from different functional areas of the organization (such as manufacturing, finance, and marketing) to work on a special project. Each employee has two direct supervisors: the line manager from her or his specific functional area and the project manager. Exhibit 10.7 shows a matrix organization with four special project groups (A, B, C, D), each with its own project manager. Because of the dual chain of command, the matrix structure presents some unique challenges for both managers and subordinates.

Advantages of the matrix structure include the following:

- *Teamwork.* By pooling the skills and abilities of various specialists, the company can increase creativity and innovation and tackle more complex tasks.
- *Efficient use of resources.* Project managers use only the specialized staff they need to get the job done instead of building large groups of underused personnel.
- *Flexibility.* The project structure is flexible and can adapt quickly to changes in the environment; the group can be disbanded quickly when it is no longer needed.
- *Ability to balance conflicting objectives.* The customer wants a quality product and predictable costs. The organization wants high profits and the development of technical capability for the future. These competing goals serve as a focal point for directing activities and overcoming conflict. The marketing representative can represent the customer, the finance representative can advocate high profits, and the engineers can push for technical capabilities.

matrix structure (project management)
An organizational structure that combines functional and product departmentalization by bringing together people from different functional areas of the organization to work on a special project.

CHAPTER 10 Designing Organizational Structures **287**

- *Higher performance.* Employees working on special project teams may experience increased feelings of ownership, commitment, and motivation.
- *Opportunities for personal and professional development.* The project structure gives individuals the opportunity to develop and strengthen technical and interpersonal skills.

Disadvantages of the matrix structure include the following:

- *Power struggles.* Functional and product managers might have differing goals and management styles.
- *Confusion among team members.* Reporting relationships and job responsibilities might be unclear.
- *Lack of cohesiveness.* Team members from different functional areas might have difficulty communicating effectively and working together as a team.

Although project-based matrix organizations can improve a company's flexibility and teamwork, some companies are trying to unravel complex matrix structures that create limited accountability. For example, during the first year as CEO of Hewlett-Packard, Mark Hurd worked diligently to untangle the complex matrix structure implemented by his predecessor, Carly Fiorina. The reason Hurd gave for tossing out Fiorina's matrix management structure, which muddied responsibilities, was to give business heads more control of their units. "The more accountable I can make you, the easier it is for you to show you're a great performer," says Hurd. "The more I use a matrix, the easier I make it to blame someone else."[5]

Committee Structure

committee structure
An organizational structure in which authority and responsibility are held by a group rather than an individual.

In committee structure, authority and responsibility are held by a group rather than an individual. Committees are typically part of a larger line-and-staff organization. Often the committee's role is only advisory, but in some situations the committee has the power to make and implement decisions. Committees can make the coordination of tasks in the organization much easier. For example, Novartis, the huge Swiss pharmaceutical company, revamped the structure of its committees, which report to its board of directors. The company reflects best practices in global corporate governance. Novartis has four permanent committees reporting to the board: the chairman's committee, the

Concept *in Action*

Matrix structures combine functional and product departmentalization where many employees report to at least two managers. Bayer AG of Germany (the makers of Bayer Aspirin) uses a matrix structure. Discuss what criteria determine how many subordinates a manager can manage.

JENS SCHLUETER/AFP/GETTY IMAGES/NEWSCOM

Exhibit 10.7 Matrix Organization

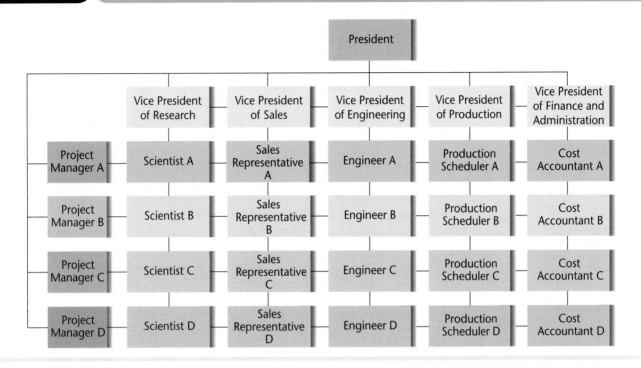

compensation committee, the audit and compliance committee, and the corporate governance committee. The chairman's committee deals with business matters arising between board meetings and is responsible for high-level appointments and acquisitions. The compensation committee looks at the remuneration of board members, whereas the audit and compliance committee oversees accounting and financial reporting practices. The corporate governance committee's duties include focusing on board nominations, board performance evaluations, and possible conflicts of interest.[6]

Committees bring diverse viewpoints to a problem and expand the range of possible solutions, but there are some drawbacks. Committees can be slow to reach a decision and are sometimes dominated by a single individual. It is also more difficult to hold any one individual accountable for a decision made by a group. Committee meetings can sometimes go on for long periods of time with little seemingly being accomplished.

Concept *Check*

Why does the matrix structure have a dual chain of command?

What are advantages of a matrix structure? Disadvantages?

TEAMS

LO6

One of the most apparent trends in business today is the use of teams to accomplish organizational goals. Using a team-based structure can increase individual and group motivation and performance. This section gives a brief overview of group behaviour, defines work teams as specific types of groups, and provides suggestions for creating high-performing teams.

Understanding Group Behaviour

Teams are a specific type of organizational group. Every organization contains groups, social units of two or more people who share the same goals and cooperate to achieve those goals. Understanding some fundamental concepts related to group behaviour and group processes provides a good foundation for understanding concepts about work teams. Groups can be formal or informal in nature. Formal groups are designated and sanctioned by the organization; their behaviour is directed toward accomplishing organizational goals. Informal groups are based on social relationships and are not determined or sanctioned by the organization.

Formal organizational groups, like the sales department at Dell Computers, must operate within the larger Dell organizational system. To some degree, elements of the larger Dell system, such as organizational strategy, company policies and procedures, available resources, and the highly motivated employee corporate culture, determine the behaviour of smaller groups, like the sales department, within Dell. Other factors that affect the behaviour of organizational groups are individual member characteristics (e.g., ability, training, personality), the roles and norms of group members, and the size and cohesiveness of the group. Norms are the implicit behavioural guidelines of the group, or the standards for acceptable and non-acceptable behaviour. For example, a Dell sales manager may be expected to work at least two Saturdays per month without extra pay. Although this isn't written anywhere, it is the expected norm.

group cohesiveness
The degree to which group members want to stay in the group and tend to resist outside influences.

Group cohesiveness refers to the degree to which group members want to stay in the group and tend to resist outside influences (such as a change in company policies). When group performance norms are high, group cohesiveness will have a positive impact on productivity. Cohesiveness tends to increase when the size of the group is small, individual and group goals are similar, the group has high status in the organization, rewards are group based rather than individual based, and the group competes with other groups within the organization. Work group cohesiveness can benefit the organization in several ways, including increased productivity, enhanced worker self-image because of group success, increased company loyalty, reduced employee turnover, and reduced absenteeism. Southwest Airlines is known for its work group cohesiveness. On the other hand, cohesiveness can also lead to restricted output, resistance to change, and conflict with other work groups in the organization.

The opportunity to turn the decision-making process over to a group with diverse skills and abilities is one of the arguments for using work groups (and teams) in organizational settings. For group decision making to be most effective, however, both managers and group members must understand its strengths and weaknesses (see Exhibit 10.8).

Work Groups versus Work Teams

work groups
The groups that share resources and coordinate efforts to help members better perform their individual jobs.

We have already noted that teams are a special type of organizational group, but we also need to differentiate between work groups and work teams. Work groups share resources and coordinate efforts to help members better perform their individual

---

Exhibit 10.8 Strengths and Weaknesses of Group Decision Making

STRENGTHS	WEAKNESSES
• Groups bring more information and knowledge to the decision process.	• Groups typically take a longer time to reach a solution than an individual takes.
• Groups offer a diversity of perspectives and, therefore, generate a greater number of alternatives.	• Group members may pressure others to conform, reducing the likelihood of disagreement.
• Group decision making results in a higher-quality decision than does individual decision making.	• The process may be dominated by one or a small number of participants.
• Participation of group members increases the likelihood that a decision will be accepted.	• Groups lack accountability, because it is difficult to assign responsibility for outcomes to any one individual.

duties and responsibilities. The performance of the group can be evaluated by adding up the contributions of the individual group members. **Work teams** require not only coordination but also collaboration, the pooling of knowledge, skills, abilities, and resources in a collective effort to attain a common goal. A work team creates synergy, causing the performance of the team as a whole to be greater than the sum of team members' individual contributions. Simply assigning employees to groups and labelling them a team does not guarantee a positive outcome. Managers and team members must be committed to creating, developing, and maintaining high-performance work teams. Factors that contribute to their success are discussed later in this section.

work teams
Like a work group, but also requires the pooling of knowledge, skills, abilities, and resources to achieve a common goal.

Types of Teams

The evolution of the team concept in organizations can be seen in three basic types of work teams: problem-solving, self-managed, and cross-functional. **Problem-solving teams** are typically made up of employees from the same department or area of expertise and from the same level of the organizational hierarchy. They meet on a regular basis to share information and discuss ways to improve processes and procedures in specific functional areas. Problem-solving teams generate ideas and alternatives and may recommend a specific course of action, but they typically do not make final decisions, allocate resources, or implement change.

problem-solving teams
Usually members of the same department who meet regularly to suggest ways to improve operations and solve specific problems.

Many organizations that experienced success by using problem-solving teams were willing to expand the team concept to allow team members greater responsibility in making decisions, implementing solutions, and monitoring outcomes. These highly autonomous groups are called **self-managed work teams**. They manage themselves without any formal supervision, taking responsibility for setting goals, planning and scheduling work activities, selecting team members, and evaluating team performance.

self-managed work teams
Teams without formal supervision that plan, select alternatives, and evaluate their own performance.

In 2006, over 70 percent of production workers were members of an empowered or self-directed work team.[7] One example is at Chrysler's pickup truck assembly plant

Making Ethical Choices

TEAM SPIRIT—OH, REALLY?

You work in the HR department of a corporation that focuses on training and organizational development. Over the next year, you will be creating a division devoted to managing virtual teams that are responsible for developing new training materials or updating existing ones. The job is organized so that you are spending your first year being mentored by your boss, the vice president of HR.

With full understanding of the benefits technology brings to virtual teams, you are also aware of the need for trust among members of virtual teams. The first project you are following is a virtual team tasked with updating one of the corporation's most sought-after guides. The HR vice president appointed all team members and assigned one person as the team leader. None of the team members knows the others, and the team leader is the only team member who has direct contact with your boss. In following the team's work, you realize that no one knows exactly what each member has contributed, because members are not in contact with each other. Their only contact is with the team leader.

Your sense is that the team leader is taking full credit for all the work. Not only is she the only one with direct contact to your boss, she lives in the same area as the corporation's headquarters. The other team members are located across the country. Your sense is confirmed when only the team leader is invited to the annual awards dinner and at the dinner receives singular acknowledgment for her work on updating the guide.

ETHICAL DILEMMA: How can the vice president of HR, and eventually you, determine whether each team member pulled his or her weight or whether the team leader had to step in to complete or redo the guide?

SOURCES: Sirkka L. Jarvenpaa and Dorothy E. Leidner, "Communication and Trust in Global Virtual Teams," *Journal of Computer-Mediated Communication*, June 1998, http://www.ascusc.org; Carla Joinson, "Managing Virtual Teams: Keeping Members on the Same Page without Being in the Same Place Poses Challenges for Managers," *HR Magazine*, June 2002, http://www.findarticles.com; and Charlene Marmer Solomon, "Managing Virtual Teams," *Workforce*, June 1, 2001, http://www.findarticles.com.

in Saltillo, Mexico, where self-directed work teams comprising 10 to 12 employees take on a set of tasks and tools, including specified maintenance, quality control, and productivity and safety jobs. Team members rotate among different tasks every few hours and are encouraged to find ways to cut time and wasted effort. Those whose jobs become redundant as a result are reassigned. Production has increased to about 38 vehicles an hour from 30, all without additional hiring or overtime.[8] A more extreme version of self-managing teams can be found at W. L. Gore, the company that invented Gore-Tex fabric and Glide dental floss. The three employees who invented Elixir guitar strings contributed their spare time to the effort and persuaded a handful of colleagues to help them improve the design. After working three years entirely on their own—without asking for any supervisory or top management permission or being subjected to any kind of oversight—the team finally sought the support of the larger company, which they needed to take the strings to market. Today, W. L. Gore's Elixir has a 35 percent market share in acoustic guitar strings.[9]

cross-functional team
Members from the same organizational level, but from different functional areas.

An adaptation of the team concept is called a **cross-functional team**. These teams are made up of employees from about the same hierarchical level, but different functional areas of the organization. Many task forces, organizational committees, and project teams are cross-functional. Often the team members work together only until they solve a given problem or complete a specific project. Cross-functional teams allow people with various levels and areas of expertise to pool their resources, develop new ideas, solve problems, and coordinate complex projects. Both problem-solving teams and self-managed teams may also be cross-functional teams. Read the Expanding Around the Globe box for an example of how General Electric is implementing—and succeeding with—global cross-functional teams.

Expanding Around the Globe

HARNESSING TALENT TO HARNESS THE WIND

Many companies boast a global workforce, but few are as skilled at mobilizing experts from diverse disciplines and locales in pursuit of a common goal as General Electric. GE executives are encouraged to think beyond the boundaries of their particular business. They come together frequently for training or joint projects. Executives are apt to move among units several times in their careers, letting them build up a rich network of internal contacts. There's also a tradition of plucking people from their day jobs for other projects. At any given time, thousands of GE employees are on so-called bubble assignments—lending their skills to another function or business that pays their salaries for the duration of the project.

James Lyons, a chief engineer at the GE Global Research Center, is the fulcrum for GE's Wind Energy project. The 30-year veteran has brought in engineers from other units and navigated cultural hurdles worldwide. He has recruited materials experts from down the hall who developed the composites for the fan blades of the GE90 aircraft engine; design teams in South Carolina and Salzbergen, Germany; engineers from Ontario, who are tackling the generators; Bangalore researchers who are drafting analytical models and turbine system design tools; and Shanghai engineers who conduct high-end simulations. Chinese researchers design the microprocessors that control the pitch of the blade. And technicians in Munich have created a smart turbine that can calculate wind speeds and signal other turbines to pitch their blades for maximum electricity production. Lyons keeps his global team focused with e-mails, teleconferences, and clear deadlines.

One way he builds team spirit is to foster familiarity. In addition to regular teleconferences, engineers take stints working in other parts of the operation. That has meant trading engineers from Bangalore and Salzbergen, for example, for a week or two at a time. Along with learning about the core design tools being created in Bangalore or the actual products being made in Salzbergen, they establish better lines of communication. With its $2 billion in annual revenues, the far-flung Wind Energy team is getting results. Among the innovations so far is a new generation of land-based wind turbines with new blade and advanced control technologies for customers who want to generate energy on sites where space is limited. One unit designed for offshore locations sits 30 storeys above the ocean, has turbine blades each longer than a football field, and can power 1,400 average American homes a year. Current projects range from a wind farm in Inner Mongolia to working on smaller turbines that could help provide clean water to villages in developing countries.[10]

Thinking Critically

1. What challenges do you think face James Lyons in managing his global Wind Energy team?
2. Would you be interested in participating in such a geographically widespread team? Why or why not?

SOURCES: Diane Brady, "Reaping the Wind: GE's Energy Initiative Is a Case Study in Innovation without Borders," *Business Week*, October 11, 2004, p. 201; Patricia Sellers, "Blowing in the Wind: To Build a Better Wind Turbine, General Electric Built a Global Team of Researchers in Germany, China, India, and the U.S.," *Fortune*, July 25, 2005, p. 130.

Apple Computer's CEO Tim Cook uses an organic structure to develop new products like the iMac computer. Organic structures allow companies like Apple to succeed in rapidly changing environments. Why else do you think that Apple has chosen an organic structure?

Building High-Performance Teams

A great team must possess certain characteristics, so selecting the appropriate employees for the team is vital. Employees who are more willing to work together to accomplish a common goal should be selected, rather than employees who are more interested in their own personal achievement. Team members should also possess a variety of skills. Diverse skills strengthen the overall effectiveness of the team, so teams should consciously recruit members to fill gaps in the collective skill set. To be effective, teams must also have clearly defined goals. Vague or unclear goals will not provide the necessary direction or allow employees to measure their performance against expectations. Next, high-performing teams need to practise good communication. Team members need to communicate messages and give appropriate feedback that seeks to correct any misunderstandings. Feedback should also be detached, that is team members should be careful to critique ideas rather than criticize the person who suggests them. Nothing can degrade the effectiveness of a team like personal attacks. Lastly, great teams have great leaders. Skilled team leaders divide work up so that tasks are not repeated, help members set and track goals, monitor their team's performance, communicate openly, and remain flexible to adapt to changing goals or management demands.

THE INFORMAL ORGANIZATION

LO7

Up to this point in the chapter, we have focused on formal organizational structures that can be seen in the boxes and lines of the organization chart. Yet many important relationships within an organization do not show up on an organization chart. Nevertheless, these relationships can affect the decisions and performance of employees at all levels of the organization.

The network of connections and channels of communication based on the informal relationships of individuals inside the organization is known as the **informal organization**. Informal relationships can be between people at the same hierarchical

informal organization
The network of connections and channels of communication based on the informal relationships of individuals inside an organization.

Smart managers understand that not all of a company's influential relationships appear on the organization chart. Off the chart, there exists a web of informal personal connections between workers, across which vital information and knowledge pass constantly. Using social network analysis software and communication-tracking tools, managers are able to map and quantify the normally invisible relationships that form between employees. How might identifying a company's informal organization aid managers in fostering teamwork, motivating employees, and boosting productivity?

level or between people at different levels and in different departments. Some connections are work-related, such as those formed among people who car-pool or ride the same train to work. Others are based on non-work commonalties, such as belonging to the same religious group or health club, or having children who attend the same school.

Functions of the Informal Organization

The informal organization has several important functions. First, it provides a source of friendships and social contact for organization members. Second, the interpersonal relationships and informal groups help employees feel better informed about and connected with what is going on in their company, thus giving them some sense of control over their work environment. Third, the informal organization can provide status and recognition that the formal organization cannot or will not provide employees. Fourth, the network of relationships can aid the socialization of new employees by informally passing along rules, responsibilities, basic objectives, and job expectations. Finally, the organizational grapevine helps employees to be more aware of what is happening in their workplace by transmitting information quickly and conveying it to places that the formal system does not reach.

Informal Communication Channels

The informal channels of communication used by the informal organization are often referred to as the grapevine, the rumour mill, or the intelligence network. Managers need to pay attention to the grapevines in their organization, because their employees increasingly put a great deal of stock in the information that travels along it. A recent survey found that many business leaders have their work cut out for them in the speeches and presentations they give employees. Survey participants were asked if they would believe a message delivered in a speech by a company leader or one that they heard over the grapevine. Forty-seven percent of those responding said they would put more credibility in the grapevine. Only 42 percent said they would believe senior leadership, and another 11 percent indicated they would believe a blend of elements from both messages.[11] Perhaps even more interesting is how accurate employees perceive their company grapevine to be: 57 percent gave it favourable ratings. "The grapevine may not be wholly accurate, but it is a very reliable indicator that something is going on," said one survey respondent.[12]

With this in mind, managers need to learn to use the existing informal organization as a tool that can potentially benefit the formal organization. An excellent way of putting the informal organization to work for the good of the company is to bring informal leaders into the decision-making process. That way, at least the people who use and nurture the grapevine will have more accurate information to send it.

THE FUTURE OF ORGANIZATIONAL STRUCTURES

LO8

To improve organizational performance and achieve long-term objectives, some organizations seek to re-engineer their business processes or adopt new technologies that open up a variety of organizational design options, such as virtual corporations and virtual teams. Other trends that have strong footholds in today's organizations include outsourcing and managing global businesses.

Re-engineering Organizational Structure

Periodically, all businesses must re-evaluate the way they do business. This includes assessing the effectiveness of the organizational structure. To meet the formidable challenges of the future, companies are increasingly turning to re-engineering—the complete redesign of business structures and processes to improve operations. An even simpler definition of re-engineering is "starting over." In effect, top management asks, "If we were a new company, how would we run this place?" The purpose of re-engineering is to identify and abandon the outdated rules and fundamental assumptions that guide current business operations. Every company has many formal and informal rules based on assumptions about technology, people, and organizational goals that no longer hold. Thus, the goal of re-engineering is to redesign business processes to achieve improvements in cost control, product quality, customer service, and speed. The re-engineering process should result in a more efficient and effective organizational structure that is better suited to the current (and future) competitive climate of the industry.

re-engineering
The complete redesign of business structures and processes to improve operations.

The Virtual Corporation

One of the greatest challenges for companies today is adapting to the technological changes that are affecting all industries. Organizations are struggling to find new organizational structures that will help them transform information technology into a competitive advantage. One alternative that is becoming increasingly prevalent is the virtual corporation, which is a network of independent companies (suppliers, customers, even competitors) linked by information technology to share skills, costs, and access to one another's markets. This network structure allows companies to come together quickly to exploit rapidly changing opportunities. These are the key attributes of a virtual corporation:

virtual corporation
A network of independent companies linked by information technology to share skills, costs, and access to one another's markets; allows the companies to come together quickly to exploit rapidly changing opportunities.

- *Technology.* Information technology helps geographically distant companies form alliances and work together.
- *Opportunism.* Alliances are less permanent, less formal, and more opportunistic than in traditional partnerships.
- *Excellence.* Each partner brings its core competencies to the alliance, so it is possible to create an organization with higher quality in every functional area and to increase competitive advantage.

- *Trust.* The network structure makes companies more reliant on one another and forces them to strengthen relationships with partners.
- *No borders.* This structure expands the traditional boundaries of an organization.

In the concept's purest form, each company that links with others to create a virtual corporation is stripped to its essence. Ideally, the virtual corporation has neither a central office nor an organization chart, no hierarchy, and no vertical integration. It contributes to an alliance only its core competencies, or key capabilities. It mixes and matches what it does best with the core competencies of other companies and entrepreneurs. For example, a manufacturer would only manufacture, while relying on a product design company to decide what to make and a marketing company to sell the end result.

Although companies that are purely virtual organizations are still relatively scarce, many companies are embracing several of the characteristics of the virtual structure. One great example is Cisco Systems. Cisco has 34 plants that produce its products, but the company owns only two of them. Human hands touch only 10 percent of customer orders. Less than half of all orders are processed by Cisco employees. To the average customer, the interdependency of Cisco's suppliers and inventory systems makes it look like one huge, seamless company.

Virtual Teams

Technology is also enabling corporations to create virtual work teams. Geography is no longer a limitation when employees are considered for a work team. Virtual teams mean reduced travel time and costs, reduced relocation expenses, and utilization of specialized talent regardless of employee location.

When managers need to staff a project, all they need to do is make a list of required skills and a general list of employees who possess those skills. When the pool of employees is known, the manager simply chooses the best mix of people and creates the virtual team. Special challenges of virtual teams include keeping team members focused, motivated, and communicating positively despite their location. If feasible, at least one face-to-face meeting during the early stages of team formation will help with these potential problems.

Outsourcing

Another organizational trend that continues to influence today's managers is outsourcing. For decades, companies have outsourced various functions. For example, payroll functions such as recording hours, benefits, wage rates, and issuing pay deposits have been handled for years by third-party providers. Today, however, outsourcing includes a much wider array of business functions: customer service, production, engineering, information technology, sales and marketing, janitorial services, maintenance, and more. Outsourcing is evolving from a trend to a way of doing business.

Companies outsource for two main reasons: cost reduction and labour needs. Often, to satisfy both requirements, companies will outsource work to companies in foreign countries. It seems that nearly every day an article in the business press mentions global outsourcing. That is because more and more companies are integrating global outsourcing into their business strategy.

Structuring for Global Mergers

Recent mergers creating mega companies raise some important questions regarding corporate structure. How can managers hope to organize the global pieces of these huge, complex new companies into a cohesive, successful whole? Should decision making be centralized or decentralized? Should the company be organized around geographic markets or product lines? And how can managers consolidate distinctly different corporate cultures? These issues and many more must be resolved if mergers of global companies are to succeed.

HOT inks

Go to
www.google.ca
and, using the search words "virtual corporation concepts," read about new approaches by Canadian companies.

Concept *in Action*

In today's high-tech world, teams can exist anyplace where there is access to a wireless network. With globalization and outsourcing on the rise, organizations are increasingly utilizing virtual teams to coordinate people and projects—often from halfway around the world. Unlike coworkers in traditional teams, members of virtual teams rarely meet in person, working from different locations and even from different continents. What practical benefits do virtual teams offer to businesses and employees?

Beyond designing a new organizational structure, one of the most difficult challenges when merging two large companies is uniting the cultures and creating a single business. Failure to effectively merge cultures can have serious effects on organizational efficiency.

Concept *Check*

How does technology enable companies to organize as virtual corporations?

What are some organizational issues that must be addressed when two large companies merge?

GREAT IDEAS TO USE NOW

How is organizational structure relevant to you? A common thread linking all of the companies profiled in this chapter is you, the consumer. Companies structure their organizations to facilitate achieving their overall organizational goals. To be profitable, companies must have a competitive advantage, and competition is based on meeting customer expectations. The company that best satisfies customer wants and demands is the company that will lead the competition.

When companies make changes to their organizational structures, they are attempting to increase in some way their ability to satisfy the customer. For example, several of the companies profiled in this chapter were consolidating or centralizing parts of their operation. Why? Those companies hope to become more efficient and reduce costs, which should translate into better customer service and more reasonable prices. Some companies are decentralizing operations, giving departments or divisions more autonomy to respond quickly to changes in the market or to be more flexible in their response to customer demands. Many companies are embracing new information technology because it brings them closer to their customers faster than was previously possible. Internet commerce is benefiting consumers in a number of ways. When you buy books at www.amazon.ca or use www.ebay.ca to sell a used bicycle, you are sending the message that the virtual company is a structure you will patronize and support. Increasing globalization and use of information technology will continue to alter the competitive landscape, and the big winner should be the consumer, in terms of increased choice, increased access, and reduced price!

Summary of Learning Outcomes

LO1 Identify the five structural building blocks that managers use to design organizations.

To build an organizational structure, companies first must divide the work into separate jobs and tasks (division of labour). Managers then group related jobs and tasks together into departments (departmentalization). Five basic types of departmentalization (see Exhibit 10.1) are commonly used in organizations:

- *Functional*: Based on the primary functions performed within an organizational unit
- *Product*: Based on the goods or services produced or sold by the organizational unit
- *Process*: Based on the production process used by the organizational unit
- *Customer*: Based on the primary type of customer served by the organizational unit
- *Geographic*: Based on the geographic segmentation of organizational units

The relationships within the organization must be established by determining how many layers of management there will be and who will report to whom (managerial hierarchy and span of control). Finally, it must be decided at what level the organizational decisions should be made (centralization/decentralization).

LO2 Examine the tools companies use to establish relationships within their organizations.

The managerial hierarchy (or the management pyramid) comprises the levels of management within the organization, and the managerial span of control is the number of employees the manager directly supervises. In daily operations, individuals in line positions are directly involved in the processes used to create goods and services. Individuals in staff positions provide the administrative and support services that line employees need to achieve the company's goals. Line positions in organizations are typically in areas such as production, marketing, and finance. Staff positions are found in areas such as legal counselling, managerial consulting, public relations, and human resource management.

LO3 Show how the degree of centralization/ decentralization can be altered to make an organization more successful.

In a highly centralized structure, top management makes most of the key decisions in the organization with very little input from lower-level employees. Centralization lets top managers develop a broad view of operations and exercise tight financial controls. In a highly decentralized organization, decision-making authority is pushed down the organizational hierarchy, giving lower-level personnel more responsibility and power to make and implement decisions. Decentralization can result in faster decision making and increased innovation and responsiveness to customer preferences.

LO4 Describe the differences between a mechanistic and organic organization.

A mechanistic organization is characterized by a relatively high degree of work specialization, rigid departmentalization, many layers of management (particularly middle management), narrow spans of control, centralized decision making, and a long chain of command. This combination of elements results in a tall organizational structure. In contrast, an organic organization is characterized by a relatively low degree of work specialization, loose departmentalization, few levels of management, wide spans of control, decentralized decision making, and a short chain of command. This combination of elements results in a flat organizational structure.

The most popular traditional organizational structure is the "line-and-staff organization." It is designed with direct, clear lines of authority and communication flowing from the top managers downward.

In recent decades, companies have begun to expand beyond traditional departmentalization methods and use matrix, committee, and team-based structures. Matrix structures combine two types of traditional organizational structures (for example, geographic and functional). Matrix structures bring together people from different functional areas of the organization to work on a special project. As such, matrix organizations are more flexible, but because employees report to two direct supervisors, managing matrix structures can be extremely challenging. Committee structures give authority and responsibility to a group rather than to an individual. Committees are part of a line-and-staff organization and often fulfill only an advisory role. Team-based structures also involve assigning authority and responsibility to groups rather than individuals, but different from committees, team-based structures give these groups autonomy to carry out their work.

Work groups share resources and coordinate efforts to help members better perform their individual duties and responsibilities. The performance of the group can be evaluated by adding up the contributions of the individual group members. Work teams require not only coordination but also collaboration, the pooling of knowledge, skills, abilities, and resources in a collective effort to attain a common goal. Four types of work teams are used: problem solving, self-managed, cross-functional, and virtual teams. Companies are using teams to improve individual and group motivation and performance.

The informal organization is the network of connections and channels of communication based on the informal relationships of individuals inside the organization. Informal relationships can be between people at the same hierarchical level or between people at different levels and in different departments. Informal organizations give employees more control over their work environment by delivering a continuous stream of company information throughout the organization, thereby helping employees stay informed.

Reengineering is a complete redesign of business structures and processes in order to improve operations in the areas of cost control, product quality, customer service, and speed.

The virtual corporation is a network of independent companies (suppliers, customers, even competitors) linked by information technology to share skills, costs, and access to one another's markets. This network structure allows companies to come together quickly to exploit rapidly changing opportunities.

Many companies are now using technology to create virtual teams. Team members may be down the hall or across the ocean. Virtual teams mean that travel time and expenses are eliminated and the best people can be placed on the team regardless of where they live. Sometimes, however, it may be difficult to keep virtual team members focused and motivated.

Outsourcing business functions—both globally and domestically—is evolving from a trend to regular business practice. Companies choose to outsource either as a cost-saving measure or as a way to gain access to needed human resource talent. To be successful, outsourcing must solve a clearly articulated business problem, and managers must closely match third-party providers with their company's actual needs.

LO5 Discuss the traditional and contemporary organizational structures companies are using.

LO6 Summarize why companies are using team-based organizational structures.

LO7 Explain how the informal organization affects the performance of the company.

LO8 List some of the trends that are influencing the way businesses organize.

Key Terms

Experiential Exercises

1. Evaluate your leadership skills. If you want to evaluate your own leadership skills, go to www.humanlinks.com/skilhome.htm and scroll down to "Managerial Skills." By taking the self-assessment quizzes offered here, you will gain insight into your ability to manage virtual teams, test your ability to think logically and analogically, and even test your perceptions about management. Companies are seeking managerial leaders who have leadership traits that will guide employees through the competitive business landscape.

2. Draw an organization chart of the company you work for, your college or university, or a campus student organization. Show the lines of authority and formal communication. Describe the informal relationships that you think are important for the success of the organization.

3. How would you restructure a large mechanistic organization to be more customer-friendly and to increase customer satisfaction? Choose a specific organization and give a detailed plan to accomplish your organizational goals.

4. Using a search engine such as Google or Yahoo! to search for the term "company organizational charts," find at least three examples of organizational charts for corporations, nonprofits, or government agencies. Analyze each entity's organizational structure. Is it organized by function, product/service, process, customer type, or geographic location?

5. At either the *Business Week,* www.businessweek.com, *Fortune,* www.fortune.com, or *Forbes,* www.forbes.com website, search the archives for stories about companies that have re-engineered. Find an example of a re-engineering effort that succeeded and one that failed and discuss why. Also visit the BPR Online Learning Center at www.prosci.com to answer the following questions: What is benchmarking and how can it help companies with business process re-engineering (BPR)? What were the key findings of the best-practices surveys for change management and benchmarking?

6. Visit the *Inc.* magazine website, www.inc.com and use the search engine to find articles about virtual corporation. Using a search engine, find the website of at

least one virtual corporation and look for information about how the company uses span of control, informal organization, and other concepts from this chapter.

7. Managing change in an organization is no easy task, as you've discovered in your new job with a consulting company that specializes in change management. To get up to speed, go to Bpubs.com, the Business Publications Search Engine, www. bpubs.com, and navigate to the Change Management section of the Management Science category. Select three articles that discuss how companies approached the change process and summarize their experiences.

8. After managing your first project team, you think you might enjoy a career in project management. The Project Management Institute is a professional organization for project managers. Its website, www.pmi.org, has many resources about this field. Start at the Professional Practices section to learn what project management is, then go to the professional Development and Careers pages. What are the requirements to earn the Project Management Professional designation? Explore other free areas of the site to learn more about the job of project manager. Prepare a brief report on the career and its opportunities. Does what you've learned make you want to follow this career path?

Review Questions

1. What is division of labour? Specialization?
2. What does the organizational chart show?
3. What are the five basic types of departmentalization that are commonly found in organizations?
4. What is managerial hierarchy? Span of control (span of management)?
5. What is the difference between a centralized and decentralized organization?
6. What are a line organization, line-and-staff organization, committee structure, and matrix structure?
7. What is the informal organization? What are its functions?
8. What is a virtual corporation? What are virtual teams?

CREATIVE THINKING CASE

Reitmans Structure Case

Go into any power centre or shopping mall in Canada and you will see a Reitmans and probably more than one of their banners. Reitmans (Canada) Ltd. operates more than 950 stores under the names Reitmans, Smart Set, RW & CO., Thyme Maternity, Cassis, Penningtons, and Addition Elle. The total number of stores has declined a bit, but profits are strong and the stock price is going up. Herman and Sarah Reitman set up a small department store in Montreal in the early 1900s, opened a second store in 1926, incorporated in 1947, and set up the current structure in 1980.

The company sells women's apparel, moderately priced; most of the goods are private label (their own brands). Private labels can offer higher quality at a lower price than "name brands." The goods are made all over the world, including some sewn in Canada. The various store names (banners) are targeted to different consumer groups. Young women might not want to shop at Penningtons but love Cassis. Over time, new banners are struck and some of the old ones fade away. Your mom might remember Dalmys, Antels, or Cactus, all banners that have been abandoned since the 1990s. The latest trend is online retailing; each banner has its own e-store.

Reitmans describes itself as a large publicly traded company with a strong family culture. The list of directors (H. Jonathan Birks, Samuel Minzberg, Howard Stotland, Stephen J. Kauser, Jeremy H. Reitman, John J. Swidler, Max Konigsberg, Stephen F. Reitman, and Robert S. Vineberg) includes two direct descendants of the founders. Notice anything about the list?

Most retailers operate an in-store system similar to Reitmans. The entry positions are sales associates who are organized into teams, which may have a team leader. Assistant managers open and close stores, and each store will have a manager who is responsible for that location. Above the store managers are district managers and a central staff in Montréal responsible for the brand. All product is distributed through a central warehouse, also in Montréal. In total, Reitmans has about 11,000 employees, 7,000 of whom are part-time.

If you drop by a Reitmans store (any banner), you will see that the customers are mostly women. The staff are almost all women. Reitmans promotes from within, so the chances are good that the team leaders, assistant manager, and manager (the full-time positions) are women. This trend continues into the district management and more than 50 percent of the banner vice-presidents are women. Five of seven banner presidents are women. But, only three of fourteen corporate staff are women and, as you should have noticed, all the company directors are men (September 1, 2011 data). *The Globe and Mail* reported in early 2011 that only 42 percent of senior officers at Reitmans were women.

Should this matter? Organizational structure may be reflected in employee morale and perception of the company. Employee attitudes can have an impact on customer satisfaction and sales. Employees sometimes tell their stories on the Internet. The words of Reitmans employees seem to be mixed. Many employees report that it's a great place to work with flexible hours, a great bonus plan, and a family feel. (The word "gossip" figures prominently.) Others complain that they are required to buy the latest styles and wear them to work. One employee said she had four different managers, seven assistant managers, and four team leaders in less than four years working in the same store. Through the four years she was paid the same wage as the newest employees.

These last comments are a common complaint in the retail sector where reliance on part-timers is central to the profitability of the company. In high unemployment, part-timers are easily replaced but quality can be negatively impacted by high turnover and inconsistent training.

Thinking Critically

1. Describe the corporate structure at Reitmans. Can you draw an organization chart?

2. What alternative structures could be tried at Reitmans?

3. Do you think the gender mix of the organization could be a problem?

4. Do the comments suggest anything about an informal organization at Reitmans? At the corporate level? At the store level?

5. Would you describe Reitmans structure as organic? Why or why not?

SOURCES: Jantzi, "Corporate Social Responsibility Ranking," *The Globe and Mail*, April 3, 2009; RateMyEmployer.ca, "Reitmans (Canada) Limited," http://www.ratemyemployer.ca/employer/employer.aspx?l=en&empID=962; Reitmans, "Annual Information Form," Montreal, 2010; Reitmans, "Annual Information Form," Montreal, 2011; Reitmans, "Annual Report," Montreal, 1998; Reitmans, "The Reitmans Story," http://www.reitmans.ca/about/the_company.aspx?lang=en.

Making the Connection

Motivating Employees

In this chapter, we'll look at the third step in the process of management—*motivating* employees toward the accomplishment of organizational goals. As we saw in Chapter 10, *organizational* structures are designed to support the accomplishment of the overall *plans* of the company. But these plans cannot be accomplished, appropriate structure or not, if the individuals responsible for their implementation are not committed to the outcome. As we've said numerous times, without the final critical success factor—*gaining employee commitment*—none of the critical success factors can be accomplished. This is, therefore, perhaps our most important management function but, unfortunately, also one of the most difficult. We're dealing with human beings, not push-button machines, and, therefore, it is extremely important that managers understand what makes people tick and treat them in a way that recognizes how important they are to the organization's success. As Richard Varela of Island Pacific Adventures states in the opening vignette, special people are what separates Island Pacific from its competitors in the guided tour market. And how does that happen? "You invest in your employees. You treat them as number one. And you celebrate in their successes."

It's easy to see how important it is to gain the commitment of your employees. Have you ever walked into a restaurant, gone up to a service counter in a store, or called a company's customer service department on the phone and been served by an employee who didn't appear to be overjoyed to answer your questions? Most of us have. The important question here is—did you just assume that the employee was having a bad day and not let it affect your perception of the company, or did it enter your mental database and register as a less-than-pleasurable experience with that company as a whole? Probably the latter. We all see our contact with employees in different companies as a contact with the company, and one

employee's attitude as the company's attitude—consciously or not. As customers, we see it in a very integrative way—we see it as the whole company. As managers in that company, we need to recognize that and focus on understanding our employees' needs to gain their commitment. Recent research, discussed in this chapter, demonstrates that employee turnover has a significant impact on customer satisfaction. Employee turnover results when employee commitment is low; therefore, the higher the commitment, the greater the likelihood that customer needs will be met. Again, our opening vignette is a great example of this. Varela recognizes that "positive word of mouth is the result of customer satisfaction, which in turn is a result of employee motivation." Varela believes that selecting the right employees is key to his company's success. He clearly sees the connection between employee commitment and *meeting customer needs*, and inevitably the *financial performance* of the company.

In this chapter, we discuss different motivation theories that will help you understand what motivates individuals to work harder to please the customer. But everyone is different. Therefore, a manager must play a truly integrative role here. He or she must see each employee as an individual but also in the context of how that person fits into the larger organization. Managers must integrate the different theories to find a style that works both for them and for their employees. They must also consider how their different policies in each of the functional areas affect their employees. It is very difficult to gain someone's true commitment to a job if they don't believe in what the organization is doing—if they feel its *marketing* is disingenuous, its *financial* policies are unfair, or its *operations* are unsafe, for example. Just as it is essential that managers understand how to gain the commitment of all of the different individuals that make up their team, as many different personalities are needed to make a successful business work, it is also important to remember that these people with different skills and motivations must work together as one within an organization they believe in.

You'll learn that when a company shows commitment to its employees, it gets commitment in return—something discovered initially through the Hawthorne experiments, when researchers saw that employees performed better when they felt that management was concerned for their welfare. A commitment to education and training—one of the trends in employee motivation discussed in the chapter—goes a long way toward showing employees that they are valued and that the organization is a place where they can grow to their full potential. The trends of employee ownership and work–life benefits are other examples.

Remember as you learn the different theories of motivation to keep in mind that the manager's job here is to gain employee commitment to achieve the other factors critical to a successful business. Each of the success factors is achieved through people, and thus the people at all levels in the organization must be motivated to achieve these success factors. They must be committed to the organization's success for it to happen.

One factor not discussed so far, but integral to achieving this success, is the external environment. The external environment can and does have concrete implications on the work environment, as well as affecting the mindset that people bring to work every day, thereby affecting their levels of motivation. Managers must therefore take into consideration the elements in the external environment that might affect employee motivation. Examples are the *political* environment and its effect on legislation pertaining to employment standards; the *economy* and its effect on job security and levels of pay; the *social* environment and the resulting expectations that people have regarding the work environment and the policies of the company toward things like sustainability, for example; and the *technological* environment and how it changes the demands of different jobs. One obvious instance of the effect of the environment that is discussed in the chapter is the effect of culture on motivation. The societal culture of different countries makes certain motivation theories inapplicable. As a company hires a more diverse workforce, it gains the benefit of a better understanding of its diverse customers—especially if it competes in the *international* marketplace—but it also becomes even more necessary to understand workers' individualities to gain their commitment to work toward the goals of the organization.

chapter 11

Motivating Employees

LEARNING OUTCOMES

1 Explain the basic principles of Frederick Taylor's concept of scientific management.

2 Summarize what Elton Mayo's Hawthorne studies revealed about worker motivation.

3 Discuss Maslow's hierarchy of needs and Clayton Alderfer's ERG theory of motivation, and how these needs relate to employee motivation.

4 Identify how McGregor's Theories X and Y and Ouchi's Theory Z are used to explain worker motivation.

5 Explain the basic components of Herzberg's motivator-hygiene theory.

6 Describe how three contemporary theories of employee motivation offer insights into improving employee performance.

7 Discuss how managers can redesign existing jobs to increase employee motivation and performance.

8 List some of the initiatives organizations are using today to motivate and retain employees.

ISLAND PACIFIC ADVENTURES INVESTS IN ITS EMPLOYEES

Island Pacific Adventures offers tours and expeditions into caves at Horne Lake on Vancouver Island, but founder Richard Varela says the tours aren't really the company's product. The valuable commodity the company actually offers customers is time with its guides. Varela believes these special people are what separates Island Pacific from its competitors in the guided tour market. And how does that happen? "You invest in your employees. You treat them as number one. And you celebrate in their successes," he says.

Think about the last time you went on vacation to a new place and wanted to know what to do and see. You might first search the Internet for information about the destination. When you get there you might visit the tourist centre or brochure racks in the hotel lobby. The next step could be to ask someone—and that's where "word of mouth" promotion comes into play. Varela recognizes that positive word of mouth is the result of customer satisfaction, which in turn is a result of employee motivation. And selecting the right employees is Varela's key to success.

He hires from local colleges and universities, looking for candidates whose goals fit with the kinds of employment he can offer. Varela spends most of the interview learning about what the student wants from a job. He will pass on candidates with perfect education and experience if they want higher pay, different hours, or more authority than Island Pacific Adventures offers. He knows they won't be happy in the job.

As a result, new hires may not know everything about guiding in caves. But Island Pacific uses peer-based training to increase the effectiveness of the whole team. Once a week, the staff gathers at what's called a TNT session—Tuesday Night Training—for pizza, beer, and learning. Sessions are lead by employees making presentations on skills at which they excel. This peer-based training communicates the idea that every employee can do the job, and reminds new staff members that one day they will be leading these discussions.

That day comes quickly, since 30 to 40 high school students join Island Pacific Adventures every fall as volunteers, and first-year employees train and supervise these teens. Passing knowledge along is a great way to reinforce training, so the rookie staffers and the students learn together.

Work at the company is fun, too. Guides meet new people, get out into the fresh air, explore some of North America's deepest and longest caves, and see incredible rock crystal formations. The TNT sessions are part of this

PHOTO COURTESY OF LEE WHITE AND HORNE LAKE REGIONAL AND PROVINCIAL PARKS

atmosphere, featuring camaraderie and activities that connect with college-aged employees.

Island Pacific rewards achievement, too, but not with cash. Eligible employees draw a prize randomly from a bag. The items are donated, with the young people in mind, by local merchants. A $20 bonus is spent quickly, but a $20 backpack is used all winter.

As this company's experience shows, success comes from motivated staff and volunteers. Smart managers recognize that their customers have choices. The same product may be available next door, but it's motivated employees who love their work and are having fun that make the difference.[1]

THINKING CRITICALLY

As you read this chapter, consider the following questions:

1. What is the correlation between motivated employees and productivity?

2. What are some strategies companies can use to motivate employees?

SOURCES: www.hornelake.com/pdfs/RV%20West.pdf/; www.hornelake.com/; www.go2hr. ca/ForbrEmployers/BCSuccessStories/HorneLakeAdventures/tabid/993/Default.aspx/; www. hornelake.com/waiver.pdf/; www.hornelake.com/volunteers.htm/; Used with permission from Horne Lake Regional and Provincial Parks.

motivation
Something that prompts a person to release his or her energy in a certain direction.

need
The gap between what is and what is required.

want
The gap between what is and what is desired.

intrinsic rewards
The rewards that are part of the job itself.

extrinsic rewards
The rewards that are external to the job.

People can be a company's most important resource. They can also be the most challenging resource to manage well. Employees who are motivated and work hard to achieve personal and organizational goals can become a crucial competitive advantage for a company. The key then is to understand the process of motivation, what motivates individuals, and how an organization can create a workplace that allows people to perform to the best of their abilities. *Motivation* is the set of forces that prompt a person to release energy in a certain direction. As such, motivation is essentially a need- and want-satisfying process. A *need* is best defined as the gap between what is and what is required. Similarly, a *want* is the gap between what is and what is desired. Unsatisfied needs and wants create a state of tension that pushes (motivates) individuals to practise behaviour that will result in the need being met or the want being fulfilled. That is, motivation is what pushes us to move from where we are to where we want to be because expending that effort will result in some kind of reward.

Rewards can be divided into two basic categories: intrinsic and extrinsic. *Intrinsic rewards* are part of the job and are valued by the individual; things such as satisfaction, contentment, a sense of accomplishment, confidence, and pride. By contrast, *extrinsic rewards* are external to the job and valued by the individual, including pay raises, promotions, bonuses, prestigious assignments, and so forth. It is important to note that for the rewards to be a motivating factor they must be valued by the individual. Exhibit 11.1 illustrates the motivation process.

Successful managers are able to marshal the forces to motivate employees to achieve organizational goals. And just as there are many types of gaps between where organizations are and where they want to be, there are many motivational theories from which managers can draw to inspire employees to bridge those gaps. In this chapter, we will first examine motivational theories that grew out of the industrial revolution and early ideas of organizational psychology. Then we will examine

Exhibit 11.1 Model of Motivation

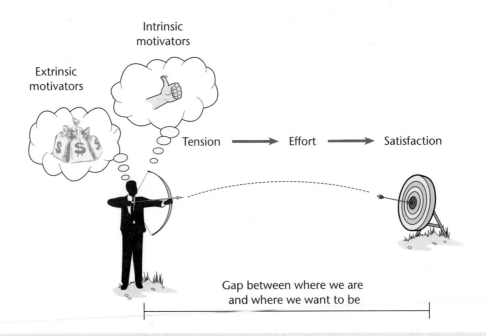

needs-based theories and more contemporary ideas about employee motivation like equity, expectancy, goals, and reinforcement theories. Finally, we will show you how managers are applying these theories in real-world situations.

EARLY THEORIES OF MOTIVATION

How can managers and organizations promote enthusiastic job performance, high productivity, and job satisfaction? Many studies of human behaviour in organizations have contributed to our current understanding of these issues. A look at the evolution of management theory and research shows how managers have arrived at the practices used today to manage human behaviour in the workplace. We will discuss a sampling of the most influential of these theorists and research studies in this section.

FREDERICK TAYLOR'S SCIENTIFIC MANAGEMENT

LO1

One of the most influential figures of the classical era of management, which lasted from about 1900 to the mid-1930s, was Frederick W. Taylor, a mechanical engineer sometimes called the "father of **scientific management**." Taylor's approach to improved performance was based on economic incentives and the premise that there is "one best way" to perform any job. As a manager at the Midvale and Bethlehem Steel companies in Philadelphia in the early 1900s, Taylor was frustrated at the inefficiency of the labourers working in the mills.

Convinced that productivity could be improved, Taylor studied the individual jobs in the mill and redesigned the equipment and the methods used by workers. Taylor timed each job with a stopwatch and broke down every task into separate movements. He then prepared an instruction sheet telling exactly how each job should be done, how much time it should take, and what motions and tools should be used. Taylor's ideas led to dramatic increases in productivity in the steel mills and resulted in the development of four basic principles of scientific management:

scientific management
A system of management developed by Frederick W. Taylor and based on four principles: developing a scientific approach for each element of a job, scientifically selecting and training workers, encouraging cooperation between workers and managers, and dividing work and responsibility between management and workers according to who can better perform a particular task.

1. Develop a scientific approach for each element of a person's job.
2. Scientifically select, train, teach, and develop workers.
3. Encourage cooperation between workers and managers, so that each job can be accomplished in a standard, scientifically determined way.
4. Divide work and responsibility between management and workers according to who is better suited to each task.

Taylor published his ideas in *The Principles of Scientific Management*. His pioneering work vastly increased production efficiency and contributed to the specialization of labour and the assembly line method of production. Taylor's approach is still being used nearly a century later in companies such as United Parcel Service (UPS), where industrial engineers maximize efficiency by carefully studying every step of the delivery process, looking for the quickest possible way to deliver packages to customers. Though Taylor's work was a giant step forward in the evolution of management, it had a fundamental flaw in that it assumed that all people are motivated primarily by economic factors. Taylor's successors in the study of management found that motivation is much more complex than he envisioned.

THE HAWTHORNE STUDIES

LO2

The classical era of management was followed by the *human relations era*, which began in the 1930s and focused primarily on how human behaviour and relations affect organizational performance. The new era was ushered in by the Hawthorne studies,

Henry Ford incorporated Taylor's scientific management principles to develop a mass production manufacturing system that produced the Model T car. The team responsible for the process first developed a materials list (all the parts needed to produce the Model T) and then decided how the production process would take place. How did incorporating the principles of scientific management increase the efficiencies of mass production?

© BETTMANN/CORBIS

Hawthorne effect
The phenomenon that employees perform better when they feel singled out for attention or feel that management is concerned about their welfare.

which changed the way many managers thought about motivation, job productivity, and employee satisfaction. The studies began when engineers at the Hawthorne Western Electric plant decided to examine the effects of varying levels of light on worker productivity—an experiment that might have interested Frederick Taylor. The engineers expected brighter light to lead to increased productivity, but the results showed that varying the level of light in either direction (brighter or dimmer) led to increased output from the experimental group. In 1927, the Hawthorne engineers asked Harvard professor Elton Mayo and a team of researchers to join them in their investigation.

From 1927 to 1932, Mayo and his colleagues conducted experiments on job redesign, length of workday and workweek, length of break times, and incentive plans. The results of the studies indicated that improvements in performance were tied to a complex set of employee attitudes. Mayo claimed that both experimental and control groups from the plant had developed a sense of group pride because they had been selected to participate in the studies. The pride that came from this special attention motivated the workers to increase their productivity. Supervisors who allowed the employees to have some control over their situation appeared to increase the workers' motivation further. These findings gave rise to what is now known as the Hawthorne effect, which suggests that employees will perform better when they feel singled out for special attention or feel that management is concerned about employee welfare. The studies also provided evidence that informal work groups (the social relationships of employees) and the resulting group pressures have positive effects on group productivity. The results of the Hawthorne studies enhanced our understanding of what motivates individuals in the workplace. They indicate that, in addition to the personal economic needs emphasized in the classical era, social needs play an important role in influencing work-related attitudes and behaviours.

MASLOW'S HIERARCHY OF NEEDS

Another well-known theorist from the behavioural era of management history, psychologist Abraham Maslow, proposed a theory of motivation based on universal human needs. Maslow believed that each individual has a hierarchy of needs, consisting of physiological, safety, social, esteem, and self-actualization needs, as shown in Exhibit 11.2.

Maslow's theory of motivation contends that people act to satisfy their unmet needs. When you're hungry, for instance, you look for and eat food, thus satisfying a basic physiological need. Once a need is satisfied, its importance to the individual diminishes, and a higher level need is more likely to motivate the person.

According to **Maslow's hierarchy of needs**, the most basic human needs are physiological needs, that is, the needs for food, shelter, and clothing. In large part, it is the physiological needs that motivate a person to find a job. People need to earn money to provide food, shelter, and clothing for themselves and their families. Once people have met these basic needs, they reach the second level in Maslow's hierarchy, which is safety needs. People need to feel secure, to be protected from physical harm, and to avoid the unexpected. In work terms, they need job security and protection from work hazards. Many companies provide their permanent employees with the job security they need by having no-layoff policies.[2] When times are good, these companies are careful about bloating the workforce; and when times are bad, they use creative ways to keep the staff working until business improves.

Physiological needs and safety are physical needs. Once these are satisfied, individuals focus on needs that involve relationships with other people. At Maslow's

Maslow's hierarchy of needs
A theory of motivation developed by Abraham Maslow; it holds that humans have five levels of needs and act to satisfy their unmet needs. At the base of the hierarchy are fundamental physiological needs, followed in order by safety, social, esteem, and self-actualization needs.

Exhibit 11.2 Maslow's Hierarchy of Needs

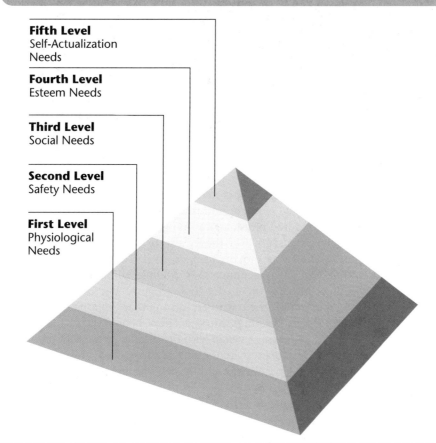

Fifth Level
Self-Actualization
Needs

Fourth Level
Esteem Needs

Third Level
Social Needs

Second Level
Safety Needs

First Level
Physiological
Needs

© CORBIS/GLOW IMAGES

third level are social needs, or needs for belonging (acceptance by others) and for giving and receiving friendship and love. Informal social groups on and off the job help people satisfy these needs. At the fourth level in Maslow's hierarchy are esteem needs, which are needs for the respect of others and for a sense of accomplishment and achievement. Satisfaction of these needs is reflected in feelings of self-worth. Praise and recognition from managers and others in the company contribute to the sense of self-worth.

Finally, at the highest level in Maslow's hierarchy are self-actualization needs, or needs for fulfillment, for living up to one's potential, and for using one's abilities to the utmost. Many mid- and upper-level managers, who have satisfied all of the lower order needs, are driven by very personal self-actualization goals.

Managers who accept Maslow's ideas attempt to improve employee motivation by modifying organizational and managerial practices to increase the likelihood that employees will meet all levels of needs. Maslow's theory has also helped managers understand that it is hard to motivate people by appealing to already satisfied needs. For instance, overtime pay might not motivate employees who earn a high wage and value their leisure time.

Maslow's theory is not without criticism, however. Maslow claimed that a higher level need was not activated until a lower-level need was met. He also claimed that a satisfied need is not a motivator. A farmer who has plenty to eat is not motivated by more food (the physiological hunger need). Research has not verified these principles in any strict sense. The theory also concentrates on moving up the hierarchy without fully addressing moving back down it. The theory does not distinguish between the differences across cultures. For example, some cultures put social needs before all the others. Also, the theory does not recognize that some people choose to have careers that do not provide them with an earning that supports the basic needs (e.g., an actor that does little paid acting). Another criticism of Maslow's theory is that studies have shown that there is some overlap with the middle levels; they are not as distinct as the model shows. Despite these limitations, Maslow's ideas are very helpful for understanding the needs of people at work and for determining what can be done to satisfy them.

Alderfer's ERG Theory

To align Maslow's theory mostly closely to empirical research, Clayton Alderfer developed the **ERG theory** (Existence, Relatedness, Growth). **Existence** relates to the

ERG theory
A theory of motivation developed by Clayton Alderfer that better supports empirical research than Maslow's hierarchy of needs theory. The three components of the model are existence, relatedness, and growth.

existence
The concern for basic material existent motivators.

Exhibit 11.3 Alderfer's ERG Theory

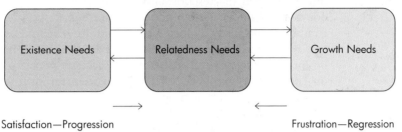

Satisfaction—Progression   Frustration—Regression

SOURCE: http://www.envisionsoftware.com/articles/erg_theory.html. Used with permission from David Russell and Envision Software, Inc.

concern with basic material existent motivators. **Relatedness** concerns interpersonal relations. **Growth** relates to personal growth. Exhibit 11.3 shows Alderfer's ERG theory.

The existence needs are similar to Maslow's physiological and safety needs. The relatedness needs are similar to social and external esteem needs in Maslow's theory. The growth stage is comparable to Maslow's self-actualization and internal esteem needs. The differences between the two theories include the following:

- Alderfer recognizes that there can be overlap of needs.
- Maslow allows for only one need to be pursued at one time; Alderfer allows for different levels being pursued simultaneously.
- ERG theory accounts for differences in cultures and better explains that there are different need orders for different people.
- Maslow assumes that people will stay at one level and then move on to the next (progression-satisfaction model). Alderfer acknowledges that if a higher-order need is not met and the person becomes frustrated, the person will want to increase satisfaction by moving to a lower-order need (frustration-regression model).

relatedness
The concern for interpersonal relations.

growth
The concern for personal growth.

HOT *links*

How do you keep employees satisfied? The Business Research Lab has a series of articles on this topic at www.busreslab.com/tips/tipses.htm

MCGREGOR'S THEORIES X AND Y

LO4

Douglas McGregor, one of Maslow's students, influenced the study of motivation with his formulation of two contrasting sets of assumptions about human nature—Theory X and Theory Y.

The **Theory X** management style is based on a pessimistic view of human nature and assumes the following:

- The average person dislikes work and will avoid it if possible.
- Because people don't like to work, they must be controlled, directed, or threatened with punishment to get them to make an effort.
- The average person prefers to be directed, avoids responsibility, is relatively lacking in ambition, and wants security above all else.

This view of people suggests that managers must constantly prod workers to perform and must closely control their on-the-job behaviour. Theory X managers tell people what to do, are very directive, like to be in control, and show little confidence in employees. They often foster dependent, passive, and resentful subordinates.

In contrast, a **Theory Y** management style is based on a more optimistic view of human nature and assumes the following:

- Work is as natural as play or rest. People want to and can be self-directed and self-controlled and will try to achieve organizational goals they believe in.
- Workers can be motivated by using positive incentives and will try hard to accomplish organizational goals if they believe they will be rewarded for doing so.
- Under proper conditions, the average person not only accepts responsibility but seeks it out. Most workers have a relatively high degree of imagination and creativity and are willing to help solve problems.

Theory X
A management style formulated by Douglas McGregor that is based on a pessimistic view of human nature and assumes that the average person dislikes work, will avoid it if possible, prefers to be directed, avoids responsibility, and wants security above all.

Theory Y
A management style formulated by Douglas McGregor that is based on a relatively optimistic view of human nature; assumes that the average person wants to work, accepts responsibility, is willing to help solve problems, and can be self-directed and self-controlled.

Managers who operate on Theory Y assumptions recognize individual differences and encourage workers to learn and develop their skills. An administrative assistant might be given the responsibility for generating a monthly report. The reward for doing so might be recognition at a meeting, a special training class to enhance computer skills, or a pay increase. In short, the Theory Y approach builds on the idea that worker and organizational interests are the same. The SAS Institute, a leader in business intelligence and analytics, has successfully created a corporate culture based on Theory Y assumptions. With a four percent turnover rate and a recruitment ratio of 200 applicants for each open position, the success of this culture is evident. VP Human Resources Jeff Chambers claims that employee retention has more to do with the company's environment than any other factor:

"The two key concepts are flexibility and trust. We have a flat organizational structure so usually an employee is no more than four to five levels away from the CEO. And we treat people like adults and allow them to do their jobs. We hire hard and then manage easy. Just leave them alone and trust them to do the right thing for the company."[3]

Theory Z

Theory Z
A theory developed by William Ouchi that combines North American and Japanese business practices by emphasizing long-term employment, slow career development, moderate specialization, group decision making, individual responsibility, relatively informal control over the employee, and concern for workers.

William Ouchi (pronounced O Chee), a management scholar at the University of California, Los Angeles, has proposed a theory that combines North American and Japanese business practices. He calls it Theory Z. Exhibit 11.4 compares the traditional North American and Japanese management styles with the Theory Z approach. Theory Z emphasizes long-term employment, slow career development, moderate specialization, group decision making, individual responsibility, relatively informal control over the employee, and concern for workers. Theory Z has many Japanese elements, but reflects North American cultural values.

Exhibit 11.4 Differences in Management Approaches

FACTOR	TRADITIONAL NORTH AMERICAN MANAGEMENT	JAPANESE MANAGEMENT	THEORY Z (COMBINATION OF NORTH AMERICAN AND JAPANESE MANAGEMENT)
Length of employment	Relatively short term; worker subject to layoffs if business is bad	Lifetime; layoffs never used to reduce costs	Long term but not necessarily lifetime; layoffs "inappropriate"; stable, loyal workforce; improved business conditions don't require new hiring and training
Rate of evaluation and promotion	Relatively rapid	Relatively slow	Slow by design; manager thoroughly trained and evaluated
Specialization in a functional area	Considerable; worker acquires expertise in single functional area	Minimal; worker acquires expertise in organization instead of functional areas	Moderate; all experience various functions of the organization and have a sense of what's good for the company rather than for a single area
Decision making	On individual basis	Input from all concerned parties	Group decision making for better decisions and easier implementation
Responsibility for success or failure	Assigned to individual	Shared by group	Assigned to individual
Control by manager	Very explicit and formal	More implicit and informal	Relatively informal but with explicit performance measures
Concern for workers	Focuses on work-related aspects of worker's life	Extends to whole life of worker	Is relatively concerned with worker's whole life, including the family

SOURCE: Based on information from Jerry D. Johnson, Austin College. Dr. Johnson was a research assistant for William Ouchi.

In the past decade, admiration for Japanese management philosophy, which centres on creating long-term relationships, has declined. The cultural beliefs of groupthink, of not taking risks, and of employees not thinking for themselves, are passé. Such conformity has limited Japanese competitiveness in the global marketplace. Today, there is a realization that Japanese companies need to be more proactive and nimble to prosper.

The average profitability of a Japanese company on the Tokyo Stock Exchange declined from about 9 to 1 percent in the past decade. This is often attributed partially to Japanese management philosophy. Sony, Hitachi, and other big companies are moving away from lifetime employment and now emphasize information disclosure, profitability, and management accountability.

HERZBERG'S MOTIVATOR-HYGIENE THEORY

LO5

Another important contribution to our understanding of individual motivation came from Frederick Herzberg's studies, which addressed the question, "What do people really want from their work experience?" In the late 1950s, Herzberg surveyed numerous employees to find out what particular work elements made them feel exceptionally good or bad about their jobs. The results indicated that certain job factors are consistently related to employee job satisfaction, whereas others can create job dissatisfaction. According to Herzberg, **motivating factors** (also called *job satisfiers*) are primarily intrinsic job elements that lead to satisfaction. **Hygiene factors** (also called *job dissatisfiers*) are extrinsic elements of the work environment. A summary of motivating and hygiene factors appears in Exhibit 11.5.

One of the most interesting results of Herzberg's studies was the implication that the opposite of satisfaction is not dissatisfaction. Herzberg believed that proper management of hygiene factors could prevent employee dissatisfaction, but that these factors could not serve as a source of satisfaction or motivation. Good working conditions, for instance, will keep employees at a job but won't make them work harder. Poor working conditions, which are job dissatisfiers, on the other hand, might make employees quit. According to Herzberg, a manager who wants to increase employee satisfaction needs to focus on the motivating factors, or satisfiers. A job with many satisfiers will usually motivate workers, provide job satisfaction, and prompt effective performance, but a lack of job satisfiers doesn't always lead to dissatisfaction and poor performance. Instead, a lack of job satisfiers might merely lead to workers doing an adequate job rather than their best.

Although Herzberg's ideas have been widely read and his recommendations implemented at numerous companies over the years, there are some very legitimate concerns about his work. Although his findings have been used to explain employee motivation, his studies actually focused on job satisfaction, a different concept from motivation,

motivating factors
Intrinsic job elements that lead to worker satisfaction.

hygiene factors
Extrinsic elements of the work environment that do not serve as a source of employee satisfaction or motivation.

HOT *links*

What are ways to motivate your employees without raising their pay?
Visit www.biztrain.com/motivation/stories/20ways.htm

Concept *Check*

What did Elton Mayo's studies reveal about employee productivity?

How can a manager use an understanding of Maslow's hierarchy to motivate employees?

How do the Theory X, Theory Y, and Theory Z management styles differ?

What is the difference between Herzberg's hygiene factors and motivating factors?

Exhibit 11.5	Herzberg's Motivating and Hygiene Factors

MOTIVATING FACTORS	HYGIENE FACTORS
Achievement	Company policy
Recognition	Supervision
Work itself	Working conditions
Responsibility	Interpersonal relationships at work
Advancement	Salary and benefits
Growth	Job security

Concept in Action

Being square has been a hip competitive advantage for on-site tech-support company Geek Squad since 1994. The company's 24-hour computer-support taskforce consists of uniformed double agents in squad-car-painted geekmobiles on a critical mission: to save frantic customers from computer viruses, crashes, and the blue screen of death. According to Herzberg's motivator-hygiene theory, what effect might Geek Squad's artfully geeky work environment have on employee satisfaction?

Sustainable Business, Sustainable World

PEPSICO

Maybe you're a Coke drinker, but after you read this you might change your mind, or at least change your mind about the type of company you'll want to work for …

If you look on PepsiCo's website under Careers, you'll see a section titled "Why Work @ PepsiCo." There, you will find under "Culture" the words "Performance with Purpose." Those words mean a lot to PepsiCo and are a big part of why employees are motivated to perform. In the company's words: "Blaze new trails. Never settle for second best. Succeed together, celebrate and do something bigger. That's what performing with purpose is all about. Around the world, we're committed to giving people the taste they crave and the nutrition they need. We dream globally and act locally—constantly innovating to sustain our planet, our people, our communities and our business practices. New markets mean new ways of doing business, and new ways of addressing health concerns, cultural differences and environmental challenges. Every day is an adventure, and an opportunity for personal and professional growth."

The research is clear on this—workers today want to go to work, and are motivated to work harder in organizations where they feel they are making a difference—not just somewhere they will get a paycheque. Companies that commit to sustainable business practices are these kinds of companies, where you can feel that your performance does indeed have a purpose.

In terms of sustainability, performance with purpose at PepsiCo means "delivering sustainable growth by investing in a healthier future for people and our planet." In its "Values & Philosophy" the company says: "We are committed to delivering sustained growth through empowered people acting responsibly and building trust."

This commitment is reflected in several areas of PepsiCo's stated purpose: human sustainability—encouraging people to live healthier; environmental sustainability—protecting the Earth's natural resources; talent sustainability—investing in employees to help them succeed; responsible and sustainable sourcing—improving procurement practices around the globe; the PepsiCo Foundation—providing grants to organizations in the areas of health, environment, and education; PepsiCo contributions—funding programs, organizations, and disaster assistance efforts focused on underserved populations; and made transparent through sustainability reporting—detailing the company's impacts and achievements.

Sustainability efforts motivate employees to work harder as it means that effort has a purpose, and PepsiCo exemplifies this in every way.

Thinking Critically

1. Do you think people really care about a company's sustainability efforts or do you think that money is the bigger motivator?
2. Have you thought about the kind of company you want to work for, or the kind of business you want to build? Is it one where you will find rewarding work that is meaningful to you and where you can make a difference in the world? Check out Pepsi's Refresh Project at www.refresheverything.com and see how you can start making a difference today!

SOURCE: http://www.pepsico.com. Used with permission from PepsiCo.

though related to it. Other criticisms focus on the unreliability of Herzberg's method, the fact that the theory ignores the impact of situational variables, and the assumed relationship between satisfaction and productivity. Nevertheless, the questions raised by Herzberg about the nature of job satisfaction and the effects of intrinsic and extrinsic factors on employee behaviour have proved a valuable contribution to the evolution of theories of motivation and job satisfaction.

CONTEMPORARY VIEWS ON MOTIVATION **LO6**

The early management scholars laid a foundation that enabled managers to understand their workers better and how best to motivate them. Since then, new theories have given us an even deeper understanding of worker motivation. Three of these theories are explained in this section: the expectancy theory, the equity theory, and the goal-setting theory.

Expectancy Theory

One of the best-supported and most widely accepted theories of motivation is expectancy theory, which focuses on the link between motivation and behaviour. According to **expectancy theory**, the probability that an individual will act in a particular way depends on how strongly that person believes the act will have a particular outcome, and on whether they value that outcome. The degree to which an employee is motivated depends on three important relationships, shown in Exhibit 11.6.

1. The link between *effort and performance*, or the strength of the individual's expectation that a certain amount of effort will lead to a certain level of performance.
2. The link between *performance and outcome*, or the strength of the expectation that a certain level of performance will lead to a particular outcome.
3. The link between *outcomes and individual needs*, or the degree to which the individual expects the anticipated outcome to satisfy personal needs. Some outcomes have more valence, or value, for individuals than others do.

Based on the expectancy theory, managers should do the following to motivate employees:

- Determine the rewards valued by each employee.
- Determine the desired performance level and then communicate it clearly to employees.
- Make the performance level attainable.
- Link rewards to performance.
- Determine what factors might counteract the effectiveness of an award.
- Make sure the reward is adequate for the level of performance.

expectancy theory
A theory of motivation that holds that the probability of an individual's acting in a particular way depends on how strongly that person believes the act will have a particular outcome, and on whether they value that outcome.

Exhibit 11.6 How Expectations Can Lead to Motivation

equity theory
A theory of motivation that holds that worker satisfaction is influenced by employees' perceptions about how fairly they are treated compared to their coworkers.

goal-setting theory
A theory of motivation based on the premise that an individual's intention to work toward a goal is a primary source of motivation.

management by objectives (MBO)
A systematic approach where individuals are given clear, specific objectives and goals to achieve that are consistent with those of the organization.

Concept *Check*

Discuss the three relationships central to expectancy theory.

Explain the comparison process that is a part of equity theory.

How does goal-setting theory contribute to our understanding of motivation?

Equity Theory

Another contemporary explanation of motivation, **equity theory** is based on individuals' perceptions about how fairly they are treated compared to their coworkers. Equity means justice or fairness, and in the workplace it refers to employees' perceived fairness of the way they are treated and the rewards they earn. Employees evaluate their *own outcomes* (e.g., salary, benefits) in relation to their *inputs* (e.g., number of hours worked, education, and training) and then compare the outcomes-to-inputs ratio to one of the following:

1. Their past experience in a different position in the current organization
2. Their past experience in a different organization
3. Another employee's experience inside the current organization
4. Another employee's experience outside the organization

According to equity theory, if employees perceive that an inequity exists, they will make one of the following choices:

- *change their work habits* (exert less effort on the job)
- *change their job benefits and income* (ask for a raise, steal from the employer)
- *distort their perception of themselves* ("I always thought I was smart, but now I realize I'm a lot smarter than my coworkers")
- *distort their perceptions of others* ("Joe's position is really much less flexible than mine")
- *look at the situation from a different perspective* ("I don't make as much as the other department heads, but I make a lot more than most graphic artists")
- *leave the situation* (quit the job)

Managers can use equity theory to improve worker satisfaction. Knowing that every employee seeks equitable and fair treatment, managers can make an effort to understand an employee's perceptions of fairness and take steps to reduce concerns about inequity.

Goal-Setting Theory

Goal-setting theory is based on the premise that an individual's intention to work toward a goal is a primary source of motivation. Once set, the goal clarifies for the employee what needs to be accomplished and how much effort will be required for completion. The theory has three main components:

1. Specific goals lead to a higher level of performance than do more generalized goals ("do your best").
2. More difficult goals lead to better performance than do easy goals (provided the individual accepts the goal).
3. Feedback on progress toward the goal enhances performance.

Feedback is particularly important, because it helps the individual identify the gap between the *real* (the actual performance) and the *ideal* (the desired outcome defined by the goal). Given the trend toward employee empowerment in the workplace, more and more employees are participating in the goal-setting process.

A separate but related topic is the organized approach to management, management by objectives (MBO). First outlined by Peter Ducker in 1954, it allows management to focus on achievable goals to realize the best possible results with the resources available. One of the primary

MARCI ANDREWS, HEALTHPOD BABY

You're having breakfast with some friends. The conversation turns to problems that you are having and how to fix them. You wish that someone would come up with a product to do what you have imagined, and you wait for it to happen. That's what most of us do, but it's not what Marci Andrews did. And not waiting is precisely how great entrepreneurial ventures are born.

Marci Andrews is the president of b.l.i.s. inc.—which stands for "because life is special"—and that really says everything you need to know about why her "star product" HealthPod Baby has been such a success. HealthPod Baby is "essentially a souped-up daytimer" in a "sturdy nylon-covered, zip-closed binder" that allows parents to record and store "all of a child's health information … in a single package that can easily be popped into a diaper bag or purse." As it is described on the company's website, it is a "brilliant idea to help you keep it all together … to help you plan, to help you educate, to help you to ensure that you get the best possible care for your baby … to keep everything together so that you can stay together … " precisely "because life is special."

If you don't have children, it might be hard to imagine why there is a need for such a product. As Marci described it in Rebecca Eckler's "Mommy Blogger Boo-Boo Diary" published in the *Globe & Mail* in October, 2006: "No longer do you have one doctor from the time you were born until adulthood … There's a whole breed of parents now that only go to walk-in clinics and you always get a new doctor." Today, it has become the responsibility of the parent to keep track of their child's health information, and as Marci puts it: "You'd be surprised how many mothers we've talked with who write down what doctors say on the back of receipts." This is definitely a product "whose time has come."

Marci's story is a lesson for all of us with ideas. It takes a lot of hard work to make a dream a reality, but it's worth it. With a business degree and experience in the consumer products field with companies like Procter & Gamble, Marci knew they had to do their due diligence. According to Marci: "It took two and a half years and consultations with hundreds of parents and a crew of 20 medical professionals." And it also took a lot of "leg-work." Marci and her partners, Jana Sinclair and Nancy Scott, would travel to different cities, visit a Starbucks and ask mothers there where they shopped, then go and cold-call the stores. And it paid off. To date, more than 8,000 HealthPods have been sold, the product has been endorsed by doctors, and it was even featured on DisneyFamily.com as one of the "Top 10 Pregnancy Essentials" in 2009.

No wonder Marci was named to the "Top 40 Under 40" in 2009 in *Avenue Calgary* magazine. Her advice to other young entrepreneurs? "Connect with people who will endorse your product," and persevere. "We found you really have to work to keep the vision in front of you, and at times it's very frustrating. But dig in, keep at it and above all, maintain your enthusiasm. If you've done your homework, and it's a good product, you'll get there." Entrepreneurship is all about motivation. The idea is just not enough if you aren't motivated to see it through. Thank goodness for parents out there that Marci Andrews was.

Thinking Critically

1. Where does the motivation come from to pursue an idea and make it a reality? What special ingredient does Marci Andrews have that caused her to act?
2. Do you think the amount of due diligence taken by Marci is really necessary, or should entrepreneurs "just do it"?

SOURCES: http://www.healthpod.ca, used with permission from Marci Andrews; http://www.avenuecalgary.com/top-40-under-40/marciandrews; "Top 10 Pregnancy Essentials," Disney Family.com, http://www.family.go.com/products/article-641953-top-pregnancy-essentials-t/6/.

---

principles of MBO is that the focus is on the results, not the activities. For MBO to work, it is imperative that everyone in the organization understands the objectives and goals of the organization and their roles and responsibilities to achieve them. It is important that performance reviews are conducted periodically to ensure that individuals are achieving the objectives and goals.

FROM MOTIVATION THEORY TO APPLICATION

LO7

The material presented thus far in this chapter demonstrates the wide variety of theorists and research studies that have contributed to our current understanding of employee motivation. Now we turn our attention to more practical matters: to ways in which these concepts can be applied in the workplace to meet organizational goals and improve individual performance.

Reinforcing Behaviour (Contingencies of Reinforcement)

Reinforcement is described as the application of consequences in response to behaviour. According to B. F. Skinner's operant learning theory, the premise behind reinforcement

Expanding Around the Globe

MOTIVATION IS CULTURE BOUND

Most motivation theories in use today were developed in the United States.[4] Of those that were not, many have been strongly influenced by the U.S. theories. In Canada, although to a lesser extent than in the United States, there is a relatively strong emphasis on individualism. This has led to expectancy and equity theories of motivation: theories that emphasize rational, individual thought as the primary basis of human behaviour. The emphasis placed on achievement is not surprising, given a willingness to accept risk and high concern for performance, but several motivation theories do not apply to all cultures.

Maslow's theory does not often hold outside of Canada and the United States. For instance, in countries whose citizens on average rate higher on uncertainty avoidance (such as Greece and Japan) as compared to those lower on uncertainty avoidance (such as Canada), security motivates employees more strongly than does self-actualization. Employees in high uncertainty-avoidance countries often consider job security and lifetime employment more important than holding a more interesting or challenging job. Also contrasting with the U.S. and, to a lesser extent, the Canadian pattern, social needs often dominate the motivation of workers in countries such as Denmark, Norway, and Sweden, whose residents stress the quality of life over materialism and productivity.

When researchers tested Herzberg's theory outside the United States, they encountered varied results. In New Zealand, for example, supervision and interpersonal relationships appear to contribute significantly to satisfaction and not merely to reducing dissatisfaction. Similarly, researchers found that citizens of Canada, Asia, Europe, Latin America, the Republic of Panama, and the West Indies cited certain extrinsic factors as satisfiers more frequently than did their American counterparts. The factors that motivate employees might not spark the same motivation in employees in other cultures.

Even the expectancy theory, considered a well-accepted contemporary motivation theory, does not always hold up in other cultures. Some of the major differences among the cultural groups include the following:

1. Citizens of English-speaking countries rank higher than average on individual achievement and lower on the desire for security.
2. Citizens of French-speaking countries, although similar to those of English-speaking countries, give greater importance to security and somewhat less to challenging work.
3. Northern Europeans have less interest in "getting ahead" and work recognition goals, instead placing more emphasis on job accomplishment. In addition, they have more concern for people and less for the organization as a whole (it is important that their jobs not interfere with their personal lives).
4. Latin Americans and southern Europeans find individual achievement somewhat less important; southern Europeans place the highest emphasis on job security, whereas citizens of both groups of countries emphasize fringe benefits.
5. Germans rank high on security and fringe benefits, and among the highest on "getting ahead."
6. The Japanese, although placing a low priority on advancement, also rank second highest on challenge and lowest on autonomy, with a strong emphasis on good working conditions and a friendly working environment.

Expectancy theories are universal to the extent that they do not specify the types of reward that motivate a given group of workers. Managers themselves must determine the level and type of reward most sought after by a particular group.[5]

is that consequences *influence* behaviour. The rules of consequences describe the outcomes that typically occur:

1. Introducing a positive consequence increases or maintains desired behaviours.
2. Removing a negative consequence increases or maintains desired behaviours.
3. Introducing a negative consequence (punishment) decreases behaviours.
4. Activities that do not give positive or negative consequences decrease behaviours.

Say, for example, that you have an employee who is consistently meeting or exceeding his or her sales targets. You might consider giving that person a bonus (positive reinforcement), but when this person no longer meets the targets, you remove the bonus (extinction). On the other hand, you might have other employees who are not meeting their sales targets, and so you give them warnings whenever they don't meet their targets (punishment). When the employees meet the targets, you no longer give the warnings (negative reinforcement). See Exhibit 11.7 for a visual of reinforcing behaviours.

Several factors are important with respect to using reinforcement strategies. Positive reinforcement must be clearly contingent on specific behaviour, diversity must be considered with respect to the choice of reinforcer, and other sources of reinforcement within the workforce must be taken into consideration (e.g., peer pressure).

Exhibit 11.7 | Reinforcing Behaviours

	Introduce Consequences	Remove Consequences
Increase or Maintain Behaviour	Positive	Negative
Decrease or Remove Behaviour	Punishment	Extinction

Motivational Job Design

How might managers redesign or modify existing jobs to increase employee motivation and performance? The following three options have been used extensively in the workplace:

- *Job enlargement.* The horizontal expansion of a job, through an increase in the number and variety of tasks that a person performs, is called job enlargement. Increasing task diversity can enhance job satisfaction, particularly when the job is mundane and repetitive in nature. A potential drawback to job enlargement is that employees might perceive that they are being asked to work harder and do more with no change in their level of responsibility or compensation. This can cause resentment and lead to dissatisfaction.
- *Job enrichment.* Job enrichment is the vertical expansion of an employee's job. Whereas job enlargement addresses the breadth or scope of a job, enrichment is an attempt to increase job depth by providing the employee with more autonomy, responsibility, and decision-making authority. In an enriched job, the employee can use a variety of talents and skills and has more control over the planning, execution, and evaluation of the required tasks. In general, job enrichment has been found to increase job satisfaction and reduce absenteeism and turnover.
- *Job rotation.* Also called *cross-training*, job rotation is the shifting of workers from one job to another. This might be done to broaden an employee's skill base or because an employee has ceased to be interested in or challenged by a particular

job enlargement
The horizontal expansion of a job based on an increase in the number and variety of tasks that a person performs.

job enrichment
The vertical expansion of a job based on an increase in the employee's autonomy, responsibility, and decision-making authority.

job rotation
The shifting of workers from one job to another; also called cross-training.

Concept *in Action*

With employees clocking longer hours at work, office romances have become more frequent and less taboo than in the past. Regular collaboration between dedicated colleagues can very easily spill over into lunch breaks, happy hour, or even after-hours work assignments. While such tight teamwork raises fewer eyebrows today, companies concerned about workplace distractions and dramatic breakups often frown upon interoffice dating. How might managers utilize reinforcement theory to discourage employees from pursuing office trysts?

ANTONIO MO/PHOTODISC/GETTY IMAGES

job. The organization might benefit from job rotation, because it increases flexibility in scheduling and production; employees can be shifted to cover for absent workers or changes in production or operations. It is also a valuable tool for training lower-level managers in a variety of functional areas. Drawbacks of job rotation include an increase in training costs and decreased productivity while employees are getting "up to speed" in new task areas.

Work-Scheduling Options

As companies try to meet the needs of a diverse workforce and retain quality employees, while remaining competitive and financially prosperous, managers are challenged to find new ways of keeping workers motivated and satisfied. Increasingly popular are alternatives to the traditional work schedule, such as the compressed workweek, flextime, job sharing, and telecommuting.

One option for employees who want to maximize their leisure hours, indulge in three-day weekends, and avoid commuting during morning and evening rush hours is the *compressed* workweek. Employees work the traditional 40 hours but fit those hours into a shorter workweek. Most common is the 4-40 schedule, whereby employees work four 10-hour days a week. Organizations that offer this option claim benefits ranging from increased motivation and productivity to reduced absenteeism and turnover.

Another scheduling option, called *flextime*, allows employees to decide what their work hours will be. Employees are generally expected to work a certain number of hours per week but have some discretion as to when they arrive at work and when they leave for the day.

Job sharing is a scheduling option that allows two individuals to split the tasks, responsibilities, and work hours of one 40-hour-per-week job. Though used less frequently than flextime and the compressed workweek, this option can also provide employees with job flexibility. The primary benefit to the company is that it gets "two for the price of one"—the company can draw on two sets of skills and abilities to accomplish one set of job objectives.

Telecommuting is a work-scheduling option that allows employees to work from home via a computer that is linked with their office, headquarters, or colleagues. It is the fastest growing of the four scheduling options.

HSBC, like many Canadian companies, recognized that its policies and practices around work–life balance were important in the competition for talent. They now offer flextime and job sharing to assist employees in meeting both their professional and their personal responsibilities.

Many companies have found themselves in a similar position to that of HSBC: recognizing that their policies and practices around work–life balance—important for an employer competing for talent in a small pool—could be enhanced and improved. And although some employers might not have accepted this challenge, HSBC took it as an opportunity to improve its policies related to work-life and change its culture to be more supportive and flexible.

Although each of these work scheduling options might have some drawbacks for the sponsoring organizations, the benefits far outweigh the problems. For this reason, not only is the number of companies offering compressed work increasing, so is the number of companies offering other options.

Recognition, Empowerment, and Economic Incentives

All employees have unique needs that they seek to fulfill through their jobs. Organizations must devise a wide array of incentives to ensure that a broad spectrum of employee needs can be addressed in the work environment, thus increasing the likelihood of motivated employees. A sampling of these motivational tools is discussed here.

Formal recognition of superior effort by individuals or groups in the workplace is one way of enhancing employee motivation. Recognition serves as positive feedback and reinforcement, letting employees know what they have done well and that

job sharing
A scheduling option that allows two individuals to split the tasks, responsibilities, and work hours of one 40-hour-per-week job.

telecommuting
An arrangement in which employees work at home and are linked to the office by phone, fax, and computer.

their contribution is valued by the organization. Recognition can take many forms, both formal and informal. Some companies use formal awards ceremonies to acknowledge and celebrate their employees' accomplishments. Others take advantage of informal interactions to congratulate employees on a job well done and offer encouragement for the future. Recognition can take the form of an employee-of-the-month plaque, a monetary reward, a day off, a congratulatory e-mail, or a verbal "pat on the back."

As described in Chapter 9, employee empowerment, sometimes called employee involvement or participative leadership, involves delegating decision-making authority to employees at all levels of the organization. Employees are given greater responsibility for planning, implementing, and evaluating the results of decisions. Empowerment is based on the premise that human resources, especially at lower levels in the company, are an underutilized asset. Employees are capable of contributing much more of their skills and abilities to organizational success if they are allowed to participate in the decision-making process and are given access to the resources needed to implement their decisions.

Any discussion of motivation has to include the use of monetary incentives to enhance performance. Currently, companies are using a variety of variable-pay programs, such as piece-rate plans, profit sharing, gain sharing, and bonuses, to encourage employees to be more productive. Unlike the standard salary or hourly wage, variable pay means that a portion of an employee's pay is linked directly to an individual or organizational performance measure. In *piece-rate pay plans*, for example, employees are paid a given amount for each unit they produce, directly linking the amount they earn to their productivity. *Profit-sharing plans* are based on overall company profitability. Using an established formula, management distributes some portion of company profits to all employees. *Gain-sharing* plans are incentive programs based on group productivity. Employees share in the financial gains attributed to the increased productivity of their group. This encourages them to increase productivity within their specific work area regardless of the overall profit picture for the organization as a whole. A *bonus* is simply a one-time lump-sum monetary reward.

Concept *Check*

Explain the difference between job enlargement and job enrichment.

What are the four work scheduling options that can enhance employee performance?

Are all employees motivated by the same economic incentives? Explain.

Making Ethical Choices

VOLUNTEERISM—OR SELF BENEFIT

You join a large financial institution that encourages and promotes employee volunteerism, allowing employees one day a month, or up to 12 days a year, to volunteer for a cause of their choosing. Shortly after you start working there as a junior teller, your boss' wife is diagnosed with a particularly aggressive form of breast cancer which carries a very poor prognosis. Realizing it will win you kudos with your boss, you choose the local chapter of a foundation—a breast cancer charity that sponsors an annual Race for the Cure—for your company-sponsored volunteer work.

In addition to working at the foundation's office one day a month, you spend your own time actively soliciting other staffers at your company to sign up for the charity walk in a few months' time. Impressed with your qualities of tireless dedication, your boss puts your name forward for promotion to junior bank officer, well before the customary two years of service normally required for being considered for promotion.

Using a Web search tool, locate articles about this topic and then write responses to the following questions. Be sure to support your arguments and cite your sources.

ETHICAL DILEMMA: Your company is generous in its approach to employee volunteerism. It gives you paid time off and you acquire enhanced job skills through your volunteer activities. Have you just been smart in recognizing the value of volunteering for a charity that you know will earn your boss' personal appreciation? Or are you taking unfair advantage of your boss' vulnerability and manipulating the situation?

SOURCES: Margarita Bauza, "Companies Find Volunteering Makes Good Business Sense," *Detroit Free Press*, November 20, 2005, http://galenet.thomsonlearning.com; "Deloitte Volunteer IMPACT Survey Reveals Link Between Volunteering and Professional Success," *Internet Wire*, June 3, 2005, http://galenet.thomsonlearning.com; Charley Hannagan, "Can Work Help?" *Post-Standard*, Syracuse, NY, September 30, 2005, p. C1.

THE FUTURE OF MOTIVATION

This chapter has focused on understanding what motivates people and how employee motivation and satisfaction affect productivity and organizational performance. Organizations can improve performance by investing in people. In reviewing the ways in which companies are currently choosing to invest in their human resources, we can spot four trends:

1. Education and training
2. Employee ownership
3. Work–life benefits
4. Nurturing knowledge workers

All of the companies making the *Canada's Top 100 Employers* list know the importance of treating employees properly. They all have programs that allow them to invest in their employees through programs such as these and many more. Today's businesses also face the challenge of increased costs of absenteeism.

Education and Training

Companies that provide educational and training opportunities for their employees reap the benefits of a more motivated, as well as a more skilled, workforce. Employees who are properly trained in new technologies are more productive and less resistant to job change. Education and training provide additional benefits by increasing employees' feelings of competence and self-worth. When companies spend money to upgrade employee knowledge and skills, they convey the message "we value you and are committed to your growth and development as an employee."

Employee Ownership

A recent trend that seems to have levelled off is employee ownership, most commonly implemented as employee stock ownership plans, or ESOPs. ESOPs are not the same as stock options, however. In an ESOP, employees receive compensation in the form of company stock. Recall that stock options give employees the opportunity to purchase company stock at a set price, even if the market price of the stock increases above that point. Because employees are compensated with stock, over time they can become the owners of the company. Behind employee ownership programs is the belief that employees who think like owners are more motivated to take care of customers' needs, reduce unnecessary expenses, make operations smoother, and stay with the company longer.

Work–Life Benefits

Another growing trend in the workplace involves companies helping their employees to manage the numerous and sometimes competing demands in their lives. Organizations are taking a more active role in helping employees achieve a balance between their work responsibilities and their personal obligations. The desired result is employees who are less stressed, better able to focus on their jobs, and therefore, more productive. Many companies provide work–life benefits for employees. For example, some companies offer telecommuting, part-time positions, job sharing, subsidized childcare, eldercare referral, and on-site fitness centres.

Nurturing Knowledge Workers

Most organizations have specialized workers, and managing them all effectively is a big challenge. In many companies, knowledge workers (now two-fifths of the workforce) might have a supervisor, but they are not "subordinates." They are "associates." Within their area of knowledge, they are supposed to do the telling. As knowledge is

Concept in Action

Companies sometimes create unusual perks to help attract and retain talented workers. Timberland employees receive a $3000 subsidy to buy a hybrid automobile. Worthington Industries offers workers on-site haircuts for just $4. And at SC Johnson, retirees receive a lifetime membership to the company fitness centre. What trends are emerging in the ways companies seek to motivate workers and keep them happy on the job?

MONKEY BUSINESS IMAGES/SHUTTERSTOCK

effective only if specialized, knowledge workers are not homogeneous, particularly the fast-growing group of knowledge technologists, such as computer systems specialists, lawyers, programmers, and others. And because knowledge work is specialized, it is deeply splintered.

A knowledge-based workforce is qualitatively different from a less skilled workforce. True, knowledge workers are still a minority, but they are fast becoming the largest single group. And they have already become the major creator of wealth. Increasingly the success, indeed the survival, of every business will depend on the performance of its knowledge workforce. The challenging part of managing knowledge workers is finding ways to motivate proud, skilled professionals to share expertise and cooperate in such a way as to advance the frontiers of their knowledge for the benefit of the shareholders and society in general. To achieve that auspicious goal, several companies have created what they call "communities of practice." Schlumberger Limited, an oilfield services company, uses this innovative tool to motivate its highly technical knowledge workers.

Concept Check

What benefits can an organization derive from training and educational opportunities, stock ownership programs, and work–life benefits?

How are knowledge workers different from traditional employees?

GREAT IDEAS TO USE NOW

We've come a long way from the days of Taylor's scientific management. Organizations now offer a wide variety of incentives to attract and retain high-quality employees. A knowledgeable, creative, committed, and highly skilled workforce provides a company with a source of sustainable advantage in an increasingly competitive business environment. What does that mean to you? It means that companies are working harder than ever to meet employee needs. It means that when you graduate from college or university, you may choose a prospective employer on the basis of its daycare facilities and fitness programs as well as its salaries. It means that you need to think about what motivates you. Would you forgo a big salary to work for a smaller company that gives you lots of freedom to be creative and make your own decisions? Would you trade extensive health coverage for a share of ownership in the company? Most organizations try to offer a broad spectrum of incentives to meet a variety of needs, but each company makes trade-offs, and so will you in choosing an employer. Do a little research on a company you are interested in working for (paying particular attention to its corporate culture); then use the first exercise in the "Experiential Exercises" to help you determine how well your values fit with the company's values.

Summary of Learning Outcomes

LO1   **Explain the basic principles of Frederick Taylor's concept of scientific management.**

Scientific management is based on the belief that employees are motivated by economic incentives and that there is "one best way" to perform any job. The four basic principles of scientific management developed by Taylor are as follows:

1. Develop a scientific approach for each element of a person's job.
2. Scientifically select, train, teach, and develop workers.
3. Encourage cooperation between workers and managers, so that each job can be accomplished in a standard, scientifically determined way.
4. Divide work and responsibility between management and workers according to who is better suited to each task.

LO2   **Summarize what Elton Mayo's Hawthorne studies revealed about worker motivation.**

The pride that comes from special attention motivates workers to increase their productivity. Supervisors who allow employees to have some control over their situation appear to increase the workers' motivation further. The Hawthorne effect suggests that employees will perform better when they feel singled out for special attention or feel that management is concerned about their welfare.

LO3   **Discuss Maslow's hierarchy of needs and Clayton Alderfer's ERG theory of motivation, and how these needs relate to employee motivation.**

Maslow believed that each individual has a hierarchy of needs, consisting of physiological, safety, social, esteem, and self-actualization needs. Managers who accept Maslow's ideas attempt to increase employee motivation by modifying organizational and managerial practices to increase the likelihood that employees will meet all levels of needs. Maslow's theory has also helped managers understand that it is hard to motivate people by appealing to already satisfied needs.

ERG theory (Existence, Relatedness, and Growth) overlaps Maslow's needs. Alderfer did not hold that each of the needs was necessarily separate, and an individual could work on more than one need at a time. Maslow theory states that one must satisfy a lower-level need before moving onto the next need (satisfaction-progression) model, whereas Alderfer allows for people to become frustrated at a level and seek satisfaction by moving to a lower-level need (frustration-regression model).

LO4   **Identify how McGregor's Theories X and Y and Ouchi's Theory Z are used to explain worker motivation.**

Douglas McGregor influenced the study of motivation with his formulation of two contrasting sets of assumptions about human nature—designated Theory X and Theory Y. Theory X says people don't like to work and will avoid it if they can. Because people don't like to work, they must be controlled, directed, or threatened to get them to make an effort. Theory Y says that people want to be self-directed and will try to accomplish goals that they believe in. Workers can be motivated with positive incentives. McGregor personally believed that Theory Y assumptions describe most employees and that managers seeking to motivate subordinates should develop management practices based on those assumptions.

William Ouchi's Theory Z combines North American and Japanese business practices. Theory Z emphasizes long-term employment, slow career development, and group decision making. The recent decline of the Japanese economy has resulted in most North American companies moving away from Japanese management practices.

Frederick Herzberg's studies indicated that certain job factors are consistently related to employee job satisfaction, whereas others can create job dissatisfaction. According to Herzberg, motivating factors (also called satisfiers) are primarily intrinsic job elements that lead to satisfaction, such as achievement, recognition, the (nature of) work itself, responsibility, advancement, and growth. What Herzberg termed hygiene factors (also called dissatisfiers) are extrinsic elements of the work environment, such as company policy, relationships with supervisors, working conditions, relationships with peers and subordinates, salary and benefits, and job security. These are factors that can result in job dissatisfaction if not managed well. One of the most interesting findings of Herzberg's studies was that the opposite of satisfaction is not dissatisfaction. Herzberg believed that proper management of hygiene factors could prevent employee dissatisfaction but that these factors could not serve as a source of satisfaction or motivation.

LO5 Explain the basic components of Herzberg's motivator-hygiene theory.

According to expectancy theory, the probability that an individual will act in a particular way depends on how strongly that person believes the act will lead to a certain level of performance, whether that performance will have a particular outcome, and whether they value that outcome. Equity theory is based on individuals' perceptions about how fairly they are treated compared to their coworkers. Goal-setting theory states that employees are highly motivated to perform when specific goals are established and feedback on progress is offered.

LO6 Describe how three contemporary theories of employee motivation offer insights into improving employee performance.

The horizontal expansion of a job by increasing the number and variety of tasks that a person performs is called job enlargement. Increasing task diversity can enhance job satisfaction, particularly when the job is mundane and repetitive in nature. Job enrichment is the vertical expansion of an employee's job to provide the employee with more autonomy, responsibility, and decision-making authority. Other popular motivational tools include work-scheduling options, employee recognition programs, empowerment, and variable-pay programs.

LO7 Discuss how managers can redesign existing jobs to increase employee motivation and performance.

Today, companies are using several key tactics to motivate and retain workers. First, companies are investing more in employee education and training, which make workers more productive and less resistant to job change. Second, managers are offering employees a chance for ownership in the company. This can strongly increase employee commitment. Third, enlightened employers are providing work–life benefits to help employees achieve a better balance between work and personal responsibilities. Finaly, businesses are also recognizing the importance of managing knowledge workers.

LO8 List some of the initiatives organizations are using today to motivate and retain employees.

Key Terms

equity theory 318
ERG theory 312
existence 312
expectancy theory 317
extrinsic rewards 308
goal-setting theory 318
growth 313
Hawthorne effect 310

hygiene factors 315
intrinsic rewards 308
job enlargement 321
job enrichment 321
job rotation 321
job sharing 322
management by objectives (MBO) 318
Maslow's hierarchy of needs 311

Experiential Exercises

1. The accompanying table lists 17 personal characteristics and 13 institutional values you might encounter at a company. Select and rank-order the 10 personal characteristics that best describe you; do the same for the 10 institutional values that would be most evident in your ideal workplace. Test your fit at a company by seeing whether the characteristics of the company's environment match your top 10 personal characteristics.

THE CHOICE MENU

RANK ORDER (1–17) YOU ARE	RANK ORDER (1–13) YOUR IDEAL COMPANY OFFERS
____ 1. Flexible	____ 1. Stability
____ 2. Innovative	____ 2. High expectations of performance
____ 3. Willing to experiment	____ 3. Opportunities for professional growth
____ 4. Risk taking	____ 4. High pay for good performance
____ 5. Careful	____ 5. Job security
____ 6. Autonomy seeking	____ 6. A clear guiding philosophy
____ 7. Comfortable with rules	____ 7. A low level of conflict
____ 8. Analytical	____ 8. Respect for the individual's rights
____ 9. Team oriented	____ 9. Informality
____10. Easygoing	____10. Fairness
____11. Supportive	____11. Long hours
____12. Aggressive	____12. Relative freedom from rules
____13. Decisive	____13. The opportunity to be distinctive, or different from others
____14. Achievement oriented	
____15. Comfortable with individual responsibility	
____16. Competitive	
____17. Interested in making friends at work	

2. How are job satisfaction and employee morale linked to job performance? Do you work harder when you are satisfied with your job? Explain your answer.

3. Review the assumptions of Theories X, Y, and Z. Under which set of assumptions would you prefer to work? Is your current or former supervisor a Theory X, Theory Y, or Theory Z manager? Explain by describing the person's behaviour.

4. Think about several of your friends who seem to be highly self-motivated. Talk with each of them and ask them what factors contribute the most to their motivation. Make a list of their responses and compare them to the factors that motivate you.

5. Both individual motivation and group participation are needed to accomplish certain goals. Describe a situation you're familiar with in which cooperation achieved a goal that individual action could not. Describe one in which group action slowed progress and individual action would have been better.

6. Using expectancy theory, analyze how you have made and will make personal choices, such as a major area of study, a career to pursue, or job interviews to seek.

7. If you're looking for 1,001 ways to motivate or reward employees, Bob Nelson can help. Visit the "Recognition" resources section of his Nelson Motivation site at www.nelson-motivation.com to get some ideas you can put to use to help you do a better job, either as an employee or as a manager.

8. More companies are offering their employees stock ownership plans. To learn the differences between an employee stock ownership plan (ESOP) and stock options, visit the National Center for Employee Ownership (NCEO), at www.nceo.org, and the Foundation for Enterprise Development (FED), at www.fed.org.

   Which stock plan would you rather have? Why? Also visit the "Ownership Culture" area of the NCEO site. What does research on employee ownership indicate? Cite specific examples.

9. Open-book management is one of the better known ways to create a participatory work environment. More than 2000 companies have adopted this practice, which involves sharing financial information with non-management employees and training them to understand financial information. Does it really motivate employees and improve productivity? Do a search for this topic at the NCEO site, www.nceo.org. You'll find survey results, case studies, related activities, and links that will help you answer this question.

10. Use a search engine to find companies that offer "work–life benefits." Link to several companies and review their employee programs in this area. How do they compare? Which benefits would be most important to you if you were job hunting, and why?

Review Questions

1. Summarize the following:
   - Frederick Taylor's scientific management
   - Hawthorne studies
   - Maslow's hierarchy of needs
   - Alderfer's ERG theory
   - McGregor's Theories X and Y
   - Ouchi's Theory Z
   - Herzberg's motivator-hygiene theory

2. Explain E > P > O of expectancy theory. How does this explain employee behaviour?

3. What are the choices available when an employee feels that there is unfairness on the job?

4. How can the use of goal-setting theory lead to motivation?

5. Explain
   - job enlargement, job enrichment, and job rotation;
   - work-scheduling options and how they can be a motivator; and
   - how motivation is affected by recognition, empowerment, and economic incentives.

6. Explain how the following affect employee motivation:
   - education and training opportunities
   - employee ownership
   - work–life benefits
   - the nurturing of knowledge workers

CREATIVE THINKING CASE

Demotivating Your Top Producer

The Max Call Centre had been home to Sandy Rolf for many years. She had a good salary, excellent bonus system (cash and other incentives), and a reasonable benefits package and pension plan. Sandy's job was outbound cold calls to bring customers back to the company. Many of us would cringe at the thought of spending eight hours a day doing this. Sandy loved it, as she said, "my two favourite things, talking on the phone and making money." As a top producer in the area, she received gift certificates in the hundreds of dollars for various local merchants, as well as her base salary and commissions. She was celebrated at company functions by upper management, received congratulatory e-mails and plaques, and was honoured at departmental meetings. Her managers could not say enough positive things about her.

So what did the company ultimately do to reward this loyal and valued employee? They outsourced her job. As a result of an executive decision, the department no longer existed. Sandy was told not to worry, she still had a job. The job turned out to be fielding inbound calls, most of which were complaints against the company for perceived wrongs against the customer.

Sandy's health began to deteriorate because of extreme stress, and the once happy, outgoing, fun-loving woman now spent most of her leisure time sleeping, watching TV, and avoiding her friends and family.

Research suggests that small pleasures (e.g., a job you enjoy) are more likely to yield long-term joy than high-profile positive events. "It's the frequency and not the intensity of the positive events in your life that leads to happiness, like comfortable shoes or a single malt scotch," according to Daniel Gilbert, a Harvard University psychology professor. By going to a job she loved, Sandy experienced happiness and job satisfaction on a daily basis. Now that this situation had changed, her happiness and motivation levels dropped, leaving Sandy in a depressed state, struggling for the energy and interest even to access the online job search sites.

Thinking Critically

1. Using the motivation theories in the chapter, explain why Sandy was so motivated in a job such as cold calling.

2. Given that she still had a salary, benefits, and a pension plan, why did she become so extremely unmotivated after the change?

SOURCE: Judy Stoffman, "You're Happy. Imagine That!: Why People Are So Bad at Predicting What Will Make Them Feel Good," *Toronto Star*, May 21, 2006, D4.

Part 4

Functional Areas of Business

Making the Connection

Managing Human Resources and Labour Relations

In this section of the text, we will take a look at the internal environment of a business or, more simply, the functional areas of a business. These areas are what most people think of when they think of a business or a career in business—*human resources*, *marketing*, *operations*, and *accounting* and *finance*.

Before we take a look inside each of the functional areas in detail, in separate chapters, one very important message must be communicated clearly at the outset. Even though each of these areas is discussed separately in different chapters of introductory textbooks, and later in separate courses in business schools, they cannot act separately if the business is to be successful. They are all part of the integrated business model that has been the central theme of this text. Each of these areas must work together to make the business successful overall. For example, a company cannot design and market a product for which it does not have the human, operational, and financial resources. Just imagine The Bay attempting to produce a new all-terrain vehicle and introduce it to the market. It could perhaps alter its store setup to sell the vehicle, but does it have the facilities and people skills to produce it? Would it even have the financial resources to put toward this type of endeavour, considering the tight budgets most businesses are working with today to keep their core business alive?

It should be clear from Chapter 9, which deals with management and planning, that all decisions made at the tactical level in the functional areas come from decisions made at a higher *strategic* level that affect the whole company. As discussed in Chapter 7 as well, top management first scans the external environment by using the PESTI model to look for opportunities and threats, and matches those with the strengths and weaknesses of the company in the different functional areas to decide the direction for the company. It

is therefore unlikely that a decision like this one would ever be made by The Bay. Even if there were opportunities in the market for ATVs, it would not match with the strengths of the company. Financial resources would therefore not be released for this type of project to begin with.

In this chapter, we'll take a look at our first functional area. The old adage "last but not least" certainly applies here. As we discussed earlier, gaining the *commitment of employees* is the most critical factor, because all of the other four critical success factors are achieved through the people in the company. Without a strong human resource area and the strong commitment of the employees toward organizational goals, the company simply cannot be successful in any functional area or overall.

The business environment today provides many challenges for the human resource manager. In the *political* environment, regulations govern many aspects of the human resource function, such as how workers can be selected (e.g., drug testing, human rights legislations governing the application and interview process). The mix of people hired is also regulated for some companies through employment equity legislation. Issues relating to diversity are critically important, because without a diverse workforce, companies will have a difficult time both understanding the *global* marketplace and, subsequently, designing products and marketing plans to appeal to this multifaceted society. Therefore, companies must consider this trend toward greater diversity in the make-up of society very seriously, taking proactive steps rather than just reacting to government legislation. In the *economic* environment, organizations are competing not only for customers but also for a shrinking pool of qualified job applicants, and they must also pay attention to the salaries of the competition to remain competitive. In the *social* environment, workers are seeking to better balance their home and work lives, making it more critical and more difficult to gain commitment in the traditional ways; and the aging workforce is also creating difficulties as well as opportunities. The *technological* environment is reshaping how work is done, offering options to human labour and changing the nature of many jobs and the skills required to do them. Technology also affects how the human resource department does its job. You'll find many examples both in the chapter and in trying to find a job yourself, such as using the Internet to recruit workers and using specially designed software to pick out key phrases from resumés to sort through them more quickly.

An environmental factor that has a dramatic impact on how a company operates is the presence of unions. This is a very integrative factor, as it has implications for all the environmental factors and all the areas of the business. It is political, because legislation governs how unions become involved with a group of workers and how the union-management relationship works; it is social, because the culture and attitude of the workers affect how they view unions and whether they would want to work in a unionized environment; it is technological, because the union contract could impact the rights of management to use technology if it replaces workers; and it is economic, because a unionized workplace often has less flexibility and higher compensation costs than a non-unionized environment, and that can impact a company's competitiveness. Unions can therefore affect the financial success of the company, and they can definitely signal an issue with respect to worker commitment when the workers feel compelled to have a third party represent them with management. This point stresses the importance of management operating with the commitment of the workers foremost in its mind if it wishes to operate without a union. It is management's job to create a work environment that gains commitment and loyalty, where the human resource policies are so worker-focused that unions are the last thought on the workers' minds.

As with the other functional areas, the main basis for all decisions in the human resource area is the company's goals and strategy. The role of the human resource area is to provide the right numbers of the right kinds of people in the right places at the right times to assist the other functional areas to help the organization achieve its objectives. To do this, the human resource area must work very closely with marketing, operations, and finance to understand their objectives and thus their human resource requirements. It must also understand the jobs that need to be done to determine the skills that it must recruit and train for.

One area in which human resources must work especially closely with finance is employee compensation and benefits. Because of the relative size of this expense, it has a tremendous impact on the bottom line on the one hand, but on the other it also affects the level of commitment from employees. Therefore, an integrative approach must be taken in determining compensation. This matter is becoming more important as workers are changing jobs more often.

Compensation is just one decision area in which the human resource manager must develop and implement policies in an integrative way to create a more committed workforce. For example, one common approach in recruitment and selection is to promote first from within. This practice shows employees that the organization is committed to them, which is an essential ingredient in gaining commitment from employees. Another particularly integrative way to increase commitment is by offering telecommuting. The technological environment has made telecommuting possible, thus improving the productivity of workers and saving companies money. This, in turn, has helped companies retain key people who would otherwise have to leave. In training and development as well, the organization can show its commitment to the employees by helping them to achieve their potential. Again, employees will be more committed to an organization that shows commitment to them in its human resource policies. This effort to train and develop employees makes them both better at their jobs and more loyal, which translates into being more *innovative*, providing greater *quality*, and working harder to meet and exceed *customer needs*, thereby allowing the organization to achieve *financial performance* both through lower turnover and through greater customer satisfaction.

chapter 12

Managing Human Resources and Labour Relations

LEARNING OUTCOMES

1 Discuss the human resource management process, and how human resource needs are determined.

2 Explain how companies recruit applicants.

3 Summarize how companies select qualified applicants.

4 List some of the types of training and development programs that organizations offer to their employees.

5 Show how performance appraisals are used to evaluate employee performance.

6 Analyze the various methods for compensating employees.

7 Explain how labour–management relations are different in a unionized environment.

8 Describe some of the key laws and federal agencies affecting human resource management and labour relations.

9 List some of the trends and issues affecting human resource management and labour relations.

ELDERLY MOTORIST "HITS" PICKETER

In March 2009, a driver tried to manoeuvre his car into the parking area of the Windsor Raceway in Ontario when his way was blocked by picketing security guards. The 81-year-old motorist tried to work his way slowly through the line, but ended up with a picketer as a hood ornament. After a short drive, he stopped, and the striker was able to get off the hood unhurt. Neither man was charged in the incident.

The security guards were on strike because their employer wanted to eliminate nine full-time positions and reduce wages by $5 an hour. All 16 local members of the Service Employees Union International had voted to strike. Theirs had been solid full-time jobs at $18 an hour. Some had families with children heading off to university, others had new mortgages and other lifestyle demands. They felt that a cut from full-time to part-time employment, and from $18 to $13 an hour, would have turned their careers into casual jobs. In addition, management had refused the union's demand for severance pay of three weeks' wages for every year worked.

The strike was settled on April 3, 2009, after four weeks, which is short for private-sector strikes in the current labour era. The jobs were cut, but the nine laid off staff received two weeks' pay for every year worked, along with some other benefits. The union described the result this way: "Sure it was a tough decision, but this strike was first and foremost about dignity and respect. We were victorious in the end—after four weeks on the picket line we achieved a significantly improved package," said Rick Berthiaume, a 38-year employee.

In Canada, labour laws are provincial; most provincial statutes provide for one week's severance per year worked, and there are other restrictions, so it's important to know the laws of the province in which you work or employ people. The application of common law (laws created through litigation and precedent) may result in severance packages of a month's pay or more for every year worked, depending on the job, the occupation, and other factors. Anyone involved in a job termination—whether employer or employee—may be wise to consult a lawyer, especially in the case of long-term employees. Most big companies are very careful in layoff situations.

Union contracts can affect many aspects of how labour laws are applied and interpreted, and the complexity of labour agreements may be one of the reasons many organizations try to avoid unions. Union density (the percentage of workers who are members of a union) in Canada is over 30 percent, compared to about 12 percent in the United States. This is down from mid-20th century peak levels near 40 percent in both countries. Today in Canada, more women than men are in unions, as are more government employees than private-sector workers.

This is no coincidence, as large private-sector organizations have taken steps to democratize the workplace and reduce the perceived need for unions. You can find union-like access to justice (grievance procedures, labour-management committees, etc.) in non-union workplaces. All these changes have made a difference in public opinion.

THE CANADIAN PRESS/TIBOR KOLLEY

The 81-year-old man may have been a member of a union in his prime, but on that day in March the picketer was in his way, preventing him from going about his business. For the picketer, his job and dignity were at stake. The workplace can be a very emotional place, for managers, employees, and customers.[1]

THINKING CRITICALLY

As you read this chapter, consider the following questions:

1. Why is proper human resource management important?

2. The phrase "labour relations" is used to denote the relationship between unions and management. Has its definition expanded today?

3. How can workers be protected in non-unionized environments?

SOURCES: "Windsor Raceway Security Guard Strike Settled," Windsor Raceway, April 3, 2009, http://www.windsorraceway.com/%5Cpdf%5Csspr.pdf; Dalson Chen, "Raceway Strike Ends With Deal, Job Cuts," The Windsor Star, April 4, 2009, http://www2.canada.com/windsorstar/news/story.html?id=19f376f7-78b0-4991-9b44-9880e833067b; "Elderly Motorist Warned After Picket Line Mishap," The Windsor Star, March 12, 2009, http://www2.canada.com/windsorstar/news/story.html?id=fc0c4be0-1eb2-4f45-911c-02db3379b291; "Our History," SEIU Local 2 BGPWU, http://seiu.crackmethod.com/?page_id=157; The View From Local 2, Volume 9, Issue 1, September 2009, http://seiu.crackmethod.com/wp-content/uploads/2011/05/View-Sep-2009.pdf.

JUPITERIMAGES/POLKA DOT/THINKSTOCK

As business expands around the globe, human resource managers need to develop communication systems and training strategies that build teamwork among diverse employees who may be located around the world. What human resource challenges are caused by increasing globalization of Canadian companies?

Human resource management is receiving increasing attention as our economy shifts from manufacturing to service- and knowledge-based businesses. Human resource management and labour relations involve acquisition, development, use, and maintenance of a human resource (HR) mix (people and positions) to achieve strategic organizational goals and objectives. Successful human resource management is based on a company's ability to attract and hire the best employees, equip them with the knowledge and skills they need to excel, compensate them fairly, and motivate them to reach their full potential and perform at high levels. Today's business environment presents numerous challenges to effectively managing employees:

- *Technology continues to advance, which places great importance on knowledge workers, especially when demand outstrips the supply of high-talent individuals.*
- *Global business operations involve rapid data transfer and necessitate accelerated decision making by executive and technical employees.*
- *The workforce is increasingly more diversified and multicultural, which places increased emphasis on communication and cultural understanding.*
- *Work life and family priorities are more difficult to balance as dual worker families populate the labour force.*
- *Employment and labour laws continue to greatly influence employee recruitment and hiring, compensation decisions, and employee retention and turnover in both union and non-union organizations.*

Each day, human resource experts and front-line supervisors deal with these challenges while sharing responsibility for attracting and retaining skilled, motivated employees. Whether faced with a large or small human resource problem, supervisors need some understanding of difficult employee relations issues, especially if there are legal implications.

In this chapter, you will learn about the elements of the human resource management process, including human resource planning and job analysis and design, employee recruitment and selection, training and development of employees, performance planning and evaluation, and compensation of the workforce. The chapter also describes labour unions and their representation of millions of Canadian workers in construction, manufacturing, transportation, and service-based industries.

LO1 ACHIEVING HIGH PERFORMANCE THROUGH HUMAN RESOURCE MANAGEMENT

human resource management (HRM)
The process of hiring, developing, motivating, and evaluating employees to achieve organizational goals.

Human resource management (HRM) is the process of hiring, developing, motivating, and evaluating employees to achieve organizational goals. The goals and strategies of the company's business model form the basis for making human resource management decisions. HR practices and systems compose the company's human resource decision support system that is intended to make employees a key element for gaining competitive advantage. To this end, the HR management process involves the activities sequenced as shown in Exhibit 12.1:

- Job analysis and design
- Human resource planning and forecasting

Exhibit 12.1 Human Resource Management Process

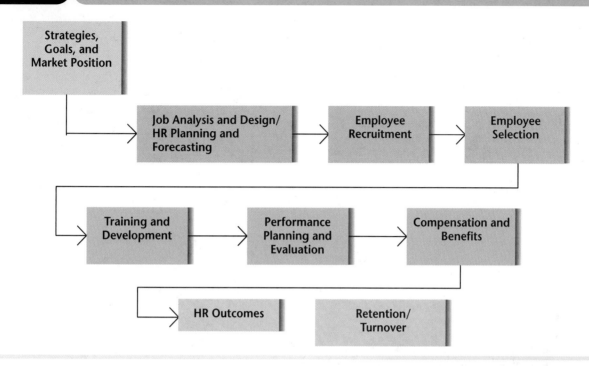

- Employee recruitment
- Employee selection
- Training and development
- Performance planning and evaluation
- Compensation and benefits

Concept *Check*

Define human resource management.

Describe the human resource management process.

The human resource management process shown in Exhibit 12.1 encourages the development of high performance employees. The process is sequential because employees can't be trained and paid until selected and placed in jobs, which follows recruitment, which is preceded by human resource planning and job analysis and design. Good HR practices used along this sequence foster performance improvement, knowledge and skill development, and loyal employees who desire to remain with the organization.

HR Planning and Job Analysis and Design

Two important, and somewhat parallel, aspects of the human resource management process are determining the employee needs of the company and the jobs to be filled. Companies need to have the right number of people, with the right training, in the right jobs, to do the organization's work when it needs to be done. Human resource specialists are the ones who must determine future human resource needs and assess the skills of the company's existing employees to see if new people must be hired or existing ones retrained.

Creating a strategy for meeting future human resource needs is called **human resource (HR) planning**. Two important aspects of HR planning are job analysis, and forecasting the company's people needs. The HR planning process begins with a review of corporate strategy and policy. By understanding the mission of the organization, planners can understand its human resource needs.

Human resource planners must know what skills different jobs require. Information about a specific job is typically assembled through a job analysis, a study of the tasks required to do a job well. This information is used to specify the essential skills, knowledge, and abilities.

human resource (HR) planning
Creating a strategy for meeting future human resource needs.

job analysis
A study of the tasks required to do a particular job well.

Exhibit 12.2 Job Description

Position: College Recruiter
Reports to: Vice President of Human Resources

Location: Corporate Offices
Classification: Salaried/Exempt

Job Summary: Member of HR corporate team. Interacts with managers and department heads to determine hiring needs for college graduates. Visits 20 to 30 college and university campuses each year to conduct preliminary interviews of graduating students in all academic disciplines. Following initial interviews, works with corporate staffing specialists to determine persons who will be interviewed a second time. Makes recommendations to hiring managers concerning best-qualified applicants.

Job Duties and Responsibilities:

Estimated time spent and importance

15 percent	Working with managers and department heads, determines college recruiting needs.
10 percent	Determines colleges and universities with degree programs appropriate to hiring needs to be visited.
15 percent	Performs college relations activities with numerous colleges and universities.
25 percent	Visits campuses to conduct interviews of graduating seniors.
15 percent	Develops applicant files and performs initial applicant evaluations.
10 percent	Assists staffing specialists and line managers in determining who to schedule for second interviews.
5 percent	Prepares annual college recruiting report containing information and data about campuses, number interviewed, number hired, and related information.
5 percent	Participates in tracking college graduates who are hired to aid in determining campuses that provide the most outstanding employees.

Job Specification (Qualifications):

Bachelor's degree in human resource management or a related field. Minimum of two years of work experience with the company in HR or department that annually hires college graduates. Ability to perform in a team environment, especially with line managers and department heads. Very effective oral and written communication skills. Reasonably proficient in Excel, Word, and Windows computer environment and familiar with PeopleSoft.

---

job description
The tasks and responsibilities of a job.

job specification
A list of the skills, knowledge, and abilities a person must have to fill a job.

The tasks and responsibilities of a job are listed in a job description. The skills, knowledge, and abilities a person must have to fill a job are spelled out in a job specification. These two documents help human resource planners find the right people for specific jobs. A sample job description is shown in Exhibit 12.2.

HR Planning and Forecasting

Forecasting an organization's human resource needs, known as an HR *demand forecast*, is an essential aspect of HR planning. This process involves two forecasts:

1. Determining the number of people needed by some future time (in one year, for example).
2. Estimating the number of people currently employed by the organization who will be available to fill various jobs at some future time. This is an *internal* supply forecast.

By comparing human resource demand and supply forecasts, a future personnel surplus or shortage can be determined and appropriate action taken. WestJet, a low-cost airline, has continuously added planes and routes that require adding personnel. In contrast, some other airlines have reduced flights and decreased employee head count. In both cases, the companies had to forecast the number of employees needed, given their respective competitive positions with the industry. Exhibit 12.3 summarizes the process of planning and forecasting an organization's people needs.

contingent workers
Persons who prefer temporary employment, either part- or full-time.

Many companies with employee shortages are hiring contingent workers, or persons who prefer temporary employment, either part- or full-time. Post-secondary students and retired persons make up a large portion of Canada's contingent workforce. Other people who want to work but don't want to be permanent employees can join a temporary employment

Concept *Check*

Distinguish between job analysis, job description, and job specification.

Describe the job analysis and design process.

What is the process for human resource forecasting?

Exhibit 12.3 Human Resource Planning Process

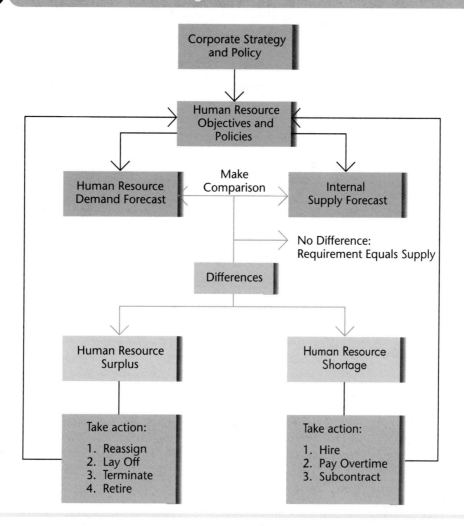

agency. A temporary employment agency performs staffing, training, and compensation functions by contracting with a business to provide employees for a specified period. A company with a shortage of accountants can rent or lease an accountant from the temporary employment agency for the expected duration of the shortage.

EMPLOYEE RECRUITMENT

LO2

When a company creates a new position or an existing one becomes vacant, it starts looking for people with qualifications that meet the requirements of the job. Two sources of job applicants are the internal and external labour markets. The internal labour market consists of employees currently employed by the company; the external labour market is the pool of potential applicants outside the company.

Internal Labour Market

Internal recruitment can be greatly facilitated by using a human resource information system containing a skills inventory, or a computerized employee database of information about an employee's previous work experience, education and certifications, job and career preferences, performance, and attendance. Promotions and job transfers are the most common results of internal recruiting. Most companies, including WestJet

Airlines, UPS, and Walmart, follow a policy of promotion from within and try to fill positions with their existing employees. The internal search for job applicants usually means that a person must change his or her job. People are typically either promoted or transferred.

External Labour Market

If qualified job candidates cannot be found inside the company, the external labour market must be tapped. **Recruitment** is the attempt to find and attract qualified applicants in the external labour market. The type of position determines which recruitment method will be used and which segment of the labour market will be searched. Boeing will not recruit an experienced engineer in the same way that it would recruit an admin support person.

Non-technical, unskilled, and other nonsupervisory workers are recruited through newspaper, radio, and sometimes even television help-wanted ads in local media. Starbucks placed ads in the *Beijing Youth Daily* to attract workers for its Beijing coffee shops. Entry-level accountants, engineers, and systems analysts are commonly hired through post-secondary campus recruitment efforts. Each year, the Canadian financial institutions send recruiters across Canada to campuses that have a business program. Another very creative recruitment method has been student groups setting up "speed-networking" events. During these events, potential employees have a few minutes with students and then the students move to the next table to meet the next recruiter.

A company that needs executives and other experienced professional, technical, and managerial employees may employ the services of an executive search company. The hiring company pays the search company a fee equivalent to one to four months of the employee's first-year salary. Many search companies specialize in a particular occupation, industry, or geographic location.

Many companies participate in local job fairs. A **job fair** is typically a one-day event held at a convention centre to bring together thousands of job seekers and hundreds of companies searching for employees. Some companies conduct a **corporate open house**.

---

recruitment
The attempt to find and attract qualified applicants in the external labour market.

Looking for a job? Check out www.workopolis.ca

job fair
An event, typically one day, held at a convention centre to bring together thousands of job seekers and hundreds of companies searching for employees.

corporate open house
Persons are invited to an open house on the premises of the corporation. Qualified applicants are encouraged to complete an application before leaving.

Concept *in Action*

Job fairs bring together hundreds of employers and thousands of job seekers. Job fairs are one of the ways human resource managers identify employees from the external job market. What are some of the benefits of job fairs to employers and potential employees?

TORONTO STAR/GETSTOCK.COM

Persons attend the open house, are briefed about various job opportunities, and are encouraged to submit a job application on the spot or before leaving the employer's premises.

Electronic Job Boards

An increasingly common and popular recruiting method involves using the Internet. Nearly all large and medium-sized businesses now use online recruiting by either drawing applicants to their own website or utilizing the services of a job board, such as Monster.ca, Career-Mosaic.com, Hotjobs.ca, or CareerPath.ca. To review and evaluate thousands of online resumés and job applications, companies depend on software to scan and track applicant materials and gather from them critical information for applicant selection.

EMPLOYEE SELECTION

LO3

selection
The process of determining which persons in the applicant pool possess the qualifications necessary to be successful on the job.

After a company has attracted enough job applicants, employment specialists begin the selection process. **Selection** is the process of determining which persons in the applicant pool possess the qualifications necessary to be successful on the job. The steps in the employee selection process are shown in Exhibit 12.4. An applicant who can jump over each step, or hurdle, will very likely receive a job offer; thus, this is known as the successive hurdles approach to applicant screening. Alternatively, an applicant can be rejected at any step or hurdle. Selection steps or hurdles are described below:

1. *Initial screening.* During the initial screening, an applicant usually completes an application form and has a brief interview of 30 minutes or less. The application form includes questions about education, work experience, and previous job duties. A personal resumé may be substituted for the application form. If the potential employer believes that the potential employee is suitable, then the next step is the interview. The interview is normally structured, consisting of a

Exhibit 12.4 Steps of the Employee Selection Process

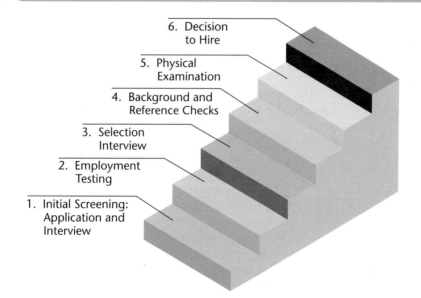

6. Decision to Hire
5. Physical Examination
4. Background and Reference Checks
3. Selection Interview
2. Employment Testing
1. Initial Screening: Application and Interview

short list of specific questions. For example: Are you familiar with any accounting software packages? Did you supervise anyone in your last job? Did you use a company car when making sales calls?

2. *Employment testing.* Following the initial screening, an applicant may be asked to take one or more employment tests, such as the Wonderlic Personnel Test, a mental-ability test. Some tests are designed to measure special job skills, others measure aptitudes, and some are intended to capture personality characteristics. The Myers-Briggs Type Indicator is a personality and motivational instrument widely used on college campuses as an aid in providing job and career counselling as well as assisting a student in selecting his or her major. In recent years, some companies have begun to use a test that assesses emotional intelligence. Frequently called the e-quotient, the emotional intelligence quotient reveals how well a person understands his or her own emotions and the emotions of others, and how he or she behaves based on this understanding.

3. *Selection interview.* The tool most widely used in making hiring decisions by Intel, Merck, and other companies is the selection interview, an in-depth discussion of an applicant's work experience, skills and abilities, education, and career interests. For managerial and professional positions, an applicant may be interviewed by several persons, including the line manager for the position to be filled. This interview is designed to determine an applicant's communication ability and motivation. It is also a means for gathering additional factual information from the applicant such as college major, years of part-time work experience, computer equipment used, and reason for leaving the last job. The applicant may be asked to explain how to solve a particular management problem or how she or he provided leadership to a group in a previous work situation when an important problem had to be solved quickly. United Airlines asks prospective flight attendants how they handled a conflict with a customer or coworker in a previous job.

   Carolyn Murray, a recruiter for W. L. Gore and Associates, makers of Gore-Tex, says she pays little attention to a candidate's carefully scripted responses to her admittedly easy questions. Instead, she listens for a casual remark that reveals the reality behind an otherwise thought-out reply. Using a baseball analogy, Carolyn's examples of how three job candidates struck out are presented in Exhibit 12.5.[2]

4. *Background and reference check.* If applicants pass the selection interview, companies may examine their background and check their references. Some potential employers carefully research applicants' backgrounds, particularly their legal history, reasons for leaving previous jobs, and even creditworthiness. Retail companies, where employees have extensive contact with customers, tend to be very careful about checking applicant backgrounds. It is important to note that reference checks must be carried out in accordance with current regulations and legislations. Two other issues are important regarding reference checks: their reliability, and the fact that some companies do not provide reference checks because of potential liability matters.

   The increasing popularity of social networks can provide much information about the person. Potential employers can search these social networks to find out more about the candidate. It cannot be stressed enough that anyone posting information should be very careful what information they provide on these social networks.

5. *Physical exams.* Companies frequently require job candidates to have a medical check-up to ensure they are physically able to perform a job. In Canada, drug testing can be conducted only after a conditional offer of employment has been extended. If the new employee tests positive, he or she will probably still be hired unless there is undue hardship to the company as a result. If the condition turns out to be an addiction, the employee will be treated under the new employer's benefit plan, and any issues as a result of the addiction become performance management issues.[3]

Concept *Check*

What are the steps in the employee selection process?

Describe some ways in which applicants are tested.

Exhibit 12.5 Striking Out with Gore-Tex

THE PITCH (QUESTION TO APPLICANT)	THE SWING (APPLICANT'S RESPONSE)	THE MISS (INTERVIEWER'S REACTION TO RESPONSE)
"Give me an example of a time when you had a conflict with a team member."	"Our leader asked me to handle all of the FedExing for our team. I did it, but I thought that FedExing was a waste of my time."	"At Gore, we work from a team concept. Her answer shows that she won't exactly jump when one of her teammates needs help."
"Tell me how you solved a problem that was impeding your project."	"One of the engineers on my team wasn't pulling his weight, and we were closing in on a deadline. So I took on some of his work."	"The candidate may have resolved the issue for this particular deadline, but he did nothing to prevent the problem from happening again."
"What's the one thing that you would change about your current position?"	"My job as a salesman has become boring. Now I want the responsibility of managing people."	"He's probably not maximizing his current territory, and he is complaining. Will he find his next role 'boring' and complain about that role, too?"

6. *Decision to hire.* If an applicant progresses satisfactorily through all the selection steps, a decision to hire the individual is made. The decision to hire is nearly always made by the manager of the new employee.

EMPLOYEE TRAINING AND DEVELOPMENT

LO4

To ensure that both new and experienced employees have the knowledge and skills to perform their jobs successfully, organizations invest in **training and development** activities. Training and development involves learning situations in which the employee acquires additional knowledge or skills to increase job performance. Training objectives specify performance improvements, reductions in errors, job knowledge to be gained, and/or other positive organizational results. Training is done either on or off the job. The process of creating and implementing training and development activities is shown in Exhibit 12.6.

training and development
Activities that provide learning situations in which an employee acquires additional knowledge or skills to increase job performance.

Exhibit 12.6 Employee Training and Development Process

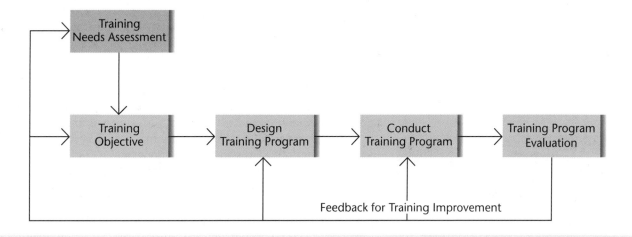

orientation
Training that prepares a new employee to perform on the job; includes information about job assignments, work rules, equipment, and performance expectations, as well as about company policies, salary and benefits, and parking.

For the latest news in the human resources field and to learn how the HR field is gaining in importance, see the Canadian Council of Human Resources Association website at www.cchra.ca/en

on-the-job training
Training in which the employee learns the job by doing it with guidance from a supervisor or an experienced coworker.

job rotation
Reassignment of workers to several different jobs over time so that they can learn the basics of each job.

apprenticeship
A form of on-the-job training that combines specific job instruction with classroom instruction.

articling
Working in an accredited environment to apply theoretical knowledge learned through formal education and develop professional judgment.

mentoring
A form of on-the-job training in which a senior manager or other experienced employee provides job- and career-related information to a protégé.

programmed instruction
A form of computer-assisted off-the-job training.

simulation
A scaled-down version or mock-up of equipment, process, or work environment.

New employee training is essential and usually begins with orientation, which entails getting the new employee ready to perform on the job. Formal orientation (often a half-day classroom program) provides information about company policies, salary and benefits, and parking. Although this information is very helpful, the more important orientation is about job assignments, work rules, equipment, and performance expectations provided by the new employee's supervisor and coworkers. This second briefing tends to be more informal and can last for several days or even weeks.

On-the-Job Training

Continuous training for both new and experienced employees is important to keep job skills fresh. Job-specific training, designed to enhance a new employee's ability to perform a job, includes on-the-job training, during which the employee learns the job by doing it with guidance from a supervisor or experienced coworker.

On-the-job training takes place at the job site or workstation and tends to be directly related to the job. This training involves specific job instructions, coaching (guidance given to new employees by experienced ones), special project assignments, or job rotation. Job rotation is the reassignment of workers to several different jobs over time. It is not uncommon for management trainees to work sequentially in two or three departments, such as customer service, credit, and human resources, during their first year on the job.

An apprenticeship usually combines specific on-the-job instruction with classroom training. It might last as long as four years and can be found in the skilled trades of carpentry, plumbing, and electrical work. For many business graduates (e.g., accounting, as well as other degrees such as law), the graduates must complete an articling position where they continue their education and are given on-the-job training.

With mentoring, another form of on-the-job training, a senior manager or other experienced employee provides job and career-related information to a protégé. Inexpensive and providing instantaneous feedback, mentoring is becoming increasingly popular with many companies. For an example of mentoring for cultural orientation, explore the Expanding Around the Globe box.

Off-the-Job Training

Even with the advantages of on-the-job training, many companies recognize that it is often necessary to train employees away from the workplace. With off-the-job training, employees learn their duties away from the job. There are numerous popular methods of off-the-job training. Frequently, it takes place in a classroom, where cases, role-play exercises, films, videos, lectures, and computer demonstrations are utilized to develop workplace skills.

Web-based technology is being increasingly used along with more traditional off-the-job training methods. E-learning and e-training involve online computer presentation of information for learning new job tasks. Many companies with widely dispersed employees deliver training materials electronically to save time and travel costs. For example, transportation companies deliver technical and safety training through programmed instruction, a computer-assisted, self-paced, and highly structured training method that presents trainees with concepts and problems using a modular format. Software makes sure that employees receive, undergo, and complete, as well as sign off on, various training modules.

Computer-assisted training is also done using a simulation, a scaled-down version of a manufacturing process or even a mock cockpit of a jet airplane. Air Canada uses a training simulator for pilots to practise hazardous flight manoeuvres or learn the controls of a new aircraft in a safe, controlled environment with no passengers. The simulator allows for more direct transfer of learning to the job.

Concept *Check*

Describe several types of on-the-job training.

What are the advantages of programmed instruction and simulation?

How is technology impacting off-the-job training?

Expanding Around the Globe

EMPLOYEES ON THE (INTERNATIONAL) MOVE

Is an international job assignment a step up the ladder to a more rewarding career path or a potential minefield of professional and family risk?

The answer depends as much on an employee's family situation as his or her ambition, according to a new survey that explores worldwide employee-relocation trends. And it also depends on how well the company supports and handles a transfer to an international location.

Working abroad at one of the Canadian or foreign multinational companies can be exciting and look good on your resumé. Increasing numbers of recent college graduates and experienced professionals are offered opportunities for overseas work assignments ranging from a few days to 24 months, or longer. But acclimating to a new country and culture, as well as a new work environment, can be daunting and involves some unique challenges. According to GMAC Global Relocation Services, an assignment and mobility consulting service that helps employees settle in a foreign country, retaining expatriate talent remains an enormous challenge for companies. With attrition rates at least double that of non-expatriate employees, about 21 percent of overseas employees left their companies during an international assignment.

Expatriates face other challenges aside from the demands of work:

- choosing schools for children
- securing housing
- finding medical facilities
- opening bank accounts
- finding transportation and obtaining a driver's licence
- completing government forms
- locating stores that sell familiar foods
- learning about community and entertainment offerings

With 1200 to 1500 employees working outside of their home countries at any given time, KPMG International, one of the world's largest accounting firms with a presence in 144 countries, attempts to deal with employee relocation adjustment issues by utilizing a "buddy" system. At work, the KPMG Global Code of Conduct, entitled "Performance with Integrity," sets out guidelines of ethical conduct that KPMG requires of all its employees worldwide. The code applies equally to partners and employees of all KPMG member companies regardless of their title or position.

To ease the social and cultural burden for new expatriates, the company links the employee to a buddy for one-on-one support during the length of their assignment, which is typically 24 months. Timothy Dwyer, national director for international human resource advisory services at KPMG, points out that buddies—who usually do not have a direct working relationship with the new expatriate— function in a social role outside of work. They help the new employee and the family resolve the myriad of problems that can arise.

KPMG places a high value on the buddy support role, which is taken into account when performance evaluations are conducted each year. By creating a sense of shared identity within and outside of the organization, KPMG's international employees are more likely to stay on the job.[4]

Thinking Critically

1. The buddy system at KPMG is a value-added human resource service that is intangible and difficult to assess; nevertheless, it is important to identify and measure its benefits and costs. What do you think these are and how would you measure them?
2. What are the top four or five job qualifications an employee should have to be considered for an overseas assignment?

SOURCE: Eric Krell, "Budding Relationships," *HR Magazine*, vol. 50, June, 2005, pp. 114–118, http://findarticles.com/p/articles/mi_m3495/is_6_50/ai_n14700370/?tag=content;col1.

PERFORMANCE PLANNING AND EVALUATION

LO5

Along with employee orientation and training, new employees learn about performance expectations through performance planning and evaluation. Managers provide employees with expectations about the job. These are communicated as job objectives, schedules, deadlines, and product and/or service quality requirements. Typically as an employee performs job tasks, the supervisor periodically evaluates the employee's efforts. A **performance appraisal** is a comparison of actual performance with expected performance to assess an employee's contributions to the organization and to make decisions about training, compensation, promotion, and other job changes. In some organizations, not only does the immediate supervisor evaluate the subordinate's performance, but others might as well. These could include a self-appraisal by the employee, a subordinate appraisal of an immediate supervisor, or an appraisal by a peer, a team, and customers. The typical performance planning and appraisal process is shown in Exhibit 12.7 and is described below:

1. Performance standards are established.
2. The employee works to meet the standards and expectations.

performance appraisal
A comparison of actual performance with expected performance to assess an employee's contributions to the organization.

Exhibit 12.7 | Performance Planning and Evaluation

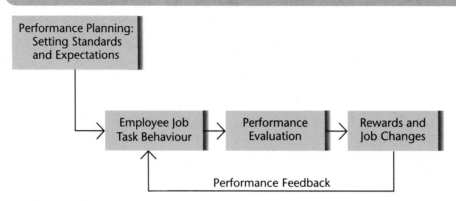

Performance Planning: Setting Standards and Expectations

Employee Job Task Behaviour → Performance Evaluation → Rewards and Job Changes

Performance Feedback

Concept *Check*

What are the steps in the performance planning and appraisal process?

What purposes do performance appraisals serve?

Describe some sources of information for the performance appraisal.

3. The employee's supervisor evaluates the employee's work in terms of quality and quantity of output and various characteristics such as job knowledge, initiative, relationships with others, and attendance and punctuality.
4. Following the performance evaluation, reward (pay raise) and job change (promotion) decisions can be made.
5. Rewards are positive feedback, providing reinforcement or encouragement for the employee to work harder in the future.

Information for performance appraisals can be assembled using rating scales, supervisor logs of employee job incidents, and reports of sales and production statistics. Regardless of the source, performance information should be accurate and a record of the employee's job behaviour and efforts. Performance appraisals serve a number of purposes, but they are most often used to make decisions about pay raises, training needs, advancement opportunities, and employee terminations.

Concept *in Action*

During a typical performance appraisal, a manager evaluates an employee's performance, comparing actual performance to expected performance goals. At most companies, feedback comes from work teams, peers, and customers to help employees develop perspective on their management style and skills. How does the performance appraisal help the employee and the organization?

© FANCY/VEER/CORBIS/GLOW IMAGES

Creating the Future of Business

JEFF NUGENT, CONTINGENT WORKFORCE SOLUTIONS INC.

Founder, President, and CEO of Contingent Workforce Solutions (CWS) Jeff Nugent runs one of Canada's fastest growing companies; fast enough to top 2011's *PROFIT HOT 50* ranking of Canada's Top New Growth Companies. Located in an industrial park in Mississauga, the company's offices aren't what you'd expect from a top ranking company, but this is CWS's fourth move to larger space in as many years. The company's revenue increased 10,330 percent from 2008 to 2011—yes, you read it right—with sales over $10 million in 2010. And according to Jeff, quoted in the August 21, 2011, issue of *Profit* magazine: "We see a whole whack of growth happening," as the company expands into new markets in Europe, Asia, and elsewhere; opportunities have "presented themselves through social-media channels."

The secret to Jeff's success seems to be applying creative approaches to building a company that is "both exceptionally lean and completely scalable." This was always his goal, right out of university. He originally took a job as an independent sales agent for an IT-staffing company, working with temporary workers. It gave him valuable "insight into the support that employers and employees need" in the contingent labour world.

The environment was also ripe for the combination of software and consulting services Jeff provides; companies were moving from the inflexible overhead of permanent employees to more agile temporary and contract workers. Conversely, the demographics of the workforce had also shifted in Jeff's favour as baby boomers and younger generations sought out self-employment as a more flexible career choice. What Jeff saw as a key opportunity was CWS's ability to help companies deal with how to manage their growing temporary labour force while significantly reducing the costs, and the employment and tax law risks of using contract labour. And what an opportunity it was. According to Jeff: "That was my 'Aha!' moment.

I realized there was a need, at the enterprise level, for services that manage clients' entire contract workforces. I had expertise in that space. I saw the trend happening and thought, 'With my skill set, I could do it.' "

After graduating with a business degree in 1995 and gaining extensive experience in the field, Jeff started the venture in 2008, with money from his savings and three young kids at home. He said it was "terrifying," but he had confidence. CWS's combination of "hyper-talented employees and smart technology" proved a great foundation for success. The company's model "is relatively simple: the staff tells clients what they must do to streamline the management of their contingent workers and comply with regulations. And CWS's software, called SimplicityVMS, automates everything from time-sheet management to tax compliance, all while giving clients a real-time view of their spending on contract workers. The software, designed by Jeff, has been instrumental in its success, as it frees up CWS's staff to provide value-added consulting, enabling the company to bring in very high revenues relative to its employee base. In separating its software out into its own operating unit, CWS has turned a typical cost centre into a profit centre by bringing in business from a lot of companies that didn't require CWS's consulting services, but had a need for it's software.

Jeff's story is one of seizing an opportunity in an area of strength. Capitalizing on a classic SWOT analysis, he saw the opportunity, he understood the market, and, most importantly, he had the guts and the entrepreneurial spirit to make it work to ensure success—that is, incredible success.

Thinking Critically

1. How much of a factor do you think environmental trends played in CWS's success?
2. What trends from our PESTI model did Jeff seize upon, and do you think they are trends that are here to stay? Why or why not? What other factors account for the explosive growth of the company?

SOURCES: http://www.cwsolutions.ca; http://www.profitguide.com/article/42499.

EMPLOYEE COMPENSATION AND BENEFITS

LO6

Compensation, which includes both pay and benefits, is closely connected to performance appraisal. Employees who perform better tend to get bigger pay raises. Several factors affect an employee's pay:

1. *Pay structure and internal influences.* Wages, salaries, and benefits usually reflect the importance of the job. The jobs that management considers more important are compensated at a higher rate; president, chief engineer, and chief financial officer are high-paying jobs. Likewise, different jobs of equal importance to the company are compensated at the same rate. For instance, if a drill-press operator and a lathe operator are considered of equal importance, they might both be paid $25 per hour.

2. *Pay level and external influences.* In deciding how much to pay workers, the company must also be concerned with the salaries paid by competitors. If competitors are paying much higher wages, a company might lose its best employees. Larger companies conduct salary surveys to see what other companies are paying. Wage and salary surveys conducted by Statistics Canada, for example, can also be useful.

An employer can decide to pay at, above, or below the going rate. Most companies try to offer competitive wages and salaries within a geographic area or an industry. If a company pays below-market wages, it might not be able to hire skilled people. The level, or competitiveness, of a company's compensation is determined by the company's financial condition (or profitability), efficiency, and employee productivity, as well as the going rates paid by competitors.

Types of Compensation

There are two basic types of compensation: direct and indirect. Direct pay is the wage or salary received by the employee; indirect pay consists of various employee benefits and services. Employees are usually paid directly on the basis of the amount of time they work, the amount they produce, or some combination of time and output. Hourly rates of pay or a monthly salary are considered base pay, or an amount of pay received by the employee regardless of output level.

The following are the most common types of compensation:

- *Hourly wages.* These will vary depending on the positions and job market. Each province and territory in Canada is responsible to set a "minimum hourly wage."
- *Salaries.* Managerial and professional employees are usually paid an annual salary on either a biweekly or a monthly basis.
- *Piecework and commission.* Some employees are paid according to how much they produce or sell. A car salesperson might be paid $500 for each car sold or a 3 percent commission on the car's sale price. Thus, a salesperson who sold four cars in one week at $500 per car would earn $2000 in pay for that week. Alternatively, a 3 percent commission on four cars sold with total sales revenue of $70,000 would yield $2100 in pay.

Increasingly, companies are paying employees by using a base wage or salary and an incentive. The incentive feature is designed to increase individual employee, work group, and/or organizational performance. Incentive pay plans are commonly referred to as variable or contingent pay arrangements.

- *Accelerated commission schedule.* A salesperson could be paid a commission rate of 3 percent on the first $50,000 of sales per month, 4 percent on the next $30,000, and 5 percent on any sales beyond $80,000. For a salesperson who made $90,000 of sales in one month, the monthly pay would be as follows:
  3 percent × $50,000 = $1500
  4 percent × $30,000 = $1200
  5 percent × $10,000 = $ 500
  $90,000 → $3200
- *Bonus.* A bonus is a payment for reaching a specific goal; it may be paid on a monthly, quarterly, or annual basis. A bank with several offices or branches might set monthly goals for opening new accounts, making loans, and customer service. Each employee of a branch that meets all goals would be paid a monthly bonus of $100. Although the bonuses are paid to the employees individually, the employees must function as an effective, high-performing group to reach the monthly goals.
- *Profit sharing.* A company that offers profit sharing pays employees a portion of the profits over a preset level. For example, profits beyond 10 percent of gross sales might be shared at a 50 percent rate with employees. The company retains the remaining profits. All employees might receive the same profit shares, or the shares might vary according to base pay.

Making Ethical Choices

KEEPING SECRETS

Working on national security issues for a consulting company with the Canadian Security Intelligence Service contracts has been both exciting and increasingly stressful. The excitement comes from the actual work of investigating and evaluating potential terrorist threats to Canada. The stress is a result of a greatly increased workload and much closer scrutiny of your work. When you started your job in June, 40- to 45-hour weeks were common. Since the increased terrorist attacks around the world, your workload has increased dramatically, and you now must work 55 to 65 hours per week. Managers appear to be monitoring employees' activities and paying closer attention to their mental state for evidence of instability. Along with your fellow workers, you are concerned that the heightened security measures might change the policies with regard to confidentiality of medical records.

Because the consulting company's culture doesn't support open discussion, you don't feel comfortable talking with your colleagues or your supervisor about the stress you are experiencing. Instead, you seek counsel from HR and are given names of several psychotherapists who participate in the company's employee assistance plan. You assume that your visit to HR and the subject of that visit are as secret as the nature of your work. Your psychotherapist has advised you that your visits and the content of all sessions are confidential.

You begin to sense that your supervisor is aware of your 90-minute absences, even though you made sure to schedule visits to the therapist on a different day and different time each week. The idea that your supervisor might know you are seeking psychological counselling only increases your stress level.

ETHICAL DILEMMA: Does your employer have the right to know about your visits to a psychotherapist?

SOURCES: Tybe Diamond, "American Psychoanalytic Association Files a Lawsuit to Challenge the Bush Administration HIPPA Abuses," e-mail, April 14, 2003; "Protecting Privacy and Personal Security—Our World's Need for a Careful Balance and the 10 Commandments of Ethical Surveillance," *PRNewswire*, September 13, 2001, http://www.findarticles.com; and Jonathan A. Segal, "Security vs. Privacy: To Ensure a Secure Environment for All Workers Avoid Violating the Privacy of Any One Individual," *HR Magazine*, February 2002, http://www.findarticles.com.

- *Fringe benefits.* **Fringe benefits** are indirect compensation and include pensions, health insurance, vacations, and many others. Some fringe benefits are required by law (e.g., paid vacations and holidays, employment insurance and Canada or Québec Pension Plan [CPP or QPP]; EI and CPP/QPP are paid at least in part by the employer).

fringe benefits
Indirect compensation, such as pensions, health insurance, and vacations.

Many employers also offer fringe benefits not required by law. Among these are paid time off (e.g., extra vacations, sick days), insurance (health care, disability, life, dental, vision, and accidental death and dismemberment), pensions and retirement savings accounts, and stock purchase options.

Some companies with numerous fringe benefits allow employees to mix and match benefit items or select items based on individual needs. This is a flexible, or cafeteria-style, benefit plan. A younger employee with a family might desire to purchase medical, disability, and life insurance, whereas an older employee might want to put more benefit dollars into a retirement savings plan. All employees are allocated the same number of benefit dollars but can spend these dollars on different items and in different amounts.

Concept *Check*

How does a company establish a pay scale for its employees?

What is the difference between direct and indirect pay?

UNDERSTANDING LABOUR RELATIONS IN A UNIONIZED ENVIRONMENT

LO7

A **labour union** is an organization that represents workers in dealing with management over issues involving wages, hours, and working conditions. The labour relations process that produces a union–management relationship consists of three phases: union organizing, negotiating a labour agreement, and the day-to-day administering of the agreement. In Phase 1, a group of employees within a company might form a union on

labour union
An organization that represents workers in dealing with management over issues involving wages, hours, and working conditions.

Determining a president or CEO's fair salary isn't easy. CEOs are responsible for making decisions that can impact thousands of employees and dramatically increase or decrease the value of a company. Christine Magee's compensation package would have to reflect her responsibilities as president of Canada's largest retailer of mattresses, Sleep Country Canada. Her responsibilities include 240 corporate stores in 17 regional markets. How do you think executive salaries should be determined?

collective bargaining
The process of negotiating labour agreements that provide for compensation and working arrangements mutually acceptable to the union and to management.

their own, or an established union may target an employer and organize many of the company's workers into a local labour union. The second phase constitutes collective bargaining, which is the process of negotiating labour agreements that provide for compensation and working arrangements mutually acceptable to the union and to management.

Finally, the third phase of the labour relations process involves the daily administering of the labour agreement, primarily through the handling of worker grievances and other workforce management problems that require interaction between managers and labour union officials.

Modern Labour Movement

local union
A branch or unit of a national union that represents workers at a specific plant or in a specific geographic area.

national union
A union that consists of many local unions in a particular industry, skilled trade, or geographic area and thus represents workers throughout an entire country.

A local union is a branch or unit of a national union that represents workers at a specific plant or over a specific geographic area. In conformance to national union rules, local unions determine the number of local union officers, procedures for electing officers, the schedule of local meetings, financial arrangements with the national organization, and the local's role in negotiating labour agreements.

The largest national union is the Canadian Union of Public Employees (CUPE), with more than half a million members across Canada. CUPE represents workers in airlines, education, emergency services, health care, libraries, municipalities, public utilities, social services, transportation, and universities. Under the CUPE national union are the various local unions (e.g., CUPE local 774 in Abbotsford, British Columbia).

The three main functions of the local union are collective bargaining, worker relations and membership services, and community and political activities. Collective bargaining generally takes place every two or three years. Local union officers and shop stewards oversee worker-management relations on a day-to-day basis. A shop steward is an elected union official who represents union members to management when workers have issues. For most union members, his or her primary contact with the union is through union officials at the local level.

shop steward
An elected union official who represents union members to management when workers have issues.

Negotiating Collective Agreements

A union contract is created through collective bargaining. Typically, both management and union negotiating teams consist of a few people. One person on each side is the chief spokesperson.

Bargaining begins with union and management negotiators setting a bargaining agenda, a list of contract issues that will be discussed. Much of the bargaining over the specific details takes place through face-to-face meetings and the exchange of written proposals. Demands, proposals, and counterproposals are exchanged during several rounds of bargaining. The resulting contract must then be approved by top management and by union members. The collective bargaining process is shown in Exhibit 12.8.

The union contract is a legally binding agreement that typically covers such issues as union security, management rights, wages and benefits, job security, and grievance procedures. Each of these is discussed in this section.

UNION SECURITY   One of the key issues in a contract is union security. From the union's perspective, the most secure arrangement is the **closed shop**, a company where only union members can be hired. The union serves, in effect, as an employment

closed shop
A company where only union members can be hired.

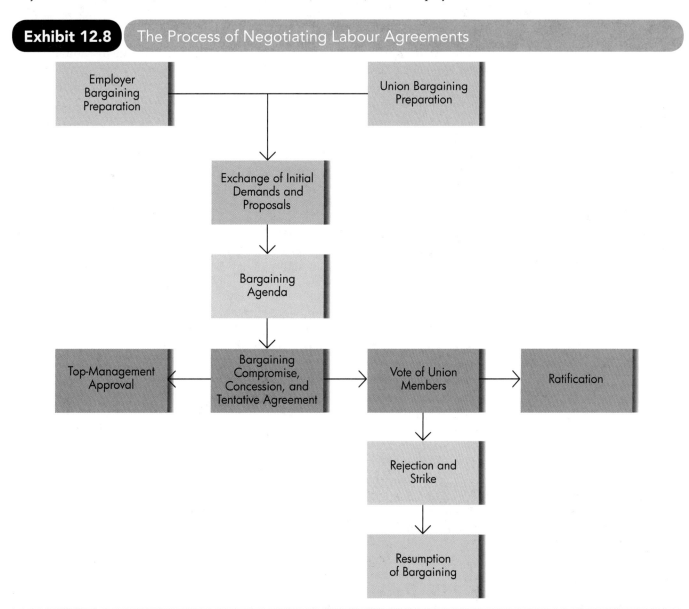

Exhibit 12.8   The Process of Negotiating Labour Agreements

CHAPTER 12 Managing Human Resources and Labour Relations

union shop
A company where non-union workers can be hired but must then join the union.

agency shop
A company where employees are not required to join the union but must pay it a fee to cover its expenses in representing them.

open shop
A company where employees do not have to join the union or pay dues or fees to the union; established under right-to-work laws.

agency for the company. Today, the most common form of union security is the **union shop**. Non-union workers can be hired, but then they must join the union, normally within 30 or 60 days.

An **agency shop** does not require employees to join the union, but to keep working at the company, employees must pay the union a fee to cover its expenses in representing them. The union must fairly represent all workers, including those who do not become members.

When employees can work at a unionized company without having to join the union, this arrangement is commonly known as an **open shop**. Workers don't have to join the union or pay dues or fees to the union.

MANAGEMENT RIGHTS When a company becomes unionized, management loses some of its decision-making abilities. But management still has certain rights that can be negotiated in collective bargaining.

One way to lessen a union's influence in the management of an organization is by having a *management rights clause* in the labour agreement. Most union contracts have one. A typical clause gives the employer all rights to manage the business except as specified in the contract. For instance, if the contract does not specify the criteria for promotions, with a management rights clause managers will have the right to use any criteria they wish. Another way to preserve management rights is to list areas that are not subject to collective bargaining. This list might secure management's right to schedule work hours, hire and fire workers, set production standards, determine the number of supervisors in each department, and promote, demote, and transfer workers.

WAGES AND BENEFITS Much bargaining effort goes into wage increases and improvements in fringe benefits. Once agreed to, they remain in effect for the life of the contract. Some contracts provide for a **cost-of-living adjustment (COLA)**, under which wages increase automatically as the cost of living goes up.

Other contracts provide for *lump-sum wage adjustments*. The workers' base pay remains unchanged for the contract period (usually two or three years), but each worker receives a bonus (or lump sum) once or twice during the contract.

The union and the employer are usually both concerned about the company's ability to pay higher wages. Its ability to pay depends greatly on its profitability. But even if profits have declined, average to above-average wage increases are still possible if labour productivity increases.

cost-of-living adjustment (COLA)
A provision in a labour contract that calls for wages to increase automatically as the cost of living rises (usually measured by the consumer price index).

In addition to requests for wage increases, unions usually want better fringe benefits. In some industries, such as steel and auto manufacturing, fringe benefits are 40 percent of the total cost of compensation. Benefits might include higher wages for overtime work, holiday work, and less desirable shifts; insurance programs (life, health and hospitalization, dental care); payment for certain non-work time (rest periods, vacations, holidays, sick time); pensions; and income maintenance plans. A fairly common income maintenance plan is a *supplementary unemployment benefits fund* set up by the employer to help laid-off workers.

JOB SECURITY AND SENIORITY Cost-of-living adjustments, supplementary unemployment benefits, and certain other benefits give employees some financial security. But most financial security is directly related to job security—the assurance, to some degree, that workers will keep their jobs. Of course, job security depends primarily on the continued success and financial well-being of the company.

Seniority, the length of an employee's continuous service with a company, is discussed in about 90 percent of all labour contracts. Seniority is a factor in job security; usually, unions want the workers with the most seniority to have the most job security.

Concept *Check*

Discuss the difference between a local and national union.

Explain the collective bargaining process.

Explain each of the following: closed shop, union shop, agency shop, and open shop.

GRIEVANCE AND ARBITRATION The union's main way of policing the contract is the grievance procedure. A **grievance** is a formal complaint, by an employee or by the union, that management has violated some part of the contract. Under a typical contract, the employee starts by presenting the grievance to the supervisor, either in person or in writing. The typical grievance procedure is illustrated in Exhibit 12.9.

If the problem isn't solved, the grievance is put in writing. The employee, one or more union officials, the supervisor, and perhaps the plant manager then discuss the grievance. If the matter still can't be resolved, another meeting takes place with higher-level representatives of both parties present. If top management and the local union president can't resolve the grievance, it goes to arbitration.

Arbitration is the process of settling a labour–management dispute by having a third party—a single arbitrator or a panel—make a decision. The arbitrator is mutually chosen by labour and management and is expected to be impartial. The decision is final and binding on the union and the employer. The arbitrator reviews the grievance at a hearing and then makes the decision, which is presented in a document called the award.

Similar to arbitration is **mediation**, the process of settling issues in which the parties present their case to a neutral mediator. The mediator (the specialist) holds talks with union and management negotiators at separate meetings and at joint sessions. The mediator also suggests compromises. Mediators cannot issue binding

grievance
A formal complaint, filed by an employee or by the union, charging that management has violated the contract.

arbitration
The process of settling a labour–management dispute by having a third party—a single arbitrator or a panel—make a decision, which is binding on both the union and the employer.

mediation
A method of attempting to settle labour issues in which a specialist (the mediator) tries to persuade management and the union to adjust or settle their dispute.

Exhibit 12.9 Typical Grievance Procedure

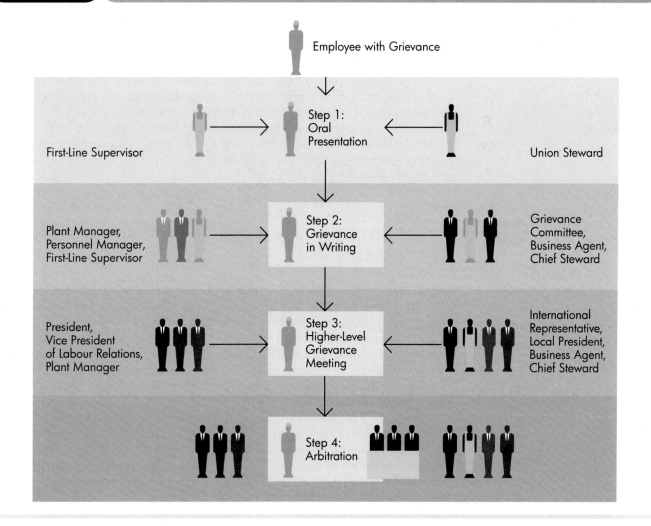

Employee with Grievance

First-Line Supervisor → **Step 1: Oral Presentation** ← Union Steward

Plant Manager, Personnel Manager, First-Line Supervisor → **Step 2: Grievance in Writing** ← Grievance Committee, Business Agent, Chief Steward

President, Vice President of Labour Relations, Plant Manager → **Step 3: Higher-Level Grievance Meeting** ← International Representative, Local President, Business Agent, Chief Steward

Step 4: Arbitration

CHAPTER 12 Managing Human Resources and Labour Relations

Exhibit 12.10	Strategies of Unions and Employers

UNION STRATEGIES		EMPLOYER STRATEGIES	
Strike:	Employees refuse to work.	Lockout:	Employer refuses to let employees enter plant to work.
Boycott:	Employees try to keep customers and others from doing business with employer.	Strike replacements:	Employer uses non-union employees to do jobs of striking union employees.
Picketing:	Employees march near entrance of business to publicize their view of dispute and discourage customers.	Mutual-aid pact:	Employer receives money from other companies in industry to cover some of income lost because of strikes.
Corporate campaign:	Union disrupts shareholder meetings or buys company stock to have more influence over management.	Shift production:	Employer moves production to non-union plant or out of country.

Concept Check

Describe the grievance procedure.

What is the distinction between arbitration and mediation?

In what ways do arbitrators act like judges?

decisions or impose a settlement on the disputing parties. Their only tools are communication and persuasion. Mediation almost always produces a settlement between the union and a company, but sometimes the process takes months or even a year, and either or both sides can reject the mediator's assistance.

Tactics for Pressuring a Contract Settlement

Virtually all labour agreements specify peaceful resolution of conflicts, usually through arbitration. However, when a contract expires and a new agreement has not been reached, the union is free to strike or engage in other efforts to exert economic pressure on the employer. A strike occurs when employees refuse to work. Likewise, the employer can put pressure on the union through a lockout or by hiring strike replacements if the union has called a strike. Some services that are seen to be critical do not have the option of a strike or lockout. Other strategies to force a contract settlement are listed in Exhibit 12.10.

LAWS AFFECTING HUMAN RESOURCE MANAGEMENT

Learn more about the Employment Equity Act by searching the Department of Justice Canada at www.justice.gc.ca

Federal laws help ensure that job applicants and employees are treated fairly and not discriminated against. Hiring, training, and job placement must be unbiased. Promotion and compensation decisions must be based on performance. These laws help all Canadians who have talent, training, and the desire to get ahead.

New legislation and the continual interpretation and reinterpretation of existing laws will continue to make the jobs of human resource managers challenging and complicated. The key laws that currently affect human resource management are shown in Exhibit 12.11.

Employers may not discriminate against persons with disability. They must make "reasonable accommodations," so that qualified employees can perform the job, unless doing so would cause "undue hardship" for the business. Altering work schedules, modifying equipment so a wheelchair-bound person can use it, and making buildings accessible by ramps and elevators are considered reasonable. Two companies often praised for their efforts to hire people with disabilities are McDonald's and IBM Canada.

Strikes are powerful union tools, usually used as a last resort when labour and management cannot reach agreement on issues such as wages, pensions, vacation time, and other benefits. In 2011 Canada Post, a Crown corporation, went on rotating strikes, and the corporation retaliated by locking out the workers. The federal government forced the two sides back to work through legislation. What other strategies are available to both unions and managements to force a contract?

JASON LEE/REUTERS/LANDOV

Exhibit 12.11	Laws Impacting Human Resource Management

LAW	PURPOSE	APPLICABILITY
Charter of Rights and Freedoms (contained in the Constitution Act of 1982)	Provides the right to live and seek employment anywhere in Canada	Takes precedence over all other laws
Human rights legislation	Provides equal opportunity for members of protected groups in areas such as accommodation, contracts, provision of goods and services, and employment	Comprises federal, provincial, and territorial laws with a common objective
Canadian Human Rights Act (1977)	Prohibits discrimination on a number of grounds	Applies to federal government agencies, Crown corporations, and businesses under federal jurisdiction
Employment Equity Act (amended in 1996)	Attempts to remove employment barriers and promote equality for the members of four designated groups: women, visible minorities, Aboriginal people, and persons with disabilities	Every employer must implement the Act and make every reasonable accommodation to ensure that people in the designated groups are represented in their organization. The degree of representation in each occupational group should reflect the Canadian workforce and be consistent with their ability to meet reasonable occupational requirements
Occupational Health and Safety Act	Designed to protect the health and safety of workers by minimizing work-related accidents and illness	All provinces, territories, and the federal jurisdiction have occupational health and safety legislation
WHMIS (Workplace Hazardous Materials Information System)	Designed to protect workers by providing information about hazardous materials in the workplace	Canada-wide legally mandated system

For some occupations, danger is part of the job description. Tallies of work-related casualties routinely identify loggers, pilots, commercial fishermen, and steel workers as holding the most deadly jobs in industry. Job fatalities are often linked to the use of heavy or outdated equipment. However, many work-related deaths also happen in common highway accidents or as homicides. What laws and agencies are designated to improve occupational safety?

© NATALIE FOBES/TERRA/CORBIS

Sustainable Business, Sustainable World

ADIDAS

Adidas, headquartered in Germany, is another example of a company ranked as one of the Top 100 most sustainable companies in the world in 2011—number 38 according to the 2011 *Global 100 Most Sustainable Corporations in the World.*

Adidas outsources most of its production, and as a result works with a very extensive, multi-layered supply chain consisting of more than 1,200 independent factories in 69 countries around the world, many of which are in China, India, Indonesia, Thailand, and Vietnam. Its ability to operate in a sustainable fashion is therefore linked very closely to the strength of its partnerships with these suppliers.

You will be happy to know that Adidas cares about how workers are treated in its suppliers' factories. They have written "Workplace Standards" to safeguard the health and safety of the workers and ensure environmentally sound operations. Adidas works with its suppliers to guide and train them, and compliance with these standards is verified by independent auditors who also evaluate the standards themselves.

According to Adidas "Performance, passion, integrity, diversity … are the core values found in sport. Sport is the soul of the Adidas Group. We measure ourselves by these values, and we measure our business partners in the same way." As a result, Adidas expects its partners in the supply chain to "conduct themselves with the utmost fairness, honesty, and responsibility in all aspects of their business."

Included in the standards are guidelines covering the use of forced labour and child labour, discrimination in recruitment and hiring, minimum wages and benefits, maximum working hours, the right to collective bargaining, disciplinary practices, and working environment standards. The standards also require its business partners to make "progressive improvement in environmental performance … integrating principles of sustainability into business decisions; responsible use of natural resources; adoption of cleaner production and pollution prevention measures; and designing and developing products, materials and technologies according to the principles of sustainability."

For example, one of the major environmental impacts in the manufacturing of shoes is the emission of volatile organic compounds (VOCs). Adidas has been working with its suppliers for over 10 years to reduce the amount of VOCs through the use of alternative and more environmentally friendly materials, and has been successful in reducing the use of VOCs by over 70 percent. It's a relief to know that with such an extensive network of suppliers Adidas is committed to changing its impact for the better.

Thinking Critically

1. The use of overseas production networks has been the subject of many sensational news stories. Does this influence your purchase decisions? Are you more likely to buy Adidas because of what you have read in this section?
2. What are your friends' opinions? Do you think the average consumer is willing to pay more for ethical goods?

SOURCE: Adidas Group, (Sustainability Statement) used with permission, http://www.adidas-group.com; http://www.global100.org.

Canada's overall employment equity record of the past decade has been mixed. The employment of women in professional occupations continues to grow, but minority representation among professionals has not significantly increased, even though professional jobs have been among the fastest-growing areas. Technical jobs have the most equitable utilization rates of minorities. Almost 400 federal and federally regulated organizations submit annual reports to Human Resources and Skills Development Canada (HRSDC) under the Employment Equity Act. The organizations are then graded on an alphabetical scale.

Concept *Check*

What are the key laws affecting employment?

What is employment equity?

THE FUTURE OF HUMAN RESOURCE MANAGEMENT

LO9

Some of today's most important trends in human resource management are dealing with the aging population, using employee diversity as a competitive advantage, improving efficiency through outsourcing and technology, and hiring employees who fit the organizational culture.

Aging Population

As discussed in Chapter 3, Canada's population is aging and life expectancy is increasing. Compound this with the recent economic developments; many people no longer see "freedom 55" as a realistic goal. Countries such as France have recently increased the retirement age because of the economic impact of retirement on the economic system.

Also, labour shortages and lack of skills is another outcome of the aging population. As the baby boomers are retiring, there are fewer and fewer people to take their position with the necessary skill bases.

Employee Diversity and Competitive Advantage

Canadian society and its workforce are becoming increasingly more diverse in terms of racial and ethnic status, age, educational background, work experience, and gender. A company with a demographic employee profile that looks like its customers may be in a position to gain a competitive advantage, which is a set of unique features of a company and its product or service that are perceived by the target market as superior to those of the competition. Competitive advantage is the factor that causes customers to patronize a company and not the competition. Many things can be a source of competitive advantage: for WestJet Airlines it is route structure and high asset utilization; for the Four Seasons Hotels it is very high quality guest services; for Toyota it is manufacturing efficiency and product durability; and for Tim Hortons it is location, service, and signature food and beverages. For these companies, a competitive advantage is also created by their HR practices.

competitive advantage
A set of unique features of an organization that are perceived by customers and potential customers as significant and superior to the competition's.

Many companies are successful because of employee diversity, which can produce more effective problem solving, a stronger reputation for hiring women and minorities, even greater employee diversity, quicker adaptation to change, and more robust product solutions because a diverse team can generate more options for improvement.[5]

In order for an organization to use employee diversity for competitive advantage, top management must be fully committed to hiring and developing women and minority individuals.

Outsourcing HR and Technology

The role of the HR professional has changed noticeably over the past 20 years. One significant change has been the use of technology in handling relatively routine HR tasks, such as payroll processing, initial screening of applicants, and benefits

How can employee diversity give a company a competitive advantage?

What are some of the advantages and disadvantages to outsourcing services?

Explain the concept of hiring for fit.

outsource
The assignment of various functions, such as human resources, accounting, or legal work, to outside organizations.

enrolments. Many businesses have purchased specialized software (SAP and Oracle/PeopleSoft) to perform the information processing aspects of many HR tasks. Other companies outsource, or contract out these tasks to HR service providers.

HR outsourcing is done when another company can perform a task better and more efficiently, thus saving costs. Sometimes HR activities are outsourced because HR requirements are extraordinary and too overwhelming to execute in-house in a timely fashion. Frequently, HR activities are simply outsourced because a provider has greater expertise.

Organizational Culture and Hiring for Fit

Regardless of general business and economic conditions, many companies are expanding operations and hiring additional employees. For many growing companies, corporate culture can be a key aspect of developing employees into a competitive advantage for the company. Corporate culture refers to the core values and beliefs that support the mission and business model of the company and guide employee behaviour. Companies frequently hire for fit with their corporate cultures. This necessitates recruitment and selection of employees who exhibit the values of the company. The companies might use carefully crafted applicant questionnaires to screen for values and behaviours that support corporate culture. In addition to cultural fit, companies are increasingly hiring for technical knowledge and skills fit to the job.

GREAT IDEAS TO USE NOW

Planning Your Career

It's never too early to start thinking about your career in business. No, you don't have to decide today, but it's important to decide fairly soon to plan your life's work. A very practical reason for doing so is that it will save you a lot of time and money. We have seen too many students who aren't really sure what they want to do after graduation. The longer you wait to choose a profession, the more credit hours you might have to take in your new field, and the longer it will be before you start earning real money.

A second reason to choose a career field early is that you can get a part-time or summer job and "test-drive" the profession. If it's not for you, you will find out very quickly.

Your school career centre can give you plenty of information about various careers in business. We also describe many career opportunities at the end of each part of this text. Another source of career information is the Internet. Go to any search engine, such as Google, Yahoo!, or Bing, and enter "careers in business," or narrow your search to a specific area such as management or marketing.

Career planning will not end when you find your first professional job. It is a lifelong process that ends only with retirement. Your career planning will include conducting a periodic self-assessment of your strengths and weaknesses, gathering information about other jobs both within the company and externally, learning about other industries, and setting career goals for yourself. You must always think about your future in business.

Human Resources Decision Making

During your professional career in business, you will likely have the opportunity to become a manager. As a manager, you will have to make many human resource decisions, including hiring, firing, promoting, giving a pay raise, sending an employee to a training program, disciplining a worker, approving a college tuition reimbursement request, and reassigning an employee to a different job. In short, you will be involved in virtually every human resource decision or activity affecting the employees you manage. Always treat people as you wish to be treated when making human resource decisions. Be fair, be honest, offer your experience and advice, and communicate frequently with your employees. If you follow this simple advice, you will be richly rewarded in your career.

Summary of Learning Outcomes

The human resource management process consists of a sequence of activities that begins with job analysis and HR planning; progresses to employee recruitment and selection; then focuses on employee training, performance appraisal, and compensation; and ends when the employee leaves the organization.

LO1 Discuss the human resource management process, and how human resource needs are determined.

Creating a strategy for meeting human resource needs is called human resource planning, which begins with job analysis. Job analysis is the process of studying a job to determine its tasks and duties for setting pay, determining employee job performance, specifying hiring requirements, and designing training programs. Information from the job analysis is used to prepare a job description, which lists the tasks and responsibilities of the job. A job specification describes the skills, knowledge, and abilities a person needs to fill the job described in the job description. By examining the human resource demand forecast and the internal supply forecast, human resource professionals can determine if the company faces a personnel surplus or shortage.

When a job vacancy occurs, most companies begin by trying to fill the job from within. If a suitable internal candidate is not available, the company begins an external search. Companies use local media to recruit non-technical, unskilled, and non-supervisory workers. To locate highly trained recruits, employers use college recruiters, executive search companies, job fairs, and company websites to promote job openings.

LO2 Explain how companies recruit applicants.

Typically, an applicant submits an application or resumé and then receives a short, structured interview. If an applicant makes it past the initial screening, he or she might be asked to take an aptitude, personality, or skills test. The next step is the selection interview, which is an in-depth discussion of the applicant's work experience, skills and abilities, education, and career interests.

LO3 Summarize how companies select qualified applicants.

Training and development programs are designed to increase employees' knowledge, skills, and abilities to foster job performance improvements. Formal training (usually classroom in nature and off-the-job) takes place shortly after being hired. Development programs prepare employees to assume positions of increasing authority and responsibility. Job rotation, executive education programs, mentoring, and special-project assignments are examples of employee development programs.

LO4 List some of the types of training and development programs that organizations offer to their employees.

LO5 Show how performance appraisals are used to evaluate employee performance.

A performance appraisal compares an employee's actual performance with the expected performance. Performance appraisals serve several purposes but are typically used to determine an employee's compensation, training needs, and advancement opportunities.

LO6 Analyze the various methods for compensating employees.

Direct pay is the hourly wage or monthly salary paid to an employee. In addition to the base wage or salary, direct pay may include bonuses and profit shares. Indirect pay consists of various benefits and services. Some benefits are required by law: unemployment insurance, workers' compensation, Canada or Québec Pension Plan, and paid vacations and holidays. Others are voluntarily made available by employers to employees. These include pensions, health and other insurance products, employee wellness programs, and college tuition reimbursement.

LO7 Explain how labour–management relations are different in a unionized environment.

Many organizations have unionized employees. A labour union is organized to represent workers in dealing with management over issues involving wages, hours, and working conditions. Contracts are negotiated that set out the responsibilities of management and the workers through collective bargaining.

LO8 Describe some of the key laws and federal agencies affecting human resource management and labour relations.

A number of federal, provincial, and territorial laws affect human resource management. These include the Charter of Rights and Freedoms (contained in the Constitution Act of 1982), the Canadian Human Rights Act (1977), the Employment Equity Act (amended in 1995), the Occupational Health and Safety Act, and the Workplace Hazardous Materials Information System.

LO9 List some of the trends and issues affecting human resource management and labour relations.

The aging population is creating many challenges in the business world. Shortages in labour and skills, and increased burden on the economic systems are just two example of the aging population.

Today, more and more companies are actively recruiting minorities. A diverse workforce often leads to increased market share and profits. Organizations are becoming proactive in their management of diversity. Companies are creating initiatives to build effective multicultural organizations.

Outsourcing is becoming more popular as a means to increase cost savings and ease of obtaining expertise. Technology continues to improve the efficiency of human resource management. It also enables companies to outsource many functions done internally in the past. In addition to normal job requirements, selected workers must have the ability to adapt to a local culture and perhaps to learn a foreign language.

Key Terms

agency shop 352
apprenticeship 344
arbitration 353
articling 344
closed shop 351
collective bargaining 350
competitive advantage 357
contingent workers 338
corporate open house 340
cost-of-living adjustment (COLA) 352
fringe benefits 349
grievance 353
human resource (HR) planning 337
human resource management (HRM) 336

job analysis 337
job description 338
job fair 340
job rotation 344
job specification 338
labour union 349
local union 350
mediation 353
mentoring 344
national union 350
on-the-job training 344
open shop 352
orientation 344
outsource 358

Experiential Exercises

1. Make telecommuting work for you. Maybe a part-time job requires too much driving time. Perhaps there are simply no jobs in the immediate area that suit you. Try telecommuting right now. Is telecommuting for you? Many people are more satisfied with their personal and family lives than before they started working at home. But telecommuting is not for every person or every job, and you'll need plenty of self-discipline to make it work for you. Ask yourself if you can perform your duties without close supervision. Think also about whether you would miss your coworkers. If you decide to give telecommuting a try, consider these suggestions to maintain your productivity:

   - *Set ground rules with your family.* Spouses and small children have to understand that even though you're in the house, you are busy earning a living. It's fine to throw in a few loads of laundry or answer the door when the plumber comes. It's another thing to take the kids to the mall or let them play games on your office PC.
   - *Clearly demarcate your work space by using a separate room with a door you can shut.* Let your family know that, emergencies excepted, the space is off-limits during working hours.
   - *If you have small children, you might want to arrange for childcare during your working hours.*
   - *Stay in touch with your coworkers and professional colleagues.* Go into the office from time to time for meetings to stay connected.

   Above all, you can make telecommuting work for you by being productive. Doing your job well, whether onsite or telecommuting, will help ensure you have a bright future.

2. The fringe benefit package of many employers includes numerous voluntarily provided items such as health care insurance, life insurance, a pension plan, tuition reimbursement, employee price discounts on products of the company, and paid sick leave. At your age, what are the three or four most important benefits? Why? Twenty years from now, what do you think will be your three or four most important benefits? Why?

3. As a corporate recruiter, you must know how to screen prospective employees. The Integrity Center website, at www.integctr.com, offers a brief tutorial on pre-employment screening, a glossary of key words and phrases, and related information. Prepare a short report that tells your assistant how to go about this process.

4. Go to the Monster Board at www.resume.monster.ca to learn how to prepare an electronic resumé that will get results. Develop a list of rules for creating effective electronic resumés, and revise your own résumé into electronic format.

5. Working as a contingent employee can help you explore your career options. Visit the Manpower website at www.manpower.com, and search for several types of jobs that interest you. What are the advantages of being a temporary worker? What other services does Manpower offer job seekers?

6. Web-based training is becoming popular at many companies as a way of bringing a wider variety of courses to more people at lower costs. The Web-Based Training

Information Center site, at webbasedtraining.com, provides a good introduction. Learn about the basics of online training at its Primer page. Then link to the Resources section, try a demo, and explore other areas that interest you. Prepare a brief report on your findings, including the pros and cons of using the Web for training, to present to your class.

7. Your 250-employee company is considering outsourcing some of its HR functions because it wants to offer a wider range of services. You've been asked to prepare a report on whether it should proceed and if so, how. Visit BuyerZone.com, www. buyerzone.com, click on HR Outsourcing and then HR Outsourcing Buyer's Guide, to learn more about why companies are going outside for this important function and the advantages and disadvantages of doing so. Summarize your finding and make a recommendation. Then use a search engine to locate two to three companies that offer HR outsourcing services. Compare them and recommend one, explaining the reasons for your choice.

Review Questions

1. Why is human resource management in today's organization instrumental in driving an organization toward its goals?

2. What is the human resource management process?

3. Why is human resource planning and forecasting so important?

4. What is recruitment? What are some recruitment methods?

5. What are the steps in employee selection?

6. Differentiate between training and development.

7. What are the steps in performance evaluation?

8. What is compensation? How is it determined?

9. Discuss the types of compensation.

10. What is a labour union?

11. How are labour agreements negotiated?

12. What are the management and union strategies for dealing with conflict?

13. What are the primary laws that affect human resource management?

14. Discuss the trends in HRM.

CREATIVE THINKING CASE

"People First" at FedEx

FedEx founder and CEO Frederick Smith wants employees to be an integral part of the decision-making process at FedEx. He believes that putting the people first leads to better service for the customer and this leads, ultimately, to higher profits for the company. The People-Service-Profit (P-S-P) focus ensures that employee satisfaction, empowerment, risk taking, and innovation are encouraged, leading to 100 percent customer satisfaction, 100 percent of the time, and resulting in corporate profits.

FedEx Canada employs more than 300,000 people in 228 countries utilizing 375 airports. On an average day, FedEx handles nearly 9 million packages generating nearly $23 billion per year. They believe the reasons for their success are echoed in their placement on *Forbes Magazine*'s "Best 100 Places to Work" and eighth most admired company in the world. To emphasize the "people first" approach, the president traded jobs with one of his couriers for a week, and had the experience televised. An unusual exercise such as this sent a clear message to customers and employees alike. "We are serious about putting people first."

To help employees with the P-S-P focus, the following processes are in place at FedEx:

- An annual employee satisfaction survey
- A promotion-from-within policy
- Employee recognition and reward programs
- Leadership evaluation (when an employee indicates a desire to advance, training and development must take place)
- Open communication including e-mail, print, broadcast and face-to-face (no restrictions across levels)
- Pay-for-performance remuneration based on management by objectives
- An employee appeal procedure and guaranteed fair treatment policies including an Open Door policy.

The P-S-P philosophy, supported by the appropriate policies, leads to motivated employees who go beyond what might be delineated in the usual job description. Corporate legend reports a story of an employee who looked after a customer's cat after the cat was inadvertently wrapped into a package by the customer. Another story describes how a FedEx manager personally flew to Ottawa to hand-deliver lifesaving medication to a customer. These examples illustrate the service commitment FedEx has encouraged and obtained from their employees. Many companies profess that "people are our greatest asset," but FedEx has managed actually to live this philosophy through their "people first" focus.

FedEx takes a pro-active approach to new markets and national cultures. Prior to entering the Chinese market, FedEx provided cultural training to their relevant employees. In the launch phase, FedEx brought training in their corporate culture to the new hires. To make their systems work, FedEx designed specifically for the Chinese cultures in order to successfully deliver their service culture. The company's particular brand of corporate social responsibility and ethics were also new to many of their Chinese employees. FedEx requires all conflicts to be disclosed and will not tolerate unethical practices. They have a commitment to made the world a better place. In countries where the residents have struggled to overcome subsistence living, translating this culture can be a challenge.

Thinking Critically

1. To maintain the culture FedEx has developed, it is important to hire employees who "fit." How might FedEx do this?

2. In international locations, is fit possible? How does FedEx seek to overcome this issue? Does this raise any new ethical debates?

3. Look at the compensation and evaluation aspects of HR. Suggest strategies for FedEx in keeping with their P-S-P focus.

SOURCES: Brenda McWillams and Gary Burkett, "Empowered Employees," *Marketing*, 3 no. 22, June 19, 2006, 40; FedEx Canada History, http://www.fedex.com/ca, accessed July 10, 2006; FedEx Philosophy, http://www.fedex.com/ca, accessed December 7, 2008; FedEx Express Facts - Canada, 2011, http://www.fedex.com/ca_english/about/overview/fastfacts/expressfactscanada.html; Strategic Global Relationships, 2011, http://www.fedex.com/ca_english/about/overview/social/strategicglobalrelation.html, Dec. 2, 2011; FedEx Canada Community Relationships, 2011, http://www.fedex.com/ca_english/about/overview/social/communityrelation.html, Dec. 2, 2011; FedEx Philosophy, 2011, http://www.fedex.com/ca_english/about/overview/philosophy.html, Dec. 2, 2011; and Alghalith, Nabil, "FedEx: Leveraging IT for a Competitive Advantage," *The Business Review*, Cambridge, 2007: 8 (1), 296–304.

Making the Connection

Marketing: The Customer Focus

In the next two chapters, we will continue to look at the functional areas of the company by examining the area of *marketing*. Marketers make decisions about what products to bring to market in conjunction with the overall *strategic* direction of the company, and then work with *operations* to design those products and allocate the resources needed to provide them—whether that be production facilities or alliances with other companies if it is a good that is being produced, or layouts and procedures to be followed if it is a service. And, of course, both marketing and operations need to work with *human resources* to make sure people with the needed skills are in place in all areas, as well as with *finance* to make sure the product is financially worthwhile for the company to pursue, and that funds will be available to pursue it. It is an integrated effort. This is evident from the example of Lexus in the chapter. The company "adopted a customer-driven approach with particular emphasis on service" by stressing "product quality with a standard of zero defects in manufacturing" and a service goal to "treat each customer as a guest in one's home." Marketing couldn't do this alone. It had to work with operations to provide this level of product quality and with human resources to provide this level of customer service. And it also needed an investment of funds to pull it all together.

But just think for a minute what would happen if there were no customer demand for the quality cars sold by Lexus? Just as the decisions that are made in the functional areas to bring a product to market are integrated, the decisions about which products to bring to market obviously have to be integrated with the outside environment—they must come ultimately from the customer. The customer is the central focal point of any successful business. Look at the critical success factors. As we've said many times, you can't achieve *financial success* if you aren't earning revenue, and you can't

earn revenue if customers aren't buying your products. And they won't buy your products if they don't at least *meet customer needs* and at best exceed their expectations. That is what this chapter is all about—understanding your customers and creating a marketing strategy that satisfies their needs.

This requires that the company keep an eye on all areas of the external environment that may affect marketing decisions, as discussed in the chapter—but particularly on the *social* environment, including demographic changes—to understand the trends that affect customer needs, as well as to better understand the different factors that influence consumer decision making. As the chapter explains, it is important to do market research to understand the customer, and advances in *technology* have made that easier. Technology has also made it possible to create a unique marketing mix for each customer; just click on Amazon.ca as a repeat customer and see what suggestions it has tailored specifically to you. The company also has to keep an eye on the *economic* environment to make sure it keeps ahead of the competition and that it takes into consideration the effect of changing incomes and interest rates, etc., as well as the *political* environment to make sure it is meeting all the requirements in its package labelling, etc.

Many concepts in this chapter are important for understanding marketing and its integrative nature. For example, in this chapter you will read about the marketing concept—focusing on customer wants and needs, and integrating the organization's activities in the functional areas to satisfy the customer, but doing so with a responsibility toward the *stakeholders*—profitably for the owners, ethically for the customer, and fairly for the employee. The marketing concept is an important integrative concept as it is the thread that ties all the marketing activities, functional areas, and the business as a whole together to stay focused on the customer and make decisions responsibly so that success is achieved with all the stakeholders in mind and all critical success factors met.

You'll also learn about relationship marketing. This is critical to the long-term success of the company—meeting the critical success factors over time by establishing long-term relationships with customers. This can be done through loyalty programs as one example, but it also requires *commitment* from your employees to be customer oriented. As discussed in the chapter, employee attitudes and actions are critical to building relationships. A good example of this is WestJet airlines. Just give them a call and chat with one of their reps, and then call another airline, and you'll see the difference in attitude toward the customer.

Target marketing is another important concept. Identifying a target market helps a company focus marketing efforts on those customers most likely to buy its products. The unique features of the product that appeal to the target group and are seen by the target group as superior to competitive offerings are the company's competitive advantage. If that competitive advantage is cost—operating at a lower cost than competitors and passing this saving on to the customer (as in Walmart)—we see another integration of marketing with the other functional areas. This cost advantage is gained through using less expensive raw materials and/or controlling overhead costs (finance), and making plant operations more efficient and/or designing products that are easier to manufacture (operations), and so on. This is achieved by these areas through people committed to this goal, often with the help of technology.

As always, you will also find a discussion of the future of business at the end of the chapter. There are many new techniques being used today that have their roots in different environmental trends—from social media to green and social marketing. This further points out the importance of understanding the customer. The influence of the customer goes far beyond what products and services to provide to how to reach them and what they want to hear.

chapter 13

Marketing: The Customer Focus

BIEBER FEVER—JUSTIN TWEETS TO PANDEMONIUM

Unless you've been hiding under a rock since 2008, you've heard of Justin Bieber. Most of us have seen the teenage Stratford, Ontario, sensation on TV and heard the story of his rise to fame by way of YouTube. But what kept him from being just another short-lived Internet sensation? Social media, and specifically Twitter, may be the answer.

Bieber's climb to stardom is a product of the Internet age, demonstrating the power of new media and perhaps heralding the decline of traditional promotional practices. Justin Bieber did not have a privileged upbringing. Early videos of the young musician were shot at a benefit held by his mom's friends to raise money to buy him a drum kit. Bieber had worn out his toy drums and they thought he was good enough for the real thing. (The cymbals were from Sabian [Chapter 4].) Some relatives couldn't make it to the show, but they still wanted to see Bieber sing and play. The videos were too big to email, so his mom put them on YouTube. The rest is history. But it almost wasn't.

The decision-makers in the recording industry didn't take YouTube sensations seriously, thinking they were no more than short-lived fads. But one man, talent manager Scooter Braun, happened across Bieber's videos and saw his potential. He became the teenage singer's manager and recorded a CD with Bieber.

But Bieber was too young to tour the bar circuit and promote his music, so he was sent off to visit DJs at radio stations with a box of CDs and his guitar. Most of the radio stations weren't playing his songs. The acoustic versions he performed on air weren't producing sales. But his popularity on YouTube continued to grow, as his primary audience was young people who used the Internet, not radio, as their primary source of entertainment and information.

Meanwhile, Bieber had started a Twitter account, and like many Twitter users, he tweeted regularly about his day. Again reaching his target customer base of young Internet users like himself, he started telling his followers what radio station he was going to the next day. And they started showing up to see him. First one or two, then more. Soon, radio stations were setting up live feeds from parking lots or nearby malls. The crowds got so large that fire marshals were concerned about safety and refused to let him appear. "Bieber fever" had taken hold, and become a pandemic.

Two stories illustrate the power of Twitter.

In March 2010, Scooter Braun was charged by police in Winston Park, New York, for refusing to tweet that Justin's appearance was cancelled because the crowd was too large. Braun and Bieber were the only two with the Twitter password, and Bieber had tweeted that he was on his way. Authorities feared injuries, and in fact there were some. Braun was charged with reckless endangerment, criminal nuisance, and endangering the welfare of a child. Def Jam records paid an $8000 fine to resolve the matter.

Lest you think Bieber is a lightweight, ask Kevin Kristopik. In 2010, he apparently drew Bieber's anger by hacking the Twitter account of one of the singer's friends. Bieber's response? He tweeted "call me or text" and included Kristopik's cell number. Kristopik's phone was bombarded with messages from Bieber's nearly five million followers, and his Twitter account was deleted. While still a teenager, Justin Bieber is a force to be taken seriously, in both his music and his use of social media.

The marketing challenge Bieber fever presents is how to use this example to market other performers or products. Did Bieber, his mom, and his manager know their customers well enough to create the sensation? Or was it a series of coincidences, and being in the right place at the right time, that led to the "accidental" creation of a social-media marketing model?[1]

THINKING CRITICALLY

As you read this chapter consider the following questions:

1. Why is understanding the target market so important for business?

2. What are some of the potential issues if a company does not identify its target market?

3. Why did Justin Bieber's fan base grow so quickly through the use of social media?

SOURCES: "Featured Artist: Justin Bieber," Whispering Rose Radio, http://www.whisperingroseradio.com/bieberlaunch.htm; Adrien Chen, "Justin Bieber Tweets Enemy's Phone Number to 4.5 Million Followers," Gawker, August 15, 2010, http://www.gawker.com/5613398/justin-bieber-tweets-enemys-phone-number-to-45-million-followers; Samul Axon, "Kid Receives 26,000 Texts After Justin Bieber Tweets Phone Number," Mashable, August 16, 2010, http://www.mashable.com/2010/08/16/justin-bieber-phone-number/; http://www.goodwinpr.com/2011/03/im-a-belieber-in-justins-marketing-team/h; http://www.hollywire.com/the-news-dump/justin-bieber-on-twitter-what-other-way-is-a-teenage-boy-going-to-talk-to-girls; "Supercharge Your Success in Life the Justin Bieber Way," Ron Karr's Business Development Blog, http://ronkarr.com/blog/supercharge-your-success-in-life-the-justin-bieber-way/; Allison Cook, "Failure to Tweet: The Bieber Effect," Online Magazine Platform, March 31, 2010, http://www.platformmag.wordpress.com/2010/03/31/failure-to-tweet-the-bieber-effect/; Justin Bieber: Never Say Never Official Site, http://www.justinbieberneversaynever.com/; Chu, J., Justin Bieber: Never Say Never, ARG Live, Toronto, 2011, 105 minutes (Documentary); Jon Azpiri, "Justin Bieber Manager Arrested: Scott Braun Arrested," NowPublic, March 25, 2010, http://www.nowpublic.com/culture/justin-bieber-manager-arrested-scott-braun-arrested-2596357.html; http://www.bestin4o.blogspot.com/2010/03/justin-bieber-biography.html; http://www.pul.se/Justin-Biebers-Manager-Gets-Off-Scot-Free-In-Kiddie-Crushing-Mall-Incident_Real-Estate-TLEMSBTALc,7F5hPIwHIDOE.

LO1

Marketing is the process of getting the right goods or services to the right people at the right place, time, and price, using the right promotion techniques. This concept is referred to as the "right" principle. We can say that marketing is finding out the needs and wants of potential buyers and customers and then providing goods and services (i.e., products—discussed in more detail in Chapter 14) that meet or exceed their expectations. Marketing is about creating exchanges. An exchange takes place when two parties give something of value to each other to satisfy their respective needs. In a typical exchange, a consumer trades money for a good or service.

To encourage exchanges, marketers follow the "right" principle. For example, if your usual retailer doesn't have the right product for you when you want it, at the right price, there will not be an exchange of money. Think about the last exchange (purchase) you made: What if the price had been 30 percent higher? What if the store or other source had been less accessible? Would you have bought anything? The "right" principle tells us that marketers control many factors that determine marketing success. In this chapter, you will learn about the marketing concept and how organizations create a marketing strategy. You will learn how the marketing mix is used to create sales opportunities. Next, we examine how and why consumers and organizations make purchase decisions. Then, we will discuss the important concept of market segmentation, which helps marketing managers focus on the most likely purchasers of their wares. We conclude the chapter by examining how marketing research and decision support systems help guide marketing decision making.

THE MARKETING CONCEPT

Companies focus on the core value proposition; a customer-based focus that identifies what is important to your customers. This is used to target the customers who will benefit most from the company's product and is the basis of why the customer should buy the company's products. The core value proposition has five value drivers:

1. *Idea:* What does your product do for the customer?
2. *Benefit:* What is the benefit to your customer?
3. *Target:* How can you segment the various customer groups? How do you reach them?
4. *Perception:* How do you want to be perceived by your customer, the public, or other stakeholders?
5. *Outcome (Reward):* What are the net results for the company?

If you study today's best organizations, you'll see that they have adopted the marketing concept, which involves identifying consumer needs and then producing the goods or services that will satisfy them while making a profit. The marketing concept is oriented toward pleasing consumers by offering value. Specifically, the marketing concept involves

- focusing on customer wants, so the organization can distinguish its product(s) from competitors' offerings;
- integrating all of the organization's activities, including production, to satisfy these wants; and
- achieving long-term goals for the organization by satisfying customer wants and needs legally and responsibly.

Today, companies of every size in all industries are applying the marketing concept. Enterprise Rent-A-Car found that its customers didn't want to have to drive to its offices. Therefore, Enterprise began delivering vehicles to customer homes or places of work. Disney found that some of its patrons really disliked waiting in lines. In response, Disney began offering FastPass at a premium price, which allows patrons to avoid standing in long lines waiting for attractions.

Companies have not always followed the marketing concept. Around the time of the Industrial Revolution in North America (1860–1910), companies had a production orientation, which meant that they worked to lower production costs without a strong desire to satisfy the needs of their customers. To do this, organizations concentrated on mass production, focusing internally on maximizing the efficiency of operations, increasing output, and ensuring uniform quality. They also asked such questions as, What can we do best? What can our engineers design? What is economical and easy to produce with our equipment?

There is nothing wrong with assessing a company's capabilities. In fact, such assessments are necessary in planning. But the production orientation does not consider whether what the company produces most efficiently also meets the needs of the marketplace. By implementing the marketing concept, an organization looks externally to the consumers in the marketplace and commits to customer value, customer satisfaction, and relationship marketing, as explained in this section.

Customer Value

Customer value is the ratio of benefits to the sacrifices necessary to obtain those benefits. The customer determines the value of both the benefits and the sacrifices. Creating customer value is a core business strategy of many successful companies. Customer value is rooted in the belief that price is not the only thing that matters. A business that focuses on the cost of production and price to the customer will be managed as though it were providing a commodity differentiated only by price. In contrast, businesses that provide customer value believe that customers will use their products.

The automobile industry also illustrates the importance of creating customer value. To penetrate the fiercely competitive luxury automobile market, Lexus adopted a customer-driven approach, with particular emphasis on service. Lexus stresses product quality with a standard of zero defects in manufacturing. The service quality goal is to treat each customer as one would treat a guest in one's home, to pursue the perfect person-to-person relationship, and to strive to improve continually. This strategy has enabled Lexus to establish a clear quality image and capture a significant share of the luxury car market.

Customer Satisfaction

Customer satisfaction is a theme that we have stressed throughout the text. Customer satisfaction is the customer's feeling that a product or service has met or exceeded expectations. Lexus consistently wins awards for its outstanding customer satisfaction. J. D. Power and Associates surveys car owners two years after they make their purchase. The Customer Satisfaction Survey is made up of four measures that each describe an element of overall ownership satisfaction at two years: vehicle quality/reliability, vehicle appeal, ownership costs, and service satisfaction from a dealer. Lexus continues to lead the industry. Lexus manager Stuart McCullough comments, "In close collaboration with our dealers, we aim to provide the best customer service, not only in the car industry, but in any industry. The J. D. Power surveys are a testament to our success in making our customers happy."[2]

At Doubletree Hotels, guests are asked to fill out a CARE card several times during their stay to let staff know how they are doing. Managers check the cards daily to solve guests' problems before they check out. Guests can

production orientation
An approach in which a company works to lower production costs without a strong desire to satisfy the needs of customers.

customer value
The ratio of benefits to the sacrifices necessary to obtain those benefits, as determined by the customer; reflects the willingness of customers to buy a product.

customer satisfaction
The customer's feeling that a product has met or exceeded expectations.

Concept in Action

Geico—the major auto insurer with the scaly mascot—famously boasts a 97 percent customer-satisfaction rating, based on an independent study conducted by Alan Newman Research. With this claim, communicated through the company's quirky and ubiquitous advertising, consumers get the message that Geico delivers quality insurance coverage at low prices. What factors do you think impact the customer-satisfaction ratings for an auto insurer like Geico?

© COURTESY OF GEICO

also use a CARE phone line to call in their complaints at the hotel. A CARE committee continually seeks ways to improve guest services. The goal is to offer a solution to a CARE call in 15 minutes. Embassy Suites goes one step further by offering a full refund to guests who are not satisfied with their stay.

Building Relationships

relationship marketing
A strategy that focuses on forging long-term partnerships with customers by offering value and providing customer satisfaction.

Relationship marketing is a strategy that focuses on forging long-term partnerships with customers. Companies build relationships with customers by offering value and providing customer satisfaction. Companies benefit from repeat sales and referrals that lead to increases in sales, market share, and profits. Costs fall because it is less expensive to serve existing customers than to attract new ones. Keeping an existing customer costs about one-fourth of what it costs to attract a new one, and the probability of retaining a customer is more than 60 percent, whereas the probability of landing a new customer is less than 30 percent.[3]

Customers also benefit from stable relationships with suppliers. Business buyers have found that partnerships with their suppliers are essential to producing high-quality products while cutting costs. Customers remain loyal to companies that provide them greater value and satisfaction than they expect from competing companies.

customer relationship management (CRM)
The processes used by organizations to track and organize information about current and prospective customers.

Customer relationship management (CRM) is the processes an organization uses to track and organize information regarding current and prospective customers. This includes information about the customers or potential customers, past history with the organization, and future prospects. Usually this involves the implementation of CRM software that can automate the data collection and correlate the data to be used later to increase customer satisfaction and sales.

Loyalty programs, sometimes referred to as frequent-buyer clubs, are an excellent way to build long-term relationships. Most major airlines have frequent-flyer programs (e.g., Air Canada's Aeroplan and WestJet's Frequent Guest Program). After flying a certain number of miles, you become eligible for a free ticket. Now, cruise lines, hotels, car rental agencies, credit card companies, and even mortgage companies give away "airline miles" with purchases. Consumers give the airline and its partners their patronage because they want the free tickets. Thus, the program helps to create a long-term relationship with the customer.

If an organization is to build relationships with customers, its employees' attitudes and actions must be customer oriented. Any person, department, or division that is not customer oriented weakens the positive image of the entire organization. An employee might be the only contact a potential customer has with the business. In that person's eyes, the employee is the business. If greeted discourteously, the potential customer might well assume that the employee's attitude represents the whole company.

Concept Check

Explain the marketing concept.

Explain the difference between customer value and customer satisfaction.

What is meant by relationship marketing?

Concept in Action

As a "guest" on WestJet, you can expect friendly, casual, yet competent service from everyone you encounter, from captain to customer service representative. How does this create customer satisfaction and value to the customer?

TORONTO STAR/GETSTOCK.COM

Building long-term relationships with customers is an excellent way for small businesses to compete against the big chains. Sometimes small companies, with few employees, are in a better position to focus on a tiny segment of the market.

CREATING A MARKETING STRATEGY

LO2

There is no secret formula for creating goods and services that provide customer value and customer satisfaction. An organization that is committed to providing superior customer satisfaction puts customers at the very centre of its marketing strategy. Creating a customer-focused *marketing strategy* involves four main steps: understanding the external environment, defining the target market, creating a competitive advantage, and developing a marketing mix. In this section, we will examine the first three steps, and in the next section, we will discuss how a company develops a marketing mix.

Understanding the External Environment

Unless marketing managers understand the external environment, a business cannot intelligently plan for the future. Thus, many organizations assemble a team of specialists to continually collect and evaluate environmental information, a process called environmental scanning. The goal in gathering the environmental data is to identify future market opportunities and threats.

environmental scanning
The process by which a company continually collects and evaluates information about its external environment.

Manufacturers of mobile devices understand the importance of environmental scanning to monitor rapidly changing consumer interests. Since the invention of the PC, techies have taken two things for granted: Processor speeds will grow exponentially, and PCs will become indistinguishable from televisions—there will be, in industry lingo, convergence. These predictions have obviously become reality. Even when computers became common, we did not understand how fast the technology—and therefore how we market—would change. Now people do many activities on their computers and other devices that were not possible just a few years ago. Communicating, for example, can be done almost anywhere, to anyone, to any device, at any time.

In general, six categories of environmental data shape marketing decisions. These categories fall out of our PESTI model of the external environment:

- *Political and legal forces*, such as changes in laws and regulatory agency activities
- *Economic forces*, such as changing incomes, inflation, and recession, along with *competitive forces* from domestic and foreign-based (*international*) companies
- *Social forces*, such as the values of potential customers and the changing roles of families, along with *demographic forces*, such as the ages, birth and death rates, and locations of various groups of people
- *Technological forces*, such as advances in communications and data retrieval capabilities

Defining the Target Market

Managers and employees focus on providing value for a well-defined target market. The target market is the specific group of consumers toward which a company directs its marketing efforts. It is selected from the larger overall market.

target market
The specific group of consumers toward which a company directs its marketing efforts.

For instance, Carnival Corporation, whose brands include Carnival Cruise Lines, Princess Cruises, and Holland America Line (among others), each have their unique target market. Carnival Cruise Lines promotes itself as the "Fun Ships," marketing to those who are looking for an active vacation; Princess Cruises to those who are seeking adventure with style; and Holland America Line markets to those who prefer a grander style of cruising.

Laura's Shoppe Canada Limited has several different types of stores, each for a distinct target market: Laura's for average-size women, Laura Petites for petite women, Laura II for plus-size women, and Melanie Lyne for upscale women's apparel featuring designer labels.

Identifying a target market helps a company focus its marketing efforts on those who are most likely to buy its products or services. Concentrating on potential customers lets the company use its resources efficiently. The target markets for some of the Marriott International brands are shown in Exhibit 13.1. Each of the brands targets a specific market, offering a variety of hotel rooms with specific amenities at prices customers are willing to pay.

Creating a Competitive Advantage

A competitive advantage, also called a differential advantage, is a set of unique features of a company and its products that are perceived by the target market as significant and superior to those of the competition. As Andrew Grove, former CEO of one of the world's largest semiconductor chip makers, Intel Corporation, says, "You have to understand what it is you are better at than anybody else and mercilessly focus your efforts on it." Competitive advantage is the factor or factors that cause customers to patronize a company and not the competition. There are three types of competitive advantage: cost, product/service differential, and niche.

competitive advantage
A set of unique features of a company and its products that are perceived by the target market as significant and superior to those of the competition; also called *differential advantage*.

Exhibit 13.1	The Target Markets for Some of the Brands of Marriott International

BRAND	TARGET MARKET
Fairfield Inn	Economizing business and leisure travellers
TownePlace Suites	Moderate-tier travellers who stay three to four weeks
SpringHill Suites	Business and leisure travellers looking for more space and amenities
Courtyard	Travellers seeking quality and affordable accommodations designed for the road warrior
Residence Inn	Travellers seeking a residential-style hotel
Marriott Hotels, Resorts, and Suites	Grounded achievers who desire consistent quality
Renaissance Hotels and Resorts	Discerning business and leisure travellers who seek creative attention to detail
Ritz-Carlton	Senior executives and entrepreneurs looking for a unique, luxurious, personalized experience

COST COMPETITIVE ADVANTAGE A company that has a cost competitive advantage can produce a product (goods and/or services) at a lower cost than all its competitors while maintaining satisfactory profit margins. Companies become cost leaders by obtaining inexpensive raw materials, making plant operations more efficient, designing products for ease of manufacture, controlling overhead costs, and avoiding marginal customers.

Over time, the cost competitive advantage might fail. Typically, if one company is using an innovative technology to reduce its costs, then others in the industry will adopt this technology and reduce their costs as well. For example, Bell Labs invented fibre optic cables, which reduced the cost of voice and data transmission by dramatically increasing the number of calls that could be transmitted simultaneously through a 5 cm cable. Within five years, however, fibre optic technology had spread through the industry, and Bell Labs lost its cost competitive advantage. Companies might also lose their cost competitive advantage if competitors match their low costs by using the same lower cost suppliers. Therefore, a cost competitive advantage might not offer a long-term competitive advantage.

DIFFERENTIAL COMPETITIVE ADVANTAGE A product/service differential competitive advantage exists when a company provides something unique that is valuable to buyers beyond simply offering a low price. Differential competitive advantages tend to be longer lasting than cost competitive advantages, because cost advantages are subject to continual erosion as competitors catch up.

The durability of a differential competitive advantage tends to make this strategy more attractive to many top managers. Common differential advantages are brand names (Lexus), a strong dealer network (Caterpillar Tractor for construction equipment), product reliability (Maytag washers), image (Holt Renfrew in retailing), and service (Federal Express). Brand names such as Coca-Cola, BMW, and Cartier stand for quality the world over. Through continual product and marketing innovations and attention to quality and value, managers at these organizations have created enduring competitive advantages. Arthur Doppelmayr, an Austrian manufacturer of aerial transport systems (Doppelmayr Lifts), believes his main differential advantage, besides innovative equipment design, is his service system, which allows the company to come to the assistance of users anywhere

cost competitive advantage
A company's ability to produce a product or service at a lower cost than all other competitors in an industry while maintaining satisfactory profit margins.

differential competitive advantage
A company's ability to provide a unique product or service with a set of features that the target market perceives as important and better than the competitor's.

Concept *in Action*

A differential competitive advantage offers a unique value to consumers. Leon's Furniture Limited has 44 retail stores and 32 franchise stores in Canada. Each year it has its "Storewide Savings Event." Considering some of the retail stores you are familiar with, what competitive advantages do they have?

TONY BOCK/GETSTOCK.COM

Sustainable Business, Sustainable World

KRAFT FOODS INC.

Kraft Foods Inc., based in the U.S.A., was ranked number 45 in the 2011 *Global 100 Most Sustainable Corporations in the World*. What makes Kraft Foods Inc. among one of the world's most sustainable companies? We'll take a look at one of its efforts—cocoa production. With a focus on customer needs, the question has to be asked: who doesn't like chocolate?

Kraft Foods Inc. diligently works to ensure the future of the world's cocoa supply to meet its customers' insatiable demand for chocolate, but more importantly, it works to make a difference in the lives of cocoa farmers, their families, and their communities.

As a global leader in chocolate, with such products as Cadbury Dairy Milk and Cote d'Or, Kraft Foods Inc. uses a lot of cocoa. In its words: "A key ingredient in our recipe for the future of cocoa is the balance for all three pillars of sustainability—economic, environment and social" —the triple bottom line. An example of this commitment is Kraft Foods Inc.'s 2010 investment of approximately $10 million to improve the quality of life for people in cocoa farming communities in West Africa, to "provide better access to education, improve family incomes, encourage responsible labour practices, and provide aid to at-risk children, while at the same time helping to protect the environment."

Kraft Foods Inc. works with the Rainforest Alliance to help farmers and farms operate in a more sustainable fashion; increasing their skills and knowledge to protect the environment while also increasing their productivity. This leads to an increase in incomes and improves living conditions in their communities. Kraft is, in fact, the largest buyer of cocoa beans from Rainforest Alliance Certified farms, which comply with rigorous environmental and social standards. Kraft Foods Inc.'s intent, by the end of 2012, was to only use Rainforest Alliance Certified cocoa in its Cote d'Or, Suchard and Marabou chocolate brands in Europe.

Kraft Foods Inc. also collaborates with the Fairtrade Foundation to work to improve the livelihoods of cocoa farmers in Ghana and other countries. The Fairtrade label means that a product has met international Fairtrade standards that help farmers in developing countries get a fairer and more stable price for their crops. Cadbury Dairy Milk Fairtrade chocolate bars have been selling in Great Britain and Ireland since 2009, and in Canada, Australia, and New Zealand since 2010. These efforts have quadrupled the volume of cocoa sold under Fairtrade terms in Ghana, generating $3.7 million in Fairtrade premiums for the farmers.

Kraft Foods Inc. is active with the Bill & Melinda Gates Foundation, helping hundreds of thousands of West African cocoa farmers lift themselves out of hunger and poverty. It is also a member of the World Cocoa Foundation (WCF), helping cocoa-farming families develop and manage effective, sustainable farming practices; in 2002, Kraft co-founded the International Cocoa Initiative (ICI) that oversees efforts to eliminate the worst forms of child labour on cocoa farms. We don't know about you, but we think that chocolate is tasting even better now!

Thinking Critically

1. If you are a chocoholic, does it matter to you where the cocoa comes from, how the farmers are treated, and how sustainably it is farmed?
2. Is Kraft Foods Inc. really focusing on the customer? Research would suggest it is— customers are increasingly looking at labels and seeking out products that are produced in sustainable ways. Are you familiar with the Rainforest Alliance and Fairtrade labels, and have you seen them on other products? If not, given today's business environment, why not?

SOURCES: Kraft Foods, http://kraftfoodscompany.com. Used with permission from Kraft Foods; The Global 100, http://www.global100.org; Rainforest Alliance, http://www.rainforest-alliance.org; Fairtrade Foundation, http://www.fairtrade.org.uk; Bill & Melinda Gates Foundation, http://www.gatesfoundation.org; World Cocoa Foundation, http://www.worldcocoafoundation.org; International Cocoa Initiative, http://www.cocoainitiative.org.

---

in the world within 24 hours. Doppelmayr uses a worldwide system of warehouses and skilled personnel prepared to move immediately in emergency cases.

niche competitive advantage
A company's ability to target and effectively serve a single segment of the market within a limited geographic area.

NICHE COMPETITIVE ADVANTAGE A company with a **niche competitive advantage** targets and effectively serves a single segment of the market within a limited geographic area. For small companies with limited resources that potentially face giant competitors, "nicheing" might be the only viable option. A market segment that has good growth potential but is not crucial to the success of major competitors is a good candidate for a niche strategy. Once a potential segment has been identified, the company needs to make certain it can defend against challengers through its superior ability to serve buyers in the segment. For example, STI Music Private Bank Group follows a niche strategy with its concentration on country music stars and entertainment industry professionals in Nashville. Its office is in the heart of Nashville's music district. STI has decided to expand its niche strategy to Miami, the epicentre of Latin music; and Atlanta. The latter is a long-time rhythm-and-blues capital and is now the centre of contemporary urban music. Both new markets have the kinds of music professionals—entertainers, record executives, producers, agents, and others—that have made STI so successful in Nashville.

Concept Check

What is environmental scanning?

What is a target market, and why should a company have one?

Explain the three types of competitive advantages, and provide examples of each.

DEVELOPING A MARKETING MIX

LO3

Once a company has defined its target market and identified its competitive advantage, it can create the **marketing mix**, that is, the blend of product offering, pricing, promotional methods, and distribution system that brings a specific group of consumers superior value. Distribution is sometimes referred to as place, so the marketing mix is based on the **four Ps (4Ps)**: product, price, promotion, and place. Every target market requires a unique marketing mix to satisfy the needs of the target consumers and meet the company's goals. A strategy must be constructed for each of the 4Ps and blended with the strategies for the other elements. Thus, the marketing mix is only as good as its weakest part. An excellent product with a poor distribution system could be doomed to failure. A successful marketing mix requires careful tailoring. For instance, at first glance you might think that McDonald's and Wendy's have roughly the same marketing mix. After all, they are both in the fast-food business. But McDonald's targets parents with young children through Ronald McDonald, heavily promoted children's Happy Meals, and playgrounds. Wendy's is targeted to a more adult crowd. Wendy's has no playgrounds, but it does have carpeting in some locations (a more adult atmosphere) and has expanded its menu to include items for adult tastes.

Product Strategy

Marketing strategy typically starts with the product. You can't plan a distribution system or set a price if you don't know what you're going to market. Marketers use the term *product* to refer to both *goods*, such as tires, stereos, and clothing, and *services*, such as hotels, hair salons, and restaurants. Thus, the heart of the marketing mix is the good or service. Creating a **product strategy** involves choosing a brand name, packaging, colours, a warranty, accessories, and a service program.

Marketers view products in a much larger context than you might imagine. They include not only the item itself but also the brand name and the company image. The names Ralph Lauren and Gucci, for instance, create extra value for everything from cosmetics to bath towels. That is, products with those names sell at higher prices than identical products without the names. Another example, Holt Renfrew's company image is one of quality and superior service. We buy things not only for what they do but also for what they mean. Product strategies are discussed further in Chapter 14.

Pricing Strategy

Pricing strategy is based on demand for the product and the cost of producing it. Some special considerations can also influence the price. Sometimes, for instance, a special introductory price is used to get people to try a new product. Some companies enter the market with low prices and keep them low, such as Carnival Cruise Lines and Suzuki cars. Others enter a market with very high prices and then lower them over time, such as producers of high-definition televisions and personal computers. You can learn more about pricing strategies in Chapter 14.

Distribution Strategy

Distribution strategy is creating the means (the channel) by which a product flows from the producer to the consumer. One aspect of distribution strategy is deciding how many stores and which specific wholesalers and retailers will handle the product in a geographic area. Cosmetics, for instance, are distributed in many different ways. Avon has a sales force of several hundred thousand representatives who call directly on consumers.

marketing mix
The blend of product offering, pricing, promotional methods, and distribution system that brings a specific group of consumers superior value.

four Ps (4Ps)
Product, price, promotion, and place (distribution), which together make up the marketing mix.

product strategy
Taking the good or service and selecting a brand name, packaging, colours, a warranty, accessories, and a service program.

pricing strategy
Setting a price based on the demand and cost for a good or service.

distribution strategy
Creating the means by which products flow from the producer to the consumer.

Concept *in Action*

© CBS/LANDOV

With their computerized profile-matching capabilities, online dating services are a high-tech way to make a love connection. Today's date-seeking singles want more than automated personals, however. They want advice from experts. At Match.com, popular psychologist Dr. Phil guides subscribers towards healthy relationships. At eHarmony.com, Dr. Neil Clark Warren helps the lovelorn find a soul mate. How do Internet dating services use various elements of the marketing mix to bolster the effectiveness of their product strategies?

promotion strategy
The unique combination of personal selling, advertising, publicity, and sales promotion to stimulate the target market to buy a product or service.

Clinique and Estée Lauder are distributed through selected department stores. CoverGirl and Del Laboratories use mostly chain drugstores and other mass merchandisers. Redken sells through beauticians. Revlon uses several of these distribution channels. Distribution is examined in detail in Chapter 14.

Promotion Strategy

Many people feel that promotion is the most exciting part of the marketing mix. Promotion strategy covers personal selling, advertising, public relations, and sales promotion. Each element is coordinated with the others to create a promotional blend. An advertisement, for instance, helps a buyer get to know the company and paves the way for a sales call. A good promotion strategy can dramatically increase a company's sales. Promotion is examined in Chapter 14.

Public relations is initiated by the company and plays a special role in promotion. It is used to create a good image of the company and its products. Bad publicity, which originates outside the company, costs nothing to send out, but it can cost a company a great deal in lost business. Good publicity, such as a television or magazine story about a company's new product, can be the result of much time, money, and effort spent by a public relations department.

Sales promotion directly stimulates sales. It includes trade shows, catalogues, contests, games, premiums, coupons, and special offers. Tim Hortons discount coupons and "Roll up the rim to win" contests, offering money and food prizes, are examples of sales promotions.

Not-for-Profit Marketing

Profit-oriented companies are not the only ones that analyze the marketing environment, find a competitive advantage, and create a marketing mix. The application of marketing principles and techniques is also vital to not-for-profit organizations. Marketing helps not-for-profit groups identify target markets and develop effective marketing mixes. In some cases, marketing has kept symphonies, museums, and other cultural groups from having to close their doors. In other organizations, marketing ideas and techniques have helped managers do their jobs better. In the private sector, the profit motive is both an objective for guiding decisions and a criterion for evaluating results. Not-for-profit organizations do not seek to make a profit for redistribution to owners or shareholders. Rather, their focus is often on generating enough funds to cover expenses. For example, organized religions do not gauge their success by the amount of money left in offering plates. The Canadian Museum of Civilization does not base its performance evaluations on the dollar value of tokens put into the turnstile.

Not-for-profit marketing is also concerned with social marketing, that is, the application of marketing to social issues and causes. The goals of social marketing are to effect social change (for instance, by creating racial harmony), further social causes (for instance, by helping the homeless), and evaluate the relationship between marketing and society (for instance, by asking whether society should allow advertising on television shows for young children). Individual organizations also engage in social marketing. Mothers Against Drunk Driving (MADD) counsels against drunk driving, and the Canadian Wildlife Federation asks for your help in protecting endangered animals and birds and their spaces.

Considering a career in marketing? See various options in marketing (or any other field) at www.workopolis.com

social marketing
The application of marketing techniques to social issues and causes; used to convince customers of ideas, attitudes, and behaviours.

Visit the website for the Canadian Museum of Civilization at www.civilization.ca

LO4

BUYER BEHAVIOUR

buyer behaviour
The actions people take in buying and using goods and services.

An organization cannot reach its goals without understanding buyer behaviour. Buyer behaviour is the actions people take in buying and using goods and services. Marketers who understand buyer behaviour, such as how a price increase will affect a product's sales, can create a more effective marketing mix.

The Canadian Red Cross, a not-for-profit organization, uses social marketing to remind families to prepare their homes and families for emergencies and disasters. What are differences and similarities in marketing in for-profit and not-for-profit organizations?

OMI AGENCY/SUN MEDIA CORPORATION

To understand buyer behaviour, marketers must understand how consumers make buying decisions. The consumer decision-making process has several steps, which are shown in Exhibit 13.2. The entire process is affected by cultural, social, individual, and psychological factors. The buying process starts with need recognition. This might be as simple as running out of coffee. Yes, I need to purchase more coffee. Or perhaps you recently got married and recognize that you need to start building equity instead of paying rent. Perhaps you are also considering starting a family. Therefore, you decide to buy your first home (Step 1 in Exhibit 13.2).

Exhibit 13.2 Consumer Decision-Making Process

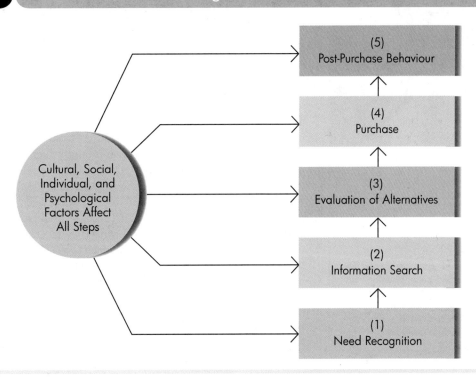

Next, you begin to gather information about financing, available homes, styles, locations, and so forth (Step 2). After you feel that you have gathered enough information, you begin to evaluate alternatives (Step 3). For example, you might eliminate all homes that cost more than $250,000 or are more than a 30-minute drive to your work. Then an offer is made and, if it is accepted, a purchase is made (Step 4). Finally, you assess the experience and your level of satisfaction with your new home (Step 5).

Influences on Consumer Decision Making

Cultural, social, individual, and psychological factors have an impact on consumer decision making from the time a person recognizes a need through post-purchase behaviour. We will examine each of these in more detail.

CULTURE Purchase roles within the family are influenced by culture. Culture is the set of values, ideas, attitudes, and symbols created to shape human behaviour. Culture is environmentally oriented. The Sami of northern Europe (Kola Peninsula of Russia, Finland, Norway, and Sweden) have developed a culture for Arctic survival. Similarly, the indigenous people of the Brazilian jungle have created a culture suitable for jungle living.

Culture, by definition, is social in nature. It is human interaction that creates values and prescribes acceptable behaviour. Thus, culture gives order to society by creating common expectations. Sometimes these expectations are codified into law; for example, if you come to a red light, you stop the car. As long as a value or belief meets the needs of society, it will remain part of the culture; if it is no longer functional, the value or belief recedes. The value that very large families are "good" is no longer held by a majority of Canadians. As Canadians live more in an urban rather than a rural environment, children are no longer needed to perform farm chores.

Culture is not static. It adapts to changing societal needs and evolving environmental factors. The rapid growth of technology has accelerated the rate of cultural change. Inventions such as the elevator made possible modern high-rise cities. Television changed entertainment patterns and family communication flows, and heightened public awareness of political and other news events. The Internet has changed how we communicate and how most of us work.

SOCIAL FACTORS Most consumers are likely to seek out the opinions of others to reduce their search and evaluation effort or uncertainty, especially as the perceived risk of the decision increases. Consumers might also seek out others' opinions for guidance on new products or services, products with image-related attributes, or products where attribute information is lacking or uninformative. Specifically, consumers interact socially with reference groups, opinion leaders, and family members to obtain product information and decision approval. All the formal and informal groups that influence the buying behaviour of an individual are that person's reference groups. Consumers might use products or brands to identify with or become a member of a group. They learn from observing how members of their reference groups consume, and they use the same criteria to make their own consumer decisions. A reference group might be a fraternity or sorority, a group you work with, or a club to which you belong.

Reference groups frequently include individuals known as group leaders, or opinion leaders—those who influence others. Obviously, it is important for marketing managers to persuade such people to purchase their goods or services. Many products and services that are integral parts of Canadians' lives today got their initial boost from opinion leaders. For example, DVDs and sport utility vehicles were embraced by opinion leaders

culture
The set of values, ideas, attitudes, and other symbols created to shape human behaviour.

reference groups
Formal and informal groups that influence buyer behaviour

opinion leaders
Those who influence others.

Concept *in Action*

Many companies target consumers reaching retirement age and other baby boomers with advertisements promoting their products. Demographic segmentation is the most common form of market segmentation. What products are specifically targeted to the following groups: age 14–25, 25–50, and over 50?

© THINKSTOCK/GETTY IMAGES

well ahead of the general public. Opinion leaders are often the first to try new products and services out of pure curiosity. They are typically self-indulgent, making them more likely to explore unproven but intriguing products and services. A great application of this concept to a successful new business is CommunityPerks profiled in the Creating the Future box in Chapter 10.

The family is the most important social institution for many consumers, strongly influencing values, attitudes, and self-concept—and buying behaviour. For example, a family that strongly values good health will have a grocery list distinctly different from that of a family that views every dinner as a gourmet event. Moreover, the family is responsible for the socialization process, the passing down of cultural values and norms to children. Children learn by observing their parents' consumption patterns, and so they will tend to shop in a similar pattern.

socialization process
The passing down of cultural norms and values to children.

Marketers should consider family purchase situations along with the distribution of consumer and decision-maker roles among family members. Ordinary marketing views the individual as both decision maker and consumer. Family marketing adds several other possibilities: Sometimes more than one family member or all family members are involved in the decision; sometimes only children are involved in the decision; sometimes more than one consumer is involved; and sometimes the decision maker and the consumer are different people. For example, a parent will select a dentist for a child to visit.

INDIVIDUAL INFLUENCES ON CONSUMER BUYING DECISIONS A person's buying decisions are also influenced by personal characteristics that are unique to each individual, such as gender, personality, and self-concept. Individual characteristics are generally stable over the course of one's life. For instance, most people do not change their gender, and the act of changing personality requires a complete reorientation of one's life.

Physiological differences between men and women result in different needs, such as health and beauty products. Just as important are the distinct cultural, social, and economic roles played by men and women and the effects that these have on their decision-making processes. Men and women also shop differently. Studies show that men and women share similar motivations in terms of where to shop—that is, seeking

Concept *in Action*

Since its launching in 2004, Facebook has become the largest Internet social network with over one billion active users as of October 2012. Originally created for Harvard university students, Facebook quickly spread to other colleges in the Boston area and then to the high schools. In September 2006, it became accessible to anyone with an email address. "Friends" are quick to share their likes and dislikes as well as any aspect of their daily lives. How can online communities influence buyer behaviour?

reasonable prices, merchandise quality, and a friendly, low-pressure environment—but they don't necessarily feel the same about shopping in general. Most women enjoy shopping; their male counterparts claim to dislike the experience and shop only out of necessity. Furthermore, men desire simple shopping experiences, stores with less variety, and convenience.

Each consumer has a unique personality. **Personality** is a broad concept that can be thought of as a way of organizing and grouping how an individual typically reacts to situations. Thus, personality combines psychological make-up and environmental forces. It includes people's underlying dispositions, especially their most dominant characteristics. Although personality is one of the least useful concepts in the study of consumer behaviour, some marketers believe that personality influences the types and brands of products purchased. For instance, the type of car, clothes, or jewellery a consumer buys can reflect one or more personality traits.

Self-concept, or self-perception, is how consumers perceive themselves. Self-concept includes attitudes, perceptions, beliefs, and self-evaluations. Although self-concept can change, the change is often gradual. Through self-concept, people define their identity, which, in turn, provides for consistent and coherent behaviour.

Self-concept combines the ideal self-image (the way an individual would like to be, called normative) and the real self-image (how an individual actually perceives him or herself, called descriptive). Generally, we try to raise our real self-image toward our ideal (or at least narrow the gap). Consumers seldom buy products that jeopardize their self-image. For example, someone who sees herself as a trendsetter wouldn't buy clothing that doesn't project a contemporary image.

PSYCHOLOGICAL INFLUENCES ON CONSUMER BUYING DECISIONS An

individual's buying decisions are further influenced by psychological factors such as perception, beliefs, and attitudes. These factors are what consumers use to interact with their world. They are the tools consumers use to recognize their feelings, gather and analyze information, formulate thoughts and opinions, and take action. Unlike the other three influences on consumer behaviour, psychological influences can be affected by a person's environment because they are applied on specific occasions. For example, you will perceive different stimuli and process these stimuli in different ways depending on whether you are sitting in class concentrating on the instructor, sitting outside of class talking to friends, or sitting in your dorm room watching television.

The world is full of stimuli. A stimulus is any unit of input affecting one or more of the five senses: sight, smell, taste, touch, and hearing. The process by which we select, organize, and interpret these stimuli into a meaningful and coherent picture is called perception. In essence, perception is how we see the world around us and how we recognize that we need some help in making a purchasing decision. People cannot perceive every stimulus in their environment. Therefore, they use selective exposure to decide which stimuli to notice and which to ignore. A typical consumer is exposed to more than 250 advertising messages a day but notices only between 11 and 20.

A belief is an organized pattern of knowledge that an individual holds as true about his or her world. A consumer might believe that Sony's camcorder makes the best home videos, tolerates hard use, and is reasonably priced. These beliefs might be based on knowledge, faith, or hearsay. Consumers tend to develop a set of beliefs about a product's attributes and then, through these beliefs, a *brand image*—a set of beliefs about a particular brand. In turn, the brand image shapes consumers' attitudes toward the product.

An attitude is a learned tendency to respond consistently toward a given object, idea, or concept, such as a brand. Attitudes rest on an individual's value system, which represents personal standards of good and bad, right and wrong, and so forth; therefore, attitudes tend to be more enduring and complex than beliefs. For an example of the nature of attitudes, consider the differing attitudes of consumers around the world toward the practice of purchasing on credit. North Americans have long been enthusiastic about charging goods and services and are willing to pay high

personality
A way of organizing and grouping how an individual reacts to situations.

self-concept
How people perceive themselves.

ideal self-image (normative)
The way an individual would like to be.

real self-image (descriptive)
How an individual actually perceives him- or herself.

perception
The process by which we select, organize, and interpret stimuli into a meaningful and coherent picture.

selective exposure
The process of deciding which stimuli to notice and which to ignore.

belief
An organized pattern of knowledge that an individual holds as true about the world.

attitude
Learned tendency to respond consistently toward a given object, idea, or concept.

interest rates for the privilege of postponing payment. To many European consumers, doing what amounts to taking out a loan—even a small one—to pay for anything seems absurd.

Types of Buying Decisions

Buying decisions are made in both the consumer markets and the business markets. Each is unique and the basic difference is the intended use of the product. The difference in the decision making is often for very different reasons.

CONSUMER PURCHASE DECISION MAKING All consumer buying decisions generally fall along a continuum of three broad categories: routine response behaviour, limited decision making, and extensive decision making (see Exhibit 13.3). Goods and services in these three categories can best be described in terms of five factors: level of consumer involvement, length of time to make a decision, cost of the good or service, degree of information search, and the number of alternatives considered. The level of consumer involvement is perhaps the most significant determinant in classifying buying decisions. **Involvement** is the amount of time and effort a buyer invests in the search, evaluation, and decision processes of consumer behaviour.

Frequently purchased, low-cost goods and services are generally associated with routine response behaviour. These goods and services can also be called low-involvement products, because consumers spend little time on searching and decision making before making the purchase. Usually, buyers are familiar with several different brands in the product category but stick with one brand. Consumers engaged in routine response behaviour normally don't experience need recognition until they are exposed to advertising or see the product displayed on a store shelf. In Chapter 14 you will see that typically these include the convenience products.

Limited decision making typically occurs when a consumer has previous product experience but is unfamiliar with the current brands available. Limited decision making is also associated with lower levels of involvement (although higher than routine decisions), because consumers do expend moderate effort in searching for information or in considering various alternatives. Suppose the children's usual brand of cereal, Kellogg's Corn Flakes, is unavailable in the grocery store. Completely out of cereal at home, the parent now must select another brand. Before making a final selection, he or she might pull from the shelf several brands similar to Kellogg's Corn Flakes (such as Cheerios) to compare their nutritional value and calories, and to decide whether the children will like the new cereal. Normally, shopping products (discussed in Chapter 14) are associated with this.

Consumers practise extensive decision making when buying an unfamiliar, expensive product or an infrequently bought item. This process is the most complex type of consumer buying decision and is associated with high involvement on the part

involvement
The amount of time and effort a buyer invests in the searches, evaluations, and decision processes of consumer behaviour.

routine response behaviour
Purchase of low-cost, frequently bought items with little search or decision making.

limited decision making
The situation in which a consumer has previous product experience but is unfamiliar with the current brands available.

extensive decision making
Purchasing an unfamiliar, expensive, infrequently bought item.

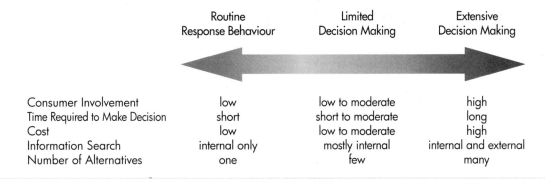

Exhibit 13.3 Continuum of Consumer Buying Decisions

	Routine Response Behaviour	Limited Decision Making	Extensive Decision Making
Consumer Involvement	low	low to moderate	high
Time Required to Make Decision	short	short to moderate	long
Cost	low	low to moderate	high
Information Search	internal only	mostly internal	internal and external
Number of Alternatives	one	few	many

of the consumer. This process resembles the model outlined in Exhibit 13.2. These consumers want to make the right decision, so they want to know as much as they can about the product category and available brands. Buyers use several criteria for evaluating their options and spend much time seeking information. Buying a home or a car, for example, requires extensive decision making; these are classified as special products (see Chapter 14).

BUSINESS-TO-BUSINESS PURCHASE DECISION MAKING Business buyer behaviour and business markets are different from consumer markets. Business markets include institutions such as hospitals and schools, manufacturers, wholesalers and retailers, and various branches of government. The key difference between a consumer product and a business product is the intended use. If you purchase a certain model of Dell computer for your home so you can surf the Internet, it is a consumer good. If a purchasing agent for MuchMusic buys exactly the same computer for a MuchMusic scriptwriter, it is a business good. Why? The reason is that MuchMusic is a business, so the computer will be used in a business environment.

CHARACTERISTICS OF THE BUSINESS-TO-BUSINESS MARKET The main differences between consumer markets and business markets are as follows:

1. *Purchase volume.* Business customers buy in much larger quantities than consumers. Think how many truckloads of sugar M&M/Mars must purchase to make one day's output of M&Ms. Imagine the number of batteries Sears buys each day for resale to consumers. Think of the number of pens the federal government must use each day.
2. *Number of customers.* Business marketers usually have far fewer customers than consumer marketers. As a result, it is much easier to identify prospective buyers and monitor current needs. Think about how few customers for airplanes or industrial cranes there are compared to the more than 4 million consumer households in Canada.
3. *Location of buyers.* Business customers tend to be much more geographically concentrated than consumers. For example, the automobile industry is concentrated in Ontario, and the oil industry is concentrated in Alberta. Suppliers to these industries often locate close to the industries to lower distribution costs and facilitate communication.
4. *Direct distribution.* Business sales tend to be made directly to the buyer, because such sales frequently involve large quantities or custom-made items like heavy machinery. Consumer goods are more likely to be sold through intermediaries, such as wholesalers and retailers.

MARKET SEGMENTATION

market segmentation
The process of separating, identifying, and evaluating the layers of a market to identify a target market.

The study of buyer behaviour helps marketing managers better understand why people make purchases. To identify the target markets that might be most profitable for the company, managers use **market segmentation**, which is the process of separating, identifying, and evaluating the layers of a market to identify a target market. For instance, a target market might be segmented into two groups: families with children and those without children. Families with young children are likely to buy hot cereals and pre-sweetened cereals. Families with no children are more likely to buy health-oriented cereals. You can be sure that cereal companies plan their marketing mixes with this difference in mind. A business market, on the other hand, might be segmented by large customers and small customers or by geographic area.

The five basic forms of consumer market segmentation are demographic, geographic, psychographic, benefit, and volume. Their characteristics are summarized in Exhibit 13.4 and are discussed in the following sections.

Exhibit 13.4 Forms of Consumer Market Segmentation

FORM	GENERAL CHARACTERISTICS
Demographic segmentation	Age, education, gender, income, race, social class, household size
Geographic segmentation	Regional location (e.g., Maritimes, Newfoundland and Labrador; Central Canada; Western Canada; Northern Canada); population density (urban, suburban, rural); city or county size; climate
Psychographic segmentation	Lifestyle, personality, interests, values, attitudes
Benefit segmentation	Benefits provided by the good or service
Volume segmentation	Amount of use (light versus heavy)

Demographic Segmentation

Demographic segmentation uses categories such as age, education, gender, income, and household size to differentiate among markets. This form of market segmentation is the most common. Statistics Canada provides a great deal of demographic data. For example, marketing researchers can use census data to find areas within cities that contain high concentrations of high-income consumers, singles, blue-collar workers, and so forth.

Many products are targeted to various age groups. Most music CDs or other music sources, Pepsi, Coke, many movies, and thousands of other products are targeted toward teenagers and persons under 25 years old. In contrast, most cruises, medical products, fine jewellery, vacation homes, and denture products are targeted toward people 50 years old and up. An example of how Frito Lay targets various age groups for three of its most popular products is shown in Exhibit 13.5.

Certain markets are segmented by gender. These include clothing, cosmetics, personal care items, magazines, jewellery, and footwear. Gillette (a subsidy company of Procter and Gamble), for example, is one of the world's best-known marketers of personal care products and has historically targeted men for the most part. Procter and Gamble was primarily targeting women prior to acquiring Gillette. The purchase of Gillette opened a new market for Procter and Gamble—the men's market.

Income is another popular way of segmenting markets. Income level influences consumers' wants and determines their buying power. Housing, clothing, automobiles, and food are among the many markets segmented by income. Michelina's frozen dinners are targeted to lower income groups, whereas Stouffer's Lean Cuisine line is aimed at higher income consumers.

demographic segmentation
The differentiation of markets through the use of categories such as age, education, gender, income, and household size.

Exhibit 13.5 Age Segmentation for Fritos, Doritos, and Tostitos

	NAME DERIVATION	YEAR INTRODUCED	MAIN INGREDIENTS	DEMOGRAPHIC	ACCORDING TO FRITO-LAY
Frito	"Little fried bits" (Spanish)	1932	Corn, vegetable oil, salt	33- to 51-year-old males	"Hunger satisfaction"
Doritos	"Little bits of gold"	1964	Corn, vegetable oil, cheddar cheese, salt	Teens, mostly male	"Bold and daring snacking"
Tostitos	"Little toasted bits" (Spanish)	1981	White corn, vegetable oil, salt	Upscale consumers born between 1946 and 1964	"Casual interaction through friends and family ... a social food that brings people together"

SOURCE: Frito-Lay

Geographic Segmentation

Geographic segmentation means segmenting markets by region of the country, city or county size, market density, or climate. *Market density* is the number of people or businesses within a certain area. Many companies segment their markets geographically to meet regional preferences and buying habits. Both Ford and Chevrolet, for instance, sell more pickup trucks and truck parts in the middle of the country than on either coast.

Psychographic Segmentation

Ethnic background, income, occupation, and other demographic variables help in developing strategies but often do not paint the entire picture of consumer needs. Demographics provide the skeleton, but psychographics add meat to the bones. **Psychographic segmentation** is market segmentation by personality or lifestyle. People with common activities, interests, and opinions are grouped together and given a "lifestyle name." For example, Harley-Davidson divides its customers into seven lifestyle segments, from "cocky misfits," who are most likely to be arrogant troublemakers, to "laid-back camper types" committed to cycling and nature, to "classy capitalists," who have wealth and privilege.

Creating the Future of Business

MICHAEL JOHNSON, SCISUPPLY INC.

We've heard the stories, we've had the nightmares—but Michael Johnson has lived through it. In 1995, Michael Johnson sustained a spinal cord injury during a high school football practice and was left with permanent paralysis from the chest down. As he puts it: "Suddenly I was classified as a quadriplegic." With such an injury, life's challenges kick into high gear, not to mention what "many people may not realize—that in addition to losing the use of your legs, paralysis also affects your bowel and bladder function."

Now before you stop reading, understand one thing—Michael turned what for most of us would have been an excuse to give up, into a very successful business—SCIsupply Inc., specializing in online sales and distribution of incontinence supplies required by people who have sustained neurological damage from spinal cord injury or disease.

Initially, as with many other people in his situation, Michael was dependent on specific medical devices, such as catheters and drainage bags, to manage his bladder. Although there are many products with different features on the market, Michael says he "... wasn't even aware of the options. [He] simply continued to use what the hospital had used when [he] was in rehab."

Michael, by chance, discovered something that suited his needs far better, and it was then that he noticed a gap in the service and delivery of these products. Having always wanted to develop a business, he entered a full-time MBA program at a Canadian university in 2008 and decided to develop an online business that served as an educational resource while also retailing the products online worldwide. His initial market was people who had sustained spinal cord injury but he soon realized, after being in business for over a year, that urinary incontinence affected more than just people with spinal cord injuries. Michael is currently in the process of rebranding to expand his market beyond this one segment.

Michael "appreciates first-hand" the importance of the products he sells, and as a result, SCIsupply "realizes that there are enough things to worry about on a daily basis; therefore, the company strives to create a system where shopping for incontinence supplies is as convenient and seamless as possible." SCIsupply takes a lot of things into consideration when deciding which brands to carry. Customers are obviously concerned with quality and value, but Michael also looks at company philosophy. He considers how interested the company is in "serving the needs of its customers after they leave the hospital and are living in the community." According to Michael, "this difference in philosophy among companies is reflected in the level of customer service,"—something else that the customer definitely cares about. SCIsupply "prides itself on being customer focused. It wants to get to know each customer and their own unique needs." It even has an automatic reorder option so a customer will never have to worry about running out of supplies.

Says Michael: "If I could offer words of inspiration (to students reading this), they would be 'Just do it'. It's very easy to doubt yourself, but there is no reward in that. It's much more rewarding, whether you succeed or fail, to follow through with your idea." And follow through he did, thankfully, for all his satisfied customers.

Thinking Critically

1. You may not have a challenge of your own like Michael's, but you may know someone who does. How important do you think Michael's understanding of the customer was to his success?

2. How did Michael's definition of his 'product' impact on his ability to see other markets to expand into?

SOURCES: http://www.scisupply.ca, and information provided personally by Michael Johnson via e-mail.

Benefit Segmentation

Benefit segmentation is based on what a product will do rather than on consumer characteristics. For years, Crest toothpaste was targeted toward consumers concerned with preventing cavities. Recently, Crest subdivided its market. It now offers many different types of toothpaste, each with a specific benefit. These include Crest Pro-Health, for people who want to prevent cavities and tartar build-up; Crest Whitening with Scope, for those that want the whitest teeth possible with the added breath freshener; Crest Sensitivity, for people with sensitive teeth; Vivid White, for people wanting whiter teeth; as well as a toothpaste that combines many of these in one tube.

Volume Segmentation

The fifth main type of segmentation is **volume segmentation**, which is based on the amount of the product purchased. Just about every product has heavy, moderate, and light users, as well as non-users. Heavy users often account for a very large portion of a product's sales. Thus, a company might want to target its marketing mix to the heavy user segment.

USING MARKETING RESEARCH TO SERVE EXISTING CUSTOMERS AND FIND NEW CUSTOMERS

How do successful companies learn what their customers value? Through marketing research, companies can be sure they are listening to the voice of the customer. **Marketing research** is the process of planning, collecting, and analyzing data relevant to a marketing decision. The results of this analysis are then communicated to management. The information collected through marketing research includes the preferences of customers, the perceived benefits of products, and consumer lifestyles.

benefit segmentation
The differentiation of markets based on what a product will do rather than on customer characteristics.

volume segmentation
The differentiation of markets based on the amount of the product purchased.

marketing research
The process of planning, collecting, and analyzing data relevant to a marketing decision.

Concept *in Action*

L. L. Bean is a world-renowned outfitter serving people who love the outdoors. Psychographic segmentation is market segmentation by personality or lifestyle. How would you describe the psychographics of L.L. Bean's customers?

© 2009 JUPITERIMAGES CORPORATION

A good place to learn more about marketing research is Quirks Marketing Research Review, www.quirks.com In addition to articles, you can link to major marketing research companies.

Research helps companies make better use of their marketing budgets. Marketing research has a range of uses from fine-tuning existing products to discovering whole new marketing concepts.

For example, everything at the Olive Garden restaurant chain, from the décor to the wine list, is based on marketing research. Each new menu item is put through a series of consumer taste tests before being added to the menu. Hallmark Cards uses marketing research to test messages, cover designs, and even the size of the cards. Hallmark's experts know which kinds of cards will sell best in which places. For instance, in geographic regions where engagement parties are popular, engagement cards sell best.

In this section, we examine the marketing research process, which consists of the following steps:

1. Define the marketing opportunity or issue.
2. Choose a research method.
3. Collect the data.
4. Analyze the research data.
5. Make recommendations to management.

Define the Marketing Opportunity or Issue

The most critical step in the marketing research process is defining the marketing opportunity or issue. This involves writing either an opportunity or a problem statement or a list of research objectives. If the opportunity or issue is not defined properly, the remainder of the research will be a waste of time and money. Two key questions can help in defining the marketing opportunity or issue correctly:

1. Why is the information being sought? By discussing with managers what the information is going to be used for and what decisions might be made as a result, the researcher can get a clearer grasp of the opportunity or issue.
2. Does the information already exist? If so, money and time can be saved, and a quick decision can be made.

Choose a Research Method

After the opportunity or issue is correctly defined, a research method is chosen. There are three basic research methods: survey, observation, and experiment.

With **survey research**, data are collected from respondents in person, at a mall, or through the Internet, by telephone, or mail to obtain facts, opinions, and attitudes. A questionnaire is used to provide an orderly and structured approach to data gathering. Face-to-face interviews might take place at the respondent's home, in a shopping mall, or at a place of business.

Observation research is research that monitors respondents' actions without direct interaction. In the fastest-growing form of observation research, researchers use cash registers with scanners that read tags with bar codes to identify the item being purchased. Technological advances are rapidly expanding the future of observation research. For example, ACNielsen has been using black boxes for years on television sets to obtain information on a family's viewing habits silently. But what if the set is on but no one is in the room? To overcome that problem, researchers will soon rely on infrared passive "people meters," which will identify the faces of family members watching the television program. Thus, the meter can duly record when the set is on and no one is watching.

In the third research method, **experiment**, the investigator changes one or more variables—price, package, design, shelf space, advertising theme, or advertising expenditures—while observing the effects of those changes on another variable (usually sales). The objective of experiments is to measure causality. For example, an experiment might reveal the impact that a change in package design has on sales.

survey research
A marketing research method in which data are collected from respondents in person, by telephone, by mail, at a mall, or through the Internet to obtain facts, opinions, and attitudes.

observation research
A marketing research method in which the investigator monitors respondents' actions without interacting directly with the respondents; for example, by using cash registers with scanners.

experiment
A marketing research method in which the investigator changes one or more variables—price, packaging, design, shelf space, advertising theme, or advertising expenditures—while observing the effects of these changes on another variable (usually sales).

Collect the Data

Two types of data are used in marketing research: primary data (using primary research), which are collected directly from the original source to have more information or to solve a problem; and secondary data (using secondary research), information that has already been collected for a project other than the current one that can help to understand a situation or solve a problem. Secondary data can come from a number of sources, among them government agencies, trade associations, research bureaus, universities, the Internet, commercial publications, and internal company records. Company records include sales invoices, accounting records, data from previous research studies, and historical sales data.

Primary data are usually gathered through some form of survey research. As described earlier, survey research often relies on interviews. See Exhibit 13.6 for the different types of surveys. Today, conducting surveys over the Internet is the fastest-growing form of survey research.

Analyze the Data

After the data have been collected, the next step in the research process is data analysis. The purpose of this analysis is to interpret and draw conclusions from the mass of collected data. Many software statistical programs, such as SAS and SPSS, are available to make this task easier for the researcher.

primary data
Information collected directly from the original source to get more information about an opportunity or to solve a problem.

secondary data
Information that has already been collected for a project, other than the current one, that can help to understand a situation or solve a problem.

HOT|inks

Find out what information Statistics Canada collects at
www.statcan.ca

Exhibit 13.6	Common Types of Survey Research
Internet surveys	Conducted on the Internet, often using respondents from huge Internet panels (persons agreeing to participate in a series of surveys).
Executive surveys	Interviews of professionals (e.g., engineers, architects, doctors, executives) or decision makers that are conducted at their place of business.
Mall-intercept surveys	Interviews with consumers that are conducted in a shopping mall or other high-traffic location. Interviews may be done in a public area of the mall, or respondents might be taken to a private test area.
Central location telephone surveys	Interviews are conducted from a telephone facility set up for that purpose. These facilities typically have equipment that permits supervisors to monitor the interviewing unobtrusively while it is taking place. Many of these facilities do national sampling from a single location. An increasing number have computer-assisted interviewing capabilities. At these locations, the interviewer sits in front of a computer terminal attached to a mainframe or personal computer. The questionnaire is programmed into the computer, and the interviewer uses the keyboard to enter responses directly.
Self-administered questionnaires	Self-administered questionnaires are most frequently employed at high-traffic locations, such as shopping malls, or in captive audience situations, such as classrooms and airplanes. Respondents are given general information on how to fill out the questionnaire and are expected to fill it out on their own. Kiosk-based point-of-service touch screens provide a way of capturing information from individuals in stores, health clinics, and other shopping or service environments. Sometimes software-driven questionnaires on diskettes are sent to individuals who have personal computers.
Ad hoc (one-shot) mail surveys	Questionnaires are mailed to a sample of consumers or industrial users, without prior contact by the researcher. Instructions are included, and respondents are asked to fill out the questionnaire and return it via mail. Sometimes a gift or monetary incentive is provided.
Mail panels	Questionnaires are mailed to a sample of individuals who have been pre-contacted. The panel concept has been explained to them, and they have agreed to participate for some period of time in exchange for gratuities. Mail panels typically generate much higher response rates than do ad hoc mail surveys.

Concept *Check*

Define marketing research.

Explain the marketing research process.

What are the three basic marketing research methods?

Make Recommendations to Management

After completing the data analysis, the researcher must prepare the report and communicate the conclusions and recommendations to management. This is a key step in the process, because marketing researchers who want their conclusions acted on must convince the manager that the results are credible and justified by the data collected. Today, presentation software provides easy-to-use tools for creating reports and presentations that are more interesting, compelling, and effective than was possible just a few years ago.

LO7 THE FUTURE OF MARKETING

To discover exactly what customers value most and to build reliable brand advocates, marketers are using innovative techniques. Social media and mobile marketing, green and social marketing, and the continued use of loyalty cards have changed marketing in the past few years and their potential is unprecedented.

Social-Media and Mobile Marketing

More marketing dollars are moving to social media and other digital marketing initiatives (as opposed to print and radio advertising). Customers are spending more time online and this is true for most demographic groups. This gives companies an opportunity not only to market to their customers but also to find new ones since the audience is so large.

Social media has given customers a platform to voice their opinions and companies are realizing their importance and the need to actively monitor them, especially concerning the public's impression of the company.

Starting in 2011, mobile marketing became a considerable presence. With numerous apps for advertising, branding, etc., technically savvy customers will continue to expect more apps that are very specific and usable.

Green and Social Marketing

green marketing
The process of selling products based on their environmental benefits.

Green marketing is the process of selling products based on their environmental benefits. This can include the product itself being environmentally friendly (e.g., solar heat collectors), or the production process or packaging being environmentally friendly (e.g., jute bags). Green marketing is growing significantly, as customers are willing to back their environmental consciousness with their spending.

Social marketing is used to convince customers of ideas, attitudes, and behaviours, not to sell the product. It seeks to influence social behaviours and to benefit the target market. Some examples of successful social marketing has been non-smoking campaigns and no hand-held cellphones while driving.

Loyalty Cards

loyalty cards
Cards issued by a manufacturer, service organization, or retailer that give discounts to loyal and frequent shoppers.

Just swipe the card at the checkout register and get a discount on tomatoes, toothpaste, or other specials. You save money, and the store builds a record that lets it know how to serve its best customers. Loyalty cards are cards issued by a service organization, retailer, or manufacturer that give discounts to loyal and frequent shoppers. Most companies require the shopper to fill out a demographic profile questionnaire before the card is issued.

Loyalty cards have been around for a few years now, and supermarket and drugstore chains are beginning to reap the benefits. With a huge amount of data being collected on shoppers, from the types of pop they buy to whether they like to shop late at night, merchants are getting smarter at tracking consumer trends. And they're changing their

Expanding Around the Globe

CHALLENGES OF CONDUCTING GLOBAL MARKETING RESEARCH

Global companies, like Research In Motion (RIM), Procter & Gamble, McDonald's, and 3M, want global marketing research to help them make good strategic marketing decisions around the world. Yet, doing marketing research in some countries is not easy.

For example, using the same questionnaire asking "How did you like the taste of the new Pizza Hut crust?" might be followed with a scale that goes (1) excellent through (7) poor. Canadians might rank the new crust at 3.3 and Asians at 1.7. Thus, the conclusion is that the Asians prefer the new crust more than the Canadians. The answer would be wrong! Asians don't like to offend others and therefore rate the new crust higher. In fact, they both liked the new crust the same!

There are many other problems in conducting global research. Cultural habits in some countries virtually prohibit communication with a stranger, particularly for women. For example, a researcher simply may not be able to speak on the phone with a housewife in an Islamic country to find out what she thinks of a particular brand. Second, in many societies, such matters as preferences for hygienic products are too personal to be shared with an outsider. In many Latin American countries, a woman may feel ashamed to talk with a researcher about her choice of a brand of sanitary pad,

hair shampoo, or perfume. Third, respondents in many cases may be unwilling to share their true feelings with interviewers because they suspect the interviewers may be agents of the government (for example, seeing information for imposition of additional taxes). Fourth, middle-class people, in developing countries in particular, are reluctant to accept their status and may make false claims to reflect the lifestyle of wealthier people. For example, in a study on the consumption of tea in India, more than 70 percent of the respondents from middle-income families claimed they used one of the several national brands of tea. This finding could not be substantiated because more than 60 percent of the tea sold nationally in India is unbranded, generic tea sold unpackaged. Fifth, many respondents, willing to cooperate, may be illiterate, so that even oral communication may be difficult.[4]

Thinking Critically

1. What cultural factors (values, attitudes, ideas, and symbols) may influence the market research conducted in a third-world country?
2. How can market researchers improve the accuracy and quality of market research conducted in a foreign country?

---

merchandise, store layout, and advertising accordingly to keep their most loyal customers spending.

Retailers estimate that 20 percent of their shoppers account for 80 percent of store sales, so finding out what their best customers want is essential. By simply scanning purchases, stores track what's selling, but when that information is tied to loyalty cards, merchants obtain richer information on who is buying what. This is the prized asset of the supermarkets' future.[5]

GREAT IDEAS TO USE NOW

> ### Concept Check
>
> How are social-media and mobile marketing changing marketing?
>
> How are green marketing and social marketing changing customers' expectations?
>
> Explain how loyalty cards are of benefit to manufacturers and retailers.

As a consumer, you participate in shaping consumer products by the choices you make and the products and services you buy. You can become a better consumer by actively participating in marketing surveys and learning more about the products you buy.

Participate in Marketing Research Surveys

All of us get tired of telephone solicitations where people try to sell us everything from new carpet to chimney cleaning. Recognize that marketing research surveys are different. A true marketing research survey will *never* involve a sales pitch, nor will the research company sell your name to a database marketer. The purpose of marketing research is to build better goods and services for you and me. Help out the researchers and ultimately help yourself. The Canadian Marketing Association (CMA) is the largest marketing association in Canada. CMA members include major financial institutions, publishers, retailers, charitable organizations, agencies, relationship marketers, and those involved in e-business and Internet marketing. A key objective of CMA is to increase consumer confidence in the marketing industry.

Making Ethical Choices

HITTING THE LONG SHOT

As a marketing manager at a beverage company, you are always looking for new products to offer—especially in the under-18 market where you are weak. A hot new drink has been a hit with kids in Japan—sales were up to 75,000 bottles a month—and it is making its way to Europe. Kidsbeer is a cola-like soft drink that is packaged to look like beer. The same colour as lager beer, the drink is formulated to pour with a beer-like foam. It includes guarana, a South American plant extract used in energy drinks. Tomomasu, the Japanese bottler, markets it with the slogan "Even kids cannot stand life unless they have a drink."

The impending arrival of such a drink has raised the ire of consumer groups outside Japan. They are alarmed that any company would glamorize drinking. Already, beer drinking is showing up in movies that target kids and teens—for example, *DodgeBall* and *HellBoy*. Says Amon Rappaport of the Marin Institute, an alcohol industry watchdog group, "The last thing we need is another product that introduces kids to drinking when the alcohol industry already spends billions doing that."

Nonetheless, you are intrigued and begin to investigate. Besides, several companies still sell candy cigarettes to kids (although some countries have banned them).

Using a Web search tool, locate articles about this topic and then write responses to the following questions. Be sure to support your arguments and cite your sources.

ETHICAL DILEMMA: Kidsbeer would boost your company's revenues, because kids love to mimic their parents' behaviour. Do you recommend it to top management?

SOURCES: "Beer-Flavored Soda Headed for Europe," *UPI NewsTrack*, September 19, 2005; "Here's Looking at You, Kid," *Food Management*, October 2005, p. 104; Andrew Adam Newman, "If the Children Can Drink Uncola, What about Unbeer?" *New York Times*, September 19, 2005, p. C8(L); Andrew Adam Newman, "Youngsters Enjoy Beer Ads, Arousing Industry's Critics," *New York Times*, February 13, 2006, p. C15(L); "Drink That Looks Like Beer Getting Popular with Kids," *Kyodo News International*, August 5, 2005.

---

cognitive dissonance
The condition of having beliefs or knowledge that are internally inconsistent or that disagree with one's behaviour.

Visit the Canadian Marketing Association at
www.the-cma.org
to learn more about how they take a leadership role in responding to consumer concerns and to learn more about their "Code of Ethics and Standards of Practice."

Understanding Cognitive Dissonance

When making a major purchase, particularly when the item is expensive and choices are similar, consumers typically experience cognitive dissonance; that is, they have beliefs or knowledge that are internally inconsistent or that disagree with their behaviour. In other words, instead of feeling happy with their new purchase, they experience doubts, feel uneasy, and wonder whether they have done the right thing. Understand that this feeling of uneasiness is perfectly normal and goes away over time. Perhaps the best way to avoid cognitive dissonance is to insist on a strong warranty or money-back guarantee. A second approach is to read everything you can find about your purchase. Go to the Internet, and use the search engines to find articles relevant to your purchase. Find Internet chat rooms about your product, and join in the discussion. And, before you buy, check out the *Consumer Reports* ratings on your product at www.consumerreports.org. For electronic products, also go to www.CNET.com and www.ZDNET.com.

Summary of Learning Outcomes

  Define the marketing concept and relationship marketing.

Marketing includes those business activities that are designed to satisfy consumer needs and wants through the exchange process. Marketing managers use the "right" principle—getting the right goods or services to the right people at the right place, time, and price, using the right promotional techniques. Today, many companies use the marketing concept. The marketing concept involves identifying consumer needs and wants and then producing goods or services that will satisfy them while making a profit. Relationship marketing entails forging long-term relationships with customers, which can lead to repeat sales, reduced costs, and stable relationships.

A company creates a marketing strategy by understanding the external environment, defining the target market, determining a competitive advantage, and developing a marketing mix. Environmental scanning enables companies to understand the external environment. The target market is the specific group of consumers toward which a company directs its marketing efforts. A competitive advantage is a set of unique features of a company and its products that are perceived by the target market as significant and superior to those of the competition.

LO2 Show how managers create a marketing strategy.

To carry out the marketing strategy, companies create a marketing mix—a blend of products, distribution systems, prices, and promotion. Marketing managers use this mix to satisfy target consumers. The mix can be applied to non-business as well as business situations.

LO3 Explain the marketing mix.

Buyer behaviour is what people and businesses do in buying and using goods and services. The consumer decision-making process consists of the following steps: recognizing a need, seeking information, evaluating alternatives, purchasing the product, judging the purchase outcome, and engaging in post-purchase behaviour. A number of factors influence the process. Cultural, social, individual, and psychological factors have an impact on consumer decision making. The main differences between consumer and business markets are purchase volume, number of customers, location of buyers, direct distribution, and rational purchase decisions.

LO4 Summarize how consumers and organizations make buying decisions.

Success in marketing depends on understanding the target market. One technique used to identify a target market is market segmentation. The five basic forms of segmentation are demographic (population statistics), geographic (location), psychographic (personality or lifestyle), benefit (product features), and volume (amount purchased).

LO5 List the five basic forms of market segmentation.

Much can be learned about consumers through marketing research, which involves collecting, recording, and analyzing data important in marketing goods and services, and communicating the results to management. Marketing researchers can use primary data, which are gathered through door-to-door, mall-intercept, telephone, the Internet, and mail interviews. The Internet is becoming a quick, cheap, and efficient way of gathering primary data. Secondary data are available from a variety of sources including government, trade, and commercial associations. Secondary data save time and money, but they might not meet researchers' needs. A huge amount of secondary data is available on the Internet. Both primary and secondary data give researchers a better idea of how the market will respond to the product. Thus, they reduce the risk of producing something the market doesn't want.

LO6 Identify how marketing research is used in marketing decision making.

There are many trends in marketing emerging, mostly because of technology and our attitudes towards the environment. These include social-media and mobile marketing, green marketing and social marketing, and the use of loyalty cards.

LO7 List some of the trends in understanding the consumer.

Key Terms

attitude 382
belief 382
benefit segmentation 387
buyer behaviour 378
cognitive dissonance 392
competitive advantage 374
core value proposition 370

cost competitive advantage 375
culture 380
customer relationship management (CRM) 372
customer satisfaction 371
customer value 371
demographic segmentation 385

Experiential Exercises

1. Can the marketing concept be applied effectively by a sole proprietorship, or is it more appropriate for larger businesses with more managers? Explain.

2. Before starting your own business, you should develop a marketing strategy to guide your efforts. Choose one of the business ideas listed, and develop a marketing strategy for the business. Include the type of market research (both primary and secondary) you will perform and how you will define your target market.

   a. Crafts store to capitalize on the renewed interest in knitting and other crafts
   b. Online corporate-training company
   c. Ethnic restaurant near your campus
   d. Another business opportunity that interests you

3. "Market segmentation is the most important concept in marketing." Why do you think some marketing professionals make this statement? Give an example of each form of segmentation.

4. Pick a specific product that you use frequently, such as a cosmetic or toiletry item, a snack food, article of clothing, book, computer program, or music CD. What is the target market for this product, and does the company's marketing strategy reflect this? Now consider the broader category of your product. How can this product be changed and/or the marketing strategy adjusted to appeal to other market segments?

5. Can marketing research be carried out in the same manner all over the world? Why or why not?

6. Visit the SRI Consulting site, www.sric-bi.com, and click on the VALS Survey link. First read about the VALS survey and how marketers can use it. Describe its value. Then take the survey to find out which psychographic segment you're in. Do you agree or disagree with the results? Why or why not?

7. How good was the marketing strategy you developed in Question 2? Using advice from the marketing section of *Entrepreneur*, www.entrepreneur.com, or other resources, revisit your marketing strategy for the business you selected and revise

the plan accordingly. (*Entrepreneur's* article "Write a Simple Marketing Plan" is a good place to start.) What did you overlook? (If you didn't do this exercise, pick one of the businesses and draft a marketing strategy by using online resources to guide you.)

8. As the number of people online continues to grow, more of the Web surfers are also buying products online. What do researchers say about the characteristics of the online market? What market segments are appearing? Visit several sites to research this topic, and then prepare a report on the demographics of online markets and other key considerations for marketers. NUA Internet Surveys is a good place to start: www.gdsourcing.ca. You'll find summaries of the latest research studies and can search for others by category. From there, you can link to the sites of market research companies. (Many research company sites require registration or subscriptions; however, you can check press releases for summaries of research findings.) Also search for "Internet marketing" or "online marketing" using search engines and business publication sites such as *Business Week, Entrepreneur,* and *Inc.*

Review Questions

1. What is marketing? What is an exchange in marketing?

2. What does the marketing concept involve?

3. What is the difference between customer value and customer satisfaction? How are these related to building relationships?

4. Why is it important for marketers to understand the external environment? What are the six general categories of the environment that marketers must evaluate?

5. What is a target market?

6. What are the various competitive advantages that a company can create?

7. What are the four variables in the marketing mix?

8. What influences consumers in their decision making?

9. What are the characteristics of the business-to-business market?

10. What is market segmentation? What are the five basic forms of consumer market segmentation?

11. What is market research, and what are the steps in the market research process?

CREATIVE THINKING CASE

Teen Power: A Force to Be Reckoned With

Cellphones, surfing gear, extreme sports, video games—these are just some of the lucrative markets where companies focus major marketing dollars on some very important consumers—teenagers. Understanding youth trends and dynamics in the constantly changing teen market remains an ongoing challenge for companies needing to know how best to spend those dollars.

That's where Teen Research Unlimited (TRU) comes in. Started by youthful entrepreneur Peter Zollo in 1982, TRU was the first company to specialize in teen-focused market research. It keeps companies in touch with teen thinking, making it possible for them to forecast trends and remain a step ahead of the competition. Based in Northbrook, Illinois, TRU has worked closely with many of the world's leading youth brands and advertising agencies, playing a key role in groundbreaking advertising and marketing campaigns, and the development of successful products and services.

Named one of the Best Gen-Y employers in 2010, TRU has worked with over two million teenagers worldwide to assemble data for use in advertising campaigns, product development, store designs, and other strategic business activities. Last year TRU conducted more than 1,000 quantitative studies as well as many quantitative research projects. TRU also applies its expertise to teen advocacy on important social issues and high-risk youth behaviours such as anti-tobacco and drug use, sexual assault, life safety, education, crisis management, and skin cancer.

So how does TRU gather its data and help its clients create effective marketing strategies? When a burgeoning fashion retailer needed ethnographic research to learn more about their target consumer, they asked TRU to help them. TRU spent months scouring malls, sitting down with shoppers, and carrying out a comprehensive national quantitative analysis to gain a well-rounded view of the client and its competitors. At project completion, TRU was able to provide its client with a strategically sound, actionable plan that built on previous strengths, addressed areas requiring improvement, and set a benchmark for future measurements.

Worldwide research in the teen markets is an industry TRU entered in 2009. They now undertake research in 40+ countries. One study showed that United Arab Emirates teens spend approximately $71 per month on clothes, more than three times the global average. In the same study, they found that North African teens plan to spend more at a higher rate than in other areas. Over half of them plan to spend more on clothes next year.

The only full-service marketing research company dedicated solely to understanding teens, TRU's initial vision remains in place today: to develop an unparalleled expertise in the teenage market and to offer clients virtually unlimited methods for researching teens. And with more businesses than ever focused on marketing to teenage consumers—Abercrombie & Fitch, PepsiCo, Nintendo, and Nokia are just some of TRU's prestigious clients—companies count on TRU's research to remain in touch with what teenagers want.

Thinking Critically

1. What makes TRU's research so important?
2. In what way is the company unique?
3. How does TRU help its customers understand their target market and create effective marketing strategies?

SOURCES: Adapted from the video "Teenage Research Unlimited," swlearning.com; Parija Bhatnagar, "More Cheese for the 'Mall Rats,'" *CNN/Money*, February 4, 2005; Ruth Laferla, "Teenagers Shop for Art of the Deal," *New York Times*, September 22, 2005; Mary Ellen Podmolik, "Teen Stores Leading the Herd," *Chicago Tribune*, January 14, 2006, p. 1; TRU corporate website, http://www.teenresearch.com, April 26, 2006; About TRU, http://www.tru-insight.com, Dec 19, 2011; S. McGinley, "UAE teens spend three times more on clothes," http://m.arabianbusiness.com/uae-teens-spend-three-times-more-on-clothes-281918.html, May 17, 2010.

Making the Connection

Creating Marketing Strategies

In this chapter, we will continue to look at the functional area of *marketing* but more specifically at the 4Ps of the marketing mix—product, price, place, and promotion. One of the keys to success in marketing is to provide something of unique *value* to the customer in order to achieve the critical success factor of *meeting their needs*. The second is to market it in such a way that you convince the customer of its benefit. They must believe that it will satisfy their needs or they won't buy it. This is where the 4Ps come in. Not only does marketing have to work with the other functional areas in an integrative fashion, as we discussed in the last chapter, but the marketing functions themselves must work together in an integrative way to convince the customer of the unique benefit of the product. For example, imagine a company that wants to promote a product that is of better quality than the competition's and therefore designs it to have the features as well as the look of higher *quality*. It then decides to promote it in ways that appeal to high-end customers, distributes it in high-end stores, but prices it below the competition's. Consumers will clearly be confused as to its quality. All four elements must give a consistent message—they must form an integrative whole—or the customer will be confused rather than convinced.

This is quite evident when you consider, as the chapter explains, that consumers make purchase decisions after considering both the tangible and intangible attributes of the product, including price. They consider the total value package—what they get at the price they have to pay. Remember, this is one of our critical success factors—providing value. Value pricing is one of the concepts discussed in this chapter. Another very integrative product concept is that of the product life cycle. It sounds like just a product concept, but the implications of what stage in the life cycle a product is at goes far beyond the product itself and into how it is priced, promoted, and distributed.

Integration is also evident in looking at product design alone. The chapter discusses how consumers buy packages of benefits; for example, Burger King sells burgers and fries, but along with that quick food preparation and cleanliness. In other words, the product design must take into consideration *human resource* and *operations* issues as well.

When new products are developed, there are also obvious connections to the other parts of our business model. New product goals are usually financially stated, for example, so that the company pursues only products that help it achieve *financial performance*, and ideas are rejected if they don't meet financial goals. The company must also determine if it has the operational facilities to produce the product, plus access to the necessary technology, human, and financial resources. New product ideas need to be checked against long-range *strategies*. Remember that planning takes place at different levels, but all levels are always connected so that they move in the same direction.

Pricing has obvious connections to *finance* of course, just as it affects the total value package for the consumer. The company must set a price that will earn a fair return for the company, but provide value to the consumer as well. This connection with finance is no more obvious than in the discussion of break-even. If the costs from operations, human resources, and marketing cannot be covered from the revenue generated by the product, then financially it is not feasible and can't be done within the current cost structure, regardless of its marketing appeal.

Place or distribution is one of the 4Ps that is, by its very nature, the most integrative since any discussion of place must combine two functional areas—operations and marketing. Distribution is typically the responsibility of operations but is critical to marketing's ability to meet the needs of the customer—getting products to customers when and where they want them. The importance placed on managing the supply chain in today's businesses, that is, the route the product takes from provider to consumer, makes these two areas inseparable. And the very fact that we are discussing supply chain management in a marketing chapter and not just an operations chapter, as is typical, makes the integrative nature of this concept very obvious.

Promotion appears to most students to be the purest form of marketing, but it is also affected by other areas of the business. For example, one of the elements of a promotional mix is personal selling. This has definite human resource implications. The sales force must be managed to communicate the intended message. And how much is spent on personal selling as opposed to other forms of promotion depends to a great extent on the financial situation of the company. As the chapter suggests, "Money, or the lack of it, is one of the biggest influences on the promotional mix." But the factors in the external environment also affect promotion—the government (*political*) sets guidelines on what can and cannot be done in advertising, the competition (*economic* environment) has to be monitored carefully to be aware of what message they are projecting versus your company's message, *social* trends will influence your advertising design and, of course, *technology* is always changing and expanding the limits of what can be done. For example, the Internet is discussed in the chapter as a potential vehicle for building a brand presence, in fact more quickly than traditional methods, and it is also a powerful tool for tailoring the message to meet the needs of specific consumers—as mentioned in the previous chapter, just go visit www.amazon.ca.

The clearest example of integration in promotion is the need for integrated marketing communications. Just as all of the 4Ps must project the same message, so must all elements of the promotional mix. If this is not done, the company risks confusing the consumer, and they will simply buy a different product. The area where there is the least control is in personal selling. You are not designing an ad with a consistent message; your salespeople are your message. Therefore, the message may not be the same every time—again you have human resource issues that must be handled very carefully to ensure consistency.

chapter 14

Creating Marketing Strategies

SCION—TOYOTA GOES YOUTHFUL

By 2001, Toyota knew it had an image problem. The Japanese automaker's vehicles were well established, respected, and popular with baby-boomers—but not with the children of that generation. These Gen-Xers were now old enough to buy their own cars, and they largely shunned Toyotas in favour of vehicles with a more youthful image and plenty of customization options, such as the Honda Civic.

High school and university parking lots were packed with Civics, and they remain popular today. The Civic is relatively inexpensive, reliable, and can be customized easily. You might see a spoiler or a hood scoop or, if you drop by after dark, the glow of neon from beneath the car. The Civic is fun and youthful; Toyotas seemed to draw an older crowd.

This trend was even visible in video games involving cars. The 2001 games featured exotic autos and some tuned-up Civics, while Toyotas, if they were seen at all, were usually parked cars to be avoided. Toyota was losing critically important entry-level market share, and the minds at Toyota knew that if the company were to remain viable it would have to start growing a base of young customers.

The reason? Toyota knows if it sells you your first car, it's more likely to also sell you your last car—and every vehicle in between. That's called creating brand loyalty, and the company's premium Lexus brand of luxury models, introduced in 1989, had the high end covered. So in 2001, Toyota started working on the Scion product line to go after young buyers. Flashy and bright, with unique designs, the cars launched across the United States in 2004, and in 2010 moved into the Canadian market.

The word "scion" means a twig or shoot, or the son of a distinguished family. That definition offers insight into the marketing strategy. Toyota is counting on Scion to bring in Generation Y and the generations to follow.

Scion's marketing tries to appeal to a couple of different age groups at once. While Lexus has separate dealerships, Scion Canada uses a "store within a store" concept inside Toyota outlets. Here's the thinking: Mom and Dad bring you to the Toyota dealer for a safe, reliable car, and you see a cool, flashy, customizable Scion over on one side. Since it's a Toyota, the parents will pay for it, buying the perceived quality of Toyota for a lower price. You get the wow factor of a car right out of a video game.

In some ways, the strategy has worked, since Scion has the youngest buyers of any brand. But sales figures suggest Scion may simply be poaching customers who would otherwise have bought Toyota-branded vehicles such as the Echo, Yaris, and Corolla. Market share numbers indicate that

overall, Toyota sales are flat (down about 2 percent from 2010 to 2011) while Honda is gaining. Scion sold well in its first few early years in the U.S., with significant growth up to 2007, but by 2010 sales had dropped to one third of what they had been at their peak.

Scion vehicles have become a bit more mainstream over the years. Customization options are still available, but the paint colours are muted and less flashy. It may be that Toyota's market strategists are looking at Canadian buyers to extend the life of the Scion brand before they have to come up with a new plan.[1]

THINKING CRITICALLY

As you read this chapter, consider the following questions:

1. What strategies can organizations use to encourage repeat customers?

2. How can getting customers at an early age help create continued success?

3. What could Toyota have done to ensure Scion wasn't simply offering an alternative to buyers who would have bought a Toyota anyway?

SOURCES: Scion Canada, http://www.scionnation.ca/scion; Scion News, http://www.scionnation.ca/scion/about/news/page/2; http://automobileretailers.com/scion/why-scion-why-now/; Jim Henry, "Can Scion Survive Success," Edmunds Inside Line, http://www.insideline.com/scion/can-scion-survive-success.html; Market Data Center, "Auto Sales," *The Wall Street Journal* online, http://online.wsj.com/mdc/public/page/2_3022-autosales.html#autosalesE; Erin Riches, "Scion Hammered by Recession, Hopes New tC Starts Bounce Back," Edmunds Auto Observer, http://www.autoobserver.com/2010/08/scion-hammered-by-recession-hopes-new-tc-starts-bounce-back.html.

The creation of a marketing mix combines the four Ps into a concise plan that will meet or exceed the target market's expectations. Organizations prepare for long-term success by creating and packaging products that add value and pricing them to meet the organization's financial objectives. The businesses must use the distribution system that enhances the value of the product and determine what methods they will use to move products to locations where consumers wish to buy them. At the same time, the organizations build demand for their products through their promotional strategies. This chapter will discuss the product, price, promotion, and place (distribution) of goods and services.

LO1

PRODUCTS—THE COMPANY'S OFFERINGS

product
In marketing, any good or service, along with its perceived attributes and benefits, that creates value for the customer.

brand
A name, design, symbol, specific colour, slogan, or any other feature that identifies a product, distinguishes it from other products, and creates a perception in the minds of consumers.

trademark
A legally exclusive design, name, or other identifying mark associated with a company's brand.

brand loyalty
A customer's preference for a particular brand that results in advocacy for that brand.

master brand
A brand that is so dominant that customers think of it immediately when a product category is mentioned.

manufacturer brand
A brand that is owned by a national or regional manufacturer; the products are widely distributed.

dealer brand
A brand that is owned by the wholesaler or retailer rather than the manufacturer.

generic brand
A brand that carries no specific name associated with a manufacturer, wholesaler, or retailer and usually comes in plain containers and sells for less than brand name products.

In marketing, a **product** is any good or service, along with its perceived attributes and benefits, that creates value for the customer. Attributes can be tangible or intangible. Among the tangible attributes are packaging and warranties, as illustrated in Exhibit 14.1. Intangible attributes are symbolic, such as brand image. People make decisions about which products to buy after considering both tangible and intangible attributes of a product. For example, when you buy a pair of jeans, you consider price, brand, store image, and style before you buy.

Products are often a blend of goods and services, as shown in Exhibit 14.2. For example, a Honda Civic (a good) would have less value without Honda's maintenance agreement (a service). Although Tim Hortons sells such goods as sandwiches and coffee, customers expect quality service as well, including quick food preparation and cleanliness. When developing a product, an organization must consider how the combination of goods and services will provide value to the customer.

Brands—It's Not Just the Name

When we think about a **brand**, many of us assume incorrectly that it refers simply to the name of a product. In fact, a brand is also a design, symbol, specific colour, slogan, or any other feature that identifies a product, distinguishes it from other products, and creates a perception in the minds of consumers. Brands are protected by a **trademark**, which is a legally exclusive design, name, or other identifying mark associated with a company's brand. No other company can use it. Two familiar brands are Lululemon's stylized omega symbol and the golden arches of McDonald's restaurants; both are highly recognizable.

Brand equity refers to the value of the company and brand names. A brand that has high awareness, perceived quality, and **brand loyalty** (customers have a strong preference for this brand and will advocate for it) among customers has high brand equity.

The four most common types of brands are master brand, manufacturer brand, dealer brand, and generic brand. A brand is so dominant that customers think of it immediately when a product category is mentioned; it is called a **master brand** (e.g., Kleenex tissue). **Manufacturer brands** (also called national brands) are owned by national or regional manufacturers, and the products are widely distributed (e.g., Maple Leaf Foods). Brands that are owned by the wholesaler or retailer rather than the manufacturer are **dealer brands** (e.g., President's Choice). **Generic brands** carry no specific name associated with a manufacturer, wholesaler, or retailer, and usually come in plain containers and sell for less than brand name products.

Classifying Consumer Products

Because most things sold are a blend of goods and services, the term *product* can be used to refer to both. After all, consumers are really buying packages of benefits that deliver value. The person who buys a plane ride on Air Canada is looking for a quick way to get

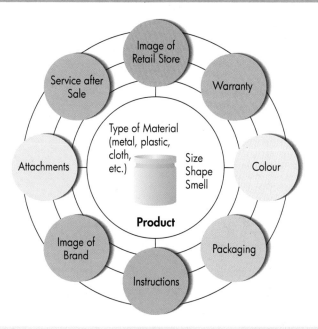

from one city to another (the benefit). Providing this benefit requires goods (a plane) and services (ticketing, maintenance, piloting, etc.).

Marketers must know how consumers view the types of product their companies sell, so that they can design the marketing mix to appeal to the selected target market. To help them define target markets, marketers have devised product categories. Products that are bought by the end user are called *consumer products* (e.g., razors, sandwiches, cars, stereos, magazines, and houses). Consumer products that get used up, such as Lay's potato chips, are called *consumer non-durables*. Those that last for a long time, such as Kenmore washing machines and Apple computers, are *consumer durables*.

Another way to classify consumer products is by the amount of effort consumers are willing to make to acquire them. The four major categories of consumer products are unsought products, convenience products, shopping products, and specialty products, as summarized in Exhibit 14.3.

Concept *Check*

What is a product?

Explain what a brand, a trademark, and brand loyalty are.

What are the different types of brands?

Exhibit 14.2 Products Are Typically a Blend of Goods and Services

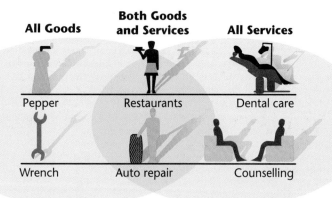

CONSUMER PRODUCT	EXAMPLES	DEGREE OF EFFORT EXPENDED BY CONSUMER
Unsought products	Life insurance Burial plots New products	No effort
Convenience products	Soft drinks Bread Milk Coffee	Very little or minimum effort
Shopping products	Automobiles Homes Vacations	Considerable effort
Specialty products	Expensive jewellery Gourmet dinners Limited-production automobiles	Maximum effort

Sustainable Business, Sustainable World

L'ORÉAL

L'Oréal is a very well known cosmetics company. Who hasn't heard the slogan for the L'Oréal Paris brand: "Because I'm Worth It"?

Those four words were written almost 40 years ago, in 1973, by a 23-year-old female copywriter who was at the time breaking new ground with an ad written strictly from a woman's viewpoint. "For the first time, the message was all about what the woman thought. It was about her self-confidence, her decision, her style." Today, of course, most successful marketing strategies consider that the female viewpoint will have a considerable impact on the purchase decision.

L'Oréal, based in France, and number 57 on the list of the 2011 *Global 100 Most Sustainable Corporations in the World*, takes that phrase very seriously in more than just its marketing efforts. Sustainable development, at L'Oréal, is considered "… a driver for responsible growth and a source of inspiration … " for its brands. Bottom line, L'Oréal believes that we are all "worth it."

As a marketing organization, L'Oréal believes that, to win the trust and confidence of consumers in the future, a responsible approach is absolutely essential. It understands some stakeholders will have concerns and in response is " … embedding sustainable consumption at each stage of the life cycle of its products." This includes sustainable innovation—integrating ethical policies in the selection of new ingredients, the development of eco-design and the use of green chemistry; and responsibly managing production, packaging, and the supply chain to reduce its environmental and social impact. To that end, the company's 2015 targets include 50 percent reductions in greenhouse gas emissions, waste, and water consumption. As reported by triplepundit.com—which stands for people, planet, profit—at L'Oréal's Brazilian operations (its third largest market) it has already "…reduced its carbon emissions by over half, (and) reduced energy consumption by 38% …"

According to triplepundit.com, L'Oréal has made some recent changes in the area of sustainability that "… may surprise you." One of those surprises is the company's use of RBT (reconstructed biological tissue), which is essentially "artificial skin," to wean away from animal testing. It has also partnered with the Environmental Protection Agency (EPA) in an effort to make animal testing obsolete.

But L'Oréal also believes, as stated on its website, that: "Consumers have a major role to play, along with the rest of society, to ensure that what is consumed today does not exceed what the world can provide tomorrow." And they have a point. All the sustainable practices in the world will simply cancel each other out if we keep consuming at such a high rate. So the big question then becomes—do you think you're "worth it"?

Thinking Critically

1. L'Oréal is quite a marketing success story. How many companies can boast a slogan that has stood the test for close to half a century? The question is, can we develop corporate policies that will allow us to sustain our way of life for centuries to come?
2. Is L'Oréal right that it is also up to consumers, or do you think corporations should shoulder most of the burden? Why or why not?

SOURCES: L'Oréal, http://www.loreal.com; The Global 100, http://www.global100.org; Triple Pundit, http://www.triplepundit.com, April 23, 2012.

Unsought products are products unknown to the potential buyer or known products that the buyer does not actively seek. New products fall into this category until advertising and distribution increase consumer awareness of them. Some goods are always marketed as unsought items, especially products we do not like to think about or care to spend money on. Life insurance, cemetery plots, medical services, and similar items require aggressive personal selling and highly persuasive advertising. Salespeople actively seek leads to potential buyers. Because consumers usually do not seek out this type of product, the company must go directly to them through a salesperson, direct mail, telemarketing, or direct-response advertising.

Convenience products are relatively inexpensive items that require little shopping effort. Soft drinks, candy bars, milk, bread, and small hardware items are examples. We buy them routinely without much planning. This does not mean that such products are unimportant or obscure. Many, in fact, are well known by their brand names—such as Pepsi-Cola, Domino's Pizza, and UPS shipping.

In contrast to convenience products, **shopping products** are bought only after a brand-to-brand and store-to-store comparison of price, suitability, and style. Examples are furniture, automobiles, a vacation in Europe, and some items of clothing. Convenience products are bought with little planning, but shopping products might be chosen months or even years before their actual purchase.

Specialty products are products for which consumers search long and hard, and for which they refuse to accept substitutes. Expensive jewellery, designer clothing, state-of-the-art stereo equipment, limited-production automobiles, and gourmet dinners fall into this category. Because consumers are willing to spend much time and effort to find specialty products, distribution is often limited to one or two sellers in a given region, such as Holt Renfrew, Gucci, or the Porsche dealer.

Classifying Business Products

Products bought by businesses or institutions for use in making other products or in providing services are called *business or industrial products*. They are classified as either capital products or expense items. **Capital products** are usually large, expensive items with a long lifespan. Examples are buildings, large machines, and airplanes. **Expense items** are typically smaller, less expensive items that usually have a life span of less than a year. Examples are printer cartridges and paper. Industrial products are sometimes further classified in the following categories:

- *Installations*. These are large, expensive capital items that determine the nature, scope, and efficiency of a company. Capital products like the Ford assembly plant represent a big commitment against future earnings and profitability. Buying an installation requires longer negotiations, more planning, and the judgments of more people than buying any other type of product.
- *Accessories*. Accessories do not have the same long-run impact on the company as installations, and they are less expensive and more standardized, but they are still capital products. Photocopy machines, IBM personal computers (PCs), and smaller machines such as Black & Decker table drills and saws are typical accessories. Marketers of accessories often rely on well-known brand names and extensive advertising as well as personal selling.
- *Component parts and materials*. These are expense items that are built into the end product. Some component parts are custom-made, such as a drive shaft for

unsought products
Products that either are unknown to the potential buyer or are known but not actively sought by the buyer.

convenience products
Relatively inexpensive items that require little shopping effort and are purchased routinely without planning.

shopping products
Items that are bought after considerable planning, including brand-to-brand and store-to-store comparisons of price, suitability, and style.

specialty products
Items for which consumers search long and hard, and for which they refuse to accept substitutes.

capital products
Large, expensive items with a long lifespan that are purchased by businesses for use in making other products or providing a service.

expense items
Items, purchased by businesses, that are smaller and less expensive than capital products and usually have a lifespan of less than one year.

product life cycle
The pattern of sales and profits over time for a product or product category; consists of an introductory stage, growth stage, maturity stage, and decline stage (that ultimately results in death of the product or product category).

an automobile, a case for a computer, or a special pigment for painting harbour buoys; others are standardized for sale to many industrial users. Intel processors for computers and cement for the construction trade are examples of standardized component parts and materials.

- *Raw materials.* Raw materials are expense items that have undergone little or no processing and are used to create a final product. Examples include lumber, copper, and zinc.
- *Supplies.* Supplies do not become part of the final product. They are bought routinely and in fairly large quantities. Supply items run the gamut from pencils and paper to paint and machine oil. They have little impact on the company's long-run profits. Bic pens, Unisource copier paper, and Pennzoil machine oil are typical supply items.
- *Services.* These are expense items used to plan or support company operations; for example janitorial cleaning and management consulting.

THE PRODUCT LIFE CYCLE

Product managers create marketing mixes for their products as they move through the life cycle. The **product life cycle** is a pattern of sales and profits over time for a product (Sunlight dishwashing liquid) or a product category (liquid detergents). As the product moves through the stages of the life cycle, the company must keep revising the marketing mix to stay competitive and meet the needs of target customers.

Stages of the Life Cycle

As illustrated in Exhibit 14.4, the product life cycle consists of the following stages:

1. *Introduction.* When a product enters the life cycle, it faces many obstacles. Although competition might be light, the *introductory stage* usually features frequent product modifications, limited distribution, and heavy promotion. The failure rate is high. Production and marketing costs are also high, and sales volume is low. Hence, profits are usually small or negative.

2. *Growth stage.* If a product survives the introductory stage, it advances to the *growth stage* of the life cycle. In this stage, sales grow at an increasing rate, profits are healthy, and many competitors enter the market. Large companies might start to acquire small pioneering companies that have reached this stage. Emphasis switches from primary demand promotion to aggressive brand advertising and communicating the differences between brands. For example, the goal changes from convincing people to buy compact DVD players to convincing them to buy Sony versus Panasonic or Sharp.

   Distribution becomes a major key to success during the growth stage, as well as in later stages. Manufacturers scramble to acquire dealers and distributors and to build long-term relationships. Without adequate distribution, it is impossible to establish a strong market position.

   Toward the end of the growth phase, prices normally begin falling and profits peak. Price reductions result from increased competition and from cost reductions from producing larger quantities of items (economies of scale). As well, most companies have recovered their development costs by now, and their priority is in increasing or retaining market share and enhancing profits.

3. *Maturity.* After the growth stage, sales continue to mount—but at a decreasing rate, and they will eventually peak. This is the *maturity stage*. Most products that have been on the market for a long time are in this stage. Thus, most marketing strategies are designed for mature products. One such strategy is to bring out several variations of a basic product (line extension). Kool-Aid, for instance, was originally offered in six flavours. Today there are many flavours, as well as sweetened and unsweetened varieties.

Exhibit 14.4   Sales and Profits during the Product Life Cycle

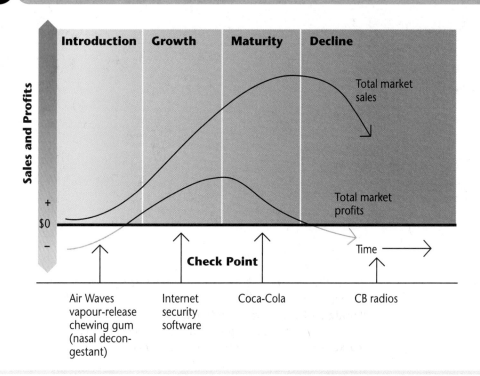

Introduction   Growth   Maturity   Decline

Total market sales

Total market profits

Sales and Profits

+

$0

−

Time

Check Point

Air Waves
vapour-release
chewing gum
(nasal decon-
gestant)

Internet
security
software

Coca-Cola

CB radios

4. *Decline (and death).* When sales and profits fall, the product has reached the decline stage. The rate of decline is governed by two factors: the rate of change in consumer tastes and the rate at which new products enter the market. An example of a product that is at the death stage in Canada is the VCR. The demand for VCRs is virtually nil (except for those who have tapes that have not been converted to DVD).

The Product Life Cycle as a Management Tool

The product life cycle can be used in planning. Marketers who understand the cycle concept are better able to forecast future sales and plan new marketing strategies. Exhibit 14.5 is a brief summary of strategic needs at various stages of the product life cycle. Marketers must be sure that a product has moved from one stage to the next before changing the company's marketing strategy. A temporary sales decline should not be interpreted as a sign that the product is dying. Pulling back marketing support can become a self-fulfilling prophecy that brings about the early death of a healthy product.

PRICING PRODUCTS RIGHT

LO3

An important part of the product development process is setting the right price. Certainly market forces can have an impact on the price of a product (e.g., supply and demand, see Chapter 2), but they are not the only influence. Price is the perceived value that is exchanged for something else. Value in our society is most commonly expressed in dollars and cents. Thus, price is typically the amount of money exchanged for a good or service. Note that perceived value refers to the time of the transaction. After you've used a product you've bought, you may decide that its actual value was less than its perceived value at the time you bought it. The price you pay for a product is based on the expected satisfaction you will receive and not necessarily the actual satisfaction you will receive.

> **Concept** *Check*
>
> What is the product life cycle?
>
> Describe each stage of the product life cycle.
>
> What are the marketing strategies for each stage of the product life cycle?

CATEGORY	INTRODUCTION	GROWTH	MATURITY	DECLINE
Marketing objectives	Encourage trial, establish distribution	Get triers to repurchase, attract new users	Seek new users or uses	Reduce marketing expenses, keep loyal users
Product	Establish competitive advantage	Maintain product quality	Modify product	Maintain product
Distribution	Establish distribution network	Solidify distribution relationships	Provide additional incentives to ensure support	Eliminate trade allowances
Promotional	Build brand awareness	Provide information	Reposition product	Eliminate most advertising and sales promotions
Pricing	Set introductory price (skimming or penetration pricing)	Maintain prices until near the end of the stage and then start to drop	Reduce prices to meet competition	Maintain prices

Although price is usually a dollar amount, it can be anything with perceived value. When goods and services are exchanged for each other, the trade is called barter. If you exchange this book for a math book at the end of the term, you have engaged in barter.

Pricing Objectives

Price is important in determining how much a company earns. The prices charged to customers times the number of units sold equals the gross revenue for the company. Revenue is what pays for every activity of the company (production, finance, sales, distribution, and so forth). What's left over (if anything) is profit. Managers strive to charge a price that will allow the company to earn a fair return on its investment.

The chosen price must be neither too high nor too low. And the price must equal the perceived value to target consumers. If consumers think the price is too high, sales opportunities will be lost. Lost sales mean lost revenue. If the price is too low, consumers may view the product as a great value, but the company may not meet its profit goals. Three common pricing objectives are maximizing profits, achieving a target return on the investment, and offering good value at a fair price.

profit maximization
A pricing objective that entails getting the largest possible profit from a product by producing it for as long as the revenue from selling the product exceeds the cost of producing it.

PROFIT MAXIMIZATION Profit maximization means producing a product for as long as the revenue from selling it exceeds the cost of producing it. In other words, the goal is to get the largest possible profit from the product. For example, suppose Carl Morgan, a builder of houses, sells each house for $300,000. His revenue and cost projections are shown in Exhibit 14.6. Notice in column 3 that the cost of building each house drops for the second through the fifth house. The lower cost per house results from two things: First, by having several houses under construction at the same time, Morgan can afford to hire a full-time crew. The crew is more economical than the independent contractors to whom he would otherwise subcontract each task. Second, Morgan can order materials in greater quantities than usual and thus get quantity discounts on his orders.

Morgan decides that he could sell 15 houses a year at the $300,000 price. But he knows he cannot maximize profits at more than seven houses a year. Inefficiencies begin to creep in at the sixth house. (Notice in column 3 that the sixth house costs more to build than any of the first five houses.) Morgan can't supervise more than seven construction jobs at once, and his full-time crew can't handle even those seven. Thus, Morgan has to subcontract some of the work on the sixth and seventh houses. To build more than seven houses, he would need a second full-time crew.

Exhibit 14.6 Revenue, Cost, and Profit Projections for Morgan's Houses

(1) UNIT OF OUTPUT (HOUSE)	(2) SELLING PRICE (REVENUE)	(3) COST OF BUILDING HOUSE	(4) PROFIT ON HOUSE	(5) TOTAL PROFIT
1st	$ 300,000	$ 276,000	$ 24,000	$ 24,000
2nd	300,000	275,000	25,000	49,000
3rd	300,000	273,000	27,000	76,000
4th	300,000	270,000	30,000	106,000
5th	300,000	270,000	30,000	136,000
6th	300,000	277,000	23,000	159,000
7th	300,000	290,000	10,000	169,000
8th	300,000	315,000	(15,000)	154,000

The exhibit also shows why Morgan should construct seven houses a year. Even though the profit per house is falling for the sixth and seventh houses (column 4), the total profit is still rising (column 5). But at the eighth house, Morgan would go beyond profit maximization. That is, the eighth unit would cost more than its selling price. He would lose $15,000 on the house, and total profit would fall to $154,000 from $169,000 after the seventh house.

ACHIEVING A TARGET RETURN ON INVESTMENT Another pricing objective used by many companies is **target return on investment**, whereby a price is set to give the company the desired profitability in terms of return on its money. Among the companies that use target return on investment as their main pricing objective are most manufacturing companies.

To get an idea of how target return works, imagine that you are a marketing manager for a cereal company. You estimate that developing, launching, and marketing a new hot cereal will cost $2 million. If the net profit for the first year is $200,000, the

target return on investment
A pricing objective where the price of a product is set so as to give the company the desired profitability in terms of return on its money.

Concept *in Action*

Some automobile makers have announced employee-discount-for-everyone prices that boosted car sales. But when the bargain blowout ended, so did sales, leaving automakers with an inventory hangover and the need to re-examine their pricing strategies. Some manufacturers switched to value pricing, slashing prices across the board while abandoning incentives like employee discounts and zero-percent financing. Why might some car buyers prefer value pricing to traditional price haggling?

GOODLUZ/SHUTTERSTOCK

Explain the concept of price.

What is meant by target return on investment, and how does it differ from profit maximization?

What is value pricing?

value pricing
A pricing strategy in which the target market is offered a high-quality product at a fair price and with good service.

return on investment will be $200,000 ÷ $2,000,000, or 10 percent. Let's say that top management sets a 15 percent target return on investment. As a net profit of $200,000 will yield only a 10 percent return, one of two things will happen: Either the cereal won't be produced, or the price and marketing mix will be changed to yield the 15 percent target return.

VALUE PRICING   Value pricing has become a popular pricing strategy. Value pricing means offering the target market a high-quality product at a fair price and with good service. It is the notion of offering the customer a good value. Value pricing doesn't mean high quality that's available only at high prices, nor does it mean bare-bones service or low-quality products. Value pricing can be used to sell a variety of products, from a $30,000 Jeep Wrangler to a $1.99 package of dinner napkins.

A value marketer does the following:

- *Offers products that perform.* This is the price of entry because consumers have lost patience with shoddy merchandise.
- *Gives consumers more than they expect.* Soon after Toyota launched Lexus, the company had to order a recall. The weekend before the recall, dealers phoned every Lexus owner that was affected and arranged to pick up their cars and provide replacement vehicles.
- *Gives meaningful guarantees.* Hyundai offers five-year, 100,000 kilometre power train protection. Michelin recently introduced a tire warranted to last 140,000 kilometres.
- *Gives the buyer facts.* Today's sophisticated consumer wants informative advertising and knowledgeable salespeople.
- *Builds long-term relationships.* The Aeroplan program, Hyatt's Passport Club, and Moen's 800-number hotline all help build good customer relations.

Product Pricing Strategies

Managers use various pricing strategies when determining the price of a product, as we explain in this section. Price skimming and penetration pricing are strategies used in pricing new products; other strategies, such as leader pricing and bundling, might be used for established products as well.

price skimming
The strategy of introducing a product with a high initial price and lowering the price over time as the product moves through its life cycle.

PRICE SKIMMING   The practice of introducing a new product on the market with a high price and then lowering the price over time is called price skimming. As the product moves through its life cycle, the price usually is lowered because competitors are entering the market. As the price falls, more and more consumers can buy the product.

Price skimming has four important advantages. First, a high initial price can be a way to find out what buyers are willing to pay. Second, if consumers find the introductory price too high, it can be lowered. Third, a high introductory price can create an image of quality and prestige. Fourth, when the price is lowered later, consumers might think they are getting a bargain. The disadvantage is that high prices attract competition.

Price skimming can be used to price virtually any new product, such as high-definition televisions, PCs, and colour computer printers. For example, the Republic of Tea has launched new Imperial Republic White Tea, which it says is among the rarest of teas. Because it is minimally processed, white tea is said to retain the highest level of antioxidants and has less caffeine than black and green teas. The company says the tea is picked only a few days each year, right before the leaves open, yielding a small harvest. The product retails for $14 per tin of 50 bags. Products don't have to be expensive to use a skimming strategy, although a skimming strategy is often used when products are expensive to bring to market and costs "sunk" in research and development need to be recovered before any profit can be made.

Dell offers new products at low prices to achieve a high sales volume. In a successful strategy to increase market share, Dell slashed prices of personal computers, requiring competitors to do the same. What pricing strategy does Dell use?

HARRY CABLUCK/AP PHOTO

PENETRATION PRICING A company that doesn't use price skimming will probably use **penetration pricing**. With this strategy, the company offers new products at low prices in the hope of achieving a large sales volume. Procter & Gamble did this with SpinBrush. Penetration pricing requires more extensive planning than skimming does, because the company must gear up for mass production and marketing. If the company significantly overestimates demand, its losses are considerable.

Penetration pricing has two advantages. First, the low initial price might induce consumers to switch brands or companies. Using penetration pricing on its jug wines, Gallo has lured customers away from Taylor California Cellars and Inglenook. Second, penetration pricing might discourage competitors from entering the market. Their costs would tend to be higher, so they would need to sell more at the same price to break even.

penetration pricing
The strategy of selling new products at low prices in the hope of achieving a large sales volume.

LEADER PRICING Pricing products below the normal markup (discussed below) or even below cost to attract customers to a store where they wouldn't otherwise shop is **leader pricing**. A product priced below cost is referred to as a **loss leader**. The customers go to the retailer and will often purchase many other products that are competitively priced, not just the loss leader. Retailers hope that this type of pricing will increase their overall sales volume and thus their profit.

Items that are leader priced are usually well known and priced low enough to appeal to many customers. They also are items that consumers will buy at a lower price, even if they have to switch brands. Supermarkets often feature coffee and bacon in their leader pricing. Department stores and specialty stores also rely heavily on leader pricing.

leader pricing
The strategy of pricing products below the normal markup or even below cost to attract customers to a store where they would not otherwise shop.

loss leader
A product priced below cost as part of a leader pricing strategy.

BUNDLING Bundling means grouping two or more related products together and pricing them as a single product. Westin Hotels' special weekend rates often include the room, breakfast, and one night's dinner. Leon's Furniture might offer a washer and dryer together for a price lower than if the units were bought separately. Rogers Communications and Shaw Cable bundle services such as telephone, Internet, and television into one package. This is not only convenient for the customer but, as the next paragraph highlights, allows the companies to sell more products.

bundling
The strategy of grouping two or more related products together and pricing them as a single product.

The idea behind bundling is to reach a segment of the market that the products sold separately would not reach as effectively. Some buyers are more than willing to buy one product but have much less use for the second. Bundling the second product to the first at a slightly reduced price thus creates some sales that otherwise would not be made. Aussie 3 Minute Miracle Shampoo is typically bundled with its conditioner, because many people use shampoo more than conditioner, so they don't need a new bottle of conditioner.

ODD-EVEN PRICING Psychology often plays a big role in how consumers view prices and what prices they will pay. Odd-even pricing (or psychological pricing) is the strategy of setting a price at an odd number to connote a bargain and at an even number to imply quality. For years, many retailers have priced their products in odd numbers—for example, $99.95 or $49.95—to make consumers feel that they are paying a lower price for the product.

Some retailers favour odd-numbered prices because they believe that $9.99 sounds much less imposing to customers than $10.00. Other retailers believe that an odd-numbered price signals to consumers that the price is at the lowest level possible, thereby encouraging them to buy more units. Neither theory has ever been proved conclusively, although one study found that consumers perceive odd-priced products as being on sale. Even-numbered pricing is sometimes used to denote quality. Examples include a fine perfume at $100 a bottle, a good watch at $500, or a Holt Renfrew coat at $3,000.

PRESTIGE PRICING The strategy of raising the price of a product so consumers will perceive it as being of higher quality, status, or value is called prestige pricing. This type of pricing is common where high prices indicate high status. In the specialty shops on Rodeo Drive in Beverly Hills, which cater to the super-rich of Hollywood, shirts that would sell for $40 elsewhere sell for at least $150. If the price were lower, customers would perceive them as being of low quality.

How Managers Set Prices

After establishing a pricing objective, managers must set a specific price for the product. Two techniques that are often used to set a price are break-even analysis and markup pricing.

BREAK-EVEN ANALYSIS Manufacturers, wholesalers (companies that buy from manufacturers and sell to retailers and institutions), and retailers (companies that sell to end users) need to know how much of a product must be sold at a certain price to cover all costs. The point at which the costs are covered and additional sales result in profit is the break-even point (or break-even quantity).

To find the break-even point, the company measures the various costs associated with the product:

- Fixed costs do not vary with different levels of output. The rent on a manufacturing facility is a fixed cost. It must be paid whether production is one unit or a million.
  - Variable costs change with different levels of output. Wages and expenses of raw materials are considered variable costs.
  - The fixed-cost contribution is the selling price per unit (revenue) minus the variable costs per unit.
  - Total revenue is the selling price per unit times the number of units sold.
  - Total cost is the total of the fixed costs and the variable costs.
  - Total profit is total revenue minus total cost.

odd-even (psychological) pricing
The strategy of setting a price at an odd number to connote a bargain and at an even number to suggest quality.

prestige pricing
The strategy of increasing the price of a product so that consumers will perceive it as being of higher quality, status, or value.

break-even point (or break-even quantity)
The price at which a product's costs are covered, so additional sales result in profit.

fixed costs
Costs that do not vary with different levels of output; for example, rent.

variable costs
Costs that change with different levels of output; for example, wages and cost of raw materials.

fixed-cost contribution
The selling price per unit (revenue) minus the variable costs per unit.

total revenue
The selling price per unit times the number of units sold.

total cost
The sum of the fixed costs and the variable costs.

total profit
Total revenue minus total cost.

Concept *Check*

What is the difference between penetration pricing and price skimming?

Explain the concept of price bundling.

Describe odd-even pricing and prestige pricing.

Knowing these amounts, the company can calculate the break-even point by using this formula:

Break-even point in units = Total fixed cost ÷ Fixed cost contribution

Let's see how this works: The typical break-even model assumes a given fixed cost and a constant variable cost. In our illustration, assume that company XYZ has fixed costs of $10,000.00 and variable costs of $1.25 for each unit produced. Assume that the company can sell up to 10, 000 units at $3.25 each before it must lower the price.

Exhibit 14.7(a) shows XYZ's break-even point and 14.7(b) shows the calculations (e.g., the variable cost increases by $1.25 for each extra unit produced and that the fixed cost does not change regardless of the number of units produced, $10,000.00).

HOT/inks

Companies are turning to Web-based, smart-pricing software to improve margins on products. Find out how one company's software works at Oracle's website,
www.oracle.com

Exhibit 14.7a Break-Even Analysis XYZ

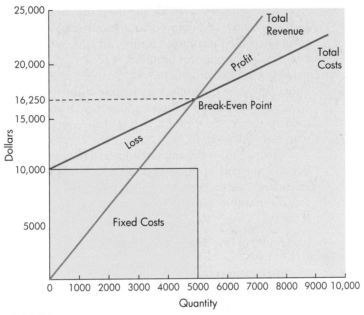

SOURCE: *Marketing*, 5th Canadian Edition - Lamb et al. Nelson

Exhibit 14.7b Cost and Revenues

QUANTITY PRODUCED AND SOLD	TOTAL FIXED COSTS PER UNIT	VARIABLE COSTS	TOTAL VARIABLE COSTS	TOTAL COSTS PER UNIT	REVENUE	TOTAL REVENUE	PROFIT OR LOSS
1,000	$ 10,000.00	1.25	$ 1,250.00	$ 11,250.00	$ 3.25	$ 3,250.00	$ (8,000.00)
2,000	$ 10,000.00	1.25	$ 2,500.00	$ 12,500.00	$ 3.25	$ 6,500.00	$ (6,000.00)
3,000	$ 10,000.00	1.25	$ 3,750.00	$ 13,750.00	$ 3.25	$ 9,750.00	$ (4,000.00)
4,000	$ 10,000.00	1.25	$ 5,000.00	$ 15,000.00	$ 3.25	$ 13,000.00	$ (2,000.00)
5,000	$ 10,000.00	1.25	$ 6,250.00	$ 16,250.00	$ 3.25	$ 16,250.00	$ -
6,000	$ 10,000.00	1.25	$ 7,500.00	$ 17,500.00	$ 3.25	$ 19,500.00	$ 2,000.00
7,000	$ 10,000.00	1.25	$ 8,750.00	$ 18,750.00	$ 3.25	$ 22,750.00	$ 4,000.00
8,000	$ 10,000.00	1.25	$ 10,000.00	$ 20,000.00	$ 3.25	$ 26,000.00	$ 6,000.00
9,000	$ 10,000.00	1.25	$ 11,250.00	$ 21,250.00	$ 3.25	$ 29,250.00	$ 8,000.00
10,000	$ 10,000.00	1.25	$ 12,500.00	$ 22,500.00	$ 3.25	$ 32,500.00	$ 10,000.00

As 14.7(b) shows, the break-even point is at 5000 units; any number below this is a loss and any number above this to 10,000 units is a profit. Exhibit 14.7(a) is a visual representation of this.

Using the break-even point formula, we see we come to the same results:

$$\text{break-even point in units} = \frac{\text{total fixed cost}}{\text{fixed cost contribution}}$$

$$= \frac{10,000}{2} = 5000$$

By using the equation, XYZ can quickly find out how much it needs to sell to break even. It can then calculate how much profit it will earn if it sells more units. A company that is operating close to the break-even point might change the profit picture in two ways. Reducing costs will lower the break-even point and expand profits. Increasing sales will not change the break-even point, but it will provide more profits.

markup pricing
A method of pricing in which a certain percentage (the markup) is added to the product's cost to arrive at the price.

activity-based costing (ABC)
ABC assigns resource costs through all the activities to either produce the product or acquire it for resale.

MARKUP PRICING One of the most common forms of pricing is markup pricing. In this method, a certain dollar amount is added to a product's cost to arrive at the retail price. (The retail price is thus *cost plus markup*.) The cost is the expense of manufacturing the product or acquiring it for resale. One way to calculate the cost is to use activity-based costing (ABC). ABC assigns resource costs through all the activities to either produce the product or acquire it for resale. For example, if a company purchases products from a supplier for resale, it would include the cost of the resources used to secure these products (e.g., ordering, shipping, inventory control, product wholesale price, etc.).

The markup is the amount added to the cost to cover expenses and leave a profit. For the purpose of discussion, there are two types of markup pricing that can be calculated: one on cost and one on selling price.

For example, if Banana Boat sunscreen costs Shoppers Drug Mart $8 and they sell it for $11

based on cost or markup-on-cost,

$$\text{markup percentage} = \frac{\text{markup amount}}{\text{item cost}} \text{ or } \frac{3}{8} = 37.5\%$$

based on selling price or markup-on-selling-price,

$$\text{markup percentage} = \frac{\text{markup amount}}{\text{selling price}} \text{ or } \frac{3}{11} = 27.3\%$$

Several elements influence markups. Among them are tradition, the competition, store image, and stock turnover. Traditionally, department stores used a 40 percent markup. But today, competition and economic conditions have forced retailers to respond to consumer demand and meet competitors' prices. A department store that tried to sell household appliances at a 40 percent markup would lose customers to discounters such as Walmart. However, a retailer trying to develop a prestige image will use markups that are much higher than those used by a retailer trying to develop an image as a discounter.

LO4

THE NATURE AND FUNCTIONS OF DISTRIBUTION

distribution (logistics)
Efficiently managing the acquisition of raw materials to the factory and the movement of products from the producer to industrial users and consumers.

Distribution (or logistics) is efficiently managing the acquisition of raw materials to the factory and the movement of products from the producer or manufacturer to industrial users and consumers. Logistics activities are usually the responsibility of the marketing department and are part of the large series of activities included in the supply chain. As discussed in Chapter 15 and later in this chapter, a supply chain is the system

Concept *in Action*

In recent years, gas prices have soared and fallen. Top producers have defended their pricing methods, citing global demand and political instability as causes of pain at the pump. What are some reasons gas prices rise and fall?

FRANK GUNN/THE CANADIAN PRESS/AP PHOTO

through which an organization acquires raw material, produces products, and delivers the products and services to its customers. Exhibit 14.8 illustrates a supply chain. Supply chain management helps increase the efficiency of logistics service by minimizing inventory and moving goods efficiently from producers to the ultimate users.

On their way from producers to end users and consumers, goods and services pass through a series of marketing entities known as a **distribution channel**. We will look first at the entities that make up a distribution channel and then will examine the functions that channels serve.

manufacturer
A producer; an organization that converts raw materials to finished products.

distribution channel
The series of marketing entities through which goods and services pass on their way from producers to end users.

Exhibit 14.8 Supply Chain

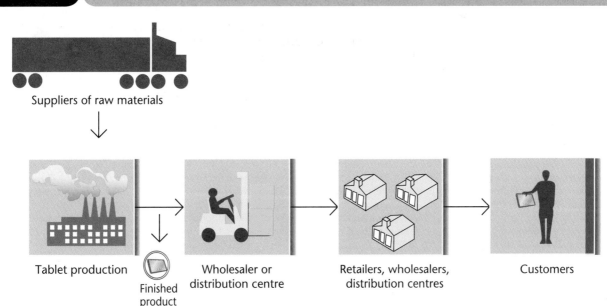

Suppliers of raw materials

Tablet production → Finished product → Wholesaler or distribution centre → Retailers, wholesalers, distribution centres → Customers

---

Marketing Intermediaries in the Distribution Channel

marketing intermediaries
Organizations that assist in moving goods and services from producers to end users.

agents
Sales representatives of manufacturers and wholesalers.

brokers
Go-betweens that bring buyers and sellers together.

industrial distributors
Independent wholesalers that buy related product lines from many manufacturers and sell them to industrial users.

A distribution channel is made up of **marketing intermediaries**, or organizations that assist in moving goods and services from producers to end users and consumers. Marketing intermediaries are in the middle of the distribution process between the producer and the end user. The following marketing intermediaries most often appear in the distribution channel:

- **Agents** *and* **brokers**. Agents are sales representatives of manufacturers and wholesalers, and brokers are entities that bring buyers and sellers together. Both agents and brokers are usually hired on commission basis by either a buyer or a seller. Agents and brokers are go-betweens whose job is to make deals. They do not own or take possession of goods.
- **Industrial distributors**. Industrial distributors are independent wholesalers that buy related product lines from many manufacturers and sell them to industrial users. They often have a sales force to call on purchasing agents, make deliveries, extend credit, and provide information. Industrial distributors are used in such industries as aircraft manufacturing, mining, and petroleum.

Creating the Future of Business

CHRIS JONES, ENTRIX SPORTS

Chris Jones founded Entrix Sports in 1995 to "create positive change for athletes through innovation." The mission of the company is "to be the Distributor of Choice in Canada by identifying and delivering innovative products to Canadians with passion and integrity." Entrix aims to achieve its mission with its own brand of the 4Ps of marketing strategy: " ... by having the best people, product, partnerships and practices." And that is exactly what it has done, through the entrepreneurial drive of its founder, Chris Jones.

What started as an invention of an undergraduate varsity football receiver looking for a football glove with a better grip has become an international company producing and distributing innovative sports products. Chris made his first pair of sports gloves in the mid '90s with his mom's help and, after experimenting, found a polymer-based material with a grip superior to leather that he made into his Gription Glove. Despite its crude construction, by 1997, Chris was supplying his gloves to the CFL, and the rest is history.

In searching for a high-end manufacturer to make his gloves, Chris met with Cutters Gloves, "an emerging world leader in grip technology and fledgling glove company." In 2000, Entrix Sports became the exclusive distributor for Cutters Gloves in Canada. This allowed Chris to start building a solid distribution network, creating relationships with professional teams, dealers, reps, suppliers, etc., to help find other innovative products "that would have a positive impact on the Canadian athlete and fit within the Entrix Sports philosophy." Some of these products in the Entrix portfolio include CEP Sportswear, MuscleTrac, Bownet, and Passback.

The story of how Chris brought CEP Compression gear to Canada is a classic story of entrepreneurial ingenuity and determination. Chris was in Finland in 2007, looking for new products to bring to Canada. He came across a small booth of a "German fellow" who wanted to show him his new insole product. Chris wasn't interested in the insoles but was intrigued by a tall compression sock that retailed

for $90. Not believing that Canadians would pay $90 for a pair of socks, not speaking any German, and not really knowing much about compression socks, Chris nonetheless thought he'd take them for a "test drive." Being a competitive flag football player, Chris tried them out in a game and loved the results. He immediately e-mailed the "German fellow" and asked for more information. After several attempts, resulting in nothing but information on the insoles, Chris went straight to the head office of the company, flew to Germany, and negotiated the rights for all of Canada. As Chris puts it: "As with many business decisions, you gather what info you can but ultimately trust your gut, or in this case, your calves."

Obviously Chris has since learned how CEP compression works and the "numerous benefits to wearing compression socks for performance, recovery and travel." And he's learned innumerable lessons on the power of innovative products and strong distribution channels.

Chris's success with Entrix resulted in him being honoured with the prestigious "Emerging Enterprise of the Year" award from the Calgary Chamber of Commerce in 2002, earned him a spot in *Calgary Inc.* magazine's "Top 40 Under 40" list in 2005, along with a nomination for Canada's Top 40 under 40 that same year, and had him recognized as one of the "40 Ways U of C Changed the World" in 2006. A long way from a football player who wanted a better grip on the ball!

Thinking Critically

1. Chris's passion for the business started from a personal story— the desire to find a solution to a problem that he himself was experiencing. How important do you think that is to entrepreneurial success? Why?
2. What other important characteristics does Chris have that make him a successful entrepreneur? What aspects of Entrix's marketing strategy are most important in its success?

SOURCES: Entrix Sports, http://www.entrixsports.ca, used with permission from Chris Jones; CEP Compression Canada, http://www.cepcompression.ca; *UMagazine* May 2006, http://www.ucalgary.ca.

- **Wholesalers.** Wholesalers are companies that sell finished goods to retailers, manufacturers, and institutions (such as schools and hospitals). Historically, their function has been to buy from manufacturers and sell to retailers.
- **Retailers.** Retailers are companies that sell goods to consumers and to industrial users for their own consumption.

At the end of the distribution channel are final consumers, like you and me, and industrial users. Industrial users are companies that buy products for internal use or for producing other products or services. They include manufacturers, utilities, airlines, railroads, and service institutions, such as hotels, hospitals, and schools.

Exhibit 14.9 shows various ways marketing intermediaries can be linked. For instance, a manufacturer may sell to a wholesaler that sells to a retailer that in turn sells to a customer. In any of these distribution systems, goods and services are physically transferred from one organization to the next. As each takes possession of the products, it may take legal ownership of them. As the exhibit indicates, distribution channels can handle either consumer products or industrial products.

wholesalers
Companies that sell finished goods to retailers, manufacturers, and institutions.

retailers
Companies that sell goods to consumers and to industrial users for their own consumption.

Alternative Channel Arrangements

Rarely does a producer use just one type of channel to move its product. It usually employs several different or alternative channels, which include multiple channels, non-traditional channels, and strategic channel alliances.[2]

Exhibit 14.9 Channels of Distribution for Industrial and Consumer Products

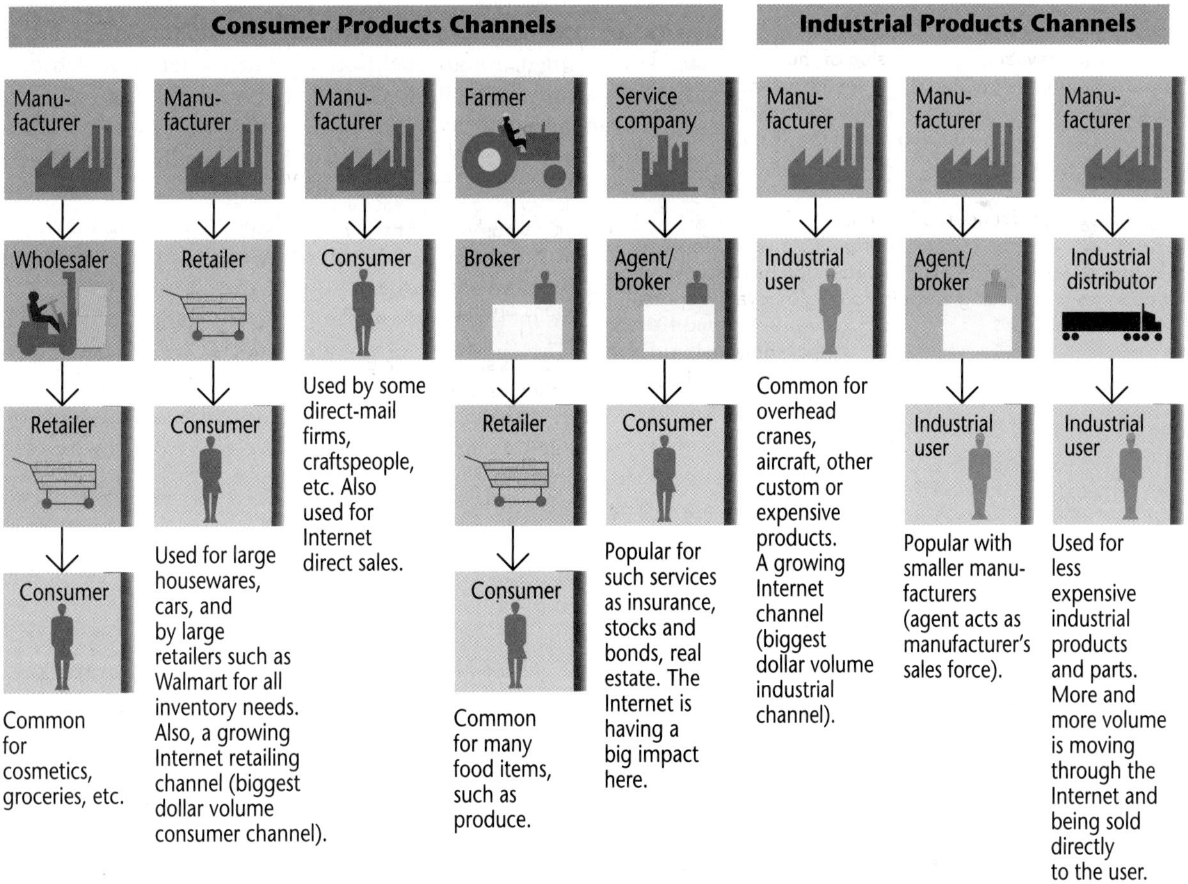

Concept *in Action*

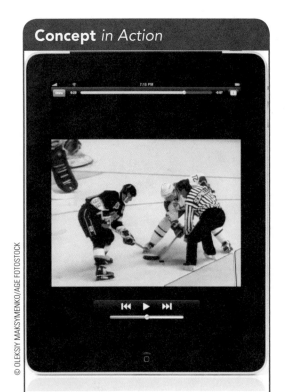

In 2009, the television networks were scrambling to stave off the end of television as we know it, as a new generation of viewers has taken to streaming shows on their mobile devices. By 2011, the television networks realized that there was no way they could stop this trend and started to distribute live streaming of their broadcasts. How might direct digital distribution upset network television's traditional distribution channel?

dual distribution (or multiple distribution)
Two or more channels that distribute the same product to target markets.

strategic channel alliances
One manufacturer using another manufacturer's previously established channel to distribute its goods.

MULTIPLE CHANNELS When a producer selects two or more channels to distribute the same product to target markets, this arrangement is called **dual distribution (or multiple distribution)**. For example, Avon, a direct supplier *of personal grooming products*, offers consumers four alternatives for purchasing products. They can contact a representative in person (the original business model), purchase on the Web, order direct from the company, or pick up products at an Avon Salon & Spa. With Avon, identical products are being distributed to existing markets by using more than one channel of distribution.

Dual channels don't always work out as planned. Tupperware finally stopped a 15-year slide in sales with new booths at shopping malls and a push onto the Internet. New buzz led to more Tupperware parties where salespeople set up shop in people's living rooms to show off plastic food storage containers and such. Then the company decided to place Tupperware in some stores with salespeople in the aisles to demonstrate the merchandise. It looked like the answer to a chronic problem: how to sell face-to-face in an era when shoppers don't have time for a door-to-door sales pitch. Tupperware also figured the move would give it a stream of potential party hosts and sales-force recruits.

But moving into stores turned out to be one of the worst disasters ever at Tupperware. It was so easy to find the company's products that interest in its parties plummeted. Fewer parties meant fewer chances to land other parties and new salespeople—which Tupperware needs to offset turnover that often hits 100 percent a year.[3]

NON-TRADITIONAL CHANNELS Often, non-traditional channel arrangements help differentiate a company's product from the competition's. For example, manufacturers may decide to use non-traditional channels such as the Internet, mail-order channels, or infomercials to sell products instead of going through traditional retailer channels. Although non-traditional channels may limit a brand's coverage, they can give a producer serving a niche market a way to gain market access and customer attention without having to establish channel intermediaries. Non-traditional channels can also provide another avenue of sales for larger companies. For example, a London publisher sells short stories through vending machines in the London Underground. Instead of the traditional book format, the stories are printed like folded maps making them an easy-to-read alternative for commuters.

Kiosks, long a popular method for ordering and registering for wedding gifts, dispersing cash through ATMs, and facilitating airline check-in, are finding new uses. Ethan Allen furniture stores use kiosks as a product locator tool for consumers and salespeople. Kiosks on some university and college campuses allow students to register for classes, see their class schedule and grades, check account balances, and even print transcripts. The general public, when it has access to the kiosks, can use them to gather information about the university.

With electronic media rapidly evolving, downloading first-run movies to cell phones may not be too far off! The changing world of electronics technology opens many doors for new, non-traditional channels.

STRATEGIC CHANNEL ALLIANCES Producers often form **strategic channel alliances**, which enable the producers to deliver products and services by using another manufacturer's already-established channel. Alliances are used most often when the creation of marketing channel relationships may be too expensive and time-consuming. Amazon and a consumer electronics store have a multiyear agreement to expand the selection of electronics available on Amazon.com. Under the agreement, Amazon.com customers have the option of purchasing items from Amazon's inventory of electronic items or from the broader selection offered by the electronic store. The arrangement benefits both companies: it allows Amazon.com to deepen its selection without increasing its own inventory expense, and it increases sales for the electronics store.

Strategic channel alliances are proving to be more successful for growing businesses than mergers and acquisitions. This is especially true in global markets where cultural differences, distance, and other barriers can prove challenging. For example, Heinz has a strategic alliance with Kagome, one of Japan's largest food companies. The companies are working together to find ways to reduce operating costs while expanding both brands' market presence globally.

The Functions of Distribution Channels

Why do distribution channels exist? Why can't every company sell its products directly to the end user or consumer? Why are go-betweens needed? Channels serve a number of functions.

CHANNELS REDUCE THE NUMBER OF TRANSACTIONS Channels make distribution simpler by reducing the number of transactions required to get a product from the manufacturer to the consumer. Assume for the moment that only four students are in your class. Also assume that your professor requires five textbooks, each from a different publisher. If there were no bookstore, 20 transactions would be necessary for all students in the class to buy the books, as shown in Exhibit 14.10. If the bookstore serves as a go-between, the number of transactions is reduced to nine. Each publisher sells to one bookstore rather than to four students. Each student buys from one bookstore instead of from five publishers.

Dealing with channel intermediaries frees producers from many of the details of distribution activity. Producers are traditionally not as efficient or as enthusiastic about selling products directly to end users as channel members are. First, producers may wish to focus on production. They may feel that they cannot both produce and distribute in a competitive way. On the other hand, manufacturers are eager to deal directly with larger retailers, such as Sport Chek. Sport Chek offers huge sales opportunities to producers.

CHANNELS EASE THE FLOW OF GOODS Channels make distribution easier in several ways. The first is by sorting, which consists of the following:

- *Sorting out.* Breaking many different items into separate stocks that are similar. Eggs, for instance, are sorted by grade and size.
- *Accumulating.* Bringing similar stocks together into a larger quantity. Twelve large Grade A eggs could be placed in some cartons and 12 medium Grade B eggs in other cartons.
- *Allocating.* Breaking similar products into smaller and smaller lots. (Allocating at the wholesale level is called **breaking bulk**.) For instance, a tank-car load of milk could be broken down into litre containers. The process of allocating generally is done when the goods are dispersed by region and as ownership of the goods changes.

Without the sorting, accumulating, and allocating processes, modern society would not exist. We would have home-based industries providing custom or semicustom products to local markets. In short, we would return to a much lower level of consumption.

A second way channels ease the flow of goods is by locating buyers for merchandise. A wholesaler must find the right retailers to sell a profitable volume of merchandise. A sporting-goods wholesaler, for instance, must find the retailers who are most likely

Concept *in Action*

An efficient distribution system allows RONA to offer customers a vast assortment of building materials, appliances, and tools economically. What do you think the distribution channels for RONA are?

breaking bulk
The process of breaking large shipments of similar products into smaller, more usable lots.

Exhibit 14.10 How Distribution Channels Reduce the Number of Transactions

Without a Marketing Intermediary:
5 publishers × 4 students = 20 transactions

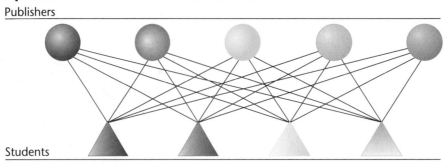

Publishers

Students

With a Marketing Intermediary:
5 publishers + 4 students = 9 transactions

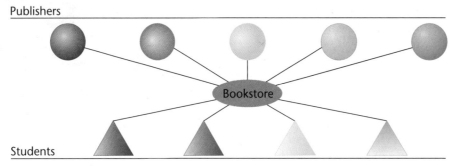

Publishers

Bookstore

Students

to reach sporting-goods consumers. Retailers have to understand the buying habits of consumers and put stores where consumers want and expect to find the merchandise. Every member of a distribution channel must locate buyers for the products it is trying to sell.

Channel members also store merchandise so that goods are available when consumers want to buy them. The high cost of retail space often means that many goods are stored by the wholesaler or the manufacturer.

CHANNELS PERFORM NEEDED FUNCTIONS The functions performed by channel intermediaries help increase the efficiency of the channel. Yet consumers sometimes feel that the go-betweens create higher prices. They doubt that these intermediaries perform useful functions. Actually, however, if channel intermediaries did not perform important and necessary functions at a reasonable cost, they would cease to exist. If companies could earn a higher profit without using certain channel members, they would not use them.

Channel intermediaries perform three general functions: transactional, logistical, and facilitating. We have already discussed logistics. Transactional functions involve contacting and communicating with prospective buyers to make them aware of goods and services that are available. Sellers attempt to explain why their offerings provide more features, benefits, and value than the competition. The third function is facilitating, which includes financing and market research. Research answers questions such as who is buying the products, where do they like to buy the items, and what the characteristics of the users are. The three basic functions that channel intermediaries perform are summarized in Exhibit 14.11.

Expanding Around the Globe

THE EASY WAY

Imagine being on the French Riviera when a massive orange ship motors in, sticking out like a sore thumb among the other white cruisers. You notice that there is an "EasyCruise.com" logo along the length of the ship. EasyGroup's venture into cruising is only one of 14 products in their line, which appeals to a budget-conscious market. Obviously the aim of founder Stelios Haji-Ioannou, Greek shipping heir, is to "get noticed."

The foundation of the Easy brand is that of low-cost living, such as EasyCruise. When Stelios Haji-Ioannou was 28 years old, he founded his global business, which began with his budget airline, EasyJet. He has been expanding the Easy brand to many discount products and services, many of which seem to have little in common. Some of the ventures include Easy movie rentals, an Easy shaving cream, Easy Internet cafés, Easy pizzas, and an Easy hotel. There's even an Easy wristwatch. "In an industry where consumers are being ripped off, if I can find a way to give them real value, I'm going to do it," he says.

Sometimes competitors feel justifiably threatened by Easy's entry into their market. Haji-Ioannou's strategy is to start price wars almost everywhere he goes, resulting in many detractors across various industries. According to Paolo Pescatore, a wireless analyst with research firm IDC, "His [Haji-Ioannou's] assumption that he can take any idea and just slap his brand on it is somewhat arrogant." Easy's mobile-phone venture illustrates this pattern; it sells SIM cards that can be put into existing handsets, and then charges for service. Initially priced at as much as 40 percent below the then-existing prices resulted in some of the competition, such as rival Carphone Warehouse, to counter with substantial discounts of their own. Orange, a heavyweight in the United Kingdom, sued Easy for using the same colour of orange that they use in their ads.[4]

Today EasyCruise offers cruise holidays to Greece and Turkey for people who want to live the easy life at reasonable prices. The company offers a variety of accommodations, from its value cabins to the spacious suites. Its target market is adventurous young people; Easy offers them an affordable and convenient way to explore the eastern Mediterranean.

Thinking Critically

1. With 15 Easy brands on the market, in many different industries, do you think that Stelios has diversified too much? Is he destroying the mystique of the brand?
2. Stelios says North America will be "Easy pickings" for the Easy Group. Do you agree? Why or why not?

SOURCES: "Easy Does It All," *Business 2.0*, August 2005, pg. 69–74; EasyCruise, "Welcome to easyCruise.com," http://www.easycruise.com/, accessed July 2012; Cool Mediterranean Cruises, "EasyCruise Mediterranean Cruises," http://www.coolmediterraneancruises.com/cruiselines/easycruise.html, accessed July 2012.

Exhibit 14.11 Marketing Channel Functions Performed by Intermediaries

TYPE OF FUNCTION	DESCRIPTION
Transaction Functions	**Contacting and promoting**: Contacting potential customers, promoting products, and soliciting orders **Negotiating**: Determining how many goods or services to buy and sell, type of transportation to use, when to deliver, and method and timing of payment **Risk taking**: Assuming the risk of owning inventory
Logistical Functions	**Physically distributing**: Transporting and sorting goods **Storing**: Maintaining inventories and protecting goods **Sorting out**: Breaking down a heterogeneous supply into separate homogeneous stocks **Accumulation**: Combining similar stocks into a larger homogeneous supply **Allocation**: Breaking a homogeneous supply into smaller and smaller lots ("breaking bulk") **Assortment**: Combining products into collections or assortments that buyers want available at one place
Facilitating Functions	**Researching**: Gathering information about other channel members and consumers **Financing**: Extending credit and other financial services to facilitate the flow of goods through the channel to the final consumer

Concept *Check*

List and define the marketing intermediaries that make up a distribution channel.

Provide an example of a strategic channel alliance.

How do channels reduce the number of transactions?

A useful rule to remember is that, although channel intermediaries can be eliminated, their functions cannot. The manufacturer must either perform the functions of the intermediaries itself or find new ways of getting them carried out. Publishers can bypass bookstores, for instance, but the function performed by the bookstores then has to be performed by the publishers or by someone else.

The Intensity of Market Coverage

All types of distribution systems must be concerned with market coverage. How many dealers will be used to distribute the product in a particular area? The three degrees of coverage are exclusive, selective, and intensive. The type of product determines the intensity of the market coverage.

When a manufacturer selects one or two dealers in an area to market its products, it is using **exclusive distribution**. Only items that are in strong demand can be distributed exclusively because consumers must be willing to travel some distance to buy them. If Dentyne chewing gum were sold in only one drugstore per city, Dentyne would soon be out of business. However, Bang and Olufsen stereo components, Jaguar automobiles, and top name designer clothing are distributed exclusively with great success. Exclusive distribution is mostly associated with specialty products and unsought products.

A manufacturer that chooses a limited number of dealers in an area (but more than one or two) is using **selective distribution**. Since the number of retailers handling the product is limited, consumers must be willing to seek it out. Timberland boots, a high-quality line of footwear, are distributed selectively. So are Sony televisions, Maytag washers, Waterford crystal, and Tommy Hilfiger clothing. When choosing dealers, manufacturers look for certain qualities. Sony may seek retailers that can offer high-quality customer service. Tommy Hilfiger may look for retailers with high-traffic locations in regional shopping malls. All manufacturers try to exclude retailers that are a poor credit risk or that have a weak or negative image. Selective distribution is mostly associated with shopping products.

A manufacturer that wants to sell its products everywhere there are potential customers is using **intensive distribution**. Such consumer goods as bread, tape, and light bulbs are often distributed intensively. Usually, these products cost little and are bought frequently, which means that complex distribution channels are necessary. Coca-Cola is sold in just about every type of retail business, from gas stations to grocery stores. Convenience products generally have intensive distribution.

exclusive distribution
A distribution system in which a manufacturer selects only one or two dealers in an area to market its products.

selective distribution
A distribution system in which a manufacturer selects a limited number of dealers in an area (but more than one or two) to market its products.

intensive distribution
A distribution system in which a manufacturer tries to sell its products wherever there are potential customers.

Concept *Check*

Name the three degrees of market coverage.

Describe the types of products that are distributed using intensive distribution.

 PROMOTION—SELLING OUR PRODUCTS

promotion
The attempt by marketers to inform, persuade, or remind consumers and industrial users to engage in the exchange process.

Very few goods or services can survive in the marketplace without good **promotion**. Marketers promote their products to build demand. Promotion is an attempt by marketers to inform, persuade, or remind customers and industrial users in order to influence their opinion or elicit a response. Once the product has been created, promotion is often used to convince target customers that it has a differential advantage over the competition. A differential competitive advantage, as explained in Chapter 13, is a set of unique features that the target market perceives as important and better than the competition's features; the advantage ideally results in purchase of the brand.

Most companies use some form of promotion, a word whose Latin root means "to move forward." Hence, actions that move a company toward its goals are promotional in nature. Because company goals vary widely, so do promotional strategies. The goal is to stimulate action. In a profit-oriented company, the desired action is for the consumer to buy the promoted item. McCain's, for instance, wants people to buy more frozen French fries. Not-for-profit organizations seek a variety of actions with their promotions. They tell us not to litter, to buckle up, and to attend the ballet.

Promotional goals include creating awareness, getting people to try products, providing information, retaining loyal customers, increasing the use of products, and identifying potential customers. Any promotional campaign may seek to achieve one or more of these goals:

Concept Check

What is the objective of a promotional campaign?

How would the promotional campaigns for a new restaurant and an established brand differ?

1. *Creating awareness.* All too often, companies go out of business because people don't know they exist or what they do. Small restaurants often have this problem. Simply putting up a sign and opening the door is rarely enough. Promotion through ads on local radio or television, coupons in local papers, flyers, and so forth can create awareness of a new business or product.

2. *Getting consumers to try products.* Promotion is almost always used to get people to try a new product or to get non-users to try an existing product. Sometimes free samples are given away.

3. *Providing information.* Informative promotion is more common in the early stages of the product life cycle. An informative promotion may explain what ingredients (like fibre) will do for your health, tell you why the product is better (high-definition television versus regular television), inform you of a new low price, or explain where the item may be bought. People typically will not buy a product or support a not-for-profit organization until they know what it will do and how it may benefit them. Thus, an informative ad may stimulate interest in a product. Consumer watchdogs and social critics applaud the informative function of promotion because it helps consumers make more intelligent purchase decisions.

4. *Keeping loyal customers.* Promotion is also used to keep people from switching brands. Slogans such as Tim Hortons' "Always Fresh" and "Intel Inside" remind consumers about the brand. Marketers also remind users that the brand is better than the competition. For years, Pepsi has claimed it has the taste that consumers prefer. Such advertising reminds customers about the quality of the product. Companies can also help keep customers loyal by telling them when a product or service is improved.

5. *Increasing the amount and frequency of use.* Promotion is often used to get people to use more of a product and to use it more often. The most popular promotion to increase the use of a product may be loyalty programs such as frequent-flyer or user programs. For example, most larger grocery stores have loyalty cards that reward customers with discounts or redeemable points.

6. *Identifying target customers.* Promotion helps find customers. One way to do this is to list a website. For instance, *Canadian Business* magazine and *Business Week* include Web addresses for more information on computer systems, corporate jets, colour copiers, and other types of business equipment to help target those who are truly interested.

The Promotional Mix

The combination of advertising, personal selling, sales promotion, and public relations used to promote a product is called the **promotional mix**. Each company creates a unique mix for each product. But the goal is always to deliver the company's message efficiently and effectively to the target audience. These are the elements of the promotional mix:

- **Advertising**: Any paid form of non-personal promotion by an identified sponsor
- **Personal sellings**: A face-to-face presentation to a prospective buyer
- **Sales promotions**: Marketing activities (other than personal selling, advertising, and public relations) that stimulate consumer buying, including coupons and samples, displays, shows and exhibitions, demonstrations, and other types of selling efforts

promotional mix
The combination of advertising, personal selling, sales promotion, and public relations used to promote a product.

advertising
Any paid form of non-personal presentation by an identified sponsor.

personal selling
A face-to-face sales presentation to a prospective customer.

sales promotions
Marketing events or sales efforts—not including advertising, personal selling, and public relations—that stimulate buying.

public relations
Any communication or activity designed to win goodwill or prestige for a company or person.

- Public relations: The linking of organizational goals with key aspects of the public interest and the development of programs designed to earn public understanding and acceptance

Ideally, marketing communications from each promotional-mix element (personal selling, advertising, sales promotion, and public relations) should be integrated. That is, the message reaching the consumer should be the same regardless of whether it comes from an advertisement, a salesperson in the field, a magazine article, or a coupon in a newspaper insert.

integrated marketing communications (IMC)
The careful coordination of all promotional activities—media advertising, sales promotion, personal selling, and public relations, as well as direct marketing, packaging, and other forms of promotion—to produce a consistent, unified message that is customer focused.

Many companies have adopted the concept of integrated marketing communications (IMC). IMC involves carefully coordinating all promotional activities—media advertising, sales promotion, personal selling, and public relations, as well as direct marketing, packaging, and other forms of promotion—to produce a consistent, unified message that is customer focused. Following the concept of IMC, marketing managers carefully work out the roles the various promotional elements will play in the marketing mix. Timing of promotional activities is coordinated, and the results of each campaign are carefully monitored to improve future use of the promotional mix tools. Typically, a marketing communications director is appointed who has overall responsibility for integrating the company's marketing communications.

Pepsi relied on IMC to launch Pepsi One. The $100 million program relied on personal selling in the distribution channels, a public-relations campaign with press releases to announce the product, and heavy doses of advertising and sales promotion. The company toured the country's shopping malls setting up Pepsi One "lounges"—inflatable couches with plastic carpeting—for random taste tests. It also produced 11,000 end-cap displays for supermarket aisles and created stand-up displays for 12-packs to spark impulse purchases. It secured Oscar-winning actor Cuba Gooding Jr. as spokesperson for the ad campaign. The ads made their debut during the World Series. The tagline for the ad campaign was "Only One has it all."

Factors That Affect the Promotional Mix

Promotional mixes vary a great deal from product to product and from one industry to the next. Advertising and personal selling are usually a company's main promotional tools. They are supported by sales promotion. Public relations helps develop a positive image for the organization and its products. The specific promotional mix depends on the nature of the product, market characteristics, available funds, and whether a push or a pull strategy is used.

The Nature of the Product

Selling toothpaste differs greatly from selling overhead industrial cranes. Personal selling is most important in marketing industrial products and least important in marketing consumer nondurables (consumer products that get used up). Broadcast advertising is used heavily in promoting consumer products, especially food and other nondurables. Print media and the Internet are used for all types of consumer products. Industrial products may be advertised through special trade magazines. Sales promotion, branding, and packaging are roughly twice as important (in terms of percentage of the promotional budget) for consumer products as for industrial products.

Market Characteristics

When potential customers are widely scattered, buyers are highly informed, and many of the buyers are brand loyal, the promotional mix should include more advertising and sales promotion and less personal selling. But sometimes personal selling is required even when buyers are well informed and geographically dispersed, as is the case with super computers and airplanes. Industrial installations and component parts may be sold to knowledgeable people with much education and work experience. Yet a salesperson must still explain the product and work out the details of the purchase agreement.

Salespeople are also required when the physical stocking of merchandise—called detailing—is the norm. Soft drinks and potato chips, for instance, are generally stocked by the person who makes the delivery, rather than by store personnel. This practice is becoming more common for convenience products as sellers try to get the best display space for their wares.

Available Funds

Money, or the lack of it, is one of the biggest influences on the promotional mix. A small manufacturer with a tight budget and a unique product may rely heavily on free publicity. The media often run stories about new products.

If the product warrants a sales force, a company with little money may turn to manufacturers' agents. They work on commission, with no salary, advances, or expense accounts. The Duncan Co., which makes parking meters, is just one of the many that rely on manufacturers' agents.

Push and Pull Strategies

Manufacturers may use aggressive personal selling and trade advertising to convince a wholesaler or a retailer to carry and sell their merchandise. This approach is known as a push strategy. The wholesaler, in turn, must often push the merchandise forward by persuading the retailer to handle the goods. A push strategy relies on extensive personal selling to channel members, or trade advertising, and price incentives to wholesalers and retailers. The retailer then uses advertising, displays, and other promotional forms to convince the consumer to buy the "pushed" products. This approach also applies to services. For example, the Jamaican Tourism Board targets promotions to travel agencies, which are members of its distribution channel.

At the other extreme is a pull strategy, which stimulates consumer demand in order to obtain product distribution. Rather than trying to sell to wholesalers, a manufacturer using a pull strategy focuses its promotional efforts on end consumers. As they begin demanding the product, the retailer orders the merchandise from the wholesaler. The wholesaler, confronted with rising demand, then places an order from the manufacturer. Thus, stimulating consumer demand pulls the product down through the channel of distribution. Heavy sampling, introductory consumer advertising, cents-off campaigns, buzz marketing, and couponing may all be used as part of a pull strategy. For example, using a pull strategy, the Jamaican Tourism Board may entice travellers to come to its island by offering discounts on hotels or airfare. The push and pull promotional strategies are illustrated in Exhibit 14.12.

Rarely does a company use a pull or a push strategy exclusively. Instead, the mix will emphasize one of these strategies. For example, pharmaceutical company Sanofi Aventis uses a push strategy by using personal selling and sampling of Allegra D, the allergy drug, to physicians and pharmacies. The company also uses print ads in consumer magazines, network TV, newspaper ads, and a website aimed at final consumers to pull the product through the channel.

SUPPLY CHAIN MANAGEMENT: INCREASING EFFICIENCY AND CUSTOMER SATISFACTION

LO6

Distribution is an important part of the marketing mix. Retailers don't sell products they can't deliver, and salespeople don't (or shouldn't) promise deliveries they can't make. Late deliveries and broken promises may mean loss of a customer. Accurate order filling and billing, timely delivery, and arrival in good condition are important to the success of the product.

detailing
The physical stocking of merchandise at a retailer by the salesperson who delivers the merchandise.

push strategy
A promotional strategy in which a manufacturer uses aggressive personal selling and trade advertising to convince a wholesaler or retailer to carry and sell its merchandise.

pull strategy
A promotional strategy in which a manufacturer focuses on stimulating consumer demand for its product, rather than on trying to persuade wholesalers or retailers to carry the product.

Exhibit 14.12 Push and Pull Promotional Strategies

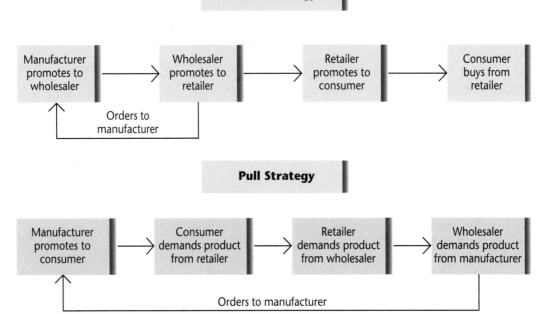

Push Strategy

| Manufacturer promotes to wholesaler | → | Wholesaler promotes to retailer | → | Retailer promotes to consumer | → | Consumer buys from retailer |

Orders to manufacturer

Pull Strategy

| Manufacturer promotes to consumer | → | Consumer demands product from retailer | → | Retailer demands product from wholesaler | → | Wholesaler demands product from manufacturer |

Orders to manufacturer

The goal of supply chain management is to create a satisfied customer by coordinating all of the activities of the supply chain members into a seamless process. Therefore, an important element of supply chain management is that it is completely customer driven. In the mass-production era, manufacturers produced standardized products that were "pushed" down through the supply channel to the consumer. In today's marketplace by contrast, products are being driven by customers who expect to receive product configurations and services matched to their unique

Making Ethical Choices

SUGAR-COATING THE TRUTH

After working really hard to distinguish yourself, you've finally been promoted to a senior account executive at a major advertising agency and placed in charge of the agency's newest account, a nationally known cereal company. Their product is one you know contains excessive amounts of sugar as well as artificial colourings, and lacks any nutritional value whatsoever. In fact, you have never allowed your own children to eat it.

Your boss has indicated that the cereal company would like to use the slogan, "It's good for you," in their new television and print advertising campaign. You know that a $2 billion lawsuit has been filed against the Kellogg and Viacom corporations for marketing junk food to young children. The suit cited "alluring product packaging, toy giveaways, contests, collectibles, kid-oriented websites, magazine ads, and branded toys and clothes." In addition, two consumer groups have brought suit against children's television network Nickelodeon for "unfair and deceptive junk-food marketing."

Your new role at the agency will be tested with this campaign. Doing a good job on it will cement your position and put you in line for a promotion to vice president. But as a responsible parent, you have strong feelings about misleading advertising targeted at susceptible children.

Using a Web search tool, locate articles about this topic and then write responses to the following questions. Be sure to support your arguments and cite your sources.

ETHICAL DILEMMA: Do you follow your principles and ask to be transferred to another account? Or do you help promote a cereal you know may be harmful to children in order to secure your career?

SOURCES: Stephanie Thompson, "Standing Still, Kellogg Gets Hit with a Lawsuit," *Advertising Age*, January 23, 2006; Stephanie Thompson, "Kellogg Co. Might as Well Have Painted a Bull's-eye on Itself," *Advertising Age*, January 23, 2006; and Abbey Klaassen, "Viacom Gets Nicked," *Advertising Age*, January 23, 2006 (all from (http://galenet. thomsonlearning.com).

needs. For example, Dell only builds computers according to its customers' precise specifications, such as the amount of RAM memory; type of monitor, modem, or CD drive; and amount of hard-disk space. The process begins by Dell purchasing partly built laptops from contract manufacturers. The final assembly is done in Dell factories in Ireland, Malaysia, or China, where microprocessors, software, and other key components are added. Those finished products are then shipped to Dell-operated distribution centres in Canada where they are packaged with other items and shipped to the customer.

Through the channel partnership, suppliers, manufacturers, wholesalers, and retailers along the entire supply chain work together toward the common goal of creating customer value. Supply chain management allows companies to respond with the unique product configuration and mix of services demanded by the customer. Today, supply chain management plays a dual role: first, as a communicator of customer demand that extends from the point of sale all the way back to the supplier, and second, as a physical flow process that engineers the timely and cost-effective movement of goods through the entire supply pipeline.

Accordingly, supply chain managers are responsible for making channel strategy decisions, coordinating the sourcing and procurement of raw materials, scheduling production, processing orders, managing inventory, transporting and storing supplies and finished goods, and coordinating customer service activities. Supply chain managers are also responsible for the management of information that flows through the supply chain. Coordinating the relationships between the company and its external partners, such as vendors, carriers and third-party companies, is also a critical function of supply chain management. Because supply chain managers play such a major role in both cost control and customer satisfaction, they are more valuable than ever.

Managing the Logistical Components of the Supply Chain

Logistics, discussed earlier, is a term borrowed from the military that describes the process of strategically managing the efficient flow and storage of raw materials, in-process inventory, and finished goods from the point of origin to the point of consumption. The supply chain team manages the logistical flow. Key decisions in managing the logistical flow are finding and procuring raw materials and supplies, production scheduling, choosing a warehouse location and type, inventory control, setting up a materials-handling system, and making transportation decisions.

Sourcing and Procurement

One of the most important links in the supply chain is between the manufacturer and the supplier. Purchasing professionals are on the front lines of supply chain management. Purchasing departments plan purchasing strategies, develop specifications, select suppliers, and negotiate price and service levels.

The goal of most sourcing and procurement activities is to reduce the costs of raw materials and supplies and to have the items available when they are needed, for production or for the office, but not before (see just-in-time manufacturing in Chapter 15).

Retailers like 1-800-Flowers.com and FTD use local florists as the backbone of their distribution networks; flowers travel from the farm to a distributor and then to a wholesaler before finally reaching the flower shop. By the time they reach consumers, flowers can be 8 to 12 days old. ProFlowers.com found this procurement system too inefficient and costly. The company developed a network-based system that transforms each domestic flower farm into a self-contained distribution facility. Growers handle everything from receiving real-time flower orders to adding personalized message cards.[5]

Production Scheduling

In traditional mass-market manufacturing, production begins when forecasts call for additional products to be made or inventory control systems signal low inventory levels. The company then makes a product and transports the finished goods to its own warehouses or those of intermediaries, where the goods wait to be ordered by retailers or customers. Production scheduling based on pushing a product down to the consumer obviously has its disadvantages, the most notable being that companies risk making products that may become obsolete or that consumers don't want in the first place.

In a customer "pull" manufacturing environment, which is growing in popularity, production of goods or services is not scheduled until an order is placed by the customer specifying the desired configuration. This process, known as mass customization, or build-to-order, uniquely tailors mass-market goods and services to the needs of the individuals who buy them. Mass customization was explained in Chapter 13. Companies as diverse as BMW, Dell Computer, Levi Strauss, Mattel, and many Web-based businesses are adopting mass customization to maintain or obtain a competitive edge.

Choosing a Warehouse Location and Type

Deciding where to put a warehouse is mostly a matter of deciding which markets will be served and where production facilities will be located. A storage warehouse is used to hold goods for a long time. For instance, Jantzen makes bathing suits at an even rate throughout the year to provide steady employment and hold down costs. It then stores them in a warehouse until the selling season.

distribution centres
Warehouses that specialize in rapid movement of goods to retail stores by making and breaking bulk.

Distribution centres are a special form of warehouse. They specialize in changing shipment sizes rather than storing goods. Such centres make bulk (put shipments together) or break bulk. They strive for rapid inventory turnover. When shipments arrive, the merchandise is quickly sorted into orders for various retail stores. As soon as the order is complete, it is delivered. Distribution centres are the wave of the future, replacing traditional warehouses. Companies simply can't afford to have a lot of money tied up in idle inventory.

Inventory Control

inventory control system
A system that maintains an adequate assortment of items to meet users' or customers' needs.

Closely interrelated with the procurement, manufacturing, and ordering processes is the inventory control system—a method that develops and maintains an adequate assortment of materials or products to meet manufacturers' or customers' demands.

Inventory decisions, for both raw materials and finished goods, have a big impact on supply chain costs and the level of service provided. If too many products are kept in inventory, costs increase—as do risks of obsolescence, theft, and damage. If too few products are kept on hand, then the company risks product shortages, angry customers, and ultimately lost sales.

Many of the chain retailers have used supply-chain technology to control inventories and dramatically raise profitability. In a matter of seconds, any store manager can tap into the chain's proprietary computer system and pull up real-time data on what products are selling best at that location or across the country.

Setting Up a Materials-Handling System

A materials-handling system moves and handles inventory. The goal of such a system is to move items as quickly as possible while handling them as little as possible. For example, Rival Material Handling Systems Inc. of Ontario specializes in the manufacture and supply of ergonomic industrial and commercial materials-handling products. By using customized materials-handling, companies operate more efficiently at lower costs.

Exhibit 14.13 | Criteria for Ranking Modes of Transportation

	HIGHEST—			—LOWEST	
Relative cost	Air	Truck	Rail	Pipe	Water
Transit time	Water	Rail	Pipe	Truck	Air
Reliability	Pipe	Truck	Rail	Air	Water
Capability	Water	Rail	Truck	Air	Pipe
Accessibility	Truck	Rail	Air	Water	Pipe
Traceability	Air	Truck	Rail	Water	Pipe

Making Transportation Decisions

Transportation typically accounts for between 5 and 10 percent of the price of goods. Physical-distribution managers must decide which mode of transportation to use to move products from producer to buyer. This decision is, of course, related to all other physical-distribution decisions. The five major modes of transportation are railroads, motor carriers, pipelines, water transportation, and airways. Distribution managers generally choose a mode of transportation on the basis of several criteria:

- *Cost*: The total amount a specific carrier charges to move the product from the point of origin to the destination
- *Transit time*: The total time a carrier has possession of goods, including the time required for pickup and delivery, handling, and movement between the point of origin and the destination
- *Reliability*: The consistency with which the carrier delivers goods on time and in acceptable condition
- *Capability*: The carrier's ability to provide the appropriate equipment and conditions for moving specific kinds of goods, such as those that must be transported in a controlled environment (for example, under refrigeration)
- *Accessibility*: The carrier's ability to move goods over a specific route or network
- *Traceability*: The relative ease with which a shipment can be located and transferred

Concept *Check*

What is the goal of supply chain management?

Describe the key decisions in managing the logistical flow.

What factors are considered when selecting a mode of transportation?

Concept *in Action*

Reliable and inexpensive, water transportation is one of the five major modes of transportation that distribution managers can use to move products from the producer to the buyer. Canada also relies on the other types of transportation to move products. What are the other four modes of transportation?

S_OLEG/SHUTTERSTOCK

THE FUTURE OF MARKETING STRATEGIES

As customer expectations increase and competition becomes fiercer, perceptive marketers will find innovative strategies to satisfy demanding consumers and establish unique products in the market at the right prices. By using new distribution strategies and harnessing new technology to hone their marketing message and reach more customers, companies can boost profits and gain a competitive edge. Some of the significant trends in marketing include increased number of computing devices and applications (apps), increased marketing dollars allotted to social media, growth in the number of buying sites that offer discounts to many different companies, such as SwarmJam and Groupon, and, job growth in supply chain management.

Not Just Traditional Products: Increased Variety of Mobile Devices

New smaller, more powerful mobile devices have become increasingly more popular and customers are demanding more apps to access information about products. Tablets, iPhone, etc., are replacing the more oversized and less functional traditional computers. Just a few years ago, laptops were taking a larger share of the market, but these are going through the product life cycle as these new devices become more compact with more real-application apps available.

Marketing Dollars Going Social

Savvy marketers are realizing the power of the social media. Its far reach and relatively low costs can give a company a very quick competitive advantage. Companies are making their websites more mobile-friendly, marketing on social sites, having specific apps built, and using direct e-mail advertising.

Bargains, Bargains: Using Technology to Save

You can check out the daily local specials offered by retailers in your area by searching SwarmJam's site. This is a collective buying site that offers great savings and even offers you rewards for recommending others to it. SwarmJam offers both fixed discounts (set discounts) and progressive discounts (as more products/coupons purchased, the more saved).

Another popular site is Groupon, which was launched in November 2008. It offers daily deals that include things to do, see, eat, and buy. Canadians can use many sites to save on products—but more importantly, by using technology, companies have the opportunity to increase their visibility and product offerings.

Supply Chain Management: Increasing Its Importance

Demand for strategic business managers, supply chain specialists, and those who provide expertise in information systems and customer-focused logistics is increasing. External partners are becoming increasingly important in the efficient deployment of supply chain management. Outsourcing, or contract logistics, is a rapidly growing segment of the distribution industry in which a manufacturer or supplier turns over the entire function of buying and managing transportation—or another function of the supply chain, such as warehousing—to an independent third party. Many manufacturers are turning to outside partners for their logistics expertise in an effort to focus on the core competencies that they do best. Partners create and manage entire solutions for getting products where they need to be, when they need to be there. Logistics partners offer staff, an infrastructure, and services that reach consumers virtually anywhere in the world. Because a logistics provider is focused, clients receive service in a timely,

Concept Check

What are the latest mobile devices and how can businesses capitalize on them?

How has social marketing changed the way businesses promote their products?

Why are more retailers outsourcing their logistics functions?

efficient manner, thereby increasing customers' level of satisfaction and boosting their perception of added value to a company's offerings.

Third-party contract logistics enable companies to cut inventories, locate stock at fewer plants and distribution centres, and still provide the same service level or even better. The companies then can refocus investment on their core business.

GREAT IDEAS TO USE NOW

Chances are that someday you will be a buyer or seller on eBay. The auction site is the largest online marketplace, with more than 100 million registered members from around the world and more than 18,000 categories of items on the auction block. Yet finding what you want or getting the best deal can be tough. Following are a few helpful tips.

A Buyer's Guide

BROWSING/SEARCHING

- Before diving in, get a solid sense of what the items you're interested in are worth. Use the "completed items" advanced search to see the prices that similar items actually sold for, or check eBay's library for the category-specific "inside scoop," which generally features a useful page titled "Factors Influencing Value."
- Search in both related and general categories, as sellers often classify their wares differently. For example, if you're looking for a CD by Elvis Costello, check classic rock, pop, and punk in addition to alternative rock.
- Be descriptive when searching. Specify dates, colours, brands, sizes, and model numbers. Try variations—if a model number has a hyphen, search both with and without it.
- Conduct searches often, as items are constantly added and removed. Save yourself from having to monitor the site on a daily basis by using the "favourite searches" service, which will notify you by e-mail when items matching your search criteria are put up for sale.
- Think eBay for retail, too. Many companies, such as Dell and Handspring, off-load surplus inventory at deep discounts, so check here before you try standard retail outlets.

BIDDING

- Don't bid if you don't intend to buy, as bids are binding contracts. Bids can be retracted only under exceptional circumstances (e.g., the seller changes the product description after you've placed your bid).
- Don't bid in the first days of an auction. Doing so merely reveals your interest and increases the likelihood of other bidders joining the fray, causing the price to rise quickly. Instead, wait until the auction is near its close (10 to 30 seconds before, depending on the speed of your Internet connection), and then bid the maximum amount you are willing to pay, regardless of any previous bids—a strategy known as sniping. To do this, open a second browser window and fill in all the relevant information, stopping just short of submitting your bid. Watch the auction wind down in the first window, and when the time is right, place your bid in the second. Don't fret—you can always use a professional sniper service to handle this for you automatically.
- Factor in shipping costs, which typically fall on the buyer. If the item is bulky or the seller lives overseas, your "bargain" might end up costing more than you bargained for.
- Try adding a penny or two to your bid. Since many bids are placed in round-number increments, this little extra something can mean the difference between winning by a nose and coming up short.

A Seller's Guide

LISTING Online auctions bring out the competitive nature in bidders, especially as the clock runs out. Bidding wars are a seller's dream; to make sure your auction gets significant play, follow these steps:

- Include specifics, such as manufacturer or product name, in both the title and the description.
- Be honest in describing imperfections. This gives buyers comfort that you're being honest and could head off conflicts later.
- Set a low initial bid amount to attract more bidders. The mere *possibility* of getting a great deal on that rare Tony Gwynn rookie card encourages competition and increases the likelihood of rival bidders' driving up the price. This can also save you money, as eBay's listing fees are based on the minimum bid you set.
- Include a picture, as most buyers are reluctant to make a big purchase sight unseen. But don't overdo it: Including too many photos, or big ones with large file sizes, slows download times and tends to frustrate buyers with dial-up connections.
- Set a "buy it now" price, which allows buyers to subvert the bidding process and nab an item outright for a predetermined amount.
- Don't set a "reserve" price, which requires bidders to meet or exceed a certain minimum. As bidders can't see this minimum price, many avoid such auctions altogether out of fear that they'll be wasting their time.
- Accept multiple forms of payment, which increases the likelihood that interested buyers will place bids.
- Pay attention to when your auction is scheduled to end. eBay auctions run 3, 5, 7, or 10 days; to get the most traffic, make sure that yours includes a full weekend and ends at a time when people will be around to bid up the price.

CLOSING THE DEAL

- Congratulate the winner by e-mail. Include the auction number, a description of the item, the amount of the winning bid, and estimated shipping charges.
- Send the item as soon as the buyer's payment clears, and alert the buyer by e-mail (be sure to include the tracking number).
- Include links to your other auctions in all e-mail correspondence with buyers; if they are satisfied with their experience, they might want to check out what else you have.[6]

Summary of Learning Outcomes

 LO1 — **Describe what is meant by a product.**

A product is any good or service, along with its perceived attributes and benefits, that creates customer value. Tangible attributes include the good itself, packaging, and warranties. Intangible attributes are symbolic, such as a brand's image. Brand loyalty plays a very important role in marketing. Brands can include master brands, manufacturer brands, dealer brands, and generic brands. Products are categorized as either consumer products or industrial products. Consumer products are goods and services that are bought and used by the end users. They can be classified as unsought products, convenience products, shopping products, or specialty products, depending on how much effort consumers are willing to exert to get them. Industrial products are those bought by organizations for use in making other products or in rendering services, and include capital products and expense items.

After a product reaches the marketplace, it enters the product life cycle. This cycle typically has four stages: introduction, growth, maturity, and decline (and possibly death). Profits usually are small in the introductory phase, reach a peak at the end of the growth phase, and then decline. Marketing strategies for each stage are listed in Exhibit 14.4.

LO2 Explain the stages of the product life cycle.

Price indicates value, helps position a product in the marketplace, and is the means for earning a fair return on investment. If a price is too high, the product won't sell well, and the company will lose money. If the price is too low, the company might lose money, even if the product sells well. Prices are set according to pricing objectives. Among the most common objectives are profit maximization, target return on investment, and value pricing.

LO3 Discuss the role of pricing and the strategies used for pricing products.

The two main strategies for pricing a new product are price skimming and penetration pricing. Price skimming involves charging a high introductory price and then, usually, lowering the price as the product moves through its life cycle. Penetration pricing involves selling a new product at a low price in the hope of achieving a large sales volume.

Pricing tactics are used to fine-tune the base prices of products. Sellers that use leader pricing set the prices of some of their products below the normal markup or even below cost to attract customers who might otherwise not shop at those stores. Bundling is grouping two or more products together and pricing them as one. Psychology often plays a role in how consumers view products and in determining what they will pay. Setting a price at an odd number tends to create a perception that the item is cheaper than the actual price. Prices in even numbers denote quality or status. Raising the price so an item will be perceived as having high quality and status is called prestige pricing.

A cost-based method for determining price is markup pricing. A certain percentage is added to the product's cost (often calculated by using activity-based costing) to arrive at the retail price. The markup is the amount added to the cost to cover expenses and earn a profit. Break-even analysis determines the level of sales that must be reached before total cost equals total revenue. Break-even analysis provides a quick look at how many units the company must sell before it starts earning a profit. The technique also reveals how much profit can be earned with higher sales volumes.

Physical distribution is efficiently managing the acquisition of raw materials to the factory and the movement of products from the producer or manufacturer to industrial users and consumers. Physical distribution activities are usually the responsibility of the marketing department and are part of the large series of activities included in the supply chain. Distribution channels are the series of marketing entities through which goods and services pass on their way from producers to end users. Distribution systems focus on the physical transfer of goods and services and on their legal ownership at each stage of the distribution process. Channels (a) reduce the number of transactions, (b) ease the flow of goods, and (c) increase channel efficiency.

LO4 Explain distribution and distribution channels.

Promotion aims to stimulate demand for a company's goods or services. Promotional strategy is designed to inform, persuade, or remind target audiences about those products. The goals of promotion are to create awareness, get people to try products, provide information, keep loyal customers, increase use of a product, and identify potential customers.

LO5 Discuss promotion, its elements, and factors that affect its use.

The unique combination of advertising, personal selling, sales promotion, and public relations used to promote a product is the promotional mix. Advertising is any paid form of non-personal promotion by an identified sponsor. Personal selling consists of a face-to-face presentation in a conversation with a prospective purchaser. Sales promotion consists of marketing activities—other than personal selling, advertising, and public relations—that stimulate consumers to buy. These activities include coupons and samples, displays, shows and exhibitions, demonstrations, and other selling efforts. Public relations is the marketing function that links the policies of the organization with the public interest and develops programs designed to earn public understanding and acceptance. Integrated marketing communications (IMC) is being used by more and more organizations. It is the careful coordination of all of the elements of the promotional mix to produce a consistent, unified message that is customer focused.

The factors that affect the promotional mix are the nature of the product, market characteristics, available funds, and whether a push or a pull strategy is emphasized. Personal selling is used more with industrial products, and advertising is used more heavily for consumer products. With widely scattered, well-informed buyers and with brand-loyal customers, a company will blend more advertising and sales promotion and less personal selling into its promotional mix. A manufacturer with a limited budget might rely heavily on publicity and manufacturers' agents to promote the product.

LO6 Illustrate how supply chain management can increase efficiency and customer satisfaction.

The goal of supply chain management is to coordinate all of the activities of the supply chain members into a seamless process, thereby increasing customer satisfaction. The logistical components of the supply chain include sourcing and procurement, production scheduling, choosing a warehouse location and type, setting up a materials-handling system, and making transportation decisions.

LO7 List some of the trends in marketing.

Four trends that we are seeing in marketing are new mobile devices and apps, increase in social marketing, more on-demand coupons, and increased opportunities in supply chain management.

Smaller and more powerful mobile devices are now available and many apps are being developed that are used to market our products. More marketing dollars are dedicated to social marketing and coupons are becoming more common over electronic sources. More opportunities for jobs are emerging in supply chain management at all levels.

Key Terms

activity-based costing (ABC) 414
advertising 423
agents 416
brand 402
brand loyalty 402
break-even point (or break-even quantity) 412
breaking bulk 419
brokers 416
bundling 411
capital products 406
convenience products 405
dealer brand 402
detailing 425
distribution centres 428
distribution channel 415
distribution (logistics) 414
dual distribution (multiple distribution) 418
exclusive distribution 422
expense items 406

fixed-cost contribution 412
fixed costs 412
generic brand 402
industrial distributors 416
integrated marketing communications (IMC) 424
intensive distribution 422
inventory control system 428
leader pricing 411
loss leader 411
manufacturer 415
manufacturer brand 402
marketing intermediaries 416
markup pricing 414
master brand 402
odd-even (psychological) pricing 412
penetration pricing 411
personal selling 423
prestige pricing 412
price skimming 410
product 402

Experiential Exercises

1. Under what circumstances would a jeans maker market the product as a convenience product? A shopping product? A specialty product?

2. Go to the library and look through magazines and newspapers to find examples of price skimming, penetration pricing, and value pricing. Make copies and show them to the class.

3. Write down the names of two brands to which you are loyal. Indicate the reasons for your loyalty.

4. Visit an online retailer such as Amazon.ca (www.amazon.ca), PCConnection.com (www.pcconnection.com), or Drugstore.com (www.drugstore.com). At the site, try to identify examples of leader pricing, bundling, odd-even pricing, and other pricing strategies. Do online retailers have different pricing considerations from "real-world" retailers? Explain.

5. Do a search on Yahoo! (www.yahoo.ca) for online auctions for a product you are interested in buying. Visit several auctions to get an idea of how the product is priced. How do these prices compare with the price you might find in a local store? What pricing advantages or disadvantages do companies face in selling their products through online auctions? How do online auctions affect the pricing strategies of other companies? Why?

6. Do some comparison shopping. One beauty of the Internet is the ability to comparison shop like never before. Tour and Internet travel companies offer many last-minute specials where travellers can save on their trips. To compare brands, features, and prices of products, go to one of these sites and any others that you have researched: www.airtransat.com, www.aircanadavacations.com, www.expedia.com, www.itravel2000.com.

7. Kick the tires before you buy. At some point you are probably going to buy a car. The Web can simplify the process, help you make an intelligent decision, and save you money. Start at www.edmunds.com. The online version of the respected car buying guide is crammed with information about new and used cars. The site offers thousands of car reviews and current loan rates.

8. Trace the distribution channel for a familiar product. Compose an e-mail explaining why the channel has evolved as it has and how it is likely to change in the future.

9. Go to a successful, independent specialty store in your area that has been in business for quite a while. Interview the manager and try to determine how the store successfully competes with the national chains.

10. Visit a local manufacturer. Interview managers to determine how its supply chain functions. Make a report to the class.

11. One of the biggest challenges for retailers is integrating their various channels to provide a seamless experience for customers, regardless of the channel. Pick two of the following companies, explore their websites, and compare the channel integration strategies: Staples (www.staples.com), Gap (www.gap.com), or Borders (www.borders.com). In addition to looking at the websites from a channel perspective, you might want to look at the company information and news sites.

12. Protect your privacy online. Here are some pointers to protect yourself against spam.

    - Use free Web-based e-mail services like Microsoft's Hotmail.com to create a second e-mail address to give out when shopping at an e-commerce site. This will prevent your corporate or primary account from being deluged with targeted spam.
    - Use websites like www.spychecker.com to check if you have unwittingly downloaded spyware—nettlesome programs that are secretly installed when you download many free programs. Visitors to Spychecker are prompted to enter the names of programs, and the site tells them whether the software contains spyware.
    - Activate your Web browser's security functions to block out cookies or alert you when a site is trying to install one on your computer. In Internet Explorer, you would go to Tools, and then click on the Internet Options command. That brings up a series of tabs, including one for Security. Moving the sliding bar to its highest setting will disable all cookies. This, however, might make it difficult to visit many popular websites, as the sites tend to require the ability to install cookies on your machine.
    - Use e-mail re-mailers like the one at www.gilc.org/speech/anonymous/remailer.html to bounce your message through a series of computers that forward it on, in theory making it untraceable. Sending anonymous e-mail through these re-mailers also reduces the odds of its being read by hackers, who try to monitor data traffic to and from companies and sites like Hotmail.
    - Use privacy software to shield the content and addresses of the websites you visit from employers and other prying eyes. One of the best such programs is available at www.anonymizer.com.

13. Think of a product that you use regularly. Find several examples of how the manufacturer markets this product, such as ads in different media, sales promotions, and publicity. Assess each example for effectiveness in meeting one or more of the six promotional goals described in the chapter. Then analyze them for effectiveness in reaching you as a target consumer. Consider such factors as the media used, the style of the ad, and ad content. Present your findings to the class.

14. Choose a current advertising campaign for a beverage product. Describe how the campaign uses different media to promote the product. Which medium is used the most, and why? What other promotional strategies does the company use for the product? Evaluate the effectiveness of the campaign. Present your results to the class.

15. The Zenith Media site at www.zenithmedia.com is a good place to find links to Internet resources on advertising. At the site, click on "Leading Corporate and Brand Sites." Pick three of the company sites listed and review them, using the concepts in this chapter.

16. Does a career in marketing appeal to you? Start your journey at Careers in Marketing, www.careers-in-marketing.com, and explore the five areas listed there: Advertising & Public Relations, Market Research, Non-Profit, Product Management, and Retailing. Which one appeals to you most, and why? Briefly describe the type of work you would be doing, the career path, and how you will prepare to enter this field (courses, part-time jobs, etc.).

Review Questions

1. What is a product? How do products create value for the buyer?
2. What are brands and brand loyalty? What are the different types of brands?
3. What are the four classifications of consumer products?
4. How are business products classified?
5. Discuss the strategies for success at each stage of the product life cycle.
6. What is the role of pricing in marketing?
7. How are product prices determined?
8. What are the various pricing strategies available to managers?
9. What is physical distribution?
10. Define *marketing intermediaries*. What are four common marketing intermediaries?
11. What is the distribution channel? What are the functions of distribution channels?
12. What are some alternative channel arrangements?
13. What are the three degrees of market coverage for consumer products?
14. Explain some of the criteria that managers must consider when deciding the mode of transportation.
15. What are the goals of promotion?
16. What is the promotional mix, and what options are available in this mix?
17. Explain integrated marketing communications (IMC).
18. List the factors that affect the promotional mix.
19. What is the goal of supply chain management? What are the logistical components of the supply chain?
20. What are some of the key decisions in managing the logistical flow of products?
21. What are some of the trends in marketing?

CREATIVE THINKING CASE

Advertisers Score with the World Cup

What sporting event is televised in 258 countries and watched by more passionate fans than any other? If you guessed the Olympics, you'd be wrong. It's the World Cup football (soccer) matches, which last a month and are held every four years. In 2010, the World Cup was held in South Africa, the first time on the continent. The plan was met with much skepticism but 3.2 million fans attended the games (most seemed to have vuvuzelas). This was the third highest attendance ever. An estimated 8 billion game views were tracked (that's person games), and Web surfers registered over 12 billion page views at www.fifaworldcup.com. Online venues such as chat rooms, blogs, and discussion boards added another media channel for fans to get more of the action. And 2010 saw the introduction of a 3-D broadcast and other innovation.

Soccer's worldwide popularity makes it a prime advertising buy for many global companies who want to get their message out to these large audiences. More than 240 million players on 1.4 million teams around the world play the game, supporting its claim to be the world's favourite sport. As the FIFA World Cup website explains, "the FIFA World Cup reaches an audience of a size and diversity that is unrivalled by any other single-sports body. Add to this a passion for the game found in all corners of the world, and you have a sporting, social, and marketing phenomenon." As a result, companies vie to become official partners with global marketing rights and custom opportunities. The 2010 FIFA World Cup official partners were Adidas, Coca-Cola, Emirates, Hyundai, Sony, and Visa. In addition, Anheuser Busch, MTN, Castrol, McDonald's, Satyam, and Continental are listed as official sponsors.

The global nature of the World Cup presents major challenges as well as opportunities for its advertisers. Unlike the Grey Cup, which focuses on Canada, the World Cup requires even greater levels of creativity to produce ads that make a strong connection with soccer fans from very diverse cultures. Ads may have to appeal to viewers in countries as different as Ireland, Mexico, Malaysia, and Bangladesh.

Companies accomplish this task in various ways. They can select the countries that see their ads. Some have one ad for all countries, whereas others customize ads. Some companies use a series of ads that create an ongoing story employing visual communication rather than relying on spoken text. In the lead-up to South Africa 2010, Anheuser-Busch, which spent more for its 2006 World Cup ads than it did for its Olympics or Super Bowl ads, re-ran its 2006 "flowing beer" commercial. People in the stands at a sporting event do the "wave," holding cards that show beer flowing from a Budweiser bottle into a glass, which then empties. The 2010 pre-event version used the idea of anticipation, the consumer anticipates the beer just as he or she does the World Cup.

In the Budweiser tradition of humour based on the sports experience, Anheuser-Busch created "The Kick" for 2010. In this ad, the game has come down to the penalty kick. First, the fans at one end of the pitch hold up cards showing a hula dancer, choreographed to distract the keeper; then, those behind the net hold up cards depicting an icy cold Budweiser to distract the player taking the kick. Go online to see the result!

"If you get too complicated, you lose people with different cultures and perspectives," says Tony Ponturo, vice president of global sports marketing for the brewer.

Thinking Critically

1. What are some of the challenges global marketers encounter when developing advertising and promotional campaigns? How does the type of product affect the promotional strategies?

2. You work for an ad agency that has a World Cup sponsor as a client. What approach would you recommend for your agency as it develops a campaign—universal, customized for each geographical region, or something else, and why?

3. Check out www.FIFA.com. What types of companies could benefit from placing ads on the FIFA website, and how can they use the Internet effectively to promote their products?

SOURCES: "Marketing & TV," Fédération Internationale de Football Association, http://www.fifa.com, May 3, 2006; Aaron O. Patrick, "World Cup's advertisers hope one size fits all," *Wall Street Journal*, March 28, 2006, p. B7; "The Wave," TV commercials, budweiser.com, http://www.budweiser.com, May 3, 2006; "World Cup advertising analysis," *Analyst Wire*, March 3, 2006, http://galenet.thomsonlearning.com; "3 billion eyes to view World Cup opener," http://www.worldcupblog.org/world-cup-2006/3-billion-eyes-to-view-world-cup-opener.html, February 26, 2009; "FIFA e-Activity Report 2010," http://www.fifa-e-activityreport.com, December 22, 2012; "TV by the Numbers," http://tvbythenumbers.zap2it.com/category/2010-fifa-world-cup-tv-ratings/, December 21, 2012; Futures sport+entertainment, 2011, "+ViewerTrack: 2010 FIFA World Cup," http://initiative.com/sites/default/files/ViewerTrack_2010_FIFA.pdf, December 22, 2011; Budweiser, "The Kick," commercial, 2010, http://www.youtube.com/watch?v=QUc0GZhwny8, December 22, 2011.

Making the Connection

Achieving World-Class Operations Management

In this chapter, we will be looking at the management of the *operations* area of a business. A classic example of both the issues related to achieving world-class operations management and the truly integrative nature of operations is Harley-Davidson. Harley-Davidson definitely epitomizes world-class operations and offers many lessons for companies struggling to get there. For years, Harley tried to sell freedom and adventure, but with a poor-quality product sold at a high price because of outdated and inefficient facilities. Its *financial performance* was extremely poor, because it simply did not *meet customer needs*—poor *quality* at a high price did not provide the customer with anything of *value*. Once it stopped trying to produce quantity and focused instead on quality, Harley turned it all around. Today, the company is a leader in quality management. But it required a view of the business as a whole—meeting the needs of the customer (*marketing*) through *committed employees* (*human resources*) and providing quality (*operations*) at the lowest cost to improve the bottom line (*finance*) while uniting all the *stakeholders* in the "Harley-Davidson family."

As explained in the chapter, sound operations management is vital to the financial success of the company because this area accounts for as much as three-quarters of the company's costs. It is a wonderful example of the integrative nature of business, as it must work very closely with the other functional areas to achieve maximum financial performance. Most obviously, operations must develop processes to provide for the demand created and forecasted by marketing, but it must also work with marketing to develop and design products so that the operations processes used to provide them are the most efficient and effective, and the distribution of those products—both an operations and a marketing issue—is done efficiently, cost-effectively, and in a manner that meets the customers' needs. Similarly, operations must work with human resources to have the

right numbers of the best-qualified people available to produce products and service customers, as well as deciding whether to replace this human effort with robots or other applications of *technology*. In fact, most of the decisions made in the operations area have wider functional implications. For example, implementing a flexible manufacturing system is expensive but needs little labour to operate and provides consistent quality products that meet individual customer specifications, whereas the choice of location can affect transportation costs and thus the final cost of the product as well as the availability and cost of labour. Choice of location also has dramatic marketing implications—for some products, customer convenience is key, as is the location of the competition. And if the location is *international*, that just magnifies the implications.

An excellent example in the chapter of the need for a successful business to integrate operations with the other functional areas is that of Designlore with its "Right the First Time" approach to designing products. Designlore recognizes the need to integrate *innovative* design that meets customer needs with traditional engineering and operations principles in order to provide products that are designed in a way that keeps all members of the supply chain satisfied, from engineering right through to the final consumer.

Another area where we can see the integration of operations with the other facets of our business model is in the external environment. Many businesses today are faced with environmental challenges in an effort to meet their operational goals. For example, in the *social* environment, consumers are expecting customized products of greater quality delivered in a timely manner at a reasonable price. This requires using whatever technology is available to allow the company to stay ahead of the competition, and improving relationships with suppliers and vendors (both important stakeholder groups), so that there is a smooth flow from provider to consumer. If consumers don't get what they want, they will simply go to the increasing number of competitors in the *global economic* environment who can often produce at a lower cost, and they will frequently do this at breakneck speed, using technology to shop over the Internet, switching their loyalties at the click of a mouse!

The technology that is available to the operations area of a business has improved tremendously. In this chapter, we outline many of these innovations. One of the most integrative examples of technology is manufacturing resource planning II (MRPII). It uses a complex computerized system to integrate data from the different departments of the company, so that they are all working as one to meet customer needs. Enterprise resource planning (ERP) takes this a step further by going outside the business and integrating information about suppliers and customers into the system. These technologies and others help to manage the supply chain so that the entire sequence, from securing inputs into the process to delivering goods to the consumer, is done in a manner that meets the needs of the customer at the highest possible level.

Operations management is also an excellent example of the management process at work. You will read in the chapter about production *planning* and *control*, and the specific tools and techniques that are used to plan and control the production process. Quality control is a particularly important issue for management in meeting the customers' needs for a quality product. Part of the process is also deciding on the layout for the production or service facility, which involves *organizing* the company's resources in the most appropriate way to produce goods or provide services to the customer efficiently. The final management function is pivotal—*motivating*—as we know that workers must be committed to the task for it all to come together. Operations managers working directly with the workers who produce the goods or services for the customers have the ultimate responsibility to gain that commitment.

In this chapter, you'll learn about many trends in operations that allow companies to both enhance innovation to meet changing customer needs in a timely manner and adapt to changes in technology. At the same time, they are improving quality and keeping costs down. One very critical trend in operations that has major integrative implications is sustainability. Because of the wide-reaching implications of this trend, we have integrated examples throughout each chapter of companies operating sustainably. Take a good look at the examples and integrate them with your understanding of business as a whole—operating sustainability is a trend that is definitely here to stay.

chapter 15

Achieving World-Class Operations Management

BOMBARDIER—USING ROBOTS INCREASES SAFETY AND QUALITY

When Bombardier Aerospace decided to create a new line of aircraft, it soon realized it also needed to create a new way of building planes. The Canadian transportation giant felt the market was ready for a short-haul jetliner it called the C Series. But assembling the plane by hand presented numerous problems, including how to work safely around its 3.7-metre-wide fuselage and how to keep costs low while quality remained high.

So management at Bombardier decided on a "clean sheet" approach—starting from the beginning and designing the manufacturing process as if it had never been done before. This process of re-engineering focused on operations management, an approach to becoming more efficient that starts at the top of an organization and flows down. It all pointed to one primary solution: robots.

Bombardier started with six robots, using them in its Mirabel and Saint-Laurent plants. At the Mirabel plant, 40 kilometres north of Montréal, the C series jets undergo final assembly by these sophisticated machines. The robots weigh about 11 tonnes each, allowing them to move and manipulate the jetliner's large pieces while riveting them together. Using the robots is expected to save Bombardier about 40 hours per assembly compared to having people do the work, reducing the production time from 57 hours per jetliner to about 17.

Says François Minville, vice-president of C Series manufacturing with Bombardier: "The use of the robots will enable us to offer a superior aircraft at the best cost to our operators." The robots can extend to nearly six metres in height, and their heavy weight provides stability that can't be matched by scaffolding or gantries. The precision of the robots' drilling and riveting is seldom achieved by humans on the repetitive tasks involved in the assembly.

The result at Bombardier will be fewer hours for employees in the assembly process, but Bombardier says no jobs will be lost. There are potential benefits for the staff as well. The thinking goes that with the robots doing the repetitive and physically difficult jobs, workers are free to learn new technologies and become more productive, while taking fewer risks and avoiding repetitive strain injuries. Ultimately, Bombardier should save time and money while increasing quality and productivity.

The clean sheet approach does not apply just to the C Series assembly techniques. The jetliner will also be much lighter than past models because Bombardier is using carbon fibre and other advanced materials to reduce the mass of

STRINGER/REUTERS

key structural and body components. A lighter plane uses less fuel to move its cargo and can help reduce pollution.

After an uncertain start to its development, the production process for the C Series is operating smoothly. As of this writing, the company has orders for more than 100 jetliners, with a sticker price of about $65 million each.[1]

THINKING CRITICALLY

As you read this chapter, consider the following questions:

1. How can a "clean sheet" approach be applied to other problems faced by businesses?

2. Bombardier talks about the benefits to employees of not having to do repetitive assembly work. Is there another side to this?

3. What are some of the benefits to Bombardier of re-engineering its aircraft manufacturing process?

SOURCES: Bombardier Aerospace, "Bombardier to Combine Efficiency and Quality in Manufacturing of CSeries Aircraft," Press Release, May 31, 2011, http://www.bombardier.com/en/aerospace/media-centre/press-releases/details?docID=0901260d8017c5c1; "Bombardier uses robots in CSeries aircraft assembly," ReinforcedPlastics.com, 18 June 2011, http://www.reinforcedplastics.com/view/18465/bombardier-uses-robots-in-cseriesaircraft-assembly/; http://www.online.wsj.com/article/BT-CO-20110531-711822.html; Canadian Manufacturing Daily Staff, "Bombardier announces US$665 million CSeries order; will use robots in assembly," June 1, 2011, http://www.canadianmanufacturing.com/general/bombardier-announces-us665-million-cseries-order-will-use-robots-in-assembly-33384; Susanna Ray and Rachel Layne, "Bombardier CSeries Gets Deal While Qatar Goes on Hold," Bloomberg, Jun 20, 2011, http://www.bloomberg.com/news/2011-06-20/bombardier-wins-one-cseries-deal-loses-second-as-qatar-retreats.html.

Finding the most efficient and effective methods of producing the goods or services it sells to customers is an ongoing focus of nearly every type of business organization. Today more than ever, changing consumer expectations, technological advances, and increased competition are all forcing business organizations to rethink where, when, and how they will produce products or services.

Manufacturers have discovered that it is no longer enough simply to push products through the factory and onto the market. Consumers demand high quality at reasonable prices. They also expect manufacturers to deliver products in a timely manner. Companies that can't meet these expectations often face strong competition from businesses that can. To compete, many manufacturers are reinventing how they make their products by automating their factories, developing new production processes, using quality control techniques, and tightening their relationships with suppliers.

Service organizations are also facing challenges. Their customers are demanding better service, shorter waits, and more individualized attention. Just like manufacturers, service organizations are using new methods to deliver what customers need and want. Banks, for example, use technology such as ATMs and the Internet to make their services more easily accessible to customers. Many universities and colleges now offer weekend and even online courses for students who find it more convenient. Tax services are filing tax returns via computer.

In this chapter, we examine how manufacturers and service companies manage and control the creation of products and services. We'll discuss production planning, including the choices companies must make concerning the type of production process they will use, the location where production will occur, the design of the facility, and the management of resources needed in production. Next, we'll explain routing and scheduling, two critical tasks for controlling production and operations efficiency. Many businesses are improving productivity by employing quality control methods and automation. We'll discuss these methods before summarizing some of the trends affecting production and operations management.

LO1 PRODUCTION AND OPERATIONS MANAGEMENT—AN OVERVIEW

production
The creation of products and services by turning inputs, such as natural resources, raw materials, human resources, and capital, into outputs, which are products and services.

operations management
Management of the production process.

Production, the creation of products and services, is an essential function in every company. Production turns inputs—such as natural resources, raw materials, human resources, and capital—into outputs, which are products and services. This process is shown in Exhibit 15.1. Managing this conversion process is the role of operations management.

In the 1980s, many Canadian industries, such as automotive and steel, lost customers to foreign competitors because their production systems could not provide the quality customers demanded. As a result, most Canadian companies, both large and small, now consider a focus on quality to be a central component of effective operations management.

The goal of customer satisfaction, closely linked to quality, is also an important part of effective production and operations. In the past, the manufacturing function in most companies was focused inward. Manufacturing had little contact with customers and didn't always understand their needs and desires. Today, however, stronger links between marketing and manufacturing have encouraged production managers to be more outwardly focused and to consider decisions in light of their effect on customer satisfaction. Service companies have also found that making operating decisions with customer satisfaction in mind can be a competitive advantage.

Concept in Action

With oil reserves second only to Saudi Arabia, Alberta is a vast supplier of crude oil worldwide. Unlike the smooth petroleum that gushes from Arabian wells, however, most of Alberta's oil has to be mined from oil-rich sands. The process is rigorous: 400-ton trucks transport excavated bitumen to crushers and mixers that separate the sands from the oil, and the resulting slurry travels kilometres of pipeline to North American refineries. What are key inputs in the mining of the oil sands?

Operations managers, the personnel charged with managing and supervising the conversion process, play a vital role in today's business. They often control about three-fourths of a company's assets (e.g., inventories, machinery, and building facilities) and make decisions that affect wages and benefits. They work closely with other major functions of the company, such as marketing, finance, accounting, and human resources, to help ensure that the company produces its goods and provides its services profitably, and continually satisfies customers. They face the challenge of combining people and other resources to produce high-quality goods and services in a timely manner and at a reasonable cost. Working with marketing, they help to decide which products to make or which services to offer. They become involved with the development and design of goods and determine what production processes will be most effective.

Exhibit 15.1	Production Process for Products and Services

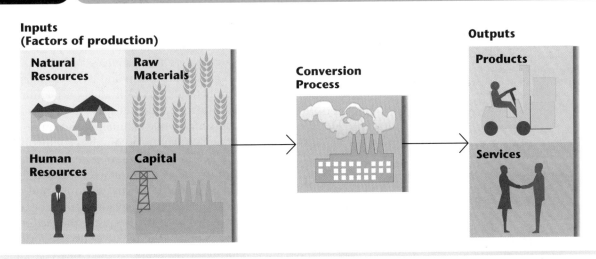

From its storied creation in post-war Italy to its big-screen immortalization in movies like *Roman Holiday* and *Quadrophenia*, the Vespa scooter has a reputation for romance, rebellion, and style. Manufactured by Italy's Piaggio, the Vespa's svelte, stainless-steel chassis and aeronautic-inspired designs are seen everywhere in Europe and more and more in Canada. The Piaggio Group presently operates factories in Italy, Spain, India, and China. What important production-planning decisions does Piaggio need to make as it considers expanding its markets?

MARIO VERIN/TIPS RM/GLOWIMAGES

Production and operations management involves three main types of decisions that are made at three different stages:

1. Production planning. The first decisions facing operations managers come at the planning stage. At this stage, managers decide where, when, and how production will occur. They obtain resources and determine site locations.
2. Production control. At this stage, the decision-making process focuses on scheduling, controlling quality and costs, and the day-to-day operations of running a factory or service facility.
3. Improving production and operations. The final stage of operations management focuses on developing more efficient methods of producing the company's goods or services.

These three types of decisions are ongoing and often occur simultaneously. In the following sections, we will take a closer look at the decisions and considerations companies face in each of these stages of production and operations management.

Gearing Up: Production Planning

An important part of operations management is **production planning**. During production planning, the company considers the resources available (e.g., natural resources, raw materials, human resources, and capital) and its own strategic goals in an effort to find the best production methods. Good production planning balances goals that might conflict, such as providing high-quality service while keeping operating costs down, or keeping profits high while maintaining adequate inventories of finished products. Sometimes it is very difficult to accomplish conflicting goals.

Production planning is a long-term process involving three phases. Strategic, long-term planning has a time frame of three to five years. It focuses on which goods to produce, in what quantity, and where they should be produced. Tactical, medium-term planning decisions cover about two years. They are concerned with the layout of the factory or service facilities, where and how to obtain the resources needed for production, and labour issues. Short-term planning, with a one-year time frame,

production planning
The aspect of operations management in which the company considers its resources and its own strategic goals in an effort to determine the best production methods.

converts these broader goals into specific production plans and materials management strategies.

Four important decisions must be made in production planning. They involve the type of production process that will be used, site selection, facility layout, and resource planning.

THE PRODUCTION PROCESS: HOW DO WE MAKE IT?

LO2

In production planning, the first decision involves which type of production process—the way in which a good is made—best fits with the company's goals and customer demands. An important consideration is the type of good or service being produced, as different goods and services will typically require different production processes. In general, there are three types of production: mass production, mass customization, and customization. In addition to production type, operations managers also classify production processes in two ways: by how inputs are converted into outputs and by the timing of the process.

ONE FOR ALL: MASS PRODUCTION Mass production, manufacturing many identical goods at once, was a product of the Industrial Revolution. Henry Ford's Model T automobile is a good example of mass production. From 1909 to 1927, more than 15 million Model T cars were produced; each was identical, right down to its colour. If you wanted a car in any colour except black, you were out of luck. Canned goods, over-the-counter drugs, and household appliances are examples of goods that are still mass produced. The emphasis in mass production is on keeping manufacturing costs low by producing highly uniform products by using repetitive and standardized processes. Mass production, therefore, relies heavily on standardization, mechanization, and specialization.

JUST FOR YOU: CUSTOMIZING GOODS In mass customization, goods are produced by using mass production techniques but only up to a point. At that point, the product or service is custom tailored to the needs or desires of individual customers. Many Canadian furniture manufacturers use mass customization to produce couches and chairs to customer specifications, usually within 30 days. The basic frames used to make the furniture are the same, but automated machinery pre-cuts the colour and type of leather or fabric ordered by each customer. These coverings are then added to the frame through mass production techniques. Dynasty Furniture Mfg. Ltd. of Mississauga, Ontario, uses mass customization for its sofas and other products. Another good example is paint. You can choose from hundreds of colours with no delay.

Customization is the opposite of mass production. In customization, the company produces unique goods or services according to the specific needs or wants of individual customers. For example, a print shop might handle a variety of projects, including newsletters, brochures, stationery, and reports. Each print job varies in quantity, type of printing process, binding, colour of ink, and type of paper. A manufacturing company that produces goods in response to customer orders is called a job shop.

Some types of service businesses also deliver customized services. Doctors, for instance, usually must consider the individual illnesses and circumstances of each patient before developing a customized treatment plan. Real-estate agents also develop a customized service plan for each customer based on the type of house the person is selling or wants to buy. The differences between mass production, mass customization, and customization are summarized in Exhibit 15.2.

production process
The way in which a good is made.

mass production
The ability to manufacture many identical goods at once.

mass customization
A manufacturing process in which goods are mass produced up to a point and then custom tailored to the needs or desires of individual customers.

customization
The production of goods or services one at a time according to the specific needs or wants of individual customers.

job shop
A manufacturing company that produces goods in response to customer orders.

Concept *Check*

What is mass production?

Differentiate mass customization from customization.

CHAPTER 15 Achieving World-Class Operations Management **447**

Exhibit 15.2 | Classification of Production Types

Mass Production	**Mass Customization**	**Customization**
Highly uniform products or services. Many products made sequentially.	Uniform standardized production to a point, then unique features added to each product.	Each product or service produced according to individual customer requirements.
Examples: Breakfast cereals, soft drinks, and iPads.	**Examples:** Dell products, tract homes, and TaylorMade golf clubs.	**Examples:** Custom homes, legal services, and haircuts.

Converting Inputs to Outputs

Production involves converting *inputs* (machinery, raw materials, parts, human resources) into *outputs* (products or services). In a manufacturing company, the inputs, the production process, and the final outputs are usually obvious. Harley-Davidson, for instance, converts steel, rubber, paint, labour, and other inputs into motorcycles. The production process in a service company involves a less apparent conversion. For example, a hospital converts the knowledge and skills of its medical personnel, along with equipment and supplies from a variety of sources, into health care services for patients. Exhibit 15.3 provides examples of the inputs and outputs used by different businesses.

There are two basic processes for converting inputs into outputs. In **process manufacturing**, the basic input (raw materials, parts) is *broken down* into one or more outputs (products). For example, bauxite (the input) is processed to extract aluminum (the output); or trees (the input) are cut into lumber (the output). The **assembly process** is just the opposite. The basic inputs, like parts, raw materials, or human resources, are either *combined* to create the output or *transformed* into the output. An airplane, for example, is created by assembling thousands of parts. Steel manufacturers use heat to transform iron and other materials into steel. In services, customers may play a role in the transformation process. For example, a tax preparation service combines the knowledge of the tax preparer with the client's information about personal finances to complete tax returns.

Production Timing

A second consideration in choosing a production process is timing. A **continuous process** uses long production runs that can last days, weeks, or months without equipment shutdowns. It is best for high-volume, low-variety products with standardized parts, such as nails, glass, and paper. Some services also use a continuous process (oil refining for example). Your local electric company is one example. Per-unit costs are low, and production is easy to schedule.

In an **intermittent process**, short production runs are used to make batches of different products. Machines are shut down to change them to make different products at different times. This process is best for low-volume, high-variety products, such as those produced by mass customization or customization. Job shops are examples of companies that use an intermittent process.

---

process manufacturing
A production process in which the basic input is broken down into one or more outputs (products).

assembly process
A production process in which the basic inputs are either combined to create the output or transformed into the output.

continuous process
A production process that uses long production runs lasting days, weeks, or months without equipment shut-downs; generally used for high-volume, low-variety products with standardized parts.

intermittent process
A production process that uses short production runs to make batches of different products; generally used for low-volume, high-variety products.

Mass customization has produced a thriving assemble-to-order society. This revolution in manufacturing is fueled, in part, by pop culture, where the compulsion to parade individuality is a hot commodity. Expressing oneself has never been easier. Consumers can design a new pair of sneakers with Vans Customs, build their own bags at Timbuk2, and customize a snowboard using the Burton Series 13 customization program—all while munching a pack of personalized M&M's candies. What developments have made mass customization a viable method of production?

COURTESY OF TIMBUK2

Although some service companies use continuous processes, most rely on intermittent processes. For instance, a restaurant preparing gourmet meals, a physician performing physical examinations or surgical operations, and an advertising agency developing ad campaigns for business clients all customize their services to suit each customer. They use the intermittent process. Note that their "production runs" might be very short—one grilled salmon or one eye exam at a time.

Concept Check

Define process manufacturing and the assembly process.

What is the difference between continuous and intermittent processes?

LOCATION, LOCATION, LOCATION: WHERE DO WE MAKE IT?

LO3

A big decision that managers must make early in production and operations planning is where to put the facility. Another determinant is who needs to access the facility (e.g., retail stores and restaurants or hospitals and schools). Another decision is whether to

Exhibit 15.3	Converting Inputs to Outputs

TYPE OF ORGANIZATION	INPUT	OUTPUT
Airline	Pilots, crew, flight attendants, reservations system, ticketing agents, customers, airplanes, fuel, maintenance crews, ground facilities	Movement of customers and freight
Grocery store	Merchandise, building, clerks, supervisors, store fixtures, shopping carts, customers	Groceries for customers
High school	Faculty, curriculum, buildings, classrooms, library, auditorium, gymnasium, students, staff, supplies,	Graduates, public service
Manufacturer	Machinery, raw materials, plant, workers, managers	Finished products for consumers and other companies
Restaurant	Food, cooking equipment, serving personnel, chefs, dishwashers, host, patrons, furniture, fixtures	Meals for patrons

have a central facility or multiple facilities (e.g., most cities with an IKEA store will only have one store, but Loblaws has multiple locations within a city). The facility's location affects operating and shipping costs and, ultimately, the price of the product or service and the company's ability to compete. Mistakes made at this stage can be expensive. Moving a factory or service facility is difficult and costly; a wrong location can result in extra costs or fewer customers. Companies must weigh a number of factors to make the right decision.

AVAILABILITY OF PRODUCTION INPUTS As we discussed earlier, organizations need certain resources to produce products and services for sale. Access to these resources, or inputs, is a huge consideration in site selection. Executives must assess the availability of raw materials, parts, and equipment for each production site under consideration. The costs of shipping raw materials and finished goods can be as much as 25 percent of a manufacturer's total cost, so locating a factory where these and other costs are as low as possible can make a major contribution to a company's success. Companies that use heavy or bulky raw materials, for example, might choose to be located near suppliers. Metal refiners want to be near ore deposits, oil refiners near oil fields, paper mills near forests, and food processors near farms.

Payroll costs can vary widely from one location to another because of differences in the cost of living, the number of jobs available, and the size, skills, and productivity of unionization of the local workforce.

Low labour costs were one reason that Globe Motors, a manufacturer of motors and power steering systems for automotive, aerospace, and defence applications, chose Portugal as the site for its production facility. In addition to low labour costs, Portugal offers manufacturers the lowest operating costs in the European Union (e.g., taxes).[2]

MARKETING FACTORS Businesses must also evaluate how their facility location will affect their ability to serve their customers. For some companies, it might not be necessary to be located near customers. Instead, the company will need to assess the difficulty and costs of distributing its goods to customers from the chosen location.

Making Ethical Choices

SWEATING IT OUT AT NEW ERA CAP

As production manager for New Era Cap, the largest North American manufacturer of ball caps (including selected NHL, NBA, and Major League Baseball teams), you supervise operations at three factories. The oldest plant, in Derby, New York, has 600 workers and produces 120,000 caps a week, the lowest production rate of the three plants. The Derby factory also has the highest worker absentee rate of any plant, with as many as 13 percent of workers calling in sick on any given day.

In an attempt to bring the Derby plant up to the same level of efficiency as the other two, you've implemented several changes in the past few years. You've introduced new production schedules, made staff cuts, and tried to reduce absentee rates.

Unhappy with the changes you've made, Derby workers went on strike 10 months ago. After New Era executives refused to settle with the striking workers' demands for reduced hours and pay raises, their union, the Communications Workers of America (CWA), issued public statements accusing the Derby plant of "sweatshop"

working conditions. At the CWA's urging, the United Students Against Sweatshops (USAS) started a campaign to get colleges and universities to boycott New Era caps. Several universities have already joined the boycott.

You are convinced that the Derby plant is not a sweatshop. You've shifted most of Derby's production to New Era's other two factories with minimal problems. The union now says it will end the strike and call off the boycott if the company grants immediate pay raises and health benefit increases to all Derby workers. You feel this is extortion.

ETHICAL DILEMMA: Should you recommend that New Era's president agree to the union's demands?

SOURCES: "New Era Union Plans Boycott," _Buffalo Business First_, July 20, 2001; "Cap Maker Shifts Production after Walkout," _Buffalo Business First_, July 16, 2001; "New Era Says 'Sweatshop' Label Is False," _Buffalo Business First_, June 4, 2002; "New Era Cap Makes New Offer to CWA Strikers," _Buffalo Business First_, February 26, 2002; all sources downloaded from http://buffalo.bizjournals.com.

Other companies might find that locating near customers can provide marketing advantages. When a factory, retail, or service centre is close to customers, the company can often offer better service at a lower cost. Other companies might gain a competitive advantage by locating their facilities so that customers can easily buy their products or services. The location of competitors might also be a factor. Businesses with more than one facility might also need to consider how far to spread their locations to maximize market coverage. Besides the familiar stand-alone Tim Hortons outlets, you can find Tim Hortons in shopping malls, highway outlets, universities, hospitals, etc.

MANUFACTURING ENVIRONMENT Another factor to consider is the manufacturing environment in a potential location. Some localities have a strong existing manufacturing base. Those areas are likely to offer greater availability of resources, such as manufacturing workers, better accessibility to suppliers and transportation, and other factors that can increase a plant's operating efficiency.

Industry Week magazine conducts a regular survey of the manufacturing climate offered by areas around the world. Each area is rated on the productivity of its manufacturing sector, the percentage of the local workforce employed in manufacturing, the contribution of manufacturing to the area's overall economy, and several other factors.

LOCAL INCENTIVES Incentives offered by countries, states, or cities might also influence site selection. Tax breaks are a common incentive. A locality might reduce the amount of taxes the company will pay on income, real estate, utilities, or payroll. Local governments also sometimes offer exemption from certain regulations or financial assistance to attract or keep production facilities in their area. For example, Portugal helped entice Globe Motors by offering 7.6 million USD in financial incentives, as well as tax breaks and assistance with employee-training programs.[3]

INTERNATIONAL LOCATION CONSIDERATIONS Like Globe Motors, many manufacturers have chosen to move much of their production to international locations in recent years. There are often sound financial reasons for considering this step. Labour costs are considerably lower in countries like Singapore, China, and Mexico. Foreign countries might also have fewer regulations governing how factories operate. A foreign location might place production closer to new markets.

Designing the Facility

After the site location decision has been made, the next focus in production planning is the facility's layout. Here, the goal is to determine the most efficient and effective design for the particular production process. A manufacturer might opt for a U-shaped production line, for example, rather than a long, straight one to allow products and workers to move more quickly from one area to another.

Service organizations must also consider layout, but they are more concerned with how it affects customer behaviour. It might be more convenient for a hospital to place its freight elevators in the centre of the building, for example, but doing so might block the flow of patients, visitors, and medical personnel between floors and departments.

There are three *main* types of facility layouts: process, product, and fixed-position layouts. All three are illustrated in Exhibit 15.4. Cellular manufacturing combines at least some aspect of the three types.

PROCESS LAYOUT: ALL WELDERS STAND HERE The **process layout** arranges workflow around the production process. All workers performing similar tasks are grouped together. Products pass from one workstation to another (but not necessarily to every workstation). For example, all grinding would be done in one area, all assembling in another, and all

What characteristics contribute to a city's manufacturing climate? Find out by reading more at *Industry Week*'s website:
www.industryweek.com

process layout
A facility arrangement in which work flows according to the production process. All workers performing similar tasks are grouped together, and products pass from one workstation to another.

Concept *Check*

Discuss how each of the following impacts the location of production:

• Availability of production inputs
• Marketing factors
• Manufacturing environment
• Local incentives
• International location considerations

Exhibit 15.4 | Facility Layouts

Process layout arranges workflow around the production process. All workers performing similar tasks are grouped together.

© RIA NOVOSTI/ALAMY

Products that require a continuous or repetitive production process use the product layout.

© LOU LINWEI/ALAMY

A fixed-position layout lets the product stay in one place while workers and machinery move to it as needed.

© JUSTIN KASE ZI2TZ/ALAMY

inspection in yet another. The process layout is best for companies that produce small numbers of a wide variety of products, typically by using general-purpose machines that can be changed rapidly to new operations for different product designs. For example, a machine shop would use a process layout as do banks and hospitals.

PRODUCT LAYOUT: MOVING DOWN THE LINE Products that require a continuous or repetitive production process use the product (or assembly line) layout. When large quantities of a product must be processed on an ongoing basis, the workstations or departments are arranged in a line with products moving along the line. Automobile and appliance manufacturers, as well as food-processing plants, usually use a product layout. Service companies may also use a product layout for routine processing operations. For example, the airline industry has people move through the system to check in themselves and their baggage.

product (assembly line) layout
A facility arrangement in which workstations or departments are arranged in a line with products moving along the line.

FIXED-POSITION LAYOUT: STAYING PUT Some products cannot be put on an assembly line or moved about in a plant. A fixed-position layout lets the product stay in one place while workers and machinery move to it as needed. Products that are difficult to move—ships, airplanes, and construction projects (e.g., office buildings, roads, mass transit systems)—are typically produced using a fixed-position layout. Limited space at a project site often means that parts of the product must be assembled at other sites, transported to the fixed site, and then assembled. Other examples of the fixed-position layout are on-site services like housecleaning services, pest control, and landscaping.

fixed-position layout
A facility arrangement in which the product stays in one place and workers and machinery move to it as needed.

CELLULAR MANUFACTURING: A START-TO-FINISH FOCUS Cellular manufacturing combines some aspects of process, product, and/or fixed-position layout. Work cells are small, self-contained production units that include several machines and workers arranged in a compact, sequential order. Each work cell performs all or most of the tasks necessary to complete a manufacturing order. There are usually between 5 and 10 workers in a cell, and they are trained to perform all of the steps in the production process. The goal is to create a team environment where team members are involved in production from beginning to end. Clothing manufacturing can use cellular manufacturing by having small work cells completing all the work of each order.

cellular manufacturing
Production technique that uses small, self-contained production units, each performing all or most of the tasks necessary to complete a manufacturing order.

PULLING IT TOGETHER: RESOURCE PLANNING

LO4

As part of the production-planning process, companies must ensure that the resources needed for production, such as raw materials, parts, and equipment, will be available at strategic moments in the production process. This can be a huge challenge. The components used to build just one Boeing airplane, for instance, number in the millions. Cost is also an important factor. In many industries, the cost of materials and supplies used in the production process amounts to as much as half of sales revenues. Resource planning is therefore a big part of any company's production strategy.

Resource planners begin by specifying which raw materials, parts, and components will be required, and when, in order to produce finished goods. To determine the amount of each item needed, the expected quantity of finished goods to be produced must be forecast. A bill of material is then drawn up that lists the items and the number of each required to make the product. Purchasing, or *procurement*, is the process of buying production inputs from various sources.

bill of material
A list of the items and the number of each required to make a given product.

purchasing
The process of buying production inputs from various sources; also called procurement.

MAKE OR BUY? Usually the first issue is the company's ability to make an item. The company must decide whether to make its production materials or buy them from outside sources. This is the make-or-buy decision. The quantity of items needed is one

make-or-buy decision
The determination by a company of whether to make its production materials or buy them from outside sources.

consideration. If a part is used in only one of many products, buying the part might be more cost-effective than making it. Buying standard items that are mass produced, such as screws, bolts, rivets, and nails, is usually cheaper and easier than producing them internally. Sometimes purchasing larger components from another manufacturing company is cost-effective as well. Also, other companies might have better quality because they produce large quantities of the product (e.g., tire manufacturers). Purchasing items from an outside source instead of making them internally is called **outsourcing**. Bombardier Inc., for example, purchases many of the components for its business aircraft (e.g., Lear) from other businesses that make them to Bombardier's specifications. If a product has special design features that need to be kept secret to protect a competitive advantage, however, a company might decide to produce those parts internally.

In deciding whether to make or buy, a company must also consider whether outside sources can provide high-quality supplies in a reliable manner. Having to shut down production because vital parts weren't delivered on time can be a costly disaster. Just as bad are inferior parts or materials, which cannot be used or can damage a company's reputation for producing high-quality goods. Therefore, companies that buy some or all of their production materials from outside sources should pay close attention to building strong relationships with quality suppliers.

INVENTORY MANAGEMENT: NOT JUST PARTS A company's **inventory** is the supply of goods it holds for use in production or for sale to customers. Deciding how much inventory to keep on hand is one of the biggest challenges facing operations managers. With large inventories, the company can meet most production and customer demands. Buying in large quantities can also allow a company to take advantage of quantity discounts. On the other hand, large inventories can tie up the company's money, are expensive to store, and can become obsolete or spoil (e.g., food).

Inventory management involves deciding how much of each type of inventory to keep on hand, and the ordering, receiving, storing, and tracking of it. The goal of inventory management is to keep down the costs of ordering and holding inventories while maintaining enough on hand for production and sales. Good inventory management enhances product quality, makes operations more efficient, and increases profits. Poor inventory management can result in dissatisfied customers, disrupted production, financial difficulties, and even bankruptcy.

There are three major costs associated with inventory: the cost of holding inventory, the cost of reordering frequently, and the cost of not keeping enough inventories on hand. The result of holding too much inventory (increased capital tied up and the physical storage used) and reordering too frequently (tracking, receiving, and re-stocking) is increased costs. The consequences of not having enough inventories when needed are just as severe. It can mean fewer sales, delayed production (and downtime for machinery and labour), and late delivery of orders. Managers must measure all three costs and try to minimize them.

To control inventory levels, managers often track the use and sales of certain inventory items. Most companies keep a **perpetual inventory**, a continuously updated list of inventory levels, orders, sales, and receipts, for all major items. Today, companies often use computers to track inventory levels, calculate order quantities, and issue purchase orders at the right times.

COMPUTERIZED RESOURCE PLANNING Many manufacturing companies have adopted computerized systems to control the flow of resources and inventory. **Materials requirement planning (MRP)** is one such system. MRP uses a master schedule to ensure that the materials, labour, and equipment needed for production are at the right places in the right amounts at the right times. The schedule is based on forecasts of demand for the company's products. It determines exactly what will be manufactured during the next few weeks or months and when the work will take place. Sophisticated computer programs coordinate all the elements of MRP. Orders are

---

outsourcing
The purchase of items from an outside source rather than making them internally.

How do companies decide whether to make or buy? Find out more at the Outsourcing Institute, a professional association where buyers and sellers network and connect:
www.outsourcing.com

inventory
The supply of goods that a company holds for use in production or for sale to customers.

inventory management
The determination of how much of each type of inventory a company will keep on hand and the ordering, receiving, storing, and tracking of inventory.

perpetual inventory
A continuously updated list of inventory levels, orders, sales, and receipts.

materials requirement planning (MRP)
A computerized system of controlling the flow of resources and inventory. A master schedule is used to ensure that the materials, labour, and equipment needed for production are at the right places in the right amounts at the right times.

placed so that materials will be available when they are needed for production. MRP helps ensure a smooth flow of finished products.

Manufacturing resource planning II (MRPII) was developed in the late 1980s to expand on MRP. It uses a complex computerized system to integrate data from many departments, including finance, marketing, accounting, engineering, and manufacturing. MRPII can generate a production plan for the company as well as management reports, forecasts, and financial statements. The system lets managers make more accurate forecasts and assess the impact of production plans on profitability. If one department's plans change, the effects of these changes on other departments are transmitted throughout the company.

Whereas MRP and MRPII systems are focused internally, enterprise resource planning (ERP) systems go a step further and incorporate information about the company's suppliers and customers into the flow of data. ERP unites all of a company's major departments into a single software program. For instance, production can call up sales information and know immediately how many units must be produced to meet customer orders. By providing information about the availability of resources, including both human resources and materials needed for production, the system allows for better cost control and eliminates production delays. The system automatically notes any changes, such as the closure of a plant for maintenance and repairs on a certain date or a supplier's inability to meet a delivery date, so that all functions can adjust accordingly. Both large and small organizations use ERP to improve operations.

manufacturing resource planning II (MRPII)
A complex, computerized system that integrates data from many departments to allow managers to forecast and assess the impact of production plans on profitability more accurately.

enterprise resource planning (ERP)
A computerized resource-planning system that incorporates information about the company's suppliers and customers with its internally generated data.

Keeping the Goods Flowing: The Supply Chain

In the past, the relationship between purchasers and suppliers was often competitive and antagonistic. Businesses used many suppliers and switched among them frequently. During contract negotiations, each side would try to get better terms at the expense of the other. Communication between purchasers and suppliers was often limited to purchase orders and billing statements.

Today, however, many companies are moving toward a new concept in supplier relationships. The emphasis is increasingly on developing a strong supply chain. The

supply chain
The entire sequence of securing inputs, producing goods, and delivering goods to customers.

Concept in Action

Walmart's retail dominance is built upon advanced logistics and inventory management. The company's vendor-managed inventory system puts the burden on suppliers to maintain stock until needed in stores. Radio frequency identification tags (RFID) help automate the flow of goods. Walmart's remarkable 2:1 sales-to-inventory ratio is expected to shrink further to a theoretical "zero inventory" state in which it won't pay for products until they're purchased by consumers. What costs are associated with keeping too much or too little inventory?

© DAVID MCNEW/GETTY IMAGES

supply chain can be thought of as the entire sequence of securing inputs, producing goods, and delivering goods to customers. If any links in this process are weak, chances are that customers—the end point of the supply chain—will end up dissatisfied.

Effective supply chain strategies reduce costs. For example, integration of the shipper and customer's supply chains allows companies to automate more processes and save time and money. Technology also improves supply chain efficiency by tracking goods through the various supply chain stages and also helping with logistics. With better information about production and inventory, companies can order and receive goods at the best time to keep inventory holding costs low but still satisfy needs.

Companies also need contingency plans for supply chain disruptions. Is there an alternative source of supply if a blizzard closes the airport so that cargo planes can't land or a drought causes crop failures? By thinking ahead, companies can avert major problems. The length and distance involved in a supply line is also a consideration. Importing parts from or outsourcing manufacturing to Asia creates a long supply chain for a manufacturer in Europe or Canada. Perhaps there are closer suppliers or manufacturers who can meet a company's needs at a lower overall cost, when transportation costs are included. Quality may also be a consideration. Companies should also reevaluate outsourcing decisions periodically.

Strategies for Supply Chain Management

Ensuring a strong supply chain requires that companies implement supply chain management strategies. Supply chain management focuses on smoothing transitions along the supply chain, with the ultimate goal of satisfying customers with quality products and services. A critical element of effective supply chain management is a close relationship with suppliers. In many cases, this means reducing the number of suppliers used and asking those suppliers to offer more services or better prices in return for an ongoing relationship. Instead of being viewed as "outsiders" in the production process, many suppliers are now seen as playing an important role in supporting the operations. They are expected to meet higher quality standards, offer suggestions that can help reduce production costs, and even contribute to the design of new products. The Expanding Around the Globe box shows the critical role of supply chain management for global companies.

TALK TO US: IMPROVING SUPPLIER COMMUNICATIONS Effective supply chain management requires the development of strong communications with suppliers. Technology, particularly the Internet, is providing new ways to do this. E-procurement, the process of purchasing supplies and materials online, is booming. Some manufacturing companies use the Internet to keep key suppliers informed about their requirements. Intel, for example, has set up a special website for its suppliers and potential suppliers. Would-be suppliers can visit the site to get information about doing business with Intel; once they are approved, they can access a secure area to make bids on Intel's current and future resource needs.

The Internet also streamlines purchasing by providing companies with quick access to a huge database of information about the products and services of hundreds of potential suppliers. Many large manufacturers now participate in *reverse auctions* online, whereby the manufacturer posts its specifications for the materials it requires. Potential suppliers then bid against each other to get the job. Reverse auctions can slash procurement costs.

Concept in Action

Manufacturing product labels for over 9,000 Estée Lauder cosmetics products would be impossible without enterprise resource planning (ERP). A daily data feed between ERP systems at Estée Lauder and label supplier Topflight ensures that machines produce only the labels necessary for the next production run. The data-transfer link is flexible enough to accommodate dynamic design changes to colours and label copy while eliminating purchase orders, invoices, and price negotiations. What quality and cost benefits does ERP deliver to manufacturers and their customers?

Expanding Around the Globe

SOPHISTICATED SUPPLY-CHAIN STRATEGIES KEEP PRODUCTS ON THE MOVE

Headquartered in Tokyo but with offices around the world, shipping company MOL is taking integrating with its customers to new levels. It is joining its customers in a series of joint ventures to build and operate dedicated ships for as long as 25 years. One such joint venture teamed MOL with a Chinese steel mill to build and sail ships bringing Brazilian iron ore and coal across the Pacific Ocean for processing.

Sophisticated supply chain systems that control every aspect of production and transportation are the key to making off-shore manufacturing work. Supply chain software monitors operations and continually makes adjustments, ensuring all processes are running at peak efficiency. By tightly mapping an entire sequence—from order to final delivery—and by automating it as much as possible, supply chain management can deliver products from across the world while at the same time cutting costs. Companies that can carry a small inventory and get paid faster improve their cash flow and profitability.

Acer, the second largest supplier of PCs and notebooks, is a Taiwanese computer and electronics maker that imports components from around the world and assembles them at factories in Taiwan and mainland China. It then reverses the flow by shipping these products to international buyers.

The synchronizing of trade is essential. If goods don't get into the stores in time, sales might be lost. Alternatively, the company might have to carry larger inventories to avoid sell-outs, but this would cut into profits. Companies need to continually monitor demand and react quickly by adjusting production. "This gets increasingly difficult when the supply chain stretches across thousands of miles and a dozen time zones," says David Bovet, managing director of Mercer Management Consulting, a Boston-based company that advises on business tactics. "There are strategies that smart companies are using to bring costs down to earth. Getting the most of lower labour costs overseas requires an emphasis on transportation, and supply-chain skills are a required core competency," he says. His advice to global manufacturers: Cooperate with shippers and integrate supply chains into one cohesive system.

The acknowledged master of supply chain dynamics is Dell, with its global logistics control room lined with big screens that monitor its shipping lanes at all times. Alongside Dell executives are representatives of its logistics suppliers for guidance and quick action if anything goes wrong.

Risk is part of international trade, and companies need to decide whether to play it safe with extra inventory or scramble if a disaster like a port strike occurs. Either way, they need to have contingency plans and be ready to react, and solid supply chain strategies will ensure they are prepared for any eventuality.[4]

Thinking Critically

1. Why are solid supply chain strategies so important?
2. What problems is a company likely to experience without such strategies in place?

Concept *in Action*

Managing an efficient supply chain is critical for businesses, especially when the product being delivered is a bouquet of fresh-cut flowers. To ensure that only the freshest, most colourful floral arrangement arrives for that special someone, Internet florist ProFlowers ships directly from the flower fields, bypassing the intermediary. This direct-from-the-grower strategy, combined with coordinated carrier scheduling and a 100 percent product-inspection policy, enables ProFlowers to deliver flowers twice as fresh as the competition's. What strategies help businesses create and maintain an effective supply chain?

FERNANDO VERGARA/AP PHOTO

electronic data interchange (EDI)
The electronic exchange of information between two trading partners.

routing
The aspect of production control that involves setting out the workflow, the sequence of machines and operations through which the product or service progresses from start to finish.

value-stream mapping
A routing technique that represents the flow of materials and information from suppliers through the factory and to customers.

scheduling
The aspect of production control that involves specifying and controlling the time required for each step in the production process.

However, there are risks with reverse auctions. For example, it can be difficult to establish and build ongoing relationships with specific suppliers using reverse auctions, because the job ultimately goes to the lowest bidder. Therefore, reverse auctions might not be an effective procurement process for critical production materials.[5] Another issue is that quality could suffer by buying at the lowest costs.

Another communications tool is **electronic data interchange (EDI)**, in which two trading partners exchange information electronically. EDI can be conducted via a linked computer system or over the Internet. The advantages of exchanging information with suppliers electronically include speed, accuracy, and lowered communication costs.

Dana Corporation, a manufacturer of auto and truck frames, has only one customer, New United Motor Manufacturing Inc. (NUMMI), a joint venture between Toyota and General Motors. In the past, NUMMI could give Dana only a six-week production forecast. A fax was sent to Dana each day updating NUMMI's needs. Dana and NUMMI then installed an EDI system that continually alerts Dana about NUMMI's purchasing requirements on an hourly basis. As a result, Dana has been able to cut its inventory, smooth its production scheduling, and meet NUMMI's needs more efficiently and rapidly.[6]

LO5 PRODUCTION AND OPERATIONS CONTROL

Every company needs to have systems in place to see that production and operations are carried out as planned and to correct errors when they are not. The coordination of materials, equipment, and human resources to achieve production and operating efficiencies is called *production control*. Two of its key aspects are routing and scheduling.

Routing: Where to Next?

Routing is the first step in production control. It sets out a workflow, that is, the sequence of machines and operations through which a product or service progresses from start to finish. Routing depends on the type of goods being produced and the facility layout. Good routing procedures increase productivity and cut unnecessary costs.

One useful tool for routing is **value-stream mapping**, where production managers "map" the flow from suppliers through the factory to customers. Simple icons represent the materials and information needed at various points in the flow. Value-stream mapping can help identify where bottlenecks might occur in the production process and is a valuable tool for visualizing how to improve production routing.

Electronics manufacturer Rockwell Collins used value-stream mapping to automate more of its purchasing operations. The company evaluated 23 areas to identify where process changes would improve efficiency. Based on the study, managers decided to automate three steps: request for quote, quote receipt and total purchase cost, and automated purchase order. The company implemented a new system that automatically sends requests for quotes to appropriate suppliers and evaluates the responses to determine which best meets Rockwell Collins' requirements. Once in place, the new systems allowed purchasing professionals to focus on strategic rather than routine purchase activities.[7]

Scheduling: When Do We Do It?

Closely related to routing is **scheduling**. Scheduling involves specifying and controlling the time required for each step in the production process. The operations manager prepares timetables showing the most efficient sequence of production and then tries to ensure that the necessary materials and labour are in the right place at the right time.

Scheduling is important to both manufacturing and service companies. The production manager in a factory schedules material deliveries, work shifts, and production processes. Trucking companies schedule drivers, clerks, truck maintenance, and repair with customer transportation needs. Scheduling at a polytechnic, college, or university entails deciding when to offer which courses, in which classrooms, with which instructors. A museum must schedule its special exhibits, ship the items to be displayed, market its services, and conduct educational programs and tours.

Scheduling can range from simple to complex. Giving numbers to customers waiting to be served in a bakery and making interview appointments with job applicants are examples of simple scheduling. Organizations that must produce large quantities of products or services, or service a diverse customer base, face more complex scheduling problems, such as an airline.

Three common scheduling tools used for complex situations are Gantt charts, the Critical Path Method (CPM), and Program Evaluation and Review Technique (PERT).

TRACKING PROGRESS WITH GANTT CHARTS Named after their originator, Henry Gantt, **Gantt charts** are bar graphs plotted on a timeline that show the relationship between scheduled and actual production. Exhibit 15.5 is an example. On the left, the chart lists the activities required to complete the job or project. Both the scheduled time and the actual time required for each activity are shown, so the manager can easily judge progress.

Gantt charts are most helpful when only a few tasks are involved, when task times are relatively long (days or weeks rather than hours), and when job routes are short and simple. One of the biggest shortcomings of Gantt charts is that they are static. They also fail to show how tasks are related. These problems can be solved, however, by using two other scheduling techniques, the CPM and PERT.

THE BIG PICTURE: CPM AND PERT To control large projects, operations managers need to closely monitor resources, costs, quality, and budgets. They also must be able to see the "big picture"—the interrelationships of the many tasks necessary to complete the project. Finally, they must be able to revise scheduling and divert resources quickly if any tasks fall behind schedule. The CPM and the PERT are related project management tools that were developed in the 1950s to help managers accomplish this.

In the **critical path method (CPM)**, the manager identifies all of the activities required to complete the project, the relationships between these activities, and the order in which they need to be completed. Then, he or she develops a diagram that uses arrows to show how the tasks are dependent on each other. The longest path through these linked activities is called the **critical path**, which determines the overall completion date. If the tasks on the critical path are not completed on time, the entire project will take longer and perhaps be completed late.

To understand better how CPM works, look at Exhibit 15.6, which shows a CPM diagram for constructing a house. All of the tasks required to finish the house and an estimated time for each have been identified. The arrows indicate the links between the various steps and their required sequence. As you will note, most of the jobs to be done can't be started until the house's foundation and frame are completed. It will take five days to finish the foundation and an additional seven days to erect the house frame. The activities linked by red arrows form the critical path for this project. It tells

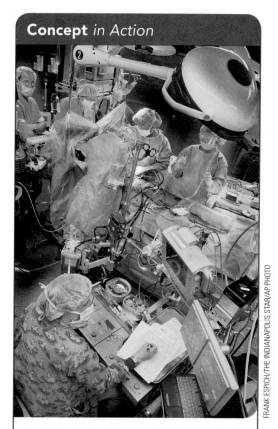
Gantt charts
Bar graphs plotted on a timeline that show the relationship between scheduled and actual production.

critical path method (CPM)
A scheduling tool that enables a manager to determine the critical path of activities for a project—the activities that will cause the entire project to fall behind schedule if they are not completed on time.

critical path
The longest path through the linked activities in a critical path method network.

Exhibit 15.5   A Typical Gantt Chart

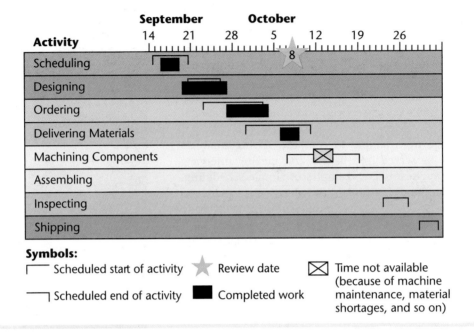

Symbols:

⌐ Scheduled start of activity	★ Review date
⌐ Scheduled end of activity	■ Completed work
⊠ Time not available (because of machine maintenance, material shortages, and so on)	

program evaluation and review technique (PERT)
A scheduling tool that is similar to the CPM method but assigns three time estimates for each activity (optimistic, most probable, and pessimistic); it allows managers to anticipate delays and potential problems and schedule accordingly.

us that the fastest possible time the house can be built is 38 days, the total time needed for all of the critical path tasks. The non-critical path jobs, those connected with black arrows, can be delayed a bit or done early. Short delays in installing appliances or roofing won't delay construction of the house, for example, because these activities don't lie on the critical path.

Like CPM, **program evaluation and review technique (PERT)** helps managers identify critical tasks and assess how delays in certain activities will affect operations or production. In both methods, managers use diagrams to see how operations and

Exhibit 15.6   A CPM Network for Building a House

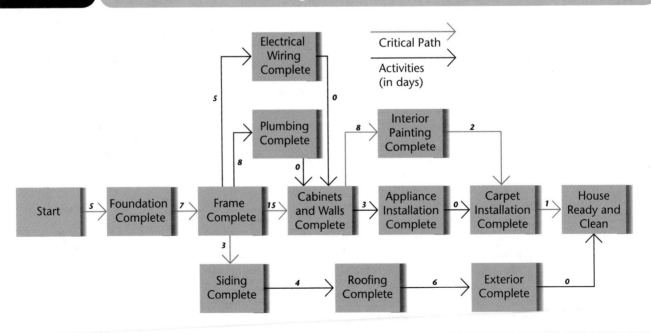

production will flow. PERT differs from CPM in one important respect, however. CPM assumes that the amount of time needed to finish a task is known with certainty; therefore, the CPM diagram shows only one number for the time needed to complete each activity. In contrast, PERT assigns three time estimates for each activity: an optimistic time for completion, the most probable time, and a pessimistic time. These estimates allow managers to anticipate delays and potential problems and schedule accordingly, as well as determine probability of different completion times.

Concept *Check*

What is production control, and what are its key aspects?

How can value-stream mapping improve routing efficiency?

Identify and describe three commonly used scheduling tools.

LO6

LOOKING FOR A BETTER WAY: IMPROVING PRODUCTION AND OPERATIONS

Competing in today's business world is challenging. To compete effectively, companies must keep production costs down. At the same time, however, it's becoming increasingly complex to produce and deliver the high-quality goods and services customers demand. Methods to help meet these challenges include quality management techniques, lean manufacturing, and automation.

Putting Quality First

Successful businesses recognize that quality and productivity must go together. Quality goods and services meet customer expectations by providing reliable performance. Defective products waste materials and time, increasing costs. Worse, poor quality causes customer dissatisfaction, which usually means lost future sales.

A consumer measures quality by how well a good serves its purpose. From the company's point of view, quality is the degree to which a good conforms to a set of predetermined standards. Quality control involves creating those quality standards, producing goods that meet them, and measuring finished products and services against them. It takes more than just inspecting goods at the end of the assembly line to ensure quality control, however. Quality control requires a company-wide dedication to managing and working in a way that builds excellence into every facet of operations.

Dr. W. Edwards Deming, an American management consultant, was the first to say that quality control should be a company-wide goal. His ideas were adopted by the Japanese in the 1950s but were largely ignored in North America until the 1970s. Deming believed that quality control must start with top management, who must foster a culture dedicated to producing quality.

Deming's concept of total quality management (TQM) emphasizes the use of quality principles in all aspects of a company's production and operations. It recognizes that all employees involved with bringing a product or service to customers—marketing, purchasing, accounting, shipping, manufacturing—contribute to its quality. TQM focuses on continuous improvement, a constant commitment to seeking better ways of doing things to achieve greater efficiency and improve quality. Company-wide teams work together to prevent problems and systematically improve key processes instead of troubleshooting problems only as they arise. Continuous improvement continually measures performance by using statistical techniques and looks for ways to apply new technologies and innovative production methods.

Quality control is the traditional means for managing quality, but many Canadian companies have moved to quality assurance, which is more comprehensive. Not only does it measure the quality against an established standard, but it also includes a commitment to doing the job right the first time. By striving to build quality into every product, companies are realizing that they can reduce costs, increase customer satisfaction, and decrease the need for quality control, placing them in a better competitive position.

quality
Goods and services that meet customer expectations by providing reliable performance.

quality control
The process of creating standards for quality, producing goods that meet them, and measuring finished products and services against them.

total quality management (TQM)
The use of quality principles in all aspects of a company's production and operations.

continuous improvement
A constant commitment to seeking better ways of doing things to achieve greater efficiency and improved quality.

quality assurance
More comprehensive than quality control, it strives for doing the job right the first time.

Another quality control method is the **Six Sigma** quality program. Six Sigma is a company-wide process that focuses on measuring the number of defects that occur and systematically eliminating them to get as close to "zero defects" as possible. In fact, Six Sigma quality aims to have every process produce no more than 3.4 defects per million. Six Sigma focuses on designing products that not only have fewer defects but also satisfy customer needs. A key process of Six Sigma is called *DMAIC*. This stands for Define, Measure, Analyze, Improve, and Control. Employees at all levels define what needs to be done to ensure quality, then measure and analyze production results by using statistics to see if the standards are met. They are also charged with finding ways of improving and controlling quality.

General Electric was one of the first companies to institute Six Sigma throughout the organization. All GE employees are trained in Six Sigma concepts, and many analysts believe this has given GE a competitive manufacturing advantage. Service companies have applied Six Sigma to their quality initiatives as well. For example, Air Canada and Canada Post have successfully implemented Six Sigma.

WORLDWIDE EXCELLENCE: INTERNATIONAL QUALITY STANDARDS The International Organization for Standardization (ISO), located in Belgium, is an industry organization that has developed standards of quality that are used by businesses around the world. ISO 9000, introduced in the 1980s, is a set of five technical standards designed to offer a uniform way of determining whether manufacturing plants and service organizations conform to sound quality procedures.

Sustainable Business, Sustainable World

THE HUDSON'S BAY COMPANY

One of the ways that a sustainable business can make the most impact is in its operations. One company that is making a real effort to be truly sustainable is the Hudson's Bay Company (HBC), Canada's largest diversified general merchandise retailer. The breadth of its commitment to sustainability can be seen on the front page of the Social Responsibility section of its corporate website: "Every day, we make choices. Some of those choices have an impact on our families and communities; some may reach around the world. At HBC, our goal is to foster and enhance sustainable business practices throughout our organization, particularly in the areas of the environment, associate wellness, community investment and ethical sourcing."

To meet its sustainability goals, HBC conducts annual audits of the company's operations to determine the amount of waste diverted from landfill, the amount of packaging and harmful PVCs in its private label products, energy consumption by store, and seven different sources of greenhouse gas (GHG) emissions. And most importantly, it continually looks for ways to improve its policies and practices.

In 2007, HBC introduced a number of new environmental improvements in its operations, including commitments to creating zero waste, recycling in its stores, preserving water, and performing lighting retrofits. In fact, HBC's head office was the first office tower in Canada to be certified zero waste by the Zero Waste International Alliance, www.zwia.org, and was archived as a case study by the Ontario Ministry of the Environment (OMOE), www.ene.gov.on.ca/environment, to serve as an example for other companies. This zero waste distinction for achieving a more than 95 percent diversion rate of waste away from landfills has been maintained, with 2010 being the fourth consecutive year of zero waste. Although not certified/audited, two other HBC office buildings and 14 of its retail locations are running a similar program. Now that's commitment.

In 2007, HBC also opened its greenest store ever, in Waterdown, Ontario. Some of the energy conservation measures include the use of two wind generators and solar panels to provide energy, a white roof to reflect heat, energy recovery ventilators, and heating/ventilating and air conditioning units that use non-ozone depleting refrigerant. Other programs instituted by HBC include its partnership with Rechargeable Battery Recycling Corporation's (RBRC) Call2Recycle program, www.call2recycle.ca, and an HBC Rewards points program under its former Zellers banner (recently purchased by and converted to Target stores) to create incentives for customers to purchase its line of reusable shopping bags, which includes rewarding points each time they decline a single-use plastic bag, regardless of the reusable bag they bring. This initiative resulted in a decline in the use of plastic shopping bags by over 54 percent in 2010!

Thinking Critically

1. Should companies become more sustainable in their operations because it's the right thing to do for our planet, because it's better for the bottom line, or both?
2. Do you think that society is becoming sufficiently more conscious that environmental sustainability will pay off in terms of more customers, or does it simply pay off in more efficient operations? Is there an integrative effect?

SOURCES: Hudsons Bay Company, http://www.hbc.com.

Concept *in Action*

The Six Sigma quality program directly involves production employees in setting quality standards and in measuring and analyzing finished goods to ensure that quality has been achieved. How can a service company (e.g., accountancy company or dry cleaners) ensure quality?

© WEST COAST SURFER/MOODBOARD/FIRST LIGHT

To register, a company must go through an audit of its manufacturing and customer service processes, covering everything from how it designs, produces, and installs its goods to how it inspects, packages, and markets them. More than 500,000 organizations worldwide have met ISO 9000 standards.

ISO 14000 is designed to promote clean production processes in response to environmental issues such as global warming and water pollution. To meet ISO 14000 standards, a company must commit to improving environmental management continually and reducing pollution resulting from its production processes. Some accredited ISO 14000 organizations include ASQR Canada, Intertek Testing Services NA Limited, and KPMG Performance Registrar Inc.

ISO 14000
A set of technical standards designed by the International Organization for Standardization to promote clean production processes to protect the environment.

Lean Manufacturing—Streamlining Production

Manufacturers are discovering that they can respond better to rapidly changing customer demands—while keeping inventory and production costs down—by adopting lean-manufacturing techniques. **Lean manufacturing** streamlines production by eliminating steps in the production process that do not add benefits customers are willing to pay for. *Non-value-added production processes* are cut, so that the company can concentrate its production and operations resources on items essential to satisfying customers. Toyota was a pioneer in developing these techniques, but today, manufacturers in many industries subscribe to the lean-manufacturing philosophy.

Another Japanese concept, **just-in-time (JIT)**, complements lean manufacturing. JIT is based on the belief that materials should arrive exactly when they are needed for production rather than being stored on-site. Relying closely on computerized systems, manufacturers determine what parts will be needed and when, and then order them from suppliers, so they arrive "just in time." Under the JIT system, inventory and products are "pulled" through the production process in response to customer demand. JIT requires close teamwork between vendors and purchasing and production personnel, because any delay in deliveries of supplies could bring JIT production to a halt.

lean manufacturing
Streamlining production by eliminating steps in the production process that do not add benefits customers are willing to pay for.

just-in-time (JIT)
A system in which materials arrive exactly when they are needed for production rather than being stored on-site.

TRANSFORMING THE FACTORY FLOOR WITH TECHNOLOGY

Technology is helping many companies improve their operating efficiency and ability to compete. Computer systems, in particular, are enabling manufacturers to automate factories in ways never before possible.

Among the technologies helping to automate manufacturing are computer-aided design and manufacturing systems, robotics, flexible manufacturing systems, and computer-integrated manufacturing.

COMPUTER-AIDED DESIGN AND MANUFACTURING SYSTEMS Computers have transformed the design and manufacturing processes in many industries. In **computer-aided design (CAD)**, computers are used to design and test new products and modify existing ones. Engineers use these systems to draw products and look at them from different angles. They can analyze the products, make changes, and test prototypes before making even one item. **Computer-aided manufacturing (CAM)** uses computers to develop and control the production process. The systems analysis determines the steps required to make the product. They then automatically send instructions to the machines that do the work. CAD/CAM systems combine the advantages of CAD and CAM by integrating design, testing, and manufacturing control into one linked computer system. The system helps design the product, control the flow of resources needed to produce the product, and operate the production process.

Cardianove Inc., a Montréal-based manufacturer of medical and surgical equipment, used CAD software to develop the world's smallest heart pump. The company says using computer-aided design cut two years off the normal design time for cardiac devices. The company's CAD program ran complex three-dimensional simulations to confirm that the design would function properly inside the human body. Cardianove Inc. tested more than 100 virtual prototypes by using the software before the top three designs were actually produced for real-life testing.[8]

ROBOTICS *Robots* are computer-controlled machines that can perform tasks independently. **Robotics** is the technology involved in designing, constructing, and operating robots. The first robot, or "steel-collar worker," was used by General Motors in 1961. Today, robots are used by many companies in many different industries.

Robots can be mobile or fixed in one place. Fixed robots have an arm that moves and does what the computer instructs. Some robots are quite simple, with limited movement for a few tasks such as cutting sheet metal and spot welding. Others are complex, with hands or grippers that can be programmed to perform a series of movements. Some robots are even equipped with sensing devices for sight and touch.

Robots usually operate with little or no human intervention. Replacing human effort with robots is most effective for tasks requiring accuracy, speed, or strength. Although manufacturers such as Bombardier, as described at the beginning of this chapter, are most likely to use robots, some service companies are also finding them useful. Some hospitals, for example, use robots to sort and process blood samples, freeing medical personnel from a tedious, sometimes hazardous, repetitive task. In many hospitals, some types of surgery are now performed with the use of robotic technology. Sometimes called computer-assisted surgery, this technology was developed to enhance the capabilities of surgeons' performance. It was in 2004 that the first person in Canada received a double bypass operation with the help of the da Vinci surgical robot in London, Ontario. In 2007, surgeons performed a coronary bypass by making four tiny incisions in the patient's chest with the use of robotics. The surgeon sat and operated the controls and was able to be more precise than with the use of more traditional methods.

computer-aided design (CAD)
The use of computers to design and test new products and modify existing ones.

computer-aided manufacturing (CAM)
The use of computers to develop and control the production process.

CAD/CAM systems
Linked computer systems that combine the advantages of *computer-aided design* and *computer-aided manufacturing*. The system helps design the product, control the flow of resources, and operate the production process.

robotics
The technology involved in designing, constructing, and operating computer-controlled machines that can perform tasks independently.

HOT *Links*

Want to know more about how robots work? Find out at science.howstuffworks.com/robot.htm

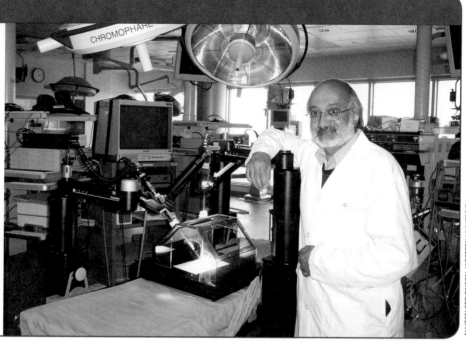

ALLISON STEVENSON, WESTERN UNIVERSITY

ADAPTABLE FACTORIES: FLEXIBLE MANUFACTURING SYSTEMS A flexible manufacturing system (FMS) automates a factory by blending computers, robots, machine tools, and materials-and-parts-handling machinery into an integrated system. These systems combine automated workstations with computer-controlled transportation devices. Automatic guided vehicles (AGVs) move materials between workstations and into and out of the system.

Flexible manufacturing systems are expensive. Once in place, however, a system requires little labour to operate and provides consistent product quality. The system can be changed easily and inexpensively. FMS equipment can be programmed to perform one job and then quickly be reprogrammed to perform another. These systems work well when small batches of a variety of products are required or when each product is made to individual customer specifications.

flexible manufacturing system (FMS)
A system that combines automated workstations with computer-controlled transportation devices—automatic guided vehicles (AGVs)—that move materials between workstations and into and out of the system.

QUICK CHANGE WITH COMPUTER-INTEGRATED MANUFACTURING Computer-integrated manufacturing (CIM) combines computerized manufacturing processes (like robots and FMS) with other computerized systems that control design, inventory, production, and purchasing. With CIM, when a part is redesigned in the CAD system, the changes are quickly transmitted both to the machines producing the part and to all other departments that need to know about and plan for the change.

computer-integrated manufacturing (CIM)
The combination of computerized manufacturing processes (such as robots and flexible manufacturing systems) with other computerized systems that control design, inventory, production, and purchasing.

Technology and Automation at Your Service

Manufacturers are not the only businesses benefiting from technology. Non-manufacturing companies are also using automation to improve customer service and productivity. Banks now offer services to customers through automated teller machines (ATMs), via automated telephone systems, and over the Internet. Retail stores of all kinds use point-of-sale (POS) terminals that track inventories, identify items that need to be reordered, and identify which products are selling well. Walmart, the leader in retailing automation, has its own satellite system connecting POS terminals directly to its distribution centres and headquarters.

Concept *Check*

Define total quality management, lean manufacturing, and just-in-time, and explain how each can help a company improve its production and operations.

How are both manufacturing and non-manufacturing companies using technology and automation to improve operations?

Creating the Future of Business

MIKE MORRICE, SUSTAINABLE WATERLOO REGION

The story of Mike Morrice and Sustainable Waterloo Region "is a story about passion" and perseverance—"not for just a particular product or service—but for a cultural shift." Mike's commitment to "community-led change is driven not by financial or personal gain, but by making measurable progress towards sustainability from the bottom up."

Mike is the cofounder and executive director of Sustainable Waterloo Region, a first-of-its-kind in Canada, not-for-profit organization that advances the environmental sustainability of organizations across the Waterloo Region through collaboration. Their flagship initiative centres on working with local organizations to help them set and make progress toward voluntary carbon reduction commitments—and it's this focus on measuring action at the community level that sets them apart. The organization is modelled after a similar organization in California called *Sustainable Silicon Valley*.

Mike didn't just wake up one day thinking that he wanted to do something different. He has always been an "independent thinker willing to challenge existing norms." In his youth, when bylaw officers cracked down on street hockey in his Montréal neighbourhood, he rallied his peers to canvas residents and had the bylaw overturned. And while attending university to receive a double degree in business and computing and computer electronics, he identified that the campus was "spinning its wheels" when it came to integrating sustainability into its decision making, so Mike spearheaded the creation of an organization called the *Campus Environmental Coalition*, which successfully worked with students and administration to find the resources for a university-wide Sustainability Office, responsible for all facets of the university's sustainability strategy—dramatically changing the way the university made operational decisions.

Mike and his friend Chris DePaul founded Sustainable Waterloo Region while working on an independent research project on carbon emission policy options while at university. The initial startup was not without hiccups. By November 2008, in the midst of a global economic crisis, their limited initial start-up funds were tapped out, but Mike and the volunteer team's passion was not. The group continued to pitch the organization "to anyone who would listen" and oversee grant applications they "weren't sure the organization would be around to collect." To build support, Mike's team committed to hosting its first event in January 2009 and was successful in getting organizations that had originally declined to be founding partners to sign up to sponsor the event. Despite a significant snowfall, 200 people attended that first event, and the rest is history. The first grant was awarded shortly thereafter.

Sustainable Waterloo Region's first initiative has linked together dozens of organizations to focus on implementing successful and cost-effective projects that result in greenhouse gas (GHG) emission reductions. Commitments to-date exceed 43,000 tonnes over the next 10 years, or the equivalent of taking almost 9,000 cars off the road! Mike is currently mentoring similar startups in other cities and is quickly becoming a Canadian leader in community-led environmental action.

Mike's achievements are inspiring. He "encourages and leads with a quiet determination, his vision never wavering. He brings fresh perspectives and optimism to a global crisis," changing the way organizations operate today and into the future. For his achievements, Mike was picked as one of Waterloo Region's inaugural Top 40 under 40 in 2009, won the LaunchPad $50K Venture Creation Competition in the Social Entrepreneurship category that same year, and was named Young Alumnus of the Year by the WLU Alumni Association in 2011. In 2012, he was named an Ashoka Fellow. If he could offer advice to budding entrepreneurs it would be to "relish the opportunity in the social and environmental challenges our culture faces; then involve others in what you want to create, and talk it into reality."

Thinking Critically

1. What is your passion? Would you have the perseverance to see it through even when it looked all but over? Do you think that this kind of passion and perseverance are necessary for an organization to create social change?
2. Do you think that organizations such as Sustainable Waterloo Region are necessary for our survival as a planet?

SOURCES: http://www.sustainablewaterlooregion.ca, and information supplied by Mike Morrice via e-mail September 15, 2011.

PHOTO COURTESY OF MIKE MORRICE

LO8 THE FUTURE OF PRODUCTION AND OPERATIONS MANAGEMENT

Some local manufacturing employment has been eliminated as manufacturers attempt to cut operating costs. Many of these jobs have been moved overseas, where manufacturers have opened new production facilities or contracted out production to foreign companies with lower operating and labour costs. Continued growth in global competition, increasingly complex products, and more demanding consumers continue to force manufacturers to plan carefully how, when, and where they produce the goods they sell. New production techniques and manufacturing technologies are vital to keeping production costs as low as possible and productivity levels high. At the same time, many companies are reevaluating the productivity of their production facilities and, in some cases, are deciding to close underperforming factories.

Non-manufacturing companies must carefully manage how they use and deploy their resources, while keeping up with the constant pace of technological change. Non-manufacturing companies must be ever vigilant in their search for new ways of streamlining service production and operations to keep their overall costs down.

Asset Management

In a tight economy, businesses must be careful about how their operating assets are used. From raw materials to inventories and manufacturing equipment, wasted, malfunctioning, or misused assets are costly. For example, one telephone company reported it had lost track of $5 billion worth of communications equipment. "I would say that every big company I have worked with has lost track of many major assets and a plethora of minor ones," said one executive. In fact, when chief financial officers of large companies were surveyed by *CFO Magazine*, 70 percent reported that asset management in their companies was "inefficient" or "erratic."[9]

Asset management software systems, many of which are Internet based, are beginning to help fix this problem. These programs automatically track materials, equipment, and inventory. They also automate inventory management, and maintenance and repairs scheduling.

Chevron has successfully implemented this type of system in its enormous production facility in Bakersfield, California. The facility is one of the largest outdoor factories in the world, stretching 160 kilometres from north to south, and containing a maze of storage tanks, filtering installations, and pipelines. In all, there are 230,000 separate pieces of equipment and machinery in hundreds of categories in the facility. To manage all of these assets, Chevron has installed an automated asset management system that schedules preventive maintenance for all equipment and tracks where surplus equipment and supplies are stored. Chevron estimates it is saving millions of dollars a year in the facility because of more effective asset management.[10]

Modular Production

Increasingly, manufacturers are relying on *modular production* to speed up and simplify production. Modular production involves breaking a complex product, service, or process into smaller pieces that can be created independently and then combined quickly to make a whole. Modular production not only cuts the cost of developing innovative products but also gives businesses a tool for meeting rapidly changing conditions. It also makes implementation of mass or pure customization strategies easier.

Johnson Controls Inc. (JCI), a manufacturer, works closely with its suppliers to build automotive interiors modularly. JCI uses 11 major components from 35 suppliers to build Jeep Liberty cockpits. The parts, designed to fit and function together, are then assembled in JCI's factory. "Our product development strategy is to build from the best capabilities and technologies in the world, but that doesn't mean they have to be owned and operated by us," says JCI vice president Jeff Edwards.[11]

Designing Products for Production Efficiency

Today's operations managers recognize that production efficiency must begin *before* the first part reaches the factory floor. As a result, many manufacturers are investing in new methods of integrating product design and engineering with the manufacturing supply chain.

Designlore of Toronto, Ontario, offers solutions and customized product design services to entrepreneurs and corporations. They specialize in taking product ideas to the finished product phase, including engineering, industrial and mechanical design, and research and development. The company prides itself on its "Right the First Time" approach, using innovative design with traditional engineering principles.

Toyota focuses design and engineering on "crossover vehicles"—car model designs that appeal to different consumer segments yet are built using many of the same components and parts. This has allowed Toyota's factories to become flexible and modular. What other industries incorporate modular production?

© MICHAEL S. YAMASHITA/ENCYCLOPEDIA/CORBIS

Concept *Check*

Explain modular production.

Why does production efficiency have to begin before the first part reaches the factory floor?

Another developing trend is the use of factory simulation tools for product design. These tools allow product designers to see the effects their designs will have on production equipment. For example, if a design calls for a specific size of drilled hole on a product, factory simulation tools will specify which particular drill bit and machine will be necessary for the task.

GREAT IDEAS TO USE NOW

As we've seen throughout this chapter, every organization produces something. Cereal manufacturers turn grains into breakfast foods. Law firms turn the skills and knowledge of lawyers into legal services. Retailers provide a convenient way for consumers to purchase a variety of goods. Colleges and universities convert students into educated individuals. Therefore, no matter what type of organization you work for in the future, you will be involved, to one degree or another, with your employer's production and operations processes.

Some employees, such as plant managers and quality control managers, will have a direct role in the production process. However, employees of manufacturing companies are not the only ones involved with production. Software developers, bank tellers, medical personnel, magazine writers, and other employees are also actively involved in turning inputs into outputs. If you manage people in these types of jobs, you'll need insight into the tools used to plan, schedule, and control production processes. Understanding production processes, resource management, and techniques for increasing productivity is vital to becoming a more valuable employee, one who sees how his or her job fits into the overall operations of the company's operating goals.

If you plan to start your own business, you'll also face many production and operations decisions. You can use the information from this chapter to help you find suppliers, design an operating facility (no matter how small), and put customer-satisfying processes in place. This information can also help you make decisions about whether to manufacture goods or rely on outside contractors for products.

Summary of Learning Outcomes

In the 1980s, many manufacturers lost customers to foreign competitors because their production and operations management systems did not support the high-quality, reasonably priced products consumers demanded. Service organizations also rely on effective operations management to satisfy consumers. Operations managers, the personnel charged with managing and supervising the conversion of inputs into outputs, work closely with other functions in organizations to help ensure quality, customer satisfaction, and financial success.

LO1 Discuss why production and operations management are important in both manufacturing and service companies.

Products are made using one of three types of production processes. In mass production, many identical goods are produced at once, keeping production costs low. Mass production, therefore, relies heavily on standardization, mechanization, and specialization. When mass customization is used, goods are produced using mass production techniques up to a point, after which the product or service is custom tailored to individual customers by adding special features. When a company's production process is built around customization, it makes many products one at a time according to the very specific needs or wants of individual customers.

LO2 List the types of production processes used by manufacturers and service companies.

Site selection affects operating costs, the price of the product or service, and the company's ability to compete. In choosing a production site, companies must weigh the availability of resources—raw materials, human resources, and even capital—needed for production, as well as the ability to serve customers and take advantage of marketing opportunities. Other factors include the availability of local incentives and the manufacturing environment. Once a site is selected, the company must choose an appropriate design for the facility. The three main production facility designs are process, product, and fixed-position layouts. Cellular manufacturing is another type of facility layout.

LO3 Describe how organizations decide where to put their production facilities and what choices must be made in designing the facility.

Production converts input resources, such as raw materials and labour, into outputs, finished products, and services. Companies must ensure that the resources needed for production will be available at strategic moments in the production process. If they are not, productivity, customer satisfaction, and quality might suffer. Carefully managing inventory can help cut production costs while maintaining enough supply for production and sales. Through good relationships with suppliers, companies can get better prices, reliable resources, and support services that can improve production efficiency.

LO4 Explain why resource-planning tasks like inventory management and supplier relations are critical to production.

Routing is the first step in scheduling and controlling production. Routing involves analyzing the steps needed in production and setting out a workflow, the sequence of machines and operations through which a product or service progresses from start to finish. Good routing increases productivity and can eliminate unnecessary costs. Scheduling involves specifying and controlling the time and resources required for each step in the production process. Operations managers use three methods to schedule production: Gantt charts, the critical path method, and program evaluation and review techniques.

LO5 Discuss how operations managers schedule and control production.

LO6 Evaluate how quality management and lean-manufacturing techniques help companies improve production and operations management.

Quality and productivity go together. Defective products waste materials and time, increasing costs. Poor quality also leads to dissatisfied customers. By implementing quality control methods, companies often reduce these problems and streamline production. Lean manufacturing also helps streamline production by eliminating unnecessary steps in the production process. When activities that don't add value for customers are eliminated, manufacturers can respond to changing market conditions with greater flexibility and ease. Many companies have moved even further by incorporating quality assurance, doing it right the first time.

LO7 Identify the roles that technology and automation play in manufacturing and service industry operations management.

Many companies are improving their operational efficiency by using technology to automate parts of production. Computer-aided design and manufacturing systems, for example, help design new products, control the flow of resources needed for production, and even operate much of the production process. By using robotics, human time and effort can be minimized. Factories are being automated by blending computers, robots, and machinery into flexible manufacturing systems that require less labour to operate. Service companies are automating operations too, using technology to cut labour costs and control quality.

LO8 List some of the trends affecting the way companies manage production and operations.

The manufacturing sector has been faced with growing global competition, increased product complexity, and more demanding customers, so manufacturers must carefully plan how, when, and where they produce the goods they sell. New production techniques and manufacturing technologies can help keep costs as low as possible. Managing assets like inventory, raw materials, and production equipment is increasingly important. Asset management software systems automatically track materials and inventory to help reduce waste, misuse, and malfunctions. Modular production allows manufacturers to produce products using high-quality parts without investments in expensive technology. Production efficiency must begin before the factory floor. Many companies are using tools that integrate product design and engineering with the manufacturing supply chain to understand the cost and quality implications of producing new products.

Key Terms

assembly process 448
bill of material 453
CAD/CAM systems 464
cellular manufacturing 453
computer-aided design (CAD) 464
computer-aided manufacturing (CAM) 464
computer-integrated manufacturing (CIM) 465
continuous improvement 461
continuous process 448
critical path 459
critical path method (CPM) 459
customization 447
electronic data interchange (EDI) 458
enterprise resource planning (ERP) 455
e-procurement 456
fixed-position layout 453
flexible manufacturing system (FMS) 465

Gantt charts 459
intermittent process 448
inventory 454
inventory management 454
ISO 9000 462
ISO 14000 463
job shop 447
just-in-time (JIT) 463
lean manufacturing 463
logistics 456
make-or-buy decision 453
manufacturing resource planning II (MRPII) 455
mass customization 447
mass production 447
materials requirement planning (MRP) 454
operations management 444
outsourcing 454
perpetual inventory 454

Experiential Exercises

1. Track a project with a Gantt chart. Your instructor has just announced a huge assignment, due in three weeks. Where do you start? How can you best organize your time? A Gantt chart can help you plan and schedule more effectively. You'll be able to see exactly what you should be doing on a particular day.

   - First, break the assignment down into smaller tasks: pick a topic, conduct research at the library or on the Internet, organize your notes, develop an outline, and write, type, and proofread the paper.
   - Next, estimate how much time each task will take. Be realistic. If you've spent a week or more writing similar papers in the past, don't expect to finish this paper in a day.
   - At the top of the page, list all of the days until the assignment is due. Along the side of the page, list all of the tasks you've identified in the order in which they need to be done.
   - Starting with the first task, block out the number of days you estimate each task will take. If you run out of days, you'll know you need to adjust how you've scheduled your time. If you know that you will not be able to work on some days, note them on the chart as well.
   - Hang the chart where you can see it.

2. Look for ways in which technology and automation are used at your school, in the local supermarket, and at your doctor's office. As a class, discuss how automation affects the service you receive from each of these organizations. Does one organization use any types of automation that might be effectively used by one of the others? Explain.

3. Pick a small business in your community. Make a list of the resources critical to the company's production and operations. What would happen if the business suddenly couldn't acquire any of these resources? Discuss strategies that small businesses can use to manage their supply chain.

4. Today's Fashions is a manufacturer of women's dresses. The company's factory has 50 employees. Production begins when the fabric is cut according to specified patterns. After being cut, the pieces for each dress style are placed into bundles, which then move through the factory from worker to worker. Each worker opens each bundle and does one assembly task, such as sewing on collars, hemming dresses, or adding decorative items such as appliqués. Then, the worker puts the bundle back together and passes it on to the next person in the production process. Finished dresses are pressed and packaged for shipment. Draw a diagram showing the production process layout in the Today's Fashions factory. What type of factory layout and process is Today's Fashions using? Discuss the pros and cons of this choice. Could Today's Fashions improve the production efficiency by using a different production process or factory layout? How? Draw a diagram to explain how this might look.

5. As discussed in this chapter, many companies have moved their manufacturing operations to overseas locations in the past decade. Although there can be sound financial benefits to this choice, moving production overseas can also raise new challenges for operations managers. Identify several of these challenges, and offer suggestions for how operations managers can use the concepts in this chapter to minimize or solve them.

6. Reliance Systems is a manufacturer of computer keyboards. The company plans to build a new factory and hopes to find a location with access to low-cost but skilled workers, national and international transportation, and favourable government incentives. As a team, use the Internet and your school library to research possible site locations, both domestic and international. Choose a location you feel would best meet the company's needs. Make a group presentation to the class explaining why you have chosen this location. Include information about the location's labour force, similar manufacturing facilities already located there, availability of resources and materials, possible local incentives, the political and economic environments, and any other factors you feel make this an attractive location. After all teams have presented their proposed locations, as a class rank all of the locations and decide the top two that Reliance should investigate further.

7. Find the supplier information websites of several companies by using the Google search engine, www.google.ca, to conduct a search for "supplier information." Visit two or three of these sites. Compare the requirements the companies set for their suppliers. How do the requirements differ? How are they similar?

8. Find out about the manufacturing environment in Canada by using www.google.ca and searching for manufacturing in Canada. You will have many options for learning more about the manufacturing opportunities.

9. Using a search engine such as www.google.ca or www.yahoo.ca, search for information about technologies like robotics, CAD/CAM systems, or ERP. Find at least three suppliers for one of these technologies. Visit their websites and discuss how their clients are using their products to automate production.

Review Questions

1. Define production and operations management.

2. What is production planning? What is the production process, and what options are available to manufacturers?

3. What are some of the considerations when determining the location of production facilities?

4. After management has decided on a location for their facilities, they need to design the facilities' layout. What are some options in the design?

5. What are the considerations in formulating resource planning?

6. What is supply chain management?

7. What is scheduling? What are the three common scheduling tools available to management?

8. Discuss some ways of improving production and operations.

9. How can technology be used to improve operating efficiencies and the ability for companies to compete?

10. Discuss the importance of asset management.

11. What is modular production?

CREATIVE THINKING CASE

Jim Brock—Fort Garry Brewing Company

Making beer is an organic process. Some of us make it at home in buckets, bathtubs, or specialized beer-making containers. When we do, we have to be extremely careful to avoid contaminants and microbes, which could make the beverage unpalatable or even dangerous. At an industrial level, the risks are much higher.

Brewmasters, like Jim Brock at Fort Garry Brewing from 1998 to 2007, are one part artisan and several parts operations manager. Every aspect of the process is computer controlled, right down to the pressure used to crack (not crush) the barley. Many factors are considered, including the age of the grain, temperature, and relative humidity on brewing day. The same goes for much of the quality control involved in brewing.

Fort Garry isn't a huge continuous process operation like Labatt or Molson Coors, but it follows the same brewing principles. Brewmasters are trained in specialty colleges in North America and Europe; many have graduate degrees in brewing, microbiology and related sciences. Jim Brock got his start on the floor at Fort Garry when the brand was resurrected by the great-grandson of the original founder. (Between times, the brewery had been sold to Molson and closed.) Jim trained with the brewmaster and studied outside his job so he could be ready to be an operations manager as well as a brewer.

More than three-quarters of the work of the brewmaster is done behind a computer, carefully planning and coordinating each brew so that quality, safety, and the flavour profile are maintained. At home, we may test the beer several times before it gets bottled. Jim only tastes it once—he opens the first bottle off the line to make sure it tastes right. Before that he has planned the brew, ordered and tested the ingredients, reviewed reports, and monitored the production process. We might be able to run to the store and pick up some ingredients or wash some extra bottles when home brewing, but at a production brewery, each step is carefully charted using both flow and dependency analysis. The only way this sort of operation is maintained is through the application of technology. A lot of barley, hops, yeast, and other ingredients are brought together in a precise manner in a pristine environment to generate the company's annual revenue of approximately $1 million.

Fort Garry Brewing suffered the loss of their re-founder in 2002 and has merged twice with other companies. Most recently (2009), the company was taken over by Russell Brewing of British Columbia for over $4 million. Despite the many corporate changes, Fort Garry's reputation as Manitoba's finest microbrewery is maintained through the development of new recipes by Jim's successors, and careful application of computers and other technology to a process dating back at least 10,000 years and organic long before the word became fashionable.

Thinking Critically

1. Research the brewing process online and construct a PERT chart for a craft brewery such as Fort Garry. Don't forget to begin your process with recipe development and end it with a customer sipping a glass in his or her home.

2. If the supply of a specific type of hops is interrupted by weather and delivery is delayed by three weeks, how could this affect your operations, assuming that hops are used in only one of your products? What should you do?

3. Over 80 percent of beer sales occur between April and September. What planning steps should Fort Garry take to anticipate this peak demand while minimizing fixed costs?

SOURCES: L. Cameron, "Mbio 4520 Industrial Processes Lab," University of Manitoba, http://www.umanitoba.ca/science/microbiology/staff/cameron/60_451.htm; MFPA, "Profile Operations," Manitoba Made, 2000, published electronically November 16, http://www.mfpa.mb.ca/uploadedFiles/Careers/jobpfs_operations_manager.pdf; "Fort Garry Brewing Company Is Vegan Friendly," Barnivore, Your Vegan beer, wine and liquor guide, 2009.

Making the Connection

Accounting for Financial Success

In the previous four chapters, we examined the functional areas of *human resources*, *operations*, and *marketing*, and saw that they must work together in a very integrative way to achieve the goals of the company. It is obvious that these three areas affect the ability of the company to *gain employee commitment*, increase the level of product *quality* and *innovativeness*, and thus *meet customer needs*, and that they therefore affect the ability of the company to *achieve financial performance*. In this chapter we will begin to look more specifically at financial performance by looking at the last functional area of *finance*, starting with how a company develops and uses financial information through the function of accounting.

It's clear from the beginning of this chapter that, regardless of your position in an organization, you need to understand accounting. It is the "financial language of businesses," and all decisions that are made in an organization eventually have financial consequences and therefore show up in the accounting information. For example, on the Income Statement (or Statement of Comprehensive Income as you'll learn later in the chapter), you might find advertising expenses and sales revenue from marketing, production and operating costs from operations, payroll and training costs from human resources, and, of course, the interest costs on debt financing to pay for it all. On the Balance Sheet (or Statement of Financial Position), you can also see the impact of each area on the numbers. For example, in the accounts payable section, there might be payments outstanding for employee wages, for marketing expenses, and for operating expenses, as well as for interest on debt financing or dividends payable to shareholders. In the current assets sections, you might find marketable securities (money invested in financial products to earn a return for a short period—a financing decision), accounts receivable from customers for invoices they have not yet paid

(a marketing decision), and inventories of goods on hand (an operating decision).

All areas of the company, and employees at all levels, must therefore understand the financial implications of the decisions they make. They must see the integration of their decisions with each area and eventually on the "bottom line." Internal accounting reports help functional areas make these decisions; for example, marketing sales reports can be used to assess how well different marketing strategies are working, and production cost reports help in efforts to control operating costs.

On the other hand, external accounting reports (such as the Income Statement/Statement of Comprehensive Income and Balance Sheet/Statement of Financial Position), which are contained in annual reports to shareholders, are used by many outside *stakeholder* groups. Potential employees use them to assess the stability of a company—and therefore job security and job prospects—before taking job offers, and potential investors use them to assess investment opportunities, just as current shareholders use them to assess the investments they have already made. These stakeholder relationships cannot be dealt with casually, particularly in light of scandals that have called into question the integrity of the accounting profession. The impact that these scandals—such as those involving Enron and Arthur Andersen (2001), WorldCom and Freddie Mac (2002), AIG (2004), and more recently Bernard L. Madoff Investment Securities LLC (2008) and Lehman Brothers (2010)—have had on the financial markets (*economic* environment) demonstrate quite clearly the far-reaching integrative impact of financial information and the importance of operating with the highest ethical standards. In fact, this demand for greater ethical conduct (*social* environment) has resulted in many new regulations (*political* environment) governing what companies can and cannot do in reporting accounting information.

The social environment has also impacted accounting statements in another way, with the trend toward sustainability. Many companies are now providing sustainability reports, often audited, along with their annual accounting statements. Check out www.pg.com for a copy of Procter & Gamble's latest sustainability report.

Of course, the *international* environment has very recently had an enormous impact on accounting. Starting in 2011, accounting rules were changed in Canada to require publicly traded companies to report by using an international set of accounting standards called IFRS. This demonstrates the integrative nature of our global economic environment, as it has become essential to have consistency in reporting standards between countries. A big reason for this is because *technology* has made the world so much smaller. Advances in technology today have also sped up the pace with which accounting information can be gathered and disseminated throughout an organization, thus giving all areas an opportunity to examine the impact of their decisions in an integrative way and focus more on the analysis of the information to make better decisions. In the remaining chapters, we'll continue with the finance area and look at these decisions in more detail.

chapter 16

Accounting for Financial Success

LEARNING OUTCOMES

1 Explain the importance of financial reports and accounting information to the targeted users.

2 Show an understanding of the accounting profession.

3 Identify the six steps in the accounting cycle.

4 Understand how a balance sheet (statement of financial position) describes the financial condition of an organization.

5 Explain the purpose of the income statement (statement of comprehensive income).

6 Describe the importance of the statement of cash flows.

7 Explain how ratio analysis is used to identify a company's financial strengths and weaknesses.

8 List some of the major trends that are impacting the accounting industry.

SHEILA FRASER—ACCOUNTANT, HERO

When you think of heroes, it's not too likely that the name of an accountant will spring to mind—with one possible exception. Sheila Fraser, Canada's auditor general from 2001 to 2011, is regarded in heroic terms by many Canadians. And it's official: in June 2011, the Pacific Institute for Public Policy declared Fraser its hero. She's also received flowers as a thank-you gift from Canadians for her role in uncovering the Sponsorship Scandal, in which it was discovered that funds paid out from 1996 to 2004 by the then-Liberal federal government for advertising to calm separatist sentiment in Québec had been misdirected. (Eventually, a public inquiry led to criminal convictions against executives whose companies billed Ottawa but did no work.)

It wasn't just the Liberals who came under her steely-eyed scrutiny. She questioned the Conservative government's spending on the 2010 G8 and G20 summits, and she even challenged the competence of the public sector integrity commissioner and the privacy commissioner. These two would normally be considered partners of the auditor general in achieving transparency in government.

Sheila Fraser isn't new to struggles or battles. Born in Dundee, Québec, she graduated from McGill University in 1972, a time when most accountants were men. It was hard for her to get an articling position with a chartered accounting firm. Finally, Ernst and Young hired the 22-year-old; nine years later she became a partner with the company. She joined the federal government as deputy auditor general in 1999, and in 2001 was appointed to a 10-year term as auditor general.

The position has its beginning in 1878, when the first auditor general was appointed, with a goal of separating public reporting from the politics of government. But that lofty ideal of an independent auditor watching over government and acting in the public interest was not reached for many years, and still the office struggles for full access to the information and data it seeks. During Fraser's term, Parliament passed several acts improving that access, and broadening the reach of the auditor general to include Crown corporations and some other related agencies. The audits that made Fraser famous may not have been possible prior to these changes.

One example of the challenges created when a political agenda is in play can be seen in the federal Long Gun Registry program. It took Fraser and her staff a lot of hard slogging through the government's books to ferret out the reality that the original projected cost of $2 million was off by 50,000 percent (that's right, it cost 500 times the

CHRIS WATTIE/REUTERS/LANDOV

estimate that had been given to the House of Commons). Another example is that many of the payments that led to the Sponsorship Scandal were made through Crown corporations. It's possible that these sorts of deals were occurring before the auditor general gained the power to audit these organizations.

The deeds of Sheila Fraser are one very public example of the importance of accountants and the need for everyone to understand financial information. The Enron, WorldCom, Livent, and Nortel scandals all relate to misrepresented financial information. Many of these would not have been revealed without brave accountants willing to become whistleblowers. Accounting might not appear to be as exciting as some business careers, but in any organization, the accountants are usually the people who know what's really going on.[1]

THINKING CRITICALLY

As you read this chapter, consider the following questions:

1. Why is understanding your finances important?

2. What are some potential issues if the accounting process is flawed or incorrect?

SOURCES: http://www.juliamorgan.ca/documents/SnapshotSheilaFraser.pdf/; http://thepacificinstitute.ca/index.php/; Jessica Bruno, "Public Sector Integrity Commissioner's Office has 'lost all credibility,' interim integrity czar tries to rebuild it," *The Hill Times* online, February 14, 2011, http://www.thehilltimes.ca/page/view/integrityoffice-02-14-2011/; Susan Munroe, "Sheila Fraser Biography," Canada Online, http://canadaonline.about.com/od/governmentspending/p/sheilafraser.htm/; http://www.newlearner.com/courses/hts/baf3m/bacproj2.htm/.

Financial information is central to every organization. To operate effectively, businesses must have a way to track income, expenses, assets, and liabilities in an organized manner. Financial information is also essential for decision making. Managers prepare financial reports by using accounting, a set of procedures and guidelines for companies to follow when preparing financial reports. Unless you understand basic accounting concepts, you will not be able to "speak" the standard financial language of business.

All of us—whether we are self-employed, work for a local small business or a multinational Fortune 100 company, or are not currently in the workforce—benefit from knowing the basics of accounting and financial statements. We can use this information to educate ourselves about companies before interviewing for a job or buying a company's shares or bonds. Employees at all levels of an organization use accounting information to monitor operations. They must also decide which financial information is important for their company or business unit, what those numbers mean, and how to use them to make decisions.

We start this chapter by discussing why accounting is important for businesses and for users of financial information. We then provide a brief overview of the accounting profession and recent problems in the industry, and the new regulatory environment. Following that, we present an overview of accounting procedures, followed by a description of the three main financial statements: the Balance Sheet (Statement of Financial Position), the Income Statement (Statement of Comprehensive Income), and the Statement of Cash Flows. Using these statements, we then demonstrate how ratio analysis of financial statements can provide valuable information about a company's financial condition. Finally, we will explore current trends affecting the accounting profession.

LO1 ACCOUNTING: MORE THAN NUMBERS

accounting
The process of collecting, recording, classifying, summarizing, reporting, and analyzing financial activities.

Accounting is the process of collecting, recording, classifying, summarizing, reporting, and analyzing financial activities. It results in reports that describe the financial condition of an organization. All types of organizations—businesses, hospitals, schools, government agencies, and civic groups—use accounting procedures. Accounting provides a framework for looking at past performance, current financial health, and possible future performance. It also provides a framework for comparing the financial positions and financial performances of different companies. Understanding how to prepare and interpret financial reports will enable you to evaluate two computer companies and choose the one that is more likely to be a good investment.

As Exhibit 16.1 shows, the accounting system converts the details of financial transactions (sales, payments, purchases, etc.) into a form that people can use to evaluate the company and make decisions. Data become information which, in turn, becomes reports. These reports describe a company's financial position at one point in time and its financial performance during a specified period. Financial reports include *financial statements*, such as the balance sheet and the income statement, and special reports, such as sales and expense breakdowns by product line.

Who Uses Financial Reports?

managerial accounting
Accounting that provides financial information that managers inside the organization can use to evaluate and make decisions about current and future operations

The accounting system generates two types of financial reports, as shown in Exhibit 16.2: internal and external. Internal reports are used within the organization. As the term implies, **managerial accounting** provides financial information that managers inside the organization can use to evaluate and make decisions about

Financial accounting information, such as asset values, sales, and inventory, helps managers in all types of organizations make business decisions that enhance organizational effectiveness and efficiency. What are some of the consequences of not understanding accounting in business?

© BONNIE KAMIN/PHOTOEDIT

current and future operations. For instance, the sales reports prepared by managerial accountants show how well marketing strategies are working. Production cost reports help departments track and control costs. Managers might prepare very detailed financial reports for their own use and provide summary reports to top management.

Financial accounting focuses on preparing external financial reports that are used by outsiders, that is, people who have an interest in the business but are not part of management. Although these reports also provide useful information for managers, they are primarily used by shareholders (the owners of the company), lenders, suppliers, investors, and government agencies to assess the financial strength of a business.

Until 2011, all Canadian companies issued their financial statements based on the Canadian **generally accepted accounting principles (GAAP)**. GAAP was used to ensure accuracy and consistency in the way financial information is reported.

financial accounting
Accounting that focuses on preparing external financial reports that are used by outsiders such as creditors, lenders, suppliers, investors, and government agencies to assess the financial strength of a business.

generally accepted accounting principles (GAAP)
The financial accounting rules, standards, and usual practices followed by accountants in Canada when preparing financial statements, until January 2011.

Exhibit 16.1   The Accounting System

Classify, summarize, and analyze data   Prepare financial reports   Use financial reports to evaluate the firm and make decisions

Exhibit 16.2 Reports Provided by the Accounting System

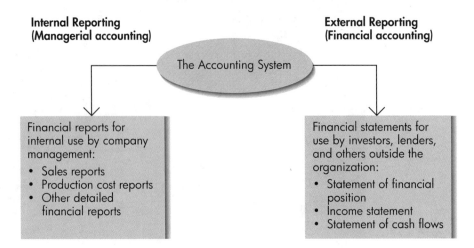

Internal Reporting (Managerial accounting)

External Reporting (Financial accounting)

The Accounting System

Financial reports for internal use by company management:

- Sales reports
- Production cost reports
- Other detailed financial reports

Financial statements for use by investors, lenders, and others outside the organization:

- Statement of financial position
- Income statement
- Statement of cash flows

International Financial Reporting Standards (IFRS)
A set of globally accepted accounting standards adopted in Canada on January 1, 2011, for public companies and those private companies that chose to adopt them.

Accounting Standards for Private Enterprises (ASPE)
The accounting framework designed to replace Canadian GAAP for private companies.

Check out what is new at the International Accounting Standards Committee:
www.iasb.org

annual report
A yearly document that describes a company's financial status and usually discusses the company's activities during the past year and its prospects for the future.

On January 1, 2011, Canada adopted the International Financial Reporting Standards (IFRS) for publicly traded companies. The adoption of the IFRS was designed to provide consistency in financial reporting internationally and replace the GAAP of over 100 countries.[2] Private companies (discussed in Chapter 8) can choose to prepare their financial statements based on IFRS or based on the Accounting Standards for Private Enterprises (ASPE), which is more similar to the former Canadian GAAP.

Some of the advantages of IFRS for public companies include lower costs associated with the preparation of financial information, consistency in reports internationally, and ease of financial comparisons with other companies. Some notable changes to IFRS include the following: revenue is called income, and, as mentioned earlier, the titles of the statements have changed—the balance sheet is called the statement of financial position, the income statement is called the statement of comprehensive income, and the cash flow statement is called the statement of cash flows.

ASPE and IFRS call for the same accounting treatment for most situations. However, there are some differences. Most of the differences in accounting standards arise from accountants having choice under one set of standards where the other set of standards only has one correct method of accounting for that kind of transaction. In some cases, IFRS allows accountants to choose options with respect to how to record a transaction and in others it is very "black and white," and vice versa.

Having the two accounting systems is realistic because stakeholders' information needs are often different for private versus public companies. Since both were derived from Canadian GAAP and both are principles to follow (not rules) they have many similarities. The Expanding Around the Globe box discusses the challenges in changing from GAAP to IFRS.

Financial statements are the chief element of the annual report, a yearly document that describes a company's financial status. Annual reports usually discuss the company's activities during the past year and its prospects for the future. Three primary financial statements included in the annual report discussed and illustrated later in this chapter are

- the balance sheet (statement of financial position);
- the income statement (statement of comprehensive income); and
- the statement of cash flows.

Concept Check

Explain who uses financial information.

Differentiate between financial accounting and managerial accounting.

Expanding Around the Globe

MOVING TOWARD ONE WORLD OF NUMBERS

Imagine being treasurer of a major multinational company with significant operations in ten other countries. Because the accounting rules in those countries don't conform to IFRS, your staff has to prepare nine sets of financial reports that comply with each host country's rules—and also translate the figures to IFRS for consolidation into the parent company's statements. It's a massive undertaking.

The Canadian Accounting Standards Board (AcSB) and the International Accounting Standards Board (IASB) worked together to develop international accounting standards that removed disparities between national and international standards, improved the quality of financial information worldwide, and simplified comparisons of financial statements across borders for both corporations and investors.

The AcSB and the IASB desired to create uniform global accounting standards. Presently, there are approximately 100 countries that use IFRS with more signing on each year. As they worked toward convergence, the board members decided to develop a new set of common standards, rather than try to reconcile the two standards.

These new standards must be better than existing ones, not simply eliminate differences. Merging GAAP and IFRS into a consistent set of international accounting standards has proven to be very difficult because of different approaches used in the two sets.

However, the convergence project is moving ahead more quickly than the sponsoring groups anticipated. Raising capital outside a corporation's home country overseas will be easier for companies because they will not have to restate their financial reports to conform to either GAAP or IFRS. Because the goal is to develop improved accounting standards, the boards take the big picture view in seeking solutions.[3]

Thinking Critically

1. Is it important to have a single set of international accounting standards for at least publicly traded companies? Defend your answer.
2. How will the change affect the accounting profession (e.g., new training, different classes at post-secondary institutions)?

THE ACCOUNTING PROFESSION

LO2

When you think of accountants, do you picture someone who works alone in a back room, hunched over a desk, scrutinizing pages and pages of numbers? Although today's accountants still must love working with numbers, they now work closely with their clients not only to prepare financial reports, but also to help them develop good financial practices. Computers have taken the tedium out of the number-crunching and data-gathering parts of the job and now offer powerful analytical tools as well. Therefore, accountants must keep up with information technology trends. The accounting profession has grown because of the increased complexity, size, and number of businesses and the frequent changes in the tax laws. There are approximately 200,000 accountants in Canada working in the private sector, public sector, or as self-employed accountants.[4]

The Accounting Designations

In Canada, there are three accounting associations that grant professional designations. They are the Canadian Institute of Chartered Accountants (CICA), the Society of Management Accountants of Canada (CMA Canada), and the Certified General Accountants Association of Canada (CGA-Canada). Each of the professional accounting associations provides specialized services and has certain educational and work experience requirements for the accountant to be granted the professional designation. The accounting professions and the services that each can provide vary between provinces. Currently the services that each provide are very much overlapped and, in some provinces, almost undistinguishable.

A **chartered accountant (CA)** typically provides tax, audit, and management services. CAs focus on the external reporting and provide an opinion as to whether the financial statements accurately reflect the company's financial health. Most CAs first work for public accounting firms and later become private accountants or financial managers.

HOT links

To find out more about the accounting profession, visit the Canadian Institute of Chartered Accountants site at
www.cica.ca
the CMA Canada site at
www.cma-canada.org
or the Certified General Accountants site at
www.cga-canada.org

chartered accountant (CA)
An accountant who typically provides tax, audit, and management services.

Concept *in Action*

CIBC

2011 Annual Report

Strong fundamentals
in a **changing world**

The financial information contained in an annual report is prepared using financial accounting standards. Lenders, suppliers, investors, and government agencies refer to the annual report to assess the financial strength of a business. What decisions can be made by reviewing a company's annual report?

certified management accountant (CMA)
An accountant who works primarily in industry and focuses on internal management accounting.

certified general accountant (CGA)
An accountant who focuses primarily on external financial reporting.

chartered professional accountant (CPA)
An accounting designation that unites the various accounting designations in Canada.

LO3

CAs generally work in four key areas: public practice, industry, government, or education. In public practice, they provide accounting and business advice to clients in areas such as small business taxation, auditing, information technology, personal finance planning, business valuation, receivership, insolvency, and forensic investigation. In industry, CAs develop financial and administrative policies, analyze information, and provide strategic leadership.

A **certified management accountant (CMA)** works primarily in industry and focuses on internal management accounting. CMAs combine their accounting expertise and business know-how with professional management skills to provide strategic financial management, strategic planning, sales and marketing, information technology, human resources, finance, and operations. According to CMA Canada,

> *Working in organizations of all sizes and types, CMAs provide an integrating perspective to business decision making, applying best management practices in strategic planning, finance, operations, sales and marketing, information technology, and human resources to identify new market opportunities, ensure corporate accountability, and help organizations maintain a long-term competitive advantage.[5]*

Certified general accountant (CGA) roles have far expanded from the primary focus on external financial reporting. CGAs also provide tax and financial advice to individuals and businesses. Many own their own accounting businesses, whereas others are employed in industry and government. According to CGA Canada,

> *CGAs work throughout the world in industry, commerce, finance, government, public practice and other areas where accounting and financial management is required. CGA clients range from major corporations and industries to entrepreneurs. Their expertise is valued in the public sector, government and the corporate world.[6]*

The requirements to become a CA, CMA, or CGA are quite extensive. Each requires a degree plus additional professional studies that cover the full spectrum of financial and business management. Candidates must also complete a period of articling (that results in real-world skills and development of practical problem-solving abilities) and, finally, pass comprehensive exams that demonstrate their knowledge of the profession.

In 2011 an initiative was introduced to merge the three accounting professions into one: **chartered professional accountant (CPA)**. While this is a national initiative, it must be approved by the accounting authorities in each of the provinces. Québec was the first to pass legislation to approve the new designation in 2012.

BASIC ACCOUNTING PROCEDURES

Using accounting principles, accountants record and report financial data in similar ways for all companies. They report their findings in financial statements that summarize a company's business transactions over a specified time period. As mentioned earlier, the three major financial statements are the balance sheet (statement of financial position), income statement (statement of comprehensive income), and statement of cash flows.

People sometimes confuse accounting with bookkeeping. Accounting is a much broader concept. *Bookkeeping*, the system used to record a company's financial transactions, is a routine, clerical process. Accountants take bookkeepers' transactions, classify and summarize the financial information, and then prepare and analyze financial reports. Accountants also develop and manage financial systems and help plan the company's financial strategy.

Concept *Check*

What are the three accounting designations in Canada?

The Accounting Cycle

The *accounting* cycle refers to the process of generating financial statements, beginning with a business transaction and ending with the preparation of the report. Exhibit 16.3 shows the six steps in the accounting cycle. The first step in the cycle is to analyze the data collected from many sources. All transactions that have a financial impact on the company—sales, payments to employees and suppliers, interest and tax payments, purchases of inventory, and the like—must be documented. The accountant must review the documents to make sure they're complete.

Next, each transaction is recorded in a *journal*, a listing of financial transactions in chronological order. Then the journal entries are recorded in *ledgers*, which show increases and decreases in specific asset, liability, and owners' equity accounts. The ledger totals for each account are summarized in a *trial balance*, which is used to confirm the accuracy of the figures. These values are used to prepare financial statements and management reports. Finally, individuals analyze these reports and make decisions based on the information in them.

assets
Things of value owned by a company.

The Accounting Equation

The accounting procedures used today are based on the three main accounting elements of assets, liabilities, and owners' equity. **Assets** are things of value owned by a company. They might be *tangible*, such as cash, equipment, and buildings, or *intangible*, such as a patent or trademarked name. **Liabilities**—also called *debts*—are what a company owes to its creditors. **Owners' equity** is the total amount of investment in the company minus any liabilities. Another term for owners' equity is *net worth*.

liabilities
What a company owes to its creditors; also called *debts*.

owners' equity
The total amount of investment in the company minus any liabilities; also called *net worth*.

Exhibit 16.3 The Accounting Cycle

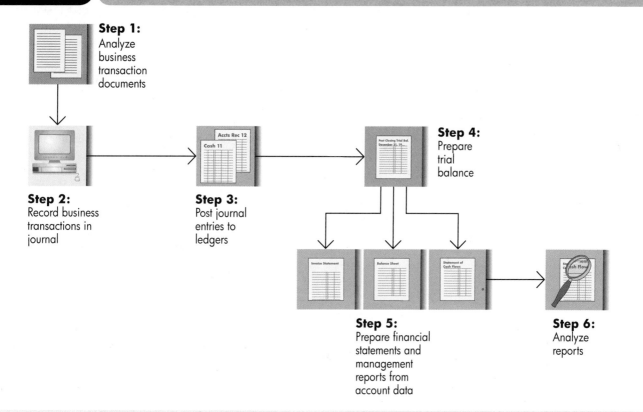

Step 1: Analyze business transaction documents

Step 2: Record business transactions in journal

Step 3: Post journal entries to ledgers

Step 4: Prepare trial balance

Step 5: Prepare financial statements and management reports from account data

Step 6: Analyze reports

The relationship among these three elements is expressed in the accounting equation:

$$\text{Assets} = \text{Liabilities} + \text{Owners' equity}$$
$$\quad\text{(own)}\qquad\text{(owe)}\qquad\text{(net worth)}$$

The accounting equation must always be in balance (that is, the total of the elements on one side of the equals sign must equal the total on the other side).

Suppose you start a bookstore and put $10,000 in cash into the business. At that point, the business has assets of $10,000 and no liabilities. This would be the accounting equation:

$$\text{Assets} = \text{Liabilities} + \text{Owners' equity}$$
$$\$10,000 = \$0 \qquad + \$10,000$$

The liabilities are zero, and owner's equity (the amount of your investment in the business) is $10,000. The equation balances.

To keep the accounting equation in balance, every transaction must be recorded as at least two entries. As each transaction is recorded, there is an equal and opposite event so that the accounts or records are changed. This method is called **double-entry bookkeeping.**

Suppose that, after starting your bookstore with $10,000 cash, you borrow an additional $10,000 from the bank. The accounting equation will change as follows:

Assets	= Liabilities + Owners' equity		
$10,000 = $0	+ $10,000	Initial equation
$10,000 = $10,000	+ $0	Borrowing transaction
$20,000 = $10,000	+ $10,000	Equation after borrowing

Now you have $20,000 in assets—your $10,000 in cash and the $10,000 loan proceeds from the bank. The bank loan is also recorded as a liability of $10,000, because it's a debt that you must repay. Making two entries keeps the equation in balance.

The T-Account

A T-account is often used to analyze financial transactions and is named such because it resembles a T.

For each financial account the company used, there is a T-account. On the left side of the T-account is the debit record (DR) and on the right side is the credit record (CR). Unlike in our normal use of the word, they are neither good nor bad; they simply represent the left side and right side of the T-account. Referring back to the accounting equations (A = L + OE), we see that assets are on the right side of the equation while liabilities and owners' equity is on the left. A simple rule is that an increase of any account is recorded in the T-account on the side corresponding to the accounting equation; a decrease is on the opposite side. Below are two visuals to help explain the debit and credit entries.

Assets = Liabilities + Owners' Equity

DEBITS (DR – DEBIT RECORD)	CREDIT (CR – CREDIT RECORD)
Increase in Assets	Increase in Liabilities or Owners' Equity
Decrease in Liabilities or Owners' Equity	Decrease in Assets
Expenses	Sales
Cost of Goods Sold (COGS)	

double-entry bookkeeping
A method of accounting in which each transaction is recorded as at least two entries, so that the accounts or records are changed.

T-account
An account that is often used to analyze financial transactions; T-accounts are named as such because they resemble a T.

Or as a T-account:

DR	CR
↑ A	↑ L or OE
↓ L or OE	↓ A
Expenses	Sales
COGS	

The Trial Balance

A **trial balance** is a list of each account and its net balance (debits minus credits for asset accounts and credits minus debits for liability and owners' equity accounts). The trial balance is not a financial statement but a system to prove the balance of the debits and credits.

Each financial transaction consists of equal debits and credits (see double-entry bookkeeping listed above). For the following example, refer to the above tables. If we purchase a computer for cash, we would increase our asset account "computer" (debit) and decrease our asset account "cash" (credit). On the other hand, if we purchased the computer and will pay the vendor in 30 days, we would record the transaction as follows: increase our account "computer" (debit) and increase our liability account "accounts payable" (credit). Once you have completed this chapter, you can try your knowledge by completing Experiential Exercise 9.

trial balance
A list of each account and its net balance.

Computers in Accounting

Computerized accounting programs do many different things. Most accounting packages offer six basic modules that handle general ledger, sales order, accounts receivable, purchase order, accounts payable, and inventory control functions. Tax programs use accounting data to prepare tax returns and tax plans. Computerized point-of-sale terminals used by many retail companies automatically record sales and do some of the bookkeeping.

Accounting and financial applications typically represent one of the largest portions of a company's software budget. Accounting software ranges from off-the-shelf programs for small businesses to full-scale customized enterprise resource planning systems for major corporations. Besides the accounting packages mentioned above, many large accounting firms have customized accounting software developed for them and their clients.

Concept *Check*

Explain the accounting equation.

Describe the six-step accounting cycle.

What role do computers play in accounting?

THE BALANCE SHEET (STATEMENT OF FINANCIAL POSITION)

LO4

The **balance sheet (statement of financial position)**, one of three financial statements generated from the accounting system, summarizes a company's financial position at a specific point in time. It reports the resources of a company (assets), the company's obligations (liabilities), and the difference between what is owned (assets) and what is owed (liabilities), which is known as owners' equity. Companies will often use the older term, balance sheet, instead of statement of financial position. balance refers to the accounting equation; both sides of the equation must be equal and therefore "balanced."

The balance sheet at December 31, 2013, for Delicious Desserts, a privately owned, imaginary bakery (therefore using ASPE), is illustrated in Exhibit 16.4. The basic accounting equation is reflected in the three totals highlighted on the balance sheet: assets of $148,900 equal the sum of liabilities and owners' equity ($70,150 + $78,750). The three main categories of accounts on the balance sheet are explained below.

balance sheet (statement of financial position)
A financial statement that summarizes a company's financial position at a specific point in time.

Exhibit 16.4 | Balance Sheet for Delicious Desserts

DELICIOUS DESSERTS, INC.

Balance Sheet as of December 31, 2013

Assets

Current Assets:			
Cash		$15,000	
Marketable securities		4,500	
Accounts receivable	$45,000		
Less: Allowance for doubtful accounts	1,300	43,700	
Notes receivable		5,000	
Inventory		15,000	
Total current assets			$ 83,200
Capital Assets:			
Bakery equipment	$56,000		
Less: Accumulated depreciation	16,000	$40,000	
Furniture and fixtures	$18,450		
Less: Accumulated depreciation	4,250	14,200	
Total fixed assets			54,200
Intangible Assets:			
Trademark		$ 4,500	
Goodwill		7,000	
Total intangible assets			11,500
Total Assets			**$148,900**

Liabilities and Owners' Equity

Current Liabilities:			
Accounts payable	$30,650		
Notes payable	15,000		
Accrued expenses	4,500		
Income taxes payable	5,000		
Current portion of long-term debt	5,000		
Total current liabilities		$60,150	
Long-term Liabilities:			
Bank loan for bakery equipment	$10,000		
Total long-term liabilities		10,000	
Total Liabilities			**$ 70,150**
Owners' Equity:			
Common shares (10,000 shares outstanding)		$30,000	
Retained earnings		48,750	
Total Owners' Equity			78,750
Total Liabilities and Owners' Equity			**$148,900**

Assets

current assets
Assets that can or will be converted to cash within the next 12 months.

Assets can be divided into three broad categories: current assets, fixed assets, and intangible assets. **Current assets** are assets that can or will be converted to cash within the next 12 months. They are important because they provide the funds used to pay the company's current bills. They also represent the amount of money the company can raise quickly. Current assets include

- *cash*—funds on hand or in a bank;
- *marketable securities (trading securities)*—temporary investments of excess cash that can readily be converted to cash;

- *accounts receivable*—amounts owed to the company by customers who bought goods or services on credit;
- *notes receivable*—amounts owed to the company by customers or others to whom it lent money; and
- *inventory*—stock of goods being held for production or for sale to customers.

The current assets are listed in order of their liquidity, the speed with which they can be converted to cash. Under ASPE, the most liquid assets come first, and the least liquid are last. Because cash is the most liquid asset, it is listed first.

Capital assets (also known as fixed assets or PPE—property, plant, and equipment) are long-term assets used by the company for more than a year. They are presented in order of declining life expectancy. These assets tend to be used in production and include land, buildings, machinery, equipment, furniture, and fixtures. Except for land, capital assets wear out and become outdated over time. Thus, they decrease in value every year. This declining value is accounted for through amortization. Amortization (also called depreciation) is the allocation of the asset's original cost to the years in which it is expected to produce revenues. A portion of the cost of a depreciable asset—a building or piece of equipment, for instance—is charged to each of the years in which it is expected to provide benefits. This practice helps match the asset's cost against the revenues it provides. As it is impossible to know exactly how long an asset will last, estimates are used. They are based on past experience with similar items or on Canada Revenue Agency's guidelines. Notice that, through 2013, Delicious Desserts has taken a total of $16,000 in amortization (depreciation) on its bakery equipment.

Intangible assets are long-term assets with no physical existence. Common examples are patents, copyrights, trademarks, and goodwill. *Patents* and *copyrights* shield the company from direct competition, so their benefits are more protective than productive. For instance, no one can use more than a small amount of copyrighted material without permission from the copyright holder. *Trademarks* are registered names that can be sold or licensed to others. One of Delicious Desserts' intangible assets is a trademark valued at $4500. Delicious Desserts' other intangible asset is goodwill of $7000. Goodwill is the value that has been paid for a company that exceeds the value of its net tangible assets. Why would any person or company pay more for a business than the value of its net tangible assets? The purchase price paid for a company is arrived at through a complex process frequently based on the potential new profit the buyer sees from access to its customers, its ideas, or other intangible assets of the company being bought.

One of the fundamental differences between ASPE and IFRS is in the presentation of assets. In our example of Delicious Desserts in Exhibit 16.4, you will notice that the order was current assets, then capital (fixed) assets, and finally intangible assets. This is because Delicious Desserts is a privately owned company that has chosen to use ASPE. If we were to use IFRS, the capital assets would be referred to as "non-current" and would be presented first and listed in order of declining life expectancy (same order as in ASPE), and then the current assets would be presented, but the order would be different—they would be presented in reverse order—inclining liquidity, with cash last. This does not change the values in any way, just the appearance changes.

Liabilities

Liabilities are the amounts a company owes to creditors. Those liabilities coming due sooner—current liabilities—are listed first on the balance sheet, followed by long-term liabilities.

Current liabilities are those due within a year of the date of the balance sheet. These short-term claims can strain the company's current assets because they must be paid in the near future. Current liabilities include the following:

- *Accounts payable.* This is the amount that the company owes for credit purchases due within a year. This account is the liability counterpart of accounts receivable.

liquidity
The speed with which an asset can be converted to cash.

capital assets
Long-term assets used by a company for more than a year, such as land, buildings, and machinery, also referred to as fixed assets or property, plant, and equipment (PPE).

amortization (depreciation)
The allocation of an asset's original cost to the years in which it is expected to produce revenues.

intangible assets
Long-term assets with no physical existence, such as patents, copyrights, trademarks, and goodwill.

goodwill
The value that has been paid for a company that exceeds the value of its net tangible assets.

current liabilities
Short-term claims that are due within a year of the date of the balance sheet.

- *Notes payable*. These are short-term loans from banks, suppliers, or others that must be repaid within a year. For example, Delicious Desserts has a six-month, $15,000 loan from its bank that is a note payable.
- *Accrued expenses*. These represent expenses, typically for wages and taxes, that have accumulated and must be paid at a specified future date within the year, although no bill has been received by the company.
- *Income taxes payable*. These are taxes owed for the current operating period but not yet paid. Taxes are often shown separately when they are a large amount.
- *Current portion of long-term debt*. This represents any repayment on long-term debt due within the year. Delicious Desserts is scheduled to repay $5000 on its equipment loan in the coming year.

Long-term liabilities come due more than one year after the date of the balance sheet. They include bank loans (such as Delicious Desserts' $10,000 loan for production equipment), mortgages on buildings, and the company's bonds sold to others.

Owners' Equity

Owners' equity (or net worth) is the owners' total investment in the business after all liabilities have been paid. For sole proprietorships and partnerships, amounts put in by the owners are recorded as capital. In a corporation, the owners provide capital by buying the company's common shares. For Delicious Desserts, the total common shares investment is $30,000. **Retained earnings** is the amount left over from profitable operations since the company's beginning. They are total profits minus all dividends (distributions of profits) paid to shareholders. Delicious Desserts has $48,750 in retained earnings.

Under IFRS, just as the order of assets is reversed, so is the order of liabilities and owners' equity. If Delicious Desserts used IFRS, owners' equity would be displayed first, then non-current liabilities (long-term liabilities), and finally current liabilities.

long-term liabilities
Claims that come due more than one year after the date of the balance sheet.

retained earnings
The amounts left over from profitable operations since the company's beginning; equal to total profits minus all dividends paid to shareholders.

Concept *Check*

What is a balance sheet (statement of financial position)?

What are the three main categories of accounts on the balance sheet, and how do they relate to the accounting equation?

How do retained earnings relate to owners' equity?

Concept *in Action*

On its balance sheet, a bakery would list its bakery equipment, furniture, and fixtures as fixed assets. The amount it owes its vendors for supplies would appear as a current liability—accounts payable—and its bank loan would be under long-term liabilities. On the income statement, you'll find a summary of revenues and expenses for a particular time period. What information can a potential investor find out from the balance sheet?

GUY SHAPIRA/SHUTTERSTOCK

Creating the Future of Business

ALYSSA RICHARD, RATEHUB.CA

Alyssa Richard, a business school graduate, left the cushy $70,000 a year consulting job in Toronto that she had been working in for two years, to start RateHub.ca. Gutsy—but smart. Alyssa's exceptional analytical skills and high-level way of thinking easily transferred to the world of web analytics and SEO (search engine optimization). It was a marriage made in mortgage heaven—she saw an opportunity in the "under-served online mortgage market in Canada" and she went for it.

RateHub.ca, founded in January 2010, is a website that compares Canadian mortgage rates to help consumers find the lowest rates. It essentially does for mortgage rates what Expedia does for travel, with the added bonus of providing a "complete and unbiased resource"— the leads obtained through its visitors—to mortgage brokers. Consumers find the best rates, mortgage brokers get more leads, and RateHub takes a piece for bringing them together—everybody wins. And with the Canadian Mortgage and Housing Corporation (CMHC) reporting that "9 out of 10 first-time home buyers are using the Internet to search for information on mortgage options," and "over 1 million local Google searches every month containing the word 'mortgage,'" that translates into big business for RateHub.

Problem is it's not as easy as it looks. Leaving a comfortable job in the corporate world is tough at any age. According to Alyssa: "When you're going from a salaried position to starting your own business, you're investing a lot of your savings and your salary goes down, sometimes even to zero." She had to make compromises but says she has no regrets. She believes "the longer you spend in a corporate job … the harder it is to start something on your own."

And the longer you enjoy a certain lifestyle, especially after buying a home and starting a family, the harder it is to start putting that money you used to enjoy into your business.

The difference with Alyssa, according to Barbara Garbens of BL Garbens Associates Inc.—a financial planning company in Toronto— is that Alyssa is mature and confident beyond her years. She took the business management knowledge she gained working in the consulting industry, applied it to her own business, and at the same time "kept her personal finances in order." Garbens suggests that for a lot of people, starting a business later in life gives them an advantage because "most people starting out need to build a network first and get some experience … (they) need to be practical and have money saved" to support themselves until the business takes off.

Time will tell, but it certainly looks like Alyssa has chosen the right time to make her move to become an entrepreneur. There's no looking back now!

Thinking Critically

1. Do you agree with Alyssa Richard or Barbara Garbens? When is the right time in life to make the leap to becoming an entrepreneur?
2. What factors do you feel have combined to help Alyssa and RateHub become a success? Which factor—the environment and market opportunity, or Alyssa's character, is the greater determinant—or are both necessary for success?

SOURCES: http://www.ratehub.ca, used with permission from Alyssa Richard; http://www.theglobeandmail.com/globe-investor/personal-finance/financial-road-map/starting-a-businessbefore-being-tied-down/article2214510/; "Interview with Alyssa Richard from RateHub.ca," Bank Nerd Blog, May 11, 2011, http://www.banknerd.ca/2011/05/11/interview-with-alyssa-richard-from-ratehub-ca/.

THE INCOME STATEMENT

LO5

The balance sheet (statement of financial position) shows the company's financial position at a certain point in time. The **income statement** (statement of comprehensive income under IFRS), the statement of earnings, or the profit and loss statement, summarizes the company's revenues and expenses and shows its total profit or loss over a period of time. Most companies prepare a monthly income statement for management and quarterly and annual statements for use by investors, creditors, and other outsiders. The primary elements of the income statement are revenues, expenses, and net income (or net loss). The income statement for Delicious Desserts for the year ended December 31, 2013, is shown in Exhibit 16.5.

Revenues

Revenues are the dollar amount of sales plus any other income received from sources such as interest, dividends, and rents. The revenues of Delicious Desserts arise from sales of its products. Revenues are determined starting with **gross sales**, the total dollar amount of a company's sales. Delicious Desserts had two deductions from gross sales. *Sales discounts* are price reductions given to customers who pay their bills early. For example, Delicious Desserts gives sales discounts to restaurants that buy in bulk and

income statement (statement of comprehensive income)
A financial statement that summarizes a company's revenues and expenses, and shows its total profit or loss over a period of time. Also known as the statement of comprehensive income, statement of earnings, and the profit and loss statement.

revenues (also called sales and income)
The dollar amount of a company's sales plus any other income it received from sources such as interest, dividends, and rents.

gross sales
The total dollar amount of a company's sales.

Exhibit 16.5 Income Statement for Delicious Desserts

DELICIOUS DESSERTS, INC.

Income Statement for the Year Ending December 31, 2013

Revenues

Gross sales	$275,000	
Less: Sales discounts	2,500	
Less: Returns and allowances	2,000	
Net sales		$ 270,500

Cost of Goods Sold

Beginning inventory, January 1	$ 18,000	
Cost of goods manufactured	109,500	
Total cost of goods available for sale	$127,500	
Less: Ending inventory December 31	15,000	
Cost of goods sold		112,500

Gross Profit		**$158,000**

Operating Expenses

Selling expenses

Sales salaries	$31,000		
Advertising	16,000		
Other selling expenses	18,000		
Total selling expenses		$ 65,000	

General and administrative expenses

Professional and office salaries	$20,500		
Utilities	5,000		
Depreciation	1,500		
Interest	3,600		
Insurance	2,500		
Rent	17,000		
Total general and administrative expenses		50,100	
Total operating expenses			115,100

Net Profit before Taxes		**$ 42,900**
Less: Income taxes		10,725
Net Profit		**$ 32,175**

pay at delivery. *Returns and allowances* is the dollar amount of merchandise returned by customers because they didn't like a product or because it was damaged or defective. Net sales is the amount left after deducting sales discounts and returns and allowances from gross sales. Delicious Desserts' gross sales were reduced by $4500, leaving net sales of $270,500.

net sales
The amount left after deducting sales discounts and returns and allowances from gross sales.

Expenses

Expenses are the costs of generating revenues. Two types are recorded on the income statement: cost of goods sold and operating expenses.

expenses
The costs of generating revenues.

cost of goods sold (COGS)
The total expense of buying or producing a company's goods or services.

The cost of goods sold (COGS) is the total expense of buying or producing the company's goods or services. For manufacturers, cost of goods sold includes all costs directly related to production: purchases of raw materials and parts, labour, and factory overhead (utilities, factory maintenance, and machinery repair). For wholesalers and retailers, it is the cost of goods bought for resale. For all sellers, cost of goods sold includes all the expenses of preparing the goods for sale, such as shipping and packaging.

The value of COGS can be calculated using

Beginning Inventories
+ <u>Inventory Purchases</u>
= Inventories Available for Sale
− <u>Ending Inventories</u>
= COGS

Delicious Desserts' cost of goods sold is based on the value of inventory on hand at the beginning of the accounting period, $18,000 (from the balance sheet of the last accounting period). During the year, the company spent $109,500 to produce its manufactured goods. This figure includes the cost of raw materials, labour costs for production workers, and the cost of operating the production area. Adding the cost of goods manufactured to the value of beginning inventory, we get the total cost of goods available for sale, $127,500. To determine the cost of goods sold for the year, we subtract the cost of inventory at the end of the period:

$$\$18,000 + \$109,500 - \$15,000 = \$112,500$$

The amount a company earns after paying to produce or buy its products but before deducting operating expenses is the gross profit. It is the difference between net sales and cost of goods sold. As service businesses do not produce goods, their gross profit equals net sales. Gross profit is a critical number for a company, because it is the source of funds to cover all the company's other expenses.

The other major expense category is operating expenses. These are the expenses of running the business that are not related directly to producing or buying its products. The two main types of operating expenses are selling expenses and general and administrative expenses. *Selling expenses* are those related to marketing and distributing the company's products. They include salaries and commissions paid to salespeople and the costs of advertising, sales supplies, delivery, and other items that can be linked to sales activity, such as insurance, telephone and other utilities, and postage. *General and administrative expenses* are the business expenses that cannot be linked to either cost of goods sold or sales. Examples of general and administrative expenses are salaries of top managers and office support staff; utilities; office supplies; interest expense; fees for accounting, consulting, and legal services; insurance; and rent. The annual depreciation on fixed (capital or non-current) assets is another operating expense. It is considered selling or general and administrative depending on the asset being amortized. Delicious Desserts' operating expenses totalled $115,100.

gross profit
The amount a company earns after paying to produce or buy its products but before deducting operating expenses.

operating expenses
The expenses of running a business that are not directly related to producing or buying its products.

Net Profit or Loss

The final figure—or bottom line—on an income statement is the net profit (or net income) or net loss. It is calculated by subtracting all expenses from revenues. If revenues are more than expenses, the result is a net profit. If expenses exceed revenues, a net loss results and is usually shown in brackets.

Several steps are involved in finding net profit or loss. (These are shown in the right-hand column of Exhibit 16.5.) First, the cost of goods sold is deducted from net sales to get the gross profit. Then, total operating expenses are subtracted from gross profit to get the net profit before taxes. Finally, income taxes are deducted to get the net profit. As shown in Exhibit 16.5, Delicious Desserts earned a net profit of $32,175 in 2013.

It is very important to recognize that profit does not represent cash. The income statement is a summary of the company's operating results during some time period. It does not present the company's actual cash flows during the period. Those are summarized in the statement of cash flows, which is discussed briefly in the next section.

net profit (net income)
The amount obtained by subtracting all of a company's expenses from its revenues, when the revenues are more than the expenses.

net loss
The amount obtained by subtracting all of a company's expenses from its revenues, when the expenses are more than the revenues.

Concept *Check*

What is an income statement (statement of comprehensive income)? How does it differ from the balance sheet (statement of financial position)?

Describe the key parts of the income statement. Distinguish between gross sales and net sales.

How is net profit or loss calculated?

LO6 | THE STATEMENT OF CASH FLOWS

statement of cash flows
A financial statement that provides a summary of the money flowing into and out of a company during a certain period, typically one year.

Choose any public Canadian company. Search its website for their financial statements, and review the balance sheet and income statement.

Concept *Check*

What is the purpose of the statement of cash flows?

Why has cash flow become such an important measure of a company's financial condition?

What situations can you cite from the chapter that support your answer?

Net profit or loss is one measure of a company's financial performance. However, creditors and investors are also keenly interested in how much cash a business generates and how it is used. The **statement of cash flows**, a summary of the money flowing into and out of a company, is the financial statement used to assess the sources and uses of cash during a certain period, typically one year. All publicly traded companies must include a statement of cash flows in their financial reports to shareholders. The statement of cash flows tracks the company's cash receipts and cash payments. It gives financial managers and analysts a way of identifying cash flow problems and of assessing the company's financial viability.

Using income statements and balance sheet data, the statement of cash flows divides the company's cash flows into three groups:

- *cash flow from operating activities*—those related to the production or purchase of the company's goods or the services performed;
- *cash flow from investment activities*—those related to the purchase and sale of assets; and
- *cash flow from financing activities*—those related to debt and equity financing.

Delicious Desserts' statement of cash flows for 2013 is presented in Exhibit 16.6. It shows that the company's cash and marketable securities have increased over the last year. Furthermore, during the year, the company generated enough cash flow to increase inventory and fixed assets and to reduce accounts payable, accruals, notes payable, and long-term debt.

LO7 | ANALYZING FINANCIAL STATEMENTS

Individually, the balance sheet, income statement, and statement of cash flows provide insight into the company's operations, profitability, and overall financial condition. By studying the relationships among the financial statements,

Exhibit 16.6 Statement of Cash Flows for Delicious Desserts

DELICIOUS DESSERTS, INC.

Statement of Cash Flows for 2013

Cash Flow from Operating Activities

Net profit after taxes	$ 32,175	
Amortization	1,500	
Decrease in accounts receivable	3,140	
Increase in inventory	(4,500)	
Decrease in accounts payable	(2,065)	
Decrease in accruals	(1,035)	
Cash provided by operating activities		$ 29,215
Cash Flow from Investment Activities		
Increase in gross fixed assets	($ 5,000)	
Cash used in investment activities		($ 5,000)
Cash Flow from Financing Activities		
Decrease in notes payable	($ 3,000)	
Decrease in long-term debt	(1,000)	
Cash used by financing activities		($ 4,000)
Net Increase in Cash and Marketable Securities		**$ 20,215**

however, one can gain even more insight into a company's financial condition and performance.

Ratio analysis involves calculating and interpreting financial ratios using data taken from the company's financial statements to assess its condition and performance. A financial ratio states the relationship between financial data on a percentage of three to five years. A company's ratios can also be compared to industry averages or to basis. For instance, current assets might be viewed relative to current liabilities or sales relative to assets. The ratios can then be compared over time, typically to those of another company in the same industry. Period-to-period and industry ratios provide a meaningful basis for comparison, so that we can answer questions such as, "Is this particular ratio good or bad?"

It's important to remember that ratio analysis is based on historical data and might not indicate future financial performance. Ratio analysis merely highlights potential problems; it does not prove that they exist. However, ratios can help managers monitor the company's performance from period to period, to understand operations better and identify trouble spots.

Ratios are also important to a company's present and prospective creditors (lenders), who want to see if the company can repay what it borrows and assess the company's financial health. Often, loan agreements require companies to maintain minimum levels of specific ratios. Both present and prospective shareholders use ratio analysis to look at the company's historical performance and trends over time.

Ratios can be classified by what they measure: liquidity, profitability, activity, and debt. Using Delicious Desserts' 2013 balance sheet and income statement (Exhibits 16.4 and 16.5), we can calculate and interpret the key ratios in each group. In Exhibit 16.7, we have summarized the calculations of these ratios for Delicious Desserts. We will now discuss how to calculate the ratios and, more important, how to interpret the ratio value.

ratio analysis
The calculation and interpretation of financial ratios using data taken from the company's financial statements to assess its condition and performance.

Liquidity Ratios

Liquidity ratios measure the company's ability to pay its short-term debts as they come due. These ratios are of special interest to the company's creditors. The three main measures of liquidity are the current ratio, the acid-test (quick) ratio, and net working capital.

liquidity ratios
Ratios that measure a company's ability to pay its short-term debts as they come due.

Concept *in Action*

How is Canadian Tire doing this quarter compared to historical results? With ratio analysis, managers can track performance. For example, the net profit margin shows how much profit is left after all expenses. Why would a company want to compare their financial ratios with the industry averages?

THE CANADIAN PRESS/MARIO BEAUREGARD

Exhibit 16.7 Ratio Analysis for Delicious Desserts at Year-End 2013

RATIO	FORMULA	CALCULATION	RESULT
Liquidity Ratios			
Current ratio	$\dfrac{\text{Total current assets}}{\text{Total current liabilities}}$	$\dfrac{\$83,200}{\$60,150}$	1.4
Acid-test (quick) ratio	$\dfrac{\text{Total current assets} - \text{inventory}}{\text{Total current liabilities}}$	$\dfrac{\$83,200 - \$15,000}{\$60,150}$	1.1
Net working capital	Total current assets – Total current liabilities	$\$83,200 - \$60,150$	$23,050
Profitability Ratios			
Net profit margin	$\dfrac{\text{Net profit}}{\text{Net sales}}$	$\dfrac{\$32,175}{\$270,500}$	11.9%
Return on equity	$\dfrac{\text{Net profit}}{\text{Total owners' equity}}$	$\dfrac{\$32,175}{\$78,750}$	40.9%
Earnings per share	$\dfrac{\text{Net profit}}{\text{Number of shares of common shares outstanding}}$	$\dfrac{\$32,175}{10,000}$	$3.22
Activity Ratio			
Inventory turnover	$\dfrac{\text{Cost of goods sold}}{\text{Average inventory}}$		
	$\dfrac{\text{Cost of goods sold}}{(\text{Beginning inventory} + \text{Ending inventory})/2}$	$\dfrac{\$112,500}{(\$18,000 + \$15,000)/2}$	6.8 times
		$\dfrac{\$112,500}{\$16,500}$	
Debt Ratio			
Debt-to-equity ratio	$\dfrac{\text{Total liabilities}}{\text{Owners' equity}}$	$\dfrac{\$70,150}{\$78,750}$	89.1%

current ratio
The ratio of total current assets to total current liabilities; used to measure a company's liquidity.

The **current ratio** is the ratio of total current assets to total current liabilities. Traditionally, a current ratio of 2 ($2 of current assets for every $1 of current liabilities) has been considered good. Whether it is sufficient depends on the industry in which the company operates. Public utilities, which have a very steady cash flow, operate quite well with a current ratio well below 2. A current ratio of 2 might not be adequate for manufacturers and merchandisers that carry high inventories and have lots of receivables. The current ratio for Delicious Desserts for 2013, as shown in Exhibit 16.7, is 1.4 (rounded up from 1.38). This means little without a basis for comparison. If the analyst found that the industry average was 2.4, Delicious Desserts would appear to have low liquidity.

acid-test (quick) ratio
The ratio of total current assets excluding inventory to total current liabilities; used to measure a company's liquidity.

The **acid-test (quick) ratio** is like the current ratio except that it excludes inventory, which is the least liquid current asset. The acid-test ratio is used to measure the company's ability to pay its current liabilities without selling inventory. The name *acid-test* implies that this ratio is a crucial test of the company's liquidity. An acid-test ratio of at least 1 is preferred, but again, what is an acceptable value varies by industry. The acid-test ratio is a good measure of liquidity when inventory cannot easily be converted to cash (for instance, if it consists of very specialized goods with a limited market). If inventory is liquid, the current ratio is better. Delicious Desserts' acid-test ratio for 2013 is 1.1. Because Delicious Desserts does not carry large inventories, the values of its acid test and current ratios are fairly close. For manufacturing companies, however, inventory typically makes up a large portion of current assets, so the acid-test ratio will be lower than the current ratio.

net working capital
The amount obtained by subtracting total current liabilities from total current assets; used to measure a company's liquidity.

Net working capital, though not really a ratio, is often used to measure a company's overall liquidity. It is calculated by subtracting total current liabilities from total current assets. Delicious Desserts' net working capital for 2013 is $23,050. Comparisons of net working capital over time often help in assessing a company's liquidity.

Profitability Ratios

To measure profitability, a company's profits can be related to its sales, equity, or shares value. Profitability ratios measure how well the company is using its resources to generate profit and how efficiently it is being managed. The main profitability ratios are net profit margin, return on equity, and earnings per share.

The ratio of net profit to net sales is the net profit margin, also called *return on sales*. It measures the percentage of each sales dollar remaining after all expenses, including taxes, have been deducted. Higher net profit margins are better than lower ones. The net profit margin is often used to measure the company's earning power. "Good" net profit margins differ quite a bit from industry to industry. A grocery store usually has a very low net profit margin, perhaps below 1 percent, whereas a jewellery store's net profit margin would probably exceed 10 percent. Delicious Desserts' net profit margin for 2013 is 11.9 percent. In other words, Delicious Desserts is earning 11.9 cents on each dollar of sales.

The ratio of net profit to total owners' equity is called return on equity (ROE). It measures the return that owners receive on their investment in the company, a major reason for investing in a company's shares. Delicious Desserts has a 40.9 percent ROE for 2013. On the surface, a 40.9 percent ROE seems quite good, but the level of risk in the business and the ROE of other companies in the same industry must also be considered. The higher the risk, the greater the ROE investors look for. A company's ROE can also be compared to past values to see how the company is performing over time.

Earnings per share (EPS) is the ratio of net profit to the number of common shares outstanding. It measures the number of dollars earned by each share. EPS values are closely watched by investors and are considered an important sign of success. EPS also indicates a company's ability to pay dividends. Note that EPS is the dollar amount earned by each share, not the actual amount given to shareholders in the form of dividends. Some earnings may be put back into the company. Delicious Desserts' EPS for 2013 is $3.22.

Activity Ratios

Activity ratios measure how well a company uses its assets. They reflect the speed with which resources are converted to cash or sales. A frequently used activity ratio is inventory turnover.

The inventory turnover ratio measures the speed with which inventory moves through the company and is turned into sales. It is calculated by dividing cost of goods sold by the average inventory. (Average inventory is estimated by adding the beginning and ending inventories for the year and dividing by 2.) Based on its 2013 financial data, Delicious Desserts' inventory, on average, is turned into sales 6.8 times each year, or about once every 54 days (365 days ÷ 6.8). The acceptable turnover ratio depends on the line of business. A grocery store would have a high turnover ratio, maybe 20 times a year, whereas the turnover for a heavy equipment manufacturer might be only 3 times a year.

Debt Ratios

Debt ratios measure the degree and effect of the company's use of borrowed funds (debt) to finance its operations. These ratios are especially important to lenders and investors. They want to make sure the company has a healthy mix of debt and equity. If the company relies too much on debt, it might have trouble meeting interest payments and repaying loans. The most important debt ratio is the debt-to-equity ratio.

The debt-to-equity ratio measures the relationship between the amount of debt financing (borrowing) and the amount of equity financing (owners' funds).

profitability ratios
Ratios that measure how well a company is using its resources to generate profit and how efficiently it is being managed.

net profit margin
The ratio of net profit to net sales; also called return on sales. It measures the percentage of each sales dollar remaining after all expenses, including taxes, have been deducted.

return on equity (ROE)
The ratio of net profit to total owners' equity; measures the return that owners receive on their investment in the company.

earnings per share (EPS)
The ratio of net profit to the number of common shares outstanding; measures the number of dollars earned by each share.

activity ratios
Ratios that measure how well a company uses its assets.

inventory turnover ratio
The ratio of cost of goods sold to average inventory; measures the speed with which inventory moves through a company and is turned into sales.

debt ratios
Ratios that measure the degree and effect of a company's use of borrowed funds (debt) to finance its operations.

debt-to-equity ratio
The ratio of total liabilities to owners' equity; measures the relationship between the amount of debt financing and the amount of equity financing (owner's funds).

It is calculated by dividing total liabilities by owners' equity. In general, the lower the ratio, the better, but it is important to assess the debt-to-equity ratio against both past values and industry averages. Delicious Desserts' ratio for 2013 is 89.1 percent. The ratio indicates that the company has 89 cents of debt for every dollar the owners have provided. A ratio above 100 percent means the company has more debt than equity. In such a case, the lenders are providing more financing than the owners.

LO8

THE FUTURE OF ACCOUNTING

The role of accountants has been changing and expanding. Although accountants still perform the important task of ensuring that a company's financial reporting conforms to accepted accounting principles, they have become a valuable part of the financial team and consult with clients on information technology and other areas as well.

The increasing complexity of today's business environment creates additional challenges for the accounting profession. As we move to a more knowledge-based economy, this creates a problem with being able to value and account for the knowledge assets. By far the most significant accounting trend is the increasing expectation of companies to not only report financial activities but also report green and social accounting. This is especially true in countries with a significant commodities-based economy such as Canada.

Accountants Expand Their Role

Moving beyond their traditional task of validating a company's financial information, accountants now take an active role in advising their clients on systems and procedures, accounting software, and changes in accounting regulations. They also delve into operating information to discover what's behind the numbers. By examining the risks and weaknesses in a company, they can help managers develop financial controls and procedures to prevent future trouble spots. For example, auditors in a manufacturing company might spend a significant amount of time on inventory, a likely problem area.

Making Ethical Choices

GROCERY COMPANIES SHELVE REVENUES AND CAN AUDITORS

As the assistant controller of a major grocery company, you work closely with the company's independent auditor. Overall, you have been pleased with your auditor's performance and believe that the company has shown high standards of integrity.

During this year's review of your company's financial reports and its internal controls, the auditor raised a question about the timing of incentive payments received from vendors and when they would be recognized as revenue. The issue of such incentive payments from vendors is a big one in the grocery industry. Several of your competitors recorded vendor payments received of $2 billion to $3 billion in 2013—more than those companies' operating profits. You are aware that your chain uses these payment receipts to manipulate earnings, choosing the supplier that offers the largest up-front incentive payments for shelf space to boost quarterly

earnings by a sizable amount. Although this is legal, it is a practice that has come under closer scrutiny in the wake of investigations of other accounting irregularities.

You are called into a meeting with the CFO and the controller to discuss what to do about the warning from the audit company that it might have a "reportable condition" relating to this situation. The CFO wants to fire the audit company and hire another one. The controller asks for your opinion.

ETHICAL DILEMMA: Should you go along with the CFO and recommend firing the audit company?

SOURCES: David Henry, "Accounting Games in the Grocer's Aisle," *Business Week*, April 14, 2003, 64; and Stephen Taub, "D&T Warned A&P Dismissed," CFO.com, September 19, 2002, http://www.cfo.com.

Sustainable Business, Sustainable World

ERNST & YOUNG

Companies release their financial statements to stakeholders to enable them to make decisions such as, "Do I want to purchase shares?" or "Should we lend them money?" But what about other kinds of statements? An increasing number of companies are preparing statements to report on their sustainability efforts, on their performance with respect to environmental and social, as well as economic performance—the "triple bottom line."

In Ernst & Young's report on climate change and sustainability: *Seven questions CEOs and boards should ask about "triple bottom line" reporting,* it says that companies that create sustainability reports are expected to show not only their successes but where they have fallen short. This may appear risky for a company's reputation, but in the long run it creates significant benefits from greater stakeholder trust, and improved risk management and greater operational efficiency from the collection and application of the data to decision making. Failing to report, it suggests, can in fact be more risky, as a company appears less transparent or lagging in its efforts. And if it reports incompletely and reporting becomes mandatory and/or standards are tightened, there will be glaring inconsistencies between earlier and later reports, drawing a company's ethics into question.

Currently, sustainability reporting is voluntary, but the trend is toward greater transparency, and standards exist for companies to follow. More than 3,000 companies worldwide issue sustainability reports, according to Harvard University's Hauser Center for Nonprofit Organizations. Sustainability reporting has been slower to take off in North America than in Europe, where companies first started producing reports nearly 20 years ago. However, more than two-thirds of the Fortune Global 500 companies publish some form of sustainability or corporate responsibility report.

There are many reasons for voluntary reporting. Pressure from external stakeholders and institutional investors is one reason.

In fact, a 2010 global Ernst & Young survey of 300 executives of large companies showed that 43 percent believe equity analysts consider factors related to climate change when valuing a company. Operational improvements may well be one of the strongest reasons. Sustainability reporting helps companies identify sustainability-related opportunities for revenue growth and cost control—"what's measured gets managed." And reputation management is an obvious reason. Research conducted by the Global Reporting Initiative (GRI) showed that 82 percent of U.S. companies and 66 percent of European companies cite transparency as the main factor influencing their corporate reputations, a higher percentage than even financial returns.

Clearly companies need to consider reporting on more than just their financial returns if they want to keep up with the demands from stakeholders in the current business environment.

Thinking Critically

1. Would seeing an audited sustainability or social responsibility report for a company influence your decision to buy its stock, all things being equal?
2. Check out the United Nations Principles for Responsible Investment (UN PRI) and see what the international investment community's views are on how environmental, social, and corporate governance (ESG) issues affect the performance of investment portfolios. Looking at the Dow Jones Sustainability Index (DJSI), launched in 1999, will also give you a sense for how the stocks of companies considered sustainability leaders perform.

SOURCES: Ernst & Young, http://www.ey.com; The Hauser Center for Nonprofit Organizations, http://www.hks.harvard.edu/hauser; Global Reporting Initiative, http://www.globalreporting.org; Principles for Responsible Investment, http://www.unpri.org; Dow Jones Sustainability Indexes, http://www.sustainability-index.com.

Accounting firms have greatly expanded the consulting services they provide clients. As a result, accountants have become more involved in the operations of their clients. This raises the question of potential conflicts of interest. Can auditors serve both the public and the client? Auditors' main purpose is to certify financial statements. Will they maintain sufficient objectivity to raise questions while auditing a client that provides them with significant consulting revenues? Can auditors review systems and methods that they recommended? According to one expert, "If the financial markets don't believe in a company's audit, the company has nothing."

Valuing Knowledge Assets

As the world's economy becomes knowledge-based rather than industrial-based, more of a company's value might come from internally generated, intangible intellectual assets. Intellectual capital is an important resource to any organization, but are we serious about actually attaching a dollar value to it? Dr. Nick Bontis, a researcher and practitioner in knowledge management, intellectual capital, and organizational learning at McMaster University in Hamilton, Ontario, discovered that the main reason cited by his research subjects for leaving their employment was that they felt they were underutilized. With voluntary turnover in Canadian organizations reaching 15 percent, we are watching these knowledge assets walk out the door.[7]

Whether and how to value intangibles are controversial issues. Some people believe that because intangibles are uncertain and risky, they do not belong on the balance sheet. Costs related to intangibles might bear no relationship to their actual value. On the other hand, placing a value on intangibles allows companies to know whether they are earning adequate returns on R&D, whether patents are worth renewing, and whether they should invest more to build brands. Clearly, there are no quick and easy solutions to this issue, which will continue to be studied in the coming years.

Green and Social Accounting

In the 1980s Professor Peter Wood suggested that there should be an attempt by accounting to factor in the environmental costs of the operations of a business. For example, in the lumber industry, trees are cut down and the wood is used to build homes, furniture, etc. These all add to the GDP but there is no financial number associated with losing the trees.

Green accounting looks at the impact on the environment whereas social accounting is more encompassing. Social accounting places a value on not only the environmental impact but also the impact on society. Often a company will include social accounting in its discussion of its corporate social responsibility.

Social accounting reports a company's contributions (or lack of) to society. By reviewing and reporting the company's business activities, social accounting focuses on how the company contributes to sustainability and the health of society.

GREAT IDEAS TO USE NOW

By now it should be very clear that basic accounting knowledge is a valuable skill to have, whether you start your own company or work for someone else. Analyzing a company's financial statements before you take a job there can tell you quite a bit about its financial health. Once you are on the job, you need to understand how to read financial statements and how to develop financial information for business operations. It's almost impossible to operate effectively in a business environment otherwise. In a small company, you will wear many hats, and having accounting skills may help you get the job. In addition, accounting will help you manage your personal finances.

If you own your own company, you can't rely on someone else to take charge of your accounting system. You must decide what financial information you need to manage your company better and to track its progress. If you can't understand the reports your accountant prepares, you will have no idea whether they are accurate.

Summary of Learning Outcomes

LO1   **Explain the importance of financial reports and accounting information to the targeted users.**

Accounting involves collecting, recording, classifying, summarizing, reporting, and analyzing a company's financial activities according to a standard set of procedures. The financial reports resulting from the accounting process give managers, employees, investors, customers, suppliers, creditors, and government agencies a way of analyzing a company's past, current, and future performance. Financial accounting is concerned with the preparation of financial reports by using generally accepted accounting principles. Managerial accounting provides financial information that management can use to make decisions about the company's operations.

Although today's accountants still must love working with numbers, they now work closely with their clients not only to prepare financial reports but also to help them develop good financial practices. Computers have taken the tedium out of the number-crunching and data-gathering parts of the job and now offer powerful analytical tools as well. Therefore, accountants must keep up with information technology trends.

In Canada, there are three accounting associations that grant professional designations. They are the Canadian Institute of Chartered Accountants (CICA), the Society of Management Accountants of Canada (CMA Canada), and the Certified General Accountants Association of Canada (CGA-Canada). Each of the professional accounting associations provides specialized services and has certain educational and work experience requirements for the accountant to be granted the professional designation. The lines of responsibility between the designations are now blurred.

LO2 Show an understanding of the accounting profession.

The accounting cycle refers to the process of generating financial statements. It begins with analyzing business transactions, recording them in journals, and posting them to ledgers. Ledger totals are then summarized in a trial balance that confirms the accuracy of the figures. Next, the accountant prepares the financial statements and reports. The final step involves analyzing these reports and making decisions.

LO3 Identify the six steps in the accounting cycle.

The balance sheet (statement of financial position) represents the financial condition of a company at one moment in time, in terms of assets, liabilities, and owners' equity. The key categories of assets are current assets, fixed assets, and intangible assets. Liabilities are divided into current and long-term liabilities. Owners' equity, the amount of the owners' investment in the company after all liabilities have been paid, is the third major category.

LO4 Understand how a balance sheet (statement of financial position) describes the financial condition of an organization.

The income statement (statement of comprehensive income) is a summary of the company's operations over a stated period of time. The main parts of the statement are revenues (gross and net sales), cost of goods sold, operating expenses (selling and general and administrative expenses), taxes, and net profit or loss.

LO5 Explain the purpose of the income statement (statement of comprehensive income).

The statement of cash flows summarizes the company's sources and uses of cash during a financial-reporting period. It breaks the company's cash flows into those from operating, investment, and financing activities. It shows the net change during the period in the company's cash and marketable securities.

LO6 Describe the importance of the statement of cash flows.

Ratio analysis is a way to use financial statements to gain insight into a company's operations, profitability, and overall financial condition. The four main types of ratios are liquidity ratios, profitability ratios, activity ratios, and debt ratios. Comparing a company's ratios over several years and comparing them to ratios of other companies in the same industry, or to industry averages, can indicate trends and highlight financial strengths and weaknesses.

LO7 Explain how ratio analysis is used to identify a company's financial strengths and weaknesses.

The accounting industry is responding to the rise in information technology in several ways. The role of accountants has expanded beyond the traditional audit and tax functions and now includes management consulting in areas such as computer systems, human resources, and electronic commerce. A major issue facing the industry is how to treat key intangible assets—knowledge assets such as patents, brands, and research and development—and whether they should be valued and included on a company's balance sheet. More and more companies are expected to report on their financial activities and to include green and social accounting.

LO8 List some of the major trends that are impacting the accounting industry.

Key Terms

accounting 478
Accounting Standards for Private Enterprises (ASPE) 480
acid-test (quick) ratio 494
activity ratios 495
amortization (depreciation) 487
annual report 480
assets 483
balance sheet (statement of financial position) 485
capital assets 487
certified general accountant (CGA) 482
certified management accountant (CMA) 482
chartered accountant (CA) 481
chartered professional accountant (CPA) 482
cost of goods sold (COGS) 490
current assets 486
current liabilities 487
current ratio 494
debt ratios 495
debt-to-equity ratio 495
depreciation (amortization) 487
double-entry bookkeeping 484
earnings per share (EPS) 495
expenses 490
financial accounting 479
generally accepted accounting principles (GAAP) 479
goodwill 487
gross profit 491

gross sales 489
income statement (statement of comprehensive income) 489
intangible assets 487
International Financial Reporting Standards (IFRS) 480
inventory turnover ratio 495
liabilities 483
liquidity 487
liquidity ratios 493
long-term liabilities 488
managerial accounting 478
net loss 491
net profit (net income) 491
net profit margin 495
net sales 490
net working capital 494
operating expenses 491
owners' equity 483
profitability ratios 495
ratio analysis 493
retained earnings 488
return on equity (ROE) 495
revenues (also called sales and income) 489
statement of cash flows 492
statement of financial position (balance sheet) 485
trial balance 485
T-account 484

Experiential Exercises

1. Learn to read financial statements. To become more familiar with annual reports and key financial statements, head for IBM's "Guide to Understanding Financials" at www.ibm.com/investor/financialguide. The material offers a good overview of financial reporting and shows you what to look for when you read these documents.

2. Prepare personal financial statements. One of the best ways to learn about financial statements is to prepare them. Put together your personal balance sheet and income statement, using Exhibits 16.4 and 16.5 as samples. You will have to adjust the account categories to fit your needs. Here are some suggestions:

   - Current assets—cash on hand, balances in savings, and chequing accounts
   - Investments—shares and bonds, retirement funds
   - Fixed assets—real estate, personal property (cars, furniture, jewellery, etc.)
   - Current liabilities—credit card balances, loan payments due in one year
   - Long-term liabilities—auto loan balance, mortgage on real estate, other loan balances that will not come due until after one year
   - Income—employment income, investment income (interest, dividends)
   - Expenses—housing, utilities, food, transportation, medical, clothing, insurance, loan payments, taxes, personal care, recreation and entertainment, and miscellaneous expenses

After you complete your personal financial statements, use them to see how well you are managing your finances. Consider the following questions:

- Should you be concerned about your debt ratio?
- Would a potential creditor conclude that it is safe or risky to lend you money?
- If you were a company, would people want to invest in you? Why or why not? What can you do to improve your financial condition?

3. Your company has been hired to help several small businesses with their year-end financial statements.

   a. Based on the following account balances, prepare the Marbella Design Enterprises balance sheet as of December 31, 2013:

Cash	$30,250
Accounts payable	28,500
Fixtures and furnishings	85,000
Notes payable	15,000
Retained earnings	64,450
Accounts receivable	24,050
Inventory	15,600
Equipment	42,750
Accumulated amortization on fixtures and furnishings	12,500
Common shares (50,000 shares outstanding)	50,000
Long-term debt	25,000
Accumulated amortization on equipment	7,800
Marketable securities	13,000
Income taxes payable	7,500

   b. The following are the account balances for the revenues and expenses of the Windsor Gift Shop for the year ending December 31, 2013. Prepare the income statement for the shop.

Rent	$ 15,000
Salaries	23,500
Cost of goods sold	98,000
Utilities	8,000
Supplies	3,500
Sales	195,000
Advertising	3,600
Interest	3,000
Taxes	12,120

4. During the year ended December 31, 2013, Lawrence Industries sold $2 million worth of merchandise on credit. A total of $1.4 million was collected during the year. The cost of this merchandise was $1.3 million. Of this amount, $1 million has been paid, and $300,000 is not yet due. Operating expenses and income taxes totalling $500,000 were paid in cash during the year. Assume that all accounts had a zero balance at the beginning of the year (January 1, 2013). Write a brief report for the company controller that includes calculation of the company's (a) net profit and (b) cash flow during the year. Explain why there is a difference between net profit and cash flow.

5. A friend has been offered a sales representative position at Draper Publications, Inc., a small publisher of computer-related books, but wants to know more about the company. Because of your expertise in financial analysis, you offer to help

analyze Draper's financial health. Draper has provided the following selected financial information:

Account balances on December 31, 2013:	
Inventory	$ 72,000
Net sales	450,000
Current assets	150,000
Cost of goods sold	290,000
Total liabilities	180,000
Net profit	35,400
Total assets	385,000
Current liabilities	75,000
Other information	
Number of common shares outstanding	25,000
Inventory at January 1, 2013	48,000

Calculate the following ratios for 2013: acid-test (quick) ratio, inventory turnover ratio, net profit margin, return on equity (ROE), debt-to-equity ratio, and earnings per share (EPS). Summarize your assessment of the company's financial performance, based on these ratios, in a report for your friend. What other information would you like to have to complete your evaluation?

6. Two years ago, Rebecca Mardon started a computer consulting business, Mardon Consulting Associates. Until now, she has been the only employee, but business has grown enough to support an administrative assistant and another consultant this year. Before she adds staff, however, she wants to hire an accountant and computerize her financial record keeping. Divide the class into small groups, assigning one person to be Rebecca and the others to represent members of a medium-sized accounting firm. Rebecca should think about the type of financial information systems her company requires and develop a list of questions for the company. The accountants will prepare a presentation, making recommendations to her as well as explaining why their company should win the account.

7. Do annual reports confuse you? Many websites can take the mystery out of this important document. See IBM's "Guide to Understanding Financials" at www.prars.com/ibm/ibmframe.html. Moneychimp's "How to Read an Annual Report" features an interactive diagram that provides a big picture view of what the report's financial information tells you: www.moneychimp.com/articles/financials/fundamentals.htm. Which site was more helpful to you, and why?

8. Can you judge an annual report by its cover? What are the most important elements of a top annual report? Go to Sid Cato's Official Annual Report website, www.sidcato.com, to find his 15 standards for annual reports and read about the reports that receive his honours. Then, get a copy of an annual report and evaluate it using Cato's 135-point scale. How well does it compare to his top picks?

9. Test your knowledge by completing the following T-account exercise:

On April 2013, XYZ was formed by a group of shareholders who contributed $250,000 for 500,000 shares in the company and appointed Mark Stevenson as the new CEO. The following transactions happened between April 1, 2013, and June 30, 2013. Please provide the T-accounts for the transactions as well as the trial balance as at June 30, 2013. From the trial balance, prepare a balance sheet for XYZ as at June 30, 2013, and an income statement for the three months ended June 30, 2013.

- April 2, 2013, Mark opened a bank account with ATB Financial and transferred $250,000 that was received from shareholders to the account.
- On April 2, Mark signed a lease agreement for an office and a nearby warehouse for a year at a rent of $2500 a month and paid $2500 for April rent and left a deposit of $2000 as damage deposit with the landlord. The lease covers all utilities as well as telephones.

- On April 3, he hired Mary as XYZ's office manager at a salary of $2000 a month, payable at the end of each month.
- On April 7, Mark purchased furniture for the office and paid $8000 for the furniture.
- On April 8, they purchased computers and printers for $5100; for use in the business.
- On April 8, they purchased $25,000 of toys for resale, which were delivered to the warehouse. The first payment of $12,500 was due on May 10, 2013, one month after delivery and the balance was paid on July 10.
- On April 15, they sold $20,000 worth of toys to various customers for cash in a trade show.
- On April 30, they paid salaries to Mary & Mark as follows:
  a. Mary $2000
  b. Mark $5000
- May 1, 2013, they paid rent as per their contract.
- On May 10, they paid the toy wholesaler.
- On May 15, they sold $10,000 more in toys to ABC, a local retailer who paid $5000 cash and will pay the balance on June 15, a month later.
- On May 30, they ordered another $15,000 in toys.
- On May 31, they paid salaries
- On June 1, they paid rent.
- On June 3, they received the toys that were ordered on May 30, and paid for them by cheque.
- On June 15, the toy retailer paid for the balance of account for toys purchased on May 15.
- On June 18, they sold another shipment of toys to ABC for $18,000 and were paid $8000 with the balance to be paid on July 18.
- On June 30, they paid salaries.
- On June 30, they counted the toys left in the warehouse, and their value based on cost of purchase was $22,000.
- XYZ depreciates the furniture over 4 years and computers over 3 years; you should provide depreciation for ¼ of the year when calculating your income for the period.

Review Questions

1. What is accounting? What is the difference between managerial and financial accounting?
2. What is IFRS? What is its function?
3. Discuss the accounting profession in terms of public versus private accountants, CAs, CMAs, and CGAs.
4. What is the accounting equation?
5. Explain the various categories of a balance sheet (statement of financial position).
6. What is the purpose of the income statement (statement of comprehensive income)? What does it include?
7. What is the purpose of a statement of cash flows?
8. What is ratio analysis?
9. Name and provide the formulas of the liquidity ratios mentioned in the chapter.
10. What do profitability ratios tell us? Which ratios are mentioned in the chapter?
11. What are activity ratios and which ones are mentioned in the chapter?
12. What do debt ratios measure? What does the debt-to-equity ratio measure?
13. What trends are happening in the accounting field?

CREATIVE THINKING CASE

Accounting: To Whom Are We Responsible?

Arthur Andersen started the accounting firm that bore his name in 1913. From the start, he embraced the highest business ethics, refusing to manipulate unsatisfactory financial results at a client's request. Andersen's motto, "Think straight, talk straight," was the foundation of the company's culture of honesty and integrity. The company was known for its disciplined and strict attention to accounting standards.

By the 1990s, the Andersen culture had strayed far from its founder's philosophy. Andersen was "a place where the mad scramble for fees had trumped good judgment," says Barbara Ley Toffler, author of *Final Accounting: Ambition, Greed and the Fall of Arthur Andersen*. These fees came not only from auditing, but increasingly from the rapidly growing consulting practices of Andersen and its industry colleagues. Business units competed with each other and were rewarded for bringing in revenues, not for evaluating a deal's risks.

The growth of consulting revenues was in itself a problem. Andersen often provided business services to the same companies it audited, earning as much from consulting as auditing. This conflict of interest placed pressure on the auditors to go along with aggressive accounting practices in order to preserve the consulting relationships and earnings.

Andersen's culture also placed a loyalty to the company before loyalty to clients or shareholders. Partners who raised questions were penalized. This attitude went straight down the line, as Toffler discovered when leading a meeting of young Andersen employees. She asked how they would respond if a supervisor told them to do something they considered wrong. Only one person spoke up: "If he insisted I do it, yes, I would." Toffler then asked if he would tell anyone about it: "No. It could hurt my career."

Turning a blind eye to accounting irregularities of clients was a common practice. Says Toffler, who—ironically—ran Andersen's business ethics consulting practice from 1995 to 1999, "High-level members of that organization knew much of what was going on." As Enron's wrongdoings became public, the company's top management became Enron's partner in duplicity instead of demonstrating the industry leadership its founder would have expected.

In June 2002, Andersen was convicted of obstruction of justice in the Enron case for shredding documents. Shannon Adlong, assistant to the lead accountant on the Enron file, described one load of material hauled away by a shredding company as "32 trunks the size of football lockers." In 2005, the Supreme Court of the United States unanimously overturned the conviction.

Regardless, the damage had been done. The process that mortally wounded Andersen has coined a new phrase, "being Enronned"—by association, the accountants were marked. The consulting company had been spun off in 2000 as Accenture and continues its worldwide operations. Arthur Andersen LLP still exists as a private corporation offering professional services, but in a very small way compared to the late 1990s. The company surrendered its licence to produce audits in 2002 and the most recent update of their website, www.andersen.com, was in 2004. According to Bloomberg *Businessweek*, Arthur Andersen had offices in 84 countries as of 2011.

Thinking Critically

1. Toffler says that Andersen executives expected that aggressive accounting would have an impact when the economy tanked but issued few warning memos and did nothing to change the culture of greed. With the benefit of hindsight, what steps could Andersen's leadership have taken to preserve the company as the accounting scandals unfolded?

2. Andersen's Enron audit team was aware of monkey business as early as 1987, when management covered up an oil-trading scandal. It also caved in to pressure to sign off on questionable deals and participated in document destruction that led to its obstruction-of-justice conviction. Suggest procedures that auditors and corporations should adopt and enforce to prevent these abuses.

3. Discuss why providing consulting services to audit clients in such areas as business strategy; financial strategy; human resources; information technology systems; and planning, design, and implementation can create a conflict of interest.

SOURCES: Greg Farrell, "Former Andersen Exec Tells of Stressful Internal Culture," *USA Today*, March 3, 2003; William J. Holstein, "Lessons of a Fallen Rival for Accounting's Big 4," *The New York Times*, February 23, 2003; Rob Walker, "Inside a Culture of Greed," *Newsday*, March 6, 2003; Unmesh Kher, "The End of Arthur Andersen?" *Time*, March 11, 2002; ARTHUR ANDERSEN LLP V. UNITED STATES (04-368) 544 U.S. 696 (2005) 374 F.3d 281, reversed and remanded, http://www.law.cornell.edu/supct/html/04-368.ZS.html, December 21, 2011; "Accenture: The Growth of a Global Leader," http://www.accenture.com/us-en/company/overview/history/Pages/growth-global-leader.aspx, accessed December 20, 2011; "Professional Services, Arthur Andersen," Bloomberg *Businessweek* 2011, http://investing.businessweek.com/research/stocks/private/snapshot.asp?privcapId=890180, December 21, 2012.

Making the Connection

Understanding Money and the Canadian Financial System

In this chapter, we will look at the *finance* area by examining where the money to run a successful business comes from. It would be wonderful if all the capital needed to operate and grow a business came from income alone. However, to move past a company's current level of income and to grow it to new heights, implementing its chosen *strategy* to achieve its *vision*, it typically must bring fresh capital in from outside. In the chapter, we introduce the role of money and financial institutions, as well as the securities markets, which provide the fuel for companies—an arena for raising capital.

Among the major *stakeholders* in any business are the owners. As discussed in previous chapters, companies must consider the impact on stakeholders of any decisions they make. Certainly the choice of how a business is financed has a tremendous impact on the owners. Particularly in the publicly traded corporation, it is critical that financial managers consider this seriously, as there is a very integrative relationship between this major stakeholder and the company's financing. Much of the company's financial resources will come from investments made by its owners—the shareholders—through the purchase of shares or stocks in the company. However, how those financial resources are managed will, in turn, affect the value of the company and the owners' stake in it, and therefore whether they would consider the company worth continuing to invest in. This affects the company's ability to raise additional money through the sale of more shares.

If the financial manager does not focus on the first of the critical success factors—achieving *financial performance*—then the shareholders will be less inclined to invest further and will perhaps even sell their shares, which could, if there is enough selling activity, drive down the price of the shares on the stock market, making the shares even less appealing to most investors. The ability to raise additional funds through the sale of shares will then be hindered. However, to achieve financial performance, we know that it is essential to achieve the other success factors as well—meeting *customer needs*, providing *quality*, encouraging *innovation*, and gaining *employee commitment*—because they are all related. So all the functional area managers—*marketing*, *operations*, and *human resources*, as well as finance, are responsible for making sure the company is successful for its stakeholders. They all have an impact on financial performance.

Companies, of course, have other options for raising capital. In the securities markets, one of the major options besides selling equity investments—a piece of ownership through shares—is to sell bonds. Selling bonds is essentially borrowing money and therefore is considered debt rather than equity financing. The balancing act that the company performs, between the amount of debt it uses to finance the company and the amount of equity, also has an impact on the financial performance of the company and, again, on its ability to raise more capital.

Whatever amount of debt it chooses to use versus equity, or the amount of bonds it sells as opposed to shares, the external environment will have an enormous impact, just as we've seen with all other aspects of the business. The external environment forms the context in which the company operates and thus affects its decisions and its success. For example, the *political* environment lays the foundation for how the company can raise capital—regulations exist surrounding the criteria that a company must meet to be able to sell its shares to the public—as well as the composition of the board of directors, the highest level of management in the company, whose main job is to protect the interests of the shareholders. The *economic* environment certainly has an impact, both from a competitive standpoint, as companies compete not only for customers but for investors as well, and from a purely economic one, as the economy affects what investments are the most attractive to investors (influencing what type of financing is likely to be the more marketable—selling shares or bonds) and the cost of debt financing to the company through interest rates. The *social* environment also impacts a company's financing. This is evident in the popularity of ethical funds—mutual funds that invest in companies that have a strong social conscience. The impact of the *technological* environment was very obvious and extreme when technological companies were the darlings of the stock market, before the "bubble burst" in 2000 and they just as dramatically fell in value. But the impact of technology is also felt in how the market operates. Each year, more and more advances are made to automate the securities exchanges. Gone are the days of traders shouting across trading floors. And finally, the *international* environment, particularly the international financial community, certainly impacts a company's financing whether it operates globally or not. You just have to think of the repercussions that the collapse of the financial markets in the U.S. have had worldwide, let alone the recent decline of major European countries, and the impact is obvious and far-reaching.

For investors, though, the markets still offer an opportunity for ordinary people like you and me to become part owners in a company and share in its success. This is all made possible by companies entering the market to raise capital to operate their businesses and, in turn, increasing value for the owners, their primary stakeholders.

chapter 17

Understanding Money and the Canadian Financial System

LEARNING OUTCOMES

1 Understand the characteristics of money and its functions.

2 Describe the basic functions of the Bank of Canada and how it manages the Canadian money supply.

3 Identify the key financial institutions and the role they play in the process of financial intermediation.

4 Outline how the Canada Deposit Insurance Corporation protects depositors' funds.

5 Summarize the role of Canadian banks in the international marketplace.

6 Distinguish between common shares and preferred shares.

7 Understand the investment advantages and disadvantages of bonds.

8 List other types of securities available to investors.

9 Describe the function of the securities markets.

10 List some of the trends that are reshaping the financial industry.

FINDING YOUR FIT: ONLINE QUESTIONNAIRE CAN HELP JOB-SEEKERS HOME IN ON THEIR INTERESTS

Chelsea Deal does mortgage calculations in her spare time. She finds finance fun, and thinks she's destined for a career in banking. So, when she's given a chance to check out the Find Your Fit questionnaire, offered to career-seekers by RBC, Canada's largest banking organization, she is keen. The questionnaire, available at RBC.com, seems to her like a good place to start a job search or see what sort of future she might have as a bank employee.

Chelsea is going into her fourth year at Saint Mary's University in Halifax. She's the first in her family to go to university, and her mom and older sister have high hopes for her. They live in Terence Bay, a small fishing village just outside Halifax. To pay for university, Chelsea works in retail. She has plenty of customer-service experience, but when the Find Your Fit survey asks her whether she'd prefer to deal with external customers or "internal partners," she leans toward the latter. She interprets it to mean she would be interacting with people in the banking industry who speak her language: mortgages, finance, and other advanced concepts she's learning.

An interesting aspect of the Find Your Fit questions is the use of phrases such as "internal partners" or "qualified" without explanations of their meanings. These words could mean different things to different people. Chelsea thinks she might be qualified for some jobs and need further training for others, but she's unsure. She'd like RBC to tell her more about what it is looking for. But she forges ahead anyway, and her answers point her toward careers involving the more technical and internal aspects of RBC.

When she finishes the process, Chelsea learns she's suited to be an "operations specialist" at RBC. The website takes her to a search engine that can show her the jobs available within the organization. She can narrow the search to type of job, geographic region, and an RBC "platform," or field of expertise, within which she'd like to work. From there, she can set up a candidate profile and submit her resume.

But Chelsea wants to finish her degree first. She's going to apply for a job at RBC or another bank when she gets closer to graduation. The questionnaire has given her some ideas about the types of jobs she might like and what further training she may need to get those jobs. It's also given her information about what banks may be looking for in their employees, and some insight into the possible careers her love of mortgage calculations could lead her to pursue.

Also informative for beginning job-seekers are the photos used to illustrate this part of RBC's website. They depict people who work for the bank's operations, which

PHOTO COURTESY OF CHRISTOPHER HARTT

include Royal Bank of Canada branches. It's easy to see how RBC expects its employees to dress. The pictures show young, earnest-looking staff members, smartly dressed in suits and ties. You'll find no "business casual" here.

By the end, Chelsea feels the Find Your Fit process might be useful for first- or second-year students who haven't picked their courses yet. For Chelsea, though, who is already familiar with the atmosphere within the banking industry, has read banks' websites and talked with alumni and professors about careers in banking, and has a good idea of how to sculpt her academic choices to improve her chances at getting the job she wants, the questionnaire hasn't been quite as valuable in clarifying career aspirations.[1]

THINKING CRITICALLY

As you read this chapter, consider the following questions:

1. What could the banking sector do to create more awareness of the career opportunities it offers?

2. What are some questions that would better clarify a person's suitability for a job in banking?

3. As the ways in which clients interact with financial institutions continue to change and evolve, what kinds of banking careers have the most long-term potential?

SOURCES: http://www.rbc.com/careers/findyourfit.html/ and personal interview - Chris Hartt.

Advanced technology, globalization of markets, and changing financial regulations are accelerating the pace of change in the financial services industry. These changes are giving businesses and consumers new options for conducting their financial transactions. The competitive landscape for financial institutions is also changing, creating new ways for these companies to increase their market share and boost profits.

Because financial institutions connect people with money, we begin this chapter with a discussion of money, its characteristics and functions, and the components of the Canadian money supply. Next we explain the role of the Bank of Canada (Canada's central bank—first introduced in Chapter 2) in managing the money supply. Then we describe different types of financial institutions (the four pillars) and their services, and the organizations that insure customer deposits. We continue with a discussion of international banking and the securities markets. Finally, we look at trends in the banking industry.

LO1 ## SHOW ME THE MONEY

money
Anything that is acceptable as payment for goods and services.

Money is anything that is acceptable as payment for goods and services. It affects our lives in many ways. We earn it, spend it, save it, invest it—and often wish we had more of it. Business and government use money in similar ways. Both require money to finance their operations. By controlling the amount of money in circulation, the Bank of Canada can promote economic and financial well-being in Canada. For this reason, money has been called the lubricant for the machinery of our economic system. Our banking system was developed to ease the handling of money.

HOT *Links*

How durable is Canadian printed money? To discover the life expectancy of Canadian bills, visit www.bankofcanada.ca/en/banknotes/

Characteristics of Money

For money to be a suitable means of exchange, it should have these key characteristics.

- *Scarcity.* Money should be scarce enough to have some value but not so scarce as to be unavailable. Pebbles, which meet some of the other criteria, would not work well as money, because they are widely available. Too much money in circulation increases prices. Central banks control the scarcity of money by limiting the quantity of money produced.
- *Durability.* Any item used as money must be durable. A perishable item such as a banana becomes useless as money when it spoils. Even early societies used durable forms of money, such as metal coins and paper money that lasted for a long time.
- *Portability.* Money must be easily moved around. Large or bulky items, such as boulders or heavy gold bars, cannot be transported easily from place to place.
- *Divisibility.* Money must be capable of being divided into smaller parts. Divisible forms of money help make possible transactions of all sizes and amounts.

Functions of Money

Using a variety of goods as money would be confusing. Thus, societies develop a uniform money system to measure the value of goods and services. For money to be acceptable, it must function as a medium of exchange, as a standard of value, and as a store of value.

As a *medium of exchange*, money makes transactions easier. Having a common form of payment in each country is much less complicated than having a barter system—where goods and services are exchanged for other goods and services. Money allows the exchange of products to be a simple process.

Money also serves as a *standard of value*. With a form of money whose value is accepted by all, goods and services can be priced in standard units. This makes it easy to measure the value of products and allows transactions to be recorded in consistent terms.

As a *store of value*, money is used to hold wealth. It retains its value over time. Someone who owns money can keep it for future use rather than exchange it today for other types of assets.

The Canadian Money Supply

The Canadian money supply has three parts: currency, demand deposits, and time deposits. The amount of money in circulation in Canada can be measured in various ways. The most common measurements are called the monetary aggregates and include these:

M1 is the narrowest measure. M1 includes all currency (bank notes and coins) plus demand deposits (personal chequing accounts) and other current accounts at banks. Other forms of currency include traveller's cheques, cashier's cheques, and money orders.

M2 is a broader measure that includes not only M1 but also personal savings accounts, other chequing accounts, term deposits, and non-personal deposits that require notice before the money can be withdrawn.

Because banks are not the only providers of deposit facilities, we can use an even broader measurement of money, *M2+ (also known as M3)*. This includes not only M1 and M2, but also all deposits at non-bank deposit institutions, such as money-market mutual funds and life insurance companies. Exhibit 17.1 shows these three measurements of the Canadian money supply.

Credit cards, sometimes referred to as "plastic money," are used as a substitute for cash and cheques. Credit cards are simply a form of borrowing. When RBC issues a credit card to a small business owner, it gives a short-term loan to the business by directly paying the seller for the business's purchases. The business pays RBC when it receives its monthly statement. Credit cards do not replace money; they simply defer payment.

currency
Bank notes and coins used as a medium of exchange.

demand deposits
Money kept in chequing accounts that can be withdrawn by depositors on demand.

time deposits
Money invested for a specific period of time.

term deposits
Deposits at a bank or other financial institution that pay interest but cannot be withdrawn on demand.

Concept *Check*

What is money, and what are its characteristics?

What are the main functions of money?

What are the components of the Canadian money supply?

Exhibit 17.1	Three Measures of the Money Stock for the Canadian Economy

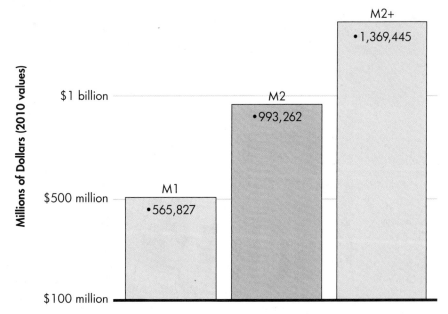

SOURCE: Adapted from Statistics Canada, Bank of Canada, Bank of Canada Review, Ottawa, "Exchange Rates, Interest Rates, Money Supply and Stock Prices," CANSIM, tables 176-0025, 176-0043, 176-0047 and 176-0064; http://www40.statcan.ca/101/cst01/econ07-eng.htm (August 18th, 2011).

LO2

THE BANK OF CANADA

Before the 20th century, there was very little government regulation of the Canadian financial system. In 1934, the Bank of Canada (also discussed in Chapter 2) was founded as a privately owned corporation. In 1938, it became a Crown corporation belonging to the federal government, with all shares held by the federal minister of finance.

The Bank of Canada is the sole issuer of bank notes in Canada and is responsible for facilitating the management of Canada's financial system. As an independent institution, the Bank of Canada has the power to create money, which is separate from the government's power to spend the money.

The Bank of Canada promotes the economic and financial welfare of Canada by

- conducting monetary policy in a way that fosters confidence in the value of money;
- supplying quality bank notes that are readily accepted and secure against counterfeiting (see Exhibit 17.2);
- promoting the safety and efficiency of Canada's financial system;
- providing efficient and effective funds-management services; and
- communicating their objectives openly and effectively and standing accountable for their actions.[2]

HOT *Links*

To learn more about how the Bank of Canada works, visit
www.bankofcanada.ca

Exhibit 17.2 | The New $100 Bank Note (Introduced in Late 2011)

The new note is

- Secure—leading-edge technology makes the bill easy to verify and hard to counterfeit
- Durable—expected to last 2.5 times as long as the older cotton-paper-based bill
- Innovative—polymer notes have less impact on the environment

USED WITH THE PERMISSION OF THE BANK OF CANADA

Exhibit 17.3 The Bank of Canada's Monetary Tools and Their Effects

TOOL	EFFECT ON ACTION	EFFECT ON MONEY SUPPLY	EFFECT ON INTEREST RATES	ECONOMIC ACTIVITY
Open market operations	Buy government securities	Increases	Lowers	Stimulates
	Sell government securities	Decreases	Raises	Slows down
Overnight rate	Raise overnight rate	Decreases	Raises	Slows down
	Lower overnight rate	Increases	Lowers	Stimulates

Carrying Out Monetary Policy

The most important function of the Bank of Canada is carrying out monetary policy. It uses its power to change the money supply to control inflation and interest rates, increase employment, and influence economic activity. Two tools used by the Bank of Canada in managing the money supply are open market operations and the overnight rate. Exhibit 17.3 summarizes the short-term effects of these tools on the economy.

In open market operations, the Canadian government issues securities to obtain the extra money needed to run the government (if taxes and other revenues aren't enough). In effect, these securities are long-term loans made by businesses and individuals to the government. When the Bank of Canada buys securities, it puts money into the economy. Banks have more money to lend so they reduce interest rates, and lower rates generally stimulate economic activity. The opposite occurs when the Bank of Canada sells government securities.

Although the bank rate still exists, the Bank of Canada is now putting more emphasis on the target for the overnight rate. The bank rate is the interest rate that the Bank of Canada charges member banks that borrow from the Bank of Canada. On the other hand, the target for the overnight rate is a signal from the Bank of Canada to the major participants in the money market as to what rate the Bank of Canada is aiming for in the market for overnight funds.[3] The target for the overnight rate (also called the Bank's key interest rate or key policy rate) is more relevant to the Canadian monetary policy. It is the average interest rate that the Bank of Canada wants to see in the overnight market (one-day loans). The overnight rate influences other interest rates (e.g., mortgage rates and consumer loans) and also affects the exchange rate of the Canadian dollar. Under the current system, the Bank of Canada will always change the target for the overnight rate and the bank rate at the same time and in the same amount.

open market operations
The purchase or sale of Canadian government securities by the Bank of Canada to stimulate or slow down the economy.

bank rate
The interest rate that the Bank of Canada charges on one-day loans to financial institutions.

target for the overnight rate
The signal to the major participants in the money market as to what the Bank of Canada is aiming for when participants borrow and lend one-day funds to each other.

Concept Check

What are the key functions of the Bank of Canada?

What tools does the Bank of Canada use in managing the money supply, and how does each affect economic activity?

THE CANADIAN FINANCIAL SYSTEM

The well-developed financial system in Canada supports our high standard of living. The Canadian financial sector is significantly integrated with different institutions offering similar financial services and products. Traditionally, this is referred to as the four pillars of the Canadian financial system—banks, trust companies, insurance companies, and investment dealers (all discussed later).

The system allows those who wish to borrow money to do so with relative ease. It also gives savers a variety of ways of earning interest on their savings. For example, a computer company that wants to build a new headquarters in New Brunswick might be financed partly with the savings of families in British Columbia. The British Columbians deposit their money in a local financial institution. That institution looks for a profitable and safe way to use the money and decides to make a real estate loan to the computer company. The transfer of funds from savers to investors enables businesses to expand and the economy to grow.

four pillars of the Canadian financial system
The four pillars of the Canadian financial system refers to banks, trust companies, insurance companies, and investment dealers.

Exhibit 17.4 | The Financial Intermediation Process

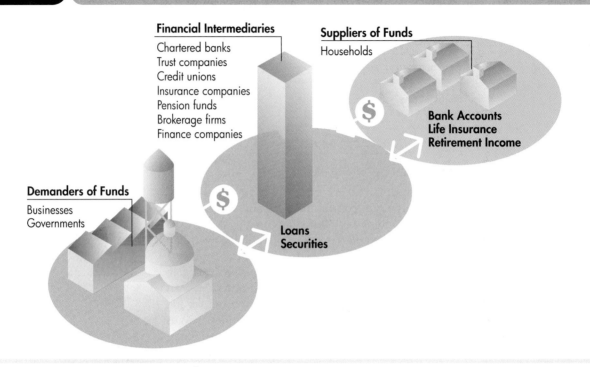

Financial Intermediaries
Chartered banks
Trust companies
Credit unions
Insurance companies
Pension funds
Brokerage firms
Finance companies

Suppliers of Funds
Households

Bank Accounts
Life Insurance
Retirement Income

Demanders of Funds
Businesses
Governments

Loans
Securities

financial intermediation
The process in which financial institutions act as intermediaries between the suppliers and demanders of funds.

Did you know that there is money unclaimed by depositors in Canada? Check out
ucbswww.bank-banque-canada.ca
to determine if you have deposits that you have forgotten about.

chartered banks
Profit-oriented financial institutions that accept deposits, make business and consumer loans, invest in government and corporate securities, and provide other financial services.

Households are important participants in the Canadian financial system. Although many households borrow money to finance purchases, they supply funds to the financial system through their purchases and savings. Overall, businesses and governments are users of funds. They borrow more money than they save.

Sometimes those who have funds deal directly with those who want them. A wealthy realtor, for example, might lend money to a client to buy a house. But most often, financial institutions act as intermediaries—or go-betweens—between the suppliers of and demanders for funds. The institutions accept savers' deposits and invest them in financial products (such as loans) that are expected to produce a return. This process, called financial intermediation, is shown in Exhibit 17.4. Households are shown as suppliers of funds, and businesses and governments are shown as demanders, but a household, business, or government can be either a supplier or a demander, depending on the circumstances.

Financial institutions are the heart of the financial system, as they are convenient vehicles for financial intermediation. They can be divided into two broad groups: depository institutions (those that accept deposits) and non-depository institutions (those that do not accept deposits).

Depository Financial Institutions

Not all depository financial institutions are alike. Most people call the place where they save their money a "bank." Some of those places are, indeed, banks, but other depository institutions include trust companies and credit unions.

CHARTERED BANKS A chartered bank is a profit-oriented financial institution that accepts deposits, makes business and consumer loans, invests in government and corporate securities, and provides other financial services. There are 21 domestic banks, 25 Canadian banks that are subsidiaries of foreign banks, and 23 foreign bank branches operating in Canada. These banks operate through approximately 8000 branches and manage more than $1.7 trillion in assets. Collectively, the chartered banks account for more than 70 percent of the total assets of the Canadian financial services sector.[4]

Customers' deposits are a chartered bank's main source of funds; the main use of those funds is loans. The differences between the interest earned on loans and the interest paid on deposits, plus fees earned from other financial services, pay the bank's costs and provide a profit. Chartered banks are corporations owned and operated by individuals or other corporations. In Canada, banks are regulated through the Bank Act.

TRUST COMPANIES A *trust company* is the only financial institution allowed to administer trusts, such as those set up to manage estates. Like banks, they operate through a network of branches and may operate under either provincial or federal legislation. When the Canadian government radically changed the financial regulations in the 1990s, this allowed banks to purchase trust companies (e.g., Toronto Dominion Bank purchased Canada Trust to become TD Canada Trust).[5]

CREDIT UNIONS AND CAISSES POPULAIRES *Credit unions and caisses populaires* are not-for-profit, member-owned financial cooperatives that operate for the benefit of the members. They are subject to provincial regulation and are usually small and locally owned, and members typically have something in common—their employer, union, professional group, or church, for example.

Chartered banks, trust companies, and credit unions offer a wide range of financial services for businesses and consumers. Typical services offered by depository institutions are listed in Exhibit 17.5. These services play an important role in helping to fuel the Canadian economy and foster individual financial security.

Non-Depository Financial Institutions

Some financial institutions provide a few banking services but do not accept deposits. These non-depository financial institutions include insurance companies, pension funds, brokerage companies, and finance companies. They serve both individuals and businesses.

INSURANCE COMPANIES Insurance companies are major suppliers of funds. Policyholders make payments (called *premiums*) to buy financial protection from the insurance company. Insurance companies invest the premiums in shares, bonds, real estate, business loans, and real estate loans for large projects.

PENSION FUNDS Corporations, unions, and governments set aside large pools of money for later use in paying retirement benefits to their employees or members. These *pension funds* are managed by the employers or unions themselves or by outside managers, such as life insurance companies, chartered banks, and private investment companies. Pension plan members receive a specified monthly payment when they reach a given age. After setting aside enough money to pay near-term benefits, pension funds invest the rest in business loans, shares, bonds, or real estate. They often invest large sums in the shares of the employer.

BROKERAGE COMPANIES A *brokerage company* buys and sells securities (shares and bonds) for its clients and gives them related advice. Many brokerage companies offer some banking services. They might offer clients a combined chequing and savings account with a high interest rate and also make loans, backed by securities, to those clients.

trust company
A financial institution that conducts the same activities as a bank but can also administer estates, trusts, pension plans, and agency contracts.

Check out the services offered by TD Canada Trust at
www.tdcanadatrust.com

credit unions and caisses populaires
Not-for-profit, member-owned financial cooperatives.

pension funds
Large pools of money set aside by corporations, unions, and governments for later use in paying retirement benefits to their employees or members.

Concept *in Action*

One of the most popular services offered by depository institutions is the automated teller machine. ATMs on post-secondary campuses make it easy for students to deposit and withdraw money. How has technology changed the way we bank in Canada today?

© THINKSTOCK/GETTY IMAGES

Exhibit 17.5 Services Offered by Depository Institutions

SERVICE	DESCRIPTION
Savings accounts	Pay interest on deposits
Chequing accounts	Allow depositors to withdraw any amount of funds at any time up to the amount on deposit
Money market deposit accounts	Savings accounts on which the interest rate is set at market rates
Certificates of deposit (CDs)	Pay a higher interest rate than regular savings accounts, provided that the deposit remains for a specified period
Consumer loans	Loans to individuals to finance the purchase of a home, car, or other expensive items
Business loans	Loans to businesses and other organizations to finance their operations
Money transfer	Transfer of funds to other banks
Electronic funds transfer	Use of telephone lines and computers to conduct financial transactions
Automated teller machines (ATMs)	Allow bank customers to make deposits and withdrawals from their accounts 24 hours a day
Debit cards	Allow customers to transfer money from their bank account directly to a merchant's account to pay for purchases
Smart cards	Cards that store monetary value and can be used to buy goods and services instead of using cash, cheques, and credit and debit cards
Online and telephone banking	Allows customers to conduct financial transactions via the Internet or through a dial-in line that operates with a bank's software

Concept Check

What is the financial intermediation process?

What are the types of depository institutions, and what services do they offer?

What are the main types of non-depository institutions?

FINANCE COMPANIES A *finance company* makes short-term loans for which the borrower puts up tangible assets (such as an automobile, inventory, machinery, or property) as security. Finance companies often make loans to individuals or businesses that cannot get credit elsewhere. To compensate for the extra risk, finance companies usually charge higher interest rates than banks do. *Consumer finance companies* make loans to individuals.

LO4

INSURING BANK DEPOSITS

Canada Deposit Insurance Corporation (CDIC)
The Canada Deposit Insurance Corporation is a federal Crown Corporation created in 1967 to provide deposit insurance and contribute to the stability of Canada's financial system.

The **Canada Deposit Insurance Corporation (CDIC)** is a federal Crown corporation created in 1967 to provide deposit insurance and to contribute to the stability of Canada's financial system. The CDIC insures eligible deposits at member institutions and reimburses depositors for the amount of their insured deposits when a member institution fails. Since 2005, the amount insured at a single member institution has been $100,000 and depositors are automatically insured for their deposits (to the maximum) if their deposits are with a member institution and in Canadian currency.

CDIC is governed by the Canada Deposit Insurance Corporation Act and is accountable to Canada's Parliament through the minister of finance. Since its creation, 43 member institutions have failed, at a cost of about $4.7 billion.[6]

Concept Check

What is the CDIC, and what are its responsibilities?

How does this encourage confidence in the Canadian economy?

LO5

INTERNATIONAL BANKING

HOT *Links*

To find out if your institution is a member of the CDIC or to see any new announcements, visit
www.cdic.ca

The financial marketplace spans the globe, with money routinely flowing across international borders. Multinational corporations need many special banking services, such as foreign currency exchange. Many Canadian banks have started expanding into trans-border and overseas markets by opening offices in the United States, Europe, Latin America, and the Far East. They provide better customer service than local banks in many countries and have access to more sources of funding.

Sustainable Business, Sustainable World

SUN LIFE FINANCIAL

Sun Life Financial is a leading Canadian-based international financial services company, offering a wide range of insurance and investment products.

It was ranked 56th on the list of the 2011 *Global 100 Most Sustainable Corporations in the World*. Only three other insurance companies in the world ranked above Sun Life, and these were based in Norway, Japan, and Britain. It also has earned a spot on the Dow Jones Sustainability Index North America, and for 10 years has been included on the FTSE4GoodIndex, which measures the performance of companies that meet globally recognized corporate responsibility measures.

Sun Life, like other financial services companies, doesn't produce a product out of a number of different production facilities or have a lot of retail outlets, so it can't focus its efforts on the sustainability of its products and/or operations in more obvious ways like some of the other companies we've looked at. So how exactly does it get such a reputation for sustainability? The company uses a lot of different forms of electronic conferencing—teleconferencing, videoconferencing, and webconferencing—to reduce the amount of travelling that they do and thus reduce the greenhouse gas emissions that would otherwise result. They also focus on making their office buildings more energy efficient and cut the amount of waste that they produce. The company also increases its efforts in sustainability indirectly through providing financing for companies that invest in green and renewable energy.

For example, in 2010, Sun Life invested approximately $270 million into renewable energy projects. In its offices, it recycles just about every kind of consumable office supply product, and larger items like office furniture are donated to charities and other institutions. In its buildings, it incorporates LEED (Leadership in Energy and Environmental Design) principles into every design. In fact, in 2010 its worldwide headquarters in Toronto received a LEED EB-O&M Gold designation.

Sun Life actually does have a sustainable "product." McLean Budden, one of Canada's oldest and most respected investment management companies, is an affiliate of Sun Life. It is a leader in SRI—sustainable, socially conscious, or ethical investing—and has developed and offers SRI funds to investors (MR Responsible Funds) that seek to maximize both financial returns and social good.

Sun Life has a very strong reason for acting in a sustainable fashion. Its business relies on what happens in the future. In fact, its financial products are sold on the assumption of a specific future. And that is exactly what sustainability is all about. According to the Report to the United Nations General Assembly of the World Commission on Environment and Development, sustainability is about "meeting the needs of the present without compromising the ability of future generations to meet their own needs." The very nature of Sun Life's business therefore demands that it operate in a sustainable fashion.

Thinking Critically

1. Can you think of any companies that would have a business model or would be in an industry that would preclude them from operating in a sustainable fashion?
2. Is there any justifiable reason for a business not to focus on sustainability? Does it make good business sense to ignore this very definite trend in the business world?
3. What other businesses can you think of, by the very nature of what they do and the industry they operate in, that would need to operate in a sustainable fashion for their very survival?

SOURCES: Sun Life Financial, http://www.sunlife.ca; The Global 100, http://www.global100.org; Dow Jones Sustainability Indexes, http://www.sustainability-index.com; FTSE The Index Company, http://www.ftse.com; LEED.net, http://www.leed.net; MFS McLean Budden Limited, http://www.mcleanbudden.com; The United Nations, http://www.un.org.

Competing against foreign banks can be difficult. Foreign banks are subject to fewer regulations, making it easier for them to undercut Canadian banks on the pricing of loans and services to multinational corporations and governments. Some governments protect their banks against foreign competition. In China, for example, the government prohibits foreign banks from acquiring more than 19.9 percent of any of its domestic financial institutions, as explained in the "Expanding Around the Globe" box.

Canadian banks play an important role in global business by providing loans to foreign governments and businesses. They also offer trade-related services. For example, Scotiabank's global cash management services help companies manage their cash flows to improve their payment efficiency and reduce their exposure to operational risks. The bank's advanced information systems enable corporate customers to access their accounts electronically throughout the world. Other Canadian banks are taking advantage of their technological expertise and information systems to sell more financial services throughout the world.

International banking can be profitable, but it's also a high-risk business. The global financial crisis beginning in 2008 resulted in many Canadian financial institutions writing down assets especially as a result of the "sub-prime mortgage" failure in the United States. Again in 2011

HOT|*inks*

Scotiabank is Canada's most international bank, with more than 12.5 million customers in more than 50 countries around the world. Check out their website at
www.scotiabank.com

Concept *Check*

What is the role of Canadian banks in international banking?

What challenges do Canadian banks face in foreign markets?

Expanding Around the Globe

BREACHING BANKING BARRIERS IN CHINA

If Citigroup's bid to purchase a majority stake in Guangdong Development Bank—with its nationwide network of over 500 branches and booming credit card business—had been successful, it would have captured the largest ownership stake held by a foreign investor in a Chinese bank and thereby gained full management control. It could have ended regulatory limits on foreign ownership of Chinese financial institutions, overcoming the current regulatory limits of 20 percent ownership for a single foreign investor in a Chinese bank and less than 25 percent for all foreign shareholders.

But the Chinese government refused to put aside the ownership rule, killing Citigroup's bid to be the first foreign company to surpass the ownership limit in a mainland lender. The government's denial indicates an increasing resistance to state-asset sales in the country. "There's real concern about losing control of the banking system and fears that the local banks have no way to compete with the more sophisticated foreign banks," said Stephan Rothlin, secretary general of the Centre for International Business Ethics in Beijing.

So Citigroup abandoned its larger stake bid in an effort to keep its bid for a smaller stake in the bank alive. China forbids foreign companies from purchasing more than 19.9 percent of a bank. Citigroup wanted 40 percent of Guangdong development as part of an investment consortium that sought an overall 85 percent stake.

The question of control is vital in China, where banks are striving to introduce modern risk-management systems after decades of uncontrolled lending. "China should pass a law to prevent 'malicious' mergers and acquisitions by overseas companies seeking monopolies," Li Deshu, the former head of the National Statistics Bureau and a ministerial-level official, said during the National People's Congress. Other critics say that foreign companies are profiteering after paying too little for their stakes. "Pricing China's big four banks only on their net assets fails to factor in the value of their brand and customers," said Shi Jianping, dean of the School of Finance at Central University of Finance & Economics.

Banking forecasters say it is doubtful that authorities will permit any of the "big four" state-owned Chinese banks to come under overseas rule any time soon. Any relaxation of the limits is more liable to concern smaller provincial and city banks, which would benefit from foreign investment and expertise.[7]

Thinking Critically

1. Why is China so reluctant to allow foreign companies a major ownership stake in their banks?
2. Why are Chinese banks attractive to foreign investors? Explain.

---

there was another global financial crisis. The 2008 crisis was primarily due to ineffective regulations and bad corporate governance; the 2011 crisis resulted primarily because of governments' fiscal irresponsibility.

INVESTOR'S CHOICE: SHARES AND BONDS

A central concern of most businesses is raising capital to finance operations and expansion. Many corporations use securities as a source of long-term financing. Securities are investment certificates that represent either equity (ownership in the issuing organization) or debt (a loan to the issuer). Corporations and governments sell securities to investors, who, in turn, take on a certain amount of risk with the hope of receiving a profit from their investment.

securities
Investment certificates issued by corporations or governments that represent either equity or debt.

Sharing the Wealth—and the Risks

Equity securities, commonly called *shares*, represent ownership in a corporation. A share is issued for each unit of ownership, and the shareholder (owner) gets a share certificate to prove ownership. If you own a share in TD Canada Trust, for example, you are a partial owner of TD Canada Trust. Your ownership interest isn't very big, because TD Canada Trust has over 800 million shares outstanding,[8] but your ownership gives you certain rights and potential rewards. The two types of equity securities are common shares and preferred shares. Each has advantages and disadvantages for investors.

COMMON SHARES *Common shares* are the most widespread form of ownership. Holders of common shares receive the right to vote on many important corporate decisions, such as who should sit on the company's board of directors and whether

Creating the Future of Business

MATT SCHNARR, AWAKE CORPORATION

Where do ideas come from for new businesses? How do you get the funding and support needed? And how do you even get the courage to go out on your own? These are all questions that entrepreneurs have to grapple with, and for Matt Schnarr and his university buddies Dan Tzotzis and Adam Deremo, they are questions they thankfully have answers to.

These three friends, all with backgrounds in big multinational consumer packaged foods companies, were as Matt puts it: "just one day sitting around having a burrito, and each of us in turn said 'I want to start my own business.' Within literally 10 seconds, we all said: 'Let's do it together' and that was that—done." That sounds pretty simple, but clearly those entrepreneurial feelings were brewing long before that fateful day. They had all launched so many brands for big companies, saw what worked and what didn't, and started saying—"here's what I'd do if this was my company" …

Coming up with the idea was another thing. As Matt describes it, they met up a week later "over beers to brainstorm." They came up with 35 ideas, shortlisted two, and finally decided to focus on caffeinated chocolate. If you are asking yourself "doesn't that already exist?" you're not alone—it's so obviously a great idea, and it actually hasn't been done, or at least not well. Back in 2008, the Mars company came out with a limited edition "Snickers Charged." Unfortunately it had a bitter aftertaste that stayed with you as long as the effect of the caffeine. The AWAKE caffeinated chocolate bar, on the other hand, offers the same caffeine as a cup of coffee with a delicious chocolate taste.

Matt and the other founders wanted to "start something we knew a little about—that leveraged our experiences and consumer insights, but was unique in the space." They certainly know about consumer packaged food products, and in the functional products category (think of vitamin water or probiotic yogurt—it brings a level of performance or function to the product) the AWAKE caffeinated chocolate bar is certainly unique.

From the idea to start a business in October 2010, to deciding on the final product in January 2011, it then took another year of working on the side while they were in their corporate jobs for Matt to be the first one to take the plunge. With a young child and a mortgage, he left his job in January 2012 to work on AWAKE full time. The beta launch was in April 2012 and they haven't looked back. AWAKE bars are currently (at time of writing) sold in Shell gas bars, Shoppers Drug Mart, Rexall pharmacies, Gateway News, and a number of other stores, and they are doing very well with minimal marketing to date.

How did they get the funding and support they needed to succeed? One of the fundamental principles of their success has been to "have coffee and meet with anybody who will meet with us, because you never know where it will go." As Matt puts it: "We know what we know and what we don't know, and we wanted the smartest people in the room." The contacts they have made and the incredible people they have been able to work with—"world class advisors" in senior positions at huge, well-known companies with priceless experience to share—astound him. And a little help from a couple of the investors on CBC's *Dragon's Den* didn't hurt either. Go to www.cbc.ca/dragonsden and check it out!

Thinking Critically

1. How often have you said "I'd do it differently if this was my company"? How many ideas for new businesses do you think are conceived that way?
2. How critical to the success of a new business do you think it is to come up with a product that is unique?
3. Momentum is an important factor in the launch of a new product. Do you think that the team of advisers the founders have been able to put together have been integral to attracting funding, or the other way around? At what point is a new business attractive to investors?

SOURCES: http://www.awakechocolate.com; http://www.facebook.com/Awakechocolate; http://twitter.ie/AWAKEEnrgyChoco; phone interview with Matt Schnarr, July 11, 2012. Used with permission from Matt Schnarr.

the company should merge with another company. In most cases, common shareholders get one vote for each share they own. Common shares also give investors the opportunity to share in the company's success, through either dividends or share price increases.

Dividends are the part of corporate profits that the company distributes to shareholders. Dividends for common shares can be paid either in cash or in additional shares (called *stock dividends*). Common share dividends are usually declared either annually or quarterly (four times a year) by a corporation's board of directors. However, these dividends are paid only after all other obligations of the company—payments to suppliers, employees, bondholders, and other creditors, plus taxes and preferred share dividends—have been met. Some companies, especially rapidly growing companies and those in high-technology industries, choose not to pay any dividends on their common shares. Instead, they reinvest their profits in more buildings, equipment, and new products in hope of earning greater profits in the future. These reinvested profits are called *retained earnings*.

One advantage of common shares ownership is its liquidity: Many common shares are actively traded in securities markets and can be bought and sold quickly. An investor can benefit by selling common shares when the price increases, or *appreciates*, above the original purchase price.

Although the returns from common share dividends and price appreciation can be quite attractive, common shareholders have no guarantee that they will get any return on their investment. Share prices are subject to many risks related to the economy, the industry, and the company. Like any commodity, the price of a specific company's shares is affected by supply and demand. The supply of shares is limited by the number of shares a company has issued, whereas demand is created by the number of investors who want to buy the shares from those who already own them. Factors that can increase demand for shares—and their price—include strong financial reports, new-product market opportunities, and positive industry trends. However, demand can fall—and a share's price drop—when negative events occur.

The threat of a lawsuit or increased government regulation of a company's industry can send share prices downward. Market conditions can also affect a company's share price. Factors like these can hold down a common share's dividends and its price, making it hard to predict the share's return. For example, Merck & Co., a major pharmaceutical company, recalled Vioxx after it was revealed that the popular painkiller could increase the risk of heart attacks and strokes. Its shares price fell 38 percent from September to December in that year and never fully regained lost ground. The result of the lawsuits from the danger of Vioxx resulted in the courts awarding injured parties compensation.[9] Factors like these can hold down a common share's dividends and its price, making it hard to predict the share's return.

PREFERRED SHARES *Preferred shares* are a second form of corporate ownership. Unlike common shareholders, preferred shareholders do not receive voting rights. However, preferred shares provide several advantages to investors that common shares do not, specifically in the payment of dividends and the distribution of assets if the company is liquidated.

The dividend for preferred shares is usually set at the time the shares are issued, giving preferred shareholders a clearer picture of the dividend proceeds they can expect from their investment. This dividend can be expressed either in dollar terms or as a percentage of the share's par (stated) value. As with common shares, the company's board of directors might decide not to pay dividends if the company encounters financial hardships. However, most preferred shares are *cumulative preferred shares*, which means that preferred shareholders must receive all unpaid dividends before any dividends can be paid to common shareholders. Suppose, for example, that a company with a $5 annual preferred dividend misses its quarterly payment of $1.25 ($5.00 ÷ 4). The following quarter, the company must pay preferred shareholders $2.50—$1.25 in unpaid preferred dividends from the previous quarter plus the $1.25 preferred dividend for the current quarter—before it can pay any dividends to common shareholders. Similarly, if the company goes bankrupt, preferred shareholders are paid off before common shareholders.

Investors like preferred shares because of the fixed dividend income. Although companies are not legally obligated to pay preferred dividends, most have an excellent record of doing so. However, the fixed dividend can also be a disadvantage, because it limits the cash paid to investors. Thus, preferred shares have less potential for price appreciation than common shares.

CASHING IN WITH BONDS

Bonds are long-term debt obligations (liabilities) of corporations and governments. A bond certificate is issued as proof of the obligation. The issuer of a bond must pay the buyer a fixed amount of money—called **interest**, stated as the *coupon rate*—on a regular schedule, typically every six months. The issuer must also pay the bondholder the amount borrowed—called the **principal**, or *par value*—at the bond's maturity date

bonds
Securities that represent a long-term debt obligation (liabilities) issued by corporations or governments.

interest
A fixed amount of money paid by the issuer of a bond to the bondholder on a regular schedule, typically every six months; stated as the *coupon rate*.

principal
The amount borrowed by the issuer of a bond; also called *par value*.

(due date). Bonds are usually issued in units of $1000—for instance, $1000, $5000, or $10,000. The two sources of return on bond investments are interest income and gains from the sale of the bonds.

Unlike common and preferred shareholders, who are owners, bondholders are creditors (lenders) of the issuer. In the event of liquidation, the bondholders' claim on the assets of the issuer comes before that of any shareholders.

Bonds do not have to be held to maturity. They can be bought and sold in the securities markets. However, the price of a bond changes over its life as market interest rates fluctuate. When the market interest rate drops below the fixed interest rate on a bond, it becomes more valuable, and the price rises. If interest rates rise, the bond's price will fall.

CORPORATE BONDS *Corporate bonds*, as the name implies, are issued by corporations. They usually have a par value of $1000. They may be secured or unsecured, include special provisions for early retirement, or be convertible to common shares.

High-yield, or **junk**, **bonds** are high-risk, high-return bonds that became popular during the 1980s, when they were widely used to finance mergers and takeovers. Today, they are used by companies whose credit characteristics would not otherwise allow them access to the debt markets. Because of their high risk, these bonds generally earn 3 percent or more above the returns on high-quality corporate bonds.

Corporate bonds can be either secured or unsecured. **Secured bonds** have specific assets pledged as collateral, which the bondholder has a right to take if the bond issuer defaults. **Mortgage bonds** are secured by property, such as land, equipment, or buildings. **Debentures** are unsecured bonds. They are backed only by the reputation of the issuer and its promise to pay the principal and interest when due. In general, debentures have a lower risk of default than secured bonds and therefore have lower interest rates. Of course, a debenture issued by a financially shaky company probably has greater default risk than a mortgage bond issued by a sound one.

Corporate bonds may be issued with an option for the bondholder to convert them into common shares. **Convertible bonds** generally allow the bondholder to exchange each bond for a specified number of shares. For instance, a $1000 par value convertible bond might be convertible into 40 shares—no matter what happens to the market price of the common shares. Because convertible bonds could be converted to shares when the price is very high, these bonds usually have a lower interest rate than non-convertible bonds.

GOVERNMENT SECURITIES Both the federal government and the provincial governments also issue bonds to finance programs. When the government of Canada borrows money on a short-term basis, it issues Treasury bills (T-bills), whereas bonds are meant to be held for a longer period.

BOND RATINGS Bonds vary in quality, depending on the financial strength of the issuer. Because the claims of bondholders come before those of shareholders, bonds are generally considered less risky than shares. However, some bonds are, in fact, quite risky. Companies can *default*—fail to make scheduled interest or principal payments—on their bonds.

Investors can use **bond ratings**, letter grades assigned to bond issues to indicate their quality or level of risk. Ratings for corporate bonds are easy to find. The two largest and best-known rating agencies are Moody's and Standard & Poor's (S&P), whose publications are in most libraries and in stock brokerages. Exhibit 17.6 lists the letter grades assigned by Moody's and S&P. A bond's rating can change with events.

high-yield (junk) bonds
High-risk, high-return bonds.

secured bonds
Corporate bonds for which specific assets have been pledged as collateral.

mortgage bonds
Corporate bonds that are secured by property, such as land, equipment, or buildings.

debentures
Unsecured bonds that are backed only by the reputation of the issuer and its promise to pay the principal and interest when due.

convertible bonds
Corporate bonds that are issued with an option that allows the bondholder to convert them into common shares.

bond ratings
Letter grades assigned to bond issues to indicate their quality, or level of risk; assigned by rating agencies such as Moody's and Standard & Poor's (S&P).

Concept *Check*

What are the advantages and disadvantages of common shares for investors and corporations?

What is a preferred share, and how is it different from a common share?

Describe the common features of all bonds and the advantages and disadvantages of bonds for investors.

Exhibit 17.6 Moody's and Standard & Poor's Bond Ratings

MOODY'S RATINGS	S&P RATINGS	DESCRIPTION
Aaa	AAA	**Prime-quality investment bonds:** Highest rating assigned; indicates extremely strong capacity to pay.
Aa A	AA A	**High-grade investment bonds:** Also considered very safe bonds, although not quite as safe as Aaa/AAA issues; Aa/AA bonds are safer (have less risk of default) than single As.
Baa	BBB	**Medium-grade investment bonds:** Lowest of investment-grade issues; seen as lacking protection against adverse economic conditions.
Ba B	BB B	**Junk bonds:** Provide little protection against default; viewed as highly speculative.
Caa Ca C	CCC CC C D	**Poor-quality bonds:** Either in default or very close to it.

LO8

PLAYING THE MARKET WITH OTHER TYPES OF SECURITIES

In addition to equity and debt, investors have several other types of securities available to them. The most popular are mutual funds, futures contracts, and options. Mutual funds appeal to a wide range of investors. Futures contracts and options are more complex investments for experienced investors.

Mutual Funds

Suppose that you have $1000 to invest but don't know which shares or bonds to buy, when to buy them, or when to sell them. By investing in a mutual fund, you can buy shares in a large, professionally managed *portfolio*, or group, of shares and bonds. A mutual fund is a financial service company that pools its investors' funds to buy a selection of securities—marketable securities, shares, bonds, or a combination of securities—that meet its stated investment goals.

Each mutual fund focuses on one of a wide variety of possible investment goals, such as growth or income. Many large financial service companies sell a wide variety of mutual funds, each with a different investment goal. Investors can pick and choose funds that match their particular interests. Some specialized funds invest in a particular type of company or asset: in one industry, such as transportation or technology; in a geographical region, such as Asia; or in an asset, such as precious metals. Mutual funds appeal to investors for three main reasons:

mutual fund
A financial service company that pools its investors' funds to buy a selection of securities that meet its stated investment goals.

- They are a good way to hold a diversified and, thus, less risky, portfolio. Investors with only $500 or $1000 to invest cannot diversify much on their own. Buying shares in a mutual fund lets them own part of a portfolio that might contain 100 or more securities.
- Mutual funds are professionally managed.
- Mutual funds might offer higher returns than individual investors could achieve on their own.

Mutual Funds

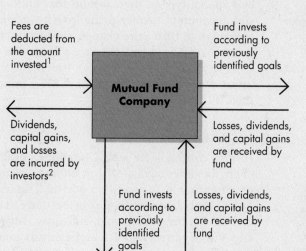

Mutual funds are professionally managed collective investments and typically include shares and bonds (both short- and long-term).

Fees are deducted from the amount invested[1]

Mutual Fund Company

Fund invests according to previously identified goals

Dividends, capital gains, and losses are incurred by investors[2]

Losses, dividends, and capital gains are received by fund

Fund invests according to previously identified goals

Losses, dividends, and capital gains are received by fund

US Dollar Funds
Investments are made in US dollars with the opportunity to benefit from the US markets.

Managed Programs
Portfolios that combine a number of mutual funds that are ready-made.

Income Funds
Investments typically include bonds, mortgages, and other fixed income securities.

Security Funds
Invest in a variety of short-term instruments such as Treasury bills and commercial paper (money market fund is an example).

Growth Funds
Investments usually include stocks (shares) and provide for the potential of higher long-term returns, but may entail greater risk.

Aggressive Growth Funds
Invest in specific market sectors or emerging economies that offer greater return potential.

Advantages of Mutual Funds

- **Convenience:** Convenient features such as consolidated statements and tax information are often available.
- **Professional Management:** Trained professionals manage investors' portfolios.
- **Liquidity:** Investors can buy and sell most funds on any business day.
- **Diversified Portfolios:** Investors can spread the investment risk over different kinds of securities and have the potential to maximize the return.

Disadvantages of Mutual Funds

- **Fees and Expenses:** Management-expense ratios (MERs) are the fees paid to the company managing the funds.
- **No Insurance:** Canadian Deposit Insurance Corporation (CDIC) does not insure mutual funds.
- **Loss of Control:** The fund managers make the decisions, not the fund holders.
- **Trading Limitations:** Unlike shares, mutual funds are priced only once a day (after the markets close).
- **Cash Holding:** The mutual fund must hold large amounts of cash to pay out when someone sells their investment in the fund.

[1] For some mutual funds, sales charges may be deducted when an investor purchases shares in the fund (or at a later date). The Securities and Exchange Commission requires that all prospective investors be provided with a booklet called the "prospectus," which clearly explains the goals, risks, expenses, and charges associated with the fund.

[2] Investors must include dividends and capital gains in current taxable income, even if they are planning to reinvest these amounts in the mutual fund.

BASED ON "HOW A MUTUAL FUND WORKS," DIAGRAM BY ADVISYS, INC.

Mutual funds are a popular way to invest in major markets, especially for people who can't follow stocks on a regular basis. Mutual funds expose investors to a basket of securities managed by a financial-services professional and fund portfolios targeted to different investor interests. Why are mutual funds so popular with investors?

Exchange-Traded Funds

exchange-traded fund (ETF)
A basket of marketable securities in a category, such as an industry sector, an investment objective, or a geographical area, or that track an index. ETFs are similar to mutual funds but trade like shares.

A relatively new type of investment, the exchange-traded fund (ETF), also called Index Participation Unit (IPU) has become very popular with investors. The world's first ETFs originated in the Toronto Stock Exchange in 1990. ETFs are considered to be a special type of mutual fund that holds a broad basket of marketable securities with a common theme, giving investors instant diversification. ETFs trade on stock exchanges so their price changes throughout the day, whereas mutual fund net asset values (NAVs) are calculated once a day, at the end of trading.

In a report released by BMO Asset Management Inc., 58 percent of Canadians are investors, but only 4 percent have ETFs; primarily because they are unfamiliar with them.[10]

Futures Contracts

futures contracts
Legally binding obligations to buy or sell specified quantities of commodities or financial instruments at an agreed-on price at a future date.

Futures contracts are legally binding obligations to buy or sell specified quantities of commodities (agricultural or mining products) or financial instruments (securities or currencies) at an agreed-on price at a future date. An investor can buy commodity futures contracts in cattle, pork bellies (large slabs of bacon), eggs, coffee, flour, gasoline, fuel oil, lumber, wheat, gold, and silver. Financial futures include Treasury securities and foreign currencies, such as the British pound or Japanese yen.

options
Contracts that entitle holders to buy or sell specified quantities of common shares or other financial instruments at a set price during a specified time.

Futures contracts do not pay interest or dividends. The return depends solely on favourable price changes. These are very risky investments, because the prices can vary a great deal.

Options

Options are contracts that entitle holders to buy or sell specified quantities of common shares or other financial instruments at a set price during a specified time. As with futures contracts, investors must correctly guess future price movements in the underlying financial instrument to earn a positive return. Unlike futures contracts, options do not legally obligate the holder to buy or sell and the price paid for an option is the maximum amount that can be lost. However, options have very short maturities, so it is easy to lose a lot of money quickly with them.

Concept *Check*

Why do mutual funds appeal to investors? Discuss some of the investment goals pursued by mutual funds.

What are futures contracts? Why are they risky investments?

How do options differ from futures contracts?

SECURITIES MARKETS

Shares, bonds, and other securities are traded in securities markets. These markets streamline the purchase and sales activities of investors by allowing transactions to be made quickly and at a fair price. They make the transfer of funds from lenders to borrowers much easier. Securities markets are busy places. On an average day, individual and institutional investors trade billions of shares in more than 10,000 companies through securities markets. They also trade bonds, mutual funds, futures contracts, and options. *Individual investors* invest their own money to achieve their personal financial goals. Institutional investors are investment professionals who are paid to manage other people's money. Most of these professional money managers work for financial institutions, such as banks, mutual funds, insurance companies, and pension funds. Institutional investors control very large sums of money, often buying shares in 10,000-share blocks. They aim to meet the investment goals of their clients. Institutional investors are a major force in the securities markets, accounting for about half of the dollar volume of equities traded.

institutional investors
Investment professionals who are paid to manage other people's money.

You have probably heard of buying on margin. Find out how this works at www.investopedia.com/university/margin/margin1.asp#axzz1VP6dqbqO

Businesses and governments also take part in the securities markets. Corporations issue bonds and shares to raise funds to finance their operations. They are also among the institutional investors who purchase corporate and government securities.

The Role of Investment Bankers and Stockbrokers

Two types of investment specialists play key roles in the functioning of the securities markets. **Investment bankers** help companies raise long-term financing. These companies act as intermediaries, buying securities from corporations and governments and reselling them to the public. This process, called **underwriting**, is the main activity of the investment banker, which acquires the security for an agreed-on price and hopes to be able to resell it at a higher price to make a profit. Investment bankers advise clients on the pricing and structure of new securities offerings, as well as on mergers, acquisitions, and other types of financing. Most Canadian banks now offer investment banking services.

A **stockbroker** is a person who is licensed to buy and sell securities on behalf of clients. Also called *account executives*, these investment professionals work for brokerage companies and execute the orders customers place for shares, bonds, mutual funds, and other securities.

Stockbrokers are the link between public companies and the investors interested in buying their shares. Before investing in securities, investors must select a stock brokerage company, select a stockbroker at that company, and open an account. Investors are wise to seek a broker who understands their investment goals and can help them pursue their objectives.

Brokerage companies are paid commissions for executing clients' transactions. Although brokers can charge whatever they want, most companies have fixed commission schedules for small transactions. These commissions usually depend on the value of the transaction and the number of shares involved.

Online Investing

Improvements in Internet technology have made it possible for investors to research, analyze, and trade securities online. Although traditional brokerage companies still dominate the investment industry, many investors use online brokerage companies for their securities transactions. Online brokerages are popular with "do-it-yourself" investors who choose their own shares and don't want to pay a full-service broker for

investment bankers
Companies that act as intermediaries, buying securities from corporations and governments and reselling them to the public.

underwriting
The process of buying securities from corporations and governments and reselling them to the public, with the aim of reselling at a higher price; the main activity of investment bankers.

stockbroker
A person who is licensed to buy and sell securities on behalf of clients.

Check online investment information at the following:
www.questrade.com
www.bmoinvestorline.com
www.tradefreedom.com

Concept *in Action*

Linking investors and public companies, stockbrokers serve a vital role in the securities marketplace. Today, most customer buy–sell orders are transacted electronically. What are the benefits of using a stockbroker?

COMSTOCK/GETTY IMAGES

Online brokerages like E*Trade and RBC Direct Investing have given rise to a new market player: the self-directed investor. These "do-it-yourselfers" take their financial futures into their own hands, buying and selling shares over the Internet for a fraction of the cost associated with traditional brokerage companies. Online investors pay commission fees as low as $4 while accessing streaming quotes and charts, financial news, and risk analyzers—all on their computer screens. What are the pros and cons of online investing?

BEN MARGOT/AP PHOTO

these services. Lower transaction costs are a major benefit. Fees at online brokerages vary depending on the number of trades a client makes and the size of the client's account. Presently, many traditional brokerage companies now have added online trading options to their list of services.

Types of Markets

primary market
The securities market where new securities are sold to the public, usually with the help of investment bankers.

Securities markets can be divided into primary and secondary markets. The primary market is where *new* securities are sold to the public, usually with the help of investment bankers. In the primary market, the issuer of the security gets the proceeds from the transaction. A security is sold in the primary market just once—when it is first issued by the corporation or government.

secondary market
The securities market where old (already issued) securities are bought and sold, or traded, among investors.

Later transactions take place in the secondary market, where *old* (already issued) securities are bought and sold, or traded, among investors. The issuers generally are not involved in these transactions. The vast majority of securities transactions take place in secondary markets, which include the organized stock exchanges, the over-the-counter securities market, and the commodities exchanges. You'll see announcements of both primary and secondary shares and bond offerings in *The Globe and Mail* and other newspapers.

broker markets or organized stock exchanges
Organizations on whose premises securities are resold by using an auction-style trading system.

Buying and Selling at Securities Exchanges

When we think of stock markets, we are typically referring to secondary markets, which handle most of the securities trading activity. The two key types of securities markets are broker markets, more commonly referred to as "organized stock exchanges" and dealer markets. Organized stock exchanges are organizations on whose premises securities are resold. They operate by using an auction-style trading system. All other securities are traded in the dealer markets.

Trading in an organized stock exchange is done by exchange members who act as agents for individual and institutional investors. To make transactions in an organized stock exchange, an individual or a company must be a member and own a "seat" on that exchange. Owners of the

How do securities markets help businesses and investors? How does an investment banker work with companies to issue securities?

How is online investing changing the securities industry?

Distinguish between primary and secondary securities markets.

limited number of seats must meet certain financial requirements and agree to observe a broad set of rules when trading securities.

The Primary Canadian Stock Exchanges

The cornerstone of the Canadian financial system is the TMX Group. The TMX Group owns and operates the two national stock exchanges, the Toronto Stock Exchange and the TSX Venture Exchange. The Toronto Stock Exchange serves the senior equity market (a broad range of established businesses from across Canada, the United States, and other countries), and the public venture equity market is served by the TSX Venture Exchange (which provides emerging companies with access to capital).

Other Exchanges Important to Canadian Businesses

Of all the foreign exchanges, the New York Stock Exchange (NYSE) is the most important to Canadian business. Canadian companies that are listed on the NYSE have access to a greater pool of potential investors because of the sheer number of people who live and invest in the United States. Only companies that meet certain minimum requirements are eligible to be listed on the NYSE.

Global Trading and Foreign Exchanges

Improved communications and the elimination of many legal barriers are helping the securities markets go global. The number of securities listed on exchanges in more than one country is growing.

Stock exchanges also exist in foreign countries. The London and Tokyo Stock Exchanges rank behind the NYSE and NASDAQ (described later). Other important foreign stock exchanges include those in Buenos Aires, Zurich, Sydney, Paris, Frankfurt, Hong Kong, and Taiwan.

Dealer Markets

Unlike broker markets, **dealer markets** do not operate on centralized trading floors but instead use sophisticated telecommunications networks that link dealers throughout

HOTLinks

To learn more about the Toronto Stock Exchange, the TSX Venture Exchange, how companies get listed on the exchanges, and the most current share price quotes, visit www.tmx.com

dealer markets
Securities markets where buy and sell orders are executed through dealers, or "market makers" linked by telecommunications networks.

Concept in Action

Once a customer order is transmitted to the trading floor, getting the most competitive price for the customer is the job of the brokerage's floor broker. Floor brokers must act quickly and aggressively to outbid other brokers. How does the traditional Toronto Stock Exchange differ from fully automated electronic trading?

RICHARD DREW/AP PHOTO

the world. Buyers and sellers do not trade securities directly, as they do in broker markets. They work through securities dealers called market makers, who make markets in one or more securities and offer to buy or sell securities at stated prices. A security transaction in the dealer market has two parts: the selling investor sells his or her securities to one dealer, and the buyer purchases the securities from another dealer (or in some cases, the same dealer).

National Association of Securities Dealers Automated Quotation (NASDAQ) system
The first electronic-based stock market and the fastest-growing part of the stock market.

NASDAQ The largest dealer market is the National Association of Securities Dealers Automated Quotation system, commonly referred to as the NASDAQ. The first electronic-based stock market, the NASDAQ is a sophisticated telecommunications network that links dealers throughout the world. Founded in 1971 with origins in the over-the-counter market (discussed below), today the NASDAQ is a separate securities exchange that is no longer part of the over-the-counter market.

over-the-counter (OTC) market
A sophisticated telecommunications network that links dealers and enables them to trade securities.

THE OVER-THE-COUNTER MARKET The over-the-counter (OTC) markets refer to those other than the organized exchanges described above. As mentioned previously, the NASDAQ, until January 2006 was part of the OTC. Today the OTC consists of dealers who make trades over the telephone and computer. It is also called the "unlisted market," or the "street market."

Market Conditions: Bull Market or Bear Market?

bull markets
Markets in which securities prices are rising.

bear markets
Markets in which securities prices are falling.

Two terms that often appear in the financial press are "bull market" and "bear market." Securities prices rise in bull markets. These markets are normally associated with investor optimism, economic recovery, and government action to encourage economic growth. In contrast, prices go down in bear markets. Investor pessimism, economic slowdown, and government restraint are all possible causes. As a rule, investors earn better returns in bull markets; they earn low, and sometimes negative, returns in bear markets.

Bull and bear market conditions are hard to predict, as seen in the economic crisis beginning in 2008. Usually, they can't be identified until after they begin. Over the past 50 years, the stock market has generally been bullish, reflecting general economic growth and prosperity. Bull markets tend to last longer than bear markets.

Concept *Check*

How do the organized share exchanges differ from the OTC market?

Explain a bull market and a bear market.

THE FUTURE OF THE FINANCIAL INDUSTRY

Once a highly regulated industry offering limited services, the banking industry continues to change. Trends influencing the direction of banking are increased use of online financial services and moves to increased fiscal responsibility by governments and corporations.

Changing the Way We Bank

To learn more about Canadian banks online, visit
www.canadabanks.net

The federal government has strict controls regulating the financial industry in Canada. These strict regulations caused Canada to be less affected by the financial crises of 2008 and 2011 than many other countries. But today, the regulations are less restrictive regarding financial business operations than they were in the latter part of the 20th century.

Today, our financial systems are using Internet technology to expand their services. "Online banking may be the critical service that enables banks to maintain their role as the dominant provider of financial services," says Paul Johnson, an analyst with International Data.[11]

Making Ethical Choices

TRIALS AND MANIPULATIONS

You have just joined a prestigious investment banking company as a junior securities analyst covering the pharmaceutical industry. Eager to make a good impression on your boss, you diligently monitor the companies your group follows and search for unique ways to get the scoop on new drugs currently under development. Rumour has it that a biotechnology company has come out with a new drug for insomnia that has the potential to be a block-buster. You've heard that other analysts, posing as doctors or patients, have called the managers of clinical trials to get inside information or have paid doctors involved in the trials to disclose confidential data. They then use what they learn in their share reports, making recommendations that can significantly impact the price of the share.

Why not go a step further, you wonder, and participate in the trial for the insomnia drug yourself? After all, you've had many sleepless nights and believe you'd qualify for the study. Not only would you help the cause of science, but you'd also get the chance to talk to doctors about the other patients in the study to find out more about the results of the trial so far.

With your boss's approval, you apply for the trial. When you arrive for your first appointment, you are asked to sign a confidentiality agreement to not disclose any treatment information based on your experiences or anything you learn about other patients.

ETHICAL DILEMMA: Should you honour the confidentiality agreement or share your findings with your boss to use in writing the share report?

SOURCES: Getta Anand and Randall Smith, "Biotech Analysts Strive to Peek Inside Clinical Tests of Drugs," *Wall Street Journal*, August 8, 2002; and Penni Crabtree, "Firm Fined for 'Creative' Research on Neurocrine," *San Diego Union-Tribune*, October 29, 2002.

One service that has given banks tremendous profit potential is online bill statements and payments. The service has benefited many businesses, such as utility companies, because it will eliminate the time-consuming and costly process of printing bills, mailing them to customers, and waiting for the cheques to arrive and clear.[12]

In 1992, the federal government reduced the various barriers and created a new framework for competition. These far-reaching changes include the ability of banks to offer a wider range of services to their customers. The deregulation of the financial industry saw financial services being consolidated, and now banks offer many of the services that were traditionally offered by industry-specific institutions. For example, insurance, brokerage services, and so on were not offered by the banks prior to the deregulation.

Increased Financial Responsibilities

After the financial crises of 2008 and 2011, it became apparent that lax regulation and irresponsible spending by governments must be controlled. Today, we see many countries using Canada as a role model for developing their financial regulations. As well, many countries, especially in the EU, have demanded governments to be more fiscally responsible.

Concept Check

How has technology changed the way we bank?

How have the changes in legislation governing financial institutions changed the way they do business?

What was the result of the financial crises of 2008 and 2011?

GREAT IDEAS TO USE NOW

After reading this chapter, you might be wondering if investing in shares or bonds is right for you. Like millions of others, you've probably read headlines about the markets' rise and fall. How can you minimize the risks while reaping the benefits of securities investments? The basic information presented in this chapter is a good starting point. It's also important to understand some of the key strategies used by successful investors.

The Time Is Now

As the S&P/TSX Composite tumbled starting in 2011, many investors panicked. They rushed to sell off their shares—often at a loss—because they believed doing otherwise would spell financial ruin.

These investors fell prey to some common mistakes of novice investors. For one thing, they got caught up in the mystique of the S&P/TSX Composite. Although it is the most publicized market indicator in Canada, it only represents the activity of approximately 220 of the roughly 1600 companies listed on the TSX.[13] A milestone on the TSX composite is just another number. It doesn't tell investors where their individual investments are going or how long the market will stay at a particular level.

The stock market has always been cyclical in nature. Share prices rise and fall depending on many factors. A bull market is almost invariably followed by a bear market. Although every investor dreams of buying a share at its low point and selling it at its peak, predicting the market's ups and downs is impossible.

Successful investors think of the stock market as a long-term investment. They know that it's important to let their investments grow over time, and they avoid falling into the trap of thinking that they should sell their shares whenever there's a market downturn. They also recognize that the best time to buy shares is when the market is at a low point.

Financial advisers suggest investing small amounts over time. Start early and invest regularly, whether the market is up or down. Don't immediately panic if the market takes a nosedive. The highs and lows will average out over time, and you'll find yourself with long-term gains.

Another reason many investors lost money in recent years is that they failed to diversify their investment portfolios. Many poured money into technology shares while ignoring the shares of businesses in other industries. When the technology boom ended, these investors were hit the hardest. Building a portfolio of individual shares in different industries can help cushion losses. Investing in mutual funds can also help spread your risk over a broad group of securities. Also, consider investing in a mix of shares and bonds. Bonds tend to rise in value as share prices drop, and vice versa, further lessening the risk of losing it all when one investment vehicle declines.

Most important, do your homework. Don't make investment decisions based only on what you find on a website or in a single magazine. It's easy to be taken in by someone hyping a share. To avoid investment scams, do your own research. Investigate the company's standing with the TSX, and look at its historic performance over a number of years. Remember, if it sounds too good to be true, it probably is!

Summary of Learning Outcomes

LO1 Understand the characteristics of money and its functions.

Money is anything accepted as payment for goods and services. For money to be a suitable means of exchange, it should be scarce, durable, portable, and divisible. Money functions as a medium of exchange, a standard of value, and a store of value. The Canadian money supply consists of currency (coins and paper money), demand deposits (chequing accounts), and time deposits (interest-bearing deposits that cannot be withdrawn on demand).

LO2 Describe the basic functions of the Bank of Canada and how it manages the Canadian money supply.

The Bank of Canada promotes the economic and financial welfare of Canada by

- conducting monetary policy in a way that fosters confidence in the value of money;
- supplying quality bank notes that are readily accepted and secure against counterfeiting;
- promoting the safety and efficiency of Canada's financial system;
- providing efficient and effective funds management services; and
- communicating their objectives openly and effectively, and standing accountable for their actions.

The Bank of Canada uses monetary policy to manage the money supply.

Financial institutions can be divided into two main groups: depository institutions and non-depository institutions. Depository institutions include chartered banks, trust companies, and credit unions and caisses populaires. Non-depository institutions include insurance companies, pension funds, brokerage companies, and finance companies. Financial institutions ease the transfer of funds between suppliers and demanders.

LO3 Identify the key financial institutions and the role they play in the process of financial intermediation.

The CDIC is a Crown corporation that insures eligible deposits at member institutions and reimburses depositors for the amount of their insured deposits when a member institution fails.

LO4 Outline how the Canada Deposit Insurance Corporation protects depositors' funds.

Canadian banks provide loans and trade-related services to foreign governments and businesses. They also offer specialized services such as cash management and foreign currency exchange.

LO5 Summarize the role of Canadian banks in the international marketplace.

Common and preferred shares represent ownership—equity—in a corporation. Common shareholders have voting rights, but their claim on profits and assets ranks behind that of holders of other securities. Preferred shareholders receive a stated dividend; it must be paid before any dividends are distributed to common shareholders.

Common shares are more risky than preferred shares. They offer the potential for increased value through growth in the share price and income through dividend payments. However, neither price increases nor dividends are guaranteed. Preferred shares are usually bought for their dividend income rather than potential price appreciation.

LO6 Distinguish between common shares and preferred shares.

Bonds are a form of debt and may be secured or unsecured. Bondholders are creditors of the issuing organization, and their claims on income and assets rank ahead of those of preferred and common shareholders. The corporation or government entity that issues the bonds must pay interest periodically and repay the principal at maturity. Bonds provide a steady source of income and the potential for price appreciation if interest rates fall below the coupon rate. However, investors also bear the risk that rising interest rates might erode the bond's price.

LO7 Understand the investment advantages and disadvantages of bonds.

Mutual funds are financial service companies that pool the funds of many investors to buy a diversified portfolio of securities. Investors choose mutual funds because they offer a convenient way of diversifying and are professionally managed. Futures contracts are legally binding obligations to buy or sell specified quantities of commodities or financial instruments at an agreed-on price at a future date. They are very risky investments, because the price of the commodity or financial instrument can change drastically. Options are contracts that entitle the holder to buy or sell specified quantities of common shares or other financial instruments at a set price during a specified time. They, too, are high-risk investments.

LO8 List other types of securities available to investors.

Securities markets allow shares, bonds, and other securities to be bought and sold quickly and at a fair price. New issues are sold in the primary market. After that, securities are traded in the secondary market. Investment bankers specialize in issuing and selling new security issues. Stockbrokers are licensed professionals who buy and sell securities on behalf of their clients.

Securities are resold on organized share exchanges, such as the Toronto Stock Exchange and regional share exchanges, and in the over-the-counter market, a telecommunications network linking dealers throughout North America. The most actively traded securities are listed on the NASDAQ system, so dealers and brokers can perform trades quickly and efficiently.

LO9 Describe the function of the securities markets.

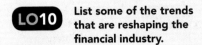

LO10 List some of the trends that are reshaping the financial industry.

By using Internet technology, banks are delivering more services online. This move is a tremendous profit potential, including online bill statements and payments. This opportunity not only reduces the costs of printing and mailing, but also gives customers access 24 hours a day.

More and more emphasis is being placed on stricter financial regulations and responsible fiscal policy by governments.

Key Terms

bank rate 513
bear markets 528
bonds 520
bond ratings 521
broker markets or organized stock exchanges 526
bull markets 528
Canada Deposit Insurance Corporation (CDIC) 516
chartered banks 514
convertible bonds 521
credit unions and caisses populaires 515
currency 511
dealer markets 527
debentures 521
demand deposits 511
exchange-traded fund (ETF) 524
financial intermediation 514
four pillars of the Canadian financial system 513
futures contracts 524
high-yield (junk) bonds 521
institutional investors 524

interest 520
investment bankers 525
money 510
mortgage bonds 521
mutual fund 522
National Association of Securities Dealers Automated Quotation (NASDAQ) system 528
open market operations 513
options 524
over-the-counter (OTC) market 528
pension funds 515
primary market 526
principal 520
secondary market 526
secured bonds 521
securities 518
stockbroker 525
target for the overnight rate 513
term deposits 511
time deposits 511
trust company 515
underwriting 525

Experiential Exercises

1. Is it really free? How much is your chequing account really costing you? Maybe more than you think. Even "free" chequing accounts aren't always a good deal when you add up extra costs such as ATM fees, lost interest, bounced-cheque charges, and other hidden expenses. Take a closer look at your current chequing account, and then comparison shop to see if you could be getting a better deal elsewhere. Here's how.

   • Ask yourself how you really use your chequing account. What's the average balance you keep in your account? How many cheques do you write in a typical month? What time of day do you do most of your banking, and where do you prefer to do it?

   • Zero in on the real cost of your current chequing account. Once you know how you use your chequing account, you can get a clearer idea of its true cost—beyond just the monthly account fee. Do you write more cheques per month than allowed by your "free" account? What is the cost of each cheque? How many times do you use the ATM instead of a branch? How much does it cost each time? Do you pay extra for overdraft protection? What does your bank charge for bounced cheques? Add in any bonuses you receive with your chequing account as well. For example, does your bank waive your credit card's annual fee for keeping your chequing account with them?

- Comparison shop. Check the websites of the major banks and credit unions in your area. Could you pay lower fees elsewhere? Could you earn interest on your chequing account at a credit union? Would you be better off paying a monthly fee with unlimited cheque-writing privileges? Crunch the numbers to find the best deal.

2. Compare brokerages. Visit the sites of two online brokerages, such as E*Trade, www.etrade.ca, or BMO, www.bmoinvestorline.com, or any others you know. Compare them for ease of use, quality of information, and other criteria you select. Summarize your findings. Which company would you prefer to use, and why?

3. Track share prices. Pick a portfolio of five companies in at least three different industries. Choose companies you know, read the financial press to find good candidates, or follow the shares on the TSX. Set up a table to track the share prices. Record the end-of-month prices for the past six months, and track the daily price movements for at least two weeks (longer is even better!). Visit the websites of these companies to view their investor relations information. Finally, monitor economic and market trends and other events that affect market conditions. Share the performance of the portfolio with your classmates. Explain your basis for selecting each share, and analyze its price changes.

4. Research the trends in the initial public offering (IPO) marketplace from 2000 to present. Then select two IPO success stories and two failures. Prepare a report for the class on their performance. What lessons about the securities markets can you learn from their stories?

5. What role do a CEO's actions/strategies have in influencing a company's share performance? Prepare a class presentation that answers this question by using both positive and negative examples from at least three companies covered in recent business news. In your presentation, discuss what your recommendations for each CEO would be.

6. At the Vanguard Group's site, www.vanguard.com, go to the page for "Personal Investors," then to the "Planning & Education" section. Read about investor education and mutual funds. After learning about the fundamentals of mutual funds, prepare a presentation for the class based on the materials.

7. You've been asked to address your investment club on socially responsible investing and how companies qualify as socially responsible. Research this topic at the websites of the Social Investment Forum, http://ussif.org/. Prepare a detailed outline of the key points you would include in the speech. How can your personal financial decisions have a positive impact on communities and the environment? Do you support socially responsible investing?

Review Questions

1. What are the characteristics of money?
2. What are the functions of money?
3. Differentiate between M1, M2, and M2+ (M3).
4. What are the roles of the Bank of Canada?
5. What are chartered banks, and what are their roles?
6. What are some of the non-depository financial institutions?
7. What agency protects depositors and to what limit?
8. Discuss the differences between common and preferred shares.
9. Discuss the use of bonds as a form of liability.
10. What are some other types of securities (other than common shares, preferred shares, and bonds)?
11. What are the securities markets? What are the two key securities markets?
12. What is the role of investment bankers and stockbrokers?
13. What are the current trends in financial institutions?

CREATIVE THINKING CASE

ING DIRECT—A Different Way to Bank

ING DIRECT began here in Canada in 1997. As they have no branches, our first introduction to the company was a television commercial announcing, "We are new here." We are all familiar with Frederik's face on television reminding us to "Save your money." ING DIRECT's business is conducted through the Internet, phone system, and ATMs. To open an account you simply mail them a cheque, payable to yourself, drawn on your existing account at another bank. And start saving your money. They have no service fees, higher interest rates on savings and lower interest rates on loans. Since 1999, ING DIRECT Funds Limited, a wholly owned subsidiary, has been selling mutual funds in all provinces except Québec. Do they make any money with this approach that is so contradictory to that of the big five banks? Actually they do. They first became profitable in 2001 and are still profitable today. ING DIRECT Canada has over 1.78 million clients, employs over 900 people and has over $38 billion in assets. In addition, they have paid out over $5 billion in interest to clients while collecting nothing in fees and service charges. ING DIRECT's goal is not to have clients waiting on hold when they phone, but when this cannot be avoided, the clients are entertained by Frederik, the spokesperson we are all familiar with.

In addition to radically different operating procedures, ING DIRECT also hopes to create a different feel to banking with their unusual ads, bright orange colour schemes and off-beat activities. For example, they wanted to show Canadians that it felt good to save as they encouraged people to adopt the savings habit by engaging in "random acts of saving." They offered free coffee, snacks, and rides on public transit in locations all across the country. ING DIRECT does not even use the word "bank" in their name but yet they are an amazingly successful bank that "believes in service, not service charges."

Thinking Critically

1. Do you think that most banking customers would choose higher interest rates and simplified loans over extra banking services? Why or why not?

2. Compare the structure of ING DIRECT and the traditional bank, such as one of the "big five." How are they alike? How are they different?

3. How might ING Direct's current strategy affect its future growth?

SOURCE: Adapted from http://www.ingdirect.ca/en/aboutus/index.html, accessed April 2, 2009, and December 21, 2011. Reprinted by permission of ING Direct.

Making the Connection

Finance: Maximizing the Value

In this chapter, we will continue to look at the *finance* area of business. The primary role of the financial manager is to maximize the value of the company for the owners, achieving the main critical success factor of *financial performance*. This, we know, cannot be done without the other four success factors, reiterating the need for managers in all departments to work closely with one another and with the finance area in particular.

As we saw in Chapter 17, the relationship between finance and the major *stakeholders*, particularly the owners, is a difficult but important one. Financial managers make many important decisions regarding the acquisition, disposition, and management of financial resources to maximize the value of the company for its owners. They must decide what projects to invest the company's money into, and how to finance those projects, whether through issuing debt—borrowing the money—or selling more shares—equity financing. Each has its own advantages and disadvantages, or rewards and risks in "finance speak." If the company chooses to use equity financing, one of the major decisions that will affect this stakeholder group is how much of the company's profit will be distributed to the shareholders in the form of a dividend. The shareholders expect a return, so if a regular dividend is not paid, then they expect the return in the form of an increased share price. This can happen only if the investing community sees potential in the value of the shares. If neither of these happens, the price of the shares will fall as shareholders sell their shares. The company must therefore consider the stakeholder response to the decisions it makes, as it will affect the company's ability to maximize its value for the owners.

As we also saw in Chapter 17, all decisions have financial consequences, but financial decisions have consequences in other areas as well. For example, policies for granting credit

affect *marketing's* ability to generate sales. Just imagine if BMW did not offer financing packages on its vehicles. Furthermore, money spent on research and development or new production facilities has an impact on what *operations* is capable of doing, just as the company's policies on payroll costs have an impact on attracting and keeping key employees (*human resources*). To make money, the company must first spend money, but it must also control that money to continue to be profitable and stay viable. A fine balance must be achieved between taking the risks and reaping the rewards—one that the finance manager must consider and that affects all areas of the company.

Cash flow provides an example of this need for integration and balance. To aid marketing in selling the company's products, the supply chain must be set up to make sure that inventory is available for customers and that credit is generally extended. However, that means that finance must balance the time that it takes to sell the inventory and then collect the accounts receivable from customers with the payments on that inventory and other expenses. If it does not do this, the company will not have enough cash coming in to pay its bills and will go bankrupt! Another example occurs with inventory. The operations area needs raw materials on hand to avoid delays in production, and marketing needs enough finished goods on hand to satisfy customers, but finance must balance these needs with the cost of carrying inventory and therefore tries to keep inventory levels at a minimum. In Chapter 15, we discussed techniques for dealing with inventory and saw that *technology* provides many new options.

Technology is just one of the many environmental factors that must be taken into account in making financial decisions. For example, as market demand changes (*social environment*), funds need to be shifted between projects.

As discussed in this chapter, the social environment has also had a significant impact on changing the role of the typical CFO in an organization—from being "just numbers people" to helping to develop and implement the company's overall *strategy* and "re-establish public trust" in the wake of recent financial scandals. As interest and exchange rates fluctuate (*economic* environment), some projects and methods of financing projects either will need to be abandoned or will become more possible. General economic conditions in domestic and world markets, like the recent global meltdown created by the sub-prime mortgage crisis (*international* environment), might cause companies to speed up or slow down the rate of investment in different projects, and government policies in the home and foreign countries (*political* environment) might make investment in certain projects more attractive than others. Finally, as technology advances and costs drop, some projects become more accessible.

In the internal business environment, when budgets are set, the finance area must work with the other functional areas to develop plans for financing the company that help it meet its strategic goals. Each area has a role to play in helping the organization achieve its strategic goals, and the resources they will need must be considered by the finance area. Finance uses various forecasts, as discussed in the chapter, to develop financial *plans* for the business to ensure that its goals are met in a way that balances risks and rewards, maximizing the value of the company for its owners.

chapter 18

Finance: Maximizing the Value

LEARNING OUTCOMES

1 Explain the roles finance and the financial manager play in the company's overall strategy.

2 Describe how a company develops its financial plans, including forecasts and budgets.

3 List the types of short- and long-term expenditures a company makes.

4 Summarize the main sources and costs of unsecured and secured short-term financing.

5 Identify and compare the two primary sources of long-term financing.

6 Understand the major types, features, and costs of long-term debt.

7 Discuss how companies issue equity and the costs to the company.

8 Understand risk, how it can be managed, and what makes a risk insurable.

9 Describe the types of insurance coverage that businesses should consider.

10 List some of the trends that are affecting the practice of financial management.

BRIAN WONG—YOUTH PLUS TALENT ADDS UP TO FINANCING

Vancouver's Brian Wong graduated with a bachelor's degree in commerce from the University of B.C. while still in his teens, and has been hailed as the youngest person ever to raise significant venture capital—even younger, at 19, than Mark Zuckerberg was when he began Facebook at age 20. The *Wall Street Journal* says Wong was the "youngest person to ever receive funding by a venture capital company." What's behind Wong's prodigious achievements?

For many young entrepreneurs, their age is a drawback. But Wong, born in 1991, has found ways to turn his youth into an asset. Seeming destined for success from the start, he worked in business development at the social content website Digg.com and was CEO of Followformation, which developed a tool to help beginning Twitter users make sense out of the service. Having quickly established himself as a leader in the youth market, Wong is now focused on a new idea: Kiip (pronounced "keep").

A "mobile rewards network," Kiip (www.kiip.me) is based on the recreational ways we use our tablets, computers, and smartphones. Kiip homes in on two facts: (1) we play games and (2) we are annoyed by pop-up ads, which Wong calls "buzz-kills."

To turn that negative into a positive, Kiip gives away prizes. Let's say you finish a stage or level of a game, and a pop-up fills your screen. But instead of being an ad, it's a notification that you've won a prize—some vitamin water, a fast-food meal, a gift card for a national retailer, or perhaps some new software. Some prizes are worth up to $100. So rather than reacting to the pop-up negatively, the player celebrates a prize, while still being exposed to a marketing message. And these prizes can be targeted to the user. For example, an algorithm can decide that if no females are playing the game, lipstick is off the prize list.

Wong got this idea from looking around a coffee shop he was in and noticing what young people were doing—playing games on their mobile devices. Tying that observation into his ongoing obsession with what young people want, he went after lining up prizes the gamers would find desirable, matching the market with the marketer.

Kiip began with $300,000 in startup capital from a mixture of angel investors and venture capitalists in October 2010. Then in March 2011, it scored $4 million in Series A venture capital from some of the same investors (True

PHOTO COURTESY OF BRIAN WONG

Ventures, Crosslink Capital, and Venture51) plus some big new ones including Hummer Winblad Venture Partners. Series A simply refers to the first round of a call for capital, which happens after a company starts to see some revenue but not enough to sustain its growth.

Venture capitalists Lars Leckie of Winblad and Phil Black of True Ventures joined the board of directors at Kiip. No doubt they want to keep an eye on their investment as well as reap some big potential returns. On investing in a virtually unproven 19-year-old, Black told the *Wall Street Journal* that "it's worth the risk with just a tiny amount of seed capital.... Our fund is set up to take modest risk on great people, investing $200,000 out of a $208 million vehicle ... the risk-reward profile is there for us."

Venture capitalists invest early in a business's life cycle and expect to make double- or triple-digit returns on that investment. Kiip has moved into new offices in San Francisco, expanded to a staff of eight, and is hiring. It continues to add new partners and games to the rewards program.

Brian Wong traded on the success of his early ideas and used his youth as an asset, which he parlayed into a multimillion-dollar corporation. Could you do what he did? Look around you; what is popular? Then look again; where is the money?[1]

As you read this chapter, consider the following questions:

1. What are some ways to finance a start-up company?

2. What would investors want to see in a financial statement to encourage them to put money into a company?

3. Brian Wong's success comes from a deep understanding of what his target consumers want. What happens when businesses focus on producing great products but don't have a clear and correct vision of who will use them?

SOURCES: Ty McMahan, "Betting Venture Capital on an Unproven 19-Year-Old," *Wall Street Journal* Blogs, August 6, 2010, http://blogs.wsj.com/venturecapital/2010/08/06/betting-venture-capital-on-an-unproven-19-year-old/; Alexia Tsotsis, "Kiip's Brian Wong on Taking Risks as Young Entrepreneur," Tech Crunch, April 12th, 2011, http://techcrunch.com/2011/04/12/kiips-brian-wong-on-taking-risks-as-young-entrepreneur/; "Brian Wong," Crunch Base, www.crunchbase.com/person/brian-wong/; Michael Arrington, "True Ventures Invests in 19-Year-Old Entrepreneur Brian Wong," Tech Crunch, August 3rd, 2010, http://techcrunch.com/2010/08/03/true-ventures-invests-in-brian-wong-teenager-kiip/; http://brianwong.com/; http://communities.canada.com/vancouversun/blogs/techsense/archive/2011/04/12/ubc-grad-brian-wong-launches-mobile-gaming-ad-model-with-real-life-rewards.aspx/; http://thegoodnetguide.com/tag/real-estate/; Wade Roush, "$300K for Kiip," Xconomy, October 28, 2010, www.xconomy.com/san-francisco/2010/10/28/300k-for-kiip/; www.kiip.me/; http://blog.kiip.me/; Gillian Shaw, "Whiz kid's startup raises $4M," *Calgary Herald*, April 18, 2011.

In today's fast-paced global economy, managing a company's finances is more complex than ever. A thorough command of traditional finance activities—financial planning, investing money, and raising funds—is only part of the job. Financial managers are more than number crunchers. As part of the top-management team, chief financial officers (CFOs) need a broad understanding of their company's business and industry, as well as leadership ability and creativity. They must never lose sight of the primary goal of the financial manager: to maximize the value of the company to its owners.

All companies, whether start-up companies with three employees or major multinational corporations with billions of dollars in annual revenue, need to manage their finances efficiently and effectively. Otherwise, the company will not have the resources it needs to pay its bills and run its daily operations or to make investments in future growth.

Financial management—spending and raising a company's money—is both a science and an art. The science part is analyzing numbers and the flow of cash through the company. The art is answering questions like these: Is the company using its financial resources in the best way? Aside from costs, why choose a particular form of financing? How risky is each option?

Whether you are a marketing manager, purchasing agent, or systems analyst, knowledge of finance will help you to do your job better. You'll be able to understand your company's financial statements, its financial condition, and management's investment and financing decisions. Financial information also provides feedback on how well you are doing and identifies problems. On a more practical note, you may be asked to prepare a budget for your department or unit. Employees who understand the financial decision-making process will be able to prepare proposals that address financial concerns. As a result, they will be more likely to get the resources they require to accomplish the company's goals.

If you own a business, you must pay close attention to financial management. Without financial plans, you may find yourself running out of cash. It's easy to get so caught up in growing sales that you neglect your billing and collection methods. In fact, managing accounts receivable is often one of the more challenging aspects of running a young company.

This chapter focuses on the financial management of a company. We'll start with an overview of the role of finance and of the financial manager in the company's overall business strategy. Next we consider the basics of financial planning: forecasts and budgets. Discussions of short- and long-term uses of funds and sources of short- and long-term financing follow. The importance of understanding and managing risk and insurance is examined, and finally, we'll look at key trends affecting financial management.

THE ROLE OF FINANCE AND THE FINANCIAL MANAGER

LO1

Any company—whether it's a two-lawyer law partnership or an integrated oil company, such as Suncor Energy—needs money to operate. To make money, it must first spend money—on inventory and supplies, equipment and facilities, and employee wages and salaries. Therefore, finance is critical to the success of all companies. It might not be as visible as marketing or production, but management of a company's finances is just as much a key to the company's success.

Financial management—the art and science of managing a company's money so that it can meet its goals—is not just the responsibility of the finance department. All business decisions have financial consequences. Managers in all departments must work closely with financial personnel. If you are a sales representative, for example, the company's credit and collection policies will affect your ability to make sales.

Revenues from sales of the company's products should be the chief source of funding, but money from sales doesn't always come in when it's needed to pay the bills. Financial managers must track how money is flowing into and out of the company (see Exhibit 18.1). They work with the company's other department managers to determine how available funds will be used and how much money is needed. Then they choose the best sources to obtain the required funding.

For example, a financial manager will track day-to-day operational data such as cash collections and disbursements to ensure that the company has enough cash to

financial management
The art and science of managing a company's money so that it can meet its goals.

HOT *Links*

What challenges do today's financial managers face? To find out, browse through recent issues of *CFO* magazine at
www3.cfo.com

Exhibit 18.1 How Cash Flows through a Business

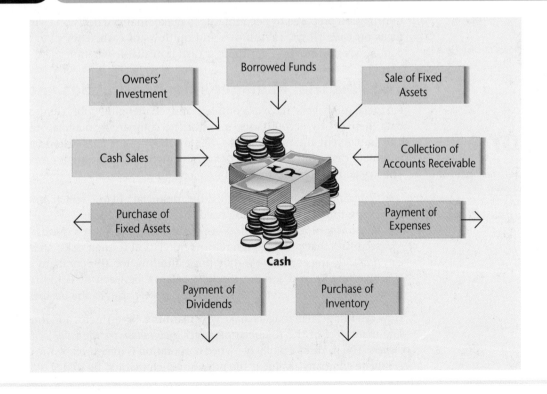

CHAPTER 18 Finance: Maximizing the Value **541**

Because all business decisions have financial consequences, managers in all departments must work closely with financial personnel. A company's credit and collection policies, for example, might impact a sales representative's ability to close a sale. Who is responsible for making key financial decisions for businesses?

© CARDINAL/CORBIS

meet its obligations. Over a longer time horizon, the manager will thoroughly study whether and when the company should open a new manufacturing facility. The manager will also suggest the most appropriate way to finance the project, raise the funds, and then monitor the project's implementation and operation.

Financial management is closely related to accounting. In most companies, both areas are the responsibility of the vice president of finance or the CFO (many of whom have an accounting designation). But the accountant's main function is to collect and present financial data. Financial managers use financial statements and other information prepared by accountants to make financial decisions. Financial managers focus on cash flows, the inflows and outflows of cash. They plan and monitor the company's cash flows to ensure that cash is available when needed.

cash flows
The inflows and outflows of cash for a company.

The Financial Manager's Responsibilities and Activities

Financial managers have a complex and challenging job. They analyze financial data prepared by accountants, monitor the company's financial status, and prepare and implement financial plans. One day they might be developing a better way to automate cash collections; the next they might be analyzing a proposed acquisition. The key activities of the financial manager are

- *financial planning*—preparing the financial plan, which projects revenues, expenditures, and financing needs over a given period;
- *investment (spending money)*—investing the company's funds in projects and securities that provide high returns in relation to their risks; and
- *financing (raising money)*—obtaining funding for the company's operations and investments and seeking the best balance between debt (borrowed funds) and equity (funds raised through the sale of ownership in the business).

How can financial managers make wise planning, investment, and financing decisions? The main goal of the financial manager is *to maximize the value of the company to its owners*. The value of a publicly owned corporation is measured by the price of its shares. A private company's value is the price at which it could be sold.

When you come across a finance term you don't understand, visit
www.financialterms.ca

To maximize the company's value, the financial manager has to consider both short- and long-term consequences of the company's actions. Maximizing profits is one approach, but it should not be the only one. Such an approach favours making short-term gains over achieving long-term goals. What if a company in a highly technical and competitive industry did no research and development? In the short run, profits would be high because research and development are very expensive, but in the long run, the company might lose its ability to compete because of its lack of new products.

This is true regardless of a company's size or point in its life cycle. David Deeds was cofounder of a company that developed an innovative computer-aided design hardware and software package for architects and engineers. He and his partners made some decisions early in the company's life to pursue opportunities such as consulting projects that generated revenue quickly. The company saw its profits grow, adding staff and offices to handle the increased business, but this sidetracked the founders from their initial vision: designing revolutionary new products to address client needs. "We managed ourselves into a niche where we could survive and make a little money but never offer anything unique or grow significantly," says Deeds. Although they built a reasonably successful small business, the desire for the quick buck overrode the long-term goal of building a $100 million company.[2]

Financial managers constantly strive for a balance between the opportunity for profit and the potential for loss. In finance, the opportunity for profit is termed **return**; the potential for loss, or the chance that an investment will not achieve the expected level of return, is **risk**. A basic principle in finance is that the higher the risk, the greater the return that is required. This widely accepted concept is called the **risk–return trade-off**. Financial managers consider many risk and return factors when making investment and financing decisions. Among them are changing patterns of market demand, interest rates, general economic conditions, market conditions, and social issues (such as environmental effects and equal employment opportunity policies).

return
The opportunity for profit.

risk
The potential for loss or the chance that an investment will not achieve the expected level of return.

risk–return trade-off
A basic principle in finance that holds that the higher the risk, the greater the return required.

> ## Concept *Check*
>
> What is the role of financial management in a company?
>
> How do the three key activities of the financial manager relate?
>
> What is the main goal of the financial manager? How does the risk–return trade-off relate to the financial manager's main goal?

FINANCIAL PLANNING: LOOKING AHEAD

LO2

As we learned in Chapter 9, companies use several types of plans to determine how to achieve organizational objectives. A company's *financial plan* is part of the overall company plan and guides the company toward its business goals and the maximization of its value. The financial plan enables the company to estimate the amount and timing of its investment and financing needs.

To prepare a financial plan, the financial manager must first consider existing and proposed products, the resources available to produce them, and the financing needed to support production and sales. Forecasts and budgets are essential to the company's financial planning. They should be part of an integrated planning process that links them to strategic plans and performance measurement.

Forecasting the Future

The financial-planning process starts with financial forecasts, or projections of future developments within the company. The estimated demand for the company's products (the sales forecast) and other financial and operating data are key inputs. At Ford Motor Company, economic analysts estimate expected production and sales for each line of cars and trucks. Then, financial analysts prepare detailed short- and long-term financial forecasts based on these assumptions.

Short-term forecasts, or *operating plans*, project revenues, costs of goods, and operating expenses over a one-year period. Using short-term forecasts, financial managers at Ford estimate the next year's expenses for inventory, labour, advertising,

short-term forecasts
Projections of revenues, costs of goods, and operating expenses over a one-year period.

long-term forecasts
Projections of a company's activities and the funding for those activities over a period that is longer than a year, typically 2 to 10 years.

and other operating activities. These estimates form the basis for cash budgets (described next), which forecast cash inflows and outflows over the same period.

Long-term forecasts, or strategic plans, cover a period that is longer than a year, typically 2 to 10 years, and take a broader view of the company's financial activities. With these forecasts, management can assess the financial effects of various business strategies: What would be the financial results of investing in new facilities and equipment? Of developing new products? Of eliminating a line of business? Of acquiring other companies? Long-term forecasts also show where the funding for these activities is expected to come from.

Lenders typically ask potential borrowers for forecasts that cover the period during which the loan will be outstanding. The forecasts are used to evaluate the risk of the loan and to see that adequate cash flow will be available to pay off the debt. Then they structure loan terms and covenants (requirements that the company comply with certain operating and financial measures during the loan period) based on those statements.

Budgets

budgets
Formal written forecasts of revenues and expenses that set spending limits based on operational forecasts; include cash budgets, capital budgets, and operating budgets.

Businesses prepare budgets to plan and control their future financial activities. **Budgets** are formal written forecasts of revenues and expenses that set spending limits based on operational forecasts. All budgets begin with forecasts. Budgets provide a way to control expenses and compare the actual performance to the forecast. By monitoring actual revenues and expenses and comparing them to budgets on a regular basis, companies

Creating the Future of Business

PATTI DIBSKI, GIBSON FINE ART

Calgary's *Avenue Magazine* described Patti Dibski, after she was named of the "Top 40 Under 40" in 2009, as someone who lives "outside of their comfort zone and welcome(s) the unfamiliar without hesitation." Sounds like a born entrepreneur to us!

Patti has definitely stepped outside what would be considered anyone's comfort zone on more than one occasion in her career path. In the early 1990s, she lived and worked for three years in Shizuoka, Japan, teaching English to executives at the Yazaki Corporation. Becoming fluent in Japanese (yes, believe it!) she also helped Japanese executives who were posted overseas with their language and culture challenges. Back in Canada, Patti worked as the national account manager for the Canadian National Railway (CNR), planning the movement of coal and coke throughout the rail system. As she puts it, her job was "a bit of a party stopper." How many young females have had jobs like that?

She left all that behind her to purchase Gibson Fine Art in 2004, and there she discovered her real comfort zone. Always a lover of art, but "not artistic at all," Patti definitely found her calling: to be an entrepreneur running a business she is passionate about. Having taken only "the odd art history class in university," she expected again to be outside her comfort zone, but that is where the true entrepreneur in her kicked in. As Patti describes it: "I could have been fearful of becoming something I wasn't, but I embraced that fear and told myself, 'I know I can learn this—I love art. Because I love it, I will spend the time learning what I need to know.' " She says the key to her success is "about not being afraid" of fear, but instead "embrac(ing) it and see(ing) it as a challenge."

And clearly she did. Patti grew the business to supply nearly 20 large corporate downtown offices with art, representing 40 artists—most local. She provided art to acute care cancer patients for their hospital rooms, through her role as vice president for Art à la Carte. And she grew her walk-in retail business from a dribble to a credible flow.

The basic idea behind Gibson's is to provide art consulting, leasing, and purchasing services to primarily corporate clients, to create "enriching environments for customer, visitors and employees." Art can be a serious and expensive investment and Gibson's helps companies find both the art and the financial approach to it that is right for them. Often that means purchasing rather than leasing the artwork, as the cost–benefit of ownership outweighs renting over longer periods of time. Gibson's supplements its services with a full-service relocation package for companies' art collections. Moving art has proven more rewarding than moving coal in more ways than one!

Thinking Critically

1. Patti Dibski is a great entrepreneur to profile in our last chapter because she sends a strong message to would-be entrepreneurs. What do you think that message is?
2. Patti's business is also a good example of the lease-or-buy decision that companies are often faced with. Why would art be more cost-effective to purchase?
3. Do you have a passion that could be your future business?

SOURCES: http://www.gibsonfineart.ca, used with permission from Patti Dibski; http://www.canada.com/calgaryherald, March 23, 2007; http://www.avenuecalgary.com/top-40-under-40.

Budgets of all types help companies plan and control their future financial activities. What types of fixed assets would a hotel chain include in its capital budget?

PHOTO COURTESY OF DELTA HOTELS LIMITED

gain critical information about operations. When variances to the budget occur, managers can analyze them to determine if they need to take steps to correct them. Suppose the owner of a small printing company sees that May sales are down and expenses are over budget because a major press broke down and the company was unable to fulfill many orders on time. This situation would require asking such questions as, How old is the press? Has it broken down before? Should the company continue to repair it or is it time to replace it? Can the company afford a new press? How would it finance the new press? A back-up plan to prevent lost orders would be another possible outcome of this budget review.

Companies use several types of budgets, most of which cover a one-year period:

What is a financial plan? Name two types of financial-planning documents.

Distinguish between short- and long-term forecasts. How are both used by financial managers?

Briefly describe three types of budgets.

- **Cash budgets** forecast the company's cash inflows and outflows, and help the company plan for cash surpluses and shortages. Because having enough cash is so critical to their financial health, many companies prepare annual cash budgets subdivided into months or weeks. Then they project the amount of cash needed in each shorter time period.
- **Capital budgets** forecast outlays for fixed assets (plant and equipment). They usually cover a period of several years and ensure that the company will have enough funds to buy the equipment and buildings it needs.
- **Operating budgets** combine sales forecasts with estimates of production costs and operating expenses to forecast profits. They are based on individual budgets for sales, production, purchases of materials, factory overhead, and operating expenses. Operating budgets then are used to plan operations: dollars of sales, units of production, amounts of raw materials, dollars of wages, and so forth.

cash budgets
Budgets that forecast a company's cash inflows and outflows and help the company plan for cash surpluses and shortages.

capital budgets
Budgets that forecast a company's outlays for fixed assets (plant and equipment), typically covering a period of several years.

operating budgets
Budgets that combine sales forecasts with estimates of production costs and operating expenses to forecast profits.

Budgets are routinely used to monitor and control the performance of a division, a department, or an individual manager. When actual outcomes differ from budget expectations, management must take action.

HOW ORGANIZATIONS USE FUNDS

To grow and prosper, a company must keep investing money in its operations. The financial manager decides how best to use the company's money. Short-term expenses support the company's day-to-day activities. For instance, an athletic-apparel maker regularly spends money to buy raw materials such as leather and fabric, and to pay employee salaries. Long-term expenses are typically for fixed assets. For the athletic-apparel maker, these would include outlays to build a new factory, buy automated manufacturing equipment, or acquire a small manufacturer of sports apparel.

Short-Term Expenses

Short-term expenses, often called *operating expenses*, are outlays used to support current selling and production activities. They typically result in current assets, which include cash and any other assets (accounts receivable and inventory) that can be converted to cash within a year. The financial manager's goal is to manage current assets so the company has enough cash to pay its bills and to support its accounts receivable and inventory.

cash management
The process of making sure that a company has enough cash on hand to pay bills as they are due and to meet unexpected expenses.

CASH MANAGEMENT: ASSURING LIQUIDITY Cash is the lifeblood of business. Without it, a company could not operate. An important duty of the financial manager is **cash management**, or making sure that enough cash is on hand to pay bills as they are due and to meet unexpected expenses.

Businesses use budgets to estimate the cash requirements for a specific period. Many companies keep a minimum cash balance to cover unexpected expenses or changes in projected cash flows. The financial manager arranges loans to cover any shortfalls. If the size and timing of cash inflows closely match the size and timing of cash outflows, the company needs to keep only a small amount of cash on hand. A company whose sales and receipts are fairly predictable and regular throughout the year needs less cash than a company with a seasonal pattern of sales and receipts. A toy company, for instance, whose sales are concentrated in the fall, spends a great deal of cash during the spring and summer to build inventory. It has excess cash during the winter and early spring, when it collects on sales from its peak selling season.

Because cash held in current accounts earns little, if any, interest, the financial manager tries to keep cash balances low and to invest the surplus cash. Surpluses are invested temporarily in marketable securities, short-term investments that are easily converted into cash. The financial manager looks for low-risk investments that offer high returns. Three of the most popular marketable securities are Treasury bills, certificates of deposit, and commercial papers. (**Commercial paper** is unsecured short-term debt—an IOU—issued by a financially strong corporation.)

commercial paper
Unsecured short-term debt—an IOU—issued by a financially strong corporation.

Companies with overseas operations face even greater cash management challenges, as the Expanding Around the Globe box explains. Developing the systems for international cash management may sound simple in theory, but in practice it's extremely complex. In addition to dealing with multiple foreign currencies, treasurers must understand and follow banking practices and regulatory and tax requirements in each country. Regulations may impede their ability to move funds freely across borders. Also, issuing a standard set of procedures for every office may not work because local business practices differ from country to country. Moreover, local managers may resist the shift to a centralized structure because they don't want to give up control of cash generated by their units. Corporate financial managers must be sensitive to and aware of local customs and adapt the centralization strategy accordingly.

marketable securities
Short-term investments that are easily converted into cash.

In addition to seeking the right balance between cash and marketable securities, the financial manager tries to shorten the time between the purchase of inventory or services (cash outflows) and the collection of cash from sales (cash inflows). The three key strategies are to collect money owed to the company (accounts receivable) as quickly as possible, to pay money owed to others (accounts payable) as late as possible without damaging the company's credit reputation, and to turn inventory quickly to minimize the funds tied up in it.

Expanding Around the Globe

FOLLOW THE MONEY

If you think it's hard to balance your chequing account, imagine trying to deal with $4 billion or more in 1400 accounts in 46 different currencies for 233 legal entities, at 145 banks worldwide! That's the job facing many financial managers at multinational companies who grapple with complex treasury operations like this on a daily basis. With so much at stake, international cash management becomes a priority for financial managers.

Many companies are seeking more efficient global cash management systems. Corporate treasurers want to identify and pool cash from overseas operations so that these cash balances can be put to work. In addition, recent regulatory changes have brought huge amounts of cash back to North America from overseas operations—and too much cash can be as much of a problem as too little. Cash is a great asset to have, but if it is earning only 1 percent pre-tax, it may not be the best financial investment. It might be advisable to invest in marketable securities in the short term.

Many financial managers are turning to a Web-based technology solution to improve their global cash pooling system. Many Canadian international companies have trouble tracking their cash; much of it may be outside North America and earning little or no interest.

Once international companies know where their cash holdings are, they can manage this cash more efficiently and profitably. Treasury managers developed budgets and goals for interest income that were tied to cash balance forecasts, exchange rates in each country, and other factors. The interest income goals establish performance benchmarks and are factored into incentive compensation. The results can be significant. Companies can also quickly identify which cash reserves are available to make an acquisition or fund a large capital project.[3]

Thinking Critically

1. Why is managing cash such an important part of a financial manager's job? Why is having too much cash a problem?
2. Once financial managers understand their cash situation, what can they do to ensure that the money is available when needed and properly invested until they do need it?

SOURCES: Adapted from Richard Gamble, "Got Cash? Who Doesn't?" Treasury & Risk Management, December 2005/January 2006, http://www.treasuryandrisk.com; Richard Gamble, Susan Kelly, and John Labate, "The 2005 Alexander Hamilton Award Winners: Cash Management; Bronze Award Winner: Honeywell International," Treasury & Risk Management, November 2005, all from http://www.treasuryandrisk.com; and Karen M. Kroll, "Treasury Today: To Centralize or Not?" Business Finance, April 2006, http://businessfinancemag.com.

MANAGING ACCOUNTS RECEIVABLE Accounts receivable represent sales for which the company has not yet been paid. Because the product has been sold but cash has not yet been received, an account receivable amounts to a use of funds. For the average manufacturing company, accounts receivable represent about 15 to 20 percent of total assets.

accounts receivable
Sales for which a company has not yet been paid.

The financial manager's goal is to collect money owed to the company as quickly as possible while offering customers credit terms attractive enough to increase sales. Accounts receivable management involves setting *credit policies*, guidelines on offering credit, and *credit terms*, specific repayment conditions, including how long customers have to pay their bills and whether a cash discount is given for quicker payment. Another aspect of accounts receivable management is deciding on *collection policies*, the procedures for collecting overdue accounts.

Setting up credit and collection policies is a balancing act for financial managers. On the one hand, easier credit policies or generous credit terms (a longer repayment period or larger cash discount) result in increased sales. On the other hand, the company has to finance more accounts receivable, and the risk of uncollectible accounts receivable rises. Businesses consider the impact on sales, timing of cash flow, experience with bad debt, customer profiles, and industry standards when developing their credit and collection policies.

Companies that want to speed up collections actively manage their accounts receivable rather than passively letting customers pay when they want to. Companies that take this approach can usually collect from anyone.

Technology plays a big role in helping companies improve their credit and collections performance. When the tech sector fell on hard times, Cisco saw its global Days Sales Outstanding (DSO) climb to a high of 47 days. The company then developed Web-based reporting tools that improved overall cash management. Managers received frequently updated accounts receivable and cash collection reports, along with real-time collection and credit reports. The new system also flagged potential problems with customers. Within nine months of implementation, Cisco exceeded its goal of reducing DSO to 30 days, slashing that number to 24 days.[4]

INVENTORY One use of funds is to buy inventory needed by the company. In a typical manufacturing company, inventory is nearly 20 percent of total assets. The cost of inventory includes not only its purchase price but also ordering, handling, storage, interest, and insurance costs.

Production, marketing, and finance managers usually have differing views about inventory. Production managers want lots of raw materials on hand to avoid production delays. Marketing managers want lots of finished goods on hand so that customer orders can be filled quickly, but financial managers want the least inventory possible without harming production efficiency or sales. Financial managers must work closely with production and marketing to balance these conflicting goals. Techniques for reducing the investment in inventory—inventory management, the just-in-time system, and materials requirement planning—were described in Chapter 15.

Long-Term Expenditures

A company also uses funds for its investments in long-lived assets—such items as land, buildings, machinery, equipment, and information systems. These are called **capital expenditures**. Unlike operating expenses, which produce benefits within a year, the benefits from capital expenditures extend beyond one year. For instance, a printer's purchase of a new printing press with a usable life of seven years is a capital expenditure. It appears as a fixed asset on the company's balance sheet. Paper, ink, and other supplies, however, are expenses. Mergers and acquisitions, discussed in Chapter 8, are also considered capital expenditures.

Companies make capital expenditures for many reasons. The most common are to expand and to replace or renew fixed assets. Another reason is to develop new products. Most manufacturing companies have a big investment in long-term assets. Bombardier Inc., for instance, puts millions of dollars a year into airplane-manufacturing facilities.

Because capital expenditures tend to be costly and have a major effect on the company's future, the financial manager must analyze long-term projects and select those that offer the best returns, while maximizing the company's value. This process is called **capital budgeting**. Decisions involving new products or the acquisition of another business are especially important. Managers look at project costs and forecast the future benefits the project will bring—for example, from increased productivity, staff reductions, and other cost savings—to calculate the company's estimated return on the investment.

For instance, consider the period during which Air Canada or WestJet Airlines is planning the purchase of new aircraft. Before going ahead, the company must consider not only its present aircraft and load factors (i.e., how many seats are typically full during any of its routes) but also the actual acquisition costs, maintenance costs, how to finance the aircraft (i.e., debt capital or equity capital), the amount that the aircraft will actually be flying (and therefore making revenue), and the anticipated payback period (i.e., how long will it take for the revenue that the aircraft generates to pay off its costs).

capital expenditures
Investments in long-lived assets, such as land, buildings, machinery, and equipment, that are expected to provide benefits extending beyond one year.

capital budgeting
The process of analyzing long-term projects and selecting those that offer the best returns while maximizing the company's value.

Concept Check

Distinguish between short- and long-term expenses.

What is the financial manager's goal in cash management? List the three key cash management strategies.

Describe the company's main motives in making capital expenditures.

LO4 OBTAINING SHORT-TERM FINANCING

How do companies raise the funding they need? They borrow money (debt), sell ownership shares (equity), and retain earnings (profits). The financial manager must assess all of these sources and choose the one most likely to help maximize the company's value.

Like expenses, borrowed funds can be divided into short- and long-term loans. A short-term loan comes due within a year; a long-term loan has a maturity greater than one year. Short-term financing is shown as a current liability on the balance sheet and is used to finance current assets and support operations. Short-term loans can be unsecured or secured.

Unsecured Short-Term Loans

Unsecured loans are made on the basis of the company's creditworthiness and the lender's previous experience with the company. An unsecured borrower does not have to pledge specific assets as security. The three main types of *unsecured short-term loans* are trade credit, bank loans, and commercial paper.

TRADE CREDIT: ACCOUNTS PAYABLE When Magna International Inc. (Magna) sells auto parts to its customers, the customers do not have to pay cash on delivery. Instead, Magna regularly bills its customers for the purchases, and they pay at a later date. This is an example of trade credit: The seller extends credit to the buyer between the time the buyer receives the goods or services and when it pays for them. Trade credit is a major source of short-term business financing. The buyer enters the credit on its books as an account payable. In effect, the credit is a short-term loan from the seller to the buyer of the goods and services. Until the customers pay Magna, Magna has an account receivable from its customers and the customers have an account payable to Magna.

BANK LOANS Unsecured bank loans are another source of short-term business financing. Companies often use these loans to finance seasonal (cyclical) businesses. For instance, a swimwear manufacturer has strong sales in the spring and summer and lower sales during the fall and winter. It needs short-term bank financing to increase inventories before its strongest selling season and to finance accounts receivable during late winter and early spring, as shown in Exhibit 18.2. The company repays these bank loans when it sells the inventory and collects the receivables.

Unsecured bank loans include lines of credit and revolving credit agreements (although in Canada most are secured). A line of credit is an agreement between a bank and a business or an individual. It specifies the maximum amount of short-term

unsecured loans
Loans for which the borrower does not have to pledge specific assets as security.

trade credit
The extension of credit by the seller to the buyer between the time the buyer receives the goods or services and when it pays for them.

accounts payable
A purchase for which a buyer has not yet paid the seller.

line of credit
An agreement between a bank and a business or person that specifies the maximum amount of short-term borrowing the bank will make available to that business or person.

Exhibit 18.2 Swimwear Manufacturer's Seasonal Cash Flows

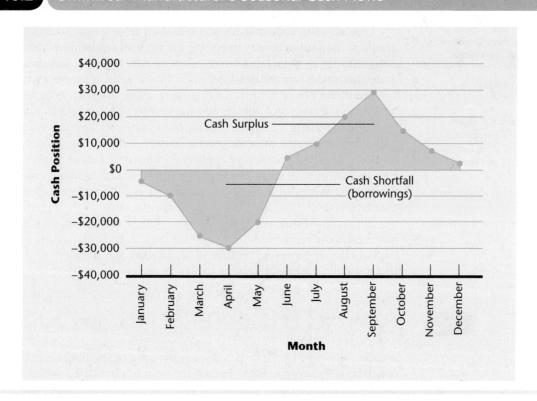

Concept Check

Distinguish between unsecured and secured short-term loans.

Briefly describe the three main types of unsecured short-term loans.

Discuss the two ways in which accounts receivable can be used to obtain short-term financing.

revolving credit agreement (or revolving line of credit)
A line of credit that allows the borrower to have access to funds again once it has been repaid.

secured loans
Loans for which the borrower is required to pledge specific assets as collateral, or security.

factoring
A form of short-term financing in which a company sells its accounts receivable outright, at a discount, to a *factor*.

When working capital is a problem, one option is factoring. Learn more about factoring by searching Export Development Canada's website at www.edc.ca

borrowing the bank will make available to the company or the individual. This allows the borrower to obtain a number of loans without reapplying each time, as long as they do not exceed the prearranged amount.

Most lines of credit are a **revolving credit agreement (or revolving line of credit)**. A revolving credit agreement allows the borrower to continue to have access to funds as long as the maximum has not been exceeded. Therefore, the business or individual can pay off the line of credit and have access to the available funds again. Most credit cards offer revolving lines of credit.

Companies often obtain annual lines of credit based on their expected seasonal needs. Then they can quickly borrow without having to reapply to the bank each time funds are needed. Suppose the swimwear manufacturer projected a cash shortfall of $80,000 for the period from February to June. The financial manager might get a $100,000 line of credit from the bank. (The extra $20,000 would be there to cover any unexpected outlays.) The company could borrow funds as needed—$10,000 in February, $25,000 in March, $30,000 in April. Then, it could gradually repay the loan as it collects cash during the summer months.

COMMERCIAL PAPER As noted earlier, *commercial paper* is an unsecured short-term debt—an IOU—issued by a financially strong corporation. Thus, it is a short-term investment for companies with temporary cash surpluses, and it is a financing option for major corporations. Corporations issue commercial paper in multiples of $100,000 for periods ranging from 3 to 270 days. Many big companies use commercial paper instead of short-term bank loans because the interest rate on commercial paper is usually 1 to 3 percent below bank rates.

Secured Short-Term Loans

Secured loans require the borrower to pledge specific assets as *collateral*, or security. The secured lender can legally take the collateral if the borrower doesn't repay the loan. Chartered banks and commercial finance companies are the main sources of secured short-term loans to business. Borrowers whose credit is not strong enough to qualify for unsecured loans use these loans.

Typically, the collateral for secured short-term loans is accounts receivable or inventory. Because accounts receivable are normally quite liquid (easily converted to cash), they are an attractive form of collateral. The appeal of inventory—raw materials or finished goods—as collateral depends on how easily it can be sold at a fair price.

Another form of short-term financing using accounts receivable is **factoring**. In this case, a company sells its accounts receivable outright to a *factor*, a financial institution (usually a chartered bank or commercial finance company) that buys accounts receivables at a discount. Factoring is widely used in the clothing, furniture, sporting goods, and appliance industries. Factoring allows a company to turn its accounts receivable into cash without worrying about collections. Because the factor assumes all the risks and expenses of collecting the accounts, companies that factor all of their accounts can reduce the costs of their credit and collection operations. Factoring is more expensive than a bank loan, however, because the factor buys the receivables at a discount from their actual value. Often a company has no choice, however, because it has neither the track record to get unsecured financing nor other collateral to pledge as security for a loan.

LO5 RAISING LONG-TERM FINANCING

A basic principle of finance is to match the term of the financing to the period over which benefits are expected to be received from the associated outlay. Short-term items should be financed with short-term funds, and long-term items should be financed with long-term funds. Long-term financing sources include both debt (borrowing) and equity (ownership). Equity financing comes either from selling new ownership interests or from retaining earnings.

Debt versus Equity Financing

Say that Bombardier plans to spend $2 billion over the next four years to build and equip new factories to make regional jets. The company's top management will assess the pros and cons of both debt and equity, and then consider several possible sources of the desired form of long-term financing.

The major advantage of debt financing is the deductibility of the interest expense for income tax purposes, which lowers its overall cost. In addition, there is no loss of ownership. The major drawback is **financial risk**: the chance that the company will be unable to make scheduled interest and principal payments. The lender can force a borrower that fails to make scheduled debt payments into bankruptcy. Most loan agreements have restrictions to ensure that the borrower operates efficiently. Lenders often use what is known as "The 6 C's of Credit" to determine the risk that the borrower will default on the debt. The 6 C's are

- Character: the past history of the borrower to repay loans.
- Capacity to pay: the ability to repay the loan.
- Capital (money): the amount of cash the borrower has access to.
- Collateral: pledge of specific assets by the borrower to the lender that becomes the lender's if the borrower defaults on the repayment of the loan.
- Conditions: issues that affect the business (e.g., economic conditions, competition, etc.)
- Confidence: the borrower addresses the concerns that the lender may have and gives reassurance that the loan will be repaid.

Equity, on the other hand, is a form of permanent financing that places few restrictions on the company. The company is not required to pay dividends or repay the investment. However, equity financing gives common shareholders voting rights that provide them with a voice in management. Equity is more costly than debt. Unlike the interest on debt, dividends to owners are not tax-deductible expenses. Exhibit 18.3 summarizes the major differences between debt and equity financing.

Financial managers try to select the mix of long-term debt and equity that results in the best balance between cost and risk. If a company's debt load gets too high, in the view of investors and securities analysts, the costs of borrowing will rise. Company policies about the mix of debt and equity vary. Some companies have high debt compared to equity. Others keep debt to a minimum. Some examples of low debt as a percentage of equity on the TSX is 1 percent at Canada Bread Co., 2 percent at Imperial Oil and Magna International, 3 percent at Reitmans Canada, and 12 percent at Laurentian Bank of Canada.[5]

Concept *in Action*

For businesses with steady orders but a lack of cash to make payroll or other immediate payments, factoring is a popular way to obtain financing. In factoring, a company sells its invoices to a third-party funding source for cash. The factor purchasing the invoices then collects on the due payments over time. Trucking companies with voluminous accounts are good candidates for factoring. Why might companies choose factoring instead of loans?

financial risk
The chance that a company will be unable to make scheduled interest and principal payments on its debt.

Concept *Check*

Discuss the major differences between debt and equity financing.

What is financial risk?

LONG-TERM DEBT FINANCING

LO6

Long-term debt is used to finance long-term (capital) expenditures. The initial maturities of long-term debt typically range between 5 and 20 years. Three important forms of long-term debt are term loans, bonds, and mortgage loans.

Exhibit 18.3   Major Differences between Debt and Equity Financing

	DEBT FINANCING	EQUITY FINANCING
Voice in management	Creditors typically have none, unless borrower defaults on payments. Creditors may be able to place restraints on management in event of default.	Common shareholders have voting rights.
Claim on income and assets	Debt holders rank ahead of equity holders. Payment of interest and principal is a contractual obligation of the company.	Equity owners have a residual claim on income (dividends are paid only after interest and any scheduled principal payments are paid) and assets. The company has no obligation to pay dividends.
Maturity	Debt has a stated maturity and requires repayment of principal by a specified maturity date.	The company is not required to repay equity, which has no maturity date.
Tax treatment	Interest is a tax-deductible expense.	Dividends are not tax-deductible and are paid from after-tax income.

term loan
A business loan with an initial maturity of more than one year; can be unsecured or secured.

A **term loan** is a business loan with an initial maturity of more than one year. Term loans generally have 5- to 12-year maturities and can be unsecured or secured. They are available from chartered banks, insurance companies, pension funds, commercial finance companies, and manufacturers' financing subsidiaries. A contract between the borrower and the lender spells out the amount and maturity of the loan, the interest rate, payment dates, the purpose of the loan, and other provisions, such as operating and financial restrictions on the borrower to control the risk of default. Term loans may be repaid on a quarterly, semiannual, or annual schedule. The payments include both interest and principal, so the loan balance declines over time. Borrowers try to arrange a repayment schedule that matches the forecast cash flow from the project being financed.

bonds
Long-term debt obligations (liabilities) issued by corporations and governments.

Bonds are long-term debt obligations (liabilities) issued by corporations and governments. Like term loans, corporate bonds are issued with formal contracts that set forth the obligations of the issuing corporation and the rights of the bondholders. Most bonds are issued in multiples of $1000 (par value) with initial maturities of 10 to 30 years. The stated interest rate, or *coupon rate*, is the percentage of the bond's par value that the issuer will pay each year as interest.

mortgage loan
A long-term loan made against real estate as collateral.

A **mortgage loan** is a long-term loan made against real estate as collateral. The lender takes a mortgage on the property, which lets the lender seize the property, sell it, and use the proceeds to pay off the loan if the borrower fails to make the scheduled payments. Long-term mortgage loans are often used to finance office buildings, factories, and warehouses. Life insurance companies are an important source of these loans. They make billions of dollars' worth of mortgage loans to businesses each year.

Concept *Check*

What is a long-term loan used for?

What is a term loan? A bond? A mortgage loan?

LO7

EQUITY FINANCING

Equity is the owners' investment in the business. In corporations, the preferred and common shareholders are the owners. A company obtains equity financing by selling new ownership shares (external financing), by retaining earnings (internal financing), or for small and growing, typically high-tech companies, through venture capital (external financing).

Selling New Issues of Common Shares

common shares
A security that represents an ownership interest in a corporation.

Common shares are securities that represent an ownership interest in a corporation. In March 2006, Tim Hortons offered 29 million shares of common shares at the initial price of $27 and began trading on the Toronto Stock Exchange and the New York Stock Exchange.

Sustainable Business, Sustainable World

ENCANA CORPORATION

The top Canadian company on the list of the 2011 *Global 100 Most Sustainable Corporations in the World*, coming in at number 12, is Encana, one of the largest energy companies in North America. Encana's business is focused on natural gas, oil and natural gas liquids, exploration, and developing resource plays using an innovative hub model that is designed to reduce production costs and environmental impacts.

As described on its website, Encana is "reshaping North America's energy portfolio by providing natural gas—a clean, affordable, abundant resource for future generations…Responsible development (is) how we do business." If finance is about maximizing value, then Encana is definitely hitting the mark in this respect, and most importantly doing so in a sustainable way by financing projects that maximize value for future generations.

Encana has created an Environmental Innovation Fund (EIF) to invest in projects that "economically improve the environmental performance of energy development through developing and implementing innovative technology." It finances "the implementation of technologies or processes that result in measurable reductions in emissions, energy, land and water use within [its] operations."

One example of this commitment can be seen at Encana's project at the Hussar Crowfoot Gas Plant near Drumheller, Alberta. With the help of the EIF, technology was piloted to provide continuous emissions surveillance, and between May 2009 and July 2010, methane and non-methane hydrocarbon concentrations in the air were monitored at Drumheller, resulting in a reduction in methane emissions of approximately 32,000 cubic feet per day, or 4,500 tonnes of carbon dioxide equivalent per year. Using the emissions

surveillance technology allowed the company to save enough gas to recover the cost of technology implementation in under two years.

Another project funded by the EIF in the Jean Marie formation in northeastern British Columbia allowed Encana to make huge advancements in the technical understanding of how to reduce greenhouse gases in some drilling operations. The project resulted in an 85 percent reduction in flaring, as well as the sale of 84,000 tonnes of carbon offsets to BC's Crown corporation, Pacific Carbon Trust. The offsets generated from the reduced flaring and carbon emissions represented the equivalent of taking 22,050 cars off the road for one year!

It is reassuring to know that one of our leading natural resource companies is so firmly committed to financing projects that will help sustain our natural resources and our environment for years to come.

Thinking Critically

1. Canada is a leader in natural resources. Can you think of other industries in which Canada takes a leadership role, and other companies in those industries that are committed to sustainability, as a benchmark for other companies to measure themselves against?

2. What other examples are there of companies around the world committed to financing research and innovation into sustainable practices to further our ability to sustain our planet and way of life?

SOURCES: http://www.encana.com, Used with permission from Encana; The Global 100, http://www.global100.org.

The Tim Hortons offering is an example of a company *going public*—its first sale of shares to the public. Usually, a high-growth company has an *initial public offering* (IPO), because it needs to raise funds to finance continuing growth. An IPO often enables existing shareholders, usually employees, family, and friends who bought the shares privately, to earn big profits on their investment. (Companies that are already public can also issue and sell additional common shares to raise equity funds.)

But going public has some drawbacks. For one thing, there is no guarantee an IPO will sell. It is also expensive. Big fees must be paid to investment bankers, brokers, lawyers, accountants, and printers. And once the company is public, it is watched closely by regulators, shareholders, and securities analysts. The company must reveal information such as operating and financial data, product details, financing plans, and operating strategies. Providing this information is often costly.

Going public can be successful when a company is well established and market conditions are right. Strong equity markets in the late 1990s and into 2000 prompted many companies, especially very young Internet-related companies, to go public. Frequently, companies that were only a year or two old rushed to go public to take advantage of market conditions. Their prices popped up to what many believed were unrealistic levels. When the recession started in 2008 and capital markets dried up, far fewer companies were willing to brave the IPO waters. Instead, they turned to other financing sources to tide them over until the market for new issues picked up.

Dividends and Retained Earnings

Dividends are payments to shareholders from a corporation's profits. A company does not have to pay dividends to shareholders, but if investors buy the shares expecting

HOT *links*

What are some of the IPOs available today? Check out the premium investor resource centre at http://ipo.investcom.com

dividends
Payments to shareholders from a corporation's profits.

share or stock dividends
Payments to shareholders in the form of more shares; can replace or supplement cash dividends.

to get dividends and the company does not pay them, the investors might sell their shares. If too many sell, the value of the shares decreases. Dividends can be paid in cash or in shares. Share dividends are payments in the form of more shares. Share dividends may replace or supplement cash dividends. After a share dividend has been paid, more shares have a claim on the same company, so the value of each share often declines.

At their quarterly meetings, the company's board of directors (with the advice of its financial managers) decides how much of the profits to distribute as dividends and how much to reinvest. A business's basic approach to paying dividends can greatly affect its share price. A stable history of dividend payments indicates good financial health. If a company that has been making regular dividend payments cuts or skips a dividend, investors start thinking it has serious financial problems. The increased uncertainty often results in lower share prices. Thus, most companies set dividends at a level they can keep paying. They start with a relatively low dividend payout ratio, so that they can maintain a steady or slightly increasing dividend over time.

retained earnings
Profits that have been reinvested in a company.

Retained earnings, profits that have been reinvested in the company, have a big advantage over other sources of equity capital: They do not incur underwriting costs. Financial managers strive to balance dividends and retained earnings to maximize the value of the company. Often the balance reflects the nature of the company and its industry. Well-established and stable companies and those that expect only modest growth, such as public utilities, financial services companies, and large industrial corporations, typically pay out much of their earnings in dividends.

Most high-growth companies, like those in technology-related fields, finance much of their growth through retained earnings and pay little or no dividends to shareholders.

Preferred Shares

preferred shares
Equity securities for which the dividend amount is set at the time the shares are issued.

Another form of equity is preferred shares. Unlike common shares, preferred shares usually have a dividend amount that is set at the time the shares are issued. These dividends must be paid before the company can pay any dividends to common shareholders. Furthermore, if the company goes bankrupt and sells its assets, preferred shareholders get their money back before common shareholders do. Preferred shares are described in greater detail in Chapter 17.

Like debt, preferred shares increase the company's financial risk because it obligates the company to make a fixed payment, but preferred shares are more flexible. The company can miss a dividend payment without suffering the serious results of failing to pay back a debt.

Preferred shares are more expensive than debt financing, however, because preferred dividends are not tax-deductible. Furthermore, because the claims of preferred shareholders on income and assets are second to those of debt holders, preferred shareholders require higher returns to compensate for the greater risk.

HOT links

Which companies are getting funding from venture capital companies? For this and other information, visit vFinance.com at
http://vfinance.com

HOT links

Find out about the Canada's Venture Capital & Private Equity Association at
www.cvca.ca

Venture Capital

As we learned in Chapter 6, *venture capital* is another source of equity capital. It is most often used by small and growing companies that aren't big enough to sell securities to the public. This type of financing is especially popular among high-tech companies that need large sums of money.

Venture capitalists invest in new businesses in return for part of the ownership, sometimes as much as 60 percent. They look for new businesses with high growth potential, and they expect a high investment return within 5 to 10 years. By getting in on the ground floor, venture capitalists buy shares at a very low price. They earn profits by selling the shares at a much higher price when the company goes public. Venture capitalists generally get a voice in management through a seat on the board of directors.

Getting venture capital is difficult, even though there are many private venture capital companies in this country. Most venture capitalists finance only about 1 to 5

Making Ethical Choices

THE FRIENDS AND FAMILY IPO PLAN

As a financial analyst at an up-and-coming high-technology company, you are involved in your most exciting project to date: helping to prepare pro forma financial statements (pro forma is a projection or estimate of what will happen in the future based on what is happening now) for the prospectus for the company's initial public offering.

During your visits to various departments, you hear rumours about promises of IPO shares for favoured customers and suppliers. Researching if this is legal, you learn your company can give up to 5 percent of its offering to anyone it chooses. Because this price is not offered to the general public, inviting these "friends and family" to buy shares at the IPO price presents an attractive opportunity. At the height of the bull market, IPO share prices were jumping an average of 65 percent on the first day. Even though times are more normal now, the growth prospects make these shares a good buy. "Companies are continuing to be approached for shares by analysts and others who wield influence," says David Helfrich, a venture capitalist.

However, some legal experts believe that allocating IPO shares to customers and vendors borders on bribery and creates conflicts of interest. Those receiving shares could feel pressured to send business to your company. Yet such practices are common; other businesses in your industry use shares to gain a competitive advantage (perhaps as a way of saying "thank you" or of obtaining obligations from people who they want help from in the future).

If your company is giving out only small allocations of shares, such as 100 to 200 shares, and the offering price is $18 to $20, the profit from flipping the shares on the first days is negligible and the potential for conflicts of interest reduced. If the invitation is for larger amounts, at what point does it become a problem?

ETHICAL DILEMMA: Should you bring this situation to your superiors' attention and urge them to develop a corporate policy that covers offers to sell shares at special prices?

SOURCES: Linda Himelstein, "CEOs to Eliot Spitzer: `Give It Back? No Way!'" *Business Week*, June 9, 2003, 113; and Linda Himelstein and Ben Elgin, "High Tech's Kickback Culture," *Business Week*, February 10, 2003, 74–77.

percent of the companies that apply. Venture capital investors, many of whom experienced losses from their investments in failed dot-coms, are less willing nowadays to take risks on very early-stage companies with unproven technology. They are looking for companies with high growth potential that are already on a demonstrated track to profitability.

As a result, other sources of venture capital, including private foundations, governments, and wealthy individuals (called *angel investors*), are helping start-up companies find equity capital. These private investors are motivated by the potential for earning a high return on their investment. Accountants, lawyers, business associates, financial consultants, bankers, and others can help the small company find an angel.

Concept Check

Define each of the following:

- Common shares
- Dividends
- Share or stock dividends
- Retained earnings
- Preferred shares
- Venture capital

MANAGING RISK AND INSURANCE

LO8

Every day, businesses and individuals are exposed to many different kinds of risk. Investors who buy shares or speculate in commodities can earn a profit, but they also take the risk of losing all or part of their money. Illness is another type of risk, involving financial loss from not only the cost of medical care but also the loss of income.

Businesses, too, are exposed to many types of risk. Market risks, such as lower demand for a product or worsening economic conditions, can hurt a company. Other risks involve customers—they could be injured on a company's premises or by a company's product. Like homes and cars owned by individuals, business property can be damaged or lost through fire, floods, and theft. Businesses must also protect themselves against losses from theft by dishonest employees. The loss of a key employee is another risk, especially for small companies.

It is impossible to avoid all risks, but individuals and businesses can minimize risks or buy protection—called insurance—against them. Although some risks are uninsurable, many others are insurable. Let's now look at basic risk concepts and the types of insurance available to cover them.

Risk Management

risk management
The process of identifying and evaluating risks and selecting and managing techniques to adapt to risk exposures.

Every business faces risks like the ones previously listed. **Risk management** involves analyzing the company's operations, evaluating the potential risks, and figuring out how to minimize losses in a cost-efficient manner. In today's complex business environment, the concern for public and employee welfare and the potential for lawsuits have both increased. Risk management thus plays a vital role in the overall management of a business.

TYPES OF RISK Individuals and companies need to protect themselves against the economic effects of certain types of risk. In an insurance sense, risk (sometimes called *pure risk*) is the chance of financial loss because of a **peril** (a hazard or a source of danger). Insurable risks include fire, theft, auto accident, injury or illness, a lawsuit, or death. **Speculative risk** is the chance of either loss or gain. Someone who buys shares in the hope of later selling it at a profit is taking a speculative risk and cannot be insured against it.

peril
A hazard or a source of danger.

speculative risk
The chance of either loss or gain, without insurance against the possible loss.

STRATEGIES TO MANAGE RISK Risk is part of life. Nevertheless, people have four major ways of dealing with it.

- *Risk avoidance.* This means staying away from situations that can lead to loss. A person can avoid the risk of a serious injury by choosing not to go skydiving. A day-care centre could avoid risk by not transporting children to and from the facility or taking them on field trips. Manufacturers who wish to avoid risks could produce only goods that have a proven track record, but these risk-avoidance strategies could stifle growth in the long run. Thus, risk avoidance is not good for all risks.
- *Risk retention (self-insurance).* This is the willingness to bear a risk without insurance, also called *risk assumption*. This offers a more practical way of handling many types of risks. Many large companies with warehouses or stores spread out over Canada might choose not to insure them. They assume that even if disaster strikes one location, the others won't be harmed. The losses will probably be less than the insurance premiums for all of the locations. Many companies retain losses, because it is cheaper to assume some risks than to insure against them. Some choose to pay small claims and insure only for catastrophic losses. Others "go naked," paying for all claims from current company funds. This is clearly the most risky strategy. A big claim could cripple the company or lead to bankruptcy.
- *Risk control (risk reduction).* This is done by adopting techniques to prevent financial losses. For example, companies adopt safety measures to reduce accidents. Construction workers are required to wear hard hats and safety glasses. Airlines keep their aircraft in good condition and require thorough training programs for pilots and flight attendants. Hotels install smoke alarms, sprinkler systems, and firewalls to protect guests and minimize fire damage.
  - *Risk transfer.* This means paying someone else to bear some or all of the risk of financial loss for certain risks that can't be avoided, assumed, or controlled to acceptable levels. One way to transfer risk is through **insurance**. Individuals and organizations can pay a fee (a *premium*) and get the promise of compensation for certain financial losses. The companies that take on the risks are called *insurance companies*.

Learn about how Catlin Canada Risk Management Services helps companies with global operations identify, measure, and manage financial risk: http://catlincanada.com/riskManagement.html

insurance
The promise of compensation for certain financial losses.

Concept *Check*

What is risk management?

What are the types of risk?

What are some strategies for managing risk?

 INSURANCE CONCEPTS

insurance policy
A written agreement that defines what the insurance covers and the risks that the insurance company will bear for the insured party.

Companies purchase insurance to cover insurable risks. An **insurance policy** is the written agreement that defines what the insurance covers and the risks that the insurance company will bear for the insured party. It also outlines the policy's benefits (the maximum amount that it will pay in the event of a loss) and the premium (the cost to the insured for coverage). Any demand for payment of losses covered by the policy is a *claim*.

Companies must constantly manage risk, which is often not foreseen. What ways can businesses manage unforeseen risks?

HAMILTON SPECTATOR/THE CANADIAN PRESS/JOHN RENNISON)

Before issuing a policy, an insurance company reviews the applications of those who want a policy and selects those that meet its standards. This underwriting process also determines the level of coverage and the premiums. Each company sets its own underwriting standards based on its experience. For instance, a life insurance company might decide not to accept an applicant who has had a heart attack within the previous five years (or to charge a 50 to 75 percent higher premium). A property insurer might refuse to issue a policy on homes near brush-filled canyons, which present above-average fire hazards.

underwriting
A review process of all insurance applications and the selection of those who meet the standards.

To get insurance, the applicant must have an insurable interest: the chance of suffering a loss if a particular peril occurs. In most cases, a person cannot insure the life of a friend, because the friend's death would not be considered a financial loss. But business partners can get life insurance on each other's lives, because the death of one of them would have a financial impact on their company.

insurable interest
An insurance applicant's chance of loss if a particular peril occurs.

Insurable Risks

Insurance companies are professional risk takers, but they won't provide coverage against all types of risk. Some risks are insurable; some are not. For instance, changes in political or economic conditions are not insurable. An insurable risk is one that an insurance company will cover. For a risk to be insurable, it must meet these criteria:

insurable risk
A risk that an insurance company will cover. It must meet certain criteria.

- *The loss must not be under the control of the insured.* The loss must be accidental—that is, unexpected and occurring by chance. Insurance companies do not cover losses purposely caused by the insured party. No insurance company will pay for the loss of a clothing store that the insured set on fire, nor will most companies pay life insurance benefits for a suicide.
- *There must be many similar exposures to that peril.* Insurance companies study the rates of deaths, auto accidents, fires, floods, and many other perils. They know about how many of these perils will occur each year. The law of large numbers lets them predict the likelihood that the peril will occur and then calculate premiums.

law of large numbers
Insurance companies' predictions of the likelihood that a peril will occur; used to calculate premiums.

Suppose that an insurance company has 150 policies in a city. The company knows from past experience that these policyholders are likely to have a total of 12 car accidents a year and that the average payment for a claim in this city has been $1000. The total claims for one year's car accidents in the city would be $12,000 (12 accidents × $1000). Thus, the company would charge each policyholder a premium of at least $80 ($12,000 ÷ 150). Profits and administrative expenses would serve to increase the premium from this base rate.

- *Losses must be financially measurable.* The dollar amount of potential losses must be known, so that the insurance company can figure the premiums. Life insurance is for a fixed amount specified at the time the policy is bought. Otherwise, the company and the beneficiary (the one who gets the funds) would have to agree on the value of the deceased's life at the time of death. Premiums have to be calculated before then, however.

- *The peril must not be likely to affect all the insured parties at the same time.* Insurance companies must spread out their risks by insuring many people and businesses in many locations. This strategy helps minimize the chance that a single calamity will wipe out the insurance company.

- *The potential loss must be significant.* Insurance companies cannot afford to insure trivial things for small amounts. Many policies have **deductibles**, amounts that the insured must pay before insurance benefits begin.

- *The company must have the right to set standards for insurance coverage.* Insurance companies can refuse to cover people with health problems such as AIDS, cancer, or heart trouble, a poor driving record, or a dangerous job or hobby. They can also charge higher premiums because of the higher risks they are covering.

deductibles
The amounts that the insured must pay before insurance benefits begin.

Premium Costs

Insurance policies must be economical—relatively low in cost compared to the benefits—so that people will want to buy them. Yet the premiums must also cover the risks that the insurance company faces. Insurance companies collect statistics on many perils. Then specially trained mathematicians called *actuaries* use the law of large numbers to develop actuarial tables, which show how likely each peril is. Actuarial tables are the basis for calculating premiums. For example, actuaries use a mortality table showing average life expectancy and the expected number of deaths per 1000 people at given ages to set life insurance premiums.

Almost every homeowner buys insurance to cover the perils of fire, theft, vandalism, and other home-related risks. With such a large pool of policyholders, homeowners' policies are usually inexpensive. Annual premiums are about 0.5 percent (or less) of the value of the home. This low cost encourages people to buy policies and thereby helps spread the insurance companies' risk over many homes throughout the country.

When setting premiums, insurers also look at the risk characteristics of certain groups to assess the probability of loss for those groups. For instance, smokers tend to die younger than non-smokers do and thus pay higher life insurance premiums. Female drivers under the age of 25 have a lower rate of accidents than male drivers, so their car insurance premiums are lower.

Insurance Providers

Insurers can be either public or private. Public insurance coverage is offered by specialized government agencies (e.g., provincial health care plans and employment insurance). Private insurance coverage is provided by privately organized (non-government) companies.

PUBLIC INSURANCE Government-sponsored insurance can be regulated by either the provinces or the federal government. These are some of the main programs:

- *Employment insurance (EI).* The employment insurance program pays laid-off workers weekly benefits while they seek new jobs. Persons who terminate their employment voluntarily or are fired for cause are generally not eligible for **employment insurance**. These programs also provide job counselling, education

employment insurance
Payment of benefits to laid-off workers while they seek new jobs.

opportunities, and placement services. The size of the weekly benefit depends on the workers' previous income. Employment insurance is funded by the employees and through contributions by the employers.

- *Workers' compensation.* The provinces and territories have laws requiring employers in many industries to fund workers' compensation insurance to cover the expenses of job-related injuries and diseases, including medical costs, rehabilitation, and job retraining if necessary. It also provides disability income benefits (salary and wage payments) for workers who can't perform their jobs. Employers can buy workers' compensation policies or self-insure. A company's premium is based on the amount of its payroll and the types of risks present in the workplace. For instance, a construction company would pay a higher premium for workers' compensation insurance than would a jewellery store.

- *Canada Pension Plan (CPP).* The Canada Pension Plan provides retirement, disability, survivor benefits, and death benefits. CPP is funded by equal contributions from workers and employers. Canadians who have paid into the plan can collect as early as age 60. The province of Québec administers its own pension plan.

- *Provincial health care.* Health care is provided to all Canadians through their respective provincial health care programs. In some provinces, the premiums are not collected separately but are included in other taxes, and in others there are direct payments to the provincial health care insurance program.

workers' compensation
Payments to cover the expenses of job-related injuries and diseases, including medical costs, rehabilitation, and job retraining if necessary.

Canada Pension Plan
Insurance that provides retirement, disability, death, and health benefits.

provincial health care
Health insurance programs provided by the provinces.

PRIVATE INSURANCE COMPANIES Private insurance companies sell property and liability insurance, health insurance, and life insurance. Generally, they can be either not-for-profit (e.g., Blue Cross) or shareholder insurance companies (e.g., Manulife Financial).

For example, all eligible residents in every province and territory can obtain Blue Cross coverage through their provincial/territorial independent member plan. Blue Cross provides products such as health care, dental care, life insurance, and disability income.

Just like other publicly owned corporations, *shareholder insurance companies* are profit-oriented companies owned by shareholders. The shareholders do not have to be policyholders, and the policyholders do not have to be shareholders. Their profits come from insurance premiums in excess of claim payments and operating expenses, and from investments in securities and real estate.

Types of Insurance

Most companies offer group health and life insurance plans for their employees as a fringe benefit. Employers typically pay some of the health insurance premiums, and employees pay the rest. The cost is usually considerably less than for individual policies, although it pays to check before signing up. For example, companies might pay for the entire cost of life insurance equal to one or two times the employee's annual salary, with an option to purchase more under the group plan, but the premiums might be more expensive than buying an individual policy.

Businesses often insure the lives of key employees, such as top executives, salespeople, inventors, and researchers, whose death could seriously limit the income or value of a company. To protect themselves, businesses buy key person life insurance, a life insurance policy that names the company as beneficiary. In the case of a partnership, which is dissolved when a partner dies, key person insurance is often bought for each partner, with the other partner named as the beneficiary, so that the surviving partner can buy the partnership interest from the estate of the deceased and continue operating.

key person life insurance
A term insurance policy that names the company as beneficiary.

PROPERTY AND LIABILITY INSURANCE Property and liability insurance is important for businesses that wish to protect against losses of property and lawsuits arising from harm to other people. *Property insurance* covers financial losses from damage to or destruction of the insured's assets as a result of specified perils, whereas *liability insurance* covers financial losses from injuries to others and damage to or destruction of others' property when the insured is considered to be the cause. It also covers the insured's legal defence fees up to the maximum amount stated in the policy. Automobile liability insurance is an example. It would pay for a fence damaged when the insured person lost control of his or her car. Commercial and product liability insurance also fall into this category.

Commercial liability insurance covers a variety of damage claims, including harm to the environment from pollution. In the case of *product liability*, if a defective furnace exploded and damaged a home, the manufacturer would be liable for the damages. If the manufacturer was insured, the insurance company would cover the losses or pay to dispute the claim in court.

Property and liability insurance is a broad category. Businesses buy many types of property and liability insurance. These protect against loss of property from fire, theft, accidents, or employee dishonesty, and financial losses arising from liability cases. Landlords and owners of business property buy *building insurance*, a type of property coverage, for protection against both property damage and liability losses. For instance, if a person broke an arm slipping on a wet floor in a hardware store, the business's insurance policy would cover any claim.

SPECIAL TYPES OF BUSINESS LIABILITY INSURANCE Businesses also purchase several other types of insurance policies, depending on their particular needs.

- *Business interruption insurance.* This optional coverage is often offered with fire insurance. It protects business owners from losses occurring when the business must be closed temporarily after property damage. **Business interruption insurance** might cover costs such as rental of temporary facilities, wage and salary payments to employees, payments for leased equipment, fixed payments (for instance, rent and loans), and profits that would have been earned during the period. *Contingent business interruption insurance* covers losses to the insured in the event of property damage to a major supplier or customer.
- *Theft insurance.* Businesses also want to protect their property against financial losses from crime. **Theft insurance** is the broadest coverage and protects businesses against losses from an act of stealing. Businesses can also buy more limited types of theft insurance.
- *Fidelity and surety bonds.* What if a company has a dishonest employee? This situation is covered by a *fidelity bond*, an agreement that insures a company against theft committed by an employee who handles company money. If a restaurant manager is bonded for $50,000 and steals $60,000, the restaurant will recover all but $10,000 of the loss. Banks, loan companies, and retail businesses that employ cashiers typically buy fidelity bonds.

  A *surety bond*, also called a *performance bond*, is an agreement to reimburse a company for non-performance of acts specified in a contract. This form of insurance is most common in the construction industry. Contractors buy surety bonds to cover themselves in case the project they are working on is not completed by the specified date or does not meet specified standards. In practice, the insurance company often pays another contractor to finish the job or to redo shoddy work when the bonded contractor fails to perform.

- *Title insurance.* A title policy protects the buyer of real estate against losses caused by a defect in the title—that is, a claim against the property that prevents the transfer of ownership from seller to purchaser. It eliminates the need to search legal records to be sure that the seller was actually the owner of (had clear title to) the property.

business interruption insurance
Covers costs such as rental of temporary facilities, wage and salary payments to employees, payments for leased equipment, fixed payments, and profits that would have been earned during that period.

theft insurance
A broad insurance coverage that protects businesses against losses from an act of stealing.

Concept *Check*

What is an insurance policy? Underwriting? Insurable interest?

What are premiums and deductibles?

What types of insurance policies are available? What is the purpose of each?

- *Professional liability insurance.* This form of insurance covers financial losses (legal fees and court-awarded damages up to specific limits) resulting from alleged malpractice by professionals in fields like medicine, law, architecture, and dentistry. *Directors and officers insurance* is a type of **professional liability insurance** designed to protect top corporate management, who have also been the target of malpractice lawsuits. It pays for legal fees and court-awarded damages up to specific limits.

professional liability insurance
Insurance designed to protect top corporate management, who have been the target of malpractice lawsuits.

THE FUTURE OF FINANCIAL MANAGEMENT

LO10

Finance has moved from a relatively isolated, inward-looking function to a unit that is heavily involved in shaping and implementing a company's overall strategic objectives. Many of the key trends shaping the practice of financial management echo those in other disciplines. For example, technology is improving the efficiency with which financial managers run their operations. The continued expansion of the financial manager's role in risk management is a natural outgrowth of the regulations in the United States, as Canadian companies that trade on the United States exchanges must adhere not only to Canadian law but also to American standards (e.g., the Sarbanes-Oxley Act).

The CFO's Role Continues to Expand

Beginning the 1990s and continuing today, CFOs have expanded their jobs beyond the ordinary finance responsibilities. No longer just numbers people, they joined top management in developing and implementing the company's strategic direction. Negotiating billion-dollar mergers and finding creative financing vehicles were all part of the day's work. They were the company's face to the Bay Street analysts, who watched to see if the company would meet each quarter's earnings estimates.

Since the economic crises of 2008 and 2011, CFOs are more highly visible and active in company management than ever before. They serve as both business partner to the chief executive and a fiduciary to the board. "Finance today is well-balanced between what I'll call the value-adding and the value-preservation aspects," says Robert Lumpkins, vice chairman and CFO of Cargill Inc. In global organizations such as Cargill, a privately owned international agricultural and industrial products company with 142,000 employees in 61 countries, finance managers must also be sensitive to cultural differences and different approaches to solving problems.[6]

Finance professionals need to have a broad view of company operations to communicate effectively with business unit managers, board members, creditors, and investors. Douglas Oberheim, a group president at Caterpillar, credits his years as CFO with providing him the broad perspective to see the company from the shareholder's viewpoint and the understanding of the importance of cross-functional activities. In addition to such traditional duties as arranging mergers and acquisitions, raising and allocating capital, and managing treasury operations, CFOs are also key players in matters pertaining to information technology, human resources, and the supply chain. Interpersonal skills are essential because they must motivate employees and encourage a positive environment that promotes accountability and ethical behaviour down through the organization. Finance managers must learn to be team players who can work with employees in other functional areas. At times finance and business unit executives have differing positions, and it takes careful negotiation to resolve issues. For example, business units may want to maintain larger cash balances than finance recommends. Educating unit managers about the cost of idle cash and establishing appropriate incentives can change corporate culture.[7]

Weighing the Risks

The job of managing a company's risk, which became even more difficult after the economic crises of 2008 and 2011, continues to be challenging for financial executives. Adding to the complexity are the volatile economy and financial markets at home and abroad. No longer does risk management focus narrowly on buying insurance to protect against loss of physical assets and interruption of business. Instead, more companies now consider enterprise risk management (ERM) a priority. ERM goes beyond just identifying, monitoring, and lowering risk to include a strategic approach to defining and managing all elements of a company's risk.

As the risk management function expands beyond its traditional role, companies recognize that ERM can make significant contributions to financial performance and shareholder returns. Because a failure in a company's risk control procedures can lead to substantial financial losses, corporate CFOs and treasurers are taking a proactive, leadership role in ERM. This requires them to get more involved with operations and form partnerships with business unit executives. "Effective risk management requires the ability to walk in the shoes of operations," says David Kelsey, senior vice president and CFO of Sealed Air Corp., a packaging products manufacturer. "Risk management can't be perceived as getting in the way of what business wants to do. Risk management needs to manage exposures, but not by creating more work or increasing costs."[8]

Companies face a wide range of risks, including

- *credit risk*—exposure to loss as a result of default on a financial transaction, or a reduction in a security's market value because of decline in the credit quality of the debt issuer;
  - *market risk*—risk resulting from adverse movements in the level or volatility of market prices of securities, commodities, and currencies; and
  - *operational risk*—the risk of unexpected losses arising from deficiencies in a company's management information, support, and control systems and procedures.

Jennifer Ceran, treasurer of eBay Inc., was an early adopter of ERM. Ceran recognized the need for the finance area to go beyond the traditional risk tasks assigned to the treasury operation, such as insurance, and take

enterprise risk management (ERM)
A company-wide, strategic approach to identifying, monitoring, and managing all elements of a company's risk.

Concept *Check*

How has the role of CFO changed since the passage of the Sarbanes-Oxley Act?

Why are improved risk management procedures important to shareholders?

Concept *in Action*

The CFO-as-busy-bean-counter image has undergone an extreme makeover, as today's financial chiefs increasingly perform highly visible decision-making roles alongside CEOs. Intense pressure for financial reporting compliance along with expectations of beating the numbers each quarter are major factors behind both the rising prominence and turnover of financial officers. And as responsibility increases, so does pay. Have CFOs become chief executive material?

COMSTOCK/THINKSTOCK

a broader view of all the risks affecting the company. Evaluating all types of risk and their impact on each other is critical to reducing overall risk for any company. As Rossini Zumwalt, assistant treasurer and director of finance at software company Symantec explains, "We identified the risks we already knew about, but what were we leaving out? It's not just the risk you know. It's the risks you don't know. We forgot the 'E' in ERM. I think that's why companies are challenged. It's important to attach the 'E,' to go beyond traditional risks."[9]

Companies are also using risk management in response to new corporate governance guidelines. Better risk management procedures are important to shareholders in the post-Enron era. They want to know that companies have taken steps to minimize risks that would affect the company's values.

GREAT IDEAS TO USE NOW

Whether you are a marketing manager, purchasing agent, or systems analyst, knowledge of finance will help you to do your job better. You'll be able to understand your company's financial statements, its financial condition, and management's investment and financing decisions. Financial information also provides feedback on how well you are doing and identifies problems. On a more practical note, you might be asked to prepare a budget for your department or unit. Employees who understand the financial decision-making process will be able to prepare proposals that address financial concerns. As a result, they will be more likely to be given the resources they require to accomplish the company's goals.

If you own a business, you must pay close attention to financial management. Without financial plans, you might find yourself running out of cash. It's easy to get so caught up in growing sales that you neglect your billing and collection methods. In fact, managing accounts receivable is often one of the more challenging aspects of running a young company. But you can't rely on revenue increases to solve your cash flow problems. Good receivables practices start with credit policies. Be choosy when it comes to offering trade credit, and check customers' credit references and payment history thoroughly. Set the initial credit limit fairly low until the customer establishes a prompt payment history. Here are some other ways to improve collections.

- Bill frequently, not just at the end of the month, so that money flows in throughout the month. Send bills when milestones are reached, such as making a presentation or completing a phase of a project.
- Clearly state payment terms, and make sure that the language on the invoice matches the contract.
- Establish regular and frequent follow-up procedures. Some companies call to notify the customer that the bill has been sent and to make sure the customer is satisfied. Weekly calls are in order for late payments.
- Try to get a firm date by which you will be paid, and be prepared to say what you will do if you aren't paid on time—for example, stopping work on a project or not shipping the next part of the order.
- Keep detailed notes of all conversations relating to a collection: your contact, date of the call, what was promised, and what you replied. You can then e-mail this as confirmation of your understanding and as another reminder.
- Monitor results of outstanding receivables collection.
- Don't fill new orders from customers who are continually delinquent.[10]

SHAWN BALDWIN/AP PHOTO

Many companies have created a new position, chief risk officer, to study risk potential and coordinate risk management procedures throughout the company. How can a company anticipate catastrophic events and minimize the devastating impact on business?

Summary of Learning Outcomes

LO1 Explain the roles finance and the financial manager play in the company's overall strategy.

Finance is the art and science involved in managing the company's money. The financial manager must decide how much money is needed and when, how best to use the available funds, and how to get the required financing. The financial manager's responsibilities include financial planning, investing (spending money), and financing (raising money). Maximizing the value of the company is the main goal of the financial manager, whose decisions often have long-term effects.

LO2 Describe how a company develops its financial plans, including forecasts and budgets.

Financial planning enables the company to estimate the amount and timing of the financial resources it needs to meet its business goals. The planning process begins with forecasts based on the demand for the company's products. Short-term forecasts project expected revenues and expenses for one year. They are the basis for cash budgets, which show the flow of cash into and out of the company and are used to plan day-to-day operations. Long-term forecasts project revenues and expenses over more than a year, typically 2 to 10 years. These strategic plans allow top management to analyze the impact of different options on the company's profits.

LO3 List the types of short- and long-term expenditures a company makes.

A company invests in short-term expenses—supplies, inventory, and wages—to support current production, marketing, and sales activities. The financial manager manages the company's investment in current assets, so that the company has enough cash to pay its bills and support accounts receivable and inventory. Long-term expenditures (capital expenditures) are made for fixed assets such as land, buildings, machinery, and equipment. Because of the large outlays required for capital expenditures, financial managers carefully analyze proposed projects to determine which offer the best returns.

LO4 Summarize the main sources and costs of unsecured and secured short-term financing.

Short-term financing comes due within one year. The main sources of unsecured short-term financing are trade credit, bank loans, and commercial paper. Secured loans require a pledge of certain assets, such as accounts receivable or inventory, as security for the loan. Factoring, or selling accounts receivable outright at a discount, is another form of short-term financing.

LO5 Identify and compare the two primary sources of long-term financing.

Financial managers must choose the best mix of debt and equity for their company. The main advantage of debt financing is the tax-deductibility of interest, but debt involves financial risk because it requires the payment of interest and principal on specified dates. Equity—common and preferred shares—is considered a permanent form of financing on which the company might or might not pay dividends. Dividends are not tax-deductible.

LO6 Understand the major types, features, and costs of long-term debt.

The main types of long-term debt are term loans, bonds, and mortgage loans. Term loans can be secured or unsecured and generally have 5- to 12-year maturities. Bonds usually have initial maturities of 10 to 30 years. Mortgage loans are secured by real estate. Long-term debt usually costs more than short-term financing because of the greater uncertainty that the borrower will be able to make the scheduled loan payments.

LO7 Discuss how companies issue equity and the costs to the company.

The chief sources of equity financing are common shares, retained earnings, and preferred shares. The cost of selling shares includes issuing costs and potential dividend payments. Retained earnings are profits reinvested in the company. For the issuing company, preferred shares are more expensive than debt, because its dividends are not tax-deductible and its claims are secondary to those of debt holders, but less expensive than common shares. Venture capital is often a source of equity financing for small and growing, typically high-tech companies.

Risk is the potential for loss or the chance that an investment will not achieve the expected level of return. Risk can be managed by identifying and evaluating the potential risks and selecting and managing techniques to adapt to risk exposures.

To get insurance, the applicant must have an insurable interest: the chance of suffering a loss if a particular peril occurs. An insurable risk is one that an insurance company will cover. To qualify, the following conditions must be met: The loss must not be under the control of the insured; there must be many similar exposures to that peril; losses must be financially measurable; the peril must not be likely to affect all the insured parties at the same time; the potential loss must be significant; and the company must have the right to set standards for insurance coverage.

LO8 Understand risk, how it can be managed, and what makes a risk insurable.

The main types of insurance that businesses should consider include property and liability, commercial liability, business interruption, theft, fidelity and surety bonds, title insurance, and professional liability insurance.

LO9 Describe the types of insurance coverage that businesses should consider.

The role of the CFO has changed, with CFOs taking the central role in overseeing corporate compliance with the various regulations and re-establishing public trust. They must balance the roles of corporate cop and strategic planner. The continued expansion of the financial manager's role in risk management is a natural outgrowth as companies face a wide range of risks, including credit, market, and operational risk. More companies are adopting risk management to identify and evaluate risks and select techniques to control and reduce risk.

LO10 List some of the trends that are affecting the practice of financial management.

Key Terms

accounts payable   549
accounts receivable   547
bonds   552
budgets   544
business interruption insurance   560
Canada Pension Plan   559
capital budgeting   548
capital budgets   545
capital expenditures   548
cash budgets   545
cash flows   542
cash management   546
commercial paper   546
common shares   552
deductibles   558
dividends   553
employment insurance   558
enterprise risk management (ERM)   562
factoring   550
financial management   541
financial risk   551
insurable interest   557
insurable risk   557
insurance   556
insurance policy   556
key person life insurance   559
law of large numbers   557

line of credit   549
long-term forecasts   544
marketable securities   546
mortgage loan   552
operating budgets   545
peril   556
preferred shares   554
professional liability insurance   561
provincial health care   559
retained earnings   554
return   543
revolving credit agreement (revolving line of credit)   550
risk   543
risk management   556
risk–return trade-off   543
secured loans   550
share or stock dividends   554
short-term forecasts   543
speculative risk   556
term loan   552
theft insurance   560
trade credit   549
underwriting   557
unsecured loans   549
workers' compensation   559

Experiential Exercises

1. Prepare a personal budget. A personal budget is one of the most valuable tools for personal financial planning. It will help you evaluate your current financial situation, spending patterns, and goals. Use the following steps to create your budget.

   Using credit card receipts, cheque records, and other documents, record your income and expenses for the past 30 days. Based on this information, develop a personal budget for the next month. Record your budget in the "Planned" column of the worksheet in Exhibit 18.4. Include scholarships or grants as other income sources.

   Track your actual income and expenses for one month. Write down everything you spend on a daily basis, or you will forget little things (like snacks) that add up over the course of a month. Record your actual totals in the "Actual" column of the worksheet.

   At the end of the budget period, compare your budget to your actual results. Record any differences between the "Planned" and "Actual" values in the "Variance" column of the worksheet. How close were you to your budget estimates? In what categories did you overspend? Where did you underspend? Did creating the budget have any impact on how you allocated your money to different categories and how you spent your money?

   Optional: Use the results of your first month's budget to project next month's income and expenses. Repeat the monitoring process.

2. The head of your school's finance department has asked you to address a group of incoming business students about the importance of finance to their overall business education. Develop an outline with the key points you would cover in your speech.

3. As a financial manager at Nature's Food Company, you are preparing forecasts and budgets for a new line of high-nutrition desserts. Why should the finance department prepare these plans for the product development group? What factors would you consider in developing your projections and assessing their impact on the company's profits?

4. You are the cash manager for a chain of sporting goods stores facing a cash crunch. To date, the chain has always paid accounts payable within the credit period. The CFO wants to consider extending payments beyond the due date. Write a memo that discusses the pros, cons, and ethics of stretching accounts payable as well as other cash-saving options to investigate.

5. You are the chief financial officer of Discovery Labs, a privately held, five-year-old biotechnology company that needs to raise $3 million to fund the development of a new drug. Prepare a report for the board of directors that discusses the types of long-term financing available to the company, their pros and cons, and the key factors to consider in choosing a financing strategy.

6. GetSmart, www.getsmart.com, is an information service that offers advice on personal loans. Try the questionnaires in each area, using different answers, to see what is necessary to qualify for that financing option.

7. If factoring accounts receivable is still a mystery to you, visit the 21st Financial Solutions site, www.21stfinancialsolutions.com. Follow the links on the home page to answer these questions: What are the advantages of factoring? What are the additional benefits, and what types of companies can use factoring to their advantage? Then summarize the factoring process.

8. Visit your bank's website to learn about the bank's products and services for corporate customers. Describe briefly each type of loan it offers. Then do the same for another financial institution.

9. Visit the Treasury Board of Canada Secretariat website at www.tbs-sct.gc.ca/tbs-sct/index-eng.asp to learn more about risk management.

Exhibit 18.4 Monthly Budget Worksheet

Name: _____

Month of _____

	Planned	Actual	Variance
Income			
Wages (take-home pay)	_____	_____	_____
Support from relatives	_____	_____	_____
Loans	_____	_____	_____
Withdrawals from savings	_____	_____	_____
Other _____	_____	_____	_____
Other _____	_____	_____	_____
(1) Total Available Income	======	======	======
Expenses			
Fixed Expenses	_____	_____	_____
Housing	_____	_____	_____
Vehicle payment	_____	_____	_____
Insurance	_____	_____	_____
Loan repayment	_____	_____	_____
Savings for goals	_____	_____	_____
Tuition and fees	_____	_____	_____
Other _____	_____	_____	_____
Subtotal, Fixed Expenses	======	======	======
Flexible Expenses			
Food	_____	_____	_____
Clothing	_____	_____	_____
Personal care	_____	_____	_____
Entertainment and recreation	_____	_____	_____
Transportation	_____	_____	_____
Telephone	_____	_____	_____
Utilities (electricity, gas, water)	_____	_____	_____
Cable TV	_____	_____	_____
Medical and dental	_____	_____	_____
Books, magazines, educational supplies	_____	_____	_____
Gifts	_____	_____	_____
Other _____	_____	_____	_____
Other _____	_____	_____	_____
Subtotal, Flexible Expenses	======	======	======
(2) Total Expenses	======	======	======
Cash Surplus (Deficit) [(1)–(2)]	======	======	======

1. What is financial management?

2. List the responsibilities of the financial manager.

3. What is the goal of the financial manager? What are risk, return, and the risk–return trade-off?

4. What are the purposes of the three types of budgets mentioned in this chapter?

5. What is cash management, and why is it important in business?

6. How can technology be used to help companies improve their credit and collection performance?

7. What are the sources of short-term financing?

8. How do companies obtain long-term financing?

9. Describe the major differences between debt and equity financing.

10. What are dividends and retained earnings?

11. What is the difference between common shares and preferred shares?

12. What is risk management? What are some strategies to manage risk?

13. What are the various types of insurance available to businesses?

CREATIVE THINKING CASE

Investors Hang Up on Vonage

Founded in 2002, Vonage quickly became a major player in Voice over Internet Protocol (VoIP) phone service. Using Internet connections instead of traditional phone lines, it offered customers an attractive flat rate of about $25 a month for calls to the United States, Canada, and many European countries. By its May IPO, Vonage had 1.7 million customers and more than half the U.S. market for Internet phone service. Vonage claimed to be the fastest-growing phone company in the United States. Revenues in 2005 were almost triple 2004 levels.

Management thought the time was right to go public and raise funds for expansion. Investors were again interested in IPOs after several years of low demand. So on May 24, 2006, it sold 31.25 million shares and raised $531 million. It also offered its individual customers—usually closed out of high-profile IPOs—the chance to buy 100 shares at the IPO price, an unusual move. So why was the Vonage IPO the worst in two years?

Timing is everything, and Vonage's timing was off. The market fell sharply on inflation concerns. The shares opened on the New York Stock Exchange at $17, fell to $14.85 by the end of the first day, and were trading below $7 by September 2006.

The offer to individual investors worked against Vonage, sending a message to some analysts that institutions were not interested in buying the stock and that Vonage needed help from its customers. Chad Brand of Peridot Capital Management considered this a "huge red flag.... If that's not a sign that nobody else wanted their stock, I don't know what is," he posted on his website. The sideways trend continued into 2007, but the share price dropped off in the second quarter, bottomed at about $1 in October, held for almost a year, then dropped to 50 cents per share. A rebound in 2010 brought the stock back up to over $45 per share in 2011 but, as of year end, the price dropped off to about $2.

Several factors negatively affected the Vonage offering. Increased competition creates pricing pressure. Rivals range from small VoIP players similar to Vonage to Internet powerhouses, including Google, Yahoo!, and MSN. Cable companies, such as Time Warner, that offer phone service bundled with television and broadband services; Verizon; and other traditional telephone service providers, are lowering prices as well. Vonage's sales were already falling in 2006, while costs-per-subscriber are rising. The company's marketing costs are very high, and the per-line cost of providing service is also rising at the same time as customer complaints about service quality are mounting. The development of Vonage World rebuilt the subscriber base in 2009. By 2011, Vonage customer base had levelled off at 1.7 million.

Regulatory uncertainty adds another layer of complexity. Telecommunications providers are campaigning to charge for carrying other company's calls. This would add to Vonage's costs. As Vonage grows, it will be required to collect sales tax and other fees, pushing customer bills well above the $25 flat rate they were expecting to pay and removing pricing advantages.

These are just a few of the issues that stand in the way of Vonage's profitability. In fact, Vonage's IPO prospectus says that it will focus on growth rather than profitability and went so far as to say that it might never become profitable. As a public company, Vonage will be under greater pressure to execute its business plan and also face close scrutiny from its investors.

1. What issues should executives of a company such as Vonage consider before deciding to go public? In your opinion, was the company ready for an IPO, and why?

2. How else could Vonage have raised funds to continue to grow? Compare the risks of raising private equity to going public.

3. Check on Vonage today. What is the stock price? The Market Cap (total value of shares of a company in the market) was $525 million in 2011 (less than the book value of assets). What is it now?

4. Do you think Vonage has a future? Why or why not?

SOURCES: David A. Gaffen, "Tale of Two IPOs," *Wall Street Journal* Online, May 24, 2006, www.wsj.com; Olga Kharif, "Vonage's Iffy IPO," *Business Week* Online, February 9, 2006, www.businessweek.com; Timothy J. Mullaney, "Vonage's Lackluster IPO," *Business Week* Online, May 24, 2006, www.businessweek.com; Shawn Young and Li Yuan, "Vonage Faces User Complaints as IPO Looms," *Wall Street Journal*, May 18, 2006, p. B1; Shawn Young and Lynn Cowan, "Vonage Lacks Voltage in Its IPO, with Weakest Debut in 2 Years," *Wall Street Journal*, May 25, 2006, p. C4; Shawn Young and Randall Smith, "How Vonage's High-Profile IPO Stumbled on the Stock Market," *Wall Street Journal*, June 3, 2006, p. A1; "Vonage Wins Computerworld Enterprise Intelligence Award for Industry Innovation," http://ir.vonage.com/releasedetail.cfm?releaseid=534163, November 24, 2011; Yahoo Finance (2011) "Vonage Holdings Corporation (VG)" http://finance.yahoo.com/q? s=VG, December 21, 2012; S. Jayson, "Are Vonage Holdings' Earnings Better Than They Look?" *The Motley Fool*, December 1, 2011.

appendix

A Basic Understanding of Our Legal Environment

THE LEGAL SYSTEM

LO1

Our legal system affects everyone who lives and does business in Canada. The smooth functioning of society depends on the law, which protects the rights of people and businesses. The purpose of law is to keep the system stable while allowing orderly change. The law defines which actions are allowed or banned and regulates some practices. It also helps settle disputes. The legal system both shapes and is shaped by political, economic, and social systems. All three levels of government—federal, provincial, and municipal—regulate various business activities as set out in the laws of Canada and the provinces.

In any society, laws are the rules of conduct created and enforced by a controlling authority, usually the government. They develop over time in response to the changing needs of people, property, and business. The legal system in Canada is thus the result of a long and continuing process. In each generation, new social problems occur, and new laws are created to solve them. For instance, the Competition Act (the successor to the Combines Investigation Act), was enacted, at least in part, to protect consumers in areas such as misleading advertising and abusive marketing practices. Other purposes of the Competition Act include

laws
The rules of conduct in a society created and enforced by a controlling authority, usually the government.

- to promote the efficiency and adaptability of the Canadian economy;
- to expand opportunities for Canadian companies to compete in the world markets (and recognize the role of foreign companies in Canada); and
- to ensure that small- and medium-sized businesses have equal opportunity to operate.

The Act also contains provisions that can be grouped under three categories: conspiracies, monopolies, and mergers.

Environmental law is an area over which the federal, provincial, and territorial governments have concurrent jurisdiction. Increased awareness of pollution and a social movement toward the protection of our environment have made this area an important public issue. The appropriate federal, provincial, and territorial Environmental Protection Acts apply to all the elements of the environment: air, land, and water.

Another area of law that is important to businesses is the Employment Equity Act. Passed in the late 1980s and last amended at the end of 2005, the act initially applied to all employers with 100 or more employees. Employment rights go beyond requiring employers to treat potential and existing employees equally, regardless of their personal characteristics (i.e., no person should be denied employment for reasons unrelated to ability). The employers, at a minimum, were encouraged to make their workforce reflect various underrepresented peoples (i.e., their organizations should reflect society as much as possible). Because of the increase of businesses geared toward social responsibility, not only did employers with 100 or more employees try to follow the Employment Equity standards, but smaller organizations did so as well.

The Employment Equity Act was amended in 1996 to include that every employer (not only those with 100 or more employees) shall implement employment equity. The amendment also states that all employers shall make reasonable accommodations to persons of one of the four designated groups (i.e., women, persons with disabilities, Aboriginal people, and visible minorities) to achieve a degree of representation that is consistent with their representation in the Canadian workforce. The Act allows employers to consider the potential employee's availability to meet reasonable occupational requirements.

Today new areas of law are developing to deal with the Internet. The increasing use of the Internet, as discussed in Chapter 4, requires that industry and the governments respond to various applicable issues, such as privacy.

© PHOTODISC COLLECTION/GETTY IMAGES

public law
The law relating to the relationship between the individual or business and the government (or its agencies).

private law
The law relating to the relationship between individuals, businesses, or individuals and businesses.

common law
The body of unwritten law that has evolved out of judicial (court) decisions rather than being enacted by a legislature; also called *case law*.

civil code
A body of written law that sets out the private rights of the citizens.

statute law (or statutory law)
Written law enacted by a legislature (municipal, provincial, territorial, or federal).

administrative law
The rules, regulations, and orders passed by boards, commissions, and agencies of government (municipal, provincial, territorial, and federal).

Public and Private Law

Public law is the law relating to the relationship between the individual or business and the government (or its agencies). The Criminal Code and the Income Tax Act are two examples at the federal level. Liquor laws are an example of public law at the provincial level.

Private law is the law relating to the relationship between individuals, businesses, or individuals and businesses. Statutes that protect one person from the harm of another are private laws.

The Main Sources of Law

Common law is the body of unwritten law that has evolved out of judicial (court) decisions rather than being enacted by legislatures. It is also called case law. It developed in England and applies to most of the English-speaking world. Common law is based on community customs that were recognized and enforced by the courts. Therefore, it is based on previous decisions. The reliance on previous decisions creates certainty and predictability.

Civil code is a body of written law that sets out the private rights of the citizens. In Québec much of what would be found in the common law of other provinces has been codified and is known as the Civil Code.

Statute law (or statutory law) is written law enacted by legislatures at all levels, from municipal, provincial, and territorial governments to the federal government. Statutes are the end result of the legislative process. Statutory laws are expected to represent the people's wishes. The particular advantage of statute law over common law is the relative ease with which the statutes can be changed.

Related to statutory law is administrative law, or the rules, regulations, and orders passed by boards, commissions, and agencies of municipal, provincial, territorial, and federal governments. The scope and influence of administrative law has expanded as the number of these government bodies has grown. Examples of the activities of regulatory agencies include the sale of securities by public companies, employment standards, and broadcasting.

Business Law

Business law is the body of law that governs commercial dealings. These laws provide a certainty within which businesses can operate, serving as guidelines for business decisions. Every businessperson should be familiar with the laws governing his or her field. Some laws, such as the Trademarks Act, apply to all businesses. Other types of business laws might apply to a specific industry, such as the Canadian Radio-television and Telecommunications Commission Act, which regulates and supervises all aspects of the Canadian broadcasting system and regulates telecommunications carriers and service providers that fall under federal jurisdiction.

business law
The body of law that governs commercial dealings.

The Court System

Canada has a highly developed court system. There are four levels of courts in Canada. The trials of most business disputes are heard in the Provincial/Territorial Superior Courts. These courts also hear appeals from Provincial Court judgments and judgments from the Provincial Administrative Tribunals. Appeals of these decisions are made to the Provincial Court of Appeal and subsequently to the Supreme Court of Canada. The Federal Court, Trial Division, and the Court of Appeals hear appeals of federally regulated Administrative Tribunals. The highest court in Canada is the Supreme Court of Canada, and it is the final court of appeal from all other Canadian courts. Also, there are specialized Federal Courts, including the Tax Court of Canada, where individuals and companies have an opportunity to settle matters relating to federal tax and revenue legislation. See Exhibit A.1 for an outline of Canada's court system.[1]

Nonjudicial Methods of Settling Disputes

Settling disputes by going to court is both expensive and time-consuming. Even if the case is settled prior to the trial, a sizable legal expense can be incurred in preparing for trial. Therefore, many companies now use private arbitration and mediation companies as alternatives to litigation. Private companies offer these services, which are a high-growth area within the legal profession.

With arbitration, the parties agree to present their case to an impartial third party and are required to accept the arbitrator's decision. Mediation is similar, but the mediator intervenes with the view of persuading the parties to adjust or settle their dispute. The mediator might or might not offer a resolution, but even if the mediator does offer a solution, neither party is bound by the mediator's decision. The mediator may suggest alternative solutions and primarily tries to help the parties negotiate a settlement. Mediation is more flexible than arbitration and allows for compromise. If the parties cannot reach a settlement, they can then go to court, an option not available in most arbitration cases.

In addition to saving time and money, corporations like the confidentiality of testimony and settlement terms in these proceedings. Arbitration and mediation also allow businesses to avoid the risks associated with going to trial. Generally speaking, once court action is initiated, the information is then public.

arbitration
A method of settling disputes in which the parties agree to present their case to an impartial third party and are required to accept the arbitrator's decision.

mediation
The intervention of a third party with a view to persuading the parties to adjust or settle their dispute.

HOT *links*

Whether we are purchasing a computer or a vehicle, it is important to fill out a bill of sale. To see what a legal bill of sale should contain to ensure that both the purchaser and the buyer are protected in case of later disagreements, go to www.lawdepot.com

Contract Law

A contract is an agreement that sets forth the relationship between parties regarding the performance of a specified action. The contract creates a legal obligation and is enforceable in a court of law. Contracts are an important part of business law. Contract law is also incorporated into other fields of business law, such as property and agency law, which we'll discuss later. Some of the business transactions that involve contracts are buying materials and property, selling goods, leasing equipment, and hiring consultants.

contract
An agreement that sets forth the relationship between parties regarding the performance of a specified action; creates a legal obligation and is enforceable in a court of law.

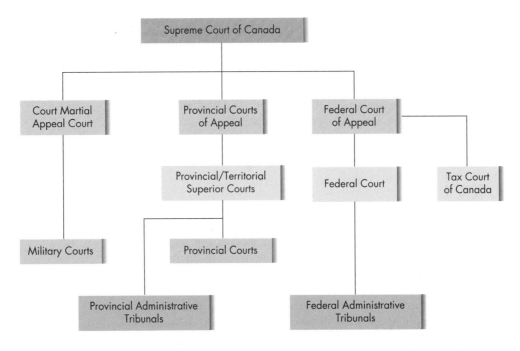

SOURCE: "Outline of Canada's Court System," http://justice.gc.ca/eng/dept-min/pub/ccs-ajc/page3.html Reproduced with the permission of the Minister of Public Works and Government Services Canada, 2012.

Concept *Check*

What are laws? List some of the laws that are important to business.

What is the difference between public and private law? Common law and civil code?

What are two ways to settle disputes without going to court?

express contract
A contract in which the terms are specified in either written or spoken words.

implied contract
A contract that depends on the acts and conduct of the parties to show agreement; the terms are not specified in writing or orally.

A contract can be an **express contract**, which specifies the terms of the agreement in either written or spoken words, or an **implied contract**, which depends on the acts and conduct of the parties to show agreement. An example of an express contract is the written contract an employee might sign that outlines the obligations of the employee and the employer. On the other hand, an implied contract exists when you order and receive a sandwich at Jason's Grill. You and the restaurant have an implied contract that you will pay the price shown on the restaurant's menu in exchange for an edible sandwich.

Michelle Sales, a 22-year-old owner of a small cosmetics company, is looking for a supplier to provide her store with inventory. She found a supplier she had confidence in, and after some negotiating, she and the supplier agree on a price of $11,000. The supplier writes up a contract, which they both sign. Has Michelle legally bought the inventory for $11,000? The answer is yes, because the transaction meets all the requirements for a valid contract.

LO2   ## CONTRACT REQUIREMENTS[2]

Businesses deal with contracts all the time, so it's important to know the requirements of a valid contract. For a contract to be legally enforceable, all of the following elements must be present.

- *Mutual agreement.* This is evidenced by the offer of one party being accepted by another party. Each party to the contract must have entered into it freely, without duress, and without improper inducements. Using physical or economic harm to force the signing of the contract—threatening injury or refusing to place another large order, for instance—invalidates a contract. Likewise, fraud—misrepresenting the essential facts of a transaction—makes a contract unenforceable. Telling a prospective used-car buyer that the brakes are new when, in fact, they have not been replaced can make the contract of sale invalid.

- *Capacity of the parties.* This refers to the legal ability of a party to enter into contracts. Under the law, minors (those who have not attained the age of majority according to the law of their province or territory), people who are mentally incompetent, and those whose judgment has been obviously impaired by drugs or alcohol cannot enter into validly enforceable contracts.
- *Legal consideration.* This is the exchange of something of legal value or benefit between the parties. Consideration can be in the form of money, goods, or giving up a legal right. Suppose that an electronics manufacturer agrees to rent an industrial building for a year at a monthly rent of $1500. Its consideration is the rent payment of $1500, and the building owner's consideration is permission to occupy the space. But if you offer to type a term paper for a friend for free and your offer is accepted, there is no contract. Your friend has not given up anything, so you are not legally bound to honour the deal.
- *Lawful object (legal purpose).* This means absence of illegality. The purpose of the contract must be legal for it to be valid. A contract cannot require performance of an illegal act. A contract to smuggle a banned substance into Canada for a specified amount of money would not be legally enforceable.
- *Legal form.* A contract can be in oral or written form, as required. Many can be oral (although a written contract provides an accurate record to the parties of their obligations). For instance, an oral contract exists when Bridge Corp. orders office supplies by phone from Ace Stationery Store and Ace delivers the requested goods. Written contracts include leases, sales contracts, and property deeds. Some types of contracts must be in writing to be legally binding.

As you can see, Michelle's inventory purchase meets all the requirements for a valid contract. Both parties have freely agreed to the terms of the contract. Michelle is not a minor and presumably does not fit any of the other categories of incapacity. Both parties are giving consideration, Michelle by paying the money and the supplier by delivering the inventory. The purchase of the inventory is a legal activity, and the written contract is in the correct form, because the cost of the inventory is over the legal amount that requires a written contract (this varies by province).

Breach of Contract

A breach of contract occurs when one party to a contract fails (without legal excuse) to fulfill the terms of the agreement. The other party then has the right to seek a remedy in the courts. There are three legal remedies for breach of contract.

breach of contract
The failure by one party to a contract to fulfill the terms of the agreement without a legal excuse.

- *Payment of damages*—money awarded to the party who was harmed by the breach of contract, to cover losses incurred because the contract wasn't fulfilled. Suppose that Ajax Roofing contracts with Fred Wellman to fix the large hole in the roof of his factory within three days, but the roofing crew doesn't show up as promised. When a thunderstorm four days later causes $45,000 in damage to Wellman's machinery, Wellman can sue for damages to cover the costs of the water damage, because Ajax breached the contract.
- *Specific performance of the contract*—a court order that requires the breaching party to perform the duties under the terms of the contract. Specific performance is a common method of settling a breach of contract. Wellman might ask the court to direct Ajax to fix the roof at the price and conditions in the contract.
- *Restitution*—cancelling the contract and returning both parties to the situation that existed before the contract. If one party fails to perform under the contract, neither party has any further obligation to the

Concept *Check*

What are the requirements for a valid contract?

What are some remedies for breach of contract?

Concept *in Action*

A contract may be verbal or written, expressed or implied. Contracts protect all parties to the contract. How do contracts protect the parties of the contract?

PRESSMASTER/PURESTOCK/GLOWIMAGES

other. Because Ajax failed to fix Wellman's roof under the terms of the contract, Wellman does not owe Ajax any money. Ajax must return the 50 percent deposit it received when Wellman signed the contract.

Summary of Learning Outcomes

LO1 **Understand how the legal system governs business transactions and settles business disputes.**

All three levels of government—federal, provincial, and municipal—regulate various business activities as set out in the laws of Canada and the provinces. Laws protect competition, the environment, employees' rights, etc. There is both public laws (the law relating to the relationship between the individual or business and the government) and there is private law (the law relating to the relationship between individuals, businesses, or individuals and businesses).

Business law is the body of law that governs commercial dealings. These laws provide a certainty within which businesses can operate, serving as guidelines for business decisions.

LO2 **Explain the required elements of a valid contract.**

A contract is an agreement that sets forth the relationship between parties regarding the performance of a specified action. For a contract to be valid there are certain conditions that are required: mutual agreement, capacity of the parties, legal consideration, legal purpose, and legal form.

Key Terms

glossary

A

absolute advantage The situation when a country can produce and sell a product at a lower cost than any other country, or when it is the only country that can provide the product. p. 136

accounting The process of collecting, recording, classifying, summarizing, reporting, and analyzing financial activities. p. 478

Accounting Standards for Private Enterprises (ASPE) The accounting framework designed to replace Canadian GAAP for private companies. p. 480

accounts payable A purchase for which a buyer has not yet paid the seller. p. 549

accounts receivable Sales for which a company has not yet been paid. p. 547

acid-test (quick) ratio The ratio of total current assets excluding inventory to total current liabilities; used to measure a company's liquidity. p. 494

acquisition The purchase of a corporation by another corporation or by an investor group; the identity of the acquired company can be lost. p. 228

activity-based costing (ABC) ABC assigns resource costs through all the activities to either produce the product or acquire it for resale. p. 414

activity ratios Ratios that measure how well a company uses its assets. p. 495

administrative law The rules, regulations, and orders passed by boards, commissions, and agencies of government (municipal, provincial, and federal). p. 574

advertising Any paid form of non-personal presentation by an identified sponsor. p. 423

agency shop A company where employees are not required to join the union but must pay it a fee to cover its expenses in representing them. p. 352

agents Sales representatives of manufacturers and wholesalers. p. 416

amortization (depreciation) The allocation of an asset's original cost to the years in which it is expected to produce revenues. p. 487

angel investors Individual investors or groups of experienced investors who provide funding for start-up businesses. p. 174

annual report A yearly document that describes a company's financial status and usually discusses the company's activities during the past year and its prospects for the future. p. 480

application service providers (ASPs) A service company that buys and maintains software on its servers and distributes it through high-speed networks to subscribers for a set period and price. p. 109

apprenticeship A form of on-the-job training that combines specific job instruction with classroom instruction. p. 344

arbitration The process of settling a labour-management dispute by having a third party—a single arbitrator or a panel—make a decision, which is binding on both the union and the employer. pp. 353, 575

articling Working in an accredited environment to apply theoretical knowledge learned through formal education and develop professional judgment. p. 344

assembly process A production process in which the basic inputs are either combined to create the output or transformed into the output. p. 448

assets Possessions of value owned by a company. p. 483

Association of Southeast Asian Nations (ASEAN) The Association of Southeast Asian Nations (ASEAN), which, as of 2012, included 10 member states. p. 139

attitude Learned tendency to respond consistently toward a given object, idea, or concept. p. 382

authority Legitimate power, granted by the organization and acknowledged by employees, that allows an individual to request action and expect compliance. p. 281

autocratic leaders Directive leaders who prefer to make decisions and solve problems on their own with little input from subordinates. p. 255

B

baby boomers Canadians born between 1946 and 1964. p. 68

balance of payments A summary of a country's international financial transactions showing the difference between the country's total payments to, and its total receipts from, other countries. p. 133

balance of trade The differences between the value of a country's exports and the value of its imports during a certain time. p. 133

balance sheet (statement of financial position) A financial statement that summarizes a company's financial position at a specific point in time. p. 485

Bank of Canada Canada's central bank, whose objective is the economic and financial well-being of Canada by creating a sound balance of growth, employment, and price stability. p. 50

bank rate The interest rate that the Bank of Canada charges on one-day loans to financial institutions. p. 513

bankruptcy The legal procedure by which individuals or businesses that cannot meet their financial obligations are relieved of some, if not all, of their debt. p. 18

barriers to entry Factors, such as technological or legal conditions, that prevent new companies from competing equally with a monopoly. p. 40

batch processing A method of updating a database in which data are collected over some time period and then processed together. p. 99

bear markets Markets in which securities prices are falling. p. 528

belief An organized pattern of knowledge that an individual holds as true about the world. p. 382

benefit segmentation The differentiation of markets based on what a product will do rather than on customer characteristics. p. 387

bill of material A list of the items and the number of each required to make a given product. p. 453

board of directors A group of people elected by the shareholders to handle the overall management of a corporation, such as setting corporate goals and policies, hiring corporate officers, and overseeing the company's operations and finances. p. 222

bond ratings Letter grades assigned to bond issues to indicate their quality, or level of risk; assigned by rating agencies such as Moody's and Standard & Poor's (S&P). p. 521

bonds Securities that represent long-term debt obligations (liabilities) issued by corporations and governments. pp. 52, 520, 552

brand A name, design, symbol, specific colour, slogan, or any other feature that identifies a product, distinguishes it from other products, and creates a perception in the minds of consumers. p. 402

brand loyalty A customer's preference for a particular brand that results in advocacy for that brand. p. 402

breach of contract The failure by one party to a contract to fulfill the terms of the agreement without a legal excuse. p. 577

break-even point (or break-even quantity) The price at which a product's costs are covered, so additional sales result in profit. p. 412

breaking bulk The process of breaking large shipments of similar products into smaller, more usable lots. p. 419

broker markets (organized stock exchanges) Organizations on whose premises securities are resold by using an auction-style trading system. p. 526

brokers Go-betweens that bring buyers and sellers together. p. 416

budgets Formal written forecasts of revenues and expenses that set spending limits based on operational forecasts; include cash budgets, capital budgets, and operating budgets. p. 544

bull markets Markets in which securities prices are rising. p. 528

bundling The strategy of grouping two or more related products together and pricing them as a single product. p. 411

business An organization that strives for a profit by providing goods and services desired by its customers. p. 12

business cycles Upward and downward changes in the level of economic activity. p. 46

Business Development Bank of Canada (BDC) Bank that provides small- and medium-sized businesses with flexible financing, affordable consulting services, and venture capital. p. 177

business interruption insurance Covers such costs as rental of temporary facilities, wage and salary payments to employees, payments for leased equipment, fixed payments, and profits that would have been earned during that period. p. 560

business law The body of law that governs commercial dealings. p. 575

business plan A formal written statement that describes in detail the idea for a new business and how it will be carried out; includes a general description of the company, the qualifications of the owner(s), a description of the product or service, an analysis of the market, and a financial plan. p. 173

buyer behaviour The actions people take in buying and using goods and services. p. 378

C

CAD/CAM systems Linked computer systems that combine the advantages of *computer-aided design* and *computer-aided manufacturing*. The system helps design the product, control the flow of resources, and operate the production process. p. 464

Canada Deposit Insurance Corporation (CDIC) A federal Crown Corporation created in 1967 to provide deposit insurance and contribute to the stability of Canada's financial system. p. 516

Canada Pension Plan Insurance that provides retirement, disability, death, and health benefits. p. 559

Canadian Charter of Rights and Freedoms Legislation that guarantees the rights and freedoms of Canadians. p. 77

capital Tools, machinery, equipment, and buildings used to produce goods and services and get them to the consumer. Sometimes refers to the money that buys machinery, factories, and other production and distribution facilities. p. 33

capital assets Long-term assets used by a company for more than a year, such as land, buildings, and machinery; also referred to as fixed assets or property, plant, and equipment (PPE). p. 487

capital budgeting The process of analyzing long-term projects and selecting those that offer the best returns while maximizing the company's value. p. 548

capital budgets Budgets that forecast a company's outlays for fixed assets (plant and equipment), typically for a period of several years. p. 545

capital expenditures Investments in long-lived assets, such as land, buildings, machinery, and equipment, that are expected to provide benefits over a period longer than one year. p. 548

capital products Large, expensive items with a long lifespan that are purchased by businesses for use in making other products or providing a service. p. 405

cartel An agreement between enterprises to lessen competition. p. 21

cash budgets Budgets that forecast a company's cash inflows and outflows and help the company plan for cash surpluses and shortages. p. 545

cash flows The inflow and outflow of cash for a company. p. 542

cash management The process of making sure that a company has enough cash on hand to pay bills as they come due and to meet unexpected expenses. p. 546

cellular manufacturing Production technique that uses small, self-contained production units, each performing all or most of the tasks necessary to complete a manufacturing order. p. 453

centralization The degree to which formal authority is concentrated in one area or level of an organization. p. 283

certified general accountant (CGA) An accountant who focuses primarily on external financial reporting. p. 482

certified management accountant (CMA) An accountant who works primarily in industry and focuses on internal management accounting. p. 482

chain of command The line of authority that extends from one level of an organization's hierarchy to the next, from top to bottom, and makes clear who reports to whom. p. 281

chartered accountant (CA) An accountant who typically provides tax, audit, and management services. p. 481

chartered banks Profit-oriented financial institutions that accept deposits, make business and consumer loans, invest in government and corporate securities, and provide other financial services. p. 514

chartered professional accountant (CPA) An accounting designation that unites the various accounting designations in Canada. p. 482

chief information officer (CIO) An executive with responsibility for managing all information resources in an organization. p. 96

circular flow The movement of inputs and outputs among households, businesses, and governments; a way of showing how the sectors of the economy interact. p. 34

civil code A body of written law that sets out the private rights of the citizens. p. 574

closed shop A company where only union members can be hired. p. 351

code of ethics A set of guidelines prepared by a company to provide its employees with the knowledge of what the company expects in terms of their responsibilities and behaviour toward fellow employees, customers, and suppliers. p. 80

coercive power Power that is derived from an individual's ability to threaten negative outcomes. p. 254

cognitive dissonance The condition of having beliefs or knowledge that are internally inconsistent or that disagree with one's behaviour. p. 392

collective bargaining The process of negotiating labour agreements that provide for compensation and working arrangements mutually acceptable to the union and to management. p. 350

command economy An economic system characterized by government ownership of virtually all resources and economic decision making by central government planning; also known as a *planned economy and central planning*. p. 36

commercial paper Unsecured short-term debt (an IOU) issued by a financially strong corporation. p. 546

committee structure An organizational structure in which authority and responsibility are held by a group rather than an individual. p. 288

common law The body of unwritten law that has evolved out of judicial (court) decisions rather than being enacted by a legislature; also called *case law*. p. 574

common shares A security that represents an ownership interest in a corporation. p. 552

competitive advantage A set of unique features of a company and its products that are perceived by the target market as significant and superior to those of the competition; also called *differential advantage*. pp. 357, 374

component lifestyle A lifestyle made up of a complex set of interests, needs, and choices. p. 64

computer network A group of two or more computer systems, as well as devices (such as printers, external hard drives, modems, and routers), linked together by communications channels to share data, commands, information, and other resources. p. 103

computer virus A computer program that copies itself into other software and can spread to other computer systems. p. 114

computer-aided design (CAD) The use of computers to design and test new products and modify existing ones. p. 464

computer-aided manufacturing (CAM) The use of computers to develop and control the production process. p. 464

computer-integrated manufacturing (CIM) The combination of computerized manufacturing processes (such as robots and flexible manufacturing systems) with other computerized systems that control design, inventory, production, and purchasing. p. 465

conceptual skills A manager's ability to view the organization as a whole, understand how the various parts are interdependent, and assess how the organization relates to its external environment. p. 262

conglomerate merger A merger or acquisition involving companies in unrelated businesses; done to reduce risk. p. 229

consensual leaders Leaders who encourage discussion about issues and then require that all parties involved agree to the final decision. p. 255

consultative leaders Leaders who confer with subordinates before making a decision but who retain the final decision-making authority. p. 256

consumer price index (CPI) A measure of retail price movements that compares a representative "shopping basket" of goods and services. p. 49

consumerism A movement that seeks to increase the rights and powers of buyers vis-à-vis sellers. p. 19

contingency plans Plans that identify alternative courses of action for very unusual or crisis situations; typically stipulate the chain of command, standard operating procedures, and communication channels the organization will use during an emergency. p. 253

contingent workers Persons who prefer temporary employment, either part- or full-time. p. 338

continuous improvement A constant commitment to seeking better ways of doing things to achieve greater efficiency and improve quality. p. 461

continuous process A production process that uses long production runs lasting days, weeks, or months without equipment shutdowns; generally used for high-volume, low-variety products with standardized parts. p. 448

contract An agreement that sets forth the relationship between parties regarding the performance of a specified action; creates a legal obligation and is enforceable in a court of law. p. 575

contract manufacturing The practice in which a foreign company manufactures private-label goods under a domestic company's brand name. p. 140

contractionary policy The use of monetary policy by the Bank of Canada to tighten the money supply by selling government securities or raising interest rates. p. 50

controlling The process of assessing the organization's progress toward accomplishing its goals; includes monitoring the implementation of a plan and correcting deviations from the plan. p. 258

convenience products Relatively inexpensive items that require little shopping effort and are purchased routinely without planning. p. 405

conventional ethics The second stage in the ethical development of individuals in which people move from an egocentric viewpoint to consider the expectations of an organization or society; also known as social ethics. p. 77

convertible bonds Corporate bonds that are issued with an option that allows the bondholder to convert them into common shares. p. 521

cooperatives Legal entities typically formed by people with similar interests, such as customers or suppliers, to reduce costs and gain economic power. A cooperative has limited liability, an unlimited lifespan, an elected board of directors, and an administrative staff; all profits are distributed to the member-owners in proportion to their contributions. p. 226

copyright A form of protection established by the government for creators of works of art, music, literature, or other intellectual property; it gives the creator the exclusive right to use, produce, and sell the creation during the lifetime of the creator and extends these rights to the creator's estate for 50 years thereafter. p. 17

core value proposition A statement of the tangible results a customer receives from using your products. p. 370

corporate culture The set of attitudes, values, and standards of behaviour that distinguishes one organization from another. p. 258

corporate governance The way in which an organization is being governed, directed, and administered. p. 75

corporate open house Persons are invited to an open house on the premises of the corporation. Qualified applicants are encouraged to complete an application before leaving. p. 340

corporate philanthropy The practice of charitable giving by corporations; includes contributing cash, donating equipment and products, and supporting the volunteer efforts of company employees. p. 75

corporation A legal entity with its own rights and responsibilities separate from its shareholders, who therefore are not personally liable for the entity's actions and liabilities. p. 220

cost competitive advantage A company's ability to produce a product or service at a lower cost than all other competitors in an industry while maintaining satisfactory profit margins. p. 375

cost of goods sold (COGS) The total expense of buying or producing a company's goods or services. p. 490

cost-of-living adjustment (COLA) A provision in a labour contract that calls for wages to increase automatically as the cost of living rises (usually measured by the consumer price index). p. 352

cost-push inflation Inflation that occurs when increases in production costs push up the prices of final goods and services. p. 49

costs Expenses incurred in creating and selling goods and services. p. 13

countertrade A form of international trade in which part or all of the payment for goods or services is in the form of other goods and services. p. 142

credit unions Not-for-profit, member-owned financial co-operatives. See also *caisses populaires*. p. 515

critical path In a critical path method network, the longest path through the linked activities. p. 459

critical path method (CPM) A scheduling tool that enables a manager to determine the critical path of activities for a project—the activities that will cause the entire project to fall behind schedule if they are not completed on time. p. 459

cross-functional teams Members from the same organizational level, but from different functional areas. p. 292

crowding out The situation that occurs when government spending replaces spending by the private sector. p. 51

Crown corporations Companies that only the provincial and federal government can set up. p. 226

culture The set of values, ideas, attitudes, and other symbols created to shape human behaviour. p. 380

currency Bank notes and coins used as a medium of exchange. p. 511

current assets Assets that can or will be converted to cash within the next twelve months. p. 486

current liabilities Short-term claims that are due within a year of the date of the balance sheet. p. 487

current ratio The ratio of total current assets to total current liabilities; used to measure a company's liquidity. p. 494

customer departmentalization Departmentalization that is based on the primary type of customer served by the organizational unit. p. 278

customer relationship management (CRM) The processes used by organizations to track and organize information about current and prospective customers. p. 372

customer satisfaction The customer's feeling that a product has met or exceeded expectations. p. 371

customer value (in marketing) The ratio of benefits to the sacrifices necessary to obtain those benefits, as determined by the customer; reflects the willingness of customers to buy a product. p. 371

customization The production of goods or services one at a time according to the specific needs or wants of individual customers. p. 447

customs regulations Regulations on products that are different from generally accepted international standards. p. 149

cyclical unemployment Unemployment that occurs when a downturn in the business cycle reduces the demand for labour throughout the economy. p. 48

D

database An electronic filing system that collects and organizes data and information. p. 97

data mart Special subset of a data warehouse that deals with a single area of data and is organized for quick analysis. p. 100

data warehouse An information technology that combines many databases across a whole company into one central database that supports management decision making. p. 100

dealer brand A brand that is owned by the wholesaler or retailer rather than the manufacturer. p. 402

dealer markets Securities markets where buy and sell orders are executed through dealers, or "market makers" linked by telecommunications networks. p. 527

debentures Unsecured bonds that are backed only by the reputation of the issuer and its promise to pay the principal and interest when due. p. 521

debt A form of business financing consisting of borrowed funds that must be repaid with interest over a stated time period. p. 174

debt ratios Ratios that measure the degree and effect of a company's use of borrowed funds (debt) to finance its operations. p. 495

debt-to-equity ratio The ratio of total liabilities to owners' equity; measures the relationship between the amount of debt financing and the amount of equity financing. p. 495

decentralization The process of pushing decision-making authority down the organizational hierarchy. p. 283

decision support system (DSS) A management support system that helps managers make decisions using interactive computer models that describe real-world processes. p. 100

decisional roles A manager's activities as an entrepreneur, resource allocator, conflict resolver, or negotiator. p. 260

deductibles The amounts that the insured must pay before insurance benefits begin. p. 558

delegation of authority The assignment of some degree of authority and responsibility to persons lower in the chain of command. p. 281

demand The quantity of a good or service that people are willing to buy at various prices. p. 42

demand curve A graph showing the quantity of a good or service that people are willing to buy at various prices. p. 42

demand deposits Money kept in chequing accounts that can be withdrawn by depositors on demand. p. 511

demand-pull inflation Inflation that occurs when the demand for goods and services is greater than the supply. p. 48

democratic leaders Leaders who solicit input from all members of the group and then allow the members to make the final decision through a vote. p. 255

demographic segmentation The differentiation of markets through the use of categories such as age, education, gender, income, and household size. p. 385

demography The study of people's vital statistics, such as their age, race and ethnicity, and location. p. 66

departmentalization The process of grouping jobs together so that similar or associated tasks and activities can be coordinated. p. 277

depreciation The allocation of an asset's original cost to the years in which it is expected to produce revenues; also referred to as *amortization*. p. 487

deregulation The removal of rules and regulations governing business competition. p. 18

detailing The physical stocking of merchandise at a retailer by the salesperson who delivers the merchandise. p. 425

devaluation A lowering of the value of a nation's currency relative to other currencies. p. 135

differential competitive advantage A company's ability to provide a unique product or service with a set of features that the target market perceives as important and better than the competitor's. p. 375

direct selling Direct selling is a popular marketing structure that connects the sellers "directly" with the customers. p. 228

distribution (logistics) Efficiently managing the acquisition of raw materials to the factory and the movement of products from the producer to industrial users and consumers. p. 414

distribution centres Warehouses that specialize in rapid movement of goods to retail stores by making and breaking bulk. p. 428

distribution channel The series of marketing entities through which goods and services pass on their way from producers to end users. p. 415

distribution strategy Creating the means by which products flow from the producer to the consumer. p. 377

dividends Payments to shareholders from a corporation's profits. p. 553

division of labour The process of dividing work into separate jobs and assigning tasks to workers. p. 277

double-entry bookkeeping A method of accounting in which each transaction is recorded as at least two entries, so that the accounts or records are changed. p. 484

dual distribution (or multiple distribution) Two or more channels that distribute the same product to target markets. p. 418

dumping The practice of charging a lower price for a product in foreign markets than in the company's home market. p. 143

E

earnings per share (EPS) The ratio of net profit to the number of common shares outstanding; measures the number of dollars earned by each share. p. 495

economic growth An increase in a nation's output of goods and services. p. 46

economic system The combination of policies, laws, and choices made by a nation's government to establish the systems that determine what goods and services are produced and how they are allocated. p. 35

economics The study of how a society uses scarce resources to produce and distribute goods and services. p. 32

effectiveness The ability to produce the desired result or good (doing the right thing). p. 248

efficiency Using the least amount of resources to accomplish the organization's goals (doing things right). p. 248

electronic data interchange (EDI) The electronic exchange of information between two trading partners. p. 458

embargo A total ban on imports or exports of a product. p. 149

employment insurance Payment of benefits to laid-off workers while they seek new jobs. pp. 558

empowerment The process of giving employees increased autonomy and discretion to make decisions, as well as control over the resources needed to implement those decisions. p. 256

enterprise portal A customizable internal website that provides proprietary corporate information to a defined user group, such as employees, supply chain partners, or customers. p. 107

enterprise resource planning (ERP) A computerized resource-planning system that incorporates information about the company's suppliers and customers with its internally generated data. p. 455

enterprise risk management (ERM) A company-wide, strategic approach to identifying, monitoring, and managing all elements of a company's risk. p. 562

entrepreneurial thinking Thinking like an entrepreneur—even those who work in a company. p. 34

entrepreneurs People with vision, drive, and creativity who are willing to take the risk of starting and managing a new business to make a profit or greatly change the scope and direction of an existing company. pp. 33, 162

environmental scanning The process in which a company continually collects and evaluates information about its external environment. p. 373

e-procurement The process of purchasing supplies and materials online by using the Internet. p. 456

equilibrium The point on the supply and demand curve at which quantity demanded equals quantity supplied. p. 43

equity A form of business financing consisting of funds raised through the sale of stock in a business. p. 174

equity theory A theory of motivation that holds that worker satisfaction is influenced by employees' perceptions about how fairly they are treated compared with their coworkers. p. 318

ERG theory A theory of motivation developed by Clayton Alderfer that better supports empirical research than Maslow's hierarchy of needs theory. The three components of the model are: existence, relatedness, and growth. p. 312

ethics A set of moral standards for judging whether something is right or wrong. p. 64

European Union (EU) Trade agreement among 27 European nations. p. 138

exchange The process in which two parties give something of value to each other to satisfy their respective needs. p. 370

exchange controls Laws that require a company earning foreign exchange (foreign currency) from its exports to sell the foreign exchange to a control agency, such as a central bank. p. 149

exchange-traded fund (ETF) A basket of marketable securities in a category, such as an industry sector, an investment objective, or a geographical area, or that track an index. ETFs are similar to mutual funds but trade like shares. p. 524

excise taxes Taxes that are imposed on specific items such as gasoline, alcoholic beverages, and tobacco. p. 22

exclusive distribution A distribution system in which a manufacturer selects only one or two dealers in an area to market its products. p. 422

executive information system (EIS) A management support system that is customized for an individual executive; provides specific information for strategic decisions. p. 101

existence (ERG theory) The concern for basic material existent motivators. p. 312

expansionary policy The use of monetary policy by the Bank of Canada to increase the growth of the money supply. p. 50

expectancy theory A theory of motivation that holds that the probability of an individual acting in a particular way depends on the strength of that individual's belief that the act will have a particular outcome and on whether the individual values that outcome. p. 317

expense items Items, purchased by businesses, that are smaller and less expensive than capital products and usually have a lifespan of less than one year. p. 406

expenses The costs of generating revenues. p. 490

experiment A marketing research method in which the investigator changes one or more variables—price, packaging, design, shelf space, advertising theme, or advertising expenditures— while observing the effects of these changes on another variable (usually sales). p. 388

expert power Power that is derived from an individual's extensive knowledge in one or more areas. p. 254

expert system A management support system that gives managers advice similar to what they would get from a consultant; it uses artificial intelligence to enable computers to reason and learn to solve problems in much the same way humans do. p. 102

exporting The practice of selling domestically produced goods to buyers in another country. p. 140

exports Goods and services produced in one country and sold in other countries. p. 132

express contract A contract in which the terms are specified in either written or spoken words. p. 576

extensive decision making Purchasing an unfamiliar, expensive, infrequently bought item. p. 383

extrinsic rewards The rewards that are external to the job. p. 308

F

factoring A form of short-term financing in which a company sells its accounts receivable outright at a discount to a *factor*. p. 550

factors of production The resources used to create goods and services, including natural resources, labour, capital, entrepreneurship, and knowledge. p. 33

federal budget deficit The condition that occurs when the federal government spends more for programs than it collects in taxes. p. 51

financial accounting Accounting that focuses on preparing external financial reports that are used by outsider stakeholders such as creditors, suppliers, investors, and government agents to assess the financial strength of a business. p. 479

financial intermediation The process in which financial institutions act as intermediaries between the suppliers and demanders of funds. p. 514

financial management The art and science of managing a company's money so that it can meet its goals. p. 541

financial risk The chance that a company will be unable to make scheduled interest and principal payments on its debt. p. 550

fiscal policy The government's use of taxation and spending to affect the economy. p. 51

fixed assets See *capital assets*. p. 487

fixed costs Costs that do not vary with different levels of output; for example, rent. p. 412

fixed-cost contribution The selling price per unit (revenue) minus the variable costs per unit. p. 412

fixed-position layout A facility arrangement in which the product stays in one place and workers and machinery move to it as needed. p. 453

flexible manufacturing system (FMS) A system that combines automated workstations with computer-controlled transportation devices—automatic guided vehicles (AGVs)—that move materials between workstations and into and out of the system. p. 465

floating exchange rates A system in which prices of currencies move up and down based upon the demand for and supply of the various currencies. p. 135

foreign direct investment Active ownership of a foreign company or of manufacturing or marketing facilities in a foreign country. p. 141

formal organization The order and design of relationships within a company; consists of two or more people working together with a common objective and clarity of purpose. p. 276

four pillars of the Canadian financial system The four pillars of the Canadian financial system refers to banks, trust companies, insurance companies, and investment dealers. p. 513

four Ps (4Ps) Product, price, promotion, and place (distribution), which together make up the marketing mix. p. 377

franchise agreement A contract setting out the terms of a franchising arrangement, including the rules for running the franchise, the services provided by the franchisor, and the financial terms. Under the contract, the franchisee is allowed to use the franchisor's business name, trademark, and logo. p. 231

franchisee In a franchising arrangement, the individual or company that sells the goods or services of the franchisor in a certain geographic area. p. 230

franchising A form of business organization based on a business arrangement between a franchisor, which supplies the product concept, and the franchisee, who sells the goods or services of the franchisor in a certain geographic area. p. 230

franchisor In a franchising arrangement, the company that supplies the product concept to the franchisee. p. 230

free trade The policy of permitting the people of a country to buy and sell where they please without restrictions. p. 136

free trade zone An area where the nations allow free, or almost free, trade with each other while imposing tariffs on goods of nations outside the zone. p. 137

free-rein (laissez-faire) leadership A leadership style in which the leader turns over all authority and control to subordinates. p. 256

frictional unemployment Short-term unemployment that is not related to the business cycle. p. 48

friendly takeover A takeover that is supported by the management and board of directors of the targeted company. p. 228

fringe benefits Indirect compensation such as pensions, health insurance, and vacations. p. 349

full employment The condition when all people who want to work and can work have jobs. p. 47

functional departmentalization Departmentalization that is based on the primary functions performed within an organizational unit. p. 277

futures contracts Legally binding obligations to buy or sell specified quantities of commodities or financial instruments at an agreed-on price at a future date. p. 524

G

Gantt charts Bar graphs plotted on a timeline that show the relationship between scheduled and actual production. p. 459

general partners Partners who have unlimited liability for all of the company's business obligations and who control its operations. p. 218

general partnership A partnership in which all partners share in the management and profits. Each partner can act on behalf of the company and has unlimited liability for all its business obligations. p. 218

generally accepted accounting principles (GAAP) The financial accounting rules, standards, and usual practices followed by accountants in Canada when preparing financial statements, until January 2011. p. 479

Generation X Canadians born between 1964 and about 1977. p. 68

Generation Y Canadians born between about 1977 and 1997. p. 67

Generation Z Canadians born from the late 1990's onward. p. 67

generic brand A brand that carries no specific name associated with a manufacturer, wholesaler, or retailer, and usually comes in plain containers and sells for less than brand name products. p. 402

geographic departmentalization Departmentalization based on the geographic segmentation of the organizational units. p. 278

geographic segmentation The differentiation of markets by region of the country, city or county size, market density, or climate. p. 386

global management skills A manager's ability to operate in diverse cultural environments. p. 262

global vision The ability to recognize and react to international business opportunities, be aware of threats from foreign competition, and use international distribution networks effectively to obtain materials and move finished products to customers. p. 130

goal-setting theory A theory of motivation based on the premise that an individual's intention to work toward a goal is a primary source of motivation. p. 318

goods Tangible items manufactured by businesses. p. 12

goodwill The value that has been paid for a company that exceeds the value of its net tangible assets. p. 487

green marketing The process of selling products based on their environmental benefits. p. 390

grievance A formal complaint, filed by an employee or by the union, charging that management has violated the contract. p. 353

gross domestic product (GDP) The total market value of all final goods and services produced within a nation's borders each year. p. 46

gross national product (GNP) The total market value of all final goods and services produced by a country regardless of where the factors of production are located. p. 46

gross profit The amount a company earns after paying to produce or buy its products but before deducting operating expenses. p. 491

gross sales The total dollar amount of a company's sales. p. 489

group cohesiveness The degree to which group members want to stay in the group and tend to resist outside influences. p. 290

growth (ERG theory) The concern for personal growth. p. 313

H

Hawthorne effect The phenomenon that employees perform better when they feel singled out for attention or feel that management is concerned about their welfare. p. 310

high-yield (junk) bonds High-risk, high-return bonds. p. 521

horizontal merger or acquisition A merger or acquisition involving companies at the same stage of the supply chain in the same industry; done to reduce costs, expand product offerings, or reduce competition. p. 229

hostile takeover A takeover that goes against the wishes of the target company's management and board of directors. p. 229

human relations skills A manager's interpersonal skills that are used to accomplish goals through the use of human resources. p. 262

human resource (HR) planning Creating a strategy for meeting future human resource needs. p. 337

human resource management (HRM) The process of hiring, developing, motivating, and evaluating employees to achieve organizational goals. p. 336

hygiene factors Extrinsic elements of the work environment that do not serve as a source of employee satisfaction or motivation. p. 315

I

ideal self-image The way an individual would like to be. p. 382

implied contract A contract that depends on the acts and conduct of the parties to show agreement; the terms are not specified in writing or orally. p. 576

import quota A limit on the quantity of a certain good that can be imported; also known as a *quantitative restraint*. p. 149

imports Goods and services that are bought from other countries. p. 132

income statement A financial statement that summarizes a company's revenues and expenses, and shows its total profit or loss over a period of time. Also known as the statement of comprehensive income, statement of earnings, and the profit and loss statement. p. 489

income taxes Taxes that are based on the income received by businesses and individuals. p. 21

industrial distributors Independent wholesalers that buy related product lines from many manufacturers and sell them to industrial users. p. 416

industry life cycle model A useful tool for analyzing the effects of an industry's evolution on competitive forces. p. 197

inflation The situation in which the average of all prices of goods and services is rising. p. 18

informal organization The network of connections and channels of communication based on the informal relationships of individuals inside an organization. p. 293

information system (IS) It's the combination of technology, people and process that an organization uses to produce, and manage information. p. 95

information technology (IT) The equipment and techniques used to manage and process information. p. 94

informational roles A manager's activities as an information gatherer, an information disseminator, or a spokesperson for the company. p. 260

infrastructure The basic institutions and public facilities upon which an economy's development depends. p. 146

initial public offer (IPO) A company's first issuance of shares to the public. p. 553

institutional investors Investment professionals who are paid to manage other people's money. p. 524

insurable interest An insurance applicant's chance of loss if a particular peril occurs. p. 557

insurable risk A risk that an insurance company will cover. It must meet certain criteria. p. 557

insurance The promise of compensation for certain financial losses. p. 556

insurance policy A written agreement that defines what the insurance covers and the risks that the insurance company will bear for the insured party. p. 556

intangible assets Long-term assets with no physical existence, such as patents, copyrights, trademarks, and goodwill. p. 487

integrated marketing communications (IMC) The careful coordination of all promotional activities—media advertising, sales promotion, personal selling, and public relations, as well as direct marketing, packaging, and other forms of promotion—to produce a consistent, unified message that is customer focused. p. 424

intensive distribution A distribution system in which a manufacturer tries to sell its products wherever there are potential customers. p. 422

interest A fixed amount of money paid by the issuer of a bond to the bondholder on a regular schedule, typically every six months; stated as the *coupon rate*. p. 520

intermittent process A production process that uses short production runs to make batches of different products; generally used for low-volume, high-variety products. p. 448

International Financial Reporting Standards (IFRS) A set of globally accepted accounting standards adopted in Canada on January 1, 2011, for public companies and those private companies that chose to adopt them. p. 480

International Monetary Fund (IMF) An international organization, founded in 1945, that promotes trade, makes short-term loans to member nations, and acts as a lender of last resort for troubled nations. p. 144

interpersonal roles A manager's activities as a figurehead, company leader, or liaison. p. 260

intranet An internal corporate-wide area network that uses Internet technology to link employees in many locations and with different types of computers. p. 105

intrapreneurs Entrepreneurs who apply their creativity, vision, and risk taking within a large corporation, rather than starting a company of their own. p. 164

intrinsic rewards The rewards that are part of the job itself. p. 308

inventory The supply of goods that a company holds for use in production or for sale to customers. p. 454

inventory control system A system that maintains an adequate assortment of items to meet a user or customer's needs. p. 428

inventory management The determination of how much of each type of inventory a company will keep on hand and the ordering, receiving, storing, and tracking of inventory. p. 454

inventory turnover ratio The ratio of cost of goods sold to average inventory; measures the speed with which inventory moves through a company and is turned into sales. p. 495

investment bankers Companies that act as intermediaries, buying securities from corporations and governments and reselling them to the public. p. 525

involvement The amount of time and effort a buyer invests in the searches, evaluations, and decision processes of consumer behaviour. p. 383

ISO 14000 A set of technical standards designed by the International Organization for Standardization to promote clean production processes to protect the environment. p. 463

ISO 9000 A set of five technical standards of quality management, created by the International Organization for Standardization, to provide a uniform way of determining whether manufacturing plants and service organizations conform to sound quality procedures. p. 462

J

job analysis A study of the tasks required to do a particular job well. p. 337

job description The tasks and responsibilities of a job. p. 338

job enlargement The horizontal expansion of a job by increasing the number and variety of tasks that a person performs. p. 321

job enrichment The vertical expansion of a job by increasing the employee's autonomy, responsibility, and decision-making authority. p. 321

job fair An event, typically one day, held at a convention centre to bring together thousands of job seekers and hundreds of companies searching for employees. p. 340

job rotation Reassignment of workers to several different jobs over time so that they can learn the basics of each job; also called *cross-training*. pp. 321

job sharing A scheduling option that allows two individuals to split the tasks, responsibilities, and work hours of one 40-hour-per-week job. p. 322

job shop A manufacturing company that produces goods in response to customer orders. p. 447

job specification A list of the skills, knowledge, and abilities a person must have to fill a job. p. 338

joint venture Two or more companies that form an alliance to pursue a particular project for a specified time period. pp. 141, 227

justice What is considered fair according to the prevailing standards of society; in the 21st century, an equitable distribution of the burdens and rewards that society has to offer. p. 77

just-in-time (JIT) A system in which materials arrive exactly when they are needed for production, rather than being stored onsite. p. 463

K

key person life insurance A term insurance policy that names the company as beneficiary. p. 559

knowledge The combined talents and skills of the workforce. p. 34

knowledge management (KM) The process of researching, gathering, organizing, and sharing an organization's collective knowledge to improve productivity, foster innovation, and gain competitive advantage. p. 111

knowledge worker A worker who develops or uses knowledge, contributing to and benefiting from information used in performing various tasks, including planning, acquiring, searching, analyzing, organizing, storing, programming, producing, distributing, marketing, or selling functions. p. 97

L

labour Economic contributions of people. p. 33

labour union An organization that represents workers in dealing with management over issues involving wages, hours, and working conditions. p. 349

law of large numbers Insurance companies' predictions of the likelihood that a peril will occur, used to calculate premiums. p. 557

laws The rules of conduct in a society created and enforced by a controlling authority, usually the government. p. 573

leader pricing The strategy of pricing products below the normal markup or even below cost to attract customers to a store where they would not otherwise shop. p. 411

leadership The relationship between a leader and the followers who want real changes resulting in outcomes that reflect their shared purposes (leading people). p. 248

leadership style The relatively consistent way that individuals in leadership positions attempt to influence the behaviour of others. p. 254

leading The process of guiding and motivating others toward the achievement of organizational goals. p. 254

lean manufacturing Streamlining production by eliminating steps in the production process that do not add benefits that customers are willing to pay for. p. 463

legitimate power Power that is derived from an individual's position in an organization. p. 254

leveraged buyout (LBO) A corporate takeover financed by large amounts of borrowed money; can be done by outside investors or by a company's own management. p. 229

liabilities What a company owes to its creditors; also called *debts*. p. 483

licensing The legal process whereby a company agrees to allow another company to use a manufacturing process, trademark, patent, trade secret, or other proprietary knowledge in exchange for the payment of a royalty. p. 140

limited decision making Situation in which a consumer has previous product experience but is unfamiliar with the current brands available. p. 383

limited liability partnership (LLP) In a limited liability partnership, each individual partner is protected from responsibility for the acts of other partners, and each party's liability is limited to harm resulting from that party's own actions. p. 218

limited partners Partners whose liability for the company's business obligations is limited to the amount of their investment. They help to finance the business and/or promote the business, but do not participate in the company's day-to-day operations. p. 218

limited partnership A partnership with one or more general partners who have unlimited liability, and one or more limited partners whose liability is limited to the amount of their investments. p. 218

line of credit An agreement between a bank and a business or person that specifies the maximum amount of short-term borrowing the bank will make available to that business or person. p. 549

line organization An organizational structure with direct, clear lines of authority and communication flowing from the top managers downward. p. 286

line positions All positions in the organization directly concerned with producing goods and services and directly connected from top to bottom. p. 286

line-and-staff organization An organizational structure that includes both line and staff positions. p. 286

liquidity The speed with which an asset can be converted to cash. p. 487

liquidity ratios Ratios that measure a company's ability to pay its short-term debts as they come due. p. 493

local area network (LAN) A network that connects computers at one site, enabling the computer users to exchange data and share the use of hardware and software from a variety of computer manufacturers. p. 104

local union A branch or unit of a national union that represents workers at a specific plant or in a specific geographic area. p. 350

logistics The management of the materials and services as they flow through an organization. p. 456

long-term forecasts Projections of a company's activities and the funding for those activities over a period that is longer than a year, typically 2 to 10 years. p. 544

long-term liabilities Claims that come due more than one year after the date of the balance sheet. p. 488

loss leader A product priced below cost as part of a leader pricing strategy. p. 411

loyalty cards Cards issued by a manufacturer, service organization, or retailer that give discounts to loyal and frequent shoppers. p. 390

M

macroeconomics The sub-area of economics that focuses on the economy as a whole by looking at aggregate data for large groups of people, companies, or products. p. 32

make-or-buy decision The determination by a company of whether to make its own production materials or buy them from outside sources. p. 453

managed service providers (MSPs) The next generation of ASPs, offering customization and expanded capabilities such as business processes and complete management of the network servers. p. 110

management The process of guiding the development, maintenance, and allocation of resources to attain organizational goals. p. 248

management by objectives (MBO) A systematic approach where individuals are given clear, specific objectives and goals to achieve that are consistent with those of the organization. p. 318

management of information systems (MIS) A discipline that involves the management of people, process, and technology around the care of information. p. 94

management support system (MSS) An information system that uses the internal master database to perform high-level analyses that help managers make better decisions. p. 100

managerial accounting Accounting that provides financial information that managers inside the organization can use to evaluate and make decisions about current and future operations. p. 478

managerial hierarchy The levels of management within an organization; typically includes top, middle, and supervisory management. p. 280

manufacturer A producer; an organization that converts raw materials to finished products. p. 415

manufacturer brand A brand that is owned by a national or regional manufacturer; the products are widely distributed. p. 402

manufacturing resource planning II (MRPII) A complex, computerized system that integrates data from many departments to allow managers to forecast and assess the impact of production plans on profitability more accurately. p. 455

market economy An economic system based on competition in the marketplace and private ownership of the factors of production (resources); also known as the *private enterprise system* or *capitalism*. p. 35

market segmentation The process of separating, identifying, and evaluating the layers of a market to design a target market. p. 384

market structure The number of suppliers in a market. p. 38

marketable securities Short-term investments that are easily converted into cash. p. 546

marketing The process of discovering the needs and wants of potential buyers and customers and then providing goods and services that meet or exceed their expectations. p. 370

marketing concept Identifying consumer needs and then producing the goods or services that will satisfy them while making a profit for the organization. p. 370

marketing intermediaries Organizations that assist in moving goods and services from producers to end users. p. 416

marketing mix The blend of product offering, pricing, promotional methods, and distribution system that brings a specific group of consumers superior value. p. 377

marketing research The process of planning, collecting, and analyzing data relevant to a marketing decision. p. 387

markup pricing A method of pricing in which a certain percentage (the markup) is added to the product's cost to arrive at the price. p. 414

Maslow's hierarchy of needs A theory of motivation developed by Abraham Maslow; holds that humans have five levels of needs and act to satisfy their unmet needs. At the base of the hierarchy are fundamental physiological needs, followed in order by safety, social, esteem, and self-actualization needs. p. 311

mass customization A manufacturing process in which goods are mass produced up to a point and then custom tailored to the needs or desires of individual customers. p. 447

mass production The ability to manufacture many identical goods at once. p. 447

master brand A brand that is so dominant that customers think of it immediately when a product category is mentioned. p. 402

materials requirement planning (MRP) A computerized system of controlling the flow or resources and inventory. A master schedule is used to ensure that the materials, labour, and equipment needed for production are at the right places in the right amounts at the right times. p. 454

matrix structure (project management) An organizational structure that combines functional and product departmentalization by bringing together people from different functional areas of the organization to work on a special project. p. 287

mechanistic organization An organizational structure that is characterized by a relatively high degree of job specialization, rigid departmentalization, many layers of management, narrow spans of control, centralized decision-making, and a long chain of command. p. 283

mediation A method of attempting to settle labour issues in which a specialist (the mediator) tries to persuade management and the union to adjust or settle their dispute. pp. 353, 575

mentoring A form of on-the-job training in which a senior manager or other experienced employee provides job- and career-related information to a protégé. p. 344

Mercosur Trade agreement between Brazil, Argentina, Uruguay, Paraguay, and Venezuela. p. 137

merger The combination of two or more companies to form a new company, which often takes on a new corporate identity. p. 228

metropolitan area network (MAN) A network that covers a larger geographic area than a LAN, but generally smaller than a WAN. p. 105

microeconomics The sub area of economics that focuses on individual parts of the economy such as households or companies. p. 32

middle management Managers who design and carry out tactical plans in specific areas of the company. p. 253

mission An organization's purpose and reason for existing; its long-term goals. p. 251

mission statement A clear, concise articulation of how the company intends to achieve its vision—how it is different from its competition and the keys to its success. pp. 200, 251

mixed economies Economies that combine several economic systems; for example, an economy where the government owns certain industries but others are owned by the private sector. p. 37

monetary policy The measures taken by the Bank of Canada to regulate the amount of money in circulation to influence the economy. p. 50

money Anything that is acceptable as payment for goods and services. p. 510

monopolistic competition A market structure in which many companies offer products that are close substitutes and in which entry is relatively easy. p. 39

monopoly A situation in which there is no competition and the benefits of a free market are lost. p. 21

mortgage bonds Corporate bonds that are secured by property, such as land, equipment, or buildings. p. 521

mortgage loan A long-term loan made against real estate as collateral. p. 552

motivation Something that prompts a person to release his or her energy in a certain direction. p. 308

motivating factors Intrinsic job elements that lead to worker satisfaction. p. 315

multiculturalism The fundamental belief that all citizens are equal regardless of their racial or ethnic backgrounds. p. 69

multinational corporations Corporations that move resources, goods, services, and skills across national boundaries without regard to the country in which their headquarters are located. p. 131

mutual fund A financial service company that pools its investors' funds to buy a selection of securities that meet its stated investment goals. p. 522

N

National Association of Securities Dealers Automated Quotation (NASDAQ) system The first electronic-based stock market and the fastest-growing part of the stock market. p. 528

national debt The accumulated total of all of the federal government's annual budget deficits. p. 51

national union A union that consists of many local unions in a particular industry, skilled trade, or geographic area and thus represents workers throughout an entire country. p. 350

nationalism A sense of national consciousness that boosts the culture and interests of one country over those of all other countries. p. 145

natural resources Commodities that are useful inputs in their natural state. p. 33

need The gap between what is and what is required. p. 308

neoliberalism A set of economic policies that believes that the economy (and therefore social policy) should be market-driven, not government-driven. p. 71

net loss The amount obtained by subtracting all of a company's expenses from its revenues, when the expenses are more than the revenues. p. 491

net profit (net income or net earnings) The amount obtained by subtracting all of a company's expenses from its revenues, when the revenues are more than the expenses. p. 491

net profit margin The ratio of net profit to net sales; also called *return on sales*. It measures the percentage of each sales dollar remaining after all expenses, including taxes, have been deducted. p. 495

net sales The amount left after deducting sales discounts and returns and allowances from gross sales. p. 490

net working capital The amount obtained by subtracting total current liabilities from total current assets; used to measure a company's liquidity. p. 494

niche competitive advantage A company's ability to target and effectively serve a single segment of the market within a limited geographic area. p. 376

non-programmed decisions Responses to infrequent, unforeseen, or very unusual problems and opportunities where the manager does not have a precedent to follow in decision-making. p. 260

North American Free Trade Agreement (NAFTA) A 1993 agreement creating a free-trade zone that includes Canada, Mexico, and the United States. p. 137

not-for-profit organization An organization that exists to achieve some goal other than the usual business goal of profit. p. 13

O

observation research A marketing research method in which the investigator monitors respondents' actions without interacting directly with the respondents; for example, by using cash registers with scanners. p. 388

odd-even (psychological) pricing The strategy of setting a price at an odd number to connote a bargain and at an even number to suggest quality. p. 412

office automation system An information system that uses information technology tools such as word-processing systems, e-mail systems, cell phones, smartphones, pagers, and facsimile (fax) machines to improve communications throughout an organization. p. 102

oligopoly A market structure in which a few companies produce most or all of the output and in which large capital requirements or other factors limit the number of companies. p. 39

one-person corporation A corporation with only one person as the shareholder; common in professional practices (e.g., medical doctors, accountants, or lawyers) and in trades (e.g. plumbers and electricians). p. 224

one-to-one marketing Creating a unique marketing mix for every customer. p. xx

online (real-time) processing A method of updating a database in which data are processed as they become available. p. 99

on-the-job training Training in which the employee learns the job by doing it with guidance from a supervisor or an experienced co-worker. p. 344

open market operations The purchase or sale of Canadian government securities by the Bank of Canada to stimulate or slow down the economy. p. 513

open shop A company where employees do not have to join the union or pay dues or fees to the union; established under right-to-work laws. p. 352

operating budgets Budgets that combine sales forecasts with estimates of production costs and operating expenses to forecast profits. p. 545

operating expenses The expenses of running a business that are not directly related to producing or buying its products. p. 491

operational planning The process of creating specific standards, methods, policies, and procedures that are used in specific functional areas of the organization; helps guide and control the implementation of tactical plans. p. 252

operations management Management of the production process. p. 444

opinion leaders Leaders who influence others. p. 380

options Contracts that entitle holders to buy or sell specified quantities of common shares or other financial instruments at a set price during a specified time. p. 524

organic organization An organizational structure that is characterized by a relatively low degree of job specialization, loose departmentalization, few levels of management, wide spans of control, decentralized decision-making, and a short chain of command. p. 285

organization chart A visual representation of the structured relationships among tasks and the people given the authority to do those tasks. p. 279

organized stock exchanges Organizations on whose premises securities are resold using an auction-style trading system. p. 526

organizing The process of coordinating and allocating a company's resources to carry out its plans. p. 253

orientation Training that prepares a new employee to perform on the job; includes information about job assignments, work rules, equipment, and performance expectations, as well as about company policies, salary and benefits, and parking. p. 334

outsource (outsourcing) The assignment of various functions, such as human resources, accounting, or legal work, to outside organizations. Also refers to the purchase of items from an outside source rather than making them internally. pp. 358, 454

over-the-counter (OTC) market A sophisticated telecommunications network that links dealers and enables them to trade securities. p. 528

owners' equity The total amount of investment in the company minus any liabilities; also called *net worth*. p. 483

P

participative leaders Leaders who share decision making with group members and encourage discussion of issues and alternatives; includes democratic, consensual, and consultative styles. p. 255

partnership An association of two or more persons who agree to operate a business together for profit. p. 218

patent A form of protection (limited monopoly) established by the government for inventors; it gives an inventor the exclusive right to manufacture, use, and sell an invention for 20 years. p. 17

payroll taxes Income taxes that are collected by the employer and remitted to the federal government, usually in the form of a deduction from the employee's pay. p. 21

penetration pricing The strategy of selling new products at low prices in the hope of achieving a large sales volume. p. 411

pension funds Large pools of money set aside by corporations, unions, and governments for later use in paying retirement benefits to their employees or members. p. 515

perception The process by which we select, organize, and interpret stimuli into a meaningful and coherent picture. p. 382

perfect (pure) competition A market structure in which a large number of small companies sell similar products, buyers and sellers have good information, and businesses can be easily opened or closed. p. 38

performance appraisal A comparison of actual performance with expected performance to assess an employee's contributions to the organization. p. 345

peril A hazard or a source of danger. p. 556

perpetual inventory A continuously updated list of inventory levels, orders, sales, and receipts. p. 454

personal selling A face-to-face sales presentation to a prospective customer. p. 423

personality A way of organizing and grouping how an individual reacts to situations. p. 382

physical distribution (logistics) The movement of products from the producer to industrial users and consumers. p. 414

planning The process of deciding what needs to be done to achieve organizational objectives, identifying when and how it will be done, and determining by whom it should be done. p. 249

Porter's Five Forces Model A model that focuses on the five forces that shape competition within an industry. p. 197

postconventional ethics The third stage in the ethical development of individuals in which people adhere to the ethical standards of a mature adult and are less concerned about how others view their behaviour than about how they will judge themselves in the long run; also known as *principled ethics*. p. 78

power The ability to influence others to behave in a particular way. p. 254

preconventional ethics A stage in the ethical development of individuals in which people behave in a childlike manner and make ethical decisions in a calculating, self-centred way, based on the possibility of immediate punishment or reward; also known as *self-centred ethics*. p. 77

preferential tariff A tariff that is lower for some nations than for others. p. 137

preferred shares Equity securities for which the dividend amount is set at the time the shares are issued. p. 554

prestige pricing The strategy of increasing the price of a product so that consumers will perceive it as being of higher quality, status, or value. p. 412

price skimming The strategy of introducing a product with a high initial price and lowering the price over time as the product moves through its life cycle. p. 410

pricing strategy Setting a price based on the demand and cost for a good or service. p. 377

primary data Information collected directly from the original source to get more information about an opportunity or to solve a problem. p. 389

primary market The securities market where new securities are sold to the public, usually with the help of investment bankers. p. 526

principal The amount borrowed by the issuer of a bond; also called *par value*. p. 520

principle of comparative advantage The concept that each country should specialize in the products that it can produce most readily and cheaply and trade those products for ones that other countries can produce more readily and cheaply. p. 136

private corporation A corporation whose number of shareholders is limited, there are normally restrictions on the transfer of shares to third parties, and its shares do not trade on a recognized stock exchange. p. 221

private law The law relating to the relationship between individuals, businesses, or individuals and businesses. p. 574

problem-solving teams Usually members of the same department who meet regularly to suggest ways to improve operations and solve specific problems. p. 291

process departmentalization Departmentalization that is based on the production process used by the organizational unit. p. 278

process layout A facility arrangement in which work flows according to the production process. All workers performing similar tasks are grouped together, and products pass from one workstation to another. p. 451

process manufacturing A production process in which the basic input is broken down into one or more outputs (products). p. 448

producer price index (PPI) An index of the prices paid by producers and wholesalers for various commodities such as raw materials, partially finished goods, and finished products. p. 49

product In marketing, any good or service, along with its perceived attributes and benefits, that creates value for the customer. pp. 370, 402

product (assembly line) layout A facility arrangement in which workstations or departments are arranged in a line with products moving along the line. p. 453

product departmentalization Departmentalization that is based on the goods or services produced or sold by the organizational unit. p. 278

product liability The responsibility of manufacturers and sellers for defects in the products they make and sell. p. 20

product life cycle The pattern of sales and profits over time for a product or product category; consists of an introductory state, growth stage, maturity stage, and decline stage (that ultimately results in death of the product or product category). p. 406

product strategy Taking the good or service and selecting a brand name, packaging, colours, a warranty, accessories, and a service program. p. 377

production The creation of products and services by turning inputs, such as natural resources, raw materials, human resources, and capital, into outputs, which are products and services. p. 444

production orientation An approach in which a company works to lower production costs without a strong desire to satisfy the needs of customers. p. 371

production planning The aspect of operations management in which the company considers its resources and its own strategic goals in an effort to determine the best production methods. p. 446

production process The way in which a good is made. p. 447

professional liability insurance Insurance designed to protect top corporate management, who have been the target of malpractice lawsuits. p. 561

profit The money left over after all expenses are paid. p. 13

profit maximization A pricing objective that entails getting the largest possible profit from a product by producing it for as long as the revenue from selling it exceeds the cost of producing it. p. 408

profitability ratios Ratios that measure how well a company is using its resources to generate profit and how efficiently it is being managed. p. 495

pro forma financial statements Projected financial statements of future values. p. 204

program evaluation and review technique (PERT) A scheduling tool that is similar to the CPM method but assigns three time estimates for each activity (optimistic, most probable, and pessimistic); it allows managers to anticipate delays and potential problems and schedule accordingly. p. 460

programmed decisions Decisions made in response to frequently occurring routine situations. p. 260

programmed instruction A form of computer-assisted off-the-job training. p. 344

promotion (in marketing) The attempt by marketers to inform, persuade, or remind consumers and industrial users to engage in the exchange process. p. 422

promotion strategy The unique combination of personal selling, advertising, publicity, and sales promotion to stimulate the target market to buy a product or service. p. 378

promotional mix The combination of advertising, personal selling, sales promotion, and public relations used to promote a product. p. 423

property taxes Taxes that are imposed on real and personal property based on the assessed value of the property. p. 21

protectionism The policy of protecting home industries from outside competition by establishing artificial barriers such as tariffs and quotas. p. 136

protective tariffs Tariffs that are imposed to make imports less attractive to buyers than domestic products are. p. 148

provincial health care Health insurance programs provided by the provinces. p. 559

psychographic segmentation The differentiation of markets by personality or lifestyle. p. 386

public corporation A corporation whose shares are widely held and available to the general public. p. 220

public law The law relating to the relationship between the individual or business and the government (or its agencies). p. 574

public relations Any communication or activity designed to win goodwill or prestige for a company or person. p. 424

pull strategy A promotional strategy in which a manufacturer focuses on stimulating consumer demand for its product rather than on trying to persuade wholesalers or retailers to carry the product. p. 425

purchasing The process of buying production inputs from various sources; also called *procurement*. p. 453

purchasing power The value of what money can buy. p. 48

pure monopoly A market structure in which a single company accounts for all industry sales and in which there are barriers to entry. p. 40

push strategy A promotional strategy in which a manufacturer uses aggressive personal selling and trade advertising to convince a wholesaler or retailer to carry and sell its merchandise. p. 425

Q

quality Goods and services that meet customer expectations by providing reliable performance. p. 461

quality assurance More comprehensive than quality control, it strives for doing the job right the first time. p. 461

quality control The process of creating standards for quality, producing goods that meet them, and measuring finished products and services against them. p. 461

quality of life The general level of human happiness based on such things as life expectancy, educational standards, health, sanitation, and leisure time. p. 12

R

ratio analysis The calculation and interpretation of financial ratios using data taken from the company's financial statements to assess its condition and performance. p. 493

real self-image How an individual actually perceives him- or herself. p. 382

recession A decline in GDP that lasts for at least two consecutive quarters. p. 46

recruitment The attempt to find and attract qualified applicants in the external labour market. p. 340

re-engineering The complete redesign of business structures and processes to improve operations. p. 295

reference groups Formal and informal groups that influence buyer behaviour. p. 380

referent power Power that is derived from an individual's personal charisma and the respect and/or admiration the individual inspires. p. 254

relatedness (ERG theory) The concern for interpersonal relations. p. 313

relationship management The practice of building, maintaining, and enhancing interactions with customers and other parties to develop long-term satisfaction through mutually beneficial partnerships. p. 53

relationship marketing A strategy that focuses on forging long-term partnerships with customers by offering value and providing customer satisfaction. p. 372

retailers Companies that sell goods to consumers and to industrial users for their own consumption. p. 417

retained earnings (in accounting) Profits that have been reinvested in a company. p. 554

retained earnings (in financial management) The amounts left over from profitable operations since the company's beginning; equal to total profits minus all dividends paid to shareholders. p. 488

return The opportunity for profit. p. 543

return on equity (ROE) The ratio of net profit to total owners' equity; measures the return that owners receive on their investment in the company. p. 495

revenue(s) (also called sales and income) The money a company earns from providing services or selling goods to customers. pp. 6, 489

revolving credit agreement (revolving line of credit) A line of credit that allows the borrower to have access to funds again once it has been repaid. p. 550

reward power Power that is derived from an individual's control over rewards. p. 254

risk (financial) The potential for loss or the chance that an investment will not achieve the expected level of return. p. 543

risk (general) The potential for losing resources, most commonly time and money, or otherwise not being able to accomplish an organization's goals. p. 13

risk management The process of identifying and evaluating risks, and selecting and managing techniques to adapt to risk exposures. p. 556

risk–return trade-off A basic principle in finance that holds that the higher the risk, the greater the return that is required. p. 543

robotics The technology involved in designing, constructing, and operating computer-controlled machines that can perform tasks independently. p. 464

routine response behaviour Purchase of low-cost, frequently bought items with little search or decision making. p. 383

routing The aspect of production control that involves setting out the workflow—the sequence of machines and operations through which the product or service progresses from start to finish. p. 458

S

sales promotions Marketing events or sales efforts—not including advertising, personal selling, and public relations— that stimulate buying. p. 423

sales taxes Taxes that are levied on goods and services when they are sold; calculated as a percentage of the price. p. 21

scheduling The aspect of production control that involves specifying and controlling the time required for each step in the production process. p. 458

scientific management A system of management developed by Frederick W. Taylor and based on four principles: developing a scientific approach for each element of a job, scientifically selecting and training workers, encouraging cooperation between workers and managers, and dividing work and responsibility between management and workers according to who can better perform a particular task. p. 309

seasonal unemployment Unemployment that occurs during specific seasons in certain industries. p. 48

secondary data Information that has already been collected for a project, other than the current one, that can help to understand a situation or solve a problem. p. 389

secondary market The securities market where old (already issued) securities are bought and sold, or traded, among investors. p. 526

secured bonds Corporate bonds for which specific assets have been pledged as collateral. p. 521

secured loans Loans for which the borrower is required to pledge specific assets as collateral, or security. p. 550

securities Investment certificates issued by corporations or governments that represent either equity or debt. p. 518

selection The process of determining which persons in the applicant pool possess the qualifications necessary to be successful on the job. p. 341

selection interview An in-depth discussion of an applicant's work experiences, skills and abilities, education, and career interests. p. 342

selective distribution A distribution system in which a manufacturer selects a limited number of dealers in an area (but more than one or two) to market its products. p. 422

selective exposure The process of deciding which stimuli to notice and which to ignore. p. 382

self-concept How people perceive themselves. p. 382

self-managed work teams Teams without formal supervision that plan, select alternatives, and evaluate their own performance. p. 291

services Intangible offerings of businesses that can't be held, touched, or stored. p. 12

share or stock dividends Payments to shareholders in the form of more shares; can replace or supplement cash dividends. p. 554

shareholders The owners of a corporation, who hold shares of stock that provide certain rights; also known as *stockholders*. p. 222

shop steward An elected union official who represents union members to management when workers have issues. p. 350

shopping products Items that are bought after considerable planning, including brand-to-brand and store-to-store comparisons of price, suitability, and style. p. 405

short-term forecasts Projections of revenues, costs of goods, and operating expenses over a one-year period. p. 543

simulation A scaled-down version or mock-up of equipment, process, or work environment. p. 344

Six Sigma A quality control process that relies on defining what needs to be done to ensure quality, measuring and analyzing production results statistically, and finding ways of improving and controlling quality. p. 462

small business A business that is independently managed, is owned by an individual or a small group of investors, is based locally, and is not a dominant company in its industry. p. 168

social investing The practice of limiting investments to securities of companies that behave in accordance with the investor's beliefs about ethical and social responsibility. p. 73

social marketing The application of marketing techniques to social issues and causes. p. 378

social responsibility The concern of businesses for the welfare of society as a whole; consists of obligations beyond those required by law or contracts. p. 70

socialism An economic system in which the basic industries are owned either by the government itself or by the private sector under strong government control. p. 37

socialization process The passing down of cultural norms and values to children. p. 381

sole proprietorship A business that is established, owned, operated, and often financed by one person. p. 216

span of control The number of employees a manager directly supervises; also called span of management. p. 281

specialization The degree to which tasks are subdivided into smaller jobs. p. 277

specialty products Items for which consumers search long and hard, and for which they refuse to accept substitutes. p. 405

speculative risk The chance of either loss or gain, without insurance against the possible loss. p. 556

staff positions Positions in an organization held by individuals who provide the administrative and support services that line employees need to achieve the company's goals. p. 286

stakeholders Individuals, groups, or organizations to whom a business has a responsibility: employees, customers, suppliers, investors, and the general public. p. 72

standard of living A country's output of goods and services that people can buy with the money they have. p. 12

statement of cash flows A financial statement that provides a summary of the money flowing into and out of a company during a certain period, typically one year. p. 492

statement of comprehensive income See *income statement*. p. 489

statement of earnings See Income. p. 489

statement of financial position See *balance sheet*. p. 485

statute law (or statutory law) Written law enacted by a legislature (municipal, provincial, or federal). p. 574

stock dividends See share dividends. p. 554

stockbroker A person who is licensed to buy and sell securities on behalf of clients. p. 525

strategic alliance A cooperative agreement between business companies; sometimes called a *strategic partnership*. p. 53

strategic channel alliances One manufacturer using another manufacturer's previously established channel to distribute its goods. p. 418

strategic giving The practice of tying philanthropy closely to the corporate mission or goals and targeting donations to regions where a company operates. p. 82

strategic planning The process of creating long-range (one to five years), broad goals for the organization and determining what resources will be needed to accomplish those goals. p. 250

strict liability A concept in product-liability laws under which a manufacturer or seller is liable for any personal injury or property damage caused by defective products or packaging that do not meet industry standards. p. 20

structural unemployment Unemployment that is caused by a mismatch between available jobs and the skills of available workers in an industry or a region; not related to the business cycle. p. 48

supervisory management (operational management) Managers who design and carry out operational plans for the ongoing daily activities of the company. p. 253

supply The quantity of a good or service that businesses will make available at various prices. p. 42

supply chain The entire sequence of securing inputs, producing goods, and delivering goods to customers. p. 455

supply chain management The process of smoothing transitions along the supply chain so that the company can satisfy its customers with quality products and services; focuses on developing tighter bonds with suppliers. p. 456

supply curve A graph showing the quantity of a good or service that a business will make available at various prices. p. 42

survey research A marketing research method in which data are gathered from respondents in person, by telephone, by mail, at a mall, or through the Internet to obtain facts, opinions, and attitudes. p. 388

SWOT analysis A SWOT analysis looks at the <u>S</u>trengths and <u>W</u>eaknesses of the company itself and the <u>O</u>pportunities and <u>T</u>hreats for the company in its external environment. p. 197

T

T-account An account that is often used to analyze financial transactions; T-accounts are named as such because they resemble a T. p. 484

tactical planning The process of beginning to implement a strategic plan by addressing issues of coordination and allocating resources to different parts of the organization; has a shorter time frame (less than one year) and more specific objectives than strategic planning. p. 252

target for the overnight rate The signal to the major participants in the money market as to what the Bank of Canada is aiming for when participants borrow and lend one-day funds to each other. p. 513

target market The specific group of consumers toward which a company directs its marketing efforts. p. 373

target return on investment A pricing objective where the price of a product is set so as to give the company the desired profitability in terms of return on its money. p. 409

tariff A tax imposed on imported goods. p. 148

technical skills A manager's specialized areas of knowledge and expertise, as well as the ability to apply that knowledge. p. 262

telecommuting An arrangement in which employees work at home and are linked to the office by phone, fax, and computer or other communication devices. p. 322

term deposits Deposits at a bank or other financial institution that pay interest but cannot be withdrawn on demand. p. 511

term loan A business loan with a maturity of more than one year; can be unsecured or secured. p. 552

theft insurance A broad insurance coverage that protects business against losses for an act of stealing. p. 560

Theory X A management style, formulated by Douglas McGregor, which is based on a pessimistic view of human nature and assumes that the average person dislikes work, will avoid it if possible, prefers to be directed, avoids responsibility, and wants security above all. p. 313

Theory Y A management style, formulated by Douglas McGregor, that is based on a relatively optimistic view of human nature; assumes that the average person wants to work, accepts responsibility, is willing to help solve problems, and can be self-directed and self-controlled. p. 313

Theory Z A theory developed by William Ouchi that combines North American and Japanese business practices by emphasizing long-term employment, slow career development, moderate specialization, group decision-making, individual responsibility, relatively informal control over the employee, and concern for workers. p. 314

time deposits Money invested for a specific period of time. p. 511

top management The highest level of managers; includes CEOs, presidents, and vice-presidents, who develop strategic plans and address long-range issues. p. 253

tort A civil or private act that harms other people or their property. p. 18

total cost The sum of the fixed costs and the variable costs. p. 412

total profit Total revenue minus total cost. p. 412

total quality management (TQM) The use of quality principles in all aspects of a company's production and operations. p. 461

total revenue The selling price per unit times the number of units sold. p. 412

trade credit The extension of credit by the seller to the buyer between the time the buyer receives the goods or services and when it pays for them. p. 549

trade deficit An unfavourable balance of trade that occurs when a country imports more than it exports. p. 133

trade surplus A favourable balance of trade that occurs when a country exports more than it imports. p. 133

trademark A legally exclusive design, name, or other identifying mark associated with a company's brand. pp. 17, 402

training and development Activities that provide learning situations in which an employee acquires additional knowledge or skills to increase job performance. p. 343

transaction-processing system (TPS) An information system that handles the daily business operations of a company. The system receives and organizes raw data from internal and external sources for storage in a database using either batch or online processing. p. 99

transfer payments Payments made to the provinces and territories by the federal government to help deliver required services such as health and education and to help equalize the wealth across Canada. p. 14

trial balance A list of each account and its net balance. p. 485

trust company A financial institution that conducts the same activities as a bank but can also administer estates, trusts, pension plans, and agency contracts. p. 515

U

underwriting The process of buying securities from corporations and governments and reselling them to the public; the main activity of investment bankers. pp. 525, 557

unemployment rate The percentage of the total labour force that is not working but is actively looking for work. p. 48

union shop A company where non-union workers can be hired but must then join the union. p. 352

unsecured loans Loans for which the borrower does not have to pledge specific assets as security. p. 549

unsought products Products that either are unknown to the potential buyer or are known but the buyer does not actively seek them. p. 405

utilitarianism A philosophy that focuses on the consequences of an action to determine whether it is right or wrong; holds that an action that affects the majority adversely is morally wrong. p. 76

V

value pricing A pricing strategy in which the target market is offered a high-quality product at a fair price and with good service. p. 410

value-stream mapping A routing technique that represents the flow of materials and information from suppliers through the factory and to customers. p. 458

variable costs Costs that change with different levels of output; for example, wages and cost of raw materials. p. 412

venture capital Financing obtained from investment companies that specialize in financing small, high-growth companies and receive an ownership interest and a voice in management in return for their money. p. 175

vertical merger or acquisition Mergers or acquisitions involving companies at different stages of the supply chain in the same industry; done to gain control over supplies of resources or to gain access to different markets. p. 229

virtual corporation A network of independent companies linked by information technology to share skills, costs, and access to one another's markets; allows the companies to come together quickly to exploit rapidly changing opportunities. p. 295

virtual private networks (VPNs) Private corporate networks connected over a public network, such as the Internet. VPNs include strong security measures to allow only authorized users to access the network. p. 108

vision statement A clear, concise picture of the company's future direction in terms of its values and purpose that is used to guide and inspire. p. 200

volume segmentation The differentiation of markets based on the amount of the product purchased. p. 387

W

want The gap between what is and what is desired. p. 308

warranty A guarantee of the quality of a good or service. p. 302

whistleblower An employee, a former employee, or any other member of an organization who reports misconduct by others in the organization to those who have the power to take corrective action. p. 81

wholesalers Companies that sell finished goods to retailers, manufacturers, and institutions. p. 417

wide area network (WAN) A network that connects computers at different sites via telecommunications media such as phone lines, satellites, and microwaves. p. 104

work groups The groups that share resources and coordinate efforts to help members better perform their individual jobs. p. 290

work teams Like a work group, but also requires the pooling of knowledge, skills, abilities, and resources to achieve a common goal. p. 291

workers' compensation Payments to cover the expenses of job-related injuries and diseases, including medical costs, rehabilitation, and job retraining if necessary. p. 559

World Bank An international bank that offers low-interest loans, as well as advice and information, to developing nations. p. 144

World Trade Organization (WTO) An organization established by the Uruguay Round in 1994 to oversee international trade, reduce trade barriers, and resolve disputes among member nations. p. 143

endnotes

Prologue

1. Marlene Caroselli, *Interpersonal Skills*, (Thomson South-Western, a part of The Thomson Corporation, 2003), The section "Getting Ahead in Business and Life" is also adapted from the above text.

2. The Persuasion self-test was created by the authors and from the following sources: *Persuade Others to Follow Your Way of Thinking*, http://www.winstonbrill.com/ bril001/html/article_index/articles/251-300/article271_body.html; *Six Unique Ways to Persuade Others*, http://www.micaworld.com/pdfs/Six%20Unique%20%20Ways%20%20Persuade%20Others.pdf; *Strategies of Influence and Persuasion*, Kenrick Cleveland, http://www.maxpersuasion.com; http://www.gowerpub.com/pdf/imppeopleconstch1.pdf; *Power Persuasion—How to Persuade People*, http://www.1000ventures.com/business_guide/crosscutings/persuading_people.html; and Wolf J. Rinke, Ph.D., CSP, *How to Persuade and Influence People*, #554 Innovative Leader Volume 11, Number 6, (2002, June) http://www.winstonbrill.com/bril001/html/article_index/articles/551-600/article554_body.html.

3. The Office Politics scale was developed by the authors and from the following sources: *Don't Sabotage Your Success!—Make Office Politics Work*, Ginsburg Wood, Karen, http://www.atlasbooks.com/markplc/00492.htm; Broderick, Cynthia A., *Play the Office Politics Game*, http://www.bankrate.com/brm/news/advice/19990914a.asp; Toupin, Edward B. *The Fairness of Office Politics … Integrity and Political Motivation!* http://www.hotlib.com/articles/show.php?t=The_Fairness_of_Office_Politics_...Integrity_and_Political_Motivation!; Vogt, Peter, *Fly Under the Radar to Absorb Delicate Office Politics*, MonsterTRAK Career Coach, http://content.monstertrak.monster.com/resources/archive/onthejob/politics; *The New Office Politics: We've Seen the Enemy at Work, and Sometimes It's Us*, Audrey Edwards, *Essence*, (2005, March), http://www.findarticles.com/p/articles/mi_ml264/is_11_35/ai_n11830673; *Assessment—Office Politics*, First Edition, http://www.course.com/downloads/courseilt/e-assessments/0619254394.pdf; and *Play Office Politics and Keep Your Soul*, http://www.createyourvision.com/playofficepolitics.htm.

4. The section on planning is adapted from: *Investing in Your Future* (Thomson South-Western, a part of The Thomson Corporation, 2007), pp. 1–10.

5. The material on Don't Let Go is adapted from Abby Marks-Beale, *Success Skills: Strategies for Study and Lifelong Learning* (Thomson South-Western, a part of The Thomson Corporation, 2007).

6. The Time Management scale was created by the authors and: *Time Management Quiz*, http://www.nus.edu.sg/osa/guidance/quiz/timemgmtquiz.html; *Manage Your Time in Ten Steps*, http://www.familyeducation.com/article/0,1120,1-263,00.html; *TimeManagement Quiz*, http://tools.monster.com/quizzes/pareto; *Stress Management, Better Health Channel*, http://www.betterhealth.vic.gov.au/bhcv2/bhcsite.nsf/pages/quiz_manage_stress?; *Stress Management Quiz*, http://www.betterhealth.vic.gov.au/bhcv2/bhcsite.nsf/pages/quiz_manage_stress?; *Time Management*, http://uwadmnweb.uwyo.edu/RanchRecr/handbook/time_management.htm; and *Time Management: Importance of Good Practice*, www.accel-team.com/techniques/time_management.html.

7. The Ability to Manage Money scale was created by your authors and: *Quiz—Can You Manage Money?*, http://collegeanduniversity.net/collegeinfo/index.cfm?catid=20&pageid=2339&affid=75; *Boston.com/Business/YourMoney*, http://www.boston.com/business/personalfinance/articles/2005/04/03can_you_manage_your_own_month?mode=PF; *Psychology of Money Management*, http://www.uwec.edu/counsel/pubs/Money.htm; *Managing Your Money*, http://www.nelliemae.com/managingmoney; *The Importance of Managing Money*, http://www.mtstcil.org/skills/budget-12.html; and *How Do You Rate as a Money Manager?*, http://cahe.nmsu.edu/pubs/_g/G-219.pdf.

8. The self-quiz on How to Study was prepared by the authors using: *EDinformatics–Education for the Information Age*, http://www.edinformatics.com/education/howtostudy.htm; *The Manila Times* (2004, March 20), http://www.manilatimes.net/national/2004/mar/20/yehey/life/20040320lif2.html; *Ten Traps of Studying—Improving Your Studying Skills—CAPS—UNC—Chapel Hill*, http://caps.unc.edu/TenTraps.html; and *Language Study Skills*, http://www.usingenglish.com/study-skills.html.

9. Julie Griffin Levitt. *Your Career: How to Make It Happen*, 5th edition (Thomson South-Western, a part of The Thomson Corporation, 2006), pp. 2–4.

10. The Assertiveness test was prepared by the authors using: *Test Your Assertive Level*, http://www.hodu.com/assertiveness-skills.shtml; *Assertive Action Plan*, http://www.headinjury.com/assertplan.html; *Assertiveness*, http://www.coping.org/relations/assert.htm; *Perception of Assertiveness as a Function of Tag Questions*, http://www.ycp.edu/besc/Journal2002/paper%201.htm; and *Assertion Training*, http://front.csulb.edu/tstevens/assertion_training.htm.

11. Levitt, p. 36.

12. Barbara Ling, http://www.riseway.com.

13. CBS, "Web Largely Untapped by Job Seekers," http://MarketWatch.com (accessed 2003, January 24).

14. Levitt, *Your Career*, 100.

15. ___, pp. 189–205.

16. ___, p. 205.

Introduction

1. http://www.theglobeandmail.com/report-on-business/rob-magazine/top-1000/the-goodbad-news-banks-and-resources-rule/article4371889.
2. Factors adapted from Fry, Stoner, and Hattwick, *Business: An Integrative Framework* (New York: McGraw-Hill, 1998).

Chapter 1

1. Service Canada, Canada Summer Jobs 2011; Service Canada, Canada Summer Jobs 2012—Frequently Asked Questions; Service Canada, Grant Application—Youth Grants 2011; Canada News Centre, Government of Canada invites employers to apply for Canada Summer Jobs 2010: Canada's Economic Action Plan creates jobs for students from coast to coast to coast; *The Globe and Mail* (2011, July 7), "Crushing Weight of Student Debt"; *Brantford Expositor* (2011, June 15), "Students get grants to create own jobs"; Public Service Commission of Newfoundland, "We're Hiring"; *Sun News*, July 25th, 2011, "Sun still not shining on student summer job market."
2. Department of Finance Canada, "Federal Transfers to Provinces and Territories," http://fin.gc.ca/access/fedprov-eng.asp (accessed 2012, December 5).
3. Walz, Genesta, "Ottawa investing $53M in clean energy projects," *Calgary Herald* (2011, July 29), p. B3.
4. Lertzman D. and H. Vredenburg, 2005, "Indigenous Peoples, Resource Extraction and Sustainable Development," *Journal of Business Ethics*, 56/3: 239–254.
5. Wilson, E.O.: 1999, *Consilience: The Unity of Knowledge*, New York: Vintage Books.
6. http://footprintnetwork.org/en/index.php/GFN/page/world_footprint/.
7. http://ucatlas.ucsc.edu/income.php.
8. Payne, D.M. and C.A. Raiborn: 2001, "Sustainable Development, The Ethics Support the Economics," *Journal of Business Ethics*, 32: 157–168.
9. DesJardins, J., 1998, "Corporate Environmental Responsibility," *Journal of Business Ethics*, 17: 825–838.
10. "Ottawa investing $53 M in clean energy projects," *Calgary Herald* (2011, July 29), p. B3.

11. Foreign Affairs and International Trade Canada, "Canadian Foreign Service Institute (CFSI)," http://international.gc.ca/ifait-iaeci/index.aspx?view=d (accessed 2011, December 8).

Chapter 2

1. Beanie Shop, Q&A, Tripod; Tripod, Peanut the Elephant; eBay.com, Beanie Babies Buying Guide, eBay.ca, Search results: Peanut Royal, SmartCollecting.com, October 08, 2000, Peanut the Royal Blue Elephant Sells for $3005; *New York Times*, July 5, 1998: CRIME; A World Gone Beanie Mad!; Badfads.com, Beanie babies; CBS News, (2009, February 11). Will Beanie Baby Craze Return?; Living in the 90s, (2010, April 15). Beanie Baby Craze.
2. Lester Thurow, "Changing the Nature of Capitalism," in *Rethinking the Future*, ed. Rowan Gibson (London: Nicholas Brealey, 1997), 228.
3. Trading Economics, "Canada's GDP Annual Growth Rate," http://www.tradingeconomics.com/canada/gdp-growth-annual (accessed on 2011, November 1).
4. Statistics Canada, "Manufacturing," http://www41.statcan.gc.ca/2009/4005/cybac4005_000-eng.htm (accessed 2011, November 1).
5. Peter Burrows, "Notebooks without Wide Margins," *Business Week*, September 5, 2005, http://www.businessweek.com, Jason Dean and Pui-Wing Tam, "The Laptop Trail," *Wall Street Journal* (2005, June 9), pp. B1, B8; and HP website, http://www.hp.com.
6. Statistics Canada, "Canada: Economic and financial data," http://www40.statcan.ca/l01/cst01/DSBBCAN-eng.htm (accessed on 2011, November 1).
7. Ray Turchansky (for Postmedia News), "World facing crisis of confidence on three economic fronts," *Calgary Herald* (2011, October 16), p. F3.
8. Pui-Wing Tam and Ann Zimmerman, "Wal-Mart's HP Elves," *Wall Street Journal* (2005, December 15), pp. B1, B4.
9. Phred Dvorak and Evan Ramstad, "TV Marriage: Behind Sony-Samsung Rivalry, an Unlikely Alliance Develops," *Wall Street Journal* (2006, January 3), pp. A1, A6.

10. James McGregor, "Advantage, China," *Washington Post*, (2005, July 31), p. B1.

Chapter 3

1. *The Globe and Mail*, (2011, May 29), "Pumping green into the grid"; *Watershed Sentinel*, (2009, April 4), "Bullfrog Power in BC"; BullfrogPower.com, Downie Interview; Bullfrogpower.com, Powered, The Straight Goods, Powell River, (2010, March 28). Bullfrog Power or Bull# percent@& Scam; http://Smartcanucks.ca, (2008, March 26). Bullfrog Power: "Taxing our Guilt."
2. "100-Calorie Snack Packs: Fad or Diet Tool?" *San Diego Union-Tribune*, (2005, October 12). pp. E1, E3.
3. Morrow, A. and Alphonso, C. "Women at Work: Still Behind on the Bottom Line," *The Globe and Mail*, http://theglobeandmail.com/news/national/women-at-work-still-behind-on-the-bottom-line/article1699176 (accessed 2011, November 10).
4. Roger Schilling, "Reaching Those Female Fans," *American Coin-Op* (2005 September), pp. 31–37.
5. *Globe and Mail*, "We're Getting Older … and Younger," (accessed 2012, May 30), pp. A8–A9.
6. "Generation Y Defined," *On-Point Marketing and Promotions*, http://onpoint-marketing.com/generation-y.htm (accessed 2006, May 23); and "Q&As from Howe and Strauss, authors of Millennials Rising," *MillennialsRising.com*, http://millenialsrising.com, (accessed 2006, May 23).
7. Desiree J. Hanford, "Long-Term Success of E-Tailers Will Hinge on 'Echo Boomers'," *Wall Street Journal*, July 27, 2005, p. B3A; and Jilian Mincer, "Generation Y Is New Territory For Financial-Service Marketers," *Wall Street Journal* (2005, September 26), p. B3A.
8. Caron Alarab, "Generation Y Spending Trends: Gotta Have It," *Detroit Free Press* (2005, August 25). http://freep.com/money/tech/youngcomps25e_20050825.htm.
9. Katherine Yung, "Generation Xers Hit Middle Age," *Houston Chronicle*, (2005, July 10), p. 3.
10. Greene, "When We're All 64," p. R1; Johnson, "Half of Boomers Hit the 50 Mark," p. 18; and Kevin Kelly, "Aging Buyers Dictate Trends," *Ward's Auto World* (2005, June).

11. Section based on Andrea Coombes, "The Case for Older Workers: Value," *San Diego Union-Tribune* (2006, January 29), p. H7; Peter Coy, "Old. Smart. Productive." *Business Week* (2005, June 27), http://businessweek.com; Ellen M. Heffes, "Dramatic Workforce Trends Require Planning Now," *Financial Executive* (2005 July/August), pp. 18–21; Patricia Kitchen, "The 4 Generation Workplace, It's Not What It Used to Be," *Newsday* (2005, August 14), p. A52; and Jennifer J. Salopek, "The New Brain Drain," *T+D* (2005 June), pp. 23–24.

12. Statistics Canada, " Census Snapshot—Immigration in Canada: A Portrait of Foreign-born Population, 2006 Census," http://statcan.gc.ca/pub/11-008-x/2008001/article/10556-eng.htm#1 (accessed November 10, 2011).

13. Canadian Heritage, Government of Canada, "What is Multiculturalism," http://pch.gc.ca/progs/multi/what_e.cfm (accessed 2006, July 11).

14. Canadian Policy Research Network, "Population Projections for 2017," http://cprn.com/en/diversity-2017.cfm (accessed 2006, April 10).

15. Statistics Canada, "Births and Birth Rate, by Province and Territory," http://www40.statcan.ca/l01/cst01/demo04a-eng.htm (accessed 2011, November 10).

16. Canadian Tire Corporation, "Canadian Tire & The Community," http://www2.canadiantire.ca/CTenglish/enreop_wrd.html (accessed 2002, May 23).

17. Sarah Ellison and Eric Bellman, "Clean Water, No Profit," *Wall Street Journal* (2005, February 3), pp. B1, B2.

18. Manulife Financial, "Corporate Giving," http://manulife.com/corporate/Corporate2.nsf/Public/corporategiving.html (accessed 2006, April 11).

19. Hemraj, Mohammed B., "Preventing Corporate Failure: The Cadbury Committee's Governance Report," *Journal of Financial Crime* (2002, October).

20. Adapted in part from Brian A. Schofield and Blair W. Feltmate, "Sustainable Development Investing," *Employee Benefits Journal* (2003, March).

21. Canadian Public Accountability Board (CPAB), "Mission and mandate," http://cpab-ccrc.ca/EN/Pages/missionMandate.aspx (accessed 2011, November 10).

22. Jennings, Marianne Moody, *Case Studies in Business Ethics*, 2nd ed.

(St. Paul, MN: West Publishing Company, 1996), pp. xx–xxiii.

23. Sankey, Derek, "Older Workers in High Demand," *Calgary Herald,* Saturday (2011, June 25), p. G1.

24. Joseph, Sarah, "Occupy Movement: Different Aims, but Untied by the Importance of Civil Protest," Monash University (2011, October 27). Retrieved from http://asiancorrespondent.com/68188/occupy-movement-different-aims-but-united-by-the-importance-of-civil-protest/ (2011, November 17).

25. Hemraj, Mohammed B., "Preventing Corporate Failure: The Cadbury Committee's Governance Report," *Journal of Financial Crime* (2002, October).

Chapter 4

1. http://www.city-data.com/canada/Meductic-Village.html; http://Sabian.com; http://www.historicplaces.ca/en/rep-reg/place-lieu.aspx?id=14831; http://www.native-artifact-consulting.com/treasures.html; http://www.trafficoutlook.com/sabian.com; http://www.webmator.com/sabian.com; http://bizinformation.co/www.sabian.com; Interview with Greg Hartt.

2. http://www.forrester.com/US+Online+Retail+Forecast+2011+To+2016/fulltext/-/E-RES60672?docid=60672.

3. Reinhardt, W., Schmidt, B., Sloep, P., & Drachsler, H. (2011). "Knowledge worker roles and actions—results of two empirical studies." *Knowledge and Process Management,* 18.3, 150–174.

4. "Electronic Trading Hubs," http://www.com-met2005.org.uk, (2006, April 4); David Luckham, "The Global Information Society and the Need for New Technology," http://www.informit.com (2006, April 4); "Trading Hubs," http://www.investni.com (2006, April 4); "Trading Hubs in Asia," *Oikono* (2005, December 6), http://www.oikono.com.

5. Zeidner, Rita, "Building a Better Intranet," *HR Magazine* (2005, November 1), p. 99.

6. Brown, James, "Hotel Group Installs Global Staff Intranet," *Computing* (2005, October 20), http://www.computing.co.uk.

7. "Executive Guides: Wireless," *Darwin Executive Guides,* http://guide.darwinmag.com/technology/communications/wireless/index.html (accessed 2003, January 31);

and "Wi-Fi," Webopedia, http://www.webopedia.com.

8. "Bluetooth® Wireless Technology Becoming Standard in Cars," *Bluetooth SIG* (2006, February 13). http://www.bluetooth.com.

9. Find VPN.com, "(VPN) Virtual Private Network FAQs," http://findvpn.com/articles/faq.php, (accessed 2003, January 31); and About.com: Computer Networking, "VPN Tutorial," http://compnetworking.about.com/library/weekly/aa010701a.htm (accessed 2003, January 24).

10. Kowalke, Mae, "Bell Canada Intros VoIP managed Services for Cisco and Nortel Enterprise Customers," *TMCnet.com* (2008, November 17), http://voipservices.tmcnet.com (accessed 2009, February 2).

11. Melymuka, Kathleen, "Far from the Mother Ship," *Computerworld* (2002, December 9), http://www.computerworld.com.

12. Section based on "Executive Guides: Knowledge Management," *Darwin Executive Guides,* http://guide.darwinmag.com/technology/enterprise/knowledge/index.html (2006, April 3).

13. SDLC—System development lifecycle.

14. "Cybercrime Cost about $400 Billion," Computer Crime Research Center (2005, July 6), http://www.crime-research.org.

15. "The Difference Between a Virus, Worm and Trojan Horse?" *Webopedia,* http://www.webopedia.com (2006, April 1).

16. "Spam Costs World Businesses $50 Billion," *InternetWeek* (2005, February 23); and "Spam Rates Rebound," *InternetWeek* (March 7, 2006), both from http://galenet.thomsonlearning.com.

17. Berinato, Scott, "The Global State of Information Security 2005," *CIO* (2005, September 15), http://www.cio.com.

18. "Security Policies 101," *Intranet Journal* (2003, January 6), http://www.intranetjournal.com.

19. Standage, Tom, "The Weakest Link" (Survey of Digital Security, Special Section), *Economist* (2002, October 26), pp. 11–16.

20. Mearian, Lucas, "IT Managers See Portable Storage Device Security Risk," *Computerworld* (2006, March 17), http://www.computerworld.com.

21. Tech Trends 2002, Volume 2, City: Deloitte & Touche LLP, Technology, Media and Telecommunications Group, http://www.deloitte.com.

22. Boyle, Matthew, "Tech in Action—The Latest Hit: CSI in Your Hard Drive," *Fortune* (2005, November 14), p. 39.

23. Boyle, Matthew, "Tech In Action—The Latest Hit: CSI in Your Hard Drive"; "Guidance Software Introduces the World's Most Complete and Advanced eDiscovery Solution," Press Release, Guidance Software Corporate Website (2006, January 30), http://www.guidancesoftware.com.

24. Bartholomew, Doug, "IT On Tap?" *Industry Week* (2005, June 1), p. 64.

25. Office of the Privacy Commissioner of Canada, "Top 10 Ways your Privacy is Threatened," http://www.privcom.gc.ca/resource/dpd/top10_e.asp (accessed 2012, July 11).

Chapter 5

1. lululemon.com, History; Stewart, M., *Business Edge Newsmagazine,* (2008, May 16), "lululemon boss rides creative wave"; FiredforNow's Blog, March 31, 2009, "Why I dislike lululemon more than ever"; *Vancouver Sun,* (2012, March 7), "*Forbes'* 2012 billionaires list includes 25 Canadians"; Advent International, lululemon athletica; Open Salon.com, (2009, April 1). A lululemon Alternative—Swadeshi Yoga Clothing.

2. Government of Canada, Department of Foreign Affairs and International Trade, "Trade Negotiations and Agreements—Why Trade Matters," http://www.dfait.maeci.gc.ca/tna-nac/ text-e.asp (accessed 2002, June 4).

3. Foreign Affairs and International Trade Canada, "Trade Matters," http://www.international.gc.ca/trade-agreements-accords-commerciaux/matters-important/index.aspx?lang=en (accessed 2011, November 5); Statistics Canada, "Imports, Exports and Trade Balance of Goods on a Balance-of-Payments Basis, by Country or Country Grouping," http://www.statcan.gc.ca/tables-tableaux/sum-som/l01/cst01/gblec02a-eng.htm (accessed 2011, November 5).

4. Foreign Affairs and International Trade Canada, "Canada Committed to Opening New Global Markets for Canadian Business," http://www.international.gc.ca/media_commerce/comm/news-communiques/2011/331.aspx?lang=eng&view=d (accessed 2011, November 5).

5. Government of Canada, Department of Foreign Affairs and International Trade, "Trade Negotiations and Agreements—Why Trade Matters," http://www.dfait.maeci.gc.ca/tna-nac/ text-e.asp (accessed 2002, June 4).

6. Statistics Canada, "Merchandise Trade of Canada *(Monthly),*" http://www.statcan.gc.ca/tables-tableaux/sum-som/l01/cst01/trad45a-eng.htm?sdi=merchandise%20trade (accessed 2009, March 13).

7. Statistics Canada, *Latest release from the Labour Force Survey (PDF),* http://www.statcan.gc.ca/subjects-sujets/labour-travail/lfs-epa/lfs-epa-eng.htm (accessed 2012, January 9).

8. "Anti-Trade/Pro-Poverty," *Fortune* (2000, January 10), p. 40.

9. "Globalization: What Americans Are Worried About," *Business Week* (2000, April 24), p. 44.

10. Council on Foreign Relations, "Mercosur: South Americas's Fractious Trade Bloc," http://cfr.org/trade/mercosur-south-americas-fractious-trade-bloc/p12762 (accessed on February 9, 2012, January 9).

11. Association Of Southeast Asian Nations, "Overview," http://aseansec.org/64.htm (accessed 2009, March 13).

12. *Business Wire,* "Global Tablet Market Will soar to U.S. $46 Billion by 2014," http://www.businesswire.com/news/home/20110105006431/en/Global-Tablet-Market-Soar-U.S.46-Billion-2014 (accessed 2012, January 11).

13. Media Awareness Network, "Canadian Content Rules (Cancon)," http://www.media-awareness.ca/english/issues/cultural_policies/canadian_content_rules.cfm (accessed 2012, January 11).

14. Government of Canada, Department of Foreign Affairs and International Trade, "About EPD, Export and Import Controls Bureau," http://www.dfait-maeci.gc.ca/~eicb/eicbintro-e.htm (accessed 2002, June 4).

15. Matthew Fisher, "Canada Seizing Prominent Role on the World Stage," *Calgary Herald* (2012, January 10), pp. A1/A3.

16. King, Neil, "A Whole New World," *Wall Street Journal* (2004, September 17), pp. R1–R2.

17. Hal Lancaster, "Global Managers Need Boundless Sensitivity, Rugged Constitutions," *Wall Street Journal* (1998, October 13).

Chapter 6

1. "About OGIO International," OGIO International website, http://www.ogio.com (accessed 2008, November 24).

2. "Famous Canadian Entrepreneurs," Westmount Collegiate Institute website, http://www.westmount.ci.yrdsb.edu.on.ca/entrepreneurs.html (accessed 2008, November 24).

3. Pennington, April Y., "Entrepreneurial Snapshot: Katrina Markoff," *Entrepreneur* (2002, November), http://www.entrepreneur.com.

4. Shook, David "Jeff Bezos: Finally Relaxing?" *Business Week Online* (2002, October 1), http://www.businessweek.com.

5. "About Us," The Jim Pattison Group website, http://www.jimpattison.com/corporate/about-us.htm (accessed 2008, November 24).

6. Katz, Gregory, "Her Daily Bread," *American Way Magazine,* July 15, 2005, p. 34; Poilane website http://www.poilane.com (2005, October 27).

7. "Are You Building an Inc. 500 Company?" *Inc. 500* (2002, October 15), http://www.inc.com/inc500.

8. "Key Small Business Statistics, July 2011," Industry Canada's website, http://www.ic.gc.ca/eic/site/sbrp-rppe.nsf/eng/h_rd02596.html (accessed 2011, November 17).

9. "Key Small Business Statistics, July 2008," Industry Canada's website, http://www.ic.gc.ca/epic/site/sbrp-rppe.nsf/en/h_rd01252e.html (accessed 2008, November 24).

10. Dulipovici, Andreea, "Small Business—Big Picture," Canadian Federation of Independent Business, http://www.cfib.ca (accessed February 9, 2006).

11. Dun & Bradstreet, "D&B 21st Annual Small Business Survey Summary Report," http://www.dnb.com.

12. McFarland, Keith, "What Makes Them Tick," *Inc. 500* (2005, October 19), http://www.inc.com.

13. McCall, Kimberly, "Then There Were Two: Should You Hire a Staff?" *Startup Journal.com* (2002, November 4), http://www.inc.com.

14. Noonan, David, "Be Your Own Master," *Newsweek* (2002, September 23), p. 61.

15. Canada Business Network, About Canada Business, http://www.canadabusiness.ca/eng/page/about/ (accessed 2011, November 28).

16. Cornwall, Jeff, "We Will Not Go Quietly," *The Entrepreneurial Mind,* June 22, 2004, http://www.belmont.edu (2005, October 27).

17. Zhao, Stacy, "Web-Based Companies Significant Part of U.S. Small Business," *Inc.com* (2005, June 7), http://www.inc.com.

18. Bailey, Jeff, "Growing Up," *Wall Street Journal*, March 27, 2002 p. R6; Case, "Trading Places," pp. 74–82; Moore, Brenda L. "Changing Classes," *Wall Street Journal* (2002, March 27), p. R8; and "Be Your Own Master."

19. Williams, Geoff. "Looks like Rain," *Entrepreneur* (2002, September), http://www.entrepreneur.com.

20. "Got ID?" *Entrepreneur*, November 2002, http://www.entrepreneur.com (accessed 2006, July).

Chapter 7

1. Slideshare.net, Porters 5 Forces Model; *Vancouver Sun,* (2011, February 24), "Smartphone Rankings"; *Yahoo Finance,* Research in Motion Ltd (RIM.TO); Van Sack, J. *Boston Herald,* (2011, August 5), "Analysts Torch BlackBerry maker's smartphone move"; http://*Berryreview.com* (2009, February 2), History of RIM, the Blackberry Smartphone; http://Wired.com, iPhone; Investing Money, Rim; BlackberryPlanetBook.com, RIM Financials 2010; The Canadian Press, July 12, 2011, "RIM's Structure goes under the microscope."

Chapter 8

1. Reuters, April 27, 2011, UDPATE 1-MTY Food to acquire Canada's Jugo Juice; *Montréal Gazette* (2011, July 7), "MTY Food Group posts lower Q2 earnings"; *Food Business Review* (2011, April 28), "MTY to acquire Jugo Juice"; Jugojuice.com, Franchise; Jugojuice.com, History; Sankey, D. (2009, August 25), *National Post,* "Good partnership Juices up Profits"; Manta.com, Jugo Juice; Calgarypuck Forms, The unofficial Calgary Flames Fan Communit, Jugo Juice vs. Booster Juice; Bogomolny, L. *Canadian Business* (2006, January 30), "Smoothie chain Booster Juice finds expanding globally is not always smooth"; http://www.Google.ca/Finance, TSE:MTY, http://www.Wikiinvest.com, MTY Food Group (TSE:MTY); TD Waterhouse Research, Overview MTY; Willis, A., *Globe Advisor* (2010, April 9), "Time is right for food court king to eat some rivals."

2. Stuart, Anne. "Where Do Great Ideas Come From?," *Inc.* (2002, October), pp. 43, 45.

3. Hofman, Mike, "The Bad Boy," *Inc.* (2002, September), pp. 78–80.

4. http://www.digitrustgroup.com (accessed 2009, March 12).

5. Canadian Co-operative Association, "*Co-op Facts and Figures,*" *About Co-ops in Canada,*" http://coopscanada.coop/en/about_co-operative/Co-op-Facts-and-Figures (accessed 2011, October 27).

6. Canadian Co-operative Association, "About Co-operatives," http://coopscanada.coop/aboutcoop/ (accessed 2005, November 1).

7. Syncrude Canada Ltd, "Syncrude Owners," http://syncrude.ca/users/folder.asp?FolderID=7101 (accessed 2011, October 25).

8. McDonald's Canada, "FAQs," http://mcdonalds.ca/en/aboutus/faq.aspx, Copyright ©2011 (accessed 2011, October 25).

9. Adler, Carlye. "How China Eats a Sandwich," *Fortune*, March 21, 2005, p. F210-B; Bennett, Julie. "Chinese Market Offers Franchise Challenges," *Startup Journal–The Wall Street Journal Online*, http://startupjournal.com; Subway corporate website, http://subway.com (accessed 2006, March 25).

10. Home Instead Senior Care, "About Us-Helping You Care for the Seniors in Your Life," http://homeinstead.com/aboutus/default.aspx (accessed 2009, March 9).

11. "Sarah Adult Day Services," *Franchise Zone,* http://entrepreneur.com/franzone/ (accessed 2006, May 31).

12. Smith, Devlin, "One Big Happy Family," (January 2003), http://entrepreneur.com.

Chapter 9

1. Oasisbags.com, Letter to our Customers (2011); http://www.oasisbags.com, About us; http://www.Oasis bags.com, blog; RBC Canadian Women Entrepreneur Awards, Robin Maloni (2011); Canada NewsWire (2010, November 30). Women Of Influence Announces 2010 RBC Canadian Woman Entrepreneur Award Winners.

2. "Now for the Hard Part," *Fortune,* (2002, November 18), pp. 95–106.

3. Procter & Gamble, http://www.pgbrands.com/Default.aspx?tabid=36&pg=1 (accessed July 12, 2012).

4. Bank, David, "Autodesk Stages Revival," *Wall Street Journal* (2005, August 19), p. B3.

5. Messmer, Max, "Surviving and Thriving as a New Manager," *National Public Accountant* (2000, June), pp. 22–24.

6. Waterstone Human Capital, "Canada's 10 Most Admired Corporate Cultures™ 2007," http://canadasmostadmired.com (accessed 2008, September 29).

7. Ramsey, Robert, "What Will You Do if the Worst Case Scenario Really Happens?" *Supervision* (2002, June), pp. 6–7.

8. McDonald, Tom, "A World of Challenges," *Successful Meetings* (2002, July), p. 25.

9. Daniels, Cora, "The Last Taboo: It's Not Sex. It's Not Drinking. It's Stress—And It's Soaring," *Fortune* (October 28, 2002), pp. 136–140; and Noonan, David, Sieder, Jill and Peraino, Kevin, "Stop Stressing Me," *Newsweek* (2001, January 29), pp. 54–56.

Chapter 10

1. Ontario Ministry of Municipal Affairs and Housing (2010, October 22), The Contact North Training Delivery System; Bates, T., (2011, April 9), New website Design for Contact North; Elearn network, (2011, June 4), Contact North Connects Aboriginal partners 15 hours and 15,000 km Apart, http://Downes.ca, Contact North; http://www.Greenstone.ca, Residential Life/Education, Jean-Louis, M., (2011, April 18), Contact North; http://Contact North.ca, New Organizational Structure at Contact North elearnnetwork.ca to Deliver Sustained Growth in Course Registrations Supported and Enhanced Student Support Services in Small, Rural and Remote Communities.

2. "Building the Right Team," *Maclean's* (2002, October 28), p. 31.

3. Ikematsu, Hiroshi, "Sony's Restructuring No Easy Task," *The Yomiuri Shimbun*, September 23, 2005; Edwards, Cliff with Lowry, Tom, Ihlwan, Moon and Hall, Kenji "The Lessons for Sony at Samsung," *Business Week*, (2005, October 10), p. 37.

4. Gooding, R. Z. and Wagner, J. A. III. "A Meta-Analytic Review of the Relationship—between Size and Performance: The Productivity and Efficiency of Organizations and Their Subunits," *Administrative Science Quarterly* (1985, December) pp. 462–481.

5. Burrows, Peter, "HP Says Goodbye to Drama; Five months in, CEO Mark Hurd's no-nonsense approach is being felt in a big way—and the Street has taken notice," *Business Week Online* (2005, September 1).

6. Novartis, "Welcome to Citizenship@ Novartis," http://www. corporatecitizenship.novartis.com (downloaded 2008, December 11).

7. Purdum, Traci, "Teaming, Take 2: Once a Buzzword, Teaming Today Is One of the Fundamentals of Manufacturing," *Industry Week* (2005, May), p. 41.

8. White, Joseph B., "LaSorda's Chrysler Challenge," *The Wall Street Journal* (2005, August 15), p. B5.

9. Deutschman, Alan. "The Fabric of Creativity: Pound for Pound, W. L. Gore Just Might Be the Most Innovative Company in America. Here's Why," *Fast Company* (2004, December), pp. 54–60.

10. Brady, Diane. "Reaping the Wind: GE's Energy Initiative Is a Case Study in Innovation without Borders," *Business Week* (2004, October 11), p. 201; Sellers, Patricia. "Blowing in the Wind: To Build a Better Wind Turbine, General Electric Built a Global Team of Researchers in Germany, China, India, and the U.S.," *Fortune* (2005, July 25), p. 130.

11. "New Study Shows That Workers Believe the Office Grapevine More Than They Do Management," *M2 Presswire* (2005, September 14).

12. Ibid.

Chapter 11

1. *Toronto Sun,* April 6, 2008, "Spelunking in an island paradise"; GO2—The Resource for People in Tourism, Success Equals Good Product, Excellent People; http:// www.hornelake.com/waiver; http:// www.hornelake.com/volunteers.

2. Clark, Kim, "No Pink Slips at the Plant," *U.S. News & World Report* (2002, February), p. 40.

3. Vanscoy, Kayte, "The Hiring Crisis," *Smart Business for the New Economy* (2000, July), p. 84–94.

4. From Alder, *International Dimensions*, pp. 174–181.

5. "Strategies for Developing an Effective Employee Absenteeism Policy," *HR Focus* (2001, September 11).

Chapter 12

1. Chen, D., "Windsor Raceway Security Guard Strike Settled," *The Windsor Star* (2009, April 04). Raceway strike ends with deal, job cuts; *The Windsor Star*, (2009, March 12). Elderly motorist warned after picket line mishap; SEIU Local 2 BGPWU, Our History—Over 100 Years of the Brewery, General, and Professional Workers' Union; The View From Local 2 (SIEU Local 2) (2009, September). Victory for Striking Workers at Windsor Raceway.

2. "Gore-Tex," *Fast Company,* (1999, January) 160. Deutschman, Alan. "What I Know Now: Terri Kelly, CEO, W. L. Gore & Associates," *Fast Company* (2005, September), p. 96; "Gore Marks 9th Year as One of Nation's Best, Company Earns #5 Position on FORTUNE Magazine '100 Best Companies to Work For' List," W. L. Gore & Associates, press release (2006, January 9), http://www.gore.com; Levering, Robert and Moskowitz, Milton "And the Winners Are ...," *Fortune* (2006, January 23), p. 89; Welch, Sara J. "GORE The Fabric of Success," Successful Meetings, (2005, May), pp. 49–51; W. L. Gore & Associates website, http:// www.gore.com (2006, February 10 & 2011, December 19); About Gore, retrieved from http:// www.gore.com/en_xx/aboutus/ index.html (2011, December 19); W. L. Gore Reviews, retrieved from http://www.glassdoor. com (2011, December 19); and Huey, J. (1994). The New Post Heroic Leadership, retrieved from http://money.cnn.com/ magazines/fortune/fortune_ archive/1994/02/21/78995/index. htm (2011, November 23).

3. Peacock, Melanie. Personal interview, conducted (2006, March 31).

4. Krell, Eric. "Budding Relationships," *HR Magazine,* vol. 50 (2005, June), pp. 114–118.

5. Cox, Taylor and Blake, Stacy, "Managing Cultural Diversity: Implications for Organizational Competitiveness," *Academy of Management Executive*, Vol. 5 (1991), pp. 45–56.

Chapter 13

1. Chu, J., *Justin Bieber: Never Say Never,* ARG Live, Toronto, 2011, 105 minutes (Documentary), http://www.whisperingroseradio. com (2012, May 3). Bieber Fever; http://www.gawker.com (2012, August 15), Justin Bieber Tweets Enemy's Phone Number to 4.5 Million Followers; KARR Associates, Supercharge Your Success in Life the Justin Bieber Way; Online Magazine platform, March 31, 2010, Failure to Tweet: The Bieber Effect; http:// www.justinbieberneversaynever. com; Azpiri, J., *Now Public* (2010, March 25), "Justin Bieber Manager Arrested: Scott Braun Arrested"; Angelo, M., *Business Insider* (2011, May 6), "Justin Bieber's Manager Gets Off Scot-Free In Kiddie-Crushing Mall Incident."

2. "Caring for the Customer Pays Off for Lexus Again," Essex Chronicle Series (2002, May 10).

3. American Marketing Association website, http://www. marketingpower.com (accessed 2003, August 28).

4. McDaniel, Carl and Gates, Roger. *Marketing Research Essentials,* 5th ed. Hoboken, NJ: John Wiley & Sons (2006), pp. 131–133.

5. D'Innocenzio, Ann. "Stores Putting Data from Loyalty Cards to Work," *Fort Worth Star Telegram* (2003, March 25).

Chapter 14

1. Scionnation.ca, April 15, 2011, "Scion Set to Reveal Concept Vehicle"; http://Automobileretailers. com, "Why Scion Why Now"; Henry, J. May 21, 2008, Edmunds Inside Line, "Can Scion Survive Success?"; *Wall Street Journal,* June 1, 2012, "Sales and Share of Total Market by Manufacturer"; Riches, E., *Edmunds Auto Observer,* August 10, 2012, "Scion Hammered by Recession, Hopes New tC Starts Bounce Back."

2. This section partially adapted from Charles Lamb, Joe Hair, and Carl McDaniel, *Marketing,* 8th ed. (Mason, OH: Thomson Publishing, 2006), pp. 402–403.

3. "A Deal with Target Put Lid on Revival at Tupperware," *Wall Street Journal,* February 18, 2004, pp. A1, A9; and "Tupperware Announces Second Quarter EPS," news release, http://www.tupperware.com (2005, July 26).

4. "Easy Does It All," *Business 2.0* (2005, August) pp. 69–74. Copyright ©2005 Time Inc. All rights reserved. Reproduced by permission.
5. "A More Profitable Harvest," *Business 2.0* (2005, May), pp. 66–67.
6. "Making the Most of eBay," *Business 2.0* (2002 June), pp. 129–130. © 2002 Time Inc. All rights reserved; *"The Company"*, eBay.ca, http://pages.ebay.ca/aboutebay/thecompany/companyoverview.html (accessed 2009, February 26).

Chapter 15

1. Bombardier, May 31, 2011, Bombardier to Combine Efficiency and Quality in Manufacturing of CSeries Aircraft; *Reinforced plastics.com* (2011, June 18), "Bombardier uses robots in CSeries aircraft assembly"; *Wall Street Journal*, May 31, 2011, "Bombardier Innovates with Robots"; *Canadian Manufacturing Daily* (2011, June 01), "Bombardier announces US$665 million CSeries order will use robots in assembly"; Ray, S. & Layne, R., Bloomberg (2011, June 20), "Bombardier CSeries Gets Deal While Qatar Goes on Hold."
2. Jusko, Jill. "Locations—Globe Motors Turns to Portugal," *Industry Week* (2002, November 1), http://industryweek.com.
3. McClenahen, John S., "The World's Best," *Industry Week* (2001, April 16), http://industryweek.com.
4. Nadel, Brian, "Chain and Command," *Fortune* (2005, July 25; Dell company website http://dell.com (2006, May 20); MOL company website, http://www.naukri.com/gpw/mol/ (2006, May 20); Acer company website http://global.acer.com (2006, May 20).
5. Verespej, Michael A. "E-Procurement Explosion," *Industry Week* (2002, March 1), http://industryweek.com.
6. McClenahen, John S., "The World's Best," *Industry Week* (2001, April 16), http://industryweek.com.
7. Varmazis, Maria, "Automation Frees Time for Strategic Activities," *Purchasing* (2005, September), p. 40.
8. Bartholomew, Doug, "Faster CAD Design Called a Lifesaver," *Industry Week* (2001, June 4), http://industryweek.com.
9. Bylinsky, Gene, "Elite Factories: They're Setting Lofty Standards in Quality Control, Preventive Maintenance, and Automation," *Fortune* (2002, September 2), p. 172B.
10. ___, "Elite Factories."
11. Stevens, Tim, "Factories of the Future—Integrated Product Development," *Industry Week* (2002, June 1), http://industryweek.com.

Chapter 16

1. Morgan, J. Homemakers (2008, January), Sheila Fraser—Canada's Auditor General, Buchanan, R. The Pacific Institute for Public Engagement (2011, June), Sheila Fraser … you are my Hero!; Bruno, J., *The Hill Times* (2011, February 14). Public Sector Integrity Commissioner's Office has "lost all credibility," interim integrity czar tries to rebuild it; Munroe, S., http://www.About.com, Sheila Fraser; http://www.Newlearner.com, Accounting Related Scandals.
2. Chartered Accountants of Canada, "Filling the GAP to IFRS: Teaching Supplements for Canada's Accounting Academics," ISBN 978-1-55385-370-1.
3. Cheney, Glenn. "FASB, IASB Agree to Push on with Convergence Effort," *Accounting Today* (2006, April 3). http://ask.elibrary.com; "FASB and IASB Reaffirm Commitment to Enhance Consistency, Comparability and Efficiency in Global Capital Markets," *Financial Accounting Standards Board* (2006, February 27), http://www.fasb.org/news; "FASB Issues Accounting Standard That Improves the Reporting of Accounting Changes as Part of Convergence Effort with IASB," *Financial Accounting Standards Board* (2005, June 1), http://www.fasb.org/news; Reason, Tim, "The Narrowing GAAP," *CFO* (2005, December 1), http://www.cfo.com.
4. The Certified General Accounts Association of Canada, "Statement delivered to the Standing Committee on Industry, Science and Technology—Review of Canada's Service Sector," February 7, 2008.
5. CMA Canada, "What is a CMA" and "About CMA," http://www.cma-canada.org (accessed 2009, March 31).
6. ___, "Overview," http://www.cga-canada.org/en-ca/aboutcgacanada/pages/_ca_about_overview.aspx (accessed 2009, March 31).
7. Papmehl, Anne, "Accounting for Knowledge: Measuring Our Intellectual Assets Helps Us Manage Them Effectively," *CMA Management*, March 2004, http://www.allbusiness.com (accessed 2006, April 1).

Chapter 17

1. http://www.rbc.com, Find your fit, Interview of Chelsea Deal by C. M. Hartt (2011, September).
2. The Bank of Canada, "Medium-Term Plan 2007–2009, Moving Forward: Building The Future Together," http://www.bankofcanada.ca/en/about/do.html (accessed 2009, March 30).
3. The Bank of Canada, "Monetary Policy–Key Interest Rate: Target for the Overnight Rate," http://www.bankofcanada.ca/en/monetary/target.html (accessed 2009, March 30).
4. Statistics Canada, "Chartered Banks," http://142.206.72.67/03/03e/03e_001a_e.htm (accessed 2005, March 8).
5. Statistics Canada, "Trust Companies," http://142.206.72.67/03/03e/03e_001b_e.htm (accessed 2005, March 8).
6. Canadian Deposit Insurance Corporation, "History of Member Institution Failures," http://www.cdic.ca/1/7/0/7/index1.shtml (accessed 2009, March 30).
7. "Overview of Economic Benefits to the United States from the Activities of International Banks," Institute of International Bankers website, http://www.iib.org (accessed 2006, June 3).
8. TD Canada Trust, "Consolidated Financial Statements–2008," http://www.td.com/ar2008/index.jsp, (accessed 2009, March 30).
9. Adams, Mike. The Health Ranger, Naturalnews Editor, "Merck Loses Vioxx Lawsuit: Jury Awards $253.4 Million to Widow," http://www.naturalnews.Com/011064.html (accessed 2009, March 30).
10. "Getting to Know ETF's" *Calgary Herald* (2011, June 26), p. F3.
11. "Online Banking Booming, Says IDC," http://www.electronicbanker.com (accessed 1999, June 2).
12. Reuters, "Top Banks Plan Online Billing Network," *The Sheboy-Gan Press* (1999, June 24), p. C5.
13. Toronto Stock Exchange, "An Exchange of Opportunity," http://www.tsx.com/en/pdf/Factsheet0607-e.pdf (accessed 2009, March 31).

Chapter 18

1. Shaw, G., *Calgary Herald* (2011, April 18), "B.C. whiz kid's startup raises $4M"; McMahan, T., *Wall Street Journal* (2011, August 6), "Betting Venture Capital on an

Unproven 19-Year-Old"; Tsotsis, A., *Tech Crunch* (2011, April 12), "Kiip's Brian Wong on Taking Risks as Young Entrepreneur"; Crunch Base, August 29, 2011, Brian Wong; Arrington, M., *Tech Crunch* (2012, August 3), "True Ventures Invests in 19-Year-Old Entrepreneur Brian Wong"; http://www.brianwong.com; *Vancouver Sun* Blogs (2011, April 12), "UBC grad Brian Wong launches Gaming Ad Model with Real Life Rewards"; Roush, W., *Xconomy* (2010, October 28), "$300K for Kiip"; Kiip.me, (2012, June 16), "How Does Kiip Work?"; http://Kiip.me, Blog.

2. Deeds, David. "Extra! Extra!" *Inc.* (2002, September), pp. 110–112.

3. Adapted from Gamble, Richard, "Got Cash? Who Doesn't?" *Treasury & Risk Management* (2005, December/2006, January), http://www.treasuryandrisk.com; Gamble, Richard, Kelly, Susan and Labate, John. "The 2005 Alexander Hamilton Award Winners: Cash Management; Bronze Award Winner: Honeywell International," *Treasury & Risk Management* (2005, November), all from http://www.treasuryandrisk.com; and Kroll, Karen M. "Treasury Today: To Centralize or Not?" *Business Finance* (2006, April), http://businessfinancemag.com.

4. Sherman, Jay and Kelly, Susan, "Uphill Racer—The 2002 Alexander Hamilton Award Winners," *Treasury & Risk Management* (2002, October), http://www.treasuryandrisk.com.

5. CanadaStock.ca, "Canadian Stocks with the Lowest Debt/Equity Ratios," retrieved from http://www.canadastock.ca/Analysis/lowest-debt-to-equity-canadian-stocks.html (2011, August 19).

6. Cummings, John, "Guiding the Global Enterprise," *Business Finance*, (2005, June), http://www.businessfinancemag.com.

7. Brannen, Laurie, "A Bird's Eye View of Finance," *Business Finance*, (2005, May); and ___, "Finance at the Forefront," *BusinessFinance* (2006, April), both from http://www.businessfinancemag.com; and Gamble, Richard, "Straddling the Great Divide," *Treasury & Risk Management* (2005, September). http://www.treasuryandrisk.com.

8. Sammer, Joanne, "What CFOs Want From Risk Management," *Business Finance* (2006, April), http://www.businessfinancemag.com.

9. Lubart, Ann, "Saving a Seat at the Table," *Treasury & Risk Management* (2005, March), http://www.treasuryandrisk.com.

10. Mochari, Ilan. How to Collect from Anyone (Even Enron)", *Inc.* (2002, September 1), pp. 67–68.

Appendix

1. Canada, Department of Justice, "Canada's Court System," http://www.justice.gc.ca/eng/dept-min/pub/ccs-ajc/page3.html.

2. Adapted from the notes of Robert Malach, LLB, LLM.

Company Index

Note: Page numbers followed by *e* refer to exhibits.

Subject Index

Note: Page numbers followed by *e* refer to exhibits.

Canadian Stock Exchanges, primary, 527
Canadian Taxpayers Federation, 58
Canadian Union of Public Employees
    (CUPE), 350
Canadian Wildlife Federation, 378
Cao, Ray, 196
Capacity, 6 C's of credit, 551
Capital
    6 C's of credit, 551
    defined, 33
Capital assets, 487
Capital budget, 545
Capital budgeting, 548
Capital expenditures, 548
Capitalism, 35
Capital & Private Equity Association, 554
Capital products, classifying, 405–406
Carbon capture and storage (CCS), 256
Careers
    as entrepreneur, 186–187
    government as, 22–23
    planning, 358
Careers in Marketing, 436
Carney, Mark, 150
Cartel, 20, 21
Carter, Rob, 97
Cash budget, 545
Cash flow
    defined, 542
    seasonal, 549e
    through business, 541e
    See also Statement of cash flow
Cash management, 546
Cellular manufacturing, facility
    design, 453
Census data, Canada, 124
Centralization, 283
Central planning, 36
Centre for International Business
    Ethics, 518
Ceran, Jennifer, 562–563
Certificates of deposit, 546
Certified general accountant (CGA), 482
Certified General Accountants
        Association of Canada
        (CGA-Canada), 481
Certified management accountant
        (CMA), 482
cfo.com, 542
CFO Magazine, 467
Chain of command, 281
Chambers, Jeff, 314
Channel intermediaries, 420–422
Character, in 6 C's of credit, 551
Characteristics of entrepreneurs
    managerial and technical knowledge,
        167–168
    personality traits, 166–167
Chartered accountants (CA), 481
Chartered banks, 515
Charter of Rights and Freedoms, 355e
Charter rights, 77
Chief Executive Officer (CEO), 96, 222,
        223e
Chief financial officer, 222, 223e
    expanding role of, 561
    responsibilities, 562e

Chief information officer (CIO), 96, 97,
        222, 223e
Chief operating officer, 222, 223e,
        279–280e
Chief risk officer, 563
Children, marketing to, 392, 426
Childs, Stephanie, 65
China
    barriers to banking in, 518
    Dell Inc. in, 148
    entrepreneurship in, 55
    manufacturing in, 47, 83–84
    setting up sandwich shop in, 234
    trade and, 37
Chouinard, Yvon, 167
Christiansen, Chris, 113
Circular flow
    defined, 28
    economics as, 34, 35e
Classic entrepreneurs, 164
Clean technology projects, 22
Client, 104
Closed Loop System, 41
Closed shop, 351–352
Cloud computing, 115
Code of Conduct for Procurement, The, 22
Code of ethics, 80
Coercive power, 254
Cognitive dissonance, 392
Cohen, Ben, 80, 318
Cohesiveness, in groups, 290
Collateral
    defined, 550
    in 6 C's of credit, 551
Collective agreements, negotiation
    about, 351
    grievance and arbitration, 353
    job security and seniority, 352
    management rights, 352
    pressuring contract settlement, 354
    union security, 351–352
Collective bargaining, 350
Command economy, 36–37, 38e
Commercial liability insurance, 560
Commercial paper, 546, 550
Commission, 348
Committee of Sponsoring Organizations
        (COSO), 115
Committee structure, of organizations,
        288–289
Commodities, natural resources, 33
Common Market of the South, 137
Common shares, 518–520
Common shares, equity financing,
        552–553
Common Threads Initiative, 167
Communication channels, in informal
        organizations, 294–295
Comparative advantage, 136
Compensation and benefits, employee,
        347–349
Competencies, determining, 200
Competition, challenges, 53–54
Competition Act, 20–21, 229
Competition Bureau, 229
Competitive advantage
    cost competitive advantage, 375

defined, 357, 374
determine, 200
differential competitive advantage,
    375–376
niche competitive advantage, 376
Competitor, government as, 16
Component lifestyle, 64
Component parts and materials, as busi-
    ness product, 405–406
Computer-aided design (CAD), 464
Computer-aided manufacturing, 464
Computer-assisted training, 344
Computer-integrated manufacturing
    (CIM), 465
Computerized resource planning,
    454–455
Computer(s)
    in accounting, 485
    ethics and, 78
    literacy, 119
    modelling, 100
    network, 103–104
    securing information, 113–117
        (see also Security, protecting
        information/computers)
    virus, 114
Concentration, corporate-level strategy,
    200
Concept in Action
    Airbus, 145
    AMJ Campbell, 206
    annual report, 482
    Apple, iPhone, 68
    Apple Computers, 293
    Ben & Jerry's, 318
    Boston Pizza, 166
    budgets, 545
    Canadian Tire, 201
    Chief information officers, 97
    chief risk officer, 563
    China, trade and, 37
    computer modelling, 100
    computer privacy, 117
    consumer price index (CPI), 49
    consumer rights, 20
    contingency plans, 251
    corporate philanthropy, 82
    corporate sponsorship, 73
    Corruption of Foreign Public Officials
        Act, 142
    customer service, 372
    dashboard software, 265
    demographic segmentation, 380
    differential competitive advantage,
        375
    distribution channels, 418, 419
    diversity, 70
    Dragon's Den, 165
    employee motivation, 325
    enterprise resource planning, 456
    entrepreneurship, 170
    expert systems, 103
    factoring, 551
    financial accounting, 479
    financial decisions, 542
    financial ratios, 493
    financial statements, 488